Fodor's 07

W9-AYY-332

ENGLAND

**Where to Stay and Eat
for All Budgets**

**Must-See Sights
and Local Secrets**

Ratings You Can Trust

Fodor's Travel Publications   New York, Toronto, London, Sydney, Auckland
www.fodors.com

FODOR'S ENGLAND 2007

Editor: Linda Cabasin

Editorial Production: Bethany Cassin Beckerlegge
Editorial Contributors: Robert Andrews, Ferne Arfin, Ruth Craig, Christi Daugherty, Adam Gold, Julius Honnor, Kate Hughes, Christina Knight, Roger Thomas, Alex Wijeratna
Maps: David Lindroth, *cartographer;* Rebecca Baer and Bob Blake, *map editors*
Design: Fabrizio La Rocca, *creative director;* Guido Caroti, *art director;* Melanie Marin, *senior picture editor*
Production/Manufacturing: Colleen Ziemba
Cover Photo (Cumbria): Look GMBH/eStock Photo

ISBN-10: 1–4000–1725–4

ISBN-13: 978–1–4000–1725–6

ISSN: 1558–870X

SPECIAL SALES

This book is available for special discounts for bulk purchases for sales promotions or premiums. Special editions, including personalized covers, excerpts of existing books, and corporate imprints, can be created in large quantities for special needs. For more information, write to Special Markets/Premium Sales, 1745 Broadway, MD 6-2, New York, NY 10019, or e-mail specialmarkets@randomhouse.com.

AN IMPORTANT TIP & AN INVITATION

Although all prices, opening times, and other details in this book are based on information supplied to us at press time, changes occur all the time in the travel world, and Fodor's cannot accept responsibility for facts that become outdated or for inadvertent errors or omissions. So **always confirm information when it matters,** especially if you're making a detour to visit a specific place. Your experiences—positive and negative—matter to us. If we have missed or misstated something, **please write to us.** We follow up on all suggestions. Contact the England editor at editors@fodors. com or c/o Fodor's at 1745 Broadway, New York, NY 10019.

PRINTED IN THE UNITED STATES OF AMERICA

10 9 8 7 6 5 4 3 2 1

Be a Fodor's Correspondent

Your opinion matters. It matters to us. It matters to your fellow Fodor's travelers, too. And we'd like to hear it. In fact, we *need* to hear it.

When you share your experiences and opinions, you become an active member of the Fodor's community. That means we'll not only use your feedback to make our books better, but we'll publish your names and comments whenever possible. Throughout our guides, look for "Word of Mouth," excerpts of your unvarnished feedback.

Here's how you can help improve Fodor's for all of us.

Tell us when we're right. We rely on local writers to give you an insider's perspective. But our writers and staff editors—who are the best in the business—depend on you. Your positive feedback is a vote to renew our recommendations for the next edition.

Tell us when we're wrong. We're proud that we update most of our guides every year. But we're not perfect. Things change. Hotels cut services. Museums change hours. Charming cafés lose charm. If our writer didn't quite capture the essence of a place, tell us how you'd do it differently. If any of our descriptions are inaccurate or inadequate, we'll incorporate your changes in the next edition and will correct factual errors at fodors.com *immediately.*

Tell us what to include. You probably have had fantastic travel experiences that aren't yet in Fodor's. Why not share them with a community of like-minded travelers? Maybe you chanced upon a pub or B&B that you don't want to keep to yourself. Tell us why we should include it. And share your discoveries and experiences with everyone directly at fodors.com. Your input may lead us to add a new listing or highlight a place we cover with a "Highly Recommended" star or with our highest rating, "Fodor's Choice."

Give us your opinion instantly at our feedback center at www.fodors.com/feedback. You may also e-mail editors@fodors.com with the subject line "England Editor." Or send your nominations, comments, and complaints by mail to England Editor, Fodor's, 1745 Broadway, New York, NY 10019.

You and travelers like you are the heart of the Fodor's community. Make our community richer by sharing your experiences. Be a Fodor's correspondent.

Happy traveling!

Tim Jarrell, Publisher

CONTENTS

PLANNING YOUR TRIP

Be a Fodor's Correspondent 3
About This Book 7
What's Where .8
Quintessential England 16
If You Like 18
Great Itineraries 22
When to Go .28
On the Calendar 29

ENGLAND

1 LONDON 33
Exploring London 36
Where to Eat .84
Pubs & Afternoon Tea 99
Where to Stay 103
Nightlife & the Arts 123
Sports & the Outdoors 135
Shopping 136
London Essentials 146

2 THE SOUTHEAST 155
Canterbury to Dover 158
Rye to Glyndebourne 171
Brighton to East Grinstead 180
Masterpieces near Tunbridge Wells . .195
Southeast Essentials 205

3 THE SOUTH 208
From Winchester to Southampton . . .211
Isle of Wight 226
Salisbury to Stonehenge 230
New Forest to Lyme Regis 243
South Essentials 257

4 THE WEST COUNTRY 260
Bristol to North Devon 264

Cornwall 281
Plymouth & Dartmoor 299
Dartmouth, Torbay & Exeter 307
West Country Essentials 317

5 THE THAMES VALLEY 320
Windsor & Environs 322
To Henley & Beyond 333
Oxford 338
Blenheim Palace to Althorp 348
Thames Valley Essentials 358

6 SHAKESPEARE COUNTRY 361
Stratford-upon-Avon 364
Around Shakespeare Country 376
Shakespeare Country Essentials 385

7 BATH & THE COTSWOLDS 388
Bath & Environs 392
The Cotswolds 407
Gloucester to the Forest of Dean 433
Bath & the Cotswolds Essentials 440

8 THE WELSH BORDERS 444
Birmingham 446
From Worcester to Dudley 458
From Shrewsbury to Chester 470
Welsh Borders Essentials 481

9 LANCASHIRE & THE PEAKS . . .484
Manchester .486
Liverpool 500
The Peak District 510
Lancashire & the Peaks Essentials . . .521

10 THE LAKE DISTRICT 525
The Southern Lakes 529
Penrith & the Northern Lakes 548
Lake District Essentials 558

11 EAST ANGLIA 562

Cambridge .564
From Ely to Bury St. Edmunds 579
Colchester & the Suffolk Coast 587
Norwich to North Norfolk 596
Lincoln, Boston & Stamford 606
East Anglia Essentials 612

12 YORKSHIRE 615
West Yorkshire & Brontë Country 618
The Yorkshire Dales 629
York 635
York Environs 644
The North Yorkshire Coast 648
The North York Moors 655
Yorkshire Essentials 658

13 THE NORTHEAST 662
Durham, Newcastle & Environs 664
Hadrian's Wall Country 679
The Far Northeast Coast 685
Northeast Essentials 690

14 WALES 693
North Wales 697
Mid-Wales 714
South Wales 723
Wales Essentials 738

UNDERSTANDING ENGLAND

England & the Performing Arts 743
Splendid Stones & Architecture 746
Books & Movies 751
Chronology 755
English Vocabulary 759
SMART TRAVEL TIPS 761
INDEX 797
ABOUT OUR WRITERS 816

CLOSEUPS

Where to See the Royals 47
Eating English 91
Vin Anglais 175
All Hail the Regent 184
Tips for Treasure Houses 200
In Search of Jane Austen 220
Ancient Sites 232
Hardy's Dorset 250
The Jurassic Coast 255
All About Arthur 283
Bath's Georgian Architecture 399
Arts and Crafts in the Cotswolds 417
Visiting Cotswold Gardens 420
Antiques & Markets 423
That Special Cotswold Stone 429
The Venice of the North 451
Cottonopolis 491
Beatles Discovered and
    Rediscovered 505
Stoke-on-Trent: The Potteries 511
Well Dressing 517
What's Real about Real Ale? 548
Poetry, Prose & the Lakes 551
Festivals & Folk Sports 556
Punting on the Cam 579
Introducing Fens & Broads 601
Popular Paths 602
Over Hills & Dales 631
The Monastic Past 646
Whitby Jet 653
All Aboard: Steam Railways 702
The Language of Cymru 718

CONTENTS

MAPS

England 10–11
London's Top Sights 38–39
London Postal Districts 40
Westminster & Royal London 43
Soho & Covent Garden 53
Bloomsbury & Legal London 57
The City 63
The South Bank 70
Kensington, Knightsbridge & Mayfair .77
Where to Eat in London 86–87
Where to Stay in London 106–107
London Shopping 140–141
The Southeast 160–161
Canterbury 162
Brighton 182
The South 214–215
Winchester 216
Salisbury 231
The West Country 266–267
Plymouth 300
Exeter 312
The Thames Valley 326–327
Oxford 339

Shakespeare Country 366
Stratford-upon-Avon 368
Bath Environs 394
Bath 396
The Cotswolds 409
The Forest of Dean 434
The Welsh Borders 450
Birmingham 452
Shrewsbury 472
Lancashire & the Peaks 490
Manchester 492
Liverpool 502
The Lake District 530–531
East Anglia 568–569
Cambridge .570
Norwich 597
Lincolnshire 607
Yorkshire 620–621
York 638
The Northeast 668
Durham 670
Wales .698–699
Cardiff 725

ABOUT THIS BOOK

Our Ratings

Sometimes you find terrific travel experiences and sometimes they just find you. But usually the burden is on you to select the right combination of experiences. That's where our ratings come in.

As travelers we've all discovered a place so wonderful that its worthiness is obvious. And sometimes superlatives don't do that place justice: you just have to be there to know. These sights, properties, and experiences get our highest rating, **Fodor's Choice,** indicated by orange stars throughout this book.

Black stars highlight sights and properties we deem **Highly Recommended,** places that our writers, editors, and readers praise again and again for consistency and excellence.

There's another category: any place we include in this book is by definition worth your time, unless we say otherwise. And we will.

Disagree with any of our choices? Care to nominate a place or suggest that we rate one more highly? Visit our feedback center at www. fodors.com/feedback.

Budget Well

Hotel and restaurant price categories from £ to £££££ are defined in the opening pages of each chapter. For attractions, we always give standard adult admission fees; reductions are usually available for children, students, and senior citizens. Want to pay with plastic? **AE, DC, MC, V** following restaurant and hotel listings indicate if American Express, Diner's Club, MasterCard, and Visa are accepted.

Restaurants

Unless we state otherwise, restaurants are open for lunch and dinner daily. We mention dress only when there's a specific requirement and reservations only when they're essential or not accepted—it's always best to book ahead.

Hotels

Hotels have private bath, phone, TV, and air-conditioning and operate on the European Plan (aka EP, meaning without meals), unless we specify that they use the Continental Plan (CP, with a continental breakfast), Breakfast Plan (BP, with a full breakfast), or Modified American Plan (MAP, with breakfast and dinner). We always list

facilities but not whether you'll be charged an extra fee to use them, so when pricing accommodations, find out what's included.

Many Listings
★ Fodor's Choice
★ Highly recommended
⊠ Physical address
♦ Directions
🏛 Mailing address
☎ Telephone
🖶 Fax
⊕ On the Web
✉ E-mail
🎫 Admission fee
☉ Open/closed times
► Start of itinerary
Ⓤ Underground (tube)
▭ Credit cards

Hotels & Restaurants
🛏 Hotel
🛌 Number of rooms
♨ Facilities
🍽 Meal plans
✕ Restaurant
🪑 Reservations
🏛 Dress code
↘ Smoking
🍷 BYOB
✕🛏 Hotel with restaurant that warrants a visit

Other
☺ Family-friendly
🔖 Contact information
⇨ See also
⊠ Branch address
☞ Take note

England, Great Britain, the United Kingdom—what's the difference? England is the largest part of Great Britain, which also includes Wales and Scotland. In fact these are three countries; Wales and Scotland have their own parliaments, with different degrees of self-government. Add Northern Ireland, and you have the political entity known as the United Kingdom, with its capital of London.

LONDON

The heart and soul of modern Britain, London is not just the nation's financial and governmental center but one of the world's great capitals. Because of that, you already know some of what to expect—mammoth museums, posh palaces, double-decker buses, iconic sights such as Big Ben and Westminster Abbey—and you won't be disappointed. But it's impossible to overlook the modern city melded with the historic one, and there are more harried commuters, noisy traffic, endless litter, and petty crime than you might expect. This is a great, rambling metropolis, and for all London's faults and high costs, the atmosphere is undeniably exhilarating, created by the presence of so many theaters, universities, powerhouse corporations, and a vast multinational population in excess of 8 million people, all scattered among villagelike neighborhoods with distinct personalities. Leicester Square is packed with tourists, Knightsbridge is populated by millionaires, Bloomsbury is filled with intellectuals, and on Fleet Street you can't swing a briefcase without hitting a lawyer. London is big, overwhelming, and cacophonous—just as it should be.

THE SOUTHEAST

The place where William the Conqueror first set foot when he arrived from France to claim the nation and build strongholds all over England, this compact green and pleasant region southeast of London stretches out to the coast. For Londoners, the area can seem all one big suburb, but for you it's much more than that. There's funky Brighton by the sea, with its artsy vibe, good restaurants, and legendary nightlife scene, all of which are largely incongruous in this area that otherwise too often languishes in the grip of chain restaurants and small, rural pubs. Still, who needs to eat when there's so much to do? You could be wandering through the medieval castles of Bodiam, Leeds, and Hever; pondering the fate of Thomas à Becket at Canterbury Cathedral; or getting gardening tips at Sissinghurst and other noted beauty spots. Around Tunbridge Wells are a cluster of historic homes, from medieval Ightham Mote to

Elizabethan Penshurst Place. It's so close to London that much of the area is day-trip material.

THE SOUTH

Here, in the counties of Hampshire, Dorset, and Wiltshire, begins the quintessential English countryside of gentle hills, green pastures, small towns, and peace and quiet. Jane Austen and Thomas Hardy are among the writers who found inspiration here, and literary pilgrims follow in their footsteps. The only cities of any size—Portsmouth and Southampton—are largely uninspiring except for some great museums such as the Portsmouth Historic Dockyard, so don't come here if you're looking for an urban scene. Instead, wonder at the mysterious stone circles of Avebury and Stonehenge, and take in the bustling towns of Winchester and Salisbury, with their imposing cathedrals. Out in the countryside, grand manors—such as Stourhead, Wilton House, and Longleat with its safari park—offer imposing evidence of the ambitions of their builders. At the area's southernmost edge, the rolling hills turn into the flat seaside landscape of Dorset, packed with Britons on holiday in the summertime, and the fossil-rich Jurassic Coast.

THE WEST COUNTRY

In poll after poll, the southwestern peninsula counties of Somerset, Devon, and Cornwall are where most Britons say they would like to live. It's easy to see why: ocean currents keep the area sunnier and warmer than the rest of the country, and many of the beaches are sandy, rather than rocky. The waves bring in the surfers, and with them comes a distinctly un-English, no-worries lifestyle, particularly in Cornwall, with its artsy coastal villages. Miles of quiet countryside are dotted with only a few pretty towns, including Wells and Exeter, and the vibrant city of Bristol, which has all the modern restaurants and good nightlife that much of the rest of the region lacks. Beyond the towns are green hills and the brooding heaths and moors of Exmoor and Dartmoor, punctuated with enigmatic stone circles and rocky outroppings that attract hikers and horseback riders.

THE THAMES VALLEY

This is bedroom-community central for Londoners, with the home-improvement stores, giant supermarkets, and real-estate agencies that come with that territory, but this is England, so the suburbs include pretty medieval towns like Windsor, where, alongside hordes of commoners, the Queen also spends most of her time (she doesn't much like Buckingham Palace, they

England

WHAT'S WHERE

say). Then there are the soaring golden spires of Oxford, which can be seen for miles in the flat countryside around that busy but lovely university town with its small rivers, excellent pubs, and bookish locals. Given the beauty of the landscape and the area's proximity to London, the area is a popular weekend escape, with good restaurants and prices to match. It's unsurprising, too, that there are plenty of stately homes, so you can explore the lives of the rich and famous at places like the over-the-top baroque Blenheim Palace.

SHAKESPEARE COUNTRY

To be fair, this is a beautiful area despite being serious tourist turf. Stratford-upon-Avon is a leafy, literary, theatrical town 100 mi north of London, and it's worth braving the tour groups and cheesy souvenir shops, particularly for anyone who loves Shakespeare. Beware: you can overdose in fairly short order. You can wander through Shakespeare's Birthplace, catch his plays at the Royal Shakespeare Theatre, stock up on his works in local bookshops, drink in Shakespeare-theme pubs . . . it never seems to end. Escape, after a while, to Warwickshire, for gentle landscape dotted with thatch-roof cottages, sleepy villages, and some noted manor houses. If that's too peaceful, you might prefer a fortress—battlemented Warwick Castle and ruined Kenilworth Castle should suffice.

BATH & THE COTSWOLDS

Pretty as a picture, the famous Cotswolds region is a small gem filled with tranquil villages, adorable golden stone cottages with neat-as-a-pin gardens, dignified churches, posh antiques shops, and salt-of-the-earth country folk keeping it all preserved in aspic. It's beautiful, but it may come to look somewhat the same: the perfect villages—Chipping Campden, Upper Slaughter, Bourton-on-the-Water—can blur together once you've soaked up all the tea and scones you've ever wanted. At that point, it's time to head to bustling Bath, which will seem like a metropolis after all those village greens. It's actually a grand Georgian town, with visible Roman history in the ruins of the mineral-spring baths, glorious 18th- and 19th-century architecture created with the local stone, and a few decent restaurants. Beyond the obvious sights, there are treasures all around here, including Hidcote Manor Gardens, Snowshill Manor, and Chastleton House.

THE WELSH BORDERS

The hills and valleys of Shropshire, Herefordshire, and Cheshire are England's breadbasket, with endless farms. This area bordering Wales has some of the country's loveliest countryside

	but it's not an exciting place, with little in the way of real sights, except for the worthwhile Industrial Revolution museums of Ironbridge Gorge. Instead, come here to get away from it all and spend a few days walking the countryside or sitting under a tree reading a book. There are a few distractions: elegant Ludlow has half-timber buildings (and excellent restaurants), and gentle Shrewsbury, with its churches and medieval buildings, is a marvelous place to spend an afternoon. Chester can pack in the tourist crowds. At the eastern edge of the area is big, multicultural Birmingham, a draw only for those interested in a modern urban experience. The city continues to press its cultural strengths—art museums, music, dance—and redeem its ugly postwar architecture with redevelopment.
LANCASHIRE & THE PEAKS 	This region contains two of England's biggest, grittiest cities, which have fans as well as detractors but are not at the top of many visitors' lists. It also has some glorious, well-known countryside and stately homes, making for two very different experiences. Liverpool still rides the coattails of the Beatles but may be breaking free a bit, since, like nearby Manchester, it has transformed some of its old docks and warehouses into interesting museums, modern malls, sleek hotels, restaurants, and condominiums. Both cities are known for buzzing nightlife, and their restaurant scenes are steadily improving, although this is still not a culinary center. In contrast, to the east are the vistas, both gentle and rugged, of the Peak District, as well as the quiet loveliness of the Wye Valley. Walkers and hikers can spend days going from village to village. Chatsworth, Haddon Hall, and Hardwick Hall, famous houses but very different from one another, are an additional draw.
THE LAKE DISTRICT 	Bordered by Scotland and the waters of Solway Firth, Morecambe Bay, and the Irish Sea, this is a startlingly beautiful area of craggy hills, wild moorland, stone cottages, and glittering silvery lakes. As you go north, the scenery becomes even more dramatic. The Lake District, now a national park, has drawn seekers of beauty since 19th-century poets and writers including William Wordsworth first made it famous. The area's enormous popularity with nature lovers and hikers means that you must head off the map to avoid crowds in summer. Still, it's the kind of place where you will chase sheep out of the road at some point, and that's part of its draw, along with literary links. High points are Wordsworth's homes at Rydal,

WHAT'S WHERE

	Grasmere, and Cockermouth, John Ruskin's abode at Coniston, and Beatrix Potter's tiny house near Hawkshead. Just don't expect sunshine—on average it rains 250 days each year.
EAST ANGLIA 	Parts of this rural, generally flat region (some find it boring) are becoming far-flung outposts of London, as city types head to Suffolk and Norfolk for homes and weekend retreats, lured by unspoiled coastline on the North Sea and leafy small towns. For visitors, the biggest lure remains Cambridge, a possible day-trip from London. You can hire a boat and go punting on the River Cam—the students will tease you if you struggle—after you explore the medieval halls of learning. Out in the countryside are the glorious cathedrals of Ely and Norwich and time-warp towns such as Tudor Lavenham and 18th-century King's Lynn, along with a few notable stately piles such as Norfolk's Holkham Hall. Londoners have encouraged the growth of quality gastro-pubs and restaurants, so you can feed your stomach as well as your eyes when you explore the peaceful Suffolk vistas immortalized by Gainsborough and Constable.
YORKSHIRE 	A wilder part of England in the north, Yorkshire is large and varied, with more appeal for lovers of the outdoors than for urban sophisticates. The ancient walled city of York, with magnificent Gothic York Minster, is deservedly prime tourist territory; nearby is Castle Howard, one of Britain's finest stately homes. Farther north are the rugged North York Moors, with the ruins of Rievaulx Abbey (Yorkshire has superb monastic remains) and irresistible villages like Hutton-le-Hole, beloved by hikers. The moors collide with the sea in spectacular fashion in places like Whitby and Robin's Head Bay. On the landlocked side of Yorkshire are the moors and dales that inspired the Brontë sisters and continue to delight walkers. Also here are the Georgian spa town of Harrogate and the revitalized former industrial city of Leeds, worth a stop if you're interested in urban revival.
THE NORTHEAST	The section of England that borders Scotland is so wild and empty that there's little to see except the spectacular countryside. This is relatively unvisited country, except for a few key sites, but some people find this remoteness appealing. You can walk or bike in the footsteps of Roman soldiers along the sturdy length of Hadrian's Wall. Slightly younger, but still old and awesome, are the castles that stand guard on the stark Northumberland coastline, including Bamburgh and Dunstanburgh.

With its winding streets and stone cathedral, Durham is a popular, perfectly preserved medieval city—in contrast with strikingly modern Newcastle. The region's liveliest city, formerly industrial Newcastle is virtually the only place in this region with lots of restaurants and bars.

WALES

Clinging to the western edge of England, Wales is green and ruggedly beautiful, with mountainous inland scenery reaching out to a magnificent coastline. With the exception of the engaging capital, Cardiff, and the tough, industrial city of Swansea (where Dylan Thomas lived and wrote), this is an entirely rural region with more sheep than people, and one more low-key and less visited except for certain beauty spots. It's worth seeking out if you appreciate things as different as bucolic market towns, industrial heritage sights, and country inns. Wales has three stunning national parks: Snowdonia, with its foot-path-beribboned mountain heights; Pembrokeshire Coast, with ocean views; and Brecon Beacons, with its windswept heights. The country is properly famous for its castles, reminders of turbulent times, including Conwy and Caernarfon. On the coast are picturesque Victorian seaside resort towns including Aberystwyth, where you can catch one of Wales's noted steam trains.

QUINTESSENTIAL ENGLAND

Pints & Pubs

Pop in for a pint at a pub to encounter what has been the center—literally the "public house"—of English social life for centuries. The basic pub recipe calls for a variety of beers on draft—dark creamy stouts like Guinness; bitter, including brews such as Tetley's and Bass; and lager, the blondest and blandest of the trio—a dart board, oak paneling, and paisley carpets. Throw in a bunch of young suits in London, a generous dash of undergrads in places such as Oxford or Cambridge, and, in rural areas, a healthy helping of blokes around the television and ladies in the corner sipping their *halves* (half pints) and having a *natter* (gossip). In smaller pubs, listen in and enjoy the banter among the regulars—you may even be privy to the occasional *barney* (harmless argument). Join in if you care to, but remember not to take anything too seriously—a severe breach of pub etiquette.

Make your visit soon: the encroachment of gastro-pubs (an ever-expanding variety of bar-restaurant hybrids) is just one of the forces challenging traditional pub culture.

Daily Rags

To blend in with the English, stash your street map, slide a folded newspaper under your arm, and head for the nearest park bench or café. Lose yourself in any one of the 11 national dailies, some now being published in tabloid size, for often well-written insight into Britain's worldview. For a dose of tabloid melodrama, choose the *Sun*, Britain's most popular newspaper. The sensational headlines are hard to miss—"Prince's Cheating Scandal" and "Empire Strikes Bark: Dogs Dress Up as Vader"—and you can safely assume that the topless model on Page 3 has helped rather than hindered the paper's success. The bi-weekly *Private Eye* offers British wit at its

If you want to get a sense of contemporary England culture, and indulge in some of its pleasures, start by familiarizing yourself with the rituals of daily life. Here are a few highlights—things you can take part in with relative ease.

best, specializing in political cartoons, punchy parodies, and satirical reporting.

A Lovely Cuppa

For almost four centuries, the English and tea have been immersed in a love affair passionate enough to survive revolutions, rations, tariffs, and lattes, but also soothing, as whistling kettles across the nation mark moments of quiet comfort in public places and in homes and offices. The ritual known as "afternoon tea" had its beginnings in the early 19th century, in the private chambers of the duchess of Bedford, where she and her "ladies of leisure" indulged in afternoons of pastries and fragrant blends. But you don't need to dress up to lift your pinky to sip the steamy brew. Department stores and tearooms across the nation offer everything from simple tea and biscuits to shockingly overpriced spreads with sandwiches and cakes that would impress even the duchess herself. And if tea is not your cup of tea, don't worry; there's no shame for those who prefer coffee with their scones and clotted cream.

Sports Fever

Whoever says England is not an overtly religious country has failed to consider the cult of sports mania that has descended on the land. Whether water events (such as Henley, Cowes, and the Head of the River Race) or a land competition (the Grand National steeplechase, the Flora London Marathon), most bring people to the edge of their seats—or more often the living room couch, thanks to satellite television. To partake in the rite, you'll need Pimm's (*the* drink for swank spectators of the Henley Royal Regatta) or beer (*the* drink for most everything else). You may experience the exhilaration yourself—which, you'll probably sense, is not for the love of a sport, but for the love of *sport* itself.

IF YOU LIKE

Castles & Stately Homes

Exploring the diversity and magnificence of England's castles and stately homes, from Norman towers to Palladian palaces, can occupy most of a blissful vacation. Whether world-famous or less-visited, owned by royalty, aristocratic families, or the National Trust, each abode has tales to tell about history or domestic life. Castles and houses are spread around the nation (with fewer stately homes in Cornwall and the Lake District), but certain clusters may help your planning. Note that most stately homes are open only from spring through fall. England's southeastern coast is lined with sturdy castles; nearby but inland, around Royal Tunbridge Wells, are treasure houses such as Hever Castle and Knole. West of Salisbury are Wilton House, Stourhead, and Longleat, and the Cotswolds have a rich assortment. England's north has gems from Peak District manors to castles on the remote northeastern coast. London visitors won't miss out, either: Buckingham and Kensington palaces, the Tower of London, and Hampton Court Palace and Windsor Castle lie within easy reach. If your itinerary extends to Wales, look for Edward I's "iron ring" of castles, including Harlech and Conwy.

- **Blenheim Palace, Thames Valley.** A baroque extravaganza touted as England's only rival to Versailles, this pile is the home of the 11th duke of Marlborough.

- **Holkham Hall, East Anglia.** A splendid 60-foot tall marble entryway and salons filled with old masters distinguish this Palladian palace.

- **Petworth House, the Southeast.** One of the National Trust's greatest treasure houses shows off magnificent art from Gainsborough and J. M. W. Turner.

Charming Villages

Year after year, armies of tourists with images of green meadows, thatched roofs, and colorful flowerbeds flock to England's countryside, for good reason. Most will find their way to famously adorable towns along the Thames, magical seaside resorts in the West Country, and a smattering of fairy-tale hamlets in the Cotswolds—a hilly area in west-central England renowned for its golden and gray stone cottages. However, torrential tourist traffic has made these once-quintessentially quaint areas a little *too* accessible for some. Steer clear of busy Cotswolds towns such as Broadway in summer (especially on weekends); Winchcombe and Snowshill are more unspoiled options. Choose a weekday to visit the Thames Valley towns, which attract Londoners. To avoid some crowds, consider the pastoral flatlands of East Anglia beyond Cambridge, where historic villages remain relatively undiscovered, or explore the Norfolk coast. The rural Welsh Borders region has tranquil landscapes and towns, or head to Wales, with its mountainside hamlets and sleepy seaside resorts.

- **Lavenham, East Anglia.** This village is full of perfectly preserved Tudor buildings, the former houses of wool merchants and weavers.

- **Ludlow, Welsh Borders.** Great restaurants and medieval and Georgian buildings cluster below a castle in this peaceful town.

- **Whitby, Yorkshire.** A ruined abbey and a cliff-lined harbor combine with a rich fishing and whaling legacy to enhance this coastal gem.

Glorious Gardens

Despite being cursed with impertinent weather and short summers, English gardeners will gladly grab a gardening tool and attack a misbehaving rose garden for just a few short months of enjoyment. The Tudors were the first to produce gardens that were more than strictly utilitarian, and since then French, Italian, Dutch, and even Japanese ideas have been imported and adapted to suit the national aesthetic. A pilgrimage to a garden is an essential part of any spring or summer trip, whether you visit a large educational garden such as Kew Gardens near London or the West Country's Eden Project; a period gem such as Arts-and-Crafts Hidcote Manor in the Cotswolds; or gardens that are part of a stately home and as lovely as the house. Green havens thrive all over England, but perhaps the most fertile hunting grounds are in Oxfordshire, Gloucestershire (including the Cotswolds), and Kent (the "Garden of England"). Some of these visions of paradise have limited hours, and most close in winter; they're all worth the trip.

- **Sissinghurst Castle Garden, Southeast.** Vita Sackville-West's masterpiece, set within the remains of a Tudor castle, is busy in summer but also spectacular in autumn.

- **Stourhead, South.** One of the country's most impressive house-and-garden combinations is an artful 18th-century sanctuary with a tranquil lake, colorful shrubs, and grottoes.

- **Wisley, Southeast.** The Royal Horticultural Society's garden splendidly blends the pretty and the practical in its inspirational displays.

Urban Action

London has everything a world capital should have—rich culture and history, thrilling art and theater scenes, world-class restaurants and sensational shopping—along with crowds, traffic, and high prices. It shouldn't be missed, but if you appreciate modern cities, fall out of the tourist trap and spend time in some of England's reviving urban centers, including those in its former industrial heartland, where blossoming multiculturalism has paved the way for a unique vibe. Football (soccer) fans might take in a match in Manchester or Liverpool, two bitter sporting rivals in the Northwest, or join hordes of fans to watch the game at a local pub. Manchester's museums are excellent, and its downtown (rebuilt after a 1996 IRA bombing) is worth a look, as are its famous clubs. Liverpool claims the Beatles sites but also the stellar museums of the Albert Dock; it's transforming itself for a stint as the European Union's Capital of Culture in 2008. See what's gentrifying in large, somewhat unlovely Birmingham, a cultural force in England.

- **Brighton, Southeast.** Bold, bright, and boisterous are the words to describe a seaside charmer that has everything from the dazzling Royal Pavilion to the trendy shops of the Lanes.

- **Bristol, West Country.** With its lively waterfront and homegrown music talent, this youthful city has vibrant nightlife as well as a long history.

- **Leeds, Yorkshire.** Another northern, former industrial city polishing its Victorian buildings, Leeds is known for its shopping arcades and youthful music scene.

IF YOU LIKE

Ancient Mysteries

Stone circles as well as ancient stone and earthen forts and mounds offer tantalizing hints about Britain's mysterious prehistoric inhabitants. The country's southwestern landscape, particularly the Salisbury Plain, Dorset, and the eastern side of Cornwall, has a notably rich concentration of these sites, perplexing mysteries that human nature compels us to try to solve. Stonehenge, the stone circle begun 5,000 years ago, stands on the wide Salisbury Plain; crowds detract from the magic, so arrive early or late to appreciate the monument's timeless power. Hypotheses about its purpose range from the scientific (ancient calendar) to the fantastic (a gift from extinct giants). Other relics—chambered tombs and mounds—dot the Avebury area to the north. Equally enigmatic are Maiden Castle, a colossal prehistoric hill fort near Dorchester, and the nearby figure of a giant carved into the hillside overlooking Cerne Abbas. Sometimes the setting of these ancient creations, such as Castlerigg Stone Circle in the Lake District, is as awesome as the surviving remains.

- **Stanton Drew Circles, West Country.** Use your imagination to visualize the vast size of the two avenues of standing stones, three rings, and burial chamber that now lie in a field.

- **Avebury Stone Circles, South.** Large and marvelously evocative, these circles surround part of the village of Avebury.

- **Vale of the White Horse, Thames Valley.** The gigantic horse here was actually carved into the chalky hillside around 1750BC.

Wonderful Walks

Britain seems to be designed with walking in mind—footpaths wind through the contours of the landscape, and popular routes are well-endowed with cozy bed-and-breakfasts and pubs. Your decisions will be what kind of landscape you prefer (coast or countryside, flat or mountainous) and how long a hike you want, though you can often do just part of a long-distance trail such as the Thames Path. Ramble through one of England's national parks (which are sprinkled with towns), and you'll generally find well-maintained trails and handy maps at local tourist information centers. The country's most famous walking spots are in the Lake District, from a short meander to a major mountain trek—but beware of summer congestion. Yorkshire's dales and moors are also popular. Cross the border to Wales, where the Brecon Beacons offer windswept uplands with easy paths, and ferocious peaks in Snowdonia National Park promise challenging hikes. Wherever you hike, always be prepared for storms or fogs.

- **Borrowdale, Lake District.** Have a color-pencil kit handy to capture the beauty of the dramatically verdant valleys and jagged peaks.

- **Peak District, Lancashire & the Peaks.** Its rocky outcrops and vaulting meadows make some people say this is the country's most beautiful national park.

- **South West Coast Path, West Country.** Spectacular is the word for the 630-mi trail that winds from Minehead in Somerset to Poole Harbour in Dorset.

Theater

There's no better antidote to an overdose of stately homes and glorious gardens than a face-to-face encounter with another British specialty, the theater. London is the heart and soul of the action: here, companies famous and lesser-known consistently churn out superb productions, from musicals and monologues to comedies and avant-garde dramas. Be sure to sample theater outside London, wherever you travel. Previews of the capital's productions often take place in Lincoln's Theatre Royal, and the Stephen Joseph Theatre in Yorkshire premieres Alan Ayckbourn's plays. Stratford-upon-Avon may be the Bard's hometown, but festivals all over the country celebrate Shakespeare's work—the best are the Ludlow Festival in the Welsh Borders and London's Shakespeare Under the Stars at Regent's Park. Brighton Dome and Windsor's Theatre Royal specialize in pantomime—theatrical entertainment with puppetry, slapstick, and music. Theatrical arts are often a major component of English festivals: see musicals at the Exeter Festival (West Country) and street theater at the Harrogate International Festival (Yorkshire). Try a university production; you may see the next big star.

- **Minack Theatre, West Country.** This open-air theater in coastal Cornwall, near Land's End and Penzance, nuzzles the slope of a sandy cliff.

- **Royal Shakespeare Theatre, Shakespeare Country.** Seeing any play by the Bard performed in his hometown is a treat.

- **Yvonne Arnaud Theatre, Guildford, the Southeast.** The productions at this theater on an island often travel to London.

Country-House Hotels

In all their luxurious glory, country-house hotels are an essential part of the English landscape, particularly in the southern part of the country. Whether you choose a converted castle, Elizabethan manor, or neoclassical retreat, these are places to indulge yourself and escape, however briefly (most are pricey), most realities of modern life. Some hotels are traditional in style, with flowery fabrics and polished wood furniture; a newer breed juxtaposes modern design with the traditional architecture. At some hotels, spas and sports—and even, alas, meeting facilities—are becoming more elaborate, but service is less stuffy. If you can't spend a night, consider just having dinner; notable chefs are turning up in more hotel kitchens. In the Thames Valley, dress up for dinner at Hartwell House or indulge in French cuisine at Le Manoir aux Quat' Saisons. The West Country's concentration includes Bovey Castle and Gidleigh Park in Dartmoor National Park, and the Cotswolds are prime ground for these retreats. One tip: before you reserve, ask if a wedding party will be using the hotel during your stay; these can take over a smaller establishment.

- **Cliveden, Thames Valley.** Live like Lord Astor for a night, taking in his palatial parlors and riverfront gardens.

- **Middlethorpe Hall, Yorkshire.** This handsome, superbly restored 18th-century mansion looks like a Gainsborough painting come to life.

- **Victoria at Holkham, East Anglia.** In the shadow of stately Holkham Hall, this Eastern-inspired hideaway provides a colorful seaside escape.

GREAT ITINERARIES

BEST OF ENGLAND: UNFORGETTABLE IMAGES 12 DAYS

London

Day 1. The capital is just the jumping-off point for this trip, so choose a few highlights that grab your interest. If it's the Changing of the Guard at Buckingham Palace, check the time to be sure you catch the pageantry. If Westminster Abbey appeals to your sense of history, arrive as early as you can. Pick a museum (many are free, so you needn't linger), whether it's the National Gallery on Trafalgar Square, the British Museum in Bloomsbury, or a smaller gem like the Queen's Gallery. Stroll Hyde Park or take a boat ride on the Thames before you find a pub or Indian restaurant for dinner. End with a play; the experience of theatergoing may be as interesting as whatever work you see.

Windsor & Cliveden

Day 2. Resplendent with centuries of treasures, Windsor Castle is favored by the Queen, and has been by rulers for centuries. Tour it to appreciate the history and wealth of the monarchy. The State Apartments are open if the Queen is not in residence, and 10 kings and queens are buried in magnificent St. George's Chapel. Time permitting, take a walk in the adjacent Great Park. If you want to live like a duke for a night, head up the valley to Cliveden, the Thames Valley's most spectacular hotel.

Logistics: Trains depart Paddington and Waterloo stations twice hourly and take less than one hour. Green Line buses depart High Street Kensington or Hyde Park Corner.

Salisbury & Stourhead

Day 3. Visible for miles around, Salisbury Cathedral's soaring spire is an unforgettable image of rural England. See the Magna Carta in the cathedral's Chapter House as you explore this marvel of medieval engineering, and walk the town path to get the view John Constable painted. Pay an afternoon visit to Stourhead to experience a grand Palladian mansion and the finest example of the naturalistic 18th-century landscaping for which England is famous.

Logistics: For trains to Salisbury, head back to London's Clapham Junction to catch a train on the Portsmouth line.

Bath & Stonehenge

Day 4. Bath's immaculately preserved, golden-stone Georgian architecture helps you recapture the late 18th century. Take time to stroll; don't miss the Royal Crescent (No. 1 may be open, allowing you to view a period interior), and sip the Pump Room's vile-tasting water as Jane Austen's characters might have. The Roman Baths are an amazing survivor of the ancient empire, complete with curses left by soldiers. There's plenty to do in Bath (museums, shopping, theater), but you might make an excursion to Stonehenge. Go early or late to avoid the worst crowds at Stonehenge, and use your imagination to appreciate this enigma.

Logistics: Trains and buses leave hourly from Salisbury to Bath.

The Cotswolds

Day 5. Antiques-shop in fairy-tale Stow-on-the-Wold and feed the ducks at the brook in Lower Slaughter for a taste of the mel-

low stone villages and dreamy green landscapes for which the area is beloved. Choose a rainy or off-season day to visit Broadway or risk jams of tourist traffic.

Logistics: Drive to make the best of the beautiful scenery. Alternatively, opt for a guided tour bus.

Oxford & Blenheim Palace

Day 6. Join a two-hour guided tour of Oxford's glorious quadrangles, chapels, and gardens to get the best access to these centuries-old academic treasures. This leaves time for a jaunt to Blenheim, a unique combination of baroque opulence (inside and out) and gorgeous parkland. For a classic Oxford experience, join students in pub crawling around Jericho, the hopping nightlife district.

Logistics: Hourly trains depart Bath for Oxford. Buses frequently depart Oxford's Gloucester Green for Blenheim Palace.

Stratford-upon-Avon

Day 7. Skip this stop if you don't care about you-know-who. Fans of Shakespeare can see his birthplace and Anne Hathaway's Cottage (walking there is a delight), then top it all off with a memorable performance at the Royal Shakespeare Theatre. Start the day early and be prepared for crowds.

Logistics: From Oxford there are direct trains and more frequent Stagecoach bus service.

Shrewsbury to Chester

Day 8. Head north to see the half-timber buildings of Shrewsbury, one of the best-preserved of England's Tudor towns. Strolling is the best way to experience it. In Chester the architecture is more or less the same (though not always authentic), but the Rows, a series of two-story shops with medieval crypts beneath, and the fine City Walls are sights you can't pass by.

Logistics: For Shrewsbury, change trains at Birmingham. The train ride to Chester is 55 minutes.

The Lake District

Days 9–10. In the area extending north beyond Kendal and Windermere, explore the English lakes on foot. This area is jam-packed with hikers in summer and on weekends, so rent a car to seek out the more isolated routes. Take a cruise on Windermere or Coniston Water, or rent a boat. If you have time for one Wordsworth-linked site, head to Dove Cottage; you can even have afternoon tea there.

Logistics: Train to Liverpool, with a switch in either Windermere and Oxenholme.

GREAT ITINERARIES

York

Day 11. This historic cathedral city is crammed with 15th- and 16th-century buildings, but don't miss York Minster and the medieval streets of the Shambles. Take in the Castle Museum; have tea at Betty's or unwind at a pub.

Logistics: By train, switch in Carlisle and Newcastle for the four-hour journey. Buses take twice as long.

Cambridge

Day 12. Spend the afternoon touring King's College Chapel and the Backs—gardens and sprawling meadows—and punting skills on the River Cam.

Logistics: For train service, switch at Leeds and again at Peterborough or Stevenage. Trains leave Cambridge for London frequently.

TIPS

❶ Train travelers should keep in mind that regional "Rovers" and "Rangers" offer unlimited train travel in 1-day, 3-day or weeklong increments. See www.nationalrail.co.uk/promotions/ for details. Also check out BritRail passes, which must be purchased before your trip.

❷ Buses are time-consuming, but more scenic and cheaper than train travel. National Express offers funfares—fares to and from London to 31 cities (including Cambridge) as low as £1 if booked more than 24 hrs in advance. Or check out low-cost Megabus.

❸ To cut the tour short, consider skipping Wales and proceed to the Lake District from Chester on Day 9. Likewise, you can forgo a visit to Cambridge if you opt for Oxford. You can add the time to your London stay.

❹ It's easy to visit Stonehenge from Salisbury, as well as from Bath.

❺ Buy theater tickets well in advance for Stratford.

STATELY HOMES & LANDSCAPES TOUR
11 DAYS

Hampton Court Palace

Day 1. Start your trip royally at this palace a half-hour from London. It's two treasures in one: a Tudor palace with magnificent baroque additions by Christopher Wren. As you walk through cobbled courtyards, Henry VIII's State Apartments and the enormous kitchens, you may feel like you've been whisked back to the days of the Tudors and William and Mary. A quiet stroll through the 60 acres of immaculate gardens—the sculpted yews look like green gumdrops—is recommended. Be sure to get lost in the 18th-century maze—if it's open (diligent maintenance leads to occasional closures).

Logistics: Tube to Richmond, then bus R68; or catch the train from Waterloo to Hampton Court Station.

Knole & Ightham Mote

Days 2–3. Clustered around Royal Tunbridge Wells south of London is the highest concentration of stately homes in England, and, as if that weren't enough, the surrounding fields of hops and colorful orchards are often wrapped in clouds of mist, creating a picture-perfect scene. We've picked two very different homes to visit, leaving you plenty of time to tour at a leisurely pace. Knole, Vita Sackville-West's sprawling childhood home, has dark, baroque rooms and a famous set of silver furniture. Ightham Mote, a moated house, is a vision from the Middle Ages. Its rooms are an ideal guide to style changes from the Tudor to Victorian eras. Spend the evening at one of the many good restaurants in Royal Tunbridge Wells.

Logistics: Take the Hastings-bound train from London's Charing Cross to Tunbridge Wells, then the bus to Knole. There is no public transportation to Ightham Mote.

Petworth House

Day 4. Priceless paintings by Gainsborough, Reynolds, and Turner (19 by Turner alone) embellish the august rooms of Petworth House, present-day home to Lord and Lady Egremont and one of the National Trust's treasures. Check out Capability Brown's 700-acre deer park or the Victorian kitchens, and for the perfect lunch, peruse the offerings in the winding lanes of Petworth town. Head to Chichester for the evening, along a route passing through the rolling grasslands and deep valleys of the South Downs.

Logistics: Train to Chichester, switching in Redhill, then bus to Petworth.

Wilton House

Day 5. Base yourself in Salisbury for two days, taking time to see the famous cathedral and to walk the town path for the best view of it. Visit neoclassical Wilton House first, where the exquisite Double Cube Room contains a spectacular family portrait by Van Dyck and gilded furniture that accommodated Eisenhower when he contemplated the Normandy invasion here. On your way back make a detour to Stonehenge to view the wide-open Salisbury Plain and ponder the enigmatic stones.

GREAT ITINERARIES

Logistics: Take a train from Chichester, with a switch in Cosham; then bus it to Wilton House.

Stourhead to Longleat House

Day 6. Day-trip west to Stourhead, to experience perhaps the most stunning house-garden combination in Europe, and either spend the day here (climb Alfred's Tower for a grand view of the house), or leave some time for nearby Longleat House—a vast, treasure-stuffed Italian Renaissance palace complete with safari park and a devilish maze. Once back in Salisbury, relax in one of New Street's many cafés.

Logistics: Bus to Warminster for Longleat; for Stourhead, take the train to Gillingham from Salisbury.

Blenheim Palace

Day 7. Home of the dukes of Marlborough and birthplace of Winston Churchill, Blenheim Palace uniquely combines exquisitely designed parklands (save time to walk) and one of the most ornate baroque structures in the world. After your visit, have afternoon tea at Blenheim Tea Rooms in adorable Woodstock. Overnight in Oxford; do your own pub crawl.

Logistics: From Salisbury, change at Bath or Basingstoke for Oxford, then catch a bus to Blenheim.

Snowshill Manor & Sudeley Castle

Days 8–9. Here you can take in the idyllic Cotswold landscape, a magical mix of greenery and mellow stone cottages and ancient churches (built with wool-trade money), along with some famous buildings. Spend the first night in Broadway to explore nearby Snowshill Manor—with its delightfully eccentric collection of Tibetan scrolls, Persian lamps, and samurai armor—

in the unspoiled village of Snowshill. If you have a car, don't linger in busy Broadway. Instead, head to Chipping Campden, one of the best-preserved Cotwolds villages, which nestles in a secluded valley. Move to another charming town, Winchcombe, on the second day. Take a stroll past honey-color stone cottages and impeccably well-kept gardens. Visit Sudeley Castle, once home to Catherine Parr (Henry VIII's last wife), a Tudor-era palace with romantic gardens (only a few rooms are now open to the public). Another option near Winchombe is Stanway House, a Jacobean manor owned by Lord Neidpath; hours are limited.

Logistics: Take a train from Oxford to Moreton-in-Marsh for Broadway, then walk to Snowshill Manor; for Sudeley Castle, take a bus from Broadway to Winchcombe, then walk.

Chatsworth House, Haddon Hall & Hardwick Hall

Days 10–11. For the final stops, head north, east of Manchester, to a more dramatic landscape. In or near the craggy Peak District, where the gentle slopes of the Pennine Hills begin their ascent to Scotland, are three of England's most renowned historic homes. Base yourself in Bakewell, and spend your first day taking in the art treasures amassed by the dukes of Devonshire at Chatsworth House. If you have any time left over, get out of Bakewell and take a walk in the hills of the Peak District National Park (maps are available at the town's tourist information center).

On the second day, devote the morning to the crenellations and boxy roofs of medieval Haddon Hall, a quintessentially English house. Give your afternoon to Hardwick

Hall, an Elizabethan stone mansion with a facade that is "more glass than wall"— a truly innovative idea in the 16th century. Its collections of period tapestries and embroideries are remarkable reminders of the splendor of the age.

Logistics: Take a train back to Oxford and then up to Manchester for the connection to Buxton; then catch a bus to Bakewell.

TIPS

❶ All stately homes, with the exception of Kensington Palace, Hampton Court Palace, and Longleat House, are closed for the winter. Most homes—not including Stourhead, Wilton House, Petworth, Snowshill Manor, and Hardwick Hall, which close for part of the week—are open daily between April through October. Confirm all hours before visiting.

❷ A car is best for this itinerary, as some houses are remote. Be sure to buy good maps.

❸ Country roads around the Peak District are hard to negotiate; be especially careful when driving to Chatsworth House, Haddon Hall, and Hardwick Hall.

❹ Look into discount passes, such as the Great British Heritage Pass (⇨ Discounts & Deals in Smart Travel Tips), which save you money on visits to multiple sites.

WHEN TO GO

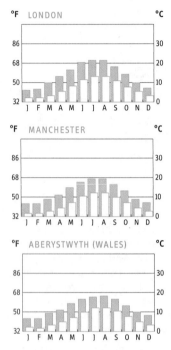

The English tourist season is year-round—with short lulls. It peaks from mid-April to mid-October, with another burst at Christmas (although many historic houses close from October to Easter). The countryside is greenest in spring, whereas in fall the northern moorlands are at their most colorful. June is a good month to visit Wales and the Lake District. During July and August, when most of the British take vacations, accommodations in popular resorts and areas are in high demand and at their most expensive. The winter cultural season in London is lively with opera, ballet, and theater among the prime attractions. Hotel rates are lower then, too, making up for the often gray skies. Museums and sights can be busy during school vacations called half-terms: these are generally the third week in October, the last week of December and first week of January, the third week of February, the last week of March, and the first week of June.

Climate

Generally, the climate in England and Wales is mild, though the weather has been volatile in recent years. Summer temperatures can reach the 90s and the atmosphere can be humid. In winter there can be heavy frost, snow, thick fog, and, of course, plenty of the rain for which the country is well known.

The following are the average daily maximum and minimum temperatures for three major cities.
🔁 Forecasts **Weather Channel** (⊕ www.weather.com).

ON THE
CALENDAR

England's top seasonal events are listed below, and any one of them could provide the stuff of lasting memories. Tickets for popular sporting events must be obtained months in advance. VisitBritain's Web site, ⊕ www.visitbritain.com, also has information about events.

From April 2006 to April 2007, the Royal Shakespeare Company is presenting the Complete Works, a festival celebrating the international impact of the great playwright. Besides presentations of all 37 plays and all known poetry by Shakespeare, there will be new writing, films, and contemporary music from visiting artists and companies. For information, check out ⊕ www.rsc.org.uk.

ONGOING Late May–Aug.	**Glyndebourne Opera** presents high-quality performances in a lovely rural setting; booking opens in April. ☏ *Box 2624, Lewes, East Sussex BN8 5UW* ☎ *01273/815000 information, 01273/813813 box office* ⊕ *www.glyndebourne.com.*
Late May– mid-Sept.	**Shakespeare Under the Stars** gives you the chance to see the Bard's plays at the Regent's Park Open Air Theatre. Performances are usually Monday through Saturday at 8, with matinees on Wednesday, Thursday, and Saturday. ⊠ *Inner Circle, London NW1* ☎ *020/ 7486–2431* ⊕ *www.openairtheatre.org.*
Mid-July– mid-Sept.	**Henry Wood Promenade Concerts,** known universally in England as "the Proms," is a celebrated series of classical-music concerts. ⊠ *Royal Albert Hall, Kensington Gore, London SW7* ☎ *020/ 7589–8212* ⊕ *www.bbc.co.uk/proms.*
WINTER Mid-Dec.	**Olympia International Show Jumping Championships** is London's main international equestrian competition, held in Olympia's Grand Hall. Tickets go on sale in June. ⊠ *London* ☎ *0870/733–0733* ⊕ *www. olympiashowjumping.com.*
Dec. 31	**New Year's Eve at Trafalgar Square** in London is a huge, freezing, sometimes drunken slosh through the fountains to celebrate the new year. Not organized by any official body, it is held in the ceremonial heart of London under an enormous Christmas tree.
Jan. 1	**New Year's Parade,** an American-style extravaganza rare in these parts, with floats and marching bands flown over from the United States, starts on the south side of Westminster Bridge around noon and finishes in Berkeley Square around 3 PM. No tickets are required. ⊠ *London* ⊕ *www.londonparade.co.uk.*

ON THE CALENDAR

SPRING	
Mid-Mar.	**British Antique Dealers' Association Fair** is large and prestigious, with many affordable pieces. ✉ *Duke of York's Headquarters, King's Rd., London SW3* ☎ *020/7589–6108, 877/872–0778 in U.S.* ⊕ *www.bada-antique-fair.co.uk.*
Mid-Mar.	**Crufts Dog Show** brings together more than 8,000 championship dogs for Britain's top canine event. ✉ *National Exhibition Centre, Birmingham* ☎ *0207/518–1012* ⊕ *www.crufts.org.uk.*
Late Mar.	The **Head of the River Boat Race** offers the spectacle of up to 420 eight-man crews dipping their 6,720 oars in the Thames as they race from Mortlake to Putney. The best view is from Surrey Bank above Chiswick Bridge (Tube to Chiswick); check *Time Out* for the starting time, which depends on the tide. The **Oxford versus Cambridge University Boat Race** takes place a week or two later, in the opposite direction but over the same 4½-mi course, carrying on a tradition going back to 1829. Around a quarter of a million people watch from the banks of the river.
Mid-Apr.	**Flora London Marathon** runners start in Greenwich and Blackheath at 9–9:30 AM and run via the Docklands, the Tower of London, and Parliament Square to the Mall. ⊕ *www.london-marathon.co.uk.*
Apr. 21	The **Queen's Birthday** earns a showy 41-gun salute at Hyde Park in London. In June, Elizabeth II's ceremonial birthday is celebrated by Trooping the Colour.
Mid-May	**Royal Windsor Horse Show,** a major five-day show-jumping event, is attended by some members of the Royal Family. ✉ *Show Office, Royal Mews, Windsor* ☎ *0870/121–5370* ⊕ *www.royal-windsor-horse-show.co.uk.*
Mid–late May	The **Chelsea Flower Show,** a prestigious four-day floral extravaganza, covers 22 acres on the Royal Hospital grounds in London's Chelsea neighborhood. Tickets can sell out well in advance of the event. ✉ *Royal Horticultural Society, Royal Hospital Rd., London SW3* ☎ *0870/906–3781* ⊕ *www.rhs.org.uk/chelsea.*
Late May	The **Hay Festival** in the Welsh border town of Hay-on-Wye gathers authors and readers from all over the world for a weeklong celebration of the town's status as the used-book capital of the world. ✉ *Hay-on-Wye* ☎ *01497/821–299* ⊕ *www.hayfestival.co.uk.*
SUMMER	
Early June	**Derby Day** is the world-renowned horse-racing event, at Epsom Downs Racecourse just south of London. ✉ *Epsom Downs, Surrey* ☎ *01372/470047* ⊕ *www.epsomderby.co.uk.*

Early June	London's **Grosvenor House Antiques Fair** is one of the most prestigious in Britain. ✉ *Grosvenor House Hotel, Park La., London W1* ☎ *020/7399–8100* ⊕ *www.grosvenor-antiquesfair.co.uk.*
Early June	**Trooping the Colour** is Queen Elizabeth's official birthday show at Horse Guards Parade, Whitehall, London. (Her actual birthday is in April.) Note that on the two previous Saturdays, there are Queenless rehearsals—the Colonel's Review and the Major General's Review. *Write for tickets from January 1 to February 28 (enclose SASE or International Reply Coupon):* ✆ *Ticket Office, Headquarters Household Division, Horse Guards, London SW1 2AX* ☎ *020/7414–2479.*
Mid-June	**Royal Ascot** is the most glamorous date in British horse racing. Usually held during the third week of June, the four-day event is graced by the Queen and other celebrities. Reserve months in advance for tickets. ✉ *Ascot Racecourse, Ascot, Berkshire* ☎ *01344/876876* ⊕ *www.ascot.co.uk.*
Late June	**Glastonbury Festival,** the biggest musical event in England, sprawls across Somerset farmland, where hundreds of bands (rock, pop, folk, and world music) perform on a half-dozen stages for three days and nights. Tickets may sell out in three hours. ☎ *0870/165–2005* ⊕ *www.glastonburyfestivals.co.uk.*
Late June–early July	**Wimbledon Lawn Tennis Championships** get bigger every year. Applications for the ticket lottery for the two-week tournament are available October through December of the preceding year. ✆ *All-England Lawn Tennis & Croquet Club, Church Rd., Wimbledon, London SW19 5AE* ☎ *020/8946–2244* ⊕ *www.wimbledon.org.*
Late June–early July	**Royal Henley Regatta** attracts premier rowers from around the world on the first weekend in July. High society lines the banks of the Thames during this four-day event. ✉ *Henley-on-Thames, Oxfordshire* ☎ *01491/572153* ⊕ *www.hrr.co.uk.*
Late June–late July	**City of London Festival** fills the City with theater, poetry, classical music, and dance performed by international artists. ☎ *020/7377–0540* ⊕ *www.colf.org.*
Early July	**Hampton Court Palace Flower Show,** a five-day event on the grounds of the palace, nearly rivals the Chelsea Flower Show for glamour. ✉ *Hampton Court Palace, East Molesey, Surrey* ☎ *0870/906–3791* ⊕ *www.rhs.org.uk/hamptoncourt.*
Early–mid-July	**Llangollen International Musical Eisteddfod** sees the little Welsh town of Llangollen overflow with music, including concerts and compe-

ON THE CALENDAR

	titions. Participants come from more than 40 nations. ✉ *Musical Eisteddfod Office, Llangollen* ☎ *01978/860000* ⊕ *www.international-eisteddfod.co.uk.*
Late July–early Aug.	The National Eisteddfod of Wales, a weeklong celebration of Welsh language and culture, is held in different Welsh cities each year. The festival features musical and literary performances. ☎ *029/2076–3777* ⊕ *www.eisteddfod.org.uk.*
Early Aug.	Cowes Regatta draws high flyers, top yachtsmen, and the occasional royal to this grand weeklong boating festival held off the Isle of Wight. ☎ *01983/295744* ⊕ *www.cowesweek.co.uk.*
Mid-Aug.	The Reading Music Festival is second only to Glastonbury in its sheer size and longevity. It takes place in two locations—Leeds and Reading (just outside of London)—over a three-day weekend, and attracts more than 100,000 mostly college-age fans to hear mostly loud rock bands. ☎ *0870/060–3777* ⊕ *www.meanfiddler.com.*
Late Aug.	International Beatles Festival sees hundreds of Beatles tribute bands descend on Liverpool for a week to play to fans. ✉ *Liverpool* ☎ *0151/236–9091* ⊕ *www.visitliverpool.com.*
Late Aug.	Notting Hill Carnival, one of the liveliest street festivals in London, includes Caribbean foods, reggae music, and street parades. ✉ *Notting Hill, London* ☎ *020/8964–0544.*
FALL Sept.	London Open House is a rare one-day chance to view historic London interiors of buildings usually closed to the public. ☎ *020/7267–7644* ⊕ *www.londonopenhouse.org.*
Mid-Sept.	Chelsea Antiques Fair is a 10-day fair with pre-1830 pieces for sale. ✉ *Old Town Hall, King's Rd., London SW3* ☎ *01444/482514* ⊕ *www.penman-fairs.co.uk.*
Mid-Oct.	Cheltenham Festival of Literature draws world-renowned authors, actors, and critics to the elegant, Regency-era town. ☎ *01242/227979* ⊕ *www.cheltenhamfestivals.co.uk.*
Nov. 5	Guy Fawkes Day commemorates a foiled 1605 attempt to blow up Parliament. Fireworks shows and bonfires are held all over the country, with the biggest celebrations in Lewes in Sussex.

London

Updated by
Ferne Arfin,
Christi
Daugherty,
Julius Honnor,
and Alex
Wijeratna

LONDON IS AN ANCIENT CITY whose history greets you at every turn. To gain a sense of its continuity, stand on Waterloo Bridge at sunset. To the east, the great globe of St. Paul's Cathedral glows golden in the fading sunlight as it has since the 17th century, still majestic amid the modern towers of glass and steel that hem it in. To the west stand the mock-medieval ramparts of Westminster, home to the "Mother of Parliaments," which has met here or hereabouts since the 1250s. Past them both snakes the swift, dark Thames, following the same course as when it flowed past the Roman settlement of Londinium nearly 2,000 years ago. If the city contained only its famous landmarks—the Tower of London, Big Ben, Westminster Abbey, Buckingham Palace—it would still rank as one of the world's top cities. But London is so much more.

A city that loves to be explored, London beckons with great museums, royal pageantry, and history-steeped houses. There's no other place like it in its agglomeration of architectural sins and sudden intervention of almost rural sights, in its medley of styles, in its mixture of the green loveliness of parks and the modern gleam of neon. Discovering it takes a bit of work, however. Modern-day London largely reflects its medieval layout, a willfully difficult tangle of streets. This swirl of spaghetti will be totally confusing to anyone brought up on the rigidity of a grid system. Even Londoners, most of whom own a dog-eared copy of an indispensable A–Z street finder, get lost in their own city. But the bewildering street patterns will be a plus for anyone who likes to get lost in atmosphere. London is a walker's city and will repay every moment you spend exploring on foot.

If you want to penetrate beyond the crust of popular knowledge, you should not only visit St. Paul's Cathedral and the Tower of London but also to set aside some time for random wandering. Walk in the city's backstreets and mews, around Park Lane and Kensington. Pass up Buckingham Palace for Kensington Palace. Take in the National Gallery, but don't forget London's "time machine" museums, such as the 19th-century home of Sir John Soane. Abandon the city's standard-issue chain stores for its wonderful markets. In such ways you can best visualize the shape of Old London, a curious city that engulfed its own past for the sake of modernity but still lives and breathes the air of history.

Today that sense of modernity is stronger than ever, as swinging-again London is one of the coolest cities in the world. Millennium fever left its trophies on the capital, with the opening of buildings and bridges and revamped museums, and the city's art, style, fashion, and dining scenes make headlines around the world. London's chefs have become superstars. Its fashion designers have conquered Paris, avant-garde artists have caused waves at the august Royal Academy of Arts, the raging after-hours scene is packed with music mavens ready to catch the Next Big Thing, and the theater continues its tradition of radical, shocking productions. In 2005, the city won the bid to host the 2012 Olympics.

Although the outward shapes may alter and the inner spirit may be warmer, the base-rocks of London's character and tradition remain the same. The British bobby is alive and well. The tall, red, double-decker

GREAT ITINERARIES

London overflows with choices: from exploring local pubs and tea rooms to taking in great theater and concerts, it's easy to fill a day. A stroll through a quiet neighborhood or a ride on the Thames may be as satisfying as seeing a world-famous museum. Below are suggestions for different experiences.

CROWNING GLORIES

This regal runaround packs more into a day than most cities can offer in a week. Hit Westminster Abbey early to avoid the crowds, then cut through St. James's Park to catch the Changing of the Guard at 11:20 at Buckingham Palace. Take a quick detour to the Tudor delights of St. James's Palace, before a promenade down the Mall past the Regency glory of Carlton House Terrace and through Admiralty Arch to Trafalgar Square. Choose from the treasures of the National Gallery, the Who's Who of the National Portrait Gallery, or a brass rubbing in the crypt of St. Martin's-in-the-Fields. This leaves a stroll down Whitehall—past Downing Street, Horse Guards Parade, and Banqueting House—to the Houses of Parliament, where you have the option of prebooking a tour, or trying to get in to see a debate. If you have any time or energy left, stroll through Green and Hyde Parks to Kensington Palace, childhood home of Queen Victoria, and (for aspiring princesses everywhere) the Royal Dress Collection.

MUSEUM MAGIC

London has one of the finest collections of museums in the world, and many are free. Some resemble hands-on playgrounds that will keep children and adults amused for hours; others take a more classical approach. One of the latter is the British Museum in Bloomsbury, an Aladdin's cave of treasures from across the world. While in the area, pop into the nearby museum of architect Sir John Soane or the Theatre Museum.

Alternatively, South Kensington's "Museum Mile" on Cromwell Road houses a triple-whammy that makes for a substantial day's-worth of diversion: the Victoria & Albert Museum, the Natural History Museum, and the Science Museum.

RETAIL THERAPY

It's not hard to shop 'til you drop in London's West End. Start with the upscale on New Bond Street, an awesome sweep of expense and elegance. In the afternoon, head to Oxford Street, which encompasses four Tube stations and is unbeatable for mass market shopping. Run the gauntlet of designers, cheap odds and ends, department stores, and ferocious pedestrians: it's seriously busy.

A more sedate but utterly fashionable experience can be found in Knightsbridge, wandering between Harvey Nichols and Harrods department stores. Head south down Sloane Street to Sloane Square and head out along King's Road, with boutiques galore. To dip into the ever-expanding world of urban chic, try an afternoon in the lively Portobello street market in Notting Hill, where you can pick up remnants of various bygone ages: glassware, furniture, art, and clothes.

buses (in an updated model) still lumber from stop to stop, although their aesthetic match at street level, the glossy red telephone booth, has been replaced by glass and steel boxes. Then there's that greatest living link with the past—the Royal Family. Don't let the tag of "typical tourist destination" stop you from enjoying the pageantry of the Windsors: the Changing of the Guard, at Buckingham Palace and at Whitehall, is one of the greatest free shows in the world.

The London you discover may include some enthusiastic recommendations from this guide, but be prepared to be taken by surprise. The best that a great city has to offer often comes in unexpected ways. The great 18th-century author Samuel Johnson said that a man who is tired of London is tired of life. Armed with energy and curiosity, you can find, to quote Dr. Johnson again, "in London all that life can afford."

EXPLORING LONDON

London grew from a wooden bridge built over the Thames in the year AD 43 to its current 600 square mi and 7 million souls in haphazard fashion, meandering from its two official centers: Westminster, seat of government and royalty, to the west, and the City, site of finance and commerce, to the east. In these two areas are most of the grand buildings that have played a central role in British history: the Tower of London and St. Paul's Cathedral, Westminster Abbey and the Houses of Parliament, Buckingham Palace, and the older royal palace of St. James's.

London's *un*official centers multiply and mutate year after year, and it would be a shame to stop only at the postcard views. Life is not lived in monuments, as the patrician patrons of the great Georgian architects understood when they commissioned the city's elegant squares and town houses. Within a few minutes' walk of Buckingham Palace, for instance, lie St. James's and Mayfair, neighboring quarters of elegant town houses built for the nobility during the 17th and early 18th centuries and now notable for shopping opportunities. Westminster Abbey's original vegetable patch (or convent garden), which became the site of London's first square, Covent Garden, is now a popular stop.

Hyde Park and Kensington Gardens, preserved by past kings and queens for their own hunting and relaxation, create a swath of parkland across the city center. A walk across Hyde Park brings you to the museum district of South Kensington, with the Natural History Museum, the Science Museum, and the Victoria & Albert Museum. If the great parks such as Hyde Park are, in Lord Chatham's phrase, "the lungs of London," then the River Thames is its backbone. The South Bank has many cultural highlights: the theaters of the South Bank Centre, the Hayward Gallery, Tate Modern, and the reconstruction of Shakespeare's Globe theater. The London Eye observation wheel here gives stunning city views, or you can walk across the Millennium or Hungerford bridges. Farther downstream is the gorgeous 17th- and 18th-century symmetry of Greenwich, and its maritime attractions.

TOP REASONS TO GO

Westminster Abbey: The most exciting church in the land is the final resting place for the men and women who built Britain.

Buckingham Palace: Not the prettiest royal palace, but a must-see for the glimpse it affords of modern royal life. Don't forget the collection of art and china at the Queen's Gallery next door.

St. Paul's Cathedral: No matter how many times you have been here, the scale and elegance of Sir Christopher Wren's masterpiece take the breath away. Climb the enormous dome for fantastic views across London.

Tower of London: The Tower is London at its majestic, idiosyncratic best. This is the heart of the kingdom, with foundations dating back nine centuries.

British Museum: If you want to journey through time and space without leaving the confines of Bloomsbury, a visit to the British Museum has hours of eye-catching artifacts from civilizations around the world.

Shakespeare's Globe Theatre: You can catch a Shakespeare play almost every night of the year in London. But watching an offering from the Bard in a re-created version of the galleried Tudor theater for which he wrote is a special thrill.

Hampton Court Palace: These buildings won over Henry VIII and became his favorite royal residence. Tudor charm, grand gardens, a wing designed by Christopher Wren, and a picturesque upstream Thames location make Hampton Court a great day out.

Tate Modern: A visit here is more of an event than the average museum stop. Tate Modern, inside a striking 1930s power station, is a hip, immensely successful addition to the London gallery landscape.

National Gallery: Whatever the collective noun is for a set of Old Masters—a palette? a canvas?—there are enough here to have the most casual art enthusiast purring with admiration. Enjoy the newly pedestrian Trafalgar Square on the doorstep.

London's central parks: It seems churlish to pick out only one. The four central parks are all within walking distance: pick St. James's Park for fairy-tale views; Green Park for hillocks and wide boulevards; Regent's Park for its open-air theater and the London Zoo; and Hyde Park for rowing on the Serpentine Lido.

Westminster & Royal London

If you have time to visit only one part of London, this is it. Westminster and Royal London might be called "London for Beginners." If you went no farther than these few acres, you would have seen many of the famous sights, from the Houses of Parliament, Big Ben, Westminster Abbey, and Buckingham Palace, to two of the world's greatest art collections, in the National and Tate Britain galleries. You can truly call

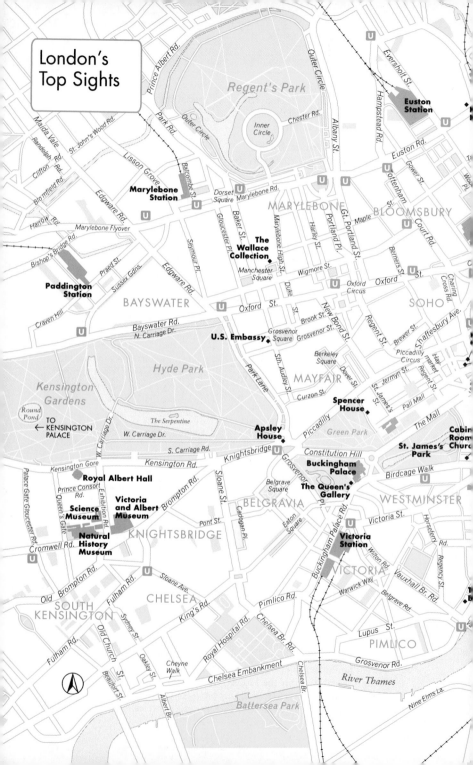

London's Top Sights

Euston Station

Regent's Park

Inner Circle

Chester Rd.

Prince Albert Rd.

Outer Circle

Outer Circle

Park Rd.

Albany St.

Hampstead Rd.

Eversholt St.

Euston Rd.

Maida Vale

Randolph Av.

St. John's Wood Rd.

Lisson Grove

Balcombe St.

Dorset Square

Marylebone Rd.

MARYLEBONE

BLOOMSBURY

Clifton

Bloomfield Rd.

Edgware Rd.

Marylebone Station

Baker St.

Marylebone High St.

Harley St.

Portland Pl.

Gt. Portland St.

Maple St.

Gower St.

Tottenham Court Rd.

Barnes St.

Court Rd.

HarroW Rd.

Marylebone Flyover

Seymour Pl.

The Wallace Collection

Manchester Square

Duke St.

Wigmore St.

Oxford St.

Oxford

St.

Charing Cross Rd.

Bishop's Bridge Rd.

Praed St.

Sussex Gdns.

Gloucester Pl.

Oxford Circus

SOHO

Paddington Station

Craven Hill

BAYSWATER

Edgware Rd.

Oxford St.

Brook St.

New Bond St.

Regent St.

Brewer St.

Shaftesbury Ave.

Bayswater Rd.

N. Carriage Dr.

Park Lane

U.S. Embassy

Grosvenor Square

Grosvenor St.

Berkeley Square

MAYFAIR

Dover St.

Piccadilly Circus

Haymarket

St. James's

Regent St.

Hyde Park

Kensington Gardens

Round Pond

TO
← KENSINGTON PALACE

The Serpentine

W. Carriage Dr.

W. Carriage Dr.

S. Carriage Rd.

Sth. Audley St.

Curzon St.

Spencer House

St. James's

Pall Mall

The Mall

Cabinet Room Church

Apsley House

Piccadilly

Green Park

St. James's Park

Knightsbridge

Constitution Hill

Constitution Hill

Birdcage Walk

Kensington Gore

Prince Consort Rd.

Royal Albert Hall

Kensington Rd.

Kensington Rd.

Sloane St.

Belgrave Square

Grosvenor Pl.

Buckingham Palace

The Queen's Gallery

WESTMINSTER

Palace Gate

Gloucester Rd.

Queen's Gate

Exhibition Rd.

Brompton Rd.

Victoria and Albert Museum

Science Museum

BELGRAVIA

Eaton Square

Cadogan Pl.

Pont St.

Belgrave Square

Buckingham Palace Rd.

Victoria St.

Victoria St.

Horseferry Rd.

Cromwell Rd.

Natural History Museum

KNIGHTSBRIDGE

Victoria Station

VICTORIA

Wilton Rd.

Vauxhall Br. Rd.

Regency St.

Old Brompton Rd.

SOUTH KENSINGTON

Fulham Rd.

Sloane Ave.

CHELSEA

King's Rd.

Sydney St.

Old Church St.

Pimlico Rd.

Royal Hospital Rd.

Chelsea Br. Rd.

Warwick Way

Belgrave Rd.

Lupus St.

PIMLICO

Beaufort St.

Oakley St.

Cheyne Walk

Chelsea Embankment

Chelsea Br.

Grosvenor Rd.

River Thames

Albert Br.

Battersea Park

Nine Elms La.

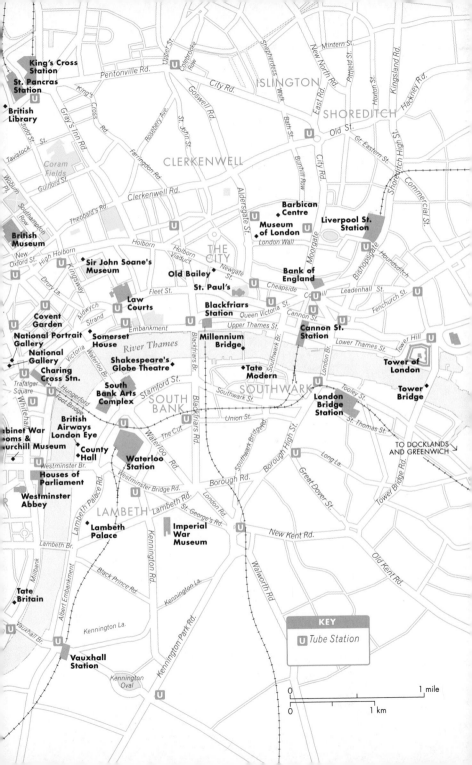

King's Cross Station
St. Pancras Station
British Library

ISLINGTON
SHOREDITCH

CLERKENWELL

Pentonville Rd.
City Rd.
Old St.

Coram Fields

Barbican Centre
Museum of London
Liverpool St. Station

British Museum

London Wall

THE CITY

Sir John Soane's Museum

Old Bailey
St. Paul's
Blackfriars Station

Bank of England

Cannon St. Station

Covent Garden
National Portrait Gallery
National Gallery
Charing Cross Stn.

Law Courts

Somerset House

Millennium Bridge

Tower of London

River Thames

Shakespeare's Globe Theatre

Tate Modern

Tower Bridge

SOUTHWARK

South Bank Arts Complex

SOUTH BANK

London Bridge Station

British Airways London Eye

Cabinet War Rooms & Churchill Museum

County Hall

Waterloo Station

TO DOCKLANDS AND GREENWICH

Houses of Parliament

Westminster Abbey

LAMBETH

Lambeth Palace

Imperial War Museum

Tate Britain

Vauxhall Station

Kennington Oval

KEY
U Tube Station

0   1 mile
0   1 km

London Postal Districts

this area Royal London, since it is bounded by the triangle of streets that make up the route that the Queen usually takes when journeying from Buckingham Palace to Westminster Abbey or to the Houses of Parliament on state occasions. The three points on this royal triangle are Trafalgar Square, Westminster, and Buckingham Palace. Naturally, in an area that regularly sees the pomp and pageantry of royal occasions, the streets are wide and the vistas long. St. James's Park lies at the heart of the triangle, which has a feeling of timeless dignity—flower beds bursting with color, long avenues of trees framing classically proportioned buildings, glimpses of pinnacles and towers over the treetops, the distant *bong!* of Big Ben counting off the hours. This is concentrated sightseeing, so pace yourself. For a large part of the year, much of Royal London is floodlighted at night, adding to the theatricality of the experience.

TIMING   It's easy to spend a few days in this area, so plan carefully. Allow as much time as you can for the three great museums—the National Gallery and the Tate Britain require *at least* two hours each, the National Portrait Gallery one to two. Westminster Abbey can take a half day—especially in summer when lines are long. In summer, you can get inside Buckingham Palace and Clarence House; a half-day's operation will be increased to a whole day if you see Spencer House (open Sundays only), the Royal Mews, or the Queen's Gallery. If the Changing of the Guard is a priority, time yourself accordingly.

GETTING HERE   Trafalgar Square—easy to access and in the center of the action—is a good place to start. Take the tube to Embankment (District and Circle lines) and walk north until you cross the Strand, or alight at Charing Cross (Bakerloo, Jubilee, and Northern lines), where the Northumberland Avenue exit deposits you on the southeast corner of the square. Practically all buses stop around here, including buses 3, 9, 11, 12, 16, 24, 29, 53, 88, 139, and 159. Alternative tube stations on the south side are St. James's Park (on the District and Circle lines), which is the best for Buckingham Palace, or the next stop, Westminster, which deposits you in the shadow of Big Ben.

Numbers in the margin correspond to numbers on the Westminster & Royal London map.

Main Attractions

❾ Buckingham Palace. Supreme among the symbols of London—indeed of Britain generally and of the Royal Family in particular—Buckingham Palace tops many must-see lists, although the building itself is no masterpiece and has housed the monarch only since Victoria (1819–1901) moved here from Kensington Palace on her accession in 1837. Its great gray bulk sums up the imperious splendor of so much of the city: stately, magnificent, and ponderous. In 1824 the palace was substantially rebuilt by John Nash, that tireless architect, for George IV, that tireless spendthrift. Compared with other great London residences, it is a fairly recent affair: the Portland stone facade dates from 1913, and the interior was renovated and redecorated after World War II bombs damaged it. The palace contains some 600 rooms, including the Ballroom and the Throne Room. The state rooms are where much of the business of royalty is played out—investitures, state banquets, and receptions for the great and good—and these

Fodor'sChoice
★

are open to the public while the Royal Family is away during the summer. The royal apartments are in the north wing; when the Queen is in, the royal standard is raised. The **Changing of the Guard**—which, with all the pomp and ceremony monarchists and children adore, remains one of London's best free shows—culminates in front of the palace. Marching to live music, the guards proceed up the Mall from St. James's Palace to Buckingham Palace. Shortly afterward, the replacement guard approaches from Wellington Barracks via Birdcage Walk. Once the old and new guards are in the forecourt, the old guard symbolically hands over the keys to the palace. ■ TIP→ **Get there by 10:30 AM to grab a spot in the best viewing section at the gate facing the palace, since most of the hoopla takes place behind the railings in the forecourt.** ⊠ *Buckingham Palace Rd., St. James's, SW1* ☎ *020/7766–7300* ⊕ *www.royal.gov.uk* ⊠ *£14, includes audio tour, credit-card reservations subject to booking charge; prebooking recommended* ⊙ *Late July–late Sept., daily 9:45–6, last admission 3:45; confirm dates, which are subject to Queen's mandate. Changing of the Guard Apr.–July, daily 11:30 AM; Aug.–Mar., alternating days only 11:30 AM* ▤*AE, MC, V* Ⓤ *Victoria, St. James's Park.*

★ ☾ ⓮ **Cabinet War Rooms & Churchill Museum.** From this small maze of bombproof underground rooms—in the back of the hulking Foreign Office—Britain's World War II fortunes were directed. During air raids, the cabinet met here, and the Cabinet Room is still arranged as if a meeting were about to convene. In the Map Room, the Allied campaign is charted. The Prime Minister's Room holds the desk from which Winston Churchill made his morale-boosting broadcasts, and the Telephone Room has his hotline to FDR. The rest of the rooms have been preserved as they were at the end of the war. The PM's "suite" of rooms for dining, cooking, and sleeping have been restored, too. By far the most exciting addition is the **Churchill Museum,** which opened in 2005 on the 40th anniversary of the great man's death. Different interactive zones explore his life and achievements—and failures, too—through objects and documents, many of which, such as his personal papers, had not been revealed to the public. ⊠ *Clive Steps, King Charles St., Westminster, SW1A* ☎ *020/7930–6961* ⊕ *www.iwm.org.uk* ⊠ *£11, includes audio tour* ⊙ *Daily 9:30–6; last admission 5* Ⓤ *Westminster.*

⓱ **Horse Guards Parade.** Once the tiltyard of Whitehall Palace, where jousting tournaments were held, the Horse Guards Parade is now notable mainly for the annual Trooping the Colour ceremony, in which the Queen takes the Royal Salute, her official birthday gift, on the second Saturday in June. (Like Paddington Bear, the Queen has two birthdays; her real one is on April 21.) There is pageantry galore, with marching bands and throngs of onlookers. At the Whitehall facade of Horse Guards, the changing of two mounted sentries known as the **mounted guard** provides what may be London's most frequently exercised photo opportunity. ⊠ *Whitehall, Westminster, SW1* ⊙ *Queen's mounted guard ceremony Mon.–Sat. 11 AM, Sun. 10 AM* Ⓤ *Westminster.*

⓬ **Houses of Parliament.** Seat of Great Britain's government, the Houses of
Fodor'sChoice Parliament are, arguably, the city's most famous and photogenic sight.
★ Facing them you see, from left to right, Big Ben—keeping watch on the

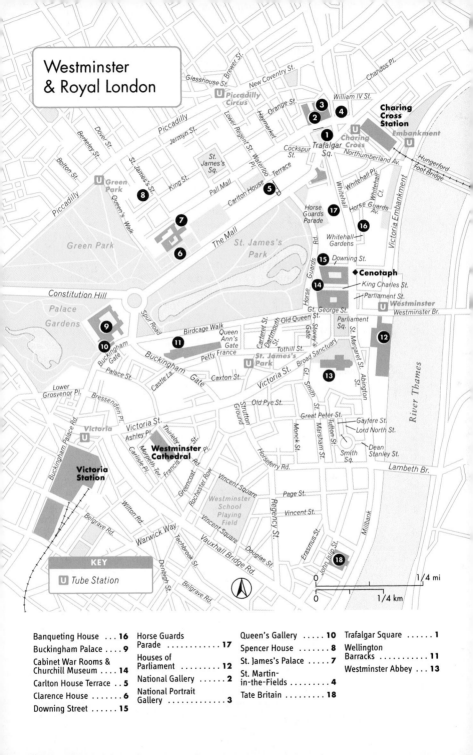

Westminster & Royal London

Piccadilly Circus

Brewer St.
Glasshouse St.
New Coventry St.
Chandos Pl.
William IV St.

Charing Cross Station

Embankment

Orange St.
Haymarket
Cockspur St.
Trafalgar Sq.
Charing Cross

Northumberland Av.
Hungerford Foot Bridge

Piccadilly
Jermyn St.
Lower Regent St.
Waterloo Pl.

St. James's St.
King St.
St. James's Sq.
Pall Mall
Carlton House Terrace

Whitehall

Horse Guards Av.

Whitehall Ct.

Victoria Embankment

Green Park

Berkeley St.
Dover St.
Bolton St.

Piccadilly

Queen's Walk

The Mall

St. James's Park

Horse Guards Parade

Whitehall Gardens

Downing St.

◆ Cenotaph

King Charles St.

Parliament St.

Constitution Hill

Palace Gardens

Spur Road

Birdcage Walk
Queen Ann's Gate

Buckingham Gate

Guards Rd.

Gt. George St.
Old Queen St.
Storey's Gate

Parliament Sq.

Westminster
Westminster Br.

St. Margaret St.

Abingdon St.

River Thames

Buckingham Gate
Castle La.
Caxton St.

Petty France
St. James's Park

Victoria St.
Broad Sanctuary

Tothill St.

Carteret St.
Dartmouth St.
Caxton St.

Lower Grosvenor Pl.
Bressenden Pl.

Victoria

Victoria St.
Ashley Pl.
Thirleby Rd.
Morpeth Ter.
Carlisle Pl.

Westminster Cathedral

Stratton Ground
Old Pye St.

Great Peter St.
Gayfere St.
Lord North St.
Dean Stanley St.
Smith Sq.

Lambeth Br.

Monck St.
Marsham St.
Tufton St.

Victoria Station

Buckingham Palace Rd.

Belgrave Rd.
Wilton Rd.

Francis St.
Greencoat Row
Rochester Row

Vincent Square

Page St.
Vincent St.

Regency St.

Westminster School Playing Field

Warwick Way
Tachbrook St.
Denbigh St.
Vauxhall Bridge Rd.
Douglas St.
Belgrave Rd.

Erasmus St.
John Islip St.
Millbank

KEY

Ⓤ Tube Station

1/4 mi

1/4 km

Banqueting House ... **16**
Buckingham Palace **9**
Cabinet War Rooms & Churchill Museum **14**
Carlton House Terrace .. **5**
Clarence House **6**
Downing Street **15**
Horse Guards Parade **17**
Houses of Parliament **12**
National Gallery **2**
National Portrait Gallery **3**
Queen's Gallery **10**
Spencer House **8**
St. James's Palace **7**
St. Martin-in-the-Fields **4**
Tate Britain **18**
Trafalgar Square **1**
Wellington Barracks **11**
Westminster Abbey ... **13**

corner—the Houses of Parliament themselves, Westminster Hall (the oldest part of the complex), and the Victoria Tower. The most romantic view of the complex is from the opposite, south side of the river, a vista especially dramatic at night when the spires, pinnacles, and towers of the great building are floodlighted green and gold. After a catastrophic fire in 1834, these buildings arose, designed in glorious, mock-medieval style by two Victorian-era architects, Sir Charles Barry and Augustus Pugin. The Palace of Westminster, as the complex is still properly called, was established by Edward the Confessor in the 11th century. It has served as the seat of English administrative power, on and off, ever since. Now virtually the symbol of London, the 1858 **Clock Tower** designed by Pugin contains the bell known as **Big Ben** that chimes the hour (and the quarters). Weighing a mighty 13 tons, the bell takes its name from Sir Benjamin Hall, the far-from-slim Westminster building works commissioner. At the other end of Parliament is the 336-foot-high **Victoria Tower.** There are two houses, the Lords and the Commons. You can see democracy in action in the Visitors' Galleries—if, that is, you're patient enough to wait in line for hours (the Lords line is shorter) or have applied in advance for the special "line of route" tour for overseas visitors in summer (late July through August and mid-September through early October). Tickets can be prebooked by phone or on the Web site; alternatively, you can take a chance and buy same-day tickets from the ticket office opposite the Houses of Parliament. The time to catch the action is Question Time—when the prime minister defends himself against the attacks of his "right honorable friends" on Wednesday between noon and 2:30 PM. For a special exhibition devoted to the history of Parliament, head to the **Jewel Tower,** across the street from Victoria Tower, on Abingdon Street. Be sure to have your name placed in advance on the waiting list for the twice-weekly tours of the **Lord Chancellor's Residence,** a popular attraction since its renovation. ⌧ *St. Stephen's Entrance, St. Margaret St., Westminster, SW1* ☎ *020/7219–4272 Commons information, 020/7219–3107 Lords information, 020/7222–2219 Jewel Tower, 020/7219–2184 Lord Chancellor's Residence, 0870/906–3773 summer tours* ⊕ *www.parliament.uk* ⌦ *Free, £7 summer tours* ⊘ *Commons Mon. 2:30–10:30, Tues. and Wed. 11:30–7:30, Thurs. 11:30–6:30, Fri. 9:30–3 although not every Fri.; Lords Mon.–Thurs. 2:30–10; Lord Chancellor's Residence Tues. and Thurs. 10:30–12:30. Closed Easter wk, late July–early Sept., 3 wks for party conference recess mid-Sept.–early Oct., and 3 wks at Christmas* Ⓤ *Westminster.*

> ### A VIEW TO REMEMBER
>
> The most romantic view of the complex is from the opposite (south) side of the river, especially dramatic at night when the spires, pinnacles, and towers are floodlighted green and gold—a fairy-tale vision only missing the presence of Peter Pan and Wendy on their way to Never-Never Land.

NEED A BREAK? The **Wesley Café** (⌧ Storey's Gate, Westminster, SW1 ☎ 020/7222–8010) is a popular budget haunt for office workers around Westminster. It's almost opposite Westminster Abbey, in the crypt of Central Hall, a former Methodist church. A meal costs around £5.

❷ National Gallery. Jan Van Eyck's *Arnolfini Marriage*, Leonardo da Vinci's

Fodor'sChoice *Virgin and Child*, Diego Velázquez's *Rokeby Venus*, John Constable's

★ *Hay Wain* . . . you get the picture. There are approximately 2,200 other paintings in this museum, many of them among the most treasured works of art anywhere. The museum's low, gray, colonnaded, neoclassical facade fills the north side of Trafalgar Square. The gallery's east wing in sleek black and white marble has cafés and improved visitor information, such as boards with a color code for different eras of paintings. The National's collection includes paintings of the early Renaissance—in the modern Sainsbury Wing—the Flemish and Dutch masters, the Spanish school, and the English tradition (notably William Hogarth, Thomas Gainsborough, George Stubbs, and Constable).

The **Micro Gallery,** a computer information center in the Sainsbury Wing, is a great place to start. You can access information on any work, choose your favorites, and print out a free personal tour map. There's another computer center in the espresso bar in the lower hall. In addition to the four mentioned above, the museum's top 10 includes Paolo Uccello's *Battle of San Romano* (children love its knights on horseback), Giovanni Bellini's *Doge Leonardo Loredan* (notice the snail-shell buttons), Sandro Botticelli's *Venus and Mars,* Michelangelo Caravaggio's *Supper at Emmaus* (almost cinematically lit), J. M. W. Turner's *Fighting Téméraire* (one of the artist's greatest sunsets), and Georges Seurat's *Bathers at Asnières.* The museum is too overwhelming to absorb in a single viewing, but the free admission encourages repeat visits. For a great time-out, head for the brasserie, Crivelli's Garden, in the Sainsbury Wing. The ultracool National Gallery Café in the east wing makes a fun stop even if you're not visiting the gallery. ⊠ *Trafalgar Sq., Westminster, WC2* ☎ *020/7747–2885* ⊕ *www.nationalgallery.org.uk* ⊠ *Free, charge for special exhibitions* ☉ *Daily 10–6, Wed. until 9; 1-hr free guided tour starts at Sainsbury Wing daily at 11:30 and 2:30, and additionally Wed. 6 and 6:30, Sat. 12:30 and 3:30* Ⓤ *Charing Cross, Leicester Sq.*

★ **❸ National Portrait Gallery.** An idiosyncratic collection that presents a potted history of Britain through its people, past and present, this museum is an essential stop for all history and literature buffs. As an art collection it is eccentric, because the subject, not the artist, is the point. Many of the faces are obscure, because the portraits outlasted their sitters' fame—not so surprising when the portraitists are such greats as Sir Joshua Reynolds, Gainsborough, Sir Thomas Lawrence, and George Romney. But the annotation is comprehensive, the layout is easy to negotiate—chronological, with the oldest at the top—and there's a separate research center for those who get hooked on particular personages. The spacious, bright galleries are accessible via a state-of-the-art escalator, which lets you view the paintings as you ascend to a skylighted space displaying the oldest works in the Tudor Gallery. At the summit, a sleek restaurant, open beyond gallery hours, will satiate skyline droolers. ⊠ *St. Martin's Pl., Covent Garden, WC2* ☎ *020/7312–2463 recorded information* ⊕ *www.npg.org.uk* ⊠ *Free, charge for special exhibitions* ☉ *Mon.–Wed., weekends 10–6, Thurs. and Fri. 10–9* Ⓤ *Charing Cross, Leicester Sq.*

★ ⑩ **Queen's Gallery.** The former chapel at the south side of Buckingham Palace is now a temple of art and rare objects, acquired by kings and queens over the centuries. The Pennethorne Gallery is dominated by the larger-than-life portrait of Charles I (Van Dyck) in equestrian mode, which almost overshadows works by Holbein, Frans Hals, Jan Vermeer, and Rubens. These contrast starkly with the frank portrait of Queen Elizabeth II by Lucian Freud in the Nash Gallery. Between and beneath the paintings are cabinets, tables, and silverwork. ■ TIP➜ **The E-gallery reveals hidden details of some artworks, allowing you to open lockets and remove a sword from its scabbard.** Admission is by timed ticket. ⊠ *Buckingham Palace, Buckingham Palace Rd., St. James's, SW1* ☎ *020/7766–7301* ⊕ *www.royal.gov.uk* ⊠ *£7.50* ⊙ *Daily 10–5:30; last admission 4:30* Ⓤ *Victoria, St. James's Park.*

☾ **St. James's Park.** With three palaces at its borders, St. James's Park is the most royal of the royal parks. It's also London's smallest, most ornamental park, as well as the oldest; it was acquired by Henry VIII in 1532 for a deer park. About 17 species of birds—including pelicans, geese, ducks, and swans (which belong to the Queen)—now breed around the lake, attracting ornithologists at dawn. Later on summer days the deck chairs (which you must pay to use) are crammed with office workers lunching while being serenaded by music from the bandstands. One of the best times to stroll the leafy walkways is after dark, with Westminster Abbey and the Houses of Parliament rising above the floodlighted lake. ⊠ *The Mall or Horse Guards approach, or Birdcage Walk, St. James's, SW1* Ⓤ *St. James's Park, Westminster.*

★ ⑱ **Tate Britain.** This museum, funded by the sugar magnate Sir Henry Tate, is a brilliant celebration of great British artists from the 16th century to the present day. Each room has a theme and includes key works by major British artists: Van Dyck, Hogarth, and Reynolds rub shoulders with Rossetti, Sickert, Hockney, and Bacon, for example. Not to be missed is the generous selection of Constable landscapes. The collection's crowning glory is the Turner Bequest, consisting of Romantic painter J. M. W. Turner's personal collection. He left it to the nation on condition that the works be displayed together. The James Stirling–designed Clore Gallery (to the right of the main gallery) opened in 1987 to fulfill his wish, and it should not be missed. You can rent an audio guide with commentaries by curators, experts, and some of the artists themselves. ⊠ *Millbank, Westminster, SW1* ☎ *020/7887–800, 020/7887–8008 recorded information* ⊕ *www.tate.org.uk* ⊠ *Free, exhibitions £3–£10* ⊙ *Daily 10–5:50* Ⓤ *Pimlico (signposted 5-min walk).*

❶ **Trafalgar Square.** This is the center of London, by dint of a plaque on the corner of the Strand and Charing Cross Road from which distances on U.K. signposts are measured. Great events, such as royal weddings, political protests, and sporting triumphs, always draw crowds to the city's most famous square. The commanding open space is built on the grand scale demanded by its central position in the capital of an empire that once reached to the farthest corners of the globe. Trafalgar Square takes its name from the Battle of Trafalgar, Admiral Lord Horatio Nelson's great naval victory over the French, in 1805. Appropriately, the domi-

Where to See the Royals

THE QUEEN AND THE ROYAL FAMILY attend some 400 functions a year, and if you want to know what they are doing on any given date, turn to the *Court Circular* printed in the major London dailies. But most people want to see the Royals in all their dazzling pomp and circumstance. For this, the best bet is the second Saturday in June, when Trooping the Colour is usually held to celebrate the Queen's official birthday. This spectacular parade begins when she leaves Buckingham Palace in her carriage and rides down the Mall to arrive at Horse Guards Parade at 11 AM exactly.

If you wish to obtain one of the 7,000 seats (no more than two per request, distributed by ballot), enclose a letter and self-addressed, stamped envelope or International Reply Coupon—January to February 28 only—to Ticket Office, Headquarters

Household Division, Horse Guards, London SW1A 2AX, ☎ 020/7414-2479. You can also just line up along the Mall with your binoculars.

Another time you can catch the Queen in all her regalia is when she and the Duke of Edinburgh ride in state to Westminster to open the Houses of Parliament. In late October or early November, the famous gilded coach is escorted by the Household Cavalry. As the Queen enters the building, the air shakes with the booming of heavy guns, and all London knows that the democratic processes have once again been renewed with all their age-old ceremony.

Should you miss seeing the Queen, or if you just want to read about the Royals, visit ⊕ www.royal.gov.uk, the official Web site of the British monarchy.

nant landmark here is **Nelson's Column,** a 145-foot-high granite perch from which E. H. Baily's 1843 statue of Nelson keeps watch. The **equestrian statue of Charles I,** looking south toward the Banqueting House, receives a wreath on the anniversary of his execution, January 30. ⊠ *Trafalgar Sq., Westminster SW1* Ⓤ *Charing Cross, Leicester Sq.*

⓭ **Westminster Abbey.** A monument to the nation's rich—and often bloody and scandalous—history, the abbey rises on the Thames skyline as one of London's most iconic sites. Nearly all of Britain's monarchs have been crowned here since the coronation of William the Conqueror on Christmas Day 1066—and most are buried here, too. The abbey's majestic main nave is packed with memories (and, often, crowds), as it has witnessed many splendid royal events. Other than the mysterious gloom of the vast interior, the first thing that strikes most people is the proliferation of statues, tombs, and commemorative tablets. In parts, the building seems more like a stonemason's yard than a place of worship. But in its latter capacity, this landmark truly comes into its own. Although attending a service is not something to undertake purely for sightseeing reasons, it provides a glimpse of the abbey in its full majesty, with the service accompanied by music from the Westminster choristers and the organ that composer Henry Purcell once played.

Fodor'sChoice
★

The current abbey is a largely 13th- and 14th-century rebuilding of the 11th-century church founded by Edward the Confessor, with one notable addition being the 18th-century twin towers over the west entrance, designed by Sir Christopher Wren and completed by Nicholas Hawksmoor. Entering by the north door to follow the one-way route through the abbey, what you see first on your left are the extravagant 18th-century monuments of statesmen in the north transept, as well as the north-transept chapels. Look up to your right to see the painted-glass rose window, the largest of its kind. At many points the view of the abbey is crowded by the many statues and screens; to your right is the mostly 19th-century choir screen (part is 13th-century), while to the left is the sacrarium, containing the medieval kings' tombs that screen the **Chapel of St. Edward** (because of its fragility the shrine is closed off, unless you take a tour with the verger—ask at the admission desk when you enter). Continuing to the foot of the Henry VII Chapel steps, you can still see the hot seat of power, the **Coronation Chair,** which has been graced by nearly every royal posterior. Then proceed into one of the architectural glories of Britain, the **Henry VII Chapel** (also known as the Lady Chapel), passing the huge white marble tomb of Elizabeth I, buried with her half-sister, "Bloody" Mary I, whose death she ordered. All around the chapel are magnificent sculptures of saints, philosophers, and kings, with mermaids and monsters carved on the choir-stall misericords (undersides), and exquisite fan vaulting above (binoculars will help you spot the statues high on the walls)—the last riot of medieval design in England and one of the miracles of Western architecture.

Continue to **Poets' Corner;** in 1400 Geoffrey Chaucer became the first poet to be buried here. There are memorials to William Shakespeare, William Blake, and Charles Dickens (who is also buried here). Outside the west front is an archway into the quiet, green **Dean's Yard** and the entrance to the **Cloisters.** If time allows, visit the **Chapter House,** a stunning octagonal room, adorned with 14th-century frescoes, where the King's Council met between 1257 and 1547. The **Abbey Museum** is in the **Undercroft,** which survives from Edward the Confessor's original church. The museum includes effigies made from the death masks and actual clothing of Charles II and Admiral Lord Nelson, among other fascinating relics. Adjoining these rooms, the **Little Cloister** is a quiet haven. Just beyond, the **College Garden,** under cultivation for more than 900 years, is planted with medicinal herbs. As you return to the abbey, look again at the truly awe-inspiring nave. Pause for the **Tomb of the Unknown Warrior,** an anonymous World War I martyr who lies buried here in memory of the soldiers fallen in both world wars.

Arrive early if possible, but be prepared to wait in line to tour the abbey. You can rent an audio guide (£3) or ask the information desk about 90-minute verger-led tours (£4). Photography is not permitted. ⊠ *Broad Sanctuary, Westminster,*

IN A HURRY?

If you're pressed for time, concentrate on these four Abbey highlights: the Coronation Chair; tombs of Elizabeth I and Mary, Queen of Scots, in the Chapel of Henry VII; Poets' Corner; and Tomb of the Unknown Warrior.

SW1 ☎ *020/7222–5152* ⊕ *www.westminster-abbey.org* 🖃 *Abbey and museum £10* ⊙ *Abbey Mon., Tues., Thurs., and Fri. 9:30–3:45, Wed. 9:30–6, Sat. 9–1:45 (closes 1 hr after last admission). Museum daily 10:30–4. Cloisters daily 8–6. College Garden Tues.–Thurs. Apr.–Sept. 10–6, Oct.–Mar. 10–4. Separate admission for Chapter House daily 10–4. Abbey closed to visitors during weekday and Sun. services* Ⓤ *Westminster.*

Also Worth Seeing

⓰ **Banqueting House.** Commissioned by James I, Inigo Jones (1573–1652), one of England's great architects, created this banqueting hall in 1619–22 out of an old remnant of the Tudor Palace of Whitehall. Influenced by Andrea Palladio's work, which he saw during a sojourn in Tuscany, Jones remade the palace with Palladian sophistication and purity. James I's son, Charles I, enhanced the interior by employing the Flemish painter Peter Paul Rubens to glorify his father all over the ceiling. These allegorical paintings, depicting a wise monarch being received into heaven, were the last thing Charles saw before he was beheaded on a scaffold outside in 1649. Phone or check the Web site for information about lunchtime concerts. 🖂 *Whitehall, Westminster, SW1A* ☎ *020/7930–4179, 0870/751–5178 recorded information, 0870/751–5187 concert tickets* ⊕ *www.hrp.org.uk* 🖃 *£4.50, includes free audio guide* ⊙ *Mon.–Sat. 10–5, last admission 4:30. Closed Christmas wk* Ⓤ *Charing Cross, Embankment, Westminster.*

❺ **Carlton House Terrace.** A glorious example of Regency architect John Nash's genius, Carlton House Terrace was built between 1812 and 1830, under the patronage of George IV (Prince Regent until George III's death in 1820). Nash was responsible for a series of West End developments, of which the white-stucco facades and massive Corinthian columns on this street may be the most imposing. Today No. 12 houses the **Institute of Contemporary Arts,** one of Britain's leading modern-art centers. 🖂 *The Mall, St. James's, W1* Ⓤ *Charing Cross.*

❻ **Clarence House.** The London home of the late Queen Elizabeth the Queen Mother for nearly 50 years, this Regency mansion is the Prince of Wales's residence. Built by John Nash for the duke of Clarence, it has remained a royal home—the present monarch, Queen Elizabeth, lived here after her marriage. The rooms have been sensitively preserved as the Queen Mother chose, with works of art from the Royal Collection. It is less palace, and more home (for Prince Charles, his wife Camilla, and his sons William and Harry), with informal family pictures and comfortable sofas. The tour (by timed ticket entry only) is of the ground-floor rooms. 🖂 *The Mall, St. James's SW1* ☎ *020/7766–7303* ⊕ *www. royal.gov.uk* 🖃 *£6* ⊙ *Aug.–mid-Oct.; call for hrs* Ⓤ *Green Park.*

⓯ **Downing Street.** The British version of the White House occupies three unassuming 18th-century houses. No. 10 has been the official residence of the prime minister since 1732. The cabinet office, hub of the British system of government, is on the ground floor; the prime minister's private apartment is on the top floor. The chancellor of the exchequer traditionally occupies No. 11. Downing Street is cordoned off, but you should be able to catch a glimpse of it from Whitehall. Just south of Downing

Street, in the middle of Whitehall, is the **Cenotaph,** a stark white mono-lith designed in 1920 by Edward Lutyens to commemorate the 1918 Armistice. ⊠ *Whitehall, Westminster, SW1* Ⓤ *Westminster.*

❼ St. James's Palace. With its scarlet-coated guard posted at the gate, this small palace of Tudor brick was a home for many British sovereigns, including the first Elizabeth and Charles I, who spent his last night here before his execution. Today it is the working office of another Charles—the Prince of Wales. Something to ponder as you look (you can't go in): foreign ambassadors to Britain are still accredited to the Court of St. James's even though it has rarely been a primary royal residence. ⊠ *Friary Court, St. James's, SW1* ⊕ *www.royal.gov.uk* Ⓤ *Green Park.*

☝ ❹ St. Martin-in-the-Fields. One of Britain's best-loved churches, St. Mar-tin's was completed in 1726; James Gibbs's classical temple-with-spire design became a familiar pattern for churches in colonial America. The church is a haven for music lovers; the Academy of St. Martin-in-the-Fields, an internationally known orchestra, was founded here, and popular lunchtime and evening concerts (free or reasonably priced) con-tinue today. ■ TIP→ **You can pop in and attend rehearsals for free, a tran-quil break from the city's bustle.** The church's fusty interior is wonderful for music making, but the wooden benches make hard seats. The Crypt is a hive of lively activity, with an excellent café and bookshop, plus the **London Brass-Rubbing Centre,** where you can make your own life-size souvenir knight, lady, or monarch from replica tomb brasses. ⊠ *Trafalgar Sq., Covent Garden, WC2* ☏ *020/7766–1100, 020/ 7839–8362 evening-concert credit-card bookings* ⊕ *www.stmartin-in-the-fields.org* ⊙ *Church daily 8–8; crypt Mon.–Sat. 10–8 (brass-rub-bing center until 6), Sun. noon–6; box office Mon.–Sat. 10–5* Ⓤ *Charing Cross, Leicester Sq.*

❽ Spencer House. Ancestral abode of the Spencers, the family of Princess Diana, this great mansion is perhaps the finest London example of 18th-century elegance on a domestic scale. The house was built in 1766 for the first earl Spencer, heir to the first duchess of Marlborough; the family hasn't lived here since 1926. The most ostentatious part of the house is the florid bow window of the Palm Room: covered with stucco palm trees, it conjures up both ancient Palmyra and modern Miami Beach. The garden, of Henry Holland design, has plantings of his era. Both the house and garden can be seen only by guided tour, so book in advance. ⊠ *27 St. James's Pl., St. James's, SW1* ☏ *020/7499–8620* ⊕ *www. spencerhouse.co.uk* 🎟 *£9* ⊙ *House: Feb.–July and Sept.–Dec., Sun. 10:45–4:45; 1-hr guided tour leaves about every 25 mins (tickets on sale Sun. at 10:30). Garden: late May–July* Ⓤ *Green Park.*

⓫ Wellington Barracks. These are the headquarters of the Queen's five reg-iments of foot guards, who protect the sovereign and patrol her palace dressed in tunics of gold-purled scarlet and tall busbies of black bearskin. The entrance to the **Guards Museum** is next to the Guards Chapel. ⊠ *Wellington Barracks, Birdcage Walk, Westminster, SW1* ☏ *020/ 7414–3428* 🎟 *£2* ⊙ *Daily 10–4; last admission 3:30* Ⓤ *St. James's Park.*

Soho & Covent Garden

Once a red-light district, the Soho of today delivers more "grown-up" than "adult" entertainment. Its theaters, restaurants, pubs, and clubs merge with the first-run cinemas of Leicester Square and the venerable venues (Royal and English National Operas) of Covent Garden to create the mega-entertainment district known as the West End. During the day, Covent Garden's historic piazza is packed with shoppers and sightseers, while Soho reverts to the business side of its lively, late-night scene—ad agencies, media, film distributors, actors, agents and casting agents all looking for each other.

A quadrilateral bounded by Regent Street, Coventry and Cranbourn streets, Charing Cross Road, and the eastern half of Oxford Street encloses Soho. This appellation, unlike the New York City neighborhood's similar one, is not an abbreviation of anything, but a blast from the past—derived from the shouts of "So-ho!" that royal huntsmen in Whitehall Palace's parklands were once heard to cry. For many years Soho was London's peep show–sex shop–brothel center. Legislation in the mid-1980s granted expensive licenses to a few such establishments and closed down the rest. Today Soho remains the address of wonderful ethnic restaurants, including those of London's Chinatown.

The Covent Garden Market became the Covent Garden Piazza in 1980. It was originally the "convent garden" belonging to the Abbey of St. Peter at Westminster (later Westminster Abbey), and still functions as the center of a neighborhood—one that has always been alluded to as "colorful." After centuries of magnificence and misery, Covent Garden became London's vegetable and flower market in the 19th century. When the produce moved to the Nine Elms Market in Vauxhall in 1974, the glass-covered market halls took on new life with stores and entertainment. Today it bustles with tourists and shoppers.

TIMING Although you may well get lost in the area's winding streets, you can whiz around both neighborhoods in an hour or you can spend all day—for shopping, lunch, and Somerset House. You might stop by Leicester Square and visit tkts, the Society of London Theatre(SOLT) half-price ticket kiosk (opens at 10 Monday through Saturday, noon Sunday), pick up tickets for later, and walk, shop, and eat in between.

GETTING HERE Take any train to the Piccadilly Circus station (on the Piccadilly and Bakerloo lines or Leicester Square and Northern lines for Soho). Get off at Covent Garden on the Piccadilly Line for Covent Garden and Embankment (Bakerloo, Northern, District and Circle lines) or Charing Cross (Northern, Bakerloo and main railway lines) for the area south of the Strand. Bus numbers 14, 19, and 38 run along Shaftesbury Avenue; 24, 29, and 176 run along Charing Cross Road; and 6, 9, 11, 13, 15, 23, 77A, 91, 139, and 176 run along the Strand.

Numbers in the margin correspond to numbers on the Soho & Covent Garden map.

Main Attractions

Courtauld Institute Gallery. One of London's most beloved art collections, the Courtauld is in the grounds of the 18th-century **Somerset House.** Founded in 1931 by textile magnate Samuel Courtauld to house his private collection, this is one of the world's finest impressionist and postimpressionist galleries, with works by masters from Bonnard to van Gogh. A déja vu moment with Cézanne, Degas, Seurat, or Monet awaits on every wall (Manet's *Bar at the Folies-Bergère* is the star), with bonus post-Renaissance works thrown in. ✉ *The Strand, Covent Garden, WC2* ☎ *020/7848–2526* ⊕ *www.courtauld.ac.uk* 🎟 *£5, free Mon. 10–2, except bank holidays;* ⊘ *Daily 10–6; last admission at 5:15* Ⓤ *Covent Garden, Holborn, Temple.*

👣 ❷ **Covent Garden Piazza.** The restored 1840 market building around which Covent Garden pivots is known as the Piazza. Inigo Jones, the King's Surveyor of Works, designed the entire area in the 1630s, including **St. Paul's Church** (known as the actors' church). Buskers perform under the church's portico, where the first scene of the play *Pygmalion* (and the musical *My Fair Lady*) take place. Inside the Piazza, the shops are mostly higher-class clothing chains, plus a couple of cafés and some knickknack stores that are good for gifts. There's the superior **Apple Market** for crafts on most days, too. If you turn right, you'll reach the indoor **Jubilee Market,** which, with its stalls of clothing, army surplus gear, and more crafts and knickknacks, is disappointingly ordinary. In summer it may seem that everyone you see around the Piazza (and the crowds are legion) is a fellow tourist, but there's still plenty of office life in the area. Londoners who shop in the area tend to head for Neal Street and the area to the left of the subway entrance rather than the touristy market itself. By the church in the square, street performers—from global musicians to jugglers and mimes—play to the crowds, as they have done since the first English Punch and Judy Show, staged here in the 17th century. ✉ *Bordered by Henrietta St., King St., Russell St., and Bedford St., Covent Garden, WC2* Ⓤ *Covent Garden.*

> **FEELING PECKISH?**
>
> Although they may set out a few tables, the coffee shops and snack bars along the Covent Garden market buildings are better for takeout than for comfortable coffee breaks or lunches. They can be overpriced and of iffy quality. Head for Soho when the munchies strike.

★ ❺ **Somerset House.** This grand 18th-century pile, constructed during the reign of George III, was designed to house government offices, principally those of the navy. The gracious rooms on the south side of the building, by the river, are free, including the Seamen's Waiting Hall and the Nelson Stair. The **Courtauld Institute Gallery** occupies most of the north building, facing the busy Strand. Cafés and a river terrace adjoin the property, and a footbridge leads on to Waterloo Bridge. In the vaults of the house is the **Gilbert Collection,** a museum with intricate works of silver, gold snuffboxes, and Italian mosaics. **The Hermitage Rooms** have treasures from the State Hermitage Museum in Russia. ✉ *The Strand, Covent Garden, WC2* ☎ *020/7845–4600, 020/*

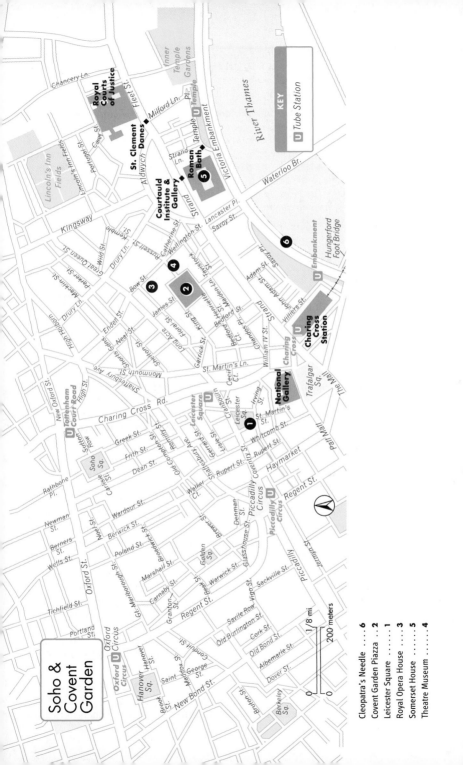

Soho & Covent Garden

KEY

U Tube Station

Cleopatra's Needle 6
Covent Garden Piazza ..2
Leicester Square 1
Royal Opera House 3
Somerset House 5
Theatre Museum 4

7485–4630 *Hermitage information* ⊕ *www.somerset-house.org.uk* ✉ *Somerset House free; galleries £5 each* ◔ *Daily 10–6; last admission at 5:15* Ⓤ *Charing Cross.*

Also Worth Seeing

❻ **Cleopatra's Needle.** Off the triangular-handkerchief Victoria Embankment Gardens is London's *very oldest thing,* predating its arbitrary namesake, and London itself, by centuries. The 60-foot red-granite obelisk was erected at Heliopolis, in lower Egypt, in about 1475 BC, then moved to Alexandria. In 1819 Mohammed Ali, the Albanian-born viceroy of Egypt, presented it to the British to commemorate Admiral Lord Nelson and the Battle of the Nile. ✉ *Embankment, Covent Garden, WC2* Ⓤ *Charing Cross, Embankment.*

❶ **Leicester Square.** Looking at the neon of the major movie houses, the fast-food outlets (plus a useful Häagen-Dazs café), and the disco entrances, you'd never guess the square was laid out around 1630. By the 19th century it was already bustling and disreputable, and now it's usually one of the few places crowded after midnight—with suburban teenagers, backpackers, and London's swelling ranks of the homeless. That said, it's not a threatening place, and the liveliness can be quite cheering. But be on your guard—any place so full of tourists and people a little the worse for wear is bound to attract pickpockets and Leicester Square certainly does. In the middle is a statue of a sulking Shakespeare, clearly wishing he were somewhere else and perhaps remembering the days when the cinemas were live theaters—burlesque houses, but live all the same. Here, too, are figures of Hogarth, Reynolds, and Charlie Chaplin. ■ TIP→ **One landmark worth visiting is tkts, the Society of London Theatre ticket kiosk, which sells half-price tickets for many of that evening's performances. It's open Monday through Saturday from 10 AM to 7 PM, and Sunday from noon to 3 PM.** ✉ *Leicester Sq., Covent Garden, WC2* Ⓤ *Covent Garden.*

♻ **London's Transport Museum.** Normally housed in the old Flower Market at the southeast corner of the Covent Garden Piazza, the museum is closed for redevelopment and not scheduled to reopen until late 2007. Most exhibits have been moved to a temporary location, the Museum Depot in the West London suburbs. The Depot is occasionally open for guided tours and open weekends. Visit the museum Web site for access information. ⊕ *www.ltmuseum.co.uk.*

❸ **Royal Opera House.** London's premier opera and ballet venue was designed in 1858 by E. M. Barry, son of Sir Charles, the architect of the House of Commons building. Without doubt, the glass-and-steel Floral Hall is the most jaw-dropping feature, and you can wander in during the day, when there may be free lunchtime concerts and events. The Amphitheatre Bar and Piazza concourse give a splendid panorama across the city. ✉ *Bow St., Covent Garden, WC2* ☎ *020/7304–4000* ⊕ *www.royaloperahouse.org* Ⓤ *Covent Garden.*

♻ ❹ **Theatre Museum.** This mostly below-ground museum aims to re-create the excitement of theater itself. There are usually programs in progress allowing children to have a giant dressing-up session. Permanent exhibits paint a history of the English stage from the 16th century to Mick Jagger's jumpsuit, with tens of thousands of theater playbills and sections on such topics as pantomime—the peculiar British theatrical tradition when men dress as ugly women, known as Panto Dames, and girls wear tights and play princes. There's a ticket desk for "real" theaters around town, plus an archive holding video recordings and audiotapes of significant British theatrical productions. ✉ *7 Russell St., Covent Garden, WC2* ☎ *020/7943–4700* ⊕ *www.theatremuseum.org* 💷 *Free* ☉ *Tues.–Sun. 10–6; last admission 5:30* Ⓤ *Covent Garden.*

Bloomsbury & Legal London

The hub of intellectual London, Bloomsbury is anchored by the British Museum and the University of London, which houses—among other institutions—the internationally ranked London School of Economics and the School of Oriental and African Studies. As a result, the streets and cafés around Bloomsbury's Russell Square are often crawling with students and professors engaged in heated conversation, while literary agents and academics surf the shelves of the antiquarian bookstores nearby.

The character of an area of London can change visibly from one street to the next. Nowhere is this so clear as in the contrast between fun-loving Soho and intellectual Bloomsbury, a mere 100 yards to the northeast, or between arty, trendy Covent Garden and—on the other side of Kingsway—sober Holborn (pronounced *hoe*-bun). Bloomsbury is known for its famous flowering of literary-arty bohemia, personified during the first three decades of the 20th century by the clique known as the Bloomsbury Group, including Virginia Woolf, E. M. Forster, Vanessa Bell, and Lytton Strachey. The second, filled with ancient buildings of the legal profession, is more interesting and beautiful than you might suppose. The Great Fire of 1666 razed most of the city but spared the buildings of legal London, and all of Holborn oozes history. Leading landmarks here are the Inns of Court, where the country's top solicitors and barristers have had their chambers for centuries.

TIMING Both Bloomsbury and Holborn are almost purely residential and should be seen by day. Bloomsbury includes the British Museum, where you could spend two hours—or two days. The Charles Dickens Museum is also worth a stop. In legal London, most of the highlights are in the architecture, with the exception of Sir John Soane's Museum. Avoid the area around King's Cross Station at night.

GETTING HERE You can walk easily around Bloomsbury, and the Russell Square Tube stop on the Piccadilly Line leaves you right at the corner of Russell Square. The best Tube stops for the Inns of Court are Holborn on the Central and Piccadilly lines or Chancery Lane on the Central Line. Tottenham Court Road on the Northern and Central lines or Russell Square (Piccadilly Line) are best for the British Museum. You can often find taxis near the British Museum or by the entrance to the hotels off Russell Square. Bus 7 is the best bus for the British Museum; for Inns of Court, take Bus 8, 17, 25, 45, 46, or 242 to High Holborn or Bus 17, 19, 38, 45, 46, 55, or 243 to Theobalds Road.

Numbers in the margin correspond to numbers on the Bloomsbury &
Legal London map.

Main Attractions

❶ British Museum. With a facade like a great temple, this celebrated treasure house, filled with plunder of incalculable value and beauty from around
the globe, occupies a ponderous Greco-Victorian building that makes
a suitably grand impression. Inside are some of the greatest relics of hu-
mankind: the Elgin Marbles, the Rosetta Stone, the Sutton Hoo Treasure—almost everything, it seems, but the Ark of the Covenant. Many
sections have been updated, particularly in ethnography, including the
impressive **Sainsbury African Galleries.** The focal point is the **Great Court,**
a brilliant techno-classical design with a vast glass roof that highlights
and reveals the museum's most well-kept secret—an inner courtyard.
The revered **Reading Room** has a blue-and-gold dome, ancient tomes,
and computer screens. If you want to navigate the highlights of the almost 100 galleries, join at least one of the free **Eyeopener** 50-minute tours
by museum guides (details at the information desk).

FodorsChoice
★

The collection began in 1753 and grew quickly, thanks to enthusiastic
kleptomaniacs during the Napoleonic Wars—most notoriously the seventh earl of Elgin, who acquired the marbles from the Parthenon and
Erechtheum in Athens during his term as British ambassador in Con-
stantinople. Here follows a highly edited résumé (in order of encounter)
of the British Museum's greatest hits: close to the entrance hall, in
Room 4, is the **Rosetta Stone,** found by French soldiers in 1799, and
carved in 196 BC with a decree of Ptolemy V in Egyptian hieroglyphics,
demotic (a cursive script developed in Egypt), and Greek. This inscription provided the French Egyptologist Jean-François Champollion with
the key to deciphering hieroglyphics. Maybe the **Parthenon Marbles** ought
to be back in Greece, but since these graceful sculptures are here, make
a beeline for them in Room 18, west of the entrance in the Parthenon
Galleries. These galleries include the spectacular remains of the Parthenon
frieze that girdled the cella of Athena's temple on the Acropolis, carved
around 440 BC. Also in the West Wing is one of the Seven Wonders of
the Ancient World—in fragment
form—in Room 21: the **Mausoleum
of Halikarnassos.** The **JP Morgan
Chase North American Gallery**
(Room 26) has one of the largest
collections of native culture outside the North American continent,
going back to the earliest hunters
10,000 years ago.

Upstairs are some of the most popular galleries, especially beloved by
children: Rooms 62–63, where the
Egyptian mummies live. Nearby are
the glittering 4th-century **Mildenhall
Treasure** and the equally splendid
8th-century Anglo-Saxon **Sutton**

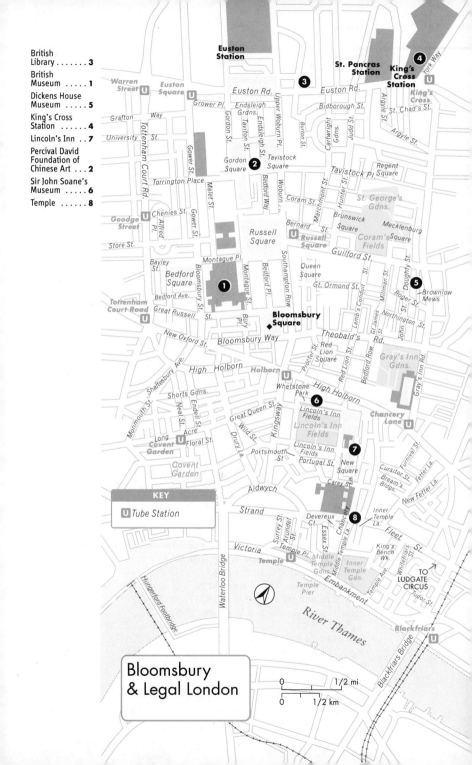

British
Library **3**

British
Museum **1**

Dickens House
Museum **5**

King's Cross
Station **4**

Lincoln's Inn . . **7**

Percival David
Foundation of
Chinese Art . . . **2**

Sir John Soane's
Museum **6**

Temple **8**

KEY

U Tube Station

Bloomsbury
& Legal London

0   1/2 mi

0   1/2 km

Hoo Treasure (with a magnificent helmet and jewelry). A more prosaic exhibit is that of Pete Marsh, sentimentally named by the archaeologists who unearthed the **Lindow Man** from a Cheshire peat marsh; poor Pete was ritually slain in the 1st century, probably as a human sacrifice. The **Korean Gallery** (Room 67) delves into the art and archaeology of the country, including precious porcelain and colorful screens. ⊠ *Great Russell St., Bloomsbury, WC1* ☎ *020/7636–1555* ⊕ *www.thebritishmuseum.ac. uk* ⊠ *Free, suggested donation £2* ⊘ *Museum Sat.–Wed. 10–5:30, Thurs. and Fri. 10–8:30. Great Court Sun.–Wed. 9–6, Thurs.–Sat. 9 AM–11 PM* Ⓤ *Holborn, Russell Sq., Tottenham Court Rd.*

NEED A BREAK? The British Museum's **Gallery Café** gets very crowded but serves a reasonably tasty menu beneath a plaster cast of a part of the Parthenon frieze. It's open daily 10 to 5. The self-service café in the Great Court concourse is open Sunday through Wednesday 9 to 5:30 and Thursday through Saturday 9 to 9.

Ⓒ ❺ **Dickens House Museum.** This is the only one of the many London houses Charles Dickens (1812–70) inhabited that's still standing. The great novelist wrote *Oliver Twist* and *Nicholas Nickleby* and finished *The Pickwick Papers* here between 1837 and 1839. The house looks exactly as it would have in Dickens's day, complete with first editions, letters, and tall clerk's desk, plus a treat for Lionel Bart fans—his score for the musical *Oliver!* Christmas is a memorable time to visit, as the rooms are decorated in traditional style. ⊠ *48 Doughty St., Bloomsbury, WC1* ☎ *020/7405–2127* ⊕ *www.dickensmuseum.com* ⊠ *£5* ⊘ *Mon.–Sat. 10–5, Sun. 11–5; last admission at 4:30* Ⓤ *Chancery La., Russell Sq.*

★ ❼ **Lincoln's Inn.** There's plenty to see at one of the oldest and most comely of the Inns of Court—from the Chancery Lane Tudor brick gatehouse to the wide-open, tree-lined Lincoln's Inn Fields and the 15th-century chapel. The wisteria-clad New Square is the city's only complete 17th-century square. ⊠ *Chancery La., Bloomsbury, WC2* ☎ *020/7405–1393* ⊠ *Free* ⊘ *Gardens weekdays 7–7; chapel weekdays noon–2:30; public may also attend Sun. service at 11:30 in chapel during legal terms* Ⓤ *Chancery La.*

★ ❻ **Sir John Soane's Museum.** Guaranteed to raise a smile from the most blasé traveler, this collection hardly deserves the burden of its dry name. Sir John, architect of the Bank of England, who lived here from 1790 to 1831, created one of London's most idiosyncratic and fascinating houses. He obviously had enormous fun with his home, having had the means to finance great experiments in perspective and scale and to fill the space with some wonderful pieces. Everywhere mirrors and colors play tricks with light and space, and split-level floors worthy of a fairground fun house disorient you. In a basement chamber sits the vast 1300 BC sarcophagus of Seti I, lighted by a skylight two stories above. ⊠ *13 Lincoln's Inn Fields, Bloomsbury, WC2* ☎ *020/7405–2107* ⊕ *www.soane. org* ⊠ *Free, Sat. tour £3* ⊘ *Tues.–Sat. 10–5; also 6–9 PM on 1st Tues. of every month; tours Sat. at 2:30* Ⓤ *Holborn.*

Also Worth Seeing

❸ **British Library.** Since 1759, the British Library had been housed in the British Museum—but space ran out in the 1990s, necessitating this grand edifice, a few blocks north of the museum, between Euston and St. Pancras stations. The collection includes 18 million volumes, and the library's treasures are on public view. ■ TIP→ **Don't miss the fine John Ritblat Gallery, which displays the Magna Carta, the Gutenberg Bible, Jane Austen's manuscripts, Shakespeare's First Folio, and musical manuscripts by George Frideric Handel and Sir Paul McCartney.** Use the headphones to listen to some interesting snippets in a small showcase of the **National Sound Archive,** such as the voice of Florence Nightingale and an extract from the Beatles' last tour interview. ⊠ *96 Euston Rd., Bloomsbury, NW1* ☏ *020/7412–7332* ⊕ *www.bl.uk* ⊠ *Free; charge for special exhibitions* ⊙ *Mon. and Wed.–Fri. 9:30–6, Tues. 9:30–8, Sat. 9:30–5, Sun. and bank holiday Mon. 11–5* Ⓤ *Euston or King's Cross.*

❷ Percival David Foundation of Chinese Art. This collection, belonging to the University of London, is dominated by ceramics from the Sung to Qing dynasties—from the 10th to the 19th century, in other words. It's on **Gordon Square,** which Virginia Woolf, the Bells, John Maynard Keynes (all at No. 46), and Lytton Strachey (at No. 51) called home for a while. ⊠ *53 Gordon Sq., Bloomsbury, WC1* ☏ *020/7387–3909* ⊕ *www. pdfmuseum.org.uk* ⊠ *Free* ⊙ *Weekdays 10:30–5* Ⓤ *Russell Sq.*

☾ ❹ King's Cross Station. Known for its 120-foot-tall clock tower, this yellow-brick Italianate building with large, arched windows was constructed in 1851–52 as the London terminus for the Great Northern Railway. Harry Potter took the Hogwarts Express to school from the imaginary platform 9¾ (platforms 4 and 5 were the actual shooting site) in the movies based on J. K. Rowling's popular novels. The station has put up a sign for platform 9¾; you can snap a picture there. ⊠ *Euston Rd. and York Way, Euston, NW1* ☏ *0845/748–4950* Ⓤ *King's Cross.*

❽ Temple. This is the collective name for the **Inner Temple** and **Middle Temple,** and its entrance, the point of entry into the City, is marked by a young (1880) bronze griffin, the **Temple Bar Memorial,** which makes a splendidly heraldic snapshot and marks the symbolic City Border. In the buildings opposite is an elaborate stone arch through which you pass into Middle Temple Lane, past a row of 17th-century timber-frame houses, and on into Fountain Court. If the Elizabethan **Middle Temple Hall** is open, don't miss its hammer-beam roof—among the finest in the land. ⊠ *Middle Temple La., Bloomsbury, EC4* ☏ *020/7427–4800* ⊙ *Weekdays 10–11 and, when not in use, 2–4* Ⓤ *Temple.*

The City

The City, as opposed to the city, is the capital's fast-beating financial heart. Behind a host of imposing neoclassical facades lie the banks and exchanges whose frantic trade determines the fortunes that underpin London—and the country. But the "Square Mile" is much more than London's Wall Street—the capital's economic engine room also has currency as a religious and political center. St. Paul's Cathedral has looked after Londoners' souls since the seventh century, and the Tower of London—that moat-surrounded royal fortress, prison, and jewel house—has taken care of beheading them. The City's maze of backstreets is also home to a host of old churches, marketplaces, and cozy pubs.

The City extends eastward from Temple Bar to the Tower of London, and north from the Thames to Chiswell Street. The pedestrian-only Millennium Bridge connects the area with the South Bank; it's well worth the walk. Twice, the City has been nearly wiped off the face of the earth. The Great Fire of 1666 necessitated a total reconstruction, in which Sir Christopher Wren had a big hand, contributing not only his masterpiece, St. Paul's Cathedral, but 49 additional parish churches. The second wave of destruction was dealt by the German bombers of World War II. The ruins were rebuilt, but slowly, and with no overall plan, leaving the City a patchwork of the old and the new, the interesting and the flagrantly awful. Since a mere 8,000 or so people call it home, the nation's financial center is deserted on weekends, with restaurants shuttered.

TIMING The "Square Mile" is as compact as the nickname suggests, with very little distance between points of interest, making it easy to dip into the City in short bursts. For full immersion in the Tower of London, set aside half a day. Allow an hour minimum for the Museum of London, St. Paul's Cathedral, and the Tower Bridge each. On weekends, without the scurrying suits, the City is nearly deserted, making it hard to find lunch—and yet this is when the major attractions are at their busiest. So if you can manage to come on a weekday, do so.

GETTING HERE The City is well-served by Underground stops. St. Paul's and Bank, on the Central Line, and Mansion House, Cannon Street, and Monument, on the District and Circle lines, deliver visitors to the heart of the City. Liverpool Street and Aldgate border the City's eastern edge, whereas Chancery Lane and Farringdon lie to the west. Barbican and Moorgate provide easy access to the theaters and galleries of the Barbican, while Blackfriars, to the south, leads to Ludgate Circus and Fleet Street.

Numbers in the margin correspond to numbers on the City map.

Main Attractions

🕒 ❼ **Millennium Bridge.** Norman Foster and sculptor Anthony Caro designed this strikingly modern, pedestrian-only bridge of aluminum and steel. The bridge connects the City—the St. Paul's Cathedral area—with the Tate Modern art gallery. On the South Bank side, the bridge marks the middle of the **Millennium Mile,** a walkway taking in a clutch of popular sights. The views from the bridge are breathtaking, with perhaps the best-ever view of St. Paul's. ✉ *Peters Hill to Bankside, The City, South Bank, EC4, SE1* Ⓤ *Mansion House, Blackfriars, or Southwark.*

🕒 ⓭ **Monument.** Commemorating the "dreadful visitation" of the Great Fire of 1666, the world's tallest isolated stone column is the work of Christopher Wren. The viewing gallery is 311 steps up the 202-foot-high structure. ✉ *Monument St., The City, EC3* ☎ *020/7626–2717* ⊕ *www. towerbridge.org.uk* 💷 *£2, combination ticket gives £1 discount off entry to Tower Bridge* 🕐 *Daily 10–5:40; hrs subject to change, phone before visiting* Ⓤ *Monument.*

★ 🕒 ❻ **Museum of London.** If there's one place to get the history of London sorted out, right from 450,000 BC to the present day, it's here—although there's a great deal to sort out: Oliver Cromwell's death mask, Queen Victoria's crinolined gowns, Selfridges' art deco elevators, and the Lord

Mayor's coach are just some of the goodies. The displays—like one of the Great Fire, a 1940s air-raid shelter, a Georgian prison cell, a Roman living room, and a Victorian street complete with fully stocked shops—are complemented by rich soundscapes that atmospherically re-create London life through the ages. ⊠ *London Wall, The City, EC2* ☎ *020/ 7600–0807* ⊕ *www.museumoflondon.org.uk* ⊠ *Free* ◷ *Mon.–Sat. 10–5:50, Sun. noon–5:50, last admission 5:30* Ⓤ *Barbican.*

❷ St. Bride's. The distinctively tiered steeple of this Christopher Wren–designed church gave rise to the shape of the traditional wedding cake. As St. Paul's (in Covent Garden) is the actors' church, so St. Bride's belongs to journalists. The crypts house a museum of the church's rich history, and a bit of Roman sidewalk. ⊠*Fleet St., The City, EC4* ☎*020/7427–0133* ⊕ *www.stbrides.com* ⊠ *Free* ◷ *Weekdays 8–6, Sat. 11–3, Sun. for services only 10–1 and 5–7:30; crypt closed Sun.* Ⓤ *Chancery La.*

❸ St. Mary-le-Bow. Christopher Wren's 1673 church has one of the most famous sets of bells—a Londoner must be born within the sound of Bow Bells to be a true cockney. The origin of that idea was probably the curfew rung on the Bow Bells during the 14th century. The name comes from the bow-shape arches in the Norman crypt. ⊠ *Cheapside, The City, EC2* ☎ *020/7248–5139* ⊕ *www.stmarylebow.co.uk* ◷ *Mon.–Thurs. 6:30–5:45, Fri. 6:30–4* Ⓤ *Mansion House.*

NEED A BREAK?

The Place Below (⊠ Cheapside, The City, EC2 ☎ 020/7329–0789), in St. Mary-le-Bow's crypt, is packed with City workers weekdays at lunchtime. The self-service vegetarian menu includes good soup and quiche. Lunches are served weekdays from 10:30 until 2:30. It's also open for breakfast.

❺ St. Paul's Cathedral. The symbolic heart of London, St. Paul's may take your breath away, even more so now that it's been spruced up for its 300th anniversary. The dome—the world's third largest—peeps through the skyline from many an angle around London. The structure is Sir Christopher Wren's masterpiece, completed in 1710 after 35 years of building, and, much later, miraculously spared (mostly) by World War II bombs. Wren's first plan, known as the New Model, did not make it past the drawing board. The second, known as the Great Model, got as far as the 20-foot oak rendering you can see here before it also was rejected. The third was accepted, with the fortunate coda that the architect be allowed to make changes as he saw fit. Without that, there would be no dome, since the approved design had a steeple. When you enter and see the dome from the inside, it may seem smaller than you expected. It *is* smaller, and 60 feet lower than the lead-covered outer dome. Beneath the lantern is Wren's famous epitaph, which his son composed and had set into the pavement, and which reads succinctly: Lector, si monumentum requiris, circumspice—"Reader, if you seek his monument, look around you." The epitaph also appears on Wren's memorial in the Crypt. Up 259 spiral steps is the **Whispering Gallery,** an acoustic phenomenon; you whisper something to the wall on one side, and a second later it transmits clearly to the other side, 107 feet away. Ascend to the **Stone Gallery,** which encircles the base of the dome. Farther up (280 feet from ground level) is the small **Golden Gallery,** around

Fodor'sChoice
★

the dome's highest point. From both these galleries (if you have a head for heights) you can walk outside for a spectacular panorama of London. The climb up the spiraling steps can be fun for older kids.

The remains of the poet John Donne, who was dean of St. Paul's for his final 10 years (he died in 1631), are in the south choir aisle. The vivacious choir-stall carvings nearby are the work of Grinling Gibbons, as are those on the organ, which Wren designed and Handel

> ### MUSICAL FRICTION
>
> The organ at St. Paul's, with its cherubs and angels, was not installed without controversy. The mighty instrument proved a tight fit, and the maker, known as Father Schmidt, and Wren nearly came to blows. Wren was reputed to have said he would not adapt his cathedral for a mere "box of whistles."

played. Behind the high altar is the **American Memorial Chapel,** dedicated in 1958 to the 28,000 GIs stationed in the United Kingdom who lost their lives in World War II. Among the famous whose remains lie in the **Crypt** are the duke of Wellington and Admiral Lord Nelson. The Crypt also has a gift shop and a café. ⊠ *St. Paul's Churchyard, The City, EC4* ☎ *020/7236–4128* ⊕ *www.stpauls.co.uk* ✉ *£9, audio tour £3.50, guided tour £3* ☉ *Cathedral Mon.–Sat. 8:30–4, closed occasionally for special services; ambulatory, Crypt, and galleries Mon.–Sat. 9–5:15. Shop and Crypt Café also open Sun. 10:30–5* Ⓤ *St. Paul's.*

❹ Temple Bar. This 1670s gateway to the City of London stands about a mile from its original site, which marked the western limit of the City. For centuries before, a simple chain or "bar" was the gateway—hence the name—followed by a stone gate (with prison above). After the Fire of London, Wren rebuilt the gate in grand Grecian Corinthian style with three arches. The Portland stone gleams with its friezes, cornices, and statues of Stuart monarchs, in its new home as a classic entrance to the square in front of St. Paul's Cathedral. As you admire the gateway's gorgeous facade, surrounded by modern office buildings, you might muse upon the grisly heads and body parts of traitors that used to adorn it more than 300 years ago. ⊠ *Paternoster Sq., The City, EC4* ⊕ *www. cityoflondon.gov.uk* Ⓤ *St. Paul's.*

★ ☾ ⓬ **Tower Bridge.** Despite its appearance, this Victorian youngster dates from 1894. Constructed of steel, then clothed in Portland stone, the bridge was built in the Gothic style to complement the Tower of London next door. It's famous for the enormous bascules, the "arms" that open to allow large ships through. The **Tower Bridge Experience** exhibition is a fun tour inside the structure to discover how one of the world's most famous bridges actually works. One highlight is the glorious view from up high on the covered walkway between the turrets. ☎ *020/7403–3761* ⊕ *www.towerbridge.org.uk* ✉ *£5.50, joint ticket available for Monument* ☉ *Daily 9:30–5:30; last admission 5* Ⓤ *Tower Hill.*

★ ☾ ⓫ **Tower of London.** Nowhere else does London's history come to life so vividly as in this minicity of 20 towers filled with heraldry and treasure, the intimate details of lords and dukes and princes and sovereigns etched in the walls (literally, in some places), and quite a few pints of

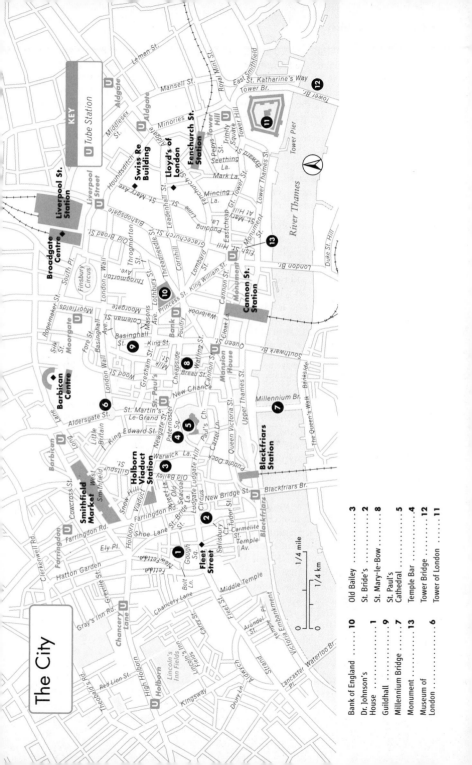

The City

KEY

Ⓤ Tube Station

Bank of England **10**

Dr. Johnson's
House **1**

Guildhall **9**

Millennium Bridge **7**

Monument **13**

Museum of
London **6**

Old Bailey **3**

St. Bride's **2**

St. Mary-le-Bow **8**

St. Paul's
Cathedral **5**

Temple Bar **4**

Tower Bridge **12**

Tower of London **11**

0   1/4 mile

0   1/4 km

royal blood spilled on the stones. ■ TIP➔ **This is one of Britain's popular sights—the Crown Jewels are here—and you can avoid lines by buying a ticket in advance on the Web site, by phone, or at any tube station; arriving before 11 can also help at busy times.** The visitor center provides an introduction to the Tower. Allow at least three hours for exploring, and take time to stroll along the battlements for a wonderful overview.

The Tower holds the royal gems because it's still one of the royal palaces, although no monarch since Henry VII has called it home. It has also housed the Royal Mint, the Public Records, the Royal Menagerie (which formed the basis of the London Zoo), and the Royal Observatory, although its most renowned and titillating function has been as a jail and place of torture and execution.

A person was mighty privileged to be beheaded in the peace and seclusion of **Tower Green** instead of before the mob at Tower Hill. In fact, only seven people were ever important enough—among them Anne Boleyn and Catherine Howard, wives two and five of Henry VIII's six; Elizabeth I's friend Robert Devereux, earl of Essex; and the nine-day queen, Lady Jane Grey, age 17. The executioner's block and ax, along with the equally famous rack, plus assorted thumbscrews, "iron maidens," and so forth, have been moved to the Royal Armouries in Leeds, Yorkshire. (Fans of this genre of heavy metal might want to pay a call on the London Dungeon attraction, just across the Thames.)

Free tours depart every half hour or so from the Middle Tower. They are conducted by the 39 Yeoman Warders, better known as Beefeaters—ex-servicemen dressed in resplendent navy-and-red (scarlet-and-gold on special occasions) Tudor outfits. Beefeaters have been guarding the Tower since Henry VII appointed them in 1485. One of them, the Yeoman Ravenmaster, is responsible for making life comfortable for the Tower ravens (six birds plus reserves)—an important duty, because if the ravens were to desert the Tower, goes the legend, the kingdom would fall. Today, the Tower takes no chances: the ravens' wings are clipped.

In prime position stands the oldest part of the Tower and the most conspicuous of its buildings, the **White Tower;** the other towers were built in the next few centuries. This central keep was begun in 1078 by William the Conqueror; Henry III (1207–72) had it whitewashed, which is where the name comes from. The spiral staircase is the only way up, and here are the **Royal Armouries,** with a collection of arms and armor. Most of the interior of the White Tower has been altered over the centuries, but the **Chapel of St. John the Evangelist,** downstairs from the armories, is a pure example of 11th-century Norman style—very rare, very simple, and very beautiful. Across the moat, **Traitors' Gate** lies to the right. Opposite Traitors' Gate is the former Garden Tower, better known since about 1570 as the **Bloody Tower.** Its name comes from one of the most famous unsolved murders in history, the saga of the "little princes in the Tower." In 1483 the uncrowned boy king, Edward V, and his brother Richard were left here by their uncle, Richard of Gloucester, after the death of their father, Edward IV. They were never seen again, Gloucester was crowned Richard III, and in 1674 two little skeletons were found under the stairs to the White Tower. The obvious conclusions have always been drawn—and were, in fact, even before the skeletons were discovered. The **New Armouries** have become a restaurant.

The most famous exhibits are the **Crown Jewels,** in the Jewel House, Waterloo Block. Moving walkways on either side of the jewels hasten progress at the busiest times. You get so close to the fabled gems you feel you could polish them (there are, however, wafers of bulletproof glass), if your eyes weren't so dazzled by the sparkle of the gems, enhanced with special lighting. Before you see them, you view a short film that includes scenes from Elizabeth's 1953 coronation. Security is tight because the jewels—even though they would be impossible for thieves to sell—are *so* priceless that they're not insured. However, they are polished every January by the crown jewelers. A brief résumé of the top jewels: finest of all is the Royal Sceptre, containing the earth's largest cut diamond, the 530-carat Star of Africa. This is also known as Cullinan I, having been cut from the South African Cullinan, which weighed 20 ounces when dug up from a De Beers mine at the beginning of the 20th century. Another chip off the block, Cullinan II, lives on the Imperial State Crown (made for Queen Victoria's coronation in 1838 and adapted to hold the large diamond); Elizabeth II wore this crown at her coronation and wears it annually for the State Opening of Parliament. Another famous gem is the Koh-i-noor, or "Mountain of Light." The legendary diamond, which was supposed to bring luck to women, came from India, and was given to the Queen in 1850. You can see it, in cutdown shape, in the late Queen Mother's Crown.

The little chapel of **St. Peter ad Vincula** is the second church on the site, and it conceals the remains of some 2,000 people executed at the Tower, Anne Boleyn and Catherine Howard among them.

Evocative **Beauchamp Tower** was built west of Tower Green by Edward I (1272–1307). It was soon designated as a jail for the higher class of miscreant, including Lady Jane Grey, who is thought to have added her Latin graffiti to the many inscriptions carved by prisoners here.

For tickets to the Ceremony of the Keys (locking of main gates, nightly between 9:30 and 10), write well in advance to the Resident Governor and Keeper of the Jewel House (at the Queen's House, address below). Give your name, the date you wish to attend (include alternate dates), and number of people (up to seven) in your party, and enclose a self-addressed, stamped envelope. ⊠ *H. M. Tower of London, Tower Hill, The City, EC3N* ☎ *0870/756–6060 recorded information and advance booking* ⊕ *www.hrp.org.uk* 🖃 *£15; joint tickets available with Kensington Palace and Hampton Court Palace* ☉ *Mar.–Oct., Tues.–Sat. 9–6, Sun. and Mon. 10–6; Nov.–Feb., Tues.–Sat. 9–5, Sun. and Mon. 10–5. Tower closes 1 hr after last admission time and all internal bldgs. close 30 mins after last admission. Free Yeoman Warder guided tours leave daily from Middle Tower (subject to weather and availability) about every 30 mins until 3:30 Mar.–Oct., 2:30 Nov.–Feb.* Ⓤ *Tower Hill.*

Also Worth Seeing

Ⓒ ❿ **Bank of England.** Known for the past couple of centuries as "the Old Lady of Threadneedle Street," the bank has been central to the British economy since 1694. Sir John Soane designed the neoclassical hulk in 1788, wrapping it in windowless walls, which are all that survive of his building. The bank's history is traced in the entertaining Bank of England Museum, around the corner on Bartholomew Lane. ⊠ *Threadneedle St., The City, EC4* ☎ *020/7601–5545* ⊕ *www.bankofengland.co.uk* 🖙 *Free* ☉ *Weekdays and Lord Mayor's Show Day (2nd Sat. in Nov.) 10–5* Ⓤ *Bank, Monument.*

❶ Dr. Johnson's House. This is where Samuel Johnson lived between 1746 and 1759, compiling his famous *Dictionary of the English Language* in the attic as his health deteriorated. The only one of Johnson's residences remaining today, its elegant Georgian lines make it exactly the kind of place you would expect the Great Bear, as Johnson was nicknamed, to live. It's a shrine to a most literary man who was passionate about London, and it includes a first edition of his dictionary among the mementos of Johnson and his friend and diarist James Boswell. ⊠ *17 Gough Sq., The City, EC4* ☎ *020/7353–3745* ⊕ *www.drjohnsonshouse. org* 🖙 *£4* ☉ *May–Sept., Mon.–Sat. 11–5:30; Oct.–Apr., Mon.–Sat. 11–5; closed bank holidays* Ⓤ *Blackfriars, Chancery La.*

❾ Guildhall. In the symbolic center of the City, the Corporation of London ceremonially elects and installs its Lord Mayor, as it has done for 800 years. The Guildhall was built in 1411, and although it failed to escape either the 1666 or 1940 flames, its core survived. The fabulous Great Hall is a patchwork of coats of arms. To the right of Guildhall Yard is the **Guildhall Art Gallery,** which includes portraits of the great and the good, cityscapes, famous battles, and a slightly cloying Pre-Raphaelite section. The construction of the gallery led to the discovery of London's only Roman amphitheater, which had lain underneath for more than 1,800 years. The 1970s west wing houses the the **Clockmakers' Company Museum,** with more than 600 timepieces. ⊠ *Gresham St., The City, EC2* ☎ *020/7606–3030, 020/7332–3700 gallery* ⊕ *www. guildhall-art-gallery.org.uk* 🖙 *Free, gallery and amphitheater £2.50* ☉ *Mon.–Sat. 9:30–5; museum weekdays 9:30–4:45; gallery Mon.–Sat. 10–5, Sun. noon–4* Ⓤ *St. Paul's, Moorgate, Bank, Mansion House.*

OFF THE
BEATEN
PATH

JACK THE RIPPER'S LONDON – *Cor blimey, guv'nor, Jack the Ripper woz here!* Several organizations offer tours of "Jack's London"—the (still) mean streets of the East End, the working-class neighborhood directly to the east of the City. Here, in 1888, the Whitechapel murders traumatized Victorian London. At the haunting hour, tour groups head out to Bucks Row and other crime scenes. Even with a large group, this can be a spooky experience. **Original London Walks** (☎ 020/7624–3978 ⊕ www.walks.com) has frequent tours leaving at 7 PM from the Tower Hill tube stop. The **Blood and Tears Walk: London's Horrible Past** (☎ 020/ 7625–5155) goes beyond Jack the Ripper and describes other murderers, as well. Tours depart from the Barbican tube; phone for times.

OFF THE
BEATEN
PATH

MUSEUM IN DOCKLANDS – This museum, in a converted quayside warehouse, focuses on the days when ships and sailors, rather than office towers, filled this part of London. The fascinating story of the old port and the river is told using films, together with interactive displays and reconstructions. ⊠ *No. 1 Warehouse, Hertsmere Rd., West India Quay,*

East End, E14 ☎ 0870/444–3857, 0870/444–3856 recorded information ⊕ www.museumindocklands.org.uk ✒ £5 (tickets valid for 1 year) ⊗ Daily 10–6, last admission 5:30 Ⓤ West India Quay.

❸ **Old Bailey.** The present-day Central Criminal Court is where legendary Newgate Prison stood from the 12th century until the early 20th century. Ask the doorman which current trial is likely to prove juicy, if you're that kind of ghoul—you may catch the conviction of the next Crippen or Christie (England's most notorious wife murderers, both tried here). The day's hearings are posted on the sign outside, but there are security restrictions, and children under 14 are not allowed in; call the information line first. *✉ Newgate St., The City, EC4 ☎ 020/7248–3277 ⊕ www.cityoflondon.gov.uk ⊗ Public Gallery weekdays 10:30–1 and 2–5 (approx.); line forms at Newgate St. entrance Ⓤ St. Paul's.*

The South Bank

Culture, history, sights: the South Bank has it all. Stretching from the Imperial War Museum in the southwest as far as the Design Museum in the east, high-caliber art, music, film, and theater venues sit alongside the likes of an aquarium, historic warships, and Borough Market, a foodie favorite. Pedestrians cross between the north and south banks using the futuristic Hungerford Bridge and the curvaceous Millennium Bridge, as they take in the compelling views of the Thames.

There's an old North London quip about needing a passport to cross the Thames, but times have changed dramatically. The Tate Modern is the star attraction, installed in a 1930s power station, with the eye-catching Millennium Bridge linking its main door across the river to the City. Near the theaters of the South Bank Centre, the British Airways London Eye observation wheel gives you a flight over the city. The South Bank of the Thames isn't beautiful, but this area of theaters and museums has Culture with a capital C. The '80s brought renovations and innovations such as Hay's Galleria and Butler's Wharf. In the '90s came the OXO Tower, the London Aquarium, and the reconstruction of Shakespeare's Globe. With the new century came the massive mushroom-like building designed by Norman Foster, which sits by the Thames near Tower Bridge; it is City Hall, which houses the London Assembly.

It's fitting that so much of London's artistic life should once again be centered on the South Bank—in the past, Southwark was the location of theaters, taverns, and cockfighting arenas. The Globe Theatre, in which Shakespeare acted and held shares, was one of several here. In truth the Globe was as likely to stage bear-baiting as Shakespeare, but today, at the reconstructed "Wooden O," you can see only the latter. Be sure to take a walk along Bankside, the embankment along the Thames from Southwark to Blackfriars Bridge.

TIMING The South Bank sprawls; block out visiting times based on locations and your interests. The Imperial War Museum demands a couple of hours, with the nearby Museum of Garden History worth an hour. The Tate Modern deserves a whole morning or afternoon to do justice to temporary exhibitions and the permanent collection. A lovely way to spend a half day is a flight on the London Eye (allow two hours), followed by a concert at the Royal Festival Hall or a performance at the National Theatre. An hour spent in the Design Museum is easily combined with a visit to HMS *Belfast*, afterward stopping by to admire the *Golden Hinde* and, farther along, City Hall. The Globe Theatre requires about two hours for the exhibition and two to three hours for a performance. Although this area is liveliest during the week, on Friday or Saturday you can stop by the Borough Market (⇨ *Shopping, below*).

GETTING HERE For the South Bank use Westminster station on the Jubilee or Northern line, from where you can walk across Westminster Bridge; Embankment on District, Circle, Northern, and Bakerloo lines, where you can walk across Hungerford Bridge; or Waterloo on the Jubilee, Northern, and Bakerloo lines, where it's a five-minute walk to the Royal Festival Hall. In the east, Tower Hill Underground on the District Line can be reached by crossing Tower Bridge; alternatively, use Tower Gateway on the Docklands Light Railway (DLR). London Bridge on the Northern and Jubilee lines is at least 20 minutes on foot from the Design Museum, but a five-minute stroll to Borough Market.

Buses that take you across Westminster Bridge toward the Imperial War Museum include 12 and 159 from Oxford Circus, and 77 from Aldwych to Lambeth Palace. For buses behind the South Bank Centre: 1 from Aldwych and Waterloo to the Imperial War Museum, 68 from Euston and Holborn, 76 from St. Paul's and Moorgate, 168 from Euston and Holborn, 171 from Holborn, 176 from Oxford Circus, and 188 from Russell Square.

To go farther downstream, near Shakespeare's Globe and the OXO Tower, take the 381 from Waterloo to Tooley Street. The new RV1 bus service links Covent Garden, South Bank, Waterloo, Bankside, London Bridge, and Tower Gateway.

For a beautiful view, commuter river services are a more leisurely way to go: the route runs from Savoy Pier to Greenland, and for the South Bank hop off at Bankside or London Bridge City. The Tate Boat service links Tate Modern with Tate Britain.

Numbers in the margin correspond to numbers on the South Bank map.

Main Attractions

★ ☾ ❺ **British Airways London Eye.** If you want a pigeon's-eye view of London, this is the place. The highest observation wheel in the world, at 500 feet, towers over the South Bank from the Jubilee Gardens next to County Hall. For 25 minutes, passengers hover over the city in a slow-motion flight. On a clear day you can take in a range of up to 25 mi, viewing London's most famous landmarks. ■ TIP→ **Buy your ticket online, over the phone, or at the ticket office in advance to avoid the long lines.** ✉ *Jubilee Gardens, South Bank, SE1* ☎ *0870/500–0600* ⊕ *www.ba-londoneye.com* 🎫 *£12.50* ☉ *June–Sept., daily 9:30 AM–10 PM; Oct.–May, daily 9:30–8* Ⓤ *Waterloo.*

❶❼ **Design Museum.** This was the first museum in the world to elevate everyday design and design classics to the status of art by placing them in their social and cultural context. Fashion, creative technology, and architecture are explored in thematic displays, and temporary exhibitions provide an in-depth focus. Take a break at the trendsetting Blueprint Café, with its own river terrace. ✉ *28 Shad Thames, South Bank, SE1* ☎ *0870/833–9955* ⊕ *www.designmuseum.org* ✑ *£7* ☉ *Mon.–Thurs. and weekends 10–5:45, last admission at 5:15; Fri. 10–10, last admission at 9:45* Ⓤ *London Bridge; DLR: Tower Gateway.*

★ ☾ ❸ **Imperial War Museum.** This museum of 20th-century warfare does not glorify bloodshed but attempts to evoke what it was like to live through the two world wars. There's hardware—a Battle of Britain Spitfire, a German V2 rocket—but also an equal amount of war art (John Singer Sargent to Henry Moore) and interactive material. One affecting exhibit, "The Blitz Experience," provides a 10-minute taste of an air raid in a street of acrid smoke, sirens, and searchlights. There's also a Holocaust exhibition. The museum is in an elegantly colonnaded 19th-century building that was once the home of the infamous insane asylum called Bedlam. ✉ *Lambeth Rd., South Bank, SE1* ☎ *020/7416–5320* ⊕ *www. iwm.org.uk* ✑ *Free* ☉ *Daily 10–6* Ⓤ *Lambeth North.*

❼ **OXO Tower.** This art deco tower has graduated from its former incarnations as power-generating station and warehouse into a vibrant community with artists' and designers' workshops, restaurants, and cafés. There's an observation deck for a super river vista (St. Paul's to the east, and Somerset House to the west). The biggest draw is martinis at the OXO Tower Restaurant. ✉ *Barge House St., South Bank, SE1* ☎ *020/ 7401–3610* ⊕ *www.oxotower.co.uk* ✑ *Free* ☉ *Studios and shops Tues.–Sun. 11–6* Ⓤ *Blackfriars, Waterloo.*

★ ☾ ❾ **Shakespeare's Globe Theatre.** A spectacular theater, this is a replica of Shakespeare's open-roof, wood-and-thatch Globe Playhouse (built in 1599 and burned down in 1613), where most of the Bard's great plays premiered. For several decades, American actor and director Sam Wanamaker worked ceaselessly to raise funds for the theater's reconstruction, 200 yards from its original site, with authentic materials and techniques; his dream was realized in 1996. The "pit," or orchestra level, can take 500 standees—or "groundlings," to use the historical term—in front of the high stage, and 1,000 can sit in the covered wooden bays. A repertory season of three or four plays is presented in summer, in daylight—and sometimes rain. Throughout the year, you can tour the theater as part of the **Shakespeare's Globe Exhibition,** an adjacent museum that provides background material on the Elizabethan theater and the construction of the modern-day Globe. There's also an exhibition at the Globe's near neighbor, the **Rose Theatre,** at 56 Park Street, which was built even earlier, in 1587. ✉ *New Globe Walk, Bankside, South Bank, SE1* ☎ *020/7401–9919 box office, 020/7902–1400 New Shakespeare's Globe Exhibition* ⊕ *www.shakespeares-globe.org* ✑ *£9 for exhibition and tour; joint ticket available with Rose Theatre* ☉ *Exhibition daily 10–5, plays May–early Oct.; call for schedule* Ⓤ *Mansion House, then walk across Southwark Bridge; Blackfriars, then walk across Blackfriars Bridge; or Southwark, then walk down to river.*

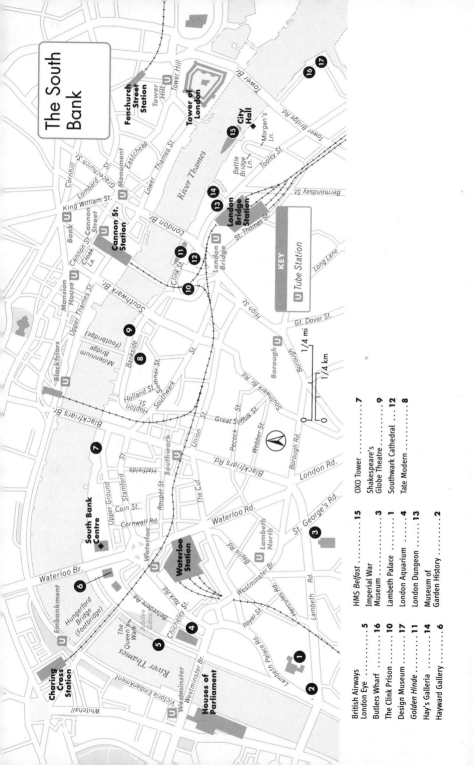

The South Bank

British Airways
London Eye **5**
Butlers Wharf **16**
The Clink Prison **10**
Design Museum **17**
Golden Hinde **11**
Hay's Galleria **14**
Hayward Gallery **6**

HMS Belfast **15**
Imperial War
Museum **3**
Lambeth Palace **1**
London Aquarium **4**
London Dungeon **13**
Museum of
Garden History **2**

OXO Tower **7**
Shakespeare's
Globe Theatre **9**
Southwark Cathedral ... **12**
Tate Modern **8**

KEY
Ⓤ Tube Station

0 ——— 1/4 mi
0 ——— 1/4 km

⑫ **Southwark Cathedral.** This cathedral (pronounced *suth*-uck) is the second-oldest Gothic church in London, next to Westminster Abbey. Look for the gaudily renovated 1408 tomb of the poet John Gower, friend of Chaucer, and for the Harvard Chapel, named after John Harvard, founder of the U.S. college, who was baptized here in 1608. Also buried here is Edmund Shakespeare, brother of William. ⊠ *Montague Close, South Bank, SE1* ☎ *020/7367–6700* ⊕ *www.southwark.anglican.org* ▭ *Free, suggested donation £4* ◉ *Daily 8–6* Ⓤ *London Bridge.*

FodorśChoice
★

⑧ **Tate Modern.** This former power station has glowered on the banks on the Thames since the 1930s, and after a dazzling renovation by Herzog de Meuron, provides a grand space for a massive collection of international modern art. The vast Turbine Hall is a dramatic entrance point. On permanent display in the galleries are classic works from 1900 to the present day, by Matisse, Picasso, Dalí, Francis Bacon, Andy Warhol, and the most-talked-about upstarts. They are arranged in themes that mix the historic with the contemporary—Landscape, Still Life, and the Nude—on different levels, reached by a moving staircase. This is a good museum for kids, who respond to the unusual space as well as the art; there are kids' programs, too. The changing exhibitions, for which there are often long lines, are always the talking point of Londoners who have their fingers on the pulse. ⊠ *Bankside, South Bank, SE1* ☎ *020/7887–8888* ⊕ *www.tate.org.uk* ▭ *Free* ◉ *Sun.–Thurs. 10–6, Fri. and Sat. 10–10* Ⓤ *Blackfriars, Southwark.*

> **WHEN TO GO**
>
> Avoid going to the Tate Modern on weekends, when visitor numbers are at their greatest. Visit during the week or join the cool crowd on Friday evenings, when it's open until 10.

Also Worth Seeing

⑯ **Butlers Wharf.** An '80s warehouse conversion of deluxe loft apartments, restaurants, and galleries, people now flock here thanks partly to London's saint of the stomach, Sir Terence Conran (also responsible for restaurants Bibendum, Mezzo, and Quaglino's). He has given it his "Gastrodrome" of four restaurants (including the fabulous Pont de la Tour), a vintner's, a deli, and a bakery. ⊠ *South Bank, SE1* Ⓤ *London Bridge or Tower Hill, then walk over bridge.*

⑩ **The Clink Prison.** Giving rise to the term "the clink," which still refers to a jail, this institution was originally the prison attached to Winchester House, palace of the bishops of Winchester until 1626. It was one of the first prisons to detain women, most of whom were called "Winchester Geese"—a euphemism meaning prostitutes. You'll discover, in graphic detail, how a grisly Tudor prison would operate on a code of cruelty and corruption. ⊠ *1 Clink St., South Bank, SE1* ☎ *020/7403–0900* ⊕ *www.clink.co.uk* ▭ *£5* ◉ *Weekdays 10–6, weekends 10–9; last admission 1 hr before closing* Ⓤ *London Bridge.*

� ⑪ ***Golden Hinde.*** Sir Francis Drake circumnavigated the globe in this little galleon, or one just like it. This exact replica made a 23-year round-the-world voyage—much of it spent along U.S. coasts, both Pacific and Atlantic—and has settled here to continue its educational purpose. ⊠ *St. Mary Overie Dock, Cathedral St., South Bank, SE1* ☎ *08700/11–8700* ⊕ *www.goldenhinde.co.uk* ☒ *£3.50, £4.50 for prebooked guided tour* ☉ *Times vary; call ahead* Ⓤ *London Bridge.*

⓮ Hay's Galleria. Once known as "London's larder" because of the edibles sold here, Hay's Galleria was reborn in 1987 as a Covent Garden–esque parade of bars and restaurants, offices, and shops, all weatherproofed by a glass atrium roof supported by iron columns. Jugglers, string quartets, and crafts stalls abound. ⊠ *Battle Bridge La., South Bank, SE1* ☎ *020/7940–7770* ⊕ *www.haysgalleria.co.uk* Ⓤ *London Bridge.*

❻ Hayward Gallery. The gray, windowless bunker has had to bear the brunt of architectural criticism over the years, but that's changed with a foyer extension that gives more daylight, more space for exhibits, a café, and better access. The highlight of the project is an elliptical mirrored glass pavilion by New York–based artist Dan Graham. The gallery encompasses a range of art media, crossing history and cultures, bridging the experimental and established. ⊠ *South Bank Centre, Belvedere Rd., South Bank, SE1* ☎ *020/7921–0813* ⊕ *www.hayward.org.uk* ☒ *Mon. £4.50, Tues.–Sun. £9* ☉ *Sat.–Mon., Thurs. 10–6, Tues. and Wed. 10–8, Fri. 10–9* Ⓤ *Waterloo.*

⓯ HMS *Belfast*. At 613 feet, this is one of the largest cruisers the Royal Navy ever had. It played an important role in the D-Day landings off Normandy. On board is a riveting outpost of the **Imperial War Museum.** ⊠ *Morgan's La., Tooley St., South Bank, SE1* ☎ *020/7940–6300* ⊕ *www.iwm.org.uk* ☒ *£8* ☉ *Mar.–Oct., daily 10–6; Nov.–Feb., daily 10–5; last admission 45 mins before closing* Ⓤ *London Bridge.*

❶ Lambeth Palace. The London residence of the archbishop of Canterbury, the senior archbishop of the Church of England since the 13th century, is closed to the public, but you can admire the Tudor gatehouse. ⊠ *Lambeth Palace Rd., South Bank, SE1* ⊕ *www.archbishopofcanterbury.org* Ⓤ *Waterloo.*

❹ London Aquarium. Here's a dark and thrilling glimpse into the waters of the world, focused around a superb three-level aquarium full of sharks and stingrays, among other common and more rare breeds. There are also educational exhibits, hands-on displays, feeding displays, and piscine sights previously unseen on these shores. ⊠ *County Hall, Riverside Bldg., Westminster Bridge Rd., South Bank, SE1* ☎ *020/7967–8000* ⊕ *www.londonaquarium.co.uk* ☒ *£9.75* ☉ *Daily 10–6; last admission at 5* Ⓤ *Westminster, Waterloo.*

⓭ London Dungeon. Here's the goriest, grisliest, most gruesome attraction in town, where realistic waxwork people are subjected in graphic detail to all the historical horrors the Tower of London merely tells you about. Tableaux depict famous bloody moments—like Anne Boleyn's decapitation and the martyrdom of St. George—alongside the torture, murder, and ritual slaughter of lesser-known victims, all to a sound track of screaming, wailing, and agonized moaning. There are displays on the Great Fire of London and Jack the Ripper. ⊠ *28–34 Tooley St., South*

Bank, SE1 ☎ *020/7403–7221* ⊕ *www.thedungeons.com* 🎟 *£14.50*
⊙ *Mid-Apr.–mid-July, daily 10–5:30; mid-July–mid-Sept., daily 10–7.30;*
mid-Sept.–mid-Nov., daily 10–5.30; mid-Nov.–mid-Apr. daily 10:30–5;
phone to confirm dates Ⓤ *London Bridge.*

❷ Museum of Garden History. The first of its kind in the world, the museum
is set in St. Mary's Church, next to Lambeth Palace. Founded in 1977,
the museum has built up one of the largest collections of historic garden tools, artifacts, and curiosities, as well as an expanding library. Alongside the museum is a replica 17th-century knot garden, a peaceful haven
of plants that can be traced back to that period. ⊠ *Lambeth Palace Rd.,*
South Bank, SE1 ☎ *020/7401–8865* ⊕ *www.museumgardenhistory.org*
🎟 *Suggested donation £3* ⊙ *Daily 10:30–5* Ⓤ *Lambeth North.*

Kensington, Knightsbridge & Mayfair

Splendid houses with pillared porches, as well as fascinating museums,
stylish squares, and glittering antiques shops, line the streets of this elegant area of the Royal Borough of Kensington. Also here is Kensington Palace (the former home of both Diana, Princess of Wales, and Queen
Victoria), which put the district literally on the map back in the 17th
century. To Kensington's east is one of the highest concentrations of important artifacts anywhere, the "museum mile" of South Kensington,
with the rest of Kensington offering peaceful strolls and a noisy main
street. Kensington first became the *Royal* Borough of Kensington (and
Chelsea) when William III, who suffered terribly from the Thames mists
over Whitehall, decided in 1689 to buy Nottingham House in the rural
village of Kensington so that he could breathe more easily. Courtiers and
functionaries and society folk soon followed where the crown led, and
by the time Queen Anne was on the throne (1702–14), Kensington was
overflowing. In a way, it still is, since most of its grand houses have been
divided into apartments, or are serving as embassies.

Hyde Park and Kensington Gardens together form by far the biggest of
central London's royal parks. It's probably been centuries since any major
royal had a casual stroll here, but the parks remain the property of the
Crown, and it was the Crown that saved them from being devoured by
the city's late-18th-century growth spurt.

Around the borders of Hyde Park are several of London's most beautiful and posh neighborhoods. To the south of the park and a short carriage ride from Buckingham Palace is the splendidly aristocratic enclave
of Belgravia. Its white-stucco buildings and grand squares—particularly
Belgrave Square—are Regency-era jewels. On the eastern border of
Hyde Park is Mayfair, which gives Belgravia a run for its money as London's wealthiest district. Two mansions here allow you to get a peek
into the lifestyles of London's rich and famous: Apsley House, the home
of the duke of Wellington, and the Wallace Collection, a mansion on
Manchester Square stuffed with great art treasures.

TIMING   The best way to approach these neighborhoods is to treat Knightsbridge shopping and the South Kensington museums as separate days
out, although the three vast museums may be too much to take in at

once. The parks are best in the growing seasons and during fall, when the foliage is turning; the summer roses in Regent's Park are stunning. On Sunday, the Hyde Park and Kensington Gardens railings all along the Bayswater Road are hung with mediocre art, which may slow your progress; this is prime perambulation day for locals.

GETTING HERE There's good tube service to these areas. On the Central Line, Marble Arch and Bond Street (also Jubilee Line) take you to the heart of Mayfair; the Hyde Park Corner stop on the Piccadilly line is at the southeast corner of the park, near Apsley House. South Kensington and Gloucester Road on the District, Circle, and Piccadilly lines are convenient stops for the South Kensington museums; Knightsbridge on the Piccadilly line leaves you close to Harrods and many retail temptations.

Numbers in the margin correspond to numbers on the Kensington, Knightsbridge & Mayfair map.

Main Attractions

★ ⑩ **Apsley House (Wellington Museum).** Once known, quite simply, as Number 1, London, this was celebrated as the best address in town. Built by Robert Adam in the 1770s, the mansion was the home of the celebrated conqueror of Napoléon, the duke of Wellington, who lived here from the 1820s until his death in 1852. The great Waterloo Gallery—scene of legendary dinners—is an orgy of opulence. Not to be missed, in every sense, is the gigantic Antonio Canova statue of a nude (but fig-leafed) Bonaparte in the entry stairwell. The free audio guide highlights the most noted works and the superb decor. The house is flanked by imposing statues: opposite is the 1828 Decimus Burton **Wellington Arch** with the four-horse chariot of peace as its pinnacle (open to the public as an exhibition area and viewing platform). Just behind Wellington Arch, and cast from captured French guns, the legendary **Achilles** statue points the way with thrusting shield to the ducal mansion from the tip of Hyde Park. ⊠ *Hyde Park Corner* ☎ *020/7499–5676* ⊕ *www.english-heritage. org.uk* ⊡ *£4.95* ⊙ *Apr.–Nov., Tues.–Sun. 10–5; Dec.–Mar., Tues.–Sun. 10–4. Also open bank holiday Mon.* Ⓤ *Hyde Park Corner.*

❼ **Harrods.** Just in case you hadn't noticed it, this well-known shopping destination outlines its domed terra-cotta Edwardian bulk in thousands of white lights at night. Owned by Mohamed Al Fayed, whose son Dodi was killed in the car crash that also claimed Princess Diana's life in 1997, the 15-acre store has wonderful, frenetic sale weeks. Don't miss the extravagant **Food Hall,** with its art nouveau tiling. ⊠ *87–135 Brompton Rd., Knightsbridge, SW1* ☎ *020/7730–1234* ⊕ *www.harrods.com* ⊙ *Mon.–Sat. 10–7, Sun. noon–6* Ⓤ *Knightsbridge.*

Ⓒ **Hyde Park.** Along with the smaller St. James's and Green parks to the east, Hyde Park started as Henry VIII's hunting grounds. Along its south side runs **Rotten Row,** once Henry's royal path to the hunt—the name is a corruption of *route du roi* (route of the king). It's still used by the Household Cavalry, who live at the **Knightsbridge Barracks**—a high-rise and a low, ugly, red block to the left. This brigade mounts the guard at the palace, and you can see them leave to perform this duty, in full regalia, at about 10:30, or await the return of the ex-guard about noon. Hyde Park is wonderful for strolling, watching the locals, or just relaxing by the **Serpentine,** the long body of water near its southern border. On the south side of the Serpentine, by the Lido, is the site of the **Diana Princess of Wales Memorial Fountain.** On Sunday, **Speakers' Corner,** in the park near Marble Arch, is an unmissable spectacle of vehement, sometimes comical, and always entertaining orators. ☎ *020/ 7298–2000* ⊕ *www.royalparks.gov.uk* ☉ *Daily 5* AM*–midnight* Ⓤ *Hyde Park Corner, Lancaster Gate, Marble Arch.*

🕑 **Kensington Gardens.** More formal than neighboring Hyde Park, Kensington Gardens was first laid out as palace grounds. The paved Italian garden at the top of the Long Water, **The Fountains,** is a reminder of this, although **Kensington Palace** itself is the main clue to its royal status, with the early-19th-century Sunken Garden north of it. Nearby is George Frampton's beloved 1912 *Peter Pan,* a bronze of the boy who lived on an island in the Serpentine and never grew up, and whose creator, J. M. Barrie, lived at 100 Bayswater Road, not 500 yards from here. The **Round Pond** is a magnet for model-boat enthusiasts and duck feeders. The fabulous **Princess Diana Memorial Playground** has specially designed structures and areas on the theme of Barrie's Neverland. ⊕ *www. royalparks.gov.uk* ☉ *Daily dawn–dusk* Ⓤ *Lancaster Gate, Queensway.*

★ ❻ **Kensington Palace.** Royals have lived here in grand style for more than 300 years, even though the palace's history has been eclipsed in the near past by the late Princess Diana, a famous resident. A walk through the State Apartments (with an excellent audio-guide device as your companion) puts in perspective the protocol-filled royal lifestyle of the past. When King William III decided in the late 17th century to make his palace at Kensington, 12 years of renovation to the original building were needed by Wren and Hawksmoor before the king and Queen Mary could move in. The palace continued to undergo refurbishment during the reigns of Queen Anne and George I and II. Kensington Palace was home to the young princess Victoria until she succeeded to the throne.

The visitor entrance to the palace is on the Garden Floor and takes you into the Red Saloon and Teck Saloon (after the Kents, the Duke and Duchess of Teck lived here), which display the **Royal Ceremonial Dress Collection** with garments dating to the 18th century. State and occasional dresses, hats, shoes, and gloves from the present Queen's wardrobe are displayed, along with some of Princess Diana's gorgeous evening gowns. Other displays interpret the symbolism of court dress and show the labor that went into producing this attire.

The King's Grand Staircase is the impressive starting point of the tour of the State Apartments; the trompe l'oeil paintings by William Kent on the walls show courtiers looking down. The Presence Chamber (used for formal receptions) is painted in Italian "grotesque" style with mythical gods. The Privy Chamber next to it received more intimate visitors. In this room, the Mortlake tapestries commissioned by Charles I represent the seasons, and the lavish painted ceiling alludes to the godlike status of monarchs. Gilt and Roman columns in the Cupola Room reminded the royal visitor that being admitted beyond the Presence Room was a mark of status. Next come the rooms where Victoria had an ultrastrict upbringing with her parents, the Duke and Duchess of Kent. Originally part of the King's Apartments, these bedrooms and dressing rooms create a pleasantly domestic scene. The King's Gallery returns to the gilded theme; here, copies of Van Dyck's Charles I portraits (the originals are at the Queen's Gallery, Buckingham Palace) dominate the scene, along with two works by Tintoretto. The tour exits via the Queen's Staircase, which leads into the garden.

The Duke and Duchess of Gloucester and Prince and Princess Michael of Kent have apartments here, as did the late Princess Margaret. A photographic exhibition, "Number 1A Kensington Palace: From Courtiers' Lodgings to Royal Home," has opened in her former apartments. ⊠ *The Broad Walk, Kensington Gardens, Kensington, W8* ☎ *0870/751–5170 advance booking and information* www.hrp.org.uk ⌑ *£11.50* ◷ Mar.–Oct., daily 10–6; Nov.–Feb., daily 10–5; last admission 1 hr before closing Ⓤ High St. Kensington.

NEED A
BREAK?

A separate building from the rest of Kensington Palace, the Orangery (⊠ The Broad Walk, Kensington Gardens, Kensington, W8 ☎ 020/7376–0239) **was built for Queen Anne in 1704–05. The setting, beneath the white-and-gold arches, is perfect for tea, light lunches, and coffee offered daily from 10 to 6.**

★ ♺ ❶ **Natural History Museum.** When you want to heed the call of the wild, explore this fun place. Don't be surprised when the dinos notice you—the fierce, animatronic Tyrannosaurus Rex senses when human prey is near and "responds" in character. Don't miss the ambitious Earth Galleries or the Creepy Crawlies Gallery, which includes a nightmarish, super-enlarged scorpion. In the basement, hands-on activities can be experienced in Investigate, which allows you to do just that, with actual objects, from old bones to bugs. The Darwin Centre showcases the museum's entire collection—all 22 million creatures—from a tiny Seychellian frog to the Komodo dragon lizard. Daily Explore tours leave from the museum's main information desk. ⊠ *Cromwell Rd., South Kensington, SW7* ☎ *020/7942–5000* ⊕ *www.nhm.ac.uk* ⌑ *Free* ◷ *Mon.–Sat. 10–5:50, Sun. 11–5:50* Ⓤ *South Kensington.*

★ ♺ **Regent's Park.** Laid out in 1812 by John Nash for the Prince Regent (hence the name), who was crowned George IV in 1820, the park was designed to re-create the atmosphere of a grand country residence close to the center of town. A walk around the Outer Circle, taking in the white-stucco terraces of grand houses facing the park, including the famous **Cumberland Terrace**, shows that it succeeds magnificently. The Inner Circle has many garden themes, the most impressive being **Queen Mary's Gardens**, a scented riot of roses in summer. From June through August, the **Regent's Park Open-Air Theatre** (☎ 0870/060–1811

> **WORD OF MOUTH**
>
> "Queen Mary's Rose Garden [in Regent's Park] was in the most magnificent bloom I have ever seen. There were so many roses they almost seemed artificial. And the aromas were intoxicating."
>
> –janis

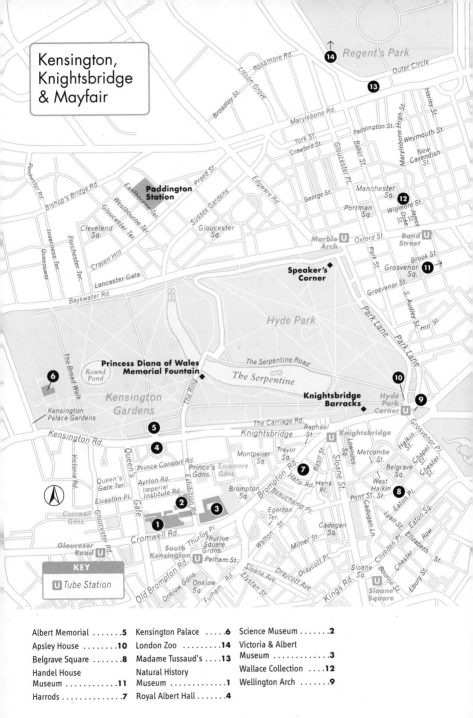

Kensington, Knightsbridge & Mayfair

Regent's Park
14
Outer Circle
13
Rossmore Rd.
Lisson Grove
Broadley St.
Harley St.
Marylebone Rd.
Weymouth St.
Paddington St.
York St.
New Cavendish St.
Crawford St.
Gloucester Pl.
Baker St.
Manchester St.
Marylebone High St.
Eastbourne Ter.
Praed St.
Paddington Station
George St.
Wigmore St.
12
James St.
Duke St.
Bishop's Bridge Rd.
Westbourne Ter.
Gloucester Ter.
Sussex Gardens
Edgware Rd.
Portman Sq.
Marble Arch ⓤ
Oxford St.
Brook St.
Bond Street ⓤ
11
Gloucester Ter.
Cleveland Sq.
Gloucester Sq.
Grosvenor St.
Grosvenor Sq.
Porchester Ter.
Craven Hill
Park St.
S. Audley St.
Hill St.
Poychester Rd.
Inverness Ter.
Queensway
Lancaster Gate
Bayswater Rd.
Speaker's Corner
Grosvenor St.
Park Lane
Park Lane
Hyde Park
The Broad Walk
6
Round Pond
Princess Diana of Wales Memorial Fountain
The Serpentine Road
The Serpentine
10
The Ring
Kensington Palace Gardens
Kensington Gardens
5
The Carriage Rd.
Knightsbridge Barracks
Hyde Park Corner ⓤ
9
Kensington Rd.
Knightsbridge
Raphael St.
Knightsbridge ⓤ
Knightsbridge
Grosvenor Pl.
Halkin St.
Victoria Rd.
Queen's Gate
4
Prince Consort Rd.
Montpelier St.
Trevor Sq.
Basil St.
Lowndes Sq.
Sloane St.
Metcombe St.
Chapel St.
Chester St.
Queen's Gate Ter.
Ayrton Rd.
Prince's Gdns.
Enismore Gdns.
7
Hans Rd.
Hans Pl.
Belgrave Sq.
Imperial Institute Rd.
Brompton Sq.
Brompton Rd.
Beauchamp Pl.
West Halkin St.
8
Elvaston Pl.
Exhibition Rd.
2
Pont St.
Cadogan Ln.
Eaton Pl.
Cornwall Gdns.
Gloucester Rd.
3
Egerton Ter.
St.
Cadogan Sq.
Lyall St.
Eaton Sq.
1
Cromwell Rd.
Thurloe Pl.
Thurloe Square Gdns.
Milner St.
Cliveden Pl.
Elizabeth St.
Glouceser Road ⓤ
South Kensington ⓤ
Pelham St.
Watton St.
Draycott Pl.
Bourne St.
Chester Row
Old Brompton Rd.
Onslow Gdns.
Onslow Sq.
Sloane Ave.
Draycott Ave.
Kings Rd.
Sloane Sq.
Sloane Square ⓤ
Ebury St.
Old Brompton Rd.
Fulham Rd.
Elystan St.
KEY
ⓤ Tube Station

Albert Memorial **5**
Apsley House **10**
Belgrave Square **8**
Handel House Museum **11**
Harrods **7**
Kensington Palace **6**
London Zoo **14**
Madame Tussaud's **13**
Natural History Museum **1**
Royal Albert Hall **4**
Science Museum **2**
Victoria & Albert Museum **3**
Wallace Collection **12**
Wellington Arch **9**

⊕ www.openairtheatre.org) mounts Shakespeare productions. The park is north of Mayfair. ☎ 020/7486–7905 ⊕ *www.royalparks.gov.uk* Ⓤ *Baker St. or Regent's Park.*

★ ☾ ❷ **Science Museum.** Hands-on exhibits make this museum enormously popular with children and adults. Highlights include *Puffing Billy* (the oldest steam locomotive in the world), and the actual *Apollo 10* capsule. A must-do attraction is the spectacular **Wellcome Wing,** devoted to contemporary science, medicine, and technology, which also has a 450-seat IMAX cinema. Special exhibitions can be great, too. ⊠ *Exhibition Rd., South Kensington, SW7* ☎ *0/870–870–4868* ⊕ *www. sciencemuseum.org.uk* ▣ *Free* ☾ *Daily 10–6* Ⓤ *South Kensington.*

★ ☾ ❸ **Victoria & Albert Museum.** Recognizable by the copy of Victoria's Imperial Crown on the lantern above the central cupola, this huge museum showcases the decorative arts of all disciplines, periods, nationalities, and tastes. Prince Albert was responsible for the genesis of this permanent version of the 1851 Great Exhibition, and Victoria laid its foundation stone in her final public London appearance in 1899. The collections of the V&A, as it's always called, are *so* all-encompassing that confusion is a hazard; select a few galleries to focus on. One minute you're gazing on the Jacobean oak, 12-foot-square four-poster Great Bed of Ware (one of the V&A's most prized possessions, given that Shakespeare immortalized it in *Twelfth Night*), and the next, you're in the 20th-century end of the equally celebrated Dress Collection, coveting a Jean Muir frock. The British Galleries provide a social context for British art and design from 1500 to 1900 (from Henry VIII through Victoria), with displays such as George Gilbert Scott's model of the Albert Memorial and the first English fork ever made (1632). Throughout the galleries are interactive corners, where you can discover, design, and build things. Free one-hour tours whirl you by some of the museum's prized treasures. The shop is the museum in microcosm, and quite the best place to buy art nouveau or arts-and-crafts gifts. ⊠ *Cromwell Rd., South Kensington, SW7* ☎ *020/7942–2000* ⊕ *www. vam.ac.uk* ▣ *Free* ☾ *Thurs.–Tues. 10–5:45; Wed. and last Fri. of month 10–10; tours daily at 10:30, 11:30, 1:30, 3:30 and Wed. at 7:30 PM* Ⓤ *South Kensington.*

❶❷ **Wallace Collection.** Assembled by four generations of marquesses of Hertford, the Wallace Collection is important, exciting, undervisited—and free. Hertford House itself, a fine late-18th-century mansion, is part of the show. The eccentric fourth marquess really built the collection, snapping up paintings by François Boucher, Jean-Honoré Fragonard, Antoine Watteau, and Nicolas Lancret for a song after the French Revolution rendered this art dangerously unfashionable. A highlight among the Gainsborough and Romney portraits is Fragonard's *The Swing,* which conjures up the 18th-century's let-them-eat-cake frivolity. Don't forget to smile back at Frans Hals's *Laughing Cavalier* in the Big Gallery. ⊠ *Hertford House, Manchester Sq., Mayfair, W1* ☎ *020/7563–9500* ⊕ *www.wallacecollection.org* ▣ *Free, charge for special exhibitions* ☾ *Daily 10–5* Ⓤ *Bond St.*

Also Worth Seeing

OFF THE
BEATEN
PATH

ABBEY ROAD STUDIOS – Strawberry Fields Forever. Here, outside the Abbey Road Studios, is the world's most famous zebra crossing. Immortalized on the Beatles' *Abbey Road* album of 1969, this footpath is a spot beloved by Beatlemaniacs and baby boomers. The studios (closed to the public) are where the Beatles recorded their entire output from "Love Me Do" on, including *Sgt. Pepper's Lonely Hearts Club Band* (1967). To see Fab Four sites, **Original London Walks** (☎ 020/7624–3978 ⊕ www.walks.com) offers two Beatles tours: The Beatles In-My-Life Walk (11:20 AM at the Baker Street Underground on Saturday and Tuesday) and the Beatles Magical Mystery Tour (10:55 AM at Underground Exit 3, Tottenham Court Road, on Sunday and Thursday), which cover nostalgic landmark Beatles spots in the city. Abbey Road is a 10-minute ride on the Jubilee tube line from central London. After you exit, head southwest three blocks down Grove End Road. ✉ *3 Abbey Rd., Hampstead, NW8* ⊕ *www. abbeyroad.co.uk* Ⓤ *St. John's Wood.*

⑤ Albert Memorial. This gleaming, neo-Gothic shrine to Prince Albert created by George Gilbert Scott epitomizes the Victorian era. Albert's grieving widow, Queen Victoria, had this elaborate confection (including a 14-foot bronze statue of the prince) erected on the spot where his Great Exhibition had stood a decade before his early death, from typhoid, in 1861. ✉ *Kensington Gore, opposite Royal Albert Hall, Hyde Park, Kensington, SW7* Ⓤ *Knightsbridge.*

⑧ Belgrave Square. The square, as well as the streets leading off it, are genuine elite territory and have been since they were built in the mid-1800s. Walk down Belgrave Place toward Eaton Place and you pass two of Belgravia's most beautiful mews: Eaton Mews North and Eccleston Mews, both fronted by grand Westminster-white rusticated entrances right out of a 19th-century engraving.

⑪ Handel House Museum. The former home of composer George Frideric Handel, where he lived for more than 30 years until his death in 1759, celebrates his genius in its fine Georgian rooms. You can linger over original manuscripts and gaze at portraits and art. Some of Handel's most famous pieces were created here, including *Messiah* and *Music for the Royal Fireworks*. Another musical star, Jimi Hendrix, lived here briefly in the 1960s (indicated by a blue plaque outside the house). ✉ *25 Brook St., Mayfair, W1* ☎ 020/7495–1685 ⊕ *www.handelhouse.org* ✎ *£5* ☉ *Tues.–Sat. 10–6, Thurs. 10–8, Sun. noon–6* Ⓤ *Bond St.*

⑭ London Zoo. Opened in 1828 and now housing animals from all over the world, this zoo has long been a local favorite. A modernization program focusing on conservation and education is under way. One highlight is the Web of Life, a conservation and education center. Recent additions include a desert swarming with locusts, meerkats perching on termite mounds, bats and hummingbirds, and an otter exhibit with underwater viewing. In a walk-through forest, you can come face-to-face with a group of black-capped squirrel monkeys. ✉ *Regent's Park, NW1* ☎ 020/7722–3333 ⊕ *www.londonzoo.co.uk* ✎ *£13.50* ☉ *Daily 10–4; last admission 1 hr before closing* Ⓤ *Camden Town, then Bus 274.*

🕙 ⑬ **Madame Tussaud's.** This is nothing more, nothing less, than the world's premier exhibition of lifelike waxwork models of celebrities. Madame T. learned her craft while making death masks of French Revolution victims and in 1835 set up her first show of the famous ones near this spot. You can see everyone from Shakespeare to Benny Hill here, but top billing still goes to the murderers in the Chamber of Horrors, who stare glassy-eyed at you—one from the electric chair. ✉ *Marylebone Rd., Regent's Park, NW1* 🕿 *0870/400–3000 for timed entry tickets* ⊕ *www.madame-tussauds.com* 🖃 *From £14.99; prices vary according to day and season, call for details, or check Web site* ☉ *Sept.–June, weekdays 10–5:30, weekends 9:30–5:30; July and Aug., daily 9:30–5:30* Ⓤ *Baker St.*

Notting Hill. Centered on the famous Portobello Road market (⇨ Shopping, *below*), this district is bordered to the west by Lansdowne Crescent—lined by "the hill's" poshest 19th-century terraced row houses—and to the east by Chepstow Road, with Notting Hill Gate and Westbourne Grove Road marking south and north boundaries. In between, the cool crowd, fashion set, and A- to B-list celebs can be spotted at the chic shops on Westbourne Grove and in the lively bars and cafés on Kensington Park Road. Ⓤ *Notting Hill Gate, Ladbroke Grove.*

❹ **Royal Albert Hall.** This famous concert hall was made possible by the Victorian public, who donated funds for the 8,000-seat auditorium. The domed hall is best known for its annual July through September Henry Wood Promenade Concerts (the "Proms"). ✉ *Kensington Gore, Kensington, SW7* 🕿 *020/7589–8212* ⊕ *www.royalalberthall.co.uk* 🖃 *Admission varies according to event* Ⓤ *South Kensington.*

❾ **Wellington Arch.** Opposite the duke of Wellington's mansion, Apsley House, this majestic stone arch dominates the busy traffic intersection that is Hyde Park Corner. Designed by Decimus Burton and built in 1828, it was created as a grand entrance to the west side of London and echoes the design of that other landmark gate, Marble Arch, at the north end of Hyde Park. Atop the arch, the Angel of Peace descends on the chariot of war. The arch has a viewing platform with panoramas over the park. ✉ *Hyde Park Corner, Mayfair, SW1* 🕿 *020/7930–2726* ⊕ *www.english-heritage.org.uk* 🖃 *£3* ☉ *Apr.–Oct., Wed.–Sun. 10–5; Nov.–Mar., Wed.–Sun. 10–4* Ⓤ *Hyde Park Corner.*

Up & Down the Thames

Downstream—meaning seaward, or east—from central London, Greenwich has enough riches, especially if the maritime theme is your thing, that you should allow a very full day to see them. Upstream, the royal palaces and grand houses that dot the area were built not as town houses but as country residences with easy access to London by river; Hampton Court Palace is the best and biggest of all.

Greenwich
8 mi east of central London.

Greenwich makes an ideal day out from central London, thanks to its historic and maritime attractions. Sir Christopher Wren's Royal Naval College and Inigo Jones's Queen's House reach architectural heights;

the Old Royal Observatory measured time for the entire planet; and the Greenwich Meridian divides the world in two. You can stand astride it with one foot in either hemisphere. The National Maritime Museum and the clipper ship *Cutty Sark* will appeal to seafaring types, and landlubbers can stroll the parkland that surround the buildings, the pretty 19th-century houses, and the weekend crafts and antiques markets.

Once, Greenwich was considered remote by Londoners, with only the river as a direct route. With transportation links in the form of the Docklands Light Railway (DLR) and the tube's Jubilee Line, getting here is easy and inexpensive. The quickest route to maritime Greenwich is the tube to Canary Wharf and the Docklands Light Rail to the Greenwich stop. However, river connections to Greenwich make the journey memorable. On the way, the boat glides past famous London sights and the ever-changing Docklands. **Ferries** (☎ 020/7987–1185 from Embankment and Tower piers, ☎ 020/7930–4097 from Westminster Pier, ☎ 020/7740–0400 from Barrier Gardens Pier, ☎ 020/7930–2062 upriver from Westminster Pier) down river from central London to Greenwich take 30 to 55 minutes and leave from different piers. You don't need to reserve. Up river to Kew, Richmond, and Hampton Court takes from 1½ hours to about 3 hours depending on tides—and depart several times a day in summer.

🌣 ***Cutty Sark.*** This sleek, romantic clipper was built in 1869, one of fleets and fleets of similar tall-masted wooden ships that plied oceanic highways of the 19th century, trading in exotic commodities—tea, in this case. The *Cutty Sark,* the only surviving clipper, was also the fastest, sailing the China–London route in 1871 in only 107 days. Now the photogenic vessel lies in dry dock, a museum of one kind of seafaring life—and not a comfortable kind for the 28-strong crew, as you'll see. The collection of figureheads is amusing, too. ⊠ *King William Walk, Greenwich, SE10* ☎ *020/8858–3445* ⊕ *www.cuttysark.org.uk* 🎟 *£4.50* 🕓 *Daily 10–5; last admission at 4:30* Ⓤ *DLR: Cutty Sark.*

★ 🌣 **National Maritime Museum.** One of Greenwich's outstanding attractions contains everything to do with the British at sea, including models, maps, globes, sextants, and uniforms (including the one Nelson died in at the 1805 Battle of Trafalgar, complete with bloodstained bullet hole). Explorers such as Captain James Cook and Robert F. Scott are celebrated, along with the valuable research gleaned from their grueling voyages. The **Queen's House,** the first Palladian building in England (1635), is home to the largest collection of maritime art in the world, including works by William Hogarth, Canaletto, and Joshua Reynolds. ⊠ *Romney Rd., Greenwich, SE10* ☎ *020/8858–4422* ⊕ *www.nmm.ac.uk* 🎟 *Free* 🕓 *Apr.–Sept., daily 10–6; Oct.–Mar., daily 10–5; last admission 4:30* Ⓤ *DLR: Greenwich.*

NEED A BREAK?

The old **Trafalgar Tavern** (⊠ Park Row, Greenwich, SE10 ☎ 020/8858–2437), with views of the Thames, is a grand place to have a pint and some upscale pub grub. In warm weather, the terrace has outdoor seating overlooking the Millennium Dome (which may reopen as a performance venue in 2007).

Old Royal Naval College. Designed by Christopher Wren in 1694 as a home for ancient mariners, these buildings became a school for young ones in 1873; today the University of Greenwich and Trinity College of Music hold classes here. The **Painted Hall,** the college's dining hall, derives its name from the baroque murals of William and Mary. In the opposite building stands the **College Chapel,** which is in a more restrained neo-Grecian style. ⊠ *King William Walk, Greenwich, SE10* ☎ *020/ 8269–4747* ⊕ *www.greenwichfoundation.org.uk* ✉ *Free, guided tours £4* ☉ *Painted Hall and College Chapel Mon.–Sat. 10–5, Sun. 12:30–5, last admission 4:15; grounds 8–6* Ⓤ *DLR: Greenwich.*

★ **Ranger's House.** This handsome, early-18th-century villa, which was the Greenwich Park Ranger's official residence during the 19th century, is hung with Stuart and Jacobean portraits. The most interesting diversion is the Wernher Collection, more than 650 works of medieval and Renaissance art (and splendid jewelry) with a north European flavor, amassed by millionaire Julius Wernher at the turn of the 20th century. ⊠ *Chesterfield Walk, Blackheath, Greenwich, SE10* ☎ *020/8853–0035* ⊕ *www.english-heritage.org.uk* ✉ *£5:30* ☉ *Apr.–Sept., Wed.–Sun. 10–6; Oct.–Mar., by appointment only* ☉ *Closed Jan. and Feb.* Ⓤ *DLR: Greenwich; no direct bus access, only to Vanbrugh Hill (from east) and Blackheath Hill (from west).*

★ ☾ **Royal Observatory.** Founded in 1675 by Charles II, this imposing institution was designed by Christopher Wren for John Flamsteed, the first Astronomer Royal. The red ball you see on its roof has been there since 1833. It drops every day at 1 PM, and you can set your watch by it, as the sailors on the Thames always have. Everyone comes here to be photographed astride the **Prime Meridian,** a brass line laid on the cobblestones at zero degrees longitude, one side being the eastern, one the western, hemisphere. An exhibit on the solution to the problem of measuring longitude includes John Harrison's famous clocks, H1–H4. ⊠ *Greenwich Park, Greenwich, SE10* ☎ *020/8858–4422* ⊕ *www.rog. nmm.ac.uk* ✉ *Free* ☉ *Apr.–Sept., daily 10–6; Oct.–Mar., daily 10–5; last admission 4:30* Ⓤ *DLR: Greenwich.*

Hampton Court Palace

☾ *20 mi southwest of central London.*

Fodor'sChoice
★

On a loop of the Thames lies Hampton Court, one of London's oldest royal palaces and more like a small town in size; you need a day to do it justice. It's actually two palaces in one—a Tudor residence and a late-17th-century baroque one—as well as a renowned garden. The magnificent Tudor brick house, with its cobbled courtyards and cavernous kitchens, was begun in 1514 by Cardinal Wolsey, the ambitious lord chancellor (roughly, prime minister) of England and archbishop of York. He wanted it to be the best palace in the land, and succeeded so well that Henry VIII grew envious, whereupon Wolsey gave Hampton Court to the king. Henry moved in during 1525, added a great hall and chapel, and proceeded to live much of his astonishing life here. Later, during the reign of William and Mary, Christopher Wren expanded the palace substantially, adding the graceful baroque south and east fronts that are highlights of the palace. Six themed routes, including Henry VIII's State

Apartments and the King William III's Apartments, help you plan your visit; special guides in period costume add to the fun.

The site beside the slow-moving Thames is idyllic, with 60 acres of ornamental gardens, lakes, and ponds, including William III's Privy Garden on the palace's south side. Its parterres, sculpted turf, and clipped yews and hollies brilliantly set off Wren's addition. Other horticultural highlights are Henry VIII's

Pond Garden and the enormous conical yews around the Fountain Garden. On the east side of the house, 544 lime trees were replanted in 2004 along the Long Water, a canal built during the time of Charles II. Perhaps best of all is the almost half-mile of paths in the fiendish maze, planted in 1714. ⊠ *East Molesey on A308* ☎ *0870/752–7777* ⊕ *www.hrp.org. uk* ⌨ *Palace, gardens, and maze £12.30, gardens only £4, maze only £3.50, park grounds free. Joint tickets available with Kensington Palace and Tower of London* ⊘ *State apartments Apr.–Oct., daily 10–6, last admission at 5; Nov.–Mar., daily 10–4:30; grounds daily 7–dusk* Ⓤ *Richmond, then Bus R68; National Rail, South West: Hampton Court Station, 35 mins from Waterloo.*

Kew Gardens

6 mi southwest of central London.

Kew Gardens, or more formally the Royal Botanic Gardens at Kew, is the headquarters of the country's leading botanical institute as well as a spectacular public garden of 300 acres and more than 30,000 species of plants. The highlights of a visit to this UNESCO World Heritage Site are the two great 19th-century greenhouses filled with tropical plants, many of which have been there as long as their housing. The bold glass roofs of the ultramodern Princess of Wales Conservatory shelter no fewer than 10 climatic zones. Two 18th-century royal ladies, Queen Caroline and Princess Augusta, were responsible for the garden's founding. The tube ride to Kew is about 40 minutes, but the gardens are very close to the stop. ⊠*Kew Rd., Kew* ☎*020/8332–5655* ⊕*www.kew.org* ⌨*£11.75* ⊘ *Gardens Apr.–Oct., weekdays 9:30–6:30, weekends 9:30–7:30; Nov.–Mar., daily 9:30–4:30* Ⓤ *Kew Gardens.*

Kew Palace and Queen Charlotte's Cottage. To this day quietly domestic Kew Palace, in Kew Gardens, remains the smallest royal palace in the land. The house offers a glimpse into the 18th century and the life of George III and his family; on display is the royal princesses' dolhouse. Originally known as the Dutch House, it was bought by King George II to provide more room for the extended Royal Family. In spring there's a romantic haze of bluebells. Note: you must purchase admission to Kew Gardens to access the palace. ⊠ *Kew Gardens, Kew* ☎ *0870/751–5179* ⊕ *www. hrp.org.uk* ⊠ *£5* ⊘ *May–Sept., daily* Ⓤ *Kew Gardens.*

NEED A BREAK?
Maids of Honour (✉ 288 Kew Rd., Kew ☎ 020/8940-2752), the most traditional of Old English tearooms, is named for the famous tarts invented here and still baked by hand on the premises. Tea is served in the afternoon, Tuesday through Saturday 2:30 to 5:30. If you can't wait for tea, and want to take some of the lovely cakes and pastries to eat at Kew Gardens or on Kew Green, the shop is open Tuesday through Saturday 9:30 to 6 and on Monday until 1 PM.

WHERE TO EAT

No longer would novelist Somerset Maugham be justified in warning, "To eat well in England, you should have breakfast three times a day." England is now one of the hottest places around for restaurants of every culinary flavor, with London at its epicenter. As anyone who reads the Sunday papers knows, London has enjoyed a huge boom in the restaurant sector. Among the city's 6,700 restaurants are "be-there" eateries, tiny neighborhood joints, gastro-pubs where young-gun foodniks find their feet, and swanky pacesetters where celebrity chefs launch their ego flights. Nearly everyone in town is passionate about food and will love telling you where they've eaten recently or where they'd like to go. You, too, will be smitten, since you will spend, on average, 25% of your travel budget on eating out. After feasting on modern British cuisine, visit one (or two) of London's fabulous pubs for a nightcap. Hit the right one on the right night and watch that legendary British reserve melt away.

This restaurant renaissance is due to talented entrepreneurs and chefs: Sir Terence Conran, Marco Pierre White, Gordon Ramsay, Jamie Oliver, and Oliver Peyton lead the list. To keep up with the whirl, each newspaper has reviewers aplenty. Read up on the top tips in the London *Evening Standard* (daily), *Time Out* magazine (weekly), or the food pages of the national newspapers, especially the weekend editions.

The thriving dining scene rests on ethnic cuisines. Thousands of Indian restaurants ensure that Londoners view access to a tasty curry as a birthright. Chinese restaurants in tiny Chinatown and beyond have been around a long time, as have Greek tavernas, and there are even more Italian restaurants than Indian. Now add Thai, Malaysian, Spanish, and Japanese cuisines to those easily found in England's capital. After all this, traditional English food appears as one more exotic cuisine.

Luckily, London also does a good job of catering to people more interested in satisfying their appetites without breaking the bank than in following the latest food fashions. The listings here strike a balance between these extremes and include hip-and-happening places, neighborhood spots, ethnic alternatives, and old favorites.

Two caveats: first, the "no-smoking" trend is sweeping the London dining scene. An outright ban on smoking in public places—such as restaurants—is imminent for 2007. Second, beware of Sunday. Many restaurants are closed, especially in the evening; likewise public holidays. Over the Christmas period, London virtually shuts down—it seems only hotels are prepared to feed travelers. When in doubt, call ahead. It's a good idea to book a table at all times.

Prices & Saving Money

London is not an inexpensive city. A modest meal for two can cost £35 (about $65) and the £100-a-head meal is not so taboo. Damage-control strategies include making lunch your main meal—the top places have bargain lunch menus, halving the price of evening à la carte—and ordering a second appetizer instead of an entrée, to which few places object. Note that an appetizer, usually known as a "starter" or "first course," is sometimes called an "entrée," as it is in France, and an entrée in England is dubbed the "main course" or simply "mains."

Ethnic restaurants have always been a good money-saving bet here, especially the thousands of Indian restaurants (curry is almost the national dish). Sandwich shops and chains proliferate: *see* Where to Refuel Around Town box, *below,* for the best bets. Seek out fixed-price menus, and watch for hidden extras on the check: cover, bread, or vegetables charged separately, and service. Many restaurants exclude service charges from the menu (which the law obliges them to display outside), then add 10% to 15% to the check, or else stamp SERVICE NOT INCLUDED along the bottom, in which case you should add the 10% to 15% yourself. Don't pay twice for service.

WHAT IT COSTS In pounds				
	£££££	**££££**	**£££**	**££**	**£**
AT DINNER	over £23	£20–£23	£14–£19	£10–£13	under £10

Prices are per person for a main course, excluding drinks, service, and V.A.T.

Bloomsbury

CHINESE ✕ **Hakkasan.** It's *Crouching Tiger* territory at this lauded Cantonese base-
££–£££££ ment restaurant off Tottenham Court Road. Ultrastylish and dimly lighted, Hakkasan is ideal for special occasions, with exquisite dim sum (lunch only), and a cracking cocktail scene. The à la carte is pricey. Its late-night days are Wednesday through Saturday (until 12:30 AM) and there's a two-hour time limit on tables. ✉ *8 Hanway Pl., Bloomsbury, W1* ☎ *020/7907–7000* ▤ *AE, MC, V* Ⓤ *Tottenham Court Rd.*

ECLECTIC ✕ **The Providores & Tapa Room.** Inventive Kiwi (New Zealand) chef Peter
★ **£££–££££** Gordon scores high with his Pacific Rim fusion cuisine in foodie-ville Marylebone. Have a sophisticated meal in the formal restaurant upstairs, or try the more relaxed ground-floor Tapa Room. On the menu you'll find venison and coriander, kangaroo loin, guava sorbet, and roast *chioca* (similar to Jerusalem artichoke). ✉ *109 Marylebone High St., Bloomsbury, W1* ☎ *020/7935–6175* ▤ *AE, MC, V* Ⓤ *Baker St.*

FRENCH ✕ **Galvin.** London's lucky to have the Galvin brothers blazing a trail
££–££££ for the bistrotdeluxe concept on Baker Street. The feted chefs, Chris
Fodor'sChoice and Jeff, forsake Michelin stars and cut loose under the brasserie ban-
★ ner. An older crowd enjoys impeccable service in a handsome salon. There's no better crab lasagna in town, and daube of venison, pork with Agen prunes, and halibut with brown shrimp are excellent. ✉ *66*

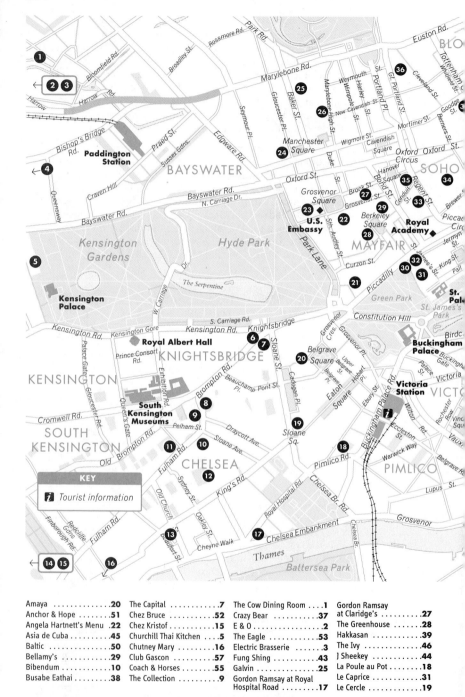

Amaya 20	The Capital 7	The Cow Dining Room 1	Gordon Ramsay
Anchor & Hope 51	Chez Bruce 52	Crazy Bear 37	at Claridge's 27
Angela Hartnett's Menu .22	Chez Kristof 15	E & O 2	The Greenhouse 28
Asia de Cuba 45	Churchill Thai Kitchen 5	The Eagle 53	Hakkasan 39
Baltic 50	Chutney Mary 16	Electric Brasserie 3	The Ivy 46
Bellamy's 29	Club Gascon 57	Fung Shing 43	J Sheekey 44
Bibendum 10	Coach & Horses 55	Galvin 25	La Poule au Pot 18
Busabe Eathai 38	The Collection 9	Gordon Ramsay at Royal	Le Caprice 31
		Hospital Road 17	Le Cercle 19

Where to Eat in London

The Ledbury **4**	Nobu **21**	The Ritz **30**	Sketch: Gallery **35**
Le Gavroche **23**	Orso **48**	River Café **14**	Tom Aikens **12**
L'Escargot **40**	Pig's Ear **13**	Rules **47**	Villandry **36**
Lindsay House **41**	PJ's Bar & Grill **11**	St. John **56**	Yauatcha **34**
Locanda Locatelli ...**24**	Plateau **62**	St. John Bread and Wine .**60**	The Wolseley **32**
Maison Bertaux **42**	Providores	Savoy Grill **49**	Zuma **6**
Momo **33**	& Tapa Room **26**	Simpson's Tavern **61**	
Moro **54**	Racine **8**	Sông Qué Café **59**	
	The Real Greek **58**		

Baker St., Bloomsbury, W1 ☎ *020/7935–4007* ▤ *AE, DC, MC, V* Ⓤ *Baker Street.*

££–££££ ✕ **Villandry.** Heaven for food lovers, this posh gourmet deli is crammed with fancy French pâtés, Continental cheeses, fruit tarts, biscuits, organic vegetables, and obscure breads galore. There's a bar, charcuterie, and fashionable dining room frequented by the extended New Labour gang. Breakfast is served from 8 AM. ⊠ *170 Great Portland St., Bloomsbury, W1* ☎ *020/7631–3131* ▤ *AE, MC, V* Ⓤ *Great Portland St.*

THAI ✕ **Crazy Bear.** Art deco styling is the draw at this glamour zone in
£–£££ Fitzrovia, ideal for cocktails in the basement lounge, and a Thai- and Asian-influenced meal upstairs. Head for the snapper with lemon zest, and end with cheesecake. ■ TIP→ **Admire the Murano chandelier, leather booths, ostrich-hide chairs, and the amazing mirrored loos.** ⊠ *26–28 Whitfield St., Bloomsbury, W1* ☎ *020/7631–0088* ⌕ *Reservations essential* ▤ *AE, MC, V* ☾ *Closed Sun.* Ⓤ *Goodge St., Tottenham Court Rd.*

★ **£** ✕ **Busabe Eathai.** It's top value for money at this superior high–turnover Thai canteen. It's fitted with bench seats and hardwood tables but is no less seductive for the communal dining. The menu includes noodles, curries, and stir-fries; try chicken with butternut squash, cuttlefish curry, or seafood vermicelli (prawn, squid, and scallops). There are busier branches near Selfridges (8–13 Bird Street) or in Soho (106–110 Wardour Street). ⊠ *22 Store St., Bloomsbury, WC1* ☎ *020/7299–7900* ⌕ *Reservations not accepted* ▤ *AE, MC, V* Ⓤ *Tottenham Court Rd.*

Chelsea

AMERICAN- ✕ **PJ's Bar & Grill.** Enter PJ's and adopt the Polo Joe lifestyle: wooden
CASUAL floors and stained glass, a slowly revolving propeller from a 1911 Vick-
££–££££ ers Vimy flying boat, and polo memorabilia. The place is relaxed and efficient, and the menu, which includes all-American staples like steaks, salads, and brownies, will please everyone except vegetarians. PJ's is open late and the bartenders can mix it all. Weekend brunch is popular with the beautiful Chelsea set. ⊠ *52 Fulham Rd., Chelsea, SW3* ☎ *020/7581–0025* ▤ *AE, DC, MC, V* Ⓤ *South Kensington.*

CONTEMPORARY ✕ **The Pig's Ear.** Royal heir Prince William came with friends and split
★ **£–£££** the bill in the first-floor dining room at this inventive gastro-pub, off the King's Road. Elbow in at the boisterous ground-floor pub area, or choose a restaurant vibe in the wood-panel salon upstairs. You'll find creative dishes on the short menu: shallot and cider soup, roast bone marrow, or skate wing and leaks are all typical, and executed . . . royally. ⊠ *35 Old Church St., Chelsea, SW3* ☎ *020/7352–2908* ⌕ *Reservations essential* ▤ *AE, DC, MC, V* Ⓤ *Sloane Sq.*

FRENCH ✕ **Gordon Ramsay at Royal Hospital Road.** The famous Mr. Ramsay whips
£££££ up a storm with white beans, lobster, foie gras, and shaved truffles. He's
Fodor'sChoice one of Britain's finest chefs, and wins the highest accolades here, where
★ tables are booked months in advance. For £90, splurge on seven courses for £70, dance through a three-course dinner; or try lunch (£40 for three courses) for a gentler check—but watch the wine and those extras. ⊠ *68–69 Royal Hospital Rd., Chelsea, SW3* ☎ *020/7352–4441 or*

020/7352–3334 ⌕ *Reservations essential* ⊟ *AE, DC, MC, V* ⊗ *Closed weekends* ⓤ *Sloane Sq.*

£££££ ✕ **Tom Aikens.** Wonder chef Tom
Fodor'sChoice Aikens trained under French legend
★ Joël Robuchon and excels at his slick modern restaurant. His constructions are intricate: many find delight with his pig's head with pork belly, poached oysters, and "piglet." There's a friendly sommelier to help navigate the hefty wine list. ✉ *43 Elystan St., Chelsea, SW3* ☎ *020/7584–2003* ⌕ *Reservations essential* ⊟ *AE, MC, V* ⓤ *South Kensington.*

££–£££££ ✕ **Racine.** There's an upscale buzz at this star of the Brompton Road dining scene. Henry Harris's chic French brasserie excels because he does the simple things well—and doesn't over charge. Classics like smoked duck with French beans or mussels with saffron mousse hit the spot. Desserts and wines by the glass are fairly priced. ✉ *239 Brompton Rd., Chelsea, SW3* ☎ *020/7584–4477* ⊟ *AE, MC, V* ⓤ *South Kensington.*

INDIAN ✕ **Chutney Mary.** London's stalwart romantic Indian holds its own as a
££–£££££ desired destination. Pan-continental dishes like Mangalore giant prawns and Goan chicken curry mingle with more familiar north Indian lamb or chicken tikka. Staff are gracious, lighting is muted, and desserts are worth a pop. ■ TIP→ **The three-course Sunday jazz brunch is good value at £16.50.** ✉ *535 King's Rd., Chelsea, SW10* ☎ *020/7351–3113* ⌕ *Reservations essential* ⊟ *AE, DC, MC, V* ⓤ *Fulham Broadway.*

The City

CONTEMPORARY ✕ **St. John.** Most people love chef Fergus Henderson's ultra-British
££–££££ cooking at this converted smokehouse in Clerkenwell. His chutzpah is
Fodor'sChoice scary: one appetizer is pig skin, and others (calf brain or pig nose and
★ tail) are marginally less extreme. Entrées like bone marrow and parsley salad can appear stark on the plate but arrive with style. Expect an all-French wine list, plus malmseys and port. Try rice pudding with plums, or traditional English Eccles cakes. ✉ *26 St. John St., The City, EC1* ☎ *020/7251–0848 or 020/7251–4998* ⌕ *Reservations essential* ⊟ *AE, DC, MC, V* ⊗ *Closed Sun. No lunch Sat.* ⓤ *Farringdon.*

££–£££ ✕ **St. John Bread & Wine.** The canteen version of St. John in Clerkenwell is a winner no matter what meal of the day: have porridge and prunes for breakfast, seed cake and a glass of Madeira for "elevenses," oxtail and horseradish for lunch, and Gloucester Old Spot ham for dinner. The scrumptious bread is baked on-site, and the wine is mainly French. ■ TIP→ **It's good before or after a stroll around nearby Old Spitalfields or Brick**

TOP 5

■ **Anchor & Hope.** London's leading gastro-pub.

■ **Le Gavroche.** Clubby haute cuisine rated London's finest dining experience.

■ **St. John.** Adventurous eaters savor the challenge of Fergus Henderson's ultra-British cooking.

■ **The Wolseley.** Viennese elegance for any budget at this grand, all-day café.

■ **Yauatcha.** Get your dim sum whenever you want it in this ultra *Sex in the City* setting.

Lane markets. ⊠ *94–96 Commercial St., The City, E1* ☎ *020/7247–8724*
⊟ *AE, MC, V* Ⓤ *Aldgate East, Liverpool St.*

ENGLISH ✕ **Coach & Horses.** Farringdon's award-winning rare-breed gastro-pub
★ **££–£££** gets it right on all levels. The inside feels like a proper English pub—retaining original wooden screens and etched glass—and there are quality ales, earnest service, and the kitchen excels through invention. You might find smoked mackerel, crispy pork belly, or Old Spot ham with fava beans and parsley sauce. ■ TIP→ Dine in the bar if you want that real English pub sensation. ⊠ *26–28 Ray St., The City, EC1* ☎ *020/7278—8990* ⊟ *AE, MC, V* Ⓤ *Farringdon.*

£–££ ✕ **Simpson's Tavern.** A bastion of tradition, this back-alley chophouse was founded in 1757 and is as "rum and raucous" as ever. It's popular with ruddy–faced City folk, who come for old-school fare: steak-and-kidney pie, liver and bacon, chump chops, potted shrimps (served in small pots with butter), or the house specialty, "stewed cheese" (cheese on toast with béchamel and Worcestershire sauce). It's shared seating and service is "idiosyncratic"—one of it's charms. ⊠ *38½ Cornhill, at Ball Ct., The City, EC3* ☎ *020/7626–9985* ⚭ *Reservations not accepted* ⊟ *AE, DC, MC, V* ۞ *Closed weekends. No dinner* Ⓤ *Bank.*

FRENCH ✕ **Plateau.** Sir Terence Conran's Plateau is an excellent choice for a Ca-
£££££ nary Wharf business meal, or for something more relaxed. In a slick all-white space, with tulip-shape chairs and floor-to-ceiling plate-glass windows overlooking Canada Square, Plateau has something for everyone; a bar, rotisserie, terrace, smoking room, and main restaurant. Mains like monkfish and leaks and sea bass and parsnip puree are mighty expensive, but this is Canary Wharf where money, it seems, is no object. ⊠ *Canada Place, Canary Wharf, The City, E14* ☎ *020/7715–7100* ⚭ *Reservations essential* ⊟ *AE, MC, V* Ⓤ *Canary Wharf.*

££££–£££££ ✕ **Club Gascon.** It's hard to find a sexier place than this in London. Maybe it's the leather-wall interior, the cut flowers, cute service, or the way the tapas-style, modern, southwestern French cuisine is served (on a rock rather than on a plate). It must be the quality of the foie gras, which you could enjoy from start to finish: feast on duck foie gras "popcorn," and then have it for pudding with grapes and gingerbread. ⊠ *57 W. Smithfield, The City, EC1* ☎ *020/7796–0600* ⚭ *Reservations essential* ⊟ *AE, MC, V* ۞ *Closed Sun. No lunch Sat.* Ⓤ *Barbican.*

GREEK ✕ **The Real Greek.** Theodore Kyriakou lifts Greek cuisine up several notches
££–£££ at this Shoreditch favorite. Push costs down with a spread of *meze* (small appetizers) and *fagakia* (mid-size dishes). Lamb sweatbreads, grilled octopus, and Ismir squid with prunes recall a real taste of the mainland, and the all-Greek wine list is worth a sniff. ⊠ *15 Hoxton Market, The City, N1* ☎ *020/7739–8212* ⚭ *Reservations essential* ⊟ *MC, V* ۞ *Closed Sun.* Ⓤ *Old St.*

MEDITERRANEAN ✕ **Moro.** Up the road from the City, near Clerkenwell and Sadler's Wells
★ **££–£££** dance theater, is Exmouth Market, a cluster of cute shops, an Italian church, and fine restaurants like Moro. The menu includes a mélange of Spanish and North African flavors. Spiced meats, Serrano hams, salt cod, and wood-fired and char-grilled offerings are the secret to Moro's success. There's a long zinc bar, the tables are small, and the only down-

CLOSE UP Eating English

IN LONDON, LOCAL COULD MEAN any global flavor, but for pure Englishness, roast beef probably tops the list. If you want the best-value traditional Sunday lunch, go to a pub. Gastro-pubs, where Sunday roasts are generally made with top-quality ingredients, are a good bet. The meat is usually served with crisp roast potatoes and carrots, and with the traditional Yorkshire pudding, a savory batter baked in the oven until crisp. A rich, dark gravy is poured on top.

Other tummy liners include shepherd's pie, made with stewed minced lamb and a mashed potato topping and baked until lightly browned on top; cottage pie is a similar dish, but made with minced beef instead of lamb. Steak-and-kidney pie is a delight when done properly: with chunks of lean beef and

ox kidneys, braised with onions and mushrooms in a thick gravy, and topped with a light puff-pastry crust.

Fish-and-chips, usually cod or haddock, comes with thick french fries. A ploughman's lunch in a pub is crusty bread, a strong flavored English cheese with bite (cheddar, blue Stilton, crumbly white Cheshire, or smooth red Leicester), and tangy pickles with a side salad garnish. As for puddings, seek out a sweet bread-and-butter pudding, served hot with layers of bread and dried fruit baked in a creamy custard until lightly crisp. And we musn't forget the English cream tea, which consists of scones served with strawberry jam and clotted cream, and sandwiches made with wafer-thin slices of cucumber—and, of course, plenty of tea.

---

side is the persistent noise. But then again, that's part of the buzz. ✉ *34–36 Exmouth Market, The City, EC1* ☎ *020/7833–8336* ✍ *Reservations essential* ▭ *AE, DC, MC, V* ☉ *Closed Sun.* Ⓤ *Farringdon.*

£–£££ ✕ **The Eagle.** The Eagle spearheaded the welcome trend toward pubs serving good meals. As *the* original '90s gastro-pub, it belongs in the "Restaurants" section by virtue of its good-value Portuguese–Spanish food. You'll find about nine dishes on the blackboard menu daily—a pasta, three vegetarian choices, and a risotto usually among them. Many places in London charge twice the price for similar food. ✉ *159 Farringdon Rd., The City, EC1* ☎ *020/7837–1353* ✍ *Reservations not accepted* ▭ *MC, V* Ⓤ *Farringdon.*

VIETNAMESE   ✕ **Sông Qué Café.** If you're in Hoxton and looking for an unpretentious
£   place to eat, this Vietnamese canteen offers outstanding value for money. Block out the scruffy Kingsland Road location and tacky decor and instead dig into papaya salad, chili squid, Vietnamese pancakes, and *pho* (beef broth with rice noodles and rare steak). ✉ *134 Kingsland Rd., The City, E2* ☎ *020/7613–3222* ▭ *AE, MC, V* Ⓤ *Old St.*

Covent Garden

CONTEMPORARY   ✕ **The Ivy.** Though pushed from the highest reaches of London's restau-
★ **£–£££££**   rant heirarchy, Ivy is still hard to get into. In a wood-panel room with

stained glass, a curious mix of celebs and out-of-towners dine on Caesar salad, salmon cakes, and English classics like shepherd's pie and rhubarb fool (stewed rhubarb and cream). For star-trekking ("Don't look now, dear, but there's Hugh Grant") this is the prime spot in London. The weekend-set lunch is a bargain at £22.50. ■ TIP→ **Try walking in off the street for a table on short notice—it's known to work.** ☒ *1 West St., Covent Garden, WC2* ☎ *020/7836–4751* ⌀ *Reservations essential* ▭ *AE, DC, MC, V* Ⓤ *Covent Garden.*

CONTINENTAL
£££££
✕ **Savoy Grill.** Ambitious chef Marcus Wareing triumphs at this bastion of power dining. Kind lighting, wood paneling, and silver-plated pillars mark the art deco interior, and assembled CEOs, press barons, and politicians have warmed to Wareing's menu. On it are braised pork belly, calves' sweetbread, an "Arnold Bennett" omelet (with smoked haddock and Gruyère béchamel sauce), and chateaubriand. ☒ *The Savoy, Strand, Covent Garden, WC2* ☎ *020/7592–1600* ⌀ *Reservations essential* ⌂ *Jacket required* ▭ *AE, MC, V* Ⓤ *Covent Garden.*

ENGLISH
★ £££
✕ **Rules.** Come, escape from the 21st century. Opened in 1798, London's oldest restaurant—and gorgeous institution—has welcomed everyone from Charles Dickens to the current Prince of Wales. It's one of the single most beautiful dining salons in London: plush red banquettes and lacquered Regency yellow walls crammed with oil paintings, engravings, and Victorian cartoons. The menu includes fine historic dishes—try roast beef and Yorkshire pudding or the steak-and-kidney pudding for a taste of the 18th century. Daily specials will, in season, include game from Rules' Teesdale estate. ☒ *35 Maiden La., Covent Garden, WC2* ☎ *020/7836–5314* ▭ *AE, DC, MC, V* Ⓤ *Covent Garden.*

ITALIAN
£–£££
✕ **Orso.** Showbiz people gravitate to the mid-range Tuscan-inspired food here in Covent Garden. It's not surprising that Orso shares the same snappy attitude as its sister restaurant, Joe Allen. The menu changes daily but always includes excellent pizza and pasta dishes plus entrées based, perhaps, on zucchini and mascarpone or roast sea bass. ☒ *27 Wellington St., Covent Garden, WC2* ☎ *020/7240–5269* ⌀ *Reservations essential* ▭ *AE, MC, V* Ⓤ *Covent Garden.*

PAN-ASIAN
£££–£££££
✕ **Asia de Cuba.** Like the trendy St. Martins Lane hotel it resides in, funky Asia de Cuba is designed by Philippe Starck. It's bold and loud—check out the dangling light bulbs, Latino music, library books, mini-TVs, and satin-clad pillars. The food is pan-Asian fusion and you're encouraged to share the family portions. The miso black cod is delicious, as is the calamari salad. Cheap, it ain't, but it's certainly disco. ☒ *45 St. Martin's La., Covent Garden, WC2* ☎ *020/7300–5588* ▭ *AE, DC, MC, V* Ⓤ *Leicester Sq.*

SEAFOOD
££–£££££
Fodor'sChoice
★
✕ **J Sheekey.** The A-list go here as an alternative to the Ivy. Sleek and discreet, and linked with Theaterland, J Sheekey is one of Londoners' favorite finds. It charms with wood paneling, alcove tables, cracked tiles, and lava-rock bar tops. Opt for jellied eels, Dover sole, fish stew, cod tongue, and famous Sheekey fish pie. ■ TIP→ **Save money with the weekend three-course lunch for £21.50; dining at the bar is romantic, too.** ☒ *28–32 St. Martin's Ct., Covent Garden, WC2* ☎ *020/7240–2565* ▭ *AE, DC, MC, V* Ⓤ *Leicester Sq.*

1

Hammersmith

FRENCH ╳ **Chez Kristof.** Chez Kristof cleans ups in Brackenbury village with this
£–£££ perfect neighborhood pitch on Hammersmith Grove. The space has a
spare look—muted greys, whites, and browns—and attracts swarms of
locals. The modern French brasserie food can be salty, but it's more hit
than miss—razor clam stew, ox cheek, pig's head or veal trotters all sing
for their supper. Go for the buzz, the terrace tables in summer, or the
relaxed but glamorous West End vibe. ✉ *111 Hammersmith Grove, Ham-*
mersmith, W6 ☎ *020/741–1177* ♢ *Reservations essential* ▤ *AE, DC,*
MC, V Ⓤ *Hammersmith.*

ITALIAN ╳ **River Café.** This canteen-style destination Italian spot started a trend
£££££ with its single-estate olive oils, simple roasts, and impeccably sourced
ingredients. Chefs Rose Gray and Ruth Rogers use ultrafresh, seasonal
ingredients, so expect salmon with Sicilian lemons, calamari with red-
pepper salsa, and pork and pancetta—plus one of London's highest checks.
But remember: if you snag an evening table, this is in distant Hammersmith, and you may be stranded if you haven't booked a cab. Note that
tables must be cleared by 11 PM. ✉ *Thames Wharf, Rainville Rd.,*
Hammersmith, W6 ☎ *020/7386–4200* ♢ *Reservations essential* ▤ *AE,*
DC, MC, V Ⓤ *Hammersmith.*

Knightsbridge

FRENCH ╳ **The Capital.** The haute cuisine is nearly peerless at this clublike din-
£££££ ing room that retains a grown-up atmosphere and formal service. Chef
Eric Chavot conjures up superb and classic French dishes. Try frogs' legs
with veal sweetbreads, foie gras with pumpkin risotto, roast pigeon and
bacon, or crab lasagna. Desserts follow the same exceptional route.
■ TIP➔ **Bargain set-price lunch menus (£29.50) are more affordable than din-**
ner (£48–£68). ✉ *22–24 Basil St., Knightsbridge, SW3* ☎ *020/7589–5171*
♢ *Reservations essential* ▤ *AE, DC, MC, V* Ⓤ *Knightsbridge.*

★ **££££** ╳ **Le Cercle.** Prepare to be wowed by knockout new French cuisine at
this ground-breaking restaurant and bar, set in a steep, slick basement
off Sloane Square. The tapas-style portions of steak tartare, foie gras,
pigs trotters, quails eggs, and wild mushrooms cry out to be shared.
■ TIP➔ **Four to six dishes generally suffice; try wines by the glass for each**
round of surprises. ✉ *1 Wilbraham Pl., Knightsbridge, SW1* ☎ *020/*
7901–9999 ♢ *Reservations essential* ▤ *AE, MC, V* ☾ *Closed Sun. and*
Mon. Ⓤ *Sloane Sq.*

££–££££ ╳ **La Poule au Pot.** Americans and the Chelsea set swoon over this candlelight corner of France in Belgravia, where exposed walls, rustic furniture, and potted roses make for romantic meals. Though not spectacular,
the country cooking is decent and rustic. The *poule au pot* (stewed chicken)
and goose with butterbeans are hearty, and there are fine classics, such
as beef bourguignonne and French onion soup, all served by a cheerful
staff. ✉ *231 Ebury St., Knightsbridge, SW1* ☎ *020/7730–7763* ♢ *Reser-*
vations essential ▤ *AE, DC, MC, V* Ⓤ *Sloane Sq.*

INDIAN ╳ **Amaya.** The demanding and hard-to-fool denizens of Knightsbridge
£–£££££ (and beyond) have anointed Amaya the new posh Indian kid on the block.

The dark-wood paneling, terra-cotta statues, rosewood candles, and sparkly chandelier set an upscale tone, but it's the spicy grilled fish and meats from the open show-kitchen that get the juices flowing. Watch the chefs produce goodies from the tandoor oven, *sigri* (a charcoal grill) and *tawa* iron skillet, but mind those prices—they're dangerously high. ✉ *Halkin Archade, 19 Motcomb St., Knightsbridge, SW1* ☎ *0870/780–8174* ⟁ *Reservations essential* ▭ *AE, DC, MC, V* Ⓤ *Knightsbridge.*

JAPANESE ✕ **Zuma.** Hats off to this fashionable, Tokyo-style Japanese restaurant.
£££££ Superbly lighted and designed, with polished granite, blond wood, and exposed pipes, it includes a bar, robata grill, and sushi counter, which takes no reservations. Try the succulent soft-shell crab, black cod wrapped in papery hoba leaf, and *wagyuu* beef. A "sake sommelier" is on hand to help navigate their 30 varieties of rice wine. ✉ *5 Raphael St., Knightsbridge, SW7* ☎ *020/7584–1010* ⟁ *Reservations essential* ▭ *AE, DC, MC, V* Ⓤ *Knightsbridge.*

Mayfair

CONTEMPORARY ✕ **Angela Hartnett's Menu.** The old-world atmosphere at these mahogany-
£££££ panel dining rooms in the English Connaught hotel is refreshed, thanks to chef Hartnett's cuisine. The modern European menu (with homage to Italy, the Mediterranean, Pays Basque, and Spain) is a far cry from the steak-and-kidney pudding and carved beef-of-old-England days of yore—although some interpretations of die-hard Connaught classics remain. Enjoy tortelli (stuffed pasta) with Swiss chard and sea bream. ✉ *The Connaught, Carlos Pl., Mayfair, W1* ☎ *020/7592–1222* ⟁ *Reservations essential* ▭ *AE, DC, MC, V* Ⓤ *Green Park.*

£££££ ✕ **Greenhouse.** Hidden behind Mayfair mansions and approached via
Fodor'sChoice a spot-lighted garden, this elegant salon is for aficionados of top-class
★ and inventive French cuisine at any price. Sit by the garden windows and feast on foie gras with espresso syrup and Amaretto foam, sea urchin panna cotta, or Limousin veal sweetbreads. The epic 90-odd page wine book spans 2,000 bins, including Château d'Yquem (1887–1990). ✉ *27A Hay's Mews, Mayfair, W1* ☎ *020/7499–3331* ⟁ *Reservations essential* ▭ *AE, DC, MC, V* ⊘ *Closed Sun. No lunch Sat.* Ⓤ *Green Park.*

FRENCH ✕ **Le Gavroche.** Chef Michel Roux Jr. inherits the family culinary gene
£££££ and outperforms at this clubby haven, which some critics rate the best
Fodor'sChoice dining in London. His mastery of classic French cuisine—formal, flow-
★ ery, decorated—makes the fixed-price lunch seem relatively affordable at £44 (with a half bottle of wine, water, and coffee included). In fact, lunch may be the best way to eat here if you don't have an expense account, which most patrons clearly do. Book at least a week in advance. ✉ *43 Upper Brook St., Mayfair, W1* ☎ *020/7408–0881* ⟁ *Reservations essential* ▭ *AE, DC, MC, V* ⊘ *Closed 10 days at Christmas. No lunch weekends* Ⓤ *Marble Arch.*

£££££ ✕ **Gordon Ramsay at Claridge's.** There's a grand and gracious atmosphere at one of London's favorite celebration restaurants (Prime Minister Tony Blair had his 50th here). Consider the three-course lunches (£30), or the opulent set dinners (£60 and £70). Try Gloucester Old Spot pork belly or foie gras and goose breast with Périgord truffle. Book months ahead—choosing a Sunday evening is more likely to yield success. Arrive early for drinks at Claridge's art deco cocktail bar, one of the sassiest in town. ⊠ *Claridge's, Brook St., Mayfair, W1* ☎ *020/7499–0099* 🕮 *Reservations essential* 🏛 *Jacket required* 🖃 *AE, MC, V* Ⓤ *Bond St.*

★ **££–££££** ✕ **Bellamy's.** The Mayfair society crowd loves this uppercrust French brasserie for simple reasons: the discreet front of house, reassuring menu, classy-but-restrained decor, and the fabulously priced all-French wine list. The menu weaves from scrambled eggs with Perigord truffles, through whitebait, coquilles St. Jacques, to entrecôte of beef, rillettes of duck, and *iles flottantes* ("floating islands"—egg custard topped with egg whites). ■ **TIP→** The entrance is through a posh delicatessen next to the restaurant. ⊠ *18–18a Bruton Pl., Mayfair, W1* ☎ *020/7491–2727* 🖃 *AE, DC, MC, V* Ⓤ *Green Park.*

ITALIAN   ✕ **Locanda Locatelli.** Chef Giorgio Locatelli has the golden touch—hence
★   the mile-long waiting list at this sexy Italian restaurant, replete with con-
£££–£££££ vex mirrors and cherry-wood dividers. The food is accomplished—superb risottos, handmade pastas, gorgeous fish, beautiful desserts. Be bold and try the nettle risotto or calves' kidney, and lose yourself in the all-Italian wine list. ⊠ *8 Seymour St., Mayfair, W1* ☎ *020/7935–9088* 🕮 *Reservations essential* 🖃 *AE, MC, V* Ⓤ *Marble Arch.*

JAPANESE   ✕ **Nobu.** Within the Metropolitan, a so-hip-it-hurts hotel, soccer (that's
££££–£££££ football to the English) stars—and *occasionally* their wives—haunt London's top celebrity hangout and pay silly money for new-style sashimi with a Peruvian touch. Nobu shifts 300 pounds of Alaskan black cod a day. Nobu Berkeley, a spin-off, rocks nearby (no reservations for parties under six), and Ubon (that's "Nobu" backwards), a sister restaurant, thrives in the east-side Canary Wharf business section. ⊠ *Metropolitan Hotel, 19 Old Park La., Mayfair, W1* ☎ *020/7447–4747* 🕮 *Reservations essential* 🖃 *AE, DC, MC, V* Ⓤ *Hyde Park.*

Notting Hill

CONTEMPORARY   ✕ **Cow Dining Room.** The faux-Dublin 1950s backroom bar at this chic
£££ gastro-pub serves rock oysters, salmon cakes, baked brill, and Cornish crab. Upstairs the chef whips up Brit specialties—roast chicken, ox tongue, lambs' kidneys, and black pudding are typical temptations. Notting Hill locals love the house special in the bar area: draft Guinness with a pint of prawns. ⊠ *89 Westbourne Park Rd., Notting Hill, W2* ☎ *020/7221–0021* 🕮 *Reservations essential* 🖃 *MC, V* Ⓤ *Westbourne Park.*

£–£££ ✕ **Electric Brasserie.** There's nowhere better for people-watching than the
Fodor'sChoice Electric on Portobello Road's market day. Go for the bustle of the in-
★   terior, too—zinc fittings, mirrors, and flattering lighting—and expect oysters, steaks, chunky sandwiches, and seafood platters. Or just settle in at the bar with a long drink. ⊠ *191 Portobello Rd., Notting Hill, W11* ☎ *020/7908–9696* 🖃 *AE, DC, MC, V* Ⓤ *Notting Hill.*

FRENCH   ✕ **The Ledbury.** Top-bracket fine dining has arrived at the doorstep of
££££–£££££ Notting Hill's ultra-high-net-worth citizens. Run by the team behind Chez Bruce in Wandsworth, Ledbury is where to go for highly refined cuisine. It's not cheap—£45 for a three-course dinner—but it's super smart

WHERE TO REFUEL AROUND TOWN

When you're on the go or don't have time for a leisurely meal—and Starbucks simply won't cut it—you might want to try a local chain restaurant or sandwich bar. The ones listed below are fairly priced and committed to quality and using fresh ingredients.

Café Rouge: A classic 30-strong French bistro chain that's been around for eons—so "uncool" that it's now almost fashionable. ⊕ www.caferouge.co.uk

Carluccio's Caffé: Affable TV chef Antonio Carluccio's chain of 12 all-day traditional Italian café/bar/food shops are freshly sourced and make brilliant stops on a shopping spree. ⊕ www.carluccios.com

Ed's Easy Diner: Overdose on made-to-order hamburgers at this chain of shiny, retro '50s-theme American diners. ⊕ www. edseasydiner.co.uk

Gourmet Burger Kitchen (aka GBK): Peter Gordon's line of burger joints is wholesome and handy, with Aberdeen Angus beef, lamb, or venison burgers. ⊕ www. gbkinfo.co.uk

Pizza Express: Serving tasty but utterly predictable pizzas, Pizza Express seems to be everywhere (there are 95 in London). Soho's branch has a cool live jazz program. ⊕ www.pizzaexpress.com

Pret a Manger: London's take-out supremo isn't just for sandwiches: there are wraps, noodles, sushi, salads, and tea cakes as well. ⊕ www.pretamanger.com

Ranoush Juice Bar: Chewy shwarmas proliferate at these late-night kebab café and juice bars (open until 3 AM daily), which serve kebabs, falafal, and tabbouleh. There are three branches in Kensington and one on Edgware Road. ⊕ www.maroush.com

Strada: Stop here for authentic pizzas baked over a wood fire, plus simple pastas and risottos. It's stylish, cheap, and packed. ⊕ www.strada.co.uk

Tootsies Grill: This superior burger joint does yummy grilled burgers, fries, salads, steaks, BLTs, and chicken spreads. There's a children's meal for £4.95. ⊕ www. tootsiesrestaurants.co.uk

Wagamama: Londoners drain endless bowls of noodles at this chain of high-tech, high-turnover, high-volume Japanese canteens. ⊕ www.wagamama.com

and professional. There's a short list of fine wines, including 20 half bottles, and seven sherries by the glass. ⊠ *127 Ledbury Rd., Notting Hill, W11* ☎ *0207/7792–9090* ▭ *AE, MC, V* Ⓤ *Westbourne Park.*

PAN-ASIAN ✕ **E&O.** If you like star-spotting, you'll enjoy E&O, one of London's
£–££££ hippest scene bars and restaurants. E&O means Eastern and Oriental, and the intelligent mix of Chinese, Japanese, Vietnamese, and Thai cuisines includes *beaucoup* vegetarian options. Don't skip the dumplings, black cod, Thai rare-beef, or mango and papaya salads. ⊠ *14 Blenheim Crescent, Notting Hill, W11* ☎ *020/7229–5454* ⌖ *Reservations essential* ▭ *AE, DC, MC, V* Ⓤ *Ladbroke Grove.*

THAI
£
✕ **Churchill Thai Kitchen.** There's a cult appeal to this super-value Thai kitchen attached to a traditional English pub. With big portions of all dishes priced at £5.85, it's a bargain for this high-end district, and full most nights. The pad thai noodles are a good bet, as are the red-and-green curries. Mind the abundant foliage in the conservatory. ⊠ *Churchill Arms, 119 Kensington Church St., Notting Hill, W8* ☎ *020/7792–1246* ▭ *MC, V* Ⓤ *Notting Hill Gate, High St. Kensington.*

St. James's

AUSTRIAN
£–££££
Fodor'sChoice
★
✕ **The Wolseley.** Enjoy grand elegance at this classic run by Messrs. Corbin and King, London's top restaurateurs. Framed with black lacquerware, the Viennese-style café begins its long, decadent days with breakfast at 7 AM and is open until midnight. Linger morning, noon, and night for Nurnberger bratwurst, Wiener schnitzel, Hungarian goulash, and, for dessert, strudel and *kaiserschmarren* (pancake with stewed fruit). It's particularly ideal for sinful pastries and weekend afternoon tea. ⊠ *160 Piccadilly, St. James's, W1* ☎ *020/7499–6996* ▭ *AE, DC, MC, V.*

CONTEMPORARY
£££–£££££
✕ **Le Caprice.** The glossy '80s Eva Jiricna interior; the perfect service; the menu, halfway between Euro-peasant and fashion plate—Le Caprice commands the deepest loyalty of almost any restaurant in London because it gets everything right. From monkfish to forest berries and white-chocolate sauce, the food has no business being so good. Frequented by the older variety of celebrity, it's also some of the best people-watching in town. ⊠ *Arlington House, Arlington St., St. James's, SW1* ☎ *020/7629–2239* ⌲ *Reservations essential* ▭ *AE, DC, MC, V* Ⓤ *Green Park.*

£££–£££££
✕ **Sketch: Gallery.** The global fashion crowd totally *gets* the unusual design aesthetic at Mourad Mazouz's gastro-emporium. "Momo's" madcap gamble is all about extremes. The lavish Gallery dining room (a true art gallery space by day) serves carbo-light contemporary cuisine to a funky beat and video projections, and turns into a club Friday and Saturday nights, as soon as staff clear the floor. There's also a bar, cakes in the Parlour Room, lunch in the Glade area, and a lauded "molecular gastronomy" (science-based cuisine) menu in the fine dining, first-floor Lecture Room, overseen by French legend Pierre Gagnaire. ⊠ *9 Conduit St., St. James's, W1* ☎ *0870/777–4488* ⌲ *Reservations essential* ▭ *AE, DC, MC, V* ☙ *Closed Sun.* Ⓤ *Oxford Circus.*

CONTINENTAL
£££££
✕ **The Ritz.** This palace of gilt, marble, mirror, and trompe l'oeil would moisten Marie Antoinette's eye. Add the view over Green Park and the Ritz's sunken garden, and it seems beside the point to eat. But the cuisine stands up to the visuals, with super-rich morsels—foie gras, lobster, truffles, caviar—all served with a flourish. Englishness is wrested from Louis XVI by a daily roast from the trolley. A three-course lunch at £45 makes the check more bearable than the £75 you would pay for the Friday and Saturday cha-cha-cha dinner-dance (a dying tradition). ⊠ *150 Piccadilly, St. James's, W1* ☎ *020/7493–8181* ⌲ *Reservations essential* ⌂ *Jacket and tie* ▭ *AE, DC, MC, V* Ⓤ *Green Park.*

NORTH AFRICAN ✗ **Momo.** It's a fun ticket, so go if you can. Mourad Mazouz—"Momo"
★ **£££** to friends—rocks beau London with his Casbah-like restaurant off Regent Street. There are Moroccan rugs, fur-skin seats, plus a DJ and often live North African music. Downstairs is the members-only Kemia Bar, and next door is Mô—a cozy Moroccan tearoom, open to all. The cuisine, although good, doesn't *quite* live up to the eclectic atmosphere, but that doesn't stop everyone having a good time. ✉ *25 Heddon St., St. James's, W1* ☎ *020/7434–4040* ⚠ *Reservations essential* ⊟ *AE, DC, MC, V* Ⓤ *Piccadilly Circus.*

Soho

CAFÉS ✗ **Maison Bertaux.** Romantics cherish this tiny, two-story '50s French
£ patisserie because nothing's changed in decades. The pastries and gooey cakes are to die for and are baked on-site; the éclairs are stuffed with light cream and the Black Forrest gâteau is studded with Morello cherries. There are savories, and cute tea services; try not to drool on the window display on the way in or out. ✉ *28 Greek St., Soho, W1* ☎ *020/7437–6007* ⊟ *No credit cards* Ⓤ *Leicester Sq.*

CHINESE ✗ **Fung Shing.** In terms of service and food, this cool-green restaurant
£–£££££ is a cut above the other Lisle–Wardour Street Chinese restaurants. Especially fine and exciting dishes are the crispy baby squid, steamed scallops, and salt-baked chicken, served on or off the bone with a bowl of broth. Reserve a table in the airy backroom conservatory. ✉ *15 Lisle St., Soho, WC2* ☎ *020/7437–1539* ⊟ *AE, DC, MC, V* Ⓤ *Leicester Sq.*

£–£££££ ✗ **Yauatcha.** It's all-day dim sum at this superbly lighted slinky Soho clas-
Fodor'sChoice sic. Expertly designed by Christian Liaigre—with a bar-length aquar-
★ ium, candles, and starry ceiling—the food's a match for the *Sex and the City* setting. There are wicked dim sum (try prawn and scallops), dumplings, and cocktails, and upstairs is a modern pastry shop. ■ TIP→ Note the 90-minute turnaround on tables, and ask to dine in the more romantic basement at night. ✉ *15 Broadwick St., Soho, W1* ☎ *020/ 7494–8888* ⚠ *Reservations essential* ⊟ *AE, MC, V* Ⓤ *Oxford Circus.*

CONTINENTAL ✗ **L'Escargot.** Everyone feels classy at this old-time Soho haunt that
★ **££–£££** serves French food in a sassy art deco ground-floor salon (there's also the Picasso Room, a first-floor formal dining area, replete with Picasso artwork). The fine wines go well with the wood-pigeon *pithiviers* (filled puff pastry), roast pheasant with juniper, or any of the grilled fish. Owned by restaurateur Marco Pierre White, L'Escargot is relaxed, reliable, grown-up, and glamorous. ✉ *48 Greek St., Soho, W1* ☎ *020/ 7437–2679* ⊟ *AE, DC, MC, V* ☯ *Closed Sun.* Ⓤ *Leicester Sq.*

IRISH ✗ **Lindsay House.** Irish chef Richard Corrigan fills up this creaky 1740s
★ Georgian Soho town house with his personality and some of the finest
£££–£££££ food in town. He's known for his invention—combining scallops with pork belly and veal sweetbreads with cauliflower. He excels with Irish beef and mash, and his white asparagus and langoustine can't be bettered. Petits fours with coffee will send you home oh-so-happy. ✉ *21 Romilly St., Soho, W1* ☎ *020/7439–0450* ⊟ *AE, DC, MC, V* ☯ *Closed Sun.* Ⓤ *Leicester Sq.*

South Bank

EASTERN
EUROPEAN
£–£££

✕ **Baltic.** To dine well in Southwark, come to this vodka-party playground. Slick white walls, wooden beams, exposed walls, and an amber chandelier make this converted coach house a sexy spot for drinks or a decent east European meal. Under the same ownership as Chez Kristof in Hammersmith, Baltic serves fine blinis (with caviar or smoked salmon) and tasty gravlax. Siberian, rye, and rose petal are but a few of the killer vodkas on offer. ✉ *74 Blackfriars Rd., South Bank, SE1* ☎ *020/7928–1111* ▤ *AE, DC, MC, V* Ⓤ *Southwark.*

ENGLISH
££–£££
Fodor'sChoice
★

✕ **Anchor & Hope.** Great things at reasonable prices come from the open kitchen at this permanently packed, no-reservations gastro-pub on the Cut: smoked sprats, and crab on toast are two standouts. It's informal, cramped, and highly original, and there are often dishes for groups (whole shoulder of lamb is a good'un.) Expect to share a table, too. ✉ *36 The Cut, South Bank, SE1* ☎ *020/7928–9898* ⚐ *Reservations not accepted* ▤ *MC, V* ☉ *Closed Sun.* Ⓤ *Waterloo, Southwark.*

FRENCH
★ **£££££**

✕ **Chez Bruce.** It's a feat to wrest the title of London's favorite restaurant from the Ivy, and even more so for a neighborhood joint south of the river on Wandsworth Common. Expect peerless yet relaxed service—and wonders from chef-proprietor Bruce Poole. Dive into the lamb's tongue, or experiment with veal, liver, and kidney, and head out with rum baba. The wines are great, the sommelier's superb, and overall it's all rather lovely. ✉ *2 Bellevue Rd., Wandsworth, SW17* ☎ *020/8672–0114* ⚐ *Reservations essential* ▤ *AE, MC, V* Ⓤ *Wandsworth Common rail.*

South Kensington

CONTEMPORARY
£££–£££££

✕ **Bibendum.** This converted 1911 Michelin tire showroom, adorned with awesome stained glass and art deco prints, remains a smooth-running, London showpiece. Chef Matthew Harris cooks with Euro-Brit flair. Try calves' brains, any risotto, Pyrenean lamb with garlic and gravy, or tripe (just as it ought to be cooked). The £28.50 fixed-price lunch menu is money well spent, especially on Sunday. ✉ *Michelin House, 81 Fulham Rd., South Kensington, SW3* ☎ *020/7581–5817* ⚐ *Reservations essential* ▤ *AE, DC, MC, V* Ⓤ *South Kensington.*

MEDITERRANEAN
££–£££

✕ **The Collection.** Enter through a spotlighted tunnel over a glass drawbridge, make your way past the style police, and find yourself engulfed by a fashionable crowd. The huge warehouse setting, with industrial wood beams and steel cables, a vast bar, and a suspended gallery, makes for great people-watching. Well-dressed wannabes peck at Mediterranean food with Japanese and Thai accents. ✉ *264 Brompton Rd., South Kensington, SW3* ☎ *020/7225–1212* ▤ *AE, MC, V* Ⓤ *South Kensington.*

PUBS & AFTERNOON TEA

Pubs

The city's pubs, public houses, or "locals" dispense beer, good cheer, and casual grub in settings that range from ancient wood-beam rooms to ornate Victorian interiors to utilitarian modern rooms. London's culinary fever has not passed pubs by, however, and gastro-pubfever is still sweeping the city. At many places, char-grills are being installed in the kitchen out back, and up front the faded wallpapers are being replaced by abstract paintings. The best of these luxe pubs are reviewed above. Some of the following also showcase nouveau pub grub, but whether you have Moroccan chicken or the usually dismal ploughman's special, do order a pint. Note that American-style beer is called "lager" in Britain, whereas the real British brew is "bitter" (usually served warm). Order up your choice in two sizes—pints or half pints. Some London pubs also sell "real ale," which is less gassy than bitters and, many would argue, has a better flavor.

In 2005, England and Wales relaxed their licensing laws and as many as 5,200 drinking establishments in London extended their opening hours. The new era marks the most notable change since 1915 of what many feel were draconian liquor laws enforced across the United Kingdom (the old laws required most pubs to close at 11 PM). And although it's controversial, the new development only translates into a modest increase in overall licensing hours.

The list below offers a few pubs selected for central location, historical interest, a pleasant garden, music, or good food, but you might just as happily adopt your own temporary local.

✕ **Black Friar.** A step from Blackfriars tube stop, this spectacular pub has an Arts and Crafts interior that is entertainingly, satirically ecclesiastical, with inlaid mother-of-pearl, wood carvings, stained glass, and marble pillars all over the place. In spite of the finely lettered temperance tracts on view just below the reliefs of monks, fairies, and friars, there is a favorable group of beers on tap from independent brewers. ✉ *174 Queen Victoria St., The City, EC4* ☏ *020/7236–5474* Ⓤ *Blackfriars.*

✕ **Dove Inn.** Read the list of famous ex-regulars, from Charles II and Nell Gwyn to Ernest Hemingway, as you wait for a beer at this very popular, very comely 16th-century riverside pub by Hammersmith Bridge. If the Dove is too full, stroll along the banks to the Old Ship or the Blue Anchor. You must be 18 to be admitted here. ✉ *19 Upper Mall, Hammersmith, W6* ☏ *020/8748–9474* Ⓤ *Hammersmith.*

✕ **George Inn.** The inn overlooks a courtyard where Shakespeare's plays were once staged. The present building dates from the late 17th century and is central London's last galleried inn. Dickens was a regular, and the George is featured in *Little Dorrit*. Entertainments include Shakespeare performances, medieval jousts, and morris dancing. ✉ *77 Borough High St., South Bank, SE1* ☏ *020/7407–2056* Ⓤ *London Bridge.*

★ ✕ **Lamb & Flag.** This 17th-century pub was once known as the Bucket of Blood because the upstairs room was used as a ring for bare-knuckle boxing. Now it's a trendy, friendly, and bloodless pub, serving food (lunchtime only) and real ale. It's on the edge of Covent Garden, off Garrick Street. ✉ *33 Rose St., Covent Garden, WC2* ☏ *020/7497–9504* Ⓤ *Covent Garden.*

1

✕ **Mayflower.** A 17th-century riverside inn with exposed beams, this is practically the very place from which the Pilgrims set sail for Plymouth Rock. The inn is licensed to sell American postage stamps. ✉ *117 Rotherhithe St., South Bank, SE16* ☎ *020/7237–4088* Ⓤ *Rotherhithe.*

✕ **Museum Tavern.** Across the street from the British Museum, this Victorian pub makes an ideal resting place after the rigors of the culture trail. This heavily restored hostelry once helped Karl Marx unwind after a hard day in the Library. He could have spent his *Kapital* on any of six beers available on tap. ✉ *49 Great Russell St., Bloomsbury, WC1* ☎ *020/7242–8987* Ⓤ *Tottenham Court Rd.*

★ ✕ **Porterhouse.** With arguably the capital's best selection of beers, this oft-crammed pub is a true institution. In the enormous, brewerylike space, you can choose from the 172 international bottles or 9 draft beers brewed by Porterhouse itself in Ireland. Irish dishes include Carlingford mussels and the "Great Craic" burger—made with Irish Angus beef and Irish cheddar. International sports on TV and live music five nights a week provide entertainment. ✉ *21–22 Maiden La., Covent Garden, WC2* ☎ *020/7379–7917* Ⓤ *Covent Garden.*

Fodor'sChoice ✕ **Prospect of Whitby.** Named after a ship, this is London's oldest river-
★ side pub, dating from 1520. Once upon a time it was called the Devil's Tavern because of the lowlife criminals—thieves and smugglers—who congregated here. Ornamented with pewter ware and nautical objects, this much-loved boozer is often pointed out from boat trips up the Thames. ✉ *57 Wapping Wall, East End, E1* ☎ *020/7481–1095* Ⓤ *Wapping.*

✕ **Sherlock Holmes.** This pub used to be known as the Northumberland Arms, and Arthur Conan Doyle popped in regularly for a pint. It figures in *The Hound of the Baskervilles*, and you can see the hound's head and plaster casts of its huge paws among other Holmes memorabilia in the bar. ✉ *10 Northumberland St., Trafalgar Square, WC2* ☎ *020/ 7930–2644* Ⓤ *Charing Cross.*

Fodor'sChoice ✕ **Spaniards Inn.** An ideal refueling point when you're on a Hampstead
★ Heath hike, this historic, oak-beam pub has a gorgeous garden, scene of the tea party in Dickens's *Pickwick Papers*. Dick Turpin, the highwayman, frequented the inn; you can see his pistols on display. Shelley, Keats, and Byron hung out here, as did Dickens. It's extremely popular, especially on Sunday, when Londoners roll up for the tasty dishes and amusing dog-washing machine in the parking lot. ✉ *Spaniards Rd., Hampstead, NW3* ☎ *020/8731–6571* Ⓤ *Hampstead.*

✕ **Star Tavern.** In the heart of elegant Belgravia, this pub has a Georgian-era facade straight off a postcard. The inside is charming, too: Victorian furnishings and two roaring fireplaces make this a popular spot to flop down with an armload of Knightsbridge shopping bags. ✉ *6 Belgrave Mews W, Belgravia, SW1* ☎ *020/7235–3019* Ⓤ *Knightsbridge.*

Fodor'sChoice ✕ **White Hart.** The drinking destination of the theater community, this
★ elegant, family-owned pub on Drury Lane is one of the best places to mix with cast and crew of the stage. A female-friendly environment, a cheery skylight above the lounge area, and well-above-average pub fare

make the White Hart one of the most sociable pubs in London. ✉ *191 Drury La., Covent Garden, WC2* ☏ *020/7242–2317* Ⓤ *Holborn.*

★ ✕ **White Horse.** This pub in well-to-do Parson's Green has a superb menu with a beer or wine chosen to match each dish. Open early for weekend brunch, too, the "Sloaney Pony" (named for its wealthy Sloane Square clientele) is enormously popular and a place to find many a Hugh Grant and Liz Hurley lookalike. The owner is an expert on cask-conditioned ale, and there are more than 100 wines to choose from. ✉ *1–3 Parson's Green, Parson's Green, SW6* ☏ *020/7736–2115* Ⓤ *Parsons Green.*

✕ **Ye Olde Cheshire Cheese.** It's a tourist trap, but it's also the most historic of all London pubs (from 1667), and it deserves a visit for its sawdust-covered floors, low wood-beam ceilings, and the 14th-century crypt of Whitefriars' monastery under the cellar bar. This was the most regular of Dr. Johnson's and Dickens's *many* locals (neighborhood pubs). ✉*145 Fleet St., The City, EC4* ☏ *020/7353–6170* Ⓤ *Blackfriars.*

Afternoon Tea

The English afternoon tea ritual has been quietly brewing among London polite society. Perhaps it's an anti-Starbucks thing, but nevertheless, it is now ever *so* fashionable to take afternoon tea.

So, what is afternoon tea, exactly? Well, it means real tea (English Breakfast, Ceylon, Indian, or Chinese—and preferably loose leaf) brewed in a china pot, and usually served with china cups and saucers and silver spoons any time between 3 and 5:30 PM daily. In particularly grand places—such as some bigger hotels—there should be elegant finger foods on a three-tier silver tea stand: bread and butter, and crustless cucumber, watercress, and egg sandwiches on the bottom; scones with clotted cream and strawberry preserve in the middle; and rich fruitcake and fancies on top.

Dress is smart casual in posh hotels. Make reservations for all these below.

✕ **Cafe at Sotheby's.** What could be better than perusing the finest art, sculpture, and antiques at this famous Mayfair auction house before afternoon tea? It's open from 9:30 AM and tends to book up days in advance. ✉ *Sotheby's Auction House, 34 New Bond St., Mayfair, W1* ☏ *020/7293–5077* ▭ *AE, DC, MC, V* ◔ *Tea weekdays 3–4:45* Ⓤ *Oxford Circus.*

✕ **Claridge's.** This is the real McCoy, with liveried footmen proffering sandwiches, scones, and superior patisseries (£31.50 for traditional tea, £40 for champagne tea) in the palatial yet genteel foyer, to the sound of the "Hungarian orchestra." ✉ *Brook St., Mayfair, W1* ☏ *020/7629–8860* ▭ *AE, DC, MC, V* ◔ *Tea served daily at 3, 5, 5:30* Ⓤ *Bond St.*

✕ **Fortnum & Mason.** Upstairs at the Queen's grocers, three set teas are ceremoniously served: standard afternoon tea (sandwiches, scones, and cakes: £22.50), old-fashioned high tea (the traditional nursery meal, adding something more robust and savory: £24.50), and champagne tea (£27.50). ✉ *St. James's Restaurant, 4th fl., 181 Piccadilly, St. James's, W1* ☏ *020/7734–8040 Ext. 2241* ▭ *AE, DC, MC, V* ◔ *Tea Mon.–Sat. 3–5:30* Ⓤ *Green Park.*

1

✗ **Harrods.** For sweet-tooths, the fourth-floor Georgian Restaurant at this well-known department store has a high tea that will give you a sugar rush for a week. ⊠ *87–135 Brompton Rd., Knightsbridge, SW3* ☎ *020/ 7730–1234* ▭ *AE, DC, MC, V* ⊙ *Tea weekdays 3:30–5:30, Sat. 4–5:30* Ⓤ *Knightsbridge.*

✗ **Kandy Tea House.** This Sri Lankan–run tiny tearoom, off Kensington Church Street, specializes in Ceylon tea. There's delightful cream tea (£8 per person) with homemade scones, clotted cream, and jam, or after-noon tea with cucumber sandwiches. ⊠ *4 Holland St., Kensington, W8* ☎ *020/7937–3001* ▭ *MC, V* ⊙ *Wed.–Fri. noon–5 PM, weekends noon–6 PM* Ⓤ *High St. Kensington.*

✗ **Patisserie Valerie at Sagne.** Scoff decadent patisseries with afternoon tea at this ever-reliable, reasonably priced, and stylish café. It's a per-fect Marylebone High Street resting point, and you'll adore the tower-ing cakes, chandelier, and murals on the walls. ⊠ *105 Marylebone High St., Marylebone, W1* ☎ *020/7935–6240* ▭ *AE, MC, V* ⊙ *Week-days 7:30 AM–7 PM, Sat. 8 AM–7 PM, Sun. 9 AM–6 PM* Ⓤ *Marylebone.*

✗ **The Ritz.** The Ritz's huge, stagy, sometimes cold and overly formal Palm Court orchestrates cake stands, silver pots, a harpist, and Louis XVI chaises, plus a great deal of rococo gilt and glitz, all for £34. Reserve four weeks ahead, more for weekends. ⊠ *150 Piccadilly, St. James's, W1* ☎ *020/7493–8181* ▭ *AE, DC, MC, V* ⊙ *Tea daily 11:30, 1:30, 3:30, and 5:30* Ⓤ *Green Park.*

✗ **The Savoy.** The glamorous Thames-side hotel does one of the most pleasant teas (£28 or £35.50). Its triple-tier cake stands are packed with goodies, and its tailcoated waiters are wonderfully polite. ⊠ *Strand, Covent Garden, WC2* ☎ *020/7836–4343* ▭ *AE, DC, MC, V* ⊙ *Tea daily 2–4, 4–6* Ⓤ *Charing Cross.*

WHERE TO STAY

It's hard to get a bargain on a London hotel. That is simply a fact of travel life. The dismal exchange rate isn't helping matters. If money is no object, though, you can have the most indulgent luxury imaginable: when it comes to pampering, few do it better than the British. Who would-n't want to relax in a brocade armchair while a frock-coated retainer serves you scones? No matter what you pay, keep in mind that rooms here tend to be much smaller than in U.S. hotels.

London has yet to get the knack of moderately priced hostelries that offer a high level of quality. Two newer hotels—Zetter Rooms and Guesthouse West—represent moves in that direction. At the budget level, B&Bs still dominate the category, and most are filled with chintz and traditional furnishings. There are also ultramodern "pod hotels," an Asian concept, such as easyHotel. These offer tiny rooms with just the basics—bed, shower, toilet—for low prices. Slightly less drastic are the chain hotels that have opened in the center of town.

If you can spend a bit of money, London is the place to do it. Prices can soar into the empyrean, but many of the best hotels are worth it. The Pelham and Covent Garden Hotel—both renovated town houses—glitter with Regency-style interiors, proving that the best hoteliers can do a great deal with even the smallest of spaces. Meanwhile, many of the grand, big-name classics have indulged in gorgeous renovations. Paying top dollar does not mean you'll get stately English grandeur—some newer places and renovations reflect neo-Bauhaus minimalism. But that's London for you—always looking for the next new thing.

Which Neighborhood?

Where you stay can affect your experience. The West End is equivalent to downtown, but there's a big difference between, say, posh Park Lane and bustling, touristy Leicester Square. Hotels in Mayfair and St. James's are central and yet distant in both mileage and sensibility from funky, youthful neighborhoods such as Notting Hill and from major tourist sights such as the Tower of London, St. Paul's Cathedral, and the Kensington museums. On the edges of the West End, Soho and Covent Garden are crammed with eateries and entertainment options. South Kensington, Kensington, Chelsea, and Knightsbridge are patrician and peaceful, which will give you a more homey feeling than anything in the West End; Belgravia is super elegant. From Bloomsbury it's a stroll to the shops and restaurants of Covent Garden, to Theatreland, and to the British Museum; Hampstead and Islington are close enough to explore easily, too. Bayswater is an affordable haven north of Hyde Park. The South Bank, with all its cultural attractions, is another option.

Reservations

Wherever you decide to stay, do reserve in advance. London is popular, and special events can fill hotels suddenly. If you arrive without a room, the **London Tourist Board Information Centres** at Heathrow, Victoria Station Forecourt, and Waterloo International Terminal can help. The **VisitLondon Accommodation Booking Service** (☎ 020/7932–2020 ⊕ www. visitlondon.com) is open weekdays 9 to 6, Saturday 10 to 2; it offers a best-price guarantee.

Prices & Money-Saving Options

London is expensive, and in the £££££ category, you can often pay considerably more than £250 per room. Finding a cheap but tolerable double room is a real coup. Look around Russell Square in Bloomsbury, around Victoria and King's Cross stations, on the South Bank, in Bayswater or Earl's Court, or farther out in Shepherd's Bush. Your cheapest option is a B&B (⇨ Bed-and-Breakfasts & Apartment Agencies, *below*) or a dorm bed in a hostel; apartments are an increasing popular choice. For other suggestions, *see* Lodging *in* Smart Travel Tips.

University residence halls offer a cheap alternative during university vacation periods. Whatever the price, *don't* expect a room that's large by American standards. **City University Hall of Residence: Walter Sickert Hall** (✉ Graham St., N1 8LA ☎ 020/7040–8822 📠 020/7040–8825 ⊕ www. city.ac.uk/ems) costs £60 for a double year-round and includes continental breakfast. **London School of Economics Vacations** (☎ 020/7955–7575 📠 0207/955–7676 ⊕ www.lsevacations.co.uk) costs £38 for a double without a toilet to £62 for a double with a toilet. You can choose from a variety of rooms in their five halls of residence around London. **University College London** (✉ Residence Manager, Campbell House, 5–10 Taviton St., WC1H 0BX ☎ 020/7679–1479 🖷 020/7388–0060) costs £35–£40 for a double and is open from mid-June to mid-September.

In any event, you should confirm *exactly* what your room costs before checking in. British hotels are obliged by law to display a price chart at the reception desk; study it carefully. In January and February you can often find reduced rates, and large hotels with a business clientele have frequent weekend packages. The usual practice these days in all but the cheaper hotels is for quoted prices to cover room alone; breakfast, whether continental or "full English," costs extra. V.A.T. (Value Added Tax—sales tax) follows the same rule, with the most expensive hotels excluding a hefty 17.5%; middle-of-the-range and budget places include it in the initial quote.

	WHAT IT COSTS In pounds				
	££££££	**££££**	**£££**	**££**	**£**
FOR 2 PEOPLE	over £250	£180–£250	£120–£179	£70–£119	under £70

Prices are for a standard double room in high season, including V.A.T., with no meals or, if indicated, CP (with continental breakfast), BP (Breakfast Plan, with full breakfast), or MAP (Modified American Plan, with breakfast and dinner).

Bayswater, Notting Hill & Shepherd's Bush

£££–£££££ 🏨 **The Portobello.** One of London's most famous hotels, the little Portobello (formed from two adjoining Victorian houses) is seriously hip, attracting as many celebrities as ordinary folk, and garnering a stellar reputation in the process. It's certainly a quirky place, with each room individually decorated with random antiques, odd-but-luscious fabrics, statuary, and heaven-knows-what thrown in with a kind of designer abandon here and there. What you'll get for your money cannot be predicted—some rooms have balconies and claw-foot bathtubs; Room 16 has a round bed and an extraordinary Victorian "bathing machine" that actor Johnny Depp is said to have once filled with champagne for his then-girlfriend Kate Moss. ✉ *22 Stanley Gardens, Notting Hill, W11 2NG* ☎ *020/7727–2777* 🖷 *020/7792–9641* ⊕ *www.portobello-hotel.co.uk* 🛏 *24 rooms ₺ Restaurant, dining room, room service, fans, in-room safes, some in-room hot tubs, minibars, cable TV, in-room VCRs, in-room data ports, bar, lounge, babysitting, dry cleaning, laundry service, concierge, Internet, business services, car rental, no-smoking rooms; no a/c in some rooms* ❙⃝❘ *CP* ⊟ *AE, MC, V* ⊘ *Closed 10 days at Christmas* Ⓤ *Notting Hill Gate.*

££££ 🏨 **K West.** Proud to be coolly modern, K West is hidden away inside an undistinguished glass-and-steel building in the bustling Shepherds Bush. The place can be a bit over-the-top and is probably unsuitable for children. The busy lobby houses the all-white K Lounge, and the minimalist approach continues in the bedrooms where dark wood, soft suede, and sleek beige walls and floors create a designer look; high-grade au-

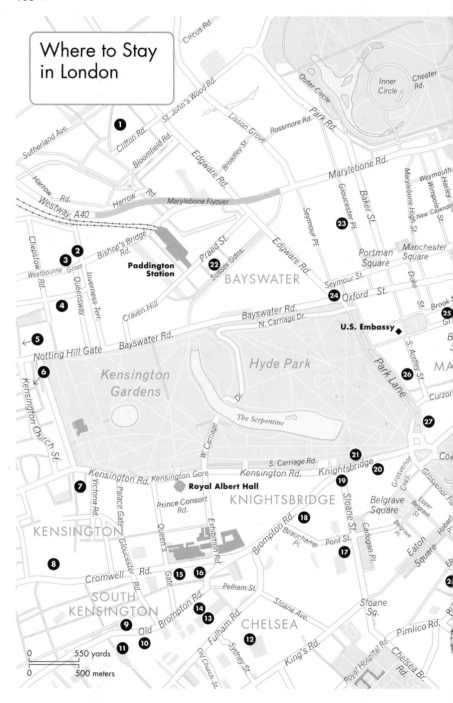

Where to Stay in London

Aster House **14**
Astons Budget Studios **9**
The Berkeley **20**
Best Western Shaftesbury **36**
Blakes **10**
The Buckingham **40**
Cadogan **17**
City Inn Westminster **30**
Claridge's **25**
The Colonnade **1**
Covent Garden Hotel **39**
The Dorchester **26**
Dukes **32**
easyHotel **8**
Five Sumner Palace **13**
The Gallery **15**
The Generator **43**
Great Eastern **47**
Guesthouse West **3**
Harlingford Hotel **42**
Hazlitt's **38**
Hotel 167 . . . . **11**
Knightsbridge Green **19**
Knightsbridge Hotel **18**
K West **6**
The Leonard **24**
Lime Tree Hotel **28**
Lincoln House Hotel **23**
London Bridge Hotel **51**
Malmaison **46**
Mandarin Oriental Hyde Park . . **21**
The Metropolitan **27**
Milestone Hotel & Apartments . . . **7**
myhotel chelsea **12**
No. 41 . . . . **31**
One Aldwych **49**
The Pavilion **22**
The Pelham **16**
The Portobello **5**
Portobello Gold **2**
Premier Travel Inn County Hall . . **53**
Primier Travel Inn Southwark . . . **52**
Renaissance Chancery Court . . . **48**
The Ritz **34**
The Rookery **45**
St. Margaret's **41**
The Savoy **50**
Soho Hotel **37**
The Stafford **33**
22 Jermyn Street **35**
Vancouver Studios **4**
The Windermere **29**
Zetter Rooms **44**

diovisual equipment replaces the stimuli of the lounge. Suites have two-person baths and drawers labeled "smut," where you'll find "adult entertainment" supplies. ⊠ *Richmond Way, Shepherd's Bush, W14 OAX* ☎ *020/7674–1000* 🖷 *020/7674–1050* ⊕ *www.k-west.co.uk* 🛏 *216 rooms, 6 suites* 🍴 *Restaurant, room service, in-room safes, minibars, cable TV with video games, in-room DVDs, in-room data ports, gym, hot tub, massage, sauna, spa, steam room, bar, dry cleaning, laundry service, Internet, meeting rooms, parking (fee), no-smoking rooms* ⊟ *AE, DC, MC, V* 🍴 *CP* Ⓤ *Shepherd's Bush (Central).*

★ **££–££££** 🔳 **Guesthouse West.** The idea behind this hip hotel is to offer high-class chic at moderate prices, and to a certain extent, it succeeds. The minimalist decor and technology—cool black-and-white photos and flat-screen TVs—are very stylish. Rooms, however, are truly tiny, and there's no room service. Nevermind, though, as the restaurant is handy and packed with locals, and the bar is a beautiful homage to the 1930s. ■ TIP→ **The hotel's relationship with a local spa and restaurant provides guests with discounts, and there are guaranteed seats for shows at the small Gate Theatre.** If you fall deeply in love with the place you can "buy" a room for £235,000, which gives you "ownership" of it for 52 days of the year. ⊠ *163–165 Westbourne Grove, Notting Hill, W11 2RS* ☎ *020/7792–9800* 🖷 *020/ 7792–9797* ⊕ *www.guesthousewest.com* 🛏 *20 rooms* 🍴 *Restaurant, cable TV, in-room DVDs, in-room data ports, Wi-Fi, bar, parking (fee), no-smoking rooms* ⊟ *AE, MC, V* Ⓤ *Notting Hill Gate.*

££–£££ 🔳 **Colonnade.** Near a canal filled with colorful narrow boats, this lovely town house rests beautifully in a quiet, residential area known as "Little Venice." From the Freud suite (Sigmund visited regularly in 1938) to the rooms with four-poster beds or balconies, you'll find rich brocades, velvets, and antiques. It's a former home, so each room is different; some are split-level. Extra touches in each are the bathrobe and slippers, bowl of apples, and CD player. The 1920s elevator and Wedgwood lobby fireplace add to the historic style of the place, but the new tapas bar is pleasantly modern. ⊠ *2 Warrington Crescent, Bayswater, W9 1ER* ☎ *020/7286–1052* 🖷 *020/7286–1057* ⊕ *www. theetoncollection.com* 🛏 *15 rooms, 28 suites* 🍴 *Restaurant, dining room, room service, in-room safes, minibars, cable TV, in-room data ports, lobby lounge, wine bar, babysitting, dry cleaning, laundry service, business services, parking (fee), some pets allowed, no-smoking rooms* ⊟ *AE, DC, MC, V* Ⓤ *Warwick Ave.*

££–£££ 🔳 **Portobello Gold.** This no-frills B&B in the heart of the Portobello Road antiques area occupies the floor above the pub and restaurant of the same name. Flat-screen TVs are mounted on the wall, and the beds take up almost the entire room in the doubles, which have their own tiny showers and basins. The best of the bunch is the split-level apartment (£££) with roof terrace, small kitchen, and soothing aquarium. The casual restaurant serves international food at reasonable prices, and there's an Internet café that charges £1 per half hour. ⊠ *95–97 Portobello Rd., Notting Hill, W11 2QB* ☎ *020/7460–4910* ⊕ *www.portobellogold.com* 🛏 *7 rooms, 1 apartment* 🍴 *Restaurant, room service, cable TV, bar, laundry service* ⊟ *MC, V* 🍴 *CP* Ⓤ *Notting Hill Gate.*

££ 🔳 **The Pavilion.** This eccentric town house is a trendy address for fashionistas, actors, and musicians. Often used for fashion shoots, the kitsch bedrooms veer wildly from Moroccan fantasy (the "Casablanca Nights" room) to acres of plaid ("Highland Fling") and satin ("Enter the Dragon"); you'll probably want to take some photos of your own. ■ TIP→ **Triples and family rooms are ideal for groups looking for space *and* style.** ✉ *34–36 Sussex Gardens, Bayswater, W2 1UL* ☎ *020/7262–0905* 🖷 *020/7262–1324* ⊕*www.pavilionhoteluk.com* ⬬*30 rooms* ⌂ *Room service, fans, cable TV, some in-room DVDs, in-room data ports, lounge, dry cleaning, laundry service, parking (fee), no-smoking rooms; no a/c* ▭ *AE, D, MC, V* ⦿⊡ *CP* ⓤ *Paddington, Edgware Rd.*

££ ⌷ **Vancouver Studios.** This little hotel in a Victorian town house is perfect for those wanting a home away from home. Rooms come with minikitchens, and you can even pre-order groceries to stock your mini-refrigerator on arrival. Each studio has daily maid service as well as room service. Some rooms have working fireplaces, and one opens onto the leafy, paved garden. ✉ *30 Prince's Sq., Bayswater, W2 4NJ* ☎ *020/7243–1270* 🖷 *020/7221–8678* ⊕ *www.vancouverstudios.co.uk* ⬬ *45 studios* ⌂ *Room service, kitchens, microwaves, refrigerators, in-room data ports, lounge, dry cleaning, laundry facilities, parking (fee); no a/c* ▭ *AE, DC, MC, V* ⓤ *Bayswater, Queensway.*

TOP 5

- **Hazlitt's.** Theater and literary types favor this 18th-century Soho retreat in prime restaurant territory.

- **Mandarin Oriental.** This exotic hotel never fails to amaze with its miles of marble and gorgeous park views.

- **Milestone.** Laid-back luxury: the fire-lighted lounge is open for drinks all night long.

- **The Rookery.** A gem amid the brash, businesslike hotels of the financial district, the Rookery charms with imported antiques.

- **Zetter Rooms.** This converted warehouse in Holborn dazzles with sleek modern style.

Bloomsbury, Covent Garden & Soho

★ £££££ ⌷ **Covent Garden Hotel.** In the midst boisterous Covent Garden, this hotel is now the London home-away-from-home for a mélange of off-duty celebrities, actors, and style mavens. The public salons keep even the most picky happy: with painted silks, style *anglais* ottomans, and 19th-century Romantic oils, they're perfect places to decompress over a glass of sherry. Guest rooms are *World of Interiors* stylish, each showcasing matching-but-mixed couture fabrics to stunning effect. ■ TIP→ **For £30 the popular Saturday-night film club includes dinner in the brasserie and a film in the deluxe in-house cinema.** ✉ *10 Monmouth St., Covent Garden, WC2H 9HB* ☎ *020/7806–1000, 800/553–6674 in U.S.* 🖷 *020/7806–1100* ⊕ *www.firmdale.com* ⬬ *55 rooms, 3 suites* ⌂ *Restaurant, room service, some in-room faxes, in-room safes, minibars, cable TV, in-room VCRs, in-room data ports, gym, spa, cinema, library, babysitting, dry cleaning, laundry service, concierge, Internet, business services, meeting rooms, car rental* ▭ *AE, MC, V* ⓤ *Covent Garden.*

£££££   ⊞ **One Aldwych.** An understated blend of contemporary and classic results in pure, modern luxury here. Flawlessly designed inside an Edwardian building, One Aldwych is coolly eclectic, with an artsy lobby, feather duvets, Italian linen sheets, and quirky touches (a TV in every bathroom, all-natural toiletries). It's the ultimate in 21st-century style, down to the awesome health club. Suites have amenities such as a private gym, a kitchen, and a terrace. Breakfast is made with organic ingredients. ■ TIP→ **The pool at One Aldwych has speakers under water that play music you can hear when you dive in.** ⊠ *1 Aldwych, Covent Garden, WC2 4BZ* ☎ *020/7300–1000* 🖷 *020/7300–1001* ⊕ *www.onealdwych. co.uk* ⇦ *93 rooms, 12 suites* ♨ *2 restaurants, room service, in-room safes, some kitchens, minibars, cable TV with movies, in-room data ports, indoor pool, health club, spa, 3 bars, cinema, shop, dry cleaning, laundry service, concierge, business services, meeting rooms, parking (fee), no-smoking floors* ▤ *AE, MC, V* Ⓤ *Charing Cross, Covent Garden.*

★ £££££   ⊞ **The Savoy.** Does this grand hotel still measure up to the history? Absolutely. The art deco rooms are especially fabulous, but all rooms are impeccably maintained, spacious, elegant, and comfortable. A room facing the Thames costs a fortune and requires an early booking, but it's worth it. If in doubt, consider that Monet painted the view of the river from such a room. Bathrooms have sunflower-size showerheads. Top-floor rooms are newer and less charming. ⊠ *Strand, Covent Garden, WC2R 0EU* ☎ *020/7836–4343* 🖷 *020/7240–6040* ⊕ *www.savoy-group.com* ⇦ *263 rooms, 19 suites* ♨ *3 restaurants, room service, in-room fax, in-room safes, minibars, cable TV with movies, in-room VCRs, in-room data ports, indoor pool, gym, hair salon, sauna, spa, steam room, 2 bars, lobby lounge, theater, shop, babysitting, dry cleaning, laundry service, concierge, Internet, business services, meeting rooms, parking (fee), no-smoking rooms* ▤ *AE, DC, MC, V* Ⓤ *Charing Cross.*

££££–£££££   ⊞ **Soho Hotel.** This redbrick, loftlike building opened its doors in 2004, making it the first upscale hotel in gritty Soho. The sleek boutique hotel's public rooms are boldly designed with bright fuschia and acid green, but the large bedrooms are much more calm, most with neutral, beige-and-cream tones, or subtle, sophisticated pinstripes, all offset by modern furniture. The bar and restaurant, Refuel, is one of the city's hot spots, and there are movie-screening rooms downstairs, in case the wide-screen TVs in the rooms aren't big enough. ⊠ *4 Richmond Mews, off Dean St., Soho, W1D 3DH* ☎ *020/7559–3000* 🖷 *020/7559–3003* ⊕ *www.sohohotel.com* ⇦ *85 rooms, 6 apartments* ♨ *Room service, in-room DVDs, in-room broadband, gym, concierge, no-smoking rooms* ▤ *AE, MC, V* Ⓤ *Tottenham Court Rd.*

££££   ⊞ **Hazlitt's.** Three connected, early-18th-century houses, one of which was the last home of essayist William Hazlitt (1778–1830), make up this charming Soho hotel. It's a disarmingly friendly place, full of personality but devoid of elevators. Robust antiques are everywhere, most beds are four-posters, and every room has a Victorian claw-foot tub in its bathroom. There are tiny sitting rooms, wooden staircases, and more restaurants within strolling distance than you could patronize in a year. ■ TIP→ **This is *the* London address of visiting antiques dealers and theater and literary types.** ⊠ *6 Frith St., Soho, W1V 5TZ* ☎ *020/7434–1771* 🖷 *020/ 7439–1524* ⊕ *www.hazlittshotel.com* ⇦ *20 rooms, 3 suites* ♨ *Room*

Fodor'sChoice
★

service, fans, minibars, cable TV, in-room VCRs, in-room data ports, dry cleaning, laundry service, concierge, Internet, meeting rooms, parking (fee), some pets allowed, no-smoking floors; no a/c in some rooms ⊟ *AE, DC, MC, V* Ⓤ *Tottenham Court Rd.*

£££–££££ 🏨 **Zetter Rooms.** By day, the area between Holborn and Clerkenwell is
Fodor'sChoice all about business, and rare is the person not wrapped head-to-toe in
★ dark wool-blend, secured neatly with a silk tie. By night, though, those
binds are loosened and it's all oh-so-trendy. London's latest "it" hotel
reflects both personalities. The dizzying five-story atrium, art deco staircase, and slick restaurant are your first indications of what to expect at
this converted warehouse: a breath of fresh air (and a little space) in London's mostly Victorian hotel scene. Rooms are smoothly done up in soft,
dove grey and vanilla fabrics, and the views from the higher floors are
wonderful. It's all lovely to look at, and a bargain by London standards.
⊠ *86–88 Clerkenwell Rd., Holborn, EC1M 5RJ* ☎ *020/7324–4444*
🖷 *020/7324–4445* ⊕ *www.thezetter.com* 📑 *59 rooms* ♢ *Restaurant,
room service, in-room safes, minibars, cable TV, in-room DVDs, in-room
data ports, bar, lobby lounge, laundry service, concierge, Internet, business services, no-smoking floors* ⊟ *AE, MC, V* Ⓤ *Farringdon.*

£££ 🏨 **Best Western Shaftesbury.** When the Best Western chain set-up house
in the midst of historic London, it did an admirable job of fitting in,
certainly using as much chrome and frosted glass as anybody could ask
for. Complimentary newspapers are scattered about, and bedrooms are
ultramodern, with neutral rugs, white walls, dark curtains, and sleek
furniture. The price reflects all of this effort, so it's not the typical Best
Western bargain, but it's pleasant and ideally situated in the heart of
Theaterland. ⊠ *65–73 Shaftesbury Ave., Piccadilly, W1D 6EX* ☎ *020/
7871–6000* 🖷 *020/7745–1207* ⊕ *www.bestwestern.com* 📑 *69 rooms*
♢ *Cable TV, in-room DVDs, in-room broadband, business services, no-
smoking rooms* ⊟ *AE, MC, V* Ⓤ *Piccadilly Circus.*

££–£££ 🏨 **The Buckingham.** This Georgian town house hotel near Russell Square
is a great bargain for the money. Its spacious, attractively designed
rooms are all studios and suites. Each has its own bijoux kitchenette,
giving you an alternative to eating in restaurants every night. All have
marble-and-granite bathrooms and plenty of amenities. Staff are friendly,
and the location is an easy walk from the British Museum and Covent
Garden. ⊠ *11–13 Bayley St., Bedford Sq., Bloomsbury, WC1B 3HD*
☎ *020/7636–2474* 🖷 *020/7580–4527* ⊕ *www.grangehotels.com* 📑 *17
rooms* ♢ *Lounge, cable TV with movies, in-room broadband, no-smoking rooms* ⊟ *MC, V* Ⓤ *Tottenham Court Rd.*

££ 🏨 **Harlingford Hotel.** The Harlingford is by far the sleekest and most contemporary of the Cartwright Gardens hotels. Bold color schemes and beautifully tile bathrooms enliven the family-run place. ■ TIP→ **The quad
rooms are an excellent choice for traveling families.** ⊠ *61–63 Cartwright Gardens, Bloomsbury, WC1H 9EL* ☎ *020/7387–1551* 🖷 *020/7383–4616*
⊕ *www.harlingfordhotel.com* 📑 *43 rooms* ♢ *In-room data ports, ten-
nis court, lounge; no a/c* ⊟ *AE, DC, MC, V* ⦿|*BP* Ⓤ *Russell Sq.*

£–££ 🏨 **St. Margaret's.** A popular hotel near the British Museum and on a
street full of budget hotels, St. Margaret's has well-lighted rooms with high
ceilings in a Georgian-era building. The friendly family that runs the hotel
is sure to welcome you by name if you stay long enough. Rooms are dec-

orated with tasteful wallpaper and a light floral touch, as well as Georgian touches such as a fireplace and beautiful cornice moldings. All have huge windows, and views of the leafy neighborhood. Internet access is free. ⊠ *26 Bedford Pl., Bloomsbury, WC1B 5JL* ☎*020/7636–4277* 📠 *020/7323–3066* ⊕ *www.stmargaretshotel.co.uk* ◆*64 rooms, 12 with bath* ♨ *Dining room, fans, cable TV, lounge, Internet, no-smoking rooms; no a/c* ⊟ *MC, V* ⍨ *BP* Ⓤ *Russell Sq.*

£ 🖼 **The Generator.** This is where the young, enthusiastic traveler comes to find fellow partiers. It's also the cleverest youth hostel in town: set in a former police barracks, its rooms are designed like prison cells, making the most of the bunk beds and dim views. The Internet café provides handy maps and leaflets. The Generator Bar has cheap drinks and a rowdy crowd, and the Fuel Stop cafeteria provides inexpensive meals. There are singles, twins, and dormitory rooms, each with a washbasin, locker, and free bed linens. Prices run from £23 per person for a double room to £17 per person for a 14-bed dorm room. ⊠ *MacNaghten House, Compton Pl. off 37 Tavistock Pl., Bloomsbury, WC1H 9SE* ☎ *020/7388–7666* 📠 *020/7388–7644* ⊕ *www.generatorhostels.com* ◆ *215 beds* ♨ *Restaurant, fans, lobby lounge, pub, sports bar, recreation room, shop, concierge, Internet, meeting rooms, airport shuttle, travel services, parking (fee), no-smoking floors; no a/c, no room phones, no room TVs* ⊟ *MC, V* ⍨ *CP* Ⓤ *Russell Sq.*

The City

£££££ 🖼 **Great Eastern.** This grand old Victorian railway hotel looks lavish and over-the-top on the outside, but inside it's all about modernity, with polished wood, neutral colors, and contemporary art. You'll want for little—there are five restaurants (serving sushi, seafood, brasserie fare, pub food, and haute cuisine), a popular bar, a gorgeous spa, and a boutique selling the covetable Ren bath products with which all the hotel's bathrooms are stocked. Rooms on the fifth and sixth floors are modern lofts, with lots of light. With all the restaurants and bars, also used by locals, this is not a retreat from bustling London life. ⊠ *Liverpool St. at Bishopsgate, The City, E2M 7QN* ☎ *020/7618–5010* 📠 *020/7618–5011* ⊕ *www.great-eastern-hotel.co.uk* ◆ *246 rooms, 21 suites* ♨ *5 restaurants, 12 dining rooms, room service, some in-room faxes, in-room safes, minibars, cable TV with video games, in-room VCRs, in-room data ports, gym, spa, 2 bars, pub, library, shop, babysitting, dry cleaning, laundry service, concierge, Internet, business services, meeting rooms, car rental, no-smoking rooms* ⊟ *AE, DC, MC, V* Ⓤ *Liverpool St.*

££££–£££££ 🖼 **The Rookery.** This is an extraordinary hotel, where each beautiful double room is decorated with a lavish, theatrical flair and an eye for history. Many have four-poster beds, each has a claw-foot bathtub, antique

Fodor'sChoice ★

carved wooden headboard, and period furnishings, including exquisite salvaged pieces. In the Rook's Nest, the hotel's duplex suite, you can relax in an antique bath in the corner of the bedroom or enjoy a magnificent view of the City's historic buildings. The conservatory, with its small patio garden, is a relaxing place to unwind. ⊠ *12 Peter's La., at Cowcross St., The City, EC1M 6DS* ☎ *020/7336–0931* 🖶 *020/7336–0932* ⊕ *www.rookeryhotel.com* ⇩ *30 rooms, 3 suites* ⟂ *Room service, fans, in-room safes, minibars, cable TV, in-room data ports, bar, lobby lounge, library, babysitting, dry cleaning, laundry service, concierge, meeting rooms, airport shuttle, car rental, parking (fee), no-smoking floors; no a/c* ⊟ *AE, DC, MC, V* Ⓤ *Farringdon.*

££££ 🏨 **Malmaison.** Part of a small chain of well-regarded U.K. boutique hotels, this Clerkenwell address is very trendy, with contemporary furnishings, clean lines, and all the extras. Stylish rooms are well-decorated in neutral cream and beige, have huge beds and CD systems with a library of music on demand, as well as satellite TVs and free broadband. It prides itself on fast, quality room service, so breakfast in bed can be a pleasure. The whole package is a business traveler's dream. ⊠ *Charterhouse Sq., The City, EC1M 6AH* ☎ *020/7012–3700* 🖶 *020/7012–3702* ⊕ *www.malmaison.com* ⇩ *95 rooms, 2 suites* ⟂ *Restaurant, room service, in-room safes, minibars, cable TV, in-room broadband, gym, bar, babysitting, dry cleaning, laundry service, concierge, meeting room, no-smoking rooms* ⊟ *AE, MC, V* ⦿⧉ *CP* Ⓤ *Barbican, Farringdon.*

£££–££££ 🏨 **Renaissance Chancery Court.** This landmark structure, built by the Pearl Assurance Company in 1914, has been transformed into a beautiful Marriott hotel. So striking is the architecture that the building was featured in the film *Howard's End.* The spacious bedrooms are popular with business travelers and the decor has a masculine edge—lots of leather and dark red fabrics. The day spa in the basement is a cocoon of peacefulness. There's marble everywhere, from the floors in public spaces to the bathrooms. The restaurant, Pearl, is known for its modern European cuisine, and the bar, in an old banking hall, has elegant soaring ceilings. ⊠ *252 High Holborn, Holborn, WC1V 7EN* ☎ *020/7829–9888* 🖶 *0207/829–9889* ⊕ *www.renaissancehotels.com/loncc* ⇩ *343 rooms, 14 suites* ⟂ *Restaurant, room service, in-room safes, minibars, cable TV with video games, in-room data ports, gym, sauna, spa, steam room, bar, lobby lounge, shop, babysitting, laundry service, concierge, business services, meeting rooms, no-smoking rooms* ⊟ *AE, MC, V* Ⓤ *Holborn.*

Kensington & South Kensington

£££££ 🏨 **Blakes.** Designed by owner Anouska Hempel, Blakes is a fantasy packed with precious Biedermeier, Murano glass, and modern pieces from around the world. Rooms hark back to the days of the British empire, and include Chinese opium dens draped in lush red fabrics, as well as bright spaces with classic colonial furnishings. The foyer sets the tone with piles of cushions, black walls, rattan, and bamboo. The exotic Thai restaurant is a trendy delight. ⊠ *33 Roland Gardens, South Kensington, SW7 3PF* ☎ *020/7370–6701* 🖶 *020/7373–0442* ⊕ *www.blakeshotels.com* ⇩ *38 rooms, 11 suites* ⟂ *Restaurant, room* *service, some in-room faxes, in-room safes, minibars, cable TV, in-room VCRs, in-room data ports, Wi-Fi, gym, bar, babysitting, dry cleaning, laundry service, concierge, Internet, business services, meeting rooms, car rental, parking (fee); no a/c in some rooms* ☰ *AE, DC, MC, V* Ⓤ *South Kensington.*

££££ 🎦 **Milestone Hotel & Apartments.** This pair of intricately decorated Vic-
Fodor'sChoice torian town houses overlooking Kensington Palace and Gardens is an
★ intimate, luxurious alternative to the city's more famous five-star hotels. Great thoughtfulness goes into the hospitality and everything is possible in this special place. You'll be offered a welcome drink upon arrival
and, if you so desire, you can return to a post-theater midnight snack
in your room or leave with a picnic for the park across the street. The
staff is friendly and efficient, but never obsequious. Each sumptuous room
is full of antiques; many have canopied beds. Our favorite is the Ascot
Room, which is filled with elegant hats of the kind worn at the famous
races. ✉ *1 Kensington Ct., Kensington, W8 5DL* ☏ *020/7917–1000*
🖷 *020/7917–1010* ⊕ *www.milestonehotel.com* ⇆ *45 rooms, 12 suites,
6 apartments* ⚹ *2 restaurants, room service, in-room fax, in-room safes,
some kitchens, minibars, cable TV with movies, in-room VCRs, gym,
hot tub, sauna, bar, lounge, babysitting, dry cleaning, laundry service,
concierge, Internet, business services, meeting rooms, some pets allowed (fee); no smoking* ☰ *AE, DC, MC, V* Ⓤ *High St. Kensington.*

££££–£££££ 🎦 **The Pelham.** Museum lovers flock to this sweet hotel across the street
from the South Kensington tube station. The Natural History, Science,
and Victoria & Albert museums are all a short stroll away, as is King's
Road. At the end of a day's sightseeing, settle down in front of the fireplace in one of the two snug drawing rooms with their honor bars. The
stylish, contemporary rooms by designer Kit Kemp have sash windows
and marble bathrooms. Some top-floor rooms have sloping ceilings
and casement windows. ✉ *15 Cromwell Pl., South Kensington, SW7
2LA* ☏ *020/7589–8288, 800/553–6674 in U.S.* 🖷 *020/7584–8444*
⊕ *www.firmdale.com* ⇆ *47 rooms, 4 suites* ⚹ *Restaurant, room service, some in-room safes, minibars, cable TV, in-room VCRs, in-room
data ports, bar, concierge, business services, meeting rooms, parking (fee)*
☰ *AE, MC, V* Ⓤ *South Kensington.*

★ £££ 🎦 **Five Sumner Place.** Once you've checked into this tall Victorian town
house on a quiet residential street, you get your own key to the front
door and make yourself at home. If the weather is pleasant, you can
enjoy the small garden. In the morning, take breakfast in the conservatory. Guest rooms are simply decorated with pleasant Victorian detail and reproduction furniture. ✉ *5 Sumner Pl., South Kensington, SW7
3EE* ☏ *020/7584–7586* 🖷 *020/7823–9962* ⊕ *www.sumnerplace.com*
⇆ *17 rooms* ⚹ *Room service, minibars, in-room broadband, in-room
data ports, parking (fee); no a/c, no smoking* ☰ *AE, MC, V* ⦿I *BP*
Ⓤ *South Kensington.*

£££ 🎦 **The Gallery.** It's a small, Edwardian world apart from the bustling city,
but it's a little pricey for what it has to offer. The Arts and Crafts–style
living room has a piano, lush carpets, and cozy fires in the winter. Decor
in the guest rooms is slightly dated, the floral fabric a bit old fashioned,
but rooms are pleasant, with solid, comfortable beds, and the bathrooms
have London's ubiquitous polished granite. ✉ *10 Queensberry Pl., South*

Kensington, SW7 2E8 ☎ *020/ 7915–0000, 800/270–9206 in U.S.* 🖷 *020/7915–4400* ⊕ *www.eeh.co. uk* ⤻ *34 rooms, 2 suites* ⚪ *Room service, some in-room faxes, in-room safes, some in-room hot tubs, some minibars, cable TV, in-room data ports, bar, dry cleaning, laundry service, concierge, Internet, meet- ing rooms, airport shuttle; no a/c in some rooms* ⊟ *AE, DC, MC, V* ✸ *BP* Ⓤ *South Kensington.*

WORD OF MOUTH

"I prefer South [Kensington] to Bloomsbury for several reasons, one of which is that it has great Tube connections, which will get you anywhere you want to go quickly, and because it's a lovely, quiet, upscale area to come home to each evening."   –MelJ

££–£££   🏠 **Aster House.** Country-casual rooms fill this delightful guesthouse. ■ TIP→ **The friendly owners go out of their way to make you feel at home and answer questions, even loaning guests a free cell phone to use while in town.** The conservatory where breakfast is served is an airy, light place, and the small garden at the back has a charming pond. Note that this is a five-story building with no elevator. ✉ *3 Sumner Pl., South Kensington, SW7 3EE* ☎ *020/7581–5888* 🖷 *020/7584–4925* ⊕ *www.welcome2london.com/asterhouse* ⤻ *14 rooms* ⚪ *Dining room, in-room safes, cable TV, lounge, Internet; no smoking* ⊟ *MC, V* ✸ *BP* Ⓤ *South Kensington.*

££–£££   🏠 **Astons Budget Studios.** These three redbrick Victorian town houses on a residential street hold studios and apartments. All accommodations have concealed kitchenettes, and the apartments (£££) have marble bath- rooms and trouser presses as well. The decor is a bit Scandinavian. ✉ *31 Rosary Gardens, South Kensington, SW7 4NH* ☎ *020/7590–6000, 800/ 525–2810 in U.S.* 🖷 *020/7590–6060* ⊕ *www.astons-apartments.com* ⤻ *43 rooms, 12 suites* ⚪ *Dining room, fans, in-room safes, kitch- enettes, microwaves, refrigerators, cable TV, in-room data ports, concierge, Internet, business services, airport shuttle, car rental, parking (fee), some pets allowed, no-smoking floors; no a/c* ⊟ *AE, MC, V* Ⓤ *Gloucester Rd.*

££   🏠 **Hotel 167.** This white-stucco, Victorian corner house just a two- minute walk from the V&A is no traditional old hostelry. With its strong abstract art pieces and black-and-white tiled floor, the lobby is unique, while the bedrooms are an unpredictable mélange of new and old furniture and colorful fabrics. The breakfast room–lounge is charm- ing, with wrought-iron furniture and sunny yellow walls. Its creative approach has been the subject of a novel ("Hotel 167" by Jane Solomon) and a song by the rock band Manic Street Preachers. ✉ *167 Old Bromp- ton Rd., South Kensington, SW5 0AN* ☎ *020/7373–3221* 🖷 *020/ 7373–3360* ⊕ *www.hotel167.com* ⤻ *18 rooms* ⚪ *Dining room, mini- bars, cable TV; no a/c* ⊟ *AE, DC, MC, V* ✸ *CP* Ⓤ *Gloucester Rd.*

£   🏠 **easyHotel.** No London hotel received more attention in 2005 than budget easyHotel. Crammed into a big white town house are 34 tiny rooms, all with double bed and private bathroom, brightly decorated in the trademark orange-and-white of the Easy chain (which includes the Internet cafés "easyeverything" and the budget airline easyJet). The idea behind the hotel is to provide quality basics (bed, sink, shower, toi- let) for little money. The tiny reception desk with one staff member can't offer much in terms of service and if you want your room cleaned, it's an additional £10 a day. The concept is a huge hit—easyHotel is fully booked months in advance. ✉ *14 Lexham Gardens, Kensington, W8 5JE* ☎ *020/7216–1717* ⊕ *www.easyhotel.com* ⬭ *34 rooms* ⚲ *Cable TV; no a/c, no room phones, no smoking* ⊟ *MC, V* Ⓜ *Gloucester Rd.*

Knightsbridge, Chelsea & Belgravia

£££££ ⬚ **The Berkeley.** The elegant Berkeley successfully mixes the old and the new in a luxurious, modern building with a splendid penthouse swimming pool. The bedrooms either have swags of William Morris prints or are art deco. All have sitting areas, CD players, and big bathrooms with bidets. There are spectacular penthouse suites with their own conservatory terraces, and others with saunas or balconies. Dining venues include Marcus Wareing's high-class Pétrus restaurant, Gordon Ramsay's excellent and extremely popular Boxwood café, the eclectic and sumptuous Blue Bar, and the whimsical Caramel Room where morning coffee and decadent doughnuts are served. ✉ *Wilton Pl., Belgravia, SW1X 7RL* ☎ *020/7235–6000, 800/637–2869 in U.S.* ⛓ *020/7235–4330* ⊕ *www.the-berkeley.com* ⬭ *103 rooms, 55 suites* ⚲ *Restaurant, room service, in-room fax, in-room safes, some kitchens, minibars, cable TV, in-room VCRs, indoor-outdoor pool, gym, hair salon, sauna, spa, Turkish bath, bar, cinema, babysitting, dry cleaning, laundry service, concierge, Internet, business services, meeting rooms, airport shuttle, car rental, parking (fee), no-smoking floors* ⊟ *AE, DC, MC, V* Ⓤ *Knightsbridge.*

★ £££££ ⬚ **Cadogan.** This is both one of London's most beautiful hotels and one of its most historically naughty. A recent overhaul means much of its old stuffiness is gone—elegant golds and creams have replaced fussy florals. The drawing room has rich, wood paneling and deep, comfortable armchairs, and is an excellent place for tea and people-watching. The sophisticated bar urges you to have a martini and a cigar. Breakfast offers the best healthy cereals and fruits alongside decadent pastries. ✉ *75 Sloane St., Chelsea, SW1X 9SG* ☎ *020/7235–7141* ⛓ *020/7245–0994* ⊕ *www.cadogan.com* ⬭ *65* ⚲ *Restaurant, room service, minibars, cable TV, in-room VCR, in-room data ports, Wi-Fi, tennis courts, bar, lounge, babysitting, dry cleaning, laundry facilities, concierge, no-smoking rooms* ⊟ *AE, MC, V.*

£££££ ⬚ **Mandarin Oriental Hyde Park.** Stay here, and the three greats of
★ Knightsbridge—Hyde Park, Harrods, and Harvey Nichols—are on your doorstep. Built in 1880, the Mandarin Oriental is one London's most elegant hotels. Bedrooms are traditional Victorian with hidden high-tech gadgets (Wi-Fi is expected in late 2006) and luxurious touches—potted orchids, delicate chocolates, and fresh fruit. The service here is legendary and includes a butler on every floor. ✉ *66 Knightsbridge, Knightsbridge, SW1X 7LA* ☎ *020/7235–2000* ⛓ *020/7235–2001* ⊕ *www.mandarinoriental.com* ⬭ *177 rooms, 23 suites* ⚲ *2 restaurants, room service, some in-room faxes, in-room safes, minibars, cable TV, in-room VCRs, in-room data ports, gym, hot tub, sauna, spa, steam room, bar, babysitting, dry cleaning, laundry service, concierge, Internet, business services, meeting rooms, airport shuttle, car rental, parking (fee), no-smoking rooms* ⊟ *AE, DC, MC, V* Ⓤ *Knightsbridge.*

£££££ ⌂ **No. 41.** This luxurious abode is not a formulaic, paint-by-numbers hotel. Its designer credentials are clear everywhere, from the unusual tiled floors to the extraordinary furnishings, which seem to have been drawn from every corner of the globe. The staff cocoons and pampers its guests—sit for a second and someone will offer you tea, cocktails, water—anything that crosses your mind can be yours in a second. Rooms, some of them split-level, are filled with high-tech gadgets to keep you in touch with the office back home. When you're not working, you can relax on the butter-soft leather sofa in front of the fireplace, recline on the exquisite bed linens and feather duvets, or luxuriate in the marble bath. A "whatever, whenever" button on the telephone connects you with the helpful, amiable staff. ⊠ *41 Buckingham Palace Rd., Victoria, SW1W 0PS ☎ 020/7300–0041 🖷 020/7300–0141 ⊕ www.41hotel. com ⇨ 14 rooms, 4 suites ⌂ Room service, in-room fax, in-room safes, some in-room hot tubs, minibars, cable TV with movies and video games, in-room broadband, in-room VCRs, in-room data ports, lounge, babysitting, dry cleaning, laundry service, concierge, Internet, business services, meeting rooms, car rental, parking (fee), no-smoking rooms ☰ AE, DC, MC, V* ◉| *CP* Ⓤ *Victoria.*

££££–£££££ ⌂ **Knightsbridge Hotel.** Just off glamorous Knightsbridge near Harrods and Harvey Nichols in quiet Beaufort Gardens, this chic hotel is well placed for shoppers. The balconied suites and regular rooms are wrapped in bold fabrics, with the beds piled high with warm duvets. All rooms have CD players, writing desks, and large granite-and-oak bathrooms. The fully loaded honor bar in the drawing room is an excellent place to unwind amid African sculptures and modern art. ⊠ *10 Beaufort Gardens, Knightsbridge, SW3 1PT ☎ 020/7584–6300, 800/553–6674 in U.S. 🖷 020/7584–6355 ⊕ www.knightsbridgehotel.co.uk ⇨ 42 rooms, 2 suites ⌂ Room service, in-room safes, minibars, cable TV, some in-room VCRs, in-room data ports, gym, bar, library, babysitting, dry cleaning, laundry service, concierge, Internet, meeting rooms, parking (fee) ☰ AE, MC, V* Ⓤ *Knightsbridge.*

£££–£££££ ⌂ **myhotel chelsea.** This small, chic hotel tucked away down a Chelsea side street is a charmer. Rooms are bijoux small, but sophisticated, with mauve satin throws atop crisp white down comforters. Tiny bathrooms are made cheery with pale pink granite countertops. Flat-screen TVs, DVD players, and in-room Wi-Fi all set the place electronically ahead of many top-level London hotels. The beauty is in the details here—there's no restaurant, but the fire-warmed bar serves light meals and tea. There's no pool, but there's an excellent spa. The guest library has DVDs and books on loan, and offers a quiet place to relax. Best of all, you can get a good deal if you book in advance via the Web site. ⊠ *35 Ixworth Pl., Chelsea, SW3 3QZ ☎ 020/7225–7500 🖷 020/7225–7555 ⊕ www. myhotels.com ⇨ 45 rooms, 9 suites ⌂ Room service, fans, in-room safes, minibars, cable TV, in-room DVDs, Wi-Fi, gym, massage, spa, bar, library, lounge, babysitting, laundry service, some pets allowed, no-smoking floors ☰ AE, D, MC, V* Ⓤ *South Kensington.*

£££ ⌂ **Knightsbridge Green.** Near Harrods and Hyde Park, this modern hotel has affordable triples and quads with sofa beds that are good for families. Rooms are rather plain and could use an update, but they have double-glaze windows that help muffle the sound of traffic on busy

Knightsbridge. Breakfast can be delivered to your room, or you could linger in the lounge over complimentary tea and coffee. ⊠ *159 Knightsbridge, Knightsbridge, SW1X 7PD* ☎*020/7584–6274* 📠*020/7225–1635* ⊕ *www.thekghotel.co.uk* ⤴ *28 rooms, 12 suites* ⚫ *In-room safes, cable TV, in-room data ports, babysitting, dry cleaning, concierge, Internet; no smoking* ⊟ *AE, DC, MC, V* Ⓤ *Knightsbridge.*

Mayfair, Marylebone & St. James's

£££££ 🏨 **The Dorchester.** Few hotels this opulent manage to be quite so charming. The glamour level is off the scale: 1,500 square yards of gold leaf and 1,100 square yards of marble. Bedrooms (some not as spacious as you might expect) have Irish-linen sheets on canopied beds, brocades and velvets, and Italian marble and etched-glass bathrooms with Floris toiletries. Furnishings throughout are opulent English country-house style, with more than a hint of art deco, in keeping with the original 1930s building. The hotel has embraced modern technology, though, and "e-butlers" help guests figure out the Web TVs in the rooms. ⊠ *Park La., Mayfair, W1A 2HJ* ☎ *020/7629–8888* 📠 *020/7409–0114* ⊕ *www. dorchesterhotel.com* ⤴ *195 rooms, 55 suites* ⚫ *3 restaurants, in-room safes, minibars, cable TV with movies, in-room VCRs, in-room data ports, gym, health club, hair salon, spa, bar, lobby lounge, nightclub, shop, babysitting, dry cleaning, laundry service, concierge, Internet, business services, meeting rooms, car rental, parking (fee), no-smoking rooms* ⊟ *AE, DC, MC, V* Ⓤ *Marble Arch, Hyde Park Corner.*

£££££ 🏨 **Dukes.** This small, exclusive, Edwardian-style hotel with a gas lantern–lighted courtyard entrance is in a discreet cul-de-sac. Overstuffed sofas, oil paintings of assorted dukes, and muted, rich colors create the perfect setting for sipping the finest dry martinis in town. ▪ TIP➔ **The hotel's trump card is that, for such a central location, it's peaceful and quiet.** The rooms are cozy with floral prints and wood everywhere. ⊠ *35 St. James's Pl., St. James's, SW1A 1NY* ☎ *020/7491–4840, 800/ 381–4702 in U.S.* 📠 *020/7493–1264* ⊕ *www.dukeshotel.co.uk* ⤴ *80 rooms, 9 suites* ⚫ *Restaurant, dining room, some in-room faxes, in-room safes, minibars, cable TV, some in-room VCRs, in-room data ports, gym, sauna, spa, steam room, bar, lobby lounge, dry cleaning, laundry service, concierge, business services, meeting rooms, parking (fee)* ⊟ *AE, DC, MC, V* Ⓤ *Green Park.*

£££££ 🏨 **The Metropolitan.** This supertrendy hotel is one of the few addresses for visiting fashion, music, and media folk in London. Its Met bar has an exclusive guest list, and the restaurant is the famed Nobu, leased by Japanese wonder-chef Nobu Matsuhisa. The lobby is sleek and postmodern, as are the bedrooms, which have identical minimalist taupe-and-white furnishings. The best rooms overlook Hyde Park, but all have a groovy minibar hiding the latest alcoholic and health-boosting beverages. ⊠ *Old Park La., Mayfair, W1K 1LB* ☎ *020/7447–1000, 800/ 337–4685 in U.S.* 📠 *020/7447–1100* ⊕ *www.metropolitan.co.uk* ⤴ *137 rooms, 18 suites* ⚫ *Restaurant, room service, in-room broadband, in-room fax, in-room safes, minibars, cable TV with movies and video games, some in-room VCRs, in-room data ports, gym, massage, bar, shop, babysitting, dry cleaning, laundry service, concierge, Inter-*

net, business services, meeting room, parking (fee), no-smoking floors ▤ *AE, DC, MC, V* Ⓤ *Hyde Park Corner.*

££££ 🏨 **The Ritz.** Uncapitalized, the word *ritz* has come to mean "posh" or "classy," and this is where the word originated. Memorialized in song by Irving Berlin, this hotel's very name conjures the kind of luxury associated with swagged curtains, handwoven carpets, and the smell of cigars, polish, and fresh lilies. The only thing that has been lost is a certain vein of moneyed naughtiness that someone like F. Scott Fitzgerald, at least, would have banked on. The bedrooms are bastions of pastel Louis XVI style, with gilded furniture and crystal chandeliers. With a ratio of two staff members to every bedroom, you're guaranteed personal service despite the hotel's massive size. ■ TIP→ **Formal dress is encouraged, and jeans are not allowed in public areas.** ✉ *150 Piccadilly, St. James's, W1J 9BR* ☎ *020/7493–8181* 🖷 *020/7493–2687* ⊕ *www. theritzhotel.co.uk* ⇆ *133 rooms* ♿ *2 restaurants, room service, some in-room faxes, in-room safes, cable TV, some in-room VCRs, in-room data ports, gym, hair salon, bar, babysitting, dry cleaning, laundry service, concierge, Internet, business services, meeting rooms, car rental, parking (fee), no-smoking rooms* ▤ *AE, DC, MC, V* Ⓤ *Piccadilly Circus.*

★ ££££ 🏨 **The Stafford.** This is a rare find: a posh hotel that offers equal parts elegance and friendliness. It's hard to check-in without meeting the gregarious manager, and his unshakable cheeriness must be infectious, for the staff are also upbeat and helpful. The location is one of the few peaceful spots in the area, down a small lane behind Piccadilly. Its 13 adorable carriage-house rooms, installed in the 18th-century stable block, are relative bargains; each individually decorated room has a cobbled mews entrance and gas-fueled fireplace, exposed beams, and CD player. The popular little American Bar has ties, baseball caps, and toy planes hanging from a ceiling modeled, presumably, on New York's 21 Club. A real find in the luxury category. ✉ *St. James's Pl., St. James's, SW1A 1NJ* ☎ *020/7493–0111* 🖷 *020/7493–7121* ⊕ *www.thestaffordhotel.co.uk* ⇆ *81 rooms* ♿ *Restaurant, dining room, cable TV, in-room data ports, bar* ▤ *AE, DC, MC, V* Ⓤ *Green Park.*

££££–£££££ 🏨 **Claridge's.** Stay here, and you're staying at a hotel legend (founded in 1812), with one of the world's classiest guest lists. The friendly, liveried staff is not in the least condescending, and the rooms are luxurious. Enjoy a cup of tea in the lounge, or retreat to the stylish bar for cocktails—or, better, to Gordon Ramsay's inimitable restaurant. The bathrooms are spacious (with enormous showerheads), as are the bedrooms (Victorian or art deco). The grand staircase and magnificent elevator complete with sofa and driver are equally glamorous. Perhaps Spencer Tracy said it best when he remarked that, when he died, he wanted to go not to heaven, but to Claridge's. ✉ *Brook St., St. James's, W1A 2JQ* ☎ *020/7629–8860, 800/637–2869 in U.S.* 🖷 *020/7499–2210* ⊕ *www. claridges.co.uk* ⇆ *203 rooms* ♿ *Restaurant, in-room fax, in-room safes, some in-room hot tubs, minibars, cable TV with movies, in-room VCRs, in-room data ports, gym, hair salon, spa, bar, lobby lounge, shop, babysitting, dry cleaning, laundry service, concierge, Internet, business services, meeting rooms, airport shuttle, car rental, parking (fee), no-smoking rooms* ▤ *AE, DC, MC, V* Ⓤ *Bond St.*

FodorsChoice ★

££££–£££££ 🏨 **The Leonard.** Four 18th-century buildings make up a stunning, relaxed, and friendly boutique hotel. Shoppers will appreciate the location, just around the corner from Oxford Street. Rooms are decorated with a judicious mix of lived-in antiques and comfortable reproductions. For more elbow room, try one of the aptly named grand suites, with their palatial sitting rooms and tall windows. The roof garden is great for warm weather, and the welcoming lobby is stocked with complimentary newspapers to read by the fire. ⊠ *15 Seymour St., Mayfair, W1H 5AA* ☎ *020/7935–2010* 🖷 *020/7935–6700* ⊕ *www.theleonard.com* 🖙 *22 rooms, 21 suites* 🖒 *Café, dining room, room service, in-room safes, some kitchens, minibars, cable TV, in-room VCRs, in-room data ports, gym, bar, lounge, babysitting, dry cleaning, laundry service, concierge, Internet, business services, meeting rooms, no-smoking rooms* ⊟ *AE, DC, MC, V* Ⓤ *Marble Arch.*

🖐 **££££** 🏨 **22 Jermyn Street.** This guesthouse is on a fashionable shopping street near Fortnum & Mason. Flexible room configurations, including sitting rooms that convert to bedrooms, mean families have plenty of space. In fact, the hotel rolls out the red carpet for children, providing anything from high chairs and coloring books to nannies and kids' bathrobes. For grown-ups, there are access to a nearby gym, complimentary newspapers, and a shoe shine. ⊠ *22 Jermyn St., St. James's, SW1Y 6HL* ☎ *020/7734–2353, 800/682–7808 in U.S.* 🖷 *020/7734–0750* ⊕ *www.22jermyn.com* 🖙 *5 rooms, 13 suites* 🖒 *Room service, in-room safes, minibars, cable TV with movies, in-room VCRs, in-room data ports, babysitting, dry cleaning, laundry service, concierge, Internet, business services, airport shuttle, car rental, parking (fee)* ⊟ *AE, DC, MC, V* Ⓤ *Piccadilly Circus.*

££ 🏨 **Lincoln House Hotel.** Just north of Oxford Street and Marble Arch, this family-run Georgian town house is done up with lots of wood and plaid. The rooms with three or four beds are more spacious and only slightly more expensive. Rooms have a slightly dated look, but are well equipped. The longer you stay, the cheaper the price. ⊠ *33 Gloucester Pl., Mayfair, W1U 8HY* ☎ *020/7486–7630* 🖷 *020/7486–0166* ⊕ *www.lincoln-house-hotel.co.uk* 🖙 *24 rooms* 🖒 *Some refrigerators, cable TV, in-room data ports, lounge, babysitting, laundry service, parking (fee); no a/c* ⫟◉⫠ *BP* ⊟ *AE, D, MC, V* Ⓤ *Marble Arch.*

South Bank

££££ 🏨 **London Bridge Hotel.** Steps away from the London Bridge rail and tube station, this thoroughly modern, stylish hotel is popular with business travelers. Most of the South Bank's attractions are within walking distance. Each sleek room is understated and contemporary. Three spacious two-bedroom apartments (£££££) come with kitchen, living room, and dining room. ⊠ *8–18 London Bridge St., South Bank, SE1 9SG* ☎ *020/7855–2200* 🖷 *020/7855–2233* ⊕ *www.london-bridge-hotel.co.uk* 🖙 *138 rooms, 3 apartments* 🖒 *Restaurant, room service, in-room safes, some kitchens, minibars, cable TV with movies, in-room broadband, gym, sauna, bar, lobby lounge, dry cleaning, laundry service, concierge, meeting rooms, parking (fee), no-smoking floors* ⊟ *AE, DC, MC, V* Ⓤ *London Bridge.*

1

££ **Premier Travel Inn County Hall.** Don't get too excited—this neighbor of the riverfront Marriott, is not next to it, but behind it, giving you a window onto the Marriott, not the Thames. Still, you get an incredible value, with the standard facilities of the cookie-cutter rooms of this chain. Best of all for families on a budget are the foldout beds that let you accommodate two kids at no extra charge. *That's* a bargain. ⊠ *Belvedere Rd., South Bank, SE1 7PB* ☎ *0870/238–3300* 🖷 *020/7902–1619* ⊕ *www.premiertravelinn.com* 📞 *313 rooms* ⚭ *Restaurant, fans, in-room data ports, bar, business services, meeting rooms, parking (fee), no-smoking floors; no a/c* 🖃 *AE, DC, MC, V* Ⓤ *Westminster.*

££ **Premier Travel Inn Southwark.** Practically riverside, this branch of the Premier Travel Inn chain has an excellent location across the cobbled road from Vinopolis, where you can do extensive wine-tastings. Rooms have desks, tea/coffeemakers, and the chain's signature 6-foot-wide beds (really two zipped together). Family rooms can accommodate four people. The nautical Anchor restaurant and pub is adjacent to the hotel. ⊠ *34 Park St., South Bank, SE1 9EF* ☎ *020/7089–2580 or 0870/990–6402* 🖷 *0870/990–6403* ⊕ *www.premiertravelinn.com* 📞 *56 rooms* ⚭ *Cable TV, in-room data ports, parking (fee), no-smoking rooms* 🖃 *AE, DC, MC, V* Ⓤ *London Bridge.*

Westminster & Victoria

� ££££ **City Inn Westminster.** In a rather stark steel-and-glass building steps from the Tate Britain, this member of a small U.K. chain has some rooms with spectacular views of Big Ben and the London Eye. Extras like floor-to-ceiling windows, CD players, and flat-screen TVs complement the contemporary, monochrome guest rooms. Cots, baby baths, Nickelodeon, special menus, and baby food are all on tap for kids. The restaurant and bar serve modern British cooking. ⊠ *30 John Islip St., Westminster, SW1P 4DD* ☎ *020/7630–1000* 🖷 *020/7233–7575* ⊕ *www.cityinn.com* 📞 *444 rooms, 16 suites* ⚭ *Restaurant, room service, in-room safes, minibars, cable TV, in-room DVDs, in-room data ports, gym, bar, lobby lounge, babysitting, dry cleaning, laundry service, concierge, Internet, business services, meeting rooms, parking (fee), no-smoking rooms* 🖃 *AE, MC, V* Ⓤ *Pimlico.*

££–£££ **Lime Tree Hotel.** On a street filled with budget hotels, the Lime Tree stands out for its gracious proprietors, the Davies family, who endeavor to provide a homey atmosphere as well as act as concierges. The flowery rooms include tea/coffeemakers. The triples and quads are suitable for families, but children under five are not allowed. The simple breakfast room covered with notes and gifts from former guests opens onto a garden. ⊠ *135–137 Ebury St., Victoria, SW1W 9RA* ☎ *020/7730–8191* 🖷 *020/7730–7865* ⊕ *www.limetreehotel.co.uk* 📞 *25 rooms* ⚭ *Fans, in-room safes; no a/c, no kids under 5* 🍽 *BP* 🖃 *MC, V* Ⓤ *Victoria.*

£–££ **Windermere Hotel.** This sweet, inexpensive hotel will not let you forget that it stands on the site of London's first B&B, which opened here in 1881. It's draped in charmingly sunny floral fabrics, kept in good taste by the antique beds and faux-antique fans in the rooms. Bathrooms are thoroughly modern, and the attached restaurant, small though it may be, is actually quite good. The Windermere is an excellent budget option. ✉ *142–144 Warwick Way, Victoria, SW1V 4JE* ☎ *020/7834–4163* 🖷 *020/7630–8831* 📞 *22 rooms* ⊕ *www.windermere-hotel.co.uk* ♨ *Room service, cable TV, in-room data ports, bar, no-smoking floors* ▭ *MC, V* Ⓤ *Victoria.*

Bed-and-Breakfasts & Apartment Agencies

If hotels are not your style, there are endless options. You can stay with London families in small, homey B&Bs for an up-close-and-personal brush with city life, relax in a pied-à-terre, or rent an entire house. The benefits of using a B&B agency are substantial—the price is cheaper than a hotel room of comparable quality, you have access to the kitchen, and yet you can usually arrange to have your breakfast prepared for you every day. The limitations are fairly minimal—there is no staff at your beck and call should you want something at odd hours, and most are not located in the very center of the city (although many are in lovely and convenient neighborhoods like Notting Hill and Kensington). Prices for attractive rooms in privately owned homes start as low as £60 a night, and go up for more central neighborhoods and larger and more luxurious homes. It's an excellent option, both for seasoned travelers and for those trying to travel well without busting their budgets.

££–££££ 🏠 **Coach House London Vacation Rentals.** Stay in the properties of Londoners who are temporarily away. Apartments and houses are primarily in Notting Hill, Kensington, and Chelsea. The extra touches—airport pickup, complimentary starter breakfast provisions, and a welcome drink with a representative—make this service personal. Homes also come with a phone number to call for help in planning your stay. ✉ *2 Tunley Rd., Balham, SW17 7QJ* ☎ *020/8772–1939* 🖷 *0870/1334957* ⊕ *www.chslondon.com* ▭ *AE, MC, V* 📞 *Payment by credit card only; 10% deposit required.*

££ 🏠 **Bulldog Club.** This reservation service offers delightful little London flats in sought-after neighborhoods. A three-year membership is about £25, with most properties available for about £105 per night. Full English breakfasts as well as other goodies are often provided. Most of the properties are in Knightsbridge, Kensington, and Chelsea. ✉ *14 Dewhurst Rd., Kensington, W14 0ET* ☎ *020/7371–3202, 877/727–3004 in U.S.* 🖷 *020/7371–2015* ⊕ *www.bulldogclub.com* ▭ *AE, MC, V.*

££ 🏠 **London B&B.** This long-established family-run agency has some truly spectacular—and some more modest—homes in central London. Check many of them out via its Web site before making a commitment. The staff here is most personable and helpful. ✉ *437 J St., Suite 210, San Diego, CA 92101* ☎ *800/872–2632* 🖷 *619/531–1686* ⊕ *www.londonbandb.com* 📞 *30% deposit required.*

££ 🏠 **Primrose Hill B&B.** This is a small, friendly B&B agency genuinely "committed to the idea that traveling shouldn't be a rip-off." Expatriate American Gail O'Farrell has family homes (to which you get your own latchkey) in or near village-y Hampstead, all of which are comfortable. So far this has been one of those word-of-mouth secrets, but now that everyone knows, book well ahead. ✉ *14 Edis St., Regent's Park, NW1 8LG* ☎ *020/7722–6869* ▭ *No credit cards.*

££ 🖼 **Uptown Reservations.** As the name implies, this B&B booking service accepts only the more upscale addresses and specializes in finding hosted homes or short-term apartments for Americans, often executives of small corporations. Nearly all of the 85 homes on its register are in Knightsbridge, Belgravia, Kensington, and Chelsea. The private homes vary, of course, but all are good-looking. Self-catering rentals—ideal for families—start at £550 per week. ✍️ *Box 50407, Chelsea, W8 5XZ* ☎ *020/7937–2001* 🖨 *020/7937–6660* ⊕ *www.uptownres.co.uk* 🖃 *AE, MC, V* ☞ *Facilities vary. Payment by bank transfer, U.S. check, or credit card; 20% deposit required.*

£–££ 🖼 **At Home in London.** This service offers rooms in private homes in Knightsbridge, Kensington, Mayfair, Chelsea, and West London. Prices are very competitive and include breakfast, and rooms are all approved by the agency. Prices start at £28 a night per room, making this a great alternative to budget hotels. ✉️ *70 Black Lion La., Hammersmith, W6 9BE* ☎ *020/8748–1943* 🖨 *020/8748–2700* ⊕ *www.athomeinlondon. co.uk* 🖃 *MC, V* ☞ *£7.50 per person booking fee.*

£ 🖼 **Host & Guest Service.** In business for 40 years, this service can find you a room based on a huge selection of B&Bs in London as well as the rest of the United Kingdom, even in rural areas. It's a great way to find excellent bargains in small hotels and guesthouses, knowing that all have been vetted by the agency. ✉️ *103 Dawes Rd., Fulham, SW6 7DU* ☎ *020/7385–9922* 🖨 *020/7386–7575* ⊕ *www.host-guest.co.uk* 🖃 *MC, V* ☞ *Full payment in advance.*

NIGHTLIFE & THE ARTS

London is a veritable utopia for excitement junkies, culture fiends, and those who like to party. Most who visit London will be mesmerized by the city's energy, which reveals itself in layers. Whether you prefer a romantic evening at the opera, rhythm and blues with fine French food, the gritty guitar riffs of east London, a pint and gourmet pizza at a local gastro-pub, or swanky cocktails and sushi at London's sexiest lair, the U.K. capital is sure to feed your fancy. Admission prices are not always bargain basement, but when you consider how much a London hotel room costs, the city's arts and nightlife diversions are a bargain.

Nightlife

As with nearly all cosmopolitan centers, the pace with which bars and clubs go in and out of fashion is mind-boggling. The phenomenon of absinthe has been replaced by bourbon's bite and the frenzy for the perfect cocktail recipe, and the dreaded velvet rope has been usurped by the doorbell-ringing mystique of members-only drinking clubs. The understated glamour of North London's Primrose Hill, which makes movie stars feel so at ease might be considered dull by the uber trendy clubgoers of London's West End, whereas the price of a pint in Chelsea would be dubbed blasphemous by the musicians and poets of racially diverse Brixton. Meanwhile, some of the city's most talked-about nightlife spots are turning out to be those attached to some of its best restaurants and hotels—no wonder when you consider the increased popularity of London cuisine in international circles.

Bars

Time was, bars were just a stopover in an evening full of fun—perhaps the pub first, then a bar, and then it's off to boogie the night away at the nearest dance club. These days, however, bars have become less pit stops and more destinations in themselves. With the addition of dinner menus, DJs, dance floors, and the still-new later opening hours, people now stay into the wee hours of the morning at many fashionable bars.

American Bar. Festooned with a chin-dropping array of club ties, signed celebrity photographs, sporting mementos, and baseball caps, this sensational cocktail bar has superb martinis. A jacket is required after 5 PM. ✉ *Stafford Hotel, 16–18 St. James's Pl., St. James's, SW1A* ☎ *020/7493–0111* ⊙ *Weekdays 11:30 AM–11 PM, Sat. noon–3 PM and 5:30–11 PM, Sun. noon–2:30 PM and 6:30–10:30* Ⓤ *Green Park.*

★ **Annex 3.** The set behind the London-based Les Trois Garcons and Loungelover (three antique dealers) now have this richly decorated den of cocktail inventions. Infused with purple-and-red decor, crystal chandeliers, and walls that resemble the side of a giant Rubic cube, the très chic Annex 3 just off Regents Street serves traditional and fruity drinks that will please most palettes (as well as Japanese-influenced modern European fare). ✉ *6 Little Portland St., Fitzrovia, W1W* ☎ *020/7631–0700* ⊙ *Mon.–Sat. noon–11 PM* Ⓤ *Oxford Circus.*

Cafe des Amis. This relaxed brasserie–wine bar near the Royal Opera House is the perfect pre- or post-theater spot—and a friendly enough place to go to on your own. More than 30 wines are served by the glass along with a good selection of cheeses. Opera buffs will enjoy the performance and production prints on the walls. ✉ *11–14 Hanover Pl., Covent Garden, WC2* ☎ *020/7379–3444* ⊙ *Mon.–Sat. 11:30 AM–11:30 PM* Ⓤ *Covent Garden.*

★ **Crazy Bear.** This sexy basement bar with cowhide stools and croc-skin tables feels like Casablanca in Fitzrovia. As you enter Crazy Bear, a spiral staircase leads to a mirrored parlor over which presides a 1947 Murano chandelier; indeed, a suitably smoky, dimly lighted backdrop for Bogey and Bergman. But don't let the opulence fool you: waitresses here are warm and welcoming to an all-ages international crowd abuzz with chatter. ✉ *26–28 Whitfield St., Fitzrovia, W1T* ☎ *020/7631–0088* ⊙ *Mon.–Sat. noon–11* Ⓤ *Goodge St.*

Dogstar. This popular South London hangout is frequented by local hipsters and counterculture types. The vibe is unpretentious and hip, and the modern Caribbean cuisine is a treat. Visual projections light up the interior and top-name DJs play cutting-edge sounds free on weekdays. Move on to the nearby dance club, Mass, and your sampling of local Brixton life will be complete. ✉ *389 Coldharbour La., Brixton, SW9* ☎ *020/7733–7515* ▣ *Free–£5* ⊙ *Mon.–Thurs. and Sun. noon–2 AM, Fri. and Sat. noon–4 AM* Ⓤ *Brixton.*

★ **Late Lounge @ Cocoon.** The "it" place of the moment, the pan-Asian restaurant Cocoon transforms itself into a sophisticated lounge (with DJ) Thursday through Saturday until 3 AM. Smack in the center of the West End on a landmark site, the Late Lounge with its soft peach decor and sanctuarylike setting serves caviar, oysters, a selection of appetizers, and desserts as well as champagne, sake, and cocktails with an Eastern twist. ⊠ *65 Regent St., St. James, W1B* ☎ *087/1332–6347* ⊗ *Thurs.–Sat. 11 PM–3 AM* Ⓤ *Piccadilly.*

Nordic. With Red Erik and Faxe draft beers, shooters called "Husky Poo" and "Danish Bacon Surprise," and crayfish tails and meatballs on the smorgasbord menu, Nordic takes its Scandinavian feel the whole way. This secluded, shabby-chic bar serves many couples cozied up among travel brochures promoting the Viking lands. The sassy, sweet Longberry is quite possibly the most perfect cocktail ever made. ⊠ *25 Newman St., Soho, W1* ☎ *020/7631–3174* ⊕ *www.nordicbar.com* ⊗ *Weekdays noon–11 PM, Sat. 6 PM–11 PM* Ⓤ *Tottenham Court Rd.*

Comedy

Amused Moose. This dark Soho basement is widely considered the best place to see breaking talent as well as household names doing "secret" shows. Ricky Gervais and Eddie Izzard are among those who have graced this stage and every summer a handful of the Edinburgh Fringe comedians preview here. The bar is open late and there's a DJ and dancing until 5 AM after the show. ⊠ *Moonlighting, 17 Greek St., Soho, W1* ☎ *020/8341–1341* 🎟 *£10.50* ⊗ *Showtimes vary, call for details* Ⓤ *Tottenham Court Rd.*

★ **Comedy Store.** Known as the birthplace of alternative comedy, the country's funniest stand-ups have cut their teeth here before being launched onto prime-time TV. Comedy Store Players entertain audiences on Wednesday and Sunday; the Cutting Edge team steps in every Tuesday; and weekends have up-and-coming comedians performing on the same stage as established talent. There's a bar with food also available. ■ TIP➡ **Tickets can be booked through Ticketmaster or over the phone.** Note that children under 18 are not admitted to this venue. ⊠ *1A Oxendon St., Soho, SW1* ☎ *0870/060–2340* 🎟 *£13–£15* ⊗ *Shows Tues.–Thurs. and Sun. 8 PM–10:15 PM, Fri. and Sat. 8 PM–10:15 PM and midnight–2:30 AM* Ⓤ *Piccadilly Circus, Leicester Sq.*

Dance Clubs

The club scene ranges from mammoth-size playgrounds to more intimate venues where you can actually hear your friends talk. Check the daily listings in *Time Out* for "club nights," which are theme nights that take place the same night every week. Another good way to learn about club nights is by picking up fliers in your favorite bar.

Fodor'sChoice **Cargo.** Housed under a series of old railway arches, this vast brick-wall ★ bar, restaurant, dance floor, and live music venue pulls an international crowd with its hip vibe and diverse music. Long tables bring people together, as does the food, which draws on global influences and is served tapas-style. ⊠ *83 Rivington St., Shoreditch, EC2* ☎ *0871/075–1741* ⊗ *Mon.–Thurs. noon–1 AM, Fri.–Sun. noon–3 AM* Ⓤ *Old St.*

The End. Co-owned by Mr. C (ex-MC of cult band the Shamen) and techhouse producer Layo, this intimate club was designed by clubbers for clubbers. Top-name DJs, a state-of-the-art sound system, and minimalist steel-and-glass decor—clubbing doesn't get much better than this. Next door, the AKA Bar (owned by same) is a stylish split-level Manhattanesque cocktail bar with excellent food. ✉ *18 West Central St., Holborn, WC1* ☎ *020/7419–9199* ⊕ *www.endclub.com* 💷 *£6–£15* ⊙ *Mon. 10 PM–3 AM, Wed. 10:30 PM–3 AM, Thurs. 10 PM–4 AM, Fri. 10 PM–5 AM, and Sat. 10 PM–7 AM. Also some Sun.* Ⓤ *Tottenham Court Rd.*

Fabric. This sprawling subterranean club has been *the* place to be for the past few years. *Fabric Live* hosts drum 'n' bass and hip-hop crews and live acts on Friday; international big-name DJs play slow sexy bass lines and cutting-edge music on Saturday. Sunday is "Polysexual Night." The devastating sound system and bodysonic dance floor ensure that bass riffs vibrate through your entire body. Get there early to avoid a lengthy queue, and don't wear a suit. ✉ *77A Charterhouse St., East End, EC1* ☎ *020/7336–8898* ⊕ *www.fabriclondon.com* 💷 *£12–£15* ⊙ *Fri. and Sun. 9:30 PM–5 AM, Sat. 10 PM–7 AM* Ⓤ *Farringdon.*

Pacha. London's version of the Ibizan superclub is in a restored 1920s dancehall next to Victoria bus station. The classic surroundings—all wood and chandeliers—don't stop the sounds from being eminently up-to-date. The crowd is slightly older than average and stylish, but not necessarily as monied as you might expect. ✉ *Terminus Pl., Victoria, SW1* ☎ *020/7833–3139* 💷 *£15–£20* ⊙ *Fri. 10 PM–4 AM, Sat. 10 PM–6 AM* Ⓤ *Victoria.*

Eclectic Music

The Borderline. This important small venue has a solid reputation for booking everything from metal to country and beyond. Oasis, Pearl Jam, Blur, Sheryl Crow, PJ Harvey, Ben Harper, Jeff Buckley, and Counting Crows have all played live here. ✉ *Orange Yard off Manette St., Soho, W1* ☎ *020/7434–9592* 💷 *£6–£15* ⊙ *Mon.–Sat. 7 PM–3 AM, Sun. 7 PM–11 PM* Ⓤ *Tottenham Court Rd.*

★ **Carling Academy Brixton.** This legendary Brixton venue has seen it all—mods and rockers, hippies and punks. Despite a capacity of almost 5,000 people, this refurbished Victorian hall with original art deco fixtures retains a clublike charm; it has plenty of bars and upstairs seating. ✉ *211 Stockwell Rd., Brixton, SW9* ☎ *0870/771–2000* 💷 *£10–£30* ⊙ *Opening hrs vary* Ⓤ *Brixton.*

★ **Union Chapel.** This old chapel has excellent acoustics and sublime architecture. The beauty of the space and its impressive multicultural programming have made it one of London's best musical venues. Performers have included Ravi Shankar, Björk, Beck, Beth Orton, and Bob Geldof, though nowadays you're more likely to hear lower-key alternative country, world music, and jazz. ✉ *Compton Terr., Islington, N1* ☎ *020/7226–1686 or 0870/120–1349* ⊕ *www.unionchapel.org.uk* 💷 *Free–£25* ⊙ *Opening hrs vary* Ⓤ *Highbury & Islington.*

Jazz

Dover Street Restaurant & Jazz Bar. Put on your blue-suede shoes and prepare to dance the night away—that is, after you've feasted from an excellent French Mediterranean menu. Fun for dates as well as groups, Dover Street Restaurant offers three bars, a DJ, and a stage with the latest live bands performing everything from Jazz to Soul to R&B, all this encircling linen-covered tables with a friendly wait staff catering to your every whim. ✉ *8–10 Dover St., Mayfair, W1X* ☎ *0871/332–4946* 💷 *£45* ⊙ *Weekdays noon–3:30 PM and 7 PM–3 AM, weekends 7 PM–3 AM* Ⓤ *Green Park.*

★ **Jazz Café.** A palace of high-tech cool in bohemian Camden—it remains an essential hangout for fans of both the mainstream end of the repertoire and hip-hop, funk, rap, and Latin fusion. Book ahead if you want a prime table overlooking the stage, in the balcony restaurant. ✉ *5 Pkwy., Camden Town, NW1* ☎ *020/7916–6060 restaurant reservations, 0870/150–0044 standing tickets* ✇ *£10–£25* ✆ *Mon.–Thurs. 7 PM–1 AM, Fri. and Sat. 7 PM–2 AM, Sun. 7 PM–midnight* Ⓤ *Camden Town.*

Pizza Express. One of the capital's most ubiquitous pizza chains also runs a great Soho jazz venue. The darkly lighted restaurant hosts top-quality international jazz acts every night. The Italian-style thin-crust pizzas are good, too, though on the small side. The Hyde Park branch has a spacious jazz club in the basement that hosts mainstream acts. ✉ *10 Dean St., Soho, W1* ☎ *020/7439–8722* Ⓤ *Tottenham Court Rd.* ✉ *11 Knightsbridge, Hyde Park Corner, Knightsbridge, W1* ☎ *020/7235–5273* Ⓤ *Hyde Park Corner* ✇ *£10–£25* ✆ *Daily from 11:30 AM for food; music Sun.–Thurs. 9 PM–midnight, Fri. and Sat. 7:30 PM–midnight.*

★ **Ronnie Scott's.** Since the '60s, this legendary jazz club has attracted big names. It's usually crowded and hot, the food isn't great, and service is slow—but the mood can't be beat, even since the sad departure of its eponymous founder and saxophonist. Reservations are recommended. ✉ *47 Frith St., Soho, W1* ☎ *020/7439–0747* ✇ *£15–£25 nonmembers, £5–£15 members, annual membership £100* ✆ *Mon.–Sat. 8:30 PM–3 AM, Sun. 7:30 PM–11 PM* Ⓤ *Leicester Sq.*

Rock

The Astoria. This balconied theater hosts cutting-edge alternative bands (punk, metal, indie guitar). Shows start early, at 7 PM most nights; the building is often cleared, following gigs, for club events. **Note that it's closed on some Tuesdays and Wednesdays.** ✉ *157 Charing Cross Rd., West End, W1* ☎ *020/7434–9592* ✇ *£8–£25* ✆ *Mon., Thurs., and Fri. 7 PM–4 AM, Tues., Wed., and Sun. 7 PM–midnight, Sat. 6 PM–4:30 AM* Ⓤ *Tottenham Court Rd.*

★ **Barfly Club.** At one of the finest small clubs in the capital, punk, indie guitar bands, and new metal rock attract a nonmainstream crowd. Weekend club nights upstairs host DJs who rock the decks. ✉ *49 Chalk Farm Rd., Camden Town, NW1* ☎ *020/7691–4244* ✇ *£5–£8* ✆ *Mon.–Thurs. 7:30 PM–midnight, Fri. and Sat. 8 PM–3 AM, Sun. 7:30 PM–11 PM* Ⓤ *Camden Town, Chalk Farm.*

Forum. The best medium-to-big-name rock performers consistently play at the 2,000-capacity club. It's a converted 1920 art deco cinema, with a balcony overlooking the dance floor. Consult the Web site for current listings. ✉ *9–17 Highgate Rd., Kentish Town, NW5* ☎ *020/7284–1001* ⊕ *www.meanfiddler.com* ✇ *£12–£25* ✆ *Opening hrs vary depending on concert schedule* Ⓤ *Kentish Town.*

The Arts

London's arts scene pushes the boundaries, whether you prefer your art classical or modern, or as a contemporary twist on a time-honored classic. Celebrity divas sing original-language librettos at the Royal Opera House; the Almeida Opera focuses on radical productions of new opera and musical theater. Shakespeare's plays are brought to life at the reconstructed Globe Theatre, and challenging new writing is produced at the Royal Court.

To find out what's showing during your stay, the weekly magazine *Time Out* (it comes out every Tuesday) is an invaluable resource. The *Evening Standard,* especially the Thursday edition, also carries listings, as do the "quality" Sunday papers and the Saturday *Independent, Guardian,* and *Times.* Leaflets and fliers are found in most cinema and theater foyers, and you can pick up the free bimonthly *London Theatre Guide* leaflet from most hotels and tourist information centers.

Classical Music

Whether it's cellist Yo-Yo Ma at the Barbican or a Mozart requiem by candlelight, you can hear first-rate musicians in world-class venues almost every day of the year. The London Symphony Orchestra is in residence at the Barbican Centre, although other top orchestras—including the Philharmonia and the Royal Philharmonic—also perform here. Wigmore Hall, a lovely venue for chamber music, is renowned for its song recitals by up-and-coming young instrumentalists. The South Bank Centre has an impressive international music season, held in the Queen Elizabeth Hall and the small Purcell Room while refurbishments, due for completion in spring 2007, close the Royal Festival Hall. Full houses are rare, so even at the biggest concert halls you should be able to get a ticket for £12. If you can't book in advance, arrive at the hall an hour before the performance for a chance at returns.

■ TIP➔ Lunchtime concerts take place all over the city in smaller concert halls, the big arts-center foyers, and churches; they usually cost less than £5 or are free, and will feature string quartets, singers, jazz ensembles, or gospel choirs. St. John's, Smith Square, and St. Martin-in-the-Fields are popular locations. Performances usually begin about 1 PM and last one hour.

A great British tradition since 1895, the **Henry Wood Promenade Concerts,** more commonly known as the "Proms" (⊕ www.bbc.co.uk/proms), lasts eight weeks, from July to September, at the Royal Albert Hall. Demand for tickets is so high you must enter a lottery. For regular Proms, tickets run £4 to £80, with hundreds of standing tickets for £4, available at the hall on the night of the concert. ■ TIP➔ The last night is broadcast in Hyde Park on a jumbo-screen, but even here a seat on the grass requires a paid ticket that can set you back around £20.

Barbican Centre. Home to the London Symphony Orchestra (www.lso.co.uk) and frequent host of the English Chamber Orchestra and the BBC Symphony Orchestra, the Barbican has an excellent season of big-name virtuosos. ⊠ *Silk St., East End, EC2* ☎ *0845/120–7518 box office, 020/7638–4141* ⊕ *www.barbican.org.uk* Ⓤ *Barbican.*

Kenwood House. Outdoor concerts are held in the grassy amphitheater in front of Kenwood House on Saturday evenings from July to late August. ⊠ *Hampstead Heath, Hampstead, NW3 7JR* ☎ *0870/333–6206* ⊕ *www.picnicconcerts.com* Ⓤ *Hampstead.*

★ **Royal Albert Hall.** Built in 1871 this splendid iron-and-glass–dome auditorium hosts a varied music program, including Europe's most democratic music festival, the Henry Wood Promenade Concerts—the Proms. The Hall is also open for daily daytime guided tours (£6). ⌂ *Kensington Gore, Kensington, SW7* ☏ *020/7589–8212* ⊕ *www.royalalberthall. com* Ⓤ *South Kensington.*

St. John's, Smith Square. This baroque church behind Westminster Abbey offers chamber-music and organ recitals as well as orchestral concerts September through July. There are occasional lunchtime recitals for £7. ⌂ *Smith Sq., Westminster, W1* ☏ *020/7222–1061* ⊕ *www.sjss.org.uk* Ⓤ *Westminster.*

★ **St. Martin-in-the-Fields.** Popular lunchtime concerts (£3.50 donation suggested) are held in this lovely 1726 church, as are regular evening concerts. ■ TIP➔ **Stop for a snack at the Café in the Crypt.** ⌂ *Trafalgar Sq., Covent Garden, WC2* ☏ *020/7839–8362* ⊕ *www.smitf.org* Ⓤ *Charing Cross.*

South Bank Centre. Due to two years' renovation work begun in 2005, the Royal Festival Hall's large-scale choral and orchestral works—including its housing of both the Philharmonia and the London Philharmonic orchestras—will be taken on by the other South Bank Centre venues such as the Queen Elizabeth Hall, which hosts chamber orchestras and A-team soloists, and the intimate Purcell Room, where you can listen to chamber music and solo recitals. ⌂ *Belvedere Rd., South Bank, SE1* ☏ *020/7960–4242* ⊕ *www.sbc.org.uk* Ⓤ *Waterloo.*

FodorśChoice **Wigmore Hall.** Hear chamber-music and song recitals in this charming ★ hall with near-perfect acoustics. Don't miss the mid-morning Sunday concerts. ⌂ *36 Wigmore St., Marylebone, W1* ☏ *020/7935–2141* ⊕ *www. wigmore-hall.org.uk* Ⓤ *Bond St.*

Contemporary Art

In the 21st century, the focus of the city's art scene has shifted from west to east, and from the past to the future. Helped by the prominence of the Tate Modern, London's contemporary art scene has never been so high profile. In public-funded exhibition spaces like the Barbican Gallery, Hayward Gallery, Institute of Contemporary Arts, Serpentine Gallery, and Whitechapel Art Gallery, London now has a modern art environment on a par with Bilbao and New York. Young British Artists (YBAs, though no longer as young as they once were)—Damien Hirst, Tracey Emin, Gary Hume, Rachel Whiteread, Jake and Dinos Chapman, Sarah Lucas, Gavin Turk, Steve McQueen, and others—are firmly planted in the public imagination. The celebrity status of British artists is in part thanks to the annual Turner Prize, which always stirs up controversy in the media during a monthlong display of the work at Tate Britain.

The South Bank, with the Tate Modern and the Hayward Gallery, may house the giants of modern art, but the East End is where the innovative action is. There are dozens of galleries in the fashionable spaces around Old Street. The Whitechapel Art Gallery continues to flourish, exhibiting exciting new British artists and, together with Jay Jopling's influential White Cube in Hoxton Square, is the new East End–art establishment.

Barbican Centre. Innovative exhibitions of 20th-century and current art and design are shown in the Barbican Gallery and **The Curve** (⌔ Free ⊙ Mon.–Sat. 11–8). ⌂ *Silk St., East End, EC2* ☏ *020/7638–8891* ⊕ *www.barbican.org.uk* ⌔ *£6–£8, tickets cheaper if booked online in* *advance* ⊙ *Mon., Wed., Fri., and Sat. 11–8, Tues. and Thurs. 11–6, Sun. noon–6* Ⓤ *Barbican.*

★ **Hayward Gallery.** This modern art gallery, a classic example of 1960s Brutalist architecture, is one of London's major venues for important touring exhibitions. ⊠ *Belvedere Rd., South Bank Centre, South Bank, SE1* ☎ *0870/165–6000* ⊕ *www.hayward.org.uk* 💷 *£7.50, Mon. half-price* ⊙ *Thurs. and Sat.–Mon. 10–6, Tues. and Wed. 10–8, Fri. 10–9* Ⓤ *Waterloo.*

Institute of Contemporary Arts. Housed in an elegant John Nash–designed Regency terrace, the three galleries have changing exhibitions of contemporary visual art. The ICA also programs contemporary drama, film, new media, literature, and photography. To visit you must be a member; a day membership costs £1.50. ⊠ *Nash House, The Mall, St. James's, SW1* ☎ *020/7930–3647 or 020/7930–0493* ⊕ *www.ica.org.uk* 💷 *Weekdays £1.50, weekends £2.50* ⊙ *Daily noon–7:30* Ⓤ *Charing Cross.*

★ **Lisson.** Owner Nicholas Logsdail represents about 40 blue-chip artists, including minimalist Sol Lewitt and Dan Graham. A new branch, Lisson New Space, down the road at 29 Bell Street features work by younger up-and-coming artists. ⊠ *52–54 Bell St., Marylebone, NW1* ☎ *020/7724–2739* ⊕ *www.lissongallery.com* 💷 *Free* ⊙ *Weekdays 10–6, Sat. 11–5* Ⓤ *Edgware Rd. or Marylebone.*

Photographer's Gallery. Britain's first photography gallery continues to program cutting-edge and provocative photography. ⊠ *5 and 8 Great Newport St., Covent Garden, WC2* ☎ *020/7831–1772* ⊕ *www.photonet. org.uk* 💷 *Free* ⊙ *Mon.–Wed., Fri., and Sat. 11–6, Thurs. 11–8, Sun. noon–6* Ⓤ *Leicester Sq.*

Royal Academy. Housed in an aristocratic mansion and home to Britain's first art school (founded in 1768), the Academy is best known for its blockbuster special exhibitions. ⊠ *Burlington House, Soho, W1* ☎ *020/ 7300–8000* ⊕ *www.royalacademy.org.uk* 💷 *From £9, prices vary with exhibition* ⊙ *Sun.–Thurs. 10–6, Fri. and Sat. 10* AM–10 PM Ⓤ *Piccadilly Circus.*

Saatchi Gallery. At this writing, Charles Saatchi's ultramodern gallery was set to reopen in the Duke of York's HQ building in Chelsea in 2007; its short-lived tenancy on the South Bank ended acrimoniously in 2005. For more information, visit the Web site. ⊠ *Duke of York's HQ, Sloane Sq., Chelsea SW3 4RY* ☎ *020/7823–2332* ⊕ *www.saatchi-gallery.co. uk* Ⓤ *Sloane Sq.*

Serpentine Gallery. In a classical 1930 tea pavilion in Kensington Gardens, the Serpentine has an international reputation for exhibitions of modern and contemporary art. ⊠ *Kensington Gardens, South Kensington, W2* ☎ *020/7402–6075* ⊕ *www.serpentinegallery.org* 💷 *Donation* ⊙ *Daily 10–6* Ⓤ *South Kensington.*

Tate Modern. This converted power station is the largest modern art gallery in the world. ■ TIP→ **The café on the top floor has gorgeous views overlooking the Thames and St. Paul's Cathedral.** ⊠ *Bankside, South Bank, SE1* ☎ *020/7887–8008* ⊕ *www.tate.org.uk* 💷 *Free–£8.50* ⊙ *Daily 10–6, Fri. and Sat. until 10* PM Ⓤ *Southwark.*

Victoria Miro Gallery. This important commercial gallery has exhibited some of the biggest names on the British contemporary art scene— Chris Ofili, the Chapman brothers, Peter Doig, to name a few. ⊠ *16*

Wharf Rd., Islington, N1 ☎ *020/7336–8109* ⊕ *www.victoria-miro. com* ✉ *Free* ⊙ *Tues.–Sat. 10–6* Ⓤ *Old St., Angel.*

★ **Whitechapel Art Gallery.** Established in 1897, this independent East End gallery is one of London's most innovative. ✉ *80–82 Whitechapel High St., East End, E1* ☎ *020/7522–7888* ⊕ *www.whitechapel.org* ✉ *Free–£8* ⊙ *Tues.–Sun. 11–6, Thurs. 11–9* Ⓤ *Aldgate East.*

★ **White Cube.** Jay Joplin's influential gallery is in a 1920s light-industrial building on Hoxton Square. Many of its artists are Turner Prize stars. ✉ *48 Hoxton Sq., East End, N1* ☎ *020/7749–7450* ⊕ *www.whitecube. com* ✉ *Free* ⊙ *Tues.–Sat. 10–6* Ⓤ *Old St.*

Dance

The **English National Ballet** and visiting international companies usually perform at the London Coliseum and at Sadler's Wells. The **Royal Ballet,** world renowned for its classical excellence, as well as innovative contemporary dance from several companies and scores of independent choreographers, can be seen at the Royal Opera House. **Royal Festival Hall** (closed for renovations until 2007) in the South Bank Centre has a fine contemporary dance program that hosts top international companies and British choreographers. **The Place** presents the most daring, cut-

★ ting-edge dance performances. **Sadler's Wells** hosts ballet companies and regional and international modern dance troupes. The city's biggest annual event, **Dance Umbrella** (☎ 020/8741–5881 ⊕ www.danceumbrella. co.uk), a six-week season in October and November, showcases international and British-based artists at venues across the city.

DANCE BOX OFFICES

London Coliseum (✉ St. Martin's La., Covent Garden, WC2N ☎ 020/ 7632–8300 Ⓤ Leicester Sq.).

The Place (✉ 17 Duke's Rd., Bloomsbury, WC1 ☎ 020/7121–1100 Ⓤ Euston).

Royal Opera House (✉ Bow St., Covent Garden, WC2 ☎ 020/7304–4000 Ⓤ Covent Garden).

Sadler's Wells (✉ Rosebery Ave., Islington, EC1 ☎ 020/7863–8000 Ⓤ Angel).

South Bank Centre (✉ Belvedere Rd., South Bank, SE1 ☎ 020/7960–4242 or 0870/380–0400 Ⓤ Embankment, Waterloo).

Film

There are many lovely movie theaters in London and several that are committed to nonmainstream cinema, notably the National Film Theatre. Most of the major houses (Odeon Leicester Square and UCI Empire) are in the Leicester Square–Piccadilly Circus area, where tickets average £10. Monday and matinees are often cheaper, at around £5 to £7, and crowds are smaller.

Curzon Soho. This comfortable cinema runs an artsy program of mixed rep and mainstream films. There's also a Mayfair branch. ✉ *99 Shaftesbury Ave., Soho, W1* ☎ *0871/871–0022* Ⓤ *Piccadilly Circus, Leicester Sq.* ✉ *38 Curzon St., Mayfair, W1* ☎ *020/7495–0500* ⊕ *www. curzoncinemas.com* Ⓤ *Green Park.*

The Electric Cinema. This refurbished Portobello Road art house screens mainstream and international movies. The emphasis is on comfort, with leather sofas, armchairs, footstools, and mini coffee tables for your popcorn. ⊠ *191 Portobello Rd., Notting Hill, W11* ☎ *020/7727–9958 information, 020/7908–9696 box office* ⊕ *www.electriccinema.co.uk* Ⓤ *Ladbroke Grove, Notting Hill Gate.*

National Film Theatre (NFT). With easily the best repertory programming in London, the NFT's three cinemas show more than 1,000 titles each year, favoring obscure, foreign, silent, classic, and short films over blockbusters. ■ TIP→ **The** *London Film Festival* **is based here at the NFT; throughout the year there are minifestivals, seminars, and guest speakers.** ⊠ *Belvedere Rd., South Bank, SE1* ☎ *020/7633–0274 information, 020/ 7928–3232 box office* ⊕ *www.bfi.org.uk/incinemas/nft/* Ⓤ *Waterloo.*

Opera

The two key players in London's opera scene are the Royal Opera (which ranks with the Metropolitan Opera in New York) and the more innovative English National Opera (ENO), which presents English-language productions at the London Coliseum. Only the Theatre Royal, Drury Lane, has a longer theatrical history than the Royal Opera House, and the current theater—the third to be built on the site since 1858—has a wonderfully restored Victorian auditorium and the Floral Hall foyer, which beautifully integrate with the Covent Garden Piazza.

The Royal Opera House struggles to shrug off its reputation for elitism and mismanagement. Ticket prices go up to £180. It has, however, made good on its promise to be more accessible—the cheapest tickets are just £4. Conditions of purchase vary; call for information. Prices for ENO are generally lower, ranging from £8 to £80. ENO sells same-day balcony seats for as little as £5.

Almeida Opera and BAC Opera (at the Battersea Arts Centre) produce festivals that showcase new opera and cutting-edge music theater. During the summer months, Holland Park Opera presents the usual chestnuts in the open-air theater of leafy Holland Park.

OPERA BOX OFFICES **Almeida Theatre** (⊠ Almeida St., Islington, N1 ☎ 020/7359–4404 Ⓤ Angel, Highbury, Islington).

BAC Opera (⊠ Lavender Hill, Battersea, SW11 ☎ 020/7223–2223 Ⓤ Clapham Junction).

English National Opera (⊠ London Coliseum, St. Martin's La., Covent Garden, WC2 ☎ 0870/145–0200 Ⓤ Leicester Sq.).

Holland Park Opera (⊠ Holland Park, Kensington High St., Kensington, W8 ☎ 020/7602–7856 Ⓤ Covent Garden).

★ **Royal Opera House** (⊠ Bow St., Covent Garden, WC2 ☎ 020/7304–4000 Ⓤ Covent Garden).

Theater

One of the special experiences the city has to offer is great theater. London's theater scene consists, broadly, of the state-subsidized companies, the Royal National Theatre and the Royal Shakespeare Company; the commercial West End, equivalent to Broadway; and the Fringe—small, experimental companies. Another category could be added: known in the weekly listings magazine *Time Out* as Off-West End, these are shows staged at the longer-established fringe theaters. Most of the West

End theaters are in the neighborhood nicknamed Theatreland, around the Strand and Shaftesbury Avenue.

The Royal Shakespeare Company and the Royal National Theatre Company often stage contemporary versions of the classics. The Almeida, Battersea Arts Centre (BAC), Donmar Warehouse, Royal Court Theatre, and the Soho Theatre attract famous actors and have excellent reputations for new writing and innovative theater. These are the places that shape the theater of the future, the venues where you can see an original production before it becomes a (more expensive) hit in the West End. From mid-May through mid-September you can see the Bard served up at the open-air reconstruction of Shakespeare's Globe Theatre on the South Bank.

Theatergoing isn't cheap. Tickets under £10 are a rarity; in the West End you should expect to pay from £15 for a seat in the upper balcony to at least £25 for a good one in the stalls (orchestra) or dress circle (mezzanine). However, as the vast majority of theaters have some tickets (returns and house seats) available on the night of performance, you may find some good deals at box offices as well as at tkts, the Society of London Theatre's discount-ticket booth. Tickets may be booked through ticket agents (extra charges may be high), at theater box offices, or over the phone by credit card; be sure to inquire about any extra fees. All the larger hotels offer theater bookings, but they tack on a hefty service charge. Fringe tickets are always considerably less expensive than tickets for West End productions.

Be *very* careful of scalpers (known locally as "ticket touts") and unscrupulous ticket agents outside theaters and in the line at tkts. They will try to sell tickets at five times the price of the ticket at legitimate box offices, and you pay a stiff fine if caught buying a scalped ticket.

Ticketmaster (☎ 0870/060–0800, 161/385–3211 from U.S. ⊕ www.ticketmaster.co.uk) sells tickets to a number of different theaters, although they charge a booking fee. You can book tickets in the United States through **Keith Prowse** (✉ 234 W. 44th St., Suite 1000, New York, NY 10036 ☎ 800/669–8687 ⊕ www.keithprowse.com).

The **Society of London Theatre** (✉ 32 Rose St., Covent Garden, London WC2 E9E5 ☎ 020/7557–6700 ⊕ www.officiallondontheatre.co.uk) operates tkts, the half-price ticket booth (no phone) on the southwest corner of Leicester Square, and sells the best available seats to performances at nearly all major theaters. It's open Monday through Saturday 10 AM to 7 PM, Sunday noon to 2 PM; there's a £2 service charge. All major credit cards are accepted. The society has good information about theatrical events.

SELECTED THEATERS

Below are some theaters known for excellent or innovative work.

★ **Almeida Theatre.** This Off-West End venue premieres excellent new plays and exciting twists on the classics. Hollywood stars often perform here. ✉ *Almeida St., Islington, N1 ☎ 020/7359–4404 ⊕ www.almeida.co. uk* Ⓤ *Angel, Highbury & Islington.*

BAC. Battersea Arts Centre has an excellent reputation for producing innovative new work. Check out Scratch, a monthly, pay-what-you-can night of low-tech cabaret theater by emerging artists. Tuesday shows also have pay-what-you-can entry. ✉ *176 Lavender Hill, Battersea, SW11* ☎ *020/7223–2223* ⊕ *www.bac.org.uk* Ⓤ *British Rail: Clapham Junction.*

Barbican Centre. B.I.T.E. (Barbican International Theatre Events) features ground-breaking dance, drama, and music theater. ✉ *Silk St., East End, EC2* ☎ *020/7638–8891* ⊕ *www.barbican.org.uk* Ⓤ *Barbican.*

Fodor'sChoice ★ **Donmar Warehouse.** Hollywood stars often perform here in diverse and daring new works, bold interpretations of the classics, and small-scale musicals. ✉ *41 Earlham St., Covent Garden, WC2* ☎ *0870/060–6624* ⊕ *www.donmar-warehouse.com* Ⓤ *Covent Garden.*

The Old Vic. American actor Kevin Spacey is the artistic director of this grand 1818 Victorian theater, one of London's oldest. Laurence Olivier called it his favorite theater. ✉ *The Cut, Southwark, SE1* ☎ *0870/060–6628* ⊕ *www.oldvictheatre.com* Ⓤ *Waterloo.*

Fodor'sChoice ★ **Open Air Theatre.** On a warm summer evening, classical theater in the pastoral, and royal Regent's Park is hard to beat for magical adventure. Enjoy supper before the performance or during intermission on the picnic lawn, and drinks in the spacious bar. ✉ *Inner Circle, Regent's Park, NW1* ☎ *0870/060–1811* ⊕ *www.openairtheatre.org* Ⓤ *Baker St., Regent's Park.*

★ **Royal Court Theatre.** Britain's undisputed epicenter of new writing, the RCT has produced gritty British and international drama since the middle of the 20th century, much of which gets produced in the West End. ■ TIP➔ **Don't miss the best deal in town—£7.50 tickets on Monday.** ✉ *Sloane Sq., Chelsea, SW1* ☎ *020/7565–5000* ⊕ *www.royalcourttheatre.com* Ⓤ *Sloane Sq.*

★ **Royal National Theatre.** Opened in 1976, the RNT has three theaters: the 1,120-seat Olivier, the 890-seat Lyttelton, and the 300-seat Cottesloe. Musicals, classics, and new plays are in repertoire. ■ TIP➔ **An adventurous new ticketing scheme means some Royal National Theatre performances can be seen for as little as £10.** It's closed Sunday. ✉ *South Bank Arts Centre, Belvedere Rd., South Bank, SE1* ☎ *020/7452–3000* ⊕ *www.nt-online.org* Ⓤ *Waterloo.*

Fodor'sChoice ★ **Shakespeare's Globe Theatre.** This faithful reconstruction of the open-air playhouse where Shakespeare worked and wrote many of his greatest plays re-creates the 16th-century theater-going experience. Standing room costs £5. The season runs May through September. ✉ *New Globe Walk, Bankside, South Bank, SE1* ☎ *020/7401–9919* ⊕ *www.shakespeares-globe.org* Ⓤ *Southwark, Mansion*

> ## WORD OF MOUTH
>
> The theater district is so lively and fun at night. It is great to eat dinner there before your show. On a quirky side note, they served ice cream in the theater during intermission—I cannot imagine that happening in Los Angeles.
>
> –littletraveler

1

House, walk across Southwark Bridge; Blackfriars, walk across Black-friars Bridge.

Soho Theatre & Writers' Centre. This sleek theater in the heart of Soho is devoted to fostering new writing and is a prolific presenter of work by emerging writers. ⊠ *21 Dean St., Soho, W1* ☎ *020/7478–0100* ⊕ *www. sohotheatre.com* Ⓤ *Tottenham Court Rd.*

Tricycle Theatre. The Tricycle is committed to the best in Irish, African-Caribbean, Asian, and political drama, and the promotion of new plays. ⊠ *269 Kilburn High Rd., Kilburn, NW6 7JR* ☎ *020/7328–1000* ⊕ *www.tricycle.co.uk* Ⓤ *Kilburn.*

SPORTS & THE OUTDOORS

Because London won the bid to host the Olympics in 2012, the city's sporting credentials and sporting facilities are receiving a massive boost. A city that was already hooked on watching football (soccer to Americans), cricket, and tennis, is waking up to the fact that joining in is fun, too. London comes into its own in summer, when the parks sprout nets and goals and painted white lines, outdoor swimming pools open, and a season of spectator events gets under way. If you feel like joining in, *Time Out* magazine, available at newsstands, is a great resource. Bring your gear, and branch out from that hotel gym.

Cricket

★ **Lord's** (⊠ St. John's Wood Rd., St. John's Wood, NW8 ☎ 020/7432–1000) has been hallowed turf for worshippers of England's summer game since 1811, a sport which has enjoyed a renaissance since England beat Australia in 2005. Tickets (by application and lottery) can be hard to procure for the five-day Test Matches (full internationals) and one-day internationals played here. Forms are sent out from mid-November. Standard Test Match tickets cost between £26 and £48. County matches (Middlesex plays here) can usually be seen by lining up on the day of the match.

Football

Three of London's football (soccer) clubs competing in the **Premier League** and the Football Association's FA Cup are particularly popular, though not always correspondingly successful: **Arsenal** (⊠ Highbury, Avenell Rd., Islington, N5 ☎ 020/7704–4040), **Chelsea** (⊠ Stamford Bridge, Fulham Rd., Fulham, SW6 ☎ 0870/300–2322), and **Tottenham Hotspur** ("Spurs"; ⊠ White Hart La., 748 High Rd., Tottenham, N17 ☎ 0870/420–5000). Try to buy tickets in advance, and don't get too carried away by the excitement a vast football crowd can generate.

Gyms

The **Central YMCA** (⊠ 112 Great Russell St., Bloomsbury, WC1 ☎ 020/7343–1700) has every facility and sport, including a 25-meter pool and a well-equipped gym. Weekly membership is £45, a "one-day taster" £15. At **The Gym Covent Garden** (⊠ 30 The Piazza, Covent Garden, WC2 ☎ 020/7379–0008), a very crowded but trendy and well-equipped central gym, the day rate is £8. The trendy yoga school **Life Centre** (⊠ 15 Edge St., Kensington, W8 ☎ 020/7221–4602) specializes in the energetic Ashtanga Vinyasa yoga technique. Classes cost £10 to £12.

Ice-Skating

★ ☾ It's hard to beat the skating experience at **Somerset House** (✉ The Strand, Covent Garden, WC2 ☎ 020/7845–4670). During December and January a rink is set up in the spectacular courtyard of this central London palace. Its popularity is enormous; if you can't get a ticket, other venues such as Hampton Court Palace and the Natural History Museum also have temporary winter rinks. Adults pay £9.50 to £12, children £6.

Running

Green Park and St. James's Park are convenient to the Piccadilly hotels. It's about 2 mi around the two parks. Hyde Park and Kensington Gardens together supply a 4-mi perimeter route, or you can do a 2½-mi run in Hyde Park if you start at Hyde Park Corner or Marble Arch and encircle the Serpentine. Near the Park Lane hotels, Regent's Park has the Outer Circle loop, measuring about 2½ mi. **London Hash House Harriers** (☎ 020/8567–5712) organizes noncompetitive hourlong group runs (£1) around interesting parts of town, with loops, shortcuts, and pubs built in. Runs start at tube stations, usually at noon on weekends during the winter, and at 7 PM on Monday during the summer.

The **Flora London Marathon** (☎ 020/7620–4117) starts at 9:30 AM on a Sunday in April, with more than 40,000 athletes running from Blackheath or Greenwich to the Mall. Entry forms for the following year are available between August and October.

Swimming

☾ **Chelsea Sports Centre** (✉ Chelsea Manor St., Chelsea, SW3 ☎ 020/7352–6985), with a 32-by-12-meter indoor pool, is just off King's Road, so it's busy, especially on weekends when it's packed with kids. Each swim costs £3. **Oasis** (✉ 32 Endell St., Covent Garden, WC2 ☎ 020/7831–1804) is just that, with a heated outdoor pool, open year-round, right in Covent Garden, and a 32-by-12-meter pool indoors. A swim costs £3.30.

Tennis

The **Wimbledon Lawn Tennis Championships,** the most prestigious of the four Grand Slam tournaments, is also one of London's most eagerly awaited annual events. To enter the lottery for show-court tickets, send a self-addressed, stamped envelope (or an international reply coupon) after August 1 and return the application form before December 31 to **All England Lawn Tennis & Croquet Club** (✆ Ticket Office, All England Lawn Tennis & Croquet Club, Box 98, Church Rd., Wimbledon, SW19 5AE ☎ 020/8946–2244). Alternatively, during the last-week-of-June, first-week-of-July tournament, tickets collected from early-departing spectators are resold (profits go to charity). These can provide grandstand seats with plenty to see: play continues until dusk. You can also line up (start as early as possible) for tickets for the outside courts.

SHOPPING

Napoléon was being scornful when he called Britain a nation of shopkeepers, but Londoners have had the last laugh. The finest emporiums are in London, still. You can shop like royalty at Her Majesty's glove maker, discover an uncommon Toby jug in a Kensington antiques shop, or find a leather-bound edition of *Wuthering Heights* on Charing Cross Road. If you have a yen to keep up with the Windsors, head for stores proclaiming they are "By Appointment" to H. M. the Queen—or to Prince Philip or the Prince of Wales. The fashion-forward crowd favors places such as Harvey Nichols or Browns of South Molton Street, whereas the most ardent fashion victims will shoot to Notting Hill, London's prime fashion location. If you have limited time, zoom in on one of the city's grand department stores, such as Harrods, Marks & Spencer, or Selfridges, where you can find enough booty for your entire gift list. Below is a brief introduction to the major shopping areas.

Apart from bankrupting yourself, the only problem you may encounter is exhaustion. London is a town of many far-flung shopping areas. ■ TIP➡ Real shophounds plan their excursions with military precision, taking in only one or two shopping districts in a day, with fortifying stops for lunch, tea, and a pint or glass of wine in the pub.

CHELSEA
Chelsea centers on King's Road, once synonymous with ultra-high fashion; it still harbors some designer boutiques, plus antiques and home furnishings stores.

COVENT GARDEN
This neighborhood has chain clothing stores and top designers, stalls selling crafts, and shops selling gifts of every type—bikes, kites, tea, herbs, beads, hats—you name it.

FULHAM
Newly popular, Fulham is divided into two postal districts, SW6 (farther away from the center of town) and SW10 (which is the closer, beyond Chelsea) on the high-fashion King's Road.

KENSINGTON
Kensington's main drag, Kensington High Street, houses some small, classy shops, with a few larger stores at the eastern end. Try Kensington Church Street for expensive antiques, plus a little fashion.

KNIGHTSBRIDGE
Knightsbridge, east of Kensington, has Harrods but also Harvey Nichols, the top clothes stop, and many expensive designers' boutiques along Sloane Street, Walton Street, and Beauchamp Place.

MARYLEBONE
Behind Oxford Street lies this quiet backwater, with Marylebone High Street as its main artery. There are restaurants, upscale delis, and designer furniture stores; chic boutiques spill over onto satellite streets.

MAYFAIR
In Mayfair are the two Bond streets, Old and New, with desirable dress designers, jewelers, and fine art. South Molton Street has high-price, high-style fashion, and the tailors of Savile Row have worldwide reputations.

NOTTING HILL
Go westward from the famous Portobello Road market and explore the Ledbury Road–Westbourne Grove axis, Clarendon Cross, and Kensington Park Road for a mix of antiques and up-to-the-minute must-haves for body and lifestyle. Toward the more bohemian foot of Portobello are Ladbroke Grove and Golborne Road, where, in among the tatty stores, Portuguese cafés, and patisseries, you can bag bargains.

REGENT STREET
At right angles to Oxford Street is Regent Street, with possibly London's most pleasant department store, Liberty, plus Hamleys, the capital's fa-

vorite toy store. Shops around once-famous Carnaby Street stock designer youth paraphernalia and 57 varieties of the T-shirt.

ST. JAMES'S Here the English gentleman buys everything but the suit (which is from Savile Row): handmade hats, shirts and shoes, silver shaving kits, and hip flasks. Nothing in this neighborhood is cheap, in any sense.

Department Stores

Debenhams (⊠ 334–348 Oxford St., Mayfair, W1 ☎ 0844/561–6161 Ⓤ Oxford Circus) has moved up the fashion stakes with the pretty, affordable, Jasper Conran collection for women. Other creations—for men, too—by in-house designers are desirable. **Harrods** (⊠ 87 Brompton Rd., Knightsbridge, SW1 ☎ 020/7730–1234 Ⓤ Knightsbridge), one of the world's most famous department stores, can be forgiven its immodest motto, *Omnia, omnibus, ubique* ("everything, for everyone, everywhere"), because it has more than 230 well-stocked departments. The food halls are stunning—so are the crowds, especially during the sales that usually run during the last three weeks of January. **Harvey Nichols** (⊠ 109 Knightsbridge, Knightsbridge, SW1 ☎ 020/7235–5000 Ⓤ Knightsbridge) is famed for five floors of ultimate fashion; every label any chic, well-bred London lady covets is here, as well as a home-furnishings department. It's also known for the restaurant, Fifth Floor. **John Lewis** (⊠ 278 Oxford St., Mayfair, W1 ☎ 020/7629–7711 Ⓤ Oxford Circus) claims as its motto "Never knowingly undersold." This traditional department store carries a good selection of dress fabrics and curtain and upholstery materials. **Liberty** (⊠ 200 Regent St., Mayfair, W1 ☎ 020/7734–1234 Ⓤ Oxford Circus), full of nooks and crannies, is famous principally for its fabulous fabrics. It also carries Eastern and exotic goods, menswear, womenswear, fragrances, soaps, and accessories. **Marks & Spencer** (⊠ 458 Oxford St., Mayfair, W1 ☎ 020/7935–7954 Ⓤ Marble Arch) is a major chain that's an integral part of the British way of life—sturdy, practical clothes and good materials. What it *is* renowned for is underwear; the English all buy theirs here. **Selfridges** (⊠ 400 Oxford St., Mayfair, W1 ☎ 0870/837–7377 Ⓤ Bond St.), huge and hip, is giving Harvey Nicks a run as London's leading fashion department store. It's packed with high-profile, popular designer clothes for everyone in the family. There's a theater ticket counter and a British Airways travel shop in the basement.

FodorśChoice ★

★

★

Specialty Stores

Antiques

★ **Alfie's Antique Market** (⊠ 13–25 Church St., Regent's Park, NW8 ☎ 020/7723–6066 Ⓤ Edgware Rd.), a huge labyrinth on several floors, has dealers specializing in anything and everything but particularly in textiles, furniture, and theater memorabilia. Closed Sunday and Monday. **Antiquarius** (⊠ 131–145 King's Rd., Chelsea, SW3 ☎ 020/7351–5353 Ⓤ Sloane Sq.), near Sloane Square, is an indoor antiques market with more than 200 stalls offering collectibles, art deco brooches, meerschaum pipes, and silver salt cellars. It's closed Sunday. **Grays Antique Market** (⊠ 58 Davies St., Mayfair, W1 ☎ 020/7629–7034 Ⓤ Bond St.) assembles dealers specializing in everything from Sheffield plates to Chippendale furniture. Bargains are not impossible, and proper pedigrees are guaranteed. ★ It's closed Saturday (except December) and Sunday. **London Silver Vaults** (✉ 53–64 Chancery La., Holborn, WC2 ☎ 020/7242–3844 Ⓤ Chancery La.) has about 40 dealers specializing in antique silver and jewelry. It's closed Saturday afternoon and Sunday.

Books, CDs & Records

BOOKS Charing Cross Road is London's "booksville," with a couple dozen antiquarian booksellers, and many mainstream bookshops, too. **Cecil Court,** off Charing Cross Road, is a pedestrian-only lane filled with specialty bookstores. **Forbidden Planet** (✉ 179 Shaftesbury Ave., Covent Garden, WC2 ☎ 020/7420–3666 Ⓤ Tottenham Court Rd.) is the place for sci-fi, fantasy, horror, and comic books. **Foyles** (✉ 113–119 Charing Cross Rd., Soho, WC2 ☎ 020/7437–5660 Ⓤ Tottenham Court Rd.) is so vast, you can find almost anything. There are two great, unique concessions: the Silver Moon for women and Ray's Jazz for music. **Gosh!** (✉ 39 Great Russell St., Bloomsbury, WC1 ☎ 020/7636–1011 Ⓤ Tottenham Court Rd.) stocks classic comics, graphic novels, manga, and independent minicomics. **Hatchards** (✉ 187 Piccadilly, St. James's, W1 ☎ 020/ 7439–9921 Ⓤ Piccadilly Circus) has a huge stock and a well-informed staff. **John Sandoe Books, Ltd.** (✉ 10 Blacklands Terr., Chelsea, SW3 ☎ 020/ 7589–9473 Ⓤ Sloane Sq.) has more than 25,000 titles that fill three dollhouse-size floors of an 18th-century house. **Marchpane** (✉ 16 Cecil Ct., Charing Cross Rd., Covent Garden, WC2 ☎ 020/7836–8661 Ⓤ Leicester Sq.) stocks rare and antique illustrated children's books with many first editions, from 18th-century volumes to Harry Potter. **Stanfords** (✉ 12 Long Acre, Covent Garden, WC2 ☎ 020/7836–1321 Ⓤ Covent Garden) specializes in travel books and maps. **Tindley & Chapman** (✉ 4 Cecil Ct., Charing Cross Rd., Covent Garden, WC2 ☎ 020/7240–2161 Ⓤ Leicester Sq.), previously Bell, Book & Radmall, still offers quality antiquarian tomes and specializes in modern first editions. **Waterstone's** (✉ 203–206 Piccadilly, St. James's, W1 ☎ 020/7851–2400 Ⓤ Piccadilly Circus) is part of an admirable chain with long hours and a program of author readings and signings. Their most upscale branch is book buying as hedonistic leisure activity, with five floors, a studio cocktail lounge with a view, and a café in the basement.

CDS & RECORDS London created the great music megastores that have taken over the globe, but don't forget to check out the many independents for a more eclectic selection. **Blackmarket** (✉ 25 D'Arblay St., Soho, W1 ☎ 020/ 7437–0478 Ⓤ Oxford Circus), a shop for vinyl lovers, stocks the hottest club music around. **HMV** (✉ 360 Oxford St., Mayfair, W1 ☎ 020/ 7514–3600 Ⓤ Bond St.), with stores all over London, tends to always be busy. Unless you know exactly what you want, the staff may seem ★ too busy grooving to be of much help. **MDC Opera Shop** (✉ 31 St. Martins La., Covent Garden, WC2 ☎ 020/7240–0270 Ⓤ Covent Garden) has staff that will guide you to the best performances of the best divas with the best conductors. **Mr CD** (✉ 80 Berwick St., Soho, W1 ☎ 020/ 7439–1097 Ⓤ Oxford Circus) stocks a wide selection for all tastes in a tiny shop where you must delve to find the bargains. **Virgin Megastore** (✉ 14–16 Oxford St., Soho, W1 ☎ 020/7631–1234 Ⓤ Tottenham

London Shopping

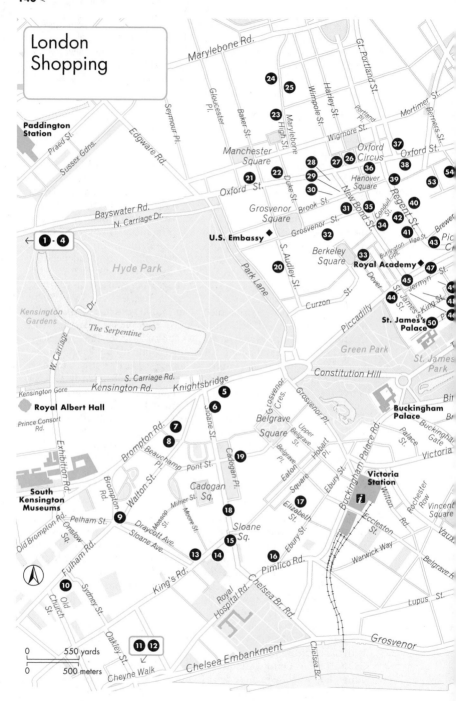

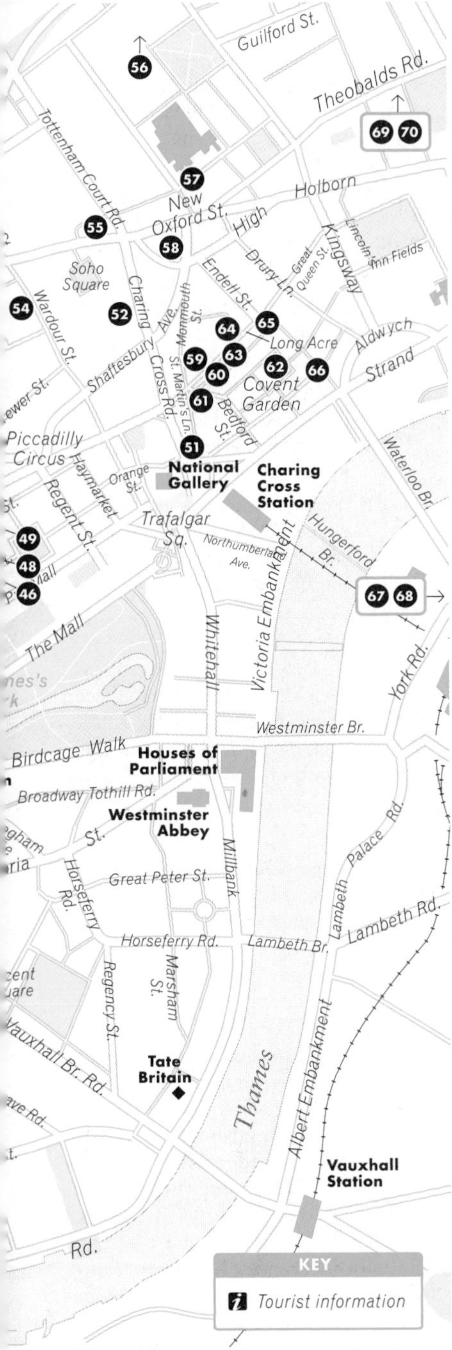

Map labels (from map):

Guilford St.

Theobalds Rd.

Tottenham Court Rd.

New Oxford St. — Holborn — High

Soho Square

Charing Cross Rd.

Wardour St.

Shaftesbury Ave.

St Martin's Ln.

Endell St.

Drury Ln.

Great Queen St.

Kingsway

Lincoln's Inn Fields

Long Acre

Aldwych

Strand

Covent Garden

Bedford St.

Waterloo Br.

Piccadilly Circus

Haymarket

Regent St.

Orange St.

National Gallery

Charing Cross Station

Trafalgar Sq.

Northumberland Ave.

Hungerford Br.

Victoria Embankment

York Rd.

The Mall

Whitehall

Birdcage Walk

Houses of Parliament

Broadway — Tothill Rd.

Westminster Abbey

Great Peter St.

Horseferry Rd.

Marsham St.

Regency St.

Lambeth Br.

Lambeth Rd.

Palace Rd.

Westminster Br.

Albert Embankment

Thames

Tate Britain ◆

Vauxhall Br. Rd.

Vauxhall Station

Rd.

KEY

ℹ *Tourist information*

Agent Provocateur **19**
Agnés B **9**
Alfie's Antique Market .**23**
Antiquaruis **11**
Aquascutum **43**
Asprey **31**
Bershka **38**
Blackmarket **54**
Browns **28**
Burberry **34**
Butler & Wilson **10**
Cath Kidston **2**
Crafts Council
Gallery Shop **56**
The Cross **1**
Daisy & Tom **12**
David Mellor **15**
Debenhams **27**
Dinny Hall **3**
Divertimenti **25**
Emma Bridgewater **24**
Favourbrook **46**
Floris **49**
Forbidden Planet **58**
Fortnum & Mason **45**
Foyles **52**
Garrard **33**
General Trading Co. ...**18**
Gosh! **57**
Grays Antique Market ..**30**
Grosvenor Prints **60**
Hamleys **40**
Harrods **7**
Harvey Nichols **5**
Hatchards **47**
HMV **42**
James Lock & Co. Ltd. ..**50**
Jigsaw **35**
Jimmy Choo **6**
John Lewis **26**
John Sandoe
Books, Ltd. **13**
Koh Samui **59**
Les Senteurs **17**
Lesley Craze Gallery ...**70**
Liberty **39**
Linley **16**
London Glassblowing
Workshop **68**
London Silver Vaults ...**69**
Lush **62**

The Map House **8**
Marchpane **61**
Marks & Spencer **21**
MDC Opera Shop **51**
Mr CD **53**
Nicole Farhi **29**
OXO Tower **67**
Ozwald Boateng **41**
Paul Smith **63**
Penhaligon's **66**
River Island **36**
Selfridges **22**
Stanfords **65**
Summerill & Bishop **4**
Tea House **64**
Thomas Goode **20**
Tindley and Chapman ..**61**
Topshop **37**
Turnbull & Asser **48**
Virgin Megastore **55**
Vivienne Westwood ...**32**
Waterstone's **44**
Zara **14**

Court Rd.), Richard Branson's pride and joy, carries music of all kinds, books, magazines, and computer games under one roof.

China & Glass

Emma Bridgewater (⊠ 81A Marylebone High St., Marylebone, W1 ☎ 020/7486–6897 Ⓤ Baker St. or Regents Park) is the home of fun and funky plates, mugs, and breakfast tableware for country-style de-★ signer kitchens. **David Mellor** (⊠ 4 Sloane Sq., Chelsea, SW1 ☎ 020/7730–4259 Ⓤ Sloane Sq.) sells practical Dartington crystal along with more unique porcelain and pottery pieces by British craftspeo-★ ple. **Divertimenti** (⊠ 33–34 Marylebone High St., Marylebone, W1 ☎ 020/7935–0689 Ⓤ Baker St. or Regents Park) specializes in beautiful kitchenware and French pot-★ tery from Provence. **Summerill & Bishop** (⊠ 100 Portland Rd., Not-

TOP 5

- **Portobello Market.** This popular market is still the best for size, variety, and sheer street theater.

- **Harrods Food Halls.** Noisy, colorful, and tempting, the food halls have long been a favorite.

- **Liberty.** The store's historic connection with William Morris and the Arts and Crafts movement is maintained in a focus on design.

- **Selfridges.** The best department store in London has an astonishing selection of goods for the whole family.

- **Hamleys.** With floor after floor of treasures for every child on your shopping list, this is *the* London toy shop.

ting Hill, W11 ☎020/7221–4566 Ⓤ Holland Park), a little piece of French country, supplies French embroidered linen, Portuguese and Tuscan stoneware, and designer culinary ware. **Thomas Goode** (⊠ 19 S. Audley St., Mayfair, W1 ☎ 020/7499–2823 Ⓤ Green Park) stocks formal china and lead crystal, including English Wedgwood and Minton, and is one of the world's top shops for these items.

Clothing

★ **Agent Provocateur** (⊠ 16 Pont St., Knightsbridge, SW1 ☎020/7235–0229 Ⓤ Knightsbridge, Sloane Sq.) is the place to go for sexy, naughty-but-nice lingerie in gorgeous fabrics and lace. **Aquascutum** (⊠ 100 Regent St., Soho, W1 ☎ 020/7675–8200 Ⓤ Piccadilly Circus) is known for its classic raincoats but also stocks expensive garments to wear underneath, for both men and women. Styles keep up with the times but are ★ firmly on the safe side. **Bershka** (⊠ 221–223 Oxford St., Marylebone, W1 ☎ 020/7025–6160 Ⓤ Oxford Circus) aims to please younger, more street-savvy shoppers than its sister Zara, owned by the same Spanish company. **Burberry** (⊠ 21–23 New Bond St., Mayfair, W1 ☎ 020/7839–5222 Ⓤ Piccadilly Circus) tries to evoke English tradition, with mahogany closets and merchandise with the trademark "Burberry Check" tartan—scarves, umbrellas, shortbread tins, and those famous raincoat linings. **Daisy & Tom** (⊠ 181–183 King's Rd., Chelsea, SW3 ☎ 020/7352–5000 Ⓤ Sloane Sq.) is for cool kids and smart parents. On one floor are high-fashion junior clothes (Kenzo, IKKS, and Polo), shoes aplenty (for newborns to 10-year-olds), a bookshop, and a soda-fountain café. **James Lock & Co. Ltd.** (⊠ 6 St. James's St., St. James, SW1 ☎ 020/7930–5849 Ⓤ Green Park, Piccadilly Circus) is a cozy shop with a full selection of classic and traditional hats. **Nicole Farhi** (✉ 158 New Bond St., Mayfair, W1 ☎ 020/7499–8368 Ⓤ Bond St.) makes contemporary yet timeless quality clothes that are standbys in many a working-woman's wardrobe; the men's collection is available at a branch

★ in Covent Garden. **River Island** (✉ 301–306 Oxford St., Soho, W1 ☎ 020/7799–4018 Ⓤ Oxford Circus) targets young and dedicated fashion followers. Prices are low and commitment to fast fashion is high.

★ There are branches throughout town. **Topshop** (✉ 214 Oxford St., Soho, W1 ☎ 020/7636–7700 Ⓤ Oxford Circus), one of the niftiest retail fashion operations for teens and women, favors top young designers. Topman is the male version of the chain.

MENSWEAR **Favourbrook** (✉ 55 Jermyn St., St. James's, W1 ☎ 020/7491–2337 Ⓤ Piccadilly Circus) tailors exquisite handmade vests, jackets, ties, and
★ cummerbunds. **Ozwald Boateng** (✉ 12A Savile Row, Mayfair, W1 ☎ 020/ 7437–0620 Ⓤ Piccadilly Circus) is one of the modern breed of bespoke tailors not on Savile Row. His made-to-measure suits are sought after by rock luminaries for their shock-color linings as well as great classic
★ cuts. **Paul Smith** (✉ 40–44 Floral St., Covent Garden, WC2 ☎ 020/ 7379–7133 Ⓤ Covent Garden) can do the job if you don't want to look
★ outlandish but you're bored with plain pants and sober jackets. **Turnbull & Asser** (✉ 71–72 Jermyn St., St. James's W1 ☎ 020/7808–3000 Ⓤ Piccadilly Circus) is *the* custom shirtmaker. Alas, the first order must be for a minimum of six shirts, from about £140 each. There are less expensive, still exquisite ready-to-wear shirts, too.

WOMENSWEAR **Agnès B** (✉ 111 Fulham Rd., South Kensington, SW3 ☎ 020/7225–3477
★ Ⓤ South Kensington) has oh-so-pretty, timeless, understated French clothing. Prices are midrange and worthy for the quality. There are branches in Marylebone High Street (W1) and Heath Street, Hampstead
★ (NW3); Floral Street (WC2) has elegant men's suits. **Browns** (✉ 23–27 South Molton St., Mayfair, W1 ☎ 020/7491–7833 Ⓤ Bond St.), the first notable store to populate the South Molton Street pedestrian mall, seems to sprout offshoots every time you visit. Well-established designers (Donna Karan, Romeo Gigli, Jasper Conran) rub shoulder pads here with funkier names (Dries Van Noten, Jean Paul Gaultier, Hussein Cha-
★ layan). The July and January sales are famous. **Jigsaw** (✉ 126–127 New Bond St., Mayfair, W1 ☎ 020/7491–4484 Ⓤ Bond St.) wins points for its reasonably priced separates, which don't sacrifice quality for fashion and suit women in their twenties to forties. **Jimmy Choo** (✉ 32 Sloane St., Knightsbridge, SW1 ☎ 020/7823–1051 Ⓤ Knightsbridge), the name on every supermodel's and fashion editor's feet, creates exquisite, elegant shoes; nothing is less than £100.

★ **Koh Samui** (✉ 65 Monmouth St., Covent Garden, WC2 ☎ 020/ 7240–4280 Ⓤ Covent Garden) stocks the clothing of about 40 hot young designers. Discover the next fashion wave before *Vogue* gets there. **Vivienne Westwood** (✉ 6 Davies St., Mayfair, W1 ☎ 020/7629–3757 Ⓤ Bond St.), one of the top British designers, produces Pompadour-punk ball gowns, Lady Hamilton vest coats, and foppish getups that still represent the apex of high-style British couture. **Zara** (✉ 65 Duke of York's Sq., King's Rd., Chelsea, SW3 ☎ 020/7901–8700 Ⓤ Sloane Sq.) has swept

Europe. The style is young and snappy, and the prices are low. Don't expect durability—these are fun pieces, for men and kids, too. There are branches around town.

Crafts

Crafts Council Gallery Shop (⊠ 44A Pentonville Rd., Islington, N1 ☏ 020/7806–2559 Ⓤ Angel) showcases a microcosm of British crafts—jewelry, glass, ceramics, and toys. A gallery at the V&A Museum has a selection of offerings. The **Lesley Craze Gallery** (⊠ 33–35 Clerkenwell Green, East End, EC1 ☏ 020/7251–9200 Ⓤ Farringdon) carries exquisite jewelry by some 100 young British designers. The adjacent Two gallery specializes in nonprecious metals and sumptuous scarves and textiles. **Linley** (⊠ 60 Pimlico Rd., Chelsea, SW1 ☏ 020/7730–7300 Ⓤ Sloane Sq.) is the outpost for Viscount Linley—the Queen's nephew and one of the finest furniture designers today. The large pieces are expensive, but small desk accessories and objets d'art are available. **London Glassblowing Workshop** (⊠ 7 The Leathermarket, Weston St., South Bank, SE1 ☏ 020/7403–2800 Ⓤ London Bridge) showcases glassblowers and designers who make decorative and practical pieces on-site. On weekdays you can see them at work, and buy or commission your own variation. In the Leathermarket are other craftspeople, most notably a silversmith and papermaker. **OXO Tower** (⊠ Bargehouse St., South Bank, SE1 ☏ 020/7401–2255 Ⓤ Southwark) holds shops and studios, open Tuesday through Sunday 11 to 6, that sell excellent handmade goods. At Gabriel's Wharf, a few steps farther west along the river, a collection of craftspeople sell porcelain, jewelry, clothes, and more.

★

Gifts

Cath Kidston (⊠ 8 Clarendon Cross, Notting Hill, W11 ☏ 020/7221–4000 Ⓤ Notting Hill Gate) translates fresh ginghams and flower-sprig cotton prints into nightclothes, bed linens, and bath wear. There are also cozy hand-knit sweaters, skirts in flouncy wools, and a children's-wear line. **The Cross** (⊠ 141 Portland Rd., Notting Hill, W11 ☏ 020/7727–6760 Ⓤ Notting Hill Gate), is big with the high-style crowd, thanks to its hedonistic, beautiful things: silk scarves, brocade bags, and jeweled baubles. **Floris** (⊠ 89 Jermyn St., St. James's, W1 ☏ 020/7930–2885 Ⓤ Piccadilly Circus) is one of London's most beautiful shops, with 19th-century glass and mahogany showcases filled with swan's-down powder puffs, cut-glass bottles, and faux tortoiseshell combs. **Fortnum & Mason** (⊠ 181 Piccadilly, St. James's, W1 ☏ 020/7734–8040 Ⓤ Piccadilly Circus), the Queen's grocer, is, paradoxically, the most egalitarian of gift stores, with plenty of luxury foods, stamped with the gold "By Appointment" crest, for less than £5. Try the teas, preserves, tins of pâté, or turtle soup. **General Trading Company** (⊠ 2 Symons St., Sloane Sq., Chelsea, SW3 ☏ 020/7730–0411 Ⓤ Sloane Sq.) "does" just about every upperclass wedding gift list, but caters also to slimmer pockets with its merchandise shipped from far shores but moored securely to English taste. **Hamleys** (⊠ 188–196 Regent St., Soho, W1 ☏ 0870/333–2455 Ⓤ Oxford Circus) is at the top of every London childs' wish list. A Regent Street institution, the shop has demonstrations, a play area, a café, and every cool toy on the planet.

Fodor'sChoice ★

Fodor'sChoice ★

Fodor'sChoice ★

Les Senteurs (⊠ 71 Elizabeth St., Belgravia, SW1 ☎ 020/7730–2322 Ⓤ Sloane Sq.), an intimate, unglossy gem of a perfumery, sells little-known yet timeless fragrances, such as Creed, worn by Eugenie, wife of Emperor Napoléon III. **Lush** (⊠ Unit 11, the Piazza, Covent Garden, WC2 ☎ 020/7240–4570 Ⓤ Covent Garden) is crammed with fresh, very

★ wacky, handmade cosmetics. **Penhaligon's** (⊠ 41 Wellington St., Covent Garden, WC2 ☎ 020/7836–2150 Ⓤ Covent Garden), established by William Penhaligon, court barber to Queen Victoria, was perfumer to Lord Rothschild and Winston Churchill. The **Tea House** (⊠ 15A Neal St., Covent Garden, WC2 ☎ 020/7240–7539 Ⓤ Covent Garden) purveys everything to do with the British national drink. Dispatch your gift list here with "teaphernalia"—strainers, trivets, infusers, and such.

Jewelry

★ **Asprey** (⊠ 167 New Bond St., Mayfair, W1 ☎ 020/7493–6767 Ⓤ Bond St.), described as the "classiest and most luxurious shop in the world," Fodor's Choice offers exquisite jewelry and gifts, both antique and modern. **Butler & Wil-**
★ **son** (⊠ 189 Fulham Rd., Chelsea, SW3 ☎ 020/7352–3045 Ⓤ South Kensington) has irresistible retro costume jewelry and is strong on diamanté, jet, and French gilt. You can also find nostalgic gowns here. There's another branch at 189 Fulham Road, South Kensington, SW3. **Dinny Hall** (⊠ 200 Westbourne Grove, Notting Hill, W11 ☎ 020/7792–3913 Ⓤ Notting Hill Gate) sells simple designs in gold and silver, including dainty gold and diamond earrings or chokers with delicate curls. There's another branch at 54 Fulham Road, SW3. **Garrard** (⊠ 24 Albemarle St., Mayfair, W1 ☎ 020/7758–8520 Ⓤ Bond St.), after sharing premises with Asprey, has returned to its original site; Jade Jagger is the designer employed by the company to draw in the younger market. Garrard is the royal jeweler, in charge of the upkeep of the Crown Jewels.

Prints

Besides print stores, browse around the gallery shops, such as those at the Tate Britain and Tate Modern. In the open air, try hunting around Waterloo Bridge along the Riverside Walk Market, at St. James's Craft Market at St. James's Church in Piccadilly, and at the Apple Market near
★ the Piazza, Covent Garden. **Grosvenor Prints** (⊠ 19 Shelton St., Covent Garden, WC2 ☎ 020/7836–1979 Ⓤ Covent Garden) sells antiquarian prints, with an emphasis on views and architecture of London—and dogs. The **Map House** (⊠ 54 Beauchamp Pl., Knightsbridge, SW3 ☎ 020/7589–4325 Ⓤ Knightsbridge) has antique maps in all price ranges, and fine reproductions of maps and prints, especially of botanical subjects and cityscapes.

Street Markets

★ **Bermondsey** is the market the dealers frequent for small antiques, which gives you an idea of its scope. The real bargains start going at 4 AM, but there'll be a few left if you arrive later. Take Bus 15 or 25 to Aldgate, then Bus 42 over Tower Bridge to Bermondsey Square; or take the tube to London Bridge and walk. ⊠ *Long La. and Bermondsey Sq., South Bank, SE1* ☉ *Fri. 4 AM–noon* Ⓤ *London Bridge.*

★ **Borough Market,** a foodie's delight, carries whole-grain, organic every-thing, mainly from Britain but with an international flavor. ⊠ *Borough High St., South Bank, SE1* ⊗ *Fri. noon–4:30, Sat. 9–4* Ⓤ *London Bridge, Borough.*

Camden Passage is hugged by curio stores and is dripping with jewelry, silverware, and other antiques. Saturday and Wednesday are when the stalls go up; the rest of the week, only the stores are open. Bus 19 or 38 or the tube will get you there. Despite the name, it's not in Camden but a couple of miles away in Islington. ⊠ *Off Upper St., Islington, N1* ⊗ *Wed. 10–2, Sat. 10–5* Ⓤ *Angel.*

Covent Garden has craft stalls, jewelry designers, clothes makers, pot-ters, and other artisans, who congregate in the undercover central area known as the Apple Market. The Jubilee Market, toward Southamp-ton Street, is less classy (printed T-shirts and the like), but on Monday the selection of vintage collectibles is worthwhile. This is more of a tourist magnet than other markets, and prices may reflect this. ⊠ *The Piazza, Covent Garden, WC2* ⊗ *Daily 9–5* Ⓤ *Covent Garden.*

FodorśChoice **Portobello Market,** London's most famous market, still wins the prize for
★ the all-round best. There are 1,500 antiques dealers here, so bargains are still possible. Nearer Notting Hill Gate, prices and quality are high-est; the middle is where locals buy fruit and vegetables and hang out in trendy restaurants. Under the Westway elevated highway is a great flea market, and more bric-a-brac and bargains appear as you walk toward Golborne Road. Take Bus 52 or the tube here. ⊠ *Portobello Rd., Not-ting Hill, W11* ⊗ *Fruit and vegetables Mon.–Wed. and Fri. 8–5, Thurs. 8–1; antiques Fri. 8–3; food market and antiques Sat. 6–4:30* Ⓤ *Lad-broke Grove, Notting Hill Gate.*

Spitalfields, an old 3-acre indoor fruit market near Petticoat Lane, has turned into Trendsville, with crafts and design shops. It also has food and clothes stalls, cafés, and performance areas. On Sunday the place comes alive, with stalls selling antique clothing, handmade rugs, and cook-ware. The resident stores have lovely things for body and home. For re-freshment, you can eat anything from tapas to Thai. ⊠ *Brushfield St., East End, E1* ⊗ *Organic market Fri. and Sun. 10–5; general market week-days 11–3, Sun. 10–5* Ⓤ *Liverpool St., Aldgate, Aldgate East.*

LONDON ESSENTIALS

Transportation

BY AIR
For information, *see* Air Travel *in* Smart Travel Tips.

AIRPORTS & London has excellent bus and train connections between its airports and
TRANSFERS downtown. For information about Heathrow, Gatwick, Stansted, and Luton airports, *see* Airports *in* Smart Travel Tips. Airport Travel Line has information on transfers between Heathrow and Gatwick and into London by bus. However, you may be directed to the numbers listed below. The Transport for London Web site has helpful information.

HEATHROW   From Heathrow, the cheapest route into London is via the Piccadilly line of the Underground. Trains on the tube run every 4 to 8 minutes from all four terminals; the 50-minute trip costs £4.30 one-way and connects with London's extensive tube system. The first train departs at around 5:13 AM (Sunday 5:57 AM) from Terminals 1, 2, 3, and 4; the last train departs from the airport at 11:49 PM (11:30 PM Sunday). The quickest way into London is the Heathrow Express train, which takes 15 minutes to and from Paddington Station in the city center; it's a main hub on the Underground. One-way tickets cost £15 for standard-express class (£26 round-trip). Daily service departs every 15 minutes from Terminals 1, 2, and 3 from around 5:12 AM (Sunday 5:08 AM), and from Terminal 4 from 5:07 AM (5:03 AM Sunday) to 12:06 AM for Terminals 1, 2, and 3, and 12:01 AM for Terminal 4.

Bus service to London is available from the Heathrow Central Bus Station. National Express A2 service costs £8 one-way, £15 round-trip; travel time is about one hour and 40 minutes. Buses leave for King's Cross and Euston, with stops at Marble Arch and Russell Square, every 30 minutes 5:30 AM to 9:45 PM from Terminal 4, 5:45 AM to 10:08 PM from Terminal 3, but can be tedious because there are more than a dozen stops en route. National Express buses leave every 30 minutes 5:40 AM to 9:35 PM to Victoria Coach Station from Heathrow Central Bus Station—connected to arrival terminals by a pedestrian underpass, and next to Heathrow Underground Station for Terminals 1–3: cost is £8 one-way.

GATWICK   The Underground does not reach all the way to Gatwick, 27 mi south of the city, so your options there are slightly more limited. You can take regular commuter train service to London Bridge and Victoria stations (approximately £11 one way), or in the opposite direction to Brighton, but it can be crowded. At the best of times there is little room for baggage. During rush hour harried commuters can be impatient with weary air travelers, and you can find yourself standing up all the way. The better option is the fast, nonstop Gatwick Express train that leaves the airport approximately every 15 minutes from 4:35 AM to 1:35 AM. The 30-minute trip costs £13 one-way standard express, £24.50 round-trip. Hourly bus service runs from Gatwick's south terminal to Victoria Station in the city center, with stops along the way at Hooley, Coulsdon, Mitcham, Streatham, Stockwell, and Pimlico. The journey takes 90 minutes and costs £11 one-way. Make sure you get on a direct bus not requiring a change—otherwise the journey could take hours.

STANSTED   Stansted, 35 mi northeast of London, serves mainly European destinations. The 45-minute journey on Stansted Express to Liverpool Street Station (with a stop at Tottenham Hale) runs every 15 minutes 8 AM to 5 PM weekdays, and every 30 minutes 5 PM to midnight and 6 AM to 8 AM weekdays, and all day on weekends. The trip costs £14.50 one-way, £24 round-trip. By bus, there's hourly service on National Express Airport bus A6 (24 hours a day) to Victoria Coach Station. The journey costs £10 one-way, £15 round-trip, and takes about 1 hour and 40 minutes. Stops include Golders Green, Finchley Road, St. John's Wood, Baker Street, Marble Arch, and Hyde Park Corner.

LUTON   From Luton (30 mi north of London), which, like Stansted, serves mainly British and European airlines, you can take a free shuttle to the nearby Luton Airport Parkway Station, from which you can take a train or bus into London. The Thameslink train service runs to several London stations, terminating at King's Cross Thameslink—an adjunct station about six blocks from the main King's Cross station. It's not the ideal station to arrive in if you're unfamiliar with London, as virtually no signs direct you to the main King's Cross station, and the neighborhood is not good. However, if you're continuing to your hotel by tube, you can walk through a connecting underground tunnel from the platforms. This is the better option. If you're going to walk to the main King's Cross Station, or if you need a taxi, ask one of the station guards for help. Do not strike out blindly on foot—the neighborhood is notorious for muggings and other petty crimes. The journey from Luton to King's Cross Thameslink Station takes about 35 minutes. Trains leave every 10 minutes or so 24 hours a day and cost £10.70 one-way, £19 round-trip. For a cheaper journey, take the Green Line 757 bus service from Luton to Victoria Station. It runs three times an hour, takes about 90 minutes, and costs around £8.

TAXIS   If you are thinking of taking a taxi from Heathrow and Gatwick, remember that they can get caught in traffic; the trip from Heathrow, for example, can take more than an hour and costs about £35. From Gatwick, the taxi fare is about £75; the ride takes about an hour and 20 minutes. From Stansted, the £75 journey takes a little over an hour. From Luton, the approximately one-hour journey should cost around £65. Your hotel may be able to recommend a car service for airport transfers; charges are usually about £35 to any of the airports. Add a tip of 10% to 15% to the basic fare.

BETWEEN AIRPORTS   For transfers between airports, allow at least two to three hours. The cheapest option is public transportation: from Gatwick to Stansted, for instance, you can catch the nonexpress commuter train from Gatwick to Victoria Station in London, take the tube to Liverpool Street Station, then catch the train to Stansted from there. To get from Heathrow to Gatwick by public transport, take the tube to King's Cross, then change to the Victoria Line, get to Victoria Station, and take the commuter train to Gatwick. Both of these trips would take about two hours.

The National Express Airport bus is the most direct option between Gatwick and Heathrow. Buses pick up passengers every 15 minutes from 5 AM to 10 PM from both airports. The trip takes 1½ to 2 hours, and the fare is £17.50 one-way, £35 round-trip. It's advisable to book tickets in advance via National Express, especially during peak travel seasons, but you can buy also tickets in the terminals. National Express also runs shuttles between all the other airports, except between Luton and Stansted. Finally, some airlines may offer shuttle services as well—check with your travel agent in advance of your journey.

TICKETS & INFORMATION   You can get discounts on many tickets if you book on the Internet. The Web site for British Airports Authority has links to all the previously mentioned services, with fare details and timetables.

🚕 Taxis & Shuttles **Airport Travel Line** ☎ 0870/574-7777. **British Airports Authority** ⊕ www.baa.co.uk. **Gatwick Express** ☎ 0845/850-1530 ⊕ www.gatwickexpress.

co.uk. **Heathrow Express** ☎ 0845/600-1515 ⊕ www.heathrowexpress.co.uk. **National Express** ☎ 0870/580-8080 ⊕ www.nationalexpress.com. **Stansted Express** ☎ 0845/850-0150 ⊕ www.stanstedexpress.co.uk. **Transport for London** ☎ 020/7222-1234 ⊕ www.tfl.gov.uk.

BY BUS

Buses, or "coaches," as long-distance services are known, operate mainly from London's Victoria Coach Station to more than 1,200 major towns and cities. Buses are about half as expensive as the train, but trips can take twice as long. For information, *see* Bus Travel *in* Smart Travel Tips.

BUS TRAVEL
WITHIN LONDON

In central London, Transport for London (TfL) buses are traditionally bright red double- and single-deckers, although there are now many privately owned buses of different colors. Not all buses run the full length of their route at all times, so check with the driver (ask as you board whether the bus travels to your destination). In central London you must purchase tickets from machines at bus stops along the routes before you board. Bus stops are clearly indicated: the main stops have a red TfL symbol on a white background. When the word REQUEST is written across the sign, you must flag the bus down. Buses are a good way to see the town, but don't take one if you're in a hurry.

London is divided into six concentric zones for tube fares: the more zones you cross, the higher the fare. The same is not true for buses, as a flat-rate fare of £1.50 applies for all bus fares. If you have a prepaid Oystercard (purchase at any tube station) the fare is only 80p. A One-Day Bus Pass for zones one through four is £3.50 (a seven-day pass is £13) but must be bought before boarding the bus, from one of the machines at bus stops, most newsagents, or underground stations.

If you're traveling on the tube as well as the bus, consider acquiring an Oystercard (an electronic smart card that you can load with as much money as you like; money is then deducted each time you use the card) or getting an off-peak one-day Travelcard (£5.30), which allows unrestricted travel on buses *and* tubes after 9:30 AM and all day on weekends and national holidays. "Peak" travelcards—those for use before 9:30 AM—are more expensive (£7.20). Kids travel free on weekends and public holidays but may be required to show proof of age for 14 to 15 years. If you're planning in advance, you can get a Visitor Travelcard—these are similar to Day Travelcards with the bonus of a booklet of money-off vouchers to major attractions (available only in the United States and Canada, for three, four, and seven days). Visitor Travelcards are available from BritRail or Rail Europe.

Traveling without a valid ticket makes you liable for an on-the-spot fine (£10 at the time of this writing), so always pay your fare before you travel. For more information, there are Transport for London Travel Information Centres at the following tube stations: Euston, Liverpool Street, Piccadilly Circus, Victoria, and Heathrow. Most are open in daytime only; call for hours.

Night Buses can prove helpful when traveling in London from 11 PM to 5 AM—these buses add the prefix "N" to their route numbers and don't run as frequently or operate on quite as many routes as day buses. You may have to transfer at one of the Night Bus nexuses: Victoria, Westminster, and either Piccadilly Circus or Trafalgar Square. For safety reasons, avoid sitting alone on the top deck of a Night Bus.

FARES & SCHEDULES 🚩 **BritRail** ☎ 877/677-1066 in U.S. ⊕ www.britrail.net. **Rail Europe** ☎ 888/274-8724 ⊕ www.raileurope.com. **Transport for London** ☎ 020/7222-1234 ⊕ www.tfl.gov.uk.

BY CAR

The major approach roads to London are motorways (six-lane highways; look for an "M" followed by a number) or "A" roads; the latter may be "dual carriageways" (divided highways), or two-lane highways. Motorways (from Heathrow, M4; from Gatwick, M23 to M25, then M3; Stansted, M11) are usually the faster option for getting in and out of town, although rush-hour traffic is horrendous. Stay tuned to local radio stations for regular traffic updates.

The simple advice about driving in London is: don't. Because the city grew as a series of villages, there was never a central street plan, and the result is a chaotic winding mass, made no easier by the one-way street systems. If you must drive in London, remember to drive on the left and stick to the speed limit (30 mph on most city streets).

An £8 "congestion charge" is levied on all vehicles entering central London (bounded by the Inner Ring Road; street signs and "C" road markings note the area) on weekdays from 7 AM to 6:30 PM, excluding bank holidays. Pay in advance or on that day until 10 PM if you're entering the central zone. You can pay by phone, mail, or Internet, or at retail outlets (look for signs indicating how and where you can pay). There are no tollbooths; cameras monitor the area. The penalty for not paying is stiff: £80 (£40 for prompt payment). For current information, check ⊕ www.cclondon.com.

BY TAXI

Taxis are expensive, but if you're with several people, they can be practical. Hotels and main tourist areas have taxi ranks; you can also hail taxis on the street. If the yellow FOR HIRE sign is lighted on top, the taxi is available. Drivers often cruise at night with their signs unlighted, so if you see an unlighted cab, keep your hand up. The fare structure is complicated, but generally fares start at £2.20 and increase by units of 20p (per 125 to 191 yards or 24.5 to 37.6 seconds) after a certain initial distance, which ranges from about 250 yards (late nights) to 381 yards (6 AM to 8 PM on weekdays). Surcharges are added around Christmas and New Year's days. Tips are extra, usually 10% to 15% per ride.

BY TRAIN

London has 15 major train stations, each serving a different area of the country, all accessible by Underground or bus. The once-national British Rail is now private companies, under National Rail, but there is a central rail information number. For further information on train travel, *see* Train Travel *in* Smart Travel Tips.

🚩 **National Rail Enquiries** ☎ 0845/748-4950 ⊕ www.nationalrail.co.uk.

1

BY UNDERGROUND (TUBE)

London's extensive Underground (tube) system has color-coded routes, clear signage, and extensive connections. Trains run out into the suburbs, and all stations are marked with the London Underground circular symbol. (In Britain, the word "subway" means "pedestrian underpass.") Trains are all one class; smoking is *not* allowed on board or in the stations. Some lines have branches (Central, District, Northern, Metropolitan, and Piccadilly), so be sure to note which branch is needed for your destination. Electronic platform signs tell you the final stop and route of the next train and how many minutes until it arrives. The zippy Docklands Light Railway runs through the Docklands with an extension to Greenwich.

FARES &
SCHEDULES

London is divided into six concentric zones (ask at Underground ticket booths for a map and booklet, which give details of the ticket options). Most tourist sights are within zone 1, but some are not—Kew Gardens, for example, is in zone 4. If you inadvertently travel into a zone for which you do not have the right ticket, you can purchase an "extension" to your own ticket at the ticket office by the barriers. This usually costs less than a pound, and merely equalizes your fare. As with buses, the cheapest way to travel is to register for an Oystercard (the city's electronic transport smart card) at any tube station. You then pay in as much as you want (usually £20), and your transport fees are deducted each time you use the card on a bus or tube. Your charges are capped at the amount of a one-day travelcard for the zones in which you've traveled. Alternatively, you can buy a travelcard (one-day or weekly) at any tube station. These allow unlimited travel on tubes, commuter trains and buses within the zones you choose (1–2, or 1–4 usually). The most expensive way to travel is by buying single fares for each leg of the journey. A single journey by tube costs £3 within zone 1 without an Oystercard, and £1.50 with an Oystercard. Note: all these fares increase regularly. For more information, including discount passes, *see By Bus.*

The tube begins running just after 5 AM Monday through Saturday; the last services leave central London between midnight and 12:30 AM. On Sunday, trains start two hours later and finish about an hour earlier. Frequency of trains depends on the route and the time of day, but normally you should not have to wait more than 10 minutes in central areas. Most tube stations are not accessible for people with disabilities. Travelers with disabilities should get the free leaflet "Access to the Underground," which lists the stations that are.

🚇 **Transport for London** ☎ 020/7222-1234 ⊕ www.tfl.gov.uk.

Contacts & Resources

ADDRESSES

Central London and its surrounding districts are divided into 32 boroughs—33, counting the City of London. More useful for finding your way around, however, are the subdivisions of London into postal districts. The first one or two letters give the location: N means north, NW means northwest, etc. The numbers aren't quite as helpful—you won't, for example, find W2 next to W3, but the general rule is that the lower numbers, such as W1 or SW1, are closest to the city center. Abbreviated (for general location) or full (for mailing information) postal codes are given for many listings in this chapter. Neighborhood names are also provided.

DISCOUNTS & DEALS

All national collections (such as the Natural History Museum, Science Museum, Victoria & Albert Museum) are free, a real bargain for museumgoers. The London Pass, a smart card, offers entry to more than 50 top attractions, such as museums and tours on boats and buses. The charge is £29 for one day, which can be reduced to £12 per day if a weekly pass is bought. There are optional discounts on travel and restaurants for a higher daily charge. London Pass is available by phone, online, or from the Britain Visitor Centre and Tourist Information Centre branches. For other discounts, *see* Discounts & Deals *in* Smart Travel Tips.

🚩 **London Pass** ☎ 0870/242-9988 ⊕ www.londonpass.com.

EMERGENCIES

For hospitals in London that provide free 24-hour accident and emergency facilities, the following are listed: in the west of London is Charing Cross Hospital; in the city center is University College Hospital; to the north of the center is the Royal Free Hospital; and on the South Bank of the city center is St. Thomas's Hospital. Bliss Chemist is open daily 9 AM to midnight. NHS Direct offers 24-hour general expert medical advice from the National Health Service. In addition, many main-street branches of Boots, a pharmacy chain, stay open late in rotation.

🚩 Emergency Services **Ambulance, fire, police** ☎ 999. **NHS Direct** ☎ 0845/4647.

🚩 Hospitals **Charing Cross Hospital** ⊠ Fulham Palace Rd., Hammersmith, W6 ☎ 020/8846-1234. **Royal Free Hospital** ⊠ Pond St., Hampstead Hampstead, NW3 ☎ 020/7794-0500. **St. Thomas's Hospital** ⊠ Lambeth Palace Rd., South Bank, SE1 ☎ 020/7928-9292. **University College Hospital** ⊠ Grafton Way, Bloomsbury, WC1 ☎ 020/7387-9300.

🚩 Late-Night Pharmacies **Bliss Chemist** ⊠ 5 Marble Arch, Bayswater, W1 ☎ 020/7723-6116.

TOUR OPTIONS

BOAT TOURS In summer, narrow boats and barges cruise London's two canals, the Grand Union and Regent's Canal. Most vessels operate on the latter, which runs between Little Venice in the west (the nearest tube is Warwick Avenue on the Bakerloo Line) and Camden Lock (about 200 yards north of Camden Town tube station). Jason's Trip operates one-way and round-trip narrow-boat cruises on this route. The London Waterbus Company operates this route year-round with a stop at London Zoo: trips run daily April through October and weekends only November through March. Canal Cruises offers three or four cruises daily March through October on the *Jenny Wren* and all year on the cruising restaurant *My Fair Lady* from Walker's Quay, Camden.

Boats cruise the Thames throughout the year, with services for both commuters and tourists; it's a great way to see the city. Most leave from Westminster Pier, Charing Cross Pier, and Tower Pier. Downstream routes go to the Tower of London, Greenwich, and the Thames Barrier; upstream destinations include Kew, Richmond, and Hampton Court. Depending on the destination, river trips may last from 30 minutes to 4 hours. For trips downriver from Charing Cross to Greenwich Pier and historic Greenwich, call Catamaran Cruisers or Westminster Passenger Services (which runs the same route from Westminster Pier). The Thames Cruises goes to Greenwich and onward to the Thames Barrier. Westminster Passenger Service (Upriver) runs through summer to Kew and Hampton Court from Westminster Pier. A Rail and River Rover ticket combines the modern wonders of Canary Wharf and Docklands development by Docklands Light Railway with the historic riverside by boat. Tickets are available year-round from Westminster, Tower, and Greenwich piers, and Dockland Light Railway stations. Transport for London (⇨ Bus Travel) should be able to give information on all companies.

Canal Cruises ☎ 020/7485-4433 ⊕ www.walkersquay.com. **Catamaran Cruisers** ☎ 020/7987-1185 ⊕ www.catamarancruisers.co.uk. **Jason's Trip** ☎ 020/7286-3428 ⊕ www.jasons.co.uk. **DLR Rail and River Rover** ☎ 020/7363-9700 ⊕ www.tfl.gov.uk. **Thames Cruises** ☎ 020/7930-3373. **Westminster Passenger Services** ☎ 020/7930-4097. **Westminster Passenger Service (Upriver)** ☎ 020/7930-2062 ⊕ www.wpsa.co.uk.

BUS TOURS Guided sightseeing tours provide a good introduction to the city from double-decker buses, which are open-top in summer. Tours run daily and depart from Haymarket, Baker Street, Grosvenor Gardens, Marble Arch, and Victoria. You may board or get off at any of about 21 stops to view the sights, and then get back on the next bus. Tickets (£16 to £20) may be bought from the driver; several companies run tours. The Original London Sightseeing Tour also offers frequent daily tours and has informative staff on easily recognizable double-decker buses. Tours depart from 8:30 AM from Baker Street (Madame Tussaud's), Marble Arch (Speakers' Corner), Piccadilly (Haymarket), or Victoria (Victoria Street) around every 12 minutes (less often outside peak summer season). The Big Bus Company runs a similar operation with a Red and Blue tour. The Red is a two-hour tour with 18 stops, and the Blue, one hour with 13. Both start from Marble Arch, Speakers' Corner. Evan Evans offers good bus tours that also visit major sights just outside the city. Another reputable agency for bus tours is Golden Tours/Frames Rickards.

Green Line, Evan Evans, and Frames Rickards offer day excursions by bus to places within easy reach of London, such as Hampton Court, Oxford, Stratford, and Bath.

Big Bus Company ☎ 020/7233-9533 ⊕ www.bigbustours.com. **Evan Evans** ☎ 020/7950-1777 ⊕ www.evanevans.co.uk. **Golden Tours/Frames Rickards** ☎ 020/7233-7030, 800/548-7083 in U.S. ⊕ www.goldentours.co.uk. **Green Line** ☎ 0870/608-7261 ⊕ www.greenline.co.uk. **Original London Sightseeing Tour** ☎ 020/8877-1722 ⊕ www.theoriginaltour.com.

PRIVATE GUIDES Black Taxi Tour of London is a personal tour by cab direct from your hotel. The price is per cab, so the fare can be shared among as many as five people. An introductory two-hour tour is £80 by day, £85 by night. You can hire a Blue Badge–accredited guide (trained by the tourist board) for walking or driving tours.

Black Taxi Tour of London ☎ 020/7935-9363 ⊕ www.blacktaxitours.co.uk. **Blue Badge tour guides** ☎ 020/7403-1115 ⊕ www.blue-badge-guides.com.

WALKING TOURS One of the best ways to get to know London is on foot. Original London Walks has theme tours devoted to the Beatles, Sherlock Holmes, Dickens, Jack the Ripper—you name it (yes, the *Da Vinci Code,* too). If horror and mystery are your interest, then the City holds plenty of that, as you may discover on a Blood and Tears tour (not suitable for younger children). Tour Guides provides themed historic walks led by accredited Blue Badge guides. Peruse the leaflets at a London Tourist Information Centre for special-interest walks.

Blood and Tears Walk ☎ 020/7625-5155. **Original London Walks** ☎ 020/7624-3978 ⊕ www.walks.com. **Tour Guides/Blue Badge** ☎ 020/7495-5504 ⊕ www.tourguides.co.uk.

VISITOR INFORMATION

The main London Tourist Information Centre at Victoria Station Forecourt is open in summer, Monday through Saturday 8 to 7 and Sunday 8 to 5; winter, Monday through Saturday 8 to 6 and Sunday 8:30 to 4; also at Heathrow Airport (Terminals 1, 2, and 3). Britain and London Visitor Centre, open weekdays 9:30 to 6:30, weekends 10 to 4, provides details about travel, accommodations, and entertainment for the whole of Britain, but you need to visit the center in person. VisitLondon, the city's tourist board, has a helpful Web site with links to other sites; you can also book a hotel on the site, with a best-price guarantee.

Britain and London Visitor Centre ✉ 1 Regent St., Piccadilly Circus, St. James's, SW1Y 4NX ☎ No phone ⊕ www.visitbritain.com. **London Tourist Information Centre** ✉ Victoria Station Forecourt, Victoria ☎ No phone. **VisitLondon** ⊕ www.visitlondon.com.

The Southeast

CANTERBURY, DOVER, BRIGHTON, TUNBRIDGE WELLS

WORD OF MOUTH

"One terrific day would be Dover/Walmer/Deal. Dover Castle takes at least half a day but Walmer and Deal Castles are very close, so you can easily do all three in one day—and all are covered by the Great British Heritage Pass. Walmer and Deal were both built by Henry VIII. Deal is a fascinating round defensive castle. Walmer . . . was converted to a grand family home with gorgeous gardens."

—janis

"I'm in the camp of those who really enjoy Brighton—the pier, beach, Lanes, and especially the Royal Pavilion. In the summer the waterfront is kitschy and fun, in the winter melancholy and atmospheric."

—John

Updated by
Christi
Daugherty

IN AN ERA WHEN EVERYTHING SMALL IS FASHIONABLE, from cell phones to digital cameras, the Southeast will inevitably have great appeal. Where ancient hedgerows have been allowed to stand, this is still a landscape of small-scale features and pleasant hills. Viewed from the air, the tiny fields, neatly hedged, form a patchwork quilt. On the ground, once away from the motorways and London commuter tract housing, the Southeast, including Surrey, Kent, and Sussex, East and West, reveals some of England's loveliest countryside. Gentle hills and woodlands are punctuated with farms and storybook villages rooted in history and with cathedral cities waiting to be explored. Rivers wind down to a coast that is alternately sweeping chalk cliff and seaside resort. This area, farthest from the unpredictable influences of the Atlantic, is England at its warmest. Fruit trees and even vineyards flourish in archetypal English landscapes and, often, atypical English sunshine.

Although it is close to London and is one of the most densely populated areas of Britain, the Southeast includes Kent, the "Garden of England." Fields of hops and acre upon acre of orchards burst into a mass of pink and white blossoms in spring and stretch away into the distance, though even here large-scale modern farming has done much to homogenize the landscape. In the Southeast, too, are ancient Canterbury, site of the mother cathedral of England, and Dover, whose chalky white cliffs and brooding castle have become symbols of Britain. Castles and stately homes, such as Petworth House and Knole, are found throughout the region.

Famous seaside towns and resorts dot the coasts of Sussex and Kent, the most famous being that eccentric combination of carnival and culture, Brighton, site of 19th-century England's own Xanadu, the Royal Pavilion. Also on the coast, the busy ports of Newhaven, Folkestone, Dover, and Ramsgate have served for centuries as gateways to continental Europe. The Channel Tunnel, linking Britain to France by rail, runs from near Folkestone.

Indeed, because the English Channel is at its narrowest here, a great deal of British history has been forged in the Southeast. The Romans landed in this area and stayed to rule Britain for four centuries. So did the Saxons—Sussex means "the land of the South Saxons." William ("the Conqueror") of Normandy defeated the Saxons at a battle near Hastings in 1066. Canterbury has been the seat of the Primate of All England, the Archbishop of Canterbury, since Pope Gregory the Great dispatched St. Augustine to convert the heathen hordes of Britain in 597. And long before any of these invaders, the ancient Britons blazed trails that formed the routes for today's modern highways.

Exploring the Southeast

For sightseeing purposes, the Southeast can be divided into four sections. The eastern part of the region takes in the cathedral town of Canterbury, as well as the port city of Dover. The next section stretches along the southern coast from Rye to Lewes. A third area reaches from the coastal city of Brighton inward to Chichester then to Guildford and East Grinstead. The fourth section takes in the spa town of Royal Tunbridge

GREAT ITINERARIES

The relatively compact Southeast is packed with points of interest. Only a scattering of sights are in and around major towns; most castles, country homes, and gardens are out in the countryside and can be difficult to reach without a car.

Numbers in the text correspond to numbers in the margin and on the Southeast, Canterbury, and Brighton maps.

IF YOU HAVE 3 DAYS

You could opt for historic 🏛 **Canterbury** ❶-❷ 🏳 as a first choice. Stay one night here, making a cathedral visit your priority. Spend the next two nights in 🏛 **Brighton** ㉖-㉜, where the Royal Pavilion is a must. Keeping Brighton as your base, you could spend a third day exploring **Lewes** ㉕, with its Tudor timber-frame buildings scattered along its steep lanes.

IF YOU HAVE 7 DAYS

Spend two nights in the ancient city of 🏛 **Canterbury** ❶-❷ 🏳. If you're traveling east from London, spend half a day at the dockyards at Chatham and the castle and cathedral in neighboring **Rochester** ㊻. In the morning, explore the cathedral and other sights in Canterbury, reserving the afternoon for a foray to the coast and **Broadstairs** ⑮, with its Dickensian associations, and

Dover ⑱. On your third morning, head south to **Sissinghurst Castle Garden**, ㊽. Overnight in 🏛 **Rye** ⑲; take in nearby **Winchelsea** ⑳ the next day; then continue west to the site of the Battle of Hastings at **Battle** ㉒, where the remains of an abbey founded by William the Conqueror mark one of the most momentous events in English history. **Hastings** ㉑ is a typical seafront town; if you're kid-free, consider heading 12 mi farther west to beautiful **Herstmonceux Castle** ㉓. From here, head to 🏛 **Brighton** ㉖-㉜, which deserves a two-night stay. While visiting this bustling seaside city, stop by more tranquil **Lewes** ㉕.

Proceeding west along the coast on your sixth morning, take in 🏛 **Arundel** ㉝ and 🏛 **Chichester** ㉞, either of which would make a wonderful place to spend the night. Arundel is dominated by Arundel Castle, whereas Chichester has a Norman cathedral in town and a Roman villa outside. For your last day, drive northeast back into Kent and choose among the historic houses around 🏛 **Royal Tunbridge Wells** ㊵. Some of the most stirring are the medieval manor house **Penshurst Place** ㊶; **Hever Castle** ㊷, with its mazes; ancient **Ightham Mote** ㊹; and **Chartwell** ㊸, home of Sir Winston Churchill.

Wells and western Kent, where the farmland is dotted with stately homes and castles. The larger towns can be easily reached by train or bus from London for a day trip. To visit most castles, grand country homes or quiet villages, though, you will need a car.

About the Restaurants

If you're in a seaside town, look for that great British staple, fish-and-chips. Perhaps "look" isn't the word—just follow your nose. In all the coastal areas, seafood, much of it locally caught, is a specialty. You can try local smoked fish (haddock and mackerel), or the succulent local oysters. Inland, sample fresh local lamb and beef. In cities such as Brighton and Tunbridge Wells, there are numerous restaurants and cafés to choose from, but out in the countryside your options will be more limited.

About the Hotels

All around the coast, resort towns stretch along beaches, their hotels standing cheek by jowl. Of the smaller hotels and guesthouses, only a few remain open year-round; most do business only from mid-April to September or October. Some hotels have all-inclusive rates for a week's stay, which is cheaper than taking room and meals by the day. Prices rise in July and August, when the seaside resorts can get solidly booked, especially Brighton, a popular conference center. Places in Brighton may not take a booking for a single night in summer or on weekends.

WHAT IT COSTS In pounds					
	££££	££££	£££	££	£
RESTAURANTS	over £22	£18–£22	£13–£17	£7–£12	under £7
HOTELS	over £160	£120–£160	£90–£119	£60–£89	under £60

Restaurant prices are for a main course at dinner. Hotel prices are for two people in a standard double room in high season, including V.A.T., with no meals or, if indicated, CP (with continental breakfast), BP (Breakfast Plan, with full breakfast), or MAP (Modified American Plan, with breakfast and dinner).

Timing

Because the counties of Kent, Surrey, and Sussex offer marvelous scenic landscapes, lovers of the open air will want to get their fill of the many outdoor attractions here. Most privately owned castles and mansions are open only between April and September or October, so it's best to tour the Southeast in the spring, summer, or early fall. Failing that, the great parks surrounding the stately houses are often open all year. If crowds tend to spoil your fun, avoid August, Sunday, and national holidays, particularly in Canterbury and the seaside towns.

CANTERBURY TO DOVER

The cathedral city of Canterbury is an ancient place that has attracted travelers since the 12th century. The city's magnificent cathedral, the Mother Church of England, remains a powerful draw. Even in prehistoric times, this part of England was relatively well settled. Saxon settlers, Norman conquerors, and the folk who lived here in late-medieval times all left their mark. From Canterbury, there's rewarding wandering to be done in the gentle Kentish countryside between the city and the busy port of Dover. Here, the landscape ravishes the eye in spring with apple blossoms, and in the autumn with lush fields ready for harvest. It is a county of orchards, market gardens, and round oasthouses with their tilted, pointed roofs, once used for drying hops (many have been converted into pricey homes).

TOP REASONS TO GO

Bodiam, Dover, Hever, and Herstmonceux castles: Take your pick: the most evocative castles in a region filled with them dazzle you with their fortitude and fascinate you with their histories.

Brighton: With its nightclubs, sunbathing, and funky, relaxed atmosphere, this is the quintessential English seaside city. From Brighton Pier to the Royal Pavilion, there's something for everyone.

Canterbury Cathedral: This massive building, a textbook of medieval architecture, inspires awe with its soaring towers and flagstone corridors. The past seems very near in such places as Trinity Chapel, where ancient stained-glass windows celebrate Thomas à Becket's miracles.

Rye: Wandering the cobbled streets of this medieval town is a pleasure, and rummaging through its antiques stores is an adventure in itself. Reward yourself afterward as the English do, with tea and scones.

Treasure houses: Here is one of England's richest concentrations of historic homes: among the superlatives are Petworth House, with its luminous paintings by Turner; sprawling Knole, with its set of silver furniture; Ightham Mote, with its Tudor chapel; and Chartwell, home of Winston Churchill.

Canterbury

▶ *56 mi southeast of London.*

Just mention Canterbury, and most people are taken back to memories of high-school English classes and Geoffrey Chaucer's *Canterbury Tales,* about medieval pilgrims making their way to Canterbury Cathedral. Judging from the tales, however, in those days Canterbury was as much a party for people on horses as it was a spiritual center. The height of Canterbury's popularity came in the 12th century, when thousands of pilgrims flocked here to see the shrine of the murdered Archbishop St. Thomas à Becket, making this southeastern town one of the most visited in England, if not Europe. Buildings that served as pilgrims' inns (and which survived World War II bombing of the city) still dominate the streets of Canterbury's center.

There is evidence of prosperous society in the Canterbury area as early as the Bronze Age (around 1000 BC). An important Roman city, an Anglo-Saxon center in the Kingdom of Kent, and currently headquarters of the Anglican Church, Canterbury remains a lively place, a fact that has impressed visitors since 1388, when Chaucer wrote his stories. Today, most pilgrims come in search of history and picture-perfect moments rather than spiritual enlightenment, and magnificently medieval Canterbury, with its ancient city walls, leaning Tudor buildings, and remnants of its Roman past, obliges.

The
Southeast

M25

Thames

Hampstead

LONDON

Hounslow

Woolwich

Thames

Windsor

Heathrow
Airport

Richmond

Sidcup

Dartford

M25

Egham

Staines

Merton

Sydenham

Bromley

Beckenham

M3

Woking

Leatherhead

Guildford

Great Bookham

Westerham

Knole

37

A246

Box Hill

M25

44

Chartwell

43

A31

36

Dorking

38

A25

**Ightham
Mote**

45

Reigate

B2027

A27

A25

A227

NORTH DOWNS

A248

Hever Castle

42

B2176

Farnham

SURREY

A3

Gatwick
Airport

M23

Penshurst Place

41

Tonbr

A26

Milford

Crawley

A264

Hartfield

Penshurst

A287

A286

A24

**East
Grinstead**

39

**Royal
Tunbridge Wells**

40

A264

A267

Haslemere

A283

A229

Horsham

A264

Handcross

A22

Wadhurst

THE

Wisborough
Green

Cuckfield

A286

WEST

Haywards Heath

Rothe

Midhurst

**Petworth
House**

Uckfield

A265

EAST

A272

35

SUSSEX

A285

Burgess
Hill

Ouse

A26

SUSSE

SOUTH

Storrington

A281

A23

23

Singleton

DOWNS

Amberley

B2139

A283

**Sculpture at
Goodwood**

Lewes

Glyndebourne

**Herstmonce
Cast**

25

**Fishbourne
Roman Palace**

33

Arundel

A27

Rodmell

24

A27

Worthing

A259

Hove

A259

Wilmington

34

Chichester

Eastbourne

Bognor Regis

English Channel

Brighton

26 — 32

see detail
map

A259

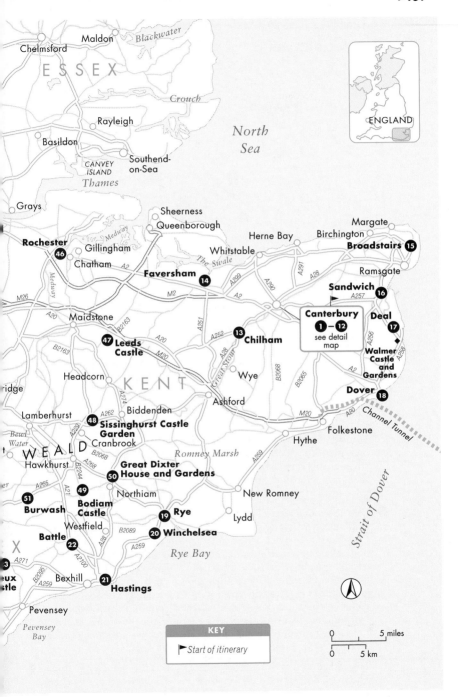

Buttermarket ..2

Canterbury
Cathedral 4

Canterbury
Roman
Museum 1

The Canterbury
Tales
Exhibition 5

Christchurch
Gate 3

Dane John
Mound 12

Eastbridge
Hospital of St.
Thomas 7

Medieval
city walls 10

Museum of
Canterbury 8

St. Augustine's
Abbey 11

Weavers'
Houses 6

West Gate
Museum 9

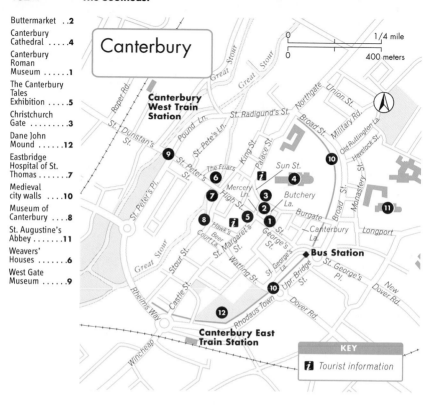

Canterbury

The absence of cars in the center brings some tranquillity to its streets, but to see Canterbury at its best, walk around early, before the tourist buses arrive, or wait until after they depart. Most major tourist sites are on one street, which crosses a branch of the River Stour in the city. The street changes name three times—beginning as St. George's Street and then becoming High Street and, finally, St. Peter's Street.

Main Attractions

❹ Canterbury Cathedral. The focal point of the city was the first of England's great Norman cathedrals. Nucleus of worldwide Anglicanism, the Cathedral Church of Christ Canterbury (its formal name) is a living textbook of medieval architecture. The building was begun in 1070, demolished, begun anew in 1096, and then systematically expanded over the next three centuries. When the original choir section burned to the ground in 1174, another replaced it, designed in the new Gothic style, with tall, pointed arches. Don't miss the *North Choir* aisle, which holds two windows that show Jesus in the Temple, the three kings asleep, and Lot's wife turned to a pillar of salt. The windows are among the earliest parts of the cathedral, but only 33 of the original 208 survive.

The cathedral was only a century old, and still relatively small, when Thomas à Becket, the archbishop of Canterbury, was murdered here in

FodorśChoice
★

1170. Becket, a defender of ecclesiastical interests, had angered his friend Henry II, who was heard to exclaim, "Who will rid me of this troublesome priest?" Thinking they were carrying out the king's wishes, four knights burst in on Becket in one of the side chapels and killed him. Two years later Becket was canonized, and Henry II's subsequent submission to the authority of the Church and his penitence helped establish the cathedral as the undisputed center of English Christianity. Becket's tomb, destroyed by Henry VIII in 1538 as part of his campaign to reduce the power of the Church and confiscate

> **WORD OF MOUTH**
>
> "I prefer atmospheric places to those that are architecturally perfect. Canterbury Cathedral was excellent in that respect. It felt mysterious and otherworldly. And from a historical standpoint, you can't beat Canterbury. The Beckett memorials are rather moving, and two of my favorites, the Black Prince and Henry IV, have gorgeous tombs. I preferred the town of Canterbury also, in spite of its touristy disposition."   –EricaS

its treasures, was one of the most extravagant shrines in Christendom. In **Trinity Chapel,** which held the shrine, you can still see a series of 13th-century stained-glass windows illustrating Becket's miracles. So hallowed was this spot that in 1376, Edward, the Black Prince, warrior son of Edward III and a national hero, was buried near it. The actual site of Becket's murder is down a flight of steps just to the left of the nave. In the corner, a second flight of steps leads down to the enormous Norman **undercroft,** or vaulted cellarage, built in the early 12th century. A row of squat pillars whose capitals dance with animals and monsters supports the roof.

If time permits, be sure to explore the **cloisters** and other small monastic buildings to the north of the cathedral. The 12th-century octagonal water tower is still part of the cathedral's water supply. The Norman staircase in the northwest corner of the Green Court dates from 1167 and is a unique example of the domestic architecture of the times. The cathedral is very popular, so arrive early or late in the day to avoid the worst crowds. ■ TIP→ You get a map and an overview of the building's history when you enter; audio guides have the most detail, or take a tour for the personal touch. ✉ *Cathedral Precincts* ☎ 01227/762862 ⊕ *www. canterbury-cathedral.org* ⊠ *£5, free for services and ½ hr before closing; £3.50 for tour, £2.95 for audio guide* ☉ *Easter–Sept., Mon.–Sat. 9–6:30, Sun. 12:30–2:30 and 4:30–5:30; Oct.–Easter, Mon.–Sat. 9–5, Sun. 12:30–2:30 and 4:30–5:30. Restricted access during services.*

NEED A BREAK? **The Custard Tart** (✉ 35A St. Margaret's St. ☎ 01227/785178), a short walk from the cathedral, serves freshly made sandwiches, pies, tarts, and cakes. You can take your choice upstairs to the seating area. It's not open for dinner.

❶ **Canterbury Roman Museum.** Below ground, at the level of the remnants of Roman Canterbury, this museum features colorful mosaic Roman pavement and a hypocaust—the Roman version of central heating. Displays of excavated objects (some of which you can hold in the Touch the Past area) and computer-generated reconstructions of Roman buildings and the marketplace help re-create the past. ⊠ *Butchery La.* ☎ *01227/ 785575* ⊕ *www.canterbury-museums.co.uk* ☑ *£2.90* ☽ *June–Oct., Mon.–Sat. 10–5, Sun. 1:30–5; Nov.–May, Mon.–Sat. 10–5; last admission at 4. Closed last wk in Dec.*

⑩ Medieval city walls. For an essential Canterbury experience, follow the circuit of the 13th- and 14th-century walls, built on the line of the Roman walls. Those to the east survive intact, towering some 20 feet high and offering a sweeping view of the town. You can access these from a number of places, including Castle Street and Broad Street.

Also Worth Seeing

② Buttermarket. Mercery Lane, with its medieval-style cottages and massive, overhanging timber roofs, runs off High Street and ends in the tiny Buttermarket, an old dairy market square with a sweet name and a dark past. Prior to the 16th century it was called "the Bullstake," because animals were tied here and tortured (a popular activity of the time known as "baiting") before they were slaughtered.

⑤ The Canterbury Tales. It's a kitschy audiovisual (and occasionally olfactory) dramatization of 14th-century English life—popular but touristy. You'll "meet" Chaucer's pilgrims at the Tabard Inn near London and view tableaus illustrating five tales. An actor in period costume often performs a charade as part of the scene. ⊠*St. Margaret's St.* ☎*01227/479227* ⊕ *www.canterburytales.org.uk* ☑ *£7.25* ☽ *Nov.–Feb., daily 10–4:30; Mar.–June, Sept. and Oct, daily 10–5; July and Aug., daily 9:30–5.*

③ Christchurch Gate. This immense gate, built in 1517, leads into the cathedral close. As you pass through, look up at the sculpted heads of two young figures: Prince Arthur, elder brother of Henry VIII, and the young Catherine of Aragon, to whom Arthur was betrothed. After Arthur's death, Catherine married Henry. Her failure to produce a male heir after 25 years of marriage led to Henry's decision to divorce her, creating an irrevocable breach with the Roman Catholic Church and altering the course of English history.

☾ ⑫ Dane John Mound. Just opposite the Canterbury East train station, this was originally part of the city defenses; now it's a park and a good place to unwind. There's a maze here, too.

⑦ Eastbridge Hospital of St. Thomas. The 12th-century building (which would now be called a hostel) lodged pilgrims who came to pray at the tomb of Thomas à Becket. It's a tiny place, fascinating in its simplicity. The refectory, the chapel, and the crypt are open to the public. ⊠ *25 High St.* ☎ *01227/462395* ⊕ *www.eastbridgehospital.org.uk* ☑ *£1* ☽ *Mon.–Sat. 10–5; last admission at 4:30.*

☾ ⑧ Museum of Canterbury. The medieval Poor Priests' Hospital is the site of this local museum, where exhibits provide an overview of the city's history and architecture from Roman times to World War II. It's a quirky place that covers everything and everyone associated with the town, including the Blitz, the mysterious death of the 16th-century writer Christopher Marlowe, and the British cartoon characters Bagpuss and Rupert

2

Bear. A renovation and expansion is under way, but the display subjects should not change. ✉ *20 Stour St.* ☎ *01227/475202* ⊕ *www.canterbury-museums.co.uk* ✍ *£3.30* ☉ *Jan.–May, Oct.–Dec., Mon.–Sat 10:30–5; June–Sept., Mon.–Sat 10:30–5, Sun. 1:30–5; last admission at 4.*

⓫ **St. Augustine's Abbey.** Augustine, England's first Christian missionary, was buried here in 597, at one of the oldest monastic sites in the country. The site remained intact for nearly 1,000 years, until Henry VIII seized the abbey in the 16th century, destroying some of the original buildings and converting others into a royal manor for his fourth wife, Anne of Cleves. A free interactive audio tour vividly puts events into context. Contemporary sculpture is placed in the grounds, and in other locations in the city, May through August. ✉ *Longport* ☎ *01227/767345* ⊕ *www.english-heritage.org.uk* ✍ *£3.70* ☉ *Apr.–Sept., daily 10–6; Oct.–Mar., Wed.–Sun. 10–4.*

❻ **Weavers' Houses.** Huguenot weavers who settled here after fleeing from religious persecution in France occupied this lopsided group of 16th-century, half-timber buildings. The houses are just past where St. Peter's Street crosses a branch of the River Stour. ✉ *St. Peter's St.*

☺❾ **West Gate Museum.** Only one of the city's seven medieval gatehouses survives, complete with twin castellated towers; it now contains this museum. Inside are medieval bric-a-brac and armaments used by the city guard, as well as more contemporary weaponry. The building became a jail in the 14th century, and you can view the prison cells. ■ TIP→ **Climb to the roof for a panoramic view of the city.** ✉ *St. Peter's St.* ☎ *01227/789576* ⊕ *www.canterbury-museums.co.uk* ✍ *£1.15* ☉ *Mon.–Sat. 11–12:30 and 1:30–3:30; last admission 1 hr before closing; closed Christmas wk and Good Fri.*

Where to Stay & Eat

★ ££–£££ ✕ **Lloyds.** The magnificent beamed barn roof of this older building remains, but the interior—stripped wooden floor, white walls enlivened by contemporary paintings—and the cooking are definitely up-to-the-minute. A crew of young chefs creates such dishes as roasted pumpkin and amaretto ravioli with Parmesan, and pheasant with kumquats and juniper berries. The ice creams are homemade. ✉ *89–90 St. Dunstan's St.* ☎ *01227/768222* ▭ *AE, MC, V.*

££–£££ ✕ **Weavers.** In the Old Weavers House, one of the Weavers' Houses on the River Stour, this popular restaurant in the center of town is an ideal place to feast in a Tudor setting. The menu lists traditional English, seafood, and pasta dishes, and a good choice of wines. ✉ *1 St. Peter's St.* ☎ *01227/464660* ▭ *AE, MC, V.*

£–£££ ✕ **The Goods Shed.** Next to Canterbury West station, this vaulted wooden space with exposed brick and stone walls was a storage shed in Victorian times. Now it's a farmers' market and restaurant offering a foodie's feast of the best Kentish food—from freshly caught fish and smoked meats to local cider and bread baked on the premises. The menu varies with the availability of the local produce, and food is served at wooden tables on a raised platform. ✉ *Station Rd. W* ☎ *01227/459153* ▭ *MC, V* ☉ *Closed Mon. No dinner Sun.*

£–££ ✗ **Tapas en las Trece.** Interesting tapas in this atmospheric small restaurant include chicken with white wine, and coriander swordfish. There are also some respectable vegetarian options. The dim lighting hides the fact that this is not quite the Mediterranean. ⊠ *13 Palace St.* ☎ *01227/762637* ▭ *AE, MC, V.*

£ ✗ **City Fish Bar.** Long lines and lots of satisfied finger-licking attest to the deserved popularity of this excellent fish-and-chips outlet in the center of town. Everything is freshly fried, the batter crisp and the fish tasty; the fried mushrooms are also surprisingly good. It closes at 7. ⊠ *30 St. Margarets St.* ☎ *01227/760873* ▭ *No credit cards.*

££–£££ ✗▥ **Falstaff Hotel.** This old coaching inn with a courtyard sits right outside Westgate. Some of the beamed and oak-furnished bedrooms overlook the River Stour; rooms have a mix of old features and new, and three have four-posters. Classic English fare at the restaurant (£££) includes grilled mackerel with cucumber and beet salad. The central location is a big plus: reserve well in advance. ⊠ *8 St. Dunstan's St., CT2 8AF* ☎ *01227/462138* 🖷 *01227/463525* ⊕ *www.english-inns.co.uk* ⇄ *47 rooms* ⌂ *Restaurant, cable TV, in-room broadband, bar, laundry service, Internet room, no-smoking rooms; no a/c* ▭ *AE, DC, MC, V* ⊙⏐ *EP.*

££–££££ ▦ **Magnolia House.** Kept in apple-pie order, this Georgian house, a 10-minute walk from the center of town, is charmingly elegant, with a lovely walled garden. Bedrooms have floral motifs and traditional furnishings; one has a four-poster. Evening meals are available from November to February by prior arrangement. To get here, follow St. Dunstan's Street until London Road and take a left; it will be three blocks on the right side. ⊠ *36 St. Dunstan's Terr., CT2 8AX* 🖷🖷 *01227/765121* ⊕ *www.magnoliahousecanterbury.co.uk* ⇄ *7 rooms* ⌂ *No a/c, no room phones, no kids under 12, no smoking* ▭ *AE, DC, MC, V* ⊙⏐ *BP.*

££–£££ ▦ **Ebury Hotel.** Friendly and family-run, this hotel earns raves for its laid-back attitude and comfortable rooms. Made up of two big Victorian buildings a 10-minute walk from central Canterbury, it has been sympathetically converted. Rooms are simply decorated but good-size (bathrooms can be a bit tiny), and beds are firm. The cozy lounge has a wood-burning fireplace, and an attractive indoor pool is perfect for hot days. The hotel's slightly old-fashioned look is not for everyone, but if you like the kind of inn that has a house labradoodle, it's perfect. There's no elevator; ask for a room on the lower floors if you have mobility problems. ⊠ *65–67 New Dover Rd. CT1 3DX* ☎ *01227/768433* 🖷 *01227/459187* ⊕ *www.ebury-hotel.co.uk* ⇄ *15 rooms* ⌂ *Restaurant, indoor pool, lounge; no a/c* ▭ *MC, V* ⊙⏐ *BP.*

££ ▦ **Cathedral Gate Hotel.** Older even than the adjoining cathedral gateway, this hotel was built as a hostelry for pilgrims in 1438. The large beams, sloping floors, and twisting corridors are evidence of its medieval origins; the plainly furnished rooms, however, have been sympathetically modernized. The bow-window restaurant looks out over the Buttermarket. A full English breakfast costs an extra £7. ⊠ *36 Burgate, CT1 2HA* ☎ *01227/464381* 🖷 *01227/462800* ⊕ *www.cathgate.co.uk* ⇄ *27 rooms* ⌂ *Restaurant, bar, some pets allowed; no a/c* ▭ *AE, DC, MC, V* ⊙⏐ *CP.*

2

££ ▦ **The White House.** Reputed to have been the house in which Queen Victoria's head coachman came to live upon retirement, the White House is a handsome Regency building on a quiet road off St. Peter's Street, between the city center and Canterbury West train station. Rooms are decorated in pastel shades with an abundance of floral patterns, and a few rooms can accommodate up to four people. ⊠ *6 St. Peter's La., CT1 2BP* ☎*01227/761836* 🖷*01227/478622* ⊕*www.canterburybreaks. co.uk* ⤴ *9 rooms* ⚲ *Lounge, no-smoking rooms; no room phones* ▭ *No credit cards* ❙⚬❙ *BP.*

Nightlife & the Arts

NIGHTLIFE Canterbury is home to a popular university, and the town's many pubs and bars are busy, often crowded with college-age folks. **Alberry's Wine Bar** (⊠ St. Margaret's St. ☎ 01227/452378), with late-night jazz and hip-hop and a trendy crowd, is the coolest place in town. **Simple Simons** (⊠ 3–9 Church La. ☎01227/762355) is known for its real ales–at least six kinds are available at any time—and its convivial setting in a wood-paneled building. **Thomas Becket** (⊠ 21 Best La. ☎01227/464384), a marvelous English pub, has a fire crackling in the winter, copper pots hanging from the ceiling, and a friendly crowd.

THE ARTS The two-week-long, mixed-arts **Canterbury Festival** (☎ 01227/452853 ⊕ www.canterburyfestival.co.uk) is held every October. The **Gulbenkian Theatre** (⊠ Giles La. ☎ 01227/769075), outside the center at the University of Kent, mounts all kinds of plays, particularly experimental works, as well as dance, music, comedy, and films. The **Marlowe** (⊠ St. Margaret's St. ☎ 01227/787787), named after the Elizabethan playwright, who was born in Canterbury, is a venue for touring drama and opera companies.

Shopping

Hawkin's Bazaar (⊠ 34 Burgate ☎01227/785809) carries an exceptional selection of traditional and modern toys and games. The **National Trust Shop** (⊠ 24 Burgate ☎ 01227/457120) stocks the National Trust line of household items, ideal for gifts.

Chilham

⑬ *5 mi southwest of Canterbury.*

The village square is filled with textbook examples of English rural architecture, with gabled windows beneath undulating roofs. The church dates from the 14th century. From this hilltop village, midway between Canterbury and Ashford on the A252 (off the A28), you can walk the last few miles of the traditional Pilgrim's Way back to Canterbury.

Where to Eat

££ ✕ **White Horse.** This 15th-century inn shadowed by Chilham's church has a pleasant beer garden and provides lunchtime and evening meals superior to the usual pub grub, with many good pasta dishes. The pub used to be a vicarage, and the ghost of a 17th-century vicar is said to regularly appear in front of the large fireplace. ⊠ *The Square* ☎ *01227/ 730355* ▭ *MC, V.*

Faversham

⑭ *9 mi west of Canterbury, 11 mi northwest of Chilham.*

In Roman times, Faversham was a thriving seaport. Today the port is hidden from sight, and you could pass through this market town without knowing it was there. Still, Faversham is a worthwhile stop for those in search of Ye Quaint Olde Englande: the town center, with its Tudor houses grouped around the 1574 guildhall and covered market, looks like a perfect stage set. There are no actual sights here, as such, but it's a lovely place to take a break and have a stroll.

Where to Stay & Eat

★ ✕⬜ **Read's.** The glorious food in this elegant restaurant is assuredly
££££–£££££ British, but puts an audacious spin on old favorites. The accent falls firmly on local ingredients, many of which come from the vegetable garden (in which you are welcome to stroll). After a main course of Kentish lamb in a fresh herb crust with mini–shepherd's pie, try the "chocoholics anonymous" dessert. Prices are fixed, with three-course lunch options at £21 and a three-course dinner costing £48. Three of the six spacious Georgian guest rooms are aptly named for the trees they overlook in the garden (Cedar, Willow, and Chestnut). A complimentary decanter of sherry in each room is a nice touch. ⊠ *Macknade Manor, Canterbury Rd. ME13 8XE* ☎ *01795/535344* 🖷 *01795/591200* ⊕ *www.reads.com* 🛏 *6 rooms* ⚲ *Restaurant, bar; no a/c, no smoking* ▤ *AE, DC, MC, V* ⊗ *Restaurant closed Sun. and Mon.* ⵌ *BP.*

££ ✕⬜ **Sun Inn.** This pretty, clapboard pub (£) dates to the 1400s. It's a traditional place that still follows the old local tradition of hanging up hops in September; their pleasant, wheaty scent fills the room. Its guest rooms are neatly done in neutral colors, and are well priced given the quality. ⊠ *10 West St.* ☎ *01795/535098* ⊕ *www.sunfaversham.co.uk* 🛏 *9 rooms* ⚲ *Restaurant, bar; no a/c* ▤ *MC, V* ⵌ *BP.*

£–££ ✕⬜ **The White Horse Inn.** Mentioned in Chaucer's *Canterbury Tales,* this 15th-century coaching inn outside Faversham on the old London-to-Dover road (now A2) retains much of its traditional character. The pale blue guest rooms have antique furniture. In addition to the friendly bar, there's an excellent restaurant (££–£££) in what used to be a courtroom; you might find shark steak on the list of daily specials. ⊠ *The Street, Boughton ME13 9AX* ☎ *01227/751343* 🖷 *01227/751090* ⊕ *www. whitehorsecanterbury.co.uk* 🛏 *13 rooms* ⚲ *Restaurant, bar; no a/c* ▤ *AE, MC, V* ⵌ *BP.*

Broadstairs

⑮ *25 mi east of Faversham, 17 mi east of Canterbury.*

Like other Victorian seaside towns such as Margate and Ramsgate on this stretch of coast, Broadstairs was once the playground of vacationing Londoners. Charles Dickens spent many summers here between 1837 and 1851 and wrote glowingly of its bracing freshness. Today grand 19th-century houses line the waterfront. In the off-season Broadstairs is a peaceful retreat, but day-trippers pack the town in July and August.

One of Dickens's favorite abodes was **Bleak House,** perched on a cliff overlooking Viking Bay, where he wrote much of *David Copperfield* and drafted *Bleak House,* after which the building was later renamed. His study and other rooms have been preserved. Displays explore local history, including the wrecks at nearby Goodwin Sands, and the cellars have exhibits about smuggling, a longtime local activity. ✉ *Fort Rd.* ☎ *01843/ 862224* ☜ *£3* ⊙ *Late-Feb.–June and Sept.–mid-Dec., daily 10–6; July and Aug., daily 10–9.*

What is now the **Dickens House Museum** was originally the home of Mary Pearson Strong, on whom Dickens based the character of Betsey Trotwood, David Copperfield's aunt. There's a reconstruction of Miss Trotwood's room, a few objects that once belonged to the Dickens family, and prints and photographs commemorating Dickens's association with Broadstairs. There's more Dickens memorabilia in Rochester, where he also lived. ✉ *2 Victoria Parade* ☎ *01843/863453* ⊕ *www. dickenshouse.co.uk* ☜ *£2.30* ⊙ *Apr.–Oct., daily 2–5.*

Where to Stay

£ ⊞ **Admiral Dundonald Hotel.** An ivy-covered Georgian building, the Admiral has just the right Olde English look. Inside the decor is a good mix of antiques and modern pieces, and the mood is both friendly and, in the lounge, a bit formal. Rooms are neat and simply decorated, and the location at the edge of the town center is handy. ✉ *43 Belvedere Rd., CT10 1PF* ☎ *01843/862236* ➶ *12 rooms* ⌂ *No a/c, no room phones* ▭ *MC, V* ⎟⊙⎟ *BP.*

Nightlife & the Arts

Each June, Broadstairs holds a **Dickens Festival** (☎ 01843/865265), lasting about a week, with readings, people in Dickensian costume, a Dickensian cricket match, a Victorian bathing party, and Victorian vaudeville, among other entertainments. Aficionados of the author are also drawn to another Christmas Dickens festival in Rochester.

Sandwich

⑯ *11 mi south of Broadstairs, 12 mi east of Canterbury.*

The coast near Canterbury holds three of the ancient **Cinque Ports** (pronounced sink ports), a confederacy of ports along the southeast seaboard whose heyday lasted from the 12th through the 14th centuries. These towns, originally five in number (hence *cinque,* from the Norman French for "five")—Sandwich, Dover, Hythe, Romney, and Hastings— are rich in history and are generally less crowded than the other resorts of Kent's northeast coast.

In Saxon times Sandwich stood in a sheltered bay; it became the most important of the Cinque Ports in the Middle Ages and later England's chief naval base. From 1500 the port began to silt up, however, and the town is now 2 mi inland, though the River Stour still flows through it. The 16th-century checkerboard barbican (gatehouse) by the toll bridge is one of many medieval and Tudor buildings here; Strand Street has many half-timber structures.

Deal

⑰ *7 mi south of Sandwich, 8 mi northeast of Dover.*

The large seaside town of Deal is famous in history books as the place where Caesar's legions landed in 55 BC, and it was from here that William Penn set sail in 1682 on his first journey to the American colony he founded, Pennsylvania.

Deal Castle, erected in 1540 and intricately built to the shape of a Tudor rose, is the largest of the coastal defenses constructed by Henry VIII. A moat surrounds its gloomy passages and austere walls. The castle museum has exhibits about prehistoric, Roman, and Saxon Britain. ✉ *Victoria Rd.* ☎ *01304/372762* ⊕ *www.english-heritage.org.uk* 🎫 *£3.90* ☉ *Apr.–Sept., daily 10–6.*

Walmer Castle and Gardens, one of Henry VIII's fortifications, was converted in 1708 into the official residence of the lord warden of the Cinque Ports, and it now resembles a cozy country house. Among the famous lord wardens were William Pitt the Younger; the duke of Wellington, hero of the Battle of Waterloo, also lived here from 1829 until his death here in 1852 (a small museum contains memorabilia); and Sir Winston Churchill. Except for when the lord warden is in residence, the drawing and dining rooms are open to the public, and attractive gardens and a grassy walk fill what was the moat. ✉ *A258, 1 mi south of Deal* ☎ *01304/364288* ⊕ *www.english-heritage.org.uk* 🎫 *£6.20* ☉ *Mar., daily 10–4; Apr.–Sept., daily 10–6; Oct., Wed.–Sun. 10–4.*

> **HENRY'S CASTLES**
>
> Why did Henry VIII rapidly (1539–1542) build sturdy forts along the southern coast? After enraging the Pope and Europe's Catholic monarchs with his marriages and by seizing control of the wealthy monasteries, he prepared for a possible invasion. It did not come. Today you can bike or walk along the beachfront between Deal and Walmer Castles.

Dover

⑱ *7 mi south of Walmer Castle, 78 mi east of London.*

The busy passenger port of Dover has for centuries been Britain's gateway to Europe. Its chalk **White Cliffs** are a famous and inspirational sight, though you may find the town itself a bit disappointing; the savage bombardments of World War II and the shortsightedness of postwar developers left the city center an unattractive place. Roman legacies include a lighthouse, adjoining a stout Anglo-Saxon church. The **Roman Painted House,** believed to have been a hotel, includes some wall paintings, along with the remnants of an ingenious heating system. ✉ *New St.* ☎ *01304/203279* 🎫 *£2* ☉ *Apr.–Sept., Tues.–Sat. 10–5, Sun. 2–5.*

★ ☺ Spectacular **Dover Castle,** towering high above the ramparts of the White Cliffs, was a mighty medieval castle, and it has served as an important strategic center over the centuries, even in World War II. Most of the

2

castle, including the keep, dates to Norman times. It was begun by Henry II in 1181 but incorporates additions from almost every succeeding century. There's a lot to see here besides the castle rooms: exhibits, many of which will appeal to kids, include the Siege of 1216, the Princess of Wales Regimental Museum, and Castle Fit for a King. ■ TIP→ **Take time to tour the secret wartime tunnels, a medieval and Napoleonic-era system that was used as a World War II command center during the evacuation of Dunkirk in 1940.** ☒ *Castle Rd.* ☎ *01304/211067* ⊕ *www.english-heritage.org. uk* ☒ *£9.50* ☉ *Feb. and Mar., daily 10–4; Apr.–Sept., daily 10–6; Oct., daily 10–5; Nov.–Jan., Thurs.–Mon. 10–4.*

Where to Stay

£ ☒ **Number One Guest House.** This popular, family-run guesthouse with garage parking is a great bargain. Wallpapers and porcelain collections decorate the cozy corner terrace home built in the early 19th century, and you can even have breakfast in your room. The walled garden has a fine view of the castle. ☒ *1 Castle St., CT16 1QH* ☎ *01304/202007* 🖷 *01304/214078* ⊕ *www.number1guesthouse.co.uk* ⟿ *4 rooms* ♢ *No a/c, no room phones* ⊟ *No credit cards* ⦿| *BP.*

RYE TO GLYNDEBOURNE

From Dover, the coast road winds west through Folkestone (a genteel resort, small port, and Channel Tunnel terminal), across Romney Marsh (reclaimed from the sea and famous for its sheep and, at one time, its ruthless smugglers), to the delightful medieval town of Rye. The region along the coast is noted for Winchelsea, the history-rich sites of Hastings and Herstmonceux, and the Glyndebourne Opera House festival, based outside Lewes, a town celebrated for its architectural heritage. One of the three steam railroads in the Southeast services part of the area: the Romney, Hythe, and Dymchurch Railway.

Rye

★ ⓳ *68 mi southeast of London, 34 mi southwest of Dover.*

With cobbled streets and ancient timbered dwellings, Rye is an artist's dream. Once a port (the water retreated, and the harbor is now 2 mi away), the town starts where the sea once lapped at its ankles and then winds its way to the top of a low hill that overlooks the Romney Marshes. Virtually every building in the little town center is intriguingly old; some places were smugglers' retreats. Rye is known for its many antiques stores and antiquarian bookstores, and also for its sheer pleasantness. This place can be easily walked without a map, but if you prefer guidance, the local tourist office has an interesting audio tour of the town as well as maps.

The diminutive **Rye Castle Museum,** below the remains of the castle wall, displays watercolors and examples of Rye pottery, for which the town was famous. ☒ *3 East St.* ☎ *01797/226728* ⊕ *www.rye.org.uk* ☒ *£1.90, £2.90 including Ypres Tower* ☉ *Apr.–Oct., Mon., Thurs., Fri. 2–5, weekends 10:30–1; last admission 30 mins before closing.*

At the top of the hill at the center of Rye, the **Church of St. Mary the Virgin** is a classic English village church in a number of architectural styles. ■ TIP➡ **You can climb the tower to see amazing views.** The turret clock dates to 1561 and still keeps excellent time. ⌧ *Church Sq.* ☉ *Daily 10–4.*

Down the hill past Church Square, **Ypres Tower** was originally built as part of the town's fortifications (now largely gone) in 1249; it later served as a prison. The stone chambers hold a rather random collection of local items, such as smuggling bric-a-brac and shipbuilding mementos. ⌧ *Gungarden* ☎ *01797/226728* ⌧ *£1.90, £2.90 including Rye Castle* ☉ *Apr.–Oct., Thurs.–Mon. 10–1 and 2–5; Nov.–Mar., weekends 10:30–3:30; last admission 30 mins before closing.*

Something about **Lamb House,** an early 18th-century house, attracts writers. The novelist Henry James lived here from 1898 to 1916. E. F. Benson, onetime mayor of Rye and author of the witty *Lucia* novels (written in the 1920s and 1930s, with some set in a town based on Rye), was a later resident. The ground-floor rooms contain some of James's furniture and personal belongings. ⌧ *West St.* ☎ *01892/890651* ⊕ *www. nationaltrust.org.uk* ⌧ *£3* ☉ *Apr.–Oct., Thurs. and Sat. 2–6; last admission at 5:30.*

Several miles outside Rye, **Tenterden Vineyard** is one of Britain's leading wine producers. The Chapel Down wines have won awards, including one for a sparkling wine. You must join a one-hour guided tour to view the grounds, after which you are free to peruse the herb garden, plant center, shop, and the restaurant, the Grapevine Bistro. ⌧ *Small Hythe* ☎ *01580/763033* ⊕ *www.newwavewines.co.uk* ⌧ *£4.30* ☉ *June–Sept., daily 10–5; May and Oct., weekends 10–5.*

> ### MERMAID CALLING
>
> Mermaid Street in Rye is one of the original cobbled streets that heads steeply from the top of the hill to the former harbor. Its name, according to local lore, came from the night a sailor who had sipped a few too many walked down it. He swore he heard a mermaid call him down to the sea.

Where to Stay & Eat

££–£££ ✕ **Landgate Bistro.** Although definitely a bistro, this restaurant in a small shop unit near one of the ancient gateways is serious about its food. Fish is always a good choice, or you can opt for the duck soaked in a tangy port sauce or griddle-cooked cutlets of venison with winter vegetables. A fixed-price menu (£18 for three courses) is available Tuesday through Thursday. ⌧ *5–6 Landgate* ☎ *01797/222829* ▭ *DC, MC, V* ☉ *Closed Sun. and Mon., last wk in Dec., and 1st wk in Jan. No lunch.*

£££££ ✕▦ **The Mermaid.** Once the headquarters of a smuggling gang, this classic half-timber inn has served Rye for nearly six centuries. Sloping floors, oak beams, low ceilings, and a huge open hearth in the bar testify to great age: the inn was rebuilt in 1420, though it dates from 1156. Rooms vary in size; some have four-posters. The decor is a bit dated for the price, but the history keeps the crowds coming in. The main restaurant (££££–£££££) allows you to soak up the period details while choosing from an extensive English menu. In summer you can have tea in the Tudor Tearoom for a rather steep price. ⊠ *Mermaid St., TN31 7EY* ☎ *01797/223065* 🖨 *01797/225069* ⊕ *www.mermaidinn.com* 🛏 *31 rooms* ⚒ *Restaurant, bar, meeting room; no a/c* ⊟ *AE, MC, V* ⏐◯⏐ *BP.*

£££–££££ 🏨 **Jeake's House.** Antiques and books fill the cozy bedrooms of this rambling 1689 house, and print fabrics and brass or mahogany beds add charm. The snug, painted-and-paneled parlor has a wood-burning stove for cold days. Breakfast, which might include deviled kidneys, kippers, or vegetarian nuggets, is served in a galleried room formerly used for Quaker meetings. Book well in advance. ⊠ *Mermaid St., TN31 7ET* ☎ *01797/222828* 🖨 *01797/222623* ⊕ *www.jeakeshouse.com* 🛏 *11 rooms, 10 with bath* ⚒ *Bar, some pets allowed (fee); no a/c, no kids under 8* ⊟ *MC, V* ⏐◯⏐ *BP.*

££–£££ 🏨 **The Old Vicarage.** Roses frame the door of this bayfront Georgian house in a peaceful location close to the church in the center of town. The sunny rooms combine Victorian, Edwardian, and French furniture. You can breakfast on homemade bread, scones, and locally produced eggs and bacon in a dining room that overlooks a garden. ⊠ *66 Church Sq., TN31 7HF* ☎ *01797/222119* 🖨 *01797/227466* ⊕ *www.oldvicaragerye.co.uk* 🛏 *4 rooms* ⚒ *No a/c, no room phones, no kids under 8, no smoking* ⊟ *No credit cards* ⊘ *Closed last wk in Dec.* ⏐◯⏐ *BP.*

Shopping

Rye has great antiques shops, perfect for an afternoon of rummaging, with the biggest cluster at the foot of the hill near the tourist information center. The English can find bargains; it's harder for Americans, given the exchange rate. The town still has a number of potteries. **Black Sheep Antiques** (⊠ 72 The Mint ☎ 01797/224508) has a superior selection of antique crystal and silver. **Collectors Corner** (⊠ 2 Market Rd. ☎ 01797/225796) sells a good mix of furniture, art and silver.

Of Rye's working potteries, **Cinque Ports Pottery** (⊠ The Monastery, Conduit Hill ☎ 01797/222033) is one of the best. **David Sharp Pottery** (⊠ 55 The Mint ☎ 01797/222620) specializes in the ceramic name plaques that are a feature of the town.

Winchelsea

➋⓪ *2 mi southwest of Rye, 71 mi southeast of London.*

Like Rye, Winchelsea perches prettily atop its own small hill amid farmland. Its historic houses, some with clapboards, are appealing, and it has a splendid (though damaged) church built in the 14th century with Caen stone from Normandy. This was once a walled town, and some of the original town gates still stand. Winchelsea was built on a grid system devised in 1283, after the sea destroyed an earlier settlement at the foot of the hill. The sea later receded, leaving the town high and dry.

Where to Stay & Eat

£ ✕🏨 **The New Inn.** This 18th-century hostelry in the heart of town is an excellent place to stop for a pub lunch (££) or a bed for the night. The quiet, refurbished rooms have deep-pile carpets and pleasant views. The bar serves up juicy roasts and quaffable cask ales, and there's a warming log fire. ⊠ *German St.* ☎ *01797/226252* ⟿ *6 rooms* ⌂ *Restaurant; no a/c, no room phones* ⊟ *AE, MC, V* ⦿ *BP.*

Hastings

㉑ *9 mi southwest of Winchelsea, 68 mi southeast of London.*

This big, sprawling Victorian seaside town will always be associated with the 1066 Norman invasion, when William, duke of Normandy, landed his troops at Pevensey Bay, a few miles west of town, and was met by King Harold's army. A vicious battle ensued. Though it was called the Battle of Hastings, it actually took place 6 mi away at a town now called, well, Battle. Harold's troops had just fought Vikings near York and marched across the country to take on the Normans. Utterly exhausted, Harold never stood a chance, and William became known as William the Conquerer.

Hastings later flourished as a Cinque Port and in the 19th century became one of England's many popular resorts. This is when it got its current looks, which are, particularly from a distance, lovely. Tall row houses painted in lemony hues cover the cliffs around the deep blue sea, and the views from the hilltops are extraordinary. The old town, east of the pier, offers a glimpse into the city's 16th-century past. It has been through difficult times in recent decades, as have many English seaside resorts, and the town developed a reputation as a rough place. However, a gentrification movement has encouraged a slow climb back to respectability. All visitors may notice, though, is that it's a handsome place, and the seafront has all the usual English accoutrements—fish-and-chips shops, candy stores, shops selling junk, miniature golf, and rocky beaches that stretch for miles. ■ TIP➡ Walk to the edge of town away from the castle, and you can often have the beach all to yourself. Below the East Cliff, tall, black wooden towers called **net shops,** unique to the town, are still used for drying fishermen's nets, and selling fresh seafood.

You can take the West Hill Cliff Railway from George Street precinct to the atmospheric ruins of the Norman **Hastings Castle,** built by William the Conqueror in 1069. All that remains are fragments of the fortifications, some ancient walls, and a number of gloomy dungeons. Nevertheless, you get an excellent view of the chalky cliffs, the coast, and the town below. "The 1066 Story" retells the Norman invasion using audiovisual technol-

BEACH HUTS

Beach huts are as English as clotted cream. Rows of tiny, cheerfully painted, one-room wooden huts brighten the shoreline in Sussex (look for them at the edges of Hastings and Brighton) and elsewhere. The huts originated in the Victorian wheeled bathing machines that were rolled into the water so that women could swim modestly behind them. Eventually the wheels came off, and they and similar structures became favored for storage and as a windbreak. Many huts lack electricity or plumbing but are beloved for their adorableness. Some are rented; others are owned, and prices can be high.

Vin Anglais

ENGLISH WINE? Indeed, the English wine industry, ridiculed for years, is beginning to be taken more seriously. English vineyards, mostly in Surrey, Sussex, and Kent, have seen boom years, boosted by the changing climate. The summer of 2003 yielded a particularly good vintage in southeast England; while the Mediterranean grape harvest was damaged by drought, the weather in England was almost perfect for wine production. Chalky soils in the region are similar to those in the Champagne region of France, and with the success of English sparkling wines, vineyards like Biddenden (near Sissinghurst), Tenterden (next to Rye), and Carr Taylor (Hastings) have attracted the attention of French wine houses. Many vineyards turn out decent whites, often using frost-resistant German grape varieties; some have even produced good wines based on Pinot Noir and Chardonnay grapes. So go ahead: ask for local wines as you're dining in the region.

ogy. ✉ *West Hill* ☎ *01424/781112* ⊕ *www.discoverhastings.co.uk* ✑ *£3.40* ⊗ *Easter–Sept., daily 10–5; Oct.–Easter, daily 11–3; last admission 30 mins before closing.*

☺ Waxworks and exhibits recall the history of smuggling at **Smuggler's Adventure,** in a labyrinth of caves and passages a 5- or 10-minute walk above Hastings Castle. ✉ *St. Clement Caves* ☎ *01424/422964* ⊕ *www.smugglersadventure.co.uk* ✑ *£6.40* ⊗ *Easter–Sept., daily 10–5:30; Oct.–Easter, daily 11–4:30; last admission 30 mins before closing.*

Carr Taylor Vineyards are well-known locally for their traditional methods of bottled fermentation, also known as *Méthode Champenoise.* The store also stocks fruit wines, ranging from strawberry to apricot, and mead—a wine of medieval origin—made following the *very* sweet Carr Taylor recipe with fermented grapes, apple juice, and honey. Take the A21 north from Hastings for 3 mi, turn onto the A28, and follow the signs. ✉ *Westfield, Hastings* ☎ *01424/752501* ⊕ *www.carr-taylor. com* ✑ *Free* ⊗ *Daily 10–5; closed last wk of Dec.*

Where to Stay & Eat

££–££££ ✕ **Bonaparte's.** A hands-on approach to food distinguishes this slightly haughty seafront restaurant, which has dark walls and booths for dining. Owner Bob Bone shoots his own game and buys fish fresh from the market to create dishes such as game pie in beer and wine sauce and halibut steak with crayfish tails. His inventive vegetarian choices include a Tibetan roast with buckwheat, spinach, mushrooms, and walnuts. ✉ *64 Eversfield Pl., St. Leonards* ☎ *01424/712218* ▭ *AE, DC, MC, V* ⊗ *Closed Mon. No lunch Sun.*

£ ▣ **Eagle House.** This guesthouse in St. Leonards, just west of Hastings's city center, is in a large Victorian building with a lovely garden. It's a quirky place with somewhat dated decor, but the guest rooms have Victorian touches. The restaurant uses fresh produce from local farms. ✉ *12 Pevensey Rd., St. Leonards TN38 0JZ* ☎ *01424/430535* ✆ *01424/*

437771 ⊕ www.eaglehousehotel.co.uk ⤺ 18 rooms ⌂ Restaurant; no a/c ▭ AE, DC, MC, V ⦿ BP.

Battle

⑳ *7 mi northwest of Hastings, 61 mi southeast of London.*

Battle is the actual site of the crucial Battle of Hastings, at which, on October 14, 1066, William of Normandy and his army trounced King Harold's Anglo-Saxon army. Today it's a sweet, quiet town, and a favorite of history buffs.

The ruins of **Battle Abbey,** the great Benedictine abbey William the Conqueror erected after his victory, still convey the sense of past conflict. A memorial stone marks the high altar, which stood on the spot where Harold II was killed. Despite its historical significance, this abbey was not spared Henry VIII's wrath, and it was largely destroyed during his dissolution of the monasteries. A visitor center (set to open in fall 2006) has an audiovisual presentation about the battle and its impact on England. You can still take the 1-mi-long walk around the edge of the battlefield and see the remains of many of the abbey's buildings. The **Abbot's House** (closed to the public) is now a girls' school. ⊠ *High St.* ☎ *01424/773792 ⊕ www.english-heritage.org.uk ⤢ £5.50 ⊙ Apr.–Oct. daily 10–6; Nov.–Mar., daily 10–4.*

Where to Stay & Eat

££££ ✕⌂ **Powder Mills Hotel.** On 150 acres of parkland, this Georgian house, close to Battle Abbey, adjoins the 1066 battlefield. Among the bedrooms lavishly furnished in country-house style are one used by the duke of Wellington and another supposedly haunted by a "lady in white." The seafood receives high marks at the Orangery Restaurant (£££–£££££). There's a fixed-price menu at lunch and dinner. ⊠ *Powdermill La., TN33 0SP* ☎ *01424/775511* ⤢ *01424/774540 ⊕ www.powdermillshotel. com* ⤺ *40 rooms ⌂ Restaurant, cable TV, pool, fishing, meeting rooms, some pets allowed; no a/c ▭ AE, DC, MC, V ⦿ BP.*

£££ ✕⌂ **Little Hemingfold Hotel.** Forty acres of fields and woodland, including a trout lake and a grass tennis court, provide the main enticement of this informal, early-Victorian farmhouse hotel. Guest rooms, done in simple country style, are bright and serene, and there's a piano in one of the sitting rooms. The fixed-price dinner in the candlelighted restaurant (££££–£££££) uses homegrown fruit and vegetables; the menu changes daily. The hotel is 2 mi south of Battle off the A2100. ⊠ *Hastings Rd., Telham TN33 0TT* ☎ *01424/774338* ⤢ *01424/775351 ⊕ www.littlehemingfoldhotel.co.uk* ⤺ *12 rooms ⌂ Restaurant, tennis court, lake, boating, fishing, croquet, bar, lounge, some pets allowed; no a/c, no kids under 7 ⊙ Closed Jan.–mid-Feb. ▭ AE, MC, V ⦿ BP.*

££ ⌂ **Farthings Farm.** This friendly B&B in a fanciful, white Edwardian farmhouse, 2 mi outside Battle, is a real find. The owners are friendly and chatty, the light-filled house has books, games, and a garden for diversions, and the views over the surrounding hills are wonderful. Bedrooms are simply but tastefully decorated. You can walk to Battle from here in 20 minutes on the 1066 Walk footpath. Dinner is available if you book in advance. ⊠ *Off B2204, Catsfield TN33 9BA* ☎ *01424/773107*

⊕ *www.farthingsfarm.co.uk* ⟿ *2 rooms* ⚓ *Lounge; no a/c* ▭ *No credit cards* ⬤ *BP.*

Herstmonceux Castle

★ ㉓ *11 mi southwest of Battle, 61 mi southeast of London.*

At last, a proper fairy-tale castle, with a banner waving from one tower and a glassy moat crossed by what was, surely, once a drawbridge—everything, in fact, except knights in armor. For true castle lovers, Herstmonceux is a fabled name. The redbrick structure was originally built by Sir Roger Fiennes (ancestor of actor Ralph Fiennes) in 1444, although it was altered in the Elizabethan age and again early in the 20th century, after it had largely fallen to ruin. Canada's Queen's University owns the castle, so only part of it is open for guided tours. Highlights include the magnificent ballroom, a medieval room, and the stunning Elizabethan-era staircase. ■ TIP→ Take time to explore the grounds, including the formal walled garden, lily-covered lakes, follies, and miles of woodland—the perfect place for a picnic on a sunny afternoon. Or you can try the scones in the castle's tea shop and watch the outside from within. ⊠ *Hailsham* ☎ *01323/834481* ⊕ *www.herstmonceux-castle.com* ⚏ *Castle tours £2.50, grounds £5* ⊙ *Mid-Apr.–Oct., daily 10–6; Oct., daily 10–5; last admission 1 hr before closing.*

Where to Eat

£££–££££ ✕ **The Sundial.** This 17th-century brick farmhouse holds a popular French restaurant run by chef Vincent Rongier and his wife, Mary. The extensive, frequently changing menu lists imaginative choices: foie gras and truffles vie with smoked salmon from the Shetland Isles. The fixed-price options are a good value. ⊠ *Gardner St., Herstmonceux* ☎ *01323/832217* ▭ *DC, MC, V* ⊙ *Closed Mon. No dinner Sun.*

Wilmington

㉔ *9 mi southwest of Herstmonceux Castle, 7 mi west of Pevensey on A27.*

Wilmington has a famous landmark. High on the downs to the south of the village (signposted off A27), a 226-foot-tall white figure, known as the **Long Man of Wilmington,** is carved into the chalk; he has a staff in each hand. His age is a subject of great debate, but some researchers think he might have originated in Roman times.

☺ Designed for children, **Drusilla's Park** is a great small zoo, with gardens, a miniature railroad, an adventure playground, and animals, including lemurs, meerkats, crocodiles and penguins. The zoo is 1½ mi west of Wilmington in the Cuckmere Valley. Admission price varies by season and there are family rates. ⊠ *A27, Alfriston* ☎ *01323/874100* ⊕ *www.drusillas.co.uk* ⚏ *£10–£11.75* ⊙ *Apr.–Oct., daily 10–6; Nov.–Mar., daily 10–5; last admission 1 hr before closing.*

Where to Stay

£££ ⌂ **Crossways Hotel.** This whitewashed house with 2 acres of gardens is near the Long Man of Wilmington, under the hills of the South Downs by the river Cuckmere. The interior is decorated in warm, upbeat colors that contrast with the antiques the owners have collected. Convenient for walking, the hotel is also only a 15-minute drive from Glyndebourne. ⊠ *Lewes Rd., BN26 5SG* ☏ *01323/482455* 🖷 *01273/487811* ⊕ *www. crosswayshotel.co.uk* ➫ *7 rooms* ⚄ *No a/c* ⊟ *AE, MC, V* ⧖ *BP.*

Lewes

★ ㉕ *10 mi northwest of Wilmington, 8 mi northeast of Brighton, 54 mi south of London.*

The town nearest to the celebrated Glyndebourne Opera House, Lewes is so rich in architectural history that the Council for British Archaeology has named it one of the 50 most important English towns. A walk is the best way to appreciate its appealing jumble of building styles and materials—flint, stone, brick, tile—and the secret lanes (called "twittens") behind the castle, with their huge beeches. Here and there are smart antiques shops and secondhand-book dealers. Most of the buildings in the center date to the 18th and 19th centuries.

Something about this town has always attracted rebels. It was once the home of Thomas Paine (1737–1809), whose pamphlet *Common Sense* advocated that the American colonies break with Britain, and was also favored by Virginia Woolf and the Bloomsbury Group, the early-20th-century group of countercultural artistic innovators.

Today Lewes' beauty and proximity to London mean that the counter-culture crew can't really afford to live here anymore, but its rebel soul still peeks through from time to time, particularly on Guy Fawkes Night (November 5), the anniversary of Fawkes's attempt to blow up the Houses of Parliament in 1605. The celebration is known countrywide for its massive bonfires and drunken enthusiasm. Flaming tar barrels are rolled down High Street and into the River Ouse; costumed processions fill the streets. Guy Fawkes Night here is enthusiastically anti-Catholic (Fawkes was a Catholic fanatic), if tongue-in-cheek. Although the Pope is burned in effigy, he is not alone; figures from popular culture and politics are also burned, in the spirit of (dark-humored) fun.

High above the valley of the River Ouse stand the majestic ruins of **Lewes Castle**, begun in 1100. For a panoramic view of the surrounding region, climb the keep. The **Barbican House Museum** inside the castle includes a sound-and-light show and the Town Model, a re-creation of Lewes in the 19th century. ⊠ *169 High St.* ☏ *01273/486290* ⊕ *www.sussexpast. co.uk* ✉ *£4.60, £6 includes Anne of Cleves House* ☉ *Tues.–Sat. 10–5:30 or dusk; Sun., Mon., and holidays 11–5:30 or dusk; last admission 30 mins before closing; closed Mon. in Jan.*

The 16th-century **Anne of Cleves House,** a fragile, timber-frame building, holds a notable collection of Sussex ironwork and other items of local interest, such as Sussex pottery. A famous painting of the local Guy Fawkes procession is also here. The house was part of Anne of Cleves's divorce settlement from Henry VIII, but she did not live in it. To get to the house, walk down steep, cobbled Keere Street, past lovely Grange Gardens, to Southover High Street. ⊠ *52 Southover High St.* ☏ *01273/ 474610* ⊕ *www.sussexpast.co.uk* ✉ *£3.10, £6 includes Lewes Castle*

2

⊙ *Mar.–Oct., Tues.–Sat. 10–5, Sun., Mon., and holidays 11–5; Nov.–Feb., Tues.–Sat. 10–5; last admission at 4.*

Of interest to Bloomsbury fans, **Monk's House** was the home of novelist Virginia Woolf and her husband, Leonard Woolf, who purchased it in 1919. Leonard lived here until his death in 1969. Rooms in the small cottage include Virginia's study and her bedroom. Artists Vanessa Bell (Virginia's sister) and Duncan Grant helped decorate the house. ✉ *C7, off A27, 3 mi south of Lewes, Rodmell* ☎ *01892/890651* ⊕ *www. nationaltrust.org.uk* 🎟 *£2.90* ⊙ *Apr.–Oct., Wed. and Sat. 2–5:30.*

Art and life mixed at **Charleston,** the farmhouse Vanessa Bell bought in 1916 and decorated with Duncan Grant (who resided here until 1978), fancifully painting the walls, doors, and furniture. The house became a refuge for writers and artists of the Bloomsbury Group and displays ceramics and textiles of the Omega Workshop—in which Bell and Grant participated—and paintings by Picasso and Renoir as well as by Bell and Grant. ✉ *Off A27, 7 mi east of Lewes, Firle* ☎ *01323/811265* ⊕ *www. charleston.org.uk* 🎟 *£6.50, gardens only £2.50* ⊙ *Mar.–June, Sept., and Oct., Wed. and Sat. 11:30–6, Thurs., Fri., Sun., and national holidays 2–6; July and Aug., Wed.–Sat. 11:30–6, Sun. and national holidays 2–6; last admission at 5.*

Where to Stay & Eat

£££££ ✗ **Circa.** Fascinatingly different food without pretentiousness is the attraction at this ambitious restaurant. Global-fusion dishes such as six-mushroom tortellini with yam crunch and seared blue-fin tuna with yuzu (a Japanese citrus fruit) dressing are presented by helpful staff in modern surroundings. The marginally simpler lunch menu is a good value at £13 for two courses. ✉ *145 High St.* ☎ *01273/471777* 🖃 *MC, V* ⊙ *Closed Sun. and Mon.*

££££–£££££ ✗🖼 **Horsted Place.** This luxurious manor-house hotel sits on 1,100 acres, a few minutes' drive from Glyndebourne. Built as a private home in 1850 with Gothic-revival elements by Augustus-Charles Pugin, it was owned by a friend of the Queen's until the 1980s, and Elizabeth was a regular visitor. Today it is richly furnished in country-house style and has a magnificent Victorian staircase and a Gothic library with a secret door that leads to a courtyard. The dining room (*£££–££££*), also Gothic, prepares such elegant fare as roasted quail cutlet. ✉ *Little Horsted TN22 5TS, 2½ mi south of Uckfield, 6 mi north of Lewes* ☎ *01825/750581* 🖶 *01825/750459* ⊕ *www.horstedplace.co.uk* ↘ *15 rooms, 5 suites* 🕭 *Restaurant, cable TV with movies, golf privileges, tennis court, croquet, library, business services, meeting rooms; no a/c* 🖃 *AE, DC, MC, V* ⦿ *BP.*

£££££ 🖼 **Shelleys.** A 17th-century building, this hotel on the hilly main road is a traditional overnight stop for Glyndebourne operagoers. Public rooms are on the grand scale, lavishly furnished with antiques, and the garden is a joy. The hotel is known for its old-fashioned but friendly service. ✉ *High St., BN7 1XS* ☎ *01273/472361* 🖶 *01273/483152* ⊕ *www.shelleys-hotel.com* ↘ *19 rooms* 🕭 *Restaurant, bar, meeting rooms, some pets allowed; no a/c* 🖃 *AE, DC, MC, V* ⦿ *BP.*

££ ⊡ **Berkeley House.** In a smart town house in one of Lewes's Georgian terraces, Berkeley House is a small, welcoming B&B. Rooms are spacious and homey, if somewhat beige, and full English breakfasts are made using free-range eggs from a local farmer. ⊠ *2 Albion St., BN7 2ND* ☎ *01273/476057* 🖷 *01273/479575* ⊕ *www.berkeleyhousehotel.co. uk* ⟋⟍*3 rooms* ⚘ *No a/c* ☰ *AE, DC, MC, V* ⊌ *BP.*

Nightlife & the Arts

NIGHTLIFE Lewes has a relatively young population and a nightlife scene to match; there are also many lovely old pubs. It's the home of the excellent Harveys Brewery, and most local pubs serve its concoctions. Try the **Brewers' Arms** (⊠ 91 High St. ☎ 01273/475524), a good pub with a friendly crowd. **The King's Head** (⊠ 9 Southover High St. ☎ 01273/474628), a traditional pub, has a good menu with game and fish dishes.

THE ARTS **Glyndebourne Opera House** (⊠ Glyndebourne, near Lewes ☎ 01273/ 813813 ⊕ www.glyndebourne.com) is one of the world's leading opera venues. Nestled beneath the downs, Glyndebourne combines first-class productions, a state-of-the-art auditorium, and a beautiful setting. Seats are *very* expensive (£25–£140) and often difficult to acquire, but they're worth every penny to aficionados, some of whom wear evening dress and bring a hamper for a picnic in the gardens. The main season runs from mid–May to the end of August. The Glyndebourne Touring Company performs here in October, when seats are cheaper and slightly easier to obtain.

Shopping

Antiques shops offer temptation along the busy High Street. Lewes also has plenty of tiny boutiques and independent clothing stores vying for your pounds. **Adamczewski** (⊠ 88 High St. ☎ 01273/470105) is a marvelous throwback to the days when everything was made by hand. Its homemade soaps, scents, and even hand-hewn brooms are works of art. **Cliffe Antiques Centre** (⊠ 47 Cliffe High St. ☎ 01273/473266) is a great place for one-stop antiques shopping, with a fine mix of vintage English prints, estate jewelry, and art at reasonable prices. Classic bone china and antique glass are the center of attention at **Loius Potts & Co.** (⊠ 43 Cliffe High St. ☎ 01273/472240).

BRIGHTON TO EAST GRINSTEAD

The self-proclaimed belle of the coast, Brighton is an upbeat, funky, old-new sprawl. It started in the 16th century as a tiny fishing village called Brighthelmstone, with a thriving herring fleet, but had no claim to fame until a certain Dr. Russell sent his patients there for its dry, bracing, crystal-clear air in the late 18th century. Today the city is colorful, a bit hippyish, young, and endlessly entertaining—a mix of pop culture and carnival. It has been dubbed "London-by-Sea" because so many Londoners have moved here since the 1990s, bringing with them upscale restaurants, big nightclubs, bookshops, expensive boutiques, and loud bars. Their presence gives the city character: there's much more to this place than its sights and the sea.

Outside of town, the soft green downs of Sussex and Surrey hold stately homes you can visit, including Arundel Castle, Petworth House, and Polesden Lacey. Along the way, you'll discover the largest Roman villa in Britain, the bustling city of Guildford, and Chichester, whose cathedral is a poem in stone.

Brighton

9 mi southwest of Lewes, 54 mi south of London.

For more than 200 years, Brighton has been England's most interesting seaside city, and today it is more vibrant, eccentric, and cosmopolitan than ever. A rich cultural mix—Regency architecture, specialty shops, sidewalk cafés, lively arts, and a flourishing gay scene—make it unique and always unpredictable.

It could be said that Brighton owes its fame and fortune to seawater. In 1750 physician Richard Russell published a book recommending seawater treatment for glandular diseases. The fashionable world flocked to Brighton to take Dr. Russell's "cure," and sea bathing became a popular pastime. Few places in the south of England were better for it, since Brighton's broad beach of smooth pebbles stretches as far as the eye can see. It has been popular with sunbathers ever since. The next windfall for the town was the arrival of the Prince of Wales (later George IV). "Prinny," as he was called, created the Royal Pavilion, a mock-Asian pleasure palace that attracted London society. The visitors triggered a wave of villa-building. Today the elegant terraces of Regency houses are today among the town's greatest attractions. The coming of the railroad set the seal on Brighton's popularity: the luxurious *Brighton Belle* brought Londoners to the coast within an hour.

Londoners are still and flocking to Brighton in ever-growing numbers. Combined with the local university students, the effect is to make this a trendy, young, laid-back city that does, occasionally, burst at its own seams. Property values have skyrocketed in recent years, but all visitors are likely to notice is the good shopping, excellent restaurants, attractive beach, and wild nightlife. Brighton is also carving out a name for itself as the place to go if you're looking for hotels with leopard-print fabrics, party nights, and strange designs.

One sad note: the city's West Pier, a delicate match to the main Pier in terms of popularity and beauty, decayed for decades as the city leaders squabbled over what could be done to fix it. In 2004 a rough storm damaged it beyond repair.

Main Attractions

Beach. The foundation of everything in Brighton is its broad beach, which spreads smoothly from one end of town to the other. In the summer sunbathers, swimmers, and hawkers selling ice cream and toys pack the shore; in the winter people stroll at the water's stormy edge, walking their dogs and searching for seashells. It's a stone beach—covered in a thick blanket of large, smooth pebbles. ■ TIP→ **If you plan on swimming, bring a pair of rubber swimming shoes, as the stones are hard on bare feet.**

Brighton Museum and Art Gallery . . .**29**

Brighton Pier **26**

The Lanes **30**

Royal Pavilion **28**

Sea Life Centre **31**

The Steine . . .**27**

Volk's Electric Railway **32**

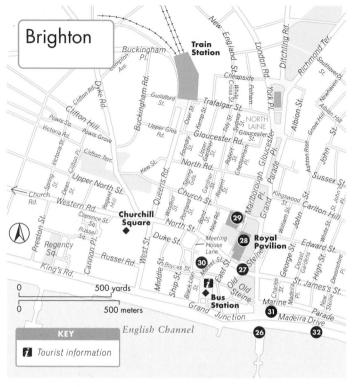

29 Brighton Museum and Art Gallery. The grounds of the Royal Pavilion contain this museum, whose buildings were designed as a stable block for the prince regent's horses. The museum includes especially interesting art nouveau and art deco collections. Look out for Salvador Dalí's famous sofa in the shape of Mae West's lips, and pause at the Balcony Café for its bird's-eye view over the 20th-century Art and Design Gallery. ✉ *Church St.* ☎ *01273/290900* ⊕ *www.brighton.virtualmuseum.info* ▣ *Free* ⊘ *Tues. 10–7, Wed.–Sat. 10–5, Sun. 2–5.*

★ **26 Brighton Pier.** Opened in 1899, the pier is an amusement park set above the sea. In the early 20th century it had a music hall and entertainment; today it has carnival rides and game arcades, along with clairvoyants, henna tattoo artists, and greasy food stalls. In the summer, it is always packed with children, by day, and teenagers, by night. ☎ *01273/609361* ⊕ *www.brightonpier.co.uk* ⊘ *Mid-Sept.–June, daily 10 AM–midnight; July–mid-Sept., daily 9 AM–2 AM.*

30 The Lanes. This maze of alleys and passageways was once the home of fishermen and their families. Closed to vehicular traffic, the area's cobbled streets are filled with interesting restaurants, boutiques, and antiques shops. Fish and seafood restaurants line the heart of the Lanes, at Market Street and Market Square. ⊠ *Bordered by West, North, East, and Prince Albert Sts.*

NEED A BREAK? On the street adjacent to the bus stop, and less than a five-minute walk from the Royal Pavilion, the **Mock Turtle** (⊠ 4 Pool Valley ☎ 01273/328380) is a great old-fashioned, homey café. Alongside a decent selection of teas and coffees are four types of rarebit, homemade soup, and scones. It's closed Monday.

★ ❷❽ **Royal Pavilion.** The most remarkable building on the Steine is this domed and pinnacled fantasy. Planned as a simple seaside villa and built in the fashionable classical style of 1787 by architect Henry Holland, the Pavilion was rebuilt between 1815 and 1822 by John Nash for the prince regent (later George IV), who wanted an exotic, Eastern design with opulent Chinese interiors. Today period furniture and ornaments, some given or lent by the current Royal Family, fill the interior. The two great set pieces are the **Music Room,** styled in the form of a Chinese pavilion, and the **Banqueting Room,** with its enormous flying-dragon "gasolier," or gaslight

> **WE DO NOT APPROVE**
>
> When Queen Victoria came to the throne in 1837, she so disapproved of the Royal Pavilion that she stripped it of its furniture and planned to demolish it. Fortunately, the local council bought it from her, and today the palace looks much as it did in its Regency heyday.

chandelier, a revolutionary invention in the early 19th century. In the kitchens, palm-tree columns support the ceilings. The upstairs bedrooms contain a selection of cruel caricatures of the prince regent, most produced during his lifetime. The gardens, too, have been restored to Regency splendor, following John Nash's naturalistic design of 1826. ■ TIP➔ For an elegant time-out, retire to one of the Pavilion's bedrooms, where a tearoom serves snacks and light meals. ⊠ *Old Steine* ☎ *01273/290900* ⊕ *www.royalpavilion.org.uk* ☒ *£7.50* ☉ *Oct.–Mar., daily 10–5:15; Apr.–Sept., daily 9:30–5:45; last admission 45 mins before closing.*

❷❼ **Steine.** One of the centers of Brighton's action is the Steine (pronounced steen), a large open area close to the seafront. This was a river mouth until the Prince of Wales had it drained in 1793.

Also Worth Seeing

⏱ ❸❶ **Sea Life Centre.** Near Brighton Pier, this aquarium has a large number of sea-dwelling creatures—from sharks to sea horses—in more than 30 marine habitats. It also has a giant-turtle convalescence center. Allow two hours to see it. ⊠ *Marine Parade* ☎ *01273/604234* ⊕ *www. sealifeeurope.com* ☒ *£9.50* ☉ *Apr.–Oct., daily 10–5; Nov.–Mar., daily 10–4.*

⏱ ❸❷ **Volk's Electric Railway.** Built by inventor Magnus Volk in 1883, this was the first public electric railroad in Britain. In summer you can take the 1¼-mi trip along Marine Parade. ⊠ *Marine Parade* ☎ *01273/292718* ☒ *£1.40 one-way, £2.40 round-trip* ☉ *Late-Mar.–Sept., weekdays 10:30–5, weekends 10:30–6.*

All Hail the Regent

THE TERM "REGENCY" comes from the last 10 years of the reign of George III (1811–20), who was deemed unfit to rule because of his mental problems. Real power was officially given to the prince of Wales, also known as the prince regent, who became King George IV and ruled until his death in 1830. Throughout his regency, George spent grand sums indulging his flamboyant tastes in architecture and interior decorating—while failing in affairs of state. The distinctive architecture of the Royal Pavilion is a prime, if extreme, example of the Regency style, popularized by architect John Nash (1752–1835) in the early part of the 19th century. The style is characterized by a diversity of influences—French, Greek, Italian, Persian, Japanese, Chinese, Roman, Indian—you name it. Nash was George IV's favorite architect, beloved for his interest in Indian and Asian designs and for his neoclassical designs, as evidenced in his plans for Regent's Park and its terraces in London.

Where to Stay & Eat

££££–£££££   ✕ **One Paston Place.** One of Brighton's best restaurants, this elegant but unstuffy place offers fine French food in a small but uncrowded room, elegantly decorated with cream linens and gilded mirrors. The fixed-price lunch (£16–£19) is the best bargain, although dinner is more leisurely. Main courses of locally raised lamb and freshly caught seafood come with creative but unfussy sauces. Dining here is an event, so jacket and tie are recommended. ✉ *1 Paston Pl.* ☎ *01273/606933* ▭ *AE, MC, V* ☾ *Closed Sun. and Mon.*

£££–££££   ▣ **Nounou.** Inspired by contemporary Moroccan and French cuisine, this polished, romantic restaurant has made headlines in Brighton for its delightful, unique fare. Dishes combines the best French techniques with Moroccan specialties such as tagine of lamb with *merquez* (a spicy lamb sausage) sausage and couscous. Grilled scallops on lemongrass risotto make a great starter. ✉ *St. George's Rd.* ☎ *01273/682200* ▭ *AE, MC, V* ☾ *Closed Sun. and Mon.*

£££–££££   ✕ **Seven Dials.** A former bank houses a restaurant that's both striking and surprisingly laid-back. Sophisticated modern English cuisine rules the menu, with choices such as roasted rump of lamb given a new look when served with eggplant caviar and an olive and rosemary sauce. It's worth blowing your diet for the desserts. Business groups and couples gravitate to this place. ✉ *1 Buckingham Pl.* ☎ *01273/885555* ⬧ *Reservations essential* ▭ *AE, MC, V.*

££–£££   ✕ **Brighton Rock Beach House.** Come here for a tongue-in-cheek take on a classic New England–beach bar that could have been lifted whole off Cape Cod and dropped in central Brighton. The menu is just as American, with Maine crab cakes, New England clam chowder, and irresistible lobster cheesecake. The mood is pure beach: some tables are outside, surrounded by driftwood (although this is Brighton, so there's no sand). Cool jazz plays as you eat. ✉ *6 Rock Pl.* ☎ *01273/601139* ▭ *MC, V.*

£–£££   ✕ **Nia Café.** In the funky North Laine area, Nia has views down Trafalgar Street from its pavement tables. Besides good coffees and leaf teas, excellent café food is available all day, from simple (but freshly made) sandwiches to fillets of cod stuffed with wild mushrooms served with a lemony spinach salad. The decor is basic, but large windows and fresh flowers make it friendly. Nia is also near the station, which is handy if you have time to kill before a train or you need to reenergize before sightseeing. ☒ 87–88 *Trafalgar St.* ☎ *01273/671371* ▤ *MC, V.*

££   ✕ **Terre à Terre.** This inspiring vegetarian restaurant is popular, so come early for a light lunch or a more sophisticated evening meal. The Jerusalem artichoke soufflé, cranberry-olive couscous, and an eclectic choice of salads should satisfy most palates. ☒ *71 East St.* ☎ *01273/ 729051* ▤ *AE, DC, MC, V* ☉ *No lunch Mon.; closed Mon. and no lunch Tues. and Wed. in winter.*

££££–£££££   ✕▣ **Blanch House.** A theatrical experience as much as a night's rest, this boutique hotel sets itself apart with eclectic, clever theme rooms, including a '70s-style Boogie Nights room (with animal print wallpaper) and elaborate Moroccan and Renaissance rooms. Beds are queen- and king-size, and bathrooms are stylish. The hip cocktail bar (the owner is a former manager of London's Groucho Club) and sleek modern restaurant complete the picture. The restaurant's (£££££) set-price lunches are a good value, and its contemporary international menu lists dishes such as seared pancetta-wrapped scallops and grilled rabbit in a creamy leek vinaigrette. ☒ *17 Atlingworth St., BN2 1PL* ☎ *01273/603504* ▤ *01273/ 689813* ⊕ *www.blanchhouse.co.uk* ⇨ *9 rooms, 3 suites* ⚘ *Restaurant, in-room data ports, massage, bar, meeting rooms; no a/c* ▤ *MC, V* �🍽 *BP.*

££££–£££££   ✕▣ **Drakes.** It's easy to miss the low-key sign for this elegant, modern hotel, tucked away amid the frilly houses on Marine Parade on the seafront. Inside, everything is cool, calm, and sleekly designed. The lobby is dark and sophisticated, and each guest room has its own style, with handmade wallpaper, firm beds covered in luxurious linens, well-designed bathrooms, and art everywhere. Some "feature" rooms have quirky touches, including claw-foot tubs in front of the bedroom windows. Gingerman, the hotel restaurant, has a huge local following for its modern British cuisine (£27 and £32 for two or three courses). ☒ *43–44 Marine Parade* ☎ *01273/696934* ⊕ *www.drakesofbrighton. com* ⇨ *20 rooms* ⚘ *Restaurant, cable TV with movies, in-room data ports, lounge, bar, business services* ▤ *AE, DC, MC, V.*

££££   ✕▣ **Hotel du Vin.** At this outpost of a stylish minichain near the seafront, rooms are crisply modern, with pampering touches such as Egyptian linens and large "monsoon" showers. The bistro restaurant (£££–££££) offers classic fare that makes use of local seafood, and the extensive wine list includes many good values. The wine bar will satisfy connoisseurs (special events take place throughout the year), and you can have a cigar from the cigar gallery before you play billiards. ☒ *Ship St., BN1 1AD*

☎ 01273/718588 ⊟ 01273/718599 ⊕ *www.hotelduvin.com* 🗢 *34 rooms, 3 suites* ⚘ *Restaurant, billiards, wine bar, meeting rooms; no a/c* ⊟ *AE, DC, MC, V.*

★ **£££££** 🖻 **Grand Hotel.** The city's most famous hotel and a Brighton landmark, the Grand sits on the seafront, a huge, creamy Victorian wedding cake of a building dating from 1864. It's both imposing and elegant, with high-ceiling public rooms richly decorated with enormous chandeliers and plenty of marble. The spacious bedrooms are traditional in style, with luxurious drapes and large bathrooms. It's famous in Britain for having survived an IRA bombing attack in 1984 that targeted Prime Minister Margaret Thatcher and killed five people, although Thatcher survived unscathed. Having tea at the Grand is a Brighton tradition, and highly recommended. ✉ *King's Rd., BN1 2FW* ☎ *01273/224300* ⊟ *01273/224321* ⊕ *www.grandbrighton.co.uk* 🗢 *200 rooms, 3 suites* ⚘ *Restaurant, minibars, cable TV with movies, in-room data ports, indoor pool, gym, massage, sauna, steam room, lounge, nightclub, business services, meeting rooms, some pets allowed (fee); no a/c in some rooms* ⊟ *AE, DC, MC, V* �†◎† *BP.*

££££–£££££ 🖻 **Nineteen.** A calm oasis of white, this guesthouse is filled with contemporary art and chic designer accessories. Beds are supported on platforms of glass bricks that filter an ocean-blue light. Massages, yoga sessions, and manicures are pampering amenities. There's a basement kitchen with snacks for guests. ✉ *19 Broad St., BN2 1TJ* ☎ *01273/675529* ⊟ *01273/675531* ⊕ *www.hotelnineteen.co.uk* 🗢 *8 rooms* ⚘ *In-room VCRs, massage, some pets allowed; no a/c, no kids, no smoking* ⊟ *MC, V* �†◎† *BP.*

£££–££££ 🖻 **Pelirocco.** Here the imaginations of designers have been given free rein, and the result is a vicarious romp through pop art and rock and roll. Rooms have themes: there's the leopard-print pin-up parlor (Betty's Boudoir), a boxing ring (Ali's Room), and the futuristic Bubble Suite with a plunge bath and mirrored ceiling. It's all way over the top, so you'll either love this place or hate it. ✉ *10 Regency Sq., BN1 2FG* ☎ *01273/327055* ⊟ *01273/733845* ⊕ *www.hotelpelirocco.co.uk* 🗢 *18 rooms, 1 suite* ⚘ *Room TVs with video games, in-room broadband, in-room data ports, bar, no-smoking rooms; no a/c, no kids under 12 on weekends* ⊟ *AE, MC, V* �†◎† *BP.*

££–££££ 🖻 **Brighton Wave.** This sleekly designed hotel is all about relaxation. Beds are big and covered in soft, white linens; rooms are painted in restful pale shades of blue and white; and breakfast is served in bed. The look is minimal without being cold, and service hits just the right note of friendliness and helpfulness. ✉ *10 Madeira Pl., BN2 1TN* ☎ *01273/676794* ⊕ *www.brightonwave.com* 🗢 *8 rooms* ⚘ *Cable TV, in-room DVD, Wi-Fi* ⊟ *AE, DC, MC, V* �†◎† *BP.*

££–£££ 🖻 **Granville Hotel.** Three grand Victorian buildings facing the sea make up this hotel. Guest rooms, heavily decorated with a theme (themed rooms are a Brighton fad), include the pink-and-white Brighton Rock and the art deco Noel Coward rooms. Dadu, the hotel's restaurant, is worth a stop. ✉ *124 King's Rd., BN1 2FY* ☎ *01273/326302* ⊟ *01273/728294* ⊕ *www.granvillehotel.co.uk* 🗢 *24 rooms* ⚘ *Restaurant, coffee shop, some in-room hot tubs, in-room broadband, bar, meeting rooms, some pets allowed; no a/c, no smoking* ⊟ *AE, DC, MC, V* �†◎† *BP.*

££ ⊞ **The Dove.** Washes of light and an uncluttered look are the keynotes of this immaculate Regency house. Rooms at the front have enormous bay-window views across the square, and you can see the sea from the narrow balconies. There's no elevator, and the stairs to the attic rooms are steep. Breakfast includes vegetarian options. ⊠ *18 Regency Sq., BN1 2FG* ☎ *01273/779222* 🖷 *01273/746912* ⊕ *www.thedovehotel.co.uk* 🛏 *9 rooms* ⌂ *Dining room; no a/c* ⊟ *AE, DC, MC, V* ⏐⏐ *BP.*

Nightlife & the Arts

NIGHTLIFE Brighton is a techno hub, largely because so many DJs have moved here from London. Clubs and bars present live music most nights, and on weekends the entire town can be a bit too raucous for some tastes. This is not a quiet seaside town; it's a seafront city. Try the popular **Above Audio** (⊠ 10 Marine Parade ☎01273/606906) in an art deco building east of Brighton Pier. Specialty nights at the **Funky Buddha Lounge** (⊠ 169 Kings Rd., Arches ☎ 01273/725541) are at the forefront of Brighton's underground, with funk and acid disco blasting out to a fairly sophisticated crowd. Small, friendly, and unfailingly funky, the **Jazz Place** (⊠ 10 Ship St. ☎ 01273/328439) can get a little cramped but makes up for it with cool, jazzy attitude. **The Zap Club** (⊠ 189–192 King's Rd., Arches ☎01273/202407), under the arches right on the beach, is Brighton's most well-established club, but no longer as trendy as it once was.

THE ARTS The three-week-long **Brighton Festival** (☎ 01273/706771 ⊕ www. ★ brighton-festival.org.uk), one of England's biggest and liveliest arts festivals, takes place every May in venues around town. The more than 600 events include drama, music, dance, and visual arts.

The **Brighton Dome** (⊠ New Rd. ☎01273/709709), just west of the Royal Pavilion, was converted from the prince regent's stables in the 1930s. It includes a theater and a concert hall that stage pantomime (a British theatrical entertainment with songs and dance) and classical and pop concerts. The **Gardner Arts Centre** (⊠ Off A27, Falmer ☎01273/685861), on the University of Sussex campus a few miles northeast of town, presents plays, concerts, and cabaret. The **Theatre Royal** (⊠ New Rd. ☎ 01273/328488), close to the Royal Pavilion, has a gem of an auditorium that is a favorite venue for shows on their way to or fresh from London's West End.

The **Cinematheque** (⊠ 9–12 Middle St. ☎ 01273/384300 ⊕ www. cinematheque.org) screens sub-art-house oddities, obscurities and rarities. The elegant 1910 **Duke of York's Picture House** (⊠ Preston Circus ☎01273/626261), a 10-minute walk north of the main train station, is one city option for art-house movies.

Shopping

The main shopping area to head for is **the Lanes,** especially for antiques or jewelry. It also has clothing boutiques, coffee shops, and pubs. Across North Street from the Lanes lies the **North Laine,** a network of narrow streets full of little stores, less glossy than those in the Lanes, but fun, funky, and exotic.

Colin Page (⊠ 36 Duke St. ☎ 01273/325954), at the western edge of the Lanes, stocks a wealth of antiquarian and secondhand books at all prices. The **Pavilion Shop** (✉ 4–5 Pavilion Bldgs. ☎ 01273/292798), next door to the Royal Pavilion, carries well-designed toys, trinkets, books and cards—all with a loose Regency theme—and high-quality fabrics, wallpapers, and ceramics based on material in the Pavilion itself. **Oliviers and Co.** (✉ 23A East St. ☎ 01273/739840) sells beautiful, if expensive, tapenades, flavored oils, soaps, candles and pots—all with an olive content or theme. The old-fashioned **Pecksniff's Bespoke Perfumery** (✉ 45–46 Meeting House La. ☎ 01273/723292) mixes and matches ingredients to suit your wishes. **Simultane** (✉ 52 Ship St. ☎ 01273/777535), a boutique near the waterfront, displays women's fashions from its own label—contemporary looks inspired by the styles of the 1940s and '50s—and clothing from other designers. **Souk Trading** (✉ 4 Little East St. ☎ 01273/776477) supplies an authentic taste of Marrakech for reasonable prices; check out superb lamps, candlesticks, pots, and mirrors.

Arundel

㉝ *23 mi west of Brighton, 60 mi south of London.*

The little hilltop town of Arundel is dominated by its great castle, the much-restored home of the dukes of Norfolk for more than 700 years, and an imposing neo-Gothic Roman Catholic cathedral—the duke is Britain's leading Catholic peer. The town itself is full of interesting old buildings and well worth a stroll.

Begun in the 11th century, vast **Arundel Castle** remains rich with the history of the Fitzalan and Howard families and with paintings by Van Dyck, Gainsborough, and Reynolds. It suffered destruction during the Civil War and was remodeled during the 18th century and the Victorian era. The keep, rising from its conical mound, is as old as the original castle, whereas the barbican and the Barons' Hall date from the 13th century. The castle interior was reconstructed in the fashionable Gothic style of the 19th century. Among the treasures are the rosary beads and prayer book used by Mary, Queen of Scots, in preparing for her execution. The castle's ceremonial entrance is at the top of High Street, but you enter at the bottom, close to the parking lot. ✉ *Mill Rd.* ☎ *01903/882173* ⊕ *www.arundelcastle.org* ✑ *£12, grounds only £6.50* ☉ *Apr.–Oct., Sun.–Fri. noon–5 (grounds open 1 hr earlier); last admission at 4.*

Where to Stay & Eat

£–££ ✗ **Black Rabbit.** This renovated 18th-century pub is a find, and you must persevere along Mill Road to find it. Its location by the River Arun, with views of the castle and a bird sanctuary, makes it ideal for a summer lunch. There's a good selection of real ales and an all-day restaurant. ✉ *Mill Rd., Offham* ☎ *01903/882828* ▤ *DC, MC, V.*

★

££££–£££££ ▦ **Amberley Castle.** The lowering of the portcullis every night at midnight is a sure sign that you're in a genuine medieval castle, one that celebrated its 900th birthday in 2003. Across the dry moat, present-day luxury dominates. Antiques and rich drapery furnish the individually designed bedrooms, and many have lattice windows, beamed ceilings, and curtained four-posters. You can dine in either the Queens restaurant, beneath a 12th-century barrel-vaulted ceiling, or amid suits of armor in the Great Room. ✉ *5 mi north of Arundel, off B2139, Amberley BN18 9LT* ☎ *01798/*

831992 📠 *01798/831998* ⊕ *www.amberleycastle.co.uk* 🛏 *20 rooms* ⚘ *Restaurant, in-room hot tubs, in-room VCRs, putting green, tennis court, bar, meeting rooms; no a/c, no kids under 12* ▤ *AE, DC, MC, V* ◑ *CP.*

£££–££££ 🏨 **Norfolk Arms Hotel.** Like the cathedral and the castle in Arundel, this 18th-century coaching inn on the main street was built by one of the dukes of Norfolk. Some rooms are small (the hotel dubs them "cozy"), but those in an annex in the courtyard block hold bigger, modern rooms. Many are decorated in a frilly style. ✉ *22 High St., BN18 9AD* ☎ *01903/ 882101* 📠 *01903/884275* ⊕ *www.norfolkarmshotel.com* 🛏 *34 rooms* ⚘ *Restaurant, 2 bars, business services, meeting rooms, some pets allowed (fee); no a/c* ▤ *AE, DC, MC, V* ◑ *BP.*

Nightlife & the Arts

The **Arundel Festival** (☎ 01903/883690 ⊕ www.arundelfestival.co.uk) presents drama productions and classical and pop concerts in and around the castle grounds for 10 days in August or September.

Chichester

34 *10 mi west of Arundel, 66 mi southwest of London.*

The Romans founded Chichester, the capital city of West Sussex, on the low-lying plains between the wooded South Downs and the sea. The city walls and major streets follow the original Roman plan. This cathedral town, a good base for exploring the area, is a well-respected theatrical hub, with a reputation for attracting good acting talent during its summer repertory season.

Norman **Chichester Cathedral,** near the corner of West and South streets, stands on Roman foundations and includes sections from later periods, such as a freestanding bell tower from the 15th century. Inside, a glass panel reveals Roman mosaics uncovered during restoration. Other treasures are the wonderful Saxon limestone reliefs of the raising of Lazarus and Christ arriving in Bethany, both in the choir area. Among the outstanding contemporary artworks are a stained-glass window by Marc Chagall, a colorful tapestry by John Piper, and a painting by Graham Sutherland. ✉ *West St.* ☎ *01243/782595* ⊕ *www.chichestercathedral. org.uk* 💷 *£3 suggested donation* ☉ *Easter–Sept., daily 7:15–7; Oct.–Easter, daily 7:15–6. Tours Mon.–Sat. at 11:15 and 2:30.*

Chichester's architecture is mainly Georgian, and its 18th-century stone houses give it a wonderful period appearance. One of the best is **Pallant House,** built in 1712 as a wine merchant's mansion. At that time, its state-of-the-art design showed the latest in complicated brickwork and superb wood carving. Appropriate antiques and porcelains furnish the faithfully restored rooms. The **Pallant House Gallery,** attached to the house, showcases a small but important collection of mainly modern British art. Admission includes entry to the **Hans Fiebusch Studio,** nearby in St. Martin's Square, with an exact re-creation of the St. John's Wood (London) studio of this exiled German artist (1898–1998) who was the last member of the so-called degenerate art group. ✉ *9 N. Pallant* ☎ *01243/774557* ⊕ *www.pallant.org.uk* 💷 *£4* ☉ *Tues.–Sat. 10–5, Sun. and national holidays 12:30–5.*

In 1960, workers digging a water-main ditch uncovered a Roman wall; so began nine years of archaeological excavation of the **Fishbourne Roman Palace,** the remains of the largest, grandest Roman villa in Britain. Intricate mosaics (including Cupid riding a dolphin) and painted walls lavishly decorate what is left of many of the 100 rooms of the palace, built in the 1st century AD, possibly for local chieftain Tiberius Claudius Togidubnus. It's a glimpse of high living, Roman-leader style. You can explore the sophisticated bathing and heating systems, and the only example of a Roman garden in northern Europe. A good on-site museum displays artifacts from the site and puts the building into historical perspective. The palace is ½ mi west of Chichester. ⊠ *Salthill Rd., Fishbourne* ☎ *01243/785859* ⊕ *www.sussexpast.co.uk* ✎ *£5.20* ⊗ *Mar.–July, Sept., and Oct., daily 10–5; Aug., daily 10–6; Nov.–mid-Dec. and Feb., daily 10–4; mid-Dec.–Jan., weekends 10–4.*

★ Twenty acres of woodland provide a backdrop for **Sculpture at Goodwood,** a collection of contemporary British sculpture specially commissioned by the Hat Hill Sculpture Foundation. A third of the approximately 40 exhibits change annually, and walks through green fields connect the pieces, sited to maximize their effect. The park is 3 mi north of Chichester, signposted on the right off A286. ⊠ *Hat Hill Copse, Goodwood* ☎ *01243/538449* ⊕ *www.sculpture.org.uk* ✎ *£10* ⊗ *Easter–Oct., Tues.–Sun. and national holidays 10:30–5.*

It's worth a stop in Singleton, a secluded village 5 mi north of Chichester, to see the excellent **Weald and Downland Open Air Museum,** a sanctuary for historical buildings. Among the 45 structures moved to 50 acres of wooded meadows are a cluster of medieval houses, a working water mill, a Tudor market hall, and an ancient blacksmith's shop. ⊠ *A286* ☎ *01243/811363* ⊕ *www.wealddown.co.uk* ✎ *£8* ⊗ *Apr.–Oct., daily 10:30–6; Nov., Dec., mid-Feb.–Mar., daily 10:30–4; Jan.–mid-Feb., weekends and Wed. 10:30–4:30; last admission 1 hr before closing.*

Where to Stay & Eat

£££ ✕ **Comme Ça.** Its location, about a five-minute walk across the park from the Chichester Festival Theatre, makes this attractively converted pub a pleasant spot for a meal before a performance. Bunches of dried hops, suspended from the ceiling, and antique children's toys decorate the dining room. The owner, Michel Navet, is French, and his chef produces authentic French dishes. The fixed-price lunch menu offers two courses for £18 or three for £21. ⊠ *67 Broyle Rd.* ☎ *01243/788724* ▭ *AE, DC, MC, V* ⊗ *Closed Mon. No dinner Sun. No lunch Tues.*

£££ ⛉ **Ship Hotel.** Built in 1790, this architecturally interesting hotel near the Chichester Festival Theatre was originally the home of Admiral Sir George Murray, one of Admiral Nelson's right-hand men. Among the outstanding elements are the flying (partially freestanding) staircase and colonnade. The house has been carefully restored to its 18th-century elegance after spending time as a dental clinic and then an antiques shop, before World War II. Reproduction period furniture fills the pastel guest rooms, which are simpler than the public areas. Prices rise steeply during the Glorious Goodwood horse race in July. ⊠ *North St., PO19 1NH* ☎ *01243/778000* ⎙ *01243/788000* ⊕ *www.shiphotel.com* ⛬ *36* *rooms ☆ Restaurant, cable TV, bar, meeting rooms, some pets allowed; no a/c ☰ AE, DC, MC, V ⦿ BP.*

Nightlife & the Arts

The **Chichester Festival Theatre** (✉ Oaklands Park ☎ 01243/781312 ⊕ www.cft.org.uk) presents classics and modern plays from May through September and is a venue for touring companies the rest of the year. Built in 1962, it has an international reputation for innovative performances and attracts theatergoers from across the country, including London.

Petworth House

35 *13 mi northeast of Chichester, 12 mi northwest of Arundel, 54 mi south of London.*

Fodor'sChoice
★

One of the National Trust's greatest treasures, the imposing 17th-century home of Lord and Lady Egremont holds an outstanding collection of English paintings by Gainsborough, Reynolds, and Van Dyck, as well as 19 oil paintings by the great proponent of Romanticism J. M. W. Turner, who often visited Petworth and immortalized it in luminous drawings. A 13th-century chapel is all that remains of the original manor house. The celebrated landscape architect Capability Brown (1716–83) added a 700-acre deer park. Other highlights include Greek and Roman sculpture and Grinling Gibbons wood carvings, such as those in the spectacular Carved Room. Six

> ### A TEMPTING TOWN
>
> After you visit Petworth House, take time to explore the small town of Petworth, a jewel studded with narrow old streets and timbered houses. Temptation awaits, too: this is a center for fine antiques and collectibles, with many excellent shops.

rooms in the servants' quarters, among them the old kitchen, are open to the public, and the Servants Block serves light lunches. You can reach the house off A272 and A283 (parking lots are off the latter). Between 11 and 1 visits are by guided tour only. ✉ *Petworth* ☎ *01798/342207 ⊕ www.nationaltrust.org.uk 🎫 £8, gardens only £3 ⊙ House Apr.–late Oct., Sat.–Wed. 11–5; last admission at 4:30. Gardens late Mar.–late Oct., Sat.–Wed. 11–6; Nov.–mid-Dec., Wed.–Sat. 10–3:30. Park daily 8–dusk.*

Guildford

36 *22 mi north of Petworth House, 28 mi southwest of London, 35 mi north of Chichester.*

Guildford, the largest town in Surrey and the county's capital, is a busy commuter town with a noted theater, but it retains a faint 18th-century air. Gabled merchants' houses line the steep, pleasantly provincial High Street, filled with upscale fashion and household shops. The remains of its old Norman castle are tucked away in a peaceful garden off High Street, and the large clock on the town's old guildhall adds charm.

Displays in the **Guildford Museum,** in the old castle building, include interesting exhibits on local history and archaeology, as well as memorabilia of Charles Dodgson, better known as Lewis Carroll, the author of *Alice in Wonderland.* Dodgson spent his last years in a house on nearby Castle Hill. He was buried in the Mount Cemetery, up the hill on High Street. **Castle Arch,** all that remains of the entrance of the old castle, displays a slot for a portcullis. Beyond the arch lie the remains of the castle. ⊠ *Quarry St.* ☎ *01483/444751* ⊕ *www.guildfordmuseum.co. uk* ⊠ *Free* ⊙ *Mon.–Sat. 11–5.*

Guildford Cathedral, looming on its hilltop across the River Wey, is only the second Anglican cathedral to be built on a new site since the Reformation in the 1500s. It was consecrated in 1961. The redbrick exterior is severely simple, whereas the interior, with its stone and plaster, looks bright and cool. It was used in the filming of the movie *The Omen.* ⊠ *Stag Hill* ☎ *01483/547860* ⊕ *www.guildford-cathedral.org* ⊠ *Donation accepted, tours £3 (call in advance)* ⊙ *Daily 8:30–5:30.*

Fodor'sChoice ★ In a nation of gardeners and garden-goers, **Wisley,** the Royal Horticultural Society's showpiece, is one of England's most popular gardens. Both an ornamental and scientific center, it claims to have greater horticultural diversity than any other garden in the world. Founded by businessman and inventor George Ferguson Wilson in 1878, Wisley has expanded to 240 innovative, colorful acres. The alpine meadow in spring, the lilies, the rose gardens, and the year-round conservatories are highlights, along with a center that sells more than 10,000 types of plants. The garden, near Woking, is 10 mi northeast of Guildford. ⊠ *A3, Woking* ☎ *01483/224234* ⊕ *www.rhs.org.uk/gardens/wisley* ⊠ *£7.50* ⊙ *Mar.–Oct., weekdays 10–6, weekends and national holidays 9–6; Nov.–Feb., weekdays 10–4:30, weekends 9–4:30.*

Where to Stay & Eat

££–££££ ✕ **Café de Paris.** An 18th-century building holds this busy, family-owned French restaurant and brasserie. The menu focuses on game and fish: try the venison in red-wine sauce, grilled tuna steak, or the wild-mushroom risotto, but leave enough room for a sorbet. The brasserie has a fine blackboard menu, and there's a fixed-price menu at lunchtime (£12.50). ⊠ *35 Castle St.* ☎ *01483/534896* ⊟ *AE, MC, V.*

£ ✕ **Rumwong.** On the incredibly long menu, the Thai name of each dish appears with a clear English description. Good choices are the fisherman's soup, a spicy mass of delicious saltwater fish in a clear broth, or *yam pla muek,* a hot salad with squid. The restaurant runs an Asian supermarket next door. ⊠ *16–18 London Rd.* ☎ *01483/536092* ⊟ *MC, V* ⊙ *Closed Mon.*

★ **££££** ✕▣ **Angel Posting House and Livery.** Guildford was famous for its old coaching inns, and this luxurious, 500-year-old hotel is the last of them. The courtyard, where coaches and horses clattered to a stop, still opens to the sky, and light lunches are offered here in summer. Individually designed guest rooms have attractive fabrics, reproductions of antiques, and marble-lined bathrooms; 10 are in a modern annex. There's a salon with a fireplace and minstrel's gallery, and the 13th-century stone-vaulted crypt serves as the backdrop for fine modern British food (£32 for fixed-price menu). ✉ *91 High St., GU1 3DP* ☎ *01483/564555* 🖷 *01483/533770* ⊕ *www.slh.com/angel* 🛏 *21 rooms* ☖ *Restaurant, coffee shop, in-room data ports, gym, health club, spa, meeting rooms, some pets allowed (fee); no a/c* ▭ *AE, DC, MC, V.*

££ 🏠 **Old Great Halfpenny.** Surrounded by well-maintained grounds, this 16th-century half-timbered house looks like something out of a picture book; it's a real find. The owners are decorators and gardeners, so the place is impeccably done, from top to bottom. Rooms have comfortable antique beds, and you can have breakfast on the patio in the summertime. ✉ *Halfpenny La., St. Martha GU3 3HJ, 5 mi north of Guildford* ☎ *01483/567835* 🛏 *2 rooms* ☖ *No a/c, no phone in room* ▭ *No credit cards* ⦶ *CP.*

Nightlife & the Arts

The **Yvonne Arnaud Theatre** (✉ Millbrook ☎ 01483/440000), a horseshoe-shape building on an island in the River Wey, frequently previews West End productions; it also has a restaurant. The smaller Mill Studio showcases more intimate productions.

Great Bookham

㊲ *8 mi northeast of Guildford, 25 mi southwest of London.*

Fine old buildings fill Great Bookham, including a well-preserved 12th-century church. **Polesden Lacey,** a gorgeous, creamy yellow Regency mansion built in 1824, contains impressive collections of furniture, paintings, porcelain, and silver. Edwardian society hostess Mrs. Ronald Greville is responsible for the lavish interiors; the future King George VI stayed here for part of his honeymoon in 1923. In summer, open-air theatrical performances are given on the grounds. On sunny summer days, you can wander its elegant gardens, or rent croquet equipment from the house (book in advance) and take advantage of its smooth lawns. ✉ *Off A246* ☎ *01372/458203* ⊕ *www.nationaltrust. org.uk* 🎟 *£9, grounds only £6* ☉ *House mid-Apr.–Oct., Wed.–Sun. and national holidays 11–5; grounds daily 11–6 or dusk.*

> **EMMA'S COUNTRY**
>
> Great Bookham may have been the Highbury of Jane Austen's *Emma,* according to some literary scholars. You can ponder this as you stroll through the town or as you take in the scenery from nearby Box Hill, where Emma famously snubbed Miss Bates.

EN ROUTE As you make your way southeast to Tunbridge Wells via Dorking (about 28 mi), you'll pass **Box Hill** (✉ A24 ☎ 01306/885502 ⊕ www. nationaltrust.org.uk), where Jane Austen's characters in *Emma* went for their picnic. Its lovely views of the South Downs make it a favorite spot for walkers still (there's an information center on the summit). At the bottom of Box Hill, the Burford Bridge Hotel was where Keats wrote the last sections of *Endymion.*

Dorking

38 *6 mi south of Great Bookham, 29 mi south of London.*

The southeasterly route to Royal Tunbridge Wells leads to the commuter town of Dorking, a pleasant neighborhood that has inspired the pens of many writers. The cemetery holds the remains of the writer George Meredith (1828–1909). On the wide High Street stands the White Horse Inn, or the Marquis o' Granby, as Dickens dubbed it in *The Pickwick Papers.*

Where to Stay

££££–£££££ ⊞ **Burford Bridge.** Romantic historical associations abound at this beautifully sited hotel at the foot of Box Hill, next to the Mole River. Here Keats completed *Endymion,* and Lord Nelson spent his last hours with Emma Hamilton before the battle of Trafalgar; Robert Louis Stevenson, Sheridan, and Wordsworth are among other past visitors. There has been an inn here since the 13th century, though the oldest parts of the existing building date from around 1600. Oak beams and antiques give a cozy feel to the public areas; rooms are more contemporary. The gardens are bordered by the river. ⌂ *Box Hill, RH5 6BX* ☎ *0870/4008283* 🖷 *01306/880386* ⊕ *www.macdonaldhotels.co.uk* ⇗ *57 rooms* ♿ *Restaurant, cable TV, pool, croquet, Internet room, meeting rooms; no a/c in some rooms* ⊟ *AE, DC, MC, V* ❧ *BP.*

East Grinstead

39 *15 mi southeast of Dorking, 32 mi south of London.*

The small country town of East Grinstead claims the longest continuous run of 14th-century timber-frame buildings in the country. Six miles to the east is the village of Hartfield, where A. A. Milne wrote his Winnie the Pooh stories in the 1920s.

★ A well-preserved family country house dating from the 1890s and set in a beautiful hillside garden, **Standen** typifies the Arts and Crafts movement. Designed by the influential architect Philip Webb (1831–1913), it contains a wealth of William Morris carpets, wallpapers, and fabrics, and even original electric-light fittings. The house is 2 mi south of East Grinstead. ⊠ *Off B2110* ☎ *01342/323029* ⊕ *www.nationaltrust.org.uk* 🖾 *£6.80, garden only £4* ⊗ *House late Mar.–Oct., Wed.–Sun. 11–5. Garden late Mar.–Oct., Wed.–Sun. 11–6.*

At lush **Nymans Garden,** exotic plants collected by the gardener Ludwig Messel beginning in 1885 mingle with more homely varieties. Spring is the time to appreciate the rhododendrons and the rare Himalayan magnolias in the romantic walled garden; in summer the roses are lovely. The surrounding estate has wildflowers and woodland walks. ⊠ *B2114, Handcross, 10 mi southwest of East Grinstead* ☎ *01444/400321* ⊕ *www.nationaltrust.org.uk* 🖾 *£7* ⊗ *Mid-Feb.–early Nov., Wed.–Sun. 11–6 or dusk; Nov.–mid-Feb., weekends 11–4.*

Where to Stay & Eat

£££££ ⊞ **Gravetye Manor.** This Elizabethan stone mansion, built in 1598, stands on a hilltop site in 1,000 acres of grounds landscaped by William

TAKE A HIKE

For those who prefer to travel on their own two feet, the Southeast offers long sweeps of open terrain that makes walking a pleasure. Ardent walkers can explore all or part of the North Downs Way (153 mi) and the South Downs Way (106 mi), following ancient paths along the tops of the downs—the undulating treeless uplands typical of the area. Both trails give you wide views over the countryside. The North Downs Way follows part of the old Pilgrim's Way to Canterbury that so fascinated Chaucer. The South Downs Way crosses the chalk landscape of Sussex Downs, with parts of the route going through deep woodland. Along the way, charming little villages serve the walkers cool ale in inns that have been doing precisely that for centuries. The 30-mi (north–south) Downs Link joins the two routes. Along the Kent coast, the Saxon Shore Way, 143 mi from Gravesend to Rye, passes four Roman forts along its way. Guides to these walks are available from the Southeast England Tourist Board (⊕ www. visitsoutheastengland.com); also check the National Trails Web site (⊕ www.nationaltrail.co.uk).

Robinson (1838–1935), the noted gardener who lived here and created fine naturalistic gardens. Restored with oak paneling and ornamental plaster ceilings, it represents the epitome of the luxurious English country-house hotel; guest rooms are spacious and flower-bedecked. The superb if expensive restaurant (fixed-price menu £52; reservations essential) favors seafood and has an excellent wine list. Two-night breaks, including meals, are better value. ✉ *Off B2110, 5 mi south of East Grinstead, RH19 4LJ* ☎ *01342/810567* 🖷 *01342/810080* ⊕ *www.gravetyemanor. co.uk* ⇨ *18 rooms* ⚭ *2 restaurants, cable TV, lake, fishing, croquet, bar, meeting rooms; no a/c, no kids under 7 except infants* 🖃 *MC, V.*

MASTERPIECES NEAR TUNBRIDGE WELLS

England is famous for its magnificent stately homes and castles, but many of them are scattered across the country. Within a 15-mi radius of Tunbridge Wells, however, in that area of hills and hidden dells known as the Weald, lies a wealth of architectural wonder in historic homes, castles, and gardens: Penshurst Place, Hever Castle, Chartwell, Knole, Ightham Mote, Leeds Castle, Sissinghurst Castle Garden, Bodiam Castle, Great Dixter House and Gardens, and Rudyard Kipling's Batemans.

Royal Tunbridge Wells

40 *13 mi east of East Grinstead, 39 mi southeast of London.*

Nobody much bothers with the "Royal" anymore, but Tunbridge Wells is no less regal because of it. For whatever reason, this historic bedroom community has been the butt of jokes for years. "Disgusted of Tunbridge Wells" was the national name for anybody who complained at length about small problems. It's seen as conservative and upper-middle class—

and so it is. But that doesn't make the town any less attractive and handy as a base for exploring the region.

The city owes its prosperity to the 17th- and 18th-century passion for spas and mineral baths. In 1606 a mineral-water spring was discovered here, drawing legions of royal visitors looking for eternal health. Tunbridge Wells reached its zenith in the mid-18th century, when Richard "Beau" Nash presided over its social life. The buildings at the lower end of High Street are mostly 18th century, but as the street climbs the hill north, changing its name to Mount Pleasant Road, structures become more modern.

A good place to begin a visit is at the **Pantiles,** a famous promenade with colonnaded shops near the spring on one side of town. Its odd name derives from the Dutch "pan tiles" that originally paved the area. Now bordered on two sides by busy main roads, the Pantiles remains an elegant, tranquil oasis, and the site of the actual well. ■ TIP→ **You can still drink the waters when a "dipper" (the traditional water dispenser) is in attendance, from Easter through September.**

The **Church of King Charles the Martyr** (⊠ Chapel Pl.), across the road from the Pantiles, dates from 1678, when it was dedicated to Charles I, who had been executed by Parliament in 1649. Its plain exterior belies its splendid interior; take special note of the beautifully plastered baroque ceiling.

Tunbridge Wells Museum and Art Gallery, at the northern end of Mount Pleasant Road, contains a rather scattered but interesting jumble of local artifacts, prehistoric relics, and Victorian toys, as well as an exhibition of Tunbridge Ware pieces: small, wooden items inlaid with tiny pieces of colored woods. ⊠ *Civic Centre, Mount Pleasant Rd.* ☎ *01892/554171* ⊕ *www.visittunbridgewells.com* ⊠ *Free* ☉ *Mon.–Sat. 9:30–5, Sun. 10–4.*

OFF THE
BEATEN
PATH

ALL SAINTS CHURCH – This modest 13th-century church holds one of the glories of 20th-century church art. The building is awash with the luminous yellows and blues of 12 windows by Marc Chagall (1887–1985), commissioned as a tribute by the family of a young girl who was drowned in a sailing accident in 1963. The church is 4 mi north of Tunbridge Wells; turn off A26 before Tonbridge and continue a mile or so east along B2017. ⊠ *B2017, Tudeley* ☎ *0870/744–1456* ⊠ *Free* ☉ *Daily 9–6 or dusk.*

Where to Stay & Eat

★
£££–£££££

✕ **Thackeray's House.** This mid-17th-century tile-hung house, once the home of Victorian novelist William Makepeace Thackeray, is now an elegant restaurant known for creative French cuisine. Specialties include honey-and-dill–glazed duck and roasted salmon with herb crust and calamari noodles. The lunchtime menu du jour is a very good value at £13.95 for two courses. ⊠ *85 London Rd.* ☎ *01892/511921* ⊟ *AE, MC, V* ☉ *Closed Mon. and last wk in Dec. No dinner Sun.*

£££–££££

✕ **Gracelands Palace.** This weird and wonderful place is a temple to Chinese food and, well, Elvis. Owner Paul Chan is famous in the region for his cabaret of Elvis songs and a fixed-price menu (£15–£19) of Szechuan and Cantonese fare. Pictures of Chan and Elvis decorate the building;

it's packed most nights with cheerful fans. ⊠ *3 Cumberland Walk* ☎ *01892/540754* ☰ *AE, MC, V* ☺ *Closed Sun. No lunch Mon.*

£–££ ✕ **Himalayan Gurkha Restaurant.** It's not what you might expect to find in the cozy confines of Tunbridge Wells, but the Nepalese cuisine of this friendly spot is popular with locals. Spicy mountain dishes are cooked with care in traditional clay ovens or barbecued on flaming charcoal. Vegetarian options are appealing, too. ⊠ *31 Church Rd.* ☎ *01892/527834* ☰ *MC, V.*

£–££ ✕ **Mount Edgcumbe Restaurant and Bar.** To some degree, the attraction of this creative restaurant above the old town center is the fact that it's in a candlelighted cave. The fact that it's carved out of the limestone foundation of the Mount Edgcumbe Hotel means that it's a very nice cave indeed. On the menu are Southeast Asian dishes such as chicken *satay* and *beef randang* (beef simmered in spices and coconut milk). ⊠ *The Common, TN4 8BX* ☎ *01892/526823* ☰ *MC, V.*

£££–£££££ ✕⊡ **Hotel du Vin.** Formerly a private house, this elegant sandstone building dating from 1762 has been transformed into a chic boutique hotel with polished wood floors and luxurious armchairs and sofas. Oriental rugs give public rooms an air of warmth that is both intimate and grand, and guest rooms are modern, with pampering bathrooms. The Burgundy Bar stocks a fine selection of wines from the eponymous region of France. The contemporary menu in the bistro (£££) changes daily but is strong on creamy soups and crisp salads. ⊠ *Crescent Rd., near Mount Pleasant Rd., TN1 2LY* ☎ *01892/526455* 🖷 *01892/512044* ⊕ *www.hotelduvin.com* ⤿ *36 rooms* ☸ *Restaurant, cable TV, billiards, 2 bars, meeting rooms; no a/c* ☰ *AE, DC, MC, V.*

£££–££££ ⊡ **Spa Hotel.** The Goring family, which also runs the noted Goring Hotel in London, owns this plush hotel. Carefully chosen traditional furnishings and details help maintain the country-house flavor of the 1766 Georgian mansion, although guest rooms come with many modern extras. There are superb views from the 15-acre grounds across the town and into the Weald of Kent. The traditional English fare of the Chandelier Restaurant is popular with locals. ⊠ *Mount Ephraim, TN4 8XJ* ☎ *01892/520331* 🖷 *01892/510575* ⊕ *www.spahotel.co.uk* ⤿ *69 rooms* ☸ *Restaurant, cable TV, Wi-Fi, tennis court, indoor pool, 2 gyms, hair salon, sauna, spa, croquet, bar, meeting rooms, some pets allowed; no a/c in some rooms* ☰ *AE, DC, MC, V.*

££–£££ ⊡ **Old Parsonage.** This friendly guesthouse, 2 mi south of Tunbridge Wells via A267, stands at the top of a quiet lane beside the village church. Built in 1820, the Georgian manor has lovely antique furniture, a dining room with oak refectory table, and a big conservatory for afternoon tea. Two pubs and a restaurant lie within a short walk of the house. ⊠ *Church La., Frant TN3 9DX* 🖷🖷 *01892/750773* ⊕ *www.theoldparsonagehotel. co.uk* ⤿ *3 rooms* ☸ *Croquet, some pets allowed; no a/c, no room phones, no kids under 7* ☰ *MC, V* ⊧ *BP.*

Penshurst Place

★ ❹❶ *7 mi northwest of Royal Tunbridge Wells, 33 mi southeast of London.*

At the center of the adorable hamlet of Penshurst stands one of England's finest medieval manor houses, hidden behind tall trees and walls.

Although it has a 14th-century hall, Penshurst is mainly Elizabethan and has been the family home of the Sidneys since 1552, giving it particular historical interest. The most famous Sidney is the Elizabethan poet, Sir Philip, author of *Arcadia*. The **Baron's Hall,** topped with a chestnut roof, is the oldest and one of the grandest halls to survive from the early Middle Ages. Family portraits, furniture, tapestries, and armor help tell the story of this house that was first inhabited in 1341 by Sir John de Pulteney, the very wealthy four-times London mayor. The grounds include a toy museum, gift shop, and the 11-acre walled Italian Garden, which displays tulips and daffodils in spring, roses in July, and mistletoe during the winter months. The house is off Leicester Square, which has late-15th-century half-timber structures adorned with soaring brick chimneys. ⊠ *Off B2188; from Tunbridge Wells, follow A26 and B2176* ☎ *01892/870307* ⊕ *www.penshurstplace.com* ✉ *£7.50 for house tour, grounds only £6* ⊙ *Mar., weekends noon–5:30; Apr.–Oct., daily noon–5. Grounds daily 10:30–6. Last admission 30 mins before closing.*

Where to Stay & Eat

££–££££ ✕ **Spotted Dog.** This pub first opened its doors in 1520 and hardly appears to have changed. Its big inglenook fireplace and heavy beams give it character, and the good food and friendly crowd make it a pleasure to visit. ⊠ *Smarts Hill* ☎ *01892/870253* ▭ *MC, V.*

£££–££££ ⊡ **Rose and Crown.** Originally a 16th-century inn, this hotel on the main street in Tonbridge (5 mi east of Penshurst, 5 mi north of Tunbridge Wells) has low-beam ceilings and good Jacobean woodwork in the snug, inviting bar and the restaurant. Guest rooms in the main building are traditionally furnished, whereas rooms in the newer annex are more modern in style. ⊠ *125 High St., Tonbridge TN9 1DD* ☎ *01732/357966* 🖶 *01732/357194* ⊕ *www.rose-andcrownhotel.co.uk* 🛏 *50 rooms* ⌂ *Restaurant, café, cable TV, bar, laundry service, concierge, meeting rooms, free parking; no a/c* ▭ *AE, MC, V* ⸙ *BP.*

Hever Castle

42 *3 mi west of Penshurst, 10 mi northwest of Royal Tunbridge Wells, 30*
FodorsChoice *mi southeast of London.*
★

For some, 13th-century Hever fits the stereotype of what a castle should look like: all turrets and battlements, the whole encircled by a water lily–bound moat. For others, it's too squat in structure (and perhaps too renovated). Here, at her childhood home, the unfortunate Anne Boleyn, second wife of Henry VIII and mother of Elizabeth I, was courted and won by Henry. He loved her dearly for a time but had her beheaded in 1536 after she failed to give birth to a son. He then gave Boleyn's home to his fourth wife, Anne of Cleves, as a

> **WORD OF MOUTH**
>
> "Knole is huge and takes several hours to see. Hever isn't as large a house, but the grounds are enormous and the gardens alone take at least 1.5 to 2 hours. By the way, also very near Hever are Chartwell and Penshurst Place—both of which are much more interesting than Leeds Castle."   –janisj

2

present. Famous though it was, the castle fell into disrepair in the 19th century. American millionaire William Waldorf Astor acquired Hever in 1903, and the Astor family owned it until 1983. Astor built a Tudor village to house his staff (it's now a hotel for corporate functions) and created the stunning gardens, which include an excellent maze, a water maze, ponds, playgrounds, tea shops, gift shops, plant shops—you get the picture. In summer activities are nonstop here, with jousting, falconry exhibitions, country fairs, making this one of southern England's most rewarding castles to visit. ⊠ *Off B2026, Hever* ☎ *01732/865224* ⊕ *www.hevercastle.co.uk* ⊠ *£9.80, grounds only £7.80* ☉ *Castle Apr.–Oct., daily noon–6; Mar. and Nov., daily noon–4. Grounds Apr.–Oct., daily 11–6; Mar. and Nov., daily 11–4. Last admission 1 hr before closing.*

Chartwell

43 *9 mi north of Hever Castle, 12 mi northwest of Tunbridge Wells, 28 mi southeast of London.*

This grand Victorian mansion with views over the Weald was the home of Sir Winston Churchill from 1924 until his death in 1965. Virtually everything has been kept as it was when he lived here, with his pictures, books, photos, and maps. There's even a half-smoked cigar that the World War II prime minister never finished. Churchill was an amateur artist, and his paintings show a different side of the crusty politician. ■ TIP➔ **Be sure to explore Chartwell's rose gardens and take one of the country walks.** ⊠ *Off B2026, Westerham* ☎ *01732/866368* ⊕ *www.nationaltrust. org.uk* ⊠ *£7.50, garden and studio only £4* ☉ *Late Mar.–June and Sept.–early Nov., Wed.–Sun. 11–5; July and Aug., Tues.–Sun. 11–5. Last admission at 4:15.*

Knole

44 *8 mi east of Chartwell, 11 mi north of Royal Tunbridge Wells, 27 mi southeast of London.*

Fodor'sChoice ★

The town of Sevenoaks lies in London's commuter belt, a world away from the baronial air of its premier attraction, Knole, the grand, beloved home of the Sackville family since the 16th century. Begun in the 15th century and enlarged in 1603 by Thomas Sackville, Knole, with its complex of courtyards and buildings, resembles a small town. You'll need most of an afternoon to explore it thoroughly. The house is noted for its tapestries, embroidered furnishings, and the most famous set of 17th-century silver furniture to survive. Most of the salons are in the pre-baroque mode, rather dark and armorial. Paintings on display include family por-

> **A ROOM PER DAY**
>
> Knole was purchased in 1456 by Thomas Bouchier, the Archbishop of Canterbury, for just £266. He made it fit for "a prince of the church," reputedly planning it as a "calendar house" with 7 courtyards, 52 staircases, and 365 rooms. The house has had many renovations since then, but remains decidedly large.

CLOSE UP

Tips for Treasure Houses

THROUGHOUT THE SOUTHEAST you can wander through the gorgeous homes of the wealthy and the formerly wealthy. Castles, manor houses, and mansions open their doors every year to thousands of visitors. The carpets and gardens may be trampled, family photos gawked at: given all of that, why do the owners (dukes, viscounts, and others) do it? Well, they need the money. Wonderful though it is to inherit vast tracts of countryside and paintings by Rembrandt and Gainsborough, it's also unbelievably expensive, and family fortunes tend not to last as long as family manors.

Hundreds of other homes and castles are owned by the National Trust or English Heritage, organizations that raise part of the money needed to maintain them through entrance fees. Here are some things to keep in mind when you visit:

Houses and castles are unique. What you get for your entrance fee differs enormously. You may be free to wander at will, or you may be organized into groups like prisoners behind enemy lines. In some homes guides are chatty family members (these may be the most memorable tours); in others they're bored local teenagers.

Sometimes the exterior of a building may be spectacular, but the interior dull. It's also true that the gardens and grounds may be just as (or more) interesting than the house, and you'll want to save time to explore them. Our individual reviews alert you to these instances.

Passes may save you money. If you plan to see lots of houses and castles, it might be cheaper to buy a pass, such as Visit Britain's Great British Heritage Pass, or to join an organization such as the National Trust (⇨ Discounts & Deals *in* Smart Travel Tips) and thus get free entry. Check entrance fees against your itinerary to be sure what you will save.

Opening hours are seasonal and change. Hours can change abruptly, so call the day before. Many houses are open only from April to October, and they may have extremely limited hours. In other cases the houses have celebrated parks and gardens that are open much of the year. Consider a trip in shoulder seasons if you can't take the crowds that inevitably pack the most popular houses; or explore lesser-known abodes. You'll still have a great time.

Transportation can be a challenge. If you don't have a car, plan transportation in advance. Some places are tucked deep in the countryside; others are more accessible.

Consider a stay at a property. To get even more up close and personal, you can rent a cottage from the National Trust (⊕ www.nationaltrustcottages. co.uk) or English Heritage (⊕ www. english-heritage.org.uk/ holidaycottages). You could stay in the servants' quarters, a lodge, or even a lighthouse. Some privately owned houses have cottages for rent on their estates; their Web sites generally have this information. Also ⇨ Lodging *in* Smart Travel Tips. This can make your trip even more memorable.

traits by 18th-century artists Thomas Gainsborough and Sir Joshua Reynolds. The magnificently florid staircase was a novelty in its Elizabethan heyday. Vita Sackville-West grew up at Knole and set her novel *The Edwardians*, a witty account of life among the gilded set, here. Encompassed by a 1,000-acre deer park, the house lies in the center of Sevenoaks, opposite St. Nicholas Church. To get there from Chartwell, drive north to Westerham, then pick up A25 and head east for 8 mi. ⊠ *Off A225* ☏ *01732/450608* ⊕ *www.nationaltrust.org.uk* 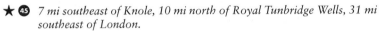 *House £6.80, gardens £2.50* ☉ *Late Mar.–early Nov., Wed.–Sun. and national holidays 11–4, last admission at 3:30; gardens May–Sept., 1st Wed. of each month 11–4, last admission at 3.*

Ightham Mote

★ **㊺** *7 mi southeast of Knole, 10 mi north of Royal Tunbridge Wells, 31 mi southeast of London.*

Finding Ightham Mote requires careful navigation, but it's worth the effort to see a vision right out of the Middle Ages. To enter this outstanding example of a small manor house, you cross a stone bridge over one of the dreamiest moats in England. This moat, however, does not relate to the "mote" in the name, which refers to the role of the house as a meeting place, or "moot." Ightham (pronounced *i*-tem) Mote's magical exterior has changed little since the 14th century, but within you'll find that it encompasses styles of several periods, Tudor to Victorian. The Great Hall is an antiquarian's delight, both comfy and grand, and the Tudor chapel, drawing room, and billiards room in the northwest quarter are highlights. Take time to explore the 14-acre garden and the woodland walks or to eat at the restaurant. To reach the house from Sevenoaks, follow A25 east to A227 (8 mi) and follow the signs. ⊠ *Off A227, Ivy Hatch, Sevenoaks* ☏ *01732/810378* ⊕ *www.nationaltrust.*  *org.uk*  *£8.50* ☉ *Mid-Mar.–Oct., Mon., Wed.–Fri., and Sun.: house 10:30–5:30, garden 10–5:30. Estate daily all year, dawn–dusk.*

Rochester

㊻ *15 mi north of Ightham Mote, 28 mi southeast of London.*

Positioned near the confluence of the Thames and the River Medway, this town has a history of Roman, Saxon, and Norman occupation, all of which have left architectural remains, including the vast castle at the town center. Novelist Charles Dickens called Rochester home for over a decade, until his death in 1870. Unfortunately, the Charles Dickens Centre in Eastgate House on High Street is closed, although you can still stroll through the garden and see the exterior of the Swiss-style chalet where he wrote. Plans are afoot to reopen the center, but nothing definite is known at this writing.

The impressive ruins of **Rochester Castle** are a superb example of Norman military architecture. The keep, built in the 1100s using the old Roman city wall as a foundation, is 125 feet high, the tallest in England. It's been shored up but left without floors, so that from the bottom you can see to the open roof and study the complex structure. At the shop you can pick up well-researched guides to the building. ☒ *Boley Hill* ☎ *01634/402276* ⊕ *www.english-heritage.org.uk* 🎫 *£4.50* ⊙ *Apr.–Sept., daily 10–6; Oct.–Mar., daily 10–4; last admission 30 mins before closing.*

In AD 604, Augustine of Canterbury ordained the first English bishop in a small cathedral on the site of **Rochester Cathedral.** The current cathedral, England's second-oldest, is a jumble of architectural styles. Much of the original Norman building (1077) remains, including the striking west front, highly carved portal, and the tympanum above the doorway. Some medieval art survives, including a 13th-century Wheel of Fortune on the choir walls; it's a reminder of how difficult medieval life was. ☒ *Boley Hill* ☎ *01634/843366* 🎫 *£2 donation suggested* ⊙ *Mon.–Sat. 7:30–6, Sun. 7:30–5.*

The buildings and 47 retired ships at the **Historic Dockyard** across the River Medway from Rochester constitute the country's most complete Georgian to early Victorian dockyard. The dockyard's origins go back to the time of Henry VIII; some 400 ships were built here over the centuries. There's a guided tour of the submarine HMS *Ocelot,* the last warship to be built for the Royal Navy at Chatham. ☒ *Chatham* ☎ *01634/ 823807* ⊕ *www.chdt.org.uk* 🎫 *£11.50* ⊙ *Mid-Feb.–Oct., daily 10–6 (or dusk if earlier).*

Where to Stay

££ 🏨 **Gordon House Hotel.** This friendly guesthouse in central Rochester is a well-priced option. Rooms are done in creamy colors, and some have Victorian architectural details; most have antiques. You can have a cup of tea and relax in the ground-floor lounge after a busy day of sightseeing. ☒ *91 High St., ME1 1LX* ☎ *01634/814769* ⇌ *12 rooms* ♿ *Lounge; no a/c* ⊟ *MC, V* ⫶⊙⫶ *BP.*

Nightlife & the Arts

Rochester sponsors a **Dickensian Christmas Festival** (☎ 01634/306000) on the first weekend in December. Thousands of people in period dress participate in reenactments of scenes from the author's novel, *A Christmas Carol.* There's a candlelight procession, mulled wine and roasted chestnuts, and Christmas carols at the cathedral. Another important Dickens festival takes place in Broadstairs (40 mi east).

Leeds Castle

47 *12 mi south of Rochester, 19 mi northwest of Royal Tunbridge Wells, 40 mi southeast of London.*

The bubbling River Medway runs through Maidstone, Kent's county seat, with its backdrop of chalky downs. Nearby, the fairy-tale stronghold of Leeds Castle commands two small islands on a peaceful lake. Dating to the 9th century and rebuilt by the Normans in 1119, Leeds (not to be confused with the city of Leeds in the north of England; this one is named after a local village) became a favorite home of many medieval English queens. Henry VIII liked it so much he had it converted from a fortress into a grand palace. The interior doesn't match the glories of the much-photographed exterior, although there are fine paintings and furniture, plus a curious dog-collar museum. The outside attractions are more impressive and include a maze, a grotto, an aviary of native and exotic birds, and woodland gardens. The castle is 5 mi east of Maidstone. ⊠ *A20* ☎ *01622/765400* ⊕ *www.leedscastle.org. uk* ☞ *13; grounds only £10.50* ☉ *Apr.–Oct., daily 10–5; Nov.–Mar., daily 10–3. Castle closed last Sat. in June and 1st Sat. in July.*

Sissinghurst Castle Garden

48 *10 mi south of Leeds Castle, 53 mi southeast of London.*

Fodor'sChoice
★

One of the most famous gardens in the world, Sissinghurst rests deep in the Kentish countryside around the remains of a moated Tudor castle. Unpretentiously beautiful, quintessentially English, the gardens were laid out in the 1930s around the remains of part of the castle by writer Vita Sackville-West (one of the Sackvilles of Knole) and her husband, the diplomat Harold Nicolson. Sackville-West's study and library are open limited hours. ■ TIP→ **Good times to visit the grounds are June and July, when the roses are in bloom.** The White Garden, with its white flowers and silver-gray foliage, is a classic, and the herb garden and cottage garden show Sackville-West's knowledge of plants. Children may feel restricted in the gardens, and strollers (push chairs, in Britain) are not allowed. From Leeds Castle, make your way south on B2163 and A274 through Headcorn, then follow signs. For those without a car, take a train from London's Charing Cross station and transfer to a bus in Staplehurst. Direct buses operate on Tuesday and Sunday between May and August; at other times, take the bus to Sissinghurst village and walk the remaining 1¼ mi. ⊠ *A262, Cranbrook* ☎ *01580/710701* ⊕ *www.nationaltrust.org.uk* ☞ *£8.50* ☉ *Mar.–Nov., Mon., Tues., and Fri. 11–6:30, weekends 10–6:30; last admission at 5:30. Admission often restricted because of limited space; a timed ticket system may be in effect, usually May–July.*

Biddenden Winery and Cider Works, 3½ mi east of Sissinghurst on the A262, cultivates 9 types of grapes on 22 acres, with a focus on the German Ortega, Huxelrebe, Bacchus, and Reichensteiner varieties. Kids can sample farm-pressed apple juice, while adults indulge in the free wine-tasting. ⊠ *Biddenden* ☎ *01580/291726* ⊕ *www.biddendenvineyards. com* ☞ *Free* ☉ *Mon.–Sat. 10–5, Sun. 11–5; closed Christmas wk and Sun. in Jan. and Feb.*

Where to Stay & Eat

£ ✕ **Claris's Tea Shop.** Claris's, near Sissinghurst Castle Garden, serves traditional English teas in a half-timber room and displays attractive English crafts items. The Cream Tea set includes scones with butter, fresh cream, preserves, and a pot of tea for £4. There's a garden for summer, and a gift shop stocks china and glass. ⊠ *1–3 High St., Biddenden* ☎ *01580/291025* ▭ *No credit cards* ☉ *Closed Mon. No dinner.*

£ ▦ **Frogshole Oast.** This converted 18th-century rural oasthouse has three kilns that were once used for drying hops. The house still has many period features, and the rooms and sitting area have some antiques. There's a garden and a natural duck pond. ⊠ *Sissinghurst Rd., 2 mi east of Sissinghurst Castle Garden, Biddenden TN27 8HB* ☎☎ *01580/*

291935 ✒ *hartley@frogsholeoast.freeserve.co.uk* ↩ *3 rooms* △ *No a/c, no room TVs* ⊺❘ *BP.*

EN
ROUTE
As you leave Sissinghurst Castle Garden, continue south along A229 through Hawkhurst, a little village that was once the headquarters of a notorious gang of smugglers. Turn left onto the B2244 and left at the Curlew pub to arrive in the tiny Sussex village of Bodiam.

Bodiam Castle

★ ℂ ㊾ *9 mi south of Cranbrook, 15 mi southeast of Royal Tunbridge Wells, 57 mi southeast of London.*

Immortalized in paintings, postcards, and photographs, the ruins of Bodiam Castle rise out of the distance like a piece of medieval legend. Its turrets, battlements, wooden portcullis, glassy moat, and 2-feet-thick walls survive, but all that was within them is long gone. Built in 1385 to withstand a threatened French invasion, it was "slighted" (partly demolished) during the English Civil War of 1642–46 and has been uninhabited ever since. Still, you can climb the towers to take in sweeping countryside views, and kids can run around in and around the castle. The castle schedules organized activities for kids during school holidays. ⊠ *Off B2244, Bodiam* ☎ *01580/830436* ⊕ *www.nationaltrust.org.uk* ⊡ *£4.60* ☼ *Mid-Feb.–Oct., daily 10–5 or dusk; Nov.–mid-Feb., weekends 10–4 or dusk; last admission 1 hr before closing.*

Great Dixter House & Gardens

㊿ *3 mi east of Bodiam, 18 mi southeast of Royal Tunbridge Wells, 60 mi southeast of London.*

Combining a large timber-frame hall with a cottage garden on a grand scale, this place will get your green thumbs twitching. The house dates to 1464 and was restored in 1910 by architect Edwin Lutyens, who also designed the garden. From these beginnings, the late horticulturist and writer Christopher Lloyd, whose home this was, developed a series of "garden rooms" and a dazzling herbaceous Long Border. There's a nursery on-site. ⊠ *Off A28, Northiam* ☎ *01797/252878* ⊕ *www.greatdixter.co.uk* ⊡ *£7.50, gardens only £6* ☼ *Apr.–Oct., Tues.–Sun. 2–5 (gardens open at 11 late Apr.–Sept.).*

Burwash

㉛ *13 mi west of Northiam, 14 mi south of Royal Tunbridge Wells, 58 mi southeast of London.*

Burwash, a pretty Sussex village, is known for its association with writer Rudyard Kipling. Close by, between Burwash Common and the River Dudwell, was the setting for Kipling's *Puck of Pook's Hill.*

Kipling lived from 1902 to 1936 at **Bateman's,** a beautiful 17th-century house a half mile south of the village. Many of the rooms, including Kipling's study, look as they did when the writer lived here, and you can also see his Rolls Royce. In the garden, a water mill still grinds flour (most Saturdays in summer at 2 PM). ⊠ *Off A265* ☎ *01435/882302*

2

⊕ *www.nationaltrust.org.uk* 🖾 *£6* ⊙ *Mar., weekends 11–4, garden only; late Mar.–Oct., Sat.–Wed. 11–5 (house) and 11–5:30 (grounds); last admission 1 hr before closing.*

Sports & the Outdoors

The reservoir at **Bewl Water** has aquatic sports, waterside walks, bicycle rentals, boat trips, and an adventure playground. There's a £2.50–£5 parking fee. ⊠ *Off B2099, 5 mi north of Burwash* ☎ *01892/890661* ⊕ *www.bewl.co.uk* ⊙ *Open daily 9–sunset.*

SOUTHEAST ESSENTIALS

Transportation

BY AIR

Gatwick Airport, 27 mi south of London, has direct flights from many U.S. cities and is more convenient for this region than Heathrow. The terminal for the British Rail line is in the airport buildings, and there are connections to major towns in the region. *See* London Essentials *in* Chapter 1 for information about transfers from Gatwick to London.

🖪 **Gatwick Airport** ⊠ M23, Junction 9, Crawley ☎ 0870/000–2468 ⊕ www.baa.co.uk.

BY BUS

National Express serves the region from London's Victoria Coach Station. Trips to Brighton and Canterbury take two hours; to Chichester, about three hours. For regional bus transport inquiries, contact Traveline. Maps and timetables are available at bus depots, train stations, local libraries, and tourist information centers.

FARES & SCHEDULES 🖪 **National Express** ☎ 0870/580–8080 ⊕ www.nationalexpress.com. **Traveline** ☎ 0870/608–2608 ⊕ www.traveline.org.uk.

BY CAR

Major routes radiating outward from London to the Southeast are, from west to east, M23/A23 to Brighton (52 mi); A21, passing by Royal Tunbridge Wells to Hastings (65 mi); A20/M20 to Folkestone; and A2/M2 via Canterbury (56 mi) to Dover (71 mi).

A car is the easiest way to get to the stately homes and castles in the region. A good link route for traveling through the region, from Hampshire across the border into Sussex and Kent, is A272 (which becomes A265). It runs through the Weald, which separates the North Downs from the more inviting South Downs. Although smaller roads forge deeper into the downs, even the main roads take you through lovely countryside. The main route east from the downs to the Channel ports and resorts of Kent is A27. To get to Romney Marsh (across the Sussex border in Kent), take A259 from Rye. Be warned that more traffic tickets are issued per traffic warden in Brighton than anywhere else in the country.

BY TRAIN

South Eastern trains serve the area from London's Victoria and Charing Cross (for all areas) and Waterloo (for the west). From London, the trip to Brighton takes about one hour by the fast train, and to Dover, almost two hours. South West Trains also runs service to Guildford. The line running west from Dover passes through Ashford, where you can change trains for Hastings and Eastbourne. There are connections from Eastbourne for Lewes, and from Brighton for Chichester. For all information, call National Rail Enquiries. For railway nostalgia, Steam Dreams runs the *Cathedrals Express* steam train several times a year from London Victoria to Canterbury. Round-trip tickets start at £45.

CUTTING COSTS A Network Railcard costing £20, valid throughout the southern and southeastern regions for a year, entitles you and three companions to one-third off many off-peak fares.

FARES & 🛈 **National Rail Enquiries** ☎ 0845/748–4950 ⊕ www.nationalrail.co.uk. **National Rail-**
SCHEDULES **card** ⊕ www.railcard.co.uk. **South Eastern Trains** ☎ 08706/030405 ⊕ www.setrains. co.uk. **Steam Dreams** ☎ 01483/209888 ⊕ www.steamdreams.co.uk.

Contacts & Resources

EMERGENCIES
🛈 **Ambulance, fire, police** ☎ 999. **Royal Sussex County Hospital** ✉ Eastern Rd., Brighton ☎ 01273/696955. **Canterbury Hospital** ✉ Ethelbert Rd., Canterbury ☎ 01227/766877.

INTERNET
Internet cafés are easy to find in the bigger towns but are rare in the countryside. Similarly, hotels in towns are more likely to have broadband than those in rural areas. Throughout the region Wi-Fi is not common, although Brighton has a few hotspots.
🛈 Internet Cafés **Brighton Internet** ✉ 54 Elm Grove, Brighton ☎ 01273/691688. **Curve Internet** ✉ 44-47 Gardner St., Brighton ☎ 01273/603031. **Canterbury Library** ✉ High St., Canterbury ☎ 01227/452747.

TOUR OPTIONS
BUS TOURS City Sightseeing's hop-on, hop-off bus tour of Brighton leaves Brighton Pier on Grand Junction Road every 20 to 30 minutes and lasts about an hour. It operates mid-June through August; the cost is £6.50.
🛈 **City Sightseeing** ☎ 01789/294466 ⊕ www.city-sightseeing.com.

PRIVATE GUIDES The Southeast England Tourist Board (⇨ Visitor Information) arranges private tours with qualified Blue Badge guides. The Canterbury Guild of Guides provides walking guides who have a specialized knowledge of the city and its surrounding area. Tours are at 2 PM every day between Easter and October, with an additional tour at 11:30 AM from Monday to Saturday, during July and August. Tour tickets cost £4.50 and are sold at the Information Center, where the walks begin.
🛈 **Canterbury Guild of Guides** ✉ Arnett House, Hawks La. ☎ 01227/459779 ⊕ www. canterbury-walks.co.uk.

VISITOR INFORMATION
Tourism Southeast can give you information on tours and excursions. The office is open Monday through Thursday 9 to 5:30 and Friday 9 to 5. Local tourist information centers (TICs) are normally open Monday

through Saturday 9:30 to 5:30, but hours vary seasonally; offices are listed below by town.

🛈 **Southeast England Tourist Board** ⊠ The Old Brew House, 1 Warwick Park, Royal Tunbridge Wells TN2 5TU ☎01892/540766 🖷01892/511008 ⊕www.visitsoutheastengland. com. **Arundel** ⊠ 61 High St., BN18 9AJ ☎ 01903/882268 ⊕ www.sussex-by-the-sea. co.uk. **Brighton** ⊠10 Bartholomew Sq., BN1 1JS ☎ 0906/7112255 ⊕ www.visitbrighton. com. **Canterbury** ⊠ 12–13 Sun St., CT1 2HX ☎ 01227/378100 ⊕ www.canterbury.co.uk. **Chichester** ⊠29A South St., PO19 1AH ☎01243/775888 ⊕www.chichester.gov.uk. **Dover** ⊠ The Old Town Gaol, Biggin St., CT16 1DL ☎ 01304/205108. **Guildford** ⊠ 14 Tunsgate, GU1 3QT ☎ 01483/444333 ⊕ www.guildford.gov.uk. **Hastings** ⊠ Queens Sq., Priory Meadow, TN34 1TL ☎ 01424/781111 🖷 2 The Stade ☎ 01424/781111 ⊕ www.visithastings. com. **Lewes** ⊠ 187 High St., BN7 2DE ☎ 01273/483448 ⊕ www.lewes.gov.uk. **Maidstone** ⊠ Town Hall, Middle Row, High St., ME14 1TF ☎ 01622/602169 ⊕ www.tour-maidstone.com. **Royal Tunbridge Wells** ⊠ The Old Fish Market, the Pantiles, TN2 5TN ☎ 01892/515675 ⊕ www.visittunbridgewells.com. **Rye** ⊠ The Heritage Centre, Strand Quay, TN31 7AY ☎ 01797/226696 ⊕ www.rye-tourism.co.uk.

The South

WINCHESTER, SALISBURY & STONEHENGE

WORD OF MOUTH

"People often combine Stonehenge with Salisbury . . . . I was just in Salisbury again a couple
of weeks ago. Salisbury is a lovely town with a
beautiful cathedral. I took the tour of the cathedral's tower; it was fantastic."

—P_M

"Don't pass on Stonehenge! For me, Stonehenge
has been the highlight of four visits to England and
it is not at all 'disappointing' or 'overcommercial-
ized,' nor is it accessible 'only by guided tour' . . . .
Even if you go during regular hours, you are not
really kept that far away—you can still see the
stones well."

—Daisy54

Updated by
Robert
Andrews

CATHEDRALS, STATELY HOMES, STONE CIRCLES—the South, made up of Hampshire, Dorset, and Wiltshire counties, holds all kinds of attractions, and not a few quiet pleasures. Two important cathedrals, Winchester and Salisbury (pronounced *sawls*-bree), are here, as are stately homes—Longleat, Stourhead, and Wilton House, among them—intriguing market towns, and hundreds of haunting prehistoric remains, two of which, Avebury and Stonehenge, should not be missed. These are just the tourist-brochure superlatives. Like those who migrate here from every corner of the country in search of upward mobility, anyone spending time in these parts should rent a bike or a car and set out to discover the back-road villages—*not* found in those brochures. After a drink in the village pub and a look at the cricket game on the village green, stretch out in a field for a nap.

Close to London, the green fields of Hampshire divide the cliffs and coves of Devon and Cornwall to the west from the hustle and bustle of the big city. If you have a coastal destination in mind, you may see this as farmland to rush through, but hit the brakes—there's plenty to see.

One of the area's many historical highlights was when Alfred the Great, teaching religion and letters, made Winchester the capital of 9th-century England and helped lay plans for Britain's first navy, sowing the seeds of the Commonwealth. This well-preserved market town is dominated by its cathedral, an imposing edifice dotted with the Gothic tombs of 15th-century bishops. Winchester is a good center from which to visit quiet villages where so many of England's once great personages, from Florence Nightingale to Lord Mountbatten, lived or died. Jane Austen and her works are enduringly popular, and the road to her home at Chawton has become a much-trodden path.

Beyond the gentle, gardenlike landscape of Hampshire, you can explore the somewhat harsher terrain of Salisbury Plain. Two monuments, millennia apart, stand sentinel over the plain. One is the 404-foot-tall stone spire of Salisbury Cathedral, which dominates the entire Salisbury valley and has been immortalized in oil by John Constable. Not far away is the most imposing and dramatic prehistoric structure in Europe: Stonehenge. The many theories about its construction and purpose only add to its attraction, which endures despite the hordes of visitors.

Other districts have their own pleasures, and many have literary or historical associations. Turn your sights to the Dorset heathland, the countryside explored in the novels of Thomas Hardy. This district is spanned by grass-covered chalk hills—the downs—wooded valleys, and meadows through which course meandering rivers. Along the coastline are fossil-rich Lyme Regis, where the tides and currents strike fear into the hearts of sailors, and Cowes, on the Isle of Wight—Queen Victoria's favorite getaway—where colorful flags flutter from sleek yachts.

The South has been quietly central to England's history for well over 4,000 years, occupied successively by prehistoric man, the Celts, the Romans, the Saxons, and the modern British. History continues to be made here. On D-Day, Allied forces sailed for Normandy this coast; nearly 40 years later, British forces set out to recover the Falklands.

Exploring the South

The wide-open, wind-blown inland county of Wiltshire offers a sharp contrast to the tame, sequestered villages of Hampshire and Dorset and the self-important bustle of coastal Southampton and Portsmouth. You may not want to spend much time in these two ports; instead, spend your nights in the more compelling towns of Salisbury and Winchester.

The obvious draw outside Salisbury is Stonehenge, but you're also within reach of an equally interesting prehistoric monument, Avebury. From there, you can swing south to the cultivated woodlands of the New Forest. The southern coast of Dorset is another major area, with a couple of popular holiday resorts, Bournemouth and Weymouth, and a string of ancient sites: Corfe Castle, Maiden Castle, and Cerne Abbas. Lyme Regis, on the Devon border at the center of the wide arc of Lyme Bay, is a favorite holiday destination in this area. It provides a gateway to the World Heritage Site called the Jurassic Coast, with its fossil-rich cliffs from Swanage in the east to Exmouth in the west.

About the Restaurants

In summer, and especially on summer weekends, visitors can overrun the restaurants in small villages, so either book a table in advance or be prepared to wait. The more popular or upscale the restaurant, the more critical a reservation is. For local specialties, try fresh-grilled river trout or sea bass poached in brine, or dine like a king on the New Forest's renowned venison. Hampshire is noted for its pig and sheep farming, and you might zero in on pork and lamb dishes on local restaurant menus.

About the Hotels

Modern hotel chains are well represented, and in rural areas you can choose among elegant country-house hotels, traditional coaching inns (updated to different degrees), and modest guesthouses. Some seaside hotels do not accept one-night bookings in summer. If you plan to visit Cowes on the Isle of Wight during Cowes Week, the annual yachting jamboree in late July or early August, book well in advance.

WHAT IT COSTS In pounds				
	££££	£££	£££	££	£
RESTAURANTS over £22	£18–£22	£13–£17	£7–£12	under £7
HOTELS over £160	£120–£160	£90–£119	£60–£89	under £60

Restaurant prices are for a main course at dinner. Hotel prices are for two people in a standard double room in high season, including V.A.T., with no meals or, if indicated, CP (with continental breakfast), BP (Breakfast Plan, with full breakfast), or MAP (Modified American Plan, with breakfast and dinner).

Timing

Don't plan to visit the cathedrals of Salisbury and Winchester on a Sunday, when your visit will be restricted, or during services, when it won't be appreciated by worshipers. Places such as Stonehenge and Longleat House attract plenty of people at all times; bypass such sights on weekends or public holidays. In summer the coastal resorts of Bournemouth

GREAT ITINERARIES

With limited time, you may want to combine the most sights with the least amount of traveling.

Numbers in the text correspond to numbers in the margin and on the South, Winchester, and Salisbury maps.

IF YOU HAVE 3 DAYS

If you're coming from London or southeast England, 🚉 **Winchester** ❶-❾ ▶ will be your first stop. It's a quiet, solid town, conducive to walking about, with the great cathedral at its heart. Spend a night here, then move west to another cathedral city, 🚉 **Salisbury** ㉑-㉙. Surely few cathedrals have a more beautiful setting than this town—worth a two-night stay to take in the sights and nearby **Stonehenge** ㊲. Even closer to Salisbury are **Wilton House** ㉚ and its gardens, which you can see on your way to visit the village of **Shaftesbury** ㉛, and two more country estates, **Stourhead** ㉝ and **Longleat House** ㉞. The former holds—many believe—the most beautiful garden in England; the latter marries an African game park with a famous Elizabethan house.

IF YOU HAVE 5 DAYS

After a day touring 🚉 **Winchester** ❶-❾ and nearby **Chawton** ⓫, indelibly associated with Jane Austen, return to overnight in the cathedral city. The next morning, head for the south coast and **Portsmouth** ⓬ to take in its historic ships and the Royal Naval Museum. Spend the next two nights in 🚉 **Salisbury** ㉑-㉙ to discover the city and the marvels surrounding it, including **Wilton House** ㉚ and **Stonehenge** ㊲. Head south again to **Wimborne Minster** ㊷, a town dwarfed by the twin towers of its great church. If you have time, head farther south to see the jagged ruins of **Corfe Castle** ㊹. Spend your last two days in the area around 🚉 **Dorchester** ㊺, a must for fans of Thomas Hardy, although even without this literary connection it would be a captivating town, with the excavations of a Roman villa and an amphitheater just outside. Also nearby is the grassy site of **Maiden Castle** ㊼, an evocative prehistoric settlement. North of town, the chalk giant at **Cerne Abbas** ㊻ provides more links with the distant past.

and Weymouth are crowded; it may be difficult to find the accommodations you want. The Isle of Wight, too, gets its fair share of summer visitors, especially during the weeklong Cowes Regatta in late July or early August, and you may wait longer for the ferries. The New Forest is most alluring in spring and early summer (for the foaling season) and fall (for the colorful foliage), whereas summer can be busy with walkers and campers. In fall, take waterproof boots for the puddles.

FROM WINCHESTER TO SOUTHAMPTON

From the cathedral city of Winchester, 70 mi southwest of London, you can meander southward to the coast, stopping at the bustling ports of Southampton and Portsmouth to explore their maritime heritage. From either port you can strike out for the restful shores of the Isle of Wight, vacation home of Queen Victoria and thousands of modern-day Britons.

Winchester

▶ *70 mi southwest of London, 14 mi north of Southampton.*

Winchester is among the most historic of English cities, and as you walk the graceful streets and wander the many gardens, a sense of the past envelops you. Although it is now merely the county seat of Hampshire, for more than four centuries Winchester served as England's capital. Here, in AD 827, Egbert was crowned first king of England, and his successor, Alfred the Great, held court until his death in 899. After the Norman Conquest in 1066, William I ("the Conqueror") had himself crowned in London, but took the precaution of repeating the ceremony in Winchester. William also commissioned the local monastery to produce the Domesday Book, a record of the general census begun in 1085. The city remained the center of ecclesiastical, commercial, and political power until the 13th century, when that power shifted to London. Winchester still preserves some of its past glory even if some fast-food outlets and retail chains have moved onto High Street.

Main Attractions

❼ City Museum. Across from the cathedral, the museum interprets Winchester's past through displays of Celtic pottery, Roman mosaics, Saxon jewelry and coins, and reconstructed Victorian shops. ⊠ *The Sq.* ☎ *01962/ 848269* 🖾 *Free* ☉ *Apr.–Oct., Mon.–Sat. 10–5, Sun. noon–5; Nov.–Mar., Tues.–Sat. 10–4, Sun. noon–4.*

❷ Close. Nearly enveloping the cathedral, this area contains neat lawns and the Deanery, Dome Alley, and Cheyney Court.

❻ Great Hall. A few blocks west of the cathedral, this hall is all that remains of the city's Norman castle. Here the English Parliament met for the first time in 1246; Sir Walter Raleigh was tried for conspiracy against King James I and condemned to death in 1603 (although he wasn't beheaded until 1618); and Dame Alice Lisle was sentenced to death by the brutal Judge Jeffreys for sheltering fugitives, after Monmouth's Rebellion in 1685. Occupying one corner of the Great Hall is a huge and gaudy sculpture of Victoria, carved by Sir Alfred Gilbert (responsible for *Eros* in Piccadilly Circus) to mark the Queen's Golden Jubilee in 1887. But the hall's greatest relic hangs on its west wall: King Arthur's Round Table has places for 24 knights and a portrait of Arthur bearing a remarkable resemblance to King Henry VIII. In fact, the table dates back no further than the 13th century and was repainted by order of Henry on the occasion of a visit by the Holy Roman Emperor Charles V; the real Arthur was probably a Celtic cavalry general who held off the invading Saxons after the fall of the Roman Empire in the 5th or 6th century. The Tudor monarchs revived the Arthurian legend for political purposes. Take time to wander through Queen Eleanor's Medieval Garden—a re-creation of a noblewoman's shady retreat. ⊠ *Castle Hill* ☎ *01962/846476* 🖾 *Free* ☉ *Mar.–Oct., daily 10–5; Nov.–Feb., daily 10–4.*

TOP REASONS TO GO

Salisbury Cathedral: You may be stunned by the sight of one of England's most spectacular cathedrals; try a tour around the roof and spire for a fascinating angle on this must-see monument.

Stonehenge: Despite mixed reports of just how impressive this greatest of all prehistoric stone circles actually is, don't put off a visit. At the right time of day (early or late is best), this mystical ring can still cast a memorable spell against the backdrop of Salisbury Plain.

House and garden at Stourhead: It's the perfect combination. Acres of parkland, landscaped in the 18th century, induce feelings of Arcadian bliss. There are classical temples, a folly, and gorgeous vistas over the lake, as well as a Palladian mansion to explore.

The New Forest: Get away from it all in the South's most extensive wilderness—crisscrossed by myriad trails that are ideal for horseback riding, hiking, and biking.

Historic Dockyard, Portsmouth: Rule, Britannia! Immerse yourself in the country's seafaring history, including an informative and fascinating tour around Nelson's flagship, HMS *Victory*, conducted by naval personnel.

Literary trails: Jane Austen, Thomas Hardy, and John Fowles have all made this part of Britain a happy stomping ground for book buffs, with a concentration of sights in Chawton, Dorchester, and Lyme Regis. The Isle of Wight was particularly popular with Victorian literati, notably Tennyson.

3

❸ **King's Gate.** On St. Swithun Street on the south side of the Close, this structure was built in the 13th century and is one of two gates remaining from the original city wall. **St. Swithun's Church** is built over King's Gate.

★ ❶ **Winchester Cathedral.** The city's greatest monument, begun in 1079 and consecrated in 1093, presents a sturdy, chunky appearance in keeping with its Norman construction, so that the Gothic lightness within is even more breathtaking. Its tower, transepts, and crypt, and the inside core of the great Perpendicular nave, reveal some of the world's best surviving examples of Norman architecture. Other features, such as the arcades, the presbytery (behind the choir, holding the high altar), and the windows, are Gothic alterations carried out between the 12th and 14th centuries. Little of the original stained glass has survived, however, thanks to Cromwell's Puritan troops, who ransacked the cathedral in the 17th century during the English Civil War, but you can still see the sumptuously illuminated 12th-century Winchester Bible in the Library and Triforium Gallery.

Among the many well-known people buried in the cathedral are William the Conqueror's son, William II ("Rufus"), mysteriously murdered in the New Forest in 1100; Izaak Walton (1593–1683), author of *The Compleat Angler*, whose memorial window in Silkstede's Chapel was paid for by "the fishermen of England and America"; and Jane Austen,

The South

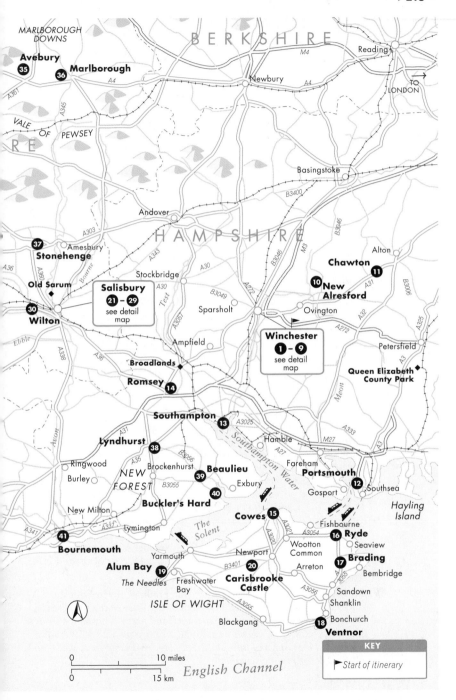

MARLBOROUGH DOWNS

B E R K S H I R E

M4

Reading

Avebury **35**

36 Marlborough

A4

Newbury

A4

TO LONDON

A361

A345

A4

VALE OF PEWSEY

RE

Basingstoke

B3400

Andover

H A M P S H I R E

B3046

M3

Alton

37 Stonehenge

Amesbury

A303

A343

A30

Stockbridge

B3046

Chawton

11

A36

A360

Old Sarum

Salisbury
21 – 29
see detail
map

A30

B3049

A272

10 New
Alresford

A31

B3006

30 Wilton

Sparsholt

Ovington

A32

A325

Eble

A338

A36

Ampfield

Winchester
1 – 9
see detail
map

A272

Petersfield

A3

Broadlands

Romsey **14**

Meon

Queen Elizabeth
County Park

Southampton **13**

A3025

Hamble

A27

M27

A333

A3

Lyndhurst **38**

A31

A35

Brockenhurst

B3056

Beaulieu

Exbury

Fareham

Portsmouth

Ringwood

NEW

B3055

39

Southampton Water

Gosport

12 Southsea

Burley

FOREST

40

Hayling
Island

New Milton

Buckler's Hard

Cowes **15**

Fishbourne

A341

A337

Lymington

The
Solent

Newport

A3054

16 **Ryde**

Seaview

41

Bournemouth

Yarmouth

Wootton
Common

Brading

Alum Bay **19**

B3401

20

Arreton

Bembridge

The Needles

Freshwater
Bay

Carisbrooke
Castle

A3056

Sandown

ISLE OF WIGHT

A3055

Shanklin

Blackgang

18 Bonchurch

Ventnor

0 ___ 10 miles

English Channel

0 ___ 15 km

KEY
▶ *Start of itinerary*

City Mill **8**

City Museum . . . **7**

Close **2**

Great Hall **6**

King's Gate/
St. Swithun's
Church **3**

St. Giles's Hill . . . **9**

Westgate **5**

Winchester
Cathedral **1**

Winchester
College **4**

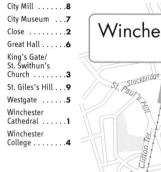

whose grave lies in the north aisle of the nave. Firmly in the 20th century, Antony Gormley's evocative statue, *Sound II* (1986), looms in the crypt, as often as not standing in water (as it was designed to do), because of seasonal flooding. You can also explore the bell tower—with views as far as the Isle of Wight in fair weather—and other recesses of the building on a tour. Special services or ceremonies may mean the cathedral is closed to visits, so telephone first to avoid disappointment. ⊠ *The Close, Cathedral Precincts* ☎ *01962/857200* ⊕ *www.winchester-cathedral.org.uk* ⊠ *£4; Library and Triforium Gallery £1, bell tower tour £4* ⊗ *Mon.–Sat. 8:30–6, Sun. 12:30–3:30, longer for services. Free tours on the hr Mon.–Sat. 10–3, bell tower tours May–Sept., weekdays 2:15, Sat. 11:30 and 2:15; Oct.–Apr., Wed. 2:15, Sat. 11:30 and 2:15.*

Also Worth Seeing

❽ City Mill. This working 18th-century water mill, complete with small island garden, is at the east end of High Street. Part of the premises is a National Trust gift shop open year-round, and part is a hostel. ⊠ *Bridge St.* ☎ *01962/870057* ⊕ *www.nationaltrust.org.uk* ⊠ *£3.20* ⊗ *Mar., weekends 11–5; Apr. and July–Dec., daily 11–5; May and June, Wed.–Sun. 11–5. Call for milling schedule.*

9 St. Giles's Hill. To top off a tour of Winchester, you can climb this hill for a panoramic view of the city. A walk down High Street and Broadway will bring you to the hill.

5 Westgate. At the top of High Street, this fortified medieval structure was a debtor's prison for 150 years, and now holds a motley assortment of items relating to Tudor and Stuart times. Suits of armor—examples can be tried on—and the opportunity to make brass rubbings make it popular with kids, and you can take in a view of Winchester from the roof. ⊠ *High St.* ☎ *01962/848269* ▭ *Free* ☉ *Apr.–Oct., Mon.–Sat. 10–5, Sun. noon–5; Feb. and Mar., Tues.–Sat. 10–4, Sun. noon–4.*

4 Winchester College. One of England's oldest "public" (i.e., private) schools was founded in 1382 by Bishop William of Wykeham, who has his own chapel in Winchester Cathedral. The school chapel is notable for its delicately vaulted ceiling. Among the original buildings still in use is Chamber Court, center of college life for six centuries. Notice the "scholars"—students holding academic scholarships—clad in their traditional gowns. ⊠ *College St.* ☎ *01962/621209* ⊕ *www.winchestercollege.co. uk* ▭ *£3.50* ☉ *1-hr tours Mon., Wed., Fri., and Sat. 10:45, noon, 2:15, and 3:30; Tues. and Thurs. 10:45 and noon; Sun. 2:15 and 3:30.*

ST. SWITHUN WEATHER

St. Swithun (died AD 862) is interred in Winchester Cathedral, although he requested outdoor burial. Legend says that when his body was transferred inside from the cathedral's churchyard, it rained for 40 days. Since then, folk wisdom says that rain on St. Swithun's Day (July 15) means 40 more days of wet weather. (Elsewhere in England the name is spelled "Swithin.") Near St. Swithun's Church at King's Gate, at 8 College Street, is the house where Jane Austen died on July 18, 1817, three days after writing a comic poem about the legend of St. Swithun's Day (copies are usually available in the cathedral).

Where to Stay & Eat

£££££ ✕ **Chesil Rectory.** The timbered and gabled building may be old English— 15th- or 16th-century—but the cuisine is essentially French, mixing classic recipes with local ingredients. On the fixed-price menu, starters such as Jerusalem artichoke soup elegantly complement such main courses as fillet of Hampshire beef Rossini with white truffle pomme purée and Madeira sauce. Service and the antique charm of the surroundings match the quality of the food. ⊠ *1 Chesil St.* ☎ *01962/851555* ▭ *AE, DC, MC, V* ☉ *Closed Sun. and Mon. No lunch Tues.*

££–£££ ✕ **Loch Fyne.** This excellent, fairly priced seafood restaurant, part of a small chain in England and Scotland, has a modern interior behind the 15th-century facade. Inside, the floor-to-ceiling windows create an airy space for dining, and the cheerful service is relaxing. Fish is the center of attention, from peppered mackerel pâté with oatcakes to solid main courses including perfectly poached haddock atop creamed spinach. ⊠ *18 Jewry St.* ☎ *01962/872930* ⌁ *Reservations essential* ▭ *AE, MC, V.*

£–££ ✕ **The Royal Oak.** Try a half pint of draft bitters or dry cider at this lively traditional pub, which claims to have Britain's oldest bar (it has a Saxon wall). The two no-smoking areas—a rarity in British pubs—are in the cellar and on the upper level. Bar meals are served until 9 PM. ✉ *Royal Oak Passage, off High St.* ☎ *01962/842701* ▭ *AE, MC, V.*

£ ✕ **Cathedral Refectory.** The bold, modern style of this self-service eatery next to the cathedral helps make it a refreshing lunch or snack stop. The menu ranges from traditional soups to cottage pie and fish dishes, but do sample the local "trenchers." This thick bread was used in medieval times as a plate from which to eat meat; once soaked in the meat juices, the bread was passed down to the poor. Today the trenchers, soaked in toppings such as pesto or ham and goat's cheese, are grilled. ✉ *Inner Close* ☎ *01962/857200* ▭ *MC, V* ☺ *No dinner.*

££££ ✕▦ **Hotel du Vin.** Rooms in this elegant redbrick Georgian town house are richly furnished in crisp modern style, with Oriental rugs enhancing the polished wooden floors. Egyptian-cotton bed linens, huge baths, and power showers make for a luxurious stay. The many eclectic wine selections in the stylish bistro (£££–££££) complement traditional French and English fare such as poached fillet of sole and chargrilled rib-eye steak with french fries. Call to arrange a private wine-tasting session. In summer, food is served in the walled garden. ✉ *14 Southgate St., S023 9EF* ☎ *01962/841414* 🖷 *01962/842458* ⊕ *www.hotelduvin.com* ⟿ *24 rooms ♻ Restaurant, cable TV, in-room data ports, bar, meeting rooms; no a/c* ▭ *AE, DC, MC, V.*

★ £££ ✕▦ **Wykeham Arms.** This old place is conveniently central, near the cathedral and the college. Bedrooms at the inn itself are cozy and full of quirky knickknacks, with period touches; those across the road in the St. George annex are slightly larger. The bars, happily cluttered with prints and pewter, make use of old school desks for tables. A good wine list sets off the French and English dishes at the restaurant (££–££££), which is popular with locals. ✉ *75 Kingsgate St., SO23 9PE* ☎ *01962/ 853834* 🖷 *01962/854411* ✑ *wykehamarms@accommodating-inns. co.uk* ⟿ *14 rooms ♻ Restaurant, 2 bars, some pets allowed, no-smoking rooms; no a/c, no kids under 14* ▭ *AE, DC, MC, V* ⦿ *BP.*

£££££ ▦ **Lainston House.** Dating from 1668, this elegant country-house hotel in a 63-acre park is discreetly secluded, an obvious attraction for such eminent guests as Margaret Thatcher, who stayed here to write her memoirs. Inside, cedar and oak paneling and other restored 17th-century details adorn the public rooms. Bedrooms, many of which are beamed, are done in warm colors and rich fabrics. Ground-floor suites have access to the gardens, and a converted stable holds luxury rooms. The hotel is 2½ mi northwest of Winchester. ✉ *Off B3049, Sparsholt SO21 2LT* ☎ *01962/863588* 🖷 *01962/776672* ⊕ *www.exclusivehotels. co.uk* ⟿ *50 rooms ♻ Restaurant, some in-room hot tubs, 2 tennis courts, gym, croquet, meeting rooms, helipad, some pets allowed; no a/c in some rooms* ▭ *AE, DC, MC, V* ⦿ *BP.*

££££ ▦ **Winchester Royal.** Formerly a bishop's house and then a convent, this classy hotel lies within easy reach of the cathedral on a quiet side street. Bedrooms, decorated with floral fabrics and dark wood, surround a large inner garden; rooms in the main building have more period features. You can have a good lunch in the bar or a fuller meal in the Conservatory Restaurant. ✉ *St. Peter St. near High St., S023 8BS* ☎ *01962/840840* 🖷 *01962/841582* ⊕ *www.forestdale.com* ⟿ *75 rooms ♻ Restaurant,* *cable TV, Wi-Fi, bar, business services, meeting rooms, some pets allowed (fee); no a/c* 🖃 *AE, DC, MC, V* 🍴 *BP.*

££ 🖵 **Enmill Lane.** As B&Bs go, this one is first class, with historic character and a modern ethos. The big, converted barn in the peaceful countryside 3 mi west of the center of Winchester makes a good base for exploring nearby villages and the South Downs. The rooms are freshly decorated in neutral tones and filled with personality—not to mention refrigerators stocked with drinks and nibbles—and breakfast includes fresh fruit and such delicacies as fresh duck eggs. ⊠ *Enmill La., Pitt SO22 5QR* ☎ *01962/856740* 🖨 *01962/854219* ⊕ *www.enmill-barn.co.uk* ⇩ *2 rooms* ⚬ *Refrigerator, tennis court, billiards, no-smoking rooms; no a/c, no room phones* 🖃 *No credit cards* 🍴 *BP.*

Shopping

A complete list of local antiques stores is available from the **Winchester Tourist Information Centre** (⊠ The Guildhall, Broadway ☎ 01962/840500). **King's Walk**, off Friarsgate, has a number of stalls selling antiques, crafts, gift items, and bric-a-brac. **The Jays' Nest** (⊠ King's Walk ☎ 01962/865650) specializes in silver and china. **P&G Wells** (⊠ 11 College St. ☎ 01962/852016), the oldest bookshop in town, stocks new titles and carries a small selection of secondhand books and prints in an annex in nearby Kingsgate Street.

Britain's largest **farmers' market** (☎ 01420/588671 ⊕ www. hampshirefarmersmarkets.co.uk), held in Middle Brook Street on the second and the last Sunday of each month, specializes in local produce and goods that are grown, reared, baked, or caught in Hampshire or within 10 mi of its borders. Look for Dexter beef, the products of water buffalo and Manx Loughton sheep, and walking sticks made from local wood. In September the market is the focal point of Hampshire Hog Day, the hog being the symbol of Hampshire.

> **OPEN-AIR MARKETS**
>
> Exploring a local market can provide a unique sense of place; for a complete list of those in the South, ask Tourism South East (⇨ Visitor Information *in* South Essentials, *below*). Among the best are Winchester's, Salisbury's traditional city market (Tuesday and Saturday), Kingsland Market in Southampton for bric-a-brac (Thursday), and a general country market (Wednesday) at Ringwood, near Bournemouth.

New Alresford

❿ *8 mi northeast of Winchester, by A31 and B3046.*

New Alresford (pronounced *awls*-ford) has a village green crossed by a stream and some Georgian houses and antiques shops. The village is the starting point of the **Watercress Line,** a 10-mi railroad reserved for steam locomotives that runs to Alton. The line (named for the watercress beds formerly in the area) takes you on a nostalgic tour through reminders of 19th-century England. ⊠ *Railway Station* ☎ *01962/733810* ⊕ *www. watercressline.co.uk* 🎫 *£10* ⊙ *May–Sept., daily departures; Mar., Apr., and Oct., weekends and national holidays; call for details.*

In Search of Jane Austen

A TOUR OF "JANE AUSTEN COUNTRY" in the South of England and beyond can enhance the experience of reading Austen's novels. Thanks to recent film adaptations of *Sense and Sensibility, Emma, Persuasion,* and *Pride and Prejudice,* the great author has captured another audience eager to peer into her decorous 18th- and early-19th-century world. By visiting one or two main locales—such as Chawton and Winchester—it is possible to imagine hearing the tinkle of teacups raised by the likes of Elinor Dashwood and Mr. Darcy. Serious Janeites will want to retrace her life—starting out in the hamlet of Steventon, southwest of Basingstoke, where she spent her first 25 years, then moving on to Bath, Southampton, Chawton, and Winchester.

Jane Austen country—a pleasant landscape filled with intimately scaled villages—is a perfectly civilized stage on which her characters organized visits to stately homes and husband-hunting expeditions. As Austen described this terrain in *Emma,* "It has a sweet view—sweet to the eye and the mind. English verdure, English culture, English comfort." Entering that world, you find that its heart is the tiny Hampshire village of Chawton. Here, at a former bailiff's cottage on her brother's estate—now a museum—Austen produced three of her greatest novels. Her daily 6-mi walks often took her to Chawton Manor—her brother's regal Jacobean mansion, now Chawton House Library, a center for the study of 16th–18th-century women's literature (for a consultation, call ☎ 01420/541010 or see ⊕ www.chawton.org)—or to nearby Lyards Farm, where her

favorite niece, Anna Lefroy (thought to be the model for Emma Woodhouse), came to live in 1815. A bit farther away is Great Bookham—closely identified with the "Highbury" of *Emma*—and nearby lies Box Hill (to the east of A24 between Leatherhead and Dorking), the probable inspiration for the locale of the famous walking expedition that left Miss Woodhouse in tears.

Driving southwest from Chawton, take A31 for about 15 mi to Winchester, where you can visit Austen's austere grave within the cathedral; then take in No. 8 College Street, where her battle with Addison's disease ended with her death on July 18, 1817. Heading 110 mi southwest you can visit Lyme Regis, the 18th-century seaside resort on the Devon border where Austen spent the summers of 1804–05. Here, at the Cobb, the stone jetty that juts into Lyme Bay, Louisa Musgrove jumps off the steps known as Granny's Teeth—a turning point in Chapter 12 of *Persuasion.* Northwest of Winchester by some 60 mi is Bath, the elegant setting that served as the backdrop for some of Austen's razor-sharp observations. The Jane Austen Centre explores the relationship between Bath and the writer.

"It is the only place for happiness, " Austen once said of the county of Kent, some 150 mi to the east of Chawton. "Everybody is rich there." Godmersham Park, another of her brother's estates (off the A28 between Canterbury and Ashford), offered her an escape to the countryside. The magnificent redbrick mansion is privately owned, but you can take a nearby public footpath to pass the little Grecian temple where she completed *Sense and Sensibility.*

Chawton

🔟🔟 *8 mi east of New Alresford.*

Jane Austen (1775–1817) lived the last eight years of her life in the village of Chawton; she moved to Winchester only during her final illness. The site has always drawn literary pilgrims, but with the ongoing release of successful films based on her novels, the popularity of the town among visitors has grown enormously. Here, in an unassuming redbrick house, Austen revised *Sense and Sensibility,* created *Pride and Prejudice,* and worked on *Emma, Persuasion,* and *Mansfield Park.*

★ Now a museum, the rooms of **Jane Austen's House** retain the atmosphere of restricted gentility suitable to the unmarried daughter of a clergyman. In the left-hand parlor, Jane would play her piano every morning, then repair to her mahogany writing desk in the family sitting room—leaving her sister Cassandra to do the household chores ("I find composition impossible with my head full of joints of mutton and doses of rhubarb," Jane wrote). In the early 19th century, the road near the house was a bustling thoroughfare, and one traveler reported that a window view proved that the Misses Austen were "looking very comfortable at breakfast." Jane was famous for working through interruptions, but one protection against the outside world was the famous door that creaked. She asked that its hinges remain unattended to because they gave her warning that someone was coming. ✉ *Signed off A31/A32 roundabout* ☎ *01420/83262* ⊕ *www.janeaustenmuseum.org.uk* 💷 *£4.50* ☉ *Mar.–Dec., daily 11–4:30; Jan. and Feb., weekends 11–4:30; last admission 30 mins before closing.*

Portsmouth

1️⃣2️⃣ *24 mi south of Chawton, 77 mi southwest of London.*

This industrial, largely charmless city was England's naval capital and principal port of departure for centuries. It still has a substantial shipping industry, but the main attraction for travelers are the ferries that set off from here for Europe and the Isle of Wight. Portsmouth also has an extraordinary collection of maritime memorabilia, including well-preserved warships that date back to medieval times. Much of the city is not particularly pleasant, so use common sense before venturing on foot into parts of town that look questionable. Still, the newly developed Gunwharf Quays and the soaring Spinnaker Tower are indications that better days may lie ahead for this weary old coastal town.

FodorśChoice ★ The city's most impressive attraction, the **Portsmouth Historic Dockyard,** includes an unrivaled collection of historic ships and the comprehensive Royal Naval Museum (a great place to learn about British naval hero Admiral Lord Horatio Nelson). The dockyard's youngest ship, **HMS *Warrior 1860,*** was England's first ironclad battleship. Admiral Nelson's flagship, **HMS *Victory,*** has been painstakingly restored to appear as she did at the battle at Trafalgar (1805). You can inspect the cramped gun decks, visit the cabin where Nelson entertained his officers, and stand on the spot where he was mortally wounded by a French sniper. Visits aboard the *Victory* are by guided tour only and may entail a long wait. The **Mary Rose,** former flagship of the Tudor navy, which capsized and sank in the harbor in 1545, was raised in 1982. Described in the 16th century as "the flower of all the ships that ever sailed," the *Mary Rose* is now housed in a special enclosure, where water continuously sprays her timbers to prevent them from drying out and breaking up. Exhibits in the intriguing *Mary Rose* Museum display more than 1,200 artifacts from the ship. The **Royal Naval Museum** has a fine collection of painted figureheads, extensive exhibits about Nelson and the battle of Trafalgar, and galleries of paintings and mementos recalling naval history from King Alfred to the present. **Action Sta-**

> ## RULING THE SEAS
>
> Island that it is, Great Britain invested heavily in its Royal Navy, to defend its shores and, eventually, to access its far-flung empire. The first dry dock in Europe was built in 1495 in Portsmouth, by order of Henry VII. His son, Henry VIII, greatly built up the navy early in his reign, but it was still a smaller force than the Spanish Armada, whose attack the English beat back famously in 1588, during the reign of Elizabeth I. It would take another century for England to make its navy the largest, and the world's most powerful, a rank it held up to World War II.

tions, an interactive attraction, gives you insight into life in the modern Royal Navy and tests your sea legs with tasks such as piloting boats through gales. **Dockyard Apprentice** showcases the skills of the shipbuilders and craftsmen who constructed and maintained the naval vessels, with illustrations of rope-making, sail-making, caulking, signals, and knots. ☒ *Historic Dockyard, Portsmouth Naval Base* ☎ *023/ 9286–1512* ⊕ *www.historicdockyard.co.uk* ☐ *£16 includes harbor tour; valid for return visits* ☉ *Apr.–Oct., daily 10–5:30; Nov.–Mar., daily 10–5; last admission 1 hr before closing.*

NEED A BREAK?

After a slog around the Historic Dockyard you can find rest and replenishment, including seafood, at the harborside **Still & West Country House** (☒ Bath Sq. ☎ 023/9282–1567), a pub with outdoor seating. It faces the Spice Island Inn, another pub.

Newly erected on the lively Gunwharf Quays development of shops and bars, **Spinnaker Tower** provides a striking visual focus on Portsmouth's skyline. The slender structure, with the form of a mast and billowing sail, rises to a height of 541 feet. An elevator whisks you to three viewing platforms 330 feet high, for thrilling all-around views over the harbor and up to 20 mi beyond. ☒ *Gunwharf Quays* ☎ *023/9285 7520* ⊕ *www.spinnakertower.co.uk* ☐ *£4.95* ☉ *Sun.–Fri. 10–5, Sat. 10–10.*

In the popular **D-Day Museum,** in nearby Southsea, exhibits reconstruct the planning and logistics involved in the D-Day landings, as well as the actual invasion on June 6, 1944. The museum's centerpiece is the Overlord Embroidery ("Overlord" was the code name for the invasion), a 272-foot-long tapestry with 34 panels illustrating the history of World War II, from the Battle of Britain in 1940 to D-Day and the first days of the liberation. ⊠ *Clarence Esplanade, Southsea* ☎ *023/9282–7261* ⊕ *www.ddaymuseum.co.uk* ✉ *£5.50* ⊙ *Apr.–Oct., daily 10–5:30; Nov.–Mar., daily 10–5; last admission 30 mins before closing.*

The highlight of **Submarine World** is the tour with an ex-submariner of the World War II submarine HMS *Alliance,* from the cramped quarters to the engine room. The museum fills you in on submarine history and lets you view Portsmouth Harbour through a periscope. There are plenty of subs, weapons, and diving paraphernalia around the large site. From Portsmouth Harbour, take the ferry to Gosport and walk along Millennium Promenade past the huge sundial clock. ⊠ *Haslar Jetty Rd., Gosport* ☎ *023/9252–9217* ⊕ *www.rnsubmus.co.uk* ✉ *£6.50* ⊙ *Apr.–Oct., daily 10–5:30; Nov.–Mar., daily 10–4:30.*

In a former arms depot near Submarine World, **Explosion!** (the name given to the Museum of Naval Firepower) gathers together munitions, mines, and missiles in relating the history of armaments used at sea. The museum also tells the story of the many locals who manufactured them. Interactive exhibits help you understand what it's like to do nautical things such as walk on a seabed. ⊠ *Priddy's Hard, Gosport* ☎ *023/9250–5600* ⊕ *www.explosion.org.uk* ✉ *£5.50* ⊙ *Apr.–Oct., daily 10–5:30; Nov.–Mar., Thurs. and weekends 10–4:30.*

Portchester Castle incorporates the walls of a Roman fort built more than 1,600 years ago; these are the most complete set of Roman walls in northern Europe. In the 12th century the castle (now in ruins) was built inside the impressive fortifications. From the keep's central tower you can take in a sweeping view of the harbor and coastline. ⊠ *Off A27, near Fareham* ☎ *023/9237–8291* ⊕ *www.english-heritage.org.uk* ✉ *£3.70* ⊙ *Apr.–Sept., daily 10–6; Oct.–Mar., daily 10–4.*

Where to Stay & Eat

£££££ ✕ **Bistro Montparnasse.** Modern paintings on terra-cotta walls add a contemporary touch to this bustling restaurant. The reasonable, fixed-price menu may include prawn and lentil bisque, or roasted rump of lamb with caramelized parsnip and garlic purée. ⊠ *103 Palmerston Rd., Southsea* ☎ *023/9281–6754* ▭ *AE, MC, V* ⊙ *Closed Sun. and Mon.*

££–£££ ✕ **Lemon Sole.** Seafood doesn't get much fresher than this. After ordering your appetizer and bread from the waiter, you head over to the amply stocked fish bar to choose your main course, which will be priced by its weight. You also select a cooking method, sauces such as citrus or mushroom and fennel, and side dishes. Ask for the sauce on the side, as it can overpower the dish. Fish, meat, and vegetarian options also appear on a menu. This place is better for grown-ups than for kids. ⊠ *123 High St.* ☎ *023/9281–1303* ▭ *AE, DC, MC, V* ⊙ *Closed Sun.*

££ ✕▭ **Sally Port.** This timber-frame old tavern opposite the cathedral in Old Portsmouth has subtle nautical associations, such as the top spar around which the Georgian staircase is built; the 40-foot mast is said to have come from a frigate. Sloping floors and marine pictures are additional details. The street-level bar and first-floor restaurant (open Friday and Saturday; £–£££) provide good light meals or fuller fare, such as sea bass, Dover sole, steaks, and lamb fillets. Rooms are comfortable and equipped with washbasins and showers; toilets are shared. ✉ *57–58 High St., PO1 2LU* ☎ *023/9282–1860* 🖷 *023/9282–1293* 🛏 *10 rooms without bath* 🕭 *Restaurant, bar; no a/c* ⊟ *AE, DC, MC, V* ⊠ *BP.*

£££ 🖭 **Westfield Hall.** Portsmouth is well supplied with chain offerings, but this pleasant smaller establishment has personal service and character. It occupies two converted early-20th-century houses close to the water in the resort of Southsea. Rooms (seven are on the ground floor) have large bay windows and are restfully furnished in greens and creams; three sitting rooms provide a place to relax. ✉ *65 Festing Rd., off Eastern Parade, PO4 0NQ* ☎ *023/9282–6971* 🖷 *023/9287–0200* ⊕ *www. whhotel.info* 🛏 *26 rooms* 🕭 *Dining room, cable TV, in-room data ports, Wi-Fi, no-smoking rooms; no a/c* ⊟ *AE, DC, MC, V* ⊠ *BP.*

£ 🖭 **Sailmaker's Loft.** This low-key B&B in Portsmouth's old town makes a handy option, not least because it's close to the water and some rooms have excellent sea views. It's also convenient to many sights. Rooms are simply decorated but pleasant and full of light; doubles have private bathrooms (singles share a bath), and the owners are friendly. ✉ *5 Bath Sq., PO1 2JL* ☎ *023/9282–3045* 🖷 *023/9229–5961* ✍ *sailmakersloft@aol. com* 🛏 *4 rooms, 2 with bath* 🕭 *No a/c* ⊟ *No credit cards* ⊠ *BP.*

The Outdoors

Queen Elizabeth Country Park, part of an Area of Outstanding Beauty in the South Downs, has 1,400 acres of chalk hills and shady beeches with scenic hiking trails. You can climb to the top of Butser Hill (888 feet) to take in a splendid view of the coast. The park lies 12 mi north of Portsmouth, and 4 mi south of the Georgian market town of Petersfield, in a wide valley between wooded hills and open downs. Check the Web site for guided walks and programs. ✉ *A3* ☎ *023/9259–5040* ⊕ *www. hants.gov.uk/countryside/qecp* 🏷 *Free; car park £1, Sun. £1.50* 🕙 *Park open 24 hrs; visitor center (including café and shop) Apr.–Oct., daily 10–5:30; Nov.–Mar. daily 10–4:30. Closed early to mid-Jan.*

Southampton

⑬ *21 mi northwest of Portsmouth, 25 mi southwest of Salisbury, 79 mi southwest of London.*

Seafaring Saxons and Romans used Southampton's harbor, Southampton Water, as a commercial trading port for centuries, and the city thrived, becoming one of England's wealthiest. But Plymouth eventually supplanted it, and Southampton has been going downhill ever since. Still, it remains England's leading passenger port, and as the home port of Henry V's fleet bound for Agincourt, the *Mayflower,* the *Queen Mary,* and the ill-fated *Titanic,* along with countless other great ocean liners of the 20th century, Southampton has one of the richest maritime traditions in England. Much of the city center is shoddy, having been hastily rebuilt after World War II bombing, but bits of the city's history peek out from between modern buildings. The Old Town retains its medieval air, and considerable parts of Southampton's castellated town walls remain. Other attractions include a decent art gallery, extensive parks, and a couple of good museums. The Southampton International Boat Show, a 10-day event in mid-September, draws huge crowds.

Incorporated in the town walls are a number of old buildings, including **God's House Tower,** originally a gunpowder factory and now an archaeology museum. Displays focus on the Roman, Saxon, and medieval periods of Southampton's history, and an interactive computer allows virtual access to the archaeological collections. ⊠ *Winkle St.* ☏ *023/8063–5904* ⊕ *www.southampton.gov.uk* ✉ *Free* ☉ *Apr.–Oct., Tues.–Fri. 10–noon and 1–5, Sat. 10–noon and 1–4, Sun. 2–5; Nov.–Mar., Tues.–Fri. 10–4, Sat. 10–noon and 1–4, Sun. 1–4.*

Mayflower Park and the Pilgrim Fathers' Memorial (⊠ Western Esplanade) commemorate the departure of 102 passengers on the North America–bound *Mayflower* from Southampton on August 15, 1620. A plaque also honors the 2 million U.S. troops who left Southampton in World War II.

The **Southampton Maritime Museum** brings together models, mementos, and items of furniture from the age of the great clippers and cruise ships, including a wealth of memorabilia relating to the *Titanic*—footage, photos, crew lists, etc. Boat buffs will relish plenty of vital statistics dealing with the history of commercial shipping. ⊠ *Bugle St.* ☏ *023/8022–3941* ⊕ *www.southampton.gov.uk* ✉ *Free* ☉ *Apr.–Oct., Tues.–Fri. 10–1 and 2–5, Sat. 10–1 and 2–4, Sun. 2–5; Nov.–Mar., Tues.–Fri. 10–4, Sat. 10–1 and 2–4, Sun. 1–4.*

Where to Stay & Eat

££–£££ ✕ **Langleys.** At this busy bistro convenient to Southampton's docks, dishes such as Breton fish soup and fillet steak with local shellfish share the menu with Mediterranean fare. Modern art adorns the walls, and ceiling fans keep things cool in summer. The Garden Room Cafe and Terrace makes an appealing lunchtime stop. ⊠ *10–11 Bedford Pl.* ☏ *023/8022–4551* ▤ *MC, V* ☉ *Closed Sun. No lunch Sat.*

££–£££ ✕ **Oxford Brasserie.** This informal place gets lively in the evening, but it's calmer at lunchtime. Fresh fish is always available (the fixed-price menus are a particularly good value), along with French and international fare. The tile floor and cream-color walls hung with paintings are straightforward and not gimmicky. ⊠ *33–34 Oxford St.* ☏ *023/8063–5043* ▤ *AE, DC, MC, V* ☉ *Closed Sun. No lunch Sat.*

£££ ⊞ **Dolphin Hotel.** Originally a Georgian coaching inn—although there's been an inn of some sort on this site for seven centuries—the Dolphin has seen such illustrious visitors as Queen Victoria, Lord Nelson, and Jane Austen. Many of the traditional trappings have been replaced by sleek, modern furnishings, with works of art up and down the stairs and in every bedroom, where beds have individually styled headboards and white Egyptian-cotton duvets. The Oak Bar and Bleu Restaurant serve bar snacks and full meals, respectively. ⊠ *35 High St., SO14 2HN* ☏ *023/8033–9955* ☐ *023/8033–3650* ⊕ *www.thedolphin.co.uk* ⇱ *70 rooms* ♿ *Restaurant, bar, in-room data ports, business services, meeting rooms, some pets allowed; no a/c* ▤ *AE, DC, MC, V* ⫝̸ *BP.*

Nightlife & the Arts

The **Mayflower Theatre** (⊠ Commercial Rd. ☏ 023/8071–1811) is among the larger theaters outside London; the Royal Shakespeare Company and Barnum on Ice are among the organizations that have packed the house.

The **Nuffield Theatre** (☎ 023/8067–1771), at Southampton University, has a repertory company and also hosts national touring groups.

Romsey

⑭ *10 mi northwest of Southampton.*

This small town on the River Test has an authentic Norman abbey church and, in the marketplace, an iron bracket said to have been used to hang two of Cromwell's soldiers. The flint-and-stone house near the marketplace, known as King John's Hunting Box, dates from the 13th century. Florence Nightingale is buried under a simple stone in East Wellow churchyard in Romsey, near her former house at Embley Park.

Broadlands, outside Romsey, was the home of the late Lord Mountbatten (1900–79), uncle of Queen Elizabeth II, and is undoubtedly the grandest house in Hampshire. Ornate plaster moldings and paintings of British and Continental royalty decorate the 18th-century Palladian mansion, which also contains an exhibition tracing Lord Mountbatten's distinguished career in the navy and in India. Landscape designer Capability Brown laid out the gardens, and the wide lawns sweep down to the banks of the River Test. In 1947 the Queen and the Duke of Edinburgh spent their honeymoon here, and Prince Charles and the late Princess Diana spent a few days here after their wedding in 1981. ⊠ *A3090 Romsey bypass* ☎ *01794/505010* ⊕ *www.broadlands.net* ⊠ *£8* ☉ *July and Aug., daily 1–5:30; last tour at 4.*

Where to Stay

£££ 🏨 **Corus Hotel Romsey.** A good place to stay if you're visiting Broadlands, this modern hotel is behind the original thatched building. Some bedrooms have floral themes and are paneled in pine, whereas others are plainer; many have balconies. Dining is in the oak-beam Potters Pub or the Garden Restaurant. ⊠ *3 mi east of Romsey, Ampfield SO51 9ZF* ☎ *023/8026–6611 or 0870/609–6155* 🖶 *023/8025–1359* ⊕ *www. corushotels.com* 🛏 *54 rooms* ♿ *Restaurant, cable TV with movies, Wi-Fi, sauna, pub, business services, meeting rooms, some pets allowed; no a/c in some rooms* ▤ *AE, DC, MC, V.*

ISLE OF WIGHT

A slightly tattered, slightly romantic place, this island sometimes gets so crowded it seems that it might sink beneath the weight of the throngs of summer visitors. Its appealingly dusty Victorian look comes courtesy of Queen Victoria, who put the Isle of Wight (pronounced white) on the map by choosing it for the site of Osborne House. She lived here as much as she could, and ultimately she died here. Perhaps understandably, islanders are fiercely chauvinistic; like Tennyson, who lived here until tourist harassment drove him away, they resent the crowds of tourists. But every season the day-trippers arrive—thanks to the ferries, hovercraft, and hydrofoils that connect the island with Southampton, Portsmouth, Southsea, and Lymington. People come to this 23-mi-long island for its holiday resorts—Ryde, Bembridge, Ventnor,

Freshwater (stay away from tacky Sandown and Shanklin)—its rich vegetation, narrow lanes, thatched cottages, curving bays, sandy beaches, and walking paths. The fabulous ocean air, to quote Tennyson, is "worth six pence a pint." All is not sea and sails, however. There is splendid driving to be done in the interior of the island, in such places as Brading Down, Ashley Down, and Mersely Down, and the occasional country house to visit, none more spectacular than Queen Vicky's own Osborne House.

3

Cowes

⓯ *11 mi northwest of Ryde.*

If you embark from Southampton, your ferry will cross the Solent channel and dock at Cowes, a magic name in the sailing world and internationally known for the Cowes Week annual yachting festival, held in July or August. Fifty years ago, the Cowes Regatta was a supreme event; the world's most famous figures crowded the green lawns of the Royal Yacht Squadron. Although its elegance is a thing of the past, the Cowes Regatta remains an important yachting event. At the north end of High Street, on the Parade, a tablet commemorates the 1633 sailing from Cowes of two ships carrying the first English settlers of the state of Maryland.

Queen Victoria's **Osborne House,** designed by Prince Albert after a villa in the stodgiest Italian Renaissance style, holds enormous interest for anyone drawn to the domestic side of history. After Albert's death in 1861 the queen spent much of her time here, mourning her loss in relative seclusion. In this massive pile, one sees the engineer manqué in Prince Albert and his clever innovations—including a kind of central heating—as well as evidence of Victoria's desperate attempts to give her children a normal but disciplined upbringing. A carriage ride will take you to the Swiss Cottage, a superior version of a playhouse, especially built for the children. The antiques-filled state rooms have scarcely been altered since Victoria's death here in 1901. The house and grounds—which can be quite crowded during July and August—were used as a location for the 1998 movie *Mrs. Brown.* ⊠ *Off A3021, 1 mi southeast of Cowes* ☎ *01983/200022* ⊕ *www.english-heritage.org.uk* ✍ *£9.50, grounds only £5.50* ◷ *Apr.–Sept., daily 10–5; Oct., daily 10–4; Nov.–Mar., Wed.–Sun. prebooked guided tours only, last tour at 2:30.*

Where to Stay

£££ 🏨 **New Holmwood Hotel.** This Best Western hotel occupies an unrivaled location above the Esplanade—ideal for watching yachters in the Solent. The three sitting rooms include one with an open fire on winter evenings and one for nonsmokers, and the sun terrace and pool take full advantage of fine weather. Patterned fabrics contrast with plain walls in the guest rooms. ⊠ *Queens Rd., Egypt Point PO31 8BW* ☎ *01983/ 292508* 🖶 *01983/295020* ⊕ *www.newholmwoodhotel.co.uk* ⇩ *26 rooms* ⚲ *Restaurant, cable TV, in-room data ports, pool, bar, meeting rooms, some pets allowed; no a/c* ⊟ *AE, DC, MC, V* ¶⊙¶ *BP.*

Ryde

⑯ *11 mi southeast of Cowes.*

The town of Ryde has long been one of the Isle of Wight's most popular summer resorts, with several family attractions. After the construction of Ryde Pier in 1814, elegant town houses sprang up along the seafront and on the slopes behind, commanding fine views of the harbor. In addition to its long, sandy beach, Ryde has a large boating lake (you can rent rowboats and pedal boats) and children's playgrounds. To get here from Cowes, leave on A3021, then follow the signs on A3054.

Where to Stay & Eat

£££££ ✕▦ **Priory Bay Hotel.** This hotel, part of which dates to medieval times, has been sympathetically developed in country-house style. Lawns and woodlands on the 70-acre estate, as well as a beach, help make for a pampered, private sojourn. Antiques furnish the public rooms, and guest rooms are light-filled and airy. On the grounds are nine chalets, four of them with kitchens; pets are allowed in these. The Island Room restaurant serves modern European cuisine, including such dishes as chargrilled asparagus risotto, and fillet of beef with wild mushrooms, creamed celeriac (a root vegetable) mash, and a Madeira jus. In summer you can dine on the terrace overlooking the sea and golf course. ⊠ *Priory Dr., Seaview PO34 5BU* ☎ *01983/613146* 🖷 *01983/616539* ⊕ *www. priorybay.co.uk* ⇥ *16 rooms, 9 chalets* ⚬ *2 restaurants, 6-hole golf course, 2 tennis courts, pool, beach, bar, business services, meeting rooms, some pets allowed; no a/c* ⊟ *AE, MC, V* � *BP.*

££–£££££ ✕▦ **Seaview Hotel.** A strong maritime flavor defines this smart hotel, a converted house dating to around 1800, in the heart of a harbor village just outside Ryde. Antiques, original watercolors, and bold fabrics furnish the guest rooms. The main attractions, however, are the restaurants (£££), which specialize in seafood and fresh island produce. Try the hot crab ramekin, baked with cream and tarragon with a cheese topping, to start, and don't pass up desserts; whiskey bread and butter pudding is a must. For a fee, guests can use the well-equipped Isle of Wight Sports Club nearby. ⊠ *High St., Seaview PO34 5EX* ☎ *01983/612711* 🖷 *01983/613729* ⊕ *www.seaviewhotel.co.uk* ⇥ *17 rooms, 2 cottages* ⚬ *2 restaurants, room service, in-room VCRs, in-room data ports, 2 bars, some pets allowed, no-smoking rooms* ⊟ *AE, DC, MC, V* 101 *BP.*

Brading

⑰ *3 mi south of Ryde on A3055.*

In Brading, St. Mary's Church, dating from Norman times, contains monuments to the local Oglander family, whose ancestor from Normandy served William the Conqueror. Next to the Old Town Hall stands the 16th-century rectory, said to be the oldest dwelling on the island; it now holds **Brading: The Experience,** which includes a wax museum, a chamber of horrors, and a collection of stuffed animals. ⊠ *46 High St.* ☎ *01983/407286* ⊕ *www.bradingtheexperience.co.uk* 🎟 *£6.50* ☺ *Easter–Oct., daily 10–5:30; Nov.–Easter, daily 10:30–5.*

The remains of the substantial 3rd-century **Brading Roman Villa,** a mile south of Brading, include splendid mosaic floors and a well-preserved heating system. There's a high-tech shelter for the mosaics, as well as a visitor center and café. ☒ *Off A3055* ☏ *01983/406223* ☞ *£3.95* ☉ *Mar.–Oct., daily 9:30–6; Nov.–Feb., daily 10–4.*

Ventnor

18 *11 mi south of Ryde.*

The south coast resorts are the sunniest and most sheltered on the Isle of Wight. Handsome Ventnor rises from such a steep slope that the ground floors of some of its houses are level with the roofs of those across the road. The **Ventnor Botanic Gardens,** laid out over 22 acres, contain more than 3,500 species of trees, plants, and shrubs. The impressive greenhouse includes banana trees and a waterfall, and a pavilioned visitor center puts the subtropical and display gardens into context. ☒ *Undercliff Dr.* ☏ *01983/855397* ⊕ *www.botanic.co.uk* ☞ *Free* ☉ *Jan. and Feb., weekends 10–4; Mar.–Oct., daily 10–6; Nov. and Dec., Tues.–Thurs. 10–3, weekends 10–4.*

Alum Bay & the Needles

19 *19 mi northwest of Ventnor, 18 mi southwest of Cowes.*

At the western tip of the Isle of Wight is the island's most famous natural landmark, the **Needles,** a long line of jagged chalk stacks jutting out of the sea like monstrous teeth, with a lighthouse at the end. It's part of the Needles Pleasure Park, which has mostly child-oriented attractions. Adjacent is **Alum Bay,** accessed from the Needles by chairlift. Here you can catch a good view of the multicolor sand in the cliff strata or take a boat to view the lighthouse.

Dimbola Lodge was the home of Julia Margaret Cameron (1815–79), the eminent Victorian portrait photographer and friend of Lord Tennyson. A gallery includes more than 60 examples of her work, and there's a bookshop and café. ☒ *Terrace La., Freshwater Bay* ☏ *01983/756814* ⊕ *www.dimbola.co.uk* ☞ *Gallery £4* ☉ *Tues.–Sun. and national holiday Mon. 10–5; open daily during school summer vacation.*

Where to Stay

££££ ☒ **Farringford Hotel.** For more than 40 years this splendid 18th-century house was the home of the Victorian poet laureate Alfred, Lord Tennyson. Now a gracious hotel on 33 acres of parkland, it also includes self-catering accommodations. Victorian mahogany and rich damask fabrics reign supreme in the bedrooms in the main house. ☒ *Bedbury La., near Alum Bay, Freshwater Bay PO40 9PE* ☏ *01983/752500* ☐ *01983/756515* ⊕ *www.farringford.co.uk* ☜ *15 rooms, 23 suites, 5 apartments, 4 cottage rooms* ☝ *2 restaurants, 9-hole golf course, tennis court, pool, croquet, lawn bowling, some pets allowed (fee); no a/c* ☐ *AE, DC, MC, V* ☉❘ *BP.*

Carisbrooke Castle

★ **20** *14 mi east of Alum Bay, 1¼ mi southwest of Newport, 5 mi south of Cowes.*

Standing above the village of Carisbrooke, this castle built by the Normans and enlarged in Elizabethan times had its moment of historical glory when King Charles I was imprisoned here during the English Civil War. Note the small window in the north curtain wall through which he tried unsuccessfully to escape. A museum holds items from his incarceration. You can stroll along the battlements and visit the well house, where donkeys draw water from a deep well. The castle is a short distance outside the Isle of Wight's modern-day capital, Newport. ⊠ *Off B3401* ☎ *01983/522107* ⊕ *www.english-heritage.org.uk* ✉ *£5.50* ⊙ *Apr.–Sept., daily 10–5; Oct.–Mar., daily 10–4.*

SALISBURY TO STONEHENGE

STOURHEAD, AVEBURY & STONEHENGE

The roster of famous sights in this area begins in the attractive city of Salisbury, renowned for its glorious cathedral, then loops west around Salisbury Plain, up to Avebury, and back to Stonehenge. A trio of stately homes reveals the ambitions and wealth of the builders—Wilton House with its Inigo Jones–designed state rooms, Stourhead and its exquisite gardens, and the Italian Renaissance pile of Longleat. Your own transportation is essential to see anything beyond Salisbury.

Salisbury

25 mi northwest of Southampton, 55 mi southeast of Bristol, 90 mi southwest of London.

The silhouette of Salisbury Cathedral's majestic spire signals your approach to this historic city long before you arrive. Although the cathedral is the principal interest in the town, and the Cathedral Close one of the country's most atmospheric spots (best experienced on a foggy night), Salisbury has much more to see, not least its largely unspoiled—and relatively traffic-free—old center. Here are stone shops and houses that grew up in the shadow of the great church over the centuries. You're never far from any of the three rivers that meet here, or from the bucolic water meadows that stretch out to the west of the cathedral and provide the best views of it.

Salisbury did not become important until the early 13th century, when the seat of the diocese was transferred here from Old Sarum, the original settlement 2 mi to the north, of which only ruins remain. In the 19th century, novelist Anthony Trollope based his tales of ecclesiastical life, notably *Barchester Towers*, on life here, although his fictional city of Barchester is really an amalgam of Salisbury and Winchester. The local tourist office organizes walks—of differing lengths for varying stamina—to lead you to the treasures.

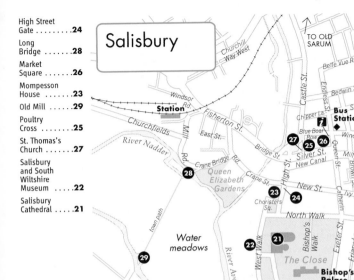

High Street
Gate **24**

Long
Bridge **28**

Market
Square **26**

Mompesson
House **23**

Old Mill **29**

Poultry
Cross **25**

St. Thomas's
Church **27**

Salisbury
and South
Wiltshire
Museum **22**

Salisbury
Cathedral **21**

KEY

🛈 Tourist information

Main Attractions

Cathedral Close. Salisbury's close forms probably the finest backdrop of any British cathedral, with its smooth lawns and splendid examples of architecture from many periods (except modern) creating a harmonious background. Some of the historic houses are open to the public.

㉓ Mompesson House. One of Britain's most appealing Queen Anne houses, dating from 1701, sits on the north side of Cathedral Close. There are no treasures per se, but some fine original paneling and plasterwork, as well as a fascinating collection of 18th-century drinking glasses, are highlights. Tea and refreshments are served in a walled garden. ✉ *The Close* ☎ *01722/335659* ⊕ *www.nationaltrust.org.uk* 🎟 *£4.40* ⊗ *Apr.–Oct., Sat.–Wed. 11–5; last admission 4:30.*

Old Sarum. Massive earthwork ramparts in a bare sweep of Wiltshire countryside are all that remain of the impressive Iron Age hill fort, which was successively taken over by Romans, Saxons, and Normans (who built a castle and cathedral within the earthworks). The site was still fortified in Tudor times, though the population had mostly decamped in the 13th century for the more amenable site of New Sarum, or Salisbury. You can clamber over the huge banks and ditches and take in the bracing views over the chalk downland. ✉ *Off A345, 2 mi north*

Ancient Sites

PREHISTORIC MONUMENTS DOT Britain's landscape, silent but tantalizing reminders of civilizations long vanished. Ceremonial stone circles, barrows used for burials, and Iron Age hill forts attract endless speculation about the motives and methods of their ancient builders. The South contains not only 5,000-year-old Stonehenge, one of the great treasures of Britain and, indeed, Europe, but also an abundance of other sites, some of them overlaid with reminders of other eras. At Old Sarum, near Salisbury, the earthwork ramparts of an Iron Age hill fort survive, although Romans and Normans took over the site. The evocative Avebury Stone Circles surround part of a village; nearby is the West Kennett Long Barrow, a chambered tomb. Close to Dorchester, Maiden Castle is a stone and earth hill fort with ramparts that enclose 45 acres. If all this fuels your imagination, the shop at Stonehenge sells plenty of books with plenty of theories, and the Salisbury and South Wiltshire Museum in Salisbury and the Alexander Keiller Museum in Avebury provide helpful background. Start by visiting one site, and you may find yourself rerouting your trip to seek out others.

of Salisbury ☎ *01722/335398* ⊕ *www.english-heritage.org.uk* ✉ *£2.90* ☉ *Apr.–June and Sept., daily 10–5; July and Aug., daily 9–6; Oct., daily 10–4; Nov.–Mar., daily 10–3.*

㉒ Salisbury and South Wiltshire Museum. Models and exhibits at the Stonehenge Gallery of this museum arm you with helpful background information for a visit to the famous stones. Also on view are collections of costumes, lace, embroidery, and Wedgwood, all dwarfed by the medieval pageant figure of St. Christopher, a 14-foot-tall, red-cloaked giant and his companion hobbyhorse, Hob Nob. ✉ *The King's House, 65 The Close* ☎ *01722/332151* ⊕ *www. salisburymuseum.org.uk* ✉ *£4* ☉ *July and Aug., Mon.–Sat. 10–5, Sun. 2–5; Sept.–June, Mon.–Sat. 10–5.*

㉑ Salisbury Cathedral. Salisbury is dominated by the towering cathedral, a soaring hymn in stone. It is unique among cathedrals in that it was conceived and built as a whole, in the amazingly short span of 38 years (1220–58). The spire, added in 1320, is the tallest in England and a miraculous feat of medieval engineering—even though the point, 404 feet above the ground, is 2½ feet off vertical. For a fictional, keenly imaginative reconstruction of the drama underlying such an achievement, read William Golding's novel *The Spire.* The excellent model of the cathedral in the north transept, the "arm" of the church to your left as you look toward the altar, shows the building about 20 years into construction, and makes clear the ambition of Salisbury's medieval builders. For all their sophistication, the height and immense weight of the great spire have always posed structural problems. In the late 17th century Sir Christopher Wren was summoned from London to strengthen the spire, and in the mid-19th century Sir George Gilbert Scott, a leading

Fodor's Choice
★

Victorian Gothicist, undertook a major program of restoration. He also initiated a clearing out of the interior and removed some less-than-sympathetic 18th-century alterations. Despite this, the interior seems spartan and a little gloomy, but check out the remarkable lancet windows and sculpted tombs of crusaders and other medieval heroes. The clock in the north aisle—probably the oldest working mechanism in Europe, if not the world—was made in 1386. ■ TIP→ **You can join a free 45-minute tour of the church leaving two or more times a day, and there are tours to the roof and spire at least once a day.** The cloisters are the largest in England, and the octagonal **Chapter House** contains a marvelous 13th-century frieze showing scenes from the Old Testament. In the Chapter House you can also see one of the four original copies of the **Magna Carta,** the charter of rights the English barons forced King John to accept in 1215; it was sent here for safekeeping in the 13th century. ⊠ *Cathedral Close* ☎ *01722/555120* ⊕ *www.salisburycathedral.org.uk* ⊠ *Cathedral £4 requested donation, roof tour £4.50, Chapter House free* ☉ *Cathedral mid-June–Aug., Mon.–Sat. 7:15–7:15, Sun. 7:15–6:15; Sept.–mid-June, daily 7:15–6:15. Chapter House mid-June–Aug., Mon.–Sat. 9:30–6:45, Sun. noon–5:30; Sept.–Oct. and Mar.–mid-June, Mon.–Sat. 9:30–5:30, Sun. noon–5:30; Nov.–Feb., Mon.–Sat. 10–4:30, Sun. noon–4:30. Access to cathedral restricted during services.*

Also Worth Seeing

㉔ High Street Gate. On the north side of the Cathedral Close is one of the four castellated stone gateways built to separate the close from the rest of the city. Passing through it, you enter into the heart of the modern town.

㉘ Long Bridge. For a classic view of Salisbury, head to the Long Bridge and the town path. From High Street walk west to Mill Road, which leads you across Queen Elizabeth Gardens. Cross the bridge and continue on the town path through the water meadows along here you can find the very spot where John Constable set down his easel to create that 19th-century icon, *Salisbury Cathedral,* now hung in the Constable Room of London's National Gallery.

㉖ Market Square. One of southern England's most popular markets fills this square on Tuesday and Saturday. Permission to hold an annual fair here was granted in 1221, and that right is still exercised for four days every October, when the Charter Fair takes place. A narrow side street links Poultry Cross to Market Square.

㉙ Old Mill. Reached via a 20-minute walk along the town path southwest of the town center, this mill, dating from the 12th century, makes a pleasant destination. It is now a restaurant and coffee shop under the same management as the Old Mill Hotel next door. ⊠ *Town Path, West Harnham.*

㉕ Poultry Cross. One of Salisbury's best-known landmarks, the hexagonal Poultry Cross is the last remaining of the four original medieval market crosses, and dealers still set up their stalls beside it. ⊠ *Silver St.*

㉗ St. Thomas's Church. This church contains a rare medieval doom painting of Judgment Day, the best-preserved and most complete of the few such works left in Britain. Created around 1470 and covering the chancel arch, the scenes of heaven and hell served to instill the fear of damnation into the congregation. ■ TIP→ **It's best seen on a spring or summer evening when the light through the west window illuminates the details.** ⊠ *Silver St.* ☎ *01722/322537* 🎫 *Free* ⊙ *Apr.–Oct., Mon.–Sat. 9:30–6, Sun. noon–6; Nov.–Mar., Mon.–Sat. 9:30–3:30, Sun. noon–6.*

NEED A BREAK?

In a lively, central location but away from traffic, **Polly Tearooms** (⊠ 8 St. Thomas's Sq. ☎ 01722/336037) provides relief from sightseeing fatigue in the form of lemon curd gâteaux (cakes), Wiltshire cream teas, and freshly ground coffee. It's closed Sunday.

Where to Stay & Eat

££–£££ ✗ **Haunch of Venison.** This wood-panel tavern opposite the Poultry Cross has been going strong for more than six centuries, and brims with period details, such as the mummified hand of an 18th-century card player still clutching his cards, found by workmen in 1903. You can fortify yourself with any of 40-odd malt whiskies, and choose between simple bar food or more substantial meals in its stylish upstairs restaurant **One Minster Street,** where the menu includes pave of beef with seared foie gras and truffle-scented jus. ⊠ *1 Minster St.* ☎ *01722/411313* 🖃 *MC, V.*

££–£££ ✗ **LXIX Bar and Bistro.** A stone's throw from the cathedral, this convivial and relaxed bistro has a cool, modern style, making it an ideal spot for a light lunch or dinner. The menu lists everything from fish cakes and pastas to sea bass and steaks. ⊠ *69 New St.* ☎ *01722/340000* 🖃 *AE, DC, MC, V* ⊙ *Closed Sun. and last wk in Dec.*

££ ✗ **Harper's.** Always buzzing, this second-floor restaurant overlooking Market Square has a friendly, neighborhood feel. The mainly English and French dishes include Scotch salmon and New Forest venison casserole with mustard mash, and there are good-value lunches and earlybird dinners. ⊠ *7 Ox Row* ☎ *01722/333118* 🖃 *AE, DC, MC, V* ⊙ *Closed Sun. Oct.–May. No lunch Sun. June–Sept.*

££ ✗ **Lemon Tree.** It's just a few steps from Cathedral Close and the High Street Gate to this light, airy bistro. Dishes range from spinach and ricotta pancakes to pork fillets panfried with apricots and pine nuts. You can sit in the small, busy conservatory or in the garden. ⊠ *90–92 Crane St.* ☎ *01722/333471* 🖃 *AE, MC, V* ⊙ *Closed Sun.*

★ ££££ ✗🖼 **Howard's House.** If you're after complete tranquillity, head for this early-17th-century house 10 mi west of Salisbury, set on 2 acres of grounds in the Nadder valley. French windows lead from the tidy lawns into the restaurant (*£££££*), which lists sophisticated contemporary fare on its set-price menus, for example Cornish scallop risotto, and desserts include passion fruit curd soufflé. The inviting sitting room mixes pastels and bright fabrics, and the soothing bedrooms use subtle colors. ⊠ *Off B3089, Teffont Evias SP3 5RJ* ☎ *01722/716392* 🖨 *01722/716820* ⊕ *www.howardshousehotel.co.uk* 🛏 *9 rooms* ⌂ *Restaurant, meeting rooms, some pets allowed (fee); no a/c* 🖃 *AE, DC, MC, V* 🍴*BP.*

££££ ✗🖼 **Red Lion Hotel.** A former coaching inn—parts of the building date from 1220—this centrally located hotel in the Best Western consortium makes a good base for exploring the city on foot. It's packed with old clocks and other relics from its long past. Rooms are in either modern or antique style, with an abundance of drapery and rich red, gold, and blue colors. Room 22 has a restored fireplace dating from the inn's original construction. The Vine restaurant (£££££; reservations essential) serves mainly modern British dishes such as roast pork with mustard sauce. ⊠ *Milford St., SP1 2AN* ☎ *01722/323334* 🖷 *01722/325756* ⊕ *www.theredlion.co.uk* 🖙 *51 rooms* 🖒 *Restaurant, cable TV, Wi-Fi, business services, meeting rooms; no a/c* ⊟ *AE, DC, MC, V.*

£££ 🖼 **White Hart.** Behind the pillared portico and imposing classical facade of this 17th-century hotel very near the cathedral lie cozily old-fashioned yet spacious public rooms. The muted cream-and-brown color scheme complements the unhurried pace, and the functional bedrooms (of various sizes) are grouped around the inner courtyard. ⊠ *1 St. John St., SP1 2SD* ☎ *0870/400–8125 or 01722/327476* 🖷 *01722/412761* ⊕ *www.macdonaldhotels.co.uk* 🖙 *68 rooms* 🖒 *Restaurant, bar, business services, meeting rooms, some pets allowed (fee); no a/c* ⊟ *AE, DC, MC, V* 🍽 *BP.*

££ 🖼 **Cricket Field House Hotel.** As the name suggests, this modernized gamekeeper's cottage overlooks a cricket ground, allowing you to puzzle over the intricacies of the game at leisure. Some rooms are in the main house and others in the pavilion annex, but all are individually furnished in soft shades. The hotel is on the main A36 road, a mile or so west of Salisbury's center. ⊠ *Wilton Rd., SP2 9NS* ☎ *01722/322595* ⊕ *www.cricketfieldhousehotel.co.uk* 🖙 *14 rooms* 🖒 *Dining room; no a/c, no kids under 14, no smoking* ⊟ *AE, MC, V* 🍽 *BP.*

£ 🖼 **Wyndham Park Lodge.** This solid Victorian house in a quiet part of town (off Castle Street) provides an excellent place to rest and a good breakfast, as well as a garden. Furnishings are in keeping with the period, with antiques and elegant patterned wallpapers and drapes, and one room has its own patio. ⊠ *51 Wyndham Rd., SP1 3AB* ☎ *01722/416517* 🖷 *01722/328851* ⊕ *www.wyndhamparklodge.co.uk* 🖙 *4 rooms* 🖒 *Cable TV, in-room DVD; no room phones, no a/c, no smoking* ⊟ *MC, V* 🍽 *BP.*

Nightlife & the Arts

★ The **Salisbury Festival** (⊠ 75 New St. ☎ 01722/332241 ⊕ www.salisburyfestival.co.uk), held in May and June, has outstanding classical concerts, recitals, plays, and outdoor events. The **Salisbury Playhouse** (⊠ Malthouse La. ☎ 01722/320333) presents high-caliber drama all year and is the main venue for the Salisbury Festival.

Sports

Hayball's Cycle Shop (⊠ 26–30 Winchester St. ☎ 01722/411378) rents bikes for about £10 per day or £55 per week, with a £25 cash deposit.

Shopping

Ellwood Books (⊠ 38 Winchester St. ☎ 01722/322975) stocks all kinds of tax-free secondhand books, including some rare first editions. **Reeve the Baker** (⊠ 2 Butcher Row ☎ 01722/320367) is a great independent bakery with goodies ranging from lamb pastries to apple dumplings. **Wat-**

sons (⊠ 8–9 Queen St. ☎ 01722/320311) specializes in Aynsley and Wedgwood bone china, Waterford and Dartington glass, Royal Doulton, and fine ornaments. The buildings, dating from 1306 and 1425, have their original windows and an oak mantelpiece.

Wilton

③⓪ *4 mi west of Salisbury.*

Five rivers—the Avon, the Bourne, the Nadder, the Wylye, and the Ebble—wind from Salisbury into the rich heart of Wiltshire. Following the valley of the Nadder will lead you to the ancient town of Wilton, from which the county takes its name. A market is held here every Thursday, and the Wilton Carpet Factory Shop draws visitors (Wilton is renowned for its carpets), but the main attraction is Wilton House.

★ The home of the 17th earl of Pembroke, **Wilton House** would be noteworthy if it contained no more than the magnificent 17th-century state rooms designed by Inigo Jones, Ben Jonson's stage designer and the architect of London's Banqueting House. John Webb rebuilt the house in neoclassical style after fire damaged the original Tudor mansion in 1647. In fine weather, the lordly expanse of sweeping lawns that surrounds the house, bisected by the River Avon and dotted with towering oaks and a gracious Palladian bridge, is a quintessential English scene. Wilton House contains the Single Cube Room (built as a perfect 30-foot cube) and one

> ### DOUBLE CUBE ROOM
>
> Adorned with gilded furniture by William Kent, Wilton House's Double Cube was where Eisenhower prepared plans for the Normandy invasion during World War II. It has been used in many films, including *The Madness of King George* and Emma Thompson's adaptation of *Sense and Sensibility.*

of the most extravagantly beautiful rooms in the history of interior decoration, the aptly named Double Cube Room. The name refers to its proportions (60 feet long by 30 feet wide and 30 feet high), evidence of Jones's classically inspired belief that beauty in architecture derives from harmony and balance. The room's headliner is the spectacular Van Dyck portrait of the Pembroke family. Other delights at Wilton House include old master paintings, an exhibition of 7,000 toy soldiers, and the Wareham Bears (200 dressed teddy bears). ■ TIP→ **Be sure to explore the extensive gardens; children will appreciate the large playground.** ⊠ *Off A30* ☎ *01722/746729* ⊕ *www.wiltonhouse.co.uk* ☞ *£9.75, grounds only £4.50* ☉ *House mid-Apr.–Sept., Sun.–Fri. 10:30–5:30; grounds mid-Apr.–Sept., daily 10:30–5:30; last admission 4:30.*

Shaftesbury

③① *18 mi west of Wilton, 22 mi west of Salisbury.*

The old village of Shaftesbury—the model for the town of Shaston in Thomas Hardy's *Jude the Obscure*—lies on a ridge overlooking Blackmore Vale just inside the Dorset county border. From the top of **Gold**

Hill, a steep, relentlessly picturesque street lined with cottages, you can catch a sweeping view of the surrounding countryside. Although Gold Hill is something of a tourist cliché (it has even appeared in TV commercials), it's still well worth visiting.

Sherborne

③² *15 mi west of Shaftesbury.*

Once granted cathedral status, until deferring to Old Sarum in 1075, this unspoiled market town is awash with medieval buildings honed from the honey-color local stone. The focal point of the winding streets is the abbey church. Also worth visiting here are the ruins of the 12th-century Old Castle and Sherborne Castle with its grounds.

The glory of **Sherborne Abbey,** a warm, "old gold" stone church, is the delicate and graceful 15th-century fan vaulting that extends the length of the soaring nave and choir. ("I would pit Sherborne's roof against any contemporary work of the Italian Renaissance," enthused Simon Jenkins, in his *England's Thousand Best Churches.*) If you're lucky you might hear "Great Tom," one of the heaviest bells in the world, pealing out from the bell tower. Guided tours are offered in summer on Tuesday (10:30) and Friday (2:30), or by prior arrangement. ⊠ *Abbey Close* ☎ *01935/812452* ⊕ *www.sherborneabbey.com* ✉ *£2 suggested donation, guided tour free or £3 by prior arrangement* ☉ *Apr.–Sept., daily 8–6; Oct.–Mar., daily 8–4.*

Sherborne Castle, built by Sir Walter Raleigh in 1594, remained his home for 10 years before it passed to the custodianship of the Digby family. The interior has been remodeled in 19th-century Gothic style, and ceilings have splendid plaster moldings. After admiring the extensive collections of Meissen and Asian porcelain, stroll around the lake and landscaped grounds, the work of Capability Brown. The house is a half mile southeast of town. ⊠ *Off A352* ☎ *01935/813182* ⊕ *www. sherbornecastle.com* ✉ *£8, gardens only £4* ☉ *Apr.–Oct., Tues.–Thurs., Sun., and national holiday Mon. 11–5, Sat. 2:30–5.*

Where to Stay

£ 🏠 **The Alders.** A quiet, unspoiled village 3 mi north of Sherborne contains this B&B, an old stone house with a walled garden. The lounge has an inglenook fireplace, and the bedrooms are modern and cheerfully decorated. The house displays the owner's watercolors and sleek pottery, which you can view while tasting homemade jam during breakfast at the farmhouse table. Nearby pubs provide evening meals. ⊠ *Sandford Orcas DT9 4SB* ☎ *01963/220666* 🖷 *01963/220106* ⊕ *www. thealdersbb.com* ⇨ *3 rooms* ⚘ *No smoking* 🚫 *No credit cards* ⍓ *BP.*

Stourhead

③³ *15 mi northeast of Sherborne, 30 mi west of Salisbury.*

Close to the village of Stourton lies one of Wiltshire's most breathtaking sights—Stourhead, a country-house-and-garden combination that has few parallels for beauty anywhere in Europe. Most of Stourhead was built between 1721 and 1725 by Henry the Magnificent, the wealthy banker Henry Hoare. Many rooms in the Palladian mansion contain Chinese and French porcelain, and some have furniture by Chippendale. The elegant library and floridly colored picture gallery were built for the cultural development of this exceedingly civilized family. Still, the house takes second place to the adjacent gardens designed by Hoare's son, Henry Hoare II, which are the most celebrated example of the English 18th-century taste for "natural" landscaping. Temples, grottoes, and bridges have been placed among shrubs, trees, and flowers to make the grounds look like a three-dimensional oil painting. A walk around the artificial lake (1½ mi) reveals changing vistas that conjure up the 17th-century landscapes of Claude Lorrain and Nicolas Poussin. ■ TIP→ **The best time to visit is early summer, when the massive banks of rhododendrons are in full bloom, but the gardens are beautiful at any time of year.** You can get a fine view of the estate from Alfred's Tower, a 1772 folly (a structure built for picturesque effect). In summer there are occasional concerts, sometimes accompanied by fireworks and gondoliers on the lake. A restaurant and plant shop are on the grounds. From London by train, get off at Gillingham and take a five-minute cab ride to Stourton. ⊠ *Off B3092, northwest of Mere, Stourton* ☎ *01747/841152* ⊕ *www. nationaltrust.org.uk* 🖾 *£10.40, house only £6.20, gardens only £6.20* ☉ *House mid-Mar.–Oct., Fri.–Tues. 11:30–4:30 or dusk; last admission 30 mins before closing; gardens daily 9–7 or dusk.*

Where to Stay & Eat

£££ ✕🏠 **Spread Eagle Inn.** You can't stay at Stourhead, but this popular hostelry, built at the beginning of the 19th century at the entrance to the landscaped park, is the next best thing (and guests are admitted free to the house and gardens). Bedrooms are elegant and understated, with some period features. The restaurant (££) serves traditional English fare, from braised venison to chicken and tarragon pie, and there are seafood and vegetarian choices. ⊠ *Northwest of Mere, Stourton BA12 6HQ* ☎ *01747/840587* 🖨 *01747/840954* ⊕ *www.spreadeagleinn.com* 🛏 *5 rooms* 🛇 *Restaurant, bar; no a/c* ⊟ *DC, MC, V* ▮⊙▮ *BP.*

Longleat House

★ ☺ ㉞ *6 mi north of Stourhead, 19 mi south of Bath, 27 mi northwest of Salisbury.*

Home of the marquess of Bath, Longleat House is one of southern England's most famous private estates, and possibly the most ambitiously, even eccentrically, commercialized, as evidenced by the presence of a drive-through safari park (open since 1966) with giraffes, zebras, rhinos, and lions. The blocklike Italian Renaissance building was completed in 1580 (for just over £8,000, an astronomical sum at the time) and contains outstanding tapestries, paintings, porcelain, and furniture, as well as notable period features such as the Victorian kitchens, the Elizabethan minstrels' gallery, and the great hall with its massive wooden beams. Giant antlers of the extinct Irish elk decorate the walls, while tours of the present Lord Bath's occasionally raunchy murals—described as "keyhole glimpses into my psyche," ranging from philosophical subjects to depictions of the kama sutra—can be booked separately at the front desk (free). Besides the safari park, Longleat has a butterfly garden, a miniature railway, an extensive (and fairly fiendish) hedge maze, and an adventure castle, all of which make it extremely popular, particularly in summer and during school vacations. ■ TIP→ **You can easily spend a whole day here, in which case it's best to visit the house in the morning, when tours are more relaxed, and the safari park in the afternoon.** Call to confirm opening hours in winter. ⊠ *Off A362, Warminster* ☎ *01985/844400* ⊕ *www.longleat.co.uk* 🖘 *House and safari park £19, house £10, safari park £10, gardens and grounds £3* ⊙ *House Jan.–Mar., weekends and school vacations 11–3; Apr.–Sept., daily 10–5:30; Oct.–Dec., daily 11–3; guided tours only, call for times. Safari park Apr.–Oct., weekdays 10–4, weekends and school vacations 10–5. Other attractions Apr.–Oct., daily 11–5:30.*

Where to Stay & Eat

★ ££££ ✕⌷ **Bishopstrow House.** This Georgian house has been converted into a luxurious but refreshingly relaxed hotel that combines antiques and fine carpets with modern amenities such as whirlpool baths and CD players. There's an airy conservatory, and the lavish, chintz-filled guest rooms overlook either the 27-acre grounds or an interior courtyard. The Mulberry restaurant creates imaginative modern European meals (£££££ fixed-price menus) with a penchant for the piquant. Bishopstrow House is 1½ mi out of town. ⊠ *Boreham Rd., Warminster BA12 9HH* ☎ *01985/ 212312* 🖷 *01985/216769* ⊕ *www.bishopstrow.co.uk* 🖘 *32 rooms* ⌃ *Restaurant, some in-room hot tubs, golf privileges, 2 tennis courts, 2 pools (1 indoor), gym, hair salon, sauna, spa, fishing, croquet, bar, piano bar, business services, meeting rooms, helipad, some pets allowed; no a/c* ⊟ *AE, DC, MC, V* ❙◯❙ *BP.*

┌─
│ **EN**
│ **ROUTE**

Four miles west of Avebury, on A4, **Cherhill Down** is a prominent hill carved with a vivid white horse and topped with a towering obelisk. It's one of a number of hillside etchings in Wiltshire, but unlike the others, this one isn't an ancient symbol—it was put there in 1780 to indicate the highest point of the downs between London and Bath. The views from the top are well worth the half-hour climb. (The best view of the horse is from A4, on the approach from Calne.)

Avebury

㉟ *25 mi northeast of Longleat, 27 mi east of Bath, 34 mi north of Salisbury.*

★ The village of Avebury was built much later than the stone circles that brought it fame. The **Avebury Stone Circles** are one of England's most evocative prehistoric monuments—not so famous as Stonehenge, but all the more powerful for their lack of commercial exploitation. The stones were erected around 2500 BC, some 500 years after Stonehenge was started but about 500 years before that much smaller site assumed its present form. As with Stonehenge, the purpose of this stone circle has never been ascertained, although it most likely was used for similar ritual purposes. Unlike Stonehenge, however, there are no astronomical alignments at Avebury, at least none that have survived. The main site consists of a wide, circular ditch and bank, about 1,400 feet across and over half a mile around; it actually surrounds part of the village of Avebury. Entrances break the perimeter at roughly the four points of the compass, and inside stand the remains of three stone circles. The largest one originally had 98 stones, although only 27 remain. Many stones on the site were destroyed centuries ago, especially in the 17th century when they were the target of religious fanaticism. Some were pillaged to build the thatched cottages you see flanking the fields. You can walk around the circles at any time; early morning and early evening are recommended. Be sure to visit the nearby Alexander Keiller

Museum. ⊠ *1 mi north of A4* ☎ *No phone* ⊕ *www.english-heritage. org.uk* ⊡ *Free* ⊗ *Daily.*

In the **Alexander Keiller Museum,** finds from the Avebury area, and charts, photos, models, and home movies taken by the archaeologist Keiller himself, put the Avebury Stone Circles and the site into context. Recent revelations suggest that Keiller, responsible for the excavation of Avebury in the 1930s, may have adapted the site's layout more in the interests of presentation than authenticity. The exhibits are divided between the **Stables Gallery,** showing excavated finds, and the more child-friendly, interactive **Barn Gallery.** ⊠ *1 mi north of A4* ☎ *01672/539250* ⊕ *www. english-heritage.org.uk* ⊡ *£4.20* ⊗ *Apr.–Oct., daily 10–6; Nov.–Mar., daily 10–4.*

The Avebury monument lies at the end of **Kennett Stone Avenue,** a sort of prehistoric processional way leading to Avebury. The avenue's stones were spaced 80 feet apart, but only the half mile nearest the main monument survives intact. The lost stones are marked with concrete.

Where to Stay & Eat

£–££ ✗ **Waggon and Horses.** A 16th-century thatched building created in part with stones taken from the Avebury site, this traditional inn and pub is beside the traffic circle linking A4 and A361, a two-minute drive from the prehistoric circle. Dickens mentioned the building in the *Pickwick Papers.* Excellent lunches and dinners are served beside a fire; homemade dishes include beef and Stilton pie, curries, and casseroles, or you can opt for a sandwich. In high season it's somewhat of a tourist hub. ⊠ *Beckhampton* ☎ *01672/539418* ⊟ *AE, MC, V* ⊗ *No dinner Sun.*

££ ◫ **Manor Farm.** Views of Avebury's monoliths straggling across the field greet you from the windows of this 18th-century farmhouse right in the heart of the village. Rooms are spacious, light, and elegantly furnished, and guests have their own sitting room. The bathroom is separate, but for your exclusive use as only one room is rented at a time. Breakfast choices include Scotch pancakes with bacon, scrambled eggs with smoked salmon, and kippers. ⊠ *High St., SN8 1RF* ☎ *01672/539294* ⇌ *2 rooms, no bath* ⚫ *No kids under 12* ⊟ *No credit cards* ⦿ *BP.*

EN ROUTE

Prehistoric relics dot the entire Avebury area; stop at the **West Kennett Long Barrow,** a chambered tomb dating from about 3250 BC, 1 mi east of Avebury on A4. As you turn right at the traffic circle onto A4, **Silbury Hill** rises on your right. This man-made mound, 130 feet high, dates from about 2500 BC and is the largest of its kind in Europe. Excavations over 200 years have provided no clue as to its original purpose, but the generally accepted notion is that it was a massive burial chamber.

Marlborough

36 *7 mi east of Avebury, 28 mi north of Salisbury.*

The attractive town of Marlborough developed as an important staging post on the old London–Bath stagecoach route. Today it is better known for its unusually wide main street, its Georgian houses—these replaced the medieval town center, which was destroyed in a great fire in 1653—and its celebrated public school. The grounds of the school, on the west side of town, enclose a small, man-made hill called Castle Mound, or Maerl's Barrow, which gave the town its name. This was said to be the grave of Merlin, King Arthur's court wizard, but it is clearly much older than the period when the historic Arthur may have lived.

Where to Stay

£££ 🏨 **Ivy House.** This redbrick Georgian house on colonnaded High Street makes an excellent touring base. Public rooms are clubby, and the traditionally styled bedrooms in the main part of the building are richly decorated, some with exposed beams or arches; others are predominantly beige and cream. A courtyard bar serves light meals, and a more formal restaurant has views overlooking the terrace. ⊠ *43 High St., SN8 1HJ* ☎ *01672/515333* 🖷 *01672/515338* ⊕ *www.ivyhousemarlborough. co.uk* ⇌ *28 rooms* ⚫ *Restaurant, cable TV, bar, meeting room; no a/c* ⊟ *AE, DC, MC, V* ⦿ *BP.*

Stonehenge

37 *21 mi south of Marlborough, 8 mi north of Salisbury.*

Fodor'sChoice
★

Mysterious and ancient, Stonehenge has baffled archaeologists for centuries. One of England's most visited monuments, the circle of giant stones that sits in lonely isolation on the wide sweep of Salisbury Plain still has the capacity to fascinate and move those who view it. Sadly, though, it is now enclosed by barriers after incidents of vandalism, and amid fears that its popularity could threaten its existence. Visitors are kept on a path a short distance away from the stones, so that you can no longer walk among the giant stones or see up close the prehistoric carvings, some of which show axes and daggers. But if you visit in the early morning, when the crowds have not yet arrived, or in the evening, when the sky is heavy with scudding clouds, you can experience Stonehenge as it once was: a mystical, awe-inspiring place.

Stonehenge was begun about 3000 BC, enlarged between 2100 and 1900 BC, and altered yet again by 150 BC. It has been excavated and rearranged several times over the centuries. The medieval term "Stonehenge" means "hanging stones." Many of the huge stones that ringed the center were brought here from great distances, but it is not certain by what ancient form of transportation they were moved. The original 80 bluestones (dolerite), which made up the two internal circles, originated in the Preseli mountains, on the Atlantic coast of Wales. They may have been moved by raft over sea and river, and then dragged on rollers across country—a total journey of 130 mi as the crow flies, but closer to 240 by the practical route. Every time a reconstruction of the journey has been attempted, though, it has failed. The labor involved in quarrying, transporting, and carving these stones is astonishing, all the more so when you realize that it was accomplished about the same time that the major pyramids of Egypt were built.

Although some of the mysteries concerning the site have been solved, the reason Stonehenge was built remains unknown. It is fairly certain that it was a religious site, and that worship here involved the cycles of the sun; the alignment of the stones to point to sunrise at midsummer and sunset in midwinter makes this clear. The druids certainly had nothing to do with the construction: the monument had already been in existence for nearly 2,000 years by the time they appeared. Most historians think Stonehenge may have been a kind of neolithic computer, with a sophisticated astronomical purpose—an observatory of sorts.

A paved path for visitors skirts the stones, ensuring that you don't get very close to the monoliths. Bring a pair of binoculars to help make out the details more clearly. It pays to walk all about the site, near and far, to get that magical photo and to engage your imagination. Romantics may want to view Stonehenge at dawn or dusk, or by a full moon. Your ticket entitles you to an informative audio tour, but in general, visitor amenities at Stonehenge are limited, especially for such a major tourist attraction. ■ TIP→ **Through some tour companies and English Heritage itself, which manages the site, you can arrange access to the inner circle outside of regular hours. English Heritage requires an application and payment of £12 well in advance.** There are plans to improve the site by replacing the too-busy, too-close highway with a tunnel. A new visitor center is in the works for 2008.

Buses leave from the Salisbury bus station for Stonehenge at 11, noon, 1, and 2 (confirm times); buy an Explorer ticket on board for £6.50. There's no place to leave luggage, though. Other options are a taxi or an organized tour. Visitors coming by car from Marlborough should join A345 south for Stonehenge, turning west onto A303 at Amesbury. The monument stands near the junction with A344. ✉ *Junction of A303 and A344/A360, near Amesbury* ☎ *0870/333–1181, 01722/343834 for information about private access outside regular hrs* ⊕ *www.english-heritage.org.uk* ✍ *£5.50* ◷ *Mid-Mar.–May and Sept.–mid-Oct., daily 9:30–6; June–Aug., daily 9–7; mid-Oct.–mid-Mar., daily 9:30–4.*

NEW FOREST TO LYME REGIS
FAR FROM THE MADDING CROWD

Tucked southwest of Southampton, the New Forest was once the hunting preserve of William the Conqueror and his royal descendants. Thus protected from the deforestation that has befallen most of southern England's other forests, this wild, scenic expanse offers great possibilities for walking, riding, and biking. West of here stretches the green, hilly, and largely unspoiled county of Dorset, the setting for most of the books of Thomas Hardy, author of *Far from the Madding Crowd* and other classic Victorian-era novels. "I am convinced that it is better for a writer to know a little bit of the world remarkably well than to know a great part of the world remarkably little," he wrote, as he immortalized the towns, villages, and fields of this idyllically rural area, not least the country capital, Dorchester, an ancient agricultural center. Other places of historic interest such as Maiden Castle and the chalk-cut giant of Cerne Abbas are interspersed with the bustling seaside resorts of Bournemouth and Weymouth. You may find Lyme Regis (associated with another writer, John Fowles) and the villages along the route closer to your ideal of rural England. The Jurassic Coast is the place to search for fossils.

Lyndhurst

38 *26 mi southeast of Stonehenge, 18 mi southeast of Salisbury, 9 mi west of Southampton.*

Lyndhurst is famous as the capital of the New Forest. To explore the depths of this natural wonder, take A35 out of Lyndhurst (the road continues southwest to Bournemouth). To get here from Stonehenge, head south along A360 to Salisbury, then follow A36, B3079, and continue along A337 another 4 mi or so. The New Forest **Visitor Information Centre** (✉ High St. ☎ 023/8028–2269) in the town's main car park is open daily year-round. Fans of Lewis Carroll's *Alice in Wonderland* should note that Alice Hargreaves (*née* Liddell), the inspiration for the fictional Alice, is buried in the **churchyard at Lyndhurst.**

The **New Forest** (⊕ www.thenewforest.co.uk) consists of 150 square mi of mainly open, unfenced countryside interspersed with dense woodland, a natural haven for herds of free-roaming deer, cattle, and, most famously, hardy New Forest ponies. The forest was "new" in 1079, when William the Conqueror cleared the area of farms and villages and turned it into his private hunting grounds. Although some popular spots can get crowded in summer, there are ample parking lots, picnic areas, and campgrounds. Miles of walking trails crisscross the region.

Where to Stay & Eat

££ **White Buck Inn.** This traditional forest lodge makes a welcome stop for refreshment or an overnight stay. The extensive menu relies on local fare, such as braised breast of pheasant and venison casserole. In summer you can sit in the spacious garden, where there are regular barbecues. Live Dixie jazz plays on Thursday evenings. Guest rooms vary from functional to plush chambers themed along Elizabethan or Indian lines, and all enjoy garden views. ⊠ *Bisterne Close, Burley, 7 mi west of Lyndhurst BH24 4AJ* ☎ *01425/402264* ⊟ *01425/403588* ✐ *whitebuckinn@accommo-dating-inns.co.uk* ➥ *7 rooms* ⚒ *Restaurant, bar* ⏲*⏲ BP* ☰ *AE, MC, V.*

£££ 🖾 **Lyndhurst Park Hotel.** Perched at the edge of the New Forest, this hotel resembles a sprawling country manor house but is a modern establishment with plenty of in-room conveniences such as a trouser press. Rooms are smallish but adequate, and not too chintz-filled; you can upgrade to one with a four-poster bed. Year-round, the 17 acres of grounds, which include three ponds, are great for a stroll. The hotel frequently hosts business conferences and is used to international customers. ⊠ *High St., SO43 7NL* ☎ *023/8028–3923* ⊟ *023/8028–2127* ⊕ *www. lyndhurstparkhotel.co.uk* ➥ *59 rooms* ⚒ *Restaurant, cable TV, Wi-Fi, tennis court, pool, sauna, bar, no-smoking rooms* ☰ *AE, MC, V* ⏲*⏲ BP.*

Sports & the Outdoors

HORSEBACK RIDING The New Forest was created for riding, and there's no better way to enjoy it than on horseback. You can arrange a ride at the **Forest Park Riding Stables** (⊠ Rhinefield Rd., Brockenhurst ☎ 01590/623429 ⊡ £25 for 1 hr). The **New Park Manor Stables** (⊠ New Park, Brockenhurst ☎ 01590/ 623919 ⊡ £30 for 1 hr) gives full instruction.

WALKING The **New Forest** is fairly domesticated, and the walks it provides are not much more than easy strolls. For one such walk (about 4 mi), start from Lyndhurst and head directly south for Brockenhurst, a commuter village. The path goes through woods, pastureland, and leafy river valleys—and you may even see some New Forest ponies.

Beaulieu

39 *7 mi southeast of Lyndhurst.*

The unspoiled village of Beaulieu (pronounced *byoo*-lee) has three major attractions in one. **Beaulieu,** with a ruined abbey, a stately home, and an automobile museum, can satisfy different interests. In 1204 King John established **Beaulieu Abbey** for the Cistercian monks, who gave their new home its name, which means "beautiful place" in French. It was badly damaged as part of the suppression of Catholicism during the reign of Henry VIII, leaving only the cloister, the doorway, the gatehouse, and two buildings. A well-planned exhibition in one building re-creates daily life in the monastery. **Palace House** incorporates the abbey's 14th-century gatehouse and has been the home of the Montagu family since they purchased it in 1538, after the dissolution of the monasteries. In this stately home you can see drawing rooms, dining halls, and fine family portraits. The present Lord Montagu is noted for his work in establishing the **National Motor Museum,** which traces the development of motor transport from 1895 to the present. You can see more than 250 classic cars, buses, and motorcycles. Museum attractions include a monorail, audiovisual presentations, and a trip in a 1912 London bus (weekends only in winter, excluding January). ⊠ *Off B3056* ☎ *01590/ 612345* ⊕ *www.beaulieu.co.uk* ⛩ *Abbey, Palace House, and Motor Museum £15.50, joint ticket with Buckler's Hard £18.50* ⊙ *May–Sept., daily 10–6; Oct.–Apr., daily 10–5; last admission 40 mins before closing.*

Buckler's Hard

 2 mi south of Beaulieu.

Among the interesting places around Beaulieu is the museum village of Buckler's Hard, a restored 18th-century hamlet of 24 brick cottages, leading down to an old shipyard on the Beaulieu River. There's a small hotel here, too. The fascinating **Maritime Museum** tells the story of Lord Nelson's favorite ship, HMS *Agamemnon*, which was built here of New Forest oak. Exhibits and model ships trace the town's shipbuilding history. Also part of the museum are four building interiors in the hamlet that re-create 18th-century village life. Easter through October, you can arrange to take a cruise on the Beaulieu River. ☎ *01590/616203* ⊕ *www.bucklershard.co.uk* ✆ *£5.50, joint ticket with Beaulieu £18.50* ⊙ *Easter–Sept., daily 10:30–5; Oct.–Easter, daily 11–4.*

> **WORD OF MOUTH**
>
> "You will love Beaulieu . . . But also stop at Buckler's Hard, only a couple of miles outside of Beaulieu. This is the most fascinating village . . . It is where they used to build ships on the main street and slide them down to the water. Plus several of the cottages are open with furnishings . . . If you do have some time, just drive along some of the lanes in the New Forest—it is just so lovely.
>
> –Janis

EN ROUTE From Beaulieu, take any of the minor roads leading west through wide-open heathland to Lymington and pick up A337 for the popular seaside resort of Bournemouth, a journey of about 18 mi.

Bournemouth

 30 mi southwest of Southampton, 30 mi south of Salisbury, 30 mi east of Dorchester.

The beach resort of Bournemouth was founded in 1810 by Lewis Tregonwell, an ex-army officer who had taken a liking to the area when stationed there some years before. He settled near what is now the Square and planted the first pine trees in the steep little valleys—or chines—cutting through the cliffs to the famous Bournemouth sands. The scent of fir trees was said to be healing for consumption (tuberculosis) sufferers, and the town grew steadily. Gardens laid out with trees and lawns link the Square and the beach. This is an excellent spot to relax and listen to music wafting from the Pine Walk bandstand. Regular musical programs take place at the Pavilion and at the Winter Gardens (home of the Bournemouth Symphony Orchestra) nearby.

Taking the zigzag paths through the leafy public gardens, you can descend to the seafront, where Bournemouth Pier juts into the channel from the pristine sandy beach. Bournemouth has 7 mi of beaches, and the waters are said to be some of southern England's cleanest. If you're not tempted to swim, you can stroll the promenade behind the beach.

Concerts and shows are staged at the **Bournemouth International Centre** (⊠ Exeter Rd. ☎ 0870/111–3000), which includes a selection of restaurants and bars, and a swimming pool. For an old-fashioned tea, try the **Cumberland Hotel** (✉ E. Overcliffe Dr. ☎ 01202/290722), which serves outdoors in summer.

On the corner of Hinton Road stands **St. Peter's** parish church, easily recognizable by its 200-foot-high tower and spire. Lewis Tregonwell, founder and developer of Bournemouth, is buried in the churchyard. Here, too, is the elaborate tombstone of Mary Shelley, author of *Frankenstein* and wife of the great Romantic poet Percy Bysshe Shelley, whose heart is buried with her.

★ The **Russell-Cotes Art Gallery and Museum,** a late Victorian mansion perched on top of East Cliff, overflows with Victorian paintings and miniatures, cases of butterflies, and treasures from Asia, including an exquisite suit of Japanese armor. Members of the Russell-Cotes family, wealthy hoteliers who traveled widely, collected the items. Fine landscaped gardens surround the house. ✉ *East Cliff* ☎ *01202/451858* ⊕ *www.russell-cotes.bournemouth.gov.uk* ⌑ *Free* ☉ *Tues.–Sun. 10–5.*

Where to Stay & Eat

££–££££ ✕ **West Beach.** Superbly positioned right on the marine promenade, close to Bournemouth Pier and with views over sand and sea, this place also has the best seafood in town. The menu usually lists oven-roasted fillet of cod, pan-seared tuna loin, and shellfish (oysters, mussels, lobster). Nonfish dishes include game pie and herb-crusted steak. The simple wooden tables and large glass front lend a modern, minimalist feel. Live jazz bands serenade on alternate Thursday evenings, and there's a narrow deck outside for eating alfresco. In summer, you can pick up baguettes and other snacks from the adjacent takeout. ✉ *Pier Approach* ☎ *01202/587785* ▤ *AE, MC, V* ☉ *Closed Sun. and Mon.*

££–£££ ✕ **Alcatraz Brasserie.** This family-owned Italian restaurant has a surprisingly sleek dining room, as well as a relaxing open-air patio dining space with garden views. Food tends toward traditional Italian favorites—pasta with carbonara sauce, lasagna, and the like—and is reliably good. ✉ *127 Old Christchurch Rd.* ☎ *01202/553650* ▤ *AE, MC, V.*

★ **£££££** ✕▦ **Chewton Glen.** Once the home of Captain Frederick Marryat, author of *The Children of the New Forest,* this early-19th-century country house on extensive grounds is now a luxurious hotel that ranks among Britain's most acclaimed—and most expensive. All the rooms are decorated in rich fabrics, with an eye to the minutest detail, and the plush spa provides the latest treatments. The restaurant, the Marryat Room (£££££), is worth a pilgrimage—the fixed-price menu concentrates on classic meat and seafood dishes enlivened with contemporary elements, and there's a choice of more than 500 wines. Chewton Glen is 12 mi east of Bournemouth. ✉ *Christchurch Rd., New Milton BH25 6QS* ☎ *01425/275341, 800/344–5087 in U.S.* ▤ *01425/272310, 800/398–4534 in U.S.* ⊕ *www.chewtonglen.com* ⇖ *59 rooms* ♿ *Restaurant, cable TV, in-room data ports, 9-hole golf course, 4 tennis courts, 2 pools (1 indoor), gym, spa, croquet, business services, meeting rooms, helipad; no a/c in some rooms, no kids under 5* ▤ *AE, DC, MC, V.*

£££–££££ ✕▦ **Langtry Manor Hotel.** Edward VII built this house for his mistress Lillie Langtry in 1877, and the hotel still preserves some Edwardian style, even in the newer annex. Rooms are as frilly as you might expect, with floral fabrics, frosted-glass light fixtures, thick carpets, and heavy curtains. Unsurprisingly, this is one of the most popular places in Dorset for weddings. In the formal restaurant (£££££; fixed-price menu), lacy tablecloths, silver cutlery, and other details set off the dishes, which are mainly British with French trimmings and include Lillie's Meringue Swans for dessert. There's an Edwardian banquet every Saturday. Guests have access to a nearby health club. ✉ *26 Derby Rd., East Cliff BH1 3QB* ☎ *01202/553887* 🖷 *01202/290115* ⊕ *www.langtrymanor.com* ➪ *27 rooms* & *Restaurant, in-room data ports, meeting rooms; no a/c* ⊟ *AE, DC, MC, V* ⊚I *BP.*

3

Nightlife & the Arts
In late June, Bournemouth holds a weeklong music festival, **Bournemouth Live** (☎ 01202/451195), with jazz and blues, choirs, brass bands, and orchestras, some from overseas.

Wimborne Minster

42 *7 mi northwest of Bournemouth via A341.*

The impressive minster of this quiet market town makes it seem like a miniature cathedral city. The crenellated and pinnacled twin towers of **Wimborne Minster** present an attractive patchwork of gray and reddish-brown stone. The church's Norman nave has zigzag molding interspersed with carved heads, and the Gothic chancel has tall lancet windows. ■ TIP➔ **See the chained library (accessed via a spiral staircase), a survivor from the days when books were valuable enough to keep on chains.** Look out for the 14th-century astronomical clock on the inside wall of the west tower. ✉ *High St.* ☎ *01202/884753* ⊕ *www.wimborneminster. org.uk* 🖾 *£1.50 donation requested for church, chained library free* ☉ *Church Mar.–Dec., Mon.–Sat. 9:30–5:30, Sun. 2:30–5:30; Jan. and Feb., Mon.–Sat. 9:30–4, Sun. 2:30–4. Chained library Easter–Oct., weekdays 10:30–12:30 and 2–4; Nov.–Easter, Sat. 10–12:30.*

The **Priest's House Museum,** on the main square in a Tudor building with a garden, includes rooms furnished in period styles and a Victorian kitchen. It also has Roman and Iron Age exhibits, including a cryptic, three-faced Celtic stone head. ✉ *23 High St.* ☎ *01202/882533* 🖾 *£3* ☉ *Apr.–Oct., Mon.–Sat. 10–4:30; also open 2 wks after Christmas.*

Kingston Lacy, a grand 17th-century house built for the Bankes family (who had lived in Corfe Castle), was altered in the 19th century by Sir Charles Barry, co-architect of the Houses of Parliament in London. The building holds a choice picture collection with works by Titian, Rubens, Van Dyck, and Velásquez, as well as the fabulous Spanish Room, lined with gilded leather and topped with an ornate Venetian ceiling. There's also a fine collection of Egyptian artifacts. Parkland with walking paths surrounds the house. ✉ *B3082, 1½ mi northwest of Wimborne Minster* ☎ *01202/883402* ⊕ *www.nationaltrust.org.uk* 🖾 *£9, park and garden only £4.50* ☉ *House mid-Mar.–Oct., Wed.–Sun. 11–5, last admission*

4. Garden and park Feb.–mid-Mar., weekends 10:30–4; mid-Mar.–Oct., daily 10:30–6; Nov. and Dec., Fri.–Sun. 10:30–4.

Where to Eat

£££ ✕ **Primizia.** The low ceiling, tangerine walls, and tile floor lend this popular bistro an intimate feel. From the menu, which shows French and Italian influences, try the smoked salmon with mango and onion salsa or the saffron and dill risotto with king prawns and scallops. ✉ *26 Westborough* ☎ *01202/883518* ▭ *MC, V* ⊘ *Closed Sun. and Mon.*

Blandford Forum

㊸ *11 mi northwest of Wimborne Minster.*

Endowed with perhaps the handsomest Georgian town center in the southwest, this market town of brick and stone on the River Stour was Thomas Hardy's "Shottesford Forum." The Church of St. Peter and St. Paul, with an imposing cupola and dating from 1739, deserves a look.

Where to Stay & Eat

★ **£££** ✕▦ **Museum Inn.** It's worth making the detour 9 mi northeast of Blandford Forum to find this characterful inn known for fine contemporary British fare. Despite a stylish transformation, the building remains in harmony with its 17th-century beginnings, retaining its flagstone floors and inglenook fireplace. Bedrooms are rustic but smart. Good fresh food, from grilled calves' liver to slow-roasted Dorset Down lamb shoulder is available daily in the bar, or, on Friday night, Saturday night, and Sunday afternoon in the more formal Shed restaurant (£££). ✉ *Farnham DT11 8DE* ☎ *01725/516261* 🖷 *01725/516988* ⊕ *www.museuminn. co.uk* ⤴ *8 rooms* ♿ *Restaurant, bar, some pets allowed; no a/c, no kids under 8* ▭ *MC, V* ○| *BP.*

Corfe Castle

★ **㊹** *20 mi south of Blandford Forum, 15 mi south of Poole, 6 mi south of Wareham.*

One of the most impressive ruins in Britain, Dorset's Corfe Castle overlooks the appealing gray limestone village of Corfe. The castle site guards a gap in the surrounding Purbeck Hills and has been fortified since at least 900. The present ruins are of the castle built between 1105, when the great central keep was erected, and the 1270s, when the outer walls and towers were built. It owes its ramshackle state to Cromwell's soldiers, who blew up the castle in 1646 during the Civil War, after Lady Bankes led its defense during a long siege. ✉ *A351* ☎ *01929/481294* ⊕ *www.nationaltrust.org.uk* 🎟 *£5* ⊘ *Mar. and Oct., daily 10–5; Apr.–Sept., daily 10–6; Nov.–Feb., daily 10–4.*

▌ OFF THE
BEATEN
PATH

CLOUDS HILL – A tiny, spartan, brick-and-tile cottage served as the retreat of T. E. Lawrence (Lawrence of Arabia) before he was killed in a motorcycle accident on the road from Bovington in 1935. The house remains very much as he left it, with photos and memorabilia from the Middle East. It's particularly atmospheric on a gloomy day, as there's no electric light. ✉ *8 mi northwest of Corfe, off B3390, Wareham*

☎ 01929/405616 ⊕ www.nationaltrust.org.uk ⊠ £3.50 ☺ Apr.–Oct.,
Thurs.–Sun. and national holiday Mon. noon–5 or dusk.

Where to Stay & Eat

★ ££ ✕ **The Fox.** An age-old pub, the Fox has a fine view of Corfe Castle from
its flower garden. There's an ancient well in the lounge bar and more
timeworn stonework in an alcove, as well as a pre-1300 fireplace. The
bar cheerfully doles out soups and sandwiches, as well as steaks and fish
dishes, but things can get uncomfortably congested in summer. ⊠ West
St., Corfe ☎ 01929/480449 ⊟ MC, V.

££ ⊡ **Castle Inn.** This thatched hotel, 10 mi west of Corfe and a five-minute
walk from the sea, has a flagstone bar and other 15th-century features.
Bedrooms are individually furnished, some with four-posters, and there's
an extensive garden to sit in, including a rose garden. A lengthy bar menu
is available daily, and on Saturday evenings the good restaurant has an
à la carte menu. Satisfying walks are nearby. ⊠ Main Rd., West Lulworth BH20 5RN ☎ 01929/400311 ⊟ 01929/400415 ⊕ www.
thecastleinn-lulworthcove.co.uk ⟿ 15 rooms, 12 with bath ⌂ Restaurant, bar, some pets allowed; no a/c, no phones in some rooms ⊟ AE,
DC, MC, V ⊺⊙⊺ BP.

Dorchester

45 21 mi west of Corfe on A351 and A352, 30 mi west of Bournemouth,
43 mi southwest of Salisbury.

In many ways Dorchester, the Casterbridge of Thomas Hardy's novel
The Mayor of Casterbridge, is a traditional southern country town. The
town owes much of its fame to its
connection with Hardy, whose
bronze statue looks westward from
a bank on Colliton Walk. Born in
a cottage in the hamlet of Higher
Bockhampton, about 3 mi northeast
of Dorchester, Hardy attended
school in the town and was apprentice to an architect here.

Dorchester has many reminders of
the Roman presence in the area.
The Romans laid out the town
about AD 70, and a walk along
Bowling Alley Walk, West Walk,
and Colliton Walk follows the ap-
proximate line of the original
Roman town walls. On the north
side of Colliton Park lies an excavated Roman villa with a marvelously preserved mosaic floor.

To appreciate the town's character, visit the Wednesday market in
Market Square, where you can find

> **BLOODY JUSTICE**
>
> Dorchester is associated with Mon-
> mouth's Rebellion of 1685, when
> Charles II's illegitimate son, the
> duke of Monmouth, led a rising
> against his unpopular uncle,
> James II. The rebellion was ruth-
> lessly put down, and the chief jus-
> tice, Lord Jeffreys, arrived from
> London to try the rebels and sym-
> pathizers for treason. A bullying
> drunkard, Jeffreys was the proto-
> typical hanging judge, and stories
> of his mass executions lingered for
> centuries throughout the South.
> The trials became known as the
> Bloody Assizes (assizes are court
> sessions). Jeffreys's courtroom in
> Dorchester was in what is now the
> Antelope Hotel on South Street.

Hardy's Dorset

AMONG THIS REGION'S PROUDEST CLAIMS is its connection with Thomas Hardy (1840–1928), one of England's most celebrated novelists. If you read some of Hardy's novels before visiting Dorset–re-created by Hardy as his part-fact, part-fiction county of Wessex–you may well recognize some places immediately from his descriptions. The tranquil countryside surrounding Dorchester is lovingly described in *Far from the Madding Crowd*, and Casterbridge, in *The Mayor of*

Casterbridge, stands for Dorchester itself. Any pilgrimage to Hardy's Wessex begins at the author's birthplace in Higher Bockhampton, 3 mi east of Dorchester. Salisbury makes an appearance as "Melchester" in *Jude the Obscure*. Walk in the footsteps of Jude Fawley by climbing Shaftesbury–"Shaston"–and its steeply Gold Hill, a street lined with charming cottages. Today, many of these sights seem frozen in time, and Hardy's spirit is ever present.

handcrafted items and Dorset delicacies such as Blue Vinney cheese (which some connoisseurs prefer to Blue Stilton). Things have changed a bit since the days when, to quote Hardy, "Bees and butterflies in the cornfields at the top of the town, who desired to get to the meads at the bottom, took no circuitous route, but flew straight down High Street . . ."

The labyrinthine **Dorset County Museum** contains ancient Celtic from nearby Maiden Castle and Roman remains from town, a rural crafts gallery, and a local-history gallery. It's better known for its large collection of Hardy memorabilia. A gallery focusing on the nearby Jurassic Coast opened in 2006. ⊠ *High West St.* ☎ *01305/262735* ⊕ *www. dorsetcountymuseum.org* 🎫 *£6* ⊘ *July–Sept., daily 10–5; Oct.–June, Mon.–Sat. 10–5.*

The small thatch-and-cob **Hardy's Cottage**, where the writer was born in 1840, was built by his grandfather and is little altered since that time. From here Thomas Hardy would make his daily 6-mi walk to school in Dorchester. Among other things, you can see the desk at which the author completed *Far from the Madding Crowd.* ⊠ *½ mi south of Blandford Rd. (A35), Higher Bockhampton* ☎ *01305/262366* ⊕ *www.nationaltrust.org.uk* 🎫 *£3* ⊘ *Apr.–Oct., Sun.–Thurs. 11–5 or dusk.*

Thomas Hardy lived in **Max Gate** from 1885 until his death in 1928. An architect by profession, Hardy designed the house, in which the dining room and the light, airy drawing room are open to the public. He wrote much of his poetry here and many of his novels, including *Tess of the d'Urbervilles* and *The Mayor of Casterbridge.* ⊠ *Allington Ave., 1 mi east of Dorchester on A352* ☎ *01305/262538* ⊕ *www.nationaltrust. org.uk* 🎫 *£2.80* ⊘ *Apr.–Sept., Mon., Wed., and Sun. 2–5.*

The **Maumbury Rings** (⊠ Maumbury Rd.), the remains of a Roman amphitheater on the edge of town, were built on a prehistoric site that later
served as a place of execution. (Hardy's *Mayor of Casterbridge* contains
a vivid evocation of the Rings.) As late as 1706, a girl was burned at
the stake here.

The popular **Dinosaur Museum** has life-size models, interactive displays,
and a hands-on Discovery Gallery. ⊠ *Icen Way, off High East St.*
☎ *01305/269741* ⊕ *www.thedinosaurmuseum.com* ⊠ *£6* ⊙ *Apr.–Oct.,
daily 9:30–5:30; Nov.–Mar., daily 10–4:30.*

It's hardly what you might expect from a small county town, but the
informative and well-displayed **Tutankhamun Exhibition,** in a former
Catholic church, re-creates the young pharaoh's tomb and treasures in
all their glory. The ticket gives you a half-price reduction to visit the small
Mummies Exhibition next door, showing the process of mummification
with copies of mummies. ⊠ *High West St.* ☎ *01305/269571* ⊕ *www.
tutankhamun-exhibition.co.uk* ⊠ *£6, Mummies Exhibition £3.80*
⊙ *Apr.–Oct., daily 9:30–5:30; Nov.–Mar., weekdays 9:30–5, weekends 10–5; last admission 30 mins before closing.*

**NEED A
BREAK?**

Drop into **Potters Café-Bistro** (⊠ 19 Durngate St. ☎ 01305/260312), occupying a 17th-century cottage, for teas, coffees, and delicious cakes and pastries,
as well as sandwiches and light lunches of fish pie or tortellini. The courtyard
garden is pleasant in summer.

Fine 19th-century gardens enhance an outstanding example of 15th-cen-
tury domestic architecture at **Athelhampton House and Gardens,** 5 mi east
of Dorchester and 1 mi east of Puddletown. Thomas Hardy called this
place Athelhall in some of his writings, referring to the legendary King
Aethelstan, who had a palace on this site. The current house includes
the Great Hall, with much of its original timber roof intact, the King's
Room, and the Library, with oak paneling and more than 3,000 books.
The 10 acres of landscaped gardens contain water features and the
Great Court with its 12 giant yew pyramids. ⊠ *A35* ☎ *01305/848363*
⊕ *www.athelhampton.co.uk* ⊠ *£8* ⊙ *Mar.–Oct., Sun.–Thurs. 10–5;
Nov.–Feb., Sun. 10:30–dusk.*

Where to Stay & Eat

££–£££ ✕ **6 North Square.** Just behind the County Museum, this pleasant neighborhood brasserie makes an ideal stop for a relaxed lunch or evening
meal. The menu may list homemade terrine for starters, and pan-fried
sirloin served with blue vinny cream sauce, and sesame crusted salmon
with king prawns and salsa for main courses. The atmosphere is intimate without being chi-chi, the tiled floor lending a Continental air. ⊠ *6
North Sq.* ☎ *01305/267679* ☰ *MC, V* ⊙ *Closed Sun.*

★ **£££** ✕▣ **Yalbury Cottage.** A thatch roof and inglenook fireplaces add to the
appeal of this 300-year-old cottage, 2½ mi east of Dorchester and close
to Hardy's birthplace. The restaurant's three-course fixed-price menu
(£32) of superior modern British and European fare might include
thyme-poached quail breasts with seared foie gras, or pan-fried wild sea-
bass with Lyonnaise potatoes and an orange butter sauce. Functional

but comfortable bedrooms are available in an extension overlooking gardens or adjacent fields. ⊠ *Lower Bockhampton DT2 8PZ* ☎ *01305/262382* 🖶 *01305/266412* ⊕ *www.yalburycottage.com* 🛏 *8 rooms* ♨ *Restaurant, in-room DVDs, some pets allowed (fee); no a/c, no smoking* ⊟ *AE, MC, V* ⊘ *Closed 2 wks Jan. No lunch* ¶◎¶ *BP.*

★ **£££** 🏨 **Casterbridge Hotel.** Small but full of character, this Georgian building (1790) reflects its age with period furniture and elegance. Guest rooms—one with its own patio—are individually and impeccably furnished in traditional style, and the conservatory overlooks a courtyard garden. A congenial husband-and-wife team owns and runs the hotel. ⊠ *49 High East St., DT1 1HU* ☎ *01305/264043* 🖶 *01305/260884* ⊕ *www.casterbridgehotel.co.uk* 🛏 *15 rooms* ♨ *In-room data ports, bar; no a/c* ⊟ *AE, MC, V* ¶◎¶ *BP.*

The Outdoors

From April through October the **Thomas Hardy Society** (✉ Box 1438, Dorchester DT1 1YH ☎🖶 01305/251501 ⊕ www.hardysociety.org) organizes walks that follow in the steps of Hardy's novels. Readings and discussions accompany the walks, which take most of a day.

OFF THE BEATEN PATH

POUNDBURY – Owned by the Duchy of Cornwall and under the aegis of the Prince of Wales, this model village a mile west of Dorchester on B3150 is a showcase of Prince Charles' vision of urban planning and community living. The emphasis is on conservation and energy efficiency; private houses coexist with shops, offices, small-scale factories, and leisure facilities. Central Pummery Square is dominated by the colonnaded Brownsword Hall. Here you'll find the pub and restaurant Poet Laureate (named after Ted Hughes [1930–98], ☎ 01305/251511), where there are weekly jazz gigs, and Dorchester's Farmer's Market, held the first Saturday of the month. For more information consult the **Duchy of Cornwall office** (Middle Farm, Poundbury, Dorchester, Dorset DT1 3RS ☎ 01305/250533, www.princeofwales.gov.uk).

Cerne Abbas

🔢 *6 mi north of Dorchester.*

The village of Cerne Abbas, worth a short exploration on foot, has some Tudor houses on the road beside the church. Nearby you can also see the original village stocks. Tenth-century **Cerne Abbey** is now a ruin, with little left to see except its old gateway, although the nearby Abbey House is still in use.

Cerne Abbas's main claim to fame is the colossal and unblushingly priapic **figure of a giant,** cut in chalk on a hillside overlooking the village. The 180-foot-long giant carries a huge club, and may have originated as a tribal fertility symbol long before Roman times; authorities disagree. His outlines are formed by 2-foot-wide trenches. The present giant is thought to have been carved in the chalk about AD 1200. The best place to view the figure is from the A352 itself, where you can park in any of numerous nearby turnouts.

Maiden Castle

★ **47** *2 mi southwest of Dorchester.*

After Stonehenge, Maiden Castle is the most important pre-Roman archaeological site in England. It's not an actual castle but an enormous, complex hill fort of stone and earth with ramparts that enclose about 45 acres. England's mysterious prehistoric inhabitants built the fort, and many centuries later it was a Celtic stronghold. In AD 43 invading Romans, under the general (later emperor) Vespasian, stormed the fort. Finds from the site are on display in the Dorset County Museum in Dorchester. To experience an uncanny silence and sense of mystery, climb Maiden Castle early in the day (access to it is unrestricted). Leave your car at the lot at the end of Maiden Castle Way, a 1½-mi lane signposted off the A354. ⊠ *A354.*

Weymouth

48 *8 mi south of Dorchester.*

Dorset's main coastal resort, Weymouth, is known for its wide, safe, sandy beaches and its royal connections. King George III took up sea bathing here for his health in 1789, setting a trend among the wealthy and fashionable people of the day. Popularity left Weymouth with many fine buildings, including the Georgian row houses lining the esplanade. Striking historical details clamor for attention: a wall on Maiden Street, for example, holds a cannonball that was embedded in it during the Civil War. Nearby, a column commemorates the launching of United States forces from Weymouth on D-Day.

Where to Eat

££–£££ ✕ **Perry's.** A busy, family-run restaurant right by the harbor, Perry's specializes in simple dishes using the best local seafood. Try the lobster or crab, or grilled fillet of turbot with leeks, new potatoes, and shellfish sauce. Meat dishes, such as roast fillet of beef, are tasty, too. ⊠ *The Harbourside, 4 Trinity Rd.* ☎ *01305/785799* ⊟ *AE, MC, V* ✆ *No lunch Mon. and Sat.; no dinner Sun. Sept.–Easter.*

£–££ ✕ **Old Rooms.** A fisherman's pub full of maritime clutter and low beams, this popular choice has great views over the harbor. The long menu is strongest on steaks, but pastas and meat pies are other choices. There's a separate dining area, or you can mix with the locals at the bar. ⊠ *7 Cove Row* ☎ *01305/771130* ⊟ *MC, V.*

Isle of Portland

49 *4 mi south of Weymouth.*

A 5-mi-long peninsula jutting south from Weymouth leads to the Isle of Portland, well known for its limestone. The peninsula is the eastern end of the unique geological curiosity known as **Chesil Beach**—a 200-yard-wide, 30-foot-high bank of pebbles that decrease in size from east to west. The beach extends for 18 mi. A powerful undertow makes swimming dangerous, and tombstones in local churchyards attest to the many shipwrecks the beach has caused.

Abbotsbury

50 *10 mi northwest of Weymouth.*

Pretty Abbotsbury is at the western end of Chesil Beach. A lagoon outside the village serves as the **Abbotsbury Swannery,** a famous breeding place for swans. Introduced by Benedictine monks as a source of meat in winter, the swans have remained for centuries, building new nests every year in the soft, moist eelgrass. ⊠ *New Barn Rd.* ☎ *01305/871858* ⊕ *www.abbotsbury-tourism.co.uk* ⊠ *£7.50* ◷ *Mid- Mar.–Sept., daily 10–6; Oct., daily 10–5; last admission 1 hr before closing.*

On the hills above Abbotsbury stands the **Hardy Monument**—dedicated to Sir Thomas Masterman Hardy, Lord Nelson's flag captain at Trafalgar, to whom Nelson's dying words, "Kiss me, Hardy, " were addressed. The monument lacks charm, but in clear weather you can scan the whole coastline between the Isle of Wight and Start Point in Devon. ⊠ *Black Down, Portesham* ☎ *01297/561900* ⊕ *www.nationaltrust.org.uk* ⊠ *£1* ◷ *Apr.–Sept., weekends 11–5. Closed in bad weather.*

Where to Stay & Eat

££££ ✕▥ **Manor Hotel.** The pedigree of this honey-color hotel and restaurant goes back more than 700 years—note its flagstone floors, oak paneling, and beamed ceilings. English and French seafood and game dishes are specialties of the restaurant (£££££); the fixed-price menu changes daily. Some of the rooms, individually decorated in pastel colors and furnished with antiques, have sea views, and Chesil Beach is a few minutes' walk away. Self-catering facilities are available. ⊠ *Beach Rd., 3 mi west of Abbotsbury, West Bexington DT2 9DF* ☎ *01308/897785* 🖨 *01308/897035* ⊕ *www.themanorhotel.com* ➦ *13 rooms* ⌂ *Restaurant, playground; no a/c* ⊟ *AE, MC, V* ⎆◯⎆ *BP.*

Lyme Regis

51 *19 mi west of Abbotsbury.*

"A very strange stranger it must be, who does not see the charms of the immediate environs of Lyme, to make him wish to know it better," wrote Jane Austen in *Persuasion.* Judging from the summer crowds, most people appear to be not at all strange. The ancient, scenic town of Lyme Regis and the so-called Jurassic Coast are highlights of southwest Dorset. The crumbling seaside cliffs in this area are especially fossil rich.

Lyme Regis is famous for its curving stone breakwater, **The Cobb,** built by King Edward I in the 13th century to improve the harbor. The duke of Monmouth landed here in 1685 during his ill-fated attempt to overthrow his uncle, James II. The Cobb figured prominently in the movie *The French Lieutenant's Woman,* based on John Fowles's novel set in Lyme Regis, as well as in the film version of Jane Austen's *Persuasion.* Fowles is Lyme's most famous current resident.

CLOSE UP

The Jurassic Coast

FOSSILS AND FOSSIL HUNTING are the lure for visitors to the coast that stretches for 95 mi between Studland Bay in the east to Exmouth (Devon) in the west. This cliff-lined coast encompasses 185 million years of the Earth's geological history, for which it has been granted World Heritage Site status. Fossils formed in the distant past are continuously being uncovered here as parts of the crumbly cliffs erode, and good examples of ammonites and dinosaur traces can be seen in museums in Dorchester and Lyme Regis. Though it is dubbed "Jurassic Coast," there are also examples of older Triassic and younger Cretacous rocks. As a rule, the older rocks can be seen in the western parts of the coast, and younger rocks form the cliffs to the east. A good path that traces the whole coast allows you to explore the area at close quarters.

Fossil hunters are free to pick and chip away at the rocks, the best stretch being within 6 mi on either side of Lyme Regis (the beach below Stonebarrow Hill, east of Charmouth, is especially fruitful). As signs along the seafront warn, the best place to find fossils is not at the rockface but on the shore. Check weather conditions and tides—collecting on a falling tide is best, and the ideal time to do it is in winter, when heavy storms are continuously uncovering new areas.

To spot the most commonly found fossils, ammonites (chambered cephalopods from the Jurassic era, related to today's nautilus), just look down hard at the shingle (large gravel) on the beach and inspect the gaps between rocks and boulders. Ammonites are usually preserved in either calcite or iron pyrite ("fools gold"); shinier, more fragile specimens may be found in aragonite. Visit the museums in Lyme to remind you what to look for: the lustrous spirals are similar in heft and size to a brass coin, most smaller than a 10p coin. Other fossils to be found include sea urchins, white oyster shells, and coiled worm tubes.

If you want to leave nothing to chance, hook up with a pro: information on guided walks is available from the tourist office and the Philpot Museum in Lyme Regis. Publications are also available for sale in the tourist offices of Lyme Regis, Weymouth, and Dorchester; they can also tell you about coastal boat trips.

☺ The small but child-friendly **Marine Aquarium** offers the usual up-close look at creatures aquatic, from conger eels to spider crabs. ⊠ *End of the Cobb* ☎ *01297/444230* 💷 *£2.50* ☉ *Easter–Oct., daily 10–5.*

In a gabled and turreted Victorian building, the lively **Philpot Museum** contains engaging items that illustrate the town's maritime and domestic history, as well as a section on local writers and a good selection of local fossils. ⊠ *Bridge St.* ☎ *01297/443370* ⊕ *www.lymeregismuseum. co.uk* 💷 *£2.20* ☉ *Apr.–Oct., Mon.–Sat. 10–5, Sun. 11–5; Nov.–Mar., Sat. 10–5, Sun. 11–5, also weekdays 10–5 during school holidays.*

☺ The **Dinosaurland Fossil Museum,** in a former church, displays an excellent collection of local fossils and gives the background on regional geology and how fossils develop. Although the museum is aimed at children, most people find it informative. Ask here about guided fossil-hunting walks. The **Lyme Regis Fossil Shop** on the ground floor sells books and fascinating fossils from around the world as well as reproductions of fossils, some fashioned into jewelry or ornaments. ⊠ *Coombe St.* ☎ *01297/443541* ⊕ *www.dinosaurland.co.uk* 🖾 *£4* ☉ *July and Aug., daily 10–6; Sept.–June, daily 10–5.*

> **EVEN KIDS DIG IT**
>
> In 1810 a local child named Mary Anning dug out a complete ichthyosaur near Lyme Regis (it's on display in London's Natural History Museum). Anning's obsession with Jurassic remains left her labeled locally as the "fossil woman"; throughout her life she made many valuable discoveries that were sought by museums and collectors.

Where to Stay & Eat

£–££ ✕ **Bell Cliff Restaurant.** This friendly little place at the bottom of Lyme's main street makes a great spot for a light lunch or tea, although it can get noisy and cramped. Apart from teas and coffees, you can order seafood, including whitebait, plaice, and the chef's salmon fish cakes, or a gammon steak (a thick slice of cured ham) or leek and mushroom crumble. ⊠ *5–6 Broad St.* ☎ *01297/442459* ⊟ *MC, V* ☉ *No dinner Oct.–June.*

£££–££££ ✕🖾 **Alexandra.** Magnificently sited above the Cobb, the Alexandra is a rambling, old-fashioned haven with a genteel, unhurried air. Informal lunches and teas are served in a conservatory that overlooks an expanse of lawn. The formal restaurant (*£££££*) has an impressive wine list to complement the fixed-price dinners, with entrées such as grilled plaice and minions of beef with glazed field mushrooms. Depending on the cost, some guest rooms have a restrained elegance and others are purely functional, although you're almost guaranteed a view over garden and sea. Bathrooms are on the small side. ⊠ *Pound St., DT7 3HZ* ☎ *01297/442010* 🖶 *01297/443229* ⊕ *www.hotelalexandra.co.uk* 🖘 *26 rooms* △ *Restaurant, bar, some pets allowed (fee); no a/c* ⊟ *MC, V* ☉ *Closed late Dec.–Jan.* ⏋◯⏝ *BP.*

£ 🖾 **Coombe House.** Tucked away on one of the oldest lanes in Lyme (dating from the 16th century), this simple B&B has genial hosts and spacious, modern guest rooms in pastel shades. Breakfast, which includes homemade jams, is brought to your room. ⊠ *41 Coombe St., DT7 3PY* 🖶🖶 *01297/443849* ⊕ *www.coombe-house.co.uk* 🖘 *2 rooms* △ *No a/c, no room phones, no smoking* ⊟ *No credit cards* ⏋◯⏝ *BP.*

Sports & the Outdoors

The 72-mi **Dorset Coast Path** (⊠ South West Coast Path Association, Bowker House, Lee Mill Bridge, Ivybridge, Devon PL21 9EF ☎ 01752/896237 ⊕ www.swcp.org.uk) runs east from Lyme Regis to Poole, bypassing Weymouth and taking in the quiet bays, shingle beaches, and low chalk cliffs of the coast. Some highlights are Golden Cap, the highest point on the South Coast; the Swannery at Abbotsbury; Chesil Beach; and Lulworth Cove (between Weymouth and Corfe Castle). Villages and isolated pubs dot the route, as do many rural B&Bs.

SOUTH ESSENTIALS

Transportation

BY AIR

The small international airport at Southampton is useful for flights to the Channel Islands and some European destinations.

Southampton International Airport ⊠ M27, Junction 5 ☎ 0870/040-0009 ⊕ www.southamptonairport.com.

BY BOAT & FERRY

Wightlink operates a car-ferry service between the mainland and the Isle of Wight. The crossing takes about 30 minutes from Lymington to Yarmouth; 35 minutes from Portsmouth to Fishbourne. The company also operates catamaran service between Portsmouth and Ryde (15 minutes). Red Funnel runs a car-ferry (one hour) and hydrofoil service (25 minutes) between Southampton and Cowes. Hovertravel has a hovercraft shuttle between Southsea (Portsmouth) and Ryde (10 minutes).

FARES & SCHEDULES   **Hovertravel** ☎ 01983/811000 or 023/9281-1000 ⊕ www.hovertravel.co.uk. **Red Funnel** ☎ 0870/444-8898 ⊕ www.redfunnel.co.uk. **Wightlink** ☎ 0870/582-7744 ⊕ www.wightlink.co.uk.

BY BUS

National Express buses at London's Victoria Coach Station on Buckingham Palace Road depart hourly for Bournemouth (2½ hours) and Southampton (2½ hours), and every 2 hours for Portsmouth (2 hours, 15 minutes) and Winchester (2 hours). There are three buses daily to Salisbury (about 3 hours). Solent Blue and Stagecoach Hampshire Bus operate a comprehensive service in the Southampton, New Forest, Winchester, and Bournemouth areas. Southern Vectis covers the Isle of Wight. Traveline can provide information about travel in the region.

CUTTING COSTS   Wilts (Wiltshire) & Dorset Bus Co. offers both one-day Explorer and seven-day Busabout tickets; ask about the Goldrider tickets offered by Stagecoach, and Rover tickets offered by Solent Blue and Southern Vectis.

FARES & SCHEDULES   **National Express** ☎ 0870/580-8080 ⊕ www.nationalexpress.com. **Solent Blue** ☎ 023/8061-8233 ⊕ www.solentblueline.com. **Southern Vectis** ☎ 0870/608-2608 ⊕ www.islandbuses.info. **Stagecoach Hampshire Bus** ☎ 0845/121-0180 ⊕ www.stagecoachbus.com. **Traveline** ☎ 0870/608-2608 ⊕ www.traveline.org.uk. **Wilts (Wiltshire) & Dorset Bus Co.** ☎ 01722/336855 ⊕ www.wdbus.co.uk.

BY CAR

The South is linked to London and other major cities by a well-developed road network, which includes M3 to Winchester (59 mi from London) and Southampton (77 mi); A3 to Portsmouth (70 mi); and M27 along the coast, from the New Forest and Southampton to Portsmouth. For Salisbury, take M3 to A303, then A30. A31 and A35 connect Bournemouth to Dorchester and the rest of Dorset.

ROAD
CONDITIONS
Driving is easy in this area. In northeast Hampshire and in many parts of neighboring Wiltshire there are lanes overhung by trees and lined with thatched cottages and Georgian houses. Often these lanes begin near the exits of main highways. Salisbury Plain has long, straight roads surrounded by endless vistas; the challenge here is staying within the speed limit.

BY TRAIN

South West Trains serves the South from London's Waterloo Station. Travel times average 1 hour to Winchester, 1¼ hours to Southampton, 2 hours to Bournemouth, and 2¾ hours to Weymouth. The trip to Salisbury takes 1½ hours, and Portsmouth about 2 hours. There is at least one fast train every hour on all these routes. For local information throughout the region, contact National Rail Enquiries.

CUTTING COSTS
A Network card (@20), valid throughout the South and Southeast for a year, entitles you to one-third off particular fares.

FARES &
SCHEDULES
🚹 **National Rail Enquiries** ☎ 0845/748–4950 ⊕ www.nationalrail.co.uk. **South West Trains** ☎ 0845/748–4950 ⊕ www.southwesttrains.co.uk.

Contacts & Resources

EMERGENCIES

🚹 **Ambulance, fire, police** ☎ 999. **Dorset County Hospital** ✉ Williams Ave., Dorchester ☎ 01305/251150. **Queen Alexandra Hospital** ✉ Southwick Hill Rd., Cosham, Portsmouth ☎ 023/9228–6000. **St. Mary's Hospital** ✉ Parkhurst Rd., Newport, Isle of Wight ☎ 01983/524081. **Salisbury District Hospital** ✉ Odstock Rd., Salisbury ☎ 01722/336262. **Southampton General Hospital** ✉ Tremona Rd., Southampton ☎ 023/8077–7222.

INTERNET

Public libraries in all the cities and many of the smaller towns of the region offer free Internet access. Salisbury's tourist office also has a terminal for brief use (*see* Visitor Information, *below*, for address). Increasing numbers of hotels and B&Bs offer Internet connections, and many also provide a Wi-Fi facility.

🚹 Internet Cafés **Online Café** ✉ 163 Elm Grove, Southsea, Portsmouth ☎ 023/9283–1106. **Salisbury Online** ✉ 14 Endless St., above the Endless Life café, Salisbury ☎ 01722/421328 ⊕ www.salisburyonline.co.uk. **Jamie's Internet Café** ✉ 10 Parchment St., Winchester ☎ 01962/870880 ⊕ www.jamiesinternetcafe.org.uk.

TOURS

City Sightseeing has three daily Stonehenge tours from Salisbury, April through October, costing £15 (check for availability). There are more frequent daily tours of Bournemouth and of Portsmouth from late May through September, both costing £6.50. A. S. Tours arranges day tours of Stonehenge and Avebury, year-round, in six-seater minibuses. Salisbury City Guides runs daily summer (weekends in winter) walks in Salisbury. The Guild of Registered Tourist Guides maintains a directory of qualified Blue Badge guides who can meet you anywhere in the region for private tours. Local organizations such as Wessexplore can also arrange Blue Badge tours.

🔲 **A. S. Tours** ☎ 01980/862931. **City Sightseeing/Guide Friday** ☎ 01708/866000 ⊕ www.city-sightseeing.com. **Guild of Registered Tourist Guides** ☎ 020/7403-1115 ⊕ www.blue-badge.org.uk. **Salisbury City Guides** ☎ 01722/320349 ⊕ www. salisburycityguides.co.uk. **Wessexplore** ☎01722/326304 ⊕www.dmac.co.uk/wessexplore.

VISITOR INFORMATION

Tourism South East can field general inquiries and put you in touch with local information centers, which are normally open Monday through Saturday 9:30 to 5:30, with reduced hours in winter.

🔲 **Tourism South East** ✉40 Chamberlayne Rd., Eastleigh S050 5JH ☎ 023/8062-5400 🖷 023/8062-0010 ⊕ www.visitsoutheastengland.com. **Avebury** ✉ Avebury Chapel, Green St., SN8 1RE ☎ 01672/539425 ⊕ www.kennet.gov.uk. **Bournemouth** ✉ Westover Rd., near bandstand, BH1 2BU ☎0845/051-1700 ⊕www.bournemouth.co.uk. **Dorchester** ✉11 Antelope Walk, DT1 1BE ☎01305/267992 ⊕www.westdorset.com. **Lyme Regis** ✉ Guildhall Cottage, Church St., DT7 3BS ☎ 01305/442138 ⊕ www.westdorset.com. **Lyndhurst** ✉Main Car Park, High St., S043 7NY ☎023/8028-2269 ⊕www.thenewforest. co.uk. **Marlborough** ✉ Car Park, George La., SN8 1EE ☎ 01672/513989. **Portsmouth** ✉ The Hard, PO1 3QJ ☎ 023/9282-6722 ⊕ www.visitportsmouth.co.uk ✉ Clarence Esplanade, Southsea PO5 3PB ☎ 023/9282-6722. **Ryde** ✉ Western Esplanade, PO33 2LW ☎ 01983/813818 ⊕ www.islandbreaks.co.uk. **Salisbury** ✉ Fish Row, off Market Sq., SP1 1EJ ☎01722/334956 ⊕ www.visitsalisbury.com. **Sherborne** ✉3 Tilton Ct., Digby Rd., DT9 3NL ☎ 01935/815341 ⊕ www.westdorset.com. **Southampton** ✉ 9 Civic Centre Rd., SO14 7FJ ☎ 023/8083-3333 ⊕ www.southampton.gov.uk. **Winchester** ✉ The Guildhall, Broadway, SO23 9LJ ☎ 01962/840500 ⊕ www.visitwinchester.co.uk..

The West Country

SOMERSET, DEVON, CORNWALL

WORD OF MOUTH

"The most scenic part of Devon, in my opinion, is the north coast. If you have time, don't miss the Lynmouth/Lynton area. The Valley of the Rocks has some of the best coastal views in England."

—Steve_James

"Cornwall is all about rugged scenery on the north coast; bracing Champagne-like air, beautiful gardens, and charming fishing villages on the south coast; plus Celtic history and the odd pirate."

—londonengland

"The water [in St. Ives] is a lush shade of blue, reminiscent of the Mediterranean. It is a little touristy, but for the British. Sort of like Cape Cod for New Englanders."

—socialworker

www.fodors.com/forums

Updated by
Robert
Andrews

LEAFY, NARROW COUNTRY ROADS all around the southwest lead through miles of buttercup meadows and cider apple orchards to mellow villages of stone and thatch and heathery heights overlooking the sea. This can be one of England's most relaxing regions to visit. The secret of exploring it is to ignore the main highways and just follow the signposts—or, even better, to let yourself get lost, which won't be difficult. The village names alone are music to the ears: there's Tintinhull, St. Endellion, and Huish Episcopi—just to name a few hamlets that *haven't* been covered below.

Somerset, Devon, and Cornwall are the three counties that make up the long southern peninsula known as the West Country. Each has its own distinct flavor, and each comes with a regionalism that borders on patriotism. Somerset is noted for its subtly rolling green countryside; Devon's wild and dramatic moors—bare, boggy, upland heath dominated by heathers and gorse—contrast with the restfulness of its many sandy beaches and coves; and Cornwall has managed to retain a touch of its old insularity, despite the annual invasion of thousands of people lured by the Atlantic waves or the ripples of the English Channel.

Bristol is where you come across the first unmistakable burrs of the western brogue. Its historic port retains a strong maritime air, and Georgian architecture and a dramatic gorge create a backdrop to what has become one of Britain's most dynamic cities. You might weave south through the lovely Chew Valley on your way to the cathedral city of Wells. The county's lush countryside is best seen in a cloak of summer heat when its orchards give ample shade, and its old stone houses and inns welcome you with a breath of coolness. Abutting the north coast are the Quantock and Mendip hills, and heather-covered Exmoor, the setting for R. D. Blackmore's historical romance, *Lorna Doone.*

Devon, farther west, is famed for its wild moorland—especially Dartmoor, supposed home of the mysterious beast in Sir Arthur Conan Doyle's novel *The Hound of the Baskervilles,* and actual home of ponies and an assortment of strange tors: rocky outcroppings eroded into weird shapes. Devon's large coastal towns are as interesting for their cultural and historical appeal—many were smugglers' havens—as for their scenic beauty. Some propagandists of east Devon speak of the "red cliffs" of Devon in contrast to the more famous "white cliffs of Dover." Parts of south Devon, on the other hand, resemble some balmy Mediterranean shore—hence its soubriquet, the English Riviera.

Cornwall, England's southernmost county, has a mild climate, and here you are never more than 20 mi from the sea. The county has always regarded itself as separate from the rest of Britain, and the Arthurian legends really took root in Cornwall, not least at Tintagel Castle, the legendary birthplace of Arthur. High, jagged cliffs line Cornwall's Atlantic coast—the dangerous and dramatic settings that Daphne du Maurier often wrote eloquently about—and indeed pose a menace to passing ships. The south coast, Janus-like, is filled with sunny beaches, delightful coves, and popular resorts. England's last outposts, the flower-filled Isles of Scilly, claim the most hours of sunshine in the country.

Exploring the West Country

A circular tour of the West Country covers a large territory, from the bustling city of Bristol, two hours by car from London, to the remote and rocky headlands of Devon and Cornwall to the west. Stark contrasts abound in this peninsula, and the farther west you travel, the more the sea becomes an overwhelming presence. On the whole, the northern coast is more rugged, the cliffs dropping dramatically to tiny coves and beaches, whereas the south coast shelters many more resorts and wider expanses of sand. The crowds gravitate to the south, but there are plenty of remote inlets and estuaries along this southern shore, and you don't need to go far to find a degree of seclusion.

Unless you confine yourself to a few towns—for example, Exeter, Penzance, and Plymouth—you will be at a huge disadvantage without your own transportation. The region has a few main arteries, but you should take minor roads whenever possible, if only to see the real West Country at a leisurely pace. Rail travelers can make use of a fast service connecting Exeter, Plymouth, and Penzance, and there's also a good network of bus services.

About the Restaurants & Hotels

The more established restaurants are often completely booked on a Friday or Saturday night, so reserve well in advance; the same is true for hotels and other lodgings. Room availability can be limited on the coasts during August. Accommodations include national hotel chains, represented in all the region's principal centers, as well as ancient inns and ubiquitous bed-and-breakfast places. Many farmhouses also rent out rooms—offering tranquillity in rural surroundings—but these lodgings are often difficult to reach without a car. It's worth finding out about weekend and winter deals that many hotels offer. For information about regional food specialties, *see* the On the Menu box, *below.*

		WHAT IT COSTS In pounds			
	££££££	££££	£££	££	£
RESTAURANTS	over £22	£18–£22	£13–£17	£7–£12	under £7
HOTELS	over £160	£120–£160	£90–£119	£60–£89	under £60

Restaurant prices are for a main course at dinner. Hotel prices are for two people in a standard double room in high season, including V.A.T., with no meals or, if indicated, CP (with continental breakfast), BP (Breakfast Plan, with full breakfast), or MAP (Modified American Plan, with breakfast and dinner).

Timing

In July and August, traffic chokes the roads leading into the West Country. Somehow the region squeezes in all the "grockles," or tourists, and the chances of finding a remote oasis of peace and quiet are severely curtailed. The beaches heave with sunseekers, and the resort towns are either bubbling with zest or unbearably tacky, depending on your point of view. If you must visit in summer, your best option is to find a secluded hotel and make brief excursions from there. Try to avoid traveling on Saturday, when weekly rentals start and finish and the roads

GREAT ITINERARIES

The West Country requires some time to explore. Four days provide only a limited view of Somerset and Devon, and you should avoid excessive traveling. Even a week would not do the region justice, but it would let you push on into Cornwall.

Numbers in the text correspond to numbers in the margin and on the West Country, Plymouth, and Exeter maps.

IF YOU HAVE 4 DAYS

Spend your first morning in **Bristol** ❶ ➤, moving on to 🏨 **Wells** ❸ for your first night's stop. Visit **Glastonbury** ❹ the next day, before meeting up with the M5 to take you on to 🏨 **Exeter** ❺–❻ for your second night. After exploring the city, drive southwest to **Plymouth** ❸–❹, which has some attractions despite its modest appearance. Then explore **Dartmoor,** one of England's last wildernesses. Specific targets on or around Dartmoor include Castle Drogo, an impressive 20th-century version of a medieval castle, near **Chagford** ❹; **Lydford Gorge** ❹, a secluded corridor of torrents and gushing waterfalls; and **Cotehele House and Quay** ❹, one of Britain's least altered medieval houses. Spend your third overnight in 🏨 **Dartmouth** ❹. The next day you could enjoy the sea air here and in the nearby "Riviera" region of **Torbay** ❺.

IF YOU HAVE 7 DAYS

Once out of **Bristol** ❶ ➤, tour the northern coast of Somerset and Devon, making stops at **Dunster** ❻, site of a turreted and battlemented castle, and the twin towns of **Lynton** and **Lynmouth** ❽, in a narrow cleft.

Continue on to your overnight destination, the cliff-top village of 🏨 **Clovelly** ❿. The second day, continue into Cornwall to take in **Tintagel** ⓬, which presents a dramatic sight perched on its black rock above the waves. Enjoy a refined seafood lunch in **Padstow** ⓮ and make a stop in **Newquay** ⓯ if you want to sample the beaches of this seaside resort. Pull into 🏨 **St. Ives** ⓱ for your second night; the town has much to offer in the way of art. After taking in St. Ives the third day, set out for the tip of the peninsula, **Land's End** ⓲. Head for your next overnight, 🏨 **Penzance** ㉑. Nearby, the island fortress of St. Michael's Mount demands closer inspection. Now make a brief sortie into the **Lizard Peninsula** ㉒, basing yourself in the resort of 🏨 **Falmouth** ㉓, which has plenty of accommodations as well as a brace of castles—the imposing Pendennis and its sibling across the estuary, **St. Mawes** ㉕. On your fifth day, begin by exploring seaside **Charlestown** ㉗, leaving the main part of the day for the eye-popping plant collection of the **Eden Project** ㉘, outside St. Austell. Spend the night either in 🏨 **Fowey** ㉙, still a thriving commercial and sailing port, or in 🏨 **Plymouth** ❸–❹. Explore Plymouth in the morning and then track north to Dartmoor, making a stop at Castle Drogo, near **Chagford** ㊻; spend your sixth night in 🏨 **Exeter** ❺–❻. Once you've soaked up the sights of this historic city, head up the M5, swinging east to see the majestic ruins of the abbey in 🏨 **Glastonbury** ❹ and the cathedral at nearby **Wells** ❸.

are jammed with vehicles; the August bank holiday (the last weekend of the month) is notorious for congested roads. Otherwise, fall and spring are good times to escape the crowds, although the water may be too cold for swimming and there is often a strong ocean breeze. Most properties that don't accept business year-round open for Easter and close in late September or October. Those that remain open have reduced hours. Winter has its own appeal: the Atlantic waves crash dramatically against the coast, and the austere Cornish cliffs are at their most spectacular.

The most notable festivals are Padstow's Obby Oss, a traditional celebration of the arrival of summer that takes place around May 1; the Cornish-theme, weeklong Golowan Festival in Penzance in late June; the Exeter Arts Festival in July; and the St. Ives Festival of Music and the Arts for eight days in mid-September. In addition, many West Country maritime towns host regattas over summer weekends. The best times to visit Devon are late summer and early fall, during the end-of-summer festivals, especially popular in the towns of eastern Dartmoor.

BRISTOL TO NORTH DEVON

Starting out from Bristol, your journey takes you south to the cathedral city of Wells and continues on via Glastonbury, possibly the Avalon of Arthurian legend. Taunton, to the west, is the capital of cider country and was the focus of fierce skirmishes during the English Civil War. Proceed west along the Somerset coast into Devon, skirting the moorlands of Exmoor and tracing the northern shore via Clovelly.

Bristol

 120 mi west of London, 46 mi south of Birmingham, 13 mi northwest of Bath.

The West Country's biggest city, Bristol has in recent years become one of the country's most vibrant centers, with a thriving cultural scene encompassing some of the best contemporary art, theater, and music. Buzzing bars, cafés, and restaurants, and a largely youthful population make it an attractive place to spend time. The city also trails a great deal of history in its wake. It can be called the "birthplace of America" with some confidence, for John Cabot and his son Sebastian sailed from the old city docks in 1497 to touch down on the North American mainland, which he claimed for the English crown. The city had been a major center since medieval times, but in the 17th and 18th centuries it became the foremost port for trade with North America. Bristol was the home of William Penn, developer of Pennsylvania, and a haven for John Wesley, whose Methodist movement played a role in colonial Georgia.

Now that the city's industries no longer rely on the docks, the historic harbor along the River Avon has been largely given over to pleasure craft. Arts and entertainment complexes, museums, stores, and restaurants fill the quayside, reflecting Bristol's fast-moving, modern face. The pubs and

TOP REASONS TO GO

A coastal walk: Pick almost any stretch of coast in Devon and Cornwall for a close encounter with the sea—raging or calm, it's always invigorating. For high, dramatic cliff scenery, choose the Exmoor coast around Lynmouth or the coast around Tintagel; for a gentler, undulating landscape, the area around Beer is perfect.

Riding or hiking on Dartmoor: Get away from it all in southern England's greatest wilderness—an empty, treeless expanse dotted with lonely, rocky outcrops called tors. Frequent organized walks are advertised at visitor centers, which also have lists of pony-trekking operations.

Seafood in Padstow: Celebrity chef Rick Stein rules the roost in this small Cornish port, and any of his establishments will strongly satisfy, though the Seafood Restaurant has the wow factor. A pre- or post-dinner stroll around the harbor, jammed with fishing boats and riotous with gulls, will allow you to soak up the spirit of this congenial town.

Tate St. Ives: There's nowhere better to absorb the local arts scene than this offshoot of London's Tate in the pretty seaside town of St. Ives. The building is half the fun—its design echoes the cylindrical gas holder that once stood here—and a marvelous rooftop café claims views over Porthmeor Beach.

A visit to Eden: It's worth the journey west for Cornwall's Eden Project alone: a wonderland of plant life, magnificently sited in a former clay pit. Two gigantic geodesic "biomes" are filled with bushes, cacti, and trees from around the world, and the elaborate outdoor plantations are equally engaging. You can spend a whole day here.

Wells Cathedral: A perfect example of medieval craftsmanship, the building is a stunning spectacle, not least for its richly sculpted west front dominating a swath of manicured lawn. Come at the end of the day when Evensong is performed to experience its lofty interior at its most evocative.

clubs here draw the under-25 set and make the area fairly boisterous (and best avoided) on Friday and Saturday nights.

Main Attractions

@Bristol. The rebuilt Harbourside area has three science- and nature-theme attractions with innovative exhibits. Explore provides a "hands-on, minds-on" experience of science, and Wildwalk includes interactive natural-history exhibits and a walk through a rain forest aflutter with exotic birds and butterflies. An IMAX cinema shows mostly science-related films. Open spaces linking the sites act as a venue for live performances and multimedia activities, with shops, cafés, and restaurants nearby. ⊠ *Anchor Rd.* ☎ *0845/345–1235* ⊕ *www.at-bristol.org.uk* ⊠ *£8 for Explore @Bristol, £7 for Wildwalk, £6.50 or £7.50 for IMAX, £11.50–£13 for 2-attraction ticket, £17.50 for 3-attraction ticket* ☉ *Weekdays 10–5, weekends and school vacations 10–6.*

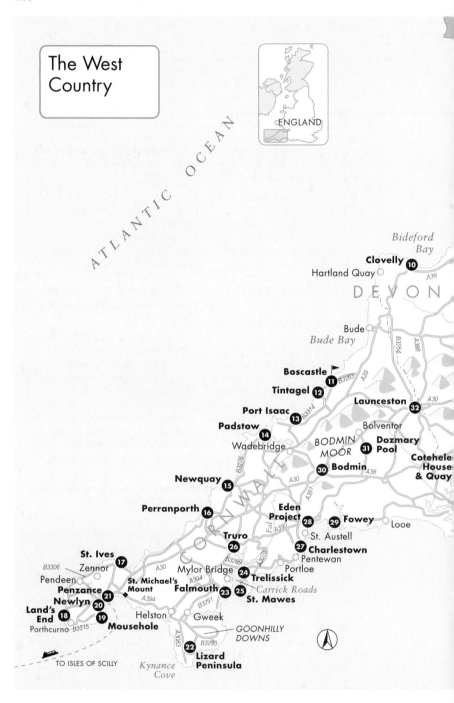

The West
Country

ENGLAND

ATLANTIC OCEAN

Bideford Bay

Clovelly **10**
Hartland Quay

D E V O N

Bude
Bude Bay

Boscastle **11** *B3263*

Tintagel **12**

Launceston **32**

Port Isaac **13** *B3314*

Bolventor

Padstow **14**

Wadebridge

BODMIN MOOR

Dozmary **31** Pool

Cotehele House & Quay

30 Bodmin *A38*

Newquay **15**

A30

Perranporth **16**

Eden Project **28**

29 Fowey

Looe

St. Austell

Truro **26**

27 Charlestown

Pentewan

St. Ives **17**

Zennor

B3306

Mylor Bridge

Portloe

Pendeen

Penzance

St. Michael's Mount

A394

Falmouth **23** **24** Trelissick

25

Carrick Roads

St. Mawes

Newlyn **21**

A394

Land's End **18** **20** **19**

Helston

Gweek

Porthcurno *B3315*

Mousehole

A3083

GOONHILLY DOWNS

B3293

22

TO ISLES OF SCILLY

Kynance Cove

Lizard Peninsula

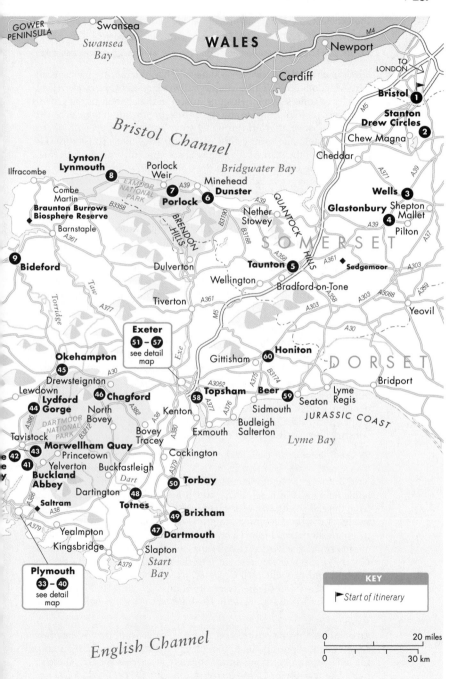

GOWER
PENINSULA

Swansea

Swansea Bay

WALES

Newport

M4

TO
LONDON

Cardiff

Bristol ❶

**Stanton
Drew Circles** ❷

Chew Magna

Bristol Channel

Lynton/
Lynmouth ❽

Porlock
Weir

Bridgwater Bay

Minehead

Cheddar

A371

A39

A39

M5

Ilfracombe

Combe
Martin

EXMOOR
NATIONAL
PARK

Porlock ❼

A39

Dunster ❻

Nether
Stowey

Wells ❸

Shepton
Mallet

B3358

Glastonbury ❹

Pilton

A37

Braunton Burrows
Biosphere Reserve

BRENDON
HILLS

B3190

B3188

QUANTOCK

A39

S O M E R S E T

Barnstaple

A361

❾
Bideford

Dulverton

Wellington

Taunton ❺

Sedgemoor

A361

A358

A303

A303

A3088

A361

A359

Yeovil

Taw

A377

Tiverton

Bradford-on-Tone

A303

A30

Torridge

M5

A361

Okehampton

❹❺
Drewsteignton

A30

Gittisham

Honiton ❻⓿

D O R S E T

Exeter
❺❶ – ❺❼
see detail
map

A3052

Topsham ❺❽

Beer ❺❾

Bridport

Exe

A376

B3174

Lewdown

**Lydford
Gorge** ❹❹

❹❻**Chagford**

North
Bovey

A382

Kenton

A377

Seaton

Lyme
Regis

A386

A30

DARTMOOR
NATIONAL
PARK

A386

B3212

Bovey
Tracey

A38

Exmouth

Sidmouth

Budleigh
Salterton

JURASSIC COAST

Tavistock

❹❷
❹❸ **Morwellham Quay**

Princetown

A380

A379

Lyme Bay

❹❶ Yelverton

Buckfastleigh

Cockington

**Buckland
Abbey**

Dart

Dartington

❹❽
Totnes

❺⓿ **Torbay**

Saltram

A38

❹❾ **Brixham**

A379

Yealmpton

❹❼ **Dartmouth**

Plymouth
❸❸ – ❹⓿
see detail
map

Kingsbridge

Slapton

A379

*Start
Bay*

English Channel

KEY

▶ *Start of itinerary*

0 ———— 20 miles

0 ———— 30 km

NEED A
BREAK? The excellent café-restaurant upstairs at the **Watershed Media Centre** (⊠ 1 Canon's Rd. ☎ 0117/927–5100) overlooks part of the harborside. Sandwiches, salads, and hot snacks are served during the day, along with coffees and cakes.

☾ **British Empire and Commonwealth Museum.** This museum, in engineer Isambard Kingdom Brunel's 19th-century railway station by the modern Temple Meads train station, helps put Bristol in the context of the growth of Britain's colonial empire and the trading organization that succeeded it. It's an absorbing whirl through history and geography, with photographs, slides, and grainy film of missionaries and memsahibs. The darker side of the story of the empire is not ignored, with space devoted to slavery, the Opium Wars, and the transportation of convicts to Australia. The interactive exhibits appeal to children. ⊠ *Station Approach, Temple Meads* ☎ *0117/925–4980* ⊕ *www.empiremuseum.co.uk* ☑ *£6.95* ☾ *Daily 10–5; last admission 4:30.*

★ **Church of St. Mary Redcliffe.** Queen Elizabeth I called the rib-vaulted, 14th-century church "the fairest in England." It was built by Bristol merchants who wanted a place in which to pray for the safe (and profitable) voyages of their ships. A chapel holds the arms and armor of Sir William Penn, father of the founder of Pennsylvania. The church is a five-minute walk from Temple Meads train station toward the docks. ⊠ *Redcliffe Way* ☎ *0117/929–1487* ☑ *Free* ☾ *Mon.–Sat. 9–5 (until 4 in winter), Sun. 8–8.*

Clifton Suspension Bridge. In the Georgian suburb of Clifton—a sort of Bath in miniature—you can take in a monument to Victorian engineering, the 702-foot-long bridge that spans the Avon Gorge. Work began on Isambard Brunel's design in 1831, but the bridge was not completed until 1864. Adjacent to the Bristol end of the bridge, the **Clifton Suspension Bridge Visitor Centre** (☎ 0117/974–4664 ⊕ www.clifton-suspension-bridge.org.uk) has an exhibition on the bridge and its construction. ⊠ *Suspension Bridge Rd., Clifton.*

★ **SS *Great Britain*.** On view in the harbor is this restored vessel, the first iron ship to cross the Atlantic. Built by the great English engineer Isambard Brunel in 1843, it remained in service until 1970, first as a transatlantic liner and ultimately as a coal storage hulk. On board, everything from the galley to the officers' quarters comes complete with sounds and smells of the time. Moored alongside is a replica of the *Matthew,* the tiny craft that carried John Cabot to North America in 1497. Your ticket admits you to the **Dockyard Museum,** which presents the history of the *Great Britain*; you can descend into the ship's dry dock for a view of the hull and propeller. ⊠ *Great Western Dockyard, Gas Ferry Rd.* ☎ *0117/926–0680* ⊕ *www.ssgreatbritain.org* ☑ *£7.50* ☾ *Apr.–Oct., daily 10–5:30; Nov.–Mar., daily 10–4:30; last entry 1 hr before closing.*

Also Worth Seeing

Arnolfini. In a prime position on Bristol's waterfront, this is one of the country's most prestigious contemporary-art venues, with a reputation for uncovering interesting and innovative yet accessible art. There's a lively bar and bistro. ⊠ *16 Narrow Quay* ☎ *0117/917–2300* ⊕ *www. arnolfini.org.uk* ☑ *Free* ☾ *Gallery daily 10 AM–8 PM.*

Bristol Zoo Gardens. Along the leafy expanse of Clifton Downs is one of the country's most famous zoos. More than 300 animal species live in 12 acres of landscaped gardens; the Seal and Penguin Coasts, with underwater viewing, are rival attractions for Gorilla Island, Bug World, and Twilight World. ✉ *Clifton Down* ☎ *0117/974–7399* ⊕ *www.bristolzoo. org.uk* 🎫 *£10* ⊙ *June–Aug., daily 9–5:30; Sept.–May, daily 9–5.*

New Room. Among the Dissenters from the Church of England who found a home in Bristol were John Wesley and Charles Wesley, and in 1739 they built the New Room, a meeting place that became the first Methodist chapel. Its simplicity contrasts both with the style of Anglican churches and with the modern shopping center hemming it in. Call ahead to arrange a tour that can include **Charles Wesley's House** (a 10-minute walk away), an 18th-century town house where the Wesleys lived. ✉ *Broadmead* ☎ *0117/926–4740* ⊕ *newroombristol.org.uk* 🎫 *Free, tour of New Room and house £8, New Room only £4* ⊙ *Mon.–Sat. and national holidays 10–4.*

OFF THE BEATEN PATH

TYNTESFIELD – The National Trust is restoring this extravagant, 35-bedroom Victorian Gothic-Revival mansion. You can see the house, garden, and chapel at your own pace; entry, by timed ticket, can't be guaranteed on the busiest days. For the full story of the house's history and renovation, prebook a guided tour (Sun. and Wed. at 10:30). Besides magnificent woodwork, stained glass, tile, and original furniture and fabrics, the house contains the modern conveniences of the 1860s, such as a heated billiard table. Tyntesfield is 7 mi south of Bristol. ✉ *Wraxall* ☎ *01275/858675, 0870/241–4500 for tours* ⊕ *www. nationaltrust.org.uk* 🎫 *£9, gardens only £4.50; guided tour £13.80 (National Trust members £5.80)* ⊙ *House early Apr.–Oct., Sat.–Mon. and Wed. 11–4:30 (chapel opens 10:30); gardens mid-Mar.–Oct., Sat.–Mon. and Wed. 10–5:30.*

Where to Stay & Eat

For a notable overture to your West Country excursion, you might book a night at Thornbury Castle, 12 mi north of Bristol in Thornbury (⇨ Berkeley Castle *in* Chapter 7).

£££–££££ ✕ **Bell's Diner.** A local institution, this bistro in the Montpelier area occupies a converted corner shop and has polished wood floors and prints of Bristol on its pale gray walls. The inventive Mediterranean menu changes daily and includes organic and wild ingredients, as well as toothsome desserts such as prune and Armagnac soufflé. Bell's is rather hidden—take A38 (Stokes Croft) north, then turn right on Ashley Road and immediately left at Picton Street, which will lead you to York Road. ✉ *1 York Rd.* ☎ *0117/924–0357* 🍽 *AE, MC, V* ⊙ *Closed Sun. and Dec. 24–30. No lunch Sat. and Mon.*

£££–££££ ✕ **Juniper.** Inventive takes on traditional English cuisine, such as wild duck with braised red cabbage, are the order of the day in this cozy neighborhood restaurant with a blackboard menu that changes with the seasons. Modern art adorns the walls, and lilac tablecloths contrast with white painted brickwork. ✉ *21 Cotham Rd. S* ☎ *0117/942–1744* 🍽 *AE, MC, V* ⊙ *No dinner Sun., no lunch Mon.–Sat.*

£–£££ ✕ **Old India.** Bristol's former stock exchange has found a new role as a fashionable Indian eatery. All the opulent trimmings have been restored, including the mahogany paneling, rich drapes, tiled staircase, and elegant statuary. It's the perfect setting for classic Indian cuisine and innovative dishes such as *niljiri korma* (chicken breast in a mild curry sauce with rose petals) and *macchi mazadaar* (salmon with mustard seeds, coconut, curry leaves, and tamarind water). The two-course lunch and pretheater menus are a particularly good deal. ⊠ *34 St. Nicholas St.* ☏ *0117/922–1136* ⊟ *MC, V* ⊘ *Closed Sun.*

£–££ ✕ **Wagamama.** Part of a chain that has expanded from London, this centrally located noodle bar at the bottom of Clifton is a convenient spot for nourishing chicken ramen (soup and noodles topped with grilled chicken breast) or *ebi raisukaree* (wok-fried tiger prawns in a coconut and lime curry sauce). White walls and plain wooden tables make a minimalist statement. Helpings are abundant, and the service is fast and courteous. ⊠ *63 Queens Rd.* ☏ *0117/922–1188* ⊟ *AE, DC, MC, V.*

£ ✕ **Boston Tea Party.** Despite the name, this laid-back and vaguely eccentric place is quintessentially English, and ideal for a relaxed lunch away from the nearby rigors of the Park Street shopping scene. Good sandwiches and generous bowls of salad as well as some light hot dishes can be taken away or eaten in the backyard or the upstairs sofa salon. ⊠ *75 Park St.* ☏ *0117/929–8601* ⊟ *MC, V* ⊘ *No dinner Sun.–Wed.*

££££ ✕▦ **Hotel du Vin.** This hip Anglo-French minichain has an ambitious outlet in the Sugar House—six former sugar-refining warehouses built in 1728 when the River Frome ran right outside the front door—close to the docklands and the city center. Rooms are crisply contemporary in style, with CD and DVD players and huge showers, but retain many original industrial features. The restaurant (*£££*) has an extensive wine list—visit the cellar for a private tasting session—and the menu entices with modern but robust French flavors. A good-value, fixed-price lunch is offered. ⊠ *Narrow Lewins Mead, BS1 2NU* ☏ *0117/925–5577* ⊞ *0117/925–1199* ⊕ *www.hotelduvin.com* ⇨ *40 rooms* ⌂ *Restaurant, cable TV, Wi-Fi, billiards, bar, meeting rooms* ⊟ *AE, DC, MC, V.*

£££ ▦ **Victoria Square Hotel.** In a mellow Georgian building overlooking one of Clifton's leafiest, loveliest squares, this Best Western hotel makes an excellent base for exploring Bristol. Rooms are decorated in neutral colors and are well equipped, most with modern bathrooms; rooms 228 and 247 open directly onto a small walled garden. Some rooms, however, are a bit cramped; those on the top floor are accessed via steep stairs (there's no elevator). ⊠ *Victoria Sq., Clifton BS8 4EW* ☏ *0117/973–9058* ⊞ *0117/970–6929* ⊕ *www.vicsquare.com* ⇨ *40 rooms* ⌂ *Restaurant, cable TV, Wi-Fi, bar, parking (fee), meeting rooms; no a/c, no smoking* ⊟ *AE, MC, V* ⦿| *BP.*

££ ▦ **Naseby House Hotel.** On a tree-lined street in the heart of elegant Clifton, this Victorian hotel is not far from Bristol's major sights. The basement holds the plushest, most expensive bedroom, with a four-poster and a French door opening onto the garden. Period pieces fill the sitting room, and the breakfast room is also impressive. ⊠ *105 Pembroke Rd., BS8*

3EF 🖨 *0117/973–7859* ⊕ *www.nasebyhousehotel.co.uk* ⇆ *14 rooms* ♿ *Some pets allowed; no a/c* ▭ *MC, V* ⟊ *BP.*

£ 🏨 **Tyndall's Park Hotel.** There are no frills in this Victorian hotel, just plain, clean rooms, mostly on the small side. On the other hand, it has a great location, just off Whiteladies Road and close to the museum and the city-center shops of Park Street. A sitting room of generous proportions compensates for the diminutive bedrooms, and the building is light and well maintained. ✉ *4 Sunderland Pl., BS8 1NA* 🖨 *0117/973–5407* 🖨 *0117/973–7965* ⊕ *www.tyndallsparkhotel.co.uk* ⇆ *15 rooms* ♿ *No a/c* ▭ *MC, V* ⟊ *BP.*

Nightlife & the Arts

The **Bristol Old Vic** (✉ King St. 🖨 0117/987–7877), the country's oldest continuously working theater, dates to 1766. Performances, from classics to new works, are staged in three spaces. **St. George's** (✉ Great George St. off Park St. 🖨 0845/402–4001), a former church built in the 18th century, serves as one of the country's leading acoustic venues for classical, jazz, and world music. Lunchtime concerts are scheduled. The **Watershed Media Centre** (✉ 1 Canon's Rd. 🖨 0117/927–5100) by the harborfront has a movie theater that shows excellent international films.

Sports

The **Badminton Horse Trials** (🖨 0870/242–3436) are held annually during four days in April or May at the duke of Beaufort's magnificent estate in Badminton, 12 mi northeast of Bristol.

EN ROUTE The area south of Bristol is notable for its scenery and walks, attractive villages, and ancient stone circles. Take A38 (follow signs for the airport) and then turn left onto B3130 and B3114 to the villages of Chew Magna and Chew Stoke. At Chew Magna note the gargoyles on the church. Continue on to Chew Valley Lake, a reservoir in a drowned valley surrounded by woods.

Stanton Drew Circles

❷ *6 mi south of Bristol, 10 mi west of Bath.*

Three rings, two avenues of standing stones, and a burial chamber make up the Stanton Drew Circles, one of the grandest and most mysterious monuments in Britain, dating from 3000 to 2000 BC. It's far less well known than Stonehenge and other circles, however. Excavations beneath the circles in 1997 revealed evidence of another site, from around 3000 BC, consisting of a wood henge, or timber circle. The great size of the circles suggests that the site was once as important as Stonehenge for its ceremonial functions, although little of great visual impact remains. ■ **TIP→ The site lies in a field reached through a farmyard—wear sturdy shoes to visit it.** English Heritage supervises the stones, which stand on private land. Access is given at any reasonable time, and a small admission may be requested. To get here from Chew Magna, turn east on B3130; the circles are just east of the village of Stanton Drew. ✉ *B3130, Stanton Drew* 🖨 *0117/975–0700* ⊕ *www.english-heritage.org.uk.*

Wells

❸ *16 mi south of Stanton Drew Circles, 22 mi south of Bristol, 132 mi west of London.*

England's smallest cathedral city, with a population of 10,000, lies at the foot of the Mendip Hills. Although it feels more like a quiet country town than a city, Wells contains one of the masterpieces of Gothic architecture, its great cathedral—the first to be built in the Early English style. The city's name refers to the underground streams that bubble up into St. Andrew's Well within the grounds of the Bishop's Palace. Spring water has run through High Street since the 15th century. Seventeenth-century buildings surround the ancient marketplace in the city center. Wells has market days on Wednesday and Saturday.

★ The great west towers of the medieval **Cathedral Church of St. Andrew,** the oldest surviving English Gothic church, can be seen for miles. Dating from the 12th century, the cathedral derives its beauty from the perfect harmony of all of its parts, the glowing colors of its original stained-glass windows, and its peaceful setting among stately trees and majestic lawns. To appreciate the elaborate west front facade, approach the building on foot from the cathedral green, accessible from Market Place through a great medieval gate called "penniless porch" (named after the beggars who once waited here to collect alms from worshipers). The cathedral's west front is twice as wide as it is high, and some 300 statues of kings and saints adorn it. Inside, vast inverted arches—known as scissor arches—were added in 1338 to stop the central tower from sinking to one side. The cathedral also has a rare and beautiful medieval clock, the second-oldest working clock in the world, consisting of the seated figure of a man called Jack Blandifer, who strikes a bell on the quarter hour while mounted knights circle in a joust. Near the clock is the entrance to the Chapter House—a small wooden door opening onto a great sweep of stairs worn down on one side by the tread of pilgrims over the centuries. Free 45-minute guided tours begin at the information desk. Tours are suspended April through October during Quiet Hour between noon and 1 PM. A cloister restaurant serves tea, coffee, and cakes. ⊠ *Cathedral Green* ☎ *01749/674483* ⊕ *www. wellscathedral.org.uk* 🎫 *£5 suggested donation* ☉ *Apr.–Sept., daily 7–7; Oct.–Mar., daily 7–6.*

> **NEED A BREAK?**
>
> **Goodfellows Patisserie** (⊠ 5 Sadler St. ☎ 01749/673866), a little French café near the cathedral, serves exquisite cakes and pastries that complement various chocolate concoctions and excellent coffee.

The Bishop's Eye gate leading from Market Place takes you to the magnificent, moat-ringed **Bishop's Palace,** which has most of the original 12th- and 13th-century residence. You can also see the ruins of a late-13th-century great hall. The hall lost its roof in the 16th century because Edward VI needed the lead it contained. ⊠ *Market Pl.* ☎ *01749/678691* ⊕ *www.bishopspalacewells.co.uk* 🎫 *£5* ☉ *Apr.–Oct., weekdays 10:30–6, Sun. noon–6 (may also open Sat. 10:30–6); last admission at 5.*

To the north of the cathedral, the cobbled **Vicar's Close**, one of Europe's oldest streets, has terraces of handsome 14th-century houses with strange, tall chimneys. A tiny medieval chapel here is still in use.

OFF THE BEATEN PATH

WOOKEY HOLE CAVES – Signs in Wells's town center direct you 2 mi north to limestone caves in the Mendip Hills that may have been the home of Iron Age people. Here, according to ancient legend, the Witch of Wookey turned to stone. You can tour the caves and an underground lake (a sound-and-light show keeps things lively), and visit a museum, a working paper mill, and a penny arcade full of Victorian amusement machines. There's plenty for kids. ☎ *01749/672243* ⊕ *www.wookey.co.uk* ▨ *£10.90* ☉ *Apr.–Oct., daily 10–5:30; Nov.–Mar., daily 10:30–4:30.*

Where to Stay & Eat

£–££ ✕ **Ask.** Part of an Italian chain of informal trattorias, this place has a marvelous location next to the cathedral and Bishop's Palace—the back window overlooks the Palace gardens. The premises are old but the large glass front admits plenty of light. Tasty pastas and pizzas dominate the menu, though the salads are worth sampling. One good option is *insalata di salmone,* a salad with mixed greens, oak-roasted salmon, red onions, cucumber, and cherry tomatoes in an orange and tarragon dressing. ⊠ *Market Pl.* ☎ *01749/677681* ⊟ *AE, DC, MC, V.*

££££ ✕▥ **Swan Hotel.** A former coaching inn built in the 15th century, the Swan faces the cathedral. Bedrooms, furnished with antiques, are done in subtle, restful colors; some have four-poster beds (including No. 40, which has a view of the cathedral to die for), and 15 are in an adjacent converted stable block, the Coach House. Check the rooms first: those in the Coach House can be dark and cramped, and some facilities need modernization. There's no elevator. The restaurant (£££–££££) prepares traditional English roasts and fish dishes and displays costumes owned by the great Victorian actor Sir Henry Irving. ⊠ *11 Sadler St., BA5 2RX* ☎ *01749/836300* 🖷 *01749/836301* ⊕ *www.swanhotelwells.co.uk* ⤶ *50 rooms* ⚘ *Restaurant, in-room data ports, Wi-Fi, bar, meeting rooms; no a/c* ⊟ *AE, DC, MC, V* ❙⊙❙ *BP.*

£££ ✕▥ **The Crown.** This hotel has been a landmark in Wells since the Middle Ages, and in 1695 William Penn was arrested here for preaching without a license. A sense of the building's age remains, although most guest rooms (with the exception of four rooms with four-posters) are furnished in simple styles more modern than traditional and have whirlpool baths or full-body massage showers. The Penn Bar serves sandwiches, salads, and hot dishes. You can try the more comfortable French bistro, Anton's (££–£££), for choices such as wild boar sausages and rump of lamb. ⊠ *Market Pl., BA5 2RP* ☎ *01749/673457* 🖷 *01749/679792* ⊕ *www. crownatwells.co.uk* ⤶ *15 rooms* ⚘ *Restaurant, bar, some pets allowed; no a/c, no room phones* ⊟ *AE, MC, V* ❙⊙❙ *BP.*

££ ✕▥ **Ancient Gate House.** The guest rooms of the Rugantino restaurant run by Franco Rossi and his sons make a convenient base. The premises, dating to 1473, incorporate the Great West Gate and are full of character. There's an ancient stone staircase, and many rooms have four-posters. You can dine well on Italian or English dishes, made largely from local produce, in the restaurant (££–£££)—scampi with white-wine sauce is a specialty, and the fixed-price menus are appealing. Breakfast may be across the street at the White Hart. ✉ *20 Sadler St., BA5 2SE* ☏ *01749/672029* 🖷 *01749/670319* ⊕ *www.ancientgatehouse.co.uk* ➥ *9 rooms* ⚘ *Restaurant, bar, some pets allowed; no a/c* ➂ *AE, MC, V* ⎥⊙⎢ *BP.*

Glastonbury

★ ➍ *5 mi southwest of Wells, 27 mi south of Bristol, 27 mi southwest of Bath.*

A town steeped in history, myth, and legend, Glastonbury lies in the lee of Glastonbury Tor, a grassy hill rising 520 feet above the drained marshes known as the Somerset Levels. The Tor is supposedly the site of crossing ley lines (hypothetical alignments of significant places), and, in legend, Glastonbury is identified with Avalon, the paradise into which King Arthur was reborn after his death. Partly because of these associations but also because of its world-class rock-music festival, the town has acquired renown as a New Age center, mixing crystal-gazers with druids, yogis, and hippies, variously in search of Arthur, Merlin, Jesus—and even Elvis.

At the foot of **Glastonbury Tor** is **Chalice Well,** the legendary burial place of the Grail. It's a stiff climb up the Tor, but your reward is the fabulous view across the Vale of Avalon. At the top stands a ruined tower, all that remains of **St. Michael's Church,** which collapsed after a landslide in 1271.

The ruins of the great **Glastonbury Abbey,** in the center of town, are on the site where, according to legend, Joseph of Arimathea built a church in the 1st century. A monastery had certainly been erected here by the 9th century, and the site drew many pilgrims. The ruins are those of the abbey completed in 1524 and destroyed in 1539, during Henry VIII's dissolution of the monasteries. A sign south of the Lady Chapel marks the sites where Arthur and Guinevere were supposedly buried. The worthwhile visitor center has a scale model of the abbey as well as carvings and decorations salvaged from the ruins. ✉ *Magdalene St.* ☏ *01458/832267* ⊕ *www. glastonburyabbey.com* 💷 *£4.50* ◷ *Feb., daily 10–5; Mar., daily 9:30–5:30; Apr., May, and Sept., daily 9:30–6; June–Aug., daily 9–6; Oct., daily 9:30–5; Nov., daily 9:30–4:30; Dec. and Jan., daily 10–4:30; last admission 30 mins before closing.*

☾ The **Somerset Rural Life Museum** occupies a Victorian farmhouse and the large, 14th-century Abbey tithe barn. More than 90 feet in length,

TALE OF THE GRAIL

According to tradition, Glastonbury was where Joseph of Arimathea brought the Holy Grail, the chalice used by Jesus at the Last Supper. Centuries later, the Grail was said to be the objective of the quests of King Arthur and the Knights of the Round Table. When monks claimed to have found the bones of Arthur and Guinevere at Glastonbury in 1191, the popular association of the town with the mythical Avalon was sealed. Arthur and Guinevere's presumed remains were lost to history after Glastonbury Abbey was plundered for its riches in 1539.

the barn once stored the one-tenth portion of the town's produce that was owed to the church. Exhibits illustrate 19th-century farming practices, and there's a cider-apple orchard nearby. Events designed for children take place most weekends during school holidays. ■ TIP→ **For a good walk, take the scenic footpath from the museum that leads up to the Tor, a half mile east.** ☒ *Chilkwell St.* ☎ *01458/831197* ⊕ *www.somerset.gov. uk/museums* 🎫 *Free* ☼ *Apr.–Oct., Tues.–Fri. 10–5, weekends 2–6; Nov.–Mar., Tues.–Sat. 10–5.*

Where to Stay

££–££££ 🏨 **George and Pilgrims Hotel.** Pilgrims en route to Glastonbury Abbey stayed here in the 15th century. Today the ancient, stone-front hotel is equipped with modern comforts but retains its flagstone floors, wooden beams, and antique furniture; three rooms have four-posters. The rooms, newly refurbished, come in different shapes and sizes. The better ones are spacious and furnished with antiques, others are smaller, and those in the newer part of the building lack character but are cheaper. ☒ *1 High St., BA6 9DP* ☎ *01458/831146* 🖶 *01458/ 832252* ⊕ *www.georgeandpilgrims.activehotels.com* ⬎ *12 rooms* ♻ *Restaurant, bar, meeting rooms, some pets allowed (fee); no a/c* 🖃 *MC, V* ¶◎¶ *BP.*

★ £££ 🏨 **Number 3.** This elegant Georgian town house next to the abbey grounds has log fires in the winter and a terrace and walled garden for summer relaxation. Grouped around the garden, the spacious bedrooms are individually styled, with mostly pastel color schemes, traditional furniture, and drapes behind the beds. Three rooms are in the separate Garden House, and the Blue Room overlooks the abbey ruins and, through the trees, Glastonbury Tor. Generous breakfasts might include fresh fruit salad, ham and cheese, yogurt, and croissants. ☒ *3 Magdalene St., BA6 9EW* ☎ *01458/832129* 🖶 *01458/834227* ⊕ *www. numberthree.co.uk* ⬎ *5 rooms* ♻ *No a/c, no smoking* ¶◎¶ *CP.*

Nightlife & the Arts

Held annually a few miles away in Pilton, the **Glastonbury Festival** (☎ 01749/890470 ⊕ www.glastonburyfestivals.co.uk) is England's biggest and perhaps best rock festival. For three days over the last weekend in June, it hosts hundreds of bands—established and up-and-coming—on five stages. Pick up an issue of *New Musical Express* for the lineup. Tickets are steep—around £125—and sell out months in advance; they include entertainment, a camping area, and service facilities.

EN ROUTE West of Glastonbury, take A39 and A361 toward Taunton to cross the Somerset Levels, marshes that were drained by open ditches (known as "rhines") for peat digging, an industry that is now heavily restricted. The broad, marshy expanse of **Sedgemoor** is where, in 1685, the troops of James II routed those of his nephew, the duke of Monmouth, in the last battle fought on English soil; a flagstaff and memorial stones indicate the site. R. D. Blackmore's novel *Lorna Doone,* published in 1869, is set during Monmouth's Rebellion.

ON THE MENU

From cider to cream teas, many specialties tempt your palate in the West Country. Lamb, venison, and, in Devon and Cornwall, seafood are favored in restaurants, which have improved markedly, notably through the influence of Rick Stein's seafood-based culinary empire in Padstow, in Cornwall. In many towns the day's catch is unloaded from the harbor and transported directly to eateries. The catch varies by season, but lobster is available year-round, as is crab, stuffed into sandwiches at quayside stalls and in pubs. Seafood is celebrated at fishy frolics that include the Newlyn Fish Fair (late August) and Falmouth's Oyster Festival (early October).

Somerset is the home of Britain's most famous cheese—the ubiquitous cheddar, from the Mendip Hills village. Do try to taste real farmhouse cheddar, made in the traditional barrel shape known as a truckle.

Devon's caloric cream teas consist of a pot of tea, homemade scones,

and lots of thickened clotted cream and strawberry jam (clotted, or specially thickened cream, is a regional specialty and is sometimes called Devonshire cream).

Cornwall's specialty is the pasty, a pastry shell filled with chopped meat, onions, and potatoes. The pasty was devised as a handy way for miners to carry their dinner to work; today's versions are generally pale imitations of the original, though you can still find delicious home-cooked pasties if you're willing to search a little.

For liquid refreshment, try scrumpy, a homemade dry cider that is refreshing but carries a surprising kick. Look out, too, for perry, similar to cider but made from pears. English wine, similar to German wine, is made in Somerset (you may see it on local menus), and in Cornwall you can find a variant of age-old mead made from local honey.

Taunton

⑤ *22 mi southwest of Glastonbury, 50 mi southwest of Bristol, 18 mi northeast of Exeter.*

Somerset's principal town lies in cider-making country in the fertile Vale of Taunton. Two of the loveliest examples of the county's famous pinnacled and battlemented churches, **St. James** and **St. Mary Magdalene,** overlook the county cricket ground in the center of town. Taunton is most celebrated for its cider, the traditional beverage in these parts. Beware—it can be far more potent than beer. In the fall, some cider mills open their doors to visitors. The grounds of **Sheppys,** a farm and cider museum, have orchards and a fishpond and are always open for picnickers. There's a café (summer only) and farm shop, too. ⊠ *Three Bridges, on A38 west of Taunton, Bradford-on-Tone* ☎ *01823/461233*

⊕ *www.sheppyscider.com* ▨ *Museum £2* ۩ *Easter–Christmas, Mon.–Sat. 8:30–6, Sun. 11–1; Christmas–Easter, Mon.–Sat. 8:30–6.*

Where to Stay & Eat

ff–fff ✕ **Brettons.** This small, casual spot serves light lunches, such as pastas and curries, and more substantial dinners, including monkfish wrapped in ham and pesto, pheasant with roasted pears, and vegetarian choices. It's a 10-minute walk from the center of town. ⊠ *49 East Reach* ☎ *01823/256688* ▤ *MC, V* ۩ *Closed Sun. No lunch Sat. and Mon.*

★ **fffff** ✕▦ **The Castle.** The battlements and turrets of this 300-year-old stone building look particularly fine from April to June, when the 150-year-old wisteria covering the facade is in flower. Rooms are individually decorated with chintz and period furniture. The excellent restaurant (*fffff*; closed Sunday evening) has creative, daily-changing, fixed-price menus of traditional and modern British food. Specialties include slow-roasted duck and Brixton scallops. Softer on the wallet, the informal Brazz dishes up pastas, salads, and deluxe burgers. ⊠ *Castle Green, TA1 1NF* ☎ *01823/272671* ☎ *01823/336066* ⊕ *www.the-castle-hotel.com* ⇆ *39 rooms, 5 suites* ⌂ *2 restaurants, in-room data ports, bar, meeting rooms, some pets allowed (fee); no a/c* ▤ *AE, DC, MC, V* ۩ *BP.*

EN ROUTE North of Taunton you can see the outlines of the **Quantock and Brendon hills.** Herds of red deer live in the beech-covered eastern Quantocks. Climb to the top of the hills for a spectacular view of the Vale of Taunton Deane and, to the north, the Bristol Channel.

Dunster

6 *21 mi northwest of Taunton, 43 mi north of Exeter.*

Lying between the Somerset coast and the edge of Exmoor National Park, Dunster is a picture-book village with a broad main street. The eight-sided yarn-market building on High Street dates from 1589.

Dunster Castle, a 13th-century fortress remodeled in 1868–72, dominates the village from its site on a hill. Parkland and unusual gardens with subtropical plants surround the building, which has fine plaster ceilings and a magnificent 17th-century oak staircase. The climb to the castle from the parking lot is steep. ⊠ *Off A39* ☎ *01643/823004* ⊕ *www.nationaltrust.org.uk* ▨ *£7.50, gardens only £4.10* ۩ *Castle mid-Mar.–Oct., Sat.–Wed. 11–5; 1st wk*

TAKE A HIKE

Britain's longest national trail, the awesome South West Coast Path, wraps around the coast of the peninsula for 630 mi from Minehead (near Dunster, Somerset) to South Haven Point, near Poole (Dorset). To complete the entire trail takes about 56 days. Some parts, notably the Tarka Trail section in North Devon, are open to cyclists. The **South West Coast Path Association** (⊠ Bowker House, Lee Mill Bridge, Ivybridge, PL21 9EF ☎ 01752/896237 ⊕ www. swcp.org.uk) has information about the trail. Another Web site, ⊕ **www.southwestcoastpath. com,** suggests walks as short as a few hours.

Nov., Sat.–Wed. 11–4. Gardens mid-Mar.–Oct., daily 10–5; Nov.–mid-Mar., daily 11–4.

Exmoor National Park

20 mi northwest of Taunton.

Less wild and forbidding than Dartmoor to its south, 267-square-mi Exmoor National Park is no less majestic for its bare heath and lofty views. The park extends right up to the coast and straddles the county border between Somerset and Devon. Some walks offer spectacular views over the Bristol Channel. Although it is interwoven with cultivated farmland and pasturage, Exmoor can be desolate. Taking one of the more than 700 mi of paths and bridleways through the bracken and heather (at its best in the fall), you might glimpse the ponies and red deer for which the region is noted. ■ TIP→ **Be careful: the proximity of the coast means that mists and squalls can descend with alarming suddenness.**

The national park visitor centers at Combe Martin, County Gate, Dulverton, Dunster, and Lynmouth have information and maps. The free Exmoor Visitor news sheet lists guided walks; they may have a theme (archaeology or deer, for example), and most cost £3–£5. If you're walking on your own, check the weather, take water and a map, and tell someone where you're going. *Exmoor National Park Authority* ⊠ *Exmoor House, Dulverton TA22 9HL* ☎ *01398/323665* ⊕ *www. exmoor-nationalpark.gov.uk* ⌕ *Free.*

Porlock

❼ *6 mi west of Dunster, 45 mi north of Exeter.*

Buried at the bottom of a valley, with the slopes of Exmoor all about, the small, unspoiled town of Porlock lies near "Doone Country," setting for R. D. Blackmore's swashbuckling saga *Lorna Doone.* Porlock had already achieved a place in literary history by the late 1790s, when Samuel Taylor Coleridge declared it was a "man from Porlock" who interrupted his opium trance while the poet was composing "Kubla Khan." The 36-mi **Coleridge Way** (⊕ www.exmoor-nationalpark.gov.uk) trail passes through the Quantock and Brendon hills and part of Exmoor, from Nether Stowey (site of Coleridge's farmhouse) to Porlock.

The small harbor in the town of **Porlock Weir** is the starting point for an undemanding 2-mi walk along the coast through chestnut and walnut trees to **St. Culbone,** reputedly the smallest and most isolated church in England. Saxon in origin, it has a small Victorian spire and is lighted by candles. It would be hard to find a more enchanting spot.

Where to Stay & Eat

£££–££££ ✕▦ **Andrews on the Weir.** Calling itself a restaurant with rooms, this waterfront Georgian hotel is pure relaxed English country house with touches of glamour. Guest rooms have print drapes and patchwork quilts. The ambitious contemporary restaurant (£32 for two courses) takes advantage of seafood, Exmoor lamb, and duckling, and you can expect unusual desserts, such as iced parfait with banana sorbet and mocha sauce, and excellent local cheeses. ✉ *Porlock Weir, TA24 8PB* ☎ *01643/863300* 🖷 *01643/863311* ⊕ *www.andrewsontheweir.co.uk* 🛏 *5 rooms* ♨ *Restaurant, bar, some pets allowed; no a/c, no kids under 12* ═ *MC, V* ☯ *Closed Mon., Tues., and Jan.* ⊄⊖⊦ *BP.*

EN ROUTE As you're heading west from Porlock to Lynton, the coast road A39 mounts **Porlock Hill,** an incline so steep that signs encourage drivers to "keep going." The views across Exmoor and north to the Bristol Channel and Wales are worth it. A less steep but quieter and equally scenic route up the hill on a toll road is accessed from Porlock Weir.

Lynton & Lynmouth

8 *13 mi west of Porlock, 60 mi northwest of Exeter.*

A steep hill separates this pretty pair of Devonshire villages, which are linked by a cliff railway. Lynmouth, a fishing village at the bottom of the hill, crouches below 1,000-foot-high cliffs at the mouths of the East and West Lynne rivers. Lynton is higher up. To 19th-century visitors, the place evoked an Alpine scene. The grand landscape of Exmoor lies all about, with walks to local beauty spots: Watersmeet, the Valley of the Rocks, or Hollerday Hill, where rare feral goats graze.

Water and a cable system power the 862-foot **cliff railway** that connects Lynton with Lynmouth by a ride up a rocky cliff; riders get fine views over the harbor. Inaugurated in 1890, it was the gift of publisher George Newnes, who also donated Lynton's imposing Town Hall, near the top station on Lee Road. ✉ *Lee Rd., Lynton* ☎ *01598/753908* ⊕ *www. cliffrailwaylynton.co.uk* 🛏 *£2.75 round-trip* ☯ *Mid-Feb.–mid-July and mid-Sept.–mid-Nov., daily 9–7; mid-July–mid-Sept., daily 9–9.*

Exmoor Coast Boat Cruises runs boat trips around the dramatic Devon coast from Lynmouth Harbour. A one-hour excursion takes in Lee Bay, Woody Bay, and the Valley of the Rocks; between April and late July, you can experience the clamorous birdlife on the cliffs. Other cruises include mackerel fishing trips (£12). ✉ ☎ *01598/753207* 🛏 *£9* ☯ *Easter–Oct.*

Where to Stay & Eat

£££–££££ ✕⊡ **Rising Sun.** A 14th-century inn and a row of thatched cottages make up this hotel with great views over the Bristol Channel. One cottage is said to have hosted the poet Percy Bysshe Shelley during his honeymoon. In the main building, corridors and creaking staircases lead to cozy rooms decorated in stylish print or solid fabrics and furnished with new pine or older wooden pieces. The traditional restaurant (*££££–£££££*) specializes in local cuisine such as Devonshire beef fillet, and there's a superb game menu December through February. ✉ *Harbourside, Lynmouth EX35 6EG* ☎ *01598/753223* 🖷 *01598/753480* ⊕ *www. risingsunlynmouth.co.uk* 🛏 *15 rooms, 1 cottage* ♨ *Restaurant, in-room data ports, fishing, bar; no a/c, no kids under 7* ═ *MC, V* ⊄⊖⊦ *BP.*

★ ££–£££ ⊡ **Shelley's Hotel.** The second of Lynmouth's two hotels that claim to be Percy Bysshe Shelley's honeymoon haunt does not have such a fine location or quite as much character as the Rising Sun, but it's more spacious and modern inside. Bright rooms have big windows and good views, and the service is cheerfully efficient. Shelley and his 16-year-old bride, Harriet Westbrook, apparently left without paying their bill—although the poet later mailed £20 of the £30 owed. During his nine-week sojourn in Lynmouth, Shelley found time to write his polemical *Queen Mab.* ⌂ *8 Watersmeet Rd., Lynmouth EX35 6EP* ☎ *01598/753219* 🖷 *01598/753751* ⊕ *www.shelleyshotel.co.uk* ⤵ *11 rooms* ♿ *Restaurant, bar, no-smoking rooms; no a/c* ▭ *MC, V* ⏿ *BP.*

OFF THE
BEATEN
PATH **Braunton Burrows Biosphere Reserve.** Bird-watching and miles of trails through the dunes are the draws at this sanctuary on the north side of the Taw estuary, a UNESCO-designated biosphere reserve. Empty stretches of sand dunes have vistas of marram grass and the sea, and bird-watching is first-class, especially in winter. The flora is most colorful between May and August. The reserve warden can advise you about organized walks. Talks are held in the **Countryside Centre** (⌂ Caen car park, Braunton ☉ Easter–Oct., Mon.–Sat. 10–4). The reserve is 18 mi southwest of Lynton. ⌂ *Off B3231, 2 mi west of Braunton* ☎ *01271/ 812552 for warden* ☲ *Free* ☉ *Daily 24 hrs.*

Bideford

❾ *28 mi southwest of Lynton, 49 mi northwest of Exeter.*

The confluence of the rivers Taw and Torridge feeds broad Bideford Bay. Bideford lies on the Torridge, which you can cross either by the 14th-century 24-arch bridge or by the more modern structure to reach the scenic hillside and the town's elegant houses. The area was a mainstay of 16th-century shipbuilding; the sturdy vessels of Sir Francis Drake were built here. From the Norman era until the 18th century, the port was the property of the Grenville family, whose most celebrated scion was Sir Richard Grenville (circa 1541–91), commander of the seven ships that carried the first settlers to Virginia, and later a key player in the defeat of the Spanish Armada.

Clovelly

❿ *12 mi west of Bideford, 60 mi*
FodorśChoice *northwest of Exeter.*
★

Lovely Clovelly always seems to have the sun shining on its flower-lined cottages and stepped and cobbled streets. Alas, its beauty is well known, and day-trippers can overrun the village in summer. Perched precariously among cliffs, a steep, cobbled road—tumbling down at such an angle that it's closed to cars—leads to the toylike harbor with its 14th-century quay. The climb back has been likened to the struggles of Sisyphus, but, happily, from Easter through October a

DONKEYS AT WORK

Donkey stables, donkey rides for kids, and abundant donkey souvenirs in Clovelly recall the days when these animals played an essential role in town life, carrying food, packages, and more up and down the village streets. Even in the 1990s, donkeys helped carry bags from the hotels. Today sledges do the work, but the animals' labor is remembered.

Land Rover service will (for a small fee) take you to and from the parking lot at the top. Allow about two hours (more if you stop for a drink or a meal) to take in the village. A fine 10-mi walk is a cliff-top hike along the coast from Hartland Quay, near Clovelly, down to Lower Sharpnose Point, just above Bude.

You pay £4.75 to park and use the **Clovelly Visitor Centre** (⌨ Off A39 ☎ 01237/431781 ⊕ www.clovelly.co.uk); this is the only way to enter the village if you arrive by car. The fee includes admission to a fisherman's cottage in the style of the 1930s and an exhibition about Victorian writer Charles Kingsley, who lived here as a child. All the buildings in the village are owned by the Clovelly Estate Company. People arriving by bicycle or on foot do not pay to enter. ■ TIP➔ **To avoid the worst crowds, visit on weekdays, preferably before or after school summer vacation. If you must visit in summer, arrive early or late in the day.**

Where to Stay & Eat

££££ ✕⌨ **Red Lion Hotel.** One of only two hotels in this coastal village, the 18th-century Red Lion sits right on the harbor. Guest rooms, some small, are decorated along a nautical theme; all have sea views. The climb up through Clovelly is perilously steep, but guests can bring cars via a back road to and from the hotel. The sophisticated restaurant (£20 and £25 fixed-price menus at dinner) specializes in seafood dishes and home-made ice creams and sorbets. ⌨ *The Quay, EX39 5TF* ☎ *01237/ 431237* 📠 *01237/431044* ⊕ *www.clovelly.co.uk* 🛏 *11 rooms* ⌂ *Restaurant, 2 bars; no a/c* ⊟ *AE, DC, MC, V* ⎢⎜⎢ *BP.*

CORNWALL

COAST & MOOR

Cornwall stretches west into the sea, with plenty of magnificent coastline to explore. One way to discover it all is to travel southwest from Boscastle and the cliff-top ruins of Tintagel Castle, the legendary birthplace of Arthur, along the north Cornish coast to Land's End. This predominantly cliff-lined coast, interspersed with broad expanses of sand, has many tempting places to stop, including Padstow (for a seafood feast), Newquay (a surfing and tourist center), or St. Ives, a delightful artists' colony. From Land's End, the westernmost tip of Britain, known for its savage land- and seascapes and panoramic views, turn northeast, stopping in the popular seaside resort of Penzance, the harbor city of Falmouth, and a string of fishing villages including Charlestown and Fowey. The Channel coast is less rugged than the northern coast, with more sheltered beaches. Leave time to visit the Eden Project, with its large, surrealistic-looking conservatories in an abandoned clay pit, and to explore the boggy, heath-covered expanse of Bodmin Moor.

The predominantly cliffy northern coast is interspersed by broad expanses of sand that attract surfers, and tourist concentrations at Newquay and Padstow, while the Channel coast is less rugged, with more sheltered beaches.

Boscastle

▶ **⓫** *15 mi north of Bodmin, 30 mi south of Clovelly.*

In tranquil Boscastle, some of the stone and slate cottages at the foot of the steep valley date from the 1300s. A good place to relax, the town is centered around a little harbor and set snug within towering cliffs. Nearby, 2 mi up the valley of the Valency, is St. Juliot's, the "Endelstow" referred to in Thomas Hardy's *A Pair of Blue Eyes*—the young author was involved with the restoration of this church while he was working as an architect. In 2004 terrible floods washed down through the town, but rebuilding has erased much of the damage.

Where to Stay

££ ⌧ **The Old Rectory.** Thomas Hardy stayed here, in what is now a delight-
Fodor'sChoice ful B&B, while restoring St. Juliot's church, and this is where he first
★ met his wife-to-be, Emma, the rector's sister-in-law. The stone house, set in 3 acres of lush grounds, has been in the same family for five generations, and updates are mainly in Victorian style. At the rear of the building, the Old Stable has a wood-burning stove and a separate entrance. Breakfast may include organic produce from the kitchen garden. ⌧ *Off B3263, St. Juliot, Boscastle PL35 0BT* ☎☎ *01840/250225* ⊕ *www.stjuliot.com* ⤴ *4 rooms, 2 with bath* ⸢ *Croquet, some pets allowed (fee); no a/c, no room phones, no kids under 12, no smoking* ⊟ *MC, V* ☺ *Closed Dec.–mid-Feb.* ⍭ *BP.*

Tintagel

⓬ *5 mi southwest of Boscastle.*

The romance of Arthurian legend thrives around Tintagel's ruined castle on the coast. Ever since the somewhat unreliable 12th-century chronicler Geoffrey of Monmouth identified Tintagel as the home of Arthur, son of Uther Pendragon and Ygrayne, devotees of the legend cycle have revered the site. In the 19th century, Alfred, Lord Tennyson described Tintagel's Arthurian connection in *The Idylls of the King*. Today the village itself has more than its share of tourist junk—including Excaliburgers. Never mind: the headland around Tintagel is splendidly scenic.

The **Old Post Office**, a 14th-century stone manor house with yard-thick walls, smoke-blackened beams, and an undulating slate-tile roof, has been restored to its Victorian appearance, when one room served as a post office. ⌧ *3–4 Tintagel Centre* ☎ *01840/770024* ⊕ *www. nationaltrust.org.uk* ⍰ *£2.60* ☺ *Late Mar.–late July and Sept., Sun.–Fri. 11–5:30; late July–Aug., daily 11–5:30; Oct., Sun.–Fri. 11–4.*

Fodor'sChoice Although all that remains of the ruined cliff-top **Tintagel Castle**, legendary
★ birthplace of King Arthur, is the outline of its walls, moats, and towers, it requires only a bit of imagination to conjure up a picture of Sir Lancelot and Sir Galahad riding out in search of the Holy Grail over the narrow causeway above the seething breakers. Archaeological evidence, however, suggests that the castle dates from much later—about 1150, when it was the stronghold of the earls of Cornwall. Long before that, Romans may have occupied the site. The earliest identified remains

All About Arthur

LEGENDS CONCERNING KING ARTHUR have resonated through the centuries, enthusiastically taken up by writers and poets from 7th-century Welsh and Breton troubadours to Tennyson and Mark Twain in the 19th century, and T. H. White in the 20th century. The historical Arthur was probably a Christian Celtic chieftain battling against the heathen Saxons in the 6th century, although most of the tales surrounding him have a much later setting, thanks to the vivid but somewhat fanciful chronicles of his exploits by medieval scholars.

The virtuous warrior-hero of popular myth has always been treated with generous helpings of nostalgia for a golden age. For Sir Thomas Malory (circa 1408–71), author of *Le Morte d'Arthur*, the finest medieval prose collection of Arthurian romance, Arthur represented a lost era of chivalry and noble romance before the loosening of the traditional bonds of feudal society and the gradual collapse of the medieval social order.

Places associated with Arthur and his consort Guinevere, the wizard Merlin, the knights of the Round Table, and the related legends of Tristan and Isolde (or Iseult) can be found all over Europe, but the West Country claims the closest association. Arthur was said to have had his court of Camelot at Cadbury Castle (17 mi south of Wells) and to have been buried at Glastonbury.

Cornwall in particular holds the greatest concentration of Arthurian links, notably his supposed birthplace, Tintagel, and the site of his last battle, on Bodmin Moor. However tenuous the links—and, barring the odd, somewhat ambiguous inscription, there is nothing in the way of hard evidence of Arthur's existence—the Cornish have taken the Once and Future King to their hearts, and his spirit is said to reside in the now-rare bird, the Cornish chough.

---

here are of Celtic (AD 5th-century) origin, and these may have some connection with the legendary Arthur. Legends aside, nothing can detract from the castle ruins, dramatically set off by the wild, windswept Cornish coast, on an island joined to the mainland by a narrow isthmus. (There are also traces of a Celtic monastery here.) Paths lead down to the pebble beach and a cavern known as **Merlin's Cave.** Exploring Tintagel Castle involves some arduous climbing on steep steps, but even on a summer's day, when people swarm over the battlements and a westerly Atlantic wind sweeps through Tintagel, you can feel the proximity of the distant past. ⊠ *Castle Rd., ½ mi west of village* ☎ *01840/770328* ⊕ *www.english-heritage.org.uk* 🎫 *£4.30* ☉ *Apr.–Sept., daily 10–6; Oct., daily 10–5; Nov.–Mar., daily 10–4.*

Displays in the **Arthurian Centre** provide background to the story of King Arthur. Highlights include Arthur's Stone, dated to 540 BC, and a woodland walk to the site of Arthur's "last battle." There's also a gift shop and tea garden. The center is 5 mi southeast of Tintagel Castle, on the edge of Bodmin Moor. ✉ *Slaughterbridge, Camelford* ☎ *01840/212450* ⊕ *www.arthur-online.com* 🎫 *£2.50* ⊗ *Easter–Oct., daily 10–dusk.*

Port Isaac

⑬ *5 mi southwest of Tintagel.*

A mixture of granite, slate, and whitewashed cottages tumbles precipitously down the cliff to the tiny harbor at Port Isaac, still dedicated to the crab and lobster trade. Low tide reveals a pebbly beach and rock pools. Relatively unscathed by tourists, it makes for a peaceful and secluded stay. For an extra slice of authentic Cornwall life, you can hear the local choir sing shanties at the harborside on Friday nights in summer.

Where to Stay & Eat

£££–££££ ✕ **Slipway Hotel.** This 16th-century inn on the harborfront has low ceilings, exposed timbers, and steep staircases that lead to rooms with simple but stylish modern furnishings. The split-level restaurant (*£££*), held up by unusual slate pillars, serves supremely fresh fish, lobster, and crab dishes. ✉ *Harbourfront, PL29 3RH* ☎ *01208/880264* 🖷 *01208/880408* ⊕ *www.portisaachotel.com* ↣ *10 rooms* ⚺ *Restaurant, bar, some pets allowed (fee); no a/c* ⊟ *MC, V* ⊗ *Closed Jan.–mid-Feb.* ⍾⊙⍿ *BP.*

Padstow

⑭ *10 mi southwest of Port Isaac.*

A small fishing port at the mouth of the Camel River, Padstow attracts attention and visitors as a center of culinary excellence, largely because of the presence here since 1975 of pioneering seafood chef Rick Stein. He has made Padstow a stop on any foodie's itinerary. Stein's empire includes two restaurants, a café, a fish-and-chips joint (gentler on the wallet), a delicatessen on South Quay, a patisserie, a cooking school (classes fill up months in advance), a gift shop, and some elegant accommodations.

Even if seafood is not your favorite fare, Padstow is worth visiting. The cries of seagulls fill its lively harbor, a string of fine beaches lies within a short ride—including some choice strands highly prized by surfers—and two scenic walking routes await: the Saints Way across the peninsula to Fowey, and the Camel Trail, a footpath and cycling path that follows the river as far as Bodmin Moor.

Where to Stay & Eat

££££–£££££ ✕ **St. Petroc's Hotel and Bistro.** This cream-color bistro in an old house is Rick Stein's French-inspired take on his Seafood Restaurant—simpler, less expensive (*£££*), and with more options for carnivores and vegetarians. Diners and hotel guests have use of the sunny walled garden. The well-equipped bedrooms are individually decorated with stylish modern pieces. ✉ *4 New St., PL28 8EA* ☎ *01841/532700* 🖷 *01841/532942* ⊕ *www.rickstein.com* ↣ *10 rooms* ⚺ *Restaurant, bar, some pets allowed (fee); no a/c* ⊟ *AE, MC, V* ⍾⊙⍿ *BP.*

££££–£££££ ✕ **The Seafood Restaurant.** Rick Stein's flagship restaurant (*££££–£££££*; Fodor'sChoice reservations essential), just across from where the lobster boats and ★ trawlers unload their catches, has built its reputation on the freshest fish and high culinary artistry. The fixed-price dinners are the best option, and may include stir-fried razor clams with black beans and grilled hake with asparagus and a cream and caviar sauce. Don't want to move after your meal? Book one of the sunny, individually designed guest rooms done in clean-lined modern or plush traditional style; ask for one overlooking the harbor. ⊠ *Riverside, PL28 8BY* ☎ *01841/532700* 🖷 *01841/532942* ⊕ *www.rickstein.com* ☞ *14 rooms* ♿ *Restaurant, minibars, some pets allowed (fee); no a/c* 🖃 *AE, MC, V* ⫯⊘⫯ *BP.*

£££££   🏨 **St. Edmund's House.** The most luxurious Rick Stein venture has a sophisticated minimalist style. Excellently equipped, the bedrooms have polished wooden floors, in-room DVD players, and French doors facing the harbor. Booking here guarantees a dinner table at the Seafood Restaurant, where breakfast is taken, but you should reserve as far ahead as possible. ■ TIP→ **If the price here is too steep but you want to stay in Stein lodging, check out the few simple rooms above Rick Stein's Café.** ⊠ *St. Edmond's La., PL28 8BZ* ☎ *01841/532700* 🖷 *01841/532942* ⊕ *www.rickstein.com* ☞ *6 rooms* ♿ *Minibars, cable TV, some pets allowed (fee); no a/c* 🖃 *AE, MC, V* ⊘ *Closed 1 wk around Christmas* ⫯⊘⫯ *BP.*

Sports & the Outdoors

BIKING   Bikes of all shapes and sizes can be rented at **Trail Bike Hire** (⊠ South Quay ☎ 01841/532594), at the start of the Camel Trail.

SURFING   **Harlyn Surf School** (⊠ 23 Grenville Rd. ☎ 01841/533076) can arrange half- to five-day surfing courses.

WALKING   The **Saints Way,** a 30-mi inland path between Padstow and the Camel Estuary on Cornwall's north coast to Fowey on the south coast, follows a Bronze Age trading route, later used by Celtic pilgrims to cross the peninsula. Several relics of such times can be seen along the way. Contact the tourist offices in Padstow or Fowey or the Cornwall Tourist Board for information.

Newquay

🕖 *14 mi southwest of Padstow, 30 mi southwest of Tintagel.*

The biggest, most developed resort on the north Cornwall coast is a fairly large town established in 1439. It was once the center of the trade in pilchards (a small herringlike fish), and on the headland you can still see a white hut where a lookout known as a "huer" watched for pilchard schools and directed the boats to the fishing grounds. Newquay has become Britain's surfing capital, and in summer young California-dreaming devotees can pack the wide, cliff-backed beaches.

Perranporth

🕖 *8 mi south of Newquay, 13 mi northwest of Truro.*

Past the sandy shores of Perran Bay, Perranporth is one of Cornwall's most popular seaside spots and becomes extremely busy in high season, though it's easier to escape the crowds here than in Newquay. The swells off this 3-mi stretch of beach attract swarms of surfers, too. The

BEACH BASICS

The beaches lining parts of the peninsula have made the West Country one of England's main family vacation destinations. Natives don't mind the water's temperature, but foreigners, especially those pampered by the warm waves of the Mediterranean, are not so eager to brave the elements. Swimming here is a bracing experience that sometimes leaves you shivering and breathless. At most resorts, red and yellow flags show the limits of safe swimming. If you see a blue flag, you can be confident that the beach and sea are unpolluted. The Blue Flag scheme, which rewards cleanliness, water quality, easy access, and facilities, is run by the Foundation for Environmental Education and is used across Europe, the Caribbean, South Africa, and parts of North America. This region of England has the biggest concentration of winners—30 beaches in 2006. There can be strong undertows, and beware of fast-moving tides.

The northern coast of the peninsula has the region's best surfing beaches, and Cornwall, especially Newquay, is the center of a thriving surfing industry. Go ahead and give it a try: it's easy to rent equipment (including wet suits), and plenty of places offer lessons.

best times to visit are the beginning and end of the summer. Enchanting coastal walks extend along the dunes and cliffs.

St. Ives

🄗 *20 mi southwest of Perranporth on A30, 10 mi north of Penzance.*

James McNeill Whistler came here to paint his landscapes, Daphne du Maurier and Virginia Woolf to write their novels. Today sand, sun, and superb art continue to attract thousands of vacationers to the fishing village of St. Ives, named after Saint Ia, a 5th-century female Irish missionary said to have arrived on a floating leaf. The town has long played host to a well-established artists' colony, and there are plenty of craftspeople, too. ■ TIP→ **Day-trippers often crowd St. Ives, so it's best to park away from the center.**

The studio and garden of Dame Barbara Hepworth (1903–75), who pioneered abstract sculpture in England, are now the **Barbara Hepworth Museum and Sculpture Garden.** London's prominent Tate gallery runs the museum. The artist lived here for 26 years. ⊠ *Trewyn Studio, Barnoon Hill* 🕾 *01736/796226* ⊕ *www.tate.org.uk* 🖃 *£4.75, combined ticket with Tate St. Ives £8.75* ⊙ *Mar.–Oct., daily 10–5:30; Nov.–Feb., Tues.–Sun. and national holidays 10–4:30.*

★ The spectacular **Tate St. Ives** displays the work of artists who lived and worked in St. Ives, mostly from 1925 to 1975, and has selections from the rich collection of the Tate in London. It occupies a modernist building—a fantasia of seaside deco-period architecture with a panoramic view of rippling turquoise ocean. The rooftop café is excellent, for the food and views. ✉ *Porthmeor Beach* ☎ *01736/796226* ⊕ *www. tate.org.uk* ✍ *£5.75, combined ticket with Barbara Hepworth Museum and Sculpture Garden £8.75* ◷ *Mar.–Oct., daily 10–5:30; Nov.–Feb., Tues.–Sun. and national holidays 10–4:30.*

> ### SURFERS WELCOME
>
> The four-story Tate St. Ives, at the base of a cliff fronted by Porthmeor Beach, may be the only art museum with special storage space for visitors' surfboards.

NEED A BREAK?

One of Cornwall's oldest pubs (built in 1312), the harborfront **Sloop Inn** (✉ The Wharf ☎ 01736/796584) serves simple lunches as well as evening meals in wood-beam rooms that display the work of local artists. If the weather's good, you can eat at the tables outside.

At the **St. Ives Society of Artists Gallery,** local artists display selections of their current work for sale in the former Old Mariners' Church. The Crypt is rented out for private exhibitions. ✉ *Norway Sq.* ☎ *01736/ 795582* ⊕ *www.stivessocietyofartists.com* ◷ *Mid-Mar.–May and Oct., Mon.–Sat. and national holidays 10:30–5:30; June–Sept., Mon.–Sat. 10:30–5:30, Sun. 1–5:30.*

Where to Stay & Eat

£££–££££ ✕**Porthminster Beach Café.** Unbeatable for its location alone—on the broad, golden sands of Porthminster Beach—this sleek modern eatery prepares imaginative lunches, teas, and evening meals you can savor while you take in the marvelous vista across the bay. Typical choices are Cornish crab fritters; spicy braised lamb tagine with roasted couscous, and cumin-fried almonds; and Barbary duck with seared foie gras on parsnip puree. The sister Porthgwidden Beach Café, in the Downalong area of town, has a smaller and cheaper but equally varied menu. ✉ *Porthminster Beach* ☎ *01736/795352* ▭ *AE, MC, V* ◷ *Closed Nov.–Easter.*

££££–£££££ ✕▥ **Garrack Hotel.** A family-run, ivy-clad hotel with panoramic sea views from its hilltop location, the Garrack is relaxed and undemanding. Some rooms are furnished in traditional style; others are more modern. The excellent restaurant (£££–££££) specializes in local fish, including grilled or sautéed lobster, as well as Cornish lamb. Breads are made in-house, and the wine list features some Cornish vineyards. ✉ *Burthallan La., TR26 3AA* ☎ *01736/796199* 🖨 *01736/798955* ⊕ *www.garrack.com* ⇆ *18 rooms* ⚬ *Restaurant, in-room data ports, indoor pool, gym, sauna, bar; no a/c* ▭ *AE, DC, MC, V* ⦿ *BP.*

£££ ▥ **Primrose Valley Hotel.** Blending the features of an Edwardian villa with clean-lined modern style, this family-friendly hotel with easygoing, young management has a great location a few steps up from Porthminster Beach. Guest rooms are bright and contemporary, and though some are on the small side, the hotel seems spacious and has a large lounge that opens onto the veranda. Early evening meals are available June through September. There's an extra charge for sea-facing rooms with balconies, and a minimum one-week stay is required in July and August. ✉ *Porthminster Beach, TR26 2ED* 🖷🖷 *01736/794939* ⊕ *www. primroseonline.co.uk* ➷ *10 rooms* ⟂ *Dining room (June–Sept.), bar, Wi-Fi; no a/c, no smoking* ⊟ *MC, V* ⟋⟍ *BP.*

£–££ ⊡ **Cornerways.** Everything in St. Ives seems squeezed into the tiniest of spaces, and this cottage B&B in the quiet Downalong quarter is no exception. The light, tastefully converted rooms are pleasingly simple in design, with neutral colors enlivened by modern art; the more expensive have sea views. Most rooms are named after characters in Daphne du Maurier's novels (she once stayed in one of them). Fresh local fish is offered at breakfast, and the galleries are minutes away. ✉ *1 Bethesda Pl., TR26 1PA* 🖷 *01736/796706* ⊕ *www.cornerwaysstives.com* ➷ *6 rooms* ⟂ *No a/c, no smoking* ⊟ *No credit cards* ⟋⟍ *BP.*

EN ROUTE The winding B3306 coastal road southwest from St. Ives passes through some of Cornwall's starkest yet most beautiful countryside. Barren hills crisscrossed by low stone walls drop abruptly to granite cliffs and wide bays. Evidence of the ancient tin-mining industry—the remains of smokestacks and pumping houses—is everywhere. Now a fascinating mining heritage center, the early-20th-century **Geevor Tin Mine** was the only mine left in the St. Just district by the 1930s. At its peak Geevor employed 400 men, but in 1985 the collapse of the world tin market wiped Cornwall from the mining map. Wear suitably sturdy footwear for the surface and underground tours. A museum, shop, and café are on the site. ✉ *B3306, Pendeen* 🖷 *01736/788662* ⊕ *www.geevor.com* ✉ *£7.50* ⊙ *Apr.–Oct., Sun.–Fri. 10–5; Nov.–Mar., Sun.–Fri. 10–4; last admission 1 hr before closing.*

Land's End

★ ⑱ *10 mi southwest of St. Ives, 10 mi west of Penzance.*

The coastal road, B3306, ends at the western tip of Britain at what is, quite literally, Land's End. The sea crashes against the rocks here and lashes ships battling their way around the point. ■ TIP➜ **Approach from one of the coastal footpaths for the best panoramic view.** Over the years, sightseers have caused some erosion of the paths, but new ones are constantly being built, and Cornish "hedges" (granite walls covered with turf) have been planted to prevent erosion. The scenic grandeur of Land's End remains undiminished, although the point draws crowds of people from all over the world. The Land's End Hotel here is undistinguished, though ⟳ the restaurant has good views. A low-key theme park, the **Land's End Experience** (🖷 0870/458–0099), runs a poor second to nature.

Mousehole

★ ⑲ *7 mi east of Land's End, 3 mi south of Penzance.*

On B3315 between Land's End and Penzance, Mousehole (pronounced *mow*-zel, with the first syllable rhyming with "cow") merits a stop—and plenty of people do stop—to see this archetypal Cornish fishing village of tiny stone cottages. It was the home of Dolly Pentreath, supposedly the last native Cornish speaker, who died in 1777.

FOUR DAYS IN CORNWALL

Here's a trip if you want to see some highlights of Cornwall. Traveling down along the North Devon coast, stop at the harbor village of **Boscastle** ⓫ before steeping yourself in Arthurian legends at **Tintagel** ⓬, ideally taking a coastal walk here. Overnight in 🏨 **Padstow** ⓮ and dine on excellent seafood (reserve ahead). The next day, head for **St. Ives** ⓱, popular with art lovers and beach fans, and push on to the dramatic scenery of the country's westernmost tip, **Land's End** ⓲. Stay in 🏨 **Penzance** ㉑ for your second night; from here you can visit the island castle of **St.**

Michael's Mount. Then either follow the coast around to tour the scenic **Lizard Peninsula** ㉒, or head straight for Pendennis Castle in **Falmouth** ㉓. Across the Carrick Roads estuary basin, explore the Roseland Peninsula, spending your third night in 🏨 **St. Mawes** ㉕, which has a fine castle. Start early the next day to visit the **Eden Project** ㉘, a must for anyone with even a passing interest in greenery, and then choose between two superb country piles: Victorian Lanhydrock, near **Bodmin** ㉚, and **Cotehele House** ㊷, a Tudor manor house.

4

Newlyn

 2 mi north of Mousehole.

Long the county's most important fishing port, Newlyn is very much a working town, in contrast to St. Ives. The Fish Fair takes over the town for a weekend at the end of August, for tastings and entertainments. Newlyn became the magnet for a popular artists' colony at the end of the 19th century, but few of the fishermen's cottages that attracted artists to the area remain. To see the works of the Newlyn School, drop by the Penlee House Gallery in Penzance.

Penzance

 1½ mi north of Newlyn, 10 mi south of St. Ives.

Superb views over Mount's Bay are one lure of this popular, unpretentious seaside resort. It's a good base for exploring the area but does get very crowded in summer. The town's isolated position has always made it vulnerable to attack from the sea. During the 16th century, Spanish raiders destroyed most of the original town, and the majority of old buildings date from as late as the 18th century. The main street is Market Jew Street, a folk mistranslation of the Cornish expression "Marghas Yow," which means "Thursday Market." Where Market Jew Street meets Causeway Head is Market House, constructed in 1837, an impressive, domed granite building that now serves as a bank.

The former main street and one of the prettiest thoroughfares in Penzance, **Chapel Street** winds down from Market House to the harbor. Its predominantly Georgian and Regency houses suddenly give way to the extraordinary **Egyptian House,** whose facade recalls ancient Egypt. Built around 1830 as a geological museum, today it houses vacation apartments. Across Chapel Street is the 17th-century **Union Hotel,** where in 1805 the death of Lord Nelson and the victory of Trafalgar were first announced from the minstrels' gallery in the assembly rooms. Near the Union Hotel on Chapel Street is one of the few remnants of old Penzance, the **Turk's Head,** an inn said to date from the 13th century.

The small collection at the **Penlee House Gallery and Museum,** in a gracious Victorian house in a park, focuses on paintings by members of the so-called Newlyn School from about 1880 to 1930. These works evoke the life of the inhabitants of Newlyn, mostly fisherfolk. The museum also covers 5,000 years of West Cornwall history through archaeology, decorative arts, costume, and photography exhibits. ✉ *Penlee Park* ☎ *01736/363625* ⊕ *www.penleehouse.org.uk* 🏷 *£3, Sat. free* ⊙ *May–Sept., Mon.–Sat. 10–5; Oct.–Apr., Mon.–Sat. 10:30–4:30; last admission ½ hr before closing.*

★ Rising out of Mount's Bay just off the coast, the spectacular granite and slate island of **St. Michael's Mount** is one of Cornwall's greatest natural attractions. The 14th-century castle perched at the highest point—200 feet above the sea—was built on the site of a Benedictine chapel founded by Edward the Confessor. In its time, the island has served as a church (Brittany's island abbey of Mont St. Michel was an inspiration), a fortress, and a private residence. The castle rooms you can tour include the Chevy Chase Room—a name probably associated with the Cheviot Hills or the French word *chevaux* (horses), after the hunting frieze that decorates the walls of this former monks' refectory. The battlements also offer wonderful views. Around the base of the rock are buildings from medieval to Victorian, but they appear harmonious. Fascinating gardens surround the Mount, and many kinds of plants flourish in its microclimates. To get to the island, walk the cobbled causeway from the village of Marazion or, when the tide is in during the summer, take the ferry. There are pubs and restaurants in the village, but the island also has a café and restaurant. ■ TIP→ Wear stout shoes for your visit to this site, which is unsuitable for anyone with mobility problems. The climb to the castle is steep. ✉ *3 mi east of Penzance on A394, Marazion* ☎ *01736/710507* ⊕ *www. stmichaelsmount.co.uk* 🏷 *Castle £6, garden £3, £1.20 for ferry each way* ⊙ *Castle late Mar.–Oct., weekdays and Sun. 10:30–5.30. Garden May and June, weekdays 10–5:30; July–Oct., Thurs. and Fri. 10–5:30; last admission 4:45; Nov.–Mar., phone for hrs.*

OFF THE BEATEN PATH

ISLES OF SCILLY – Fondly regarded in folklore as the lost land of Lyonesse, this compact group of more than 100 islands 30 mi southwest of Land's End is equally famed for the warm summer climate and ferocious winter storms. In fair weather, you can find peace, flowers—wild, cultivated, and subtropical—swarms of seabirds, and unspoiled beaches galore. If you have time, take the 2½-hour ferry service from Penzance; otherwise there's plane and helicopter service. These all arrive at the largest of the five inhabited islands, St. Mary's, which has the bulk of the lodgings, from palatial retreats to humble but comfortable B&Bs.

Where to Stay & Eat

£££–££££ ✕**Abbey Restaurant.** Sleekly modern, this restaurant has garnered enthusiastic plaudits with a short, intriguing contemporary menu that highlights fresh seafood and local meat. Starters might include pigeon and pork terrine with onion marmalade and toasted brioche, followed by such dishes as grilled lemon sole with eggplant caviar. Among the exquisite desserts are and croissant and butter pudding with apricots and pear sorbet. ✉ *Abbey St.* ☎ *01736/330680* ▤ *AE, MC, V* ☉ *Closed Dec., Jan., and Mon.; also Tues. Feb.–May and Sept.–Nov.; Wed. in Feb. and Nov. No lunch Tues.–Thurs.*

£££–££££ ✕**Harris's.** Seafood is the main event in the two small, boldly colored rooms of this restaurant off Market Jew Street. The menu showcases whatever the boats bring: crab Florentine, grilled on a bed of spinach with cheese sauce, is usually available. Meat dishes might include grilled guinea fowl stuffed with goat cheese. The semiformal style is intimate, elegant, and traditional. ✉ *46 New St.* ☎ *01736/364408* ▤ *AE, MC, V* ☉ *Closed Sun., also Mon. Nov.–May, and 4 wks Nov.–Mar.*

★ **££–£££** ✕**Admiral Benbow Inn.** One of the town's most famous inns, the 15th-century Admiral Benbow was once a smugglers' pub—look for the figure of a smuggler on the roof. Seafaring memorabilia, a brass cannon, model ships, and figureheads fill the place. In the restaurant area, decorated to resemble a ship's galley, you can dine on seafood or a steak-and-Guinness pie. ✉ *46 Chapel St.* ☎ *01736/363448* ▤ *MC, V.*

★ **£££££** ▥**Abbey Hotel.** Owned by former 1960s model–icon Jean Shrimpton and her husband, this small, Wedgwood-blue-colored 17th-century hotel off Chapel Street is marvelously homey. Books fill the drawing room, and antiques and chintzes decorate many of the rooms, most of which have harbor views; there's also a small, comfortable apartment. ✉ *Abbey St., TR18 4AR* ☎ *01736/366906* 🖷 *01736/351163* ⊕ *www.theabbeyonline.co.uk* ⚲ *6 rooms, 1 apartment* ♨ *Dining room, some pets allowed; no a/c* ▤ *AE, MC, V* ◉| *BP.*

££ ▥**Union Hotel.** Strong on historical and nautical details, this central lodging housed the town's assembly rooms, where news of Admiral Nelson's victory at Trafalgar and of the death of Nelson himself were first announced from the minstrels' gallery in 1805. The bar, lounge, and dining rooms retain their Georgian elegance. However, the guest rooms, in traditional style, could use updating; some have tired-looking carpets and old-fashioned prints. A number have window seats, with views over Mount's Bay. Breakfast is served in the restored assembly rooms. ✉ *Chapel St., TR18 4AE* 🖷 *01736/362319* ⊕ *www.unionhotel.co.uk* ⚲ *28 rooms* ♨ *Dining room, 2 bars; no a/c* ▤ *MC, V* ◉| *BP.*

£–££ ▥**Camilla House.** This flower-bedecked Georgian house stands on a road parallel to the promenade, close to the harbor. Guest rooms are cheerfully decorated; those at the front have sea views. The owners are great sources of local information and can help with ferry crossings and flights to the Isles of Scilly. Evening meals are available on request. ✉ *12 Regent Terr., TR18 4DW* 🖷 *01736/363771* ⊕ *www.camillahouse-hotel.co.uk* ⚲ *8 rooms* ♨ *Dining room, in-room data ports, Wi-Fi, bar; no a/c, no room phones, no smoking* ▤ *AE, MC, V* ◉| *BP.*

Nightlife & the Arts

★ The open-air **Minack Theatre** perches high above a beach 3 mi southeast of Land's End and about 6 mi southwest of Penzance. The slope of the cliff forms a natural amphitheater, with bench seats on the terraces and the sea as a magnificent backdrop. Different companies present plays from classic dramas to modern comedies afternoons and evenings in summer. An exhibition center tells the story of the theater's creation. ⊠ *Off B3315, Porthcurno* ☎ *01736/810181* 🖃 *Exhibition center £3, performances £6 and £7.50* ☉ *Apr.–Oct., daily 9:30–5:30; Nov.–Mar., daily 10–4. Exhibition center closed during matinees, currently May–Sept., Wed. and Fri. noon–4:30.*

Sports & the Outdoors

Many ships have foundered on Cornwall's rocky coastline, resulting in an estimated 3,600 shipwrecks. The area around Land's End has some of the best diving in Europe, in part because the convergence of the Atlantic and the Gulf Stream here results in impressive visibility and unusual subtropical marine life. **Undersea Adventures** (⊠ 7 Hayle Industrial Park, Hayle ☎ 01736/751066) offers courses and guided dives for beginners and experts.

Lizard Peninsula

★ ㉒ *23 mi southwest of Penzance*

The southernmost point on mainland Britain, this peninsula is a government-designated Area of Outstanding Natural Beauty. The rocky, dramatic coast is the highlight, as the interior is flat and boring. There's no coast road, unlike Land's End, so the peninsula is best explored on foot. The beaches are good. With no large town (Helston is the biggest, and is not a tourist center), it's far less busy than Land's End. The huge, eerily rotating dish antennae of the Goonhilly Satellite Communications Earth Station are visible from the road as it crosses Goonhilly Downs, the backbone of the peninsula.

A path close to the tip of the peninsula plunges down 200-foot cliffs to the tiny **Kynance Cove,** with its handful of pint-size islands. The sands here are reachable only during the 2½ hours before and after low tide. The peninsula's cliffs are made of greenish serpentine rock, interspersed with granite; souvenirs of the area are carved out of the stone.

Falmouth

㉓ *7 mi northeast of Gweek, 12 mi south of Truro.*

The bustle of this resort town's fishing harbor, yachting center, and commercial port only adds to its charm. In the 18th century, Falmouth was the main mail-boat port for North America, and in Flushing, a village across the inlet, you can see the slate-covered houses built by prosperous mail-boat captains. A ferry service now links the two towns. On Custom House Quay, off Arwenack Street, is the King's Pipe, an oven in which seized contraband was burned.

The granite and oak-clad **National Maritime Museum Cornwall** by the harbor is an excellent place to come to grips with Cornish maritime heritage, weather lore, and navigational science. You can view the collection of 140 or so boats, examine the tools associated with Cornish boatbuilders, and study the prospect across to Flushing from the lighthouse-like Lookout, which is equipped with maps, telescopes, and binoculars. In the glass-fronted Tidal Zone below sea level, you come face to face with the sea itself. In summer, you can reach the museum by ferry from Falmouth's Prince of Wales Pier. ⊠ *Discovery Quay* ☎ *01326/313388* ⊕ *www.nmmc. co.uk* ⊠ *£7* ⊘ *Daily 10–5.*

At the end of its own peninsula stands the formidable **Pendennis Castle**, built by Henry VIII in the 1540s and improved by his daughter, Elizabeth I. You can explore the defenses developed over the centuries. In the Royal Artillery Barracks, the Key to Cornwall exhibit explores the castle's history and its connection to Cornwall and England. The castle has sweeping views over the English Channel and across the water known as Carrick Roads to St. Mawes Castle, designed as a companion fortress to guard the roads. ⊠ *Pendennis Head* ☎ *01326/316594* ⊕ *www.english-heritage.org.uk* ⊠ *£4.80* ⊘ *Apr.–June and Sept., Sun.–Fri. 10–5, Sat 10–4; July and Aug., Sun.–Fri. 10–6, Sat 10–4; Oct.–Mar., daily 10–4.*

Where to Stay & Eat

££–£££ ✕ **Pandora Inn.** Four miles north of Falmouth, this thatched pub on a creek is a great retreat, with both a patio and a moored pontoon for summer dining. Maritime memorabilia and fresh flowers provide decoration, and you can eat in the bar (lunch or dinner) or in the candlelighted restaurant (dinner only). The menu highlight is fresh seafood—try the roast sea bream—though there's a good selection of game in winter. ⊠ *Restronguet Creek, Mylor Bridge* ☎ *01326/372678* ⊟ *MC, V.*

★ **££–£££** ✕ **Seafood Bar.** Head down an alley off the quay to get to this restaurant with a fish tank for a window. Beyond the door is the very best local seafood, with such choices as thick crab soup, Helford River oysters, or scallops from Falmouth Bay. ⊠ *Quay St.* ☎ *01326/315129* ⊟ *MC, V* ⊘ *Closed Sun. and Mon. Oct.–Easter. No lunch.*

££££–£££££ ⊞ **St. Michael's Hotel.** Colorful subtropical gardens sweep down to the water at this seaside hotel in a long, low, white building overlooking Falmouth Bay. The public areas and guest rooms are sleek and contemporary, and the staff welcomes families. Treatments in the spa's four rooms are state of the art. ⊠ *Stracey Rd., TR11 4NB* ☎ *01326/312707* 🖷 *01326/211772* ⊕ *www.corushotels.com* ⇌ *61 rooms, 3 suites* ⚒ *2 restaurants, indoor pool, spa, gym, hot tub, sauna, bar, meeting rooms; no a/c* ⊟ *AE, MC, V* ⦿ *BP.*

Trelissick

㉔ *6 mi north of Falmouth.*

Trelissick has a ferry terminal as well as colorful Trelissick Garden, owned by the National Trust. The **King Harry Ferry** (☎ 01872/862312 ⊕ www.kingharryferry.co.uk), a chain-drawn car ferry, runs to the scenically splendid Roseland Peninsula three times hourly every day. From its decks you can see up and down the Fal, a deep, narrow river with steep, wooded banks. The river's great depth provides mooring for old ships waiting to be sold; these mammoth shapes lend a surreal touch to the riverscape.

St. Mawes

㉕ *16 mi east of Falmouth by road, 1½ mi east by sea, 11 mi south of Truro by ferry.*

At the tip of the Roseland Peninsula is the quiet, unspoiled village of St. Mawes, where subtropical plants thrive. The peninsula itself is a lovely backwater with old churches, a lighthouse, and good coast walking. One or two sailing and boating options are available in summer, but most companies operate from Falmouth.

The well-preserved Tudor-era **St. Mawes Castle,** outside the village, has a cloverleaf shape that makes it seemingly impregnable, yet during the Civil War, its Royalist commander surrendered without firing a shot. (In contrast, Pendennis Castle held out at this time for 23 weeks before submitting to a siege.) ✉ *A3078* ☎ *01326/270526* ⊕ *www.english-heritage.org.uk* 🎫 *£3.60* ☼ *Apr.–June and Sept., Sun.–Fri. 10–5; July and Aug., Sun.–Fri. 10–6; Oct., daily 10–4; Nov.–Mar., Fri.–Mon. 10–4.*

> ### WORD OF MOUTH
>
> "We love the area around St. Mawes. You could spend your entire trip sipping cold white wine and watching all the activity in the harbor, but there are lots of things to see and do in the area. St. Just in Roseland has a very pretty church in a lovely location. Lots of fishing villages to visit." –rickmay

★ North of St. Mawes on A3078 is **St. Just in Roseland,** one of the most beautiful spots in the West Country. This tiny hamlet made up of stone cottage terraces and a 13th-century church is set within a subtropical garden, often abloom with magnolias and rhododendrons on a summer's day. St. Just in Roseland is 9 mi south of Truro.

Where to Stay & Eat

★ **£££££** ✕🏠 **Lugger Hotel.** It's worth the winding drive on some of Cornwall's narrowest roads to get to this chic hideaway by the water in a tiny fishing village. Several 17th-century cottages have been transformed in an eclectic modern style with bleached Portuguese wood and subdued hues. Seafood is a good choice at the excellent restaurant (£££££; fixed-price menu), which overlooks the diminutive harbor. There's a terrace for drinks and sunbathing, and on either side of the hotel, the rugged coastline tempts you with exhilarating walks. The Lugger is 8 mi east of St. Mawes and 12 mi southeast of Truro. ✉ *Portloe TR2 5RD* ☎ *01872/501322* 🖷 *01872/501691* ⊕ *www.luggerhotel.com* 🛏 *21 rooms* ⚒ *Restaurant, in-room data ports, spa; no a/c* ⊟*AE, MC, V* ⎆*BP.*

★ **£££££** ✕🏠 **Tresanton Hotel.** It's the Cornish Riviera, Italian style: this former yachtsman's club, owned by Olga Polizzi, daughter of grand hotelier Charles Forte, makes for a luxuriously relaxed stay. Decorated in sunny whites, blues, and yellows, with terra-cotta pots on the terrace, the Tresanton seems distinctly Mediterranean, and the yacht and speedboat available in summer to guests reinforce the jet-set spirit. In the restaurant (£££££; fixed-price menu), the Italian-inspired menu includes steamed langoustine with fettuccine. The same owner has converted Endsleigh House, a country manor in Tavistock, Devon, with equal panache. ⊠ *Lower Castle Rd., TR2 5DR* ☎ *01326/270055* 🖷 *01326/270053* ⊕ *www.tresanton.com* ⇌ *27 rooms, 2 suites* ♿ *Restaurant, boating, fishing, bar, cinema, meeting rooms; no a/c* ⊟ *AE, MC, V* ☉ *BP.*

EN ROUTE	The shortest route from St. Mawes to Truro is via the King Harry Ferry. The longer way swings in a circle on A3078 for 19 mi through countryside where subtropical shrubs and flowers thrive. It takes you past Portloe and the 123-foot-tall church tower in Probus, which flaunts gargoyles and pierced stonework.

Truro

26 *12 mi north of Falmouth, 19 mi north of St. Mawes.*

Truro is a compact, elegant Georgian city, nestled in a crook at the head of the River Truro. Although Bodmin is the county seat, Truro is Cornwall's only real city; it's a good option mostly for food and shopping, and for cathedral and museum buffs. For an overview of the Georgian house fronts, take a stroll down steep, broad Lemon Street. The 18th-century facades are of pale stone—unusual for Cornwall, where granite predominates. Like Lemon Street, Walsingham Place is a typical Georgian street, a curving, flower-lined pedestrian oasis.

Truro Cathedral, the **Cathedral Church of St. Mary,** dominates the city. Although comparatively modern (built 1880–1910), it evokes a medieval church, with an exterior in early-English Gothic style. The interior is filled with relics from the 16th-century parish church that stood on this site, part of which has been incorporated into a side chapel. An open, cobbled area called High Cross lies in front of the west porch, and the city's main shopping streets fan out from here. ⊠ *14 St. Mary's St.* ☎ *01872/276782* ⊕ *www.trurocathedral.org.uk* 🖂 *£3 suggested donation, tours £1* ☉ *Mon.–Sat. 7:30–6, Sun. 9–7; tours Easter–Oct., Mon.–Thurs. and Sat. at 11, Fri. at 11:30, also weekdays at 2 during school vacations.*

The **Royal Cornwall Museum,** in a Georgian building, displays some fine examples of Cornwall-inspired art, a sampling of Cornish archaeology, an absorbing hodgepodge of local history, and an extensive collection of minerals. There's a restaurant (Stingi Lulu's) and shop. ⊠ *River St.* ☎ *01872/272205* ⊕ *www.royalcornwallmuseum.org.uk* 🖂 *Free* ☉ *Mon.–Sat. 10–5.*

Where to Stay & Eat

££££ ✕🖭 **Alverton Manor.** A former bishop's house and then a convent, this up-to-date hotel is efficient and atmospheric, with a chapel that serves as a conference room. Guest rooms are large and have French cherrywood furniture. Quiet elegance is the keynote of the public areas, and in the Terrace restaurant (£30 fixed-price menu), standards are kept high with the use of local produce in traditional and modern English recipes. ⊠ *Tregolls Rd., TR1 1ZQ* ☎ *01872/276633* 🖷 *01872/222989* ⊕ *www.connexions.co.uk/alvertonmanor* ➪ *33 rooms* ♻ *Restaurant, cable TV, in-room data ports, bar, meeting rooms, some pets allowed (fee); no a/c* ⊟ *AE, MC, V* ☺ *May be closed 4 days over New Year* ⅋ *BP.*

Charlestown

㉗ *15 mi east of Truro.*

This port was built by a local merchant in 1791 to export the huge reserves of china clay from St. Austell, 1 mi to the north, and it became one of the ports from which 19th-century emigrants left for North America. Charlestown has managed to avoid overdevelopment since its heyday in the early 1800s. Its Georgian harbor often appears in period film and television productions.

★ The sprawling, popular **Lost Gardens of Heligan** have something for all garden lovers, as well as an intriguing history. Restored in the early 1990s by former rock producer Tom Smit (the force behind the Eden Project) after decades of neglect, they were begun by the Tremayne family in the late 18th century. In Victorian times the gardens displayed exotic plants from around the British Empire. The Jungle Garden contains surviving plants from this era. The Italian Garden and walled Flower Gardens are delightful, but don't overlook the extensive fruit and vegetable gardens or Flora's Green, bordered by a ravine. It's easy to spend half a day here. ■ TIP→ Travel via St. Austell to avoid confusing country lanes. ⊠ *B3273, Pentewan* ☎ *0176/845100* ⊕ *www.heligan.com* 🖅 *£7.50* ☺ *Mar.–Oct., daily 10–6; Nov.–Feb., daily 10–5.*

Where to Stay

★ ££ 🖫 **T'Gallants.** This cheerfully refurbished Georgian house directly behind the harbor takes its name from top gallant, one of the sails of a square-rigged sailing ship. Ask for a south-facing room to enjoy the tranquil morning view. The garden at the front is ideal for afternoon tea, and bag lunches are sometimes available from the (separately run) tearoom. ⊠ *6 Charlestown Rd., PL25 3NJ* ☎ *01726/70203* ⊕ *www.t-gallants.co.uk* ➪ *7 rooms* ♻ *No a/c; no smoking* ⊟ *AE, MC, V* ⅋ *CP.*

Eden Project

㉘ *3 mi northeast of Charlestown.*

Fodor'sChoice
★

Spectacularly set in a former china clay pit, the Eden Project presents the world's major plant systems in microcosm. The crater contains more than 70,000 plants, many belonging to rare or endangered species, from three climate zones. Plants from the temperate zone are outdoors, and those from other zones are housed in biomes—hexagonally paneled geodesic domes—that are the largest conservatories in Britain. In one dome, olive and citrus groves mix with cacti and other plants indigenous to a warmer temperate climate. The tropical dome steams with heat, resounds to the gushing of a waterfall, and blooms with exotic flora. The emphasis is on conservation and ecology, but free of any moralizing. A free shuttle, the Land Train, helps the footsore, and well-informed guides provide information. An entertaining exhibition in the visitor center gives you the lowdown on the project, and the Core, an education center, provides amusement and instruction for children. Extra attractions include open-air concerts in summer, and an ice-skating rink in winter. ■ TIP→ **To avoid the biggest crowds, visit on a Friday or Saturday, early in the morning, or after 2; you need at least half a day to see everything.** ⊠ *Bodelva, signposted off A30, A390, and A391, St. Austell* ☎ *01726/811911* ⊕ *www.edenproject.com* ⊠ *£13.80* ⊙ *Apr.–Oct., daily 10–6; Nov.–Mar., daily 10–4:30; last admission 1½ hrs before closing.*

Fowey

㉙ *7 mi northeast of the Eden Project, 10 mi northeast of Charlestown.*

Nestled in the mouth of a wooded estuary, Fowey (pronounced Foy) is still very much a working china clay port as well as a focal point for the sailing fraternity. Increasingly, it's also the favored home of the rich and famous. Good and varied eating and sleeping options abound; these are most in demand during Regatta Week in mid-August and the annual Daphne du Maurier Festival in mid-May. The Bodinnick Ferry takes cars as well as foot passengers across the river for the coast road on to Looe.

Where to Stay & Eat

££–£££ ✕ **Sam's.** You should be prepared to wait at this small and buzzing bistro with a rock-and-roll flavor. Diners squeeze onto benches and into booths to savor dishes made with local seafood, including a majestic bouillabaisse, or just a simple "Samburger." ⊠ *20 Fore St.* ☎ *01726/832273* ⊲ *Reservations not accepted* ⊟ *MC, V* ⊙ *Closed 2 or 3 wks in Jan. No lunch Sun.*

£££££ ▥ **Fowey Hall.** A showy Victorian edifice, all turrets, castellations, and elaborate plasterwork, this friendly, relaxed hotel with 5 acres of gardens is very family centered—despite the abundance of antiques. Guest rooms are spacious, and there are great facilities for children. You can dine in the sumptuously oak-panel Hansons or in the less formal Palm Court, which opens onto the terrace. ⊠ *Hanson Dr., PL23 1ET* ☎ *01726/833866* 🖷 *01726/834100* ⊕ *www.foweyhallhotel. co.uk* ⟳ *20 rooms, 12 suites* ⟑ *2 restaurants, cable TV with movies, in-room VCRs or DVDs, indoor pool, Ping-Pong, bar, babysitting, meeting rooms; no a/c* ⊟ *AE, MC, V* ⫲ *BP.*

Sports & the Outdoors

Between May and September, **Fowey River Canoe Expeditions** (⊠ 17 Passage St. ☎ 01726/833627) runs daily canoe trips up the tranquil River Fowey, the best way to observe the abundant wildlife.

> **WORD OF MOUTH**
>
> "We totally fell in love with Fowey . . . It was our base for visiting both the Eden Project and the Lost Gardens of Heligan. Fowey hangs on the side of a very steep hillside . . . lots of steps everywhere. There are lovely outings on the estuary and the river by boat . . . The water was crystal clear—I used to watch the fishermen pulling up their lobster pots from right below my hotel window!"
>
> –tod

Bodmin

30 *12 mi north of Fowey.*

Bodmin, the county seat, was the only Cornish town recorded in the 11th-century Domesday Book, William the Conqueror's census. During World War I, the Domesday Book and the Crown Jewels were sent to Bodmin Prison for safekeeping. From the Gilbert Memorial on Beacon Hill, you can see both of Cornwall's coasts.

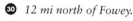 ★ One of Cornwall's greatest country piles, **Lanhydrock** gives a look into the lives of the privileged rich in the 19th century. The former home of the powerful, wealthy Robartes family was originally constructed in the 17th century but was totally rebuilt after a fire in 1881. The granite exterior remains true to its original form, however, and the long picture gallery in the north wing, with its barrel-vaulted plaster ceiling depicting 24 biblical scenes, survived the devastation. A small museum in the north wing shows photographs and letters relating to the family. The house's endless pantries, sculleries, dairies, nurseries, and linen and livery cupboards bear witness to the immense amount of work involved in maintaining this lifestyle. Nine hundred acres of wooded parkland border the River Fowey, and in spring the gardens present an exquisite ensemble of magnolias, azaleas, and rhododendrons. Allow two hours to see the house and more time to stroll the grounds. ⊠ *3 mi southeast of Bodmin, signposted off A30, A38, and B3268* ☎ *01208/73320* ⊕ *www.nationaltrust.org.uk* ⊡ *£9, grounds only £5* ⊗ *House mid-Mar.–Sept., Tues.–Sun. and national holidays 11–5:30; Oct., Tues.–Sun. 11–5; garden daily 10–6; last admission 30 mins before closing.*

Dozmary Pool

31 *10 mi northeast of Bodmin.*

For a taste of Arthurian legend, follow A30 northeast out of Bodmin across the boggy, heather-clad granite plateau of Bodmin Moor, and turn right at Bolventor to get to Dozmary Pool. A lake rather than a pool, it was here that King Arthur's legendary magic sword, Excalibur, was supposedly returned to the Lady of the Lake after Arthur's final battle.

Where to Stay

££–£££ ✕▥ **Jamaica Inn.** This inn near the middle of Bodmin Moor was made famous by Daphne du Maurier's 1936 novel of the same name, and it makes a good base for excursions onto the moor. Originally a farmstead, Cornwall's best-known pub incorporates a reproduction of du Maurier's study and a smugglers' museum, both worth a look. The bedrooms are functional and traditional in style, and four have four-posters. The bar–restaurant offers filling pub grub—steaks, grills, Cajun chicken and the like. ⊠ *Off A30, Bolventor PL15 7TS* ☎ *01566/86250* 🖷 *01566/ 86177* ⊕ *www.jamaicainn.co.uk* ↪ *16 rooms* ⟁ *Restaurant, bar; no a/c* ▤ *AE, MC, V* ⋈ *BP.*

Launceston

 25 mi northwest of Plymouth.

Cornwall's ancient capital, Launceston, on the eastern side of Bodmin Moor, retains parts of its medieval walls, including the South Gate. For a superb view of the surrounding countryside, climb to the hilltop ruins of 14th-century **Launceston Castle.** ☎ *01566/772365* ⊕ *www.english-heritage.org.uk* ☞ *£2.30* ☉ *Apr.–June and Sept., daily 10–5; July and Aug., daily 10–6; Oct., daily 10–4.*

Where to Stay & Eat

££££–£££££ ✕⌂ **Lewtrenchard Manor.** Paneled rooms, stone fireplaces, leaded-glass windows, and handsome gardens enhance this spacious 1620 manor house on the northwestern edge of Dartmoor. Victorian hymn writer Sabine Baring Gould is responsible for the eclectic mix of architectural styles. Prints, chintzes, and upholstered furniture create comfort in the individually decorated guest rooms. The restaurant (£37 fixed-price menu), with its big log fire and family portraits, serves modern English fare such as rabbit with polenta, as well as good, fresh fish caught an hour away. ✉ *Between Launceston and Okehampton, Lewdown EX20 4PN* ☎ *01566/783222* 🖶 *01566/783332* ⊕ *www.lewtrenchard.co.uk* ⛵ *14 rooms* ⌂ *Restaurant, in-room data ports, croquet, bar, meeting rooms, some pets allowed (fee); no a/c* ⊟ *AE, DC, MC, V* ⍾ *BP.*

PLYMOUTH & DARTMOOR

Just over the border from Cornwall is Plymouth, an unprepossessing city but one with a historic old core and splendid harbor that recall a rich maritime heritage. North of Plymouth, you can explore the vast, boggy reaches of hilly Dartmoor, the setting for the Sherlock Holmes classic *The Hound of the Baskervilles*. It's a place to hike or go horseback riding away from the crowds.

Plymouth

48 mi southwest of Exeter, 124 mi southwest of Bristol, 240 mi southwest of London.

Devon's largest city has long been linked with England's commercial and maritime history. The Pilgrims sailed from here to the New World in the *Mayflower* in 1620. Although much of the city center was destroyed by air raids in World War II and has been rebuilt in an uninspiring style, there are worthwhile sights. A harbor tour is also a good way to see the city.

Sound Cruising Ltd (✉ Hexton Quay, Hooe ☎ 01752/408590) runs harbor and river sightseeing trips all year; boats depart every 30 minutes in peak season from Phoenix Wharf (Tuesday through Thursday only in winter; call to check). **Tamar Cruising** (✉ Cremyll Quay, Cremyll, Torpoint ☎ 01752/822105) has harbor cruises and longer scenic trips

Barbican **37**

Hoe **33**

Mayflower
Steps **38**

Merchant's
House **39**

National
Marine
Aquarium **40**

Plymouth
Dome **35**

Royal
Citadel **36**

Smeaton's
Tower **34**

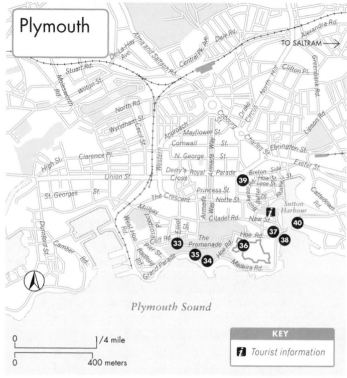

KEY

ⓘ *Tourist information*

on the Rivers Tamar and Yealm between Easter and October. Boats leave
from the Mayflower Steps and Cremyll Quay.

Main Attractions

�37 Barbican. East of the Royal Citadel is the Barbican, the oldest surviving
section of Plymouth. Here, Tudor houses and warehouses rise from a
maze of narrow streets leading down to the fishing docks and harbor.
Many of these buildings have become antiques shops, art shops, and
bookstores. It's worth a stroll.

�33 Hoe. From the Hoe, a wide, grassy esplanade with crisscrossing walkways high above the city, you can take in a magnificent view of the inlets, bays, and harbors that make up Plymouth Sound.

★ ♡ **㊵ National Marine Aquarium.** This excellent aquarium, on a central harborside site, presents aqueous environments, from a freshwater stream
to a seawater wave tank and a huge "shark theater." Not to be missed
are the extensive collection of sea horses, part of an important breeding program, and the chance to walk under sharks in the Mediterranean tank. ■ TIP→ **Try to visit at shark-feeding time, which takes place three
times a week.** Explorocean, highlights undersea technology with demonstrations and hands-on gizmos, and there's a 3-D cinema. ✉ *Rope
Walk, Coxside* ☎ *01752/600301* ⊕ *www.national-aquarium.co.uk*

✈ *£9.50* ⊗ *Apr.–Oct., daily 10–6; Nov.–Mar., daily 10–5; last admission 1 hr before closing.*

36 **Royal Citadel.** This huge citadel was built by Charles II in 1666 and still operates as a military center. ⊠ *End of the Hoe* ☎ *0870/225–4950* ⊕ *www.english-heritage.org.uk* ✈ *£3.50* ⊗ *May–Sept., Tues. 1¼-hr guided tours at 2:30.*

Saltram. An exquisite 18th-century home with many of its original furnishings, Saltram was built around the remains of a late Tudor mansion. Its jewel is one of Britain's grandest neoclassical rooms, a vast, double-cube salon designed by Robert Adam and adorned with paintings by Sir Joshua Reynolds, first president of the Royal Academy of Arts, who was born nearby in 1723. The Axminster carpet was created for the room. Fine plasterwork adorns many rooms, and three have their original Chinese wallpaper. Admission to the house is by timed ticket. The outstanding garden includes rare trees and shrubs. There is a restaurant in the house and a cafeteria in the Coach House. Saltram is 3½ mi east of Plymouth city center. ⊠ *South of A38, Plympton* ☎ *01752/333500* ⊕ *www.nationaltrust.org.uk* ✈ *£8, garden only £4* ⊗ *House late Mar.–Oct., Sat.–Thurs. noon–4:30; last admission 3:45. Garden Mar.–Oct., Sat.–Thurs. 11–4:30; Nov.–Feb., Sat.–Thurs. 11–4.*

Also Worth Seeing

38 **Mayflower Steps.** By the harbor you can visit the Mayflower Steps, where the Pilgrims embarked in 1620; the **Mayflower Stone** marks the exact spot. They had sailed from Southampton but had to stop in Plymouth because of damage from a storm.

39 **Merchant's House.** Near the Barbican, just off the Royal Parade, this largely 18th-century house is a museum of local history. ⊠ *33 St. Andrew's St.* ☎ *01752/304774* ✈ *£1.30* ⊗ *Apr.–Sept., Tues.–Fri. 10–1 and 2–5:30, Sat. 10–1 and 2–5.*

35 **Plymouth Dome.** Next to Smeaton's Tower, the Dome has an exhibition that takes in exploration, battles, and the Blitz in its overview of local history; plenty of high-tech reconstructions add interest. One section covers the construction and rebuilding of Smeaton's Tower. Kids appreciate it, and it makes a great haven on a wet afternoon. ⊠ *Hoe Rd.* ☎ *01752/603300* ⊕ *www.plymouthdome.info* ✈ *£4.75, £6.50 includes Smeaton's Tower* ⊗ *Easter–Oct., daily 10–5; Nov.–Easter, Tues.–Sat. 10–4; last admission 1 hr before closing.*

34 **Smeaton's Tower.** This lighthouse, transferred here at the end of the 19th century from its original site 14 mi out to sea, provides a sweeping vista over Plymouth Sound and the city as far as Dartmoor. ⊠ *Hoe Rd.* ☎ *01752/603300* ⊕ *www.plymouthdome.info* ✈ *£2.25, £6.50 includes Plymouth Dome* ⊗ *Easter.–Oct., daily 10–4; Nov.–Easter, Tues.–Sat. 10–3.*

Where to Stay & Eat

£££££ ✕ **Tanners.** One of the city's oldest buildings, the 15th-century Prysten House, is the setting for the highly regarded, inventive cuisine of brothers Chris and James Tanner. On the eclectic, fixed-price menus are such lunch options as spinach and cauliflower lasagna; evening choices include steamed sea bass with ginger. One of the two lattice-windowed rooms has a well in it, and the other is hung with tapestries. The courtyard is ideal for alfresco dining. ⊠ *Finewell St.* ☎ *01752/252001* ⌂ *Reservations essential* ▤ *AE, MC, V* ⊘ *Closed Sun.*

£££–££££ ✕ **Piermasters.** Fresh seafood landed at nearby piers, notably squid, mussels, and oysters, appears high on the menu at this Barbican eatery. The decoration is basic seafront, with a tiled floor and wooden tables. There are fixed-price menus at lunch and dinner, or you can choose individual selections. ⊠ *33 Southside St.* ☎ *01752/229345* ▤ *AE, MC, V* ⊘ *Closed Sun. and 10 days over Christmas.*

£££££ ▥ **Copthorne Hotel Plymouth.** This businesslike, modern chain hotel downtown delivers the expected comforts and amenities but is not special. Guest rooms are contemporary in style, with a coral, turquoise, and cream color scheme. Bentley's is a no-smoking brasserie. Special deals can lower the price. ⊠ *Armada Way, PL1 1AR* ☎ *01752/224161* ▤ *01752/670688* ⊕ *www.millenniumhotels.com* ↰ *135 rooms* ⌂ *Restaurant, bar, cable TV with movies, in-room data ports, Wi-Fi, bar, business services, meeting rooms, parking (fee); no a/c* ▤ *AE, DC, MC, V* ⱢⓄⱢ *BP.*

££ ▥ **Bowling Green Hotel.** Friendly and unpretentious, this Victorian house overlooks Sir Francis Drake's bowling green on Plymouth Hoe. Pine pieces and floral print fabrics decorate the guest rooms. The house is convenient for shopping and sightseeing. ⊠ *9–10 Osborne Pl., Lockyer St., PL1 2PU* ☎*01752/209090* ▤*01752/209092* ⊕*www.bowlinggreenhotel. com* ↰ *12 rooms* ⌂ *In-room data ports, Wi-Fi, parking (fee); no a/c* ▤ *MC, V* ⱢⓄⱢ *BP.*

Nightlife & the Arts

Plymouth's **Theatre Royal** (⊠ Royal Parade ☎ 01752/267222) presents ballet, musicals, and plays by some of Britain's best companies.

EN
ROUTE

From Plymouth, you have a choice of routes northeast to Exeter. If rugged, desolate, moorland scenery appeals to you, take A386 and B3212 northeast across Dartmoor. There is plenty to stir the imagination.

Dartmoor National Park

10 mi north of Plymouth, 13 mi west of Exeter.

Even on a summer's day the scarred, brooding hills of this sprawling wilderness appear a likely haunt for such monsters as the hound of the Baskervilles, and it seems entirely fitting that Sir Arthur Conan Doyle set his Sherlock Holmes thriller in this landscape. Sometimes the wet, peaty wasteland vanishes in rain and mist, although in clear weather you can see north to Exmoor, south over the English Channel, and west far into Cornwall. Much of Dartmoor consists of open heath and moorland, unspoiled by roads—wonderful walking and horseback-riding territory but an easy place to lose your bearings. Dartmoor's earliest inhabitants left behind stone monuments and burial mounds that help you envision prehistoric man roaming these pastures. Ponies, sheep, and birds are the main animals to be seen.

Several villages scattered along the borders of this 368-square-mi reserve—one-third of which is owned by Prince Charles—make useful bases for hiking excursions. Accommodations include simple inns and some elegant havens. **Okehampton** is a main gateway, and **Chagford** is a good base for exploring North Dartmoor. Other scenic spots include **Buckland-in-the-Moor,** a hamlet with thatched-roof cottages, **Widecombe-in-the-Moor,** whose church is known as the Cathedral of the Moor, and **Grimspound,** the Bronze Age site featured in Conan Doyle's most famous tale. Transmoor Link buses connect most of Dartmoor's towns and villages. Park information centers include the main **High Moorland Visitor Centre** in Princetown and centers in Newbridge, Postbridge, and Haytor. The park also works with tourist information centers in Ivybridge, Okehampton, Tavistock, and Totnes. ✉ *High Moorland Visitor Centre, Tavistock Rd., Princetown PL20 6QF* ☎ *01822/890414* ⊕ *www.dartmoor-npa.gov.uk.*

STAY ON A FARM

Do you plan to travel by car and want to be far from tourist resorts, traffic jams, and general hubbub? One way to experience the authentic rural life in Somerset, Devon, and Cornwall is to stay on a farm. Southwest Tourism's Web site (⊕ www.naturesouthwest.co.uk) gives details about working farms that supply accommodation—including bed-and-breakfasts and house rentals—throughout the region. Other reference points are Discover Devon (⊕ www.discoverdevon.com), for farms in Devon, and Cornish Farm Holidays (⊕ www.cornish-farms.co.uk), for Cornwall.

Sports & the Outdoors

This is a great area for horseback riding; many towns have stables for guided rides. Hiking is popular, but longer hikes in the bleak, unpeopled region of Dartmoor—for example, the tors south of Okehampton—are appropriate only for the most experienced walkers. The areas around Widgery Cross, Becky Falls, and the Bovey Valley, and the short but dramatic walk along Lydford Gorge, have wide appeal, as do the many valleys around the southern edge of the moors. Guided hikes (£3–£6) are available through the park; reservations are not needed for most, but you can check with the High Moorland Visitor Centre in Princetown. Tourist information centers can help you decide what to do; another source is the **Dartmoor National Park Authority** (✉ Parke, Haytor Rd., Bovey Tracey, Newton Abbot TQ13 9JQ ☎ 01626/832093 ⊕ www.dartmoor-npa.gov. uk).

Buckland Abbey

❹ *8 mi north of Plymouth.*

This 13th-century Cistercian monastery became the home of Sir Francis Drake in 1581. Today it is filled with mementos of Drake and the Spanish Armada and has a restaurant. From Tavistock, take A386 south to Crapstone and then head west. ✉ *Yelverton* ☎ *01822/853607* ⊕ *www.nationaltrust.org.uk* ✎ *£7, grounds only £3.70* ☉ *Mid-*

Feb.–mid-Mar. and Nov., weekends 2–5; late Mar.–Oct., Fri.–Wed. 10:30–5:30; early Dec.–mid-Dec., weekends 11–5; last admission 45 mins before closing.

Cotehele House & Quay

★ ㊷ *4 mi west of Buckland Abbey, 15 mi north of Plymouth.*

Just over the border in Cornwall, this was formerly a busy port on the River Tamar, but it is now usually visited for the well-preserved late-medieval manor, home of the Edgcumbe family for centuries. The house has original furniture, tapestries, embroideries, and armor, and there are impressive gardens, a restored mill, and a quay museum. A limited number of visitors are allowed per day, so arrive early and be prepared to wait. Choose a bright day, because the rooms have no electric light. Shops, a crafts gallery, and a restaurant provide other diversions. ⊠ *St. Dominick, north of Saltash, signposted off A390* ☎ *01579/352739* ⊕ *www.nationaltrust.org.uk* ✉ *£8, gardens and mill only £4.80* ⊙ *House mid-Mar.–Sept., Sat.–Thurs. 11–4:30; Oct., Sat.–Thurs. 11–4. Mill mid-Mar.–June and Sept., Sat.–Thurs. 1–5:30; July and Aug., daily 1–5:30; Oct., Sat.–Thurs. 1–4:30. Gardens daily 10:30–dusk.*

Morwellham Quay

㊸ *2 mi east of Cotehele House & Quay, 5 mi southwest of Tavistock, 18 mi north of Plymouth.*

In the 19th century, Morwellham (pronounced More-*wel*-ham) Quay was England's main copper-exporting port, and it has been carefully restored as a working museum, with quay workers and coachmen in costume, and a copper mine open to visitors. ⊠ *Off A390, on a minor road off B3257* ☎ *01822/832766, 01822/833808 recorded information* ⊕ *www.morwellham-quay.co.uk* ✉ *Apr.–Oct. £8.90, Nov.–Mar. £6* ⊙ *Easter–Oct., daily 10–5:30; Nov.–Easter, daily 10–4:30; last admission 2 hrs before closing.*

Where to Stay & Eat

★ ✕🛏 **Horn of Plenty.** A "country house hotel and restaurant" is the way
££££–£££££ this establishment in a Georgian house describes itself. The restaurant (no lunch Monday) has magnificent views across the wooded, rhododendron-filled Tamar Valley. Peter Gorton's sophisticated cooking takes its inspiration from around the world; panfried sea bass with crushed Cornish new potatoes and a white-wine saffron sauce is a typical main course. There are three-course, fixed-price menus (£42), the best value being Monday's potluck menu (£25). A converted coach house and the main house contain sumptuously furnished guest rooms, many with balconies. ⊠ *3 mi west of Tavistock on A390, Gulworthy PL19 8JD* ☎🛏 *01822/832528* ⊕ *www.thehornofplenty.co.uk* ⇥ *8 rooms, 2 suites* ⚴ *Restaurant, in-room DVDs, minibars, meeting rooms, some pets allowed, no-smoking rooms; no a/c* ⊟ *AE, MC, V* 🍽 *BP.*

Lydford Gorge

★ ⓭ *12 mi north of Morwellham Quay, 7 mi north of Tavistock, 9 mi east of Launceston, 24 mi north of Plymouth.*

The River Lyd has carved a spectacular 1½-mi-long chasm through the rock at Lydford Gorge, outside the pretty village of Lydford, midway between Okehampton and Tavistock on the edge of Dartmoor. Two paths follow the gorge past gurgling whirlpools and waterfalls with names such as the Devil's Cauldron and the White Lady. Sturdy footwear is recommended. Although the walk can be quite challenging, the paths can still get congested during busy periods. From Launceston, continue east along A30, following the signs. ⊠ *Off A386, Lydford* ☎ *01822/820320* ⊕ *www.nationaltrust.org.uk* ✆ *£5 Apr.–Oct., £3 mid-Feb.–Mar., free Nov.–mid-Feb.* ☉ *Apr.–Sept., daily 10–5; Oct., daily 10–4; Nov.–Mar., daily 11–3:30 (walk restricted to main waterfall).*

Where to Stay & Eat

£££–££££ ✕ **Dartmoor Inn.** Locals and visitors alike make a beeline for this 16th-century pub, a good spot for snacks such as farmhouse sausages and mashed potatoes or for something more substantial fare like a fish casserole. Fixed-price, two-course lunches and suppers are a good value during the week. The pub is at the Lydford junction. ⊠ *A386, Lydford* ☎ *01822/820221* ▭ *AE, MC, V* ☉ *Closed Mon. No dinner Sun.*

££–£££ ▥ **Castle Inn.** The heart of Lydford village, this 16th-century inn is next to Lydford Castle. Rose trellises frame its rosy brick facade, and the public rooms are snug, lamp-lighted, and full of period clutter. Vivid colors are used in the guest rooms; one room has its own roof garden. ⊠ *1 mi off A386, Lydford EX20 4BH* ☎ *01822/820241* ▭ *01822/820454* ⊕ *www.castleinnlydford.co.uk* ↪ *9 rooms* ⟁ *Restaurant, bar, some pets allowed (fee); no a/c* ▭ *AE, MC, V* ⱺ *BP.*

Sports & the Outdoors

Cholwell Stables (⊠ *Mary Tavy* ☎ *01822/810526*) has one- or two-hour horseback rides through some of Dartmoor's wilder tracts. Riders of all abilities are escorted, and equipment is provided. The stables are about 6 mi south of Lydford; call for directions.

Okehampton

⓭ *8 mi northeast of Lydford Gorge, 28 mi north of Plymouth, 23 mi west of Exeter.*

This town at the confluence of the Rivers East and West Okement is a good base for exploring North Dartmoor. It has numerous pubs and cottage tearooms (giving you a chance to have a Devon cream tea), as well as a helpful tourist office. On the riverbank a mile southwest of the town center, the jagged ruins of the Norman **Okehampton Castle** occupy a verdant site with a picnic area and woodland walks. ☎ *01837/52844* ⊕ *www.english-heritage.org.uk* ✆ *£3* ☉ *Apr.–June and Sept., daily 10–5; July and Aug., daily 10–6.*

The three floors of the informative **Museum of Dartmoor Life** contain models, a working waterwheel, and photos of traditional farming methods. ⊠ *3 West St.* ☎ *01837/52295* ⊕ *www.museumofdartmoorlife.eclipse. co.uk* ⌨*£2.50* ⊙ *Easter–Oct., Mon.–Sat. 10:15–4:30; Nov.–Easter, Mon. and Fri. 10:15–4:30; may close for lunch.*

Sports & the Outdoors

Skaigh Stables Farm (⊠ Skaigh La., near Okehampton, Belstone ☎ 01837/ 840917, 01837/840429 evenings) arranges horseback rides by the hour, half-day and full day from Easter through September.

Chagford

46 *9 mi southeast of Okehampton, 30 mi northeast of Plymouth.*

Chagford, once a tin-weighing station, was an area of fierce fighting between the Roundheads and the Cavaliers during the Civil War. Although officially a "town" since 1305, Chagford is more of a village, with old taverns grouped around a seasoned old church and a curious "pepper-pot" market house on the site of the old Stannary Court. With a handful of cafés and shops to browse around, it makes a convenient base from which to explore North Dartmoor.

The intriguing **Castle Drogo,** east of Chagford across A382 above the Teign Gorge, looks like a medieval fortress, complete with battlements, but construction actually took place between 1910 and 1930. Designed by Sir Edwin Lutyens for Julius Drewe, a wealthy grocer, the castle is only half finished (funds ran out). Inside, this magisterial pile combines medieval grandeur and early-20th-century comforts like the large bathrooms. ■ TIP➔ **You can play croquet on the lawn and take in awesome views over Dartmoor.** Take the A30 Exeter–Okehampton road to reach the castle, which is 4 mi northeast of Chagford and 6 mi south of A30. ⊠ *Drewsteignton* ☎ *01647/433306* ⊕ *www.nationaltrust.org.uk* ⌨ *£7, grounds only £4.50* ⊙ *Castle early Mar., weekends 11–4; mid-Mar.–Oct., Wed.–Mon. 11–5; early Nov., Wed.–Mon. 11–4; mid-Dec., weekends noon–4 or dusk. Grounds early Mar., weekends 10:30–4:30; mid-Mar.–Oct., daily 10:30–5:30; early Nov., daily 10:30–4:30; early Nov.–mid-Dec., Fri.–Sun. 11–4 or dusk.*

★ The **Devon Guild of Craftsmen,** the southwest's most important contemporary arts and crafts center, is in a converted 19th-century building on the edge of Dartmoor in the town of Bovey Tracey, 10 mi southeast of Chagford and 14 mi southwest of Exeter. The center has excellent exhibitions of local, national, and international crafts as well as a craft shop and café. ⊠ *Riverside Mill, Bovey Tracey* ☎ *01626/832223* ⊕ *www.crafts.org.uk* ⌨ *Free* ⊙ *Daily 10–5:30.*

■ **NEED A BREAK?**   **The Old Cottage Tea Shop** (⊠ 20 Fore St., Bovey Tracey ☎ 01626/833430), is the real deal, perfect for a light lunch or, even better, a cream tea served on bone china. Warm scones come in baskets, with black currant and other homemade jams and plenty of clotted cream.

Where to Stay & Eat

★ **£££££** ✕📠 **Gidleigh Park.** One of England's foremost hotels and restaurants, lauded in poetry by Ted Hughes, occupies an enclave of landscaped gardens and streams up a lengthy, winding private drive at the edge of Dartmoor. Antiques and luxurious country-house furnishings fill the long, half-timber Tudor-style residence, and the extremely pricey contemporary French restaurant (about £75 prix-fixe; reservations essential), directed by chef Michael Caines, has been showered with culinary awards. You may see why when you dig into the roast Gressingham duckling with garlic and cabbage. The locally pumped spring water is like no other. ⊠ *Gidleigh Park, TQ13 8HH* ☎ *01647/432367* 🖷 *01647/432574* ⊕ *www.gidleigh.com* 🛏 *14 rooms, 1 estate cottage* ♿ *Restaurant, putting green, tennis court, croquet, meeting rooms, helipad, some pets allowed; no a/c* ▭ *AE, DC, MC, V* ⏱ *MAP.*

★ **£££££** 📠 **Bovey Castle.** With the grandeur of a country estate and the facilities of a top modern hotel, Bovey Castle, built in 1906 for Viscount Hambledon, has it all. On its vast grounds, the hotel has an outstanding golf course and 24 mi of riverbank that can be used for salmon fishing. There is a resident pianist, and children have a dedicated barn filled with games. Enormous fireplaces and oak-panel rooms give a sense of early-20th-century pomp to the public rooms; bedrooms are luxurious, and even some of the bathrooms have great views across the valley. ⊠ *Off B3212, North Bovey TQ13 8RE* ☎ *01647/445016* 🖷 *01647/445020* ⊕ *www.boveycastle.com* 🛏 *65 rooms* ♿ *Restaurant, 18-hole golf course, 3 tennis courts, indoor pool, lake, fishing, spa, croquet, cinema, business services, some pets allowed (fee); no a/c* ▭ *AE, MC, V* ⏱ *BP.*

££ 📠 **Easton Court.** Discerning travelers such as C. P. Snow, Margaret Mead, John Steinbeck, and Evelyn Waugh—who completed *Brideshead Revisited* here—made this their Dartmoor home-away-from-home. The Tudor thatched-roof house has a garden and simple but elegant cottage-style rooms in an Edwardian wing; all rooms have views over the Teign Valley. ⊠ *Easton Cross, TQ13 8JL* ☎ *01647/433469* 🖷 *01647/433654* ⊕ *www.easton.co.uk* 🛏 *5 rooms* ♿ *No a/c, no kids under 10, no smoking* ▭ *MC, V* ⏱ *BP.*

DARTMOUTH, TORBAY & EXETER

Sheltered by the high mass of Dartmoor to the west, the yachting center of Dartmouth and the area known as the English Riviera, Torbay, enjoy a mild, warm climate. To the north is Exeter, Devon's county seat, an ancient city that has retained some of its medieval character despite wartime bombing. From Exeter you can explore south to Exmouth.

Dartmouth

47 *35 mi east of Plymouth, 35 mi south of Exeter.*

An important port in the Middle Ages, Dartmouth is today a favorite haunt of yacht owners. Traces of its past include the old houses in Bayard's Cove near Lower Ferry, the 16th-century covered Butterwalk, and the two castles guarding the entrance to the River Dart. The Royal Naval College, built in 1905, dominates the town.

£££–£££££ ✕ **New Angel.** John Burton Race, TV celebrity chef, has a restaurant in this prime spot by the waterfront; it's yet another sign of the country's ongoing food revolution. The menu is British and European, with an emphasis on local fare such as Brixham turbot grilled with béarnaise sauce or roast best end of Blackawton lamb with an herb crust. Open in the mornings for coffee and croissants, this place is relaxed and family-friendly. ⊠ *2 S. Embankment* ☎ *01803/839425* ⌂ *Reservations essential* ⊟ *AE, MC, V* ۞ *Closed Mon. No dinner Sun.*

££££–£££££ ⊡ **Royal Castle Hotel.** This hotel has truly earned the name "Royal"— several monarchs have slept here. Part of Dartmouth's historic waterfront (and consequently a hub of activity), it was built in the 17th century, reputedly of timber from wrecks of the Spanish Armada. Fireplaces and beamed ceilings are traditional features. Rooms come in different sizes and styles, but all are thoughtfully and richly furnished, with a liberal sprinkling of antiques. Number 6 has its own priest hole, a secret room used to hide Roman Catholic priests, and the pricier rooms facing the river have hot tubs. ⊠ *11 The Quay, TQ6 9PS* ☎ *01803/ 833033* ☒ *01803/835445* ⊕ *www.royalcastle.co.uk* ⇥ *25 rooms* ⌂ *Restaurant, cable TV, Wi-Fi, some hot tubs, 2 bars, meeting rooms, some pets allowed; no a/c* ⊟ *AE, MC, V* ۞⃝ *BP.*

EN ROUTE Two ferries cross the River Dart at Dartmouth; in summer, lines can be long, and you may want to try the inland route, heading west via A3122 to Halwell and then taking A381 north to Totnes. An attractive, relaxed approach to Dartmouth is by boat down the Dart from Totnes.

Totnes

48 *9 mi northwest of Dartmouth, 28 mi southwest of Exeter.*

This busy market town preserves some of its past, and on summer Tuesdays some shopkeepers dress in Elizabethan costume. Market day proper is Friday, when the town's status as a center of alternative medicine and culture becomes especially clear; Totnes is also celebrated for its many secondhand bookshops. The historic buildings include a guildhall and St. Mary's Church. You can climb up the hill in town to the ruins of **Totnes Castle**—a fine Norman motte and bailey design—for a wonderful view of Totnes and the River Dart. ☎ *01803/864406* ⊕ *www. english-heritage.org.uk* ⊡ *£2.40* ۞ *Apr.–June and Sept., daily 10–5; July and Aug., daily 10–6; Oct., daily 10–4.*

۞ Steam trains of the **South Devon Railway** run through 7 mi of the wooded Dart Valley between Totnes and Buckfastleigh, on the edge of Dartmoor. ⊠ *Near Totnes, Littlehempston* ☎ *0845/345–1420* ⊕ *www. southdevonrailway.org* ⊡ *£8.80 round-trip* ۞ *Easter–Oct., daily; call for winter times, including specials at Christmas and New Year's.*

££ ✕⊡ **Cott Inn.** The exterior of this inn—a long, low, thatched building— has remained almost unchanged since 1320. Flagstone floors, thick ceiling beams, and open fireplaces are other signs of age. The snug bedrooms, tucked beneath the eaves, are furnished in modern style. Good rustic

English meals are available from the restaurant (££–££££), and there's a carvery with roasted meats; you can eat more informally in the bar, which has three real ales on tap. ✉ *2 mi west of Totnes on A385, Dartington TQ9 6HE* ☎*01803/863777* ☷*01803/866629* ⊕*www.thecottinn. co.uk* ↳ *5 rooms* ⌂ *Restaurant, bar; no a/c* ➿ *MC, V* ⍾ *BP.*

Nightlife & the Arts

★ One of the foremost arts centers of the West Country, **Dartington Hall** (✉ Dartington ☎ 01803/847070 ⊕ www.dartingtonarts.org.uk) lies 2 mi northwest of Totnes. Renovated in 1925 by the American millionaire Dorothy Elmhirst and her husband, the medieval estate was an experimental school before it evolved into an arts and education center. There are concerts, a respected summer school of classical music with master classes and performances, film screenings, and exhibitions, usually with a contemporary slant. The gardens, free year-round, are the setting for outdoor performances of Shakespeare in summer. There's a café, and you can stay overnight in some rooms in the hall.

Shopping

Near Dartington Hall, 15 stores and two restaurants in and around an old cider press make up the **Dartington Cider Press Centre** (✉ Shinners Bridge, Dartington ☎ 01803/847500), which markets handmade Dartington crystal glassware, kitchenware, high-quality crafts, books, and toys from Devon and elsewhere. The farm shop sells fudge, ice cream, and cider, and Cranks is an excellent vegetarian restaurant.

Brixham

49 *10 mi southeast of Totnes by A385 and A3022.*

Brixham, at the southern point of Tor Bay, has kept much of its original charm, partly because it is still an active fishing village. Much of the catch goes straight to restaurants as far away as London. Sample fish-and-chips on the quayside, where there is a (surprisingly petite) full-scale reproduction of the vessel on which Sir Francis Drake circumnavigated the world.

Torbay

50 *5 mi north of Brixham via A3022, 23 mi south of Exeter.*

The most important resort area in South Devon, Torbay envisions itself as the center of the "English Riviera." Since 1968, the towns of Paignton and Torquay (pronounced tor-*kee*) have been amalgamated under the common moniker of Torbay. Torquay is the supposed site of the hotel in the popular British television comedy *Fawlty Towers* and was the home of mystery writer Agatha Christie. Fans should check out the exhibition devoted to Christie at the town museum; Torre Abbey Mansion, with the writer's reconstructed study, is closed until 2008.

The town has shed some of its old-fashioned image in recent years, with modern hotels, luxury villas, and apartments that climb the hillsides above the harbor. Still, Torquay is more like Brighton's maiden aunt in terms of energy and fizz, though a pubs-and-clubs culture makes an appearance on Friday and Saturday nights. Palm trees and other semi-tropical plants (a benefit of being near the warming Gulf Stream) flourish in the seafront gardens. The sea is a clear and intense blue, and in summer the whole place has the unmistakable air that was once called Continental.

Torbay's **beaches,** a mixture of sand and shingle (coarse gravel), have won awards for their water quality and facilities, and can get very crowded in summer. Apart from the central Torre Abbey Sands, they are scattered around town, often separated by the crumbly red cliffs characteristic of the area. To sun and swim, head for Anstey's Cove, a favorite spot for scuba divers, with more beaches farther along at neighboring Babbacombe.

> ### FAWLTY TOWERS
>
> John Cleese was inspired to write the TV series *Fawlty Towers* after he and the Monty Python team stayed at a hotel in Torquay while filming the series *Monty Python's Flying Circus* in the early 1970s. The "wonderfully rude" owner became the model for Basil Fawlty, the exasperated, accident-prone manager in the series. The owner died in 1981, but his hotel, the Gleneagles, is still going strong—though happily nothing like the chaotic Fawlty Towers.

Just outside Torbay lies a chocolate-box Devon village, **Cockington,** which has thatched cottages, a 14th-century forge, and the square-towered Church of St. George and St. Mary. Repair to the Old Mill for a café lunch or head to the Drum Inn, designed by Sir Edwin Lutyens to be an archetypal pub. On the village outskirts lies Cockington Court—a grand estate with shops and an eatery. Cockington has, however, more than a touch of the faux: cottages that don't sell anything put up signs to this effect.

Where to Stay & Eat

★ £££ ✕ **Capers.** A place for anyone who likes enthusiasm along with the food, this small, select restaurant goes in for serious cooking. Local fish ranks high on the menu, accompanied by vegetables and herbs grown by the chef. Try sea bass with sautéed potatoes, or curried crayfish risotto. ✉ *7 Lisburne Sq.* ☎ *01803/291177* ⊟ *AE, MC, V* ⊙ *Closed Mon. (Oct.–Easter), Sun. and 2 wks Jan. No lunch.*

£country£ ✕▥ **Mulberry House.** Dining at this simple but sophisticated restaurant with rooms is like dining in someone's private home; the furnishings are light and airy, and service is personable. Local fish and meat and vegetarian dishes are always on the menu, for example mushroom parcels with a creamy herb sauce, and Brixham sole. (The restaurant, £21–£24 for fixed-price menus, is closed Sunday evening and lunch Monday through Thursday; it's open only to overnight guests Monday and Tuesday evenings.) Upstairs, guest rooms are bright and well cared for, with plants and antiques. One has a private bathroom adjacent to the room. ✉ *1 Scarborough Rd., TQ2 5UJ* ⊕ *www.mulberryhousetorquay. co.uk* ☎ *01803/213639* ⇨ *3 rooms* ⌂ *Restaurant; no smoking* ⊟ *No credit cards.*

£££££ ▥ **The Imperial.** This enormous pile perched above the sea, overlooking Torbay, exudes Victorian splendor. Magnificent gardens surround the property, and the interior of the 1866 hotel is, well, imperial, with chandeliers, marble floors, and the general air of a bygone world. Most of the traditionally furnished bedrooms are large and comfortable, and many have balconies. ⊠ *Park Hill Rd., TQ1 2DG* ☎ *01803/294301* 🖷 *01803/298293* ⊕ *www.paramount-hotels.co.uk* ⇱ *152 rooms, 17 suites* ⸜ *2 restaurants, cable TV with movies, tennis court, 2 pools (1 indoor), health club, sauna, squash, business services, meeting rooms; no a/c* ⊟ *AE, DC, MC, V* ⍓ *BP.*

££ 🏨 **Fairmount House Hotel.** Near the village of Cockington, on the edge of Torquay, this relaxed, family-run Victorian hotel has a pleasant, south-facing garden. Guest rooms are solidly furnished; two have direct access to the garden, as does the Conservatory Bar. ⊠ *Herbert Rd., Chelston, Torquay TQ2 6RW* ☎☎ *01803/605446* ⊕ *www.fairmounthousehotel.co.uk* ⇱ *8 rooms* ⸜ *Dining room, bar, some pets allowed (fee); no a/c, no room phones* ⊟ *MC, V* ⍓ *BP.*

Exeter

23 mi north of Torbay, 48 mi northeast of Plymouth, 85 mi southwest of Bristol, 205 mi southwest of London.

Devon's county seat, Exeter, has been the capital of the region since the Romans established a fortress here 2,000 years ago. Evidence of the Roman occupation remains in the city walls. Although it was heavily bombed in 1942, Exeter retains much of its medieval character, as well as examples of the gracious architecture of the 18th and 19th centuries.

Main Attractions

★ ⑤ **Cathedral of St. Peter.** At the heart of Exeter, the great Gothic cathedral was begun in 1275 and completed almost a century later. Its twin towers are even older survivors of an earlier Norman cathedral. Rising from a forest of ribbed columns, the nave's 300-foot stretch of unbroken Gothic vaulting is the longest in the world. Myriad statues, tombs, and memorial plaques adorn the interior. In the minstrels' gallery, high up on the left of the nave, stands a group of carved figures singing and playing musical instruments, including bagpipes. The **Close,** a pleasant green space for relaxing, surrounds the cathedral. Don't miss the 400-year-old door to No. 10, the bishop of Crediton's house, ornately carved with angels' and lions' heads. ⊠ *Cathedral Close* ☎ *01392/285983* ⊕ *www.exeter-cathedral.org.uk* 🎫 *£3.50 suggested donation* ☉ *Daily 9:30–5. Free guided tours Apr.–Oct., weekdays at 11 and 2:30, Sat. at 11, Sun. at 4; July–Sept., Mon.–Sat. at 12:30.*

OFF THE
BEATEN
PATH

POWDERHAM CASTLE – Seat of the earls of Devon, this notable stately home 8 mi south of Exeter is famed for its staircase hall, a soaring fantasia of white stuccowork on a turquoise background, constructed in 1739–69. Other sumptuous rooms, adorned with family portraits by Sir Godfrey Kneller and Sir Joshua Reynolds, were used in the Merchant Ivory film *Remains of the Day.* A tower built in 1400 by Sir Philip Courtenay, ancestor of the current owners, stands in the deer park. The restaurant serves traditional English fare, and there's a farm shop and plant

Cathedral of
St. Peter **51**

Custom House . **56**

Guildhall **53**

Mol's Coffee
House **52**

Quay House ... **57**

Rougemont
Gardens **55**

Royal Albert
Memorial
Museum **54**

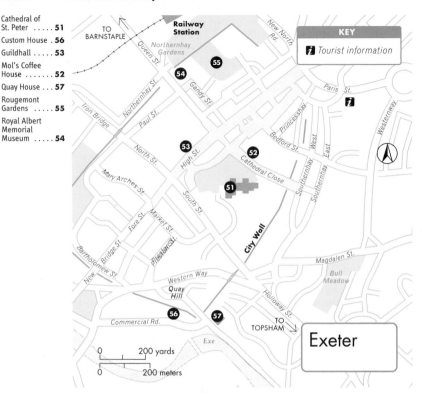

center. ⊠ *A379, Kenton* ☎ *01626/890243* ⊕ *www.powderham.co.uk*
🎫 *£7.45, £4.90 grounds only* ⊗ *Apr.–Oct., Sun.–Fri. 10–5:30.*

54 **Royal Albert Memorial Museum.** This museum houses natural-history displays, superb Exeter silverware, and the work of some West Country
artists. There is also an excellent international gallery and a fine archaeological section. The museum is the focus of a multiyear redevelopment
plan designed to increase its appeal. ⊠ *Queen St.* ☎ *01392/665858*
⊕ *www.exeter.gov.uk* 🎫 *Free* ⊗ *Mon.–Sat. 10–5.*

Also Worth Seeing

56 **Custom House.** Exeter's historic waterfront on the River Exe was the center of the city's medieval wool industry, and the Custom House, built
in 1682 on the quay, attests to the city's prosperity. Victorian warehouses
flank the city's earliest surviving brick building.

53 **Guildhall.** Just behind the Close, this is said to be the oldest municipal
building in the country still in use. The current hall, with its Renaissance
portico, dates from 1330, although a guildhall has occupied this site since
at least 1160. Its timber-braced roof, one of the earliest in England, dates
from about 1460. ⊠ *High St.* ☎ *01392/665500* 🎫 *Free* ⊗ *Weekdays
10:30–1 and 2–4, Sat. 10–noon (alternate Sat. only in winter), unless
in use for a civic function.*

⑳ Mol's Coffee House. With its half-timber facade bearing the coat of arms of Elizabeth I, this building (now a map shop), on the corner of Cathedral Close, is redolent of bygone times. It is said that Sir Francis Drake met his admirals here to plan strategy against the Spanish Armada in 1588.

㊲ Quay House. This late-17th-century stone warehouse houses the Heritage Centre, with documents on the maritime history of the city and an audiovisual display. ⊠ *The Quay* ☎ *01392/271611* ⌨ *Free* ☉ *Apr.–Oct., daily 10–5; Nov.–Mar., weekends 11–4.*

NEED A BREAK?

At the **Prospect Inn** (⊠ The Quay ☎ 01392/273152) you can contemplate the quayside comings and goings over a pint of real ale and a hot or cold meal. The nautical theme comes through in pictures and the ship's wheel hanging from the ceiling.

㊳ Rougemont Gardens. These gardens behind the Royal Albert Memorial Museum were laid out at the end of the 18th century. The land was once part of the defensive ditch of Rougemont Castle, built in 1068 by decree of William the Conqueror. The gardens contain the original Norman gatehouse and the remains of the Roman city wall, the latter forming part of the ancient castle's outer wall; nothing else remains of the castle. ⊠ *Off Queen St.*

Where to Stay & Eat

★ £££££ ✕ **St. Olaves.** One of the finest dining spots in the West Country, this restaurant in a Georgian house with a walled garden is part of St. Olaves Court Hotel. From the fixed-price, seasonal menus, you might try terrine of wild duck, guinea fowl, and wild mushrooms or the baked monkfish stuffed with prawns and tarragon. The bar menu is a cheaper lunchtime option. ⊠ *Mary Arches St.* ☎ *01392/217736* ▭ *MC, V.*

££–£££ ✕ **Carved Angel Café.** This fashionable café-bistro facing the cathedral across the green has high-quality sandwiches, wraps, and cakes, as well as good coffee and freshly squeezed juices during the day (no reservations at lunchtime). Warm-hued walls set off the thick oak chairs and tables, and you can unwind to cool modern music. In the evening, choose from an eclectic menu that might include risotto of ratatouille with a Parmesan and pesto sauce; a three-course fixed-price menu is available Monday through Thursday. Service, usually good, can be interminably slow when things get busy. ⊠ *21A Cathedral Yard* ☎ *01392/210303* ▭ *MC, V* ☉ *No dinner Sun.*

£–££ ✕ **Hansons.** Near the cathedral, this old-fashioned spot is ideal for lunch, coffee, or snacks when you're seeing the sights. You can also sample one of Devon's famous cream teas, served with jam, scones, and clotted cream, or show up earlier for a cooked English breakfast. ⊠ *1 Cathedral Close* ☎ *01392/276913* ▭ *AE, DC, MC, V* ☉ *Closed Sun. No dinner.*

★ £–££ ✕ **Herbie's.** A mellow stop for lunch or dinner, this friendly, no-frills vegetarian restaurant is ideal for unwinding over leisurely conversation. You can snack on pita bread with hummus, or tackle the carrot and cashew nut loaf or Caribbean coconut and black-pea rundown (a spicy stew). All wines and the superb ice cream are organic. ⊠ *15 North St.* ☎ *01392/258473* ▭ *MC, V* ☉ *Closed Sun. No dinner Mon.*

£–££   ✕ **Ship Inn.** Here you can lift a tankard of stout in the very rooms where Sir Francis Drake and Sir Walter Raleigh enjoyed their ale. Drake, in fact, once wrote, "Next to mine own shippe, I do most love that old 'Shippe' in Exon." The pub dishes out casual bar fare, and the upstairs restaurant serves good sausage and mashed potatoes, and baked cod with tarragon and wine. ✉ *St. Martin's La.* ☎ *01392/272040* ▤ *MC, V.*

★   ✕▥ **Royal Clarence Hotel.** Perfectly located within the Cathedral Close,
££££–£££££   this antique establishment was acquired in 2003 by master chef Michael Caines (of Gidleigh Park fame), who has successfully transformed it into an upscale boutique hotel. The lime-light rests firmly on the ultrachic restaurant (£££–££££), with its French-accented contemporary fare. A more relaxed café-bar (easier on the wallet) serves coffee, snacks, and meals all day; there's live jazz some evenings. Public areas reflect the restaurant's clean-lined, modern style, and the beautifully designed bedrooms come with state-of-the-art technology, though some are small and viewless. ✉ *Cathedral Yard, EX1 1HD* ☎ *01392/319955 hotel, 01392/223638 restaurant* 🖷 *01392/439423* ⊕ *www.abodehotels.co.uk* ⇆ *53 rooms* ⚴ *Restaurant, 2 bars, in-room DVDs, Wi-Fi, gym, spa, meeting rooms, some pets allowed (fee); no a/c* ▤ *AE, DC, MC, V.*

> ### RIGHT ROYAL
>
> Opposite the cathedral, the 1769 Royal Clarence Hotel was England's first inn to be described as a "hotel"—a designation applied by an enterprising French manager. It is named after the duchess of Clarence, who stayed here in 1827 on her way to visit her husband, the future William IV.

£££–££££   ✕▥ **Hotel Barcelona.** This hip, classy hotel (part of the Alias mini-chain)
Fodor$Choice   occupies the old redbrick eye hospital, as the long corridors and big el-
★   evators testify. Bright, Gaudí-esque furnishings and ornaments from the 1930s to the 1960s give the rooms flair, and the aquamarine bathrooms with mosaic tiling are luxurious. You can find Spanish and other Mediterranean flavors in the pavilion-like bistro-restaurant, Café Paradiso. ✉ *Magdalen St., EX2 4HY* ☎ *01392/281000* 🖷 *01392/281001* ⊕ *www.hotelbarcelona-uk.com* ⇆ *46 rooms* ⚴ *Restaurant, cable TV with movies, in-room VCRs, in-room data ports, nightclub, meeting rooms, some pets allowed (fee); no a/c* ▤ *AE, DC, MC, V.*

££   ✕▥ **White Hart.** Guests have been welcomed to this inn since the 15th century, and it is said that Oliver Cromwell stabled his horses here. Beyond the lovely cobbled entrance, the main building retains all the trappings of a period inn—beams, stone walls, courtyard—but there are also fully modern bedrooms in one wing. The hotel has a casual bar-restaurant (£–£££) where you can order such traditional English dishes as salmon and lamb casserole with dumplings. ✉ *66 South St., EX1 1EE* ☎ *01392/279897* 🖷 *01392/250159* ⊕ *www.pubswithrooms.co.uk* ⇆ *55 rooms* ⚴ *Restaurant, bar, wine bar; no a/c* ▤ *AE, DC, MC, V* ⏉◯⏉ *BP.*

££   ▥ **Georgian Lodge.** There's nothing fancy in this quiet hotel close by Exeter Central train station, just clean, modern, and functional rooms, small but more than adequate for a night or two. The main benefit is the location in a calm Georgian square, just a stroll away from all the sights. ⊠ *5 Bystock Terr., EX4 4HY* ☎ *01392/213079* ⊕ *www.exeterhotels. com* ⇄ *8 rooms* ⌂ *Wi-Fi; no a/c, no smoking* ⊟ *MC, V* ⎜◎⎜ *BP.*

Nightlife & the Arts

Among the best known of the West Country's festivals, the **Exeter Festival** (☎ 01392/265205) mixes musical and theater events each July. Some of London's best companies often stage plays at the **Northcott Theatre** (⊠ Stocker Rd. ☎ 01392/493493).

Shopping

Many of Exeter's most interesting shops are along Gandy Street, off the main High Street drag, with several good food and clothes outlets. Exeter was the silver-assay office for the West Country, and the earliest example of Exeter silver (now a museum piece) dates from 1218; Victorian pieces are still sold. The Exeter assay mark is three castles. **Bruford's of Exeter** (⊠ 17 The Guildhall Centre, Queen St. ☎ 01392/254901) stocks antique jewelry and silver.

Sports & the Outdoors

Saddles and Paddles (⊠ 4 Kings Wharf, the Quay ☎ 01392/424241) rents bikes, kayaks, and canoes and is handily placed for a 7-mi route along the scenic Exeter Canal Trail, which follows the River Exe and the Exeter Ship Canal.

Topsham

58 *4 mi southeast of Exeter on B3182.*

This town, full of narrow streets and hidden courtyards, was once a bustling port, and it remains rich in 18th-century houses and inns. Occupying a 17th-century Dutch-style merchant's house beside the river, the **Topsham Museum** has period-furnished rooms and eclectic displays about everything from local history to wildlife; note the memorabilia belonging to the late actress Vivien Leigh. ⊠ *25 The Strand* ☎ *01392/ 873244* ⊡ *Free* ⊙ *Easter–Oct., Mon., Wed., and weekends 2–5.*

★ The 16-sided, nearly circular **A la Ronde,** surely one of the most unusual houses in England, was built in 1798 by two cousins inspired by the Church of San Vitale in Ravenna, Italy. Among the 18th- and 19th-century curiosities here is an elaborate display of feathers and shells. The house is 5 mi south of Topsham. ⊠ *Summer La., on A376 near Exmouth* ☎ *01395/265514* ⊕ *www.nationaltrust.org.uk* ⊡ *£5* ⊙ *Apr.–Oct., Sun.–Thurs. 11–5:30; last admission at 5.*

EN ROUTE
The **Jurassic Coast** (⊕ www.jurassiccoast.com), from Exmouth to Studland Bay in Dorset, 95 mi to the east, has been designated a World Heritage Site because of the rich geological record of ancient rocks and fossils exposed here. The reddish, grass-topped cliffs of the region are punctuated by quiet seaside resorts such as Budleigh Salterton, Sidmouth, and Seaton. For more information about the Jurassic Coast, *see* Lyme Regis *in* Chapter 3.

Beer

❺❾ *22 mi east of Topsham, 26 mi east of Exeter, 33 mi south of Taunton.*

Beer, just outside Seaton, was once a favorite smugglers' haunt, and this fishing village has remained fairly unchanged. It was the source of the white stone used for numerous Devon churches, Exeter Cathedral, and, farther afield, Winchester Cathedral, Westminster Abbey, and the Tower of London. A tour of the **Beer Quarry Caves,** worked from Roman times until 1900, explores the impressive underground network. A small exhibition includes tools and examples of carved stone. ⊠ *Quarry La.* ☎ *01297/680282* ⊕ *www.beerquarrycaves.fsnet.co.uk* 🎫 *£5.50* ⊙ *Easter–Sept., daily 10–5:30; Oct., daily 11–4:30; last tour 30 mins before closing.*

Honiton

❻⓪ *10 mi northwest of Beer on A3052/A375, 19 mi south of Taunton.*

Handsome Georgian houses line Honiton's long High Street. Modern storefronts have intruded, but the original facades remain at second-floor level. For 300 years the town was known for lace-making, and the industry was revived when Queen Victoria selected the fabric for her wedding veil in 1840. Lace has not been made here commercially since the early 20th century, but individuals keep up the craft.

After viewing the glorious collection of lace at **Allhallows Museum**—in what is claimed to be the town's oldest building—it's worth delving into the antiques shops where prized early examples are sold. ⊠ *High St.* ☎ *01404/44966* ⊕ *www.honitonmuseum.co.uk* 🎫 *£2* ⊙ *Easter–Oct., weekdays 9:30–4:30, Sat. 9:30–1.*

Where to Stay & Eat

££–£££ ✕ **The Holt.** For a satisfying lunch or dinner, try this pub and restaurant at the bottom of the High Street. Downstairs is a vibrant, chattery pub with soft orange walls and fine Otter real ales; the buzz wafts upstairs, where you can dine on such dishes as home-smoked salmon with asparagus and deep-fried poached egg, and lamb cutlets. ⊠ *178 High St.* ☎ *01404/47707* ☰ *MC, V* ⊙ *No dinner Sun.*

£££££ ✕🛏 **Combe House.** Rolling parkland surrounds this luxurious Elizabethan manor house. From the imposing Great Hall, with its huge, open fireplace, to the spacious, individually decorated bedrooms, the emphasis is on country-house style that unites antiques and modern comfort. The restaurant (£40 fixed-price menu) prepares such sophisticated creations as saddle of rabbit with black pudding ravioli and Jerusalem artichoke velouté, and there's a wide-ranging wine list. Hotel guests can fish on a 1½-mi stretch of the River Otter and explore Gittisham, just west of Honiton, once described as "the ideal English village" by Prince Charles. There's a two-night minimum stay on weekends. ⊠ *Gittisham EX14 3AD* ☎ *01404/540400* 🖷 *01404/46004* ⊕ *www.thishotel.com* 🛏 *14 rooms, 1 suite* ⚫ *Restaurant, fishing, meeting rooms, some pets allowed (fee); no a/c* ☰ *MC, V* ⦿ *BP.*

Shopping

Honiton has several dozen fine antiques stores. The **Lace Shop** (⊠ 44 High St. ☎ 01404/42416) has everything needed for lace-making and examples of old and new work for sale.

WEST COUNTRY ESSENTIALS

Transportation

BY AIR

Bristol International Airport, a few miles southwest of the city on the A38, has flights to and from destinations in Britain and Europe. Continental runs a direct daily service between Bristol and New York. Plymouth has a small airport 3 mi from town. Exeter International Airport is 5 mi east of Exeter, 2 mi from the M5 motorway. Newquay Airport, 5 mi east of town, has daily flights to London Stansted and London Gatwick. All four airports have flights to the Isles of Scilly in summer; Land's End Airport also connects daily, and British International operates helicopter flights to the islands from Penzance. Isles of Scilly Travel (⇨ By Boat & Ferry) runs the Skybus air service to St. Mary's from Land's End, Newquay, and, from March through September, Southampton, Bristol, and Exeter. Budget airline Ryanair flies from Newquay to London's Stansted airport, and Air Southwest flies in and out of Bristol.

🖪 **Bristol International Airport** ⊠ Bridgwater Rd., Lulsgate, Bristol ☎ 0870/121–2747 ⊕ www.bristolairport.co.uk. **British International** ⊠ Penzance Heliport, A30, Penzance ☎ 01736/363871 ⊕ www.scillyhelicopter.co.uk. **Exeter International Airport** ⊠ M5, Junction 29, Exeter ☎ 01392/367433 ⊕ www.exeter-airport.co.uk. **Newquay Airport** ⊠ St. Mawgan, Newquay ☎ 01637/860600 ⊕ www.newquay-airport.co.uk. **Plymouth City Airport** ⊠ Crownhill, Plymouth ☎ 01752/204090 ⊕ www.plymouthairport.com. **Skybus** ⊠ Land's End Airport, St. Just ☎ 0845/710–5555, 01736/334220 outside U.K. ⊕ www.ios-travel.co.uk.

BY BOAT & FERRY

Isles of Scilly Travel operates ferries from Penzance to St. Mary's at least four times weekly from late March through early November. Travel time is 2 hours and 40 minutes, and the trip can be rough.

🖪 **Isles of Scilly Travel** ☎ 0845/710–5555, 1736/334220 outside U.K. ⊕ www.ios-travel.co.uk.

BUS TRAVEL

National Express buses leave London's Victoria Coach Station for Bristol (2½ hours), Exeter (4¼ hours), Plymouth (4¾ hours), and Penzance (about 9 hours). Megabus offer a cheap, though not very comfortable, way of getting between Plymouth, Exeter, and London.

The bus company Stagecoach Devon covers mainly South Devon. First runs most of the services in North Devon, in Plymouth, and throughout Cornwall. Truronian operates in West Cornwall. Ask any of these companies about money-saving one-, three-, and seven-day Explorer passes good for unlimited travel. Buses serve the main towns, but it's best to have a car if you want to explore off the beaten path. For public transportation information, contact Traveline.

FARES & SCHEDULES ⚑ **First** ☎ 0845/600-1420 ⊕ www.firstgroup.com. **Megabus** ☎ 0900/160-0900 ⊕ www.megabus.com. **National Express** ☎ 0870/580-8080 ⊕ www.nationalexpress. com. **Stagecoach Devon** ☎ 0870/608-2608 ⊕ www.stagecoachbus.com. **Traveline** ☎ 0870/608-2608 ⊕ www.traveline.org.uk. **Truronian** ☎ 01872/273453 ⊕ www. truronian.co.uk.

CAR TRAVEL

The fastest route from London to the West Country is via the M4 and M5 motorways, bypassing Bristol (115 mi) and heading south to Exeter, in Devon (172 mi). Allow two hours at least to drive to Bristol from London, three to Exeter. Taking the M3 and A303 route is shorter and more scenic, but you may encounter delays. The main roads heading west are A30—which burrows through the center of Devon and Cornwall all the way to Land's End at the tip of Cornwall—A39 (near the northern shore of the peninsula), and A38 (near the southern shore of the peninsula, south of Dartmoor and taking in Plymouth). West of Plymouth, there are few main roads, which results in heavy traffic in summer. Still, having a car give you maximum freedom to explore rural areas.

ROAD CONDITIONS Driving can be tricky, especially as you travel farther west. Most small roads are twisting country lanes flanked by high stone walls and thick hedges that severely restrict visibility.

TRAIN TRAVEL

First Great Western and South West Trains serve the region from London's Paddington and Waterloo stations; contact National Rail Enquiries for details. Average travel time to Exeter is 2½ hours; to Plymouth, 3½ hours; and to Penzance, about 5½ hours.

CUTTING COSTS Regional Rail Rover tickets provide 8 days' unlimited travel throughout the West Country in any 15-day period, and localized Rovers cover Devon or Cornwall.

⚑ **National Rail Enquiries** ☎ 0845/748-4950 ⊕ www.nationalrail.co.uk.

Contacts & Resources

EMERGENCIES

⚑ Ambulance, fire, police ☎ 999. **Derriford Hospital** ✉ Derriford, Plymouth ☎ 01752/777111. **Royal Cornwall Hospital (Treliske)** ✉ A390, Higher Town, Truro ☎ 01872/250000. **Royal Devon and Exeter Hospital** ✉ Barrack Rd., Exeter ☎ 01392/411611.

INTERNET

If your hotel or B&B cannot supply an Internet connection, you'll find cafés and public libraries in all the major centers where you can get online. Broadband is widespread and Wi-Fi increasingly so.

⚑ Internet Cafés **Bristol Life** ✉ 27 Baldwin St., Bristol ☎ 0117/945-9926 ⊕ www. internet-exchange.co.uk. **Exeter Central library** ✉ Castle St., Exeter ☎ 01392/384206. **Carp Internet Café** ✉ 32 Frankfort Gate, Plymouth ☎ 01752/221777.

TOUR OPTIONS

South West Tourism (⇨ Visitor Information) and local tourist information centers have lists of qualified guides. West Country Tour Guides
(Blue Badge) offers walking tours around Plymouth's old town and can
arrange tours throughout Devon and Cornwall.

🄵 **West Country Tourist Guides (Blue Badge)** ☎ 01579/370224 ⊕ www.luxsoft.
demon.co.uk/awctg.

VISITOR INFORMATION

Local tourist information centers are usually open Monday through Saturday 9:30 to 5:30; they are listed after the regional offices below by
town. The Exeter tourist office will move to the Princesshay development in summer 2007; at this writing the address was not set, but the
phone may remain the same.

🄵 **South West Tourism** ✉ Woodwater Park, Pynes Hill, Exeter EX2 5WT ☎ 0870/442-
0880 🖷 0870/442-0881 ⊕ www.visitsouthwest.co.uk. **Cornwall Tourist Board** ✉ Pydar
House, Pydar St., Truro TR1 1EA ☎ 01872/322900 🖷 01872/322895 ⊕ www.
cornwalltouristboard.co.uk. **Devon Tourist Information Service** ☏ Box 55, Barnstaple EX32 8YR ☎0870/608-5531, 1392/382168 from outside the U.K. ⊕www.discoverdevon.
com. **Somerset Visitor Centre** ✉ Sedgemoor Service Station, M5 Southbound ☎ 01934/
750833 🖷 01934/750646 ⊕ www.somerset.gov.uk.

Bristol ✉ The Annexe, Wildscreen Walk, Harbourside, BS1 5DB ☎ 0906/711-2191 50p
per min, 0845/408-0474 accommodations line, 870/444-0654 from outside U.K. ✉ Galleries Shopping Centre, Broadmead ☎ No phone ⊕ www.visitbristol.co.uk. **Exeter**
✉ Civic Centre, Paris St., EX1 1JJ ☎ 01392/265700 ⊕ www.exeter.gov.uk. **Falmouth** ✉ 11
Market Strand, TR11 3DF ☎ 01326/312300 ⊕ www.go-cornwall.com. **Glastonbury**
✉ The Tribunal, 9 High St., BA6 9DP ☎ 01458/832954 ⊕ www.glastonburytic.co.uk.
Isles of Scilly ✉ Hugh St., Hugh Town, St. Mary's, TR21 0LL ☎ 01720/422536 ⊕ www.
simplyscilly.co.uk. **Penzance** ✉ Station Approach, TR18 2NF ☎ 01736/362207 ⊕ www.
go-cornwall.com. **Plymouth** ✉ Plymouth Mayflower, 3-5 The Barbican, PL1 2LR ☎ 01752/
266030 ⊕ www.visitplymouth.co.uk. **St. Ives** ✉ The Guildhall, Street-an-Pol, TR26 2DS
☎ 01736/796297 ⊕ www.go-cornwall.com. **Taunton** ✉ Paul St., TA1 3XZ ☎ 01823/336344
⊕ www.tauntondeane.gov.uk. **Truro** ✉ City Hall, Boscawen St., TR1 2NE ☎ 01872/274555
⊕ www.truro.gov.uk. **Wells** ✉ Town Hall, Market Pl., BA5 2RB ☎ 01749/672552
⊕ www.wells-uk.com.

The Thames Valley

5

WORD OF MOUTH

"Windsor Castle looks like a castle outside, but inside is mostly reasonably sumptuous apartments and the like. At a pinch, your sons could indulge a few military fantasies. . . . I've always found the castle a bit girly: it is, after all, where Her Maj prefers to live, and is a working royal palace."
—flanneruk

"Most folks who say Oxford is 'industrial' have not been there. Either Cambridge or Oxford is fine—wonderful in fact . . . But if you also want to visit things outside the city, Oxford is better. Blenheim Palace is just up the road and easy by local bus."
—janisj

Updated by
Christi
Daugherty

THE AREA JUST WEST OF LONDON—including the prosperous country-side of Berkshire and Oxfordshire—is called the Thames Valley for the river that winds through it on its way to the sea, a river as significant in history as the Seine or the Danube. The Thames River floods meadows in spring and fall and ripples past places holding significance not just for England but also the world. In Runnymede, on a riverside greensward, the Magna Carta was signed, a crucial step in the Western world's progress toward democracy.

Travelers to London are in luck that such rich historical treasures are within an easy day trip of the city. Anyone who wants to understand the mystique of the British monarchy should visit Windsor, 45 minutes from London by train and home to the medieval and massive Windsor Castle, the Queen's favorite home. Farther upstream, the quadrangles and spires of Oxford are the hallmarks of one of the world's most famous universities. Within 10 mi of Oxford are the storybook village of Woodstock and Blenheim Palace, one of the grandest houses in all the land.

The railroads and motorways carrying traffic to and from London have turned much of this area into commuter territory, but you can still find timeless villages and miles of relaxing countryside. The stretches of the Thames near Marlow, Henley, and Sonning-on-Thames are lovely, with rowing clubs, piers, and sturdy waterside cottages and villas. It all conspires to make this a wonderful find, even for experienced travelers.

Exploring the Thames Valley

A great place to begin an exploration of the Thames Valley is the town of Windsor, home to the Queen's favorite palace. From there you can follow the river to Henley-on-Thames, site of the famous regatta, and then make a counterclockwise sweep west to Ewelme, the countryside immortalized by Kenneth Grahame's *The Wind in the Willows*. Next, you can head north to Oxford, and end with a visit to some stately homes and palaces.

About the Restaurants

Londoners weekend here, and where they go, stellar restaurants follow. Windsor, Henley, and Great Milton claim some of Britain's best tables. Simple pub food, as well as classic French cuisine, can be enjoyed in waterside settings at many restaurants beside the Thames. Even in towns away from the river, well-heeled commuters and Oxford professors support top-flight establishments. Reservations are strongly recommended, especially on weekends.

About the Hotels

From converted country houses to refurbished Elizabethan inns, the region's accommodations are rich in history and distinctive in appeal. Many hotels cultivate traditional gardens and retain a sense of the past with impressive collections of antiques. Book ahead, particularly in summer; you're competing for rooms with many Londoners in search of a getaway.

WHAT IT COSTS In pounds				
£££££	**££££**	**£££**	**££**	**£**
RESTAURANTS over £22	£18–£22	£13–£17	£7–£12	under £7
HOTELS over £160	£120–£160	£90–£119	£60–£89	under £60

Restaurant prices are for a main course at dinner. Hotel prices are for two people in a standard double room in high season, including V.A.T., with no meals or, if indicated, CP (with continental breakfast), BP (Breakfast Plan, with full breakfast), or MAP (Modified American Plan, with breakfast and dinner).

Timing

As with all of England, the depths of winter are not the ideal time to visit, as the winter chill can chase you indoors. High summer is lovely, but droves of visitors have the same effect on some travelers as bad weather. If crowds trouble you, but you relish a bit of sunshine, consider visiting in late spring or early fall, when the weather is not too bad, and the crowds have headed home for the school year. Book tickets and accommodations well in advance for Henley's Royal Regatta at the cusp of June and July or Ascot's Royal Meeting in mid-June. Visiting at Eton and the Oxford colleges is much more restricted during term time (generally September to late March and late April to mid-July). Most stately homes are open March through September or October only—call in advance if you're planning an itinerary. Avoid any driving in the London area during afternoon and morning rush hours.

WINDSOR & ENVIRONS

Windsor Castle is one of the jewels of the area known as Royal Windsor, but a journey around this section of the Thames has other classic pleasures. The town of Eton holds the eponymous public school, Ascot has its famous racecourse, and Cliveden is a stately home turned into a very grand hotel. At Runnymede you can honor an early step toward democracy.

Windsor

▶ ❶ *21 mi west of London.*

Only a small part of old Windsor—the settlement that grew up around the town's famous castle in the Middle Ages—has survived. The charming town is not what it was in the time of Sir John Falstaff and the *Merry Wives of Windsor*, when it was famous for its convivial inns—in 1650, it had about 70 of them. Only a handful remain, with the others replaced, it seems, by endless tea shops. Windsor can feel overrun by tourists in the high season, but, even so, romantics will appreciate narrow, cobbled Church Lane and noble Queen Charlotte Street, opposite the castle entrance.

★ The imposing turrets and towers of **Windsor Castle** are visible for miles. From William the Conqueror to Queen Victoria, the kings and queens of England added towers and wings to the brooding structure, and it's now the largest inhabited castle in the world. Despite the multiplicity

GREAT ITINERARIES

With a car, you can see all the places outlined below on day trips from London, but it's worth staying at that perfect riverside inn or village hotel and settling in for a night or more. The area offers the greatest pleasure to those willing to leave the main roads to explore the smaller towns.

Numbers in the text correspond to numbers in the margin and on the Thames Valley and Oxford maps.

IF YOU HAVE 3 DAYS

Begin at ⊞ **Windsor ❶** ►, where royalty is the predominant note, and spend a morning visiting the castle, leaving part of the day for Eton College and Windsor Great Park. The next day, follow the river upstream, taking in the village of **Marlow ❻**, where the pubs offer decent snacks for lunch. Head toward **Henley-on-Thames ❼**, where the Thames forms a harmonious dialogue with the medieval buildings alongside, and easy and tranquil walks beckon upstream or down. Reserve the last morning for scholarly ⊞ **Oxford ❶ –㉔**, with an afternoon visit to nearby **Woodstock ㉖**—a lovely English village—and **Blenheim Palace ㉗**,

birthplace of Winston Churchill and one of the most spectacular houses in England.

IF YOU HAVE 5 DAYS

Make your base at ⊞ **Windsor ❶** ► for your first night. From there you can take excursions to **Ascot ❹**, for some of England's finest horse racing, and, to the north, **Cliveden ❺**. For your second night, consider staying in ⊞ **Henley-on-Thames ❼**, from which it's an easy trip to the aristocratic **Mapledurham House ❾** and a cluster of attractive Thames-side villages, such as **Sonning-on-Thames ❽** and **Dorchester-on-Thames ㉚**. Reserve the third day and night for the medieval wonders of ⊞ **Oxford ❶ –㉔**; on your fourth day head for the nearby 18th-century village of ⊞ **Woodstock ㉖**, site of magisterial **Blenheim Palace ㉗**. For the final day, swing eastward to the town of **Great Milton ㉛** for perhaps the grandest luncheon of your English trip, at Le Manoir aux Quat' Saisons. Next, pay a call on one or two of a trio of stately homes: Waddesdon Manor near **Aylesbury ㉜**, **Woburn Abbey ㉞**, or **Althorp ㉟**.

5

of hands involved in its design, the palace manages to have a unity of style and character. The most impressive view of Windsor Castle is from the A332 road, coming into town from the south.

William the Conqueror began work on the castle in the 11th century, and Edward III modified and extended it in the mid-1300s. One of Edward's largest contributions was the enormous and distinctive **Round Tower.** Finally, between 1824 and 1837, George IV transformed the still essentially medieval castle into the fortified royal palace you see today. Most of England's kings and queens have demonstrated their undying attachment to the castle, the only royal residence in continuous use by the Royal Family since the Middle Ages.

As you enter the castle, **Henry VIII's gateway** leads uphill into the wide castle precincts, where you are free to wander. Across from the entrance is the exquisite **St. George's Chapel** (closed Sunday). Here lie 10 of the kings of England, including Henry VI, Charles I, and Henry VIII (Jane Seymour is the only one of his six wives buried here). One of the noblest buildings in England, the chapel was built in the Perpendicular style popular in the 15th and 16th centuries, with elegant stained-glass windows, a high, vaulted ceiling, and intricately carved choir stalls. The colorful heraldic banners of the Knights of the Garter—the oldest British Order of Chivalry, founded by Edward III in 1348—hang in the choir. The ceremony in which the knights are installed as members of the order has been held here with much pageantry for more than five centuries.

The **North Terrace** provides especially good views across the Thames to Eton College, perhaps the most famous of Britain's exclusive "public" boys' schools. From the terrace, you enter the **State Apartments,** which are open to the public when the Queen is not in residence (call in advance to see if they're open). Queen Elizabeth uses the castle far more than any of her predecessors did. It has become a sort of country weekend home. As such, it's a rather sleepy place most of the time.

■ TIP→ To see it come magnificently alive, check out the Windsor Castle Changing of the Guard, which takes place at 11 AM weekdays and Saturday from April through July and on odd-numbered weekdays and Saturday from August through March. Because the dates are changeable, it's a good idea to confirm the exact schedule before traveling to Windsor. When the Queen is in town, the guard and a regimental band parade through town to the castle gate; when she is away, a drum-and-fife band takes over.

Although a devastating fire in 1992 gutted some of the State Apartments, hardly any works of art were lost. Phenomenal repair work restored the **Grand Reception Room,** the **Green and Crimson Drawing Rooms,** and the **State and Octagonal dining rooms.** A green oak hammer-beam (a short horizontal roof beam that projects from the tops of walls for support) roof looms magnificently over the 600-year-old **St. George's Hall,** where the Queen gives state banquets. The State Apartments contain priceless furniture, including a magnificent Louis XVI bed and Gobelin tapestries; and paintings by Canaletto, Rubens, Van Dyck, Holbein, Dürer, and del Sarto. The high points of the tour are the **Throne Room** and the **Waterloo Chamber,** where Sir Thomas Lawrence's portraits of Napoléon's victorious foes line the walls. You can also see arms and armor and an exhibition on the restoration of Windsor Castle.

☾ **Queen Mary's Doll's House,** on display to the left of the entrance to the State Apartments, is a perfect miniature Georgian palace-within-a-palace, created in 1923. Electric lights glow, the doors all have tiny little keys, and water pours from the small faucets. A miniature library holds Lilliputian-size books especially written for the young Queen by famous authors of the 1920s. ☎ *020/7766–7304 tickets, 01753/831118 recorded information* ⊕ *www.royalresidences.com* ✉ *£13.50 for Precincts, State Apartments, Gallery, St. George's Chapel (closed Sun.), Albert Memorial Chapel, and Doll's House; £7 when State Apartments*

TOP REASONS TO GO

Windsor Castle: The mystique of eight successive royal houses of the British monarchy permeates Windsor, where a fraction of the current Queen's vast wealth is displayed in heraldic splendor.

Mapledurham House: While at this house that inspired "Toad Hall" from *The Wind in the Willows,* you can picnic on the grounds and drink in the views of the sleepy countryside.

Oxford: While scholars' noses are buried in their books, you get to sightsee among Oxford University's ancient stone buildings. Be on the

lookout for gargoyles around New College: the evil little creatures are wickedly creative. Try your luck at punting, too. You'll either proudly exhibit your balance and strength, or take a humiliating plunge into a slow-moving river. Every big splash is greeted with a cheer by the students lounging on the shore.

Blenheim Palace: The only British historic home to be named a World Heritage Site has fine 18th-century architecture, stunning gardens, and remembrances of Winston Churchill. For a memorable treat, attend an outdoor summer concert.

5

are closed ☻ *Mar.–Oct., daily 9:45–5:15, last admission at 4; Nov.–Feb., daily 9:45–4:15, last admission at 3.*

Just outside the castle, on St. Albans Street, the royal horses are kept in the **Royal Mews,** along with carriages, coaches, and splendid crimson and gold harnesses. The **Jubilee Garden,** created in 2002, has a stone bandstand used for concerts on summer Sunday afternoons. The garden begins at the main gates and extends to St. George's Gate on Castle Hill.

Windsor Great Park, the remains of an ancient royal hunting forest, stretches for some 8 mi (about 5,000 acres) south of Windsor Castle. Much of it is open to the public and can be seen by car or on foot, including its geographical focal points, the romantic 3-mi **Long Walk,** designed by Charles II to join castle and park, and **Virginia Water,** a 2-mi-long lake. The park contains one of Queen Victoria's most treasured residences, **Frogmore House** (☎ 020/7766–7305 ⊕ www.royalresidences.com ☞ House, gardens, and mausoleum £5.50 ☻ May and Aug., selected days only; check Web site or phone, 10–5:30). The sprawling white mansion is still a retreat for the Royal Family. Nearby, at the Royal Mausoleum at Frogmore, two famous royal couples are buried: inside, Victoria and Albert; outside, the Duke and Duchess of Windsor. It's open only a few days a year. The main horticultural delight of Windsor Great Park, the exquisite **Savill Garden** (⊠ Wick La., Englefield Green, Egham ☎ 01753/847518 ⊕ www.savillgarden.co.uk ☞ £3.50–£5.50 ☻ Mar.–Oct., daily 10–6; Nov.–Feb., daily 10–4), contains a tremendous diversity of trees and shrubs.

The extensive theme park **Legoland,** 2 mi outside Windsor, does everything you could imagine with Lego building bricks. Kids can play on ingenious models and try the rides and interactive games. There's a lake-

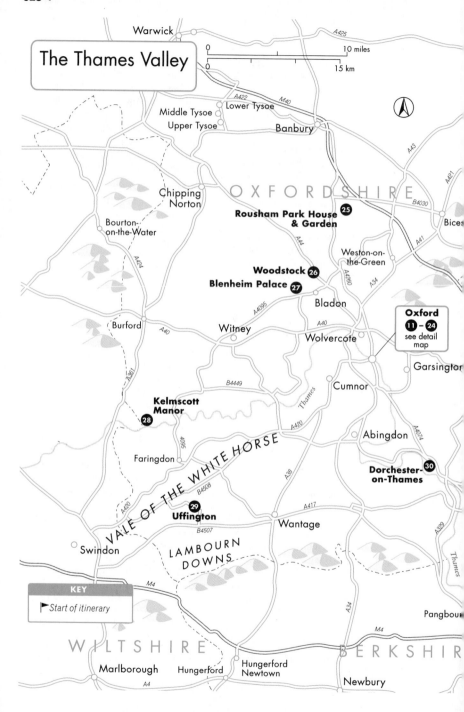

The Thames Valley

Warwick

A425

0 | 10 miles
0 | 15 km

A422 *M40*

Middle Tysoe Lower Tysoe
Upper Tysoe Banbury

A43 *A421*

OXFORDSHIRE *B4030*

Chipping
Norton

Bourton-
on-the-Water

**Rousham Park House
& Garden** 25 Bices

A44

Weston-on-
the-Green

Woodstock 26
Blenheim Palace 27

A4260 *A34*

Bladon

Burford *A40* Witney *A40* Wolvercote

A4095

Oxford
11 – 24
see detail
map

Garsington

B4449 Cumnor

Thames

**Kelmscott
Manor**
28

B4449

A420 Abingdon *A4074*

4095

VALE OF THE WHITE HORSE

Faringdon

**Dorchester-
on-Thames** 30

A38

A417

B4508

29
Uffington Wantage *A329*

B4507

Swindon LAMBOURN
DOWNS

Thames

Pangbour

M4

KEY

▶ *Start of itinerary*

WILTSHIRE BERKSHIR

Marlborough Hungerford Hungerford
Newtown Newbury

A4

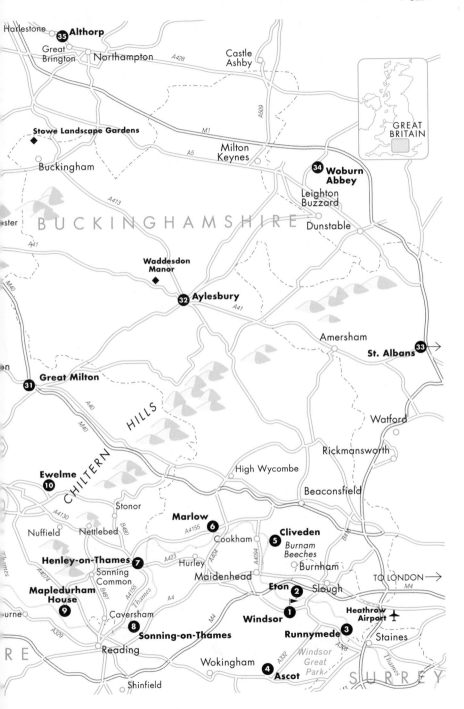

side picnic area, 150 acres of parkland, and several restaurants. ✉ *Wink-field Rd.* ☎ *08705/040404* ⊕ *www.legoland.co.uk* 🎫 *£23–£29* ⊙ *Mid-Mar.–June, Sept., and Oct., weekdays 10–5, weekends 10–6; July and Aug., daily 10–7.*

Where to Stay & Eat

Bray, a tiny village 6 mi outside Windsor, is known for its restaurants more than anything else.

★ **£££££** ✕ **Fat Duck.** One of the top restaurants in the country, this extraordinary Bray establishment packs in fans of hyper creative cuisine every night. Chef Heston Blumenthal delights in unusual taste combinations, from mango and Douglas fir sorbet to smoked bacon and egg ice cream. The fixed-price menu lists plenty of good choices, such as foie gras spiced with Szechuan peppercorn and mead, and lasagna of langoustine with pig's trotter and truffle. Lunch from Monday through Saturday, with a £50 fixed-price menu, is cheaper than the £80 per person charged at night (as is Blumenthal's Hinds Head pub just across the road). Like the food, the interior blends traditional and contemporary elements—modern art, exposed brick walls, and ancient wooden beams. ✉ *High St., Bray-on-Thames* ☎ *01628/580333* ⊕ *www.fatduck.co.uk* 🔖 *Reservations essential* ▤ *AE, DC, MC, V* ⊙ *Closed Mon. No dinner Sun.*

£££££ ✕ **Hinds Head.** The Fat Duck's esteemed chef Heston Blumenthal also owns this traditional pub across the road, where he sells less extreme dishes to a more laid-back crowd at somewhat more reasonable prices. The atmosphere is relaxed, and the look of the place is historic, with polished wood walls, brick fireplaces, and comfortable leather chairs. The food is a brilliant modern take on traditional English cuisine, so there's oxtail and kidney pudding, and rump steak with bone-marrow sauce and triple-cooked fries. The approachable menu makes this place less intimidating than the Fat Duck, and the dress code is as casual as the mood. ✉ *High St., Bray-on-Thames* ☎ *01628/626151* ▤ *MC, V.*

£££££ ✕ **Strok's Restaurant.** In Sir Christopher Wren's House Hotel—a mansion built in 1676 by the architect who designed St. Paul's Cathedral—Strok's offers an ever-changing continental menu and a Thames-side wooden terrace that swells with crowds in summer. Dishes may include roasted lamb with hummus and couscous, slathered in a minty yogurt sauce, or cod rice cakes sprinkled with Parmesan and lime juice. ✉ *Thames St. at Eton Bridge* ☎ *01753/861354* ▤ *AE, DC, MC, V.*

££–£££ ✕ **Two Brewers.** Locals congregate in the two small low-ceiling rooms of this 17th-century pub. Children are not welcome, but adults will find a suitable collection of wine, espresso, and local beer, plus an excellent little menu with dishes from grilled salmon to chili and pasta. Reservations are essential on Sunday, when the pub serves a traditional roast. ✉ *34 Park St.* ☎ *01753/855426* ▤ *AE, MC, V* ⊙ *No dinner Fri.*

> **TIME FOR A CUPPA**
>
> This is a tea-and-scones town, so having some in one of Windsor's many charming tearooms simply feels right. After taking in the castle's art and wandering the town's winding medieval lanes, a nice "cuppa," as the locals call it, is just perfect.

££££££ ✕🖼 **Oakley Court.** A romantic getaway with plenty of pampering amenities, this Victorian-era Gothic mansion stands on landscaped grounds beside the Thames, 3 mi west of Windsor. Its bristling towers and spires have been used in several films, including *The Rocky Horror Picture Show,* and *Dracula*; note, however, that half the rooms are in a modern annex. The Oakleaf restaurant (£££–£££££) serves continental cuisine in plush surroundings. ✉ *Windsor Rd., Water Oakley SL4 5UF* ☎ *01753/609988* 🖷 *01628/637011* ⊕ *www.moathousehotels.com* ↪ *106 rooms, 12 suites* ♿ *Restaurant, room service, in-room safes, minibars, room TVs with movies, in-room data ports, 9-hole golf course, putting green, 2 tennis courts, indoor pool, gym, hot tub, sauna, spa, steam room, billiards, croquet, bar, lobby lounge, dry cleaning, laundry service, concierge, business services, meeting rooms, no-smoking rooms; no a/c in some rooms* ▭ *AE, DC, MC, V.*

££££££ ✕🖼 **Stoke Park Club.** On a 350-acre estate 4 mi southwest of Windsor, Stoke Park can make Windsor Castle, off in the distance, seem almost humble in comparison. Architect James Wyatt perfected this version of neoclassical grandeur when he built the house for the Penn family in 1791. Antiques, paintings, and original prints decorate the elegant bedrooms. The Park Restaurant (££££) serves traditional English cuisine. *Goldfinger, Wimbledon,* and *Bridget Jones's Diary* were partly filmed here. Check ahead for special packages, which include a full English breakfast, three-course table d'hôte dinner, or both. ✉ *Park Rd., Stoke Poges SL2 4PG* ☎ *01753/717171* 🖷 *01753/717181* ⊕ *www.stokeparkclub.com* ↪ *21 rooms* ♿ *2 restaurants, cable TV, in-room data ports, 27-hole golf course, 13 tennis courts, indoor pool, fitness classes, gym, hair salon, hot tub, massage, spa, steam room, fishing, croquet, squash, 2 bars, lounge, shops, meeting rooms* ▭ *AE, DC, MC, V.*

£££££ 🖼 **The Castle Hotel.** You get an exceptional view of the Changing of the Guard from this Georgian hotel, parts of which date back much further to its start in the 16th century as a coaching inn. All rooms have recently been renovated and modernized—broadband brings modern life to the historic atmosphere. In the older section guest rooms have gently tilting floors, whereas elsewhere it's smooth elegance, with tasteful fabrics in neutral tones juxtaposed against original architectural detail. The cozy lounges have beamed ceilings and plush, antique furnishings—perfect for afternoon tea. To take advantage of lower prices, book a weekend leisure break with breakfast or half board. ✉ *High St., SL4 ILJ* ☎ *0870/400–8300* 🖷 *01753/830244* ⊕ *www.macdonaldhotels.co.uk* ↪ *111 rooms* ♿ *2 restaurants, room service, minibars, cable TV, some in-room broadband, bar, lounge, laundry service, meeting rooms, no-smoking rooms; no a/c in some rooms* ▭ *AE, DC, MC, V.*

££££ 🖼 **Ye Harte & Garter Hotel.** The location couldn't be better—right across the street from Windsor Castle, with a good view of it from many rooms. Some rooms have balconies and others have whirlpool tubs. Expect a muted rose tone and floral prints in the rooms, which vary in size. The hotel has Albert's Fish and Chips shop and the stodgy Victorian Restaurant and Carvery. It also hosts amusing medieval banquets in its dungeon. ✉ *31 High St., SL4 1PH* ☎ *01753/863426* 🖷 *01753/830527* ⊕ *www.harteandgarter.com* ↪ *58 rooms* ♿ *3 restaurants, some in-room* *hot tubs, some minibars, cable TV, bar, dry cleaning, laundry service, meeting rooms; no a/c* ⊟ *AE, DC, MC, V.*

££ ⊡ **Alma Lodge.** This friendly little bed-and-breakfast in an early Victorian town house is just one of many that can be booked through the Windsor tourist office. Ornate ceilings and ornamental fireplaces are some of the house's original features, and each well-maintained room is decorated in an uncluttered Victorian style. ⊠ *58 Alma Rd., SL4 3HA* ☎ *01753/862983* ⊕ *www.almalodge.co.uk* ⤳ *4 rooms* ⚬ *Some pets allowed; no a/c, no room phones, no smoking* ⊟ *MC, V* ⦿ *BP.*

⟳ ££ ⊡ **Langton House** This big Victorian mansion on a quiet, leafy lane in central Windsor was a residence for Queen Victoria's local governmental officials. Today it's a comfortable guesthouse with spacious rooms decorated with antiques and modern furniture. Guests have access to a small kitchen with refrigerator, toaster, microwave, and kettle. The lounge has a TV, video library, and games. This place is very child-friendly, with supplies for babies including travel cots, high chairs, and a baby monitor. ⊠ *46 Alma Rd., SL4 3HA* ☎ *01753/858299* ⊕ *www. langtonhouse.co.uk* ⤳ *4 rooms* ⚬ *Cable TV, Wi-Fi, kitchen; no smoking* ⊟ *MC, V* ⦿ *BP.*

Nightlife & the Arts

Windsor's **Theatre Royal** (⊠ 10th St. ☎ 01753/853888), where productions have been staged since 1910, is one of Britain's leading provincial theaters. It puts on plays and musicals year-round, including a pantomime for the six weeks after Christmas.

Concerts, poetry readings, and children's events highlight the two-week **Windsor Festival** (☎ 01753/714364 ⊕ www.windsorfestival.com), usually held in early September or October, with events occasionally taking place in the castle.

Sports & the Outdoors

From March through September, **John Logie Motorboats** (⊠ Barry Ave. ☎ 07774/983809) rents motorboats and rowboats by the half hour and hour.

Windsor Cycle Hire (⊠ Alexandra Gardens, Alma Rd. ☎ 01753/830220) rents bikes, skateboards, scooters, and in-line skates.

Shopping

Most Windsor stores are open Sunday as well as the rest of the week, particularly the antiques stores along Peascod Street, High Street, and King Edward Court. The **Windsor Royal Station shopping center** (⊠ Central Train Station ☎ 01753/797070) includes Jaeger, Pied-à-Terre, and an outpost of the quintessential London department store, Liberty.

Eton

❷ *23 mi west of London, linked by a footbridge across the Thames to Windsor.*

Some observers may find it symbolic that almost opposite Windsor Castle—which embodies the continuity of the royal tradition—stands Eton, a school that for centuries has educated many future leaders of the country. With its single main street leading from the river to the famous school, the old-fashioned town itself is much quieter than Windsor.

★ The splendid redbrick Tudor-style buildings of **Eton College**, founded in 1440 by King Henry VI, border the north end of High Street; signs warn drivers of BOYS CROSSING. During the college semesters, the schoolboys dress in their distinctive pinstripe trousers, swallow-tailed coats, and stiff collars (top hats have not been worn by the boys since the 1940s) to walk to class, and it's all terrifically photogenic. The Gothic **Chapel** rivals St. George's at Windsor in size and magnificence, and is both impressively austere and intimate. Beyond the cloisters are the school's playing fields where, according to the duke of Wellington, the Battle of Waterloo was really won, since so many of his officers had learned discipline and strategy during their school days there. The **Museum of Eton Life** has displays on the school's history. You can also take a guided tour of the school and chapel. ⊠ *Main entrance Brewhouse Yard* ☎ *01753/ 671177* ⊕ *www.etoncollege.com* ⊠ *£3.80, £4.90 with tour* ☉ *Mar.–mid-Apr., July, and Aug., daily 10:30–4:30; mid-Apr.–June and Sept., daily 2–4:30; guided tours mid-Mar.–Sept., daily at 2:15 and 3:15.*

Where to Stay & Eat

££–££££ ✕ **Gilbey's Bar & Restaurant.** Just over the bridge from Windsor, this restaurant at the center of Eton's Antiques Row serves a fine, changing menu of inspired English fare, from cod, cheddar, and chive fish cakes to lamb with black pudding and spiced cabbage. Well-priced French wines are a specialty. The conservatory is a particularly pleasant place to sit in fine weather. ⊠ *82–83 High St.* ☎ *01753/854921* ☰ *AE, DC, MC, V.*

££ ✕ **The George Inn & Eatery.** This stylish pub has stripped pine floors, wooden tables, and a menu of contemporary cuisine. You might opt for the spicy Thai beef salad or the more traditional sausage and mashed potatoes in onion gravy. The terrace is a relaxing spot for a summertime pint. ⊠ *77 High St.* ☎ *01753/861797* ☰ *AE, MC, V.*

££££ ✕⌷ **Christopher Hotel.** Sister to Sir Christopher Wren's Hotel in Windsor, this former coaching inn on the main shopping street has spacious rooms in the main building as well as in the courtyard mews. All are done in traditional style, but the courtyard rooms have more privacy. The fine Renata's restaurant (££–£££), serving dinner every day except Sunday, has a modern European menu. ⊠ *110 High St., SL4 6AN* ☎ *01753/852359* ☐ *01753/830914* ⊕ *www.christopher-hotel.co.uk* ⌂ *33 rooms* ⌂ *Restaurant, room service, cable TV, bar, meeting room, some pets allowed, no-smoking rooms* ☰ *AE, DC, MC, V.*

Runnymede

❸ *6 mi east of Windsor.*

A giant step in the history of democracy was taken at Runnymede on the Thames outside Egham. Here King John, under his barons' compulsion, signed the Magna Carta in 1215, affirming at least in theory that individuals had the right to justice and liberty. There's not much to see here, though. On the wooded hillside, in a meadow given to the United States by Queen Elizabeth in 1965, stands a **memorial to President John F. Kennedy.** Nearby is another memorial, a classical temple in style, erected by the American Bar Association for the 750th anniversary of the signing. There is no visitor center at Runnymede, just informational plaques and a parking lot (small charge). The site is on the south side of A308; on the opposite bank of the Thames are the ruins of the 11th-century St. Mary's Priory and the 2,000-year-old Ankerwycke Yew. ⊠ *A308, Egham* ☎ *01784/432891* ⊕ *www.nationaltrust.org.uk.*

Ascot

❹ *10 mi southwest of Runnymede, 8 mi southwest of Windsor, 28 mi southwest from London.*

The town of Ascot (pronounced *as*-cut) has for centuries been famous for horse racing and for style. Queen Anne chose to have a racecourse here, and the first race meeting took place in 1711. The impressive show of millinery for which the Royal Meeting, or Royal Ascot, is also known was immortalized in Cecil Beaton's Ascot sequence in *My Fair Lady,* in which osprey feathers and black and white silk roses transformed Eliza Doolittle into a grand lady.

Renovated in 2005, **Ascot Racecourse** (⊠ A329 ☎ 01344/622211 racecourse, 01344/876876 credit-card hotline ⊕ www.ascot.co.uk) looks more gloriously upper class than ever. The races run regularly from June through December. The Royal Ascot takes place annually in June. ■ TIP➔ Tickets to all races can be purchased online and by phone. However, if you're hankering to go during the Royal Ascot, purchase your tickets well in advance. Tickets generally go on sale in January, but call or check the Web site for details. Prices range from £7 for standing room on the heath, to £60 for seats in the stands.

Where to Stay

££££ 🏨 **McDonald Berystede Hotel and Spa.** With its turrets and half-timbering, this Victorian-era hotel is a magnificent neo-Gothic fantasy on 9 acres of traditional British countryside. Inside, every square inch pays homage to the horsey culture of Ascot, and horse and jockey prints line the walls. Most of the rooms are pleasantly standard (in the annex); a few (in the main house) are nothing short of extraordinary. There's also a luxurious indoor pool and a high-tech gym. The Hyperion restaurant serves modern British cuisine. ⊠ *Bagshot Rd., SL5 9JH* ☎ *0870/400–8111* 🖷 *01344/872301* ⊕ *www.mcdonaldhotels.co.uk* 🛏 *119 rooms, 10 suites* ⚒ *Restaurant, room service, cable TV, in-room broadband, indoor-outdoor pool, spa, gym, croquet, bar, lounge, library, babysitting, dry cleaning, laundry service, meeting rooms, some pets allowed, no-smoking rooms; no a/c* 🖃 *AE, DC, MC, V* ⏱◖ *BP.*

Cliveden

❺ *8 mi northwest of Windsor, 16 mi north of Ascot, 26 mi west of London.*

Described by Queen Victoria a "bijou of taste," this magnificent country mansion has for more than 300 years lived up to its Georgian heritage as a bastion of aesthetic delights. The house, set in 376 acres of gardens and parkland above the River Thames, was rebuilt for the Duke of Sutherland by Sir Charles Barry in 1861; the Astors, who purchased it in 1893, made it famous. In the 1920s and '30s the Cliveden Set met here at the strongly conservative (not to say fascist) salon presided over by Nancy Astor, who—though she was an American—was the first woman to sit in Parliament, in 1919. Cliveden now belongs to the National Trust, which leases it as a *very* exclusive hotel. The public can visit the spectacular grounds that run down to bluffs overlooking the Thames and, by timed ticket, three rooms in the house. ⊠ *Off A404, Taplow, near Maidenhead* ☎ *01628/605069, 01494/755562 recorded information* ⊕ *www.nationaltrust.org.uk* 🖾 *Grounds £7.50* ⊙ *Grounds mid-Mar.–Oct., daily 11–6; Nov. and Dec., daily 11–4. House Apr.–Oct., Thurs. and Sun. 3–5:30. Restaurant in Orangery mid-Mar.–Oct., Wed.–Sun. 11–5; Nov.–mid-Dec., Fri.–Sun. 11–2:30.*

Where to Stay & Eat

£££££ ✕🏨 **Cliveden.** If you've ever wondered what it would feel like to be an
Fodor'sChoice Edwardian grandee, splurge for a stay at this stately home, one of
★ Britain's grandest hotels. Cliveden's opulent interior includes portraits such as Sargent's portrait of Nancy Astor (in the Great Hall), suits of armor, and a richly paneled staircase. The plush traditional bedrooms each bear the name of someone famous who has stayed here. Since people lease many of the rooms, you may feel you're in a home rather than a hotel. Waldo's (£££££), one of three restaurants, serves excellent contemporary British and French cuisine. ⊠ *Off A404 near Maidenhead, Taplow SL6 0JF* ☎ *01628/668561* 🖶 *01628/661837* ⊕ *www. clivedenhouse.co.uk* 🛏 *38 rooms, 1 cottage* ♨ *3 restaurants, room service, in-room safes, cable TV with movies, in-room VCRs, in-room data ports, 3 tennis courts, indoor-outdoor pool, gym, hair salon, 2 outdoor hot tubs, massage, sauna, spa, steam room, boating, billiards, horseback riding, squash, lounge, library, babysitting, dry cleaning, laundry service, concierge, meeting rooms, some pets allowed, no-smoking rooms; no a/c in some rooms* ➦ *AE, DC, MC, V* ⧀ *BP.*

Outdoors

Cliveden Boathouse (⊠ Off A404 near Maidenhead, Taplow ☎ 01628/ 668561) at Cliveden hotel has three vintage boats that ply the Thames. The champagne sunset cruise is the most affordable at £45 per person; you can rent the boats, too.

TO HENLEY & BEYOND
"WIND IN THE WILLOWS" COUNTRY

This stretch of the Thames Valley, from Marlow to Ewelme, is literally the stuff of fairy tales. Walking through its fields and along its waterways, it's easy to see how it inspired Kenneth Grahame's classic 1908 children's book *The Wind in the Willows.* Whether by boat or on foot, you can discover some of the region's most delightful scenery here. On each bank are fine wooded hills, with spacious homes, greenhouses, flower beds, and neat lawns that stretch to the water's edge. Grahame wrote his book in Pangbourne, while his illustrator, E. H. Shepard, used the great house at Mapledurham as the model for Toad Hall. It all still has the power to inspire.

Marlow

6 *7 mi west of Cliveden, 15 mi northwest of Windsor.*

Just inside the Buckinghamshire border, Marlow overflows with Thames-side prettiness. The unusual suspension bridge was built in the 1830s by William Tierney Clark, architect of the bridge linking Buda and Pest. Marlow has a number of striking old buildings, particularly the privately owned Georgian houses along Peter and West streets. In 1817 the Romantic poet Percy Bysshe Shelley stayed with friends at 67 West Street and then bought **Albion House** on the same street. His second wife, Mary, completed her Gothic novel *Frankenstein* here. **Marlow Place**, on Station Road, dates from 1721 and has been home to several princes. Marlow hosts its own miniregatta in mid-June for one day. The town is a good base from which to join the Thames Path to Henley-on-Thames. On summer weekends, tourism can often overwhelm the town.

Swan-Upping (☎ 01628/523030), a traditional event that dates back 800 years, takes places in the third week of July. By bizarre ancient laws, the Queen owns the country's swans, so each year swan-markers in skiffs start from Sunbury-on-Thames, catching the new cygnets and marking their beaks to establish ownership. The Queen's swan keeper, dressed in scarlet livery, presides over this colorful ceremony.

Where to Stay & Eat

££££ ✗ **Vanilla Pod.** Beamed ceilings and warm, vanilla-hue walls cocoon French-inspired cuisine by chef Michael Macdonald. Some of the best choices are the glazed chicken—embraced by layers of honey, coriander, and fennel—and the poached sea bass with vanilla and saffron. For dessert, indulge in the crème caramel with orange salsa and strawberry salad. The £18.50 fixed-price lunch menu offers a fantastic bargain, and the seven-course *menu gourmand* for £45 is a tour de force. ⊠ *31 West St.* ☎ *01628/898101* ⌂ *Reservations essential* ▤ *AE, MC, V.*

££££–£££££ ✗▥ **Compleat Angler.** Fishing aficionados might consider this luxurious, 17th-century Thames-side inn the ideal place to stay. The name comes from Isaak Walton's 1653 masterpiece of angling advice and philosophy, which he wrote in this area. Plenty of fishy touches enhance the decor; most rooms and the Riverside Restaurant (with outstanding cooking from chef Dean Timpson ££££) have views over the Thames. A cozy conservatory serves afternoon tea. ⊠ *Marlow Bridge, Bisham Rd., SL7 1RG* ☎ *0870/400–8100* ▤ *01628/486388* ⊕ *www. compleatangler-hotel.co.uk* ⇆ *61 rooms, 3 suites* ⌂ *2 restaurants, room service, minibars, cable TV with video games, boating, fishing, 2 bars, lounge, meeting rooms, some pets allowed (fee), no-smoking rooms; no a/c* ▤ *AE, DC, MC, V.*

Henley-on-Thames

7 *7 mi southwest of Marlow on A4155, 8 mi north of Reading, 36 mi west of central London.*

Henley's fame is based on one thing: rowing. The Henley Royal Regatta, held at the cusp of June and July on a long, straight stretch of the River

Thames, has made the little riverside town famous throughout the world. Townspeople launched the Henley Regatta in 1839, initiating the Grand Challenge Cup, the most famous of its many trophies. The best amateur oarsmen from around the globe compete in crews of eight, four, or two, or as single scullers. For many spectators, however, the social side of the event is far more important and on par with Royal Ascot and Wimbledon. Elderly oarsmen wear straw boater hats; businesspeople entertain clients and everyone admires the ladies' fashions.

The town is set in a broad valley between gentle hillsides. Henley's historic buildings, including half-timber Georgian cottages and inns (as well as one of Britain's oldest theaters, the Kenton), are all within a few minutes' walk. The river near Henley is alive with boats of every shape and size, from luxury cabin cruisers to tiny rowboats.

The 16th-century "checkerboard" tower of **St. Mary's Church** overlooks Henley's bridge on Hart Street. If the church's rector is about, ask permission to climb to the top to take in the superb views up and down the river. The adjacent **Chantry House,** built in 1420, is one of England's few remaining merchant houses from the period. It is an unspoiled example of the rare timber-frame design, with upper floors jutting out. ⊠ *Hart St.* ☎ *01491/577062* 🖾 *Free* ☉ *Church services or by appointment.*

🐌 The handsome **River & Rowing Museum** focuses not just on the history and sport of rowing but on the Thames and the town itself. One gallery interprets the Thames and its surroundings as the river flows from its source to the ocean; another explores Henley's history and the regatta. Galleries devoted to rowing display models and actual boats, from Greek triremes to lifeboats to sleek modern rowing boats. A *Wind in the Willows* exhibit evokes the settings of the famous children's book. David Chipperfield's striking building, combining traditional oak and modern steel, takes full advantage of its riverside location. ⊠ *Mill Meadows* ☎ *01491/415600* ⊕ *www.rrm.co.uk* 🖾 *£6* ☉ *May–Aug., daily 10–5:30; Sept.–Apr., daily 10–5.*

Where to Stay & Eat

££–£££ ✕ **Three Tuns Foodhouse.** What used to be a tiny pub has been redone into a delightful, antiques-filled eatery. On the menu, panfried scallops with saffron and fennel share space with chicken with thyme potatoes and Scottish chanterelle mushrooms. ⊠ *5 Market Pl.* ☎ *01491/573260* 🗈 *Reservations essential* 🖃 *MC, V.*

££££ ✕🏨 **Red Lion.** Ivy-draped and dignified, this redbrick 16th-century hotel overlooks the river and the town bridge. Guests have included King Charles I; Samuel Johnson, the 18th-century critic, poet, and lexicographer; and the duke of Marlborough, who used it as a base during the building of Blenheim Palace. Rooms are furnished with antiques, and some bedrooms have river views. The restaurant (£££) serves traditional fare such as roast pheasant or beef fillet with leek and Stilton mousse; the bar has a lighter menu. ⊠ *Hart St., RG9 2AR* ☎ *01491/572161* 🖷 *01491/410039* ⊕ *www.redlionhenley.co.uk* 🗨 *26 rooms* ⚹ *Restaurant, room service, cable TV, in-room data ports, bar, lobby lounge,* *babysitting, dry cleaning, laundry service, Internet room, meeting rooms; no a/c* ⊟ *AE, MC, V* ⊖ *BP.*

£££–££££ ✕⊡ **White Hart Hotel & Nettlebed Restaurant.** The focus at this modern gastro-pub with guest rooms is delectable food, prepared with fresh, local ingredients by chef-owner Chris Barber, who spent a decade as personal chef to Prince Charles. With its three-course set menu (£35) and five-course tasting menu (£55), the restaurant is pricier and more formal than the bistro, but both have the same caliber of friendly, professional staff. The soothing, light-filled guest rooms, done in olive green, gray, cream, and dark chocolate, are contemporary in style. ⊠ *A4130, Nettlebed RG9 5DD, 5 mi west of Henley-on-Thames* ☎ *01491/ 641245* ⎙ *01491/649018* ⊕ *www.whitehartnettlebed.com* ⇆ *12 rooms* ♿ *Restaurant, room service, in-room data ports, lounge, pub, dry cleaning, laundry service, meeting rooms, no-smoking rooms; no a/c* ⊟ *AE, MC, V* ⊖ *CP.*

££££ ⊡ **Hotel du Vin.** The small British Hotel du Vin chain of boutique hotels is known for its clever use of unique buildings, and in Henley a sprawling old brick brewery became a design showplace. Bedrooms have beige carpeting and white-washed walls—everything else is black. The original brewery windows appear in strange places, and staircases contort to fit the space. Deep bathtubs, firm beds, and a minimalist ethic make this modern hotel a pleasure. ⊠ *New St., RG9 2BP* ☎ *01491/848400* ⊕ *www.hotelduvin.com* ⇆ *43 rooms* ♿ *Restaurant, room service, cable TV, in-room data ports, bar* ⊟ *AE, MC, V.*

££££ ⊡ **Thamesmead House Hotel.** Neutral tones and simple, clean-lined furnishings create restful bedrooms in this sophisticated guesthouse across the bridge from the center of Henley. The helpful staff are knowledgeable about local eateries and attractions. ⊠ *Remenham La., RG9 2LR* ☎ *01491/574745* ⎙ *01491/579944* ⊕ *www.thamesmeadhousehotel. co.uk* ⇆ *6 rooms* ♿ *In-room safes, cable TV, in-room data ports, lounge; no a/c, no kids under 10, no smoking* ⊟ *AE, MC, V* ⊖ *BP.*

££ ⊡ **Alftrudis.** This sweet Victorian house in central Henley is a real find. Its three guest rooms are neatly decorated in whites and creams, beds are comfortable, and owner Sue Lambert offers a wealth of information about the area. Book well in advance at this popular place. ⊠ *8 Norman Ave., Henley-on-Thames RG9 1SG* ☎ *01491/ 573099* ⊕ *www.alftrudis.co.uk* ⇆ *3 rooms* ♿ *Cable TV, Wi-Fi* ⊟ *No credit cards* ⊖ *BP.*

Nightlife & the Arts

A floating stage and spectacular events draw a dress-code abiding crowd to the upscale **Henley Festi-**

WALK THE CHILTERNS

Part of the Chiltern Hills is an Area of Outstanding Beauty (⊕ www. chilternsaonb.org), a nature reserve that stretches over 320 square mi, taking in chalk hills, valleys, forests, lakes, and pretty towns. Its springtime bluebell woods are famed for their soft blue carpets of flowers, and its autumn colors are glorious. You'll likely drive in and out of the Chilterns as you explore the area, or you could walk part of the circular 124-mi Chiltern Way. A 13-mi section of the path starts in Henley, runs north through the Hambleden Valley, and returns to Henley via the Assendons.

val (☎ 01491/843404 ⊕ www.henley-festival.co.uk) during the week after the regatta in July. Book tickets ahead.

Sports & the Outdoors

ROWING **Henley Royal Regatta** (☎01491/572153 ⊕www.hrr.co.uk), a series of rowing competitions that draw participants from many countries, takes place in late June and early July each year. Large tents go up, especially along both sides of the unique straight stretch of river here known as Henley Reach (1 mi, 550 yards), and every surrounding field becomes a parking lot. The most prestigious place for spectators is the Stewards' Enclosure, but admission here is by invitation only. Fortunately, there is plenty of space on the public towpath from which to watch the early stages of the races. If you want to attend, make your plans and book a room months in advance (500,000 attend the race, including members of the Royal Family). Each day, the racing pauses twice, at noon for luncheon and at 4 for tea. *See* Thames Valley Essentials, *below,* for places to rent your own boat.

Sonning-on-Thames

❽ *5 mi south of Henley-on-Thames, 4 mi northeast of Reading.*

It is plausible that Sonning's reputation as the prettiest village on the Thames goes back as far as its Saxon bishops. The 18th-century bridge, the Georgian houses, the mill so old that it's mentioned in the 11th-century Domesday Book, and the black, white, and yellow cottages make it a perfect riverside idyll.

Where to Stay & Eat

£££££-£££££ ✕▣ **French Horn.** Elegance is the keynote of this Thames-side hotel with a graceful willow tree and calming river views. Guest rooms, some in the main building and others in cottages, are spacious. Most have sitting rooms, and the light green walls and rose-festooned fabrics are typically English. The restaurant (££–£££) serves inspired French cooking. ⊠ *Thames St., RG4 6TN* ☎ *0118/969–2204* 🖷 *0118/944–2210* ⊕ *www.thefrenchhorn.co.uk* ⇆ *11 rooms, 10 suites* ⑆ *Restaurant, some minibars, in-room data ports, bar, lobby lounge, laundry service, meeting rooms; no a/c in some rooms* ▤ *AE, DC, MC, V* ¶◎¶ *BP.*

Mapledurham House

★ **❾** *5 mi west of Sonning-on-Thames, 10 mi southwest of Henley-on-Thames.*

The section of the Thames from Caversham to Mapledurham inspired Kenneth Grahame's *The Wind in the Willows,* which began as a bedtime story for Grahame's son Alastair while the family lived at Pangbourne. Some of E. F. Shepard's illustrations are of specific sites along the river—none more fabled than this redbrick Elizabethan mansion, bristling with tall chimneys, mullioned windows, and battlements, which became the inspiration for Shepard's vision of Toad Hall. The Eyston family, descendants of longtime owners of the estate, still lives at Mapledurham, and the house seems warm and friendly even with all the family portraits, magnificent oak staircases, and Tudor plasterwork ceilings. There's also a 15th-century water mill—the last working grain mill on the river. On summer weekends you can reach the house by a **Thames River Cruises** (☎ 0118/948–1088) boat from Caversham Promenade in Reading. The boat leaves at 2 PM, and travel time is about 45 minutes. You can linger at one of the 11 rental cottages around the estate (£265–£620 a week). ⊠ *Mapledurham, near Reading* ☎ *0118/972–3350* ⊕ *www.mapledurham.co.uk* 🔁 *House and mill £7, house only £4.50, grounds and mill £3.50* ☉ *Easter–Sept., weekends 2–5:30.*

Ewelme

 12 mi north of Mapledurham House, 10 mi northwest of Henley-on-Thames off A4130.

This lovely, unspoiled village near the town of Benson, in Oxfordshire, has picture-book almshouses, church, and a school—one of the oldest in Britain—huddled close together. All date back more than 500 years. The church shelters the carved alabaster tomb of Alice, duchess of Suffolk, the granddaughter of medieval poet Geoffrey Chaucer. Jerome K. Jerome, author of the humorous book *Three Men in a Boat,* describing a 19th-century Thames-side vacation, is also buried here.

OXFORD

With arguably the most famous university in the world, Oxford has been a center of learning since 1167, with only the Sorbonne preceding it. It doesn't take more than a day or two to explore its winding medieval streets, snap some gorgeous photographs of its ivy-covered stone buildings, and ancient churches and libraries, and even take a punt down one of its placid, picturesque waterways. The town center is quite compact and walkable, and at its heart is Oxford University. Alumni of this prestigious institution include 47 Nobel prize winners, 25 British Prime Ministers (including Prime Minister Tony Blair), and 28 foreign presidents (including former U.S. President Bill Clinton), along with poets, authors, and artists such as Percy Bysshe Shelley, Oscar Wilde, and W. H. Auden. Save for its modern storefronts, the city looks much as it has for hundreds of years, in part because Adolf Hitler had vague plans to make it his European capital and so spared it from bombings. Victorian writer Matthew Arnold described Oxford's "dreaming spires," a phrase that has become famous. Students rush past you on the sidewalks on the way to their exams, clad with marvelous antiquarian style in their requisite mortar caps, flowing dark gowns, stiff collars, and crisp white bow ties.

Oxford is 55 mi northwest of London, at the junction of the Thames and Cherwell rivers. The city is more interesting and more cosmopolitan than Cambridge, and although it's also bigger, its suburbs are not remotely interesting to visitors. The interest is all at the center, where the old town curls around the grand stone buildings, good restaurants, and historic pubs.

Exploring Oxford

Oxford University is not one easily identifiable campus, but a sprawling mixture of more than 39 colleges scattered around the city center,

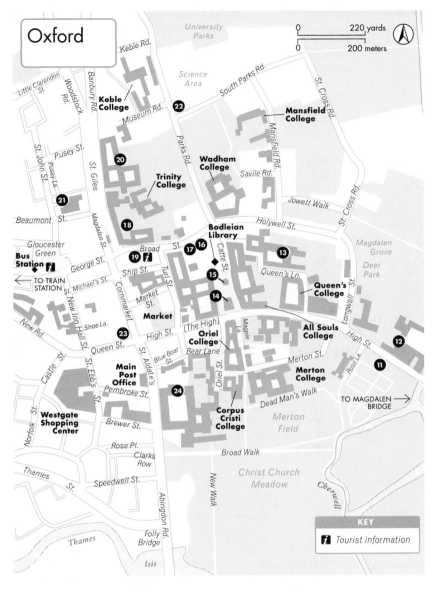

Oxford

University Parks

Science Area

Keble Rd.

Keble College

Museum Rd.

Mansfield College

South Parks Rd.

St. Cross Rd.

Little Clarendon St.

Woodstock Rd.

Banbury Rd.

Pusey St.

St. Giles

St. John St.

Pusey La.

Magdalen St.

Parks Rd.

Mansfield Rd.

Wadham College

Savile Rd.

Jowett Walk

Trinity College

Beaumont St.

Gloucester Green

Bus Station

← TO TRAIN STATION

George St.

New Inn Hall St.

New Rd.

St. Michael's St.

Cornmarket

Ship St.

Broad St.

Turl St.

Bodleian Library

Catte St.

Holywell St.

Magdalen Grove

Deer Park

St. Cross Rd.

Longwall St.

Queen's Ln.

Queen's College

Market St.

Market

(The High)

High St.

Magpie La.

All Souls College

High St.

Rose La.

Castle St.

Queen St.

St. Aldate's

Blue Boar St.

Shoe La.

Oriel College

Bear Lane

Oriel St.

Merton St.

Merton College

Dead Man's Walk

TO MAGDALEN BRIDGE →

Norfolk St.

St. Ebb's St.

Main Post Office

Pembroke St.

Westgate Shopping Center

Brewer St.

Corpus Cristi College

Merton Field

Rose Pl.

Clarks Row

Thames St.

Speedwell St.

Abingdon Rd.

Broad Walk

New Walk

Christ Church Meadow

Cherwell

Thames

Folly Bridge

Isis

0 — 220 yards
0 — 200 meters

KEY

🛈 Tourist information

Ashmolean Museum . . .**21**

Balliol College **18**

Carfax Tower **23**

Christ Church **24**

Magdalen College **12**

Museum of the
History of Science **17**

New College **13**

Oxford Story
Exhibition **19**

Oxford University Museum
of Natural History **22**

Radcliffe Camera and
Bodleian Library **15**

Sheldonian Theatre . . .**16**

St. John's College **20**

University Church of
St. Mary the Virgin **14**

University of Oxford
Botanic Garden **11**

each with its own distinctive identity and focus. Oxford students live and study at their own college, and also use the centralized resources of the over-arching university. The individual colleges are deeply competitive. Most of the grounds and magnificent dining halls and chapels are open to visitors, though the opening times (displayed at the entrance gates) vary greatly. Some colleges are open only in the afternoons during university terms; when the undergraduates are in residence, access is often restricted to the chapels and dining rooms (called halls) and sometimes the libraries, too, and you are requested to refrain from picnicking in the quadrangles. All are closed certain days during exams, usually from mid-April to late June. ■ TIP➔ **The best way to gain access is to join a walking tour led by a Blue Badge guide. These two-hour tours leave up to five times daily from the Tourist Information Centre.** As you walk through this scholastic wonderland, take in the Gothic gargoyles glaring down everywhere; after all, this was the home of both Lewis Carroll and J. R.R. Tolkien.

The St. Clement's parking lot before the roundabout that leads to Magdalen (pronounced *maud*-lin) Bridge is the best option for public parking (fee).

Main Attractions

㉑ Ashmolean Museum. Britain's oldest public museum contains among its priceless collections (all university-owned) many Egyptian, Greek, and Roman artifacts uncovered during archaeological expeditions conducted by the university. Michelangelo drawings and an extraordinary statuary collection are highlights, as is the Alfred Jewel. This ancient piece features a large semiprecious stone set in gold carved with the words AELFRED MEC HEHT GEWYRCAN, which translates from old English as "Alfred ordered me to be made." The piece dates from the reign of King Alfred the Great (ruled 871–899). ⊠ *Beaumont St.* ☏ *01865/278000* ⊕ *www.ashmol.ox.ac.uk* ◺ *Free* ☼ *Tues.–Sat. 10–5, Sun. noon–5.*

⑱ Balliol College. The wooden doors between the inner and outer quadrangles of Balliol (founded 1263) still bear scorch marks from 1555 and 1556, when during the reign of Mary ("Bloody Mary"), Bishops Latimer and Ridley and Archbishop Cranmer were burned alive on huge pyres in Broad Street for their Protestant beliefs. A cross on the roadway marks the spot. The **Martyrs' Memorial** at St. Giles and Beaumont Street also commemorates the three men. ⊠ *Broad St. and St. Giles* ☏ *01865/277777* ⊕ *www.balliol.ox.ac.uk* ◺ *£1* ☼ *Daily 2–5.*

㉓ Carfax Tower. Passing through Carfax, where four roads meet, you can spot this tower, all that remains of **St. Martin's Church,** where Shakespeare stood as godfather for William Davenant, who himself became a playwright. Every 15 minutes, little mechanical "quarter boys" mark the passage of time on the tower front. You can climb up the dark stairwell for a good view of the town center. ⊠ *Corner of Carfax and Cornmarket* ☏ *01865/792653* ◺ *£1.50* ☼ *Apr.–Oct., daily 10–5:30; Nov.–Mar., daily 10–4:30.*

㉔ Christ Church. Built in 1546, the college of Christ Church is referred to by its members as "The House." This is the site of Oxford's largest quadrangle, Tom Quad, named after the huge bell (6¼ tons) that hangs in the Christopher Wren–designed gate tower and rings 101 times at five past nine every evening in honor of the original number of Christ Church scholars. The vaulted, 800-year-old chapel in one corner has been Oxford's cathedral since the time of Henry VIII. The college's medieval dining hall contains portraits of many famous alumni, including John Wesley, William Penn, and 13 of Britain's prime ministers. A reproduction of this room appears in the banquet scenes at Hogwarts School in the *Harry Potter* films. Lewis Carroll was a teacher of mathematics here for many years; a shop opposite the meadows on St. Aldate's sells Alice paraphernalia. ✉ *St. Aldate's* ☎ *01865/276150* ⊕ *www.chch.ox.ac.uk* 💷 *£4* ☉ *Mon.–Sat. 9–5:30, Sun. 1–5:30.*

> ## WORD OF MOUTH
>
> "Oxford is an astoundingly beautiful place. I would simply wander, seeing as many of the college chapels and cloisters as possible. Christ Church Chapel . . . is a must-see. Magdalen College has a deer park but also something called Addison's Walk, which is an idyllic place as well."
>
> –Guy 18

Christ Church Picture Gallery. This connoisseur's delight in Canterbury Quadrangle exhibits works by the Italian masters as well as Hals, Rubens, and Van Dyck. Drawings in the 2,000-strong collection are shown on a changing basis. ✉ *Oriel Sq.* ☎ *01865/276172* ⊕ *www.chch.ox. ac.uk* 💷 *£3* ☉ *Apr.–Sept., Mon.–Sat. 10:30–5, Sun. 2–5; Oct.–Mar., Mon.–Sat., 10:30–1 and 2–4:30, Sun. 2–4:30.*

★ ⑫ **Magdalen College.** Founded in 1458, with a handsome main quadrangle and a supremely monastic air, Magdalen (pronounced: *"maud-lin"*) is one of the most impressive of Oxford's colleges and attracts its most artistic students. Alumni include such diverse people as Cardinal Wolsey, P.G. Wodehouse, Edward Gibbon, Oscar Wilde, Dudley Moore, and U.S. Supreme Court Justice David Souter. The school's large, square tower is a famous local landmark. A stroll around the Deer Park and along Addison's Walk is a good way to appreciate the place. ✉ *High St.* ☎ *01865/276000* ⊕ *www.magd.ox.ac.uk* 💷 *£3* ☉ *July–Sept., daily noon–6; Oct.–June, daily 1–6.*

⑬ **New College.** One of the university's best known and oldest colleges (dating to 1379), New College stands alongside New College Lane, known for its Italianate Bridge of Sighs. Its grounds are big and enticing, with acres of soft green grass and pristinely maintained gardens. The college buildings, in ivory stone, are partly enclosed by the medieval city wall, and feature one of the city's best displays of Gothic gargoyles. Famous alumni include the actors Hugh Grant and Kate Beckinsale. ✉ *Holywell St.* ☎ *01865/279555* ⊕ *www.new.ox.ac.uk* 💷 *Easter–Sept. £2, Oct.–Easter free* ☉ *Easter–Sept., daily 11–5; Oct.–Easter, daily 2–5.*

★ ⑮ **Radcliffe Camera and Bodleian Library.** This vast library is Oxford's most spectacular building, built in 1737–49 by James Gibbs in Italian baroque style. It's usually surrounded by crowds of tourists with digital cameras trained at its golden walls. The Camera contains part of the Bodleian

Library's enormous collection, which was begun in 1602 and has grown to more than 6 million volumes. Much like the Library of Congress in the United States, it contains a copy of every book printed in Great Britain (not all are held in this building, which is the library's public face). Although only students and professors are allowed inside the Camera, the general public may step into another part of the Bodleian, the Divinity School. This superbly vaulted room dates to 1462. In the *Harry Potter* films, some interior scenes at Hogwarts School take place in the Bodleian, including the Divinity School. ✉ *Broad St.* ☎ *01865/277224 for information on tour* 🌐 *www.bodley.ox.ac.uk* 🎫 *£4, extended tour £7* ⏲ *Tours of Bodleian Mar.–Oct., weekdays at 10:30, 11:30, 2, and 3; Sat. at 10:30 and 11:30; Nov.–Feb., weekdays at 2 and 3; Sat. at 10:30 and 11:30. Children under 14 not admitted. Divinity School weekdays 9–4:45, Sat. 9–12:30.*

LIBRARIES OF OLD

Disappointed that you can't get inside Radcliffe Camera? Those eager to see the inside of another scholarly library, this one medieval in vintage, can check out the library at Merton College, on Merton Street.

⑳ **St. John's College.** One of Oxford's most attractive campuses, St. John's has seven quiet quadrangles (which you first enter through a low wooden door) surrounded by elaborately carved, cloisterlike buildings. This college dates to 1555, when it was founded by a merchant named Sir Thomas White. His heart is buried in the chapel and, by tradition, students curse as they walk over it. The Canterbury Quad represented the first example of Italian Renaissance architecture in Oxford, and the Front Quad includes the buildings of the old St. Bernard's Monastary. St. John's is Tony Blair's alma mater and Oxford's wealthiest college, with an estimated endowment of half a billion dollars. ✉ *St. Giles* ☎ *01865/277300* 🌐 *www.sjc.ox.ac.uk* ⏲ *Daily 1–dusk.*

NEED A BREAK?

The Eagle and Child pub (✉ 49 St. Giles ☎ 01865/302925) is a favorite not only for its good ales and historical feel, but also for its literary associations. This was the meeting place of C. S. Lewis, J. R. R. Tolkien, and their circle of literary friends who called themselves the "Inklings." The pub is so close to St. John's College, and such a favorite of its students, that the college purchased it, although it remains open to the public.

⑯ **Sheldonian Theatre.** This fabulously ornate theater is where Oxford's impressive graduation ceremonies are held, conducted almost entirely in Latin. Dating to 1663, it was the first building designed by Sir Christopher Wren when he served as professor of astronomy. The D-shape theater has pillars, balconies, and an elaborately painted ceiling. Outside, stone pillars are topped by 18 massive stone heads, sculpted in the 1970s to replace originals destroyed by air pollution. ✉ *Broad St.* ☎ *01865/277299* 🌐 *www.sheldon.ox.ac.uk* 🎫 *£1.50* ⏲ *Mon.–Sat. 10–12:30 and 2–4:30; mid-Nov.–Feb., closes at 3:30. Closed for 10 days at Christmas and Easter and for degree ceremonies and events.*

⑭ University Church of St. Mary the Virgin. Seven hundred years' worth of funeral monuments crowd this church, including the tombstone of Amy Robsart, the wife of Robert Dudley, Elizabeth I's favorite. One pillar marks the site of Thomas Cranmer's trial under Bloody Mary for his marital machinations on behalf of Henry VIII. From the top of the church's 14th-century tower, you get a panoramic view of the city's skyline with nearly every architectural style since the 11th century. The Convocation House, a part of the church accessible from Radcliffe Square, serves generous portions of warm food—cafeteria style—under the room in which the charity OxFam was founded. ⊠ *High St.* ☎ *01865/279111* ⊕ *www. university-church.ox.ac.uk* ✉ *Church free, tower £2* ⊙ *Sept.–June, Mon.–Sat. 9–5, Sun. noon–5; July and Aug., Mon.–Sat. 9–6, Sun. noon–6; last admission to tower 30 mins before closing.*

Also Worth Seeing

⑰ Museum of the History of Science. The Ashmolean, the world's oldest public museum, was originally housed in this 1638 building, which now holds scientific and mathematical instruments, from astrolabes to quadrants to medical equipment. You can also visit the restored 18th-century chemical laboratory in the basement. ⊠ *Broad St.* ☎ *01865/277280* ⊕ *www.mhs.ox.ac.uk* ✉ *Free* ⊙ *Tues.–Sat. noon–4, Sun. 2–5.*

☾ ⑲ Oxford Story Exhibition. This kitschy presentation in a converted warehouse revisits 800 years of Oxford life with models, sounds, and smells. You ride through the exhibition in small cars shaped like medieval students' desks. It's history made easy. ⊠ *6 Broad St.* ☎ *01865/728822* ⊕ *www.oxfordstory.org.uk* ✉ *£7.25* ⊙ *July and Aug., daily 9:30–5; Sept.–June, Mon.–Sat. 10–4:30, Sun. 11–4:30.*

㉒ Oxford University Museum of Natural History. Eclectic collections relating to entomology, geology, mineralogy, and zoology are stored in this massive Victorian Gothic structure. Among the myriad exhibits are local dinosaur remains and the head and left foot of a dodo bird. The museum is across the street from the Rhodes House, in which hangs a portrait of former president Bill Clinton, who attended University College on High Street. ⊠ *Parks Rd.* ☎ *01865/272950, 01865/270949 recorded information* ⊕ *www.oum.ox.ac.uk* ✉ *Free* ⊙ *Daily noon–5.*

⑪ University of Oxford Botanic Garden. Founded in 1621 as a physic (healing) garden, this is the oldest of its kind in the British Isles. The compact but diverse garden displays 7,000 species from lilies to palms in greenhouses, a small walled garden, and special gardens (such as rock and bog gardens) outside the walled area. ⊠ *Rose La.* ☎ *01865/286690* ⊕ *www.botanic-garden.ox.ac.uk* ✉ *Free* ⊙ *Mar., Apr., and Oct., daily 9–5; May–Sept., daily 9–6; Nov.–Feb., daily 9–4:30..*

Where to Eat

The Old Bank and Old Parsonage hotels also have worthwhile restaurants.

★ ✗ **Le Petit Blanc.** Raymond Blanc's sophisticated brasserie, a hipper
££££–£££££ cousin of Le Manoir aux Quat' Saisons in Great Milton, is the finest place to eat in Oxford. The changing menu always lists innovative, vi-

sually stunning adaptations of bourgeois French fare, sometimes with Mediterranean or Asian influences. Try the herb pancakes with mushrooms, Gruyère, and ham. The set menus here are a good value. ⌧ 71–72 *Walton St.* ☎ 01865/510999 ▭ *AE, DC, V.*

££–££££ ✕ **Fishers.** This is widely viewed as the city's best seafood restaurant, and everything is remarkably fresh. Seafood is available grilled, fried, broiled, or resting comfortably on the half-shell. The atmosphere is bustling but relaxed; it's often fully booked. ⌧ 25–37 St. Clements St. ☎ 01865/ 243003 ⌕ Reservations essential ▭ MC, V.

££–££££ ✕ **Gee's.** With its glass-and-steel framework, this former florist's shop just north of the town center makes a charming dining room. The constantly changing menu features locally raised meats and vegetables in modern versions of traditional English dishes. ⌧ 61 Banbury Rd. ☎ 01865/553540 ▭ AE, MC, V ⤶ No smoking.

££–£££ ✕ **Du Liban.** From the outside this restaurant looks unassuming—it's approached up some stairs beneath a modest sign. Inside, Lebanese music swirls, the atmosphere is lively and jovial, and the students and university workers share big plates of hummus and stuffed grape leaves. After meals, diners smoke hookah pipes (which the English wonderfully call "hubbly bubblies") as bellydancers shake and shimmy between the tables. All good fun, and the food is reliably fresh and good. ⌧ 1–5 Bond St. ☎ 01865/310066 ▭ MC, V.

£–££ ✕ **Grand Café.** Golden-hue tiles, columns, and antique marble tables make
Fodor'sChoice this café both architecturally impressive and an excellent spot for a light
★ meal or leisurely drink. Pop in for early afternoon tea, as the tasty menu lists sandwiches, salads, and tarts along with a good selection of coffee and tea. ⌧ 84 High St. ☎ 01865/204463 ▭ AE, DC, MC, V.

★ **£–££** ✕ **Trout Inn.** More than a century ago, Lewis Carroll took three children on a Thames picnic. "We rowed up to Godstow, and had tea beside a haystack," he told a friend at Christ Church; "I told them the fairy tale of Alice's adventures in Wonderland." The haystacks are gone, but you can still stop at the creeper-covered Thames-side pub 2 mi north of the city center for mixed grills and baked trout. There's a corner devoted to Carroll, and a "Morse Bar" with ample Inspector Morse memorabilia, as the fictional inspector often drank here. ⌧ 195 Godstow Rd., Wolvercote ☎ 01865/302071 ▭ AE, DC, MC, V.

Where to Stay

Oxford is pricey; for the cheapest lodging, contact the tourist information office for B&Bs in locals' homes.

£££££ ▦ **Old Bank Hotel.** From its sleek lobby to the 20th-century British paintings on display and the modern furnishings in the guest rooms, the former Barclay's Bank has brought some style to a city that favors the traditional. Oxford's most centrally located hotel holds the contemporary Quod Bar and Grill, serving creative pastas and dishes such as duck confit. ⌧ 92–94 High St., OX1 4BN ☎ 01865/799599 ⎙ 01865/ 799598 ⊕ www.oxford-hotels-restaurants.co.uk ⇨ 42 rooms ⌂ Restaurant, room service, in-room safes, cable TV, in-room DVDs, in-room broadband, bar, lounge, babysitting, dry cleaning, laundry service, meeting room, free parking, no-smoking rooms ▭ AE, DC, MC, V.

£££££ 🏨 **The Randolph.** A 19th-century neo-Gothic landmark, the hotel faces both the Ashmolean and the Martyrs' Memorial. If their parents are feeling generous, undergraduates are treated to tea in the Morse Bar or dinner in the Spires Restaurant. Scenes from PBS's Inspector Morse *Mystery* series and the film *Shadowlands* were shot here. ⊠ *Beaumont St., OX1 2LN* ☎ *0870/400–8200* 🖷 *01865/791678* ⊕ *www.macdonald-hotels. co.uk* 🛏 *151 rooms* ⅄ *Restaurant, room service, fans, minibars, cable TV, in-room data ports, bar, lobby lounge, laundry service, concierge, business services, Internet room, meeting rooms, parking (fee), some pets allowed (fee), no-smoking floors; no a/c* ⊟ *AE, DC, MC, V.*

★
££££–£££££ 🏨 **Old Parsonage.** This hotel, a 17th-century gabled stone house in a small garden next to St. Giles Church, provides a dignified escape from the surrounding city center. Dark-wood paneling in the soft, red lobby and the guest rooms' tasteful chintzes and marble baths were completely refurbished in 2005. Memorable meals by an open fire (or in the walled garden terrace in summer) keep people coming back. Afternoon teas with scones and clotted cream are excellent. ⊠ *1 Banbury Rd., OX2 6NN* ☎ *01865/310210* 🖷 *01865/311262* ⊕ *www.oxford-hotels-restaurants. co.uk* 🛏 *26 rooms, 4 suites* ⅄ *Restaurant, room service, in-room safes, in-room broadband, bar, lobby lounge, dry cleaning, laundry service, business services, meeting rooms, car rental, free parking, no-smoking rooms; no a/c* ⊟ *AE, DC, MC, V.*

££££ 🏨 **Malmaison Oxford Castle.** This is the place everybody's talking about: a boutique hotel inside an artfully converted, 19th-century prison. Much of the design remains sympathetic to the past. Rooms are divided into the old prison wings—"A Wing" rooms are comfortable in size, "C Wing" rooms include two semicircular suites. With its metal doors, exposed brick walls, and clever embrace of its incarcerating past, this hotel is not for all. You half expect guests to come out and bang their spoons on the white metal railing if breakfast isn't served on time. But they won't, and breakfast is always served on time. ⊠ *3 Oxford Castle, OX1 1AY* ☎ *01865/248432* 🖷 *01845/365–4247* ⊕ *www.malmaison.com* 🛏 *86 rooms, 8 suites* ⅄ *Restaurant, bar, room service, cable TV, in-room broadband, in-room DVDs, Wi-Fi, dry cleaning, laundry service, spa, business services, meeting rooms, no-smoking rooms* ⊟ *AE, MC, V* ⌊◯⌉ *BP.*

££££ 🏨 **Royal Oxford Hotel.** This post–new millennium hotel is a few steps from the train station. Rooms are bright, light, and modern, with contemporary Ikea-style furniture. Bathrooms are tiny but well-equipped. Tea- and coffeemakers, and hospitality trays of chocolates, fruit, and biscuits are welcome touches. ⊠ *17 Park End St., OX1 1HR* ☎ *01865/ 248432* 🖷 *01865/250049* ⊕ *www.royaloxfordhotel.co.uk* 🛏 *26 rooms* ⅄ *Restaurant, room service, cable TV, Wi-Fi, dry cleaning, laundry service, business services, Internet room, meeting rooms, parking (fee), no-smoking rooms; no a/c* ⊟ *AE, MC, V* ⌊◯⌉ *BP.*

£££ 🏨 **Bath Place Hotel.** Down a cobbled alleyway off Holywell Street, 17th-century weavers' cottages have been converted into a small hotel. A number of rooms have four-poster beds; nearly all have slanting floors and exposed beams. Some rooms have their own entrances, and others are in the main building. There's only a breakfast room, but the adjacent Turf Tavern serves ale and bar food. ⊠ *4–5 Bath Pl., OX1 3SI* ☎ *01865/*

5

791812 🖷*01865/791834* ⊕*www.bathplace.co.uk* ↵*14 rooms* ♿*Fans, minibars, bar, laundry service, free parking, some pets allowed; no a/c, no smoking* ▭*AE, DC, MC, V* ⦿|*CP.*

££ ⛭ **Brown's Guest House.** This redbrick Victorian at the edge of central Oxford is a good bet in a town that has precious few affordable guest-houses. Rooms are spacious and neatly decorated, with comfortable beds (most rooms have two) and lots of light. The breakfast room is big and homey, and the food is good and hearty. The only downside is the 15-minute walk or a bus ride into the center. ✉ *281 Iffley Rd., OX4 4AQ* ☎ *01865/791812* 🖷 *01865/791834* ⊕ *www.brownsguesthouse.co.uk* ↵ *8 rooms* ♿ *Cable TV* ▭ *No credit cards* ⦿| *BP.*

££ ⛭ **Newton Guest House.** A big, handsome Victorian mansion just a five–minute walk from all of Oxford's action, Newton is a sprawling, friendly place. Decent-size rooms are brightly decorated with lemony walls and red curtains; some have original Victorian features. The breakfast menu is more varied than that of some guesthouses, with cereals and croissants, along with the usual eggs and bacon. This is one of the best deals in the city center, so book early. ✉ *82 Abingdon Rd., OX1 4PL* ☎ *01865/240561* 🖷 *01865/244647* ✎ *newton.house@btinternet. com* ↵ *11 rooms* ♿ *Cable TV* ▭ *No credit cards* ⦿| *BP.*

££ ⛭ **Victoria House Hotel.** Basic, modern rooms at a low (for Oxford) price are the draw at this no-nonsense hotel aimed at the business set. Don't expect breakfast here, but at your doorstep is a fine selection of cafés. The downstairs Mood bar attracts the trendy with its resident DJ; on weekends, clubbers use the hotel as a base. This is a lively place—if you were hoping for a quiet weekend, this is not it. ✉ *29 George St., OX1 2AY* ☎ *01865/727400* 🖷 *01865/727402* ⊕ *www.victoriahouse-hotel.co.uk* ↵ *14 rooms* ♿ *Bar; no a/c, no smoking* ▭ *AE, DC, MC, V.*

Nightlife & the Arts

Nightlife

Nightlife in Oxford centers around student life, which in turns centers around the local pubs, though you may find a few surprises, too. **Frevd** (✉ 119 Walton St. ☎ 01865/311171), in a renovated neoclassical church, serves light meals and cocktails as well as nightly live jazz or funk. The **Kings Arms** (✉ 40 Holywell St. ☎ 01865/242369), popular with students and fairly quiet during the day, carries excellent local brews as well as inexpensive pub grub. **Raoul's** (✉ 32 Walton St. ☎ 01865/ 553732) is a trendy cocktail bar in the equally trendy Jericho neighborhood. The **Turf Tavern** (✉ Bath Pl. ☎ 01865/243235), off Holywell Street, includes a higgledy-piggledy collection of little rooms and outdoor space good for a quiet drink and inexpensive pub food.

The Arts

FESTIVALS & **Choral music** at the city's churches is a calming way to spend the early
CONCERTS evening. Drop by weekdays during term time at 6 PM at Magdalen (except Tuesday) or New College (except Wednesday) to hear evensong.

The **Jacqueline Du Pre Music Building** (✉ St. Hilda's College ☎ 01865/ 276821), endowed with the city's best acoustics, showcases rising talent at recitals. **Music at Oxford** (☎ 01865/242865), an acclaimed series of weekend classical concerts, takes place mid-September through June in such surroundings as Christ Church Cathedral and Sir Christopher Wren's Sheldonian Theatre. At the **Oxford Coffee Concerts** (⊠ Holywell Music Room, Holywell Rd.), a program of Sunday chamber concerts, string quartets, piano trios, and soloists present baroque and classical pieces in a 1748 hall. Reasonably priced tickets are available from the **Oxford Playhouse** (⊠ Beaumont St. ☎ 01865/305305).

Blenheim Palace (☎ 01993/811091, ⊕ www.blenheimpalace.com) in nearby Woodstock puts on marvelous classical and pop concerts in summer, sometimes combined with fireworks displays. ■ TIP➜ **If you happen to be in town when one is on, pack a picnic of Champagne, Kent strawberries, and fresh Henley cream, and head out for a true, elegant English summertime experience.**

OPERA   The **Garsington Opera** (⊠ Garsington ☎ 01865/361636), a well-regarded event staged in a covered outdoor auditorium, uses Garsington Manor's magical gardens as a backdrop for classic and little-known operas each June and July. The manor is 5 mi southeast of Oxford; you can dine in the Great Barn.

THEATERS   During term time, undergraduate productions are often given in the colleges or local halls. In summer, outdoor performances may take place in quadrangles or college gardens. Look for announcement posters.

New Theatre (⊠ George St. ☎ 0870/606–3500), Oxford's main theater, stages plays, opera, ballet, pantomime, and concerts. It's the second home of the Welsh National Opera and the Glyndebourne Touring Opera. **Old Fire Station** (⊠ 40 George St. ☎ 01865/297170), an alternative theater, showcases student productions, small-scale opera, and new musicals. The **Oxford Playhouse** (⊠ Beaumont St. ☎ 01865/305305) is a serious theater presenting classic and modern dramas.

Sports & the Outdoors

Biking
Bikes can be rented at **Bike Zone** (⊠ 6 Market St. ☎ 01865/728877).

Punting

Fodor'sChoice   You may choose, like many an Oxford student, to spend a summer afternoon **punting,** while dangling your Champagne bottle in the water to ★   keep it cool. Punts—shallow-bottomed boats that are poled slowly up the river—can be rented in several places.

From mid-March through mid-October, **Cherwell Boathouse** (⊠ Bardwell Rd. ☎ 01865/515978), a punt station and restaurant a mile north of the heart of Oxford, will rent you a boat and, if you wish, someone (usually an Oxford student) to punt it. Rentals are £10–£12 per hour; £50–£60 per day. At the foot of **Magdalen Bridge** (⊠ High St. ☎ 01865/515978) you can rent a punt for £10 an hour, plus a £25 refundable deposit. At the St. Aldates Road end of Folly Bridge, **Salter's Steamers** (☎ 01865/243421) rents out punts and skiffs (rowboats) for £10 per hour, £30 per half day, and £50 per day. Their chauffeured punts are

£35 per hour. Three-hour jazz cruises cost £15 and include an onboard performance by the Royal Castle Jazz Band.

Spectator Sports

At the end of May, during **Oxford's Eights Week,** men and women rowers from the university's colleges compete to be "Head of the River." Because the river is too narrow for teams of eight to race side by side, the boats set off, 13 at a time, one behind another. Each boat tries to catch and bump the one in front. Spectators can watch all the way.

Oxford University Cricket Club competes against leading county teams and, each summer, the major foreign team visiting Britain. In the middle of the sprawling University Parks—itself worthy of a walk—the club's playing field is truly lovely.

Shopping

Small shops line High Street, Cornmarket, and Queen Street, and the Clarendon and Westgate centers, which lead off them, have branches of several nationally known stores. **Alice's Shop** (⊠ 83 St. Aldate's
★ ☎ 01865/723793) sells all manner of *Alice in Wonderland* paraphernalia. **Blackwell's** (⊠ 48–51 Broad St. ☎ 01865/792792), family-owned and -run since 1879, stocks an excellent selection of books. The **Covered Market** (⊠ Off High St.) is a good place for a cheap sandwich and a leisurely browse; the smell of pastries follows you from cobbler to jeweler to cheese-monger. **Shepherd & Woodward** (⊠ 109–113 High St. ☎ 01865/249491), a traditional tailor, specializes in university gowns, ties, and scarves. The **University of Oxford Shop** (⊠ 106 High St. ☎01865/ 247414), run by the university, sells authorized clothing, ceramics, and tea towels, all emblazoned with university crests.

BLENHEIM PALACE TO ALTHORP

The River Thames takes on a new graciousness as it flows along the borders of Oxfordshire for 71 mi; each league it increases in size and importance. Three tributaries swell the river as it passes through the landscape: the Windrush, the Evenlode, and the Cherwell. Tucked among the hills and dales are one of England's impressive stately homes, an Edenic village, and a former Rothschild estate. Closer to London in Hertfordshire is St. Albans, with its cathedral and Roman remains.

Rousham Park House & Garden

㉕ *15 mi north of Oxford.*

Wonderfully uncommercialized Rousham Park House & Garden has an expansive 18th-century English landscape park as well as the austere, gray Dormer family mansion, built in 1635. The design of gardener William Kent (1685–1748) is still preserved in the park, where there are paths, groves and meadows, and walled gardens. Longhorn cattle add an exotic touch to the English landscape. Tickets are sold on an honesty system through a vending machine. ■ TIP➔ **There's no shop and no tearoom, so bring a picnic and plenty of water.** Children under 15 are not allowed, nor are dogs. ⊠ *Rousham, near Steeple Aston* ☎ *01869/ 347110* ⊕ *www.rousham.org* ✉ *House £4, garden £3* ☉ *Gardens daily 10–4:30; house Apr.–Sept., Wed. and Sun. 2–4:30.*

Shopping

Serious fashionistas and bargain hunters head for the white clapboard storefronts at **Bicester Village Outlet Shopping** (⊠ 50 Pingle Dr., off A41, Bicester ☎ 01869/323200 ⊕ www.bicestervillage.com) to scoop up European luxury brands like Versace and Jaeger at cut-rate prices. British highlights include Aquascutum, Burberry, Gieves & Hawkes, Waterford Wedgwood, Molton Brown, and Penhaligon's. It's like shopping at a half-price sale on London's Bond Street, but Bicester Village is 7½ mi from Rousham. The Bicester town tourist office is within the outlet.

Woodstock

★ ㉖ *8 mi northwest of Oxford on A44.*

5

Handsome 17th- and 18th-century houses line the trim streets of Woodstock, at the edge of the Cotswolds. It's best known for nearby Blenheim Palace, and in the summer, tour buses clog the village's ancient streets. On a quiet fall or spring afternoon, however, Woodstock is a sublime experience: a mellowed 18th-century church and town hall mark the central square, and along its back streets you can find flower-bedecked houses and quiet lanes right out of a 19th-century etching. The public bus route No. 20 runs (usually every half hour) between Oxford to Woodstock and costs £1.90.

Where to Stay & Eat

★ ✕⊡ **The Feathers.** Flowery, antiques-bedecked guest rooms fill this styl**££££–£££££** ish hotel in the heart of town. Feathers was created from five 17th-century houses, and its elegant courtyard is favored for a summertime meal. In winter, log fires make the public rooms cozy. The seasonal menu and upscale dining room are worth the restaurant's hefty prices (££££). You might opt for lamb served with goat-cheese ravioli or seared scallops and eggplant caviar. Note when checking out that an optional 10% service charge for lodging appears on your bill. ⊠ *Market St., OX20 1SX* ☎ *01993/812291* 🖷 *01993/813158* ⊕ *www.feathers.co.uk* ➳ *20 rooms, 5 suites* ⚥ *Restaurant, café, room service, lounge, dry cleaning, laundry service, meeting rooms; no a/c* ▤ *AE, DC, MC, V* ⋈ *BP.*

££££–£££££ ⊡ **The Bear.** This is an archetypal English coaching inn, with Tudoresque wood paneling, beamed ceilings, wattle-and-daub walls, and blazing fireplaces in winter. The guest rooms, overlooking either a quiet churchyard or the town square, have plenty of carved oak; the duplex suites would make a Stuart king feel at home, thanks to their timbered loft-balconies and gargantuan four-posters. Legend has it that the Bear is where Richard Burton finally popped the question to Elizabeth Taylor. ⊠ *Park St., OX20 1SZ* ☎ *0870/400–8202* 🖷 *01993/813380* ⊕ *www. macdonaldhotels.co.uk* ➳ *48 rooms, 6 suites* ⚥ *Restaurant, room service, minibars, cable TV, bar, laundry service, meeting rooms, no-smoking rooms; no a/c* ▤ *AE, DC, MC, V* ⋈ *BP.*

££ 🏠 **Blenheim Guest House & Tea Rooms.** The Cinderella of all British hotels, this small three-story guesthouse stands in the quiet village cul-de-
sac that leads to the back gates of Blenheim Palace. Its facade still bears
a Victorian-era banner that says VIEWS AND POSTCARDS OF BLENHEIM,
and there's a storefront tearoom. The unassuming guest rooms have modern furnishings, but the Marlborough room is unique—its bathroom offers a view of Blenheim. ⊠ *17 Park St., OX20 1SJ* ☎ *01993/813814*
🖷 *01993/813810* ⊕ *www.theblenheim.com* ⤶ *6 rooms* ⌂ *Tea shop,
laundry service; no a/c, no smoking* ▭ *MC, V* ⦿ *BP.*

Blenheim Palace

㉗ *8 mi northwest of Oxford via A44 to A4095.*

Fodor's Choice
★

So grandiose is Blenheim's masonry and so breathtaking are its articu-
lations of splendor that it was named a World Heritage Site, the only
historic house in Britain to receive the honor. Built by Sir John Vanbrugh
in the early 1700s, Blenheim was given by Queen Anne and the nation
to General John Churchill, first duke of Marlborough. The exterior is
mind-boggling, with its huge columns, enormous pediments and obelisks,
all exemplars of English baroque. Inside, lavishness continues in monumental extremes. In most of the opulent rooms, great family portraits
look down at sumptuous furniture, tapestries illustrating important
battles, and immense pieces of silver. For some visitors, however, the most
memorable room is the small, low-ceiling chamber where Winston
Churchill (his father was the younger brother of the then-duke) was born
in 1874; he is buried in nearby Bladon.

Sir Winston wrote that the unique beauty of Blenheim lay in its perfect adaptation of English parkland to an Italian palace. Indeed the 2,000
acres of grounds, the work of Capability Brown, 18th-century England's
most gifted landscape gardener, are arguably the best example of the
"cunningly natural" park in the country. Brown declared that his object at Blenheim was to "make the Thames look like a small stream
compared with the winding
Danube." At points he almost succeeds—the scale of these grounds
must be seen to be believed. At
dusk, flocks of sheep are let loose
to become living mowers for the
magnificent lawns. Tucked away
here is the Temple of Diana, where
Winston Churchill proposed to his
future wife, Clementine. Blenheim's
formal gardens include notable
water terraces and an Italian garden with a mermaid fountain, all
built in the 1920s.

The Pleasure Gardens, reached by
a train that stops outside the main
entrance to the palace, contain some
child-pleasers: a butterfly house,

giant hedge maze, playground, and giant chess set. The herb and lavender garden is also delightful. The train runs every 30 minutes from 11
until 5. ⊠ *Woodstock* ☎ *01993/811325* ⊕ *www.blenheimpalace.com*
▨ *Palace, park, and gardens: mid-Feb.–mid-May and mid-Sept.–mid-
Dec. £12; June–mid-Sept. £14; park and gardens only £7 or £9, depending on season* ☉ *Palace mid-Feb.–mid-Dec., daily 10:30–4:45; park daily
9–4:45; special events, fairs, and concerts throughout year.*

**EN
ROUTE**
After taking in Blenheim Palace, stop by **Bladon,** 2 mi southeast of
Woodstock on A4095 and 6 mi northwest of Oxford, to see the small,
tree-lined churchyard that is the burial place of Sir Winston Churchill.
His grave is all the more impressive for its simplicity.

Kelmscott Manor

㉘ *20 mi southwest of Oxford.*

Behind its dignified 16th- and 17th-century exterior, limestone Kelmscott Manor was, in its Victorian heyday, a site of social unrest as well
as domestic disarray. Here, artist, writer, and socialist William Morris
(1834–96) launched his anti-industrial Arts and Crafts movement. His
wife, Jane, openly cohabited with her lover, the painter Dante Gabriel
Rossetti (1828–82), Morris's business partner. Today the house displays
textiles, furniture, and ceramics by Morris and his associates. Morris
died at Kelmscott and is buried in the local churchyard. ⊠ *Off A417,
Kelmscott, Lechlade* ☎ *01367/252486* ⊕ *www.kelmscottmanor.co.uk*
▨ *£8.50, garden £2* ☉ *Apr.–Sept., Wed. 11–1 and 2–5; Apr.–June and
Sept., 3rd Sat. 2–5; July and Aug., 1st and 3rd Sat. 2–5.*

Uffington & the Vale of the White Horse

㉙ *7 mi southeast of Kelmscott Manor, 18 mi southwest of Oxford, 9 mi
northeast of Swindon.*

Stretching up into the foothills of the Berkshire Downs between Swindon and Oxford is a wide fertile plain known as the Vale of the White
Horse. Here, off B4507, cut into the turf of the hillside to expose the
underlying chalk, is the 374-foot-long, 110-foot-high **figure of a white
horse,** an important prehistoric site. Some historians believed that the
figure might have been carved to commemorate King Alfred's victory
over the Danes in 871, whereas others dated it to the Iron Age, around
750 BC. More current research suggests that it is at least 1,000 years older,
created at the beginning of the second millennium BC. **Uffington Castle,** above the horse, is a prehistoric fort. English Heritage maintains these
sites. To reach the Vale of the White Horse from Oxford, follow A420,
then B4508 to the village of Uffington.

The 85-mi **Ridgeway National Trail** (⊕ www.nationaltrail.co.uk), which
runs from south of Aylesbury to near Avebury, passes through the area.

Where to Stay

££–£££ ▦ **The Craven B&B.** Rose-filled gardens and antiques-filled rooms are
among the traditional elements at this pretty thatch-roof, 17th-century
cottage on the outskirts of Uffington. Bedrooms have beamed ceilings

and country-cottage prints. Family photographs and the shared kitchen table at breakfast time keep the B&B convivial. Creative seasonal menus are available for dinner (guests only). ✉ *Fernham Rd., Uffington SN7 7RD* ☎ *01367/820449* ⊕ *www.thecraven.co.uk* ⇆ *6 rooms, 4 with bath* ⚘ *Dining room, lounge, laundry service; no a/c, no room phones, no room TVs, no smoking* ▤ *MC, V* ⦿⦿ *BP.*

Dorchester-on-Thames

㉚ *15 mi east of Uffington, 7 mi southeast of Abingdon, 9 mi southeast of Oxford.*

An important center in Saxon times, when it was the seat of a bishopric, Dorchester merits a visit chiefly because of its ancient abbey, but also because it's a charming little town. The main street, once a leg of the Roman road to Silchester, has timber houses, thatch cottages, and ancient inns. Crossing the Thames at Day's Lock and turning left at Little Wittenham takes you on a bucolic and historic walk past the remains of the village's Iron Age settlements. Pricey and alluring antiques shops line the High Street.

In addition to secluded cloisters and gardens, **Dorchester Abbey** has a spacious church (1170) with traceried medieval windows and a lead baptismal font. The great tower was rebuilt in 1602, but incorporated the old 14th-century spiral staircase. If you climb the tower you can take in sweeping views of verdant pastures, graceful willows, and water meadows. The abbey is a popular concert venue. ✉ *Off A4074* ☎ *01865/ 340007* ⊕ *www.dorchester-abbey.org.uk* ✑ *Free* ☉ *May–Sept., daily 8:30–7; Oct.–Apr., daily 8:30–dusk, except during services.*

Where to Stay

££ ⊞ **George Hotel.** Overlooking Dorchester Abbey, this 500-year-old hotel was built as a coaching inn—there's an old coach parked outside—and it retains whitewashed walls, exposed beams, and log fires. Each room has an individual style and two have four-poster beds. All are tastefully decorated in taupe and russet hues. The modern rooms in the annex have less character. ✉ *23 High St., OX10 7JX* ☎ *0870/752–2235* 🖨 *01865/ 341620* ⊕ *www.thegeorgedorchester.co.uk* ⇆ *17 rooms* ⚘ *Restaurant, room service, in-room data ports, pub, dry cleaning, laundry facilities, meeting rooms, free parking, some pets allowed, no-smoking rooms; no a/c* ▤ *AE, DC, MC, V* ⦿⦿ *CP.*

Great Milton

㉛ *8 mi northeast of Dorchester-on-Thames, 7 mi southeast of Oxford.*

With adorable thatch cottages built of local stone and a single street about a mile long with wide grass verges, this is another historic stop on the literary pilgrim's route. The poet John Milton, author of *Paradise Lost* (1667), was married in the local church, which holds an unusual collection of old musical instruments. The town's fine restaurants are a haunt of culinary pilgrims.

HIKING & BIKING ALONG THE THAMES

The Thames Valley is a great area to explore by foot or bike. It's not too hilly, and pubs and easily accessible lodgings dot the riverside and small towns. The Thames is almost completely free of car traffic along the Thames Path, a 180-mi national trail that traces the river from the London flood barrier to the river's source near Kemble, in the Cotswolds. The path follows towpaths from the outskirts of London, through Windsor, to Oxford and Lechlade. Good public transportation in the region makes it possible to start and stop easily anywhere along this route. In summer the walking is fine and no special gear is necessary, but in winter the path often floods—check before you head out.

The Countryside Agency has been charting and preserving Thames paths for years and offers publications about them. For maps and advice, contact the National Trails Office or the Ramblers' Association. The Chiltern Conservation Board promotes walking in the Chilterns peaks.

Biking is perhaps the best way to see the Chilterns. Routes include the 98-mi Thames Valley Cycle Route from London to Oxford, the 200-mi Oxfordshire Cycleway around the county's countryside, and the 85-mi Ridgeway Path from Uffington that follows the Chilterns; the National Trails Office has information. The 180-mi Thames Path also has plenty of biking opportunities.

CONTACTS & RESOURCES

Chiltern Conservation Board (☎ 01844/271300 ⊕ www.chilternsaonb.org). **Chiltern Way** (☎ 01494/771250 ⊕ www.chilternsociety.org.uk). **Countryside Agency** (☎ 01242/521381 ⊕ www.countryside.gov.uk ✉ London ☎ 020/7340-2900). **National Trails Office** (☎ 01865/810224 ⊕ www.nationaltrail.co.uk). **Ramblers' Association** (☎ 020/7339-8500 ⊕ www.ramblers.org.uk). **Sustrans (Thames Valley Cycle Route)** (☎ 0117/903-0504 ⊕ www.sustrans.org.uk).

Where to Stay & Eat

£££££
Fodor'sChoice
★

✕🏨 **Le Manoir aux Quat' Saisons.** Standards are high at this 15th-century stone manor house, which has luxurious rooms in occasionally over-the-top styles ranging from pink rococo fantasy to chic yellow chinoiserie (most rooms have private gardens and working fireplaces, too). It has one of the country's finest kitchens (complete with cooking school; £££££), and Chef Raymond Blanc's epicurean touch shows at every turn. Decide among the innovative French creations or treat yourself to the *menu gourmand*—eight courses of haute cuisine for £95. A stroll through the hotel's herb and Japanese gardens is de rigueur. ✉ *Church Rd., OX44 7PD* ☎ *01844/278881* 🖶 *01844/278847* ⊕ *www.manoir.com* 🛏 *32 rooms ⅙ Restaurant, room service, in-room safes, cable TV, in-room data ports, croquet, lounge, babysitting, dry cleaning, laundry service, concierge, meeting rooms, car rental, kennel, no-smoking rooms; no a/c in some rooms ▭ AE, DC, MC, V* ⵋ *CP.*

Aylesbury

32 *17 mi northeast of Great Milton, 22 mi east of Oxford, 46 mi northwest of London.*

Aylesbury makes a good base for exploring the surrounding countryside. It's a charming historic town with a 13th-century church, surrounded by small Tudor lanes and cottages.

Fodor's Choice
★

Many of the regal residences created by the Rothschild family throughout Europe are gone now, but **Waddesdon Manor** remains, a vision of the 19th century at its most sumptuous. G. H. Destailleur built the house in the 1880s for Baron Ferdinand de Rothschild in the style of a French chateau, with perfectly balanced turrets and towers and walls of creamy stone. Inside it was lovingly furnished over the course of 35 years with Savonnerie carpets, Sèvres porcelain, furniture made by Riesener for Marie Antoinette, and paintings by Rubens, Watteau, Gainsborough, and Reynolds. The gardens are equally extraordinary, with an aviary, colorful plantings, and winding trails with allow panoramic views. In the restaurant you can dine on English or French fare and order excellent Rothschild wines if your pocketbook can take the hit. ⊠ *Waddesdon, on A41 near Aylesbury* ☎ *01296/653226* ⊕ *www.waddesdon.org.uk* ✉ *House and grounds £11, grounds £4* ⊙ *House Apr.–Oct., Wed.–Sun. and national holidays Mon. 11–4; gardens Jan.–Mar., weekends 10–5; Apr.–late Dec., Wed.–Sun. and national holidays Mon. 10–5.*

★ A superb example of a Georgian garden, **Stowe Landscape Gardens** was created for the Temple family by the most famous gardeners of the 18th century. Capability Brown, Charles Bridgeman, and William Kent all worked on the land to create 980 acres of pleasing greenery in the valleys and meadows. More than 30 striking monuments, follies, and temples dot the landscape of lakes, rivers, and pleasant vistas. Stowe House, at its center, is now a fancy school with some magnificently restored rooms; it's closed to the public, apart from occasional tours (arranged in advance by phone). The gardens are about 3 mi northwest of Buckingham, which is a half mile from Aylesbury. ⊠ *Stowe Ave., off 422 Buckingham–Banbury Rd., Buckingham* ☎ *01280/822850* ⊕ *www.nationaltrust.org.uk* ✉ *£5 gardens only; £12 house and gardens* ⊙ *Mar.–Oct., Wed.–Sun. 10–5:30; Nov.–Feb., weekends 10–4.*

Where to Stay & Eat

££–£££ ✕▦ **Five Arrows.** Fancifully patterned brick chimneys and purple gables decorate this baroque building next to the main entrance of Waddesdon Manor. Constructed to house the manor's workers, it now holds a hotel with traditional-style bedrooms that are sweet, if small. The delightful suites in the Courtyard Stables are big enough for families, or couples who just want to stretch out a little. A fine restaurant (££–£££) and pub serves inspired modern fare with a Mediterranean twist; the wine list is excellent. The in-house "wine pub" is a regular award winner. ⊠ *High St., Waddesdon HP18 0JE* ☎ *01296/651727* 🖷 *01296/658596* ⊕ *www.waddesdon.org.uk* ➣ *9 rooms, 2 suites* ⚑ *Restaurant, bar; no a/c, no smoking* ▭ *MC, V* ❑ *BP.*

£££££ ▦ **The Grove.** This epitome of the modern country-house hotel—a hybrid 18th-century manor house and 21st-century wing—has a perfect balance of old-fashioned charm and contemporary style. In the manor house, luxurious touches include Victorian claw-foot bathtubs and ostrich feather–top four-poster beds. Rooms in the modern wing are sleek, with white lacquered furniture. All the rooms have gadgetry and modern technology galore, including plasma-screen TVs. Some have balconies with views of the gardens. The spa is perfectly pampering, and the mood throughout is all about elegant relaxation. ⊠ *Off Exit 19 of M25, Chandler's Cross WD3 4TG, 14 mi east of Aylesbury* ☎ *01923/807807* 📠 *01923/221008* ⊕ *www.thegrove.co.uk* 🛏 *211 rooms, 16 suites* ⌂ *Restaurant, room service, in-room safes, minibars, cable TV, in-room CD/DVD, in-room broadband, 18-hole golf course, 2 tennis courts, indoor-outdoor pool, gym, hair salon, hot tub, sauna, spa, steam room, croquet, bar, lounge, library, dry cleaning, laundry service, concierge, meeting rooms; no-smoking rooms* ▤ *AE, D, MC, V.*

£££££ ▦ **Hartwell House.** Part Jacobean, part Georgian, this magnificent stately home offers formal luxury in a soothing countryside setting. The elegant building is decorated with a masterful touch—chandeliers, original oil paintings, and carved ceilings adorn the ornate public areas, and bedrooms with well chosen antiques and comfortable beds are suitably grand. Some rooms have direct access to the gardens, which sprawl over 90 acres of landscaped parkland, perfect for strolls. This is the kind of place where you must dress to impress for dinner. ⊠ *Oxford Rd. (A418), HP17 8NL* ☎ *01296/747444* 📠 *01296/747450* ⊕ *www.hartwellhouse.com* 🛏 *46 rooms* ⌂ *Restaurant, room service, in-room data ports, 2 tennis courts, indoor pool, gym, hair salon, hot tub, sauna, spa, steam room, fishing, croquet, bar, lounge, library, dry cleaning, laundry service, concierge, meeting rooms, car rental, some pets allowed, no-smoking floor; no a/c, no kids under 8* ▤ *AE, MC, V.*

St. Albans

③③ *25 mi east of Aylesbury, 27 mi northwest of London.*

A lively town on the outskirts of London, St. Albans is known for its historic cathedral, and it also holds reminders of its long history. From AD 50 to 440, the town then known as Verulamium was one of the largest communities in Roman Britain. You can explore this past in the Verulamium museum and splendid Roman sites around the area. The bucolic surrounding countryside is where George Bernard Shaw was inspired. Every Wednesday and Saturday, the Market Place on St. Peter's Street comes alive with traders from all over England. St. Albans is 30 minutes by fast train from St. Pancras Station in central London. The estimable Campaign for Real Ale (CAMRA), which lobbies for the protection and development of traditional English ales, holds an annual beer festival here in late September.

Medieval pilgrims came from far and wide to hilltop **St. Albans Cathedral** to honor its patron saint, a Roman soldier turned Christian martyr. Construction of the impressive, mainly Norman cathedral began in the early 11th century, but the nearly 300-foot-long nave dates from 1235. The tower is even more historic, and contains bricks from ancient Roman buildings. ⊠ *Holywell Hill at High St.* ☎ *01727/860780* ⊕ *www.stalbanscathedral.org.uk* ✉ *Free* ⊘ *Daily 8–5:45; guided tours weekdays 11:30 and 2:30, Sat. 11:30 and 2, Sun. 2:30.*

With exhibits on everything from Roman food to burial practices, the **Verulamium Museum**, on the site of the ancient Roman city, explores life 2,000 years ago. The re-created Roman rooms contain colorful mosaics that are some of the finest in Britain. Every second weekend of the month, "Roman soldiers" invade the museum and demonstrate the skills of the Imperial Army. ⊠*St. Michael's St.* ☎*01754/768837* ⊕*www.verulamium. co.uk* ✉ *£3.40* ⊘ *Mon.–Sat. 10–5:30, Sun. 2–5:30.*

Verulamium Park, adjacent to the Verulamium Museum, contains the usual—playground, wading pool, lake—and the unusual—**Roman ruins** that include part of the Roman town hall and a hypocaust, a central-heating system. The hypocaust dates to AD 200 and included one of the first heated floors in Britain. Brick columns supported the floor, and hot air from a nearby fire was drawn underneath the floor to keep bathers warm. ⊠ *St. Michael's St.* ☎ *01754/768837* ⊕ *www.verulamium.co. uk* ✉ *Free* ⊘ *Hypocaust Mon.–Sat. 10–5:30, Sun. 2–5:30.*

Imagination can take you back to AD 130 and to a Roman stage drama as you walk around the ruins of the **Roman Theater**, one of the few in this country. Next to the theater are the ruins of a Roman town house, shops, and a shrine. ⊠ *Bluehouse Hill* ☎ *01727/835035* ✉ *£2* ⊘ *Easter–Nov., daily 10–5; Dec.–Easter, daily 10–4.*

Hatfield House, an outstanding brick mansion surrounded by formal gardens, stands as a testament to the magnificence of Jacobean architecture. Robert Cecil, earl of Salisbury, built Hatfield in 1611, and his descendants still live here. The interior, with its dark wood paneling, lush tapestries, and Tudor and Jacobean portraits, reveals much about the era. Perhaps the finest feature is the ornate Grand Staircase, with carved wooden figures on the banisters. Friday is Connoisseurs' Day; entrance is £10.50 and includes an extended tour and a view of additional gardens. The **Elizabethan Banquet** (☎ 01707/262055 ⊕ www. theoldpalace.co.uk ✉ £40 ⊘ Tues., Fri., and Sat. 7:30 PM–11 PM) is a hearty five-course dinner accompanied by kitschy entertainment from King Henry VIII, Queen Elizabeth I, minstrels, and jokers. ⊠ *Hatfield, 6 mi east of St. Albans, off A1* ☎ *01707/287010* ⊕ *www.hatfield-house.co.uk* ✉ *House, gardens, and park £8 (£10.50 on Fri.), gardens £5, park £3* ⊘ *Easter–Sept., mansion daily noon–4, west gardens daily 11–5:30, east gardens Fri. 11–6; guided tours weekdays only.*

From 1906 to his death in 1950, the famed Irish playwright George Bernard Shaw lived in the small village of Ayot St. Lawrence. Today his small Edwardian home, **Shaw's Corner,** remains much as he left it. The most delightful curiosity is his little writing hut in the garden, which can be turned to face the sun. ⊠ *Off Hill Farm La., Ayot St. Lawrence, 9 mi northeast of St. Albans* ☎ *01438/820307, 01494/755567 recorded*

information ⊕ *www.nationaltrust.org.uk* 🖼 *£4* ⊗ *House Apr.–Oct.,
Wed.–Sun. 1–5; gardens Apr.–Oct., Wed.–Sun. noon–5:30.*

Where to Stay & Eat

£ ✕ **Waffle House.** Indoors or outside, you can have a great budget meal
at the 16th-century Kingsbury Watermill, near the Verulamium Museum.
The organic flour for the high-quality, sweet and savory Belgian waf-
fles comes from Redbournbury Watermill just north of the city; daily
specials add variety. In the main dining room, you can see the wheel churn
the water of the River Ver. ⊠ *Kingsbury Watermill, St. Michael's St.*
☎ *01727/853502* 🖭 *MC, V.*

£ ✕ **Ye Olde Fighting Cocks.** Some claim this is England's oldest pub, although that's a contentious category. Still, this octagonal building certainly looks suitably aged. The building was moved to this location in
the 16th century, but the foundations date back to the 8th century. The
small rooms with low ceilings make a cozy stop for a pint and simple
pub grub. Be prepared for crowds. ⊠ *16 Abbey Mill La.* ☎ *01727/869152*
🖭 *MC, V.*

££££–£££££ ✕🏠 **St. Michael's Manor.** The Newling Ward family has owned this luxurious 16th-century manor house in the heart of St. Albans for three
generations. The 5 acres of grounds, complete with a lake, add a sense
of seclusion, and plush furniture helps make the antiques- and paint-
ing-filled public areas inviting. The ruffled Victorian-style bedrooms are
equipped with thoughtful extras like complimentary bottled water, fruit,
and cookies. The conservatory restaurant (£££££) has a daily set menu
of modern British cuisine, including items like cutlets of spring lamb with
confit tomato jus. ⊠ *Fishpool St., AL3 4RY* ☎ *01727/864444* 🖷 *01727/
848909* ⊕ *www.stmichaelsmanor.com* ⇆ *22 rooms* ♿ *2 restaurants,
room service, cable TV, fishing, croquet, bar, lounge, babysitting, dry
cleaning, laundry service, meeting room, no-smoking rooms; no a/c*
🖭 *AE, DC, MC, V* ⏐⏐ *BP.*

Woburn Abbey

☾ ❸❹ *30 mi west of St. Albans, 10 mi northeast of Aylesbury.*

Still the ancestral residence of the duke of Bedford, Woburn Abbey houses
countless Grand Tour treasures and old master paintings, including 20
stunning Canalettos that practically wallpaper the crimson dining salon,
and excellent works by Gainsborough and Reynolds. The Palladian
mansion contains a number of etchings by Queen Victoria, who left them
behind after she stayed here. Outside, nine species of deer roam the
grounds that include an antiques center and small restaurant. The adjacent, **Woburn Safari Park** is a popular drive-through wildlife experience, home to big game from around the world. Jeep tours, walks with
elephants, and other special packages are available. There are plenty of
play areas, a boating lake with swan boats, and walkabouts with small
animals such as wallabies. ⊠ *Woburn* ☎ *01525/290666* ⊕ *www.
woburnabbey.co.uk* 🖼 *House and deer park £10.50, safari £16.50 in
summer, £8 off-season; abbey grounds £3* ⊗ *Jan.–Mar. and Oct., weekends 11–4; Apr.–Sept., Mon.–Sat. 11–4, Sun. 11–5.*

Where to Stay & Eat

££££–£££££  **The Inn at Woburn.** This modern hotel with traditional pine furnishings is in the center of Woburn village, a small Georgian town. Bedrooms are uncluttered and comfortable, with hot-beverage makers. Olivier's (££–£££) serves contemporary British cuisine with an Italian accent, and the pub is a snug place for a pint. Ask about packages that include entrance to Woburn Abbey and Safari Park. ⊠ *George St., Woburn MK17 9PX* ☎ *01525/290441* 🖷 *01525/290432* ⊕ *www.theinnatwoburn. com* 🍴 *51 rooms, 7 suites △ Restaurant, room service, some in-room safes, minibars, cable TV, in-room data ports, bar, lobby lounge, dry cleaning, laundry service, meeting rooms, some pets allowed, no-smoking rooms; no a/c* ▤ *AE, DC, MC, V.*

Althorp

35 *5 mi west of Northampton, 27 mi northwest of Woburn Abbey.*

Deep in the heart of Northamptonshire sits Althorp, the ancestral home of the Spencers, the family of Diana, Princess of Wales. Here, on a tiny island within the estate park, is Diana's final resting place. Back in 1765 Horace Walpole described the setting as "one of those enchanted scenes which a thousand circumstances of history and art endear to a pensive spectator." As it turns out, Princess Diana and her siblings found the house ugly and melancholy, calling it "Deadlock Hall." What the house does have are rooms filled with Van Dycks, Reynoldses, and Rubens— all portraits of the Spencers going back 500 years—and an entry hall that architectural historian Nikolaus Pevsner called "the noblest Georgian room in the country." To these attractions, Earl Spencer has added a visitor center devoted to Diana, which includes her wedding dress, childhood memorabilia, and an exhibition on her charitable work. A percentage of ticket income is donated to the Diana Princess of Wales Memorial Fund. On the west side of the estate park is Great Brington, the neighboring village where the church of **St. Mary the Virgin** (🕑 Daily noon–5) holds the Spencer family crypt; it's best reached by the designated path from Althorp. ⊠ *Rugby Rd., off A428* ☎ *01604/770107* ⊕ *www.althorp.com* 🎟 *£12* 🕑 *July–Sept., daily 11–5; closed Aug. 31.*

THAMES VALLEY ESSENTIALS

Transportation

BY AIR

The Thames Valley is convenient to major airports in London (⇨ Air Travel *in* Smart Travel Tips).

BY BUS

If you haven't rented a car, traveling by bus is the second best way to explore the Thames Valley. The Oxford Bus Company, Megabus and the Oxford Tube offer service to Oxford several times an hour during rush hour, and hourly throughout the night. Pick-up points in London are Victoria train and bus stations, and Baker Street and Marble Arch by the Underground stops. The Oxford Bus Company also offers "The Airline," round-trip shuttle service from Oxford to Gatwick (£25) and Heathrow (£18) every half hour.

Other local bus services, such as Stagecoach, link the towns between Oxford and Henley with services to Heathrow Airport and London. Reading Buses also connect Oxford and Reading to the airports, and First of Bracknell serves the smaller towns of Berkshire. For information about buses and other forms of public transportation, contact Traveline.

CUTTING COSTS The Oxford Bus Company offers a one-day ticket (£4) and a seven-day Freedom ticket (£12), for unlimited bus travel within Oxford.

FARES & 🗹 **First** ☎ 01344/868688 ⊕ www.firstgroup.com. **Megabus** ⊕ www.megabus.co.uk.
SCHEDULES **Oxford Bus Company** ☎ 01865/785400 ⊕ www.oxfordbus.co.uk. **Reading Buses** ☎ 0118/959-4000 ⊕ www.reading-buses.co.uk. **Stagecoach Oxford Tube** ☎ 01865/772250 ⊕ www.stagecoachbus.com/oxfordshire. **Traveline** ☎ 0870/608-2608 ⊕ www.traveline.org.uk.

BY CAR
The M4 and M40 radiate west from London, bringing Oxford (56 mi) and Reading (41 mi) within an hour's drive, except during rush hour. Although the roads are good, this wealthy section of the commuter belt has heavy traffic, even on the smaller roads. Parking in towns can be a problem, too, so allow plenty of time.

BY TRAIN
Trains to Oxford (1 hour) and the region depart from London's Paddington station. Ascot (¾ hour) is easily accessible from London: trains leave Waterloo on the half hour. Trains to St. Albans (30 minutes) leave from St. Pancras Station. For timetables, call or log on to National Rail Enquiries's Web site.
🗹 **National Rail Enquiries** ☎ 0845/748-4950 ⊕ www.nationalrail.co.uk.

Contacts & Resources

EMERGENCIES
The John Radcliffe Hospital is accessible by Bus 13 from Carfax Tower in Oxford or from the A40.
🗹 **Ambulance, fire, police** ☎ 999. **John Radcliffe Hospital** ⊠ Headley Way, Oxford ☎ 01865/741166. **Princess Christian's Hospital** ⊠ 12 Clarence Rd., Windsor ☎ 01753/853121.

INTERNET
There are relatively few Internet cafés in this region, most in and around Oxford. Internet access is nearly impossible to find in the smaller villages. In those areas, your best bet will be your hotel, although the general rule seems to that only more expensive properties offer access. Even then, broadband is still relatively rare, and Wi-Fi virtually unheard of.
🗹 Internet Cafés **Mices Internet Shop** ⊠ 118 High St., Oxford ☎ 01865/515955. **Wired To** ⊠ 138 Magdalen Rd., Oxford ☎ 01865/727770.

TOUR OPTIONS

BOAT TOURS   One ideal way to see the Thames region is from the water. Water-based tours can range from 30 minutes to all day. Hobbs and Sons covers the Henley Reach and also rents boats if you want to take the active approach. Salter's Steamers runs daily steamer cruises, mid-May to mid-September from Windsor, Oxford, Abingdon, Henley, Marlow, and Reading. Thames River Cruises conducts outings from Caversham Bridge in Reading, Easter through September. French Brothers operates river trips from the Promenade in Windsor, and from Runnymede going as far as Hampton Court.

The Environment Agency's Visit Thames Web site and telephone hotline provide information about boating, fishing, and walking the Thames. **Environment Agency Visit Thames** ☎0845/601–5336 ⊕www.visitthames.com. **French Brothers** ⊠ The Promenade, Windsor ☎ 01753/851900 ⊕ www.boat-trips.co.uk. **Hobbs and Sons** ⊠ Station Rd., Henley-on-Thames ☎ 01491/572035 ⊕ www.hobbs-of-henley.com. **Salter's Steamers** ⊠ Folly Bridge, Oxford ☎ 01865/243421 ⊕ www.salterssteamers.co.uk. **Thames River Cruises** ⊠ Caversham Bridge, Reading ☎ 0118/948–1088 ⊕ www.thamesrivercruise.co.uk.

BUS TOURS   City Sightseeing runs guided, open-top bus tours of Windsor for £6 (daily mid-March–October, weekends only November–late December) and of Oxford for £9 (year-round).
City Sightseeing ☎ 01865/790522 ⊕ www.city-sightseeing.com.

WALKING TOURS   Two-hour guided walking tours leave the Oxford Tourist Information Centre (⇨ Visitor Information) at 11 and 4 daily. Tickets (£6.50, £7.50 on Saturday) include admission to some colleges. Saturday tours include Christ Church. An Inspector Morse walking tour is offered at 1:30 on Saturday (£7), and ghost tours (£5.50) run June–September and October 31 on Friday and Saturday at 8 PM. The information center also sells pamphlets detailing walking tours.

Blue Badge guides provide theme walking tours (£4) of Windsor and Eton that start at the Windsor Tourist Information Centre (⇨ Visitor Information). Tours run mid-April–August on weekends at 10:30 AM. You can also purchase self-guided walking pamphlets for 50p each.

For a memorably different way to tour Windsor, take a 30-minute (£19) or one-hour (£38) horse-drawn carriage tour run by Orchard Poyle. Tours leave from the Harte & Garter Hotel in central Windsor and tour the town and Windsor Great Park.
Orchard Poyle Carriage Rides ⊠ South Gates, Wick La., Englefield Green TW20 0XA ☎ 01784/435983 ⊕ www.orchardpoyle.co.uk.

VISITOR INFORMATION

Aylesbury ⊠ 8 Bourbon St., HP20 2RR ☎ 01296/330559. **Henley-on-Thames** ⊠ King's Arms Barn, Kings Rd., RG9 2DG ☎ 01491/578034 ⊕ www.visit-henley.co.uk. **Marlow** ⊠ 31 High St., SL7 1AU ☎ 01628/483597. **Oxford** ⊠ 15/16 Broad St., OX1 3AS ☎ 01865/726871 ⊕ www.oxford.gov.uk. **Oxford University** ⊕ www.ox.ac.uk. **St. Albans** ⊠ Town Hall, Market Pl., AL3 5DJ ☎ 01727/864511 ⊕ www.stalbans.gov.uk. **Windsor** ⊠24 High St., SL4 1LH ☎01753/743900 ⊕www.windsor.gov.uk. **Woburn** ⊠Old St. Mary's Church, Bedford St., MK17 9PJ ☎ 01525/290631. **Woodstock** ⊠ Park St., Oxfordshire Museum, OX20 1SN ☎ 01993/813632.

Shakespeare Country

STRATFORD-UPON-AVON & ENVIRONS

WORD OF MOUTH

"What Stratford does have . . . is a beautiful river setting, a great theater, old buildings, and delightful walks. Most visitors have only enough time . . . to walk from the coach park or train station to the Birthplace. If they stayed longer and visited Anne Hathaway's Cottage by *walking* from the center across the fields, or visited Charlecote Park, they might return home with happier memories!"

–bellini

"[Collegiate Church of St. Mary] is just a short walk from Warwick Castle, and worth every step. Beautiful church, especially the Beauchamp Chapel . . . . You can climb the tower—but be warned that it's a narrow and completely dark spiral staircase. Views from the top are nice."

–Amanda

www.fodors.com/forums

Updated by
Christi
Daugherty

YOU GET NEW INSIGHT INTO WILLIAM SHAKESPEARE when you visit the stretch of country where he was born and raised. The hills of sculpted farmland may look nothing like the forested countryside of the 16th century, but some sturdy Tudor houses that Shakespeare knew survive to this day. You can walk down streets he might have traveled up and cross streams where, as a child, he might have dangled his feet in the cool water. There's beauty in this—and also the possibility of tourist overkill. Stratford-upon-Avon, with its carefully preserved Shakespeare sites and the theaters of the famed Royal Shakespeare Company, veers toward becoming "Shakespeare World." Still, it's a fascinating place, and there's much more to see—castles, churches, and countryside—in this famously lovely part of Britain.

Warwickshire—the county of which Stratford is the southern nexus—is a land of sleepy villages, thatch-roof cottages, and solitary farmhouses. It was the birthplace of the image of England that has been spread around the world by the works of Shakespeare. Driving down its country lanes is one of the best ways of exploring this area. Stop in at Charlecote, a grand Elizabethan manor house, and Baddesley Clinton, a superb example of late-medieval domestic architecture. Other treasure houses are Ragley Hall, Coughton Court, and Broughton Castle, brimming with art and antiques; Compton Verney is a stately home that has been converted to an art gallery. Warwick Castle, a huge fortress, provides a glimpse into the country's turbulent history.

The price you pay for visiting Stratford is being caught among vast crowds of people, especially in peak season when the volume of visitors and the commercialization can be too much. If the hurlyburly overwhelms you, take a hint from the young Shakespeare. He often turned his back on the town and followed the Avon through quiet meadows and peaceful villages. You, too, can wander though a tranquil landscape and spend an afternoon picnicking in peace by a quiet river.

Exploring Shakespeare Country

Stratford-upon-Avon, the heart of this small region, is surrounded by tiny villages, some with Shakespearean connections. The countryside around these hamlets is littered with stately "piles," as the British call the sprawling mansions built over the centuries. Many are open to the public, and each requires a half day to explore. To the north lie two magnificent castles, Warwick and Kenilworth. The town of Warwick has much to offer besides its castle, and it's worth a protracted jaunt.

About the Restaurants

Although Stratford has few restaurants serving the most sophisticated cuisine, many reasonably priced bistros and unpretentious eateries offer a broad choice of international fare. For finer options, seek out one of the better hotels, which have drawn some of the foremost chefs from London and beyond. Warwick and Kenilworth have some excellent restaurants, and the countryside has many old pubs where the home cooking is memorable.

GREAT ITINERARIES

Stratford-upon-Avon is ideal for day visits or as a convenient base. If you have only a day here, arrive early and confine your visit to two or three Shakespeare Birthplace Trust properties, a few other town sights, a pub lunch, and a walk along the river, capped off by a stroll to the cottage of Anne Hathaway.

Numbers in the text correspond to numbers in the margin and on the Shakespeare Country and Stratford-upon-Avon maps.

IF YOU HAVE 2 DAYS

🚉 **Stratford-upon-Avon** ❶-❾ ⚑ deserves at least a full day and a drama-packed night at the Royal Shakespeare Theatre. Five historic properties are must-sees: three are in town—**Shakespeare's Birthplace** ❶, on Henley Street, **Nash's House and New Place** ❸, and **Hall's Croft** ❻—whereas the others—**Anne Hathaway's Cottage** ❼ and **Mary Arden's House** ❿—are just a few minutes out of town. After your Stratford sojourn, spend the next day touring selected sights, including the mansions of **Baddesley Clinton** ⓭, **Packwood House** ⓬, and **Charlecote Park** ⓱. In between, take in some of the villages nearby, ideal for lunch.

Spend your second night back in Stratford or in one of the inns along the way.

IF YOU HAVE 4 DAYS

After two days spent touring 🚉 **Stratford-upon-Avon** ❶-❾ ⚑ and the Shakespeare-linked attractions of the immediate vicinity—including **Henley-in-Arden** ⓫—you will be ready for a change of scene. Dedicate your third day to visiting two or three of the stately houses within easy driving distance. Plan your route along minor roads to take in some off-the-beaten-track hamlets. Nearest of these is fetching **Welford-on-Avon** ㉑, hugging the river as it loops west from Stratford. A short distance north, on either side of the village of **Alcester** ㉒, an appealing one-horse town, lie two notable country houses, Palladian **Ragley Hall** ㉓ and Elizabethan **Coughton Court** ㉔, each surrounded by inviting parkland. Head to 🚉 **Warwick** ⓮ for the night, devoting the next morning to exploring the town's medieval castle. Other lower-key attractions are worth an hour or two. If castles are your thing, see ruined **Kenilworth Castle** ⓯, a short drive north.

About the Hotels

Stratford holds the highest concentration of lodgings in the area, from bed-and-breakfasts to hotels. Here you can find accommodations to fit every wallet, and for the most part they are well maintained. The best establishments are the older, centrally located ones, often with fine period architecture; national chains own most of these. Because Stratford is *so* popular with theatergoers, book well ahead whenever possible. Most hotels offer discounted two- and three-day packages. Outside town, some top-notch country hotels guarantee discreet but attentive service—at very fancy prices. At the other end of the scale, almost every village has a gnarled old inn with rooms at reasonable rates, or you can book a B&B through the local Tourist Information Centre.

WHAT IT COSTS In pounds				
£££££	**££££**	**£££**	**££**	**£**
RESTAURANTS	over £22	£18–£22	£13–£17	£7–£12	under £7
HOTELS	over £160	£120–£160	£90–£119	£60–£89	under £60

Restaurant prices are for a main course at dinner. Hotel prices are for two people in a standard double room in high season, including V.A.T., with no meals or, if indicated, CP (with continental breakfast), BP (Breakfast Plan, with full breakfast), or MAP (Modified American Plan, with breakfast and dinner).

Timing

In Stratford, avoid visits on weekends and school holidays, and take in the main Shakespeare shrines in the early morning to see them at their least frenetic. One high point of Stratford's calendar is the Shakespeare Birthday Celebrations, usually on the weekend nearest to April 23. If you visit during this time, make hotel reservations as early as possible. Warwick Castle, too, usually brims with visitors, and you should arrive early in the day to beat the rush. Some country properties fill up quickly on weekends, and most close in winter. Some stately homes have limited hours even in summer, and many close in winter.

STRATFORD-UPON-AVON

➤ Even under the weight of busloads of visitors, Stratford has somehow hung on to much of its ancient character and can, on a good day, still feel like an English market town. It's on the banks of the slow-flowing River Avon, close to Birmingham, 37 mi to the northwest, and not far from London, 102 mi to the southeast.

Around here, it doesn't take long to figure out who's the center of attention. Born in a half-timber, early-16th-century building in the center of Stratford on April 23, 1564, Shakespeare died on April 23, 1616, his 52nd birthday, in a more imposing house at New Place. Although he spent much of his life in London, the world still associates him with "Shakespeare's Avon." Here, in the years between his birth and 1587, he played as a young lad, attended grammar school, and married Anne Hathaway; and here he returned, as a prosperous man. You can see his birthplace on Henley Street; his burial place in Holy Trinity Church; Anne Hathaway's Cottage; his mother's home at Wilmcote; New Place and the neighboring Nash's House, home of Shakespeare's granddaughter.

Take Antonio's advice (*Twelfth Night,* act 3, scene 3) and "beguile the time, and feed your knowledge with viewing the town"—or with seeing a play at the Royal Shakespeare Theatre. By the 16th century Stratford was a prosperous market town with thriving guilds and industries. Half-timber houses from this era have been preserved, and they are set off by later architecture, such as the elegant Georgian storefronts on Bridge Street, with their 18th-century porticoes and arched doorways.

TOP REASONS TO GO

Shakespeare in Stratford: To see a play by Shakespeare in the town where he was born—and perhaps after you've visited his birthplace or other sites—is a magical experience. The Royal Shakespeare Company's productions are often outstanding.

A stroll to Anne Hathaway's Cottage: Taking a walk here from Stratford—it's a little over a mile—is as memorable as seeing the home of Shakespeare's wife. In spring and summer, flowers and soft green grass surround the path. The thatched cottage itself has rare period furniture and lush gardens.

Warwick Castle: Taking in the history—and some modern kitsch—at this sprawling medieval castle is a fun day out and great for the whole family. The castle is more than just the armory, great hall, and Tussauds waxworks. Expect year-round activities and events from jousting tournaments to demonstrations of falconry.

Kenilworth Castle: Exploring the sprawling, red-stone ruins of Kenilworth helps you appreciate the great amount of history that took place here, from the castle's massive Norman keep to buildings constructed for a visit from Elizabeth I. Cromwell may have ravaged this fortress, but it still commands the countryside.

6

Exploring Stratford-upon-Avon

The town is easily manageable on foot. Most sights cluster around Henley Street (off the roundabout as you come in on the A3400 Birmingham road), High Street, and Waterside, which skirts the public gardens through which the River Avon flows. Bridge Street and Sheep Street (parallel to Bridge) are Stratford's main thoroughfares and the site of most banks, shops, and eating places. The town's tourist office lies at Bridgefoot, between the canal and the river, next to Clopton Bridge— "a sumptuous new bridge and large of stone"—built in the 15th century by Sir Hugh Clopton, once lord mayor of London and one of Stratford's richest and most philanthropic residents.

The **Shakespeare Birthplace Trust** runs the main places of Shakespearean interest: Anne Hathaway's Cottage, Hall's Croft, Mary Arden's House, Nash's House and New Place, and Shakespeare's Birthplace. They have similar opening times, and you can buy a combination ticket to the three in-town properties or to all five properties, or pay separate entry fees if you want to visit only one or two. The trust hosts events by the Tudor Group, costumed interpreters who give demonstrations and talks about subjects such as how Tudor England celebrated Christmas. ☏ *01789/ 204016* ⊕ *www.shakespeare.org.uk* ✉ *Joint ticket to 5 properties £14; joint ticket to Shakespeare's Birthplace, Hall's Croft, and Nash's House–New Place £11.*

Main Attractions

★ ❼ **Anne Hathaway's Cottage.** The most picturesque of the Shakespeare Trust properties, on the western outskirts of Stratford, was the family home of

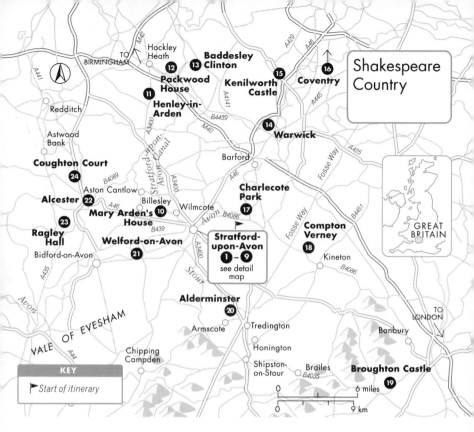

the woman Shakespeare married in 1582. The "cottage," actually a substantial Tudor farmhouse, has latticed windows and a grand thatch roof. Inside is period furniture including a rare carved Elizabethan bed; outside is a garden planted in lush Victorian style with herbs and flowers. In a nearby field the **Shakespeare Tree Garden** has 40 trees mentioned in the playwright's works, a yew maze, and sculptures with Shakespearean themes. ■ TIP→ **The best way to get here is to walk, especially in late spring when the apple trees are in blossom.** There are two main footpaths, one via Greenhill Street by the railroad bridge, the other leaving from Holy Trinity Church up Old Town and Chestnut Walk. ⊠ *Cottage La., Shottery* ☎ *01789/204016* ⊕ *www.shakespeare.org.uk* ⊡ *£5.50, Shakespeare Trust 5-property ticket £14* ⊙ *Apr., May, Sept., and Oct., Mon.–Sat. 9:30–5, Sun. 10–5; June–Aug., Mon.–Sat. 9–5, Sun. 9:30–5; Nov.–Mar., Mon.–Sat. 10–4, Sun. 10:30–4; last entry 30 mins before closing.*

❻ Hall's Croft. One of the finest surviving Jacobean (early 17th-century) town houses, this impressive residence has a delightful walled garden. Tradition has it that Hall's Croft was the home of Shakespeare's elder daughter Susanna and her husband, Dr. John Hall, whose dispensary is on view along with the other rooms, all containing Jacobean furniture of heavy oak and some 17th-century portraits. Restoration of the house is under way, and some exhibits are being remounted. Some rooms may

be closed when you visit. ✉ *Old Town* ☎ *01789/204016* ⊕ *www.
shakespeare.org.uk* 💷*£3.75, Shakespeare Trust ticket for 3 in-town properties £11, 5-property ticket £14* ⊘ *Nov.–Mar., daily 11–4; Apr., May,
Sept., and Oct., daily 11–5; June–Aug., Mon.–Sat. 9:30–5, Sun. 10–5;
last entry 30 mins before closing.*

⑧ Holy Trinity Church. The burial place of William Shakespeare, this 13th-
century church sits on the banks of the Avon, with a graceful avenue of
lime trees framing its entrance. Shakespeare's final resting place is in the
chancel, rebuilt in 1465–91 in the late Perpendicular style. He was buried
here not because he was a famed poet but because he was a lay rector of
Stratford, owning a portion of the township tithes. On the north wall of
the sanctuary, over the altar steps, is the famous marble bust created by
Gerard Jansen in 1623. Along with the Droeshout engraving in the First
Folio, this is one of only two known contemporary portraits of Shakespeare. Rigidly stylized in the Elizabethan mode, the bust offers a more
human, even humorous, perspective when viewed from the side. Also in
the chancel are the graves of Shakespeare's wife, Anne; his daughter Susanna; his son-in-law, John Hall; and his granddaughter's husband,
Thomas Nash. Nearby, the Parish Register is displayed, containing both
Shakespeare's baptismal entry (1564) and his burial notice (1616).
✉ *Trinity St.* 💷 *Small fee for chancel* ⊘ *Mar., Mon.–Sat. 9–5, Sun.
12:30–5; Apr.–Oct., Mon.–Sat. 8:30–6, Sun. 12:30–5; Nov.–Feb.,
Mon.–Sat. 9–4, Sun. 12:30–5; last admission 20 mins before closing.*

❸ Nash's House and New Place. This is the home of Thomas Nash, who
married Shakespeare's last direct descendant, his granddaughter Elizabeth Hall. The heavily restored house has been furnished in 17th-cen-
tury style, and it also contains a local museum. In the gardens (where
there's an intricately laid-out Elizabethan knot garden) are the foundations of **New Place,** the house in which Shakespeare died in 1616. Built
in 1483 "of brike and tymber" for a lord mayor of London, New Place
was Stratford's grandest piece of real estate when Shakespeare bought
it in 1597 for £60; tragically it was torn down in 1759. The man responsible for this, Reverend Francis Gastrell, had already shown his ire
at the hordes of Shakespeare-related sightseers by cutting down a mulberry tree said to have been planted by the Bard himself. That act of
vandalism put the townspeople into such an uproar that they stoned his
house. Today a tree claimed to be a descendant of the unfortunate mulberry stands in the middle of the lawn. The **Great Garden** of New Place,
beyond the knot garden, has a sculpture trail with bronze works inspired
by Shakespeare's plays. ✉ *Chapel St.* ☎ *01789/204016* ⊕ *www.
shakespeare.org.uk* 💷*£3.75, Shakespeare Trust ticket for 3 in-town properties £11, 5-property ticket £14* ⊘ *Nov.–Mar., daily 11–4; Apr., May,
Sept., and Oct., daily 11–5; June–Aug., Mon.–Sat. 9:30–5, Sun. 10–5;
last entry 30 mins before closing.*

❾ Royal Shakespeare Theatre. The Stratford home of the Royal Shakespeare Company (RSC), amid lovely gardens along the River Avon, presents some of the finest productions of Shakespeare's plays. The company
has existed since 1879, established by brewer Charles Edward Flower;
its original home burned down in 1926. Six years later the current

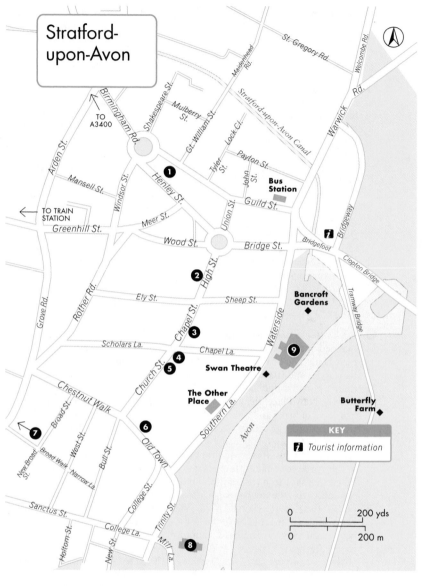

Stratford-upon-Avon

Anne Hathaway's
Cottage 7

Guild Chapel 4

Guildhall 5

Hall's Croft 6

Harvard House 2

Holy Trinity Church 8

Nash's House
and New Place 3

Royal
Shakespeare Theatre 9

Shakespeare's
Birthplace 1

building was erected. Starting in May or June 2007, the theater will close for three years. During that time there will be no tours of the original theater, and action will switch to the RSC's other theaters, including the adjacent **Swan Theatre,** the only part of the Victorian theater to survive the 1926 fire. This theater follows the lines of Shakespeare's original Globe and is one of the most exciting performing spaces in Britain. Beside the Swan, an art gallery has theater-related exhibitions and portraits and depictions of scenes from the plays. After spring 2007, the main home of the RSC will be the temporary **Courtyard Theatre.** The theater is behind **The Other Place,** a modern auditorium used primarily for contemporary productions. ✉ *Waterside* ☎ *0870/609–1110 ticket hotline, 01789/296655 information, 01789/403405 tours* 🖷 *01789/403413 box office* ⊕ *www.rsc.org.uk* 🎫 *Tour £5* ☉ *Tour weekdays (except matinee days; book well in advance) 1:30 and 5:30; matinee days 5:30 and after show; Sun. noon, 1, 2, and 3. No tours when shows are being prepared. Gallery Mon.–Sat. 9:30–6:30, Sun. noon–4:30.*

❶ **Shakespeare's Birthplace.** A half-timber house typical of its time, the playwright's birthplace has been altered and restored since he lived here but remains a much-visited shrine. You enter through the **Shakespeare Centre,** the headquarters of the Shakespeare Birthplace Trust, which is a favorite with scholars, who head straight for the library; other visitors spend their time at the informative exhibition. Furnishings in the house reflect comfortable middle-class Elizabethan domestic life. Shakespeare's father, John, a glove maker and wool dealer, purchased the house; a reconstructed

> ### WILL FOR SALE
>
> In 1847 two widowed ladies were maintaining Shakespeare's birthplace in a somewhat ramshackle state. With the approach of the tercentennial of the playwright's birth, and in response to a rumor that the building was to be purchased by P. T. Barnum and shipped across the Atlantic, the city shelled out £3, 000 for the relic. It was tidied up and made the main attraction for the stream of Shakespeare devotees that was steadily growing into a torrent.

workshop shows the tools of the glover's trade. An auction notice describes the property as it was when it was offered for sale in 1847. You can also see the signatures of earlier pilgrims cut into the windowpanes, including those of Mark Twain and Charles Dickens. ✉ *Henley St.* ☎ *01789/204016* ⊕ *www.shakespeare.org.uk* 🎫 *£7, Shakespeare Trust ticket for 3 in-town properties £11, 5-property ticket £14* ☉ *Nov.–Mar., Mon.–Sat. 10–4, Sun. 10:30–4; Apr. and May, Mon.–Sat. 10–5, Sun. 10:30–5; June–Aug., Mon.–Sat. 9–5, Sun. 9:30–5; Sept. and Oct., Mon.–Sat. 10–5, Sun. 10:30–5; last entry 30 mins before closing.*

Also Worth Seeing

Almshouses. Immediately beyond the Guildhall on Church Street is a delightful row of timber-and-daub almshouses. These were built to accommodate the poor by the Guild of the Holy Cross in the early 15th century and still serve as housing for pensioners. ✉ *Church St.*

Bancroft Gardens. Between the Royal Shakespeare Theatre and Clopton Bridge lie these well-tended expanses of lawns and flower beds. The swans gliding gracefully along the river are permanent residents, coexisting with the pleasure craft on the river and the nearby canal. The centerpiece of the gardens is the **Gower Memorial statue,** designed in 1888 by Lord Gower, and adorned with bronze figures of Hamlet, Lady Macbeth, Falstaff, and Prince Hal—symbols of philosophy, tragedy, comedy, and history, respectively. ⊠ *Off Waterside.*

At Cox's Yard Tea Shop (⊠ Bridgefoot ☎ 01789/404600), next to Bancroft Gardens in the town center, linger over tea and a scone for a relaxing break before more sightseeing or a riverside walk.

Butterfly Farm. Come here to see Europe's largest display of butterflies, a mock rain forest, and spiders, caterpillars, and insects from all over the world. It's a two-minute walk past the Bridgefoot footbridge. ⊠ *Swan's Nest La.* ☎ *01789/299288* ⊕ *www.butterflyfarm.co.uk* ⊠ *£4.95* ⊙ *June–Aug., daily 10–6; Sept.–May, daily 10–dusk.*

❹ Guild Chapel. This chapel is the noble centerpiece of Stratford's Guild buildings, including the Guildhall, the Grammar School, and the almshouses—all structures well known to Shakespeare. The ancient structure was rebuilt in the late Perpendicular style in the first half of the 15th century, thanks to the largesse of Stratford resident Hugh Clopton. The otherwise plain interior includes fragments of a remarkable medieval fresco of the Last Judgment. The bell, also given by Sir Hugh, still rings as it did to tell Shakespeare the time of day. ⊠ *Chapel La. at Church St.* ☎ *01789/293351* ⊠ *Free* ⊙ *Daily 9–5.*

❺ Guildhall. Dating to 1416–18, the Guildhall is occupied by **King Edward's Grammar School,** which Shakespeare probably attended as a boy; it's still used as a school. On the first floor is the Guildhall proper, where traveling acting companies came to perform. Many historians believe that it was after seeing the troupe known as the Earl of Leicester's Men in 1587 that Shakespeare got the acting bug and set off for London. Upstairs is the classroom in which he is reputed to have learned "little Latin and less Greek." A brass plate at its far end records the traditional position of Master Will's seat. Students use the classroom today, so visits may be made by prior arrangement only, during after-school hours or vacation time. Contact the tourist information office to schedule a visit. ⊠ *Church St.*

❷ Harvard House. This is the grand, half-timber, 16th-century home of Katherine Rogers, mother of the John Harvard who founded Harvard University in 1636. The twin-gabled facade, dating from about 1600, is one of Stratford's glories. Note the exterior beams carved with fleurs-de-lis in relief, the sculpted human faces on the corbels, and the bear and staff (symbols of the Warwick earls) on the bracket heads. Inside, the **Museum of British Pewter** displays pewter toys, tankards, and teapots, dating from Roman times to the present. ⊠ *High St.* ☎ *01789/ 204507* ⊕ *www.shakespeare.org.uk* ⊠ *£2.75, free if you have a 3- or 5-property ticket* ⊙ *May, June, and Sept.–Nov., Fri.–Sun. 11:30–4:30; July and Aug., Thurs.–Sun. 11:30–4:30.*

Teddy Bear Museum. A diversion from Shakespeareana, this museum contains hundreds of the furry creatures in all shapes and sizes from around the world, including Paddington Bear and bears previously owned by Margaret Thatcher and Tony Blair. ✉ *19 Greenhill St.* ☎ *01789/293160* ⊕ *www.theteddybearmuseum.com* ✉ *£2.95* ⊙ *Daily 9:30–5:30.*

Where to Eat

£££–£££££ ✕ **Callands.** Brightly painted and cheerful, this restaurant wins high marks for outstanding contemporary cuisine with international influences and for good-value fixed-price menus (£20 for a pretheater dinner, for example). You might start with tomato and paprika soup or Thai fish cakes with sweet dipping sauce, and move on to crab risotto, Moroccan-spice chicken, or grilled whole lemon sole. Friday is lobster night. ✉ *13–14 Meer St.* ☎ *01789/269304* ⊟ *AE, MC, V.*

★ **£££–££££** ✕ **Restaurant Margaux.** One of the best places for good food in town, Margaux resembles a simple, cozy bistro with its two floors, darkwood furniture, and white walls. The sophisticated menu lists quail and foie gras ravioli with leeks, and char-grilled tuna with crab beignet (a fritter) and saffron dressing; for dessert, try the pistachio and strawberry parfait. ✉ *6 Union St.* ☎ *01789/269106* ⚖ *Reservations essential* ⊟ *MC, V.*

££–£££ ✕ **Lambs of Sheep Street.** Sit downstairs to appreciate the hardwood floors and oak beams of this local epicurean favorite. The modern updates of tried-and-true dishes include roast chicken with lime butter and char-grilled sausages with leek mash. Daily specials keep the menu seasonal. The two- and three-course fixed-price menus are good deals. ✉ *12 Sheep St.* ☎ *01789/292554* ⚖ *Reservations essential* ⊟ *AE, MC, V.*

££–£££ ✕ **Russons.** A 16th-century building holds a quaint dining room that's a favorite with theatergoers. The fare, though reasonably priced, doesn't skimp on quality. On the daily-changing menu, chalked on a blackboard, are English specialties such as roast lamb and guinea fowl. ✉ *8 Church St.* ☎ *01789/268822* ⚖ *Reservations essential* ⊟ *AE, MC, V* ⊙ *Closed Mon.*

££–£££ ✕ **The Vintner.** The imaginative, bistro-inspired menu varies each day at this café and wine bar. Shoulder of lamb is a popular main course; tapas are also popular, and a children's menu is available. To dine before curtain time, arrive early or make a reservation. The building, largely unaltered since the late 1400s, has lovely flagstone floors and oak beams. ✉ *5 Sheep St.* ☎ *01789/297259* ⊟ *AE, MC, V.*

££ ✕ **Embargo.** Leather booths and a lounge bar enhance this breezy venue for contemporary fare. Fish specials, slow-roasted lamb with garlic mashed potatoes and rosemary gravy, and tagliatelle with roast peppers, goat cheese, and pesto are good dinner choices. Crispy shredded duck with plum sauce and cucumbers in a tortilla and a steak baguette appear on the lunch menu; one late-night snack is a small coriander hamburger and chunky fries with garlic mayonnaise. ✉ *1 Shakespeare St.* ☎ *01789/262233* ⊟ *MC, V.*

££ ✕ **Opposition.** Pre- and posttheater meals are offered at this informal, family-style restaurant in a 16th-century building on the main dining street near the theater. The American and modern European dishes on the menu win praise from the locals. Try the roasted chicken breast with banana and basmati rice, wild mushroom pizza, or blood sausage salad. ⊠ *13 Sheep St.* ☎ *01789/269980* ⊟ *MC, V.*

£–££ ✕ **Black Swan.** Known locally as the Dirty Duck, one of Stratford's most celebrated pubs has attracted actors since Garrick's days. Its little veranda overlooks the theaters and the river. You can sample English grill specialties as well as bar meals such as mussels and fries. Few people come here for the food, which is mediocre: the real attraction is the ambience and the other customers. ⊠ *Southern La.* ☎ *01789/ 297312* ⊟ *AE, MC, V* ⊗ *No dinner Sun.*

Where to Stay

The Ettington Park Hotel and the Fox & Goose, both near Alderminster, are excellent rural hotels a few miles from Stratford. Another is Pear Tree Cottage, near Mary Arden's House in Wilmcote.

££££ 🏨 **Alveston Manor.** This redbrick Elizabethan manor house surrounded by lawns and a terrace has ancient elements as well as a pampering spa. A few Tudor-style rooms in the main building have four-poster beds; in the rear of the hotel are most of the rooms, modern and done up in sea green and beige. Legend says the grounds were the setting for the first production of *A Midsummer Night's Dream*. The Alveston is across the river from the Royal Shakespeare Theatre. ⊠ *Clopton Bridge, CV37 7HP* ☎ *08704/008181* 🖷 *01789/414095* ⊕ *www.macdonald-hotels. co.uk* ⇱ *110 rooms, 4 suites* ⚭ *Restaurant, room service, cable TV, in-room data ports, indoor pool, spa, bar, 2 lounges, dry cleaning, laundry service, meeting rooms, free parking, some pets allowed (fee), no-smoking rooms* ⊟ *AE, DC, MC, V* ⊺◎⊺ *BP.*

££££ 🏨 **Menzies Welcombe Hotel & Golf Course.** With its mullioned bay windows, gables, and tall chimneys, this hotel in an 1886 neo-Jacobean-style building evokes the luxury of bygone days. You can relax in the clubby bar or the Italianate garden terrace. Public rooms such as the Great Hall, with its wood paneling, chandeliers, and marble fireplace, complement the spacious main-house guest rooms, all with period-style furnishings and some with garden views. Garden rooms in the adjacent building are comfortable but not as big. The fancy Trevelyan Restaurant (jacket and tie required) relies on a French foundation to present English cuisine. The hotel is a 10-minute drive from Stratford. ⊠ *Warwick Rd., CV37 0NR* ☎ *01789/295252* 🖷 *01789/414666* ⊕ *www. menzies-hotels.co.uk* ⇱ *64 rooms* ⚭ *2 restaurants, room service, cable TV, in-room data ports, 18-hole golf course, tennis court, pool, gym, fishing, bar, lounge, babysitting, dry cleaning, laundry service, meeting rooms, car rental, free parking, no-smoking rooms; no a/c* ⊟ *AE, D, MC, V* ⊺◎⊺ *BP.*

★ ££££ 🏨 **Shakespeare Hotel.** Built in the 1400s, this Elizabethan town house in the heart of town is a vision right out of *The Merry Wives of Windsor,* with its five gables and long, stunning, black-and-white half-timber facade. The comfortably modernized interiors have a touch of luxury; Shakespeareana and old playbills decorate in the public areas. Upstairs, rooms are named after the characters from Shakespeare's plays and the actors who have portrayed them. Hewn timbers carved with rose-and-thistle patterns decorate some rooms; all have CD play-

ers. ⊠ *Chapel St., CV37 6ER* ☎ *0870/400–8182* 🖷 *01789/415411*
⊕ *www.macdonald-hotels.co.uk* 🛏 *64 rooms, 6 suites* ♨ *Restaurant,
room service, cable TV, bar, lounge, laundry service, meeting rooms, parking (fee), some pets allowed (fee), no-smoking rooms; no a/c* ☰ *AE, DC,
MC, V.*

£££–££££ 🏨 **Holiday Inn Stratford-upon-Avon.** This good-value, modern chain
hotel's best selling points are its excellent location in the center of the
historic district, on the banks of the Avon, and its views across the river
and town center. It also has plenty of modern amenities. Rooms are large
and have plenty of light, but bathrooms are a bit of a squeeze. Furnishings are inexpensive and cheerful; the management planned some refur-
bishing in 2006–07. Children are welcomed enthusiastically (if you
don't appreciate kids, you might find this place annoying). Ask for
rooms away from the elevators, as those can be a bit noisy, and call well
in advance to check on special rates. ⊠ *Bridgefoot, CV37 6VR* ☎ *01789/
279988* 🖷 *01789/298589* ⊕ *www.holidayinn.com* 🛏 *251 rooms, 2 suites*
♨ *Restaurant, room service, indoor pool, health club, bar, Wi-Fi, business services, no-smoking rooms* ☰ *AE, MC, V* ⦿ *BP.*

£££–££££ 🏨 **Stratford Victoria.** Despite its name, the Victoria is actually quite
modern. It may lack the period charm of older hotels, but its up-to-date
facilities, spacious rooms, and ample grounds make it a good option for
those for whom Tudor beamed ceilings are nothing more than something to bump your head into. Rooms, all in dark wood with burgundy
and green color schemes, come in several shapes: some have four-poster
beds or accommodate four people, others are geared to business travel.
Guests can use the leisure facilities, including an indoor pool, at a sister hotel, the Stratford Manor, 3 mi away. ⊠ *Arden St., CV37 6QQ*
☎ *01789/271000* 🖷 *01789/271001* ⊕ *www.marstonhotels.com* 🛏 *102
rooms* ♨ *Restaurant, room service, cable TV, in-room data ports, gym,
hot tub, massage, bar, lounge, babysitting, laundry service, meeting
rooms, broadband, free parking, no-smoking floors; no a/c* ☰ *AE, DC,
MC, V* ⦿ *BP.*

★ £££ 🏨 **White Swan.** Exposed beams,
low ceilings, and winding corridors
make this cozy hotel a delight for
those who like a little authenticity.
It claims to be the oldest building
in town, and the look of the exterior (circa 1450) reinforces that
boast. Each room is individually
decorated, and although fabrics are
not luxurious, admirable effort has
been made to avoid traditional
chintz. Heavy antiques mix with
reproductions; some rooms have
fireplaces, and some have four-
poster beds. Bathrooms are tucked
into what little space is available. The popular pub, a traditional English boozer with ancient beams, attracts visitors and locals. ⊠ *Rother*

> ### THE PUB'S THE THING
>
> Take a break from Shakespeare.
> Having a pint of ale at the White
> Swan, on a cool night when the
> fires are lit and the mood is jovial,
> is a true English experience. You
> never know which direction the
> conversation will turn. Or stop by
> another of Stratford's pubs, such
> as the Black Swan (also known as
> the Dirty Duck).

St., CV37 6NH ☎ *01789/297022* 🖷 *01789/26877* ⊕ *www.thewhiteswanstratford.co.uk* ⟲ *41 rooms* ♿ *Restaurant, room service, some in-room data ports, meeting rooms, free parking; no a/c in some rooms* ▭ *MC, V* ⫶○⫶ *BP.*

££ ⊞ **Penryn House.** Traditional English prints and furnishings as well as some simple modern pieces fill this choice at the low end of the price category. The helpful proprietors, Robert and Anne Dawkes, take pride in the hearty breakfast, which can accommodate vegetarians. The B&B is an easy walk from the city center, Anne Hathaway's Cottage, and the rail station. ⊠ *126 Alcester Rd., CV37 9DP* ☎ *01789/293718* 🖷 *01789/266077* ⊕ *www.penrynguesthouse.co.uk* ⟲ *7 rooms, 6 with bath* ♿ *Laundry service, free parking; no a/c, no smoking* ▭ *MC, V* ⫶○⫶ *BP.*

££ ⊞ **Stratheden Hotel.** One advantage of this family-run budget choice is its location in the center of town. Wall-to-wall carpeting and flowery bedspreads decorate the simple rooms; one has a canopy bed previously owned by Victorian novelist Marie Corelli. The spacious rooms have either a shower or tub, and all have coffeemakers. Garret rooms are smaller but charming. ⊠ *5 Chapel St., CV37 6EP* ☎☎ *01789/297119* ⟲ *9 rooms* ♿ *Babysitting, parking (fee), no-smoking rooms; no a/c* ▭ *MC, V* ⫶○⫶ *BP.*

££ ⊞ **Victoria Spa Lodge.** This good-value B&B lies 1½ mi outside town, within view of the Stratford Canal. The grand, clematis-drape building dates from 1837; you can see Queen Victoria's coat of arms in two of its gables. Dark-wood and plain white furnishings decorate the lounge–breakfast room and spacious guest rooms. ⊠ *Bishopton La., Bishopton, CV37 9QY* ☎ *01789/267985* 🖷 *01789/204728* ⊕ *www.victoriaspa.co.uk* ⟲ *7 rooms* ♿ *Free parking; no a/c, no room phones, no smoking* ▭ *MC, V* ⫶○⫶ *BP.*

★ £ ⊞ **Heron Lodge.** Just a half mile outside of Stratford town center, this B&B combines budget accommodation in a family home with luxurious service. Rooms are individually decorated, and the conservatory is perfect for an afternoon cup of tea. Owners Chris and Bob Heaps are serious about breakfast, serving pancakes made from a family recipe; locally sourced ingredients—from tea to jam and sausages—appear on the menu. You can also get a top-quality English breakfast. ⊠ *260 Alcester Rd., CV37 9JQ* ☎ *01789/299169* ⊕ *www.heronlodge.com* ⟲ *5 rooms* ♿ *Lounge, free parking; no a/c, no kids under 5, no smoking* ▭ *AE, MC, V* ⫶○⫶ *BP.*

Nightlife & the Arts

Festivals

The **Stratford-upon-Avon Shakespeare Birthday Celebrations** (⊠ Shakespeare Centre, Henley St., Stratford-upon-Avon, CV37 6QW ☎ 01789/415536 ⊕ www.shakespeare.org.uk) take place on and around the weekend closest to April 23 (unless Easter occurs during that time). The events, spread over four days, include a formal reception, lectures, free concerts, processions, and a special performance of a play. For tickets for the three-course birthday luncheon in the marquee on the Avon Paddock, write the Shakespeare Birthday Celebrations secretary at the address above, call, or check the Web site.

★ Starting in April 2006 and running until April 2007, the yearlong **Complete Works of Shakespeare Festival** (⊕ www.rsc.org.uk), sponsored by the Royal Shakespeare Company, will present the entire Shakespearean canon from sonnets to plays. Other British groups and many international companies will participate in this ambitious undertaking, and film, opera, music, and dance events will complement the theatrical activities. ■ TIP→ This is a major event, so be sure to book tickets and lodgings well in advance.

The **Mop Fair,** dating from medieval times, takes place on or around October 12, traditionally the time when laborers and apprentices from the surrounding area came to seek work. They carried implements of their trades so that prospective employers could identify them. The fair still attracts entertainers and fairground amusements.

Theater

Fodor'sChoice ★ The **Royal Shakespeare Company** (⊠ Waterside, Stratford-upon-Avon, CV37 6BB ☎ 0870/609–1110 ticket hotline, 01789/296655 general information 🖷 01789/403413 ⊕ www.rsc.org.uk) performs Shakespeare plays year-round in Stratford, as well as in other venues around Britain. Stratford's Royal Shakespeare Theatre is the home of the RSC, one of the finest repertory troupes in the world and long the backbone of the country's theatrical life. Although the company's main stage will close for three years beginning in spring 2007, performances will take place at a temporary space. In September and October, visiting companies perform opera, ballet, and musicals. The Swan Theatre, behind the Royal Shakespeare Theatre, stages plays by Shakespeare contemporaries such as Christopher Marlowe and Ben Jonson. In the Other Place, the RSC performs some of its most adventurous work. Prices usually are £7 to £45. Book ahead, as seats go fast, but day of performance (two per person to personal callers only) and returned tickets are often available. You can book tickets from London with **Ticketmaster** (☎ 0870/534–4444 ⊕ www.ticketmaster.co.uk), operating 24 hours a day. You can book tickets in the United States (a 20% surcharge applies) with **Keith Prowse** (☎ 212/398–1430 or 800/669–8687 ⊕ www.keithprowse.com).

> ## THE SHOW GOES ON
>
> After years of complaints and controversy, the Royal Shakespeare Company is building a new main stage in Shakespeare's hometown. The Royal Shakespeare Theatre will close from spring 2007 until 2010 for major reconstruction, but performances will continue. During that time, the main home of the RSC will be the Courtyard Theatre, a prefabricated, temporary 1,000-seat theater, down Southern Lane toward Holy Trinity Church. It's opening in 2006 for the Complete Works festival. The stage configuration will be similar to what is planned for the new space.

Sports & the Outdoors

Avon Cruises (⊠ The Boatyard, Swan's Nest La. 🖷 01789/267073) rents boats and provides half-hour river excursions for an escape from the crowds; the company can arrange longer trips from Easter to October. **Bancroft Cruises** (⊠ Moathouse, Bridgefoot ☎ 01789/269669) runs half-hourly excursions on the river. Hour-long trips farther afield can also be scheduled.

Shopping

Chain stores and shops sell tourist junk, but this is also a good place to shop for high-quality (and high-price) silver, jewelry, and china. There's an open market (great for bargains) every Friday in the Market Place at Greenhill and Meer streets. **Antique Arms & Armour** (⊠ Poet's Arbour, Sheep St. ☎ 01789/293453) sells antique swords, sabers, and armor. The **Antique Market** (⊠ Ely St.) contains 50 stalls of jewelry, silver, linens, porcelain, and memorabilia. **B&W Thornton** (⊠ 23 Henley St. ☎ 01789/269405), above Shakespeare's Birthplace, stocks Moorcroft pottery and glass. **Chaucer Head Bookshop** (⊠ 21 Chapel St. ☎ 01789/415691) is the best of Stratford's many secondhand bookshops. The **Shakespeare Bookshop** (⊠ 39 Henley St. ☎ 01789/201820), run by the Shakespeare Birthplace, carries Elizabethan plays, Tudor history books, children's books, and general paraphernalia.

AROUND SHAKESPEARE COUNTRY

This section of Warwickshire is marked by gentle hills, green fields, slow-moving, mirrorlike rivers, quiet villages, and time-burnished halls, castles (Warwick and Kenilworth are the best examples), and churches.

Mary Arden's House

 3 mi northwest of Stratford, 8 mi southwest of Warwick.

A Tudor farmhouse on this bucolic site in tiny Wilmcote was long believed to have been the home of Mary Arden, Shakespeare's mother. In 2000, researchers discovered that it was actually the former home of Adam Palmer, and the farmhouse was renamed Palmer's Farm. However, other evidence revealed that Mary Arden lived in a modest house on the adjoining Glebe Farm, and that house has now assumed the name Mary Arden's House. The Tudor farmhouse and farm form the **Shakespeare Countryside Museum,** with crafts exhibits, a café, and a garden. Rare breeds of poultry, longhorn cows, and Cotswold sheep live on the grounds, and the museum has demonstrations of farm-

COUNTRY WALKS

The gentle countryside here rewards exploration on foot. Ambitious walkers can try the 26-mi Arden Way loop that takes in Henley-in-Arden and the Forest of Arden. On the 3 mi from Stratford to Wilmcote and Mary Arden's House, you can see beautiful scenery and ancient houses. Parkland with trails surrounds many stately homes such as Charlecote Park, Coughton Court, and Ragley Hall. Even Stratford can be the base for easy walks along the River Avon, and the path bordering the Stratford-upon-Avon Canal provides an escape from the throngs. The Stratford Tourist Information Centre has pamphlets with walks.

ing techniques from the last 400 years. A small falcon and owl exhibit is here, too. ☒ *Off A3400, Wilmcote* ☎ *01789/204016, 01789/293455 information on special events* ⊕ *www.shakespeare.org.uk* ☒ *£6, Shakespeare Trust 5-property ticket £14* ⊙ *Nov.–Mar., Mon.–Sat. 10–4, Sun. 10:30–4; Sept., Oct., Apr., and May, Mon.–Sat. 10–5, Sun. 10:30–5; June–Aug., Mon.–Sat. 9:30–5, Sun. 10–5; last entry 30 mins before closing.*

Where to Stay

★ £ 🏠 **Pear Tree Cottage.** This lovely guesthouse, just around the corner from Mary Arden's House, occupies a 16th-century cottage that retains its beamed ceilings, flagstone floors, and exposed brick walls. The small garden provides an ideal place to relax. Rooms, decorated in a flowery country style, have coffeemakers and some antique furnishings, and guests have access to the kitchen and the living room. The apartments are ideal for longer stays. Shakespeare's parents owned Pear Tree Cottage in the late 1500s. ☒ *7 Church Rd., Wilmcote CV37 9UX* ☎ *01789/205889* 🖷 *01789/262862* ⊕ *www.peartreecot.co.uk* 🛏 *5 rooms, 2 apartments* ♨ *Some in-room VCRs, lounge; no a/c, no kids under 3, no smoking* ▤ *No credit cards* ⊙ *Closed Jan.* ⦿| *BP.*

EN ROUTE — From Wilmcote, continue west for 1½ mi on minor roads to reach **Aston Cantlow.** Shakespeare's parents, Mary Arden and John Shakespeare, got married at the small country church here. Stop for a lunch or dinner of creative pub food and good wine at the relaxed **King's Head** (☒ Bearley Rd., Aston Cantlow ☎ 01789/488242); reserve in advance.

Henley-in-Arden

⓫ *6 mi north of Mary Arden's House, 8 mi northwest of Stratford.*

A brief drive out of Stratford on the A3400 will take you under the Stratford-upon-Avon Canal aqueduct to pretty Henley-in-Arden, whose wide main street is an architectural pageant of many periods. This area was once the Forest of Arden, where Shakespeare set one of his greatest comedies, *As You Like It.* Among the buildings to look for are the former Guildhall, dating from the 15th century, and the White Swan pub, built in the early 1600s.

Packwood House

⓬ *5 mi north of Henley-in-Arden, 12 mi north of Stratford-upon-Avon.*

Packwood House draws garden enthusiasts to its re-created 17th-century gardens, highlighted by an ambitious topiary Tudor garden in which yew trees depict Jesus' Sermon on the Mount. The house combines red-brick and half-timbering, and its tall chimneys are also typical of the period. Exquisite collections of 16th-century furniture and textiles in the interior's 20th-century version of Tudor architecture make this one of the area's finest historic houses open to the public. ☒ *Off B4439, 2 mi east of Hockley Heath* ☎ *01564/783294* ⊕ *www.nationaltrust. org.uk* ☒ *£6.20, garden only £3.20, combined ticket with Baddesley Clinton £9.80* ⊙ *House Mar.–Oct., Wed.–Sun. noon–4:30. Garden Mar., Apr., and Oct., Wed.–Sun. 11–4:30; May–Sept., Wed.–Sun. 11–5:30.*

Baddesley Clinton

★ **⑬** *2 mi east of Packwood House, 15 mi north of Stratford-upon-Avon.*

"As you approach Baddesley Clinton, it stands before you as the perfect late medieval manor house. The entrance side of grey stone, the small, creeper-clad Queen Anne brick bridge across the moat, the gateway with a porch higher than the roof and embattled—it could not be better." So wrote the eminent architectural historian Sir Nikolaus Pevsner, and the house lives up to his praise. Set off a winding back-road, the manor retains its great fireplaces, 17th-century paneling, and three priest holes (secret chambers for Roman Catholic priests, who were hidden by sympathizers when Catholicism was banned in the 16th and 17th centuries). The café is an idyllic spot for tea and cakes. Admission to the house is by timed ticket. ■ TIP➡ Ask about reservations for evening tours on Wednesday and Thursday; you may even be able to include dinner. ✉ *Rising La., off A4141 near Chadwick End* ☎ *01564/783294* ⊕ *www.nationaltrust.org.uk* 🎟 *£6.80, garden only £3.40, combined ticket with Packwood House £9.80* ⊙ *House Mar., Apr., and Oct., Wed.–Sun. 1:30–5; May–Sept., Wed.–Sun. 1:30–5:30. Garden Mar., Apr., and Oct., Wed.–Sun. noon–5; May–Sept., Wed.–Sun. noon–5:30; Nov.–mid-Dec., Wed.–Sun. noon–4:30.*

Warwick

⑭ *7½ mi southeast of Baddesley Clinton, 4 mi south of Kenilworth, 9 mi northeast of Stratford-upon-Avon.*

Most famous for Warwick Castle—that vision out of the feudal ages—the town of Warwick (pronounced *wa*-rick) is an interesting architectural mix of Georgian redbrick and Elizabethan half-timbering. Much of the town center has been spoiled by unattractive postwar development, but look for the 15th-century half-timber **Lord Leycester Hospital,** which has provided a home for old soldiers since the earl of Leicester dedicated it to that purpose in 1571. Within the complex are a chapel and a fine courtyard, complete with a wattle-and-daub balcony and 500-year-old gardens. Try a cream tea in the Brethren's Kitchen. ✉ *High St.* ☎ *01926/491422* 🎟 *£3.20* ⊙ *Apr.–Sept., Tues.–Sun. 10–5; Oct.–Mar., Tues.–Sun. 10–4.*

Crowded with gilded, carved, and painted tombs, the **Beauchamp Chapel** of the **Collegiate Church of St. Mary** is the essence of late-medieval and Tudor chivalry—although it was built (1443–64) to honor the somewhat-less-than-chivalrous Richard Beauchamp, who consigned Joan of Arc to the flames. Colored bosses (projecting blocks), fan tracery, and flying ribs distinguish the chapel, which holds many monuments to the Beauchamps (several of whom became earl of Warwick), including Richard Beauchamp's impressive effigy in bronze and the alabaster table tomb of Thomas Beauchamp and his wife. Robert Dudley, earl of Leicester, adviser and favorite of Elizabeth I, is also buried here. There's a brass-rubbing center, and you can climb the tower in summer. It's a five-minute walk from Warwick Castle. ✉ *Church St., Old Sq.* ☎ *01926/403940* ⊕ *www.saintmaryschurch.co.uk* 🎟 *Free* ⊙ *Apr.–Oct., daily 10–6; Nov.–Mar., daily 10–4:30.*

★ ☾ The vast bulk of medieval **Warwick Castle** rests on a cliff overlooking the Avon—"the fairest monument of ancient and chivalrous splendor which yet remains uninjured by time," to use the words of Sir Walter Scott. Its two soaring towers can be seen for miles: the 147-foot-high Caesar's Tower, built in 1356, and the 128-foot-high Guy's Tower, built in 1380. The towers bristle with battlements, and their irregular forms allowed defenders to

shoot from numerous points. The castle's most powerful commander was Richard Neville, earl of Warwick, known during the 15th-century Wars of the Roses as the Kingmaker. Warwick Castle's monumental walls now enclose an armory with one of the best collections of medieval armor and weapons in Europe, as well as state rooms with historic furnishings and paintings by Peter Paul Rubens, Anthony Van Dyck, and other old masters. Twelve rooms are devoted to an imaginative Madame Tussaud's wax exhibition, "A Royal Weekend Party—1898" (the Tussaud's Group owns the castle). Another exhibit displays the sights and sounds of a great medieval household as it prepares for an important battle. At the Mill and Engine House, you can see the turning water mill and the engines used to generate electricity early in the 20th century. Below the castle, along the Avon, strutting peacocks patrol 60 acres of grounds elegantly landscaped by Capability Brown in the 18th century. ■ TIP→ **You could spend a full day exploring everything, so arrive early to beat the crowds. There are sometimes coupons on the castle's Web site for £5 off ticket prices.** Lavish medieval banquets (extra charge) and special events, including festivals, jousting tournaments, and a Christmas market, take place throughout the year, and a restaurant in the cellars serves lunch. Head to the bridge across the river to get the best view of the castle. ✉ *Castle La. off Mill St., Warwick* ☎ *01926/495421, 08704/422000 24-hr information line* ⊕ *www.warwick-castle.co.uk* ☑ *Nov.–Feb. £13.95, Mar.–mid-July £15.95, mid-July–Oct. £17.95* ☉ *Apr.–July and Sept., daily 10–6; Aug., weekdays 10–6, weekends 10–7; Oct.–Mar., daily 10–5.*

NEED A BREAK?   After a vigorous walk around the ramparts at Warwick Castle, you can drop by the cream, crimson, and golden vaulted, 14th-century **Undercroft** (☎ 01926/ 495421) for a refreshing spot of tea or a hot meal from the cafeteria.

☾ The half-timber Oken's House, near the castle entrance, houses the **Warwickshire Doll Museum** and its large collection of antique dolls, toys, and games. Note that it's open only on Saturday in winter. ✉ *Castle St.* ☎ *01926/495546* ☑ *£1* ☉ *Easter–Oct., Mon.–Sat. 10–5, Sun. 11–5; Nov.–Easter, Sat. 10–dusk.*

☾ Kids as well as adults appreciate **St. John's House,** a Jacobean building; beautiful gardens surround it. Inside are period costumes and scenes of domestic life, as well as a Victorian schoolroom. ✉ *Smith St.* ☎ *01926/*

6

412132 ⌨ *Free* ⊙ *May–Sept., Tues.–Sat. 10–5, Sun. 2:30–5; Oct.–Apr., Tues.–Sat. 10–5.*

Where to Stay & Eat

£££ ✕ **Findon's.** The imaginative menu at this posh Georgian town-house restaurant takes its inspiration from Asia and Europe as well as England. Among the delicious choices are Gressingham duck with blackberry and green peppercorn sauce, and scallops with apple couscous, creamed sweet potatoes, and lime broth. The terrace is a lovely spot to dine in summer. For the best deal, try the fixed-price menus. ✉ *7 Old Sq.* ☎ *01926/411755* ⊟ *MC, V* ⊙ *Closed Sun.*

££ ✕▥ **Rose and Crown.** Stripped pine floorboards, red walls, big wooden tables, and solidly good food and drink set the tone at this contemporary pub (*££–£££*) with rooms on the town's main square. The deli board lists marinated anchovies, crayfish tails, and fruit and cheese; other options are coq au vin with sweet potato and ginger puree, and Aberdeen rump steak and chips. Bedrooms are simple but clean and modern. All in all, this is a decent value for a pint and a meal or a moderately priced room. ✉ *30 Market Pl., CV34 4SH* ☎ *01926/411117* ⊕ *www.peachpubs. com* ⇌ *5 rooms* ⌂ *Restaurant, in-room data ports, meeting rooms; no a/c, no smoking* ⊟ *MC, V* ⅩⓄⅠ *CP.*

££ ▥ **Lord Leycester Hotel.** Built in 1726, this house with an appealing central location became a hotel in 1925, and signs of age and history abound. The small, comfortably furnished rooms and even smaller bathrooms with showers are not to everyone's taste. ✉ *17 Jury St., CV34 4EJ* ☎ *01926/491481* ⌨ *01926/491561* ⊕ *www.lord-leycester.co.uk* ⇌ *49 rooms* ⌂ *2 restaurants, room service, room TVs with movies, some in-room data ports, bar, lounge, babysitting, laundry service, meeting rooms, free parking, some pets allowed (fee), no-smoking rooms; no a/c* ⊟ *AE, DC, MC, V* ⅩⓄⅠ *BP.*

Kenilworth Castle

★ ⑮ *5 mi north of Warwick.*

The sprawling, graceful red ruins of Kenilworth Castle loom over the green fields of Warwickshire, surrounded by the low grassy impression of what was once a lake that surrounded it completely. The top of the keep (central tower) has commanding views of the countryside, one good indication of why this was such a formidable fortress from 1120 until it was dismantled by Oliver Cromwell after the Civil War in the mid-17th century. Still intact are its keep, with 20-foot-thick walls; its great hall built by John of Gaunt in the 14th century; and its curtain walls, the low outer walls forming the castle's first line of defense. Even more so than Warwick Castle, these ruins reflect English history. In 1326, King Edward II was imprisoned here and forced to renounce the throne, before he was transferred to Berkeley Castle and allegedly murdered with a red-hot poker. Here the ambitious Robert Dudley, earl of Leicester, one of Elizabeth I's favorites, entertained her four times, most notably in 1575 with 19 days of sumptuous feasting and revelry. A new exhibition discusses the relationship between Leicester and Elizabeth. Sir Walter Scott's novel *Kenilworth* (1821) presented tales about the earl and

Elizabeth, adding to a national fascination with the castle. This is a good place for a picnic and contemplation of the passage of time. The fine gift shop sells excellent replicas of tapestries and swords. ⊠ *Off A452, Kenilworth* ☎ *01926/852078* ⊕ *www.english-heritage.org.uk* ⊠ *£5.90* ⊗ *Apr.–Sept., daily 10–6; Oct., daily 10–5; Nov.–Mar., daily 10–4.*

Where to Eat

££££–£££££ ✕ **Restaurant Bosquet.** This Victorian town-house restaurant serves fixed-price menus cooked by the French *patron,* with regularly changing à la carte selections. Try the veal or venison with wild mushrooms, and don't pass up the delicious desserts. Bosquet is mainly a dinner spot, although lunch is available by prior reservation. There's no fixed-price menu on Saturday. ⊠ *97A Warwick Rd.* ☎ *01926/852463* ▭ *AE, MC, V* ⊗ *Closed Sun., 3 wks in Aug., last wk in Dec. No dinner Mon.*

£–££ ✕ **Clarendon Arms.** A location close to Kenilworth Castle helps make this pub a good spot for lunch. You can order fine home-cooked food at the small bar downstairs. A larger, slightly pricier restaurant upstairs serves complete meals, from English roasts to more international fare. ⊠ *44 Castle Hill* ☎ *01926/852017* ▭ *AE, DC, MC, V.*

Coventry

 7 mi northeast of Warwick, 16 mi northeast of Stratford-upon-Avon.

Coventry, which thrived in medieval times as a center for the cloth and dyeing industries, is where, according to lore, a naked Lady Godiva allegedly rode through the streets in the 11th century to protest high taxes. In the 19th century the city became an industrial powerhouse, and the first British automobiles were manufactured here (the Coventry Transport Museum heralds the now largely lost British auto industry). In World Wars I and II, Coventry was a center for weapons manufacturing, a fact that made it a favorite German target. On November 14, 1940, it suffered one of the worst air raids of the war: hundreds died, and the historic St. Michael's Cathedral was destroyed. Rapid postwar rebuilding was done in the cold architectural style of the 1950s and '60s, therefore Coventry is not a pretty town today; but it attracts history buffs and those who honor its past.

Before World War II, Coventry, like York and Canterbury, was virtually defined by its cathedral. After the war, to raise national morale, Sir Basil Spence was given the task of building a new cathedral. Wisely, he made no attempt to re-create the lost building. The striking, modern **Coventry Cathedral,** completed in 1962, stands beside the ruins of the blitzed St. Michael's, a powerful symbol of rebirth and reconciliation. Outside the sandstone building is Sir Jacob Epstein's *St. Michael Defeating the Devil*; the modern artworks inside include Graham Sutherland's stunning 70-foot-high tapestry, *Christ in Glory,* and unusual abstract stained glass. The visitor center in the undercroft shows a film about the cathedral; there's also a charred cross wired together from timbers from the bombed building. ⊠ *Priory Row* ☎ *024/7622–1200* ⊕ *www. coventrycathedral.org.uk* ⊠ *Suggested cathedral donation £3, visitor center £2* ⊗ *Daily 9–5, services permitting.*

Charlecote Park

⑰ *13 mi south of Coventry, 6 mi south of Warwick.*

This celebrated house in the village of Hampton Lucy was built in 1572 by Sir Thomas Lucy to entertain Queen Elizabeth I (in her honor, the house is shaped like the letter "E"). Shakespeare knew the house and may even have poached deer here. Standing at the edge of a glassy lake, the redbrick manor is striking and sprawling. It was renovated in neo-Elizabethan style by the Lucy family during the mid-19th century; a carved ebony bed is one of many spectacular pieces of furniture. The Tudor gatehouse is unchanged since Shakespeare's day, and a collection of carriages, a Victorian kitchen, and a small brewery occupy the outbuidings. Indulge in a game of croquet near the quirky, Victorian-era summer hut, or explore the deer park landscaped by Capability Brown. ⌧ *B4086, off A429, Hampton Lucy* ☏ *01789/ 470277* ⊕*www.nationaltrust.org.uk*

> ### BARD'S REVENGE?
>
> According to tradition, Shakespeare was caught poaching deer at Charlecote Park soon after his marriage and fled to London. Years later he supposedly retaliated by portraying Sir Thomas Lucy in *Henry IV Part 2* and the *Merry Wives of Windsor* as the foolish Justice Shallow. Some historians doubt the reference, but Shakespeare does mention the "dozen white luces"—which figure in the Lucy coat of arms—and Shallow does tax Falstaff with killing his deer.

⌦ *£6.90, grounds only £3.50* ☉ *House Mar.–Nov., Fri.–Sun. noon–5. Gardens Mar.–Oct., Fri.–Tues. 11–6; Nov.–mid-Dec., weekends 11–4.*

Compton Verney

⑱ *6 mi southeast of Charlecote Park.*

A neoclassical country mansion remodeled in the 1760s by Robert Adam, Compton Verney opened in 2004 as an art museum with more than 800 works. The house, set in 120 acres of parkland landscaped by Capability Brown, was decaying when the Peter Moores Foundation purchased it in 1993 and created a trust to raise money to purchase art. The artworks are intriguingly varied and beautifully displayed in restored rooms: British folk art and portraits, textiles, Chinese pottery and bronzes, southern Italian art from 1600 to 1800, and German art from 1450 to 1600 are the main focus. Special exhibitions round out the program. ⌧ *Off B4086, near Kineton* ☏ *01926/645500* ⊕ *www. comptonverney.org.uk* ⌦ *£6* ☉ *Mid-Mar.–Oct., daily 10–5.*

Broughton Castle

⑲ *8 mi southeast of Compton Verney, 18 mi southeast of Stratford-upon-Avon.*

Once owned by the great chancellor and patron William of Wykeham (whose descendants live there still), this regal redbrick, moated mansion dates to 1300, and it was remodeled in Tudor times. The inside is rich with fireplaces, plasterwork, and exquisite furniture. High points include the Great Chamber, the chapel, and a fine collection of Chinese wall-paper. The house's opening hours are limited, as it is home to members of the Twistleton-Wykeham-Fiennes family, which, understandably, shortened its length family name to "Fiennes" in the 1960s. Broughton appeared in the movie *Shakespeare in Love* as the home of Viola de Lesseps—a nice touch given that actor Joseph Fiennes, who played Shakespeare in the film, is the owner's cousin. ✉ *B4035, Broughton* ☎ *01295/276070* ⊕ *www.broughtoncastle.com* 💷 *£6* ☉ *Mid-May–June and early–mid-Sept., Wed. and Sun. 2–5; July and Aug., Wed., Thurs., and Sun. 2–5; national holiday Mon. 2–5.*

Alderminster

⑳ *5 mi south of Stratford-upon-Avon on A3400.*

Alderminster is one of the most interesting of the so-called "Stour villages"—those places so characteristic of Shakespeare Country, strung along the winding route of the River Stour south of Stratford. The main street holds an unusual row of old stone cottages, and the church has a Norman nave and a tower dating from the 13th century. Although the interior of the church has been much restored, it's worth a peek for the carved faces between the arches and the old altar stone.

Other Stour villages include Honington, Shipston-on-Stour, and Tredington. A village green anchors Honington, where a lovely five-arched bridge crosses the river. Shipston, the largest of the group, is an old sheep-market town, its handsome batch of Georgian houses formerly owned by wealthy wool merchants. Tredington, an exquisite nutshell of a village, has an old stone church.

Where to Stay & Eat

★ **✕▥ Ettington Park Hotel.** This luxurious Victorian Gothic mansion with
££££–£££££ a modern wing, built on land owned by the Shirley family since the 12th century, is a peaceful retreat for theatergoers who don't want to cope with Stratford's crowds. Some of the individually decorated rooms have four-poster beds; you can also choose the unusual Kingmaker and Shakespeare suites. The oak-panel restaurant (fixed-price menu; £££££) offers extremely good modern British cuisine. For a break, take tea or a whisky in antiques-filled public rooms or stroll in the 40-acre grounds, which contain the ruins of a 12th-century church. ✉ *Off A3400, Alderminster CV37 8BU* ☎ *01789/450123* 🖷 *01789/450472* ⊕ *www. handpicked.co.uk/ettingtonpark* 🛏 *37 rooms, 11 suites* ♿ *Restaurant, room service, cable TV, in-room data ports, 2 tennis courts, indoor pool, gym, hot tub, sauna, spa, fishing, croquet, bar, lounge, library, babysitting, dry cleaning, laundry service, meeting rooms, helipad; no a/c* ☰ *AE, DC, MC, V* ⨀| *BP.*

★ **£££** **✕▥ Fox & Goose.** A quirky style and fabulous, fresh food make this place in the wee, unspoiled village of Armscote, 8 mi south of Stratford, more than just a pub with rooms. Everything is in place for relaxation: Victorian claw-foot tubs with candles, a CD player, and a satisfying English breakfast served until noon. Rooms are themed around Clue (Cluedo in England) characters: Colonel Mustard's room is yellow, and Miss Scarlet's Boudoir is red and dimly lighted. The gastro-pub downstairs (££) serves a daily-changing fusion menu. ⊠ *Armscote CV37 8DD* 🕾🕾 *01608/682293* ⊕ *www.foxandgoose.co.uk* 🛌 *4 rooms* ♨ *Pub, meeting room; no a/c, no room phones* ▤ *MC, V* ⌾ *BP.*

Welford-on-Avon

㉑ *8 mi northwest of Alderminster, 4 mi southwest of Stratford-upon-Avon.*

Welford, off B439, is most famous for its May Day revelry, when Morris dancers wearing costumes and bells perform around the maypole on the green. To reach the maypole, go straight through town to High Street. The partly Norman church, reached by taking a right at the Bell Inn, has an ancient lych-gate (a covered gate at the entrance to graveyards). Close by the church are pretty timber and whitewashed thatched cottages. A lovely riverside path calls out for an afternoon of exploring.

Where to Eat

£–££ ✕ **Bell Inn.** This quiet spot has a flagstone public bar with an open fire, and a conservatory and garden in which to enjoy the generous portions of casual food such as fish and chips, lasagna, and sausage on mashed potatoes. ⊠ *High St.* 🕾 *01789/750353* ▤ *MC, V.*

Alcester

㉒ *8 mi northwest of Welford, 8 mi west of Stratford-upon-Avon.*

The small market town of Alcester (pronounced *al*-ster) holds ancient buildings and Tudor houses. Search out the narrow **Butter Street,** off High Street, site of the 17th-century Churchill House, and on Malt Mill Lane (off Church Street) the **Old Malt House,** dating from 1500.

Where to Stay & Eat

£££££ ✕⊡ **Billesley Manor.** Cozy public rooms with fireplaces and antiques and 11 acres of grounds with a topiary garden enhance this 16th-century manor house, now a luxurious retreat with the requisite spa. The bedrooms retain period features and are richly decorated in modern or traditional country style; some have four-poster beds. The excellent wine list complements the wood-panel restaurant's sophisticated food (££££–£££££), which includes honey-glaze lamb and chicken breast stuffed with Brie and apricots. ⊠ *Off A46, Billesley B49 6NF, near Alcester* 🕾 *01789/279955* 🖳 *01789/764145* ⊕ *www.billesleymanor.co.uk* 🛌 *69 rooms, 2 suites* ♨ *Restaurant, room service, cable TV, in-room data ports, tennis court, indoor pool, gym, sauna, spa, croquet, babysitting, dry cleaning, laundry service, meeting rooms, no-smoking rooms; no a/c* ▤*AE, D, MC, V* ⌾*BP.*

Ragley Hall

㉓ *2 mi southwest of Alcester.*

James Wyatt and other outstanding architects worked on Ragley Hall, a Palladian-style mansion with more than 100 rooms. Inside are architectural and decorative treasures as well as magnificent views of the parkland laid out by Capability Brown in the 1750s. The Great Hall has fine baroque plasterwork by James Gibb, and there are portraits by Joshua

Reynolds and Dutch masters, among others, as well as some striking 20th-century murals by Graham Rust. This is the ancestral home of the marquesses of Hertford, the third of whom figured in Thackeray's *Vanity Fair* and the fourth of whom collected many of the treasures in London's Wallace Collection. ■ TIP→ Let the kids blow off extra energy in the adventure playground and picnic area. Adults should save room for a cream tea at Hooke's coffeehouse, overlooking the rose garden. ⊠ *Off A435 and A46* ☎*01789/762090* ⊕*www.ragleyhall.com* ⊡*£7* ⊙ *House Apr.–Sept., Thurs.–Sun. 10–6. Park Apr.–Sept., daily 10–6.*

Coughton Court

㉔ *2 mi north of Alcester, 8 mi northwest of Stratford*

A grand Elizabethan manor house, Coughton Court is the home of the Catholic Throckmorton family, as it has been since 1409. The impressive gatehouse, the centerpiece of a half-timber courtyard, contains a fine fan-vaulted ceiling and memorabilia, including the dress worn by Mary, Queen of Scots at her execution. There are children's clothes and a Gunpowder Plot exhibition, and you can wander in the excellent formal gardens and along a river and lake. ⊠ *A435* ☎ *01789/400777* ⊕ *www.coughtoncourt.co.uk* ⊡ *£8.60, gardens only £5.90, parking £1* ⊙ *Apr.–Sept., Wed.–Sun. 11–5; Oct., weekends 11:30–5.*

SHAKESPEARE COUNTRY ESSENTIALS

Transportation

BY AIR

Warwickshire is convenient to major airports in London (⇨ Airports *in* Smart Travel Tips) and Birmingham (⇨ Airports *in* Smart Travel Tips).

BY BOAT & FERRY

For information about the Stratford towpath and canal, contact British Waterways.

🗂 **British Waterways** ☎ 01564/784634 ⊕ www.waterscape.com.

BY BUS

National Express serves the region from London's Victoria Coach Station with eight buses daily to the Stratford region. Flightlink buses run from London's Heathrow and Gatwick airports to Warwick, and Stagecoach serves local routes throughout the Stratford, Birmingham, and Coventry areas.

FARES & SCHEDULES 🗂 **Flightlink** ☎ 0870/580-8080 ⊕ www.nationalexpress.com. **National Express** ☎ 0870/580-8080 ⊕ www.nationalexpress.com. **Stagecoach** ☎ 01788/535555 or 0845/600-1314 ⊕ www.stagecoachbus.com.

BY CAR

Stratford lies about 100 mi northwest of London; take M40 to Junction 15. The town is 37 mi southeast of Birmingham by A435 and A46 or by M40 to Junction 15. Main roads provide easy access between towns, but one pleasure of this rural area is exploring the smaller "B" roads, which lead deep into the countryside.

BY TRAIN

First Great Western Link and Virgin Trains serve the area. Four direct trains (two in the morning and two in the afternoon) from London's Paddington Station take two hours to reach Stratford; these avoid a change at Leamington Spa. Two direct trains return from Stratford each evening. On Sunday in winter there are no direct trains. You can travel by train *and* bus using the Shakespeare Connection Road & Rail Link from Euston Station to Coventry, then a City Sightseeing bus (⇨ Tour Options).

The Shakespeare Connection trip takes two hours, and there are four departures on weekdays—the three that would allow you to catch an evening performance in Stratford are at 9:15 AM, 10:45 AM, and 4:55 PM; Saturday departures are at 9:05 AM, 10:35 AM, and 5:05 PM; the Sunday departure is at 9:45 AM. There's a train to London after performances, usually at 11:15 PM. Schedules can change, so call to confirm times. National Rail Enquiries has further information.

DISCOUNTS & DEALS A seven-day Heart of England Rover ticket is valid for unlimited travel within the region; contact National Rail Enquiries for purchasing information. Visit First Great Western's Web site, or phone the company, to find out about Stratford-related packages and deals; these change regularly.

FARES & SCHEDULES **National Rail Enquiries** ☎ 0845/748–4950 ⊕ www.nationalrail.co.uk. **First Great Western Link** ☎ 01789/293127 ⊕ www.firstgreatwestern.co.uk/link. **Virgin Trains** ☎ 0845/722–2333 ⊕ www.virgin.co.uk/trains.

Contacts & Resources

EMERGENCIES

Ambulance, fire, police ☎ 999. **Stratford-upon-Avon Hospital** ✉ Arden St., Stratford-upon-Avon ☎ 01789/205831. **Warwick Hospital** ✉ Lakin Rd., Warwick ☎ 01926/495321.

INTERNET

Outside the main towns (Stratford and Warwick) in this area, if there's no Internet access in your hotel or B&B, there's little chance of finding a way to check your e-mail. Broadband is relatively rare in hotels in this region, and Wi-Fi is very rare indeed.

 Internet Cafés **Java Cafe** ✉ 28 Greenhill St., Stratford-upon-Avon ☎ 01789/29263400. **Stratford Leisure & Visitor Centre** ✉ Bridgefoot, Stratford-upon-Avon ☎ 01789/268826. **The King's Head** ✉ 39 Saltisford, Warwick ☎ 01926/775177.

TOUR OPTIONS

The Heart of England Tourist Board (⇨ Visitor Information) arranges tours throughout the region. City Sightseeing runs guided tours of Stratford (£8.50), Coventry (£5.50), and trips to Warwick Castle from Stratford (£19.50). The tours don't include admission to the Stratford sights (most of which are within walking distance in town), so some people find the tour isn't the best value. The two-hour Shakespeare's Life in Stratford walk (£6), led by actors, begins at 10:30 AM on Saturday October through March, Thursday and Saturday April through September, and Thursday, Saturday, and Sunday July through September.

🎭 **City Sightseeing** ☎ 01789/294466 ⊕ www.city-sightseeing.com. **Shakespeare's Life in Stratford Walk** ☎ 01789/403405.

VISITOR INFORMATION

Tourist information centers are normally open Monday through Saturday 9:30 to 5:30, but times vary according to season.

🎭 **Heart of England Tourist Board** ✉ Larkhill Rd., Worcester WR5 2EZ ☎ 01905/761100 🖨 01905/763450 ⊕ www.visitheartofengland.com. **Shakespeare Country** ☎ 0870/160–7930 ⊕ www.shakespeare-country.co.uk. **Coventry** ✉ Bayley La., CV1 5RN ☎ 024/7622–7264 ⊕ www.coventry.org. **Kenilworth** ✉ Kenilworth Library, 11 Smalley Pl., CV8 1QG ☎ 01926/852595. **Stratford-upon-Avon** ✉ Bridgefoot, CV37 6GW ☎ 0870/160–7930 ⊕ www.stratford-upon-avon.co.uk. **Warwick** ✉ Court House, Jury St., CV34 4EW ☎ 01926/492212 ⊕ www.warwick-uk.co.uk.

6

Bath & the Cotswolds

WORD OF MOUTH

"Crowds in the Cotswolds are a bit of a myth. Most visitors come in for the day—a period that lasts from 11-ish to 4:30. They congregate in half a dozen honeypots. . . . The pleasures are small ones: scenery that's best appreciated on foot, endless small villages with lived-in churches and pubs—and the world's densest concentration of gardens. Glamour and excitement we don't do here . . . . Civilization is what we specialize in."
—flanneruk

"We loved Westonbirt Arboretum. It's just a short drive north of Bath. The trees were magnificent, and each one is identified . . . . An entire day could be spent there, but we only had a few hours. Hidcote Manor Gardens in the Cotswolds is worth a visit also."
—nini

Updated by
Robert
Andrews

THE ROLLING UPLANDS OF THE COTSWOLD HILLS represent the quintessence of rural England, as immortalized in countless books, paintings, and films. This blissfully unspoiled region, deservedly popular with visitors, occupies much of the county of Gloucestershire, in west-central England, with slices of neighboring Oxfordshire, Worcestershire, and Somerset. Together these make up a sweep of land stretching from Shakespeare Country in the north almost as far as the Bristol Channel in the south. On the edge of the area are three historic towns that have absorbed, rather than compromised, the flavor of the Cotswolds: Bath, among the most alluring small cities in Europe, offering up "18th-century England in all its urban glory," to use a phrase by writer Nigel Nicolson; Regency-era Cheltenham—like Bath, a spa town with remarkably elegant architecture; and Gloucester, which holds an outstanding medieval cathedral and gives access to the ancient Forest of Dean, on the western edge of the area.

Bath rightly boasts of being the best-planned town in England. Although the Romans founded the city when they discovered here the only true hot springs in England, its popularity during the 17th and 18th centuries ensured its aesthetic immortality. Bath's fashionable period luckily coincided with one of Britain's most creative architectural eras, producing virtually an entire town of stylish buildings. The city powers have been wise enough to make sure that Bath is kept spruce and welcoming. In the past, Thomas Gainsborough, Lord Nelson, and Queen Victoria traveled here to sip the waters, which Charles Dickens described as tasting like "warm flatirons." Today people come to walk in the footsteps of Jane Austen, to visit Bath Abbey and the excavated Roman baths, or shop in an elegant setting.

North of Bath are the Cotswolds—a region that more than one writer has called the very soul of England. Is it the sun, or the soil? The pretty-as-a-picture villages with the perfectly clipped hedges? The mellow, centuries-old, stone-built cottages festooned with honeysuckle? Whatever the reason, this idyllic region, which from medieval times grew prosperous on the wool trade, remains a vision of rural England. Here are time-defying churches, sleepy hamlets, and ancient farmsteads so sequestered that they seem to offer everyone the thrill of personal discovery. Hidden in sheltered valleys are fabled abodes—Sudeley Castle, Stanway House, and Snowshill Manor among them. The Cotswolds can hardly claim to be undiscovered, but, happily, the area's poetic appeal has a way of surviving the tour buses, crowds, and antiques shops that sometimes pierce its timeless tranquillity. Here you can taste the glories of the old English village—its stone slate roofs, low-ceiling rooms, and gardens; its atmosphere is as thick as honey, and equally as sweet.

Exploring Bath & the Cotswolds

The region's major points of interest—Bath, the Cotswold Hills, and the Gloucester–Cheltenham axis—are one way to organize your explorations. Bath, in the southwestern corner of this area, is a good place to start; it can also be visited on a day out from London. The Cotswold Hills, about two hours by car from London, cover some of southern England's most beautiful terrain, with which the characteristic stone cottages throughout the area are in perfect harmony. To the west of the Cotswolds lie the city of Gloucester and Cheltenham, a former spa town; beyond them, between the River Severn and the border of Wales, is the Forest of Dean. The road from Gloucester to Bath takes you by the castle at Berkeley.

About the Restaurants

Good restaurants dot the region, thanks to a steady flow of fine chefs seeking to cater to wealthy locals and waves of demanding visitors. The country's food revolution is in full evidence here. Restaurants have never had a problem with a fresh food supply: excellent regional produce, salmon from the Rivers Severn and Wye, local lamb and pork, venison from the Forest of Dean, and pheasant, partridge, quail, and grouse in season. Also look for Gloucestershire Old Spot pork, bacon, and sausage on area menus.

About the Hotels

The hotels of this region are among Britain's most highly rated—from bed-and-breakfasts in village homes and farmhouses to luxurious country-house hotels. Many hotels present themselves as deeply traditional rural retreats, but some have opted for a sleeker, fresher style, with boldly contemporary or minimalist furnishings. Spas are becoming increasingly popular at these hotels, too. Book ahead whenever possible, especially if you want to visit Bath during the two weeks in May and June when the Bath International Music Festival hits town, or Cheltenham in mid-March when the National Hunt Festival takes place. Brace yourself for some high prices. B&Bs are a cheaper alternative to the fancier hotels, and most hotels offer two- and three-day packages. Note that most lodgings in Bath require a two-night minimum stay on weekends and national holidays. Also keep in mind when making reservations that hotels can front on heavily trafficked roads; ask for quiet rooms.

WHAT IT COSTS In pounds				
£££££	**££££**	**£££**	**££**	**£**
RESTAURANTS over £22	£18–£22	£13–£17	£7–£12	under £7
HOTELS over £160	£120–£160	£90–£119	£60–£89	under £60

Restaurant prices are for a main course at dinner. Hotel prices are for two people in a standard double room in high season, including V.A.T., with no meals or, if indicated, CP (with continental breakfast), BP (Breakfast Plan, with full breakfast), or MAP (Modified American Plan, with breakfast and dinner).

Timing

This area contains some of England's most popular destinations, and you would do well to avoid weekends in the busier areas of the Cotswolds. During the week, even in summer, you may hardly see a soul in the more remote spots. Bath is particularly congested in summer, when students flock to its language schools. On the other hand, Gloucester and Cheltenham are workaday places that can absorb many tour buses comfortably; Cheltenham does, however, get full at festival time and during race meetings. Note that the private properties of Hidcote Manor, Snowshill

GREAT ITINERARIES

You can get a taste of Bath and the Cotswolds in three days; a weeklong visit gives you plenty of time for the slow wandering this small region deserves.

Numbers in the text correspond to numbers in the margin and on the Bath Environs, Bath, the Cotswolds, and the Forest of Dean maps.

IF YOU HAVE 3 DAYS

A day in 🖼 **Bath** ① - ⑫ ▶ will enable you to tour the Roman Baths, followed by a whirl around Bath Abbey. In the afternoon, stroll along the river or canal, view the ceramics and silverware in the Holburne Museum, and then cross town to the Royal Crescent for a promenade. Heading out early for **Cheltenham** ⑯, whose Regency architecture and fashionable shops will occupy a morning. After lunch, drive northeast on B4632 through **Winchcombe** ⑰, near which are historic **Sudeley Castle** ⑱ and treasure-filled **Snowshill Manor** ⑳. A stop in **Broadway** ㉑ will allow you to sample its prettiness, or you can press on to that Cotswold showpiece, 🖼 **Chipping Campden** ㉒. Now head south on the A429 through the classic Cotswold villages of **Moreton-in-Marsh** ㉔ and **Stow-on-the-Wold** ㉓, where cottage pubs are sandwiched between antiques shops. Nearby, don't miss the smaller places such as 🖼 **Lower and Upper Slaughter** ㉗. For your final afternoon, head westward on A436 to **Gloucester** ㊱, with its National Waterways Museum.

IF YOU HAVE 7 DAYS

Two days in 🖼 **Bath** ① - ⑫ ▶ will give you time to explore this

Georgian treasure. Outside Bath, make sure you see **Castle Combe** ⑬, "the prettiest village in England," or **Lacock** ⑭. On your third day, head north to swank 🖼 **Cheltenham** ⑯ and walk its Regency-era terraces. Overnight there, then start out on a circuit of the best of the Cotswold villages and countryside; Cheltenham's tourist office has useful information. Take a look at **Winchcombe** ⑰ and explore the impressive grounds of **Sudeley Castle** ⑱ and **Stanway House** ⑲ (the latter has limited hours). Nearby **Snowshill Manor** ⑳ is in an unspoiled village. The popular Cotswold center of **Broadway** ㉑ lies a couple of miles to the north, on A44. You might head to Stratford-upon-Avon for some Shakespeare; it's 15 mi north of Broadway.

Spend your fourth night in that Cotswold gem, 🖼 **Chipping Campden** ㉒, from which it is an easy drive to the "garden rooms" of **Hidcote Manor Garden** ㉓. From here, head south through **Moreton-in-Marsh** ㉔ and **Stow-on-the-Wold** ㉕. South of Stow, kids may enjoy **Bourton-on-the-Water** ㉖ and **Northleach** ㉘. **Chedworth Roman Villa** ㉛ recalls the area's importance in Roman times—nearby **Cirencester** ㉜ was Corinium, an important provincial capital. Pick a rural retreat for your fifth night, perhaps around 🖼 **Lower and Upper Slaughter** ㉗. In the morning, an outing eastward might take in idyllic **Bibury** ㉚ and the wool town of **Burford** ㉙. Driving west from Cirencester on A417, stop in the model village of **Owlpen** ㉞, immaculate **Painswick** ㉝, and the market town of **Tetbury** ㉟.

7

Manor, and Sudeley Castle close in winter. Hidcote Manor Garden is at its best in spring and fall, Bowood Gardens in May.

BATH & ENVIRONS

Anyone who listens to the local speech of Bath will note the inflections that herald the closeness of England's West Country. The city, however, has strong links with the Cotswold Hills stretching north, and the Georgian architecture and mellow stone that are such a feature of Bath recall the stone mansions and cottages of that region. The hinterland of the county of Somerset has plenty of gentle, green countryside.

Bath

★ ▶ *13 mi southeast of Bristol, 115 mi west of London.*

"I really believe I shall always be talking of Bath . . . Oh! who can ever be tired of Bath," enthused Catherine Morland in Jane Austen's *Northanger Abbey,* and today thousands of people heartily agree with the sentiments expressed by the great 19th-century author. One of the delights of staying in this city, a UNESCO World Heritage Site, is being surrounded by magnificent 18th-century architecture, a lasting reminder of the vanished world described by Austen. In the 19th century Bath lost its fashionable luster and slid into a refined gentility that is still palpable. Although the 20th century saw some slight harm from World War II bombing and slightly more from urban renewal, the damage was halted before it could ruin the city's Georgian elegance.

This doesn't mean that Bath is a museum. It's lively, with good dining and shopping, excellent art galleries and museums, the remarkable excavated Roman baths, and theater, music, and other performances all year. Many people rush through Bath in a day, but there's enough to do to merit an overnight stay—or more. It does get crowded in summer; the sheer volume of sightseers may hamper your progress on a stroll.

The Romans put Bath on the map in the 1st century, when they built a temple here, in honor of the goddess Minerva, and a sophisticated network of baths to make full use of the mineral springs that gush from the earth at a constant temperature of 116°F (46.5°C). The remains of these baths are one of the city's glories. Visits by Queen Anne in 1702 and 1703 brought attention to the town, and soon 18th-century "people of quality" took it to heart. Bath became the most fashionable spa in Britain. The architect John Wood created a harmonious city, building graceful terraces (row houses), crescents (curving rows of houses), and villas of the same golden local limestone used by the Romans. His son, called John Wood the Younger, also designed notable buildings in the city. Assembly rooms, theaters, and pleasure gardens were built to entertain the rich and titled when they weren't busy attending the parties of Beau Nash (the city's master of ceremonies and chief social organizer, who helped increase Bath's popularity) and having their portraits painted by Gainsborough.

TOP REASONS TO GO

A drink in a Cotswold pub: The classic pubs here press all the right buttons—low wooden beams, horse brasses, inglenook fireplaces, and hanging tankards. Log fires in winter and beer gardens in summer are further enticements. Many pubs date back 300 years or more, but some have added smart dining areas. Most now offer tea and coffee, and also welcome children.

Finding the perfect village: With their golden stone cottages, Cotswold villages tend to be improbably picturesque; the hamlets of Upper and Lower Slaughter are among the most seductive. Part of the fun is to take almost any scenic lane or head for any evocatively named cluster of houses on the map.

Gloucester Cathedral: The Great East Window, Whispering Gallery, and cloisters are especially noteworthy in this ancient monument, one of the country's finest cathedrals. Elsewhere, look out for the Whispering Gallery and for the settings of scenes in the Harry Potter movies.

Hidcote Manor Gardens: In a region rich with imaginative garden displays, Hidcote lays good claim to be the most eminent. Exotic shrubs from around the world and the famous "garden rooms" are the highlights of this Arts-and-Crafts masterpiece.

Roman Baths, Bath: Take a break from the town's Georgian elegance and return to its Roman days on a fascinating tour around this beautifully preserved bath complex, built around the country's only hot spring.

Shopping in Cheltenham: The grand Regency terraces of Cheltenham, worth a look in themselves, make a wonderful setting for "country chic" boutiques, antiques shops, and gift stores that attract people from the entire region.

Soon it may be possible to relive the experience of the Romans and Georgians by bathing in the hot sprints at the Thermae Bath Spa, a much-delayed venture that may finally open in late 2006 or 2007.

Main Attractions

❷ **Bath Abbey.** Dominating Bath's center, this 15th-century edifice of golden, glowing stone has a splendid west front, with carved figures of angels ascending ladders on either side. Notice, too, the miter, olive tree, and crown motif, a play on the name of the current building's founder, Bishop Oliver King. More than 50 stained-glass windows fill about 80% of the building's wall space, giving the interior an impression of lightness. The abbey was built in the Perpendicular (English late-Gothic) style on the site of a Saxon abbey, and the nave and side aisles contain superb fan-vaulted ceilings. There are six services on Sunday. In the **Heritage Vaults,** accessible from outside the building (the entrance is in the abbey's south wall, off Abbey Churchyard), you can see an audiovisual presentation of the abbey's history, along with a reconstruction of the Norman cathedral that preceded it, various pieces of statuary, and a pe-

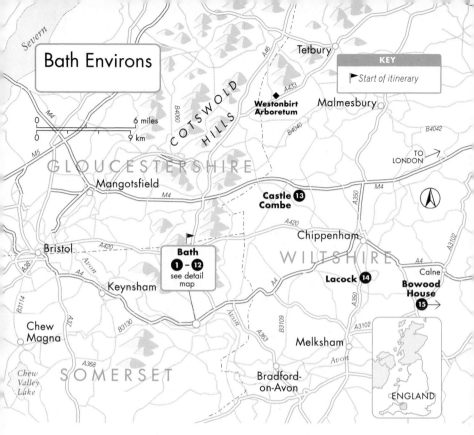

tition from 4th-century Bath, which includes what is thought to be the first mention of the word "Christian" in Britain. ✉ *Abbey Churchyard* ☎ *01225/422462* ⊕ *www.bathabbey.org* ✑ *Abbey £3 donation, Heritage Vaults free* ⊙ *Abbey Apr.–Oct., Mon.–Sat. 9–6, Sun. 1–2:30 and 4:30–5:30; Nov.–Mar., Mon.–Sat. 9–4:30, Sun. 1–2:30. Heritage Vaults Mon.–Sat. 10–4.*

★ ❾ **Circus.** John Wood designed the masterful Circus, a circle of curving, perfectly proportioned Georgian houses interrupted just three times for intersecting streets. Wood died shortly after work on the Circus began; his son, the younger John Wood, completed the project. Notice the carved acorns atop the houses: Wood nurtured the myth that Prince Bladud founded Bath, ostensibly with the help of an errant pig rooting for acorns (this is one of a number of variations of Bladud's story), and the architect adopted the acorn motif in a number of places. A garden fills the center of the Circus. The painter Thomas Gainsborough (1727–88) lived at No. 17 from 1760 to 1774.

★ ❹ **Holburne Museum.** One of Bath's gems, this elegant 18th-century building houses a small but superb collection of 17th- and 18th-century decorative arts, ceramics, and silverware. Highlights include paintings by Gainsborough (*The Byam Family*, on indefinite loan) and George Stubbs

(*Reverend Carter Thelwall and Family*), and Rachmaninoff's Steinway piano. In its original incarnation as the Sydney Hotel, the house was one of the pivots of Bath's high society, which came to perambulate in the pleasure gardens (Sydney Gardens) that still lie behind it. One visitor was Jane Austen, whose main Bath residence was No. 4 Sydney Place, a brief stroll across the road from the museum. ⊠ *Great Pulteney St.* ☎ *01225/466669* ⊕ *www.bath.ac.uk/holburne* ⊠ *£5.50* ☉ *Mid-Jan.–mid-Dec., Tues.–Sat. 10–5, Sun. and national holidays 11–5.*

⑧ Jane Austen Centre. The one place in Bath that gives Austen any space provides a briefly diverting exhibition about the influence of the city on her writings; *Northanger Abbey* and *Persuasion* are both set primarily in the city. Displays give a pictorial introduction, and the digitally enlarged panorama of Bath in 1800 by Robert Havell helps put Austen's world in context. The cozy Georgian house, a few doors up from where the writer lived in 1805 (one of several addresses she had in Bath at different times), also includes the Austen-themed Regency Tearoom, open to the public. ■ TIP→ **You can buy tickets here for Jane Austen walking tours, which leave from the Abbey Churchyard at 11 on weekends. A tour ticket entitles you to a 20% reduction for entry to the exhibition.** ⊠ *40 Gay St.* ☎ *01225/443000* ⊕ *www.janeausten.co.uk* ⊠ *£5.95, tours £4.50* ☉ *Mar.–Oct., daily 10–5:30; Nov.–Feb., Sun.–Fri. 11–4:30, Sat 10–5:30.*

> ### JANE IN BATH
>
> Though born and brought up in Hampshire, Jane Austen had close connections with Bath and lived here from 1801 to 1806. She was never overly fond of the place, peppering her letters with caustic comments about it (interspersed with gossip and effusions on bonnets and trimmings). Austen wrote her sister Cassandra that she left "with what happy feelings of escape." However, she is thought to have fallen in love here, and she received her only known offer of marriage while in Bath.

★ ⑦ Museum of Costume and Assembly Rooms. In its role as the **Assembly Rooms,** this neoclassical building was the leading center for social life in 18th-century Bath, with a schedule of dress balls, concerts, and choral nights. Jane Austen came here often, and it was here, in the Ballroom, that Catherine Morland had her first, disappointing encounter with Bath's beau monde in *Northanger Abbey;* the Octagon Room was the setting for an important encounter between Anne Elliot and Captain Wentworth in *Persuasion.* Built by John Wood the Younger in 1771, the building was badly damaged by wartime bombing in 1942 but was faithfully restored. Today the Assembly Rooms house the entertaining **Museum of Costume,** displaying costumes from Jacobean times up to the present (audio guide included). Throughout the year, classical concerts are given in the Ballroom, just as they were in bygone days. ⊠ *Bennett St.* ☎ *01225/477789* ⊕ *www.museumofcostume.co.uk* ⊠ *£6.50; combined ticket with Roman Baths, valid 7 days, £13* ☉ *Mar.–Oct., daily 11–6; Nov.–Feb., daily 11–5; last admission 1 hr before closing.*

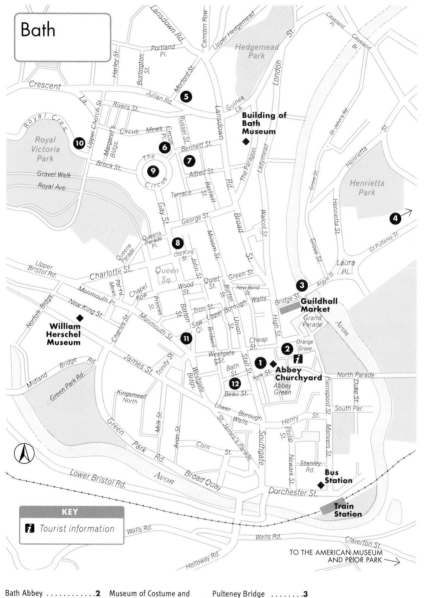

Bath

Bath Abbey **2**

The Circus **9**

Holburne Museum **4**

Jane Austen Centre **8**

Museum of
Bath at Work **5**

Museum of Costume and
Assembly Rooms **7**

Museum of
East Asian Art **6**

Number 1
Royal Crescent **10**

Pulteney Bridge **3**

Roman Baths
& the Pump Room **1**

Theatre Royal **11**

Thermae Bath Spa **12**

KEY

🛈 Tourist information

A GOOD WALK

This hour-long stroll takes in Bath's architectural showpieces. Start in the traffic-free Abbey Churchyard, a lively piazza (often filled with musicians and street artists) dominated by Bath Abbey and the Roman Baths complex. Work your way east to Grand Parade and look out over flower-filled gardens and the River Avon, crossed by the graceful, Italianate Pulteney Bridge. Stroll over the shop-lined bridge to gaze up the broad thoroughfare of Great Pulteney Street; then cross back over the bridge and head east up Bridge Street, turning right at High Street to follow up Broad Street and its northern extension, Lansdown Road. Turn left onto Bennett Street, passing the 18th-century Assembly Rooms and the Museum of Costume. Bennett Street ends at the Circus, an architectural tour de force compared by some to an inverted Colosseum. The graceful arc of Bath's most dazzling terrace, the Royal Crescent, embraces a swath of green lawns at one end of Brock Street. Return to the Circus and walk south down Gay Street, which brings you past dignified Queen Square, with its obelisk, to the Theatre Royal. Wander east from here along tiny alleys packed with stores, galleries, and eating places, back to your starting point at Abbey Churchyard, where you could have a well-earned sit-down and tea at the Pump Room.

7

🔟 **Number 1 Royal Crescent.** The majestic arc of the Royal Crescent, much
Fodor'sChoice used as a film location, is the crowning glory of Palladian architecture
★ in Bath; Number 1 offers you a glimpse inside this splendor. The work of John Wood the Younger, the 30 houses fronted by 114 columns were laid out between 1767 and 1774. A house in the center is now the Royal Crescent Hotel. On the corner of Brock Street and the Royal Crescent, Number 1 Royal Crescent has been turned into a museum and furnished as it might have been at the turn of the 19th century. The museum crystallizes a view of the English class system—upstairs all is elegance, and downstairs is a kitchen display. ☎ 01225/428126 ⊕ www.bath-preservation-trust.org.uk ⊠ £5 ☉ Feb.–Oct., Tues.–Sun. and national holidays 10:30–5; Nov., Tues.–Sun. 10:30–4; last admission 30 mins before closing.

❸ **Pulteney Bridge.** Florence's Ponte Vecchio inspired this 18th-century span, one of the most famous landmarks in the city and the only work of Robert Adam in Bath. It's unique in Great Britain because shops line both sides of the bridge.

Queen Square. Houses and the Francis Hotel surround the garden in the center of this small, peaceful square. An obelisk designed by the older John Wood and financed by Beau Nash celebrates the 1738 visit of Frederick, Prince of Wales.

❶ **Roman Baths & the Pump Room.** The hot springs have drawn people here
Fodor'sChoice since prehistoric times, so it's quite appropriate to begin an exploration
★ of Bath at this excellent museum on the site of the ancient city's temple

complex and primary "watering hole." Here the Roman patricians would gather to immerse themselves, drink the mineral waters, and socialize. With the departure of the Romans, the baths fell into disuse and were partially covered. When bathing again became fashionable, the site was reopened; the magnificent Georgian building now standing was erected at the end of the 18th century. During the 19th century, almost the entire Roman bath complex was rediscovered and excavated, and the museum displays relics of the temple once dedicated to Sulis Minerva. Exhibits include a mustachioed, Celtic-influenced Gorgon's head, fragments of colorful curses invoked by the Romans against some of their neighbors, and information about Roman bathing practices. The **Great Bath** is now roofless, and the statuary and pillars belong to the 19th century, but much remains from the original complex, and the steaming, somewhat murky waters are undeniably evocative. ■ TIP→ **On August evenings, you can take torch-lighted tours of the baths.**

Adjacent to the Roman bath complex is the famed **Pump Room,** built 1792–96, a rendezvous place for members of 18th-century and 19th-century Bath society, who liked to check on the new arrivals to the city. Here Catherine Morland and Mrs. Allen "paraded up and down for an hour, looking at everybody and speaking to no one," to quote from Jane Austen's *Northanger Abbey.* Today you can take eat in the elegant space—or you can simply, for a small fee, taste the fairly vile mineral water. ✉ *Abbey Churchyard* 🕾 *01225/477785* ⊕ *www.romanbaths. co.uk* ✉ *Pump Room free, Roman Baths £10, £11 in July and Aug. with audio guide; combined ticket with Museum of Costume and Assembly Rooms (valid 7 days) £13* ◷ *Mar.–June, Sept., and Oct., daily 9–6; July and Aug., daily 9 AM–10 PM; Nov.–Feb., daily 9:30–5:30; last admission 1 hr before closing.*

NEED A BREAK? The quiet courtyard of two adjacent cafés, the **Café René and Café Parisien** (✉ 2 Shires Yard, off Broad St. 🕾 01225/447147) is handy for coffee or a lunchtime baguette. You can linger in the **Pump Room** (✉ Abbey Churchyard 🕾 01225/444477) for morning coffee or afternoon tea after seeing the Roman Baths.

⑪ Theatre Royal. George Dance the Younger designed this magnificent auditorium, which opened in 1805 and was restored in 1982 as a vision in damson plush, raspberry-stripe silk, and gold grisaille. ✉ *Saw Close* 🕾 *01225/448844* ⊕ *www.theatreroyal.org.uk* ✉ *Tour £4* ◷ *Tours 1st Sat. of month at 11 and following Wed. at noon; call to confirm.*

Also Worth Seeing

American Museum and Gardens. A Greek-revival (19th-century) mansion in a majestic setting on a hill southeast of the city holds the first museum of American decorative arts to be established outside the United States. Some galleries are furnished rooms (bedrooms, parlors, and a morning room), and others contain objects—in silver, pewter, and glass, for example—dating from the 17th to 19th centuries. Several rooms are devoted to folk art, Native American culture, and quilts. The parkland includes a reproduction of George Washington's garden at Mount Vernon. ✉ *Warminster Rd. (A36), Claverton Down, 2½ mi southeast of Bath* 🕾 *01225/460503* ⊕ *www.americanmuseum.org* ✉ *Museum, special*

CLOSE UP

Bath's Georgian Architecture

BATH WOULDN'T BE BATH without its distinctive 18th-century Georgian architecture, much of which was conceived by John Wood the Elder (1704–54), an antiquarian and architect obsessed. Wood saw Bath as a city destined for almost mythic greatness along the lines of Winchester and Glastonbury. Arriving in Bath in 1727, he sought an architectural style that would do justice to his concept, and found it in the Palladian style, made popular in Britain by Inigo Jones. For building material, he looked no further than the local golden limestone. Influenced by nearby ancient stone circles as well as round Roman temples, Wood broke from convention in his design for Bath's Circus, a circle of houses broken only three times for intersecting streets. After the death of Wood the Elder, John Wood the Younger (1728–82) carried out his father's plans for the Royal Crescent, an obtuse crescent of 30 interconnected houses. Today you can stop in at No. 1 Royal Crescent for a look at one of these homes—it's like eavesdropping on the 18th century.

exhibitions, and grounds £6.50; special exhibitions and grounds £4 ⊙ *Museum: late Mar.–July, Sept., and Oct., Tues.–Sun. and national holidays noon–5; Aug., daily noon–5; late Nov.–mid-Dec., Tues.–Sun. and national holidays noon–4:30.*

Building of Bath Museum. This absorbing museum in the Georgian Gothic–style Countess of Huntingdon's Chapel is an essential stop on any exploration of Bath, particularly for fans of Georgian architecture. It explains and illustrates the evolution of the city, with examples of everything from window design and wrought-iron railings to marquetry and other interior ornamentation. ⊠ *The Paragon* ☎ *01225/333895* ⊕ *www.bath-preservation-trust.org.uk* ☑ *£4* ⊙ *Mid-Feb.–Nov., Tues.–Sun. and national holidays 10:30–5. Last entry 45 mins before closing.*

➎ Museum of Bath at Work. The core of this industrial-history collection, which gives a novel perspective on the city, is a complete engineering works and fizzy drinks factory, relocated to this building. It once belonged to Bath entrepreneur Jonathan Bowler, who started his many businesses in 1872. The tour includes the original clanking machinery and offers glimpses into Bath's stone industry and cabinetmaking. ⊠ *Julian Rd.* ☎ *01225/318348* ⊕ *www.bath-at-work.org.uk* ☑ *£4* ⊙ *Apr.–Oct., daily 10:30–5; Nov.–Mar., weekends 10:30–5; last admission at 4.*

➏ Museum of East Asian Art. Intimate galleries on three floors finely display ancient and modern pieces from China, Japan, Korea, and Southeast Asia. Highlights are graphic 19th-century watercolors depicting the Chinese idea of hell, Chinese ivory figures, and Japanese lacquerware. ⊠ *12 Bennett St.* ☎ *01225/464640* ⊕ *www.meaa.org.uk* ☑ *£3.50* ⊙ *Tues.–Sat. 10–5, Sun. noon–5; last admission at 4:30.*

Prior Park. A vision to warm Jane Austen's heart, Bath's grandest house lies a mile or so southeast of the center, with splendid views over the

Georgian townscape. Built around 1738 by John Wood the Elder of honey-color limestone, the Palladian mansion was the home of local business-man (he owned a stone quarry) and philanthropist Ralph Allen (1693–1764), whose guests included such luminaries as poet Alexan-der Pope and novelists Henry Fielding and Samuel Richardson. Today it is a Roman Catholic school and the interior is not open to the pub-lic, but you may wander through the beautiful grounds, designed by Ca-pability Brown and embellished with a Palladian bridge and lake. ■ TIP→ There is no parking lot here or in the vicinity: unless you relish the uphill trudge, take a taxi or use the frequent bus service (Nos. 2 or 4 from the center). ☒ *Ralph Allen Dr.* ☎ *01225/833422* ⊕ *www.nationaltrust. org.uk* ☒ *£4.50* ⊙ *Feb.–Nov., Wed.–Mon. 11–5:30 or dusk; Dec. and Jan., Fri.–Sun. 11–dusk; last admission 1 hr before closing.*

⓬ **Thermae Bath Spa.** The only place in Britain where you can bathe in nat-ural hot spring water, and in an open-air rooftop location as well, this state-of-the-art complex designed by Nicholas Grimshaw consists of a Bath-stone building surrounded by a glass curtain wall. Set to open (after years of delay) in late 2006 or 2007, the spa has four luxurious floors offering the latest spa treatments. Close by, the Cross Bath and the Hot Bath, two 18th-century thermal baths, have been brought back into use; there's also a café and shop. You can book in advance or call on the day. ☒ *Hot Bath St.* ☎ *01225/331234* ⊕ *www.thermaebathspa.com* ☒ *£19 for 2 hrs, £29 for 4 hrs, £45 all day; extra charges for treat-ments* ⊙ *Daily 9 AM–10 PM; last entry at 8 PM.*

William Herschel Museum. In this modest Bath town house, using a hand-made telescope of his own devising, William Herschel (1738–1822) identified the planet Uranus. This small museum devoted to his studies and discoveries contains his telescopes, the workshop where he cast his speculum metal mirrors, musical instruments of his time (Herschel was the organist at Bath's Octagon Chapel), and the tiny garden where the discovery of Uranus was made. ☒ *19 New King St.* ☎ *01225/446865* ⊕ *www.bath-preservation-trust.org.uk* ☒ *£3.50* ⊙ *Mid-Jan.–mid-Dec., Mon., Tues., Thurs., and Fri. 1–5, weekends 11–5; last admission at 4:30.*

Where to Stay & Eat

Among hotel restaurants, Pimpernel's, in the Royal Crescent Hotel, is outstanding; the Olive Tree, in the Queensberry Hotel, is noteworthy.

££–££££ ✕ **Hole in the Wall.** Escape from Bath's busy-ness at this relaxed eatery serving sophisticated modern English fare in an 18th-century town house. At the bottom of a flight of stairs, the unfussy, stone-tile dining area—warmed by a generous open fire in winter—exudes calm and poise. It's the perfect environment to indulge in such dishes as grilled Devon oysters, panfried Gloucester beef, and roast partridge with braised cab-bage. Cheeses come with sultana and honey bread. Pretheater meals are a good value. ☒ *16 George St.* ☎ *01225/425242* ▭ *AE, DC, MC, V* ⊙ *No lunch Sun.*

£££ ✕ **Number 5 Bistro.** An ideal spot for a light lunch, this airy bistro, dec-orated with plants and framed posters, is just over Pulteney Bridge from the center of town. The menu changes daily but includes soups and such dishes as crostini (toasted bread) of goat's cheese and grilled rib of beef with red wine and shallots. You can bring your own wine on Monday and Tuesday. ⊠ *5 Argyle St.* ☎ *01225/444499* ⊟ *AE, DC, MC, V.*

££–£££ ✕**Firehouse Rotisserie.** California comes to Bath. Tex-Mex, Pacific Rim, and creole influences are also evident on the menu, which features dishes from the rotisserie and grill, such as stone-baked fillets of sea bass with oregano, and mesquite-grilled loin of pork with griddled corn cakes. Brick-fired pizzas come with enticing toppings such as spicy Baja chicken with avocado salsa. Rustic decor, wooden floors and tables, and an easy, sociable vibe set the scene. ⊠ *2 John St.* ☎ *01225/482070* ⊟ *AE, MC, V* ⊗ *Closed Sun.*

££–£££ ✕**Pump Room.** The 18th-century Pump Room, next to the Roman Baths, serves morning coffee, lunches of steak sandwiches or chicken and lamb dishes, and afternoon tea, often to music by a string trio. Do sample the English cheese board and homemade Bath biscuits. The Terrace Restaurant has views over the Baths and is also open occasionally for dinner (there are fixed-price menus, and reservations are essential). Be prepared to wait in line for a table during the day. ⊠ *Abbey Churchyard* ☎ *01225/444477* ⊟ *AE, DC, MC, V* ⊗ *No dinner except during July, Aug., Dec., and festivals.*

££–£££ ✕**Tilleys Bistro.** The meat and vegetarian menus of this intimate, bow-windowed eatery present an alluring selection of hot and cold dishes offered in small, medium, and large portions. Choices include French onion soup, roast lamb studded with garlic, and veal Tilleys—panfried veal stuffed with Gruyère cheese and topped with asparagus wrapped in Parma ham. Pretheater meals are available starting at 6 PM. ⊠ *3 N. Parade Passage* ☎ *01225/484200* ⊟ *MC, V* ⊗ *Closed Sun.*

££ ✕**Demuths.** This is the region's top spot for high-class vegetarian cuisine at reasonable prices. Inspiration from around the world shows in such satisfying concoctions as Keralan *thali*—coconut and vegetable curry with cauliflower *bhaji* (a mildly spiced side dish) and coriander rice—and sweet potato and *haloumi* (an eastern Mediterranean cheese with mint leaves in it) salad. The dining rooms, on two floors, are small without being crowded, and there's usually a soft jazz soundtrack. ⊠ *2 N. Parade Passage* ☎ *01225/446059* ⊟ *MC, V.*

££ ✕**Sally Lunn's.** A well-done magnet for visitors, this popular spot near Bath Abbey occupies the oldest house in Bath, dating to 1482. It's famous for the Sally Lunn bun (served here since 1680), actually a light, semisweet bread. You can choose from more than 40 sweet and savory toppings to accompany your bun, or turn it into a meal with such dishes as trencher pork (served with bread that holds the juices) with sherry and brandy sauce. Daytime diners can view the small kitchen museum in the cellar (free, 30p for nondining visitors). ⊠ *4 N. Parade Passage* ☎ *01225/461634* ⊟ *MC, V* ⊗ *No dinner mid-Dec.–early Jan.*

££ ✕**Strada.** The former home of Richard "Beau" Nash—the dictator of fashion for mid-18th-century society in Bath—and his mistress Juliana Popjoy provides an elegant setting for this outpost of a reliable chain of Italian eateries. Pizzas and pasta appear on the menu with dishes based on traditional classics, including braised lamb shank with olive oil and sage potato puree in tomato sauce. You can dine on the ground floor or in the Georgian drawing room upstairs. ✉ *Beau Nash House, Saw Close* ☎ *01225/337753* ▤ *AE, MC, V.*

£–££ ✕ **Jazz Café.** Dine to a background of jazz classics in this cramped but buzzing café, with check tablecloths and a workaday atmosphere. Daily specials might be goulash, Mediterranean bean cassoulet, or spinach and ricotta pancakes. Famous for its all-day breakfasts, the café is also a good spot for a quick lunch, with soups, salads, sandwiches, and good vegetarian choices. Last orders are taken at 9 PM. ✉ *Kingsmead Sq.* ☎ *01225/329002* ▤ *AE, MC, V* ☉ *No dinner Sun.*

★ **£££££** ✕⊡ **Royal Crescent Hotel.** At the heart of the monumental Royal Crescent, this lavishly converted house is an architectural treasure, with prices to match. The furnishings are consistent with the building's period elegance, and a Palladian villa in the garden provides extra lodging. If some bedrooms are on the small side, the ample luxuries, including a pampering spa, compensate. The hotel's superb Pimpernel's restaurant (£45–£55 fixed-price dinner menus) has won consistent praise for modern British fare incorporating influences from Europe and the Far East. You can dine alfresco in summer. ✉ *16 Royal Crescent, BA1 2LS* ☎ *01225/823333, 888/295–4710 in U.S.* ▤ *01225/339401, 888/295–4711 in U.S.* ⊕ *www.royalcrescent.co.uk* ⇆ *31 rooms, 14 suites* ⚘ *Restaurant, cable TV, in-room data ports, indoor pool, gym, sauna, spa, croquet, bar, library, meeting rooms, free parking, some pets allowed (fee)* ▤ *AE, DC, MC, V* ⦿ *CP.*

£££–£££££ ✕⊡ **Queensberry Hotel.** Intimate and elegant, this boutique hotel in a
FodorśChoice residential street near the Circus occupies three 1772 town houses built
★ by John Wood the Younger for the marquis of Queensberry. Renovations have preserved the Regency stucco ceilings and cornices and marble tile on the fireplaces, and each room is individually decorated in contemporary style. Four secluded, terraced gardens invite a summer aperitif. Downstairs, the semiformal, sleek, and understated Olive Tree (£££–££££) serves top-notch English and Mediterranean dishes. ✉ *Russel St., BA1 2QF* ☎ *01225/447928* ▤ *01225/446065* ⊕ *www.thequeensberry.co.uk* ⇆ *26 rooms, 3 suites* ⚘ *Restaurant, cable TV, in-room data ports, Wi-Fi, bar, meeting rooms, free parking; no a/c* ▤ *AE, MC, V.*

££££–£££££ ⊡ **Dukes Hotel.** Refurbishment of this Palladian-style mansion has revealed the true Georgian grandeur of its rooms. Elegant bedrooms are individually decorated in English-, French-, or Italian-inspired style, and some have elaborate plasterwork or large windows facing the street. Note that some rooms are on the fourth story, and there is no elevator. The airy Cavendish Restaurant relies on locally sourced and organic ingredients. ✉ *Great Pulteney St. (entrance on Edward St.), BA2 4DN* ☎ *01225/787960* ▤ *01225/787961* ⊕ *www.dukesbath.co.uk* ⇆ *12 rooms, 5 suites* ⚘ *Restaurant, cable TV, in-room data ports, bar, meeting room, some pets allowed (fee); no a/c* ▤ *AE, DC, MC, V* ⦿ *BP.*

£££–££££ ⊡ **Bath Paradise House.** Don't be put off by the 10-minute uphill walk from the center of Bath—you'll be rewarded by a wonderful prospect of the city from the upper stories of this Georgian guesthouse. Cool pastels and traditional furnishings decorate the rooms attractively, and there are open fires in winter and a lush garden for spring and summer.

Rooms 3 and 5 have the best views; Nos. 11 and 12 open straight onto the garden. If the full English breakfast is too daunting, indulge in coffee and croissants in bed. ⊠ *88 Holloway, BA2 4PX* ☎ *01225/317723* 🖷 *01225/482005* ⊕ *www.paradise-house.co.uk* 🖙 *11 rooms* ⚿ *Croquet, bar, free parking; no a/c, no smoking* ⊟ *AE, MC, V* ⊘◯⊘ *BP.*

ʒʒ–ʒʒʒʒ 🎦 **Harington's Hotel.** It's rare to find a compact hotel in the cobblestoned heart of Bath, and this informal lodging converted from a group of Georgian town houses fits the bill nicely. The surprisingly quiet bedrooms aren't spacious, there are no views from the windows, and the parking facilities can be tricky to find, but these minuses are outweighed by the polite but friendly service and the central location. The bar serves snacks all day. Note that this three-story building has no elevator. ⊠ *Queen St., BA1 1HE* ☎ *01225/461728* 🖷 *01225/444804* ⊕ *www.haringtons. co.uk* 🖙 *13 rooms* ⚿ *Cable TV, Wi-Fi, bar, parking (fee), no-smoking rooms; no a/c* ⊟ *AE, MC, V* ⊘◯⊘ *BP.*

ʒʒʒ 🎦 **Three Abbey Green.** A majestic sycamore tree dominates the gorgeous square, just steps away from Bath Abbey, that is home to this welcoming B&B with spacious rooms in pastel shades. Parts of the building date from 1689, but contemporary design lightens the traditional tone. The Lord Nelson room is extra big, with a four-poster, separate sitting area, and handsome fireplace; there are also family rooms. The only downsides are Bath's perennial shortage of parking space—though there are car parks nearby—and the occasional noise at night. The hosts are ready with tips for visiting the city and beyond. ⊠ *3 Abbey Green, BA1 1NW* ☎ *01225/428558* 🖷 *01225/316669* ⊕ *www.threeabbeygreen.com* 🖙 *6 rooms* ⚿ *Wi-Fi; no a/c, no smoking* ⊟ *MC, V* ⊘◯⊘ *BP.*

ʒʒ–ʒʒʒ 🎦 **Cranleigh.** In a quiet location on the hill high above the city center, this Victorian guesthouse has wonderful views from the back of the building. Rooms are richly decorated, and large breakfasts—pancakes with maple syrup, kippers, scrambled eggs with smoked salmon, and vegetarian options—are served in the dining room, which overlooks the garden. There's a £7.50 charge for the hot tub. ⊠ *159 Newbridge Hill, BA1 3PX* ☎ *01225/310197* 🖷 *01225/423143* ⊕ *www.cranleighguesthouse. com* 🖙 *9 rooms* ⚿ *In-room data ports, outdoor hot tub, free parking; no a/c, no kids under 5, no smoking* ⊟ *MC, V* ⊘◯⊘ *BP.*

ʒʒ–ʒʒʒ 🎦 **Marlborough House.** A warm and informal welcome greets all who stay at this family-run Victorian establishment, close to the center of town. Each room charms with period furniture, fresh flowers, and antique beds. Leisurely breakfasts are positively encouraged; choose from home-baked muffins, scones, yogurts, pancakes, and French toast; all the food is organic, and vegans and those with special diets will find their needs amply supplied. ⊠ *1 Marlborough La., BA1 2NQ* ☎ *01225/ 318175* 🖷 *01225/466127* ⊕ *www.marlborough-house.net* 🖙 *7 rooms* ⚿ *Wi-Fi, bar, some pets allowed (fee); no a/c, no smoking* ⊟ *AE, DC, MC, V* ⊘◯⊘ *BP.*

ʒ–ʒʒ 🎦 **Albany Guest House.** Homey and friendly, this Edwardian house, close to Victoria Park and the center of town, has simply furnished rooms with a floral motif. The contemporary, parchment- and plum-color attic room is the largest and best. Homemade vegetarian sausages are an option at breakfast. ⊠ *24 Crescent Gardens, BA1 2 NB* ☎ *01225/*

313339 ⊕ *www.albanybath.co.uk* ⟿ *4 rooms, 2 with shower* ⟳ *Free parking; no a/c, no room phones, no kids under 7, no smoking* ⊟ *No credit cards* ⟨◎⟩ *BP.*

Nightlife & the Arts

BARS & PUBS   The small, brown and beige **Beau Bar** (⊠ 34 Monmouth St. ☏ 01225/444770), behind the Theatre Royal, serves the best cocktails in town (it's closed Sunday). Pub aficionados will relish the friendly, unspoiled ambience of the oak-panel **Old Green Tree** (⊠ 12 Green St. ☏ 01225/448259), a great spot for a pint.

FESTIVALS   The **Bath International Music Festival** (⊠ Bath Festivals Box Office, 2
★   Church St., Abbey Green ☏ 01225/463362 ⊕ www.bathfestivals.org. uk), held for two weeks in May and June, presents concerts (classical, jazz, and world music), dance performances, and exhibitions in and around Bath, many in the Assembly Rooms and Bath Abbey.

The weeklong **Bath Literature Festival** (⊠ Bath Festivals Box Office, 2 Church St., Abbey Green ☏ 01225/463362 ⊕ www.bathlitfest.org.uk) in early March features readings and talks by writers, mostly in the 18th-century Guildhall on High Street.

The **Jane Austen Festival** (☏ 01225/443000 ⊕ www.janeaustenfestival. co.uk) celebrates the great writer with films, plays, walks, and talks during a week in late September.

THEATER   The **Theatre Royal** (⊠ Box Office, Saw Close ☏ 01225/448844), a Regency playhouse, has a year-round program that often includes pre- or post-London tours. You have to reserve the best seats well in advance, but you can line up for same-day standby seats or standing room. ■ TIP➜ Check the location—sight lines can be poor.

Sports & the Outdoors

To explore the River Avon by rented punt or canoe, head for the **Bath Boating Station** (⊠ Forester Rd. ☏ 01225/312900), behind the Holburne Museum. It's open April through September.

Shopping

Bath has excellent small, family-run, and specialty shops; many close on Sunday. The shopping district centers on Stall and Union streets (modern stores), Milsom Street (traditional stores), and Walcot Street (arts and crafts). Leading off these main streets are alleyways and passages lined with galleries and antiques shops.

★   **Bartlett Street Antique Centre** (⊠ Bartlett St. ☏ 01225/466689) has more than 100 showcases and stands selling every kind of antique imaginable, including silver, porcelain, and jewelry. **Beaux Arts Ceramics** (⊠ 12–13 York St. ☏ 01225/464850) carries the work of prominent potters. The covered **Guildhall Market** (⊠ Entrances on High St. and Grand Parade), open Monday through Saturday 9 to 5, is the place for everything from jewelry and gifts to delicatessen food, secondhand books, bags, and batteries; there's a café, too. **Margaret's Buildings** (⊠ Halfway between the Circus and Royal Crescent) is a lane with gift shops and several stores selling secondhand and antiquarian books.

Castle Combe

13 *12 mi northeast of Bath, 5 mi northwest of Chippenham.*

Fodor'sChoice
★

This Wiltshire village lived a sleepy existence until 1962, when it was voted the Prettiest Village in England—without any of its inhabitants knowing that it had even been a contender. The village's magic is that it's so toylike, so delightfully all-of-a-piece: you can see almost the whole town at one glance from any one position. It consists of little more than a brook, a pack bridge, a street (which is called the Street) of simple stone cottages, a market cross from the 13th century, and the Perpendicular-style church of St. Andrew. The grandest house in the village (actually, on its outskirts) is the Upper Manor House, built in the 15th century by Sir John Fastolf; it was Dr. Dolittle's house in the 1967 Rex Harrison film and is now the Manor House Hotel.

Where to Stay & Eat

★ ££££ ✕⌂ **Manor House Hotel.** The partly 14th-century manor house, outside the village in a 23-acre park, is a baronial swirl of solid chimney stacks, carvings, and columns. Inside, a stone frieze depicts characters from Shakespeare's Falstaff plays, to commemorate the fact that Sir John Fastolf, thought to be the model for the character, was lord of this manor. Antiques abound and bedrooms have lavish bathrooms; some rooms are in mews cottages. The Bybrook restaurant serves imaginative fixed-price meals (£49.50)—try Wiltshire lamb with warm apple and rosemary jelly. ⊠ *Castle Combe SN14 7HR* ☎ *01249/782206* 🖷 *01249/782159* ⊕ *www.exclusivehotels.co.uk* ⌁ *48 rooms* ⌂ *Restaurant, in-room data ports, 18-hole golf course, tennis court, bar, meeting rooms, helipad; no a/c* ⊟ *AE, DC, MC, V.*

Lacock

14 *3 mi south of Chippenham, 8 mi southeast of Castle Combe.*

Fodor'sChoice
★

This lovely Wiltshire village owned by the National Trust is the victim of its own charm, its unspoiled gabled and stone-tile cottages drawing tour buses aplenty. Off-season, however, Lacock slips back into its profound slumber, the mellow stone and brick buildings little changed in 500 years and well worth a wander. Besides Lacock Abbey, there are a few antiques shops, the handsome church of St. Cyriac (built with money earned in the wool trade), a 14th-century tithe barn, and a scattering of pubs that serve bar meals in atmospheric surroundings.

Well-preserved **Lacock Abbey** reflects the fate of many religious establishments in England—a spiritual center became a home. The abbey, at the town's center, was founded in the 13th century and closed down during the dissolution of the monasteries in 1539, when its new owner, Sir William Sharington, demolished the church and converted the cloisters, sacristy, chapter house, and monastic quarters into a private dwelling. His last descendant, Mathilda Talbot, donated the property as well as Lacock itself to the National Trust in the 1940s. The abbey's grounds are also worth a wander, with a Victorian woodland garden and an 18th-century summerhouse. Harry Potter fans, take note: Lacock Abbey was

7

used for some scenes at Hogwarts School in the film *Harry Potter and the Sorcerer's Stone.* The **Fox Talbot Museum** in a 16th-century barn at the gates of Lacock Abbey, illustrates the early history of photography with works by pioneers in the field and also exhibits contemporary artists. The museum commemorates the work of William Henry Fox Talbot (1800–77), who developed the first photographic negative at Lacock Abbey, showing an

oriel window in his family home. Look for a copy of this and other results of Fox Talbot's experiments in the 1830s. ⊠ *Just east of A350* ☎ *01249/730459* ⊕ *www.nationaltrust.org.uk* ⊠ *Abbey, museum, gardens, and cloisters £7.80; abbey, garden, and cloisters £6.30; museum, gardens, and cloisters £4.80; museum only (winter) £3.40* ⊙ *Abbey late Mar.–Oct., Wed.–Mon. 1–5:30; museum late Feb.–Oct., daily 11–5:30; Nov.–mid-Dec. and early Jan–mid-Feb., weekends 11–4; gardens and cloisters late-Feb.–Oct., daily 11–5:30; last admission 30 mins before closing.*

Where to Stay & Eat

£££–££££ ✕▦ **Sign of the Angel.** An inn since the 15th century, this building measures up to expectations of comfortable antiquity—polished floors, gleaming silver, antiques, and cottage-style bedrooms (one room contains a bed that belonged to famous Victorian engineer Isambard Kingdom Brunel); some rooms are in an annex. The restaurant (££–£££) is known for its Stilton and walnut paté, roasts, casseroles, and desserts such as meringues with clotted cream. ⊠ *6 Church St., SN15 2LB* ☎ *01249/730230* 🖶 *01249/730527* ⊕ *www.lacock.co.uk* 🛏 *11 rooms* ♿ *Restaurant, some in-room data ports, lounge, some pets allowed; no a/c* ▭ *AE, DC, MC, V* ⊙ *Closed last wk of Dec.* ♦❙ *BP.*

Bowood House & Gardens

★ ⊛ ❶ *3 mi southeast of Chippenham, 3 mi east of Lacock.*

Dating to the mid-18th century, beautifully proportioned Bowood House sits in graceful parkland designed by Capability Brown. The family home of the marquess of Lansdowne owes its present appearance to Charles Cockerell, architect of the Ashmolean Museum at Oxford, and to Robert Adam, who was responsible for the south front, the orangery, and the splendid library and sculpture gallery. One room served as the laboratory where Joseph Priestley discovered oxygen gas in 1774. Among the treasures are Lord Byron's Albanian dress, much booty from India, and dazzling jewelry. ■ TIP➔ **The landscaped gardens, complete with Doric temple on the lake and waterfall in the woods, are at their finest in spring, when acres of rhododendrons on 2 mi of walks are in flower.** There's also an adventure playground and soft play palace for children. ⊠ *South* *of A4, Calne ☎ 01249/812102 ⊕ www.bowood-house.co.uk ✉ £7.50, rhododendron walks £4.80 (£3.80 if combined with visit to house and gardens) ⊙ House and gardens Apr.–Oct., daily 11–5:30; rhododendron walks late Apr.–early June, daily 11–6.*

THE COTSWOLDS

The Thames rises among the limestone Cotswold Hills, and a more delightful cradle could not be imagined for that historic river. The Cotswolds are among the best-preserved rural districts of England, and the quiet but lovely grays and ambers of the stone buildings here are truly unsurpassed. Much has been written about the area's towns, which age has mellowed rather than withered, but on closer inspection, the architecture of the villages differs little from that of villages elsewhere in England. Their distinction lies instead in the character of their surroundings: the valleys are deep and rolling, and cozy hamlets appear to drip in foliage from church tower to garden gate. Beyond the town limits, you may often discover the "high wild hills and rough uneven ways" that Shakespeare wrote about.

Over the centuries, quarries of honey-color stone have yielded building blocks for many Cotswold houses and churches and have transformed little towns into realms of gold. Nowhere else in Britain does that superb combination of church tower and gabled manor house shine so brightly, nowhere else are the hedges so perfectly clipped, nor the churchyards so peaceful. There's an elusive spirit about the Cotswolds, so make Chipping Campden, Moreton-in-Marsh, or Stow-on-the-Wold your headquarters for a few days, and wander for a while. Then ask yourself what the area is all about. Its secret seems shared by two things—sheep and stone. The combination is not as strange as it may sound. These were once the great sheep-rearing areas of England, and during the peak of prosperity in the Middle Ages, Cotswold wool was in demand the world over. This made the local merchants rich, but many gave back to the Cotswolds by restoring old churches (the famous "wool churches" of the region) or building rows of almshouses, of limestone now seasoned to a glorious golden-gray.

Begin with Cheltenham—the largest town in the area and a gateway to the Cotswolds, but slightly outside the boundaries—then move on to the beauty spots in and around Winchcombe. Next are Sudeley Castle, Stanway House, and Snowshill Manor, among the most impressive houses of the region; the oversold village of Broadway, which has many rivals for beauty hereabouts; Chipping Campden—the Cotswold cognoscenti's favorite; and Hidcote Manor, one of the most spectacular gardens in England. Then circle back south, down through Moreton-in-Marsh, Stow-on-the-Wold, Upper Slaughter, Lower Slaughter, Bourton-on-the-Water, and end with Bibury, Tetbury, and Owlpen. This is definitely a region where it pays to go off the beaten track to take a look at that village among the trees.

7

Cheltenham

🔞 *50 mi north of Bath, 13 mi east of Gloucester, 99 mi west of London.*

Although Cheltenham has acquired a reputation as snooty—the population (around 110,000) is generally well-heeled and conservative—it's also cosmopolitan. The town has excellent restaurants and bars, fashionable stores, and a thriving cultural life. Its primary claim to renown, however, is its architecture, rivaling Bath's in its Georgian elegance, with wide, tree-lined streets, crescents, and terraces with row houses, balconies, and iron railings. Like Bath, Cheltenham owes part of its fame to mineral springs. By 1740 the first spa was built, and after a visit from George III and Queen Charlotte in 1788, the town dedicated itself to idleness and enjoyment. "A polka, parson-worshipping place"—in the words of resident Lord Tennyson—Cheltenham gained its reputation for snobbishness when stiff-collared Raj majordomos returned from India to find that the springs—the only purely natural alkaline waters in England—were the most effective cure for their "tropical ailments."

Great Regency architectural set pieces—Lansdown Crescent, Pittville Spa, and the Lower Assembly Rooms, among them—were built solely to adorn the town. The Rotunda building (1826) at the top of Montpellier Walk—now a bank—contains the spa's original "pump room," in which the mineral waters were on draft. More than 30 statues adorn the storefronts of Montpellier Walk. Wander past Imperial Square, with its ironwork balconies, past the ornate Neptune's Fountain, and along the Promenade. In spring and summer, lush flower gardens enhance the town's buildings, attracting many visitors.

> ### FLOWERS & FESTIVALS
>
> Parts of the town may look like something out of a Gilbert and Sullivan stage set, but Cheltenham is the site of two of England's most progressive arts festivals—the Cheltenham Festival of Literature and the town's music festival—as well as a jazz fest.

From the 1880s onward, Cheltenham was at the forefront of the Arts and Crafts movement, and the **Cheltenham Art Gallery and Museum** contains fine displays of William Morris textiles, furniture by Charles Voysey, and simple wood and metal pieces by Ernest Gimson. Decorative arts, such as Chinese ceramics, are well represented, and British artists, including Stanley Spencer and Vanessa Bell, make their mark in the art gallery. Other exhibits focus on local archaeology and history; one is devoted to Edward Wilson, who traveled with Robert Scott to the Antarctic on Scott's ill-fated 1912 expedition. ⊠ *Clarence St.* ☎ *01242/ 237431* ⊕ *www.cheltenhammuseum.org.uk* 🖃 *Free* ☾ *Mon.–Sat. 10–5:20 (11–5:20 first Thurs. of month).*

The grandest of the spa buildings remaining in town, the **Pittville Pump Room** is set amid parkland, a 20-minute walk from the town center. The classic Regency structure, built in the late 1820s, now serves mainly as a concert hall and a theatrical venue but still offers its musty mineral waters to the strong of stomach. The Pump Room may not be accessi-

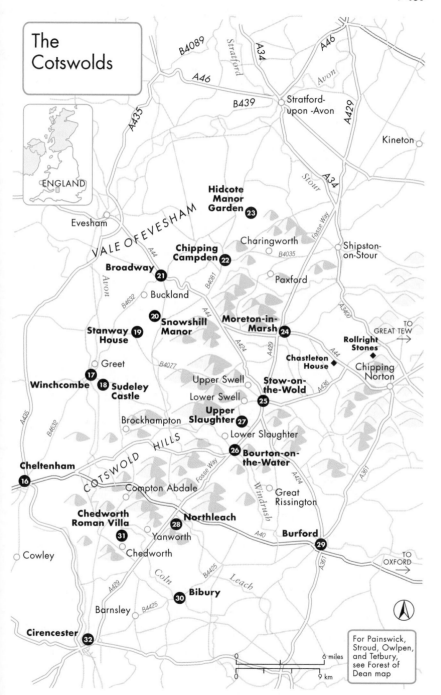

The
Cotswolds

ENGLAND

B4089

Stratford

A34

A46

Avon

A46

B439

Stratford-
upon-Avon

A429

Kineton

VALE OF EVESHAM

A44

Evesham

**Hidcote
Manor
Garden** 23

Charingworth

Stour

Fosse Way

A34

Shipston-
on-Stour

**Chipping
Campden** 22

B4035

Paxford

Broadway 21

A3400

B4632

Buckland

B4081

A44

**Moreton-in-
Marsh** 24

TO
GREAT TEW

20 **Snowshill
Manor**

Stanway 19
House

A424

A429

**Rollright
Stones**

Greet

A44

**Chastleton
House**

Chipping
Norton

17

B4077

Upper Swell

**Stow-on-
the-Wold** 25

A436

Winchcombe 18 **Sudeley
Castle**

Lower Swell

A435

B4632

Brockhampton

**Upper
Slaughter** 27

COTSWOLD HILLS

Lower Slaughter

26 **Bourton-on-
the-Water**

A424

A361

Cheltenham

Fosse Way

Windrush

Great
Rissington

16

Compton Abdale

**Chedworth
Roman Villa**

31

Northleach 28

A40

Burford 29

Cowley

Yanworth

TO
OXFORD

Chedworth

B4425

Leach

A361

Coln

A429

30 **Bibury**

Barnsley

B4425

Cirencester 32

0   6 miles

0   9 km

For Painswick,
Stroud, Owlpen,
and Tetbury,
see Forest of
Dean map

ble during functions—call to check. ✉ *E. Approach Dr., Pittville* ☎ *01242/523852* ☜ *Free* ☉ *Wed.–Mon. 10–4.*

Where to Stay & Eat

★ ✕ **Le Champignon Sauvage.** The relatively short, perfectly balanced menu
££££–£££££ at this excellent, well-established restaurant showcases contemporary French cooking. Relax in a room with cream walls and modern art as you indulge in dishes such as pressed terrine of rabbit confit followed by Cinderford lamb. Desserts, including hot fig tart, are worth the calories; you can choose among many cheeses as well. Fixed-price menus at lunch and dinner help keep the cost down. ✉ *24 Suffolk Rd.* ☎ *01242/573449* ⊟ *AE, DC, MC, V* ☉ *Closed Sun., Mon., 3 wks in June, and 10 days in Dec. and Jan.*

££–££££ ✕ **Le Petit Blanc.** In the same building as Queen's Hotel, this offshoot of renowned chef Raymond Blanc's Manoir aux Quat' Saisons in Great Milton offers French provincial cooking in contemporary surroundings that harmonize well with the good-size Regency windows. The impressive menu takes in everything from herb pancakes with mushrooms, ham, and kirsch sauce to lemon sole meunière with new potatoes. Among the lip-smacking desserts is grilled pineapple with rum baba and piña colada sauce. ✉ *The Promenade* ☎ *01242/266800* ⊟ *AE, DC, MC, V.*

££–££££ ✕ **Montpellier Wine Bar.** An ideal place for a light snack or a fuller evening meal, this busy, informal wine bar on two stories (downstairs for the more formal seating area) in Cheltenham's fashionable Montpellier shopping district serves tapas, pastas, salads, and dishes such as salmon and dill fishcakes. Get in early for fast service. ✉ *Bayshill Lodge, Montpellier St.* ☎ *01242/527774* ⊟ *AE, DC, MC, V.*

£££ ✕ **The Daffodil.** Brasserie cuisine is the focus of this former cinema that preserves the heyday of 1930s elegance. Admire the art deco trappings, sip an aperitif in the Circle Bar, and then sweep down the staircase to watch the chefs at work "on stage." Among the delightful dishes are venison marinated in gin and juniper berries. There's live jazz on Monday, when a special jazz menu is offered. ✉ *18–20 Suffolk Parade* ☎ *01242/700055* ⊟ *AE, MC, V* ☉ *Closed Sun.*

£–££ ✕ **Boogaloos.** Choose between the brightly colored, vibrant rooms upstairs or the sofa seating in the relaxed basement for lunches of salads, baked potatoes, or more substantial fare such as shredded lamb with Thai noodles. Leave room for the homemade cakes and puddings. ✉ *16 Regent St.* ☎ *01242/702259* ⊟ *MC, V* ☉ *No dinner.*

£££££ 🏠 **Cowley Manor.** Good-bye, floral prints: this Georgian mansion on 55 acres brings luxury country-house hotels into the 21st century by using modern fabrics and furniture but keeping the comfort level high enough to soothe a chic clientele. Witty sculptures and lighting complement the public rooms, bedrooms are brightly colored, and bathrooms are suitably trendy, with glass walls and large showers. Half the rooms are in the house; the rest fill a transformed stable. The spa, set into the ground, looks like a work of art. Cowley Manor is 5 mi south of Cheltenham. ✉ *Cowley GL53 9NL* ☎ *01242/870900* 🖷 *01242/870901* ⊕ *www.cowleymanor.com* ⬎ *30 rooms* ♿ *Restaurant, cable TV with movies,* in-room DVDs, in-room data ports, 2 pools (1 indoor), gym, sauna, spa, steam room, billiards ⊟ AE, DC, MC, V ⏐○⏐ CP.

£££££ ⊡ **Queen's Hotel.** Grandly dominating Imperial Gardens, this hotel in a classic Regency building has welcomed people to Cheltenham since 1838. Public areas and rooms leading off the stunning inner stairway are traditionally British (and rather old-fashioned) in style, and every bedroom is individually decorated. ⊠ *The Promenade, GL50 1NN* ☎ *0870/400–8107* ⎙ *01242/224145* ⊕ *www.thequeens-cheltenham. co.uk* ⌁ *79 rooms* ♿ *Restaurant, cable TV, in-room data ports, Wi-Fi, bar, some pets allowed (fee)* ⊟ *AE, DC, MC, V.*

£££–££££ ⊡ **Hotel Kandinsky.** A fashionably cool style that doesn't stint on the comfort factor makes a stay in this Georgian hotel (part of the trendy Alias minichain) a memorable experience at a fairly sensible price. Colorful rugs, huge potted plants, and the occasional touch of eccentricity offset the antiques in the guest rooms and clubby public rooms. A Mediterranean-style bistro and a hip basement nightclub are on the premises, and guests have access to a nearby pool and gym. ⊠ *Bayshill Rd., GL50 3AS* ☎ *01242/527788* ⎙ *01242/226412* ⊕ *www.aliashotels. com* ⌁ *48 rooms* ♿ *Restaurant, cable TV, in-room VCRs, Wi-Fi, bar, nightclub, meeting rooms; no a/c* ⊟ *AE, DC, MC, V.*

££–£££ ⊡ **Lypiatt House Hotel.** This splendid Victorian villa—a short walk from central Cheltenham in the chic Montpellier area—is an excellent B&B with attentive service. The bedrooms are spacious and have chic bathrooms. The restful drawing room is done in deep pink, and the conservatory makes a good place for a drink. ⊠ *Lypiatt Rd., GL50 2QW* ☎ *01242/224994* ⎙ *01242/224996* ⊕ *www.lypiatt.co.uk* ⌁ *10 rooms* ♿ *Bar; no a/c* ⊟ *AE, MC, V* ⏐○⏐ BP.

££ ⊡ **Abbey Hotel.** Relaxed and family-run, this hotel in a quiet terrace near the center of town offers great value. Bedrooms are simple but stylish, decorated in subtle tones, and the breakfast area overlooks the well-stocked garden. ⊠ *14–16 Bath Parade, GL53 7HN* ☎ *01242/516053* ⎙ *01242/ 513034* ⊕ *www.abbeyhotel-cheltenham.com* ⌁ *12 rooms* ♿ *Bar, no-smoking rooms; no a/c* ⊟ *AE, MC, V* ⏐○⏐ BP.

Nightlife & the Arts

The grand, late Victorian **Everyman Theatre** (⊠ Regent St. ☎ 01242/ 572573) is an intimate venue for opera, dance, concerts, and plays.
■ TIP→ You can often catch pre- or post-West End productions here, at a fraction of big city prices.

For information on the town's ambitious lineup of festivals, contact the **Festival Office** (⊠ Town Hall, Imperial Sq., Cheltenham GL50 1QA
★ ☎ 01242/227979 ⊕ www.cheltenhamfestivals.co.uk). The 10-day **Festival of Literature** in October brings together world-renowned authors, actors, and critics for hundreds of readings events. Cheltenham's famous
★ **International Festival of Music,** during the first half of July, highlights new compositions, often conducted by the composers, and classical pieces. The **International Jazz Festival,** held over five days in April and May, presents noted musicians. The **Science Festival,** which takes place over five days in June, attracts leading scientists and writers.

Sports

Important steeplechase races take place at **Cheltenham Racecourse** (⊠ Prestbury Park ☎ 01242/513014), north of the town center; the Gold Cup awards crown the last day of the National Hunt Festival in mid-March.

Shopping

This is serious shopping territory. A stroll along Montpellier Walk and then along the flower-bedecked Promenade brings you to high-quality specialty stores and boutiques. A bubble-blowing Wishing Fish Clock, designed by Kit Williams, dominates the Regent Arcade, a modern shopping area behind the Promenade. General markets are held every Sunday at the Cheltenham Racecourse and every Thursday morning off Lower High Street. An indoor antiques market is open Monday through Saturday at 54 Suffolk Road; there are other antiques shops in the Suffolk area. A farmers market takes place on the Promenade on the second and fourth Friday of the month.

Cavendish House (⊠ 32–48 The Promenade ☎ 01242/521300) is a high-quality department store with designer fashions. **Early Bird** (⊠ 5 Suffolk Rd. ☎ 01242/233507) displays antiques, faux antiques, and enticing bric-a-brac. **Laura Ashley** (⊠ 92 The Promenade ☎ 01242/580770) sells products in its distinctive, Arts-and-Crafts-influenced style, including clothes, handbags, and gift items. **Martin** (⊠ 19 The Promenade ☎ 01242/522821) carries a good stock of modern jewelry.

Winchcombe

⑰ *7 mi northeast of Cheltenham.*

The sleepy, unspoiled village of Winchcombe, once the capital of the Anglo-Saxon kingdom of Mercia, has some attractive half-timber and stone houses, as well as a clutch of appealing old inns serving food. A good place to escape the crowds, it's near Sudeley Castle and is also the start of both the Wardens' Way and Windrush Way walking trails. Almost 40 outlandish gargoyles adorn the mid-15th-century Perpendicular-style **St. Peter's Church,** a typical Cotswold wool church.

★ A bracing 2-mi walk south of Winchcombe on the Cotswold Way leads to the hilltop site of **Belas Knap,** a neolithic long barrow, or submerged burial chamber, above **Humblebee Wood. ■ TIP→ The site isn't much to see, but you hike next to and through one of the most enchanting natural domains in England, with views stretching over to Sudeley Castle.** If you have a car, take the scenic Humblebee Wood road down to the villages of Sevenhampton and Brockhampton.

A mile east of Winchcombe, at Greet, you can board a steam-hauled train of the **Gloucestershire and Warwickshire Railway,** which chugs its way along a 13-mi stretch at the foot of the Cotswolds between Toddington Station and Cheltenham Racecourse. ⊠ *Station Rd., Greet* ☎ *01242/621405* ⊕ *www.gwsr.com* ⊠ *£9.50 round-trip* ☉ *Mar.–Dec., weekends 10:30–5; daily during school holidays and some of Dec.*

Where to Stay & Eat

£££–£££ ✕⬚ **Wesley House.** Beams and stone walls distinguish this 15th-century half-timber building, a restaurant (£35–£38 fixed-price menu; no dinner Sunday) with five bedrooms. The red-carpeted dining room makes a fine backdrop for superior Mediterranean-style food; fixed-price menus include shellfish nâge and grilled Cornish lamb with *merguez* (a spicy sausage) and sweet potato puree. Upstairs, the smallish rooms have twisted beams and sloping ceilings; Almsbury has the best view, or you can opt for the Preacher's Room, where John Wesley used to stay. You may smoke only in the bar. ⊠ *High St., GL54 5LJ* ☎ *01242/602366* 🖷 *01242/609046* ⊕ *www.wesleyhouse.co.uk* 🛏 *5 rooms* 🖧 *Restaurant, in-room VCRs, bar; no a/c, no smoking* ⊟ *AE, MC, V* ⦿ *BP.*

Sudeley Castle

⓲ *1 mi southeast of Winchcombe, 9 mi northeast of Cheltenham.*

One of the grand showpieces of the Cotswolds, Sudeley Castle was the home and burial place of Catherine Parr (1512–48), Henry VIII's sixth and last wife, who outlived him by one year. Here Catherine undertook, in her later years, the education of the ill-fated Lady Jane Grey and the future queen, Princess Elizabeth. Sudeley, for good reason, has been called a woman's castle. The term "castle" is misleading, for it looks more like a Tudor-era palace, with a peaceful air that belies its turbulent history. During the 17th century, Charles I took refuge here, causing Oliver Cromwell's army to besiege the castle, leaving it in ruins until the Dent-Brocklehurst family stepped in with a 19th-century renovation. The 14 acres of gardens, which include the spectacular roses of the Queen's Garden and a Tudor knot garden, are the setting for Shakespeare performances, concerts, and other events in summer. Inside the castle, however, visitors see only the West Wing, with the Long Room and temporary exhibitions that focus on such subjects as the Tudors, the Civil War, and the Victorians. The private apartments of Lord and Lady Ashcombe, where you can see paintings by Van Dyck, Rubens, Turner, and Reynolds, are viewable only on Connoisseur Tours on Wednesday and Thursday (£15, including entry to the public rooms and a guidebook). Accommodations in 13 cottages on the grounds are booked for a minimum of four-night stays. ⊠ *Off B4632, Winchcombe* ☎ *01242/602308, 01242/604357 recorded information* ⊕ *www.sudeleycastle.co.uk* 🖾 *£7.20* ⊙ *Mar.–mid-Apr., May, and Sept.–mid-Oct., Sun.–Thurs. 10:30–5; mid- to late Apr., June–Aug., and late Oct., daily 10:30–5.*

Stanway House

★ **⓳** *5 mi northeast of Sudeley Castle, 11 mi northeast of Cheltenham.*

This perfect Cotswold manor of glowing limestone in the small village of Stanway dates from the Jacobean era. Its triple-gabled gatehouse is a Cotswold landmark, and towering windows dominate the house's Great Hall. Divided by mullions and transoms into 60 panes, these windows are "so mellowed by time"—to quote Lady Cynthia Asquith (a former chatelaine)—"that whenever the sun shines through their amber and green glass, the effect is of a vast honeycomb." They illuminate a 22-foot-long

7

shuffleboard table from 1620 and an 18th-century bouncing exercise machine. The other well-worn rooms are adorned with family portraits, tattered tapestries, vintage armchairs, and, at times, Lord Neidpath himself, the current owner. The partly restored baroque water garden has a fountain, built in 2004, that shoots up 300 feet; it's the tallest in Britain. On the grounds is a cricket pavilion built by J. M. Barrie, author of *Peter Pan*, who leased the house. To get to Stanway, take B4632 north of Winchcombe, turning right at B4077. ⊠ *Stanway* ☎ *01386/584469* ⊕ *www.stanwayfountain.co.uk* ⊠ *House and fountain £6; fountain only £4* ☉ *House and fountain: June–Aug., Tues. and Thurs. 2–5; fountain only Sat. in July and Aug. 2–5; fountain shoots at 2:45 and 4 for 30 mins.*

Snowshill Manor

★ ⑳ *4 mi northeast of Sudeley Castle, 3 mi south of Broadway, 13 mi northeast of Cheltenham.*

Snowshill is one of the most unspoiled of all Cotswold villages. Snuggled beneath Oat Hill, with little room for expansion, the hamlet is centered around an old burial ground, the 19th-century St. Barnabas Church, and Snowshill Manor, a splendid 17th-century house that brims with the collections of Charles Paget Wade, gathered between 1919 and 1956. Over the door of the house is Wade's family motto, *Nequid pereat* ("Let nothing perish"). The rooms are bursting with Tibetan scrolls, spinners' tools, ship models, Persian lamps, and bric-a-brac. The Green Room displays 26 suits of Japanese samurai armor. Children love the place. Outside, an imaginative terraced garden provides an exquisite frame for the house. ⊠ *Off A44, Snowshill* ☎ *01386/852410* ⊕ *www. nationaltrust.org.uk* ⊠ *£7.30, garden only £4* ☉ *House: late Mar.–Oct., Wed.–Sun. noon–5. Garden: late Mar.–Oct., Wed.–Sun. 11–5:30.*

Broadway

㉑ *3 mi north of Snowshill Manor, 17 mi northeast of Cheltenham.*

The Cotswold town to end all Cotswold towns, Broadway has become a favorite of day-trippers. William Morris first discovered the delights of this village, and J. M. Barrie, Vaughan Williams, and Edward Elgar soon followed. Today you may want to avoid Broadway in summer, when it's clogged with cars and buses. Named for its handsome, wide main street (well worth a stroll), the village includes the renowned Lygon Arms and numerous antiques shops, tea parlors, and boutiques. Step off onto Broadway's back roads and alleys and you can discover any number of honey-color houses and colorful gardens.

> **SEEKING SHAKESPEARE**
>
> The country delights of the area lure you to linger, but keep in mind that in the northern part of the Cotswolds, you're less than 15 mi from Stratford-upon-Avon. It's easy to detour to visit the Shakespeare sights or even see a play at the Royal Shakespeare Theatre (⇨ Chapter 6).

Among the attractions of **Broadway Tower Country Park,** on the outskirts of town, is its tower, an 18th-century "folly" built by the sixth earl of Coventry and later used by William Morris as a retreat. Exhibits describe the tower's past, and the view from the top takes in 3 counties. Peaceful countryside surrounds you on the nature trails and picnic grounds. ⊠ *Off A44* ☎ *01386/852390* 🖾 *Park free, tower £3.50* ☉ *Tower Apr.–Oct., daily 10:30–5; Nov.–Mar., weekends 10:30–4.*

Where to Stay & Eat

★ **£££££** ✕🔲 **Buckland Manor.** As an alternative to the razzmatazz of Broadway, you can splurge at this exceptional hotel 2 mi away in the idyllic hamlet of Buckland. The land was valued at £9 in the 11th-century Domesday Book, and the sprawling stone building dates back to Jacobean times. Public areas and guest rooms are plushly comfortable, with old pictures, fine rugs, and antiques everywhere. The gardens are well groomed and tranquil. In the baronial and expensive restaurant (jacket and tie required: £££££), you choose from a menu of traditional fare with some contemporary touches; monkfish comes with mussel soufflé, for example. ⊠ *Off B4632, Buckland WR12 7LY* ☎ *01386/852626* 🖾 *01386/ 853557* ⊕ *www.bucklandmanor.co.uk* 🛏 *13 rooms* ♻ *Restaurant, cable TV, putting green, tennis court, pool, croquet, bar; no a/c, no kids under 12* ⊟ *AE, DC, MC, V* 🍽 *BP.*

£££££ ✕🔲 **Lygon Arms.** Here is modern luxury in perfect symbiosis with old-fashioned charm. In business since 1532, the inn has a multigabled facade and mullioned windows dating to 1620. Inside, look for antiques-bedecked parlors, fireplaces, 18th-century paneling, and rooms that once sheltered Charles I and Oliver Cromwell. Behind the house are more modern (and less expensive) bedrooms and 3 acres of formal gardens. One restaurant, the Great Hall (£££££), complete with a minstrel's gallery, focuses on creative adaptations of traditional dishes. A good and cheaper option is the bar menu. ⊠ *High St., WR12 7DU* ☎ *01386/852255* 🖾 *01386/858611* ⊕ *www.paramount-hotels.co.uk* 🛏 *69 rooms* ♻ *2 restaurants, cable TV, in-room data ports, tennis court, indoor pool, sauna, spa, steam room, croquet, bar, business services, meeting rooms, helipad, some pets allowed (fee); no a/c in some rooms* ⊟ *AE, DC, MC, V* 🍽 *BP.*

★ **££££–£££££** ✕🔲 **Dormy House Hotel.** Guest rooms in this converted 17th-century farmhouse overlook the Vale of Evesham from high on the Cotswolds ridge, one of the region's most celebrated vistas. Luxury rules at this establishment, where you can relax by a fireplace or in one of the bars. Traditional pieces and a mixture of brass and carved bedsteads furnish the beamed bedrooms. Noted in the region, the restaurant (£££–£££££) has a superlative wine list and specializes in contemporary fare such as Cornish sea bass with with sweet potato and marsh samphire (a fleshy saltwater plant). A more economical eating option is the beamed Barn Owl bar, a gastro-pub. The hotel is 2 mi north of Broadway. ⊠ *Willersey Hill, WR12 7LF* ☎ *01386/852711* 🖾 *01386/858636* ⊕ *www. dormyhouse.co.uk* 🛏 *47 rooms* ♻ *Restaurant, café, in-room data ports, putting green, gym, sauna, steam room, billiards, croquet, 3 bars, meeting rooms, some pets allowed (fee); no a/c* ⊟ *AE, DC, MC, V* 🍽 *BP.*

7

££££ 🏠 **Mill Hay House.** If the rose garden, trout-filled pond, and pet sheep at this 18th-century Queen Anne house aren't appealing enough, then the stone-flagged floors, leather sofas, and grandfather clocks should satisfy. There are only three beautiful, pastel bedrooms at this B&B, so booking ahead is essential. It's a mile from Broadway on Snowshill Road. ✉ *Snowshill Rd., WR12 7JS* ☎ *01386/852498* 📠 *01386/858038* ⊕ *www.millhay.co.uk* 🛏 *2 rooms, 1 suite* ♻ *In-room safes, kitchenettes, no-smoking rooms; no a/c, no kids under 12* ▤ *MC, V* ⏝ *BP.*

Chipping Campden

㉒ *4 mi east of Broadway, 18 mi northeast of Cheltenham.*

Undoubtedly one of the most beautiful towns in the area, Chipping Campden, with its population of about 2,500, is the Cotswolds in a microcosm—it has St. James, the region's most impressive church; frozen-in-time streets; a silk mill that was once the center of the Guild of Handicrafts; and pleasant (and not touristy) shops. One of the area's most seductive settings unfolds before you as you travel on B4081 through sublime English countryside and happen upon the town, tucked in a slight valley. North of town is lovely Hidcote Manor Gardens.

The soaring pinnacled tower of **St. James,** a prime example of a Cotswold wool church (rebuilt in the 15th century with money from wool merchants), announces the town from a distance; it's worth stepping inside to see the lofty nave. It recalls the old saying, which became popular because of the vast numbers of houses of worship in the Cotswolds, "As sure as God's in Gloucestershire." Nearby, on Church Street, is an important row of almshouses dating from King James I's reign. ✉ *Church St.* ☎ *01386/841927* ⊕ *www.stjameschurchcampden.co.uk* 💷 *£1 donation suggested* ☉ *Mar.–Oct., Mon.–Sat. 10–5, Sun. 2–6; Feb. and Nov., Mon.–Sat. 11–4, Sun. 2–4; Dec. and Jan., Mon.–Sat. 11–3, Sun. 2–3.*

The broad High Street, lined with stone houses and shops, follows a captivating curve; in the center, on Market Street, is the **Market Hall,** a gabled Jacobean structure built by Sir Baptiste Hicks in 1627 "for the sale of local produce."

In 1902 the Guild of Handicrafts took over the **Silk Mill,** and Arts and Crafts evangelist Charles Robert Ashbee (1863–1942) brought 150 acolytes here from London, including 50 guildsmen, to revive and practice such skills as cabinetmaking and bookbinding. The operation folded in 1920, but the refurbished building houses an exhibition and workshops, including those of a silversmith, jeweler and stone carver. ✉ *Sheep St.* 💷 *Free* ☉ *Weekdays 9–5, Sat. 9–1.*

Where to Stay & Eat

£££££ ✕🏠 **Charingworth Manor.** Views of the Cotswold countryside are limitless from this 14th-century manor-house hotel a short distance outside town. Mullioned windows and oak beams enhance the sofa-filled sitting room, and bedrooms have English floral fabrics and antique and period furniture. T. S. Eliot, a guest in the 1930s, used to enjoy walking the 50 acres of grounds. The restaurant (£38 fixed-price menu), with

Arts & Crafts in the Cotswolds

CLOSE UP

THE ARTS AND CRAFTS MOVEMENT flourished throughout Britain in the late 19th and early 20th centuries, but the Cotswolds are most closely associated with it. The godfather of the movement was designer William Morris (1834–96), whose home for the last 25 years of his life, Kelmscott Manor in Gloucestershire, became the headquarters of the school. A lecture by Morris, "The Beauty of Life," delivered in Birmingham in 1880, included the injunction that became the guiding principle of the movement: "Have nothing in your houses which you do not know to be useful or believe to be beautiful."

Driven by the belief that the spirit of medieval arts and crafts was being degraded and destroyed by the mass production and aggressive capitalism of the Victorian era, and aided by a dedicated core of artisans, Morris revolutionized the art of house design and decoration. His work with textiles was particularly influential.

Many of Morris's followers were influenced by the Cotswold countryside, such as the designer and architect Charles Robert Ashbee, who transferred his Guild of Handicrafts from London to Chipping Campden in 1902. The village holds a permanent exhibition of pieces by the original group and those who followed in their wake. Their work can also be seen at Cheltenham's Art Gallery and Museum, and, in its original context, at Rodmarton Manor outside Tetbury (which Ashbee declared the finest application of the movement's ideals), and at Owlpen Manor. (Farther afield, Standen, near East Grinstead, and Blackwell, in the Lake District, are notable Arts and Crafts houses.) To see the Arts and Crafts ethic applied to horticulture, visit Hidcote Manor Garden, near Chipping Campden.

7

its low-beam ceilings, is attractive but somewhat expensive, and serves both traditional and Mediterranean-inspired dishes such as roast rump of lamb on a bean cassoulet. The hotel is 3 mi east of Chipping Campden. ✉ *Charingworth GL55 6NS* ☎ *01386/593555* 📠 *01386/593353* ⊕ *www.englishrosehotels.co.uk* 🛏 *23 rooms, 3 suites* ♿ *Restaurant, in-room safes, cable TV, tennis court, indoor pool, sauna, steam room, billiards, croquet, meeting rooms; no a/c* ▭ *AE, DC, MC, V* 🍴 *BP.*

£££££ ✕▥ **Cotswold House.** The enduring delight of this luxury hotel in the center of Chipping Campden is the elegant harmony with which the up-to-the-minute design and fittings blend into the setting of an 18th-century Cotswold manor house. From the swirling staircase in the entrance to the guest rooms studded with contemporary art and high-tech gadgetry, it's a winning formula. The lounges invite lingering, and the patio and spacious garden offer seclusion. The formal Juliana's Restaurant (*£££££*; no lunch except Sunday), where there are fixed-price menus, and the livelier and cheaper Hick's Brasserie (*£££–££££*) offer creative takes on English and Mediterranean dishes. Hick's is open all day and is worth a stop even if you aren't staying here. ✉ *The Sq., GL55 6AN* ☎ *01386/840330* 📠 *01386/840310* ⊕ *www.cotswoldhouse.com* 🛏 *21* *rooms, 8 suites ⚭ 2 restaurants, 2 bars, in-room data ports, Wi-Fi, cable TV, minibars; no a/c* ▤ *AE, DC, MC, V* ⦿ *BP.*

££ ✕▣ **Churchill Arms.** This small country gastro-pub with rooms, a mile southeast of Chipping Campden, makes for an intimate stay. Plain wooden tables and benches, sepia prints, a flagstone floor, and a roaring fire provide the backdrop for excellent food (*££–£££*). Daily specials—steamed lemon sole filled with salmon and chive mousse, and pot-roasted partridge with parsnips and red wine, for example—appear on the blackboard. Upstairs bedrooms aren't large but are nicely furnished with antiques; two are in a new wing. ⊠ *Off B4035, Paxford GL55 6XH* ☎ *01386/594000* 🖷 *01386/594005* ⊕ *www. thechurchillarms.com* ↩ *4 rooms* ⚭ *Restaurant, in-room VCRs, no-smoking rooms; no a/c* ▤ *MC, V* ⦿ *BP.*

££££ ▣ **Noel Arms Hotel.** Dating to the 14th century, the town's oldest inn was built in the heart of Chipping Campden to accommodate foreign wool traders. The building retains its exposed beams and stonework, even though it has been enlarged. The bedrooms—some in the 14th-century portion—are full of warm colors and dark oak furniture, and fully equipped with modern amenities. Breakfast can be taken in the flagstoned conservatory. The same owners run the more expensive Cotswold House; guests here have access to its facilities. ⊠ *High St., GL55 6AT* ☎ *01386/ 840317* 🖷 *01386/841136* ⊕ *www.noelarmshotel.com* ↩ *26 rooms* ⚭ *Restaurant, bar, meeting rooms, some pets allowed; no a/c* ▤ *AE, MC, V* ⦿ *BP.*

££–£££ ▣ **Badgers Hall.** Expect a friendly welcome at this antique B&B above a tearoom just across from the Market Hall. The spacious, spotless rooms have low, beamed ceilings and exposed stonework. Midweek guests are greeted with tea and scrumptious fresh scones on arrival, and the generous breakfast will set you up for the day. Book ahead. ⊠ *High St., GL55 6HB* ☎ *01386/840839* ⊕ *www.badgershall.com* ↩ *2 rooms* ⚭ *No smoking, no kids under 10* ▤ *No credit cards* ⦿ *BP.*

Shopping

At **Hart** (⊠ The Silk Mill, Sheep St. ☎ 01386/841100), descendants of an original member of the Guild of Handicrafts specialize in making silver items. **Martin Gotrel** (⊠ Camperdene House, High St. ☎ 01386/ 841360) crafts fine traditional and contemporary jewelry.

Hidcote Manor Garden

㉓ *4 mi northeast of Chipping Campden, 9 mi south of Stratford-upon-Avon.*

Fodor'sChoice
★

Laid out around a Cotswold manor house, Hidcote Manor Garden is arguably the most interesting and attractive large garden in Britain. Crowds are correspondingly large at the height of the season, but it's worthwhile anytime. A horticulturist from the United States, Major Lawrence Johnstone, created the garden in 1907 in the Arts and Crafts style. Johnstone was an imaginative gardener and widely traveled plantsman who brought back specimens from all over the world. The formal part of the garden is arranged in "rooms" without roofs, separated by hedges and often with fine topiary work and walls. Besides the variety of plants, what's impressive are the different effects created, from calm open spaces to areas packed with flowers. ■ TIP→ **Look out for one of Johnson's earliest schemes, the red borders of dahlias, poppies, fuschias, lobelias, and roses; the tall hornbeam hedges; and the Bathing Pool garden, where the pool is so wide there's scarcely space to walk.** The White Garden was probably the forerunner of the popular white gardens at Sissinghurst and Glyndebourne. ✉ *Hidcote Bartrim* ☎ *01386/438333* ⊕ *www.nationaltrust.org.uk* ▦ *£7* ◷ *Late Mar.–Sept., Mon.–Wed. and weekends 10:30–6; Oct., Mon.–Wed. and weekends 10:30–5; last admission 1 hr before closing.*

Hidcote Manor Garden borders the hamlet of **Hidcote Bartrim**, which fills another storybook Cotswold dell. A handful of thatched stone houses, a duck pond, and a well make up the center of this cul-de-sac; less than a mile away are the equally idyllic hamlet of Hidcote Boyce and a 17th-century manor, Hidcote House.

Moreton-in-Marsh

㉔ *13 mi south of Hidcote Manor Garden, 18 mi northeast of Cheltenham, 5 mi north of Stow-on-the-Wold.*

In Moreton-in-Marsh, the houses have been built not around a central square but along a street wide enough to accommodate a market. The village has fine views across the hills. One local landmark is St. David's Church, which has a tower of honey-gold ashlar. This town of about 3,500 also possesses one of the last remaining curfew towers, dated 1633; curfew dates to the time of the Norman Conquest, when a bell was rung to "cover-fire" for the night against any invaders. From Chipping Campden, take B4081 south, then A44 south and east to reach Moreton-in-Marsh. The town has train service from London daily.

Supposed to be the largest street market in the Cotswolds, the **Tuesday market** takes over the center of the main street between 8 and 4, offering a mix of household goods, fruit and veg, and some arts-and-crafts stalls, gift items, and jewelry. It's no newcomer: it was chartered in 1227.

It comes as somewhat of an architectural surprise to see the blue onion domes and miniature minarets of **Sezincote,** a mellow stone house tucked into a valley near Moreton-in-Marsh. Created in the early 19th century, the house and estate were the vision of Sir Charles Cockerell, who made a fortune in the East India Company. He employed his architect brother, Samuel Pepys Cockerell, to "Indianize" the residence with Hindu and Muslim motifs. Note the peacock-tail arches surrounding the windows of the first floor. The exotic garden, Hindu temple folly, and Indian-style bridge have appealed to visitors ever since the future George IV came to the estate in 1807 (and was inspired to create that Xanadu of Brighton, the Royal Pavilion). If you come in spring, glorious aconites and snowdrops greet you. Note that children are allowed indoors only at the owners' discretion. ✉ *Off A44* ☎ *01386/700444* ▦ *House and grounds £6, grounds £4* ◷ *House May–July and Sept., Thurs. and Fri. 2:30–6; grounds Jan.–Nov., Thurs. and Fri. and national holidays 2–6 or dusk.*

CLOSE UP

Visiting Cotswold Gardens

PERHAPS IT'S THE SHEER BEAUTY OF THIS AREA that has inspired the creation of so many superb gardens. Gardening is an English passion, and even nongardeners may be tempted by the choices large and small. The Arts and Crafts movement in Britain transformed not only interior design but also the world of gardening; at Hidcote Manor Garden, a much-visited masterpiece of the style, hedges and walls set off vistas and surround distinct themed garden rooms. Rodmarton Manor also has a garden in this style.

In the Cotswolds, as elsewhere in England, gardens often complement a stately home and deserve as close a look as the house. At Sudeley Castle, the home of Catherine Parr (Henry VIII's last wife), for example, explore the 19th-century Queen's Garden, beloved for its roses. Admirers of the naturalistic landscaping of Capability Brown can see a notable example of his large-scale work in the 2,000-acre park at Bowood House & Gardens;

the spectacular rhododendron walks here are a later, 19th-century creation. Also large in scale but entirely different is Westonbirt National Arboreturm, near Tetbury, with its magnificent collection of trees. In contrast, the 18th-century Painswick Rococo Garden, with its Gothic screen and other intriguing structures, has a pleasant intimacy. Britain wouldn't be Britain without a touch of eccentricity, and in the Cotswolds the garden at the Indian-style manor of Sezincote, with its temple to a Hindu god, supplies a satisfying blend of the stately and the exotic.

Eager to see more? The National Garden Scheme (⊕ www.ngs.org.uk) publishes annual "yellow books" that list all gardens open for individual counties and for the whole country; cost is £1–£2 for a county, £7.99 for the whole country. Bookstores sell these, too. Also *see* Discounts & Deals *in* Smart Travel Tips; depending on your itinerary, buying a pass or joining the National Trust may save you money on admissions.

OFF THE BEATEN PATH

ROLLRIGHT STONES – A reminder of the ancient civilizations of Britain can be seen about 8 mi east of Moreton, where three stone groups occupy a high position on the Wolds. The site has none of the grandeur of Stonehenge and Avebury but is almost as important. Legend gives the stones, dating from before 1500 BC, the names of the King's Men, the King Stone, and the Whispering Knights. ⊠ *Minor Rd. off A3400, 2 mi northwest of Chipping Norton* ⊕ *www.english-heritage.org.uk* 🎟 *Free; property owner may charge small fee to see King's Men* ☉ *Daily sunrise–sunset.*

Where to Stay & Eat

££££–£££££ ✕🏨 **Manor House Hotel.** Secret passages and a priest's hole testify to the age of this 16th-century building, set back from the main thoroughfare. Wing chairs and chintz-covered sofas and drapes adorn the public rooms. Bedrooms, revealing original stonework, mix stylish modern furnishings and fabrics with antiques. The Mulberry restaurant serves an adventurous fixed-price English menu (£32.50) on which you might find breast of squab pigeon with fried quail eggs; cheeses are accompanied by apricot chutney and homemade oatcakes. ✉ *High St., GL56 0LJ* ☎ *01608/650501* 📠 *01608/651481* 🌐 *www.cotswold-inns-hotels.co. uk* ⇨ *38 rooms* ⌂ *Restaurant, bar, meeting rooms, some pets allowed; no a/c* ☰ *AE, MC, V* ⏹ *BP.*

£££   ✕🛏 **Falkland Arms.** It's worth detouring a bit for this supremely appeal-
Fodor'sChoice ing pub on the village green at Great Tew (12 mi east of Moreton), where
★ you can still buy snuff and smoke a clay pipe. The bar has impressive malt whiskies, and mugs and jugs hangs from the beams. The small restaurant (££; no dinner Sunday) chalks up a traditional but creative menu. A spiral stone staircase leads to the bedrooms, which have brass bedsteads or four-posters, and traditional quilted bedcovers. Reservations are essential for both staying and eating here. From Moreton, take A44 to Chipping Norton, then A361 to B4022. ✉ *Great Tew OX7 4DB* ☎ *01608/683653* 🌐 *www.falklandarms.org.uk* ⇨ *5 rooms* ⌂ *Restaurant, bar, no-smoking rooms; no a/c, no room phones, no kids under 16* ☰ *AE, MC, V* ⏹ *BP.*

££   ✕🛏 **Bell Inn.** The coach house of this 18th-century hostelry holds spacious but modest guest rooms, still with the original beams, and furnished with period pieces, deep carpets, and comfy sofas. The pub (££) has a courtyard and garden and prepares such dishes as trout with honey and almonds and venison sausages. In summer you can join in the obscure Cotswold game of Aunt Sally, which involves hitting a moving target with something akin to a rolling pin. ✉ *High St., GL56 0AE* ☎ *01608/651688* 📠 *01608/652195* ⇨ *5 rooms* ⌂ *Restaurant, bar, some pets allowed; no a/c, no room phones* ☰ *MC, V* ⏹ *BP.*

Stow-on-the-Wold

㉕ *5 mi south of Moreton-in-Marsh, 15 mi east of Cheltenham.*

At an elevation of 800 feet, Stow is the highest town in the Cotswolds—"Stow-on-the-Wold, where the wind blows cold" is the age-old saying. Built around a wide square, Stow's imposing golden stone houses have been discreetly converted into a good number of high-quality antiques stores. The Square, as it is known, has a fascinating history. In the 18th century, Daniel Defoe wrote that more than 20,000 sheep could be sold here on a busy day; such was the press of livestock that sheep runs, known as "tures," were used to control the sheep, and these narrow streets still run off the main square. Today pubs and cafés fill the area.

Also here are St. Edward's Church and the Kings Arms Old Posting House, its wide entrance still seeming to wait for the stagecoaches that used to stop here on their way to Cheltenham. As well as being a lure for the antiques hunter, Stow is a convenient base: eight main Cotswolds roads intersect here, but all—happily—bypass the town center. The town's current population is about 2,500.

★ **Chastleton House,** one of the most complete Jacobean properties in Britain, opts for a beguilingly lived-in appearance, taking advantage of almost 400 years' worth of furniture and trappings accumulated by many generations of the single family that owned it until 1991. The house was built between 1605 and 1612 for William Jones, a wealthy wool merchant, and has an appealing authenticity: cobwebs and bric-a-brac are strewn around, wood and pewter are unpolished, upholstery uncleaned. The top floor is a glorious, barrel-vaulted long gallery, and throughout the house you can see exquisite plasterwork, paneling, and tapestries. The ornamental gardens include England's first croquet lawn (the rules of croquet were codified here in 1865) and rotund topiaries. Chastleton is 6

mi northeast of Stow, signposted off A436 between Stow and A44. ☒ *Off A436, Moreton-in-Marsh* ☎ *01608 674355, 01494/755560 for recorded information* ⊕ *www.nationaltrust.org.uk* ☒ *£6.50* ☉ *Apr.–Sept., Wed.–Sat. 1–5; Oct., Wed.–Sat. 1–4. Admission is by timed ticket, for which prebooking is advised.*

Where to Stay & Eat

£–££ ✕ **Queen's Head.** An excellent stopping-off spot for lunch or dinner, this pub has a courtyard out back that's perfect for a summer afternoon. The bench in front, under a climbing rose, makes a relaxing spot for imbibing outdoor refreshment. Besides standard pub grub, including ploughman's lunches, sandwiches, sausage and mash, and chicken pie, there are daily specials such as mushroom stroganoff. ☒ *The Square* ☎ *01451/830563* ☰ *AE, MC, V* ☉ *No dinner Sun.*

££££ ✕⊞ **Royalist Hotel.** Certified as the oldest inn in the country (AD 947), this hostelry is jammed with interesting features—witches' marks on the beams, a tunnel to the church across the road—and the owners have stylishly integrated designer bedrooms and the sleek AD 947 restaurant (£34 fixed-price menu; closed Sunday and Monday). If the elegant modern English dishes here don't appeal, the adjacent Eagle and Child (££) offers a hearty brasserie-style menu from the same kitchen. ☒ *Digbeth St., GL54 1BN* ☎ *01451/830670* ☰ *01451/870048* ⊕ *www.nichehotels. com* ⊶ *6 rooms, 2 suites* ↺ *Restaurant, 2 bars, pub, meeting rooms, no-smoking rooms; no a/c* ☰ *MC, V* ⦿ *BP.*

££ ⊞ **Number Nine.** Beyond the traditional stone and creeper exterior of this former coaching inn are unfussy, spacious bedrooms done in soothing white and pale colors. The inglenook fireplace is a draw in winter, and wholesome breakfasts include poached fruits and specialty breads. ☒ *9 Park St., GL54 1AQ* ☎ *01451/870333* ⊕ *www.number-nine.info* ⊶ *3 rooms* ↺ *No a/c, no room phones, no smoking* ☰ *MC, V* ⦿ *BP.*

Shopping

Stow-on-the-Wold is the leading center for antiques stores in the Cotswolds, with more than 40 dealers centered around the Square, Sheep Street, and Church Street.

Duncan Baggott Antiques (☒ Woolcomber House, Sheep St. ☎ 01451/ 830662) displays fine old English furniture, portraits and landscape paintings, and garden statuary and ornaments. Head for **Talbot Galleries** (☒ 7

Antiques & Markets

THE COTSWOLDS contains one of the largest concentrations of art and antiques dealers outside London. The famous antiques shops here are, it is sometimes whispered, "temporary" storerooms for the great families of the region, filled with tole-ware, treen, faience firedogs, toby jugs, and silhouettes, plus country furniture, Edwardiana, and ravishing 17th- to 19th-century furniture. The center of antiquing is Stow-on-the-Wold, in terms of volume of dealers. Other towns that have a number of antiques shops are Burford, Cirencester, Tetbury, and Moreton-in-Marsh. The Cotswolds have few of those "anything in this tray for £10" shops, however. For information about dealers and special events, contact the **Cotswold Antique Dealers' Association** (CADA; ✉ Broadwell House, Sheep St., Stow-on-the-Wold GL54 1JS ☎ 01451/810407 ⊕ www.cotswolds-antiques-art.com), which represents more than 40 dealers in the area.

As across England, many towns in the region have market days, when you can purchase local produce (including special treats from Cotswold cheeses to fruit juices), crafts, and items such as clothes, books, and toys. Attending a farmers' market or a general market is a great way to mingle with the locals and perhaps find a special treasure or a tasty treat. Head for Moreton-in-Marsh on Tuesday and Cirencester on Friday and some Saturdays; tourist information offices have information on market days, or check out **Country Markets** (⊕ www.country-markets.co.uk).

Talbot Ct. ☎ 01451/832169) if you're interested in antique maps and prints. **Roger Lamb Antiques** (✉ The Sq. ☎ 01451/831371) specializes in objets d'art and small pieces of furniture from the Georgian and Regency periods, with Regency "faux bamboo," tea caddies, and antique needlework the particular fortes.

Bourton-on-the-Water

26 *4 mi southwest of Stow-on-the-Wold, 12 mi northeast of Cheltenham.*

Bourton-on-the-Water, off A429 on the eastern edge of the Cotswold Hills, is deservedly famous as a classic Cotswold village. Like many others, it became wealthy in the Middle Ages because of wool. The little River Windrush runs through Bourton, crossed by low stone bridges; it's as pretty as it sounds. This village makes a good touring base and has a collection of quirky small museums, but in summer it can be overcrowded. A stroll through Bourton takes you past stone cottages, many converted to small stores and coffee shops.

An old mill, now the **Cotswold Motor Museum and Toy Collection,** contains more than 30 vintage motor vehicles and a collection of old advertising signs (supposedly the largest in Europe), as well as two caravans (trailers) from the 1920s, ancient bicycles, and children's toys. ✉ *Sherborne St.* ☎ *01451/821255* ⊕ *www.cotswold-motor-museum.com* 🖾 *£3.50* ☉ *Mid-Feb.–early Dec., daily 10–6.*

⟳ The **Model Railway Exhibition** displays more than 40 British and Continental trains running on 500 square feet of scenic layout. There are plenty of trains, models, and toys to buy in the shop. ⊠ *Box Bush, High St.* ☎ *01451/820686* ⊕ *www.bourtonmodelrailway.co.uk* ⊡ *£2.25* ⊘ *June–Sept., daily 11–5; Oct.–May, weekends 11–5 (limited opening in Jan.; call ahead).*

An outdoor reproduction of Bourton, the **Model Village** was built in 1937 to a scale of one-ninth; you can walk through it. ⊠ *Old New Inn* ☎ *01451/820467* ⊡ *£2.75* ⊘ *Apr.–Oct., daily 9–5:45; Nov.–Mar., daily 10–3:45* ⊕ *www.theoldnewinn.co.uk.*

Where to Stay

£££ 🏨 **The Old Manse.** Built in 1748 for the local Baptist pastor, this stone hotel is only steps away from the River Windrush. The smallish bedrooms are decorated in cream and maroon hues; one has a four-poster and a whirlpool bath, another a canopied French half-sleigh bed. Some rooms can be noisy—avoid those facing Sherborne Street if you can. Traditional English fare with a contemporary touch is served in the restaurant. There's a patio at the rear, and one at the front looking onto the river. ⊠ *Victoria St., GL54 2BX* ☎*01451/820082* ⊟*01451/810381* ⊕*www.oldmansehotel. com* ⇥ *15 rooms* ⚬ *Restaurant, bar; no a/c* ⊟ *AE, MC, V* ⦿ *BP.*

£ 🏨 **Rooftrees.** If you go for frills, flounces, and leprechauns, then this old Cotswold stone house, a 10-minute walk from the center of the village, is the place for you. Ornaments abound within, and hanging baskets and garden gnomes decorate the outside. The amiable Irish hosts dish up substantial breakfasts, and dinners (£14) are provided by arrangement. Two guest rooms have four-posters. ⊠ *Rissington Rd., GL54 2DX* ☎ *01451/821943* ⊟ *01451/810614* ⇥ *3 rooms* ⚬ *Dining room; no a/c, no room phones, no smoking* ⊟ *No credit cards* ⦿ *BP.*

Shopping

The **Cotswold Perfumery** carries many perfumes that are manufactured here, and also stocks perfume bottles and jewelry. You can exercise your olfactory skills in the Perfumed Garden, part of a prebooked factory tour that takes in the laboratory, compounding room, and bottling process. ⊠ *Victoria St.* ☎ *01451/820698* ⊡ *Factory tour £5* ⊘ *Mon.–Sat. 9:30–5, Sun. 10:30–5.*

Lower & Upper Slaughter

27 *2 mi north of Bourton-on-the-Water, 15 mi east of Cheltenham.*

Fodor'sChoice ★

To see the quieter, more typical Cotswold villages, seek out the evocatively named Lower Slaughter and Upper Slaughter (the names have nothing to do with mass murder, but come from the Saxon word *sloh*, which means "a marshy place"). Lower Slaughter is one of the "water villages," with Slaughter Brook running down the center road of the town. Little stone footbridges cross the brook, and the town's resident gaggle of geese can often be seen paddling through the sparkling water. Lower and Upper Swell are two other quiet towns to explore in the area.

Connecting the two Slaughters is **Wardens' Way** (⊕ www.cotswoldsaonb. com), a mile-long pathway that begins in Upper Slaughter at the town-center parking lot and passes stone houses, green meadows, ancient trees, and a 19th-century corn mill with a waterwheel and brick chimney. Wardens' Way continues south to Bourton-on-the-Water; the full walk from Winchcombe to Bourton is 14 mi.

Where to Stay & Eat

£££££ ✕⌂ **Lords of the Manor Hotel.** A fishing stream threads the rolling fields that surround this rambling 17th-century manor house with Victorian additions. It offers comfort and a warm welcome in a quintessential Cotswold village, with a choice of bedrooms in the main house or more modern ones in the converted granary and barn. Country-house chintzes and antiques set the style throughout, including in the acclaimed restaurant, which has a creative British-French fixed-price menu (£££££) that might list slow-roasted Scottish beef with oxtail ravioli, and butternut squash creme brûlée. ⊠ *Upper Slaughter GL54 2JD* ☎ *01451/820243* 🖷 *01451/820696* ⊕ *www.lordsofthemanor.com* 🛏 *27 rooms* ⌂ *Restaurant, in-room data ports, croquet, bar, business services, meeting rooms; no a/c* ⊟ *AE, DC, MC, V* ⦿ *BP.*

££££ ✕⌂ **Washbourne Court.** This fine 17th-century stone building, amid 4 acres of verdant grounds beside the River Wye, has flagstone floors, beams, and open fires. The bedrooms in the main building are done in a weathered country style, whereas rooms in the converted barn and cottages are more modern. Choices in the restaurant (£££££) might include poached halibut or pork with mustard puree, followed by banana and chocolate millefeuille. ⊠ *Lower Slaughter GL54 2HS* ☎ *01451/822143* 🖷 *01451/821045* ⊕ *www.washbournecourt.co.uk* 🛏 *26 rooms, 2 suites* ⌂ *Restaurant, bar; no a/c* ⊟ *AE, DC, MC, V* ⦿ *BP.*

Northleach

28 *7 mi southwest of Lower and Upper Slaughter, 14 mi southeast of Cheltenham.*

Just off the Fosse Way (and bypassed by the busy A40), little Northleach—population around 2,000—has remained one of the least spoiled of Cotswold towns. Trim cottages, many with traditional stone-tile roofs, line the streets that converge on the spacious central square. By the 13th century, Northleach had acquired substantial wealth thanks to the wool trade. The wool of the local Cotswold Lion sheep (so-called

---

COUNTRY WALKS

Short walks thread the gentle countryside around the historic towns and are a great way to appreciate the Cotswolds, an **Area of Outstanding National Beauty** (www.cotswoldsaonb.com). Tourist information centers carry walking maps and have information about longer trails. To branch out on your own, track the rivers on which many towns are built, following the **towpaths** that usually run along the water. The **Cotswold Way** (www.nationaltrail.co.uk), a national trail stretching about 100 mi between Bath and Chipping Campden, traces the ridge marking the edge of the Cotswolds and the Severn Valley and has incomparable views. You can walk just part of it.

7

because of their thick, manelike fleeces) was praised above all other by weavers in Flanders, to whom it was exported.

The 15th-century church of **St. Peter and St. Paul,** with its soaring pillars and clerestory windows, contains notable memorial brasses, monuments to the merchants who endowed the church; each merchant has a wool sack and sheep at his feet. ⊠ *Mill End* ☎ *01451/860314* ⬚ *Free, donations accepted* ⊙ *Apr.–Oct., daily 8–6; Nov.–Mar., daily 8–dusk.*

At **Keith Harding's World of Mechanical Music,** the diverting tour explores pianolas, music boxes, and other mechanical instruments from times past, which you can hear played. You can even listen to the maestros Grieg, Paderewski, Rachmaninov, and Gershwin on piano rolls. The shop stocks antique and modern music boxes and more. ⊠ *The Oak House, High St.* ☎ *01451/860181* ⊕ *www.mechanicalmusic.co.uk* ⬚ *£6* ⊙ *Daily 10–6; last tour at 5.*

Where to Stay & Eat

££ ✕⬚ **Wheatsheaf Inn.** This elegantly remodeled traditional pub has stylish, uncluttered bedrooms in soft tones, as well as a highly regarded restaurant specializing in modern British fare. On the dinner menu (££–££££) you might find wild mushroom and spinach risotto as a starter, and monkfish and Thai curry with jasmine rice as a main course. The staff is youthful and friendly. ⊠ *West End, GL54 3EZ* ☎ *01451/860244* ⬚ *01451/ 861037* ⊕ *www.wheatsheafatnorthleach.com* ⤳ *8 rooms* ⌂ *Restaurant, bar; no a/c* ☰ *MC, V* ⦿ *BP.*

££ ⬚ **Cotteswold House.** Period features—including wood beams and paneling, and a Tudor archway—abound in this typical Cotswold dwelling, once the home of a wool merchant. For a little extra, it's worth staying in the Tudor Suite, which has a four-poster, a fireplace from 1620, and a separate area with DVD and a pool table. A self-catering cottage (rented by the week) is also available. ⊠ *Market Pl., GL54 3EG* ☎⬚ *01451 860493* ⊕ *www.cotteswoldhouse.com* ⤳ *2 rooms, 1 suite* ⌂ *No smoking* ☰ *MC, V* ⦿ *BP.*

Burford

㉙ *9 mi east of Northleach, 18 mi north of Swindon, 18 mi west of Oxford.*

Burford's broad main street leads steeply down to a narrow bridge across the River Windrush. The village served as a stagecoach stop for centuries and has many historic inns; it is now a popular stop for tour buses and seekers of antiques. Hidden away at the end of a lane at the bottom of High Street is the splendid parish church of **St. John,** its interior a warren of arches, chapels, and shrines. The church was remodeled in the 15th century from Norman beginnings. Among the many monuments is one dedicated to Henry VIII's barber, Edmund Harman, that shows four Amazonian Indians; it's said to be the first depiction of native people from the Americas in Britain. Look also for the elaborate Tanfield monument and its poignant widow's epitaph. ⊠ *Church Green* ☎ *01993/822275* ⬚ *Free, donations accepted* ⊙ *Apr.–Oct., daily 9–5; Nov.–Mar., daily 9–4.*

£££ ✕⌂ **Jonathan's at the Angel.** Contemporary dishes you might see at the farmhouse-style tables of this informal brasserie (£££–££££) in a 16th-century former coaching inn include gilthead bream (a saltwater fish) with warm potato salad and saffron sauce, and venison with caramel peaches. Upstairs, the delightful guest rooms are furnished in different styles: Indian in reds and oranges, French with wooden sleigh bed, or cool-blue contemporary Italian. ⊠ *14 Witney St., OX18 4SN* ☎ *01993/822714* 🖷 *01993/822069* ⊕ *www.theangel-uk.com* 🖘 *3 rooms* ☝ *Restaurant, in-room VCRs; no a/c* ☐ *MC, V* ☉ *Closed last 2 wks of Jan. and 1st wk of Feb. Restaurant closed Mon.; no dinner Sun.* ⧆ *BP.*

££££ ⌂ **Burford House.** The family photographs and memorabilia, rugs, books and toys scattered throughout this 17th-century building make it feel more like home than a hotel. The richly decorated bedrooms, filled with antiques, come with freestanding baths and power showers. If you don't stay for lunch or afternoon tea, make sure you try the homemade damson gin, maybe in one of the intimate sitting rooms or courtyard garden. There is no dinner service. ⊠ *99 High St., OX18 4QA* ☎ *01993/823151* 🖷 *01993/823240* ⊕ *www.burford-house.co.uk* 🖘 *8 rooms* ☝ *Cable TV, in-room data ports, bar, lounge; no a/c* ☐ *AE, MC, V* ⧆ *BP.*

Bibury

③⓪ *10 mi southwest of Burford, 6 mi northeast of Cirencester, 15 mi north of Swindon.*

The tiny town of Bibury, with a population of less than 1,000, sits idyllically beside the little River Coln on B4425; it was famed Arts and Crafts designer William Morris's choice for Britain's most beautiful village. Fine old cottages, a river meadow, and the church of St. Mary's are some of the delights here. **Arlington Row** is a famously pretty group of 17th-century weavers' cottages made of stone.

££££–£££££ ✕⌂ **Swan Hotel.** Chandeliers and displays of plates and glassware adorn this mid-17th-century coaching inn on the banks of the River Coln. Guest rooms, all different though most are traditional in style, come with splendid modern bathrooms—Room 3's is dramatically tiled in black and white. The formal Gallery restaurant (open evenings and Sunday lunch) has £30 fixed-price menus with such dishes as panfried local trout, or you can dine in the cheaper Swan Café. Head to the attached Beauty Sanctuary for therapeutic and cosmetic spa treatments. ⊠ *Off B4425, GL7 5NW* ☎ *01285/740695* 🖷 *01285/740473* ⊕ *www.swanhotel.co.uk* 🖘 *18 rooms* ☝ *2 restaurants, some in-room hot tubs, spa, fishing, bar, meeting rooms, some pets allowed; no a/c* ☐ *AE, DC, MC, V* ⧆ *BP.*

Chedworth Roman Villa

③① *6 mi northwest of Bibury, 9 mi north of Cirencester, 10 mi southeast of Cheltenham.*

The remains of a mile of walls is what's left of one of the largest Roman villas in England, beautifully set in a wooded valley on the eastern fringe of the Cotswolds. Thirty-two rooms, including two complete bath suites, have been identified, and the colorful mosaics are some of the most complete in England. The visitor center and museum give a detailed picture of Roman life in Britain; they may even appeal to non-fans of the period. ■ TIP→ **Look carefully for the signs for the villa: from Bibury, go across A429 to Yanworth and Chedworth. The villa is also signposted from A40.** ⊠ *Yanworth* ☎ *01242/890256* ⊕ *www.nationaltrust.org.uk* 🖼 *£5.50* ⊗ *Apr.–late Oct., Tues.–Sun. and national holidays 10–5; Mar., Tues.–Sun. 11–4; late Oct.–mid-Nov., Tues.–Sun. 10–4.*

Cirencester

32 *9 mi south of Chedworth, 14 mi southeast of Cheltenham.*

Cirencester (pronounced sirensester) has been a hub of the Cotswolds since Roman times, when it was called Corinium; the town was second only to Londinium (London) in importance. It lay at the intersection of two major Roman roads, the Fosse Way and Ermin Street (today A429 and A417). In the Middle Ages, Cirencester grew rich on wool, which funded its 15th-century parish church. Today this old market town is the area's largest, with a population of 19,000. It preserves many mellow stone buildings dating mainly from the 17th and 18th centuries, and bow-fronted shops that still have one foot in the past.

At the top of Market Place is the magnificent Gothic parish church of **St. John the Baptist,** known as the cathedral of the "woolgothic" style. Its elaborate, three-tier, three-bay south porch, the largest in England, once served as the town hall. The chantry chapels and many coats of arms bear witness to the importance of the wool merchants, benefactors of the church. A rare example of a 15th-century wineglass pulpit sits in the nave. ⊠ *Market Pl.* ☎ *01285/659317* 🖼 *Free, £2 suggested donation* ⊗ *Mon.–Sat. 9:30–5 (9:30–4 in winter), Sun. 2:15–5.*

★ Not much of the Roman town remains visible, but the **Corinium Museum** displays an outstanding collection of Roman artifacts, including mosaic pavements, as well as full-scale reconstructions of local Roman interiors. Spacious galleries explore the town's history in Roman and Anglo-Saxon times and in the 18th century; they include plenty of hands-on exhibits. ⊠ *Park St.* ☎ *01285/655611* ⊕ *www.cotswold.gov.uk* 🖼 *£3.70* ⊗ *Mon.–Sat. 10–5, Sun. 2–5.*

Where to Stay & Eat

£££££ ✕🏠 **Barnsley House.** The former home of the late garden designer Rosemary Verey has been discreetly modernized and converted into a pricey retreat. None of the charm of the Georgian, honey-and-cream Cotswold house has been jettisoned, and the gardens continue to be an attraction. The main focus, though, is on exquisite dining (£40 and £46 fixed-price menus; no children under 12) with a strong Italian and Mediterranean influence, as in the classic *vincisgrassi*—baked pasta with Parma ham, porcini mushrooms, and truffles. Rooms are spacious and stylishly modern; bathrooms are positively extravagant, each with its own TV and CD player. Service may at times be less than you'd expect for the price. ⊠ *B4425, 4 mi northeast of Cirencester, Barnsley GL7 5EE*

CLOSE UP

That Special Cotswold Stone

IF THERE'S ONE FEATURE of the Cotswold landscape that sums up its special flavor, it's the oolitic limestone that is the area's primary building material. This stone can be seen in everything from drystone walls (whose total length in the region is said to equal or exceed that of the Great Wall of China) to snug cottages and manor houses. Even roof tiles are fashioned from the stone, contributing to a harmonious ensemble despite the different ages of the buildings.

Malleable when first quarried, and gradually hardening with age, the stone lends itself to every use. During the late-medieval heyday of the great churches funded by wool merchants, it was used to brilliant effect in the mullions, gargoyles, and other intricate decorations on ecclesiastical buildings. Some area quarries are still

active, producing stone that is used mainly for restoration and repair purposes. The varying colors of the stone are caused by impurities in the rock. They include the honey hues of the northern reaches of the Cotswolds, and modulate to a more golden tone in the central area, with a paler hue in and around Bath.

Writer and commentator J. B. Priestley, however, wrote of Cotswold stone that "the truth is that it has no color that can be described. Even when the sun is obscured and the light is cold, these walls are still faintly warm and luminous, as if they knew the trick of keeping the lost sunlight of centuries glimmering about them." Walk or drive around Cotswold villages and towns for even a day, and you will know what he meant

7

☎ *01285/740000* 🖶 *01285/740925* ⊕ *www.barnsleyhouse.com* ⇥ *10 rooms* ⚷ *Restaurant, minibars, cable TV with movies, in-room DVDs, in-room broadband, spa, bar; no a/c* ⊟ *MC, V* ¶◯¶ *CP.*

£££ ✕⊞ **Wild Duck Inn.** This family-run Elizabethan inn 3 mi south of Cirencester has richly decorated guest rooms with print fabrics and dark wood furniture. The mellow, deep-red dining room (££–££££) has an abundance of beams and oil portraits, and the menu is strong on fresh fish—try it in a beer batter—and such meat dishes as honey-roasted duck. Make room reservations well in advance, as the inn is popular. ⊠ *Ewen GL7 6BY* ☎ *01285/770310* 🖶 *01285/770924* ⊕ *www.thewildduckinn. co.uk* ⇥ *12 rooms* ⚷ *Restaurant, some pets allowed (fee); no a/c* ⊟ *AE, MC, V* ¶◯¶ *CP.*

£ ⊞ **Ivy House.** Contrary to expectations, Virginia creeper clings to this stone Victorian house, close to the center of town. The simple bedrooms have pastel colors and offer excellent value. The owners are friendly, and cyclists and walkers are welcomed. ⊠ *2 Victoria Rd., GL7 1EN* ☎🖶 *01285/656626* ⊕ *www.ivyhousecotswolds.com* ⇥ *4 rooms* ⚷ *No a/c, no room phones, no smoking* ⊟ *MC, V* ¶◯¶ *BP.*

Nightlife & the Arts

The **Brewery Arts Centre** (⊠ Brewery Ct. ☎ 01285/657181) includes a theater, exhibition space, and a café. It's also well known for its crafts studios and shop.

Sports & the Outdoors

You can indulge in water sports such as waterskiing and windsurfing at the **Cotswold Water Park,** 3 mi south of Cirencester. This group of 130 lakes covers 40 square mi and has multiple entrances. There's swimming June through September; the park also draws wildlife enthusiasts, walkers, cyclists, and horseback riders. You pay individual charges for the activities April through October, and you can rent equipment on-site. ✉ *Keynes Country Park, off B4696, Shorncote* ☎ *01285/861459* ⊕ *www.waterpark.org* ☜ *£3–£4 Apr.–Oct., £1 Nov.–Mar.* ☉ *Apr.–Oct., 9–dusk; Nov.–Mar., 9–5.*

Shopping

The **Brewery Arts Centre** (✉ Brewery Ct. ☎ 01285/657181) has studios for more than a dozen artists and craftspeople, as well as a good shop that sells their work. The **Corn Hall** (✉ Market Pl.) is the venue for an antiques market on Thursday, Friday, and Saturday, when there's also a crafts market (unless it's the fifth Saturday in the month). Every Monday and Friday, Cirencester's central **Market Place** is packed with stalls selling a motley assortment of goods, mainly household items but some local produce and crafts, too. **Rankine Taylor Antiques** (✉ 34 Dollar St. ☎ 01285/652529) concentrates on 17th- and 18th-century furniture, silver, pottery, and glass. **William H. Stokes** (✉ 6–8 Dollar St. ☎ 01285/653907) specializes in oak furniture from the 16th and 17th centuries.

Painswick

 16 mi northwest of Cirencester, 8 mi southwest of Cheltenham, 5 mi south of Gloucester.

This old Cotswold wool town of around 2,000 inhabitants has become a chocolate-box picture of quaintness, attracting day-trippers and tour buses. But come during the week and you can discover the place in relative tranquillity. The huddled gray stone houses and inns date from as early as the 14th century and include a notable group from the Georgian era. The churchyard of St. Mary's is renowned for its 99 yew trees (legend has it that the devil prevents the 100th from growing) planted in 1792.

The **Painswick Rococo Garden,** ½ mi north of town, has survived from the exuberant rococo period of English garden design (1720–60). After 50 years in its original form, the 6-acre garden became overgrown with woodland. Beginning in 1984, after the rediscovery of a 1748 painting of the garden by Thomas Robins, the garden was restored. Now you can view the original architectural structures—such as the vaguely Gothic Eagle House and Exedra—and asym-

> **SPECIAL DAYS**
>
> Painswick's annual Clypping Ceremony, on the first Sunday after September 19, has nothing to do with topiaries—the name derives from the Anglo-Saxon word "clyppan," meaning "encircle." Children with garlands make a ring around the parish church as traditional hymns are sung; the idea is to affirm the church and the faith it stands for. Another good time to visit is the town's Victorian Market Day in early July.

metrical vistas. There's also a restaurant and a shop. ✉ *B4073* ☎ *01452/ 813204* ⊕ *www.rococogarden.org.uk* 🎫 *£5* ⊙ *Mid-Jan.–Oct., daily 11–5.*

Where to Stay & Eat

££££ ✕🖭 **Painswick Hotel.** Unstuffy and friendly, this family-run hotel occupies a Georgian mansion behind Painswick's church. Beautiful fabrics and deep, vibrant colors enhance the spacious and individually designed rooms, some of which have antique four-posters and balconies. In the Old Rectory restaurant, the £30 fixed-price seasonal menu blends the traditional with the exotic—roast guinea fowl with braised bok choy and truffle gnocchi, for example; there are good local cheeses. A two-night minimum stay is required on weekends. Service can be uneven. ✉ *Kemps La., GL6 6YB* ☎ *01452/812160* 🖨 *01452/814059* ⊕ *www. painswickhotel.com* 🛏 *19 rooms* 🍴 *Restaurant, Wi-Fi, meeting rooms; no smoking, no a/c* ▭ *AE, MC, V* ❘◎❘ *BP.*

££–£££ ✕🖭 **Cardynham House.** The Cotswolds are really about the art of living, as this 15th to 16th-century former wool merchant's house demonstrates. The stylish retreat, which retains its beamed ceilings, Jacobean staircase, and Elizabethan fireplace, has four-poster beds in all rooms but one and creative theme rooms such as the Medieval Garden, Dovecote, and Arabian Nights. One pricier room has a private pool. Downstairs, the March Hare dining room (£24.50, fixed-price menu; closed Sunday and Monday) serves delicious Thai food such as red snapper curry with coconut and lime leaves. ✉ *The Cross, GL6 6XX* ☎ *01452/ 814006, 01452/813452 restaurant* 🖨 *01452/812321* ⊕ *www.cardynham. co.uk* 🛏 *9 rooms* 🍴 *Restaurant; no a/c* ▭ *AE, MC, V* ❘◎❘ *BP.*

FodorśChoice
★

Owlpen

★ ㉞ *6 mi southwest of Stroud, 13 mi west of Cirencester.*

Prince Charles described the beauty spot of Owlpen, an off-the-beaten-path hamlet, as "the epitome of the English village." First settled in Saxon days as Olla's Pen (meaning "valley"), the village centers on a church, a Tudor manor house, and pearl-gray stone cottages, all set against a hillside. A graceful grouping of tithe barns, garden buildings, and gristmill softens the seignorial bearing of the manor house.

The triple-gabled stone **Owlpen Manor** was built between 1450 and 1616, but was restored in the 1920s by local Arts and Crafts artisans, who also created some of the furnishings. Today Nicholas and Karin Mander live here with their family. Inside are oak chests fashioned by William Morris, family portraits, Georgian doorcases, painted cloths from the Tudor and Stuart eras, and Queen Margaret's Room, said to be haunted by the spirit of Margaret of Anjou, wife of Henry VI, who visited here during the Wars of the Roses. You can also explore the terraced garden with its yew topiary, the envy of gardening masters such as Gertrude Jekyll. The Cyder Press restaurant opens at noon. ▪ TIP→ **Want to linger in this idyllic place? Several cottages have been converted into guest accommodations, available for two-night or longer rentals.** ✉ *Off B4066, near Uley* ☎ *01453/860261* ⊕ *www.owlpen.com* 🎫 *£5.25, gardens only £3.25* ⊙ *May–Sept., Tues., Thurs., and Sun. 2–5.*

7

Tetbury

35 *6 mi southeast of Owlpen, 8 mi southwest of Cirencester, 12 mi south of Painswick.*

Tetbury, with about 5,300 inhabitants, claims right royal connections. Indeed, the soaring spire of the church that presides over this Elizabethan market town is within sight of Highgrove House, the Prince of Wales's abode. The town is known as one of the area's antiques centers. In the center of the village, look for the eye-catching, white-painted stone **Market House** on Market Square, dating from 1655 and built up on rows of Tuscan pillars. Various markets are held here during the week. The **Church of St. Mary** (⊠ Church St. ☎ 01666/502333), in 18th-century neo-Gothic style, has a spacious galleried interior with pews.

NEED A BREAK?

Two Toads (⊠ 19 Church St. ☎ 01666/503696) is a relaxed spot for coffee, light lunches, and cream teas. Be sure to try the delicious pastries. The small courtyard garden is open in fine weather.

Tall gate piers and spreading trees frame the family-owned **Chavenage,** a gray Cotswold-stone Elizabethan manor house. The tour includes a room with fine tapestries, where Cromwell lodged during the Civil War, and a main hall with minstrels' gallery. ⊠ *2 mi northwest of Tetbury between B4104 and A4135* ☎*01666/502329* ⊕ *www.chavenage.com* ⊡ *£6* ⊙ *May–Sept., Thurs., Sun., and national holidays 2–5.*

One of the last English country houses constructed using traditional methods and materials, **Rodmarton Manor** (built 1909–29) is furnished with specially commissioned pieces in the Arts and Crafts style. Ernest Barnsley, a follower of William Morris, worked on the house and gardens. The notable gardens—wild, winter, sunken, and white—are divided into "rooms" bounded by hedges of holly, beech, and yew. The manor is 5 mi northeast of Tetbury. ⊠ *Off A433, Rodmarton* ☎ *01285/841253* ⊕*www.rodmarton-manor.co.uk* ⊡*£7, garden only £4* ⊙*May–Sept., Wed., Sat., and national holidays 2–5.*

> **ROYAL NEIGHBORS**
>
> Prince Charles and the late Princess Diana made their home at Highgrove House, near Tetbury, in 1981. Charles set about making the 37-acre estate a showcase for traditional and organic growing methods. It's unlikely you'll run into the Prince of Wales, though, unless it's at a polo match at Cirencester or on a local hunt. Princess Anne has lived at Gatcombe Park, near Minchinhampton, since the Queen bought it for her as a wedding present in 1973.

★ The 600-acre **Westonbirt National Arboretum,** 3 mi southwest of Tetbury, contains one of the most extensive collections of trees and shrubs in Europe. The best times to come for color are in late spring, when the rhododendrons, azaleas, and magnolias are blooming, and in fall, when the maples come into their own. There's a gift shop, café, and restaurant. ⊠ *Off A433* ☎ *01666/880220* ⊕ *www.forestry.gov.uk* ⊡ *£5 Jan. and Feb; £6.50 Mar.–Sept.; £7.50 Oct.–mid-Nov., free mid-Nov.–Dec.* ⊙ *Daily 10–8 or dusk.*

Where to Stay & Eat

★ **£££** ✕ **Trouble House.** Simple but wonderfully tasty dishes are created at this relaxed, whitewashed pub with wooden floors, a low-beam ceiling, and fireplaces for cool days. Your order from the bar might be halibut baked in lemon slices with pumpkin and Parmesan mash, or classic cassoulet of duck confit. The pub is 2 mi northeast of Tetbury on the Cirencester Road. ⊠ *A433* ☎ *01666/502206* ▤ *AE, MC, V* ⊘ *Closed Mon. and last wk in Dec. No dinner Sun.*

£££££ ✕▥ **Calcot Manor.** Comfortable country-house furnishings with lots of greens and burgundies fill the main house and converted sandstone barns and stables of this family-friendly establishment with a luxurious spa. Guest rooms are airy and spacious; family suites have bunk beds in a separate room and refrigerators. The formal Conservatory restaurant (£££–££££) prepares wood-roasted meats and homemade fresh fruit sorbets and the Gumstool Inn provides farmhouse-style fare; dinner is included in the price on weekends. The hotel is 3 mi west of town. ⊠ *A4135, GL8 8YJ* ☎ *01666/890391* 🖷 *01666/890394* ⊕ *www. calcotmanor.co.uk* ↽ *24 rooms, 6 suites* ⚹ *2 restaurants, in-room data ports, tennis court, pool, gym, spa, croquet, 2 bars, meeting rooms; no a/c* ▤ *AE, DC, MC, V* ▯ᅵ *BP.*

Shopping

Tetbury is home to more than 30 antiques shops, some of which are incorporated into small malls. You'll be sure to find something from **Alchemy** (⊠ Old Chapel, Long St. ☎ 01666/505281), a cornucopia of treasures from kitchenware to jewelry, and glass. **Day Antiques** (⊠ 5 New Church St. ☎ 01666/502413) specializes in oak furniture and early pottery, metalware, and treen. **Townsend Bateson** (⊠ 51A Long St. ☎ 01666/505083) displays decorative wares and some furniture.

GLOUCESTER TO THE FOREST OF DEAN

West of the Cotswolds a rather urbanized axis connects Gloucester with Cheltenham. Despite their proximity on either side of the M5 motorway, the towns are very different; the down-to-earth Gloucester, built around docks connected to the River Severn, contrasts with the gentrified spa town of Cheltenham. North of Gloucester lies the riverside town of Tewkesbury with its imposing abbey; to the south, easily accessible from M5, stands battlemented Berkeley Castle. Southwest of Gloucester, the low-lying Forest of Dean (officially the Royal Forest of Dean), once a private hunting ground of kings, is now a recreation area for the public, with some of the country's most beautiful woodlands.

Gloucester

36 *13 mi southwest of Cheltenham, 56 mi south of Birmingham, 105 mi west of London.*

Although much of the ancient heritage of this county seat has been lost to nondescript modern stores and offices, Gloucester (population about 111,000) has a number of worthwhile sights, most notably its cathedral. The historic **Gloucester Docks,** a short walk from the cathedral along

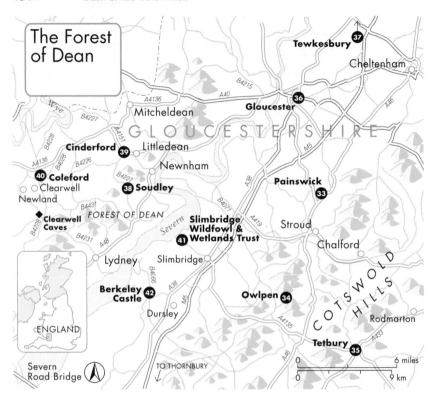

The Forest of Dean

Tewkesbury 37
Cheltenham

B4215

A4136   A40
Mitcheldean   **Gloucester** 36

GLOUCESTERSHIRE

Cinderford 39 Littledean
Newnham

40 **Coleford**
Clearwell
Newland   38 **Soudley**   **Painswick** 33

Clearwell Caves   *FOREST OF DEAN*   **Slimbridge Wildfowl & Wetlands Trust** 41   Stroud
Chalford

Lydney   Slimbridge

Berkeley Castle 42   **Owlpen** 34
Dursley   Rodmarton

COTSWOLD HILLS

ENGLAND

Tetbury 35

Severn Road Bridge   TO THORNBURY   0   6 miles
0   9 km

the canal, still function but now cater mainly to pleasure craft. The vast Victorian warehouses have been restored, and shops and cafés added, reviving the area. One warehouse is now the Antiques Centre, and others hold good museums. **Walking tours** around the docks start at the Mariners' Church in the center of the docks. ☎ *01452/396572* 🖂 *£2.50 tours* ☉ *Tours mid-June–mid-Sept., weekends at 11.*

★ Magnificent **Gloucester Cathedral,** with its soaring, elegant exterior, was originally a Norman abbey church, consecrated in 1100. Reflecting different periods, the cathedral mirrors perfectly the slow growth of ecclesiastical taste and the development of the Perpendicular style. The interior has largely been spared the sterilizing attentions of modern architects and is almost completely Norman, with the massive pillars of the nave left untouched since their completion. The fan-vaulted roof of the 14th-century cloisters is the finest in Europe, and the cloisters enclose a peaceful garden (used in the filming of *Harry Potter and the Sorcerer's Stone* for some Hogwarts School scenes). The Whispering Gallery has a permanent exhibition devoted to the splendid, 14th-century stained glass of the Great East Window, and tours of the tower (269 steps up) are available. 🖂 *Westgate St.* ☎ *01452/528095* ⊕ *www.gloucestercathedral.org.uk* 🖂 *£3 donation requested, photography permit £3. Tower tours £2.50, exhibition £2* ☉ *Daily 8–6, except during* *services and special events. Tower tours Apr.–Oct., Wed.–Fri. 2:30, Sat. and national holidays 1:30 and 2:30. Whispering Gallery Apr.–Oct., weekdays 10:30–4, Sat. 10:30–3:30.*

The **Gloucester Folk Museum,** opposite the cathedral, fills a row of fine Tudor and Jacobean half-timber houses. Exhibits on crafts and domestic life illustrate the history of Gloucester and the surrounding areas, and there's a Toys and Childhood Gallery. ⊠ *99–103 Westgate St.* ☎ *01452/396868* ⊕ *www.gloucester.gov.uk* ☒ *Free* ☉ *Tues.–Sat. 10–5.*

FodorsChoice
★

The **National Waterways Museum,** in a converted Victorian warehouse, contains examples of canal houseboats, including gaily painted "canal ware"—ornaments and utensils found on barges. Exhibits interpret the role of canals in the 18th and 19th centuries, and you can try your foot at "walking the wall"—the boatmen's way of propelling barges through tunnels with their feet. ⊠ *Llanthony Warehouse, Llanthony Rd., Gloucester Docks* ☎ *01452/318200* ⊕ *www.nwm.org.uk* ☒ *£5.95* ☉ *Daily 10–5, last admission at 4.*

From the pier outside the National Waterways Museum, boats leave for a 45-minute tour of the Gloucester Docks or all-day cruises that head as far north as Tewkesbury or south to the Severn Estuary at Sharpness. Tours take place between Easter and October: contact the **National Waterways Museum** (☎ 01452/318200) for dates and prices.

NEED A BREAK?

While you're at the docks, drop in at **Foster's** (⊠ Kimberley Warehouse, Gloucester Docks ☎ 01452/300990), a pub, wine bar, and brasserie, where you can sit on sofas or in a glassed-in, plant-filled atrium right on the quayside. Hot and cold drinks, snacks, and full meals are available.

A Georgian mansion holds **Nature in Art,** a museum dedicated to works of art inspired by nature. Exhibits are mainly contemporary, with selections by Picasso, Henry Moore, and the wildlife artist David Shepherd, but also include a Byzantine mosaic and 19th-century Asian ivory. From February through November you can watch artists at work. The museum is 2 mi north of Gloucester. ⊠ *Wallsworth Hall, A38, Twigworth* ☎ *0845/450 0233* ⊕ *www.nature-in-art.org.uk* ☒ *£4.50* ☉ *Tues.–Sun. and national holidays 10–5.*

Where to Stay & Eat

£–£££ ✕ **The New Inn.** This rambling coaching inn is a few steps down from the Cross—the historic heart of the old city where Northgate, Westgate, Southgate, and Eastgate streets meet. The galleried courtyard, overgrown with creepers, adds to the impression of age. There's an extensive carvery menu (a buffet of roasted meats, carved to order) and plenty of vegetarian choices. ⊠ *16 Northgate St.* ☎ *01452/522177* ⊟ *AE, MC, V.*

££££ 🛏 **Hatherley Manor.** On 37 acres of grounds 2 mi north of Gloucester, this 17th-century redbrick house is fairly quiet, unless a conference is going on—which happens frequently. Guest rooms are spacious and furnished in modern style with muted, earthy colors. The public rooms have retained their beams and low ceilings. ⊠ *Down Hatherley La., GL2 9QA* ☎ *0870 194/2126* 🖶 *01452/731032* ⊕ *www.macdonaldhotels.co.uk* ⊃*52 rooms* ⚘ *Restaurant, in-room data ports, croquet, bar, meet-*

ing rooms, helipad, some pets allowed (fee), no-smoking rooms; no a/c
☐ *AE, DC, MC, V* ‖◎‖ *BP.*

£–££ ☒ **Edward Hotel.** Close to the center, this lodging offers simple comfort at reasonable prices. Although the hotel was converted from three Georgian houses, the style is distinctly Edwardian, with soft reds, striped wallpaper, and period furnishings in some rooms, whereas others have a fresher, more modern feel. There's a garden, a log fire in the lounge, and parking space—a real bonus in this part of town. ☒ *88–92 London Rd., GL1 3PG* ☎*01452/525865* ☒*01452/302165* ⊕*www.edwardhotel-gloucester. co.uk* ⇨ *20 rooms* ♢ *Bar* ☐ *MC, V* ‖◎‖ *BP.*

Shopping

The locals say it's best to look in Cheltenham and buy in Gloucester, where prices are lower. The more than 100 dealers in the **Antiques Centre** (☒ 1 Severn Rd. ☎ 01452/529716) offer some good buys on items—clocks, silver, china, military collectibles, and more—in a five-floor Victorian warehouse by the Gloucester Docks. The **Beatrix Potter Gift Shop** (☒ 9 College Ct. ☎ 01452/422856), next to the Cathedral Gate, is in the house that served as a model for the tailor's house in Potter's story *The Tailor of Gloucester.* The shop sells Potter-related items and also has a small museum.

Tewkesbury

③ *12 mi northeast of Gloucester.*

Tewkesbury is an ancient town of black-and-white half-timber buildings, as well as some fine Georgian ones, on the River Avon. The stonework in the Norman **Tewkesbury Abbey** has much in common with that of Gloucester Cathedral, but this church was built in the Romanesque (12th-century) and Decorated Gothic (14th-century) styles. Its exterior makes an impressive sight, with the largest Norman tower in the world—148 feet high and 46 feet square—and the 65-foot-high arch of the west front. Fourteen stout Norman pillars and myriad gilded bosses on the roof of the nave and choir (best viewed through a mirror on wheels) grace the beautifully kept interior. ☒ *Church St.* ☎ *01684/ 850959* ⊕ *www.tewkesburyabbey.org.uk* ☒ *Requested donation £3, tours £3* ☉ *Easter–Oct., Mon.–Sat. 7:30–6, Sun. 7:30–7; Nov.–Easter, Mon.–Sat. 7:30–5:30, Sun 7:30–7; tours Apr.–Oct., daily at 11 and 2:15 (or prebook at any time).*

Where to Stay

££££ ☒ **Royal Hop Pole.** One of the most famous old English inns, the half-timber Hop Pole is mentioned in Charles Dickens's *The Pickwick Papers.* The rooms at the rear have wood beams and views of the gardens running down to the river, where there is private mooring for boats. ☒ *Church St., GL20 5RT* ☎ *01684/293236* ☒ *01684/296680* ⊕ *www. royalhoppole.co.uk* ⇨ *29 rooms* ♢ *Restaurant, bar, meeting rooms, some pets allowed; no a/c* ☐ *AE, DC, MC, V* ‖◎‖ *BP.*

£ ☒ **Abbey Antiques B&B.** If you have yearned to wake up in an antiques shop, this may be your best option. This three-story Georgian town house, just across from the abbey, has two gorgeously furnished, antiques-filled rooms above the Aladdin's cave of a shop and one apartment on the top floor. Wooden floorboards, patchwork quilts, fresh flowers in the house, and grand views of the Abbey and the Malvern Hills are added attractions. ☒ *61 Church St., GL20 5RZ* ☎ *01684/298145* ⇨ *2 rooms, 1 apartment* ⚹ *No a/c, no room phones* ▤ *No credit cards* ⎜◯⎜ *BP.*

Soudley

38 *27 mi southwest of Tewkesbury, 15 mi west of Gloucester.*

★ Soudley has a museum that provides a useful introduction to the surrounding forest. The ancient **Forest of Dean** (⊕ www.visitforestofdean. co.uk) covers much of the valley between the Rivers Severn and Wye. Although the primordial forest has long since been cut down and replanted, the landscape here remains one of strange beauty, hiding in its folds and under its hills deposits of iron, silver, and coal that have been mined for thousands of years. Of the original forest established in 1016 by King Canute, 27,000 acres are preserved by the Forestry Commission. It's still a source of timber, but parking lots and picnic grounds have been created and eight nature trails marked. ▪ TIP➔ **For a driving tour of the forest, head to Littledean, where** SCENIC DRIVE **signs direct you through the best of the forest.** To get to Littledean from Soudley, backtrack north on B4227, and turn east on A4151.

> **FOREST CUSTOMS**
>
> The ancient laws and customs of the Forest of Dean linger on. To this day, adult males born within the area formerly known as the Hundred of St. Briavels, and who have worked for a year and a day in a mine, are entitled to register as "freeminers," with the right to mine and quarry in the forest. Four elected "verderers" still meet to discuss Forest issues.

★ The **Dean Heritage Centre,** in a restored mill building in a wooded valley on the forest's eastern edge, tells the history of the forest, with reconstructions of a forester's cottage, a waterwheel, and a "beam engine" (a primitive steam engine used to pump water from flooded coal mines). Other galleries show art with local themes as well as furniture, ornaments, and the like made from local oak. Also within the grounds is a smallholding (a small farm), with a couple of resident pigs, and a charcoal burner's hut. Craftspeople work in the outbuildings. ☒ *B4227, near Cinderford* ☎ *01594/822170* ⊕ *www.deanheritagemuseum.com* ▣ *£4.50* ☉ *Apr.–Oct., daily 10–5; Nov.–Mar., daily 10–4.*

Sports & the Outdoors

The densely wooded Forest of Dean is quite special for walking, with interesting villages and monastic ruins. Many of its public footpaths are signposted, as are most of the Forestry Commission trails. There are easy walks out of Newland, around New Fancy (great view) and Mallards Pike Lake, and a slightly longer one (three hours), which takes in Wench Ford, Danby Lodge, and Blackpool Bridge. The area has picnic grounds, car parking, and, hidden away, old pubs where you can wet your whistle. For information on hiking in the Forest of Dean, contact the **Forestry Commission** (☒ Bank House, Bank St., Coleford GL16 8BA ☎ 01594/ 833057 ⊕ www.forestry.gov.uk).

Cinderford

39 *1 mi west of Littledean, 14 mi southwest of Gloucester.*

In Cinderford, a hiking trail links sculptures around Speech House, the medieval verderer's court in the forest's center, and now a restaurant and inn. The verderer was responsible for the enforcement of the forest laws. It was usually a capital offense to kill game or cut wood without authorization.

Where to Stay & Eat

£££ ✕⬚ **Speech House.** Dating from 1676, this former royal hunting lodge retains its satisfyingly creaky floors and low-beam ceilings. Rooms are traditionally furnished with striped and print fabrics; some have four-posters. The wood-panel Verderer's Court still functions four times a year, but at any other time the courtroom is a restaurant (£££) serving country platters that might include the local Gloucestershire Old Spot pork and steamed pudding with custard. Although the postal address for Speech House is the town of Coleford, it is midway between Cinderford and Coleford. ⌂ *B4226, Coleford GL16 7EL* ☎ *01594/822607* 🖶 *01594/823658* ⊕ *www.thespeechhouse.co.uk* ➦ *37 rooms* ⬭ *Restaurant, in-room data ports, golf privileges, bar, meeting rooms, some pets allowed (fee); no a/c* ⊟ *AE, DC, MC, V* ⬚ *BP.*

Coleford

40 *4 mi west of Cinderford, 10 mi south of Ross-on-Wye.*

The area around Coleford, a large village of over 8,000 people, is a maze of moss-covered rocks, huge ferns, and ancient yew trees—a shady haven on a summer's day. The **tourist information center** (☎ 01594/ 812388 ⊕ www.forestofdean.gov.uk) at Coleford (drive west from Cinderford on A4151, and then west again on B4226 and B4028) has details of picnic grounds, nature and sculpture trails, and tours of the forest.

☾ A visit to the workings in the spectacular **Clearwell Caves,** 1½ mi south of Coleford, provides insight into the region's mining for iron and coal, which went on continuously from Roman times to 1945. Ocher (for paint pigments and cosmetics) is still mined here. ⌂ *Off B4228* ☎ *01594/ 832535* ⊕ *www.clearwellcaves.com* ⬚ *£4.50, £5.50 Christmas Fantasy displays* ⊙ *Daily 10–5.*

Where to Stay & Eat

££–£££ ✕⬚ **Wyndham Arms Hotel.** This old-fashioned village inn, just a hundred yards from Clearwell Castle, has comfortable accommodations, a bar with fine wines and ales, and a restaurant (££–£££) that can rustle up sophisticated English cuisine. The frequently changing menu might include Tintern cheese soufflé, loin of venison, or panfried sea bass. Bedrooms, fairly plain but well equipped, are in the main building, where there's a suite with a beamed ceiling, or in an annex. ⌂ *The Cross, Clearwell GL16 8JT* ☎ *01594/833666* 🖶 *01594/836450* ⊕ *www. thewyndhamhotel.co.uk* ➦ *17 rooms, 1 suite* ⬭ *Restaurant, bar, no-smoking rooms; no a/c* ⊟ *MC, V.*

££ ✕⌂ **Tudor Farmhouse.** Despite its name, this former farmhouse has some sections that date to the 13th century. Polished oak staircases, mullioned windows, and a huge stone fireplace in the sitting room imbue the place with antique calm. Most of the traditionally decorated bedrooms are in a converted barn, and three have four-poster beds. The restaurant (£££) serves good-quality fare using seasonal ingredients in such dishes as fresh spinach and apple soup. Steaks, turbot, and vegetable cannelloni might also be on the menu. ✉ *High St., near Coleford, Clearwell GL16 8JS* ☎ *01594/833046 or 0800/783–5935* 🖷 *01594/837093* ⊕ *www. tudorfarmhousehotel.co.uk* 🛏 *22 rooms* ♿ *Restaurant, some pets allowed; no a/c* ☰ *AE, MC, V* ⎟⦿⎟ *BP.*

Slimbridge Wildfowl & Wetlands Trust

④ *38 mi east of Coleford (via Severn Bridge to the south), 12 mi south of Gloucester, 20 mi northeast of Bristol.*

On the banks of the River Severn, this 73-acre site encompasses rich marshland that harbors Britain's largest collection of wildfowl. Thousands of swans, ducks, and geese come to winter here; spring and early summer are the times to see cygnets, ducklings, and goslings. Trails with blinds (called "hides" in Britain) thread the preserve. The flashy visitor center has an observation tower, cinema, gift shop, and restaurant; a gallery of wildlife art presents changing exhibitions. The preserve is outside the village of Slimbridge (head west and across the little swing bridge over the Sharpness Canal). ☎ *01453/890333* ⊕ *www.wwt.org.uk* 💷 *£6.75* ⊗ *Apr.–Oct., daily 9:30–5:30; Nov.–Mar., daily 9:30–5.*

Berkeley Castle

★ **④** *4 mi southwest of Slimbridge, 17 mi southwest of Gloucester, 21 mi north of Bristol.*

Berkeley Castle, in the sleepy village of Berkeley (pronounced *bark*-ley), is perfectly preserved, down to its medieval turrets. It witnessed the gruesome murder of King Edward II in 1327—the cell in which it occurred can still be seen. Edward was deposed by his French consort, Queen Isabella, and her paramour, the earl of Mortimer. They then connived at his imprisonment and subsequent death. Roger De Berkeley, a Norman knight, began work on the castle in 1153, and it has remained in the family ever since. Magnificent furniture, tapestries, and pictures fill the state apartments, but even the ancient buttery and kitchen are interesting. The surrounding meadows, now the setting for pleasant Elizabethan gardens that include a tropical Butterfly House, were once flooded to make a formidable moat. On the last two weekends in July the castle stages a **medieval jousting tournament** (☎ 020/7482–0115 💷 *£10*), a costumed pageant with minstrels, dancing, mock battles, and archery and falconry demonstrations. File this in the corny but fun category. Ticket-holders have free entry to the castle. ✉ *Off A38, Berkeley* ☎ *01453/810332* ⊕ *www.berkeley-castle.com* 💷 *£7.50; gardens only £4; Butterfly House only £2; jousting tournament £10* ⊗ *House* *and gardens: Apr.–Sept., Tues.–Sat. and national holidays 11–4, Sun. 2–5; Oct., Sun. 2–5. Butterfly House closed Oct.*

Where to Stay & Eat

★ **££££** ✕ **Thornbury Castle.** An impressive castle-hotel, Thornbury has everything a genuine 16th-century Tudor castle needs: huge fireplaces, antiques, paintings, and mullioned windows, along with a large garden. There's also plenty of history: Henry VIII, Anne Boleyn, and Mary Tudor spent time here. The standards of comfort are famous, and the pampering touches in the plushly decorated bedrooms include well-appointed bathrooms. People come from all over to dine on sophisticated fare such as panfried turbot with roasted leeks and Champagne sauce, or lamb with ratatouille. The hotel is 12 mi north of Bristol. ⊠ *Castle St., off A38, Thornbury BS35 1HH* ☎ *01454/281182* 🖶 *01454/416188* ⊕ *www.thornburycastle.co.uk* ↩ *25 rooms* ♻ *Restaurant, in-room broadband, archery, croquet, lounge, business services, meeting rooms, some pets allowed (fee); no a/c* ⊟ *AE, DC, MC, V* ⊚ *BP.*

££ ▦ **Drakestone House.** This lovely, reasonably priced Cotswold Arts and Crafts house 3 mi east of Berkeley has wooden floors and beamed and plasterwork ceilings. Fine antiques and period furniture complement the architecture. The B&B is a member of Wolsey Lodges, an association of private homes with many distinctive properties. ⊠ *Off B4060, Stinchcombe, Dursley GL11 6AS* ☎ *01453/542140* ⊕ *www.wolsey-lodges. com* ↩ *3 rooms* ♻ *Some pets allowed; no a/c, no room phones, no room TVs, no smoking* ⊟ *No credit cards* ⊙ *Closed Dec. and Jan.* ⊚ *BP.*

BATH & THE COTSWOLDS ESSENTIALS

Transportation

BY AIR

This area is about two hours from London; Bristol and Birmingham have the closest regional airports. Bristol's airport is 8 mi south of the city; it also has limited service from New York.

🛈 **Birmingham International Airport** ⊠ A45, off Junction 6 of M42 ☎ 0870/733–5511 ⊕ www.bhx.co.uk. **Bristol International Airport** ⊠ Bridgwater Rd., Lulsgate ☎ 0870/ 121–2747 ⊕ www.bristolairport.co.uk.

BY BUS

National Express serves the region from London's Victoria Coach Station. Megabus, a budget service that you book on the Internet, serves Cheltenham and Gloucester. First covers the area around Bath. Stagecoach, Castleways, and Pulhams operate in the Gloucestershire and Cotswolds region. For all bus inquiries, call Traveline. Travel times vary; it can take about three hours to get to Burford or Cheltenham, three to four hours to get to Bath. Trains are faster. Although you can get around the Cotswolds by bus, service between some towns can be extremely limited, perhaps only twice a week.

Some bus routes to major Cotswold destinations are as follows (when not stated otherwise, routes are serviced by National Express buses and depart from London's Victoria Coach Station). Bourton-on-the-Water: take Pulhams buses from Cheltenham or Stow-on-the-Wold (no Sunday bus service in winter). Broadway: from Cheltenham, four Castleways coaches daily serve the town Monday to Saturday, and four Stagecoach coaches serve the town on Sunday. Burford (A40 turnout): Swanbrook buses leave from Cheltenham three times daily Monday to Saturday, once on Sunday; from London, change at Oxford. Cheltenham and Cirencester: buses leave London hourly. Moreton-in-Marsh: buses depart five times daily from London, changing at Cirencester. Painswick: Stagecoach buses run from Cheltenham (hourly Monday to Saturday). Stow-on-the-Wold: Pulhams buses run six times daily (not Sunday in winter) from Moreton-in-Marsh. Winchcombe: from Cheltenham, 11 Castleways buses leave daily Monday to Saturday.

FARES & SCHEDULES **Castleways** ☎ 01242/602949. **First** ☎ 0845/606-4446 ⊕ www.firstbadgerline.co. uk. **Megabus** ⊕ www.megabus.com. **National Express** ☎ 0870/580-8080 ⊕ www. nationalexpress.com. **Pulhams** ☎ 01451/820369 ⊕ www.pulhamscoaches.com. **Stagecoach** ☎ 01242/224853 ⊕ www.stagecoachbus.com. **Swanbrook** ☎ 01452/712386 ⊕ www.swanbrook.co.uk. **Traveline** ☎ 0870/608-2608 ⊕ www.traveline.org.uk.

BY CAR

M4 is the main route west from London to Bath and southern Gloucestershire; expect about a two-hour drive. From Exit 18, take A46 south to Bath. From Exit 20, take M5 north to Gloucester (25 mi), Cheltenham, and Tewkesbury; from Exit 15, take A419 to A429 north to the Cotswolds. From London, you can also take M40 and A40 to the Cotswolds.

Parking in Bath is restricted within the city, and any car illegally parked is likely to be ticketed. Fees for towed cars can be hundreds of pounds. Public parking lots in the historic area fill up early, but the Park and Ride lots on the outskirts provide shuttle service into the center. In Cheltenham and Gloucester, garage your car or leave it at your hotel and forgo the stress of finding parking and negotiating one-way streets.

BY TRAIN

First Great Western, Wales and West, Virgin, Central, and Thames trains serve the region from London's Paddington Station, or, less frequently, from Euston. Travel time from Paddington to Bath is about 90 minutes. Most trains to Cheltenham (2 hours) and Gloucester (1¾ hours) involve a change at Swindon. A three-day or seven-day Heart of England Rover ticket is valid for unlimited travel within the region.

Some pointers for reaching central Cotswold destinations by train follow. Broadway: train to Moreton-in-Marsh or Evesham, then bus or taxi locally to reach the town. Burford: train to Oxford, then bus from the Taylor Institute. Cirencester: train from London Paddington to Kemble (4 mi from town). Bourton-on-the-Water, Chipping Campden, and Stow-on-the-Wold: train to Moreton-in-Marsh, then local bus lines (some have minimal schedules). Moreton-in-Marsh is serviced by train from London Paddington daily. Local tourist offices have details.

FARES & SCHEDULES **National Rail Enquiries** ☎ 0845/748-4950 ⊕ www.nationalrail.co.uk.

Contacts & Resources

EMERGENCIES

🚹 **Ambulance, fire, police** ☎ 999. **Cheltenham General Hospital** ✉ Sandford Rd. ☎ 0845/422–2222. **Gloucester Royal Hospital** ✉ Great Western Rd. ☎ 0845/422–2222. **Royal United Hospital** ✉ Combe Park, Bath ☎ 01225/428331.

INTERNET

Internet connections are variable in the rural Cotswolds, though full facilities are increasingly offered in the region's hotels and B&Bs; Wi-Fi may be available in some or all rooms. You'll find public Internet cafés in Bath, Cheltenham, and Gloucester. Cheltenham's Everyman Theatre has free access and a wireless facility.

🚹 Internet Cafés **Click Internet Café** ✉ 13 Manvers St., Bath ☎ 01225/481008 ⊕ www. clickcafe.zen.co.uk. **Loft Internet Café** ✉ Above Moss Books, 8–9 Henrietta St., Cheltenham ☎ 01242/222947 ⊕ www.loftcybercafe.co.uk. **Smart Space Internet Café** ✉ County Bar, Everyman Theatre, Regent St., Cheltenham ☎ 01242/572573. **Surf Scorpio** ✉ 135 Eastgate St., Gloucester ☎ 01452/528030 ⊕ www.surfscorpio.co.uk.

TOUR OPTIONS

Based in Oxford, Cotswold Roaming is a stylish outfit offering tours of the Cotswolds (Tuesday and Saturday) and excursions to Bath and Castle Combe (Wednesday and Saturday) in small vehicles. The full-day tour of the Cotswolds takes in Bourton-on-the-Water, Upper Slaughter and Lower Slaughter, Chipping Campden, Sudeley Castle, and Stow-on-the-Wold. Half-day tours are also offered. The pickup point is next to the Playhouse Theatre in Beaumont Street, Oxford.

Between mid-June and mid-September, Gloucester Civic Trust organizes tours of the city (Monday to Saturday at 11 from the tourist office) and docks (weekends at 11 from near the National Waterways Museum), or by appointment at other times. City Sightseeing runs 45-minute guided tours of Bath year-round and half-day tours from Stratford-upon-Avon into the Cotswolds from Easter through September.

🚹 **City Sightseeing** ☎ 01789/299123 in Stratford, 01225/330444 in Bath ⊕ www.city-sightseeing.com. **Cotswold Roaming** ☎ 01865/308300 ⊕ www.oxfordcity.co.uk/cotswold-roaming. **Gloucester Civic Trust** ☎ 01452/501666.

VISITOR INFORMATION

The Heart of England Tourist Board is open Monday through Thursday 9 to 5:30, Friday 9 to 5. South West Tourism has information on Bath. Local tourist information centers are normally open Monday through Saturday 9:30 to 5:30, but times vary according to season. Note that Cirencester's and Stow-on-the-Wold's Web site cover the whole of the Cotswolds.

🚹 **Gloucestershire Cotswolds** ⊕ www.glos-cotswolds.com. **Heart of England Tourism** ✉ Larkhill Rd., Worcester WR5 2EZ ☎ 01905/761100 🖷 01905/763450 ⊕ www. visitheartofengland.com. **South West Tourism** ✉ Woodwater Park, Pynes Hill, Exeter EX2 5WT ☎ 0870/442–0880 🖷 0870/442–0881 ⊕ www.westcountrynow.com. **Bath** ✉ Abbey Chambers, Abbey Church Yard, BA1 1LY ☎ 0906/711–2000 (calls cost 50p per minute), 0870/444–6442, 0870/420–1278 accommodation line ⊕ www.visitbath.co.uk. **Bourton-on-the-Water** ✉ Victoria St., GL54 2BU ☎ 01451/820211. **Broadway** ✉ 1

Cotswold Ct., WR12 7AA ☎ 01386/852937. **Burford** ⊠ The Brewery, Sheep St., OX18 4LP ☎ 01993/823558 ⊕ www.oxfordshirecotswolds.co.uk. **Cheltenham** ⊠ 77 Promenade, GL50 1PP ☎ 01242/522878 ⊕ www.visitcheltenham.com. **Chipping Campden** ⊠ The Old Police Station, High St., GL55 6HB ☎ 01386/841206 ⊕ www.visitchippingcampden. com. **Cirencester** ⊠ Corn Hall, Market Pl., GL7 2NW ☎ 01285/654180 ⊕ www.cotswold. gov.uk. **Gloucester** ⊠ 28 Southgate St., GL1 2DP ☎ 01452/396572 ⊕ www.gloucester. gov.uk/tourism. **Moreton-in-Marsh** ⊠ High St., GL56 0AZ ☎ 01608/650881 ⊕ www. moreton-in-marsh.co.uk. **Painswick** ⊠ The Library, Stroud Rd., GL6 6UT ☎ 01452/813552. **Stow-on-the-Wold** ⊠ Hollis House, The Square, GL54 1AF ☎ 01451/831082 ⊕ www. cotswold.gov.uk. **Tetbury** ⊠ 33 Church St., GL8 8JG ☎ 01666/503552 ⊕ www.tetbury. org. **Tewkesbury** ⊠ 64 Barton St., GL20 5PX ☎ 01684/295027 ⊕ www. visitcotswoldsandsevernvale.gov.uk.

The Welsh Borders

BIRMINGHAM, WORCESTER, HEREFORD, SHREWSBURY, CHESTER

WORD OF MOUTH

"If you are a foodie, Ludlow is a must. . . . It's also an extremely charming old market town with a castle, river, medieval half-timbered houses, Georgian houses . . . and easy to walk around."
—caroline_edinburgh

"There's Eastnor and Goodrich Castles in Herefordshire, and if you go a little farther north to Shropshire, you'll find some wonderful castles: Ludlow, Stokesay . . . all on the Welsh Borders and set amid stunning scenery and countryside. South Shropshire is one of England's greatest secrets."
—julia_t

Updated by
Kate Hughes

SOME OF ENGLAND'S PRETTIEST COUNTRYSIDE lies along the 108-mi border with the principality of Wales, which stretches from the town of Chepstow on the Severn estuary in the south to the city of Chester in the north. Much of the land along this border, in the counties of Herefordshire, Shropshire, and southern Cheshire, is remote and tranquil. But today's rural peace belies a turbulent past. Relations between the English and the Welsh have seldom been easy, and from earliest times the English have felt it necessary to keep the "troublesome" Welsh firmly on the other side of the border. The 177-mi Offa's Dyke Path, a National Trail that runs near the border (two-thirds is in Wales), follows part of the 8th-century earthen wall built by King Offa as protection against Welsh raiders. A string of medieval castles also bears witness to this history. Many are romantic ruins; some are brooding fortresses. Built to control the countryside, they still radiate mystery and menace.

For the last 500 years or so, the people of this border country have enjoyed a peaceful existence, with little to disturb the traditional patterns of country life. In the 18th century, however, one small corner of Shropshire heralded the tumultuous birth of the Industrial Revolution. Here, in a wooded stretch of the Severn Gorge, the coke blast furnace was invented and the first iron bridge was erected (1779).

The ramifications of that technological leap led to the growth of Britain's second-largest city, Birmingham, the capital of the Midlands. Birmingham has transcended its reputation as one of the country's least attractive cities, and its active artistic life draws people who appreciate what remains of its historic civic architecture.

Herefordshire, in the south, is a county of rich, rolling countryside and river valleys, gradually opening out in the high hills and plateaus of Shropshire. North of the Shropshire hills, the gentler Cheshire plain stretches toward the great industrial cities of Liverpool and Manchester. This is dairy country, dotted with small villages and market towns, many rich in the 13th- and 14th-century black-and-white, half-timber buildings typical of northwestern England. These are the legacy of a forested countryside, where wood was easier to come by than stone. (The Victorians, however, are responsible for the more recent fashion of painting these structures black and white.) In the market towns of Chester and Shrewsbury, the more elaborately decorated half-timber buildings are monuments to wealth, dating mostly from the early Jacobean period at the beginning of the 17th century. More half-timbered structures are found in the archetypal Borders town of Ludlow, now a culinary center nestled in the lee of its majestic ruined castle.

Exploring the Welsh Borders

The main gateway to the region is bustling Birmingham, one of the best places in England for the performing arts, having redeemed itself from its reputation as a post–World War II urban disaster zone. The city of Worcester, to the south, is renowned for its proud cathedral and fine bone china. Farther south and west, along the lovely Malvern Hills, lie the peaceful spa town of Great Malvern and the prosperous agricultural city of Hereford. West of Birmingham is Bewdley, a terminus of the Severn Valley Railway, and beyond, the West Midlands—birthplace of modern British industry.

The city of Shrewsbury is near the banks of the River Severn and a cluster of Ironbridge museums interpreting the region's industrial heritage. To its south lies Ludlow, an architectural and culinary jewel; at the northwestern edge of the region is the ancient city of Chester.

About the Restaurants

Birmingham has splendid international restaurants but is probably most famous for its Indian and Pakistani eateries, the best of which are off the main roads. To dine in one of Ludlow's noted restaurants, you must book up to three months ahead for dinner (lunch is a better bet).

About the Hotels

The Welsh Borders are full of ancient inns and venerable Regency-style houses converted into hotels. Although some of these can be pricey, bargains can be found. You may have to put up with asthmatic plumbing and creaking beams that masquerade as period charm, but it's usually worth the savings. Birmingham's hotels, geared to the convention crowd, are mostly bland and impersonal, but smart; weekend rates may be up to 50% less than they would be during the week.

WHAT IT COSTS In pounds				
	££££££	££££	£££	££	£
RESTAURANTS	over £22	£18–£22	£13–£17	£7–£12	under £7
HOTELS	over £160	£120–£160	£90–£119	£60–£89	under £60

Restaurant prices are for a main course at dinner. Hotel prices are for two people in a standard double room in high season, including V.A.T., with no meals or, if indicated, CP (with continental breakfast), BP (Breakfast Plan, with full breakfast), or MAP (Modified American Plan, with breakfast and dinner).

Timing

Most attractions are open and the countryside is most appealing in the warmer weather between April and September. The Autumn in Malvern Festival takes place on weekends in October, the open-air performances at Ludlow Castle at the end of June, and the Shrewsbury International Music Festival in June and July. The Three Choirs Festival, rotating from year to year among Gloucester (2007), Worcester, and Hereford, takes place in mid-August. Most rural sights have limited opening hours in winter. Even in the towns, the majority of attractions close at 5. Working in this season's favor are the creeping mists shrouding the valleys, and the warm hearths at inns and hotels.

BIRMINGHAM

▶ The dynamic cultural life of Birmingham—the result of the museums, art galleries, theater, ballet, and symphony that thrive here—comes as a refreshing surprise. The city's visual appeal, thanks to heavy industry and German bombing during World War II, may be less than instantly evident, but treasures and historic civic architecture remain. Birming-

GREAT ITINERARIES

Although the region's main towns—Worcester, Hereford, Shrewsbury, and Chester—distill the essence of the surrounding countryside, there's much in between that should not be neglected. It would be easy to base yourself in one of these towns, but you might do better to lodge in some of the smaller centers, or in one of the remoter country inns, to absorb the full flavor of the borderlands.

Numbers in the text correspond to numbers in the margin and on the Welsh Borders, Birmingham, and Shrewsbury maps.

IF YOU HAVE 3 DAYS

The city of **Worcester** 14 makes a convenient entry to the Welsh Borders. Take a whirl around the Royal Worcester Porcelain Factory. On your second day, take A443 northwest, making a stop at the evocative ruins of **Witley Court** 25. Keep on the same road as far as **Ludlow** 40, stopping to view its magnificent castle and its Tudor, Jacobean, and Georgian buildings. Make a reservation if you want to have lunch at one of its noted restaurants. Next, head south for **Hereford** 24, with its stout Norman cathedral and numerous reminders of the city's importance as a market town. See the most interesting sights in the morning, and spend the afternoon exploring **Ross-on-Wye** 20, nearby **Goodrich** 21, dramatically poised over the River Wye, and the beauty spot of **Symond's Yat** 22.

IF YOU HAVE 7 DAYS

Devote at least a day to **Birmingham** 1–13, and don't miss the Barber Institute of Fine Arts and the Birmingham Museum and Art Gallery. After an overnight stay, head south to Worcester and the Malvern Hills. You could take a lunch break at the generously timbered village of **Ledbury** 18 before continuing on toward the Wye Valley, where the nearby ruins of the castle at **Goodrich** 21 and **Symond's Yat** 22 provide good excuses to stretch your legs. A night in **Hereford** 24 will allow you to absorb the flavor of this old market town before heading up to **Ludlow** 41 for lunch and a couple of hours' ramble around the castle and its surrounding streets. Spend the next two nights in **Worcester** 14, taking in the Malverns and, to the north, the quiet riverside town of **Bewdley** 26, with its Georgian architecture. One of the main stops is **Bridgnorth** 39, occupying a ridge high above the Severn, and within a short distance of **Ironbridge Gorge** 38, the crucible of the Industrial Revolution. You can stay near Ironbridge or visit it on a day's excursion from **Shrewsbury** 29–35. Outside Shrewsbury lies **Attingham Park** 37, an 18th-century mansion. Your last overnight—entailing a journey northward—can be spent in **Chester** 41, famous for its black-and-white buildings.

8

ham has become something of a monument to late-20th-century civic architecture—for better or worse. Mercifully, creative redevelopment and public art are increasingly making areas more attractive. The redeveloped Bullring shopping center, part of which has a striking, curving facade of 15,000 aluminum disks, is one recent creation that has won praise.

Birmingham, with a metropolitan area population of 2.6 million, lies 25 mi north of Stratford and 120 mi northwest of London. "Brum," as it's known, is one of the country's most ethnically diverse urban areas, with nearly a third of its residents from minority groups. The city first flourished in the boom years of the 19th-century's Industrial Revolution. Its inventive, hardworking citizens accumulated enormous wealth, and at one time the city had some of the finest Victorian buildings in the country (it still has some of the most ravishingly beautiful Pre-Raphaelite paintings, on view in the Birmingham Museum and Art Gallery). The surviving architectural treasures can be best reached on foot or by public transportation; it's advisable to avoid negotiating the city's convoluted road network. ■ TIP➜ **If you are driving, don't be surprised that Birmingham's inner ring road twists right through the city center.**

Exploring Birmingham

Allow a full day to visit all the sights, which gives you time to linger in the Jewellery Quarter and browse the art museums. Much of Birmingham is now pedestrian-friendly, the downtown shopping area transformed into arcades and buses-only streets. You can also explore restored canals and canal towpaths. Most of the central sights, which are well signposted, form a tight-knit group. The tourist information center, the best place to pick up a map, is close both to public bus and rail stations. Its leaflet on a Tolkien Trail details six sites in or near the city that are linked to the writer J. R. R. Tolkien, who spent 16 of his early years in and around Birmingham. You can reach the Jewellery Quarter (note that the shops here are closed on Sunday) by public transport, which is the best means for arriving at the Barber Institute and Cadbury World sites away from the center.

Main Attractions

OFF THE
BEATEN
PATH

AVONCROFT MUSEUM OF HISTORIC BUILDINGS – You can see the architecture typical of the Midlands in microcosm at this 15-acre open-air museum, which has rescued more than 25 structures from destruction. Alongside the half-timber buildings are Victorian chimneys, a collection of phone boxes, a three-seater earth closet (lavatory), and a working windmill. Avoncroft is 17 mi southwest of Birmingham. ■ TIP➜ **School groups usually arrive at the museum in the morning, making afternoons a less crowded time to visit. Wear sensible shoes.** ✉ *Stokeheath, Bromsgrove* ☎ *01527/831363* ⊕ *www.avoncroft.org.uk* ✉ *£6* ☽ *Mar., Tues.–Thurs. and weekends 10:30–4; Apr.–June, Tues.–Fri. 10:30–4:30, weekends 10:30–5; July and Aug., daily 10:30–5; Sept. and Oct., Tues.–Sun. 10:30–4; Nov., weekends 10:30–4.*

★ ❾ **Barber Institute of Fine Art.** Part of the University of Birmingham, the museum has a small but astounding collection of European paintings,

TOP REASONS TO GO

The city of Birmingham: The revamped city center shows off its superb art collections, international cuisine, and renowned Jewellery Quarter amid its full-bodied redbrick architecture, a link to its industrial heritage.

Ludlow in Shropshire: Taste the border country at every turn in the fine restaurants of this small but spirited market town, which holds quality food in high regard.

Half-timber architecture: Black-and-white, half-timber houses are a mark of pride throughout the region; there are concentrations of

buildings from medieval times to the Jacobean era in Chester, Shrewsbury, and Ludlow.

Walking on the Malverns: Take inspiration as composer Elgar did, as you stride across these hills and look across the fields and orchards to the Cotswolds in the east and misty Welsh mountains to the west.

Ironbridge Gorge: Recall the burgeoning of England's Industrial Revolution at the complex of museums within the shadow of this graceful bridge, the first of its kind in the world.

prints, drawings, and sculpture, including works by Bellini, Canaletto, Poussin, Gainsborough, Turner, Whistler, Renoir, Monet, and van Gogh. To get here, take Cross City Line train from New Street Station south to University Station, or Bus 61, 62, or 63 from the city center. ⊠ *Off Edgbaston Park Rd. near East Gate, Edgbaston* ☎ *0121/414–7333* ⊕ *www.barber.org.uk* ⊠ *Free* ☉ *Mon.–Sat. 10–5, Sun. noon–5.*

Birmingham Back to Backs. Of the 20,000 courts of back-to-back houses (constructed around a courtyard and thus backing onto each other) built in the 19th century for the city's expanding working-class population, this is the only survivor. Three houses tell the stories of families, headed by a watchmaker, a locksmith, and a glassworker, who lived here between the 1840s and the 1930s. A few rooms are available for overnight stays. Admission is by timed ticket, booked in advance; allow one hour for the tour and be prepared for steep stairs. The houses are closed the Tuesday following a national holiday. ⊠ *Hurst St., City Centre* ☎ *0121/666-7671* ⊕ *www.nationaltrust.co.uk* ⊠ *£4* ☉ *Tues.–Sun. and national holidays 10–5.*

❼ FodorśChoice ★ **Birmingham Museum and Art Gallery.** Vast and impressive, this museum holds a magnificent collection of Victorian art and is known internationally for its works by the Pre-Raphaelites. All the big names are here, including William Holman Hunt, John Everett Millais, and Dante Gabriel Rossetti—reflecting the enormous wealth of 19th-century Birmingham and the aesthetic taste of its industrialists. Galleries of metalwork, silver, and ceramics also reveal some of the city's history, and selections of contemporary art are displayed. ⊠ *Chamberlain Sq., City Centre* ☎ *0121/303–2834* ⊕ *www.bmag.org.uk* ⊠ *Free* ☉ *Mon.–Thurs. and Sat. 10–5, Fri. 10:30–5, Sun. 12:30–5.*

8

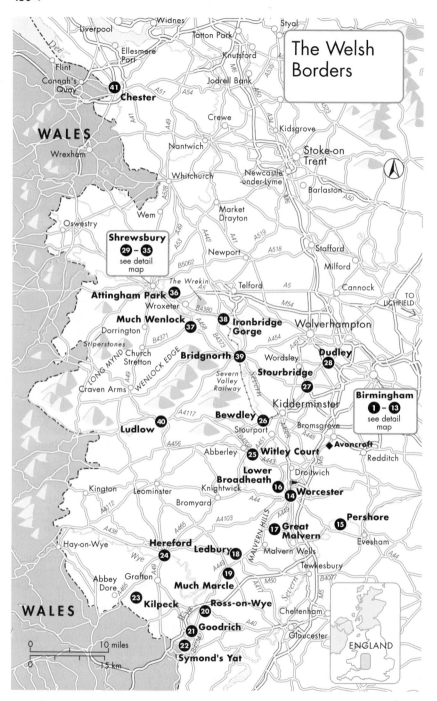

The Welsh Borders

The Venice of the North

CLOSE UP

IT MAY COME AS A SURPRISE that Birmingham has more canals in its center than Venice: its eight canals make up 34 mi of waterways. The city is at the heart of a system of waterways built during the Industrial Revolution to connect inland factories to rivers and seaports—by 1840 the canals extended more than 4,000 mi throughout the British Isles. These canals, which carried 9 million tons of cargo a year in the late 19th century and helped make the city an industrial powerhouse, have undergone extensive cleanup and renovation, and are now a tourist attraction in their own right.

A walk along the Birmingham Canal Main Line near the Gas Street Basin will bring you to modern developments such as Brindleyplace and to pubs, shops, and cafés, and you can see the city from an attractive new perspective. Contact any city tourist office for maps of pleasant walks along the towpaths and for details about canal cruises on colorfully painted barges.

❹ **Centenary Square.** Just outside the International Convention Centre and near the Birmingham Repertory Theatre and Symphony Hall, the square is at the heart of the city's cultural life. Pavement bricks of different shades form a pattern like a Persian carpet. The creamy sculpture in the center of the square, *Forward,* shows a group of people (and a factory) and represents the city's progressive outlook. The octagonal war memorial, the **Hall of Memory** was built in the neoclassical style of the 1920s. It honors the dead of World Wars I and II.

NEED A BREAK? The balcony of the redbrick **Malt House** (✉ 75 King Edward's Rd. ☎ 0121/633–4171) is just the place to linger over a drink as you watch canal life go by. Former president Bill Clinton had a beer here during the G8 Summit in 1998.

❺ **Jewellery Quarter.** For more than two centuries, jewelers have worked in the district of Hockley, northwest of the city center; today around 200 manufacturing jewelers continue the tradition, producing a third of the jewelry made in Britain. ■ TIP➔ **The Jewellery Quarter is a great place to shop for jewelry, too. The free booklet *The Jewellery Quarter in Birmingham,* from the tourist office or library, will give you the lowdown on all the history and the shops, as well as a history of the area.** The city has its own Assay Office, which hallmarks 13 million items each year with the anchor symbol denoting Birmingham origin. The ornate green and gilded Chamberlain Clock, at the intersection of Vyse Street, Warstone Lane, and Frederick Street, marks the center of the district. ✉ *Hockley* ⊕ *www.the-quarter.com.*

OFF THE BEATEN PATH **LICHFIELD CATHEDRAL** – It's worth a detour (14 mi northeast of Birmingham on A38) to explore the only English cathedral with three spires. The sandstone building, beautifully sited by a tree-fringed pool, dates mainly from the 12th and 13th centuries, and the Lady Chapel glows with some fine 16th-century stained glass from the Cistercian abbey of

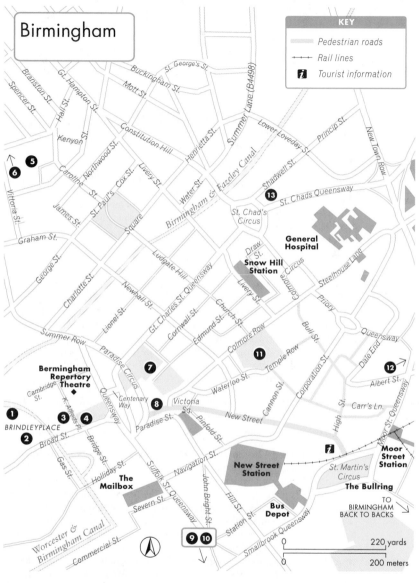

Birmingham

Barber Institute of
Fine Arts 9

Birmingham Cathedral
(St. Philip's) 11

Birmingham Museum
and Art Gallery 7

Cadbury World 10

Centenary Square 4

Ikon Gallery 2

Jewellery Quarter 5

Museum of the
Jewellery Quarter 6

National
Sea Life Centre 1

St. Chad's Roman
Catholic Cathedral 13

Symphony Hall 3

Thinktank 12

Town Hall 8

Herkenrode, near Liège, in Belgium. Half-timber houses surround the peaceful grounds, and the town itself has attractive Georgian buildings as well as the birthplace (now a museum) of lexicographer Dr. Samuel Johnson. ⊠ *19A The Close, Lichfield* ☎ *01543/306100* ⊕ *www. lichfield-cathedral.org* ✉ *Suggested donation £3* ⊗ *Daily 7:30–6:15; closes Sun. at 5 in winter.*

❻ Museum of the Jewellery Quarter. The museum is built around the workshops of Smith & Pepper, a firm that operated here for more than 80 years until 1981; little has changed since the early 1900s. The factory tour and exhibits explain the history of the neighborhood and the jeweler's craft, and you can watch jewelry being made. ⊠ *75–79 Vyse St., Hockley* ☎ *0121/554–3598* ⊕ *www.bmag.org.uk* ✉ *Free* ⊗ *Easter–Oct., Tues.–Sun. and national holidays 11:30–4; Nov.–Easter, Tues.–Sat. 11.30–4; last admission 1 hr before closing.*

❤ ⓬ Thinktank. This interactive museum in the state-of-the-art Millennium Point center allows you to explore science and the history of Birmingham over four floors of galleries. You can walk into the giant boiler of a steam engine, explore deep space, program a robot to play the drums, and perform a hip operation. The IMAX cinema and planetarium put on shows throughout the day. The museum is a 10-minute walk from Moor Street railway station. ⊠ *Curzon St., Digbeth* ☎ *0121/202–2222* ⊕ *www.thinktank.ac* ✉ *£6.95; IMAX cinema £6.50, planetarium £1* ⊗ *Daily 10–5; last admission at 4.*

Also Worth Seeing

⓫ Birmingham Cathedral. The early-18th-century cathedral of St. Philip, a few blocks from Victoria Square, contains some lovely plasterwork in its elegant, gilded Georgian interior. The stained-glass windows behind the altar, designed by the Pre-Raphaelite Edward Burne-Jones (1833–98) and executed by William Morris (1834–96), glow with a garnet hue. ⊠ *Colmore Row, City Centre* ☎ *0121/262–1840* ⊕ *www. birminghamcathedral.com* ✉ *Donation suggested* ⊗ *Daily 8:30–5.*

❿ Cadbury World. The village of Bournville (4 mi south of the city center) contains this museum devoted to—what else?—chocolate. In 1879 the Quaker Cadbury brothers moved the family business to this "factory in a garden" from the less than healthy conditions of the city; they also constructed a model village for workers. The museum traces the history of the cocoa bean and the Cadbury dynasty, and you walk through a replica rain forest. You can watch (and smell) specialties being made in the factory, enjoy free samples, and then stock up from the cut-price shop. The restaurant has specialty chocolate cakes as well as lunches. ⊠ *Off A38 (take train from New St. to Bournville Train Station), Bournville* ☎ *0121/451–4180* ⊕ *www.cadburyworld.co.uk* ✉ *£12.50* ⊗ *Feb.–Oct., daily; late Jan., Nov. and Dec., Tues.–Thurs. and weekends; times vary; reservations advised, and essential at busy times.*

❷ Ikon Gallery. This gallery, converted from a Victorian Gothic–style school, serves as the city's main venue for exhibitions of contemporary art from Britain and abroad. The bright, white interior is divided into comparatively small display areas, making the shows easily digestible.

8

If you need fortifying, however, try the attached tapas bar. ☒ *1 Oozells Sq., Brindleyplace, City Centre* ☎ *0121/248–0708* ⊕ *www.ikon-gallery. co.uk* ☜ *Free* ⊙ *Tues.–Sun. and national holiday Mon. 11–6.*

⊕ ❶ **National Sea Life Centre.** As far from the sea as you can get in Britain, this imaginatively landscaped aquarium allows a glimpse into Davey Jones's locker. An underwater tunnel lets you view sharks and stingrays up close, and there are displays of oceanic, tropical, rain forest, and freshwater marine life. Children will gravitate to the touch pools and other interactive activities. ☒ *The Water's Edge, Brindleyplace, City Centre* ☎ *0121/643–6777* ⊕ *www.sealifeeurope.com* ☜ *£11.50* ⊙ *Mid-Feb.–Oct., daily 10–5; Nov.–mid-Feb., weekdays 10–4, weekends 10–5.*

⓭ **St. Chad's Roman Catholic Cathedral.** Dating from 1841, this redbrick pile was the first Roman Catholic cathedral to be built in England after the Reformation. A. W. N. Pugin, leading architect of the Gothic Revival, designed St. Chad's, which basically consists of one lofty room—the nave—divided by soaring slender pillars and decorated in red, blue, and gold. Many furnishings are 15th century. ☒ *Queensway, City Centre* ☎ *0121/230–6208* ☜ *Free* ⊙ *Daily 8–6:30.*

❸ **Symphony Hall.** The internationally recognized City of Birmingham Symphony Orchestra won awards for its recordings under its former conductor, Sir Simon Rattle (who occasionally guest conducts). Symphony Hall occupies the same building as the International Convention Centre; as long as there is no rehearsal in progress, you can view its plush wooden and chrome interior. ☒ *Broad St., City Centre* ☎ *0121/780–3333* ⊕ *www.symphonyhall.co.uk.*

❽ **Town Hall.** Classical columns surround this mid-19th-century performance hall, a copy of the Temple of Castor and Pollux in Rome. The former home of the symphony orchestra heard the premieres of Mendelssohn's *Elijah* and Elgar's *Dream of Gerontius.* The hall is due to reopen in fall 2007 after a lengthy refurbishment. Locals have affectionately dubbed the statue of a woman in the fountain outside the building "the floozie in the Jacuzzi." ☒ *Victoria Sq., City Centre.*

Where to Eat

★ **£££££** ✕ **Paris.** Star chef Patrick McDonald has created an enclave of sophistication in the trendy Mailbox shopping center. Chocolate-color walls, oil paintings, and slinky leather chairs complement superb French-influenced food. Dishes such as roast quail salad with walnut vinaigrette, followed by loin of veal and truffled potatoes, and desserts such as prune-and-Armagnac soufflé, do not disappoint. The gourmand menu is £55. Reservations are essential on weekends. ☒ *The Mailbox, 109–111 Wharfside St., City Centre* ☎ *0121/632–1488* ▭ *AE, MC, V* ⊙ *Closed Sun. and Mon., and 2 wks in Aug.*

★ **£££££** ✕ **Simpsons.** The L-shape conservatory, which favors either the bustling kitchen activity or the peace of the garden, wraps around the inner dining space of this elegant and gleaming Georgian villa. The neutral decor, and assured and welcoming service give the senses leave to indulge house specialties, for example sea bream with citrus fruits and Aberdeenshire beef with haggis and snails. There are four luxurious theme guest rooms for those who wish to stray no further, and a cooking school. It's is a mile south of the city center. ⊠ *20 Highfield Rd., Edgbaston* ☎ *0121/454–3434* 🖃 *AE, MC, V* ⊗ *No dinner Sun.*

££–£££ ✕ **Brass House.** The city's first foundry is now a useful central place for full meals or bar snacks. Look for such traditional favorites as steak, roast ham and parsley sauce, and even the humble "chip buttie" (a sandwich filled with french fries). The pastel, marbled glass lights on the bar are an attraction in their own right. ⊠ *44 Broad St., City Centre* ☎ *0121/633–3383* 🖃 *AE, MC, V.*

££–£££ ✕ **Café Lazeez.** This spacious, warmly decorated new-wave Indian restaurant in a shopping center blends the traditional with the contemporary taste for lighter, less oily dishes. Try the Peshawari naan bread as an accompaniment to prawns with saffron rice and banana wafers or herbed breast of chicken. ⊠ *The Mailbox, 116 Wharfside St., City Centre* ☎ *0121/643–7979* 🖃 *AE, MC, V.*

★ **££–£££** ✕ **Le Petit Blanc.** An outpost of noted chef Raymond Blanc (of Le Manoir aux Quat' Saisons, near Oxford), this brasserie provides a contemporary showcase of gleaming metal, light wood, and plate glass for the excellent regional French menu. The deep-fried goat's cheese with tomato chutney is one of the fine starters; you might follow up with grilled sea trout with herb puree. ⊠ *9 Brindley Pl., City Centre* ☎ *0121/633–7333* 🖃 *AE, MC, V.*

££–£££ ✕ **Shimla Pinks.** Birmingham has some of Britain's finest Indian restaurants, and this is one upbeat choice—the name refers to the "bright young things" of India's upper classes. Both the decoration and the cooking are a mix of modern and traditional, and waiters are elegantly turbaned. Try the Assamese *jalfrezi*, pieces of meat with coriander leaves and red peppers, or *rogan josh* made from fresh tomatoes, paprika, and chili. ⊠ *214 Broad St., City Centre* ☎ *0121/633–0366* 🖃 *AE, MC, V.*

££ ✕ **Henry's.** This popular, traditional Cantonese restaurant on the edge of the Jewellery Quarter is a haven for lunch during a shopping spree. The menu lists more than 180 dishes; there's also a good-value fixed-price menu and a Sunday buffet. ⊠ *27 St. Paul's Sq., City Centre* ☎ *0121/200–1136* 🖃 *AE, MC, V.*

££ ✕ **Thai Edge.** The elegant, contemporary Asian design will draw you into this restaurant. Dishes such as *gang keow waan* (green curry cooked in coconut milk with eggplant, lime leaves, and basil) are excellent. You

---

DISCOVER BALTI

Birmingham is home to the Balti, a popular type of cuisine invented here in the mid-1970s by the Pakistani community. The name derives from an Urdu word meaning a large bucket, although the food is cooked and brought to the table in a small wok-like dish and eaten with naan bread, not rice. Curry and other spices season the meat and vegetables. The more than 30 restaurants in the "Balti Triangle" of the Moseley and Sparkbrook districts include **Punjab Paradise**, (⊠ 377 Ladypool Rd. ☎ 0121/499–4110) and **Royal Al Faisals**, (⊠ 136-40 Stoney La. ☎ 0121/449–5695).

8

can eat all you want for £13 at the Sunday lunch buffet. ⊠ *7 Oozells Sq., City Centre* ☎ *0121/643–3993* ☰ *AE, DC, MC, V.*

Where to Stay

££££–£££££ 🏨 **Macdonald Burlington Hotel.** Wood paneling, marble, and classical columns abound at this traditional hotel, and rooms are decorated with conservative dark woods and print fabrics or in a modern, minimalist style. At the sumptuous Berlioz restaurant, English dishes such as fillet steak with tomatoes and mushrooms share menu space with classic French-influenced dishes. On weekends, a full breakfast is included. ⊠ *Burlington Arcade, 126 New St., City Centre, B2 4JQ* ☎ *0121/643–9191* 🖨*0121/628–5005* ⊕ *www.burlingtonhotel.com* ➵ *112 rooms* ⌂ *Restaurant, cable TV with movies, in-room broadband, in-room data ports, gym, sauna, business services, meeting rooms, parking (fee), some pets allowed (fee); no a/c* ☰ *AE, DC, MC, V* ⍮ *BP.*

★ 🏨 **New Hall.** A tree-lined drive leads through 26 acres of gardens and
££££–£££££ open land to this moated, 12th-century manor-house-turned-country-hotel. The public rooms reflect the house's long history with touches such as the 16th-century oak paneling and Flemish glass, 18th-century chandeliers, and a stone fireplace from the 17th century. Guest rooms, most in a more modern section, are done in English country style with print fabrics and marble-tile baths. Both the formal Bridge restaurant and the more relaxed Terrace Room serve sophisticated English and French cuisine. The hotel is 7 mi northeast of the city center. ⊠ *Walmley Rd., Sutton Coldfield, Birmingham B76 1QX* ☎ *0870/333–9147* 🖨 *0870/ 333–9247* ⊕ *www.newhalluk.com* ➵ *60 rooms* ⌂ *Restaurant, cable TV with movies, Wi-Fi, 9-hole golf course, tennis court, pool, gym, hot tub, sauna, spa, croquet, bar, meeting rooms, free parking, some pets allowed; no a/c in some rooms* ☰ *AE, MC, V* ⍮ *BP.*

££££ 🏨 **Hotel du Vin & Bistro.** A Victorian eye hospital in the city center received a makeover from this *très* hip mini-chain but retains details such as the ironwork double stairway and marble columns. Beyond the imposing redbrick exterior is an inner courtyard with a fountain and garden. Bedrooms are sleek and contemporary, with huge, fluffy towels and white linens. The bistro is redolent of fin-de-siècle Paris, and in the Bubble Lounge you can indulge in more than 50 varieties of champagne. ⊠ *25 Church St., City Centre, B3 2NR* ☎ *0121/200–0600* 🖨 *0121/236– 0889* ⊕ *www.hotelduvin.com* ➵ *56 rooms, 10 suites* ⌂ *Restaurant, cable TV, in-room data ports, Wi-Fi, gym, sauna, spa, steam room, bar, meeting rooms, parking (fee); no a/c* ☰ *AE, DC, MC, V.*

£££–££££ 🏨 **Malmaison.** Retail therapy is on your doorstep at this chic, up-to-the-minute hotel in the Mailbox shopping center. Floor-to-ceiling windows light the large and airy guest rooms by day, and there's subtle lighting by night. Furnishings are smoothly modern, in rich but muted colors; bathrooms indulge you with tailor-made toiletries and soothing showers. A plush red carpet winds upstairs to the upbeat Brasserie, which concentrates on French cuisine. ⊠ *1 Wharfside St., City Centre, B1 1RD* ☎ *0121/246–5000* 🖨 *0121/246–5002* ⊕ *www.malmaison.com* ➵ *189 rooms, 10 suites* ⌂ *Restaurant, cable TV with movies, in-room broad-*

band, in-room data ports, Wi-Fi, gym, sauna, spa, steam room, meeting rooms, parking (fee) ☰ *AE, DC, MC, V.*

££–££££ ▦ **City Inn.** This bustling hotel in the canalside piazza, near the waterside nightlife scene, represents an excellent value. The crisp, modern bedrooms and bathrooms, though on the small side, are beautifully equipped and furnished in calming, neutral tones. Floors 6 and 7 have the best views. Breakfast is included in the price on weekends. ⊠ *1 Brunswick Sq., Brindleyplace, City Centre, B1 2HW* ☎ *0121/643–1003* 📠 *0121/643–1005* ⊕ *www.cityinn.com* ⬎ *238 rooms* ⅃ *Restaurant, cable TV with movies, in-room broadband, in-room data ports, gym, meeting rooms, parking (fee)* ☰ *AE, DC, MC, V.*

££–£££ ▦ **Copperfield House Hotel.** In a quiet location a few minutes' drive from Cadbury World, this family-run hotel, a converted Victorian house with secluded lawns and simple guest rooms, is nevertheless convenient to the bustle of the city center 2 mi away. The restaurant (open weekdays only) serves good English cooking, including delicious desserts. ⊠ *60 Upland Rd., Selly Park, Birmingham B29 7JS* ☎ *0121/472–8344* 📠 *0121/415–5655* ⊕ *www.copperfieldhousehotel.fsnet.co.uk* ⬎ *17 rooms* ⅃ *Restaurant, bar, free parking, some pets allowed (fee); no a/c* ☰ *AE, MC, V* ⎰⎱ *BP.*

£–££ ▦ **Fountain Court.** A five-minute drive from the city center, this cheerful family-run hotel is in a leafy, well-heeled neighborhood. Bedrooms are modern and bright, and the more traditional public rooms have darkwood furniture. ⊠ *339–343 Hagley Rd., Edgbaston, B17 8NH* ☎ *0121/429–1754* 📠 *0121/429–1209* ⊕ *www.fountain-court.net* ⬎ *23 rooms* ⅃ *Restaurant, bar; no a/c* ☰ *AE, MC, V* ⎰⎱ *BP.*

Nightlife & the Arts

Nightlife

The city's thriving nightlife scene is concentrated around Broad and Hurst streets, as well as the Brindleyplace and Mailbox areas. **Bar Epernay** (⊠ 171 Wharfside St., City Centre ☎ 0121/632–1430), a Champagne bar and brasserie in the Mailbox, has a revolving piano and central, warming brazier, making it perfect for relaxing after a day's sightseeing. **Mechu** (⊠ 59 Summer Row, City Centre ☎ 0121/212–1661), a chic drinking, dining, and dancing venue, has a roof garden. The spacious and high-dome **Old Joint Stock** (⊠ 4 Temple Row West, off Colmore Row, City Centre ☎ 0121/200–1892) serves good ales and pies. At **52° North** (⊠ Arcadian, Hurst St., City Centre ☎ 0121/622–5250), the bar specializes in classic and contemporary cocktails and mixes 14 types of martinis.

The Arts

Birmingham's performing arts companies are well regarded throughout the country. Catch a performance if you can.

BALLET The **Birmingham Royal Ballet** (⊠ Hurst St., City Centre ☎ 0870/730–1234), the second company of the Royal Ballet, is based at the Hippodrome Theatre, which also hosts visiting companies such as the Welsh National Opera.

CONCERTS
★

The distinguished **City of Birmingham Symphony Orchestra** (✉ International Convention Centre, Broad St., City Centre ☏ 0121/780–3333) performs regularly in Symphony Hall, also a venue for visiting artists.

The **City of National Exhibition Centre** (✉ M42, Junction 6, close to airport ☏ 0870/909–4133) hosts top names in rock and pop.

THEATER

The **Alexandra Theatre** (✉ Station St., City Centre ☏ 0870/607–7533) welcomes touring companies on their way to or from London's West End. The **Birmingham Repertory Theatre** (✉ Centenary Sq., Broad St., City Centre ☏ 0121/236–4455), founded in 1913, is equally at home with modern or classical work as one of England's oldest and most esteemed theater companies. The sweeping windows of the excellent cafeteria-restaurant in its foyer allow a great view over Centenary Square.

Sports & the Outdoors

Boating

Birmingham's canals provide a novel perspective on the city. You can take an hour ride on a canal barge from **Sherborne Wharf** (✉ Sherborne St., City Centre ☏ 0121/455–6163). Trips leave daily mid-April through October at 11:30, 1, 2:30, and 4, and on weekends the rest of the year, departing from the International Convention Centre Quayside.

Cricket

To watch first-class cricket at one of the country's most hallowed venues, head for **Warwickshire County Cricket Club** (✉ County Ground, Edgbaston ☏ 0870/062–1902). Tickets for test matches sell out months ahead, but those at county level are not so sought after.

Shopping

★

The glass-roof **Bullring** (✉ Between New St. and High St., City Centre ☏ 0121/632–1500) has three floors of retail enticement, including two department stores, Debenhams and the stunningly curved Selfridges, which is covered with aluminum disks. The development has been seen as another step in the city's regeneration. The **Jewellery Quarter** (✉ Hockley ☏ 0121/554–3598) has more than 100 shops that sell and repair gold and silver handcrafted jewelry, clocks, and watches. The Museum of the Jewellery Quarter sells a selection of contemporary work and provides information on artisans and retail outlets. **The Mailbox** (✉ 150 Wharfside St., City Centre ☏ 0121/632–1000), once a Royal Mail sorting office, entices with trendy shops and designer outlets such as Harvey Nichols and Armani, restaurants, and hotels.

FROM WORCESTER TO DUDLEY

In the arc of towns to the west of Birmingham and the cluster of places around the banks of the River Wye, history and tradition rub up against deepest rural England. The cathedral towns of Worcester and Hereford make great bases from which to soak up the bucolic flavor of the Malverns and Elgar country, or to view the spectacular swing of the Wye at Symond's Yat. En route, there's a taste of Georgian architecture at

Pershore and Bewdley, and reminders of the old industrial Midlands at Stourbridge and Dudley.

Worcester

⓮ *27 mi southwest of Birmingham, 118 mi northwest of London.*

Worcester (pronounced *wuss*-ter), on the River Severn in the center of Worcestershire, is an ancient cathedral city proud of its history, and in particular, of its nickname, "the Faithful City," bestowed on the town for steadfast allegiance to the crown during the English Civil War. In that conflict between king and Parliament, two major battles were waged here. The second one, the decisive Battle of Worcester of 1651, resulted in the exile of the future Charles II. Since the mid-18th century the town's name has become synonymous with the fine bone china produced here. Despite unfortunate modernization in the 1960s, some of medieval Worcester remains. This ancient section forms a convenient and pleasant walking route around the great cathedral. Worcester's mainly pedestrianized High Street runs through the center of town, from the cathedral to Foregate Street train station.

★ There are few more quintessentially English sights than that of **Worcester Cathedral,** its towers overlooking the green expanse of the county cricket ground, and its majestic image reflected in the swift-flowing—and frequently flooding—waters of the River Severn. A cathedral has stood on this site since 680, and much of what remains dates from the 13th and 14th centuries. Notable exceptions are the Norman crypt (built in the 1080s), the largest in England, and the ambulatory, a cloister built around the east end. The most important tomb in the cathedral is that of King John (1167–1216), one of the country's least-admired monarchs, who alienated his barons and subjects through bad administration and heavy taxation and in 1215 was forced to sign the Magna Carta, the great charter of liberty. The cathedral's most beautiful decoration is in the vaulted **chantry chapel of Prince Arthur,** Henry VII's elder son, whose body was brought to Worcester after his death at Ludlow in 1502. The wealthy endowed chantry chapels to enable priests to celebrate masses there for the souls of the deceased. ⊠ *College Yard at High St.* ☎ *01905/28854* ⊕ *www.cofe-worcester.org.uk* ✉ *Suggested donation £3* ⊙ *Daily 8–6.*

At the **Royal Worcester Porcelain Factory,** you can browse in the showrooms or rummage in the seconds and clearance shops; the January and July sales have especially good bargains. Tours of the factory take you to see artists at work (weekdays only) in the painting room. The **Museum of Worcester Porcelain** displays the world's largest collection of Worcester porcelain, bone china, and earthenware, representing work from the start of manufacturing in 1751 to the present. The factory lies south of Worcester Cathedral (follow Severn Street). ⊠ *Severn St.* ☎ *01905/746000* ⊕ *www.royal-worcester.co.uk* ✉ *Visitor center and 1-hr tour of factory £5; museum £5, museum, tour and visitor center £9* ⊙ *Mon.–Sat. 10–5:30, Sun. 11–5; tours weekdays 9–5.*

8

An enthralling museum focusing on the Civil War, the **Commandery** occupies a cluster of 15th-century half-timber buildings that were built as a poorhouse and later became the headquarters of the Royalist troops during the Battle of Worcester. It's closed until April 2007; call ahead. When the museum is open, an audio guide tells the story of the building, including its magnificent, oak-beam Great Hall. The Commandery is across the road from the porcelain factory, minutes from the cathedral. ⊠ *Sidbury* ☎ *01905/361821* ⊕ *www. worcestercitymuseums.org.uk.*

The wood-panel rooms in the black-and-white **Greyfriars** building, a merchant's house that dates to the 15th century, contain fine period textiles and furniture. The parlor has some rare Georgian hunting wallpaper. Admission is by timed ticket. ⊠ *Friar St.* ☎ *01905/23571* ⊕ *www. nationaltrust.org.uk* 🎟 *£3.60* ⊗ *Mar.–June and Sept.–mid-Dec., Wed.–Sat. 1–5; July and Aug., Wed.–Sun. 1–5.*

Also the location of the tourist information office, the **Guildhall**, set back behind ornate iron railings, has an 18th-century facade with gilded statues of Queen Anne, Charles I, and Charles II. Note the carving of Cromwell's head pinned up by the ears. In the Assembly Room, impressive patrician portraits hang under a painted ceiling; you can admire them while having tea and buns. ⊠ *High St.* ☎ *01905/723471* 🎟 *Free* ⊗ *Weekdays 8:30–4:30, Sat. 8:30–4.*

Where to Stay & Eat

★ **£££££** ✕ **Brown's.** A former grain mill contains this light, airy riverside restaurant. The fixed-price menu and daily specialties revolve around varied, well-prepared modern English dishes. You might start with scallops with cauliflower and cardamom puree, continue with slow braised beef with beet and horseradish relish, finishing up with a creme brulée with hazelnut shortbread. ⊠ *24 Quay St.* ☎ *01905/26263* ▤ *AE, MC, V* ⊗ *Closed Mon. No lunch Sat., no dinner Sun.*

£££–££££ ✕ **King Charles II Restaurant.** A half-timber house in which Charles II hid after the Battle of Worcester is now an oak-panel, silver-service restaurant that exudes friendliness. The cuisine is mainly French and Italian, but traditional English selections such as beef Wellington and fish dishes including Dover sole meunière also appear on the menu. ⊠ *29 New St.* ☎ *01905/22449* ▤ *AE, MC, V* ⊗ *Closed Sun.*

£££–££££ ▦ **Diglis House Hotel.** English artist John Constable was a frequent visitor to this idyllically sited 18th-century house overlooking terraced gardens and the river. Service is discreet but friendly, and furnishings are uncluttered and elegant. Choose between views over the garden or river when you dine. ⊠ *Severn St., WR1 2NF* ☎ *01905/353518* 🖷 *01905/ 767772* ⊕ *www.diglishousehotel.co.uk* ⇆ *29 rooms* ⇩ *2 restaurants, bar, Wi-Fi, meeting rooms; no a/c* ▤ *AE, MC, V* ¡◎¡ *BP.*

££ ▦ **Ye Olde Talbot Hotel.** The Olde Talbot was originally a courtroom belonging to the cathedral, which stands close by. Modern extensions supplement the 16th-century core of the building. The spacious bedrooms have double-glaze windows and are done in cream, blue, and burgundy tones with patterned fabrics. Be sure to try a cask ale in the Victorian bar. ✉ *Friar St., WR1 2NA* ☎ *01905/23573* 🖨 *01905/612760* ⊕ *www. yeoldetalbot.com* ⇱ *28 rooms* ⌂ *Restaurant, cable TV, some in-room DVDs, bar, parking (fee); no a/c* ▭ *AE, DC, MC, V* ⍾ *BP.*

Nightlife & the Arts

Huntingdon Hall (✉ Crowngate ☎ 01905/611427), a refurbished Methodist chapel founded in 1773, puts on a varied program of music, interspersed with some theater and dance. The original pews are—thankfully—provided with cushions.

Sports & the Outdoors

You can have a day at the races at **Worcester Racecourse** (✉ Pitchcroft ☎ 0870/220–2772), attractively set on the banks of the River Severn. Admission prices start at £6.

Shopping

★ **Bygones** (✉ 3 College Precincts ☎ 01905/23132) sells antiques, finely crafted items, and small gifts in silver, glass, and porcelain. **G. R. Pratley** (✉ The Shambles ☎ 01905/22678) has tables piled high with fine china, such as Royal Worcester, Wedgwood, and Spode; it's closed Thursday afternoon. The **Royal Worcester Porcelain Factory** (✉ Severn St. ☎ 01905/746000) attracts crowds to its shop, which sells seconds along with other merchandise. It's open daily.

Pershore

⓯ *8 mi southeast of Worcester.*

Peaceful and unspoiled, the market town of Pershore is in the fruitful Vale of Evesham. This is plum and asparagus country; trees are loaded down with blossoms in spring, and May sees the asparagus harvest. Georgian buildings with elegant facades flank the town's wide streets.

The nave of **Pershore Abbey** did not survive the dissolution of the monasteries, but the beautiful chancel and crossing have been preserved. The choir has a rare plowshare vault (so called because the curved panels resemble the blade of a plowshare) with soaring ribs that culminate in 41 carved bosses; no two are the same. Architect George Gilbert Scott opened up the fine lantern tower in the 1860s to reveal the internal tracery. He replaced the old bell-ringing chamber with a suspended platform that seems to float in space. ✉ *Church Row* ☎ *01386/552071* ⊕ *www. pershoreabbey.fsnet.co.uk* ⍰ *Suggested donation £2* ☼ *Apr.–Oct., Mon.–Sat. 9–5, Sun., 9–4; Nov.–Mar., daily 9–4.*

Where to Stay

££££ ⍟ **Evesham Hotel.** Definitely family-centered and upbeat, this modernized Georgian house-turned-lodging stocks an abundance of toys, games, and teddy bears for all ages; there's even a rubber duck in the bathrooms. For more sophistication, opt for one of the four theme rooms: the Aquarium, for example, has its own fish tank, and the Egyptian room sarcophagi and an impressive bed. The 2 acres of gardens make a peaceful refuge, though the hotel is close to town. Evesham is 6 mi southeast of Pershore. ✉ *Cooper's La., off Waterside, Evesham WR11 1DA*

8

☎ *01386/765566* 📠 *01386/765443* ⊕ *www.eveshamhotel.com* ⇲ *40 rooms* ⌂ *Restaurant, Wi-Fi in some rooms, indoor pool, bar, meeting rooms, some pets allowed; no a/c* ⊟ *AE, DC, MC, V* ⦶ *BP.*

Lower Broadheath

16 *10 mi northwest of Pershore, 2 mi west of Worcester.*

Southwest of Worcester lie the Malvern Hills, their long, low, purple profiles rising starkly from the surrounding plain. These hills inspired much of the music of Sir Edward Elgar (1857–1934), as well as his remark that "there is music in the air, music all around us." The village of Lower Broadheath is on B4204.

The **Elgar Birthplace Museum,** in a peaceful little garden, is the tiny brick cottage in which the composer was born. The house contains personal memorabilia, and the Elgar Centre exhibits photographs, musical scores, and letters. ⊠ *Crown East La.* ☎ *01905/333224* ⊕ *www.elgar.org* 🎫 *£5* ⊙ *Feb.–Dec., daily 11–5; last admission 45 mins before closing.*

Great Malvern

17 *9 mi south of Lower Broadheath, 7 mi south of Worcester.*

Great Malvern, off the A449, is a Victorian spa town whose architecture has changed little since the mid-1800s. Great Malvern is known both as an educational center and as a place for old folks' homes. The town also has a Winter Gardens complex with a theater, cinema, and gardens. During three days in mid-June, the agricultural **Three Counties Show** (☎ 01684/584900 ⊕ www.threecounties.co.uk) showcases rare animal breeds, equestrian events, competitions for the best cows, pigs, and sheep, and plenty of food.

FAMOUS FOR NOTHING

"The Malvern water," says Dr John Wall, "is famous for containing nothing at all." So records an early account of 1756. The famously pure Malvern spring water is still bottled in the town and exported worldwide; it is said that the Queen never travels without it.

The **Priory,** a solidly built early-Norman Benedictine abbey with later Perpendicular elements, dominates the steep streets downtown. Vertical lines of airy tracery and fine 15th-century glass decorate the building. ⊠ *Entrance opposite church* ☎ *01684/561020* ⊕ *www.greatmalvernpriory.org.uk* 🎫 *Free* ⊙ *Daily 9–5.*

Where to Stay & Eat

£££–£££££ ✕🛏 **Cottage in the Wood.** This family-run hotel sits on shady grounds high up the side of the Malvern Hills, with splendid views of the countryside. Country-house furnishings in the three buildings include floral prints and white bedspreads; rooms with a view are equipped with binoculars. The mirrored restaurant (£££–££££), which has the best of the panorama, serves modern English fare such as Herefordshire beef fillet with a leek and oxtail tart. You can choose from more than 600

ON THE MENU

Outside Birmingham, this area is all rich farming country where, for centuries, the orchards have produced succulent fruit, especially apples and plums. Hereford cider, for example, is popular because it tastes much sweeter than the cider brewed farther south in Devon. The meat and milk products, which come from the local red-and-white Hereford breed of cattle, are second to none. Cheshire cheese, one of the country's oldest cheeses, is noted for its rich, crumbly texture;

blue-veined Shropshire cheese is more unusual and worth trying. In May the sheltered Vale of Evesham is the center for the asparagus crop. Ludlow produces a formidable assortment of local meat products and is noted for its sausages.

Despite the natural bounty, formal dining establishments are few and far between in this rural area, with the notable exception of Ludlow, which has a group of superb restaurants.

wines, among them many local vintages. ⊠ *Holywell Rd., WR14 4LG* ☎ *01684/575859* 🖷 *01684/560662* ⊕ *www.cottageinthewood.co.uk* 🗪 *20 rooms* ⌂ *Restaurant, some in-room data ports, bar, meeting rooms, some pets allowed; no a/c* ▤ *AE, MC, V* � *BP.*

£–££ 🏨 **Sidney House.** In addition to having stunning views, this dignified early-19th-century hotel, run by a friendly husband-and-wife team, is near the town center. Rooms, done in pastel hues, are furnished with stripped pine and period pieces. On a clear afternoon you can sit on the terrace and gaze out over the Vale of Evesham to the Cotswolds. ⊠ *40 Worcester Rd., WR14 4AA* ☎🖷 *01684/574994* ⊕ *www.sidneyhouse.co.uk* 🗪 *8 rooms* ⌂ *Some pets allowed; no a/c, no room phones* ▤ *MC, V* ⌾ *BP.*

Nightlife & the Arts

Malvern has links with Sir Edward Elgar as well as with George Bernard Shaw, who premiered many of his plays here. The **Autumn in Malvern Festival** (☎ 01684/892277 or 01684/892289 ⊕ www.malvernfestival. co.uk) takes place on weekends throughout October and concentrates on classical music, including Elgar, as well as literary events.

Ledbury

⓲ *10 mi southwest of Great Malvern on A449.*

Among the black-and-white half-timber buildings that make up the market town of Ledbury, take special note of two late-16th-century ones: the Feathers Hotel and the Talbot Inn. Almost hidden behind the 17th-century market house, cobbled Church Lane, crowded with medieval half-timber buildings, leads to St. Michael's Church. The **Old Grammar School,** a heritage center in an old school, traces the history of local industries. It also has displays on two literary celebrities linked to the area, John Masefield and Elizabeth Barrett Browning. ⊠ *Church La.* ☎ *01531/636147* 🎟 *Free* ☉ *Apr.–Oct., daily 10:30–4:30.*

8

★ Completed in 1820, **Eastnor Castle**, a turreted, stone, Norman Revival extravaganza on the eastern outskirts of Ledbury, includes some magnificent, ornate, neo-Gothic salons designed by 19th-century architect Augustus Pugin. The Hervey-Bathurst family has restored other grand rooms, full of tapestries, gilded paintings, Regency chandeliers, and Auntie's old armchairs, making Eastnor a must-see for lovers of English interior decoration. ⊠ *A438* ☎ *01531/633160* ⊕ *www.eastnorcastle.com* ⊟ *House and grounds £7, grounds only £3* ⊙ *Mid-July and Aug., Sun.–Fri. 11–5; mid-Apr.–June and Sept., Sun. and national holiday Mon. 11–5; last admission 30 mins before closing.*

Where to Stay & Eat

£££–££££ ✕⊡ **Feathers Hotel.** You can't miss the striking black-and-white facade of this central hostelry, which dates from the 16th century. The interior has a satisfyingly antique flavor, with creaking staircases and ancient floorboards, and some rooms have four-posters. The hop-bedecked Fuggles Brasserie (named after a variety of hop) and the more formal Quills restaurant serve plenty of fresh fish, as well as lighter meals. If you're indulging, try the Herefordshire duck or beef. ⊠ *High St., HR8 1DS* ☎ *01531/635266* ⊟ *01531/638955* ⊕ *www.feathers-ledbury.co.uk* ⊷ *19 rooms* ♿ *2 restaurants, cable TV, in-room broadband, in-room data ports, Wi-Fi, indoor pool, health club, bar, meeting rooms, some pets allowed; no a/c* ⊟ *AE, MC, V* ⦿ *BP.*

> ## GREAT WALKS
>
> The Malvern Hills have climbs and walks of varying length and difficulty. The best places to start are Great Malvern and Ledbury. The Elgar Route extends for 45 mi and touches on Malvern and Worcester as it threads through the Malverns. The hilltop views across the countryside are spectacular—isolated hills rise up from the fairly flat plain, providing vistas for many miles around. The area around Ross-on-Wye has ideal walks with scenic river views. In Shropshire, Wenlock Edge and the uplands of Long Mynd south of Much Wenlock are popular places to walk. For information on hiking the Malverns, contact the Malvern or Ross-on-Wye tourist office (⇨ Visitor Information *in* Welsh Border Essentials, *below*).

Much Marcle

⑲ *4 mi southwest of Ledbury.*

Much Marcle is one of the English villages still holding the ancient annual ceremony of "wassailing"—beating the apple trees to make them fruitful in the coming year. The ritual takes place on Twelfth Night, January 6. Effigies and tombs richly endow the beautiful 13th-century church here, notably the exquisitely carved tomb of Blanche, Lady Grandison. If you have a detailed map and plenty of time, wander around and discover tiny villages down sleepy lanes overhung by hedges.

Just outside Much Marcle lies the beautiful 17th-century manor of **Hellens,** still in authentic and pristine condition. Part of the house dates from the 13th century and contains fine old-master paintings. The gloom and dust are part of the experience; candles illuminate the house, and central heating has been scorned. ⊠ *½ mi east of Much Marcle* ☎ *01531/*

660504 ⊕ *www.hellensmanor.com* ✉ *£5* ☉ *Apr.–Sept., Wed., Thurs., Sun., and national holiday Mon. 2–5; tours at 2, 3, and 4.*

Ross-on-Wye

❷⓿ *6 mi southwest of Much Marcle.*

Perched high above the River Wye, Ross-on-Wye seems oblivious to modern-day intrusions and remains at heart a small market town. Its steep streets come alive on Thursday and Saturday—market days—but they're always a happy hunting ground for antiques.

Where to Stay

£££–£££££ 🏨 **Chase Hotel.** The public areas in this well-renovated Georgian-style country-house hotel on 11 acres of grounds retain some original elements. Bedrooms in the main house are simply and comfortably furnished in pastels and print fabrics, and those in the newer wing are more modern. ✉ *Gloucester Rd., HR9 5LH* ☎ *01989/763161* 🖶 *01989/768330* ⊕ *www.chasehotel.co.uk* ✍ *36 rooms* ☖ *Restaurant, cable TV, in-room broadband, in-room data ports, gym, meeting rooms; no a/c* ▭ *AE, DC, MC, V* ⓘⓄⓘ *BP.*

Goodrich

❷❶ *3 mi south of Ross-on-Wye on B4234, 3 mi north of Symond's Yat on B4229.*

The ruins of a castle that resembles a fortress from the Rhineland dominate the village of Goodrich. Looming dramatically over the River Wye crossing at Kerne Bridge, **Goodrich Castle** from the south looks picturesque amid the green fields, but you quickly see its grimmer face from the battlements on its north side. Dating from the late 12th century, the red sandstone castle is surrounded by a deep moat carved out of solid rock, from which its walls appear to soar upward. Built to repel Welsh raiders, Goodrich was destroyed in the 17th century during the Civil War. ✉ *Off A40* ☎ *01600/890538* ⊕ *www.english-heritage.org.uk* ✉ *£4.50* ☉ *Mar.–May, daily 10–5; June–Aug., daily 10–6; Sept. and Oct., daily 10–5; Nov.–Feb., Thurs.–Mon. 10–4.*

Symond's Yat

❷❷ *3 mi south of Goodrich, 6 mi south of Ross-on-Wye.*

Outside the village of Symond's Yat ("gate"), the 473-foot-high Yat Rock commands superb views of the River Wye as it winds through a narrow gorge and swings around in a great 5-mi loop.

Kilpeck

❷❸ *15 mi northwest of Goodrich, 7 mi southwest of Hereford.*

Tucked away on a minor road off A465, the tiny hamlet of Kilpeck is blessed with one of the best-preserved Norman churches in Britain. Much of the village, along with the remains of a castle and the church, is protected as a Scheduled Ancient Monument. The red sandstone **Kilpeck**

8

church, completed in the mid-12th century, is lavishly decorated inside and out with sculpted carving exceptional for a country church. The carvings depict all manner of subjects, including animals. ⊠ *Off A465* ☎ *01981/570315* ✉ *Donations accepted* ⊙ *Daily 9–dusk.*

Hereford

㉔ *7 mi northeast of Kilpeck, 56 mi southwest of Birmingham, 31 mi northwest of Gloucester, 54 mi northeast of Cardiff.*

A busy country town, Hereford is the center of a wealthy agricultural area known for its cider, fruit, and cattle—the white-faced Hereford breed has spread across the world. It's also an important cathedral city, and the massive Norman building towers proudly over the River Wye. Before 1066, Hereford was the capital of the Anglo-Saxon kingdom of Mercia and, earlier still, the site of Roman, Celtic, and Iron Age settlements. Today people come primarily to see the cathedral but quickly discover the charms of a town that has changed slowly but unobtrusively with the passing centuries.

Built of local red sandstone with a large central tower, **Hereford Cathedral** retains some fine 11th-century Norman carvings but suffered considerable "restoration" in the 19th century. Inside, its greatest glories include a 12th-century chair, to the left of the high altar, one of the earliest pieces of furniture in the country and reputedly used by King Stephen, and some fine misericords (the elaborately carved undersides of choristers' seats). The cathedral's brass-rubbing center has copies of memorial brasses from around Britain; it's open in summer or by appointment. ⊠ *Cathedral Close* ☎ *01432/374200, 01432/374202 for brass-rubbing center hrs* ⊕ *www.herefordcathedral.org* ✉ *Suggested donation £2, tours £3.50* ⊙ *Mon.–Sat. 7:30–6:30, Sun. 8–4:30; tours Apr.–Oct., daily 11 and 2.*

★ The **Mappa Mundi and Chained Library Exhibition,** an extraordinary double attraction, includes the more than 20-square-foot parchment Mappa Mundi. Hereford's own picture of the medieval world shows the Earth as flat, with Jerusalem at its center. It's now thought that the map was originally the central section of an altarpiece dating from 1290. The chained library contains some 1,500 books, among them an 8th-century copy of the Four Gospels. Chained libraries, in which books were attached to cupboards to discourage theft, are extremely rare: they date from medieval times, when books were as precious as gold. ⊠ *Cathedral Close* ☎ *01432/374219* ⊕ *www.herefordcathedral.org* ✉ *£4.50* ⊙ *Apr.–Oct., Mon.–Sat. 10–5, Sun. 11–4; Nov., Dec., Feb., and Mar., Mon.–Sat. 10–4; last admission 30 mins before closing.*

STRANGE SHELVING

The books in the chained library are unusually stored with their spines facing inward. This is so that a book can be taken down and opened on the desk, without the chain, which is attached to the front cover, becoming entangled. Index boards at the end of the shelves indicate the titles.

The half-timber **Old House** is a fine example of domestic Jacobean architecture, furnished in 17th-century style on three floors. You can see a kitchen, dining hall, parlor, and bedrooms. Look for the dog's door between the nursery and master bedroom. ✉ *High Town* 🕾 *01432/ 260694* 🌎 *Free* 🕑 *Apr.–Sept., Tues.–Sat. 10–5, Sun. and national holiday Mon. 10–4; Oct.–Mar., Tues.–Sat. 10–5.*

The 13th-century **All Saints Church,** on the west side of High Town, contains superb canopied choir stalls and misericords, as well as an unusual Queen Anne reredos in the south chapel. There's also an excellent coffee bar and restaurant.

A farm cider house and a cooper's workshop have been re-created at the **Cider Museum,** where you can tour ancient cider cellars with huge oak vats. Cider brandy (applejack) is made here, and the museum sells its own brand, along with other cider items. ✉ *Pomona Pl. at White-cross Rd.* 🕾 *01432/354207* ⊕ *www.cidermuseum.co.uk* ✉ *£3* 🕑 *Apr.–Oct., Tues.–Sat. and national holiday Mon. 10–5; Nov.–Mar., Tues.–Sat. 11–3; last admission 1 hr before closing.*

Where to Stay & Eat

★ £ ✕ **Café @ All Saints.** The west end and gallery of this community-minded church are given over to a coffee bar and restaurant, granting a rare opportunity to indulge body and spirit at one sitting. The imaginative vegetarian menu is worth every penny, but for something lighter, try the tasty sandwiches, salads, cakes, and local ice creams. ✉ *High St.* 🕾 *01432/370415* 🍽 *MC, V* 🕑 *Closed Sun. No dinner.*

£££££ ✕🖾 **Castle House.** These conjoined Georgian villas next to the moat (all that remains of Hereford Castle) offer luxury and a warm welcome. Delicate plasterwork graces the public areas. The spacious rooms vary in style, with yellow and cream the preferred colors; each bedroom contains a decanter of cider brandy. The restaurant (££££–£££££) relies on home-grown vegetables, and meat, such as Hereford beef and Gloucester Old Spot pork, for its contemporary fare. ✉ *Castle St., HR1 2NW* 🕾 *01432/356321* 🖶 *01432/365909* ⊕ *www.castlehse.co.uk* 🛏 *10 suites, 5 rooms* ⚂ *Restaurant, refrigerators, in-room safes, cable TV, in-room VCRs, in-room broadband, bar, business services, Internet room, meeting rooms, some pets allowed; no a/c* 🍽 *AE, MC, V* 🍴 *BP.*

£ 🖾 **Grafton Villa Farm.** Warm period rooms with antiques and rich furnishings fill this peaceful, early-18th-century farmhouse 2 mi south of the city. For breakfast, choose between scrambled eggs provided by the resident hens or local bacon and sausages. ✉ *Off A49, Grafton HR2 8ED* 🕾🖶 *01432/268689* ⊕ *www.graftonvilla.co.uk* 🛏 *3 rooms* ⚂ *No a/c, no room phones, no smoking* 🍽 *No credit cards* 🍴 *BP.*

Shopping

Hereford has a market for livestock market on Wednesday and for general retail on Saturday. The stores in **Capuchin Yard** (✉ Off 29 Church St.) display crafts, including handmade shoes and knitwear; other outlets sell books, posters, and watercolors. For high-quality foods, head for the **Left Bank Village** (✉ Bridge St. 🕾 01432/349000) development and browse the delicatessen, patisserie, ice-cream parlor, and wine shop.

8

Witley Court

25 *27 mi northeast of Hereford, 10 mi northwest of Worcester.*

The romantic shell of Witley Court conjures up the Victorian heyday of the imposing stately home—a huge Italianate pile—that stood here before a fire in 1937. In contrast to this ruin, the tiny baroque parish church on the grounds is perfectly preserved. Note its parapet with balustrades, and the small golden dome over its cupola. Inside are 10 colored windows and a ceiling painted by Antonio Bellucci. Witley Court's glorious gardens are being restored, and one of the impressive fountains, the enormous Perseus and Andromeda, sends its jets skyward (April through October, weekdays at noon, 2, and 4, weekends on the hour). The Jerwood sculpture park contains works by Elizabeth Frink and Antony Gormley, among others. The house is little less than a mile outside Great Witley. ⊠ *A443, Great Witley* ☎ *01299/896636* ⊕ *www.english-heritage.org.uk* ✉ *£4.95* ⊗ *Mar.–May, Sept. and Oct., daily 10–5; June.–Aug., daily 10–6; Nov.–Feb., Thurs.–Mon. 10–4.*

Where to Stay & Eat

£££–£££££ ✕⌷ **Elms Hotel.** Formal gardens and 10 acres of grounds surround this creeper-clad Queen Anne mansion, now a luxurious, traditional country-house hotel 16 mi northeast of Worcester and near Great Witley. Gilbert White, a pupil of Sir Christopher Wren, designed the house, and public areas retain their original ornate plasterwork. All rooms are individually decorated in muted colors and include antiques. The restaurant (£££££) creates imaginative contemporary fare using local produce and herbs. ⊠ *Stockton Rd., Abberley WR6 6AT* ☎ *01299/896666* 🖷 *01299/896804* ⊕ *www.theelmshotel.co.uk* ➥ *21 rooms* ⚬ *Restaurant, in-room data ports, tennis court, croquet, meeting rooms, helipad, some pets allowed (fee); no a/c* ⊟ *AE, DC, MC, V* ⎮⊙⎮ *BP.*

Bewdley

26 *8 mi north of Great Witley, 14 mi north of Worcester, 3 mi west of Kidderminster.*

In Bewdley, an exceptionally attractive Severn Valley town, many tall, narrow-front Georgian buildings are clustered around the river bridge. The 18th-century butchers' market, the **Shambles,** now holds a museum of local history, trades, and crafts, with exhibits and demonstrations of rope-making and clay-pipe-making. Craftspeople working in wood, ceramics, and textiles occupy the nearby workshops. ⊠ *Load St.* ☎ *01299/403573* ✉ *Free* ⊗ *Apr.–Sept., daily 10–4:30; Oct., daily 11–4.*

♻ Bewdley is a southern terminus of the **Severn Valley Railway,** a steam railroad running 16 mi north along the river to Bridgnorth. It stops at a handful of sleepy stations where time has apparently stood still since the age of steam. You can get off at any of these stations, picnic by the river, and walk to the next station to get a train back. ⊠ *Railway Station* ☎ *01299/403816* ⊕ *www.svr.co.uk* ✉ *£11.80 round-trip* ⊗ *Mid-May–Sept., trains run daily; Oct.–mid-May, weekends only.*

The **Stourport Steamer Co.** has short river trips, or you can take longer journeys as far as Worcester on Wednesday from the last week in July through August. Stourport is a few miles south of Bewdley. ⊠ *Riverside Walk, Stourport* ☎ *01299/871177 or 0786/046–8792* ⊕ *www. riverboathire.co.uk* 🖃 *£4–£12* ⊙ *Mar.–mid-July and Sept., Sun.; mid-July–Aug., daily.*

Stourbridge

㉗ *8 mi northeast of Bewdley via A451, 11 mi west of Birmingham.*

Stourbridge is the home of Britain's crystal glass industry, and although the industry is in decline, exquisite glassware is still being produced. A number of shops sell "factory seconds" bargains.

Shopping

Two good shops are a mile or so north of Stourbridge on the A491 Wolverhampton road. The **Tudor Crystal** (⊠ Stewkins, Audnam ☎ 01384/392525), stocks jewelry and animals as well as a wide range of glasses

★ and decanters; it's open Monday through Saturday. The **Stuart Crystal Visitor Centre and Factory Shop** (⊠ High St., Wordsley ☎ 01384/261777), open daily, carries a good selection of gift items.

Dudley

㉘ *6 mi northeast of Stourbridge, 8 mi west of central Birmingham.*

It was in Dudley, in the 17th century, that coal was first used for smelting iron. The town subsequently became known as the capital of the Black Country, a term that arose from the air pollution caused by iron-

★ ⟁ works foundries and coal mining. The **Black Country Living Museum,** established to interpret the area's industrial heritage, consists of an entire village reconstructed of disused buildings from around the region. Among the exhibits on 26 acres are a chain-maker's house and workshop, with demonstrations of chain-making; a small trap works that made animal traps; a druggist and general store, where costumed women describe life in a poor industrial community in the 19th century; a Methodist chapel; the Bottle & Glass pub; Stables restaurant, serving such traditional delicacies as faggots and peas (a fried pork-liver dish); and a coal mine and wharf. The reconstructed brick-and-terra-cotta Rolfe Street Baths building, brought here from Smethwick, gives an overview of the Black Country. You can also sit on a hard bench and watch Charlie Chaplin in the 1920's cinema, or ride on a barge (extra charge) through a tunnel to experience the canal travel of yesteryear. ⊠ *Tipton Rd.* ☎ *0121/557–9643* ⊕ *www.bclm.co.uk* 🖃 *£11, barge trip £4.25* ⊙ *Mar.–Oct., daily 10–5; Nov.–Feb., Wed.–Sun. 10–4.*

At the **New Royal Brierley Experience,** next to the Black Country Living Museum, you can witness the making of glass (all by hand) on a factory tour, view documents and pieces from the Brierley company's 300 years of history, and browse through samples in the shop. ⊠ *Tipton Rd.* ☎ *0121/530–5600* ⊕ *www.royalbrierley.com* 🖃 *Free* ⊙ *Weekdays 9–5:30, Sat. 9–5, Sun. 10–4; self-guided factory tours weekdays, 9–5.*

8

FROM SHREWSBURY TO CHESTER
SKIRTING THE "BLACK COUNTRY"

The "peak" of this region—in terms of height—is the Wrekin, a hill geologists claim to be the oldest in the land, and a hill A. E. Housman and others have invested with some of their poetic charm. From its isolated summit you can gaze on a peaceful rural scene, quite different from most people's preconceptions of the industrial Midlands. Ironbridge, several miles from the Wrekin, has two identities, as a place as well as a thing. The thing itself is the first bridge to be made of iron, erected between 1777 and 1779. Now taken over by the Ironbridge Gorge Museum Trust, the bridge is the centerpiece of a vast Industrial Revolution–museum complex. The place is the 6-mi stretch of the Ironbridge Gorge, once an awesome scene of mining and charcoal-burning that reeked with smoke and the stench of sulfur. Ironworks forges and coal mining created the pollution that gave this region west of Birmingham its name—the Black Country—during the mid-19th century. The stretch has been transformed into a scene of idyllic beauty, scars grassed over, woodland filling the gaps left by tree-felling.

Within easy reach of Ironbridge, rural Shropshire spreads invitingly, with towns long famed as beauty spots, such as Bridgnorth and Ludlow. Around this area are two important cities of the Welsh Border region, Shrewsbury and Chester, both famous for their medieval heritage and their wealth of half-timber buildings.

Shrewsbury

47 mi northwest of Dudley, 55 mi north of Hereford, 46 mi south of Chester, 48 mi northwest of Birmingham.

One of England's most important medieval towns, Shrewsbury (usually pronounced *shrose*-bury), the county seat of Shropshire, lies within a great horseshoe loop of the Severn. It has numerous 16th-century half-timber buildings—many built by well-to-do wool merchants—plus elegant ones from later periods. Today the town retains a romantic air (indeed, there are many bridal shops, along with churches), and it can be a lovely experience to stroll the Shrewsbury "shuts." These narrow alleys overhung with timbered gables lead off the central market square, which was designed to be closed off at night to protect local residents. In summer, filled window boxes and hanging baskets make a vivid contrast to the black-and-white buildings.

Walking is an ideal way to see Shrewsbury, and traffic has been banned on some historic streets. A good starting point for a walking tour is the small square between Fish Street and Butcher Row. These streets are little changed since medieval times, when some of them took their names from the principal trades carried on there, but Peacock Alley, Gullet Passage, and Grope Lane clearly got their names from somewhere else.

㉛ Ireland's Mansion. Bear Steps is a cluster of restored half-timber buildings that link Fish Street with Market Square; this one, built in 1575 with elaborate Jacobean timbering and richly decorated with quatrefoils, is the most notable. It's not open to the public.

NEED A BREAK?

The timbered room and–if the weather is right–the courtyard at **Poppy's Tea Rooms** (✉ Milk St., off Wyle Cop ☎ 01743/272709) make a pleasant stop for coffee, teas, and some satisfying snacks. It's closed Sunday.

㉜ Quarry Park. Below Swan Hill, the manicured lawn of the park slopes down to the river. In a sheltered corner is the **Dingle,** a garden with floral displays. To reach the park from the center of town, head for Welsh Bridge and stroll along the riverbank, or walk up Claremont Hill.

㉚ St. Alkmund's. Prominent on the Shrewsbury skyline, this church is worth seeing for its dramatic and inspiring east window (1795) by Francis Eginton. Depicting Faith, the window appears as stained glass, but is in fact painted, and is a copy of Guido Reni's *Assumption of the Blessed Virgin* in Munich. ✉ *St. Alkmund's Pl., off Fish St.* ☎ *01743/244668* ⊙ *Apr.–Oct., Mon.–Sat. 10–5; Nov.–Mar., Mon.–Sat. 10–dusk.*

㉝ St. Chad. On a hilltop west of the town center, this church designed by George Steuart, the architect of Attingham Park, is one of England's most original ecclesiastical buildings. Completed in 1792, the round Georgian church is surmounted by a tower that is in turn square, octagonal, and circular—and finally topped by a dome. When being built, it provoked riots among townsfolk averse to its radical style. The interior has a fine Venetian east window and a brass Arts and Crafts pulpit. ✉ *St. Chad's Terr.* ☎ *01743/365478* ▨ *Free* ⊙ *Apr.–Oct., daily 8–5; Nov.–Mar., daily 8–1.*

㉙ St. Mary's church. The stone spire of the church, built around 1200, is one of the three tallest in England. The church merits a visit for its stained glass, collected from continental churches by a Victorian vicar, and its Victorian encaustic tiles. ✉ *St. Mary's St., off Castle St.* ☎ *01743/ 357006* ▨ *Donations welcome* ⊙ *Weekdays 10–5, Sat. 10–4.*

㉟ Shrewsbury Abbey. Now unbecomingly surrounded by busy roads, the abbey was founded in 1083 and later became a powerful Benedictine monastery. The abbey church has survived many vicissitudes and retains a 14th-century west window above a Norman doorway. The abbey figures in the Brother Cadfael whodunits by Ellis Peters; the novels provide an excellent idea of local life in the Middle Ages. To reach the abbey from the center, cross the river by the English Bridge. ✉ *Abbey Church, Abbey Foregate* ☎ *01743/232723* ⊕ *www.shrewsburyabbey.com* ▨ *Donations welcome* ⊙ *Apr.–Oct., Mon.–Sat. 10–4:30, Sun. 11:30–2:30; Nov.–Mar., Mon.–Sat. 10:30–3, Sun. 11:30–2:30.*

㉞ Shrewsbury Castle. Guarding the northern approaches to the town, the castle rises over the River Severn at the bottom of Pride Hill. Originally Norman, it was dismantled during the Civil War and later rebuilt by Thomas Telford, the Scottish engineer who designed many notable buildings and bridges in the early 19th century. The castle holds the **Shropshire Regimental Museum.** ✉ *Shrewsbury Castle, Castle Gates* ☎ *01743/ 358516* ⊕ *www.shrewsburymuseums.com* ▨ *£2* ⊙ *Mid-Feb.–Mar.*

8

Ireland's
Mansion **31**

Quarry Park . . **32**

St. Alkmund's . **30**

St. Chad **33**

St. Mary's **29**

Shrewsbury
Abbey **35**

Shrewsbury
Castle **34**

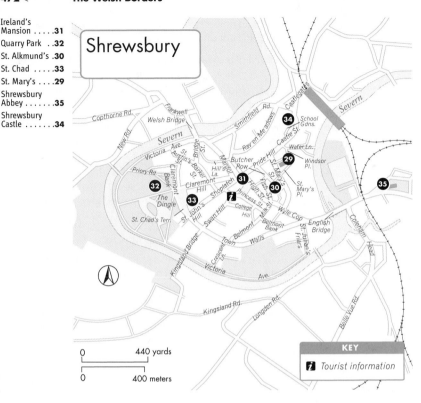

and Nov.–Dec., Tues.–Sat. and national holiday Mon. 10–4; Apr., May, Sept. and Oct., Tues.–Sat. and national holiday Mon. 10–5; June–Aug., Tues.–Sat. 10–5, Sun. and Mon. 10–4. Castle grounds daily 10–4.

Where to Stay & Eat

£££ ✕ **Draper's Hall.** The dark-wood paneling, antique furniture, and warm, intimate lighting of this distinctive 16th-century hall make it a distinctive dining spot for contemporary cuisine. You might try the lemon sole with caper butter; leave room for desserts such as caramelized pineapple with honeycomb ice cream. There are plenty of cheeses and salad choices. ⊠ *10 St. Mary's Pl.* ☎ *01743/344679* ⊟ *AE, MC, V* ☉ *Closed Sun. Jan.–Mar.*

££–£££ ✕ **The Armoury.** This smartly converted warehouse, whose arched windows overlook the river, is well stocked with books, prints, and curiosities, as well as good food, wines, and real ales. Among the appetizers are smoked haddock and salmon fishcakes. Shropshire sausages with bacon mash potato and onion gravy is a popular main course, and you can try syrup sponge cake and custard for dessert. ⊠ *Victoria Quay* ☎ *01743/340525* ⊟ *AE, MC, V.*

£££–££££ ▥ **Albright Hussey Hotel.** Lovely gardens surround this Tudor manor house, originally the home of the Hussey family, which dates back to 1524 and combines black-and-white half-timbering with a later (1560) redbrick-and-stone extension. Beams, oak paneling, four-poster beds, and antiques enhance rooms in the original building, for which you should book well ahead; those in the extension are plainer. The hotel is 2½ mi north of Shrewsbury on A5228. ⊠ *Ellesmere Rd., SY4 3AF* ☎ *01939/290571* 🖨 *01939/291143* ⊕ *www.albrighthussey.co.uk* 🛏 *19 rooms, 7 suites* ⚭ *Restaurant, in-room data ports, Wi-Fi, 2 bars, meeting rooms, some pets allowed (fee); no a/c* ☐ *AE, DC, MC, V* ⊘⊙⏐ *BP.*

££ 🖾 **The Lion Hotel.** Parts of this once-renowned coaching inn in the heart of town date to the 14th century; today the hotel envelops you in the 17th century–style luxury for which it became famous. Rooms are small and traditionally furnished, but the glorious lounge, with its high ceiling, oil paintings, and carved-stone fireplace, sets the Lion apart. Add to this the magnificent Adam Ballroom, and you can see the appeal for former guests such as Charles Dickens, Benjamin Disraeli, and King William IV. ⊠ *Wyle Cop, SY1 1UY* ☎ *01743/353107* 🖨 *01743/352744* ⊕ *www.regalhotels.co.uk/thelion* 🛏 *59 rooms* ⚭ *Restaurant, room TVs with movies, some in-room data ports, bar, lounge, business services, meeting rooms; no a/c* ☐ *AE, DC, MC, V* ⊘⊙⏐ *BP.*

££ 🖾 **Sandford House.** The hospitable Richards family runs this late-Georgian B&B close to the river and the town center. Original decorative plasterwork is still much in evidence; modern pine furnishes the bedrooms. Room 5 is seven-sided, with a beautiful molded ceiling. ⊠ *St. Julian Friars, SY1 1XL* ☎ *01743/343829* ⊕ *www.sandfordhouse.co.uk* 🛏 *19 rooms* ⚭ *Wi-Fi, some pets allowed; no a/c, no room phones, no smoking* ☐ *AE, MC, V* ⊘⊙⏐ *BP.*

Nightlife & the Arts

During the **Shrewsbury International Music Festival** (☎ 01606/872633), in June and July, the town vibrates to traditional and not-so-traditional music by groups from Europe and North America.

Shopping

The Parade (⊠ St. Mary's Pl. ☎ 01743/343178), just behind St. Mary's church, is a shopping center created from the neoclassical former Royal Infirmary, built in 1830. One of the most appealing malls in England, it has thirty attractive boutiques, a coffee shop, and a river terrace.

Attingham Park

36 *4 mi southeast of Shrewsbury.*

Built in 1785 by George Steuart (architect of the church of St. Chad in Shrewsbury) for the first Lord Berwick, this elegant stone mansion has a three-story portico, with a pediment carried on four tall columns. The building overlooks a sweep of parkland, including a deer park landscaped by Humphrey Repton (1752–1818), and there are walks by the river and in the deer park. Inside the house are painted ceilings and delicate plasterwork, a fine picture gallery designed by John Nash (1752–1835), and 19th-century Neapolitan furniture. ⊠ *B4380, off A5, Atcham* ☎ *01743/708162* ⊕ *www.nationaltrust.org.uk* 🎟 *£6.50, park and grounds only £3.30* ⊙ *House early to mid-Mar., weekends 1–5; late-Mar.–Oct., Fri.–Tues. 1–5, national holiday Mon. 11–5; last admission*

8

1 hr before closing. Park and grounds Mar.–Oct., daily 10–8; Nov.–Feb., daily 10–5.

EN
ROUTE Continuing southeast on B4380, you can see, rising on the left, the **Wrekin,** a strange, wooded, conical, extinct volcano that is 1,335 feet high. The walk to the summit, which has panoramic views, is about 5 mi. A few miles farther on, you enter the wooded gorge of the River Severn.

Much Wenlock

③⑦ *8 mi southeast of Attingham Park, 12 mi southeast of Shrewsbury.*

Much Wenlock, a town on A458, is full of half-timber buildings, including a 16th-century guildhall. The romantic ruins of Norman **Wenlock Priory** are in a topiary garden. ⊠ *High St.* ☎ *01952/727466* ⊕ *www. english-heritage.org.uk* 🎟 *£3.30* ⊙ *Mar.–May, Sept., and Oct., Thurs.–Mon. 10–5; June–Aug., daily 10–6; Nov.–Feb., Thurs.–Sun. 10–4.*

Sports & the Outdoors

The high escarpment of **Wenlock Edge** runs southwest from Much Wenlock and provides a splendid view. This is hiking country, and if a healthful walk sounds inviting, turn off B4371 through Church Stretton into Cardingmill Valley, or to the wide heather uplands on top of Long Mynd. You can park and set off on foot.

Ironbridge Gorge

★ **③⑧** *15 mi east of Shrewsbury, 28 mi northwest of Birmingham.*

Ironbridge Gorge is the name given to a group of villages south of Telford that were crucial in ushering in the Industrial Revolution. The Shropshire coalfields were of enormous importance to the development of the coke-smelting process, which helped make producing anything in iron much easier. The 10 component sections of the **Ironbridge Gorge Museum,** spread over 6 square mi, preserve and interpret the area's fascinating industrial history. ■ TIP➔ Allow at least a full day to appreciate all the major sights, and perhaps to take a stroll around the famous iron bridge or hunt for Coalport china in the stores clustered near it. If you're without a vehicle, visit on a weekend or national holiday (April through October) when a shuttle bus takes you between sites. The best starting point is the **Museum of the Gorge,** which has a good selection of literature and an audiovisual show on the gorge's history. In nearby Coalbrookdale, the **Museum of Iron** explains the production of iron and steel. You can see the blast furnace built by Abraham Darby, who developed the original coke process in 1709. Adjacent to this, the **Enginuity** exhibition is a hands-on, feet-on exploration of engineering, offering the opportunity to pull a locomotive and even "fly" a magnetic carpet. From here, drive the few miles along the river until the arches of the **Iron Bridge** come into view; it was designed by T. F. Pritchard, smelted by Darby, and erected between 1777 and 1779. This graceful arch spanning the River Severn can best be seen—and photographed or painted—from the towpath, a riverside walk edged with wildflowers and shrubs. The tollhouse on the far side houses an exhibition on the bridge's history and restoration.

A mile farther along the river is the old factory and the **Coalport China Museum** (the china is now made in Stoke-on-Trent). Exhibits show some of the factory's most beautiful wares, and craftspeople give demonstrations. Above Coalport is **Blists Hill Victorian Town,** where you can see old mines, furnaces, and a wrought-iron works. But the main draw is the re-creation of the "town" itself, with its doctor's office, bakery, grocer's, candle-maker's, sawmill, printing shop, and candy store. At the entrance you can change some money for specially minted pennies and make purchases from the shops. Shopkeepers, the bank manager, and the doctor's wife are on hand to give you advice. Craft demonstrations are scheduled in summer. ✉ *B4380, Ironbridge, Telford* ☎ *01952/884391* 🌐 *www.ironbridge.org.uk* 🎫 *Ticket to all sights £14* ⏲ *Apr.–Oct., daily 10–5; Nov.–Mar., daily 10–4.*

WORD OF MOUTH

"While visiting Ironbridge, don't miss the Blists Hill open-air museum, which is a re-created Victorian town, complete with shops, houses and even a working iron foundry." –Maria H

Where to Stay & Eat

£ ✕ **New Inn.** This Victorian building was moved from Walsall, 22 mi away, so that it could be part of the Blists Hill Victorian Town. It's a fully functioning pub, with gas lamps, sawdust on the floor, traditional ales, and old-fashioned lemonade and ginger beer. For an inexpensive meal, you can try a ploughman's lunch or a steak and kidney pudding from the butcher's store next door. Join in the daily sing-along around the piano at 1 and 3:30 (3 PM in winter). ✉ *Blists Hill Victorian Town* ☎ *01952/601010* 💳 *MC, V.*

££££ ✕🏨 **Clarion Hotel at Madeley Court, Telford.** Guest rooms in this restored 16th-century stone manor house, once the home of Abraham Darby, are rich in antiques and period furnishings. Modern rooms are available as well. The Priory Restaurant occupies the original Great Hall and serves contemporary British food; you might find medallions of pork with caramelized apples, or grilled slamon and plaice served on stir-fry vegetables on the fixed-price menu (££££). The garden has a rare example of an Elizabethan stone cube sundial. ✉ *Castlefields Way, Madeley, Telford TF7 5DW* ☎ *01952/680068* 📠 *01952/684275* 🌐 *www.choicehotelseurope.com* 🛏 *47 rooms* 🖒 *Restaurant, cable TV, some in-room data ports, bar, Internet room, Wi-Fi, meeting rooms, some pets allowed; no a/c* 💳 *AE, DC, MC, V.*

★ **££** 🏨 **Library House.** At one point the village's library, this small guesthouse on the hillside near the Ironbridge museums (and only a few steps from the bridge itself) has kept its attractive Victorian style while allowing for modern-day luxuries—a DVD library, for instance. Service is warm without being obtrusive. ✉ *11 Severn Bank, Ironbridge, Telford TF8 7AN* ☎ *01952/432299* 📠 *01952/433967* 🌐 *www.libraryhouse.com* 🛏 *4 rooms* 🖒 *Cable TV, in-room DVDs, Wi-Fi; no a/c, no room phones, no kids under 10, no smoking* 💳 *No credit cards* 🍽 *BP.*

8

Bridgnorth

 9 mi south of Ironbridge, 22 mi southeast of Shrewsbury, 25 mi west of Birmingham.

Perching perilously on a high sandstone ridge on the banks of the Severn, the market town of Bridgnorth has two distinct parts, High Town and Low Town, connected by a winding road, flights of steep steps, and—best of all—a cliff railroad. Even the tower of the Norman castle seems to suffer from vertigo, having a 17° list (three times the angle of the Leaning Tower of Pisa). Severn Valley Railway trains, which originate in Bewdley or Kidderminster, terminate here.

Ludlow

 29 mi south of Shrewsbury, 24 mi north of Hereford.

Fodor's Choice
★

Pretty Ludlow has medieval, Georgian, and Victorian buildings and a finer display of black-and-white half-timber buildings than even Shrewsbury. The Church of St. Lawrence on College Street dominates the center, its extravagant size a testimony to the town's prosperous wool trade. Cross the River Teme and climb Whitcliff for a spectacular view. The town is also a perfect example of how small rural places (the population is around 10,000) can become culinary hot spots, in this case from the buzz generated by a cluster of outstanding restaurants. The **Ludlow and the Marches Food Festival** (☎ 01584/873957 ⊕ www.foodfestival.co.uk) takes place over a weekend in mid-September and has demonstrations and tastings (including local sausages, ale, and cider).

Dating from 1085, the massive, ruined, red sandstone **Ludlow Castle** dwarfs the town; it served as a vital stronghold for centuries and was the seat of the Marcher Lords who ruled "the Marches," the local name for the border region. The two sons of Edward IV—the little princes of the Tower of London—spent time here before being dispatched to London and their death in 1483. The earl of Powys owns the castle. Follow the terraced walk around the castle for a lovely view of the countryside. ⊠ *Castle Sq.* ☎ *01584/873355* ⊕ *www.ludlowcastle.com* ☎ *£4* ☉ *Jan., weekends 10–4; Feb., Mar., and Oct.–Dec., daily 10–4; Apr.–July and Sept., daily 10–5; Aug., daily 10–7; last admission 30 mins before closing.*

OFF THE
BEATEN
PATH

STOKESAY CASTLE – This 13th-century fortified manor house built by a wealthy merchant is arguably the finest of its kind in England. Inside the main hall, the wooden cruck roof and timber staircase (a rare survival) demonstrate state-of-the-art building methods of the day. Outside, the cottage-style garden creates a bewitching backdrop for the magnificent Jacobean timber-frame gatehouse. ⊠ *Craven Arms, off A49 Shrewsbury road, 7 mi northwest of Ludlow* ☎ *01588/672544* ⊕ *www. english-heritage.org.uk* ☎ *£4.80* ☉ *Mar., Apr., Sept., and Oct., Thurs.–Mon. 10–5; May and June, daily 10–5; July and Aug., daily 10–6; Nov.–Feb., Fri.–Mon. 10–4.*

Where to Stay & Eat

£££££ ✕ **Hibiscus.** French chef Claude Bosi creates contemporary dishes with
Fodor'sChoice panache: step into the two small rooms (one stone-walled, the other oak-
★ paneled) of this 17th-century building and feast on creations such as beet-
root and orange tart, followed by Cornish turbot and roast quince, on
the changing, fixed-price menu. Book well ahead. ⊠ *17 Corve St.*
☎ *01584/872325* ⌨ *Reservations essential* ☰ *MC, V* ⊘ *Closed Sun.*
and Mon, 1st 2 wks in Jan. and 3 wks in Aug. No lunch Tues.

££££–£££££ ✕⊡ **Dinham Hall.** A converted merchant's town house dating from
1792, this hotel near Ludlow Castle formerly served as a boys' dormitory for the local grammar school. The owners have successfully integrated modern amenities—including comfortable furniture and print
fabrics—with historic elements. The deep-pink dining room (£££££) serves
creative fixed-price meals, with choices such as duck with honey and
black pepper, or Manx lamb with red cabbage. ⊠ *Off Market Sq., SY8*
1EJ ☎ *01584/876464* 📠 *01584/876019* ⊕ *www.dinhamhall.co.uk*
⌨ *10 rooms, 3 suites* ⌂ *Restaurant, meeting rooms, some pets al-*
lowed (fee), no-smoking rooms; no a/c ☰ *AE, DC, MC, V* ⦿| *BP.*

★ ✕⊡ **Mr. Underhill's.** Occupying a converted mill building beneath the cas-
££££–£££££ tle, this secluded restaurant with rooms looks onto the wooded River
Teme. Both the restaurant (closed Monday and Tuesday; reservations
essential; £££££) and rooms are informal, with plenty of pictures, and
the bright bedrooms are furnished with natural fabrics and specially designed pieces. The superb, modern-British, fixed-price menu, customized
when you book, uses only fresh seasonal ingredients. Dinner could be
halibut with coconut and ginger or local venison with red wine, elder-
berry, and thyme. Book well ahead. ⊠ *Dinham Weir, SY8 1EH* ☎ *01584/*
874431 ⊕ *www.mr-underhills.co.uk* ⌨ *6 rooms, 3 suites* ⌂ *Restau-*
rant; no a/c, no smoking ☰ *MC, V* ⦿| *BP.*

££–££££ ⊡ **The Feathers.** Even if you're not staying here, take time to admire the
extravagant half-timber facade of this building, described by the architectural historian Nicholas Pevsner as "that prodigy of timber-framed
houses." The interior is equally impressive—dripping with ornate plaster ceilings, carved oak, paneling, beams, and creaking floors. Some guest
rooms are done in modern style, but others preserve the antique look.
⊠ *The Bull Ring, SY8 1AA* ☎ *01584/875261* 📠 *01584/876030* ⊕ *www.*
feathersatludlow.co.uk ⌨ *40 rooms* ⌂ *Restaurant, cable TV with*
movies, meeting rooms, some pets allowed (fee); no a/c ☰ *AE, MC, V*
⦿| *BP.*

££ ⊡ **Hen and Chickens.** Creaking floors and sloping ceilings abound in this
18th-century former pub. Bedrooms are simply furnished, bathrooms
are sizable, and the breakfast table is laden with home-produced eggs
and preserves, as well as local sausages. ⊠ *103 Old St., SY8 1NU*
☎ *01584/874318* ⊕ *www.hen-and-chickens.co.uk* ⌨ *4 rooms* ⌂ *No*
a/c, no room phones, no kids under 10, no smoking ☰ *MC, V* ⦿| *BP.*

Nightlife & the Arts

The two-week **Ludlow Festival** (☎ 01584/872150 ⊕ www.ludlowfestival.
co.uk), starting in late June, includes Shakespeare performed near the
ruined castle and opera, dance, and concerts around town.

Chester

41 *75 mi north of Ludlow, 46 mi north of Shrewsbury.*

Cheshire is mainly a land of well-kept farms, supporting their herds of cattle, but numerous places here are steeped in history. Villages contain many fine examples of the black-and-white "magpie" type of architecture more often associated with areas to the east. The thriving center of the region is Chester, a city similar in some ways to Shrewsbury, though it has many more black-and-white half-timber buildings (some built in Georgian and Victorian times), and its medieval walls still stand.

Chester has been a prominent city since the late 1st century, when the Roman Empire expanded north to the banks of the River Dee. The original Roman town plan is still evident: the principal streets, Eastgate, Northgate, Watergate, and Bridge Street, lead out from the Cross—the site of the central area of the Roman fortress—to the four city gates, and the partly excavated remains of what is thought to have been the country's largest Roman amphitheater lie to the south of Chester's medieval castle. Since Roman times, seagoing vessels have sailed up the estuary of the Dee and anchored under the walls of Chester. The port enjoyed its most prosperous period during the 12th and 13th centuries.

History seems more tangible in Chester than in many other ancient cities. Much medieval architecture remains in the compact town center, and modern buildings have not been allowed to intrude. A negative result of this perfection is that Chester has become a favorite bus-tour destination, with gift shops, noise, and crowds. ■ TIP➔ **If you've made it this far north, consider heading on to Liverpool, if the Beatles and maritime history have any appeal.**

★ Chester's unique **Rows,** which originated in the 12th and 13th centuries, are essentially double rows of stores, one at street level and the other on the second floor with galleries overlooking the street. The Rows line the junction of the four streets in the old town. They have medieval crypts below them, and some reveal Roman foundations.

The city **walls,** accessible from several points, provide splendid views of the city and its surroundings. The whole circuit is 2 mi, but if your time is short, climb the steps at Newgate and walk along toward Eastgate to see the great ornamental **Eastgate Clock,** erected to commemorate Queen Victoria's Diamond Jubilee in 1897. Lots of small shops near this part of the walls sell old books, old postcards, antiques, and jewelry. Where the **Bridge of Sighs** (named after the enclosed bridge in Venice that it closely resembles) crosses the canal, descend to street level and walk up Northgate Street into Market Square.

> **WORD OF MOUTH**
>
> "We spent a night in Chester and fell in love with it. The city is a walled pedestrian town and is chock full of shops. If you are interested in antiquing, there are lots of shops . . . the river runs around the town and they have tours on the boats."   –Andy

Tradition has it that a church of some sort stood on the site of what is now **Chester Cathedral** in Roman times, but records indicate construction around AD 900. The earliest work traceable today, mainly in the north transept, is that of the 11th-century Benedictine abbey. After Henry VIII dissolved the monasteries in the 16th century, the abbey church became the cathedral church of the new diocese of Chester. The choir stalls reveal figures of people and dragons, and above is a gilded and colorful vaulted ceiling. In the small inner garden, a striking modern bronze statue depicts the woman of Samaria offering water to Jesus. ⊠ *St. Werburgh St., off Market Sq.* ☎ *01244/324756* ⊕ *www.chestercathedral.com* ☑ *£4 including audio guide* ◷ *Mon.–Sat. 9–5, Sun. 12:30–3:30.*

Chester Castle, overlooking the River Dee, lost its moats and battlements at the end of the 18th century to make way for the classical-style civil and criminal courts, jail, and barracks. The castle houses the **Cheshire Military Museum,** exhibiting uniforms, memorabilia, and some fine silver. ⊠ *Castle St.* ☎ *01244/327617* ☑ *£2* ◷ *Daily 10–4.*

ⓒ Well-landscaped grounds and natural enclosures make the 80-acre **Chester Zoo** one of Britain's most popular zoos, as well as the largest. Highlights include Chimpanzee Island, the jaguar enclosure, and the Islands in Danger tropical habitat. Baby animals are often on display. Eleven miles of paths wend through the zoo, and you can use the waterbus boats or the overhead train to tour the grounds. ⊠ *A41, 2 mi north of Chester* ☎ *01244/380280* ⊕ *www.chesterzoo.org* ☑ *Apr.–Oct. £13.50; Nov.–Mar. £10.50, bus £2, train £2* ◷ *Daily 10–dusk.*

Where to Stay & Eat

££–£££ ✕**Brasserie 10/16.** Flooded with natural light from a wall of windows, this brasserie has clean, elegant lines. The Mediterranean fare is well presented, too, ranging from numerous salads to sea bass with crab and tomato risotto, and beef with horseradish mashed potatoes. Indulge yourself with the local ice creams or a trio of chocolate desserts. ⊠ *Brookdale Pl.* ☎ *01244/322288* ▭ *AE, MC, V.*

££–£££ ✕**Francs.** Beyond the black-and-white half-timber exterior of this French eatery is an intimate dining area, with rustic basketwork on the walls and bentwood chairs. The menu lists choices such as fish cakes fried in a light beer batter, followed by chicken breast stuffed with garlic cheese; vegetarians might consider crepes filled with hazelnuts and leeks. Fixed-price meals are a great value, and children are welcomed with a special menu. ⊠ *14 Cuppin St.* ☎ *01244/317952* ▭ *AE, MC, V.*

★ **£££££** ✕▥**Chester Crabwall Manor.** Eleven acres of farm and parkland surround this dramatic, castellated, part-Tudor, part-neo-Gothic mansion, a good place to indulge yourself. The hotel has elegant, subtle furnishings in dusky pinks and blues and an impressive stone staircase and fireplace. In the spacious Conservatory restaurant (£££££), try such fine English fare as wild trout with Cheshire cured bacon, or loin of Welsh lamb. ⊠ *A540, Parkgate Rd., Mollington CH1 6NE* ☎ *01244/851666* ▣ *01244/851400* ⊕ *www.swallowhotels.com* ↬ *42 rooms, 6 suites*

♿ Restaurant, cable TV, in-room broadband, in-room data ports, indoor pool, health club, spa, meeting rooms, no-smoking rooms; no a/c ⊟ AE, DC, MC, V ⦿ BP.

£££££ ✕▦ **Chester Grosvenor Hotel.** At this deluxe traditional hotel in a Tudor-style building downtown, handmade Italian furniture and French silk furnishings complement the English architecture. Floris toiletries, CD players, and a luxury spa are among the pampering amenities. The elegant Arkle Restaurant (named after a celebrated racehorse; closed Monday and Sunday evening and first three weeks in January; £££££) offers a fixed-price dinner as well as a daily gastronomic menu. The wine cellar has more than 600 bins. Good, hearty food is served in the brasserie (££–££££), and the intimate library serves light lunches as well as afternoon tea. Breakfast is included in the lower, weekend leisure rates. ⊠ Eastgate St., CH1 1LT ☎ 01244/324024 🖷 01244/313246 ⊕ www.chestergrosvenor.co.uk ⟿ 80 rooms ♿ 2 restaurants, cable TV, in-room broadband, in-room data ports, health club, spa, Internet room, business services, meeting rooms, no-smoking rooms ⊟ AE, DC, MC, V.

££££ ✕▦ **Green Bough Hotel.** Chester's leafy outskirts are the setting for this memorable small hotel a mile from the town center. Furnished with antiques, including cast-iron and carved wooden beds, and decorated with Italian fabrics and wallcoverings, the individually designed guest rooms make luxurious and soothing retreats. The Olive Tree restaurant (££££–£££££) provides top-notch contemporary British fare in intimate surroundings. Head to the rooftop garden for a relaxing drink in summer. ⊠ 60 Hoole Rd., CH2 3NL ☎ 01244/326241 🖷 01244/326265 ⊕ www.greenbough.co.uk ⟿ 6 rooms, 8 suites ♿ Restaurant, bar, Wi-Fi, meeting room; no a/c, no kids under 11, no smoking ⊟ AE, DC, MC, V ⦿ BP.

££ ▦ **Grove Villa.** The location of this family-run B&B, a 19th-century house on the banks of the River Dee, enhances its appeal. Add antique furniture and a sense of calm, and you are guaranteed a soothing stay. Rooms are often priced at @60. ⊠ 18 The Groves, CH1 1SD ☎ 01244/349713 ✎ grovevilla18@btinternet.com ⟿ 3 rooms ♿ No a/c, no room phones, no smoking ⊟ No credit cards ⦿ BP.

££ ▦ **Ye Olde King's Head.** Creaky stairs and passageways lead through this centrally located black-and-white 17th-century inn to well-equipped guest rooms. Lattice windows and chunky oak beams evoke the past, and the rich fabrics and thick green carpeting provide present-day comfort; bathrooms, though, are on the small side. ⊠ 48–50 Lower Bridge St., CH1 1RS ☎ 01244/324855 🖷 01244/315693 ⟿ 8 rooms ♿ Restaurant, cable TV, bar; no a/c ⊟ MC, V ⦿ BP.

Shopping

Chester has an **indoor market** in the Forum, near the Town Hall, every day except Sunday. Watergate Street hosts antiques shops, which stock anything from small ceramic pieces and clocks to furniture. **Bookland** (⊠ 12 Bridge St. ☎ 01244/347323), in an ancient building with a converted 14th-century crypt, stocks travel and general-interest books.

Sports & the Outdoors

BOATING   **Bithell Boats** (✉ Boating Station, Souters La., The Groves ☎ 01244/325394 ⊕ www.showboatsofchester.co.uk) runs excursions on the River Dee on an excursion boat every 30 minutes daily (April through October) and hourly on weekends (November through March). Some evening cruises feature disco or live music.

WELSH BORDERS ESSENTIALS

Transportation

BY AIR

Birmingham International Airport, 6 mi east of the city center, is the country's second-busiest airport, with connections to all of Britain's major cities. Bus 900 runs to the city center every 20 minutes; a taxi will cost you around £16.

🛈 **Birmingham International Airport** ✉ A45, off Junction 6 of M42 ☎ 0870/733-5511 ⊕ www.bhx.co.uk.

BY BUS

National Express serves the region from London's Victoria Coach Station. Average travel time to Birmingham is 2¾ hours; to Chester is 5½ hours; to Hereford, and Shrewsbury, 4¼ hours; and to Worcester, 4 hours. Flightlink operates services from London's Heathrow (2¾ hours) and Gatwick (4¼ hours) airports to Birmingham.

FARES & SCHEDULES   Traveline fields all public transport inquiries. You can also contact local companies individually. For information about bus services and Rover tickets for the Birmingham area, contact the Centro Hotline. For Worcester, Hereford, Chester, and surrounding areas, contact First.

🛈 **Centro Hotline** ☎ 0121/200-2700 ⊕ www.centro.org.uk. **First (for Chester)** ☎ 01244/381461 ⊕ www.firstgroup.com. **Cheshire Bus Line** ☎ 01244/602666 ⊕ www.firstgroup.com. **First (for Worcester and Hereford)** ☎ 0870/608-2608 ⊕ www.firstgroup.com. **Flightlink** ☎ 0870/580-8080 ⊕ www.nationalexpress.com. **National Express** ☎ 0870/580-8080 ⊕ www.nationalexpress.com. **Traveline** ☎ 0870/608-2608 ⊕ www.traveline.org.uk.

BY CAR

To reach Birmingham (120 mi), Shrewsbury (150 mi), and Chester (180 mi) from London, take M40 and keep on it until it becomes M42, or else take M1/M6. M4 and then M5 from London take you to Worcester and Hereford in just under three hours. A prettier but slower route to Worcester and vicinity is M40 to Oxford and then A44, which skirts the Cotswolds.

ROAD CONDITIONS   Driving can be difficult in the region's western reaches—especially in the hills and valleys west of Hereford, where steep, twisting roads often narrow down into mere trackways. Winter travel can be grueling.

BY TRAIN

From London, Great Western and Arriva trains serve the region from Paddington Station, and Virgin, Central, and Silverlink Trains leave from Euston (call National Rail Enquiries for all schedules and information). Average travel times are Paddington to Hereford (with a change at Newport), 3 hours; to Worcester, 2¼ hours; Euston to Birmingham, 2 hours; Euston to Shrewsbury, with a change at Wolverhampton or Birmingham, 3 hours; or to Chester, with a change at Crewe, 2¾ hours. A direct local service links Hereford and Shrewsbury (1 hour), with a change at Crewe for Chester.

CUTTING COSTS West Midlands Day Ranger tickets (£13.60) and three- and seven-day Heart of England Rover tickets (£53 and £69.40) allow unlimited travel. 🛈 **National Rail Enquiries** ☎ 0845/748-4950 ⊕ www.nationalrail.co.uk.

Contacts & Resources

EMERGENCIES

🛈 **Ambulance, fire, police** ☎ 999. **Birmingham Heartlands Hospital** ✉ Bordesley Green E, Birmingham ☎ 0121/424-2000. **Countess of Chester Hospital** ✉ Liverpool Rd., Chester ☎ 01244/365000.

INTERNET

Internet cafés have not yet arrived at all of the smaller towns. However, the local public library is always a good place to try for Internet access; the tourist office will give you details, and you may have to book ahead for a time slot. The larger hotels are gradually introducing Wi-Fi. 🛈 **NetAdventure Cyber Café** ✉ 68-70 Dalton St., Birmingham ☎ 0121/693-6655, open daily until 10 PM. **Mailboxes** ✉ Shoplatch, Shrewsbury ☎ 01743/270570, closed on Saturday afternoon and Sunday. **Cafenet** ✉ 63 Watergate St., Chester ☎ 01244/401-116, open daily.

TOUR OPTIONS

Local tourist offices can recommend day or half-day tours of the region and will have the names of registered Blue Badge guides. From April to October, City Sightseeing operates daily tours of Chester in open-top buses. Walking tours of Shrewsbury depart from the tourist office (⇨ Visitor Information) daily at 2:30 from May through September and on Saturday the rest of the year (£3.50). Home James runs day trips and longer theme tours of the Shropshire area throughout the year. 🛈 **City Sightseeing** ✉ Chester ☎ 01244/347457 or 0871/666000 ⊕ www.city-sightseeing.com. **Home James** ✉ Box 1, Shrewsbury SY1 1AA ☎ 01743/242424 ⊕ www.homejames.uk.com.

VISITOR INFORMATION

Heart of England Tourism is open Monday through Thursday 9 to 5:30, Friday 9 to 5. Local tourist information centers are usually open Monday through Saturday 9:30 to 5:30. 🛈 **Heart of England Tourism** ✉ Larkhill Rd., Worcester WR5 2EZ ☎ 01905/763436 🖷 01905/763450 ⊕ www.visitheartofengland.com. **Birmingham** ✉ The Rotunda, 150 New St., B2 4PA ☎ 0870/225-0127 ⊕ www.beinbirmingham.com. **Chester** ✉ Town Hall, Northgate St., CH1 2HJ ✉ Vicar's La., CH1 1QX ☎ 01244/402111 ⊕ www.chestertourism.

com. **Great Malvern Tourist Office** ✉ 21 Church St., WR14 2AA ☎ 01684/892289 ⊕ www.malvernhills.gov.uk. **Hereford** ✉1 King St., HR4 9BW ☎ 01432/268430 ⊕ www.visitherefordshire.co.uk. **Ludlow** ✉ Castle St., SY8 1AS ☎ 01584/875053 ⊕ www.ludlow.org.uk. **Much Wenlock** ✉ The Museum, The Square, TF13 6HR ☎ 01952/727679 ⊕ www.muchwenlockguide.info. **Ross-on-Wye** ✉ Swan House, Edde Cross St., HR9 7BZ ☎ 01989/562768 ⊕ www.visitherefordshire.co.uk. **Shrewsbury** ✉ The Music Hall, The Square, SY1 1LH ☎ 01743/281200 ⊕ www.visitshrewsbury.com. **Worcester** ✉ The Guildhall, High St., WR1 2EY ☎ 01905/726311 ⊕ www.visitworcester.com.

8

Lancashire & the Peaks

MANCHESTER, LIVERPOOL & THE PEAK DISTRICT

WORD OF MOUTH

"In Manchester, have a look inside the glorious Town Hall, which has been used in movies as a stand-in for the Parliament in London. Walk down to the renovated Castlefield area, perhaps taking in the Museum of Science and Industry, and have a pint at the canalside Dukes 92. If you fancy hedonism, trot along Canal Street, home of gay and gay-friendly crowds who like to party hard."

—Nigello

"I'd choose Chatsworth. It is among the three or four grandest houses in the United Kingdom, and it looks basically like it has for the past several centuries. Also relatively close to Chatsworth is Hardwick Hall, a wonderful Elizabethan house that's well worth a visit."

—Anglophile

Updated by
Kate Hughes

FOR THOSE LOOKING FOR THE POSTCARD ENGLAND of little villages and churches, the northwest region of England might not appear at the top of a sightseeing list. Manchester today bustles with redevelopment and youth culture, and Liverpool's upcoming stint as the European Union's Capital of Culture in 2008 is bringing exciting changes; but 200 years of smokestack industry, which abated only in the 1980s, have taken a toll on the east Lancashire landscape. The region does have some lovely scenery inland, in Derbyshire (pronounced "Darbyshire")—notably the spectacular Peak District, a huge national park at the southern end of the Pennines range. In and around this area are Victorian-era spas such as Buxton, pretty towns such as Bakewell, and magnificent stately houses such as Chatsworth, Hardwick Hall, and Haddon Hall.

Manchester and Liverpool were the economic engines that propelled Britain in the 18th and 19th centuries, but they suffered decline in the mid-20th century. Both cities are sloughing off the recent past and celebrating their rich industrial and maritime heritage in their excellent museums—in imposing Victorian edifices, or, in Manchester's case, in strikingly modern buildings that are a statement in themselves. The cities have reestablished themselves as centers of sporting and musical and excellence, and as nightlife hot spots. Since 1962, the Manchester United, Everton, and Liverpool football (soccer in the United States) clubs have won everything worth winning in Britain and Europe. The Beatles launched the Mersey sound of the '60s; contemporary Manchester groups ride both British and U.S. airwaves. On the classical side of music, Manchester is also the home of Britain's oldest leading orchestra, the Hallé (founded in 1857)—just one legacy of 19th-century industrialists' investments in culture.

The Peak District is a wilder part of England, a region of crags that rear violently out of the plain. The Pennines, a line of hills that begins in the Peak District and runs as far north as Scotland, are sometimes called the "backbone of England." In this landscape of rocky outcrops and vaulting meadowland, you'll see nothing for miles but sheep, drystone (without mortar) walls, and farms, interrupted—spectacularly—by 19th-century villages and treasure houses. The delight of the Peak District is being able to ramble for days in rugged countryside but still enjoy civilization at its finest.

Exploring Lancashire & the Peak District

Manchester lies at the heart of a tangle of motorways in the northwest of England, about a half hour across the Pennines from Yorkshire. It's 70 mi from the southern part of the Lake District. The city spreads west toward the coast and the mouth of the River Mersey, where Liverpool is still centered on its port. For the Northwest's most dramatic scenery—indeed, its only real geological feature of interest—you must travel to the Peak District, a national park less than an hour's drive southeast of Manchester. England at its most grand and ducal can be seen in the Derbyshire valley of the River Wye: majestic 18th-century Chatsworth; Haddon Hall, an enchanting Tudor and Jacobean structure; and Hardwick Hall, the glory of the late Elizabethan age.

About the Restaurants

Though Manchester currently has the edge over Liverpool, dining options in both cities vary from smart café-bars offering modern British and continental fare to excellent ethnic restaurants. Manchester has one of Britain's biggest Chinatowns, and locals also savor the 40-odd Bangladeshi, Pakistani, and Indian restaurants along Wilmslow Road in Rusholme, a mile south of the city center, known as Curry Mile (check out ⊕ www.rusholmecurry.co.uk).

One local dish that has survived is Bakewell pudding (*never* called "tart" in these areas, as its imitations are elsewhere in England). Served with custard or cream, the pudding is the joy of Bakewell. Another regional creation is the hearty Lancashire hot pot, a meat stew.

About the Hotels

If your trip centers on the cities of the northwest, you may want to base yourself in Manchester (which has a better choice of accommodations, though Liverpool's are improving steadily) and make Liverpool a day trip. Because the larger city-center hotels in both cities rely on businesspeople during the week, they often markedly reduce their rates on weekends. Smaller hotels and guesthouses abound in nearby suburbs, many just a short bus ride from downtown. The Manchester Visitor Centre operates a room-booking service. The Peak District has inns, bed-and-breakfasts, and hotels, as well as a network of youth hostels. Local tourist offices have details; reserve well in advance for Easter and summer.

WHAT IT COSTS In pounds				
££££££	**££££**	**£££**	**££**	**£**
RESTAURANTS over £22	£18–£22	£13–£17	£7–£12	under £7
HOTELS over £160	£120–£160	£90–£119	£60–£89	under £60

Restaurant prices are for a main course at dinner. Hotel prices are for two people in a standard double room in high season, including V.A.T., with no meals or, if indicated, CP (with continental breakfast), BP (Breakfast Plan, with full breakfast), or MAP (Modified American Plan, with breakfast and dinner).

Timing

Manchester has a reputation as one of the wettest cities in Britain, and visiting in summer won't guarantee fine weather. Nevertheless, the many indoor sights and cultural activities here and in Liverpool means that wet or cold weather shouldn't spoil a visit. Summer is the optimum time to see the Peak District, especially because traditional festivities take place in many villages at its start. The *only* time to see the great houses of the Derbyshire Wye valley and vicinity—Chatsworth, Haddon Hall, and Hardwick Hall—is from spring through fall.

MANCHESTER

▶ Manchester's center hums with the energy of cutting-edge popular music and a swank café-bar culture. The formerly grim industrial landscape has been redeveloped since the late 1980s, in part because of events as

GREAT ITINERARIES

Greater Manchester and Merseyside form one of the most built-up areas in Britain, but motorway access between the two is fast. One of the main towns of the Peak District, Buxton, could be visited on a day trip from Manchester if you wanted to base yourself in that city. But the Peaks deserve more than just a short drive around the principal sights.

Numbers in the text correspond to numbers in the margin and on the Lancashire & the Peaks, Manchester, and Liverpool maps.

IF YOU HAVE 3 DAYS

Base yourself in Manchester ① – ⑫ ⬛ for your first night, which will give you a chance to see the central sights on your first day and take in a concert or a club that night. On the next day, journey to the green Derbyshire Wye Valley to visit two of England's most magnificent stately homes, **Haddon Hall** ㉘ and **Chatsworth House** ㉛. Spend your second night in nearby Bakewell ㉗ or Buxton ㉖. If you're traveling when these houses are closed for the season, visit Liverpool ⑬ – ㉔ for an overnight stay. Enjoy a lunch on

the Albert Dock and spend the afternoon in the museums and attractions of this dockside center.

IF YOU HAVE 7 DAYS

It's wisest to split your time between city and national park. Start by exploring Buxton ㉖ ⬛; you can overnight there or in Bakewell ㉗. Visit **Haddon Hall** ㉘ and **Chatsworth House** ㉛, both among the top stately homes in Britain, returning to Bakewell for the night. On the morning of your third day, move on to **Matlock** ㉙ and its river, and take a cable-car ride to the Heights of Abraham, or visit **Hardwick Hall** ㉚, which sums up the late Elizabethan era, before aiming for **Castleton** ㉜ and its splendid caverns. If you want to do any walking around the isolated village of **Edale** ㉝, spend the third night back in Buxton ㉖ (or in Edale itself), making an early start on the day. After walking on the moors, you can take a short drive to Manchester ① – ⑫, where a two-night stay will let you see the best of that city. Move on to enjoy your last night in Liverpool ⑬ – ㉔.

different as an IRA bombing in the city center in 1996 and the 2002 Commonwealth Games. Canals have been tidied up, cotton mills serve as loft apartments, and stylish contemporary architecture has transformed the skyline. Britain's tallest sculpture, the *B of the Bang,* at an intersection next to Manchester City Stadium, rises 184 feet in the air like a starburst of fireworks. Beetham Tower, the second-tallest building in Britain after London's Canary Wharf, opened in 2006. Bridgewater Hall and the Lowry, as well as the Imperial War Museum North, are outstanding cultural facilities. Sure, it still rains here, but the rain-soaked streets are part of the city's charm, in a bleak northern kind of way.

For most of its existence Manchester, which has a population of 2.6 million and is Britain's third-largest city, has been a thriving and prosperous place. The Romans built a fort here in AD 79 and named it Mamucium, but the city that stands today—with the imposing Town Hall, Royal Exchange, Midland Hotel, the waterways, and railway—is a product of the Industrial Revolution and the wealth it created.

It's impossible to talk about Manchester without mentioning music and football. Out of poverty and unemployment came the brash sounds of punk and the indie record labels, and a thriving club scene. The band New Order produced a unique Mancunian sound that mixed live instruments with digital sound. The now-defunct Haçienda Club marketed New Order to the world, and Manchester became the clubbing capital of England. Joy Division, Morrissey, Stone Roses, Happy Mondays, and Oasis rose to the top of the charts. The triumphant reign of the Manchester United football club, which now faces new challenges from southern rivals Arsenal and Chelsea, has kept many eyes on Manchester.

Exploring Manchester

Manchester is compact enough that you can easily walk across the city center in 40 minutes, but buses and Metrolink trams make it easy to navigate. Deansgate and Princess Street, the main thoroughfares, run roughly north to south and west to east; the lofty terra-cotta Victorian **Town Hall** sits in the middle, close to the visitor center and the fine **Manchester Art Gallery.** Dominating the skyline at the southern end of Deansgate is Manchester's newest and highest building, Beetham Tower, which houses a Hilton Hotel and marks the beginning of the **Castlefield Urban Heritage Park,** with the Museum of Science and Industry and the canal system. The **Whitworth Art Gallery** is a bus ride from downtown; otherwise, all other central sights are within easy walking distance of the Town Hall. Take a Metrolink tram 2 mi south for the Salford Quays dockland area, with the **Lowry** and the **Imperial War Museum;** you can spend half a day or more in this area. ■ TIP→ Shopping and nightlife offer great diversions in Manchester, but keep in mind that the museums are both excellent and free. Note that the city will be emptier on Sunday; many museums will be open, but some other sights are closed.

Main Attractions

❹ Castlefield Urban Heritage Park. Site of an early Roman fort, the district of Castlefield was later the center of the city's industrial boom, which resulted in the building of Britain's first modern canal in 1764 and the world's first railway station in 1830. What had become an urban wasteland has been beautifully restored into an urban park with canal-side walks, landscaped open spaces, and refurbished warehouses. The 7-acre site contains the reconstructed gate to the Roman fort of Mamucium, the buildings of the **Museum of Science and Industry,** and several of the city's hippest bars and restaurants. You can spend half a day here, including the museum. ✉ *Off Liverpool Rd., Castlefield.*

★ **Imperial War Museum North.** The thought-provoking exhibits in this striking, aluminum-clad building, which architect Daniel Libeskind described as representing three shards of an exploded globe, present the reasons for war and show its effects on society. Three Big Picture au-

TOP REASONS TO GO

The Beatles: Whether you want to relive the Fab Four's moments of glory, visit their haunts, see their childhood homes, or just buy a Beatle pencil sharpener, a magical mystery tour in Liverpool will provide it all.

Museums in Manchester and Liverpool: You don't need the excuse of rain to learn about these cities' industrial and maritime pasts, or to see the glories of English art; visit even on a sunny day. Take history lessons at the Museum of Science and Industry and the Imperial War Museum North in Manchester, and the Merseyside Maritime Museum in Liverpool. Then opt for art appreciation in the cities' galleries.

Manchester nightspots: Catch the city at night in any of its humming café-bars and pubs; strut your stuff, soak up the latest sounds, or just enjoy a good beer in a gloriously ornate Victorian pub.

Chatsworth House and Haddon Hall: Engage the past and imagine yourself as a country landowner roaming the great pile that is Chatsworth, or as a Tudor noble exercising in the intricate long gallery of the quintessentially English Haddon Hall. Each can take you a half-day—Chatsworth a day—to explore.

Walking in the Peak District: Even a short walk in Edale or High Peak reveals the rocky yet intimate scenery that is unique to the area—dales rubbing shoulders with moors, and drystone walls patterning the fields. Civilization, in the form of welcoming pubs and peaceful towns, is always close at hand; that's part of the pleasure.

diovisual shows envelop you in the sights and sounds of conflicts from 1914 to the present, and a storage system allows you to select trays of objects to view, including exhibits from the 2003 war in Iraq. A 100-foot viewing platform gives a bird's-eye view of the city. The museum is on the banks of the Manchester Ship Canal in Salford Quays, across the footbridge from the Lowry. It's a 10-minute walk from the Harbour City stop of the Metrolink tram. ⊠ *Trafford Wharf Rd., Salford Quays* ☎ *0161/836–4000* ⊕ *www.iwm.org.uk* ✉ *Free* ⊙ *Mar.–Oct., daily 10–6; Nov.–Feb., daily 10–5; last admission 30 mins before closing.*

The Lowry. This impressive arts center in Manchester's Salford Quays waterways occupies a dramatic modern building with a steel-gray metallic and glass exterior that reflects the light. L. S. Lowry (1887–1976) was a local artist, and one of the few who painted the industrial landscape. Galleries showcase Lowry's and other contemporary artists' work. The theater, Britain's largest outside London, presents an impressive lineup of touring companies. The nearest Metrolink tram stop is Harbour City, a 10-minute walk from the Lowry. ⊠ *Pier 8, Salford Quays* ☎ *0161/876–2000* ⊕ *www.thelowry.com* ✉ *Free; prices vary for theater tickets and exhibitions; tours £3* ⊙ *Building Sun. and Mon. 10–6, Tues.–Sat. 10–8, or last performance; galleries Sun.–Fri. 11–5, Sat. 10–5; tours daily 11:30, 1, and 2:30.*

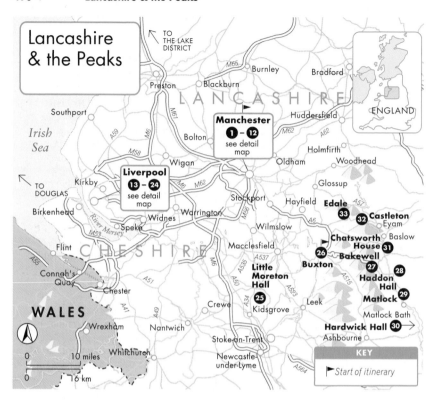

★ ❷ **Manchester Art Gallery.** Behind its impressive classical portico, this splendid museum presents its collections in both a Victorian and contemporary setting. Outstanding are the vibrant paintings by the Pre-Raphaelites and their circle, exemplified by Ford Madox Brown's masterpiece *Work* and Holman Hunt's *The Hireling Shepherd*. British works from the 18th century—*Cheetah and Stag with Two Indians* by George Stubbs, for instance—and the 20th century are also well represented. The Manchester Gallery illustrates the city's contribution to art, and the second-floor Craft and Design Gallery shows off the best of the decorative arts in ceramics and glass, metalwork, and furniture. ⊠ *Mosely St., City Centre* ☎ *0161/235–8888* ⊕ *www.manchestergalleries.org.uk* ✉ *Free* ⊙ *Tues.–Sun. and national holidays 10–5.*

❺ **Museum of Science and Industry.** The museum's five buildings, one of which is the world's oldest passenger rail station (1830), hold marvelous collections relating to the city's industrial past and present. You can walk through a reconstructed Victorian sewer, be blasted by the heat and noise of working steam engines, and see cotton looms whirring in action. The Air and Space Gallery fills a graceful cast-iron-and-glass building, constructed as a market hall in 1877. ■ TIP→ Allow at least half a day to get the most out of all the sites, which are in the Castlefield Urban Heritage Park.

Fodor's Choice
★

Cottonopolis

Manchester's spectacular rise from a small town to the world's cotton capital—with the nickname Cottonopolis—in only 100 years began with the first steam-powered cotton mill, built in 1783. Dredging made the rivers Irwell and Mersey navigable to ship coal to the factories. The world's first passenger railway opened in 1830, and construction of the Manchester Ship Canal in 1894 provided the infrastructure for Manchester to dominate the industrial world. Check out ⊕ www.industrialpowerhouse.co.uk for information about seeing more of this industrial heritage.

A few people acquired great wealth, but factory hands worked under appalling conditions. Working-class discontent came to a head in 1819 in the Peterloo Massacre, when soldiers killed 11 workers at a protest meeting. The conditions under which factory hands worked were later recorded by Friedrich Engels (coauthor with Karl Marx of the *Communist Manifesto*), who managed a cotton mill in the city. More formal political opposition to the government emerged in the shape of the Chartist movement (which campaigned for universal suffrage) and the Anti-Corn Law League (which opposed trade tariffs), forerunners of the British trade unions. From Victorian times until the 1960s, daily life for the average Mancunian was so oppressive that it bred the desire to escape, although most stayed put and endured the harsh conditions.

✉ *Liverpool Rd., main entrance on Lower Byrom Rd., Castlefield* ☎ *0161/832–2244* ⊕ *www.msim.org.uk* ✉ *Free, charges vary for special exhibitions* ⊙ *Daily 10–5.*

PumpHouse: People's History Museum. Not everyone in 19th-century Manchester owned a cotton mill or made a fortune on the trading floor. This museum recounts powerfully the struggles of working people in the city since the Industrial Revolution. The museum tells the story of the 1819 Peterloo Massacre and has an unrivaled collection of trade-union banners, tools, toys, utensils, and photographs, all illustrating the working lives and pastimes of the city's people. ✉ *Bridge St., City Centre* ☎ *0161/839–6061* ⊕ *www.peopleshistorymuseum.org.uk* ✉ *Free* ⊙ *Tues.–Sun. and national holidays 11–4:30.*

NEED A BREAK?

The brick-vaulted, waterside **Mark Addy pub** (✉ Stanley St., off Bridge St., City Centre ☎ 0161/832–4080) is a good spot to have a relaxing drink and sample an excellent spread of pâtés and cheeses. The pub is named for the 19th-century boatman who rescued more than 50 people from the River Irwell.

Royal Exchange. Throughout its commercial heyday, this was the city's most important building—the cotton market. Built with Victorian panache in 1874, the existing structure accommodated 7,000 traders. The building was refurbished and the giant glass-dome roof restored after damage by the 1996 IRA bombing. Visit to see the lunar module–inspired Royal Exchange Theatre, to have a drink in the café, or to browse

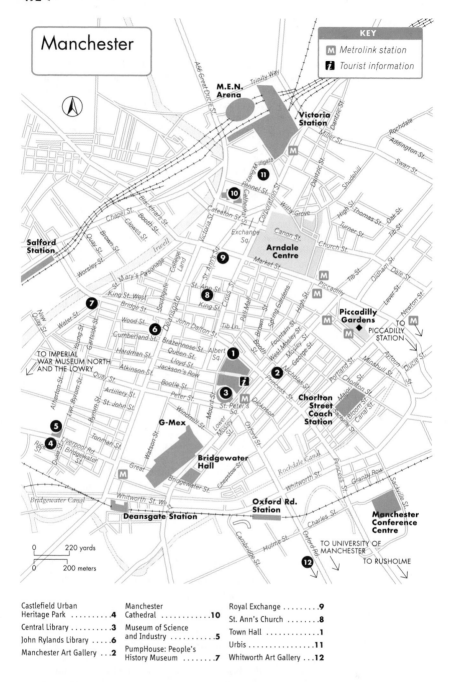

Manchester

KEY

Ⓜ Metrolink station

🛈 Tourist information

M.E.N. Arena

Victoria Station

Salford Station

Arndale Centre

Piccadilly Gardens

Piccadilly

TO PICCADILLY STATION

Chorlton Street Coach Station

TO IMPERIAL WAR MUSEUM NORTH AND THE LOWRY

G-Mex

Bridgewater Hall

Deansgate Station

Oxford Rd. Station

Manchester Conference Centre

TO UNIVERSITY OF MANCHESTER

TO RUSHOLME

Bridgewater Canal

0   220 yards

0   200 meters

Castlefield Urban Heritage Park **4**	Manchester Cathedral **10**	Royal Exchange **9**
Central Library **3**	Museum of Science and Industry **5**	St. Ann's Church **8**
John Rylands Library **6**		Town Hall **1**
Manchester Art Gallery ...**2**	PumpHouse: People's History Museum **7**	Urbis **11**
		Whitworth Art Gallery ...**12**

in the craft and clothes outlets in the arcade. ✉ *St. Ann's Sq., City Centre* ☎ *0161/834–3731* ⊕ *www.royalexchange.co.uk.*

❶ Town Hall. Manchester's exuberant Town Hall, with its imposing 280-foot-tall clock tower, speaks volumes about the city's 19th-century sense of self-importance. Alfred Waterhouse designed the Victorian Gothic building (1867–76); extensions were added just before World War II. Over the main entrance is a statue of Roman general Agricola, who founded Mamucium in AD 79. Above him are Henry III, Elizabeth I, and St. George, the patron saint of England. Murals of the city's history, painted between 1852 and 1865 by the Pre-Raphaelite Ford Madox Brown, decorate the Great Hall, with its emblazoned hammer-beam roof. Guided tours (twice a month) include the murals, but ask at the front desk: if the rooms aren't being used, you may be allowed to wander in. ✉ *Albert Sq., public entrance on Lloyd St., City Centre* ☎ *0161/234–5000* ✉ *Free; guided tours £4* ☉ *Mon.–Sat. 9–4:30; not always open to public access; see tourist office in Town Hall Extension for tour information.*

⓬ Whitworth Art Gallery. This University of Manchester–run art museum has strong collections of British watercolors, old-master drawings, and postimpressionist works, as well as wallpapers. Captivating rooms full of textiles—Coptic and Peruvian fabrics, Spanish and Italian vestments, tribal rugs, and contemporary weaving—are just what you might expect in a city built on textile manufacture. There's a bistro and a good gift shop. To get here catch any bus with a number in the 40s (except 47) on Oxford Road, or from St. Peters Square or Piccadilly Gardens. ✉ *Oxford Rd., University Quarter* ☎ *0161/275–7450* ⊕ *www.whitworth.man.ac.uk* ✉ *Free* ☉ *Mon.–Sat. 10–5, Sun. 2–5.*

Also Worth Seeing

❸ Central Library. The circular exterior of the city's main library, topped by a line of Doric columns and a massive Corinthian portico facing St. Peter's Square, is a major focus for Manchester's most prestigious civic quarter. Erected in 1930, it was at one time the biggest municipal library in the world. The vast, glass-top social sciences reading room, inspired by the Pantheon, is worth seeing. The **Library Theatre** is part of the complex. ✉ *St. Peter's Sq., City Centre* ☎ *0161/234–1900* ⊕ *www.manchester.gov.uk* ☉ *Mon.–Thurs. 9–8, Fri. and Sat. 9–5.*

❻ John Rylands Library. Now owned by the University of Manchester, this Gothic-revival masterpiece designed by Alfred Waterhouse was built by Enriqueta Augustina Rylands as a memorial to her husband, a cotton magnate. Constructed of red sandstone in the 1890s, the library resembles a cathedral. A staircase leads to the reading room, with plaster carvings, and paneled reading alcoves. The library is due to reopen late 2006 after restoration. ✉ *150 Deansgate, City Centre* ☎ *0161/275–3764 until reopening* ⊕ *www.library.manchester.ac.uk/.*

❿ Manchester Cathedral. The city's cathedral, set beside the River Irwell and originally a medieval parish church dating in part from the 15th century, is unusually broad for its length and has the widest medieval nave in Britain. Inside, angels with gilded instruments look down from the roof of the nave, and misericords in the early-16th-century choir stalls reveal intriguing carvings. The octagonal chapter house dates from 1485. ⊠ *Victoria St., Millennium Quarter* ☎ *0161/833–2220* 🖃 *Free, donations welcome* ⊕ *www.manchestercathedral.org* ⊘ *Weekdays and Sun. 9–5:30, Sat. 9–3:30.*

⑧ St. Ann's Church. Built in 1712 and sometimes wrongly attributed to Christopher Wren, St. Ann's is Manchester's oldest surviving classical building. The Lady Chapel contains *The Descent from the Cross,* a painting by Annibale Carracci (1561–1609). The verger is usually on hand to show you around. ⊠ *St. Ann's Sq., City Centre* ☎ *0161/834–0239* 🖃 *Free, donations welcome* ⊘ *Daily 9:45–4:45.*

⑪ Urbis. A high-tech museum in this striking glass-skinned triangle of a building dissects the modern urban condition with a vengeance, though with mixed success. Interactive galleries present issues of immigration, social control through design, and crime, all with a focus mainly on Manchester. ⊠ *Cathedral Gardens, Millennium Quarter* ☎ *0161/605–8200* ⊕ *www.urbis.org.uk* 🖃 *Free; temporary exhibitions £5* ⊘ *Tues.–Sun. and national holidays 10–6; last admission 1½ hrs before closing.*

Where to Eat

The city's dining scene, with everything from Indian (go to Rusholme) to modern British fare, is lively. The Manchester Food & Drink Festival, held the first two weeks of October, showcases the city's chefs and regional products with special events. Marco Pierre White's River Room at the Lowry Hotel is another excellent dining choice. The city's pubs (*see* Nightlife & the Arts, *below*) are also good for lunch or dinner.

★
££££–£££££ ✕ **Juniper.** Chef Paul Kitchings aims to surprise and delight with his innovative combinations of ingredients: scallops with raspberries and lamb with bees' pollen and curried mayonnaise, to name but a few. The £40 fixed-price menu offers three courses, but for £55 you can indulge in 12 bite- and small-size dishes. Gilt mirrors and large paintings decorate the restaurant's mint-green walls, and service is professional but friendly. Altrincham, 8 mi south of Manchester, near the airport, is easily accessible by train. ⊠ *21 The Downs, Altrincham* ☎ *0161/929–4008* ⌂ *Reservations essential* ⊟ *AE, MC, V* ⊘ *Closed Sun. and Mon. and 2 wks mid-Feb., 2 wks late Aug., 1 wk late Dec. No lunch Tues.–Thurs.*

★ **£££** ✕ **Market Restaurant.** Lace curtains, pretty china, and green basket-work chairs set the tone in this nicely old-fashioned, family-run restaurant. Food is up to the minute, though: you could start with a twice-baked crab soufflé, and follow with beef wrapped in bacon with Stilton butter and port wine gravy. Leave room for a marzipan baklava with Jersey cream. Specialty beers and excellent wines fit the bill. ⊠ *104 High St., Northern Quarter* ☎ *0161/834-3743* ⌂ *Reservations essential* ⊟ *AE, MC, V* ⊘ *Closed Sun.–Tues. No lunch Sat.*

£££ ✕ **Stock.** The Edwardian building that houses this buzzing Italian restaurant was once the city's stock exchange—hence its name and grand domed setting. Chef Enzo Mauro emphasizes the flavors of southern Italy on a menu that might list potato gnocchi with pumpkin and pancetta or pork fillet with rosemary and white wine; you can accompany this with a fine-quality wine. Bonuses are a good-value lunch deal, jazz on Friday, and occasional opera nights. ✉ *4 Norfolk St., City Centre* ☎ *0161/ 839–6644* 🖃 *AE, MC, V* 🕐 *Closed Sun.*

ff–fff ✕ **Le Petit Blanc.** Famed chef Raymond Blanc's upscale Manchester brasserie is faithful to its Parisian role models. Conversation buzzes in the relaxed yet elegant surroundings of the mostly white room. The menu combines the best traditions of French bourgeois cuisine with Asian and Mediterranean accents. Try the pasta with Roquefort sauce, celery, and toasted hazelnuts; finish up with banana and pecan toffee pudding with bitter chocolate and vanilla ice cream. Children are welcome and have their own menu. ✉ *55 King St., entrance on Chapel Walk, City Centre* ☎ *0161/832–1000* 🖃 *AE, MC, V.*

ff–fff ✕ **Mr. Thomas's Chophouse.** The city's oldest restaurant (1872) dishes out good old British favorites such as steak-and-kidney pudding, Cheshire gammon (ham), and corned beef hash. This hearty food is served in a Victorian-style room with a black-and-white-checked floor, brown ceilings, and dark green tiling. The wine list is exceptional. Mr. Sam's Chophouse in Chapel Walks is just as busy and serves similar fare. ✉ *52 Cross St., City Centre* ☎ *0161/832–2245* 🖃 *AE, MC, V.*

ff–fff ✕ **Pacific.** Designed around feng shui principles, this split-level concept restaurant fuses old and new Asian culture. The lower floor is China, the upper Thailand; each has a separate kitchen and chef. In China you can sample dim sum and à la carte dishes, with classic favorites as well as unusual delicacies such as honey-glazed eel fillets. Thailand has authentic regional cooking; try the roasted duck in red curry. ✉ *58–60 George St., City Centre* ☎ *0161/228–6668* 🖃 *AE, DC, MC, V.*

ff–fff ✕ **Simply Heathcote's.** Lancastrian chef Paul Heathcote earned his reputation as the "cook of the North" for his original, modern food. A diverse clientele that includes the pretheater crowd packs the minimalist dining room. Some signature dishes are local rib-eye steak, matured for 28 days, calves' liver with bubble and squeak (cabbage and mashed potatoes, fried), and, for dessert, strawberries with cream and meringue (called Eton Mess). ✉ *Jackson's Row, City Centre* ☎ *0161/835–3536* 🖃 *AE, MC, V.*

f–ff ✕ **Lal Haweli.** One of Rusholme's string of Indian restaurants, this bright and spacious establishment specializes in Nepalese offerings such as chicken sultani (with orange, pineapple, and chilies) and stir-fried Balti dishes from Pakistan, as well as tandooris and other Indian staples. The area, south of the city center, is easily accessible by bus. ✉ *68–72 Wilmslow Rd., Rusholme* ☎ *0161/ 248–9700* 🖃 *AE, MC, V.*

★ **f–ff** ✕ **Yang Sing.** One of Manchester's best Chinese restaurants, this place is popular with Chinese families, which is always a good sign. The menu of Cantonese dishes is huge, the dim sum are legendary, and

> **WORD OF MOUTH**
>
> If you like Indian food, you must go to Rusholme with its famous Curry Mile. There are also some excellent Chinese restaurants in Manchester." –oldie

there's plenty for the adventurous—ox tripe with black-bean sauce or shark's fin soup, for example. Vegetarians won't be disappointed, either. ✉ *34 Princess St., City Centre* ☎ *0161/236–2200* 🖃 *AE, MC, V.*

9

Where to Stay

£££££ ⊞ **The Lowry Hotel.** The strikingly modern, ergonomic Italian design of
Fodor'sChoice this glass edifice exudes luxury and spaciousness. The clean-lined pub-
★ lic and guest rooms are washed in soothing neutral tones, enlivened by
brilliant red splashes of furniture; marble bathrooms and walk-in closets enhance the bedrooms. Celebrity chef Marco Pierre White oversees
the French-inspired menu of the elegant River Room restaurant. The
hotel fronts the River Irwell across from the landmark Trinity Bridge designed
by Santiago Calatrava. ⊠ *50 Dearman's Pl., City Centre, M3 5LH*
☎ *0161/827–4000* 🖨 *0161/827–4001* ⊕ *www.thelowryhotel.com*
🛏 *157 rooms, 7 suites* ⤿ *Restaurant, cable TV with movies, in-room
DVDs, in-room broadband, in-room data ports, indoor pool, health club,
hair salon, sauna, spa, steam room, bar, business services, meeting
rooms, parking (fee), no-smoking floors* ⊟ *AE, DC, MC, V* ⍓ *BP.*

££££–£££££ ⊞ **Arora International.** The centrally located Arora occupies one of the
city's grand Victorian buildings, opposite the Manchester Art Gallery,
but its design is minimalist modern. Chunky contemporary upholstered
furnishings fill the public areas and guest rooms, where favored colors
are beiges and muted reds and purples. Five rooms, inspired by Cliff
Richard songs, contain artwork and memorabilia from Sir Cliff's own
collection, and all the luxurious bathrooms have music speakers.
⊠ *18–24 Princess St., City Centre, M1 4LY* ☎ *0161/236–8999* 🖨 *0161/
236–3222* ⊕ *www.arorainternational.com* 🛏 *141 rooms* ⤿ *Restaurant,
in-room safes, refrigerators, cable TV, in-room broadband, Wi-Fi, gym,
bar, meeting rooms* ⊟ *AE, MC, V* ⍓ *BP, EP.*

£££–£££££ ⊞ **The Midland Hotel.** The Edwardian splendor of the hotel's public
rooms still manages to shine through a contemporary makeover, evok-
ing the days when this was Manchester's railroad station hotel. High
tea (£16, book in advance) is still served in the grand lobby. Guest rooms,
with huge photos of Manchester as bedheads, are pleasant and light,
with contemporary walnut furniture and dark purple and cream furnishings. ⊠ *Peter St., City Centre, M60 2DS* ☎ *0161/236–3333* 🖨 *0161/
932–4100* ⊕ *www.qhotels.co.uk* 🛏 *298 rooms, 14 suites* ⤿ *2 restaurants, cable TV with movies, in-room safes, in-room broadband, in-room
data ports, Wi-Fi, indoor pool, gym, squash court, health club, hair salon,
sauna, 2 bars, lounge, business services, meeting rooms, parking (fee),
some pets allowed* ⊟ *AE, DC, MC, V* ⍓ *BP.*

££££ ⊞ **Malmaison Hotel.** Part of a chic minichain, this is the kind of place
that's popular with British pop stars. The striking contemporary design, inside an Edwardian facade, includes good-size, individually designed rooms plushly decorated in raspberry red, violet, and cream. The
modern extension has windows at eye and knee level. Traditional
French fare is the focus in the Brasserie. The Malmaison is a few minutes' walk from Piccadilly Station. ⊠ *Piccadilly, City Centre, M1 3AQ*
☎ *0161/278–1000* 🖨 *0161/278–1002* ⊕ *www.malmaison.com* 🛏 *169
rooms* ⤿ *Restaurant, cable TV, in-room broadband, in-room data
ports, Wi-Fi, health club, sauna, spa, steam room, bar, business services, meeting rooms, no-smoking floors, some pets allowed; no a/c*
⊟ *AE, DC, MC, V.*

££££ 🖼 **The Place Apartment Hotel.** Cast-iron columns rise side by side with palm trees in this elegantly converted former cotton warehouse with loft-style apartments. It's a good alternative for people who want the convenience of a kitchen or a second bedroom. The spacious rooms, built around an atrium, still retain the original redbrick work but are fitted out in cool blues and light-wood furniture. One- and two-bedroom apartments are available. ⊠ *Ducie St, Piccadilly City Centre, M1 2TP* ☎ *0161/778–7500* 🖨 *0161/778–7507* ⊕ *www.theplacehotel.com* ⟳ *100 apartments, 8 penthouses* ♿ *Restaurant, kitchens, cable TV, in-room DVDs, Wi-Fi, meeting rooms, parking (fee); no a/c* ⊟ *AE, DC, MC, V.*

£££–££££ 🖼 **Rossetti.** The girders, parquet flooring, and tiles of this converted Victorian textile warehouse (which used to supply floral print dresses to Queen Elizabeth II) are still here, but the feather-soft beds, Molteni furniture, and funky lights are determinedly cool. Each floor has a help-yourself breakfast bar, the café-restaurant dishes up Neapolitan pizzas, and a glitzy nightclub occupies the basement. ⊠ *107 Piccadilly, City Centre, M1 2DB* ☎ *0161/247–7744* 🖨 *0161/247–7747* ⊕ *www.aliasrossetti. com* ⟳ *56 rooms, 5 suites* ♿ *Restaurant, in-room DVDs, in-room broadband, in-room data ports, Wi-Fi, bar, nightclub, meeting rooms, parking (fee), some pets allowed; no a/c* ⊟ *AE, MC, V* ⦿ *CP.*

££–££££ 🖼 **Jurys Inn.** A good-value outpost of the Irish-based chain, Jurys has a sleek wooden lobby and contemporary design that's light and attractive. Guest rooms are spacious, and you can use a nearby health club. The location is excellent—next to Bridgewater Hall and close to shopping on King Street and the café-bar scenes on Whitworth Street and in Castlefield. ⊠ *56 Great Bridgewater St., Peter's Fields, M1 5LE* ☎ *0161/ 953–8888* 🖨 *0161/953–9090* ⊕ *www.jurysdoyle.com* ⟳ *265 rooms* ♿ *Restaurant, cable TV, in-room data ports, in-room broadband, Wi-Fi, bar, business services, meeting rooms, parking (fee), no-smoking floors* ⊟ *AE, DC, MC, V* ⦿ *BP.*

££ 🖼 **Castlefield Hotel.** This popular modern redbrick hotel sits near the water's edge in the Castlefield Basin. Public rooms are cheery and traditional, with patterned carpets and plain furnishings; subdued, warm tones help make the bedrooms restful. The leisure facilities and free breakfast make this a good value. ⊠ *Liverpool Rd., Castlefield, M3 4JR* ☎ *0161/832–7073* 🖨 *0161/837–3534* ⊕ *www.castlefield-hotel.co.uk* ⟳ *48 rooms* ♿ *Restaurant, cable TV, Wi-Fi, indoor pool, health club, sauna, bar, meeting rooms, parking (fee); no a/c* ⊟ *AE, DC, MC, V* ⦿ *BP.*

£ 🖼 **The Ox.** Friendly and relaxed, this gastro-pub with rooms is a real find for those who just want the basics. Guest rooms are simple, creamy cool and modern in style. The buzz-filled restaurant, decorated with local artwork, serves modern British cuisine. Guest ales are on tap, complemented by a good selection of wines. ⊠ *71 Liverpool Rd., Castlefield, M3 4NQ* ☎ *0161/839–7740* 🖨 *0161/839–7760* ⊕ *www.theox.co.uk* ⟳ *9 rooms* ♿ *Restaurant, bar; no a/c* ⊟ *MC, V.*

Nightlife & the Arts

Manchester vies with London as Britain's capital of youth culture but has vibrant nightlife and entertainment options for all ages. Spending time at a bar, pub, or club is definitely an essential part of any trip. For event listings, buy the *Manchester Evening News* or check out the free *Manchester Metro News* paper, usually found at tram stations.

Nightlife

The action after dark centers on the Deansgate, Northern Quarter, and Gay Village areas.

CAFÉ-BARS &
PUBS
Barça (⊠ 8–9 Catalan Sq., Castlefield ☎ 0161/839–7099) is a hip canalside bar-restaurant that has won architectural awards. **Dry Bar** (⊠ 28–30 Oldham St., Northern Quarter ☎ 0161/236–9840), the original café-bar in town, is still full of young people drinking and dancing. Whether you come to see or be seen, the **Living Room** (⊠ Deansgate, City Centre ☎ 0870/442–2537) is the city's top spot; a pianist plays in the early evening. **Obsidian** (⊠ 18–24 Princess St., City Centre ☎ 0161/238–4348) has a huge frosted-glass bar and great cocktails. **Revolution** (⊠ Arch 7, Whitworth St. W, Peter's Fields ☎ 0161/839–7558), one of the trendy bars converted from a railway arch in Deansgate Locks, is a vodka bar. **Tiger Tiger** (⊠ 5–6 The Printworks, City Centre ☎ 0161/385–8080) is the place to go for a relaxed meal and to drink or dance.

★ The **Gay Village,** which came to television in the British series *Queer as Folk,* has stylish bars and cafés along the Rochdale Canal; Canal Street is its heart. The area is not only the center of Manchester's good-size gay scene but also the nightlife center for the young and trendy. The café-bar **Manto** (⊠ 46 Canal St., Gay Village ☎ 0161/236–2667) draws a chic, mostly gay crowd to its split-level, postindustrial interior.

Fodor'sChoice
★
The Britons Protection (⊠ 50 Great Bridgewater St., Peter's Fields ☎ 0161/236–5895) stands out as a relaxed pub, with stained glass and cozy back rooms, a Peterloo Massacre mural, cask ales, and more than 230 whiskies and bourbons. **Peveril of the Peak** (⊠ 127 Great Bridgewater St., Peter's Fields ☎ 0161/236–6364), a nifty Victorian pub with a green-tile exterior, draws a crush of locals to its tiny rooms. **Sinclair's Oyster Bar** (⊠ 2 Cathedral Gates, Millennium Quarter ☎ 0161/834–0430), a half-timber pub built in the 17th century, specializes in fresh oyster dishes.

DANCE CLUBS
42nd Street (⊠ 2 Bootle St., off Deansgate, City Centre ☎ 0161/831–7108) plays retro, indie, sing-along anthems, and classic rock. **Sankey's Soap** (⊠ Beehive Mill, Jersey St., Ancoats ☎ 0161/661–9668) covers anthems, drum 'n' bass breaks, beats, and hardcore.

LIVE MUSIC
Manchester Apollo (⊠ Stockport Rd., Ardwick Green ☎ 0870/401–8000) showcases acts for all musical tastes. Major rock and pop stars appear at the **Manchester Evening News Arena** (⊠ 21 Hunt's Bank, Hunt's Bank ☎ 0870/190–8000). **The Roadhouse** (⊠ 8 Newton St., City Centre ☎ 0161/237–9789), an intimate band venue, also hosts funk and indie nights.

The Arts

FESTIVALS
During the first two weeks of July 2007, the first **Manchester International Festival** (☎ 0161/238–7300 ⊕ www.manchesterinternationalfestival. com) will present specially commissioned work from international musicians and artists. Look for events throughout the city.

FILM The city's major center for contemporary cinema and the visual arts, the **Cornerhouse** (⊠ 70 Oxford St., City Centre ☎ 0161/200–1500) has three movie screens plus galleries, a bookshop, a trendy bar, and a café. The **Odeon** (⊠ The Printworks, Exchange Square, Millennium Quarter ☎ 0871/224–4007) is a state-of-the-art 20-screen complex with an IMAX 3-D screen.

PERFORMING- Dramatically modern **Bridgewater Hall** (⊠ Lower Mosley St., Peter's
ARTS VENUES Fields ☎ 0161/907–9000) has concerts by Manchester's renowned
★ Hallé Orchestra and hosts both classical music and a varied light-entertainment program. **The Lowry** (⊠ Pier 8, Salford Quays ☎ 0870/ 787–5780) contains two theaters and presents everything from musicals to dance and performance poetry. The **Opera House** (⊠ Quay St., City Centre ☎ 0870/401–6000) is a venue for West End musicals, opera, and classical ballet. The **Palace Theatre** (⊠ Oxford St., City Centre ☎ 0870/401–6000) presents large touring shows—major plays, ballet, and opera. **Royal Northern College of Music** (⊠ 124 Oxford Rd., University Quarter ☎ 0161/907–5555) hosts classical and contemporary music concerts, jazz, and opera.

THEATER **Green Room** (⊠ 54–56 Whitworth St. W, City Centre ☎ 0161/615–0500) is an alternative space for theater, poetry, dance, and performance art. **Library Theatre** (⊠ St. Peter's Sq., City Centre ☎ 0161/236–7110) in the Central Library stages classical drama, Shakespeare, chamber musicals, and new work from local playwrights. **Royal Exchange Theatre** (⊠ St. Ann's Sq., City Centre ☎ 0161/833–9833) serves as the city's main venue for innovative contemporary theater.

Football

Football (soccer in the United States) is *the* reigning passion in Manchester. Locals support the perennially unsuccessful local club, Manchester City, and glory seekers come from afar to root for Manchester United, based in neighboring Trafford. Matches for both clubs are usually sold out months in advance, but touts (scalpers, legal here) do business outside the grounds. **Manchester City** (⊠ Rowsley St., SportCity ☎ 0870/062–1894) plays at the City of Manchester Stadium. At the **Manchester City Experience** (⊠ Rowsley St., SportCity ☎ 0870/062–1894), you can see club memorabilia, visit the players' changing rooms, and go down the tunnel to pitch side. Excluding match days, there are at least five tours daily; admission is £8.25.

★ **Manchester United** (⊠ Sir Matt Busby Way, Trafford Wharf ☎ 0870/442–1968 information line, 0870/442–1999 ticket line) has home matches at Old Trafford. You can take a trip to the Theatre of Dreams at the **Manchester United Museum and Tour** (⊠ Sir Matt Busby Way, Trafford Wharf ☎ 0870/442–1994), which tells the history of the football club. The tour (not available on match days) takes you behind the scenes, into the changing rooms and players' lounge, and down the tunnel. It's open daily 9:30 to 5; admission for the museum and tour is £9.50, museum only £6. Take the tram to the Old Trafford stop and walk five minutes.

9

Shopping

The city is nothing if not fashion conscious; take your pick from glitzy department stores, huge retail outlets, designer shops, and idiosyncratic boutiques. Famous names are centered around Exchange Square, Deansgate and King Street; the Northern Quarter provides style for younger trendsetters. **Afflecks Palace** (✉ 52 Church St., Northern Quarter ☎ 0161/834–2039) attracts Mancunian youth with four floors of bohemian glam, ethnic crafts and jewelry, and innovative gift ideas. **Barton Arcade** (✉ 51–63 Deansgate, City Centre ☎ 0161/839–3172) has specialty shopping inside a lovely Victorian arcade.

Harvey Nichols (✉ 21 New Cathedral St., City Centre ☎ 0161/828–8888), an outpost of London's chic luxury department store, is packed with designer goods and has an excellent second-floor restaurant and brasserie. The **Lowry Designer Outlet** (✉ Salford Quays ☎ 0161/848–1850), with 80 stores, has good discounts on top brands at stores such as Nike and Karen Millen. The **Manchester Craft and Design Centre** (✉ 17 Oak St., Northern Quarter ☎ 0161/832–4274) houses 16 workshop–cum–retail outlets. The world's largest **Marks & Spencer** (✉ 7 Market St., City Centre ☎ 0161/831–7341) department store offers its own brand of fashion and has an excellent food department. **Oldham Street,** in the Northern Quarter, is littered with urban hip-hop boutiques and music shops. The **Royal Exchange Shopping Centre and Arcade** (✉ St. Ann's Sq., City Centre ☎ 0161/834–3731) has three floors of restaurants and specialty shops, with antiques, Belgian chocolates, teddy bears, and more, inside the former cotton market. **The Triangle** (✉ Millennium Quarter ☎ 0161/834–8961), a stylish mall in the Victorian Corn Exchange, has more than 30 stores, including independent designer shops.

> ### CHINATOWN
>
> The large red-and-gold Imperial Chinese Arch, erected in 1987, marks Chinatown, one of the largest Chinese communities outside London. Bordered by Portland Street, Mosley Street, Princess Street, and Charlotte Street, the area really buzzes on Sunday, when traders from all over the country stock up from the supermarkets, food stalls, herbalists, and gift shops. The many restaurants here offer excellent choices of authentic Cantonese cooking, so consider a stop here when your shopping energies run low.

LIVERPOOL

A city lined with one of the most famous waterfronts in England, celebrated around the world as the birthplace of the Beatles, and still the place to catch that "Ferry 'Cross the Mersey," Liverpool has reversed a downturn in its fortunes with recent developments such as the Tate Liverpool and the refurbishment of Albert Dock. The naming of the city as the European Union's Capital of Culture for 2008 has accelerated plans for what Liverpool hopes will be a reinvention of itself as a center for culture and innovation. Themed events in 2007 will focus on Liverpool's 800th birthday. Check out ⊕ www.liverpool08.com for the latest information. In 2004, UNESCO named six historic areas in the city center a World Heritage Site, in recognition of the significance of its maritime and mercantile achievements.

Liverpool, on the east bank of the Mersey River estuary, at the point where it merges with the Irish Sea, developed from the 17th century through the slave trade. It became Britain's leading port for ferrying Africans to North America and for handling sugar, tobacco, rum, and cotton, which began to dominate the local economy after the abolition of the slave trade in 1807. Because of its proximity to Ireland, the city was also the first port of call for those fleeing famine, poverty, and persecution in that country. Liverpool was often the last British port of call for thousands of mostly Jewish refugees fleeing Eastern Europe.

Many of the best-known liner companies were based in Liverpool, including Cunard and White Star, whose best-known vessel, the *Titanic,* was registered in Liverpool. The city was dealt an economic blow in 1894 with the opening of the Manchester Ship Canal, which allowed traders to bypass Liverpool and head to Manchester, 35 mi east. Wartime bombing in the 1940s devastated the city's infrastructure, and rebuilding was uninspired. The postwar growth of air travel curtailed the services of the oceangoing liners, and Britain's entry into the European Common Market saw more trade move from the west coast to the east.

As economic decline set in, Liverpool produced its most famous export—the Beatles. The group was one of hundreds that copied the rock and roll they heard from visiting American GIs and merchant seamen in the late 1950s, and one of many that played local venues such as the Cavern (demolished but since rebuilt nearby). All four Beatles were born in Liverpool, but the group's success dates from the time they left for London. Nevertheless, the city has milked the group's Liverpool connections for all they are worth, with a multitude of local attractions such as Paul McCartney's and John Lennon's childhood homes.

Despite the roughness of parts of the city, many people visit Liverpool to tour Beatles's sites, view the paintings in the renowned art galleries, watch horse racing or soccer, and learn about the city's industrial and maritime heritage at the impressive Albert Dock area.

Exploring Liverpool

Liverpool has a fairly compact center, and you can see most of the city highlights on foot. The skyline helps orientation: the Radio City tower on **Queen Square** marks the center of the city and is a stone's throw away from the '08 Place, which gives tourist information. The Liver Birds, on top of the **Royal Liver Building,** signal the waterfront and River Mersey. North of the Radio City tower lie Lime Street station and **William Brown Street,** a showcase boulevard of municipal buildings, including the outstanding **Walker Art Gallery** and **Liverpool World Museum.** The city's other museums and the **Beatles Story** are concentrated westward on the waterfront in the **Albert Dock** area, a 20-minute walk or 5-minute bus ride away. **Hope Street,** to the east of the center, connects the city's

Albert Dock ...**20**

Anglican
Cathedral **23**

Beatles
Story **22**

Mathew
Street **16**

Merseyside
Maritime
Museum **19**

Metropolitan
Cathedral
of Christ
the King **24**

Pier Head **18**

Royal Liver
Building **17**

St. George's
Hall **14**

Tate
Liverpool **21**

Walker Art
Gallery **15**

World Museum
Liverpool **13**

two cathedrals, both easily recognizable on the skyline. Be prepared for building work in preparation for 2008. Allow yourself extra time if you want to visit **20 Forthlin Road** and **Mendips,** the childhood homes of Paul McCartney and John Lennon (closed in winter), as they lie outside the city center; they can be seen only on a prebooked tour.

Main Attractions

★ ⓴ **Albert Dock.** To understand the city's prosperous maritime past, head for waterfront Albert Dock, 7 acres of restored warehouses built in 1846. Named after Queen Victoria's consort, Prince Albert, the dock provided storage for silk, tea, and tobacco from the Far East until it was closed in 1972. Rescued by the Merseyside Development Corporation, the fine colonnaded brick warehouse buildings are England's largest heritage attraction, containing the **Merseyside Maritime Museum, Tate Liverpool,** and the **Beatles Story.** When weather allows, sit at an outdoor café overlooking the dock or take a boat trip through the docks and onto the river. Albert Dock is part of the area known as **Liverpool's Historic Waterfront.** ■ TIP→ **Much of the pedestrian area of the Albert Dock and Waterfront area is made of cobbled stone, so be sure to wear comfortable walking shoes.** ✉ *Tourist Information Centre, Merseyside Maritime Museum, Waterfront* ☏ *0906/680–6866 (calls cost 25p per minute)* ⊕ *www. albertdock.com* ☉ *Information center, daily 10–5.*

⑲ Merseyside Maritime Museum. Part of the Albert Dock complex, the museum tells the story of the port of Liverpool using models, paintings, and original boats and equipment spread across five floors; it also has a gallery on the Battle of the Atlantic and Liverpool's role during World War II. In summer full-size vessels are on display. The Transatlantic Slavery exhibition, on the human misery engendered by the slave trade, is compelling. ⊠ *Albert Dock, Waterfront* ☎ *0151/478–4499* ⊕ *www.liverpoolmuseums.org.uk* ⊠ *Free* ⊙ *Daily 10–5; last admission 4.*

Fodor'sChoice ★

> **WORD OF MOUTH**
>
> "Actually, I rather like Albert Dock. I know it's all gussied up for the visitors, but I do like the shops, and the maritime museum, and just being near the ferry dock is a joy." —Merseyheart

⑱ Pier Head. Here you can take a ferry across the River Mersey from Pierhead to Birkenhead and back. Boats leave regularly and offer fine views of the city—a journey celebrated in "Ferry 'Cross the Mersey," Gerry and the Pacemakers' 1964 hit song. It was from Pier Head that 9 million British, Irish, and other European emigrants set sail between 1830 and 1930 for new lives in the United States, Canada, Australia, and Africa. ■ TIP➡ Choose a ferry (if you're short of time) or the longer 50-minute cruise with commentary ("Scousers," as locals are known, are famous for their patter); the city views are wonderful and worth the time and money. ⊠ *Pier Head Ferry Terminal, Mersey Ferries, Waterfront* ☎ *0151/330–1444* ⊕ *www. merseyferries.co.uk* ⊠ *£2.15 round-trip, cruises £4.95* ⊙ *Ferries every 30 mins weekdays 7:45–9:15* AM *and 4:15–6:45* PM; *cruises hourly weekdays 10–3, weekends 10–6.*

⑰ Royal Liver Building. Best seen from the ferry, the 322-foot-tall Royal Liver (pronounced "lie-ver") Building with its twin towers is topped by two 18-foot-high copper birds. They represent the mythical Liver Birds, the town symbol; local legend has it that if they fly away, Liverpool will cease to exist. For decades Liverpudlians looked to the Royal Liver Society for assistance—it was originally a burial club to which families paid contributions to ensure a decent send-off. ⊠ *Water St., Waterfront.*

㉑ Tate Liverpool. An offshoot of the London-based art galleries of the same name, the Liverpool museum, a handsome conversion of existing Albert Dock warehouses, was designed in the 1990s by the late James Stirling, one of Britain's leading 20th-century architects. Galleries display changing exhibits of challenging modern art. The excellent shop sells art books, prints, and posters, and there's a children's art-play area and a dockside café-restaurant. ⊠ *The Colonnades, Albert Dock, Waterfront* ☎ *0151/702–7400* ⊕ *www.tate.org.uk* ⊠ *Free, charge for special exhibitions* ⊙ *Tues.–Sun. and national holidays 10–5:50.*

⑮ Walker Art Gallery. With a superb display of British art and some superb Italian and Flemish works, the Walker maintains its position as one of the best British art collections outside London. Particularly notable are the unrivaled collection of paintings by 18th-century Liverpudlian equestrian artist George Stubbs, and works by J. M. W. Turner, John

Fodor'sChoice ★

Constable, Sir Edwin Henry Landseer, and the Pre-Raphaelites. Modern British artists are included, too—on display is one of David Hockney's typically Californian pool scenes. Other excellent exhibits showcase china, silver, and furniture that once adorned the mansions of Liverpool's industrial barons. The Tea Room holds center stage in the airy museum lobby. ⊠ *William Brown St., City Centre* ☎ *0151/478–4199* ⊕ *www. liverpoolmuseums.org.uk* 🎟 *Free* ⊙ *Daily 10–5.*

🅬 ⑬ **World Museum Liverpool.** You can travel from the prehistoric to the space age through stunning displays in these state-of-the-art galleries. Ethnology, the natural and physical sciences, and archaeology all get their due on five floors. The World Cultures gallery colorfully illustrates the cosmopolitan history of the city. If the kids aren't grabbed by the monster bugs in the Bug House or afternoon shows in the Treasure House Theatre and Planetarium, they'll find plenty to do in the hands-on centers. ⊠ *William Brown St.* ☎ *0151/478–4393* ⊕ *www.worldmuseumliverpool. org.uk* 🎟 *Free* ⊙ *Daily 10–5.*

On the Trail of the Beatles

★ ㉒ **Beatles Story.** You can follow in the footsteps of the Fab Four at one of the more popular attractions in the Albert Dock complex. It has 18 entertaining scenes re-creating stages in their career, from the enthusiastic early days in Germany and the Cavern Club to the White Room, where "Imagine" seems to emanate from softly billowing curtains. Artifacts included are the glasses John Lennon wore when he composed "Imagine" and the blue felt bedspread used in the famous "Bed-in" in 1969. ■ TIP→ Avoid the crowds of July and August by visiting in the late afternoon. You can purchase tickets online in advance, and the store has Beatles items from CDs to wallets and alarm clocks. ⊠ *Britannia Vaults, Albert Dock, Waterfront* ☎ *0151/709–1963* ⊕ *www.beatlesstory.com* 🎟 *£8.99* ⊙ *Daily 10–6; last admission 1 hr before closing.*

⑯ **Mathew Street.** It was at the Cavern on this street that Brian Epstein, who became the Beatles' manager, first heard the group in 1961. The Cavern had opened at No. 10 as a jazz venue in 1957, but beat groups, of whom the Beatles were clearly the most talented, had taken it over. Epstein became their manager a few months after first visiting the club, and within two years the group was the most talked-about phenomenon in music. The Cavern club was demolished in 1973; it was rebuilt a few yards from the original site. At No. 5 is the Cavern Pub, opened in 1994, with Beatles memorabilia and plenty of nostalgia. ■ TIP→ At No. 31, check out the well-stocked Beatles Shop.

Mendips. The august National Trust (overseers of such landmarks as Blenheim Palace) maintains the 1930s middle-class, semidetached house that was the home of John Lennon from 1946 to 1963 and is a mustsee for Beatles pilgrims. After his parents separated, John joined his aunt Mimi here; she gave him his first guitar but banished him to play on the porch, saying, "The guitar's all very well, John, but you'll never make a living out of it." The house can be seen only on a tour, for which you must prebook a seat on the minibus that connects the site with Albert Dock (mornings) or Speke Hall (afternoons). ⊠ *251 Menlove Ave.,*

Beatles Discovered . . . and Rediscovered

BRIAN EPSTEIN WAS LED to the Beatles in 1961 by a teenager who came into his record shop, NEMS (North End Music Stores) at 12–14 Whitechapel, and asked for a record by Tony Sheridan and the Beat Brothers. He couldn't find it in his catalog, but discovered that the backing band was the Beatles, a local group, playing at the nearby Cavern Club. Epstein heard the group, and the rest is history.

History lives on, though. If the Beatles Story, Mathew Street, Mendips, and 20 Forthlin Road can't sate your Beatlemania in Liverpool, consider a **Cavern City Tours** (⇨ Bus Tours *in* Lancashire & the Peaks Essentials)

Magical Mystery Tour of the essential landmarks.

The faithful celebrate the Beatles' enduring appeal at the annual **International Beatle Week** (⊕ www.cavern-liverpool.co.uk), usually held the last week in August when what seems to be the entire city takes time out to dance, attend John and Yoko fancy-dress parties, and listen to Beatle bands from around the world. The event includes concerts, a convention, flea markets, and more. If you hold on until 2008, Cavern City Tours plans to open the Beatle-themed **Hard Day's Night Hotel**, right on Mathew Street. Yeah, yeah, yeah!

Woolton ☎ *0870/900–0256 morning tours, 0151/427–7231 afternoon tours* ⊕ *www.nationaltrust.org.uk* ✉ *£12 includes 20 Forthlin Rd. and Speke Hall gardens* ☉ *Late Mar.–Oct., Wed.–Sun. and national holidays; 4 departures a day, call for times.*

20 Forthlin Road. Paul McCartney lived with his family in this modest 1950s council house (a building rented from the local government), with its period-authentic windows, doors, and hedges, from 1955 to 1963; now it's a shrine for fans. A number of the Beatles' songs, including "Love Me Do" and "When I'm Sixty-Four," were written here. The house is viewable only on a tour, for which you must prebook a seat on the minibus that connects the site with Albert Dock (mornings) or Speke Hall (afternoons). ✉ *20 Forthlin Rd., Allerton* ☎ *0870/900–0256 morning tours, 0151/427–7231 afternoon tours* ⊕ *www.nationaltrust.org* ✉ *£12 includes Mendips and Speke Hall gardens* ☉ *Late Mar.–Oct., Wed.–Sun. and national holidays; 4 departures a day, call for times.*

Also Worth Seeing

❷❸ Anglican Cathedral. The largest church in northern Britain overlooks the city and the River Mersey. Built of local sandstone, the Gothic-style cathedral was begun in 1903 by architect Giles Gilbert Scott; it was finally finished in 1978. Take a look at the grand interior, view the exhibit of Victorian embroidery, and climb the 331-foot-tall tower. A refectory serves light meals and coffee. ✉ *St. James's Mount, City Centre* ☎ *0151/709–6271* ⊕ *www.liverpoolcathedral.org.uk* ✉ *£3.50 suggested donation, tower and embroidery exhibition £4.25* ☉ *Daily 8–6. Tower Mar.–Sept., Mon.–Sat. 11–4:30; Oct.–Feb., Mon.–Sat. 11–3:30.*

NEED A
BREAK? **Prohibition Bar & Grill** (✉ 1A Bold St., City Centre ☎ 0151/707–2333) used to be a library and a gentleman's club. Now you can sink into a huge sofa for coffee or cocktails beneath the grand domed ceiling.

㉔ Metropolitan Cathedral of Christ the King. This Roman Catholic cathedral consecrated in 1967 is a modernistic, funnel-like structure of concrete, stone, and mosaic, topped with a glass lantern. Long, narrow, blue-glass windows separate chapels, each with modern works of art. An earlier design by classically inspired architect Edwin Lutyens was abandoned when World War II began (the current design is by Frederick Gibberd), but the crypt shows some of Lutyens's work. ✉ *Mount Pleasant, City Centre* ☎ *0151/709–9222* ⊕ *www.liverpoolmetrocathedral.org.uk* 🎟 *Donations welcome* ☉ *Mon.–Sat. 8–6, Sun. 8–5.*

⑭ St. George's Hall. Built between 1839 and 1847, St. George's Hall is among the world's best Greek-Revival buildings. When Queen Victoria visited Liverpool in 1851, she declared it "worthy of ancient Athens." Today the hall serves as a home for music festivals, concerts, and fairs. Refurbishment will be underway until 2007; call for information. ✉ *Lime St., City Centre* ☎ *0151/225–5530.*

Speke Hall and Gardens. This black-and-white mansion only 6 mi from downtown Liverpool is one of the best examples of half-timbering in Britain. Built around a cobbled courtyard, the earliest part, the great hall, dates to 1490; an elaborate western bay with a vast chimneypiece was added in 1560. The house, owned by the National Trust, was heavily restored in the 19th century, though a Tudor priest hole and Jacobean plasterwork remain intact. Speke Hall is on the east side of the airport; the Airportxpress 500 bus drops you a pleasant 10-minute walk away. ✉ *The Walk, Speke* ☎ *0151/427–7231* ⊕ *www.nationaltrust.org.uk* 🎟 *£6.50, gardens only £3.50* ☉ *House late Mar.–Oct., Wed.–Sun. and national holidays 1–5:30; Nov.–early Dec., weekends 1–4:30. Gardens daily 11–5:30 or dusk. Last admission 30 mins before closing.*

Where to Eat

£££–£££££ ✗ **60 Hope Street.** The combination of a ground-floor restaurant and a cheaper basement café-bar make this a popular choice for any budget. A light, polished wood floor and blue-and-cream walls help create the uncluttered backdrop for dishes that reflect a Mediterranean clime, but found only on British shores is the deep-fried jam sandwich with condensed milk ice cream. ✉ *60 Hope St., City Centre* ☎ *0151/707–6060* ▭ *AE, MC, V* ☉ *Closed Sun. No lunch Sat. in restaurant.*

££–££££ ✗ **Blue Bar and Grill.** Expect to rub shoulders with local celebrities in this sophisticated modern restaurant and bar on the waterfront. The focal point is the beautiful Venetian crystal chandelier, a counterpoint to the original open brickwork, chunky furnishings, and plasma screens. Downstairs you can sample tapas, dim sum, and bruschetta; the fare in the upstairs gallery includes panfried goose breast and a large selection of meat and fish steaks, accompanied by different sauces. ✉ *Edward Pavilion, Albert Dock, Waterfront* ☎ *0151/709–7097* ▭ *AE, MC, V.*

££–£££ ✕ **Chung Ku.** Liverpool has a strong Chinese presence, and here you can sample Asian cuisine with a superb Merseyside view. Panoramic windows wrap around this stunning, ultramodern restaurant. Choose from 70 kinds of dim sum, or try one of the sizzling platters or something from the extensive seafood selection. The restaurant lies 2 mi east of the center on the waterfront, at the Jaguar car dealership; take the No. 1 bus from Queen Square. ⊠ *2 Columbus Quay, Riverside Dr., Otterspool* ☎ *0151/726–8191* 🖃 *AE, MC, V.*

££–£££ ✕ **Simply Heathcote's.** This chic contemporary restaurant, an outpost of chef Paul Heathcote's expanding empire, has a curved glass front, cherrywood furnishings, and a granite floor. The menu has a local accent—black pudding in beer batter, pork and leek sausages, bread and butter pudding—along with dishes from warmer climes. Vegetarians are well served, too. The restaurant is opposite the Royal Liver and Cunard buildings. ⊠ *25 The Strand, Waterfront* ☎ *0151/236–3536* 🖃 *AE, MC, V.*

£–££ ✕ **Tabac.** The warm decor and chilled-out music of this long, thin café-bar at the top of Bold Street attracts a cosmopolitan crowd. It's good for breakfasts with home-baked bread, cocktails, sandwiches, and salads, as well as daily specials such as roast chicken and cottage pie (minced beef with mashed potatoes on top). ⊠ *126 Bold St., City Centre* ☎ *0151/709–9502* 🖃 *MC, V.*

£ ✕ **Tate Café.** The Tate Liverpool's café-bar is a winner for daytime sustenance. There are dockside seats for warm summer days, and you can choose among the open sandwiches and salads, as well as dishes such as beef casserole with parsnip and potato chips (crisps, in Britain) and fruit cake with cheese and pear chutney. ⊠ *The Colonnades, Albert Dock, Waterfront* ☎ *0151/702–7580* 🖃 *MC, V* ⊙ *Closed Mon. No dinner.*

Where to Stay

With the naming of the city as the European Union's Capital of Culture in 2008, hotel options are expanding. New chains due to open in Liverpool in 2007 are the design-driven Alias and trendy Malmaison.

★ 🏨 **Hope Street Hotel.** Liverpool's boutique hotel, a converted carriage warehouse built in the style of a Venetian palazzo, puts the emphasis on traditional, natural materials and retains the exposed brickwork and cast-iron columns from the 1860s. A stunning oak staircase runs the height of the building. Light and elegant modern bedrooms have crisp white bed linens and custom-made walnut and cherry pieces, and benefit from floor heating. The London Carriage Works (£££££; fixed-price menus) concentrates on local and seasonal produce, used in such dishes as Suffolk lamb with buttered kale. ⊠ *40 Hope St., City Centre, L1 9DA* ☎ *0151/709–3000* 🖶 *0151/709–2454* ⊕ *www.hopestreethotel.co.uk* 📲 *41 rooms, 7 suites* ᐤ *Restaurant, cable TV, in-room DVDs, in-room broadband, in-room data ports, 2 bars, business services, meeting rooms, parking (fee); no a/c* 🖃 *AE, MC, V.*

£££–££££ 🏨 **Crowne Plaza Liverpool.** Many of the city's main sights are at the doorstep of this modern hotel on the waterfront next to the Royal Liver Building. A bright, bustling atrium leads to well-equipped and spacious bedrooms, done in soothing colors. Family rooms have two double

9

beds; children under 12 stay free and even get free meals in the Plaza Brasserie. Breakfast is included in the price on weekends. ⊠ *St Nicholas Place, Waterfront, L3 1QW* ☎ *0151/243–8000* ⊟ *0151/243–8111* ⊕ *www.cpliverpool.com* ⇆ *159 rooms* ⟂ *2 restaurants, room service, minibars, cable TV with movies, in-room data ports, in-room broadband, Wi-Fi, indoor pool, health club, hot tub, sauna, steam room, bar, laundry service, business services, meeting rooms, parking (fee), no-smoking rooms* ⊟ *AE, DC, MC, V.*

£££–££££ ⊞ **Liverpool City Centre Marriott Hotel.** This modern city-center hotel was the first indication of Liverpool's rise from the economic ashes. Guest rooms have cherry furniture and are decorated in gold, blue, and burgundy hues. The unbeatable location is a minute from Lime Street Station and the Walker Art Gallery. Breakfast is included on weekends. ⊠ *1 Queen Sq., City Centre, L1 1RH* ☎ *0151/476–8000* ⊟ *0151/474–5000* ⊕ *www.marriott.com* ⇆ *143 rooms, 3 suites* ⟂ *Restaurant, cable TV with movies, in-room broadband, in-room data ports, Wi-Fi, indoor pool, gym, sauna, bar, business services, meeting rooms, parking (fee)* ⊟ *AE, DC, MC, V.*

££–£££ ⊞ **Feathers Hotel.** One of a terrace of Georgian brick houses, this smart and efficient hotel close to both the city's cathedrals doesn't stint on decoration. Swags and drapes adorn the public rooms, and bedrooms have modern pine pieces and patterned fabrics in red, blue, and yellow. You can sip a drink at night in the 24-hour bar. ⊠ *119–125 Mt. Pleasant, City Centre, L3 6DX* ☎ *0151/709–9655* ⊟ *0151/709–3838* ⊕ *www.feathers.uk.com* ⇆ *81 rooms* ⟂ *Restaurant, cable TV, bar, meeting rooms, parking (fee); no a/c* ⊟ *AE, MC, V* ⊙| *BP.*

★ ££ ⊞ **Express by Holiday Inn.** The best central accommodation in terms of value, location, and style is this offering in the upper part of the Britannia Pavilion, in a converted warehouse in the heart of the waterfront district. Management is friendly and helpful, and the rich red-and-blue decor and thick carpeting reflect the style of the chain. Try for a room with views of the dock. ⊠ *Britannia Pavilion, Albert Dock, Waterfront, L3 4AD* ☎ *0151/709–1133 or 0800/434040* ⊟ *0151/709–1144* ⊕ *www.hiexpress.co.uk* ⇆ *135 rooms* ⟂ *Restaurant, cable TV with movies, in-room data ports, Wi-Fi, bar, business services, meeting room, parking (fee), some pets allowed; no a/c* ⊟ *AE, MC, V* ⊙| *BP.*

£ ⊞ **Liverpool Youth Hostel.** This hostel a few minutes' walk from Albert Dock really should change its name, because it offers modest hotel standards for bargain prices. The smart rooms (for two, four, or six people) are fully carpeted, with private bathrooms and heated towel rails. Guests must be members of the Youth Hostels Association; you can join on the spot (£15.50), but it's advisable to book well in advance. ⊠ *Chalenor St., Waterfront, L1 8EE* ☎ *0151/709–8888* ⊟ *0151/709–0417* ⊕ *www.yha.org.uk* ⇆ *106 beds* ⟂ *Cafeteria, recreation room, Internet, laundry facilities; no a/c, no room TVs* ⊟ *MC, V* ⊙| *BP.*

Nightlife & the Arts

Nightlife

Baby Cream (⊠ Atlantic Pavilion, Albert Dock, Waterfront ☎ 0151/702–5826), one of the city's newer bars, is a place where you can listen to weekend DJs. The ladies can pamper themselves in the glitzy black powder room. **Blue Bar** (✉ Edward Pavilion, Albert Dock, Waterfront ☎ 0151/709–7097), typical of the bars at the Albert Dock, attracts a funky, young professional crowd with its late hours, grill, and dockside seating. The **Cavern Club** (✉ 8–10 Mathew St., City Centre ☎ 0151/236–1965) draws many on the Beatles trail, who don't realize it's not the original spot—that was demolished years ago. The **Cavern Pub** (✉ 5 Mathew St., City Centre ☎ 0151/236–4041) merits a stop for nostalgia's sake; here are recorded the names of the groups and artists who played in the Cavern Club between 1957 and 1973. The **Philharmonic** (✉ 36 Hope St., City Centre ☎ 0151/707–2837), nicest of the city-center pubs and opposite the Philharmonic Hall, is a Victorian-era extravaganza (complete with ornate toilets) decorated in colorful marble, with comfortable bar rooms and good food. **Ye Cracke** (✉ 13 Rice St., off Hope St., City Centre ☎ 0151/709–4171), one of the city's oldest pubs, was much visited by John Lennon in the 1960s.

Fodor's Choice ★

The Arts

★ The well-regarded Royal Liverpool Philharmonic Orchestra plays its concert season at **Philharmonic Hall** (✉ Hope St., City Centre ☎ 0151/709–3789). The venue also hosts contemporary music, jazz, and world concerts, and shows classic films.

Everyman Theatre (✉ 5–9 Hope St., City Centre ☎ 0151/709–4776) focuses on works by British playwrights as well as experimental productions from around the world. The **Liverpool Empire** (✉ Lime St., City Centre ☎ 0870/606–3536) presents major ballet, opera, drama, and musical performances. **Royal Court Theatre** (✉ 1 Roe St., City Centre ☎ 0151/709–4321), an art deco building, is one of the city's most appealing sites for stand-up comedy and occasional pop and rock concerts.

Sports & the Outdoors

Horse Racing

★ Britain's most famous horse race, the Grand National steeplechase, has been run at Liverpool's **Aintree Racecourse** (✉ Ormskirk Rd., Aintree ☎ 0151/523–2600, 0151/522–2929 booking line) almost every year since 1839. The race is held in March or April. Admission on race days is £16 (for Grand National, £12–£73; book well in advance). The **Grand National Experience** (☎ 0151/523–2600 ✉ £7 ☉ Late May–mid-Oct., Tues.–Fri. 11 and 2) includes a tour of the racecourse and admission to the visitor center; advance booking is required.

Soccer

Soccer ("football" in Great Britain) matches are played on weekends and, increasingly, weekdays. Ticket prices vary, but the cheapest seats start at about £26. Tourist offices can give you match schedules and directions to the grounds. **Liverpool** (☎ 0870/444–4949, 0870/220–2345 booking line), one of England's top clubs, plays at Anfield, 2 mi north of the city center. **Everton** (☎ 0870/442–1878, 0870/7383–7866 booking line), now reestablishing their historic competitiveness, plays at Goodison Park, about ½ mi north of Anfield.

9

Shopping

★ The **Beatles Shop** (✉ 31 Mathew St., City Centre ☎ 0151/236–8066) may stock the mop-top knickknack of your dreams. **Circa 1900** (✉ 11–13 Holts Arcade, India Buildings, Water St., City Centre ☎ 0151/236–1282) specializes in authentic art nouveau and art deco pieces, from ceramics and glass to furniture. The **Stanley Dock Sunday Market** (✉ Great Howard St. and Regent Rd., City Centre) has more than 400 stalls operating each Sunday, selling bric-a-brac, clothes, and toys from 9 to 4. The **Walker Art Gallery** (✉ William Brown St., City Centre ☎ 0151/478–4199) has a small lobby shop with high-quality glassware, ceramics, and jewelry by local designers.

THE PEAK DISTRICT
BUXTON, BAKEWELL, CHATSWORTH

Heading southeast, away from the urban congestion of Manchester and Liverpool, it's not far to the southernmost contortions of the Pennine Hills. Here, about an hour from Manchester, sheltered in a great natural bowl, is the spa town of Buxton: at an elevation of more than 1,000 feet, it's the second-highest town in England. Buxton makes a convenient base for exploring the 540 square mi of the Peak District, Britain's oldest—and, some say, most beautiful—national park. "Peak" is perhaps misleading; despite being a hilly area, it contains only long, flat-top rises that don't reach much higher than 2,000 feet. Yet a trip around destinations such as Bakewell, Matlock, Castleton, and Edale, and the grand estates of Chatsworth House, Haddon Hall, and Hardwick Hall involves negotiating fairly perilous country roads, each of which repays the effort with enchanting views. Outdoor activities are popular in the Peaks, particularly caving (or "potholing"), walking, and hiking. Bring all-weather clothing and waterproof shoes.

Little Moreton Hall

★ **㉕** *20 mi southwest of Buxton, 45 mi southeast of Liverpool.*

The epitome of "magpie" black-and-white half-timber buildings, this house, in the words of Olive Cook's *The English Country House,* "exaggerates and exalts the typical and humble medieval timber-framed dwelling, making of it a bizarre, unforgettable phenomenon." Covered with zigzags, crosses, and lozenge shapes crafted of timber and daub, the house was built by the Moreton family between 1450 and 1580. The long gallery and Tudor-era wall paintings are spectacular. Little Moreton Hall lies to the west of the Peak District; to get here from Liverpool, take the M6 to the A534 east to Congleton. ✉ *A34, Congleton* ☎ *01260/ 272018* ⊕ *www.nationaltrust.org.uk* ✉ *£5.50; Mar.–Nov., Dec. £2.50* ☉ *Mar., Wed.–Sun. 11:30–4; Apr.–early Nov., Wed.–Sun. and national holidays 11:30–5; mid-Nov.–late Nov., weekends 11:30–4; early–mid-Dec., ground floor only, weekends 11:30–4.*

CLOSE UP

Stoke-on-Trent: The Potteries

THE AREA KNOWN AS THE POTTERIES, about 55 mi southeast of Liverpool, is the center of Britain's ceramic industry and still the largest clayware producer in the world. The novels of Arnold Bennett (1867–1931), including *Anna of the Five Towns*, realistically describe life in the area as an "architecture of ovens and chimneys" with an atmosphere "as black as mud." There are, in fact, six towns, now administered as "the city of Stoke-on-Trent." Wedgwood, Minton, Royal Doulton, Spode, Coalport, and other famous names carry on, as do workshops and outlets.

The most famous manufacturer, Josiah Wedgwood, established his pottery works at Etruria, near Burslem, in 1759 and created the cream-color ware (creamware), which so pleased Queen Charlotte that in 1762 she appointed him royal supplier of dinnerware. Perhaps Wedgwood's best-known innovation was his blue jasperware, decorated with white cameo figures by the British artist John Flaxman. More recent innovators include the very collectible Clarice Cliff, who strove to brighten plain whiteware in the 1920s with her colorful geometric and floral designs, notably the bold crocus pattern. Also bold and colorful were the classic art deco pieces of Susie Cooper. Four museums evocatively portray the history of this area, and factory shops sell all kinds of china.

Ceramica occupies an ornate former town hall and uses displays, videos, and interactive technology to explore the area's history, the process of creating china, and some noted companies. In Bizarreland (the name comes from Clarice Cliff's art deco designs), kids can dig for relics from the past and take a virtual ride over the Potteries. A shop sells local wares. ⊠ *Market Pl., Burslem* ☎ *01782/ 832001* ⊕ *www.ceramicauk.com* 🎟 *£3.95* ⊘ *Mon.–Sat. 9:30–5, Sun. 10:30–4:30.*

The **Gladstone Pottery Museum,** the city's only remaining Victorian pottery factory, contains examples of the old ovens, surrounded by original workshops where you can watch the traditional skills of throwing, casting, and decorating. The Flushed with Pride galleries tell the story of the toilet from the 1840s onward. ⊠ *Uttoxeter Rd., Longton* ☎ *01782/ 319232* ⊕ *www.stoke.gov.uk* 🎟 *£4.95* ⊘ *Daily 10–5; last admission 4.*

The modern **Potteries Museum and Art Gallery** displays a 5,000-piece ceramic collection of international repute and is recognized worldwide for its unique Staffordshire pottery. ⊠ *Bethesda St., Hanley* ☎ *01782/ 232323* ⊕ *www.stoke.gov.uk* 🎟 *Free* ⊘ *Mar.–Oct., Mon.–Sat. 10–5, Sun. 2–5; Nov.–Feb., Mon.–Sat. 10–4, Sun. 1–4.*

At the **Wedgwood Visitor Centre** you can learn about the history of Wedgwood, watch all stages of pottery production, and even try throwing a pot. Two self-guided tours are available: the shorter takes in the ground floor of the factory only, the longer covers both floors and includes the Coalport section. After the tour, shop in the "firsts" and "seconds" stores. ⊠ *Off A5035, Barlaston* ☎ *01782/204218* ⊕ *www. thewedgwoodstory.com* 🎟 *£7.75 and £9* ⊘ *Weekdays 9–5, weekends 10–5.*

9

Buxton

 20 mi northeast of Little Moreton Hall, 25 mi southeast of Manchester.

The Romans arrived in AD 79 and named Buxton *Aquae Arnemetiae*, loosely translated as "Waters of the Goddess of the Grove," suggesting they considered this area in the Derbyshire hills special. The mineral springs, which emerge from 3,500 to 5,000 feet below ground at a constant 82°F, were believed to cure assorted ailments; in the 18th century the town became established as a popular spa, a minor rival to Bath. You can still drink water from the ancient St. Anne's Well, and it's also bottled and sold throughout Britain.

Buxton's spa days left a notable legacy of 18th- and 19th-century buildings, parks, and open spaces that give the town an air of faded grandeur. A good place to start exploring is the **Crescent** on the northwest side of the Slopes park (the town hall is on the opposite side); almost all out-of-town roads lead toward this central green. The three former hotels that make up the Georgian-era Crescent, with its arches, Doric colonnades, and 378 windows, were built in 1780 by fashionable architect John Carr for the fifth duke of Devonshire (of nearby Chatsworth House). The thermal baths at the end of the Crescent now house a shopping center. The Crescent buildings themselves are closed to the public, except for the tourist information center.

The **Devonshire Royal Hospital,** behind the Crescent, also by John Carr, was originally a stable with room for 110 horses. In 1859 the circular area for exercising horses was covered with a massive 156-foot-wide slate-color dome and incorporated into the hospital. The University of Derby has taken over the building, which has an informal bistro open during the day; the restaurant serves excellent lunches (Monday through Thursday) and dinners (Wednesday and Thursday).

The **Buxton Museum** contains a collection of Blue John stone, a semiprecious mineral found only in the Peak District. It also displays local archaeological finds, including a few pieces from Roman times, and there's a small art gallery. The museum is on the eastern side of the Slopes. ⊠ *Terrace Rd.* ☎ *01298/24658* ⊡ *Free* ☉ *Tues.–Fri. 9:30–5:30, Sat. 9:30–5, Sun. and national holidays (Apr.–Sept. only) 10:30–5.*

The **Pavilion** (⊠ Pavilion Gardens ☎ 01298/23114), with its ornate iron-and-glass roof, was a concert hall and ballroom. Erected in the 1870s, it remains a lively place, with a plant-filled conservatory, several bars, a cafeteria, and a restaurant, surrounded by 25 acres of gardens. The Pavilion is adjacent to the Crescent and the Slopes on the west.

Buxton Opera House (⊠ Water St. ☎ 0845/127–2190), built in 1903, is one of the most architecturally exuberant structures in town. Its marble bulk, bedecked with carved cupids, is even more impressive inside. Otherwise, tours of the interior (£2.50) are conducted most Saturdays at 11 AM.

The Peak District's extraordinary geology is revealed close to Buxton at **Poole's Cavern,** a large limestone cave far beneath the 100 wooded acres of Buxton Country Park. The cave was inhabited in prehistoric times and contains, in addition to the standard stalactites and stalagmites, the source of the River Wye, which flows through Buxton. ✉ *Green La.* ☎ *01298/26978* ⊕ *www.poolescavern.co.uk* ☎ *£6.20 including 45-min guided tour. Park and visitor center free* ☉ *Mid-Feb.–Oct., daily 10–5. Tours every ½ hr; last tour at 4:45.*

Where to Stay & Eat

£££–££££ ✕▥ **Old Hall.** Friendly and central, this hotel in a refurbished 16th-century building overlooks the Opera House. The individually decorated rooms are furnished in a mixture of period and modern styles. One room, Mary's Bower, in the oldest section, retains its original ceiling moldings. The Cockerel Bar (££–£££) is popular with theatergoers who stoke up on hearty dishes or salads and hot or cold sandwiches; there's a more formal restaurant as well, with some pretheater specials. ✉ *The Square, SK17 6BD* ☎ *01298/22841* ☎ *01298/72437* ⊕ *www.oldhallhotelbuxton. co.uk* ➪ *38 rooms* ♨ *Restaurant, bar, meeting rooms, some pets allowed; no a/c* ☐ *AE, DC, MC, V* ⵏ�ⵏ *BP.*

£££–££££ ▥ **Palace Hotel.** A Victorian pile on a grand scale, the Palace dates from the halcyon days of the spa and sits on 5 acres overlooking the town center and surrounding hills. The interior reveals a sweeping staircase, marble columns, and chandeliers, but the rooms, although spacious, are a little behind the times in tone, though pleasantly furnished in greens, reds, and blues. The spa, though, is up-to-date. ✉ *Palace Rd., SK17 6AG* ☎ *01298/22001* ☎ *01298/72131* ⊕ *www.paramount-hotels.co.uk* ➪ *118 rooms, 4 suites* ♨ *Restaurant, cable TV with movies, in-room broadband, in-room data ports, indoor pool, health club, sauna, spa, steam room, bar, business services, meeting rooms, some pets allowed (fee); no a/c* ☐ *AE, DC, MC, V* ⵏⵏ *BP.*

★ **££** ▥ **Buxton's Victorian Guesthouse.** One of a terrace (a group of row houses) built by the duke of Devonshire in 1860, this beautifully and imaginatively decorated house stands a stone's throw away from the Opera House. The Oriental dining room has a dragon mural, and the bedrooms have intriguing themes such as Victorian Craftsman. Victorian and Edwardian antiques and prints furnish all the rooms. ✉ *3A Broad Walk, SK17 6JE* ☎ *01298/78759* ☎ *01298/74732* ⊕ *www.buxtonvictorian. co.uk* ➪ *7 rooms, 1 suite* ♨ *No a/c, no room phones, no kids under 4, no smoking* ☐ *AE, MC, V* ⵏⵏ *BP.*

££ ▥ **Lakenham Guest House.** This large Victorian structure retains pleasant reminders of that period. Potted plants proliferate, as do antiques, and the Victorian-style bedrooms have excellent views; the house overlooks Pavilion Gardens. ✉ *11 Burlington Rd., SK17 9AL* ☎ *01298/79209* ⊕ *www.lakenhambuxton.co.uk* ➪ *6 rooms* ♨ *Refrigerators, cable TV; no a/c, no room phones, no kids under 10* ☐ *No credit cards* ⵏⵏ *BP.*

£ ▥ **Stoneridge.** Built of stone, this Edwardian B&B close to the Opera House has been richly restored in sympathetic style. Tartan touches offset the crisp white bedrooms, which are furnished with modern pieces. Hearty breakfasts include fresh fruit, omelets, haggis, and potato scones; packed lunches, afternoon teas, and three-course evening meals can be provided on request. ✉ *9 Park Rd., SK17 6SG* ☎ *01298/26120* ⊕ *www.*

9

stoneridge.co.uk ⇝ *4 rooms* △ *Some pets allowed; no a/c, no room phones, no kids under 5, no smoking* ⊟ *No credit cards* ⓧ *BP.*

Nightlife & the Arts

★ **Buxton Opera House** (✉ Water St. ☎ 0845/127–2190) presents excellent theater, ballet, and jazz performances year-round; in late February it also hosts the annual Four-Four Time festival of world, jazz, blues, and folk music.

The renowned **Buxton Festival** (✉ Festival Office, The Square ☎ 01298/70395 ⊕ www.buxtonfestival.co.uk), held for two weeks during mid-July each year, includes opera, drama, and concerts.

Shopping

Buxton has many kinds of stores, especially around Spring Gardens, the main shopping street. Stores in the beautifully tiled **Cavendish Arcade** (✉ The Crescent), on the site of the old thermal baths, sell antiques, jewelry, fashions, and leather goods in stylish surroundings. A **market** is held in Buxton every Tuesday and Saturday.

EN ROUTE As you head southeast from Buxton on the A6, you pass through the spectacular valleys of Ashwood Dale, Wyedale, and Monsal Dale before reaching Bakewell.

Bakewell

㉗ *12 mi southeast of Buxton.*

Here, a medieval bridge crosses the winding River Wye in five graceful arches, and the 9th-century Saxon cross that stands outside the parish church reveals the town's great age. Narrow streets and houses built out of the local gray-brown stone also make Bakewell extremely appealing. Ceaseless traffic through the streets can take the shine off—though there's respite down on the quiet riverside paths. The crowds are really substantial on market day (Monday), attended by area farmers; a similarly popular traditional agricultural show takes place the first week of August. For a self-guided hour-long stroll, pick up a map at the tourist office, where the town trail begins. A small exhibition upstairs explains the landscape of the Peak District.

Where to Stay & Eat

£££ ✕ **The Prospect.** Cream and brown are the dominant colors of this intimate, wood-beam and -panel restaurant, where spacious tables, upholstered chairs, and attentive service enhance the comfort factor. If you're in the mood for tradition, opt for the Lancashire hot pot or slow-roast belly pork with parsnip mash and apple chutney. If you feel adventurous, try the chocolate torte and vodka ice cream, or the canapés and blinis that accompany the good-value fixed-price menus. ✉ *Unit 6, Theme Court, Bridge St.* ☎ *01629/810077* ⊟ *AE, MC, V* ⊗ *Closed Mon. No dinner Sun.*

£–££ ✕ **The Old Original Bakewell Pudding Shop.** Given the plethora of local rivals, it takes a bold establishment to claim its Bakewell puddings as "original," but there's certainly nothing wrong with those served here, eaten hot with custard or cream. The oak-beam dining room also turns out commendable main courses of Yorkshireman (batter pudding with meat and vegetables) and steak-and-stout pie. ⊠ *The Square* ☎ *01629/812193* ⊟ *MC, V* ☉ *Closes 6 PM winter, 7 PM summer.*

★ ✕▥ **Fischer's.** The Fischer family
££££–£££££ bought this stately Edwardian manor primarily with their restaurant in mind. On the edge of the Chatsworth estate, rooms in the main house have fancy plasterwork ceilings, antique pine furniture, and muted colors; those in the garden annex show a more contemporary style. The formal restaurant has a more expensive menu (£60, Monday to Saturday) or a menu du jour (£30–£35, Sunday to Friday). Fish often comes with fresh pastas and delicate sauces; duck, lamb, and game receive similar care. Sunday dinner is for guests only. ⊠ *Baslow Hall, Calver Rd., Baslow, DE45 1RR* ☎ *01246/583259* ⊟ *01246/583818* ⊕ *www. fischers-baslowhall.co.uk* ⇝ *11 rooms* ⚐ *Restaurant, in-room data ports, bar, meeting rooms, no-smoking rooms; no a/c, no kids under 10* ⊟ *AE, DC, MC, V* ⵙ *CP.*

££ ▥ **Haddon House Farm.** This may be a working farm, but there's nothing workaday about the fresh and imaginatively designed rooms (with themes such as Monet and Shakespeare) that the Nicholls husband-and-wife team created. The peaceful valley location, antiques, flowers, and CD players all contribute to a relaxing stay. Bathrooms have tiles hand-painted with insects and bamboo, and breakfasts are taken around the kitchen table. The location on the A6 lies between Haddon Hall and Bakewell. ⊠ *Haddon Rd., DE45 1BN* ☎ *01629/814024* ⊟ *01629/ 812759* ⊕ *www.great-place.co.uk* ⇝ *4 rooms* ⚐ *No a/c, no room phones, no kids under 5, no smoking* ⊟ *No credit cards* ⵙ *BP.*

BAKEWELL PUDDING

Bakewell is the source of Bakewell pudding, said to have been created inadvertently when, sometime in the 19th century, a cook at the town's Rutland Arms Hotel dropped some rich cake mixture over jam tarts and baked it. Every local bakery and tearoom claims an original recipe—it's easy to spend a gustatory afternoon tasting rival puddings.

Haddon Hall

28 *2 mi southeast of Bakewell.*

Fodor's Choice
★

Stately house scholar Hugo Montgomery-Massingberd has called Haddon Hall, a romantic, storybook medieval manor set along the River Wye, "the *beau idéal* of the English country house." Unlike other trophy homes that are marble Palladian monuments to the grand tour, Haddon Hall remains quintessentially English in appearance, bristling with crenellations and stepped roofs and landscaped with rose gardens. The house, built mainly in the 14th century, is famous as the setting (perhaps apocryphal) for the shocking 16th-century elopement of Dorothy Vernon and Sir John Manners during a banquet; the tale became a popular Victorian-era love story. (Dorothy and Sir John are buried in Bakewell's parish church.) Constructed by generations of the Vernon family in the Middle Ages, Haddon Hall passed into the ownership of the dukes of Rutland. After the dukes moved their county seat to Belvoir Castle, little changed in the house for hundreds of years. In the early 20th century, however, the ninth duke undertook a superlative restoration. The wider world saw the hall in Franco Zeffirelli's 1996 film *Jane Eyre*; part of the 1999 *Elizabeth,* starring Cate Blanchett, was also filmed here. The virtually unfurnished house has fine plasterwork and wooden paneling, especially in the Long Gallery, and still holds some treasures, including tapestries, and a famous 1932 painting of Haddon Hall by Rex Whistler. ⊠ *A6* ☎ *01629/812855* ⊕ *www.haddonhall.co. uk* ✉ *£7.75, parking £1* ⊙ *May–Sept., daily noon–5; Apr. and Oct., Sat.–Mon. 10:30–4:30; last admission 30 mins before closing.*

Matlock

㉙ *5 mi south of Haddon Hall, 8 mi southeast of Bakewell.*

In the heart of the Derbyshire Dales, Matlock and its near neighbor Matlock Bath are former spa towns compressed into a narrow gorge on the River Derwent. Some surviving Regency buildings in Matlock testify to its former importance, although it's less impressive an ensemble than that presented by Buxton. The surroundings, however, are particularly beautiful. The **Matlock River Illuminations,** a flotilla of lighted boats shimmering after dark along the still waters of the river, takes place on weekends late August through late October.

At Matlock Bath, 2 mi south of Matlock, river and valley views unfold from the curving line of buildings that makes up the village. Aside from riverside strolls, the major attraction is the cable-car ride across the River Derwent that takes you to the **Heights of Abraham Country Park and Caverns** on the crags above, with a visitor center and café. The all-inclusive ticket allows access to the woodland walks and nature trails of the 60-acre park, as well as entry to a cavern and a guided descent into an old lead mine, where workers toiled by candlelight. ⊠ *A6, Matlock Bath* ☎ *01629/582365* ⊕ *www.heights-of-abraham.co.uk* ✉ *£9.50, additional parking fee based on time* ⊙ *Cable car and visitor center mid-Feb.–late Feb., daily 10–4:30; late Feb.–late Mar., weekends 10–4:30; late Mar.–Oct., daily 10–5 (and later in summer).*

Where to Stay & Eat

★ ✕▣ **Riber Hall.** Awash with romantic resonance, this partly Elizabethan, **££££–£££££** partly Jacobean manor-house hotel perches above the town. Antiques and four-poster beds decorate the half-timber bedrooms; some bathrooms have whirlpool tubs. The garden is especially lovely. The restaurant (£££££ fixed-price menu) serves imaginative dishes inspired by modern French cuisine; choices might be fillet of sea bass with squid ink, followed by poached pear in saffron. There's a daily vegetarian menu. ⊠ *Off A615, DE4 5JU* ☎ *01629/582795* 🖷 *01629/580475* ⊕ *www.riber-hall.co.uk* ⌦ *14 rooms* ⚒ *Restaurant, tennis court, bar, business services, meeting rooms, some pets allowed; no a/c* ☰ *AE, MC, V* ⁋◯ *CP.*

Sports & the Outdoors

One of the major trails in the Peak District, **High Peak Trail,** runs for 17 mi from Cromford (south of Matlock Bath) to Dowlow, following the

CLOSE UP

Well Dressing

UNIQUE TO THE PEAK DISTRICT is the custom of well dressing, when certain wells or springs are decorated with elaborate pictures made of flowers. Frames up to 4 feet wide and 6 feet high, covered with a base of clay, are filled with a colorful mosaic of seeds, grasses, berries, and moss as well as flowers and flower petals, a process that involves a team of workers and takes about a week to complete. Although the designs usually incorporate religious themes such as biblical stories, they are a Christian veneer over an ancient pagan celebration of the water's life-giving powers. The well dressing and blessing ceremony, usually accompanied by a brass band, heralds the start of several days of festivities. Of the 70 or so towns and villages that continue this summertime tradition, Tissington (May), south of Matlock; Bakewell (early July); and, near Chatsworth, Eyam (late August) are among the most popular.

route of an old railroad. For information, guidebooks, guide services, and maps, contact any Peak District National Park Office.

Hardwick Hall

★ **③** *10 mi east of Matlock.*

Few houses in England evoke the late Elizabethan era as vividly as this beautiful stone mansion and all its treasures. The facade glitters with myriad windows, making it easy to see why the house came to be known as "Hardwick Hall, more glass than wall." ■ **TIP→ Choose a sunny day to see the rooms and their treasures at their best; electric lighting is limited.** The vast state apartments well befit their original chatelaine, Bess of Hardwick. By marrying a succession of four rich husbands, she had become second only to Elizabeth in her wealth when work on this house began. She took possession in 1597, and four years later made an inventory of the important rooms and their contents—furniture, tapestries, and embroideries. The wonder is that these items still remain here. Unique patchwork hangings, probably made from clerical copes and altar frontals taken from monasteries and abbeys, grace the entrance hall, and superb 16th- and 17th-century tapestries cover the walls of the main staircase and 1st-floor High Great Chamber. The collection of Elizabethan embroideries—table carpets, cushions, bed hangings, and pillowcases—is second to none. There are also fine examples of plasterwork, painted friezes, and ornamental chimneypieces. Outside, you can visit the walled gardens. Access is signposted from Junction 29 of the M1 motorway. ⊠ *Doe Lea, Chesterfield* ☎ *01246/850430* ⊕ *www.nationaltrust.org. uk* ⊡ *£7.80, gardens only £4.30; £2 parking* ☉ *House Apr.–Oct., Wed., Thurs., weekends, and national holidays 12:30–4:30; gardens Apr.–Oct., Wed.–Sun. and national holidays 11–5:30; last admission 30 mins before closing. Grounds daily 8–dusk.*

9

Chatsworth House

★ ☾ ③ *13 mi northwest of Hardwick Hall, 4 mi northeast of Bakewell.*

Glorious parkland leads to Chatsworth House, ancestral home of the dukes of Devonshire and one of England's greatest country houses. The vast expanse of greenery, grazed by deer and sheep, sets off the Palladian-style elegance of "the Palace of the Peak." Originally an Elizabethan house, Chatsworth was conceived on a grand, even monumental, scale. It was altered over several generations starting in 1686, and the architecture now has a hodgepodge look, though the Palladian facade remains splendid. The house is surrounded by woods, elaborate gardens, greenhouses, rock gardens, and the most famous water cascade in the kingdom—all designed by two great landscape artists, Capability Brown and, in the 19th century, Joseph Paxton, an engineer as well as a brilliant gardener. The gravity-fed Emperor Fountain can shoot as high as 300 feet. Perennially popular with children, the farmyard area has milking demonstrations at 3, and an adventure playground. ■ TIP→ **Plan on at least a half day to explore the grounds; avoid Sunday if you prefer not to be with the heaviest crowds. Do stop at the farm shop, which has terrific organic goodies.** A brass band plays on Sunday afternoons in July and August.

Although death duties have taken a toll on the interior grandeur, with duke after duke forced to sell off treasures to keep the place going, there is more than enough to look at. Inside are intricate carvings, Van Dyck portraits, superb furniture, and a few fabulous rooms, including the Sculpture Gallery, the library, and the Blue Drawing Room, where you can see two of the most famous portraits in Britain, Sir Joshua Reynolds's *Georgiana, Duchess of Devonshire, and Her Baby,* and John Singer Sargent's enormous *Acheson Sisters.* ✉ *Off B6012, Bakewell* ☎ *01246/582204* ⊕ *www.chatsworth-house.co.uk* ✉ *House, gardens, and Scots rooms £12, house and gardens £9.75, gardens only £6, farmyard and adventure playground £4.50; parking £1.50* ☉ *Mid-Mar.–mid-Dec., house daily 11–5:30, gardens daily 11–6, farmyard and adventure playground daily 10:30–5:30; last admission 1 hr before closing.*

Where to Eat

££–£££ ✕ **Devonshire Arms.** Inside this stone 18th-century coaching inn, which counts Charles Dickens as one of its many visitors, are antique settles, copper and brass, and great homemade fare. Typical dishes include deviled whitebait, steak-and-ale pie, and sausage and mash. Friday is fresh fish day, and on Sunday you can sample a Victorian breakfast (book ahead), which comes with Buck's Fizz—champagne and or-

PRIDE & CHATSWORTH

You may recognize the exterior and parkland of Chatsworth as Pemberley, home of Mr. Darcy, in the 2005 film version of *Pride and Prejudice.* It was Hollywood exaggeration to give him one of England's grandest country mansions, but no matter. The film also has some enticing views of the Peak District. Check ⊕ www.visitbritain.com or ⊕ www.visitprideandprejudice.com for more location information.

ange juice—and newspapers. The inn is 2 mi south of Chatsworth. ⊠ *B6012, Beeley* ☎ *01629/733259* ⊟ *AE, MC, V.*

Castleton

32 *10 mi northwest of Chatsworth, 9 mi northeast of Buxton.*

The area around Castleton, in Hope Valley, contains the most famous manifestations of the peculiar geology of the Peak District. A number of caves and mines are open to the public, including some former lead mines and Blue John mines (amethystine spar; the unusual name is a corruption of the French *bleu-jaune* (meaning "blue yellow"). The limestone caverns attract many people, which means that Castleton shows a certain commercialization and can be crowded in summer. The town was probably established by Henry II, in the mid-12th century.

It was Henry II who in 1176 added the square tower to the Norman **Peveril Castle,** whose ruins occupy a dramatic crag above the town. The castle has superb views—from here you can clearly see a curving section of the medieval defensive earthworks still visible in the town center below. Peveril Castle is protected on its west side by a 230-foot-deep gorge formed by a collapsed cave. ⊠ *Market Pl., A1687* ☎ *01433/620613* ⊕ *www.english-heritage.org.uk* ⊠ *£3.50* ⊙ *Apr., Sept., and Oct., daily 10–5; May–Aug, daily 10–6; Nov.–Mar., Thurs.–Mon. 10–4.*

Caves riddle the entire town and the surrounding area, and in the massive **Peak Cavern**—reputedly Derbyshire's largest natural cave—rope-making has been done on a great ropewalk for more than 400 years. You can also see the remains of a prehistoric village that has been excavated here. ☎ *01433/620285* ⊕ *www.devilsarse.com* ⊠ *£6.25; £11 joint ticket with Speedwell Cavern* ⊙ *Apr.–Oct., daily 10–5; Nov.–Mar., weekdays tours at noon and 2, weekends 10–5; last tour at 4.*

The area's most exciting cavern by far is **Speedwell Cavern,** where 105 slippery steps lead down to old lead-mine tunnels, blasted out by 19th-century miners. Here you transfer to a small boat for the claustrophobic ¼-mi chug through an illuminated access tunnel to the cavern itself. At this point you're 600 feet underground, in the deepest public-access cave in Britain, with views farther down to the so-called Bottomless Pit, a water-filled cavern into which the miners dumped their blasted limestone debris. A shop on-site sells items made of the Blue John mineral. Speedwell Cavern is at the bottom of Winnats Pass, 1 mi west of Castleton. ⊠ *Winnats Pass* ☎ *01433/620512* ⊕ *www.speedwellcavern.co.uk* ⊠ *£6.75; £11 joint ticket with Peak Cavern* ⊙ *Daily 10–5; last tour 1 hr before closing.*

Where to Stay

££   **Underleigh House.** Peaceful is the word for the location of this creeper-clad cottage and barn at the end of a lane in lovely walking country. The big lounge has a fireplace, and the flagstone entrance hall has one big table for breakfasts (expect local specialties such as oatcakes and black pudding). There are games for rainy days, and books, sweets, and

9

flowers in the tidy modern bedrooms. Hope is 1 mi east of Castleton on A617. ✉ *Off Edale Rd., Hope S33 6RF* ☎ *01433/621372* 🖨 *01433/ 621324* ⊕ *www.underleighhouse.co.uk* 🛏 *6 rooms* 🐾 *Some pets allowed; no a/c, no kids under 12, no smoking* ▤ *MC, V* ⵙ *BP.*

£ 🖼 **Bargate Cottage.** This cottage dating to 1650, at the top of Market Place opposite the church, is one of Castleton's B&B treasures. The kindly owners scatter rag dolls and teddy bears with abandon, and the cutesy oak-beam rooms incorporate the necessary facilities. Breakfast is served at one table, with plenty of bonhomie and hiking advice on tap. ✉ *Market Pl., S33 8WQ* ☎ *01433/620201* 🖨 *01433/621739* ⊕ *www. bargatecottage.co.uk* 🛏 *3 rooms* 🐾 *No a/c, no kids under 12, no smoking* ▤ *No credit cards* ⵙ *BP.*

▎**EN ROUTE**   Heading northwest to Edale, the most spectacular driving route is over **Winnats Pass,** through a narrow, boulder-strewn valley. Beyond are the tops of Mam Tor (where there's a lookout point) and the hamlet of Barber Booth, after which you run into Edale.

Edale

㉝ *5 mi north of Castleton.*

At Edale, you're truly in the Peak District wilds. This sleepy, straggling village, in the shadow of Mam Tor and Lose Hill and the moorlands of the high plateau known as Kinder Scout (2,088 feet), lies among some of the most breathtaking scenery in Derbyshire. England can show little wilder scenery than Kinder Scout, with its ragged edges of grit stone and its interminable leagues of heather and peat. Late summer brings a covering of reddish purple as the heather flowers, but the time to really appreciate the somber beauties of Kinder and its neighbors is in late fall or early winter, when the moors seem to brood under low clouds.

The **Old Nag's Head** (☎01433/670291) at the top of the village has marked the official start of the Pennine Way since 1965. Call in at the Hiker's Bar, sit by the fire, and tuck into hearty bar meals and warming hot toddies. On Monday and Tuesday in winter, when this pub is closed, the Ramblers' Inn, at the other end of the village, is open.

In the village, the Edale **National Park Information Centre** has maps, guides, and information on all the walks in the area. There's limited accommodation in the village (all B&B-style), but the information center can provide a list or point you toward the local youth hostel. ☎ *01433/ 670207* ⊕ *www.peakdistrict.org* ⊙ *Apr.–Oct., daily 9:30–5:30; Nov.–Mar., daily 10–5.*

Sports & the Outdoors

An extremely popular walking center, Edale is the starting point of the 250-mi-long **Pennine Way** (⊕ www.nationaltrail.co.uk), which crosses Kinder Scout. If you plan to attempt this, seek local advice first, because bad weather can make the walk treacherous. However, several much shorter routes into the Edale Valley, like the 8-mi route west to Hayfield, give you a taste of dramatic scenery.

LANCASHIRE & THE PEAKS ESSENTIALS

Transportation

BY AIR

Manchester Airport, about 10 mi south of the city, is the third-largest airport in the country. About 100 airlines serve 175 international and U.K. destinations. M56 north leads directly into Manchester via the A5103. Frequent trains run from Manchester Airport to Piccadilly Railway Station (15–20 minutes); buses go to Piccadilly Gardens Bus Station (1 hour). A taxi from the airport to Manchester city center costs between £12 and £15. For more details, call the Greater Manchester Passenger Transport Executive (GMPTE) information line.

Liverpool John Lennon Airport, about 8 mi southeast of the city at Speke, covers inland and European destinations. There's bus service to the city center every 30 minutes; contact Airportxpress 500.
🚌 **AirportXpress 500** ☎ 0870/608-2608 ⊕ www.merseytravel.gov.uk. **GMPTE information line** ☎ 0161/228-7811 ⊕ www.gmpte.com. **Liverpool John Lennon Airport** ✉ Off A561, Speke ☎ 0870/750-8484 ⊕ www.liverpooljohnlennononairport.com. **Manchester Airport** ✉ Near Junctions 5 and 6 of M56 ☎ 0161/489-3000 ⊕ www.manairport.co.uk.

BY BUS

National Express serves the region from London's Victoria Coach Station. Average travel time to Manchester or Liverpool is five hours. To reach Matlock, Bakewell, and Buxton you can take a bus from London to Derby and change to the TransPeak bus service, though you might find it more convenient to travel first to Manchester.

Chorlton Street Coach Station, a few hundred yards west of Piccadilly Railway Station in Manchester's city center, is the main bus station for regional and long-distance buses. Most local buses leave from Piccadilly Gardens Bus Station, the hub of the urban bus network. Metroshuttle operates three free circular routes around the city center; service runs every 5 to 10 minutes from 7 AM to 7 PM (Sunday 10 to 6).

In Liverpool, regional and long-distance National Express coaches use the Norton Street Coach Station, and local and cross-river buses depart from Sir Thomas Street, Queen Square, and Paradise Street.

The TransPeak service between Manchester and Derby stops at Buxton and major Peak District destinations, with departures every two hours from Manchester's Chorlton Street Bus Station. Wayfarer tickets are available for 24-hour weekdays (£8) or 48-hour weekends (£11.50).

FARES & SCHEDULES For Manchester bus information, call the GMPTE information line (⇨ By Air). For timetables and local bus (and train and ferry) service in Liverpool, call the Mersey Travel Line. For local bus information in Buxton and the Peak District, call Traveline. The *Peak District Timetable* (60p) covers all local public transportation services and is available at area tourist offices.

9

Mersey Travel Line ☎ 0870/608-2608 ⊕ www.merseytravel.gov.uk. **National Express** ☎ 0870/580-8080 ⊕ www.nationalexpress.com. **Traveline** ☎ 0870/608-2608 ⊕ www.traveline.org.uk.

BY CAR

Although a car is not be an asset in touring the centers of Manchester and Liverpool, it is helpful in getting around the Peak District. Bus service there is quite good, but a car allows the most flexibility. To reach Manchester from London, take M1 north to M6, leaving M6 at Exit 21A and joining M62 east, which becomes M602 as it enters Greater Manchester. M60 is the ring road around Manchester. Liverpool is reached by leaving M6 at the same junction, Exit 21A, and following M62 west into the city. Travel time to Manchester or Liverpool from London is 3–3½ hours. Expect heavy traffic out of London on weekends to all destinations in the northwest. The M6 toll road, Britain's first toll motorway (£3.50, £2.50 at night), which runs between Exits 4 and 11A of the M6, provides a speedier alternative to the M6.

Driving from London to the Peak District, stay on M1 until you reach Exit 29, then head west via A617/A619/A6 to Buxton. From Manchester, take A6 southeast via Stockport to Buxton, about an hour's drive.

ROAD
CONDITIONS   Roads within the region are generally very good. In Manchester and Liverpool, try to sightsee on foot to avoid parking problems in the city centers. In the Peak District, park in signposted parking lots whenever possible. In summer, Peak District traffic is very heavy; watch out for speeding motorbikes, especially on the A6. In winter, know the weather forecast as moorland roads can quickly become impassable.

BY TRAIN

Virgin Trains serves the region from London's Euston Station. Direct service to Manchester and Liverpool takes three hours. To reach Buxton from London, take the Manchester train and switch at Stockport.

There are trains between Manchester's Piccadilly Station and Liverpool's Lime Street every half hour during the day; the trip takes 50 minutes. Local service—one train an hour—from Manchester to Buxton takes one hour. Call National Rail Enquiries for timetable information.
National Rail Enquiries ☎ 0845/748-4950 ⊕ www.nationalrail.co.uk. **Virgin Trains** ☎ 0845/722-2333 ⊕ www.virgintrains.co.uk.

BY TRAM

In Manchester, Metrolink electric tram service runs through the city center and out to the suburbs. The Eccles extension has stops for the Lowry (Harbour City) and for the Manchester United Stadium (Old Trafford). Buy a ticket (cash only) from the platform machine before you board.
Metrolink ☎ 0161/205-2000 ⊕ www.metrolink.co.uk.

Contacts & Resources

EMERGENCIES

Ambulance, fire, police ☎ 999. **Royal Liverpool University Hospital** ✉ Prescot St., City Centre, Liverpool ☎ 0151/706-2000. **Manchester Royal Infirmary** ✉ Oxford Rd., University Quarter, Manchester ☎ 0161/276-1234.

INTERNET

Wi-Fi access is common in the public areas of larger city hotels, less so in the guest rooms. Broadband is available throughout the region. Internet cafés are thin on the ground in Manchester and Liverpool.

🔗 Internet Cafés **Cyberemporium** ✉ 28 High St., Buxton ☎ 01298/214455, open Tuesday through Sunday. **EasyInternet** ✉ Clayton Square Shopping Centre, City Centre, Liverpool ☎ no phone, open Monday through Saturday 10–6, Sunday 10–4. **Internet Gaming** ✉ 32 Princess St., City Centre, Manchester ☎ 0161/244–5566, open daily.

NATIONAL PARK

The Peak District National Park head office is in Bakewell. There are also regional offices.

🔗 **Peak District National Park** head office ✉ Baslow Rd., Bakewell DE45 1AE ☎ 01629/816200 ⊕ www.peakdistrict.org. **Bakewell** ☎ 01629/813227. **Castleton** ☎ 01433/620679. **Edale** ☎ 01433/670207.

BIKING Special Peak District National Park Hire Centres rent bikes for around £12 per day. The service is restricted to April through October except for Parsley Hay, which opens on weekends in winter (excluding December and January). The most accessible centers are listed below; contact a Peak District National Park Information Centre for more information.

🔗 Bike Rentals **Peak District National Park Hire Centres** ✉ Hayfield ☎ 01663/746222 ✉ Parsley Hay ☎ 01298/84493 ✉ Middleton Top ☎ 01629/823204 ⊕ www.peakdistrict.org, www.derbyshire.gov.uk.

TOUR OPTIONS

BOAT TOURS City Centre Cruises in Manchester offers a three-hour Sunday lunch round-trip on a barge to the Manchester Ship Canal.

🔗 **City Centre Cruises** ☎ 0161/902–0222 ⊕ www.citycentrecruises.co.uk.

BUS TOURS Cavern City Tours has a Beatles Magical Mystery Tour of Liverpool, departing from the Beatles Story, Albert Dock, daily at noon and at 2:30 on weekends (late June through late September, and some school holiday periods). The two-hour bus tour (£12) runs past Penny Lane, Strawberry Field, and other mop-top landmarks. You can also choose among specialized tours such as those that focus on John Lennon or Paul McCartney, or even hire a private guide.

A novel way to travel Liverpool is by YellowDuckmarines, amphibious vehicles from World War II. Tours run from mid-February to Christmas (£9.95 and £11.95) and leave from Albert Dock.

Tourist offices in Manchester and Liverpool can book you on short city coach tours that cover the main sights.

🔗 **Cavern City Tours** ✉ Mathew St., City Centre, Liverpool ☎ 0151/709–3285 ⊕ www.cavern-liverpool.co.uk. **YellowDuckmarines** ☎ 0151/708–7799 ⊕ www.theyellowduckmarine.co.uk.

WALKING TOURS In Manchester and Liverpool, Blue Badge Guides arrange dozens of different tours. Tours can be booked through the tourist offices.

🔗 **Blue Badge Guides, Liverpool** ☎ 0151/237–3925. **Blue Badge Guides, Manchester** ☎ 0161/440–0277.

VISITOR INFORMATION

General information about the region is available from the North West Tourist Board, the Heart of England Tourist Board (for Derbyshire and the Peak District), and from the Manchester Visitor Centre. Local tourist information offices are listed below by town.

🚩 Tourist Information **North West Tourism** ✉ Swan House, Swan Meadow Rd., Wigan Pier, Wigan WN3 5BB ☎ 0845/600-6040 ⊕ www.visitnorthwest.com. **Bakewell** ✉ Old Market Hall, Bridge St., DE45 1DS ☎ 01629/813227 ⊕ www.visitpeakdistrict.com. **Buxton** ✉ The Crescent, SK17 6BQ ☎ 01298/25106 ⊕ www.visitbuxton.co.uk. **Liverpool,08 Place** ✉ 36–38 Whitechapel City Centre, L1 6DZ ☎ 0151/233-2008 or 0845/601-1125, 0151/709-8111 for accommodations ✉ Merseyside Maritime Museum, Albert Dock, L3 4AQ ✉ Arrival Hall, South Terminal, John Lennon Airport ☎ 0151/907-1057 ⊕ www.visitliverpool.com. **Manchester Visitor Centre** ✉ Town Hall Extension, Lloyd St., City Centre, M60 2LA ☎ 0871/222-8223 ⊕ www.visitmanchester.com ✉ International Arrivals Hall, Manchester Airport Terminal 1 ☎ 0161/436-3344 ✉ International Arrivals Hall, Manchester Airport Terminal 2 ☎ 0161/489-6412. **Matlock** ✉ Crown Sq., DE4 3AT ☎ 01629/583388. **Matlock Bath** ✉ The Pavilion, DE4 3NR ☎ 01629/55082 ⊕ www.visitpeakdistrict.com. **Stoke-on-Trent** ✉ Victoria Hall, Bagnall St., ST1 3AD ☎ 01782/236000 ⊕ www.visitstoke.co.uk.

The Lake District

WINDERMERE, GRASMERE, KENDAL, KESWICK

WORD OF MOUTH

"I like the northern lakes region toward Keswick better than the more commercial Windermere area. Take your son to Beatrix Potter's Hill Top farm . . . this is the real thing. Acquire a taste for real gingerbread . . . in Grasmere. A boat cruise on a lake is fun. Also, don't miss the Castlerigg Stone Circle, near Keswick . . . the setting is perhaps the most dramatic anywhere."

–KidsToLondon

"Keswick is lovely. Easily takes an entire day if you like to walk. Town is very nice and, yes, we did go to the pencil museum and acutally found it quite interesting."

–SandyBrit

Updated by
Julius Honnor

"LET NATURE BE YOUR TEACHER . . ." Wordsworth's ideal comes true in this region of jagged mountains, waterfalls, wooded valleys, and stone-built villages. The poets Wordsworth and Coleridge, and other Englishmen and women of letters, found the Lake District an inspiring setting for their work, and visitors have followed ever since, to walk, go boating, or just relax and take in the views. In 1951 the Lake District National Park was created here from parts of the counties of Cumberland, Westmorland, and Lancashire. No mountains in Britain are finer in outline or give a greater impression of majesty; deeper and bluer lakes can be found, but none that fit so readily into the surrounding scene.

Perhaps it's only natural that an area so blessed with beauty should have become linked with so many prominent figures in English literature. It all may have started on April 15, 1802, when William Wordsworth and his sister, Dorothy, were walking in the woods of Gowbarrow Park just above Aira Force, and Dorothy noted in her journal that she had never seen "daffodils so beautiful." Two years later Wordsworth was inspired by his sister's words to write one of the best-known lyric poems in English, "I Wandered Lonely as a Cloud." In turn, other English Romantic poets came to the region and were inspired by its beauty. Besides Wordsworth, literary figures who made their homes in the Lake District include Samuel Taylor Coleridge, Thomas De Quincey, Robert Southey, John Ruskin, Matthew Arnold, and later, Hugh Walpole, and the children's writers Arthur Ransome and Beatrix Potter.

The Lake District is a contour map come to life, a stunning natural park beloved by outdoor enthusiasts. It covers an area of approximately 885 square mi and holds 16 major lakes and countless smaller stretches of water. You can cross it by car in about an hour, though that would be a shame. The mountains are not high by international standards—Scafell Pike, England's highest peak, is only 3,210 feet above sea level—but they can be tricky to climb. In spring, many of the higher summits remain snowcapped long after the weather below has turned mild.

This area can be one of Britain's most appealing reservoirs of calm, but not in summer. A lakeside town, however appealing, loses its charm when cars and tour buses clog its narrow streets. Similarly, the walks and hiking trails that crisscross the region seem less inviting when you share them with a crowd that churns the grass into a quagmire. In January 2005 storms felled an estimated half-million trees in the national park, an apparent ecological disaster. However, the destruction of areas of coniferous woodland may be an opportunity to re-create more indigenous mixed habitats. Despite the challenges of geography and popularity, the Lake District has managed tourism and the landscape in a manner that retains the character of both the villages and the natural environment.

Off-season visits can be a real treat. All those little inns and bed-and-breakfasts that turn away crowds in summer are eager for business the rest of the year (and their rates drop accordingly). It's not an easy task to avail yourself of a succession of sunny days in the Lake District—some statisticians allot to it about 250 rainy days a year—but when the sun breaks through and brightens the surfaces of the lakes, it is an away-from-it-all place to remember.

GREAT ITINERARIES

You could spend months tramping the hills, valleys, and fells of the Lake District, or, in three days, you could drive through the major towns and villages. The key is not to do too much in too short a time. If you are traveling by public transportation, many places will be off-limits.

Numbers in the text correspond to numbers in the margin and on the Lake District map.

IF YOU HAVE 3 DAYS

If you must tour both south and north lakes together in a short time, start in **Kendal ❶** ▶. After you've looked around the market town, move on to ▦ **Windermere and Bowness-on-Windermere ❷**, where you spend the first night. You can take a boat trip on the lake that afternoon up to **Ambleside ❹**. Next day, cross Windermere by ferry, and drive through **Hawkshead ❾** and **Coniston ❽** to rural **Elterwater ❼**, where you can have lunch in one of the fine walkers' inns thereabouts. Spend the afternoon in **Grasmere ❻** and nearby **Rydal ❺** touring the sites associated with Wordsworth, such as Rydal Mount and Dove Cottage. Your second night is in ▦ **Keswick ⓬**, and on the third day, you can loop around Derwentwater through **Borrowdale ⓭** and isolated Seatoller to **Cockermouth ⓮**,

Wordsworth's birthplace. From there it's an easy drive east to the market town of **Penrith ❿** and the M6 motorway, or north to Carlisle.

IF YOU HAVE 5 DAYS

Kendal ❶ ▶, in the southern part of the Lake District, marks the starting point, followed by a drive to ▦ **Windermere and Bowness-on-Windermere ❷** and a cruise on the lake that afternoon up to **Ambleside ❹**. The next morning you can mosey around the shops and museums in Bowness before venturing on to the **Lake District National Park Visitor Centre at Brockhole ❸**. In the afternoon, cross Windermere by ferry, stopping in **Hawkshead ❾** and **Coniston ❽**, before ending up at ▦ **Elterwater ❼**. This is a splendid place to spend the night in peaceful rural surroundings, and you can take in one of the local walks the next morning. Lunch and your overnight can be in ▦ **Grasmere ❻**, just a short distance away, giving you plenty of opportunity to explore that lovely village. From Grasmere, ▦ **Keswick ⓬** is the next overnight stop, allowing you to make a day trip into the gorgeous Borrowdale Valley and perhaps take a boat trip on Derwentwater. On the final day, you can see **Cockermouth ⓮** and **Penrith ❿**.

10

Exploring the Lake District

The Lake District is in northwest England, north of the industrial belt along the River Mersey that stretches from Liverpool to Manchester, and south of Scotland. The major gateway from the south is Kendal, and from the north, Penrith. Both are on the M6 motorway. Main-line trains stop at Oxenholme, near Kendal, with a branch linking Oxenholme to Kendal and Windermere. The Lake District National Park breaks into two reasonably distinct sections. The southern lakes and valleys contain the park's most popular destinations, incorporating the largest body of water, Windermere, as well as most of the quintessential Lakeland towns and villages: Kendal, Bowness, Ambleside, Grasmere, Elterwater, Coniston, and Hawkshead. To the north, the landscape opens out across the bleaker fells to reveal challenging (and spectacular) walking country. Here, in the northern lakes, south of Keswick and Cockermouth, you have the best chance to get away from the crowds.

About the Restaurants & Hotels

Some of the area's better restaurants are at hotels. If you aren't a guest but want to dine at the hotel, be sure to make reservations in advance. Also inquire if you want to eat in a particular room at the restaurant; guests may have priority.

If the front hall has a row of muddy boots, you've probably made the right choice for a hostelry. At the best of these hotels, people eat heartily and loll about in front of fires in the evenings, sharing an almost religious dedication to the mountains. Your choices include everything from small country inns to grand lakeside hotels; many hotels offer the option of paying a higher price that includes dinner as well as breakfast. The regional mainstay is the bed-and-breakfast, from the house on Main Street to farmhouses. Most country hotels and B&Bs gladly cater to hikers and can provide on-the-spot information. The Lake District's more than 25 youth hostels, including mountain huts and lakeside mansions, are open to anyone who purchases a membership or has a membership card from their home country's hostel association. Wherever you stay, book well in advance for summer visits, especially those in late July and August. In winter many accommodations close for a month or two. On weekends and in summer, it may be hard to find places willing to take bookings for a single night.

WHAT IT COSTS In pounds				
££££	**££££**	**£££**	**££**	**£**
RESTAURANTS over £22	£18–£22	£13–£17	£7–£12	under £7
HOTELS over £160	£120–£160	£90–£119	£60–£89	under £60

Restaurant prices are for a main course at dinner. Hotel prices are for two people in a standard double room in high season, including V.A.T., with no meals or, if indicated, CP (with continental breakfast), BP (Breakfast Plan, with full breakfast), or MAP (Modified American Plan, with breakfast and dinner).

Timing

The Lake District is one of the rainiest areas in Britain, but June, July, and August hold the best hope of fine weather and are the time for all the major festivals. You will, however, be sharing the roads, hotels, trails, and lakes with thousands of other people. If you must travel at this time, turn up early at popular museums and attractions, and expect to work to find parking. April and May, as well as September and October, are alternatives. Later and earlier in the year there will be even more space and freedom, but many attractions close, and snow on high ground may preclude serious walking without heavy-duty equipment.

TOP REASONS TO GO

Take a hike: Whether it's a demanding trek up England's highest mountain, or a gentle wander around a tarn (a small mountain lake), walking is the number-one pleasure and the way to see the Lake District at its rugged and spectacular best. Even in summer, there are fantastic opportunities to escape the crowds.

Mucking around in boats: Maybe you can't match the adventures of English children's classic *Swallows and Amazons,* but there's nowhere better for renting a small boat or taking a cruise on a vintage boat and discovering the pleasures of bobbing around on the water. You'll get a different perspective on the mountains, too. The Coniston Boating Centre is one place to start.

Wordsworth's daffodils: The Lakeland landscape has a rich literary history, in the children's books of Beatrix Potter, in the thoughtful writings of John Ruskin, and, most notably, in the poems of Wordsworth, which resonate deeper after you've seen his flowers dancing in the breeze. A stop at any of the writers' homes will enrich the experience.

Rejuvenating pints: Cumbria has some great microbreweries, and a pint of real ale in one of the region's atmospheric rural inns may never taste as good as after a long hard day up a mountain.

Sunrise at Castlerigg: The stone circle at Castlerigg, in a natural hollow ringed by peaks, is a rare reminder of the region's ancient history. Blenvathra and other mountains provides an awesome backdrop for the 38 stones. Sunrise here is magical.

THE SOUTHERN LAKES
KENDAL, WINDERMERE, GRASMERE & CONISTON

10

Among the many attractions here are the small resort towns clustered around Windermere, England's largest lake, and the area's hideaway valleys, rugged walking centers, and monuments rich in literary associations. This is the easiest part of the Lake District to reach, with Kendal, the largest town, just a short distance from the M6 motorway. An obvious route from Kendal takes in Windermere, the area's natural touring center, before moving north through Ambleside and Rydal Water to Grasmere. Some of the loveliest Lakeland scenery is to be found by then turning south, through Elterwater, Hawkshead, and Coniston.

Kendal

 70 mi north of Manchester.

The southern gateway to the Lake District is the "Auld Gray Town" of Kendal, outside the national park and less touristy than the towns to the north. The town's motto, "Wool Is My Bread," refers to its importance as a textile center in northern England before the Industrial

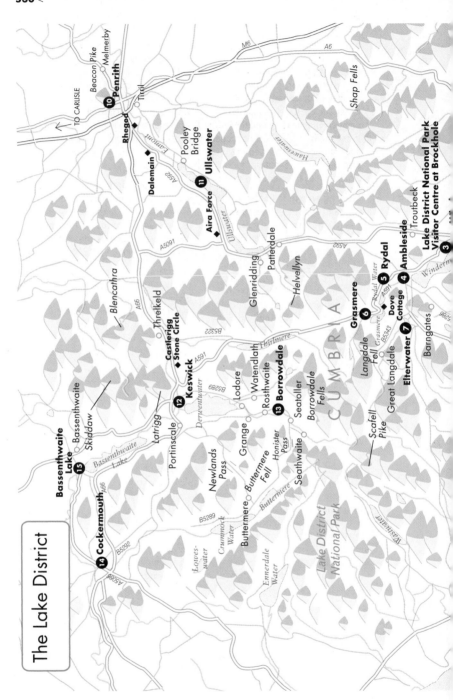

The Lake District

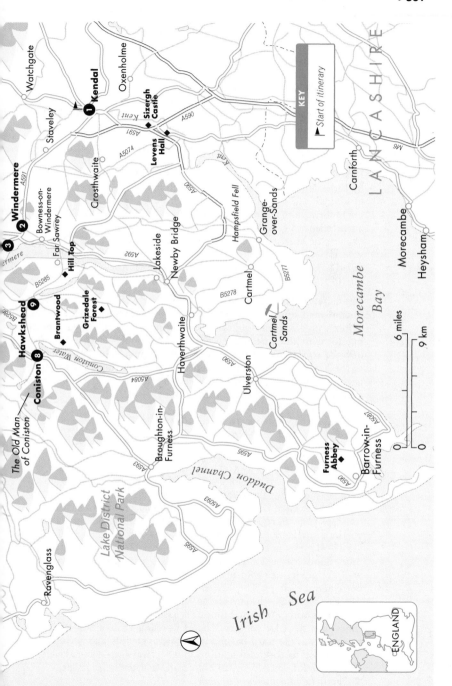

Watchgate

1 Kendal ▲

Oxenholme

Staveley

Sizergh Castle ♦

Kent

A590

A591

A5074

Levens Hall ♦

Kent

A590

Crosthwaite

Hampsfield Fell

Grange-over-Sands

2 Windermere

A591

Bowness-on-Windermere

Far Sawrey

Hill Top ♦

Newby Bridge

Lakeside

A592

Cartmel

B5278

B5277

ermere **3**

B5285

Brantwood ♦

Grizedale Forest ♦

B5286

Hawkshead

9

Haverthwaite

Cartmel Sands

Morecambe Bay

8 Coniston

Coniston Water

A5084

Ulverston

The Old Man of Coniston

Broughton-in-Furness

A593

A590

A595

A5092

Furness Abbey ♦

Barrow-in-Furness

A590

Lake District National Park

A5093

A595

Duddon Channel

Ravenglass

Irish Sea

Carnforth

L A N C A S H I R E

M6

Morecambe

Heysham

KEY

▲ *Start of itinerary*

0   6 miles

0   9 km

ENGLAND

Revolution. It was known for manufacturing woolen cloth, especially Kendal Green, which archers favored. Away from the main road are quiet courtyards and winding medieval streets known as "ginnels." Wool merchants used these for easy access to the River Kent. Nearby hills frame Kendal's gray stone houses and provide some delightful walks; you can also explore the ruins of Kendal Castle. ■ TIP→ **Pack a slab of Kendal mint cake, the local peppermint candy that all British walkers and climbers swear by to provide them with energy. It's on sale in town gift shops (and around the region).**

One of the region's finest art galleries, **Abbot Hall,** occupies a Palladian-style Georgian mansion built in 1759. The collection includes works by Victorian artist and critic John Ruskin, who lived near Coniston, and by 18th-century portrait painter George Romney, who worked (and died) in Kendal. The gallery also displays 18th-century furniture, watercolors of the region, and changing exhibitions of 20th-century art. There's an excellent café. Abbot Hall is on the River Kent, next to the parish church; the Museum of Lakeland Life is on the same site. ⊠ *Off High-gate* ☎ *01539/722464* ⊕ *www.abbothall.org.uk* ⊡ *£5, £7.50 combined ticket with Museum of Lakeland Life* ☉ *Apr.–Oct., Mon.–Sat. 10:30–5; Nov., Dec., and mid-Jan.–Mar., Mon.–Sat. 10:30–4.*

The **Museum of Lakeland Life,** in the former stable block of Abbot Hall, documents Cumbrian life over the past 300 years through excellent exhibits on blacksmithing, wheel-wrighting, farming, weaving, printing, local architecture and interiors, and regional customs. A room is devoted to the curious life of Arthur Ransome (1884–1967), author of the *Swallows and Amazons* series of children's books, set in Coniston. ⊠ *Off Highgate* ☎ *01539/722464* ⊕ *www.lakelandmuseum. org.uk* ⊡ *£3.75, £7.50 combined ticket with Abbot Hall* ☉ *Apr.–Oct., Mon.–Sat. 10:30–5; Nov., Dec., and mid-Jan–Mar., Mon.–Sat. 10:30–4.*

The **Kendal Museum** focuses on natural history and archaeology and details splendidly the flora and fauna of the Lake District. It also has displays on the region's great fell walker, Alfred Wainwright (1907–91). His famous multivolume, handwritten Lake District walking guides are sold in local book and gift shops. The interactive Kendal Castle display charts the town's history from prehistoric times into the 21st century. The museum is at the northern end of town, close to the train station. ⊠ *Station Rd.* ☎ *01539/721374* ⊕ *www.kendalmuseum.org.uk*

WAINWRIGHT IN LOVE

Alfred Wainwright, an accountant, become one of travel writing's most famous authors. First published in the 1950s and '60s, his handwritten, illustrated guides have sold more than 2 million copies; these classics are still sold in area bookstores. The gruff Wainwright seemed to want the hills to himself, yet he lovingly created a series that continues to introduce people to the Lakeland mountains. The first of his 49 books may reveal his motivation: he calls the book a "love letter" to the eastern fells. Clearly Wainwright was deep in love with the area until the end of his life.

🖼 *£2.70* ⏱ *Apr.–Oct., Mon.–Sat. 10:30–5; Nov., Dec., and mid-Feb.–Mar., Mon.–Sat. 10:30–4.*

Sizergh Castle, one of the Lake District's finest fortified houses, has a 58-foot-tall defensive peel tower that dates from 1340, when Scottish raids were feared. It has been the home of the Strickland family for more than 760 years. Expanded in Elizabethan times, the castle includes outstanding oak-paneled interiors with intricately carved chimneypieces and oak furniture. The estate has a rock garden with a large collection of ferns, two lakes, and an ancient woodland with many kinds of butterflies. Sizergh is 3½ mi south of Kendal. ✉ *Off A591, Sizergh* ☎ *015395/60070* ⊕ *www.nationaltrust.org.uk* 🖼 *£6.20, gardens only £4* ⏱ *Apr.–Oct., Sun.–Thurs.; house 1:30–5:30, gardens 12:30–5:30.*

★ **Levens Hall,** a handsome Elizabethan house and the home of the Bagot family, is famous for its topiary garden, probably the most distinctive in the world. Laid out in 1694, the garden retains its original design, and the yew and beech hedges, cut into amazingly complex shapes that resemble enormous chess pieces, rise among a profusion of flowers. The house contains a stunning medieval hall with oak paneling, ornate plasterwork, Jacobean furniture, and Cordova goat leather wallpaper. Levens Hall is 4 mi south of Kendal. ✉ *Off A590, Levens* ☎ *015395/60321* ⊕ *www.levenshall.co.uk* 🖼 *£9, gardens only £6* ⏱ *Mid-Apr.–mid-Oct., Sun.–Thurs.; house noon–5, gardens 10–5, last admission 4:30.*

Where to Stay & Eat

The Brewery Arts Centre is another good dining option in Kendal, as is the café at Abbot Hall.

£££ ✗ **The New Moon.** This small but sleek restaurant, decorated in tones of warm off-white and pale, earthy brown, has won a good local reputation for high-quality dishes. The vegetarian selections are always worthwhile, and the sometimes adventurous modern English cooking shows Mediterranean flourishes, such as a risotto of tomatoes, spinach, and asparagus. Lunch and the fixed-price early dinner (5:30–6:30) are especially good values. ✉ *129 Highgate* ☎ *01539/729254* 💳 *MC, V* ⏱ *Closed Mon.*

£ ✗ **1657 Chocolate House.** Chocolate rules at this old spot serving 38 chocolate drinks and 25 chocolate desserts. You can choose among 300 kinds of chocolates in the shop, too. Aztec Experience hot chocolate blends five spices; the milk-chocolate truffle cake is scrumptious. Servers in period costumes also deliver traditional English fare such as ploughman's lunch. Credit cards are accepted for amounts more than £10. ✉ *54 Branthwaite Brow, Finkle St.* ☎ *01539/740702* 💳 *MC, V* ⏱ *No dinner.*

£ ✗ **Waterside Wholefoods Café.** In summer, grab one of the outdoor picnic tables overlooking the River Kent and order from the delicious, filling vegetarian menu of soups, quiches, cottage pies, salads, and cakes and scones. For the full Lakeland experience, stay at Lakeland Natural, the café's inexpensive guesthouse. ✉ *2 Kent View, Waterside* ☎ *01539/729743* 💳 *MC, V* ⏱ *Closed Sun. No dinner.*

★ ££ 🏨 **Beech House Hotel.** Old-fashioned qualities combine with modern luxuries such as heated bathroom floors in this comfortable, ivy-clad

10

town house in a conservation area. Rooms are individually designed but share a common homeyness. A full English breakfast includes local smoked bacon, honey-glazed sausages, and pancakes. ⊠ *40 Greenside, LA9 4LD* ☎ *01539/720385* 🖷 *01539/724082* ⊕ *www.beechhouse-kendal.co.uk* ↪ *5 rooms* ⚭ *Minibars, Wi-Fi; no a/c* ☰ *MC, V* ⦿ *BP.*

Nightlife & the Arts

★ The **Brewery Arts Centre,** a contemporary complex in a converted brewery, includes an art gallery, theater, cinemas, and workshop spaces. It gives Kendal a good, artsy vibe. The Green Room, overlooking lovely gardens, serves lunch and dinner, and Vats Bar offers pizza and ales, lagers, and wines. In November, the Mountain Film Festival presents productions aimed at climbers and walkers. ⊠ *Highgate* ☎ *01539/725133* 🖾 *Free, except for special exhibitions* ⊙ *Mon.–Sat. 9* AM–11 PM.

Shopping

Kendal has a pleasant mix of chain names, factory outlet stores, specialty shops, and traditional markets. The most interesting stores are tucked away in the quiet lanes and courtyards around Market Place, Finkle Street, and Stramongate. There's been a **market** in Kendal since 1189, and outdoor market stalls still line the center of town along Stramongate and Market Place every Wednesday and Saturday.

Henry Roberts Bookshop (⊠ 7 Stramongate ☎ 01539/720425), in Kendal's oldest house (a 16th-century cottage), stocks a superb selection of regional books. **K Village Outlet Centre** (⊠ Lound Rd., Junction 36 of M6 ☎ 01539/732363) sells brand names at discounted prices; the best deals are at the K Shoes Factory. The **Kentdale Rambler** (⊠ 34 Market Pl. ☎ 01539/729188) is the best local store for walking boots and equipment, maps, and guides, including Wainwright's guides. **Peter Hall & Son** (⊠ Danes Rd., Staveley ☎ 01539/821633), a woodcraft workshop 4 mi north of Kendal along A591, sells ornamental bowls and wood gifts.

Windermere & Bowness-on-Windermere

❷ *10 mi northwest of Kendal.*

For a natural touring base for the southern half of the Lake District, you don't need to look much farther than Windermere, though it does get quite crowded in summer. The resort became popular in the Victorian era when the arrival of the railway made the remote and rugged area accessible. Wordsworth and Ruskin opposed the railway, fearing an influx of tourists would ruin the tranquil place. Sure enough, the railway terminus in 1847 brought with it Victorian day-trippers, and the original hamlet of Birthwaite was subsumed by the new town of Windermere, named after the lake. The day-trippers keep coming and the town has continued to flourish, despite being a mile or so from the water; the development now spreads to envelop the slate-gray lakeside village of Bowness-on-Windermere. Bowness is the more attractive, but they are so close it matters little where you stay. Bus 599, leaving every 20 minutes in summer (hourly the rest of the year) from outside Windermere train station, links the two.

★ No sights in Windermere or Bowness compete with that of **Windermere** itself. At 11 mi long, 1½ mi wide, and 200 feet deep, the lake is England's largest and stretches from Newby Bridge almost to Ambleside, filling a rocky gorge between steep, thickly wooded hills. The cold waters are superb for fishing, especially for Windermere char, a rare lake trout. In summer, steamers and pleasure craft travel the lake, and a trip across the island-studded waters, particularly the round-trip from Bowness to Ambleside or down to Lakeside, is wonderful. Although the lake's marinas and piers have some charm, you can bypass the busier stretches of shoreline (in summer they can be packed solid) by walking beyond the boathouses. Here, from among the pine trees, is a fine view across the lake. The **car ferry,** which also carries pedestrians, crosses from Ferry Nab on the Bowness side to reach Far Sawrey and the road to Hawkshead. ☎07860/813427 🚗 *Car ferry £2.50 cars, 40p foot passengers ☉ Ferries every 30 mins Mon.–Sat. 6:50 AM–9:50 PM, Sun. 9:10 AM–9:50 PM; winter until 8:50 PM.*

The **Windermere Steamboat Centre,** right beside the lake, houses the world's finest collection of Victorian and Edwardian steam- and motor-powered yachts and launches. Displays about Windermere's nautical history include the famous names of motorboat racing on the lake. The *Dolly,* built around 1850, is one of the two oldest mechanically powered boats in the world. Among the many other vessels on view are Beatrix Potter's rowing boat and a dinghy that belonged to Arthur Ransome. ▪ TIP➔ For an additional £5.50, you can take a boat ride on Windermere in an antique vessel—if the weather is good. ✉ *Rayrigg Rd., Bowness-on-Windermere* ☎ *015394/45565* ⊕ *www.steamboat.co.uk* 🚗 *£4.75 ☉ Mid-Mar.–early Nov., daily 10–5.*

Windermere Lake Cruises (☎ 015395/31188 ⊕ www.windermere-lakecruises.co.uk) employs modern launches and vintage cruisers year-round between Ambleside, Bowness, Brockhole, and Lakeside. Ticket prices vary; a Freedom of the Lake ticket (£10.50) gives unlimited travel on any of the ferries for 24 hours.

In 1900, architect H. M. Baillie Scott (1865–1945) designed **Blackwell,** a quintessential Arts and Crafts house full of carved paneling and delicate plasterwork. Lakeland birds, flowers, and trees are artfully integrated into the stained glass, stonework, friezes, and wrought iron. The house showcases exhibits of works from different periods that embody Arts and Crafts ideals. Peruse the bookshop or relax in the Tea Room overlooking Windermere. ✉ *B5360, Windermere* ☎ *015394/46139* ⊕ *www.blackwell.org.uk* 🚗 *£5.45 ☉ Apr.–Oct., daily 10:30–5; Nov., Dec., and mid-Feb.–Mar., daily 10:30–4.*

ARTS & CRAFTS TRAIL

The Arts and Crafts movement of the late 19th century flourished in the Lake District, inspired by the landscape as well as the writings of John Ruskin, who lived here. The search for meaningful style produced many artistic gems in the area's houses, churches, and hotels. At Blackwell you can purchase an Arts and Crafts Trail map and explore the best of them. Blackwell's Web site, ⊕ www.blackwell.org.uk, has extensive information about sites on the trail.

10

🕐 **The World of Beatrix Potter,** a touristy attraction aimed at kids, interprets the author's 23 tales with three-dimensional scenes of Peter Rabbit raiding Mr. McGregor's garden, Mrs. Tiggy-Winkle in her kitchen, Jemima Puddle-duck in the woods, and more. Skip it if you can and visit Potter's former home at Hill Top and the Beatrix Potter Gallery in Hawkshead. ⊠ *The Old Laundry, Crag Brow, Bowness-on-Windermere* ☎ *015394/88444* ⊕ *www.hop-skip-jump.com* ⊠ *£6* ⊘ *Easter–Sept., daily 10–5:30; Oct.–Easter, daily 10–4:30.*

★ 🕐 The excellent **Aquarium of the Lakes,** on the quayside at the southern end of Windermere, has wildlife and waterside exhibits that focus on the region. The highlights are an underwater tunnel walk along a re-created lake bed and a re-creation of a nocturnal riverbank. You can take a boat to Lakeside from the town of Windermere or drive here. ⊠ *C5062, Lakeside* ☎ *015394/30153* ⊕ *www.aquariumofthelakes.co.uk* ⊠ *£6.25* ⊘ *Apr.–Oct., daily 9–6; Nov.–Mar., daily 9–5.*

🕐 The **Lakeside & Haverthwaite Railway Company** runs vintage steam trains on the 4-mi branch line between Lakeside and Haverthwaite along the lake's southern tip; you can add on a lake cruise. Departures coincide with ferry arrivals from Windermere. ☎ *015395/31594* ⊕ *www. lakesiderailway.co.uk* ⊠ *£4.90* ⊘ *Apr.–Oct., daily 10:30–6.*

OFF THE BEATEN PATH

ORREST HEAD – To escape the traffic and have a memorable view of Windermere, set out on foot and follow the signs near the Windermere Hotel (across from the train station) to Orrest Head. The shady, uphill path winds through Elleray Wood, and after a 20-minute hike you arrive at a rocky little summit (784 feet) with a panoramic view that encompasses the Yorkshire fells, Morecambe Bay, and Troutbeck Valley.

Where to Stay & Eat

£££–££££ ✕ **Jerichos.** You can watch your meal being prepared in this stylish restaurant with an open kitchen. Choices from the modern British menu include fricassee of chicken on sage and onion mashed potatoes and sea bass on couscous. ⊠ *Birch St., Windermere* ☎ *015394/42522* ▤ *MC, V* ⊘ *No lunch. Closed Mon., last 2 wks of Nov., and 1st wk of Dec. Also closed Sun. Jan.–Mar.*

★ **£££** ✕ **Porthole Eating House.** Superb French, Italian, and traditional English dishes have been served in this intimate, whitewashed 17th-century house for more than 30 years. Delicacies on the changing menu may include char-grilled beef with pepper sauce, and risotto of wild Lakeland mushrooms. The wine cellar stocks more than 350 vintages, or you can try a glass of Taglag, the excellent local beer. Petits fours are served with coffee. The patio is ideal for alfresco dining. ⊠ *3 Ash St., Bowness-on-Windermere* ☎ *015394/42793* ▤ *AE, DC, MC, V* ⊘ *Closed Tues. No lunch Mon., Wed., and Sat.*

★ **££–£££** ✕ **Kwela's.** Delicious pan-African–influenced cuisine sets this restaurant apart from most of the more traditional eateries in the center of Windermere. Culinary influences on the changing menu stretch from Kenyan (roasted rack of lamb with tamarind sauce) to South African (*bobotie*—curried minced meat). The decor is stylish but refreshingly minimalist, with square wooden tables and natural colors. Africantinged jazz makes the scene even more mellow. ✉ *4 High St., Windermere* ☎ *015394/44954* 🖨 *015394/44192* 🖃 *MC, V.*

★ **£££££** ✕🖬 **Gilpin Lodge.** Hidden in 22 acres of tranquil grounds with two lakes and meandering paths, this family-run, rambling country-house hotel 2 mi west of Windermere pampers its guests in a low-key way. The hotel, in a converted 1901 house with two modern wings, has plush but understated public rooms furnished with sofas and rugs and warmed by log fires. Bedrooms embody contemporary rustic chic and most have sitting areas. The superb restaurant (reservations essential; fixed-price menu £££££), run by noted chef Chris Meredith, serves imaginative modern dishes using local products such as venison,

homemade sausages, and Herdwick lamb. You can use a well-equipped nearby health club, and the hotel helps arrange sports activities. ✉ *Crook Rd., off B5284, Bowness-on-Windermere LA23 3NE* ☎ *015394/88818* 🖨 *015394/88058* ⊕ *www.gilpin-lodge.co.uk* 🛏 *14 rooms* ♨ *Restaurant, room service, in-room safes, minibars, croquet, 2 lounges, Internet room, no-smoking rooms; no a/c, no kids under 7* 🖃 *AE, DC, MC, V* ⊙ *BP.*

★ **£££££** ✕🖬 **Miller Howe.** The sumptuous guest rooms in this luxurious Edwardian country-house hotel come with canopy-draped beds and binoculars that allow you to study the dazzling view across Windermere. You can relax in sitting rooms filled with fine antiques and paintings, and have afternoon tea and scones in the conservatory. The modern British restaurant (££££–£££££) serves sophisticated fare such as venison with onion and raisin compote. Guests have access to a health club, and the hotel arranges activities from archery to pony trekking. ✉ *Rayrigg Rd., Bowness-on-Windermere LA23 1EY* ☎ *015394/42536* 🖨 *015394/ 45664* ⊕ *www.millerhowe.com* 🛏 *12 rooms, 3 suites in cottage* ♨ *Restaurant, croquet, piano, airport shuttle, helipad, some pets allowed; no a/c, no kids under 8* 🖃 *AE, MC, V* ⊙ *MAP.*

£££££
Fodor'sChoice
★
✕🖬 **The Samling.** On its own sculpture-dotted 67 acres above Windermere, this place oozes exclusivity from every carefully fashioned corner. Wordsworth used to come here to pay his rent. Today the hotel is favored by the rich and famous, but it avoids the snobbishness sometimes found in such establishments. Furnishings are traditional but not fussy, service is a good mix of professional and friendly, and the lake views are fantastic. The restaurant (£££££) specializes in creative fare such as veal with caramelized sweetbread and herb risotto; it's open to nonguests for dinner, afternoon tea, and Sunday lunch. ✉ *Ambleside Rd., Windermere LA23 1LR* ☎ *015394/31922* ⊕ *www.thesamling. com* 🛏 *10 suites* ♨ *Restaurant; no a/c* 🖃 *AE, MC, V* ⊙ *BP.*

££££–£££££ ✕🖬 **The Punch Bowl.** Under the same management as the celebrated Drunken Duck Inn, the Punch Bowl is a pleasantly modern retreat in the peaceful Lyth Valley, between Windermere and Kendal. The sleek, slate-floored bar serves fine real ales alongside a bar menu with treats (££–£££) such as fish pie or roast duck, whereas the bright contemporary restaurant (£££–££££) offers a more updated selection of locally sourced cuisine, such as Cumbrian ham with ginger. Bedrooms have oak-beam, high ceilings, with chic fabric designs and big baths—there's little Lakeland chintz here. ⊠ *Off A5074, Crosthwaite, Lyth Valley LA8 8HR* ☎ *015395/68237* ⊕ *www.the-punchbowl.co.uk* ↝ *9 rooms* ⸎ *Restaurant, no-smoking rooms; no a/c* ☰ *AE, MC, V* �◉ *BP.*

£££ ✕⊡ **The Queen's Head Hotel.** Popular with locals, this 17th-century inn north of Windermere is renowned for its innovative twist on pub food such as fried fillet of sea bass with rosti potato and sautéed beans, and for real ales (fermented twice in the cask) served from what was once an Elizabethan four-poster bed. The intimate dining rooms (£££) have oak beams, flagged floors, and roaring log fires. Guest rooms are plain (though seven have four-posters) but offer splendid views and good value. ⊠ *A592, Troutbeck LA23 1PW* ☎ *015394/32174* 🖷 *015394/31938* ⊕ *www.queensheadhotel.com* ↝ *15 rooms* ⸎ *Restaurant, no-smoking rooms; no a/c, no room phones* ☰ *MC, V* ◉ *BP.*

££ ⊡ **Boston House.** Built for railway executives in 1849, this Victorian stone house designed by Augustus Pugin, on a private drive directly above the train station, is one of Windermere's oldest buildings. The friendly owners will collect you from the station on request. One of the casual, country-style bedrooms has a four-poster. ⊠ *The Terr., Windermere LA23 1AJ* ☎ *015394/43654* ⊕ *www.bostonhouse.co.uk* ↝ *5 rooms* ⸎ *No a/c, no kids under 13, no smoking* ☰ *MC, V* ◉ *BP.*

Sports & the Outdoors

Windermere Lake Holidays Afloat (⊠ Gilly's Landing, Glebe Rd., Bowness-on-Windermere ☎ 015394/43415) rents boats, from small sailboats to large cabin cruisers and houseboats.

Shopping

The best selection of shops is at the Bowness end of Windermere, on Lake Road and around Queen's Square: clothing stores, crafts shops, and souvenir stores of all kinds. At **Lakeland Jewellers** (⊠ Crag Brow, Bowness-on-Windermere ☎ 015394/42992), the local experts set semi-precious stones in necklaces and brooches. The **Lakeland Sheepskin and Leather Centre** (⊠ Lake Rd., Bowness-on-Windermere ☎ 015394/44466), which also has branches in Ambleside and Keswick, stocks moderately priced leather and sheepskin goods.

Lake District National Park Visitor Centre at Brockhole

☾ ❸ *3 mi northwest of Windermere.*

Brockhole, a lakeside 19th-century mansion with 30 acres of terraced gardens sloping down to the water, serves as the park's official visitor center and has exhibits about the local ecology, flora, and fauna. It's a good stop at the start of your visit. The gardens are at their best in spring, when daffodils cover the lawns and azaleas burst into bloom. Among the park activities are lectures, guided walks, and demonstrations of traditional crafts such as drystone wall building. Some programs are geared to children, who appreciate the adventure playground here. You can also try the croquet lawn. The bookstore carries hiking guides and maps, and you can picnic here or eat at the café-restaurant. Bus 555/556 goes to the visitor center from the Windermere train station. **Windermere Lake Cruises** (☎ 015394/43360 ⊕ www.windermere-lakecruises.co.uk) runs a ferry service to the center from Ambleside. ⊠ *A591, Ambleside Rd., Windermere* ☎ *015394/46601* ⊕ *www.lake-district.gov.uk* ✉ *Free; parking £3 half day, £4 full day, £1 out of season* ☉ *Easter–Oct., daily 10–5; early–mid-Nov., weekends 10–5.*

Ambleside

④ *4 mi north of Lake District National Park Visitor Centre at Brockhole.*

Unlike Kendal and Windermere, Ambleside seems almost part of the hills and fells. Its buildings, mainly of local stone and many built in the traditional style that forgoes the use of mortar in the outer walls, blend perfectly into their setting. The small town sits at the northern end of Windermere, making it a popular center for Lake District excursions. It has a better choice of restaurants than Windermere or Bowness, and the numerous outdoor shops are handy for fell walkers. The town does, however, suffer from overcrowding in high season. Wednesday, when the local market takes place, is particularly busy.

Bridge House, a tiny 17th-century stone cottage, perches on an arched stone bridge that spans Stone Beck. This much-photographed building holds a National Trust shop and information center. ⊠ *Rydal Rd.* ☎ *015394/35599* ✉ *Free* ☉ *Easter–Oct., daily 10–5.*

> ### LAKELAND LINGO
>
> If someone tells you to walk along the "beck" to the "force" and then climb the "fell" to the "tarn," you've just been told to hike along the stream or river (beck) to the waterfall (force) before climbing the hill or mountain (fell) to reach a small mountain lake (tarn). Also, keep in mind that town or place names in the Lake District can be the same as the name of the lake on which the town or stands. For example, Windermere is both the lake (a "mere" is a lake, in Old English) and the town.

10

NEED A BREAK?

Cozy **Sheila's Cottage** (⊠ The Slack ☎ 015394/33079), serving great homemade cakes and desserts, is a good place to gather the strength for a walk or to relax after one. Try a good-value afternoon tea with teabread or, for the full calorie replenishment, go for a hot chocolate loaded with cream.

The **Armitt Museum,** a fine local-history gallery and library, explores Ambleside's past and its surroundings through the eyes of local people such as William Wordsworth, Thomas De Quincey, Robert Southey, John Ruskin, and Beatrix Potter. You can study Beatrix Potter's natural-history watercolors or watch a Victorian lantern slide show. ⊠ *Rydal Rd.* ☎ *015394/31212* ⊕ *www.armitt.com* ✉ *£3* ☉ *Nov.–Feb., Mon.–Sat. 10–5; Mar.–Oct., daily 10–5.*

Windermere Lake Cruises (☏ 015395/31188 ⊕ www.windermere-lakecruises.co.uk) has year-round service between Ambleside, Bowness, Brockhole, and Lakeside. It's a pleasant way to experience the lake.

Where to Stay & Eat

★ **£££–££££** ✕ **Glass House.** The most stylish restaurant in town occupies a converted medieval mill with a working waterwheel, adjacent to Adrian Sankey's Ambleside Glass Works. Modern British cuisine comes with a Mediterranean twist in dishes such as fillet of beef with red-wine sauce, and salmon with a tarragon crust. You can have an elegant dinner or just sip a cappuccino in the courtyard. There's a well-priced early evening menu weekdays from 6:30 to 7:30. Note that only "well-behaved, seated-at-all-times" children are welcome. ⊠ *Rydal Rd.* ☏ *015394/32137* ⚐ *Reservations essential* ⊟ *MC, V* ⊘ *Closed Tues. and Jan.*

★ **££–££££** ✕ **Lucy's on a Plate.** This friendly café by day, restaurant by night is the perfect spot to relax, whether with mushroom stroganoff for lunch, a chocolate almond torte for afternoon tea, or grilled char for dinner by candlelight. Lucy's is famous for its puddings, and on the first Wednesday of every month a "pudding night" includes a menu of at least 30 desserts. An attached delicatessen sells high-class Cumbrian foods: sticky toffee pudding, farm cheeses, Cumberland sausage, jams, chutneys, and biscuits. ⊠ *Church St.* ☏ *015394/31191* ⊟ *MC, V.*

£–££ ✕ **Lucy 4.** You can order wine by the glass and dance to salsa music in this wine bar and bistro that caters to an upbeat crowd. Nibbling is the way to eat, with mostly Mediterranean-influenced tapas such as goat-cheese bruschetta, calamari, and feta-stuffed peppers. The same owner runs Lucy's on a Plate; the name, in case you didn't guess, is a pun on "Lucifer." ⊠ *2 St. Mary's La.* ☏ *015394/34666* ⊟ *MC, V* ⊘ *Closed Tues. and Wed. No lunch.*

★ **££–£££** ☷ **The Old Vicarage.** A quiet edge of Ambleside's old center is the peaceful setting for this excellent-value B&B in a large Victorian former vicarage. Rooms are furnished in traditional English country style, with floral and print fabrics and dark wood furniture; some are well equipped for families. A log fire, great breakfasts, and a warm welcome help make this a good deal even without the pool. ⊠ *Vicarage Rd., LA22 9DH* ☏ *015394/33364* ☷ *015394/34734* ⊕ *www.oldvicarageambleside.co.uk* ⥱ *10 rooms* ⚒ *In-room DVDs, indoor pool, sauna, lounge, piano; no a/c* ⊟ *MC, V* ⊠ *BP.*

£ ☷ **3 Cambridge Villas.** Ambleside has many inexpensive B&Bs, many clumped along Vicarage Road, but it's hard to find a more welcoming spot than this lofty Victorian house right in the center, with hosts who know a thing or two about local walks. Although space is at a premium, the rooms are pleasantly decorated with prints and wood furniture. ⊠ *Church St., LA22 9DL* ☏ *015394/32307* ⊕ *www.3cambridgevillas.co.uk* ⥱ *7 rooms, 4 with bath* ⚒ *No a/c, no room phones, no smoking* ⊟ *No credit cards* ⊠ *BP.*

Sports & the Outdoors

The fine walks in the vicinity include routes north to Rydal Mount or southeast over Wansfell to Troutbeck. Each walk will take up to a half day, there and back. Ferries from Bowness-on-Windermere dock at Am-

ON THE MENU

In Cumbria, which encompasses the Lake District, food is more than fuel for hiking. The area has earned a reputation for good country food using Herdwick lamb, beef, and game, as well as fish from the freshwater streams and lakes, such as salmon, Windermere char, and Borrowdale and Ullswater trout. Sold in one long strip, the thick pork-and-herb Cumberland sausage is another specialty. Local breads, cakes, pastries, and scones are scrumptious. Brown sugar, molasses, nutmeg, cinnamon, ginger, and rum—favorite ingredients in traditional cakes—were imported from the West Indies in exchange for wool and are integral to the cakes' flavor. Lyth Valley damsons (a kind of plum) have a nutty taste used in everything from beverages and desserts to cheese. Grasmere gingerbread is baked from a secret recipe, and Kendal mint cake (a candy marketed as survival food) has a home in many hikers' backpacks.

bleside's harbor, called Waterhead. ■ TIP➔ **You can rent rowboats here for an hour or two to escape the crowds and get a different view of the area.**

Biketreks (⊠ 2 Milans Park ☎ 015394/31245) is a good source for bike rentals.

Rydal

❺ *1 mi northwest of Ambleside.*

The village of Rydal, on the small glacial lake called Rydal Water, is rich with Wordsworthian associations. One famous beauty spot linked with the poet is **Dora's Field,** below Rydal Mount next to the church of St. Mary's (where you can still see the poet's pew). In spring the field is awash in yellow daffodils, planted by William Wordsworth and his wife in memory of their beloved daughter Dora, who died in 1847.

If there's one poet associated with the Lake District, it is Wordsworth, who made his home at **Rydal Mount** from 1813 until his death. Wordsworth and his family moved to these grand surroundings when he was nearing the height of his career, and his descendants still live here, surrounded by his furniture, books, and portraits. You can see the study in which he worked, the family dining room, and the 4½-acre garden, laid out by the poet himself, that gave him so much pleasure. ■ TIP➔ **Surrounding Rydal Mount and the areas around Dove Cottage and Grasmere are many footpaths where Wordsworth wandered. His favorite can be found on the hill past White Moss Common and the River Rothay.** Spend an hour or two walking them and you may understand why the great poet composed most of his verse in the open air. ⊠ *A591* ☎ *015394/33002* ⊕ *www.rydalmount.co.uk* ✉ *£5, garden only £2.50* ◷ *Mar.–Oct., daily 9:30–5; Nov.–Feb., Wed.–Mon. 10–4. Closed 3 wks in Jan.*

10

Grasmere

❻ *3 mi north of Rydal, 4 mi northwest of Ambleside.*

Lovely Grasmere, on a tiny, wood-fringed lake, is made up of crooked lanes in which Westmorland slate–built cottages hold shops, cafés, and galleries. The village is a focal point for literary and landscape associations because this area was the adopted heartland of the Romantic poets, notably Wordsworth and Coleridge. The Vale of Grasmere has changed over the years, but many features Wordsworth wrote about are still visible. Wordsworth lived on the town's outskirts for almost 50 years and described the area as "the loveliest spot that man hath ever known." The poet walked the hills with his guests, who included the authors Ralph Waldo Emerson and Nathaniel Hawthorne. Wordsworth, his wife Mary, his sister Dorothy, and four of his children are buried in the churchyard of **St. Oswald's,** which is on the River Rothay. The poet planted eight of the yew trees here. As you leave the churchyard, stop at the Gingerbread Shop, in a tiny cottage, for a special local treat.

★ William Wordsworth lived in **Dove Cottage** from 1799 to 1808, a prolific and happy time for the poet. During this time he wrote some of his most famous works, including "Ode: Intimations of Immortality" and *The Prelude;* he was also married here. Built in the early 17th century as an inn, this tiny house is beautifully preserved, with an oak-panel hall and floors of Westmorland slate. It first opened to the public in 1891 and remains as it was when Wordsworth lived here with his sister, Dorothy, and wife, Mary. Bedrooms and living areas contain much of Wordsworth's furniture and many personal belongings. Coleridge was a frequent visitor, as was Thomas De Quincey, best known for his 1822 autobiographical masterpiece *Confessions of an Opium Eater*—he moved in after the Wordsworths left. Your ticket includes admission to the **Wordsworth Museum,** which documents the poet's life and the literary contributions of Wordsworth and the Lake Poets. Besides seeing the poet's original manuscripts, you can hear his poems read aloud on headphones. Books, manuscripts, and artwork capture the spirit of the Romantic movement. The museum includes space for major art exhibitions. The **Jerwood Centre,** open to researchers by appointment, houses 50,000 letters and manuscripts. Afternoon tea is served at **Dove Cottage Tea Rooms and Restaurant,** also known as Villa Colombina. Opposite the tearooms, the 3°W Gallery, another Wordsworth Trust property (free; ring the bell for entry), has innovative contemporary art exhibitions. ✉ *A591, 1 mi south of Grasmere* ☎ *015394/35544* ⊕ *www. wordsworth.org.uk* 🎫 *£6.20* ⊙ *Feb.–Dec., daily 9:30–5:30.*

NEED A BREAK? At Baldry's (✉ Red Lion Sq. ☎ 015394/35301), a cheerful traditional café without too many frills, the owners serve coffee and homemade snacks, including delicious scones, cakes, pies, salads, and rarebit. Don't miss the excellent apple and almond Bakewell tart. It's not open for dinner.

Where to Stay & Eat

£££–££££ ✕ **Jumble Room Café.** This small, stone-built restaurant, dating to the 18th century, was Grasmere's first shop and is a friendly, fashionable, and colorful place, crammed with painted objets d'art. The food is an eclectic mix of international and traditional English: excellent fish-and-chips and game pie appear on the menu with Thai sweet potato ravioli. Lunches are lighter and cheaper, with good soups, and you can pop in anytime during the day for tea and cakes. ☒ *Langdale Rd.* ☎ *015394/35188* ▤ *MC, V* ☺ *Closed Mon. and Tues. Easter–Nov.; Sun. eve. and Mon.–Wed. Dec.–Easter.*

★ **£££££** ✕▦ **White Moss House.** Wordsworth purchased this comfortable house, built in 1730 to overlook Rydal Water, for his son, Willie, whose family lived here until the 1930s. Pristine public areas and bedrooms are decorated with prints and traditional pieces such as the grandfather clock at the bottom of the stairs. The current hosts, the Dixons, lavish attention on guests, but the highlight of a stay is the renowned restaurant (£££££). The menu changes daily, but the five courses of contemporary English cuisine always include a soup, local meat and fish, and a choice of British cheeses. ☒ *A591, Rydal Water LA22 9SE* ☎ *015394/35295* ⊞ *015394/35516* ⊕ *www.whitemoss.com* ⤙ *7 rooms, 1 suite* ♿ *Restaurant, fishing, lounge; no a/c* ▤ *MC, V* ☺ *Closed Dec. and Jan.* ⑩| *MAP.*

★ **£** ▦ **Banerigg House.** You don't have to spend a fortune to find appealing lakeside lodgings in Grasmere. This cozy, early-20th-century house, ¾ mi south of the village on A591, has unfussy, well-appointed rooms, most with lake views. Games and books fill the guest lounge. The B&B is walker-friendly, too, which means you get hiking advice from the owners, drying facilities for wet days, and a roaring fire when needed. ☒ *Lake Rd., LA22 9PW* ☎ *015394/35204* ⊕ *www.banerigguesthouse. co.uk* ⤙ *6 rooms, 5 with bath* ♿ *No a/c, no room phones, no room TVs, no smoking* ▤ *No credit cards* ⑩| *BP.*

Sports & the Outdoors

The most panoramic views of lake and village are from the south, from the bare slopes of Loughrigg Terrace, reached along a signposted track on the western side of the lake. It's less than an hour's walk, though your stroll can be extended by continuing around Rydal Water, passing Rydal Mount and Dove Cottage before returning to Grasmere, a 4-mi (three-hour) walk in total.

Shopping

★ The smells wafting across the churchyard draw many people to the **Grasmere Gingerbread Shop** (☒ Church Cottage ☎ 015394/35428). Since 1854 Sarah Nelson's gingerbread has been sold from this cramped 17th-century cottage, which was once the village school. The delicious treats, still made from a secret recipe, are available in attractive tins for the journey home or to eat right away. **The Stables** (☒ College St. ☎ 015394/ 35453 ☺ Closed Dec.–Easter except by appointment) antiques shop is a little Aladdin's cave piled with great books, bottles, silver candlesticks, lamps, and prints.

Elterwater

❼ *2½ mi south of Grasmere, 4 mi west of Ambleside.*

The delightful village of Elterwater, at the eastern end of the Great Langdale Valley on B5343, is a good stop for hikers. It's barely more than a cluster of houses around a village green, but from here you can choose from a selection of excellent circular walks.

Where to Stay & Eat

£££ ✕ Britannia Inn. At this family-owned, 500-year-old lodging in the heart of superb walking country, antiques, comfortable chairs, and prints and oil paintings furnish the cozy, beam public rooms. The smallish bedrooms are more modern in style, and two cottages with kitchens can be rented by the week. You can relax with a bar meal and Cumbrian ale on the terrace while taking in the village green and the rolling scenery beyond. The hearty traditional English food (££) is popular with locals, as are the many ales and whiskies. A nearby health club is available to guests. ✉ B5343, LA22 9HP ☎ 015394/37210 🖷 015394/37311 ⊕ www.britinn.net ⇨ 9 rooms, 8 with bath ⌂ Restaurant, bar, lounge, some pets allowed; no a/c ▤ MC, V ⏐◯⏐ BP.

★ **££–£££** ▢ Old Dungeon Ghyll Hotel. There's no more comforting stop after a day outdoors than the Hiker's Bar of this hotel at the head of the Great Langdale Valley. The stone floor and wooden beams echo to the clatter of hikers' boots, and the roaring stove rapidly dries out wet walking gear. The old inn has provided hospitality for more than 300 years; guest rooms are done in traditional Lakeland style with patterned carpets, botanical prints, and flowered bed linens. You can include dinner in the rate. ✉ Off B5343, Great Langdale LA22 9JY ☎☎ 015394/37272 ⊕ www.odg.co.uk ⇨ 13 rooms, 8 with bath ⌂ Restaurant, 2 bars, lounge; no a/c, no room phones, no room TVs ▤ AE, MC, V ⏐◯⏐ BP.

Sports & the Outdoors

There are access points to Langdale Fell from several places along B5343, the main road; look for information boards at local parking places. You can also stroll up the river valley or embark on more energetic hikes to Stickle Tarn or to one of the summits of the Langdale Pikes.

Coniston

❽ *5 mi south of Elterwater.*

This small lake resort and boating center attracts climbers with the peak known as the **Old Man of Coniston** (2,635 feet); it also has sites related to John Ruskin. **Coniston Water,** the lake on which Coniston stands, came to prominence in the 1930s when Arthur Ransome made it the setting for *Swallows and Amazons,* one of a series of novels about a group of children and their adventures. The lake is about 5 mi long, a tempting stretch that drew boat and car racer Donald Campbell here in 1959 to set a water-speed record of 260 mph. He was killed when trying to beat it in 1967. His body and the wreckage of *Bluebird K7* were retrieved from the lake in 2001. Campbell is buried in St. Andrew's church in Coniston, and a stone memorial on the village green commemorates him.

The **Ruskin Museum** holds fascinating and thought-provoking manuscripts, personal items, and watercolors by John Ruskin that illuminate his thinking and influence. There is also a focus on Donald Campbell; the tailfin of his *Bluebird K7,* dragged up from Coniston Water, is here. Good local-interest exhibits include copper mining, geology, lace, and

START WALKING

You can choose gentle rambles near the most popular towns and villages or challenging hikes and climbs up some of England's most impressive peaks. Information boards at parking lots throughout the region point out the possibilities. British mountaineering began in the Lake District, with its notable hikes: the famous Old Man of Coniston, the Langdale Pikes, Scafell Pike, Skiddaw, and Helvellyn are all popular, though these require experience, energy, and proper hiking boots and clothing. The Cumbria Way (70 mi) crosses the Lake District, starting at the market town of Ulverston and finishing at Carlisle. The Coast-to-Coast Walk (190 mi) runs from St. Bees on the Irish Sea through the Lake District and across the Yorkshire Dales and the North York Moors; it ends at Robin Hood's Bay at the edge of the North Sea in Yorkshire. Guidebooks to these and other Lakeland walks are available in local bookstores—don't miss Alfred Wainwright's classic guides. For short walks, consult the tourist information centers: those at Ambleside, Cockermouth, Grasmere, Kendal, Keswick, and Windermere provide maps and advice. The other main sources of information are the Lake District National Park information centers. Several climbing organizations offer guided hikes as well as technical rock climbing.

more. ⊠ *Yewdale Rd.* ☎ *015394/41164* ⊕ *www.ruskinmuseum.com* ▭ *£3.95* ☉ *Mid-Mar.–mid-Nov., daily 10–5:30; mid-Nov.–mid-Mar., Wed.–Sun. 10:30–3:30.*

★ **Brantwood,** on the eastern shore of Coniston Water, was the cherished home of John Ruskin (1819–1900), the noted Victorian artist, writer, critic, and social reformer, after 1872. The rambling, white, 18th-century house (with Victorian alterations) is on a 250-acre estate that stretches high above the lake. Here, alongside mementos such as his mahogany desk, are Ruskin's own paintings, drawings, and books. Also on display is much of the art—he was a great connoisseur—that Ruskin collected, not least superb drawings by the landscape painter J. M. W. Turner (1775–1851). A video on Ruskin's life shows the lasting influence of his thoughts, and the **Severn Studio** has rotating art exhibitions. Ruskin himself laid out the extensive grounds with gardens and woodland walks. ■ TIP→ **It's an easy drive to Brantwood from Coniston, but it's pleasant to travel here by ferry across the lake, via either the Coniston Launch or the *Gondola,* a 19th-century steam yacht. Both depart from Coniston Pier through the summer.** ⊠ *Off B5285* ☎ *015394/41396* ⊕ *www.brantwood. org.uk* ▭ *£5.50, gardens only £3.75* ☉ *Mid-Mar.–mid-Nov., daily 11–5:30; mid-Nov.–mid-Mar., Wed.–Sun. 11–4:30.*

Coniston Launch (☎ 015394/36216 ⊕ www.conistonlaunch.co.uk) connects Coniston Pier with Ruskin's home at Brantwood, offering hourly service for most of the year (service is reduced in winter) on its wooden *Ruskin* and *Ransome* launches, which run on a solar–electric power system. **Steam Yacht *Gondola*** (☎ 015394/41288 ⊕ www.nationaltrust.org.

uk) runs the National Trust's luxurious Victorian steam yacht between Coniston Pier, Brantwood, and Park-a-Moor at the south end of Coniston Water, daily from April through October.

Where to Stay & Eat

£–££ ✕ **Jumping Jenny's.** Named after Ruskin's beloved boat, the wood-beamed tearoom at Brantwood occupies the converted coach house. It has an open log fire and mountain views, and serves morning coffee, lunch (sophisticated soups, pastas, sandwiches, and salads), and afternoon tea with tasty homemade cakes. You can sit on the terrace in warmer weather. ⊠ *Off B5285* ☎ *015394/41715* ⊟ *MC, V* ⊙ *Closed Mon. and Tues. mid-Nov.–mid-Mar. No dinner.*

★ **££–£££** ✕🏠 **Sun Hotel.** Standing at the foot of the Old Man of Coniston, this country-house hotel was built at the turn of the 20th century alongside the 16th-century coaching inn that still serves as a pub. The simply furnished guest rooms, refurbished in 2006, and conservatory restaurant have exceptional mountain views. The ancient pub (££–£££), with flagstone walls and floors and exposed beams, fills up most nights with a mix of locals and climbers. The lamb hot pot is good, and the chef prepares paella in summer: take your pick of five real ales and 36 wines. ⊠ *LA21 8HQ* ☎ *015394/41248* 🖷 *015394/41219* ⊕ *www.thesunconiston.com* 🛏 *10 rooms, 9 with bath* ⚲ *Restaurant, pub, some pets allowed, no-smoking rooms; no a/c* ⊟ *MC, V* ⊺◯ *BP.*

★ **£** 🏠 **Beech Tree Guest House.** This Victorian stone house with friendly owners and a garden is within walking distance of the town center. The individually furnished rooms, some of which look out over an ancient beech tree, are done in a country theme, and breakfast is hearty and vegetarian. There's a TV in the sitting room. ⊠ *Yewdale Rd., LA21 8DX* ☎ *015394/413717* 🛏 *8 rooms, 4 with bath* ⚲ *Some pets allowed; no a/c, no room TVs, no smoking* ⊟ *No credit cards* ⊺◯ *BP.*

Sports & the Outdoors

Steep tracks lead up from the village to the **Old Man of Coniston**. The trail starts near the Sun Hotel and goes past an old copper mine to the peak, which you can reach in about two hours. It's one of the Lake District's most satisfying—not too arduous but high enough to feel a real sense of accomplishment and get some fantastic views (west to the sea, south to Morecambe Bay, and east to Windermere). Experienced hikers include the peak in a seven-hour circular walk from the village, also taking in the dramatic heights and ridges of Swirl How and Wetherlam.

★ **Coniston Boating Centre** (⊠ Lake Rd. ☎ 015394/41366 ⊕ www.lakedistrict.gov.uk) is a good place to help you enjoy the water. You can rent launches, canoes, kayaks, and wooden rowboats, or even take a sailing lesson. A picnic area and café are near the center, too.

Hawkshead

❾ *3 mi east of Coniston.*

In the Vale of Esthwaite, this small market town, with a pleasing hodge-podge of tiny squares, cobbled lanes, and whitewashed houses, is perhaps the Lake District's most picturesque village. There's a good deal more history here than in most local villages, however. The Hawkshead Courthouse, just outside town, was built by the monks of Furness Abbey in the 15th century. Hawkshead later derived much wealth from the wool trade, which flourished here in the 17th and 18th centuries. As a thriving market center, it could afford to maintain the **Hawkshead Grammar School,** at which William Wordsworth was a pupil from 1779 to 1787; he carved his name on a desk inside, now on display. A house in the village (Ann Tyson's House) claims the honor of providing the young William with lodgings. The twin draws of Wordsworth and Beatrix Potter—apart from her home, Hill Top, there's a Potter gallery—conspire to make Hawkshead overcrowded throughout the year. There may be more attention in 2007, when Renée Zellweger stars in *Miss Potter,* a movie about the writer-artist's life.

The **Beatrix Potter Gallery,** in the solicitor's offices formerly used by Potter's husband, displays an annually changing selection of the artist-writer's original watercolors and drawings, as well as information on her interests as a naturalist. Potter was a conservationist and an early supporter of the National Trust. The house looks almost as it would have done in her day. Admission is by timed ticket. ⊠ *Main St.* ☎ *015394/ 36355* ⊕ *www.nationaltrust.org.uk* ⊠ *£3.50* ⊙ *Apr.–Oct., Sat.–Wed. 10:30–4:30.*

Hill Top was the home of children's author and illustrator Beatrix Potter (1866–1943), most famous for her *Peter Rabbit* stories. The house looks much the same as when Potter bequeathed it to the National Trust, and fans will recognize details such as the porch and garden gate, old kitchen range, Victorian dollhouse, and 17th-century four-poster bed, which were depicted in the book illustrations. ■ TIP→ **Admission to this often-crowded spot is by timed ticket; you can book in advance. Try to avoid visiting on summer weekends and during school vacations.** Hill Top lies 2 mi south of Hawkshead by car or foot, though you can also approach via the car ferry from Bowness-on-Windermere. ⊠ *Off B5285, Near Sawrey* ☎ *015394/36269* ⊕ *www.nationaltrust.org.uk* ⊠ *£5.10, gardens free when house closed* ⊙ *House Easter–Oct., Sat.–Wed. 10:30–4.30; gardens and shop Easter–Oct., daily 10:30–5.*

Two miles northwest of the village (follow signs on B5285) is one of the Lake District's most celebrated beauty spots, **Tarn Hows,** a tree-lined lake. Scenic overlooks let you drink it all in, or you can take an hour to putter along the paths. A free National Trust bus runs here from Hawkshead and Coniston (Easter–October, Sunday only).

Where to Stay & Eat

£££££ ✕🖼 **Drunken Duck Inn.** After four centuries, this friendly old coaching
Fodor$Choice inn remains a fine place for food and lodging. Nestle into the cozy bar
★ with oak settles and order a tasty real ale from the Duck's Barnsgate Brewery. There's an open fire, and hops hang over the bar. The two dining spaces have dark-wood furniture and hunting prints; venison with polenta and figs is typical of the modern British fare (reservations essential in restaurant; £££). Bedrooms, bright and contemporary, make use of natural materials and have wonderful views of the Langdale

10

What's Real about Real Ale?

THE ENGLISH CAN BE PASSIONATE about their drink, as the growing interest in real ale shows. It differs from other ales by the use of natural ingredients and the fact that it is matured by fermentation in the barrel from which the ale is served. The process doesn't use carbon dioxide, so pure taste wins out over fizz. The Directory of U.K. Real Ale Breweries (⊕ www.quaffale.org.uk) lists 17 operating real-ale breweries in Cumbria, of which the Coniston Brewing Company, Barngates Brewery (at the Drunken Duck Inn) and Jennings (in Cockermouth) are three of the best. Most real ales are caramel in color and hoppy, malty, and slightly bitter to taste. A pint of ale is the usual quantity to be consumed, though a half is acceptable; you can also find it in bottles. Most pubs in the Lake District offer some sort of local brew—the better ones take enormous pride in their careful tending of the beer, from barrel to glass. Interested in the issues? Check out the Web site of the Campaign for Real Ale (⊕ www.camra.org.uk).

Pikes. The price includes afternoon tea and breakfast. The inn is 2½ mi from Ambleside and Hawkshead. ⊠ *Off B5286, Barngates LA22 ONG* ☎ *015394/36347* 🖷 *015394/36781* ⊕ *www.drunkenduckinn.co.uk* 🛏 *16 rooms* 🍴 *Restaurant, pub, no-smoking rooms; no a/c* ⊟ *AE, MC, V* 🍴 *BP* 🗣 *Reservations essential.*

££ 🔲 **Yewfield.** With the laid-back friendliness of a B&B but with most of the style of a fancier country-house hotel, this is a very good value for the money—especially if you can get one of the rooms with a great view across the valley from the front of the house. The 19th-century Gothic house, between Hawkshead and Tarn Hows, is on 30 acres of land. Breakfast is wholesome and vegetarian. ⊠ *Hawkshead Hill, LA22 0PR* ☎ *015394/36765* 🖷 *015394/36096* ⊕ *www.yewfield.co.uk* 🛏 *6 rooms, 4 apartments* 🍴 *Lounge, library, in-room DVDs; no a/c, no kids under 9* ⊟ *MC, V* ⊗ *Closed mid-Nov.–Jan.* 🍴 *BP.*

Sports & the Outdoors

Stretching southwest from Hawkshead and blanketing the hills between Coniston and Windermere, **Grizedale Forest Park** (⊠ Off B5286 ☎ 01229/860010 ⊕ www.forestry.gov.uk/grizedaleforestpark) has a thick mix of oak, pine, and larch woods criscrossed with biking and walking paths. Ninety-two outdoor sculptures are scattered beside the trails. The **Visitor Centre** has information, maps, a café, and an adventure playground.

Grizedale Mountain Bikes (⊠ Old Hall Car Park, Grizedale Forest Park Visitor Centre, off B5286 ☎ 01229/860369 ⊕ www. grizedalemountainbikes.co.uk) rents bicycles.

PENRITH & THE NORTHERN LAKES

The scenery of the northern lakes is considerably more dramatic—some would say bleaker—than much of the landscape to the south, a change that becomes apparent on your way north from Kendal to Penrith. Your easiest approach is a 30-mi drive on the A6 that takes you through the wild and desolate Shap Fells, which rise to a height of 1,304 feet. This is one of the most notorious moorland crossings in the country: even in summer it's a lonely place to be, and in winter, snow on the road can be dangerous. From Penrith the road leads to Ullswater, possibly the grandest of all the lakes; then there's a steady route west past Keswick, south through the marvelous Borrowdale Valley, and on to Bassenthwaite and Cockermouth.

Penrith

10 *30 mi north of Kendal.*

The red-sandstone town of Penrith was the capital of Cumbria, part of the Scottish kingdom of Strathclyde in the 9th and 10th centuries. It was rather neglected after the Normans arrived, and the Scots sacked it on several occasions. Penrith has been a thriving market town for centuries; the market still takes place on Tuesday, and it continues to be known for good shopping.

The tourist information center, in the Penrith Museum, has information about the historic town trail, which takes you through narrow byways to the plague stone on King Street, where food was left for the stricken, to St. Andrew's churchyard and its 1,000-year-old "hog back" tombstones (stones carved as stylized "houses of the dead"), and finally to the ruins of Penrith Castle.

The evocative remains of the 14th-century redbrick **Penrith Castle** stand high above a steep, now-dry moat. Home of the maligned Richard, duke of Gloucester (later Richard III), who was responsible for keeping peace along the border, it was one of England's first lines of defense against the Scots. By the Civil War the castle was in ruins, and the townsfolk used some of the fallen stones to build their houses. The ruins stand across from the town's train station. ⊠ *Off Castlegate* ☎ *No phone* ⊕ *www. english-heritage.org.uk* ▣ *Free* ☉ *June–Sept., daily 7:30 AM–9 PM; Oct.–May, daily 7:30–4:30.*

The **Penrith Museum,** in a 16th-century building that served as a school from 1670 to the 1970s, contains displays on the history of the Eden Valley, including Roman pottery and a medieval cauldron. The Penrith Tourist Information Centre is here. ⊠ *Robinson's School, Middlegate* ☎ *01768/212228* ▣ *Free* ☉ *Apr.–Oct., Mon.–Sat. 10–5, Sun. 1–5; Nov.–Mar., Mon.–Sat. 10–5.*

☾ **Rheged,** the name of the Celtic kingdom of Cumbria that stretched from Strathclyde in Scotland to Lancashire, is the theme of this grass-covered visitor center that looks like a Cumbrian hill from the outside. Its centerpiece, a large-format cinema, shows the historically dubious *Rheged— The Movie,* introducing Celtic warriors, Scottish raiders, and Arthurian legends. The National Mountaineering Exhibition celebrates Everest and mountaineering heroes. Shops showcase Cumbrian produce and crafts, and the Reivers restaurant has mountain views. Rheged is 2 mi southwest of Penrith and 1 mi west of Junction 40 on the M6. ⊠ *A66*

10

☎ *01768/868000* ⊕ *www.rheged.com* ✎ *Free, movie £5.95, National Mountaineering Exhibition £5.95* ◷ *Daily 10–5:30.*

Home of the Hasell family since 1679, **Dalemain,** 3 mi southwest of Penrith, began with a 12th-century peel tower built to protect the occupants from raiding Scots, and is now a delightful hodgepodge of architectural styles. An imposing Georgian facade of local pink sandstone encompasses a medieval hall and extensions from the 16th through the 18th centuries. Inside are a magnificent oak staircase, furniture dating from the mid-17th century, a Chinese drawing room, a 16th-century fretwork room with intricate plasterwork, and many fine paintings, including masterpieces by Van Dyck. The gardens are also worth a look. ✉ *A592* ☎ *01768/486450* ⊕ *www.dalemain.com* ✎ *£6, gardens only £4* ◷ *House Apr.–Oct., Sun.–Thurs. 11–4; gardens Apr.–Oct., Sun.–Thurs. 10:30–5; Nov.–mid-Dec., Feb., and Mar., Sun.–Thurs. 11–4.*

Where to Stay & Eat

★ ££ ✕⊞ **Queen's Head Inn.** Once owned by the Wordsworths, this 1719 inn is a true gem. Now the home of a brewery, the traditional pub and restaurant (££–£££) is often packed with locals sampling Tirril beers as well as guest ales on tap, 40 malt whiskies, and rare domestic and imported wines. Sophisticated meals use local produce such as farmhouse cheeses and Ullswater trout, but may include more exotic dishes, such as venison with orange and port gravy. Rambling hallways lead to small, pleasant rooms with plaid bedspreads and simple wood furniture. The inn is 2½ mi south of Penrith. ✉ *B5320, Tirril CA10 2JF* ☎ *01768/863219* ☐ *01768/863243* ⊕ *www.queensheadinn.co.uk* ⇥ *7 rooms* ⌂ *Restaurant, pub; no a/c, no room phones* ▤ *MC, V* ⦿⏐ *BP.*

Shopping

Penrith is a diverting place to shop, with its narrow streets, and arcades chockablock with family-run specialty shops. Major shopping areas include Devonshire Arcade, with its brand-name stores; the pedestrian-only Angel Lane and Little Dockray; and Angel Square. The stalls of the outdoor **market** line Dockray, Corn Market, and Market Square every Tuesday and sell fine local produce and original crafts.

The excellent **Bluebell Bookshop** (✉ 8 Angel La. ☎ 01768/866660) sometimes hosts special events and readings. **James & John Graham of Penrith Ltd.** (✉ Market Sq. ☎ 01768/862281) has a great bakery and a well-stocked delicatessen that specializes in cheese and local products. **The Toffee Shop** (✉ 7 Brunswick Rd. ☎ 01768/862008), where the Queen buys her toffee, may also have England's best fudge. **Wetheriggs Country Pottery** (✉ Clifton Dykes ☎ 01768/892733), 2 mi south of Penrith on the A6, sells handmade earthenware and stoneware from Britain's only remaining steam-powered pottery.

Ullswater

⑪ *3 mi southwest of Dalemain, 6 mi southwest of Penrith.*

Hemmed in by towering hills, Ullswater, the region's second-largest lake, draws outdoor types. Some of the finest views are from the A592

Poetry, Prose & the Lakes

THE LAKE DISTRICT'S BEAUTY has whetted the creativity of many a famous poet and artist. Here's a quick rundown of some of the writers inspired by the area's vistas.

William Wordsworth (1770–1850), one of the first English Romantics, redefined poetry by replacing the mannered style of his forerunners with a more conversational style. Many of his greatest works, such as *The Prelude*, draw directly from his experiences in the Lake District, where he spent the first 20 and last 50 years of his life. Wordsworth and his work had an enormous effect on Coleridge, Keats, Shelley, Byron, and countless other writers.

John Ruskin (1819–1900), writer, art critic, and early conservationist, was an impassioned champion of new ways of seeing. He defended contemporary artists such as William Turner and the Pre-Raphaelites. His five-volume masterwork, *Modern*

Painters, changed the role of the art critic from that of approver or naysayer to that of interpreter.

Thomas De Quincey (1785–1859) wrote essays whose impressionistic style influenced many 19th-century writers, including Poe and Baudelaire. His most famous work, *Confessions of an English Opium Eater* (1822), is an imaginative memoir of his young life, which indeed included opium addiction. He settled in Grasmere in 1809.

Beatrix Potter (1866–1943) never had a formal education; instead, she spent her childhood studying nature. Her love of the outdoors, and Lakeland scenery in particular, influenced her delightfully illustrated children's books, including *The Tale of Jemima Puddle-Duck* and *Squirrel Nutkin*. Potter also became a noted conservationist who donated land to the National Trust.

as it sticks to the lake's western shore, through the adjacent hamlets of **Glenridding** and **Patterdale** at the southern end. Lakeside strolls, tea shops, and rowboat rental all help provide the usual Lakeland experience.

10

Ullswater Steamers (☎ 017684/82229 ⊕ www.ullswater-steamers.co. uk) sends its oil-burning, 19th-century steamers the length of Ullswater between Glenridding and Pooley Bridge; it's a pleasant tour. The service operates 363 days a year from the pier at Glenridding.

At **Aira Force** (✉ Off A592, 5 mi north of Patterdale), a spectacular waterfall pounds under a stone bridge and through a wooded ravine to feed into Ullswater. From the parking lot (£2–£4 fee, depending on how long you stay), it's a 10-minute walk to the falls. Bring sturdy shoes in wet weather. Just above Aira Force in the woods of Gowbarrow Park is the spot where, in 1802, William Wordsworth's sister, Dorothy, observed daffodils that, as she wrote, " . . . tossed and reeled and danced and seemed as if they verily laughed with the wind that blew upon them." Two years later Wordsworth transformed his sister's words into the famous poem "I Wandered Lonely as a Cloud." And two centuries later, national park wardens patrol Gowbarrow Park in season to prevent tourists from picking the few remaining daffodils.

★ West of Ullswater's southern end, the brooding presence of **Helvellyn** (3,118 feet), one of the Lake District's most formidable mountains, recalls the region's fundamental character. It's an arduous climb to the top, especially via the challenging ridge known as Striding Edge, and the ascent shouldn't be attempted in poor weather or by inexperienced hikers. Signposted paths to the peak run from the road between Glenridding and Patterdale and pass by **Red Tarn,** at 2,356 feet the highest small mountain lake in the region.

Where to Stay & Eat

★ £££££ ✕⌂ **Sharrow Bay.** Sublime views and exceptional service and cuisine add distinction to this country-house hotel on the shores of Ullswater. Salons with oil paintings and fringed lamp shades represent classic Lakeland style. The bedrooms are plushly opulent, although those in the Edwardian Gatehouse and in the Bank House, an Elizabethan farmhouse about 1½ mi away, are somewhat simpler. Your sophisticated dinner (reservations essential, fixed-price menu, £££££) might include roast salmon on scallop risotto or venison with sweet potato confit. Be sure to request the lake-view dining room. Stop by for afternoon tea (£17.50). ⊠ *Howtown Rd., Pooley Bridge CA10 2LZ* ☎ *017684/86301* 🖶 *017684/86349* ⊕ *www.sharrowbay.co.uk* 🛏 *16 rooms, 8 suites* ⌂ *2 restaurants, 2 lounges, business services, some pets allowed, no-smoking rooms; no a/c in some rooms, no kids under 13* ☰ *AE, MC, V* ⍾⍥ *MAP.*

££££ ⌂ **Howtown Hotel.** Near the end of the road down the isolated eastern side of Ullswater, this gloriously quiet, welcoming hotel is low-key and low-tech, though the Ullswater Steamer does connect it to the outside world. Cut flowers, antiques, and stuffed deer heads decorate the interior, and the garden is worth a look. The restaurant serves traditional Lakeland fare, and good takeout lunches are available. Howtown is popular, so book ahead. ⊠ *4 mi south of Pooley Bridge, CA10 2ND* ☎ *017684/86514* 🛏 *13 rooms* ⌂ *Restaurant, bar, some pets allowed (fee); no a/c, no room phones, no room TVs, no kids under 7* ☰ *No credit cards* ⊗ *Closed Nov.–Mar.* ⍾⍥ *MAP.*

Keswick

⑫ *14 mi west of Ullswater.*

The great mountains of Skiddaw and Blencathra brood over the gray slate houses of Keswick (pronounced *kezz*-ick), on the scenic shores of Derwentwater. The town is a natural base for exploring the rounded, heather-clad Skiddaw range to the north, and the hidden valleys of Borrowdale and Buttermere (the latter reached by stunning Honister Pass) take you into the rugged heart of the Lake District. Nearby, five beautiful lakes are set among the three highest mountain ranges in England.

Although tourists pack its cobbled, narrow streets, Keswick doesn't have quite the Victorian charm of Windermere or Ambleside, or the specialty shops of Penrith. Its center is pedestrianized, however, and is the best spot in the Lake District to purchase mountaineering gear and outdoor clothing. There are also many hotels, guesthouses, restaurants, and pubs, but the best places are a few miles away in the countryside.

■ TIP➜ Because traffic congestion can be horrendous in summer, and parking is difficult in the higher valleys, you may want to leave your car in Keswick. The open-top Borrowdale bus service between Keswick and Seatoller runs frequently, and the Honister Rambler minibus is perfect for walkers aiming for the high fells of the central lakes; it makes many stops from Keswick to Buttermere. The Keswick Launch service on Derwentwater links to many walks as well as the Borrowdale bus service.

The handsome 19th-century **Moot Hall** has served as both the town hall and the local prison. Now it houses the main **tourist information center** for the region. It's also the place to get fishing permits for Derwentwater and Bassenthwaite. ⊠ *Market Pl.* ☎ *017687/72645* ⊗ *Mid-Mar.–Oct., daily 9:30–5.30; Nov.–mid-Mar., daily 9:30–4:30.*

☉ Borrowdale's long connection with graphite is celebrated at the **Cumberland Pencil Museum.** Legend has it that shepherds found graphite on Seathwaite Fell after a storm uprooted trees in the 16th century. The Derwent company still makes pencils here, and the museum contains the world's longest pencil, as well as displays about graphite mining and pencil making. ⊠ *Southey Works* ☎ *017687/73626* ⊕ *www.pencils.co.uk* ☜ *£3* ⊗ *Daily 9:30–4.*

★ To understand why **Derwentwater** is considered one of England's finest lakes, take a short walk from Keswick's town center to the lakeshore and follow the **Friar's Crag** path, about a 15-minute level walk from the center. This pine-tree-fringed peninsula is a favorite vantage point, with its view of the lake, the ring of mountains, and many tiny islands. Ahead, crags line the **Jaws of Borrowdale** and overhang a mountain ravine—a scene that looks as if it emerged from a Romantic painting.

For the best lake views, take a wooden-launch cruise with **Keswick-on-Derwentwater Launch Co.** (☎ 017687/72263 ⊕ www.keswick-launch.co.uk) around Derwentwater. Between late March and November, cruises set off every hour in each direction from a dock at the shore; there is also a limited winter timetable. You can also rent a rowboat here. Buy a "hop-on, hop-off" explorer ticket and take advantage of the seven landing stages around the lake that provide access to hiking trails, such as the two-hour climb up and down Cat Bells, a celebrated lookout point on the western shore of Derwentwater.

★ A Neolithic monument about 100 feet in diameter, the **Castlerigg Stone Circle** (⊠ Off A66, 4 mi east of Keswick) lies in a brooding natural hollow called St. John's Vale, ringed by magnificent peaks and ranged by sheep. The 38 stones aren't large, but the site makes them particularly impressive. Wordsworth described them as "a dismal cirque of Druid stones upon a forlorn moor." A marked route leads to a 200-foot-long path through a pasture. You can visit during daylight, no charge.

10

Where to Stay & Eat

££–£££ ╳ **Luca's.** The River Greta runs beside this stylish Italian bistro-restaurant, which is somewhat isolated at the north end of town. Choose from a great selection of pastas, risottos, and wood-fired pizzas, as well as traditional Italian dishes with meat or fish. The sauces and daily specials are imaginative. ⊠ *Greta Bridge, High Hill* ☎ *017687/74621* ⊟ *AE, MC, V* ⊘ *Closed Mon., and Sun.–Wed. Jan. and Feb. No lunch.*

££–£££ ╳ **Morrel's.** One of the town's better eating places has cinematically themed art and wooden floors that give a contemporary edge to the refurbished bar and dining area. The relaxed restaurant prepares contemporary fare: the pork fillet is stuffed with prunes and Calvados and the duck breast comes with puy lentils and black cherries. A couple of equally stylish apartments upstairs are available for short-term rentals. ⊠ *34 Lake Rd., CA12 5DQ* ☎ *017687/72666* ⊟ *MC, V* ⊘ *Closed Mon.*

★ **£–££** ╳ **Square Orange Cafe.** Young locals and windblown walkers gather here for excellent teas, cordials, and some serious hot chocolate. Music is laid-back, the walls have real paintings and photos, and there are games, good pizzas, and pints of local beer for long rainy days or cold winter nights. ⊠ *20 St. Johns St.* ☎ *017687/73888* ⊟ *No credit cards.*

£ ╳ **Lakeland Pedlar.** This colorful, cheerful café and bike shop serves inspired vegetarian and vegan cuisine: hearty breakfast burritos, Tex-Mex and Mediterranean food, and fun pizzas such as the Switchback, with sun-dried tomatoes, peppers, and crumbled blue cheese. You can also check out the fresh juices, espresso, and homemade cakes. Admire the fells (or the parking lot) from the outdoor tables or take food with you for the trail. ⊠ *Henderson's Yard, Bell Close* ☎ *017687/74492* ⊟ *MC, V* ⊘ *Closed Wed. No dinner Sept.–June.*

££££ ╳▥ **Highfield Hotel.** Slightly austere-looking and stubbornly old-fashioned, this family-run Victorian hotel overlooks the lawns of Hope Park and has lodging with great character, including turret rooms and a former chapel that holds a four-poster. The balconies of the common areas have superb valley views. The restaurant's daily-changing fixed-price menu (£££££) takes advantage of local ingredients in dishes such as roast pork with poached apricots and sea trout with sweet potatoes. No children under 8 are allowed in the restaurant. ⊠ *The Heads, CA12 5ER* ☎ *017687/72508* 🖷 *017687/72508* ⊕ *www.highfieldkeswick. co.uk* 🛏 *19 rooms* 🛎 *Restaurant, bar, no-smoking rooms; no a/c, no room phones* ⊟ *AE, MC, V* ⊘ *Closed mid-Nov.–Jan.* ▥◯▮ *MAP.*

★ **££** ▥ **Howe Keld.** Those in the know bypass the rows of cookie-cutter B&Bs and head here for budget TLC. The Fisher family puts you at ease in their comfortable, pretty town house–hotel. High-quality breakfasts are the big event; vegetarians do well here with fresh home-baked bread and pancakes, but there are also meaty Cumbrian fry-ups. Evening meals (on request) are a good value. ⊠ *5–7 The Heads, CA12 5ES* ☎ *017687/72417* ⊕ *www.howekeld.co.uk* 🛏 *15 rooms* 🛎 *Dining room, lounge, some pets allowed, no-smoking; no a/c, no room phones* ⊟ *No credit cards* ⊘ *Closed Jan.* ▥◯▮ *BP.*

Nightlife & the Arts

The **Keswick Film Club** (☎ 017687/72398) has an excellent festival in February and a program of international and classic films, screened at the

Alhambra Cinema on St. John's Street and at the Theatre by the Lake. The popular **Keswick Jazz Festival** (☎ 017687/74411), held each May, consists of four days of music. Reservations are taken before Christmas.

The resident company at the **Theatre by the Lake** (⊠ Lake Rd. ☎ 017687/ 74411) presents classic and contemporary productions year-round. Touring music, opera, and dance companies also perform. The Keswick Music Society season runs from September through January, and the Words on the Water literary festival takes place in February and March.

Sports & the Outdoors

BIKING **Keswick Mountain Bike Centre** (⊠ Southey Hill ☎ 017687/75202) rents bikes and provides information on trails; it also stocks accessories and clothing. Guided tours can be arranged with advance notice.

WATER SPORTS **Derwentwater Marina** (⊠ Portinscale ☎ 017687/72912) offers boat rentals and instruction in canoeing, sailing, windsurfing, and rowing.

Shopping

Keswick has a good choice of bookstores, crafts shops, and wool-clothing stores tucked away in its cobbled streets, as well as excellent outdoor shops. Keswick's **market** is held Saturday.

Bryson's of Keswick (⊠ 42 Main St. ☎ 017687/71222) makes more than 250 varieties of baked goods daily and is renowned for hot savory pies and ice cream. You can also sample these goodies in the tearoom. **George Fisher** (⊠ 2 Borrowdale Rd. ☎ 017687/72178), the area's largest outdoor equipment store, sells sportswear, travel books, and maps. Daily weather information is posted in the window. **Needle Sports** (⊠ 56 Main St. ☎ 017687/72227) supplies equipment for mountaineering and for rock and ice climbing. The **Viridian Gallery** (⊠ 13 St. John St. ☎ 017687/71328), a local artists' co-op, presents the paintings, prints, and ceramics of a half dozen Cumbrian artists.

EN ROUTE The most scenic route from Keswick, B5289 south, runs along the eastern edge of Derwentwater, past turnoffs to natural attractions such as Ashness Bridge, the idyllic tarn of Watendlath, the Lodore Falls (best in wet weather), and the precariously balanced Bowder Stone. Farther south is the tiny village of **Grange,** a walking center at the head of Borrowdale, where there's a riverside café.

Borrowdale

⑬ *7 mi south of Keswick.*

Fodor'sChoice ★

South of Keswick and its lake lies the valley of Borrowdale, whose varied landscape of green valley floor and surrounding crags has long been considered one of the region's most magnificent treasures. **Rosthwaite,** a tranquil farming village, and **Seatoller,** the southernmost settlement, are the two main centers (both are accessible by bus from Keswick), though they are little more than clusters of aged buildings surrounded by glorious countryside.

The steep **Borrowdale Fells** rise up dramatically behind Seatoller. Get out and walk whenever inspiration strikes. England's highest mountain, the

Festivals & Folk Sports

WITH EVERYTHING from rushbearing to Westmorland wrestling to traditional music, the Lake District hosts some of Britain's most unusual country festivals. Major festivals include the Cockermouth and Keswick carnivals (June), Ambleside rushbearing (August) and sports (July), Grasmere rushbearing (August) and sports (August), and Kendal Folk Festival (August), but some sort of event or festival happens somewhere during most weeks throughout the year. Rushbearing dates back to medieval times, when rushes covered church floors; today processions of flower-bedecked children and adults bring rushes to churches in a number of villages. Folk sports, often the highlights at local festivals, include Cumberland and Westmorland wrestling, in which the opponents must maintain a grip around each other's body. Fell running, a sort of cross-country run where the route goes roughly straight up and down a mountain, is also popular. A calendar of events is available at tourist information centers or on the Cumbria Tourist Board Web site, ⊕ www.golakes.co.uk.

3,210-foot **Scafell Pike** (pronounced *scar*-fell) is visible from Seatoller. One route up the mountain, for experienced walkers, is from the hamlet of Seathwaite, a mile south of Seatoller.

Where to Stay & Eat

£–££ ✕ **Yew Tree Restaurant.** Two 17th-century miners' cottages make up this intimate restaurant at the foot of Honister Pass. A low-beam ceiling, open fireplace, and excellent bar serving local Hesket Newmarket Brewery beers add appeal. The menu focuses on regional ingredients: Ullswater trout, Derwentwater pike, Herdwick burgers ("herdy burgers"), and wonderful Cumbrian cheeses and sausages. ⊠ *B5289, Seatoller* ☎ *017687/77634* ▭ *D, MC, V* ⊗ *Closed Mon. and 3 wks in Jan.*

£££££ 🏠 **Hazel Bank Country House.** Hikers and others appreciate the comforts of this stately, carefully restored Victorian home, which retains original elements such as the stained-glass windows. Immaculate, spacious bedrooms are done in a faux-Victorian theme, and some have four-posters and window seats. All rooms, including the sitting area, have splendid views of the Borrowdale Valley and the central Lakeland peaks. The four-course dinner for guests (included in price) focuses on local ingredients prepared with modern British flair. ⊠ *Off B5289, Rosthwaite CA12 5XB* ☎ *017687/77248* 🖨 *017687/77373* ⊕ *www.hazelbankhotel.co.uk* ⥂ *8 rooms* ♨ *Dining room, lounge, business services, Internet room; no a/c, no kids under 10, no smoking* ▭ *MC, V* ⊠ *MAP.*

EN ROUTE Beyond Seatoller, B5289 turns westward through **Honister Pass** (1,176 feet) and Buttermere Fell. Boulders line the road, which is one of the most dramatic in the region; at times it channels through soaring rock canyons. The road sweeps down from the pass to the village of Buttermere, sandwiched between Buttermere (the lake) and Crummock Water at the foot of high, craggy fells.

Cockermouth

⑭ *14 mi northwest of Seatoller.*

This small but bustling town, at the confluence of the Rivers Derwent and Cocker has a maze of narrow streets that are a delight to wander. It's a bit off the usual tourist path, and a bit bohemian. The ruined 13th-century castle is open only on special occasions. All year-round, you can tour **Jennings Brewery** (⊠ Castle Brewery ☎ 0845/129–7190 ⊕ www.jenningsbrewery.co.uk) and learn how real ales are made. From late June through July, the **Cockermouth Summer Festival** (⊕ www.cockermouth.org.uk) presents art, music, and theater in town.

Cockermouth was the birthplace of William Wordsworth (and his sister, Dorothy), whose childhood home, **Wordsworth House,** is an 18th-century town house. The restored house looks somewhat close to what the poet would have known. You see it complete with clutter, costumed interpreters, and even period cooking in the kitchen. Wordsworth's father is buried in the All Saints' churchyard, and the church has a stained-glass window in memory of the poet. ⊠ *Main St.* ☎ *01900/824805* ⊕ *www.nationaltrust.org.uk* ⊠ *£4.70* ⊗ *Apr.–June, Sept., and Oct., Tues.–Sat. 11–4:30; July and Aug., Mon.–Sat. 11–4:30; last admission 4.*

Castlegate House Gallery displays and sells an outstanding collection of works, many by Cumbrian artists. Eight exhibitions a year focus on paintings, sculpture, glass, ceramics, and jewelry. ⊠ *Castlegate* ☎ *01900/822149* ⊕ *www.castlegatehouse.co.uk* ⊗ *Mar.–Dec., Mon.–Wed., Fri., and Sat. 10:30–5, Sun. 2–5.*

Where to Stay & Eat

★ **£££** ✕ **Quince & Medlar.** Sophisticated vegetarian cuisine, served by candlelight, is the specialty at this wood-panel Georgian town house. Choose from at least six main courses, such as smoked Cumbrian cheese and mushroom roulade (a kind of stuffed soufflé); all come with seasonal vegetables. Desserts are delicious, especially the chilled cinnamon rhubarb. ⊠ *13 Castlegate* ☎ *01900/823579* ▤ *MC, V* ⊗ *Closed Sun. and Mon. No lunch.*

££ ▥ **Allerdale Court Hotel.** At this 17th-century coaching inn, which may have been home to famous mutineer Fletcher Christian, original oak beams provide a touch of old-fashioned charm, although the furnishings are mostly modern. The four rooms with four-posters verge on the regal. Pickwick's restaurant (££–£££) serves English fare with some international influences, from lamb with mint sauce to crispy ratatouille pancakes; Oscar's (££) specializes in grills, pizzas, and Italian dishes. ⊠ *20 Market Pl., CA13 9NQ* ☎ *01900/823654* ▤ *01900/823033* ⊕ *www.allerdalecourthotel.co.uk* ⇌ *28 rooms* ⚬ *2 restaurants, in-room data ports, bar, some pets allowed; no a/c* ▤ *AE, MC, V* ▥ *BP.*

10

Bassenthwaite Lake

⑮ *5 mi east of Cockermouth, 3 mi north of Keswick.*

Bassenthwaite is the only body of water officially called a lake in the Lake District; the others are known as "meres" or "waters." Bird-watchers know this less-frequented lake well because of the many species of migratory birds found here. The shoreline habitat is the best-preserved in the national park—in part because most of it is privately owned, and also because motorboats are not allowed. Posh accommodations and good restaurants dot the area, and popular walks include the climb up Skiddaw (3,054 feet), which, on a clear day, has panoramic views of the Lake District, Pennines, Scotland, and the Isle of Man from its summit.

Where to Stay & Eat

★ **££££** ✕🖫 **The Pheasant.** Halfway between Cockermouth and Keswick, this traditional 17th-century coaching inn exudes English coziness without the usual Lakeland fussiness. The tasteful, modern bedrooms have soft but comfortable beds and tiled bathrooms with large tubs, and they overlook a garden and 60 acres of forest. You can request a TV. A wood-beamed restaurant (£££–££££) serves superb English fare such as venison with mushrooms and shallots, as well as afternoon tea. Varnished walls, oak settles, and a smattering of locals enjoying the fine Jennings ale set the mood in the popular bar. ⊠ *Off A66, Bassenthwaite Lake CA13 9YE* ☎ *017687/76234* 🖷 *017687/76002* ⊕ *www.the-pheasant.co.uk* 🛏 *15 rooms, 3 suites* ⌂ *Restaurant, in-room data ports, bar, 3 lounges, business services, some pets allowed; no a/c* ═ *MC, V* ⦿❘ *BP.*

LAKE DISTRICT ESSENTIALS

Transportation

BY AIR

Manchester Airport has its own rail station with direct service to Carlisle, Windermere, and Barrow-in-Furness. Manchester is 70 mi from the southern part of the Lake District.

🛈 **Manchester Airport** ⊠ Near Junctions 5 and 6 of M56 ☎ 0161/489–3000 ⊕ www.manairport.co.uk.

BY BIKE

Cycling along the numerous bicycle paths and quiet forest roads in Cumbria is pleasurable and safe. The Cumbria Cycle Way circles the county, and for local excursions guided bike tours are often available, starting at about £25 per day. Contact local tourist offices or bike rental places for details on cycle routes.

BY BOAT & FERRY

Whether you rent a boat or take a ride on a modern launch or vintage vessels, getting out on the water is a fun (and often useful) way to see the Lake District. Check the sections on individual towns for information about additional services and boat rentals.

BY BUS

Traveline handles public transportation inquiries. National Express serves the region from London's Victoria Coach Station and from Manchester's Chorlton Street Station. Average travel time to Kendal is just over 7 hours from London; to Windermere, 7½ hours; and to Keswick, 8¼ hours. From Manchester there's one bus a day to Windermere (3½ hours); it stops in Ambleside, Grasmere, and Keswick. There's direct bus service to the Lake District from Carlisle, Lancaster, and York.

Stagecoach in Cumbria provides local service between Lakeland towns and through the valleys and high passes. Contact Traveline for an up-to-date timetable. A one-day Explorer Ticket (£6) is available on the bus and valid on all routes. Service between main tourist centers is fairly frequent on weekdays, but much reduced on weekends and bank holidays. Don't count on reaching the more remote parts of the area by bus. Off-the-beaten-track touring requires a car or strong legs.

CUTTING COSTS   The YHA Shuttle Bus operates a door-to-door service for guests at eight popular hostels in the Lakes (Easter through October only). Get on and off where you like for £2 a journey, or send your luggage ahead to the next hostel if you want to walk unencumbered. The trip from Windermere station to the Windermere or Ambleside hostel is free.

🚩 **YHA Shuttle Bus** ⊠ Ambleside Youth Hostel, Waterhead ☎ 015394/32304.

FARES & SCHEDULES   🚩 **National Express** ☎ 0870/580-8080 ⊕ www.nationalexpress.com. **Traveline** ☎ 0870/608-2608 ⊕ www.traveline.org.uk.

BY CAR

A car is a good option in the Lake District to get beyond the major towns; bus service is limited. To reach the Lake District from London, take M1 north to M6, getting off either at Junction 36 and joining A590/A591 west (around the Kendal bypass to Windermere) or at Junction 40, joining A66 direct to Keswick and the northern lakes region. Travel time to Kendal is about four hours, to Keswick five to six hours. Expect heavy traffic out of London on weekends to all destinations in the Northwest; construction work also often slows progress on M6.

ROAD CONDITIONS   Roads within the region are generally very good, although many minor routes and mountain passes can be both steep and narrow. Warning signs are normally posted if snow has made a road impassable; always listen to local weather forecasts in winter before heading out. In July and August and during the long public holiday weekends, expect heavy traffic. The Lake District has plenty of parking lots, which should be used to avoid blocking narrow lanes.

BY TRAIN

For schedule information, call National Rail Enquiries. Two train companies serve the region from London's Euston Station: take a Virgin or Northern Rail train bound for Carlisle, Edinburgh, or Glasgow and change at Oxenholme for the branch line service to Kendal and Windermere. Average travel time to Windermere (including the change) is 4½ hours. If you're heading for Keswick, you can either take the train to Windermere and continue from there by Stagecoach bus (Bus 555/556; 70 minutes), or stay on the main London–Carlisle train to Penrith Station (4

10

hours), from which Stagecoach buses (Bus X5) also run to Keswick (45 minutes). Direct trains from Manchester depart for Windermere five times daily (travel time 2 hours). First North Western runs a local service from Windermere and Barrow-in-Furness to Manchester Airport.

Train connections are good around the edges of the Lake District, especially on the Oxenholme–Kendal–Windermere line and the Furness and West Cumbria branch line from Lancaster to Grange-over-Sands, Ulverston, Barrow, and Ravenglass. However, these services aren't useful for getting around the central Lakeland region (you must take the bus or drive), and they are reduced, or nonexistent, on Sunday.

FARES & SCHEDULES   🚋 **Northern Rail** 🕿 0845/600–1159 ⊕ www.northernrail.org. **National Rail Enquiries** 🕿 0845/748–4950 ⊕ www.nationalrail.co.uk. **Virgin Trains** 🕿 0845/722–2333 ⊕ www.virgintrains.co.uk.

Contacts & Resources

EMERGENCIES

🚋 **Ambulance, fire, police** 🕿 999. **Keswick Cottage Hospital** ✉ Croswaithe Rd., Keswick 🕿 017687/72012. **Penrith New Hospital** ✉ Bridge La., Penrith 🕿 017687/245300. **Westmorland General Hospital** ✉ Burton Rd., Kendal 🕿 01539/732288.

INTERNET

Internet access in the Lakes is slow and patchy. Some of the better hotels offer access but Internet cafés are all but nonexistent.

🚋 **Internet Cafés Tea Too Ltd** ✉ 4 Windermere Bank, Lake Rd., Windermere 🕿 015394/45657. **Over The Top Café** ✉ 36 Kirkgate, Cockermouth 🕿 01900/827016.

NATIONAL PARK

The Lake District National Park head office (and main visitor center) is at Brockhole, north of Windermere. Helpful regional national-park information centers sell books and maps, book accommodations, and provide walking advice. Call regional offices before visiting, as funding cutbacks have caused many closures.

🚋 **Lake District National Park** ✉ Brockhole, A591, Ambleside Rd., Windermere 🕿 015394/46601 ⊕ www.lake-district.gov.uk. **Bowness Bay** ✉ Glebe Rd., Bowness-on-Windermere 🕿 015394/42895. **Keswick** ✉ Moot Hall, Main St. 🕿 017687/72645. **Ullswater** ✉ Beckside Car Park, Glenridding 🕿 017684/82414.

TOUR OPTIONS

BUS TOURS   Mountain Goat Holidays, Lakes Supertours, and Park Tours & Travel provide minibus sightseeing tours with skilled local guides. Half- and full-day tours, which really get off the beaten track, depart from Bowness, Windermere, Ambleside, and Grasmere.

🚋 **Lakes Supertours** ✉ 1 High St., Windermere 🕿 015394/42751 ⊕ www.lakes-supertours.co.uk. **Mountain Goat Holidays** ✉ Victoria St., Windermere 🕿 015394/45161 ⊕ www.lakes-pages.co.uk/goatmain.html. **Park Tours & Travel** ✉ The Lodge, Burnside Park, Windermere 🕿 015394/48600 ⊕ www.parktours.co.uk.

WALKING TOURS   You can find walks from gentle, literary-oriented strolls to challenging ridge hikes. The Lake District National Park (⇨ National Park) or the Cumbria Tourist Board in Windermere (⇨ Visitor Information) can put you in touch with qualified guides. Blue Badge Guides can provide experts on the area. English Lakeland Ramblers organizes single-base and inn-to-inn guided tours of the Lake District from May through October. Go Higher will take you on the more challenging routes and provides technical gear and courses on mountaineering skills.

🗐 **Blue Badge Guides** ☎ 020/7403–1115 ⊕ www.blue-badge.org.uk. **English Lakeland Ramblers** ✉ 18 Stuyvesant Oval, #1A, New York, NY 10009 ☎ 01229/587382 or 212/505–1020, 800/724–8801 in U.S. ⊕ www.ramblers.com. **Go Higher** ✉ High Dyon Side, Distington ☎ 01946/830476 ⊕ www.gohigher.co.uk.

VISITOR INFORMATION

Cumbria Tourist Board is open Monday through Thursday 9:30 to 5:30 and Friday 9:30 to 5.

🗐 **Cumbria Tourist Board** ✉ Ashleigh, Holly Rd., Windermere LA23 2AQ ☎ 015394/44444 ⊕ www.golakes.co.uk. **Youth Hostel Association England and Wales** ✉ Trevelyan House, Matlock, Derbyshire, DE4 3YH ☎ 0870/870–8808 ⊕ www.yha.org.uk. **Ambleside** ✉ Central Bldgs., Market Cross, Rydal Rd. ☎ 015394/32582. **Cockermouth** ✉ The Town Hall, Market St. ☎ 01900/822634. **Kendal** ✉ Town Hall, Highgate ☎ 01539/725758. **Keswick** ✉ Moot Hall, Market Sq. ☎ 017687/72645. **Penrith** ✉ Penrith Museum, Middlegate ☎ 01768/867466 ⊕ www.visiteden.co.uk. **Ullswater** ✉ Main Car Park, Glenridding ☎ 017684/82414. **Windermere** ✉ The Gateway Centre, Victoria St. ☎ 015394/46499 ⊕ www.visiteden.co.uk.

10

East Anglia

CAMBRIDGE, BURY ST. EDMUNDS, NORWICH, LINCOLN

WORD OF MOUTH

"King's College Chapel alone is worth the trip [to Cambridge] . . . It is considered the finest example of late medieval architecture in Europe. The stained-glass windows are breathtaking. And 'punting on the Cam' is a must. Some things to see in the area are the cathedral at Ely, ditto at Peterborough, and ruins at Bury St. Edmonds."

–jrandolph

"Suffolk and Norfolk have some delightful small towns and villages, many with very big churches built with money from the wool trade. It's not very far from London but seems to be off the main tourist track. Lavenham is charming. The houses were made from unseasoned oak, with the result that they are crooked."

–MissPrism

www.fodors.com/forums

Updated by
Julius Honnor

ONE OF THOSE BEAUTIFUL ENGLISH INCONSISTENCIES, East Anglia has no spectacular mountains or rivers to disturb the storied, quiet land, full of rural delights such as tulip fields, flint churches, and thatched-roof cottages. Occupying an area of southeastern England that bulges out into the North Sea, its counties of Essex, Norfolk, Suffolk, Lincolnshire, and Cambridgeshire are a bit cut off from the central routes and pulse of the country.

This area has been home to some of Britain's greatest thinkers, artists, and poets. John Milton, Francis Bacon, Sir Isaac Newton, Lord Byron, William Thackeray, and Alfred, Lord Tennyson were educated at Cambridge University, one of the world's most important centers of learning and arguably the world's most attractive university town. Here, Oliver Cromwell groomed his Roundhead troops, and Tom Paine, the man who wrote "These are the times that try men's souls," developed his revolutionary ideas. Here, John Constable painted *The Hay Wain,* and Thomas Gainsborough achieved eminence as England's most elegant portraitist. If East Anglia has remained rural to a large extent, its harvest of legendary minds has been just as impressive as its agricultural crops.

Despite its easy access from London, East Anglia remains relatively unfamiliar to visitors, with the notable exception of Cambridge and, to a lesser degree, North Norfolk, where the unspoiled villages have become fashionable. It was a region of major importance in ancient times, as evidenced by the Roman settlements at Colchester and Lincoln; and during the medieval era, when trade in wool with the Netherlands made East Anglian towns strong and independent. But with the lack of main thoroughfares and canals, the Industrial Revolution mercifully passed East Anglia by.

As a result of being a historical backwater, the region is enormously rich in quiet villages, presided over by ancient churches, tiny settlements in the midst of otherwise deserted fenland (lowlands), and manor houses surrounded by moats. Few parts of Britain can claim so many stately churches and half-timber houses. The towns are more like large villages; even the largest city, Norwich, has a population of only about 125,000.

If you find the region's mostly quiet, flat spaces dull, you need travel only a few miles to reach the bright lights: four splendid stately houses— Holkham Hall, Blickling Hall, Houghton Hall, and Her Majesty's own Sandringham. There are incomparable cathedrals, at Ely and Lincoln particularly, and the "finest flower of Gothic in Europe," King's College Chapel in Cambridge. These are the superlatives of East Anglia. But half the attraction of the region lies in its subtle landscapes, where the beauties of rural England appear at their enduring best.

Exploring East Anglia

For purposes of sightseeing, East Anglia can be divided into distinct areas: the central area surrounding the ancient university city of Cambridge and including the towns of inland Suffolk; the southeast, taking in the ancient Roman town of Colchester and sweeping upward along the Suffolk Heritage Coast; and the northeast, with the region's capital, Norwich, the waterways of the Broads, and the beaches and salt marshes of the North Norfolk coast. North of Cambridge, the fenland city of Ely has a magnificent cathedral rising out of the flatlands. Farther north, in Lincolnshire, are the city of Lincoln, landmarked by its tall, fluted cathedral towers, and the historic ports of King's Lynn and Boston, which flank the shallow bay known as the Wash.

About the Restaurants

In summer the coast gets so packed with people that reservations are essential at restaurants. Getting something to eat at other than regular mealtime hours is not always possible in small towns; look for cafés if you want a mid-morning or after-lunch snack.

About the Hotels

Few hotels in East Anglia have more than 100 rooms, so even the biggest hostelries offer friendly, personal service. The region is full of centuries-old, half-timber inns with rooms full of roaring fires and cozy bars. Bed-and-breakfasts are a good option in pricey Cambridge. It's always busy in Cambridge and along the coast in summer, so reserve well in advance.

WHAT IT COSTS In pounds					
	££££££	**££££**	**£££**	**££**	**£**
RESTAURANTS	over £22	£18–£22	£13–£17	£7–£12	under £7
HOTELS	over £160	£120–£160	£90–£119	£60–£89	under £60

Restaurant prices are for a main course at dinner. Hotel prices are for two people in a standard double room in high season, including V.A.T., with no meals or, if indicated, CP (with continental breakfast), BP (Breakfast Plan, with full breakfast), or MAP (Modified American Plan, with breakfast and dinner).

Timing

Summer and late spring are the best times to visit. Late fall and winter can be cold, windy, and rainy, though this is England's driest region and crisp frosty days here are beautiful. To escape crowds, avoid the popular Norfolk Broads in late July and August. The May Bumps, intercollegiate boat races, are, confusingly, held the first week of June in Cambridge. During the summer "long vac" (and also over the Easter and Christmas holidays), Cambridge is empty of its students, its life and soul. To see the city in full swing, visit from October through June, although in summer there are enjoyable festivals, notably the Strawberry Fair (mid-June), and the Folk Festival and Arts Festival (both July). The world-famous Aldeburgh Festival of music and the arts takes place in June.

CAMBRIDGE

▶ Cambridge embodies a certain genteel, intellectual, and, sometimes, anachronistically idealized image of Englishness. Think Rupert Brooke, the short-lived World War I–era poet ("There is some corner of a foreign field/That is forever England"), a Cambridgeshire lad, who called his county "The shire for Men who Understand," as well as William Wordsworth, Thackeray, Byron, Tennyson, E. M. Forster and C. S.

GREAT ITINERARIES

You need more than a few days to soak up the medieval atmosphere of Norfolk, Suffolk, and the unspoiled coastal villages. On a three-day trip, it's best to concentrate on one area, probably Cambridge and its surroundings, rather than try to cover the distances separating major sights and towns.

Numbers in the text correspond to numbers in the margin and on the East Anglia, Cambridge, Norwich, and Lincolnshire maps.

IF YOU HAVE 3 DAYS

Cambridge ①-⑱ ▶ is easy to visit even as a day trip from London—too easy, some say, to judge by the huge number of visitors year-round. It's also the best East Anglian base. Explore some of the ancient university buildings, stroll along the Backs, or punt down the River Cam. The next day, head for **Ely** ⑲ and spend an hour or two exploring its majestic cathedral before moving on to **Bury St. Edmunds** ㉔, a town with graceful Georgian streets. Spend the third day exploring the medieval Suffolk wool towns of **Sudbury** ㉑, **Long Melford** ㉒, and **Lavenham** ㉓ before returning to Cambridge.

IF YOU HAVE 7 DAYS

Start from **Cambridge** ①-⑱ ▶ and take in the medieval sights on

your first day. Spend the night and then head out to **Saffron Walden** ⑳ and northeast, overnighting in **Bury St. Edmunds** ㉔. Explore the town the next day, making time to visit the Abbey Ruins and Botanical Gardens, and then head south through **Long Melford** ㉒, **Lavenham** ㉓, and **Sudbury** ㉑ (with a quick stopover to see Gainsborough's House) to **Colchester** ㉕, the traditional base for exploring Constable Country. The next day, head for Constable's **Dedham** ㉖, then take the B1084 to **Orford** ㉘, a tiny village with a Norman church and castle and traditional smokehouses for preparing fish. Spend the next day exploring Sutton Hoo near **Woodbridge** ㉗ or **Aldeburgh** ㉙; you may also want to visit **Southwold** ㉚, a seaside town where time seems to have stood still. Travel to **Norwich** ㉛-㊴ and visit its cathedral and medieval alleys. The extensive journey northwest to **Lincoln** ㊽, where you can spend your sixth night, takes you through flat fenland. Lincoln is worthy of a day's exploration: on the way back to Cambridge the next day, opt to stop either at **Ely** ⑰, to see its great cathedral, or at **Stamford** ㊼ to visit Burghley House, an Elizabethan extravaganza.

Lewis. The exquisite King's College choir defines the traditional English Christmas, when the *Festival of Nine Lessons and Carols* is broadcast live on Christmas Eve. On top of all this tradition and history, it remains a lively city and an extraordinary center of learning and research where innovation and discovery still happen behind its ancient walls.

With the spires of its university buildings framed by towering trees and expansive meadows, its medieval streets and passages enhanced by gardens and riverbanks, the city of Cambridge is among the loveliest in England. The city predates the Roman occupation of Britain but there's confusion about when the university was founded. One story attributes its founding to impoverished students from Oxford, who came in search of eels—a cheap source of nourishment.

Keep in mind there is no recognizable campus: the scattered colleges *are* the university. The town reveals itself only slowly, filled with tiny gardens, ancient courtyards, imposing classic buildings, alleyways that lead past medieval churches, and wisteria-hung facades. Perhaps the best views are from the Backs, the green parkland that extends along the River Cam behind several colleges. Resulting from the larger size of the colleges and from the lack of industrialization in the city center, this broad, sweeping openness is just what distinguishes Cambridge from Oxford.

Exploring Cambridge

Exploring the city means, in large part, exploring the university. Each of the 25 oldest colleges is built around a series of courts, or quadrangles, whose velvety lawns are the envy of many a gardener. Since students and fellows (faculty) live and work in these courts, access is sometimes restricted, and at *all* times you are requested to refrain from picnicking in the quadrangles. Visitors are not normally allowed into college buildings other than chapels, dining halls, and some libraries; some colleges charge admission for certain buildings. The university's Web site, ⊕ www.cam.ac.uk, has information about the colleges and other institutions associated with it. Public visiting hours vary from college to college, depending on the time of year, and it's best to call or to check with the city tourist office. Colleges close to visitors during the main exam time, late May to mid-June. Term time (when classes are in session) means roughly October to December, January to March, and April to June; summer term, or vacation, runs from July to September.

■ TIP→ **When the colleges are open, the best way to gain access is to join a walking tour led by an official Blue Badge guide—many areas are off-limits unless you do.** The two-hour tours leave up to five times daily from the city tourist office. The other traditional view of the colleges is gained from a punt—the boats propelled by pole on the River Cam.

Main Attractions

⑬ Christ's College. To see the way a college has grown over the centuries you could not do better than visit here. The main gateway bears the enormous coat of arms of its patroness, Lady Margaret Beaufort, mother of Henry VII, who established the institution in 1505. It leads into a fine courtyard, with the chapel framed by an ancient magnolia. In the dining hall hang portraits of John Milton and Charles Darwin, two of the college's more famous students. You next walk past a fellows' building credited to Inigo Jones, to the spacious garden (once the haunt of Milton), and finally to a modern zigguratlike confection. ✉ *St. Andrew's St.* ☎ *01223/334900* ⊕ *www.christs.cam.ac.uk* ☯ *Term time, except exam period, daily 9:30–dusk; out of term, daily 9:30–noon.*

⑪ Corpus Christi College. If you visit only one quadrangle, make it the beautiful, serene, 14th-century Old Court here. Founded in 1352, it's

TOP REASONS TO GO

Cambridge: A walk though the colleges is grand, but the best views of the university's colleges and immaculate lawns (and some famous bridges) are from a punt on the river. Try not to let your pole get stuck in the mud.

Constable country: In the area where Constable grew up, you can walk or row downstream from the pastel-shaded village of Dedham straight into the setting of one of the English landscape painter's masterpieces at Flatford Mill.

Grand houses: When the Queen's not in residence you can visit the Royal Family's holiday home of Sandringham. If that's out of bounds, other options, including Audley End, Holkham Hall, and Burghley House, are just as spectacular.

Lincoln's old center: The ancient center of the city has a vast, soaring cathedral, a proper rampart-ringed castle, and winding medieval streets lined with small shops, restaurants, and cafés.

Wild North Sea coast: Trendy North Norfolk has enormous sandy beaches (great for walking) and opportunities to see seals and birdlife, especially on the salt marshes around Blakeney.

Lavenham: This medieval town is the most comely of the tight-knit cluster of places that did well from the wool trade: nearby are Sudbury and Long Melford. All have perhaps the region's most memorable architecture, including timber-framed houses gnarled into crookedness by age.

the longest continuously inhabited college quadrangle in Cambridge. ⊠ *King's Parade* ☎ *01223/338000* ⊕ *www.corpus.cam.ac.uk* 🖅 *Free* ☼ *Daily dawn–dusk.*

⓮ **Emmanuel College.** The master hand of architect Christopher Wren (1632–1723) is evident throughout much of Cambridge, particularly at Emmanuel, built on the site of a Dominican friary, where he designed the chapel and colonnade. A stained-glass window in the chapel has a likeness of John Harvard, founder of Harvard University, who studied here. The college, founded in 1584, was an early center of Puritan learning; a number of the Pilgrims were Emmanuel alumni, and they remembered their alma mater in naming Cambridge, Massachusetts. ⊠ *St. Andrew's St.* ☎ *01223/334200* ⊕ *www.emma.cam.ac.uk* ☼ *Daily 9–6, except exam period.*

★ ⓲ **Fitzwilliam Museum.** In a classical revival building renowned for its grand Corinthian portico, the Fitzwilliam, founded by the seventh viscount Fitzwilliam of Merrion in 1816, has one of Britain's most outstanding collections of art (including paintings by Constable, Gainsborough, the Pre-Raphaelites, and the French impressionists) and antiquities. The opulent interior displays its treasures to marvelous effect from Egyptian pieces such as inch-high figurines and painted coffins to sculptures from the Chinese Han dynasty of the 3rd century BC. Besides its archaeological collections, the Fitzwilliam contains a large display of English

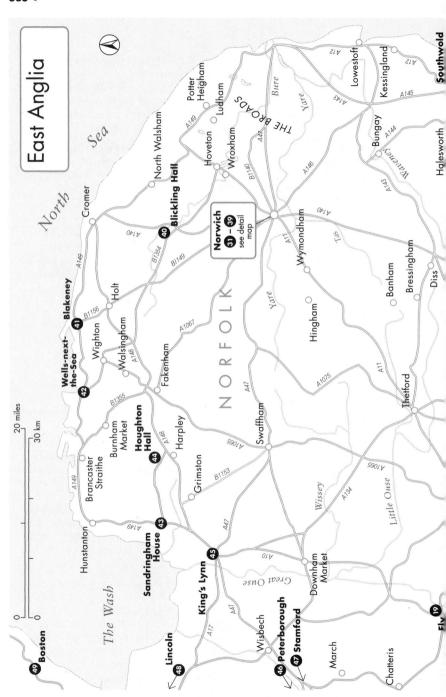

East Anglia

20 miles

30 km

North Sea

NORFOLK

THE BROADS

The Wash

The Broads

Norwich 31 – 39
see detail map

Boston 49

Lincoln

King's Lynn

Wisbech

Peterborough 46

Stamford 47

48

Sandringham House 43

Houghton Hall 44

Wells-next-the-Sea 42

Blakeney 41

Blickling Hall 40

Southwold

Ely 19

45

Hunstanton

Brancaster
Staithe

Burnham
Market

Harpley

Grimston

Downham
Market

March

Chatteris

Swaffham

Thetford

Diss

Bressingham

Banham

Hingham

Wymondham

Bungay

Halesworth

Kessingland

Lowestoft

Southwold

Walsingham

Wighton

Holt

Fakenham

Cromer

North Walsham

Potter
Heigham

Ludham

Hoveton

Wroxham

A149

A148

A149

A1065

A47

A10

A17

A47

A134

A1075

A11

A140

A11

A143

A145

A144

A143

A12

A12

A146

A1

A140

A149

A1067

A148

B1355

B1153

B1354

B1149

B1156

B1140

A47

Great Ouse

Little Ouse

Wissey

Yare

Yare

Bure

Waveney

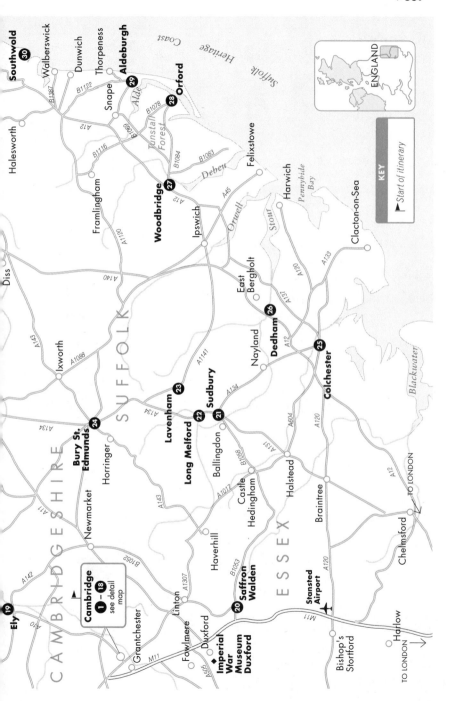

Cambridge

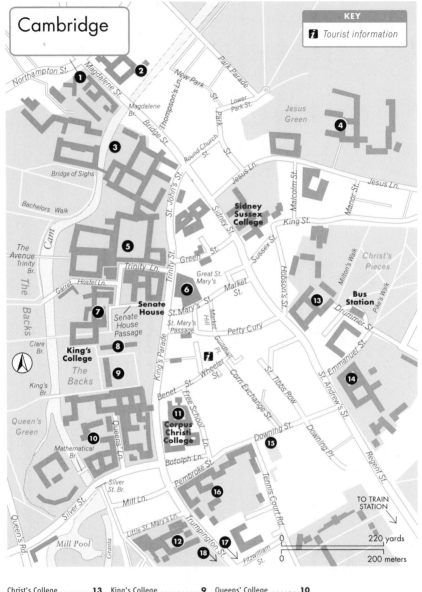

Christ's College **13**	King's College **9**	Queens' College **10**
Corpus Christi College . . .**11**	King's College Chapel **8**	St. John's College **3**
Emmanuel College **14**	Magdalene College **2**	Trinity College **5**
Fitzwilliam Museum **18**	Museum of Archaeology and Anthropology **15**	Trinity Hall College **7**
Great St. Mary's **6**		University Botanic Gardens **17**
Jesus College **4**	Pembroke College **16**	
Kettle's Yard **1**	Peterhouse College **12**	

Staffordshire and other pottery, as well as a fascinating room full of armor and muskets. ⊠ *Trumpington St.* ☎ *01223/332900* ⊕ *www.fitzmuseum. cam.ac.uk* 🖾 *Free* ⊙ *Tues.–Sat. 10–5, Sun. noon–5; contact Cambridge Tourist Information Office for guided tours.*

❻ Great St. Mary's. Known as the "university church," Great St. Mary's has its origins in the 11th century, although the current building dates from 1478. The main reason to visit is to climb the 113-foot tower, which has a superb view over the colleges and marketplace. ⊠ *Market Hill, King's Parade* ☎ *01223/741716* ⊕ *www.ely.anglican.org/parishes/ camgsm* 🖾 *Free, tower £2* ⊙ *Mon.–Sat. 9:30–5:30, Sun. noon–5:30.*

OFF THE BEATEN PATH

IMPERIAL WAR MUSEUM DUXFORD – The buildings and grounds of this former airfield, now Europe's leading aviation museum, house a remarkable collection of 180 aircraft from Europe and the United States. The **Land Warfare Hall** holds tanks and other military vehicles. The **American Air Museum,** in a striking Norman Foster–designed building, contains American combat aircraft. It honors the 30,000 Americans who were killed in action flying from Britain during World War II; Duxford itself was the headquarters of the 78th Fighter Group. A vast new exhibition, AirSpace, will open in 2007, displaying 30 aircraft. Check in advance for air shows (extra charge). The museum is 10 mi south of Cambridge, and a shuttle bus runs from Cambridge's Crowne Plaza hotel (Downing Street) to the Cambridge train station and Duxford. ⊠ *A505, Duxford* ☎ *01223/835000* ⊕ *duxford.iwm.org.uk* 🖾 *£13* ⊙ *Mid-Mar.–Oct., daily 10–6; Nov.–mid-Mar., daily 10–4.*

❹ Jesus College. Unique in Cambridge, the spacious grounds of Jesus College incorporate cloisters, a remnant of the nunnery of St. Radegund, which existed on the site before the college was founded in 1496. Cloister Court exudes a quiet medieval charm, an attribute evident in the adjacent chapel, another part of the nunnery. Victorian restoration of the building includes some Pre-Raphaelite stained-glass windows and ceiling designs by William Morris. ⊠ *Jesus La.* ☎ *01223/339339* ⊕ *www. jesus.cam.ac.uk* ⊙ *Daily 8–7, except exam period.*

❾ King's College. Founded in 1441 by Henry VI, King's College's most famous landmark is its late-15th-century chapel. Other architecture of note is the neo-Gothic Porters' Lodge, facing King's Parade, which was a relatively recent addition in the 1830s, and the classical Gibbs building. ■ TIP→ **Follow the college's Back Lawn down to the river, from where the panorama of college and chapel is one of the university's most photographed views.** Past students of King's College include the novelist E. M. Forster, the economist John Maynard Keynes, and the World War I poet Rupert Brooke. ⊠ *King's Parade* ☎ *01223/331100* ⊕ *www.kings.cam.ac.uk* 🖾 *£4, includes chapel* ⊙ *Term-time, weekdays 9:30–3:30, Sat. 9:30–3:15, Sun. 1:15–2:15; out of term, Mon.–Sat. 9:30–4:30, Sun. 10–5. Times may vary; call in advance.*

★ ❽ King's College Chapel. Based on Sainte Chapelle, the 13th-century royal chapel in Paris, this one was constructed toward the end of the 15th century and is the final, perhaps most glorious flowering of Perpendicular Gothic in Britain. Henry VI, the king after whom the college is named, oversaw the work. This was the last period before the classical architecture of the ancient Greeks and Romans, then being rediscovered by the Italians, began to make its influence felt in northern Europe. From the outside, the most prominent features are the expanses of glass, the massive flying buttresses, and the fingerlike spires that line the length of the building. Inside, the most obvious impression is of great space—the chapel has been described as "the noblest barn in Europe"—and of light flooding in from its huge windows. The brilliantly colored bosses (carved panels at the intersections of the roof ribs) are particularly intense, although hard to see without binoculars. An exhibition in the chantries, or side chapels, explains more about the chapel's construction. Behind the altar is *The Adoration of the Magi*, an enormous painting by Peter Paul Rubens, painted for a convent in Louvain. Every Christmas Eve, a festival of carols sung by the chapel's famous choir is broadcast worldwide from here. ⊠ *King's Parade* ☎ *01223/331155* ⊕ *www.kings.cam.ac.uk* ☜ *£4, includes college and grounds* ☉ *Term-time, weekdays 9:30–3:30, Sat. 9:30–3:15, Sun. 1:15–2:15; out of term, Mon.–Sat. 9:30–4:30, Sun. 10–5. Times may vary; call in advance.*

> **NEED A BREAK?**
>
> The 600-year-old **Pickerel Inn** (⊠ 30 Magdalene St. ☎ 01223/355068), one of the city's oldest pubs, makes for a good stop for a soothing afternoon pint of real ale or lager and a bowl of potato wedges. Watch for the low beams.

⑩ Queens' College. One of the most eye-catching colleges is Queens', named after Margaret, queen of Henry VI, and Elizabeth, queen of Edward IV. Founded in 1448, the college is tucked away on Queens' Lane, next to the wide lawns that lead down from King's College to the Backs. The secluded "cloister court" looks untouched since its completion in the 1540s. Queens' masterpiece is the **Mathematical Bridge**, the original version of which is said to have been built without any fastenings. The current bridge (1902) is securely bolted. ⊠ *Queens' La.* ☎ *01223/ 335511* ⊕ *www.quns.cam.ac.uk* ☜ *£1.50, free Nov.–mid-Mar. and weekdays in Oct.* ☉ *Mid-Mar.–late May, weekdays 11–3, weekends 10–4:30; late June–Sept., daily 10–4:30; Oct. weekdays 1:45–4:30, weekends 10–4:30; Nov.–mid-Mar., daily 1:45–4:30.*

❸ St. John's College. Two mythical beasts called "yales," with the bodies of antelopes and heads of goats, hold up the coat of arms and guard the gateway of Cambridge's second-largest college. St. John's was founded in 1511 by Henry VII's mother, Lady Margaret Beaufort. Its structures lie on two sites: from the main entrance, walk to the left through the courts to the 1831 "**Bridge of Sighs**," whose only resemblance to its Venetian counterpart is its covering. The windowed, covered stone bridge reaches across the Cam to the mock-Gothic New Court (1825), nicknamed "the wedding cake." If you walk through to the riverbank, you can stroll along the Backs and photograph the elegant bridge. ⊠ *St. John's St.* ☎ *01223/338600* ⊕ *www.joh.cam.ac.uk* ☜ *£2.50* ☉ *Easter–early Nov., weekdays 10–5, Sat. 9:30–5.*

❺ Trinity College. Founded in 1546 by Henry VIII, Trinity replaced a 14th-century educational foundation and is the largest college in either Cambridge or Oxford, with nearly 700 undergraduates. Many of the buildings match its size, not least its 17th-century "great court." Here the massive gatehouse holds "Great Tom," a giant clock that strikes each hour with high and low notes. The college's greatest masterpiece is Christopher Wren's library, colonnaded and seemingly constructed with as much light as stone, with wood carving by the 17th-century master Grinling Gibbons. Alumni include Sir Isaac Newton, William Thackeray, and Lords George Byron, Alfred Tennyson, and Thomas Macaulay, and 31 Nobel Prize winners. Prince Charles was an undergraduate here in the late 1960s. ⊠ *St. John's St.* ☎ *01223/ 338400* ⊕ *www.trin.cam.ac.uk* ⊠ *£2.20, free late Oct.–mid-Mar.* ⊗ *College mid-Mar.–Oct., daily 10–5, except exam period; library weekdays noon–2, Sat. in term time 10:30–12:30; hall and chapel open but hrs vary.*

> **A GIFT FOR SCIENCE**
>
> For centuries the University of Cambridge has been among the greatest universities, rivaled in Britain only by Oxford. Since the time of its most famous scientific alumnus, Sir Isaac Newton, it has outshone Oxford in the natural sciences. The university has taken advantage of its scientific prestige, pooling its research facilities with high-tech industries. As a result, Cambridge is surrounded by IT companies and has been dubbed "Silicon Fen" in comparison to California's Silicon Valley. The prosperity brought by these businesses is evident around the city.

Also Worth Seeing

❶ Kettle's Yard. Originally a private house owned by a former curator of London's Tate galleries, Kettle's Yard contains a fine collection of 20th-century art, sculpture, furniture, and decorative arts, including works by Henry Moore, Barbara Hepworth, and Henri Gaudier-Brzeska. One gallery shows changing exhibitions of modern art and crafts, and weekly concerts (term time only) and lectures attract an eclectic mix of enthusiasts. ⊠ *Castle St.* ☎ *01223/352124* ⊕ *www.kettlesyard.co.uk* ⊠ *Free* ⊗ *House mid-Apr.–mid-Sept., Tues.–Sun. 1:30–4:30; mid-Sept.–mid-Apr., Tues.–Sun. 2–4. Gallery Tues.–Sun. 11:30–5.*

❷ Magdalene College. Across Magdalene (pronounced *maud*-lin) Bridge, a cast-iron 1820 structure, lies the only one of the older colleges to be sited across the river. Magdalene Street itself is traffic-heavy, but there's relative calm inside the redbrick courts. It was a hostel for Benedictine monks for more than 100 years before the college was founded in 1542. In the second court, the college's **Pepys Library** (☎ 01223/332187 ⊗ Mid-Apr.–Aug., Mon.–Sat. 11:30–12:30 and 2:30–3:30; Oct.–Nov. and mid-Jan.–mid-Mar., Mon.–Sat. 2:30–3:30)—labeled *Bibliotecha Pepysiana*—contains the books and desk of the famed 17th-century diarist Samuel Pepys. ⊠ *Magdalene St.* ☎ *01223/332100* ⊕ *www.magd. cam.ac.uk* ⊠ *Free* ⊗ *Daily 9–6, except exam period.*

⓯ Museum of Archaeology and Anthropology. The university maintains some fine museums in its research halls on Downing Street—the wonder is that they are not better known to visitors. Geological collections at the

Sedgwick Museum and the exhibits at the Zoological Museum are extensive, but be sure to see the Museum of Archaeology and Anthropology, which houses a superb collection of ethnographic objects brought back by early explorers, including members of Captain Cook's pioneering voyages to the Pacific. ⊠ *Downing St.* ☎ *01223/333516* ⊕ *museumserver.archanth.cam.ac.uk* ◱ *Free* ⊙ *Tues.–Sat. 2–4:30.*

🖈 **Pembroke College.** Established in 1347, Pembroke has some buildings dating from the 14th century in its first court. On the south side, Christopher Wren's chapel—his first major commission, completed in 1665—looks like a distinctly modern intrusion. You can walk through the college, around a delightful garden, and past the fellows' bowling green. Outside the library you can't miss the resplendent, toga-clad statue of the precocious William Pitt the Younger; he came up to Pembroke at age 15 and was appointed prime minister of Great Britain in 1783, when he was just 24. ⊠ *Trumpington St.* ☎ *01223/338100* ⊕ *www.pem.cam.ac.uk* ⊙ *Daily 9–dusk, except exam period.*

🖈 **Peterhouse College.** The bishop of Ely founded Cambridge's oldest college in 1281. Parts of the dining hall date from 1290, although the hall is most notable for powerful, 19th-century stained glass by William Morris and his contemporaries. The adjacent church of Little St. Mary's served as the college chapel until 1632, when the current late-Gothic chapel was built. ⊠ *Trumpington St.* ☎ *01223/338200* ⊕ *www.pet.cam.ac.uk* ⊙ *Daily 9–5, except exam period.*

🖈 **Trinity Hall College.** The green parkland of the Backs is best appreciated from Trinity College's 14th-century neighbor, Trinity Hall, where you can sit on a wall by the river and watch students in punts maneuver under the ancient ornamental bridges of Clare and King's. Access to the river is down Trinity Lane, off Trinity Street. The **Senate House** (⊠ King's Parade), which stands between Clare College and Trinity Hall, is not part of a particular college. A classical building of the 1720s, it's used for graduation ceremonies and other university events. The public can't enter, but if the gate is open you can wander into the court and grounds. ⊠ *Trinity La.* ☎ *01223/332500* ⊕ *www.trinhall.cam.ac.uk* ⊙ *Daily 9:15–noon and 2–5:30, except exam period and summer term.*

🖈 **University Botanic Gardens.** Laid out in 1846, these gardens contain, besides rare specimens, conservatories and a rock garden. They are a five-minutes' walk from the Fitzwilliam Museum. ⊠ *Cory Lodge, Bateman St.* ☎ *01223/336265* ⊕ *www.botanic.cam.ac.uk* ◱ *£3* ⊙ *Feb., Mar., and Oct., daily 10–5; Apr.–Sept., daily 10–6; Nov.–Jan., daily 10–4.*

Where to Eat

£££–£££££ ✕ **Three Horseshoes.** This early-19th-century pub-restaurant in a thatched cottage has additional dining space in the conservatory. The tempting, beautifully presented dishes focus on modern British cuisine. Some fashionable culinary accoutrements—sun-dried tomatoes, prosecco with pomegranate and campari, and provencal olives—accompany chargrilled meats or roast fish. It's 3 mi west of Cambridge, about a 10-minutes' taxi ride. ⊠ *High St., Madingley* ☎ *01954/210221* ▤ *MC, V.*

ON THE MENU

Farmland and the rivers and sea provide ample bounty for the table in East Anglia. Look for area specialties, such as duckling, Norfolk black turkey, hare, and partridge, on menus around the region. In Norwich, there's no escaping the hot, bright Coleman's mustard, which is perfect smeared on some sausage and mash.

Among the culinary treats from the sea is samphire, a delicious plant that grows in the salt marshes along the North Norfolk and Suffolk coasts. The long coastline also provides tasty Cromer crabs and Yarmouth bloaters (a kind of smoked herring), whereas the Essex coast near Colchester has been producing oysters since Roman times. Brancaster and Stiffkey mussels, Sheringham lobster, and Thornham oysters are all seafood highlights worth indulging in while visiting North Norfolk. Eel, a delicacy in the Fens, is served smoked or jellied. Maldon sea salt is another famous, high-quality local product. When you're traveling the coast, sample fresh fish-and-chips on the Suffolk coast, especially in Aldeburgh, where local creations have gained national recognition.

For liquid refreshment, Adnams, Greene King, and Tolly Cobbold are major ale producers, and a pint of Suffolk cider is usually a good accompaniment to the local food. There's an equally venerable tradition in wine making in the region. The Romans first introduced vines to Britain, and they took especially well here. Today East Anglia has more than 40 vineyards; check wine lists in local restaurants.

★ **£££–££££** ✕**Midsummer House.** An elegant restaurant beside the River Cam on the edge of Midsummer Common, the gray-brick Midsummer House has a comfortable conservatory. Fixed-price menus for lunch and dinner offer sophisticated French and Mediterranean dishes. Choices might include tender roast spring lamb or seared sea scallops. ✉ *Midsummer Common* ☎*01223/369299* ⊕*www.midsummerhouse.co.uk* ⌁*Reservations essential* ▤ *AE, MC, V* ⊗ *Closed Mon. No lunch Sun.–Thurs., no dinner Sun.*

££–£££ ✕**Loch Fyne Oyster Restaurant.** Part of a small Scottish chain that harvests oysters and runs seafood restaurants, this airy, casual place across the street from the Fitzwilliam Museum is open for breakfast, lunch, and dinner. The deservedly popular oysters and other seafood—mussels, salmon, tuna, and more—are fresh and well prepared. Some good bets are the dauntingly large seafood platters. ✉ *37 Trumpington St.* ☎ *01223/362433* ⊕ *www.lochfyne.com* ▤ *AE, MC, V.*

££ ✕**River Bar & Kitchen.** Fashionable and stylish, this riverside eatery designed by Terence Conran focuses on contemporary food with the occasional Eastern influence, such as spicy lamb samosas with mint and cucumber dip and wonton prawns. At lunch, served between noon and 3, choose among the creative sandwiches. Dinner service begins at 6:30. ✉ *Quayside, off Bridge St.* ☎ *01223/307030* ⌁ *Reservations essential* ▤ *AE, MC, V* ⊗ *Closed Mon. No dinner Sun.*

££ ✕ **Vaults.** Ochre and deep red walls and metal chairs on slate floors bring a sleek, contemporary edge to the underground Vaults. The zinc-top bar with red sofas is the perfect place for lounging with a cocktail, and there is live music four nights a week. The evening menu is tapas-style: lots of small portions of an eclectic mix of international cuisine. Lunchtime menus are more traditional. ⊠ *14A Trinity St.* ☎ *01223/506090* ⌂ *Reservations essential* ▤ *AE, MC, V.*

£ ✕ **Dojo Noodle Bar.** Many highlights of Asian cuisine are represented at this trendy spot with shared tables near the river. If the different kinds of wheat, rice, or mung bean noodles aren't your thing, try a rice dish or pot stickers, tempura prawns, or chicken yakitori. ⊠ *1–2 Millers Yard, Mill La., off Trumpington St.* ☎ *01223/363471* ▤ *AE, MC, V.*

Where to Stay

There aren't many hotels downtown. For more (and cheaper) options, consider one of the numerous guesthouses on the arterial roads and in the suburbs. These start at £18 to £25 per person per night and can be booked through the tourist information center.

£££££ ▥ **Hotel Felix.** This contemporary hotel, less than a mile from the city center, has spacious bedrooms with clean-lined, stylish modern furnishings in neutral colors. The main part of the building is a converted Victorian mansion; today it contains some bedrooms as well as the sophisticated Graffiti restaurant and bar, serving Mediterranean food. Guests can use a health club and spa in the center of the city. ⊠ *Whitehouse La., off Huntingdon Rd., CB3 0LX* ☎ *01223/277977* ⊟ *01223/ 277973* ⊕ *www.hotelfelix.co.uk* ⇝ *52 rooms* ⌂ *Restaurant, room service, in-room safes, cable TV with movies, in-room data ports, lounge, babysitting, dry cleaning, laundry service, meeting rooms, free parking, some pets allowed, no-smoking rooms* ▤ *AE, DC, MC, V* ⦿ *CP.*

££££–£££££ ▥ **Crowne Plaza.** In the middle of historic Cambridge, this late-20th-century building doesn't mesh well with its older neighbors but does provide the high standard of accommodation you'd expect from this chain, as well as a top-notch location. Modern amenities such as a writing desk and trouser press enhance the colorful, contemporary rooms. ⊠ *Downing St., CB2 3DT* ☎ *01223/464466* ⊟ *01223/464440* ⊕ *www.cambridge. crowneplaza.com* ⇝ *198 rooms* ⌂ *Restaurant, room service, in-room safes, minibars, cable TV with movies, in-room broadband, gym, sauna, bar, lobby lounge, pub, babysitting, dry cleaning, laundry service, concierge, business services, meeting rooms, parking (fee), no-smoking rooms* ▤ *AE, DC, MC, V.*

£££–£££££ ▥ **De Vere University Arms Hotel.** Elegant and sympathetically modernized, the 19th-century De Vere is well placed in the city center, though space is at a premium in central Cambridge: the traditionally furnished guest rooms are comfortable but not overly large. Many rooms have views of Parker's Piece, the green backing the hotel, although you pay slightly more for these; Parker's Bar also overlooks the green. The lounge serves afternoon tea by the fireplace. As for service, the quality can vary. Guests can use a health club 2 mi away. ⊠ *Regent St., CB2 1AD* ☎ *01223/351241* ⊟ *01223/315256* ⊕ *www.devereonline.co.uk* ⇝ *116 rooms, 1 suite* ⌂ *Restaurant, room service, cable TV with* *movies, in-room data ports, 2 bars, lounge, business services, meeting rooms, parking (fee), some pets allowed (fee)* ⊟ *AE, DC, MC, V.*

£££–£££££ 🏨 **Garden Moat House Hotel.** Set among the colleges in 3 acres of private grounds, this modern hotel makes the most of its peaceful riverside location. The gardens, bar, and conservatories all overlook the Cam, as do most rooms. Request a river view when you reserve. As with many chain hotels, the service and standards are high, but the architecture exhibits a brutal use of concrete and furnishings are not particularly special. Ask about lower leisure (vacation) rates, which include breakfast. ⊠ *Granta Pl. and Mill La., CB2 1RT* ☎ *01223/259988* 🖷 *01223/316605* ⊕ *www.moathousehotels.com* 🛏 *117 rooms* ⚖ *Restaurant, room service, minibars, cable TV, Wi-Fi, indoor pool, sauna, steam room, bar, lounge, business services, meeting rooms, parking (fee), no-smoking rooms, Internet; no a/c in some rooms* ⊟ *AE, DC, MC, V.*

£££–££££ 🏨 **Arundel House Hotel.** Elegantly proportioned, this Victorian hotel made up of now-connected town houses has a fine location overlooking the River Cam, with Jesus Green in the background. The comfortable bedrooms, modern in style, have locally made mahogany furniture. Rattan chairs, trailing plants, and a patio garden add a certain cachet to meals and afternoon teas in the Victorian-style conservatory. The special weekend rates are an excellent value. ⊠ *53 Chesterton Rd., CB4 3AN* ☎ *01223/367701* 🖷 *01223/367721* ⊕ *www.arundelhousehotels. co.uk* 🛏 *102 rooms* ⚖ *2 restaurants, bar, lounge, meeting rooms, free parking, no-smoking rooms; no a/c* ⊟ *AE, DC, MC, V* ⦿ *CP.*

££ 🏨 **Ashley Hotel.** Sister to the Arundel House Hotel, this pleasant smaller establishment near the center of Cambridge was converted from a private home. Rooms with double or twin beds are decent, and you can take advantage of the facilities of nearby Arundel House, where you should go to check-in. ⊠ *74 Chesterton Rd., CB4 1ER* ☎ *01223/350059* 🖷 *01223/350900* ⊕ *www.arundelhousehotels.co.uk/ashley.html* 🛏 *16 rooms* ⚖ *Free parking; no a/c, no smoking* ⊟ *AE, DC, MC, V* ⦿ *BP.*

£ 🏨 **Sleeperz.** A low-key budget option, this hostelry right outside the train station has small bedrooms with natural wood floors, white walls, and futon beds. Most double rooms have bunk beds. The sparsely furnished accommodations are for those who want a cheap, clean place to sleep. ⊠ *Station Rd., CB1 2TZ* ☎ *01223/304050* 🖷 *01223/357286* ⊕ *www. sleeperz.com* 🛏 *25 rooms* ⚖ *Free parking; no a/c, no room phones, no smoking* ⊟ *MC, V* ⦿ *CP.*

Nightlife & the Arts

Nightlife

The city's pubs provide the mainstay of Cambridge's nightlife. The **Eagle** (⊠ Benet St. ☎ 01223/505020), first among equals, is a 16th-century coaching inn with several bars and a cobbled courtyard that's lost none of its old-time character. It's extremely busy on weekends. **Fort St. George** (⊠ Midsummer Common ☎ 01223/354327), which overlooks the university boathouses, gets the honors for riverside views. The **Free Press** (⊠ Prospect Row ☎ 01223/368337) is a small, nonsmoking, and mobile phone–free pub, attracting a student rowing clientele.

The Arts

Cambridge supports its own symphony orchestra, and regular musical events are held in many colleges, especially those with large chapels. **King's College Chapel** (☎ 01223/331447) has evensong services Tuesday through Saturday at 5:30, Sunday at 3:30. The **Corn Exchange** (✉ Wheeler St. ☎ 01223/357851), beautifully restored, presents concerts (classical and rock), stand-up comedy, musicals, opera, and ballet.

The newly spruced up **ADC Theatre** (✉ Park St. ☎ 01223/503333) hosts mainly student and fringe theater productions, including the famous Cambridge Footlights revue, training ground for much comic talent since the 1970s. The **Arts Theatre** (✉ 6 St. Edward's Passage ☎ 01223/5033333), the city's main repertory theater, was built by economist John Maynard Keynes in 1936 and supports a full program of theater, concerts, and events. It also has a good ground-floor bar and two restaurants.

The **Cambridge Folk Festival** (☎ 01223/357851 ⊕ www. cambridgefolkfestival.co.uk), spread over a late July weekend at Cherry Hinton Hall, attracts major international folk singers and groups. Camping is available on the park grounds—reservations are essential.

Sports & the Outdoors

Biking

It's fun to explore Cambridge by bike. **Geoff's Bike Hire** (✉ 65 Devonshire Rd. ☎ 01223/365629), a short walk from the railroad station, charges from £8 per day and £15 per week, or £5 for up to three hours. Advance reservations are essential in July and August. Geoff's also runs guided cycle tours of Cambridge.

Punting

You can rent punts at several places, notably at Silver Street Bridge–Mill Lane, at Magdalene Bridge, and from outside the Rat and Parrot pub on Thompson's Lane on Jesus Green. Hourly rental costs about £16 (and requires a deposit of £70). Chauffeured punting on the River Cam is also possible at most rental places. Around £12 per head is the usual rate, and your chauffeur will likely be a Cambridge student. **Scudamore's Punting Co.** (✉ Mill La. and Quayside ☎ 01223/359750) rents chauffeured and self-drive punts.

Shopping

Cambridge is a main shopping area for a wide region, and it has all the usual chain stores, many in the Grafton Centre and Lion's Yard shopping precincts. More interesting are the specialty shops found among the colleges in the center of Cambridge, especially in and around Rose Crescent and King's Parade. Bookshops, including antiquarian stores, are Cambridge's pride and joy.

All Saints Garden Art & Craft Market (✉ Trinity St.) displays the wares of local artists outdoors. **Ryder & Amies** (✉ 22 King's Parade ☎ 01223/ 350371) carries official university wear and even straw boaters.

★ The **Bookshop** (✉ 24 Magdalene St. ☎ 01223/362457) is the best local secondhand bookshop. The **Cambridge University Press bookshop** (✉ 1

11

Punting on the Cam

TO PUNT IS TO MANEUVER a flat-bottom, wooden, gondolalike boat—in this case, through the shallow River Cam along the verdant Backs behind the colleges of the University of Cambridge. One benefit of this popular activity is that you get a better view of the ivy-covered walls from the water than from the front. Mastery of the sport lies in your ability to control a 15-foot pole, used to propel the punt. Collect a bottle of wine, some food, and a few friends, and you may find yourself saying things such as, "It doesn't get any better than this." One piece of advice: if your pole gets stuck, let go. You can use the smaller paddle to go back and retrieve it.

The lazier-at-heart may prefer chauffeured punting, with food supplied. Students from Cambridge may do the work, and you get a fairly informative spiel on the colleges. For a romantic evening trip, there are illuminated punts.

Trinity St. ☎01223/333333) stands on the oldest bookstore site in Britain, with books sold here since at least 1581. **G. David** (✉ 3 and 16 St. Edward's Passage ☎ 01223/354619), near the Arts Theatre, sells antiquarian books. The **Haunted Bookshop** (✉ 9 St. Edward's Passage ☎ 01223/312913) carries a great selection of old, illustrated books and British classics. **Heffer's** (✉ 20 Trinity St. ☎ 01223/568568 ✉ Children's branch, 30 Trinity St. ☎ 01223/568551) stocks many rare and imported books.

FROM ELY TO BURY ST. EDMUNDS

This central area of towns and villages within easy reach of Cambridge is testament to the amazing changeability of the English landscape. The town of Ely is set in an eerie, flat, and apparently endless fenland, or marsh. Only a few miles south and east into Suffolk, however, all this changes to pastoral landscapes of gently undulating hills, clusters of villages, and pretty towns.

Ely

 16 mi north of Cambridge.

Ely is the "capital" of the fens, the center of what used to be a separate county called the Isle of Ely (literally "island of eels"). Until the land was drained in the 17th century, Ely was surrounded by treacherous marshland, which inhabitants crossed wearing stilts. Today Wicken Fen, a nature reserve 9 mi southeast of town (off A1123), preserves the sole remaining example of fenland in an undrained state. Enveloped by fields of wheat, sugar beets, and carrots, Ely is a small, dense town that fails to live up to the high expectations created by its big attraction, its cathedral. The shopping area and market square lie to the north and lead down to the riverside, and the medieval buildings of the cathedral grounds and the King's School (which trains cathedral choristers) spread out to the south and west. Ely's most famous resident was Oliver Cromwell, whose house is now a museum.

★ Known affectionately as the Ship of the Fens, **Ely Cathedral** can be seen for miles, towering above the flat landscape on one of the few ridges in the fens. In 1083 the Normans began work on the cathedral, which stands on the site of a Benedictine monastery founded by the Anglo-Saxon princess Etheldreda in 673. In the center of the cathedral you see a marvel of medieval construction—the unique octagonal **Lantern Tower,** a sort of stained-glass skylight of colossal proportions, built to replace the central tower after it collapsed in 1322. The cathedral is also notable for its 248-foot-long

> **DRAINING EAST ANGLIA**
>
> Large areas of East Anglia were originally barely inhabited, swampy marshes. Drainage of the wetlands by the creation of waterways was carried out most energetically in the 17th and 18th centuries. The process was far from smooth. Locals, whose fishing rights were threatened, sometimes destroyed the work. Also, as the marshland dried out, it shrunk and sank, requiring pumps to stop renewed flooding. Hundreds of windmills were used to pump water away; some of them can still be seen today.

nave, with its simple Norman arches and Victorian painted ceiling. Much of the decorative carving of the 14th-century **Lady Chapel** was defaced during the Reformation (mostly by knocking off the heads of the statuary), but enough tracery remains to show its original beauty. The fan-vaulted, carved ceiling remains intact, as it was too high for the iconoclasts to reach. The cathedral houses a superior **Stained Glass Museum** (☎ 01353/660347 ⊕ www.stainedglassmuseum.com ☞ £3.50 ☉ May–Oct., weekdays 10:30–5, Sat. 10:30–5:30, Sun. noon–6; Nov.–Apr., weekdays and Sat. 10:30–5, Sun. noon–4:30), up a flight of 41 steps. Exhibits trace the history of stained glass from medieval to modern times. ⊠ *The Gallery* ☎ *01353/667735* ⊕ *www.cathedral.ely. anglican.org* ☞ *£5.20, free on Sun.* ☉ *May–Oct., daily 7–7; Nov.–Apr., Mon.–Sat. 7:30–6, Sun. 7:30–5.*

Oliver Cromwell's House, the half-timber medieval building that was the home of Cromwell and his family, stands in the shadows of Ely Cathedral. During the 10 years he lived here, from 1636, Cromwell was leading the rebellious Roundheads in their eventually victorious struggle against King Charles I in the English Civil War. The house contains an exhibit on its former occupant and audiovisual presentations about Cromwell and about the draining of the local fens. It's also the site of Ely's tourist information center. ⊠ *29 St. Mary's St.* ☎ *01353/662062* ☞ *£3.75* ☉ *Apr.–Sept., daily 10–6; Oct.–Mar., Mon.–Sat. 10–5.*

Where to Stay & Eat

★ **£££** ✕ **Old Fire Engine House.** Scrubbed pine tables fill the main dining room of this restaurant in a converted fire station near the cathedral. Another room, used only for overflow, has an open fireplace and a polished wood floor, and also serves as an art gallery. Among the English dishes are traditional fenland recipes such as pike baked in white wine, as well as eel pie and game in season. ⊠ *25 St. Mary's St.* ☎ *01353/662582*

☰ *MC, V ⊙ Closed 2 wks at Christmas. No dinner Sun.*

££ ⌂ **Cathedral House.** Run by Jenny and Robin Farndale, this Georgian house makes a pleasant overnight stop in Ely, though a busy road runs past the house. The cozy bedrooms have antique furniture and coffeemakers, and an oriel window and handsome staircase are original features. In the back is a walled garden filled with flowers. ✉ *17 St. Mary's St., CB7 4ER* ☎ *01353/662124* ⊕ *www.cathedralhouse.co.uk* ⤴ *3 rooms, 1 cottage ⟳ No a/c, no smoking* ☰ *No credit cards* ⊙⊙ *BP.*

Saffron Walden

⓴ *30 mi south of Ely, 14 mi south of Cambridge.*

Best known for its many typically East Anglian timber-frame buildings, this town owes its name to the saffron crocus fields that used to be cultivated in medieval times and processed for their dye. The common at the east end of town has a 17th-century circular earth maze, created from space left among the crocus beds. Some buildings have elaborate pargeting (decorative plasterwork), especially the walls of the former Sun Inn on Church Street, which was used by Cromwell during his campaigns. At the other end of Church Street, the tall, imposing **St. Mary the Virgin,** built between 1450 and 1525, is the largest church in Essex.

★ Palatial **Audley End House and Gardens,** a mile or so west of Saffron Walden, is a famous example of Jacobean (early-17th-century) architecture. It was once owned by Charles II, who bought it as a convenient place to break his journey on the way to the Newmarket races. Although the house was remodeled in the 18th and 19th centuries, the original Jacobean work is still on display in the magnificent Great Hall. You can walk around the park, landscaped by Capability Brown in the 18th century, and the fine Victorian gardens. ✉ *B1383* ☎ *01799/522842* ⊕ *www.english-heritage. org.uk* 🎟 *£8.95, park only £4.60 ⊙ Apr.–Sept., Wed.–Sun., park 11–6, house noon–5; Oct., park weekends 11–5, house weekends 11–4.*

Where to Stay

£ ⌂ **Archway Guesthouse.** Opposite St. Mary's, what must be one of Britain's quirkiest B&Bs embraces the early era of rock and roll by packing its public rooms with rock memorabilia and toys from the 1950s and '60s. Bedrooms are tasteful, homey, and uncluttered, and hosts Flora and Haydn Miles are personable. ✉ *Church St., CB10 1JW* ☎ *01799/ 501500* 🖷 *01799/506003* ✉ *archwayguesthouse@ntlworld.com* ⤴ *7 rooms ⟳ No a/c, no smoking* ☰ *No credit cards* ⊙⊙ *BP.*

EN ROUTE

Hedingham Castle, between Saffron Walden and Sudbury, has a wonderful 12th-century Norman keep (main tower), built on a hill by Aubrey de Vere and designed by the archbishop of Canterbury. The highlight of the 110-foot-tall keep is the Banqueting Hall, which can be viewed from the minstrels' gallery. In summer the age of knighthood is re-created through jousts and medieval festivals. ✉ *B1058, Saffron Walden, Castle Hedingham* ☎ *01787/460261* ⊕ *www.hedinghamcastle.co.uk* 🎟 *£4.50. Special events an additional £5–£8 ⊙ Easter–Oct., Sun.–Thurs. 11–4, also the occasional Sun. in winter, call ahead to confirm.*

Sudbury

㉑ *23 mi east of Saffron Walden, 16 mi south of Bury St. Edmunds, 14 mi northwest of Colchester.*

An early silk-weaving industry (still in existence, on a smaller scale) as well as the wool trade brought prosperity to Sudbury, which has three fine Perpendicular Gothic churches and some half-timber houses. Today this town of 20,000 is the largest in this part of the Stour Valley. The Stour River was once navigable to the sea, and quays filled the town. In Charles Dicken's first novel, *The Pickwick Papers,* Sudbury was the model for the fictional Eatanswill, where Mr. Pickwick stands for Parliament. Thomas Gainsborough, one of the greatest English portrait and landscape painters, was born here in 1727; a **statue of Gainsborough** holding his palette stands on Market Hill.

The birthplace and family home of Thomas Gainsborough (1727–88), **Gainsborough's House,** refurbished and restored in 2005 and 2006, contains many paintings and drawings by the artist and his contemporaries. Although it presents a Georgian facade, with touches of the 18th-century neo-Gothic style, the building is essentially Tudor. The walled garden has a mulberry tree planted in 1620 and a printmaking workshop. The entrance is through the café and shop on Weavers Lane. ✉ *46 Gainsborough St.* ☎ *01787/372958* ⊕ *www.gainsborough.org* 🎫 *£3.50, free Tues. 1–5* ⊙ *Mon.–Sat. 10–5.*

Long Melford

㉒ *2 mi north of Sudbury, 14 mi south of Bury St. Edmunds.*

It's easy to see how this village got its name, especially if you walk the full length of its 2-mi-long main street, which gradually broadens to include green squares and trees and finally opens into the large triangular green on the hill. Long Melford grew rich on its wool trade in the 15th century, and the town's buildings are an appealing mix, mostly Tudor half-timber or Georgian. Many house antiques shops. Utility poles are banned to preserve the ancient look, although the parked cars down both sides of the street make this a fruitless exercise. Away from the main road, Long Melford returns to its resolutely late-medieval roots.

The largely 15th-century **Holy Trinity Church,** founded by the rich clothiers of Long Melford, stands on a hill at the north end of the village. Close up, the delicate flint flush-work (shaped flints set into a pattern) and huge Perpendicular Gothic windows that take up most of the church's walls have great impact, especially because the nave is 150 feet long. Much of the superb original stained glass remains, notably the Lily Crucifix window. The Lady Chapel has an unusual interior cloister. ✉ *Main St.* ☎ *01787/310845* ⊕ *www.stedmundsbury.anglican.org/ longmelford* ⊙ *Daily 10–4.*

Melford Hall, distinguished from the outside by its turrets and topiaries, is an Elizabethan house with its original banqueting hall, a fair number of 18th-century additions, and pleasant gardens. Much of the porcelain and other fine pieces here come from the *Santissima Trinidad,* a ship loaded with gifts from the emperor of China and bound for Spain that was captured by one of the house's owners in the 18th century. Children's writer Beatrix Potter, who was related to the owners, visited the house often; there's a small collection of Potter memorabilia. ⊠ *Off A134* ☎ *01787/880286* ⊕ *www.nationaltrust.co.uk* ⊡ *£4.70* ⊙ *Apr. and Oct., weekends 2–5:30; May–Sept., Wed.–Sun. 2–5:30.*

☺ A wide moat surrounds **Kentwell Hall,** a redbrick Tudor manor house with tall chimneys and domed turrets. Built between 1520 and 1550, it was heavily restored inside after a fire in the early 19th century. On some weekends from mid-April through September, costumed "servants" and "farmworkers" perform reenactments of Tudor life or life during World War II. There's also an organic farm with rare-breed farm animals. The house is a half mile north of Long Melford Green. ⊠ *Off A134* ☎ *01787/ 310207* ⊕ *www.kentwell.co.uk* ⊡ *£7.50, £7.50–£13.95 during special events, £5.30 farm and garden only* ⊙ *Apr.–June, Sun. and Tues.–Thurs. noon–5; July and Aug., daily noon–5; Sept., Sun., Wed., and Thurs. noon–5; Oct., Sun. noon–5.*

Where to Stay & Eat

££££ ╳▥ **The Bull.** The public rooms of the Bull—stone-flagged floors, bowed oak beams, and heavy antique furniture—show its long history. Throughout, the half-timber Elizabethan building is a joy, and whether you eat in the restaurant (££–£££) or the bar with its huge fireplace, service is efficient and careful. Traditional roasts mix on the menu with modern flavors, such as venison with a bitter chocolate sauce. Creature comforts and pleasant bathrooms offset the smallish size of the bedrooms, which retain their original character. ⊠ *Hall St., CO10 9JG* ☎ *01787/ 378494* ⊟ *01787/880307* ⊕ *www.thebull-hotel.com* ⊷ *23 rooms, 2 suites* ⚭ *Restaurant, bar, lounge, meeting rooms, some pets allowed, no-smoking rooms; no a/c* ⊟ *AE, DC, MC, V* ⦿ *BP.*

Lavenham

㉓   *4 mi northeast of Long Melford, 10 mi south of Bury St. Edmunds.*

Fodor'sChoice
★

Virtually unchanged since the height of its wealth in the 15th and 16th centuries, Lavenham is one of the most perfectly preserved examples of a Tudor village in England. The weavers' and wool merchants' houses occupy not just one show street but most of the town. The houses are timber-frame in black oak, the main posts looking as if they could last another 400 years, though their walls are often no longer entirely perpendicular to the ground. The town has many examples of Suffolk pink buildings, in hues from pale pink to apricot, and many of these house small galleries selling paintings and crafts. The timber-frame **Guildhall of Corpus Christi** (1529), the most spectacular building in Lavenham, dominates Market Place, a square with barely a foot in the present. The guildhall is open as a museum of the medieval wool trade. ⊠ *Market Pl.* ☎ *01787/247646* ⊕ *www.nationaltrust.org.uk* ⊡ *£3.25* ⊙ *Mar. and Nov., weekends 11–4; Apr., Wed.–Sun. 11–5; May–Oct., daily 11–5.*

The timber-frame **Little Hall,** a former wool merchant's house, shows the building's progress from its creation in the 14th century to its subsequent "modernization" through the 17th century and has a beautiful garden. ⊠ *Market Pl.* ☎ *01787/247179* ⊕ *www.littlehall.org.uk* ⊡ *£2.50* ⊘ *Easter–Oct., Wed., Thurs., and weekends 2–5:30.*

⌐
| NEED A
| BREAK?
In a haphazardly leaning old house, the **Tickle Manor Tea Room** (⊠ **17 High St.** ☎ 01787/248438) has fresh cakes and coffee as well as soup and sandwiches.

The grand 15th-century Perpendicular **Church of St. Peter and St. Paul** (⊠ Church St.), set apart from the village on a hill, was built with wool money by cloth merchant Thomas Spring between 1480 and 1520. The height of its tower (141 feet) was meant to surpass those of the neighboring churches—and perhaps to impress rival towns. The rest of the church is perfectly proportioned, with intricate wood carving.

Where to Stay & Eat

££ ✕ **The Angel.** Modern British cuisine is the draw at this popular spot overlooking Lavenham's picture-book main square. The specialty of the house—home-smoked fish—earns rave reviews. You can also just sit a spell at the scrubbed pine tables to enjoy one of the local beers on tap. Eight guest rooms are available, for about £75. ⊠ *Market Sq.* ☎ *01787/ 247388* ▤ *AE, MC, V* ⌑ *Reservations essential.*

££–££££ ✕▥ **Great House.** The town's finest "restaurant with rooms" occupies
Fodor'sChoice a 15th-century building on the medieval market square. Run by Régis
★ and Martine Crépy, the dining room (££££; reservations essential) has a fixed-price menu of European fare with a French touch. From the fireplace and wood floors of the restaurant to the walled courtyard garden, dining is a pleasure. The spacious bedrooms have sloping floors, beamed ceilings, well–appointed bathrooms, and antique furnishings. Loft rooms are especially romantic. ⊠ *Market Pl., CO10 9QZ* ☎ *01787/ 247431* ▤ *01787/248007* ⊕ *www.greathouse.co.uk* ⇆ *5 rooms* ⌂ *Restaurant, bar, lounge, babysitting, some pets allowed, no-smoking rooms, Internet; no a/c* ▤ *AE, MC, V* ⊘ *Closed Jan.* ⦿| *BP.*

££££ ▥ **Swan Hotel.** This half-timber 14th-century lodging has aging timbers, rambling public rooms, and open fires. Along corridors so low that cushions are strategically placed on beams, most of the individually styled bedrooms have rich oak cabinets, original wood paneling, and CD players. Bathrooms have been fashioned around ancient timbers and hidden rooms. The restaurant, which has its own minstrels' gallery, serves traditional English cuisine. Full-board and weekend packages can be good deals. ■ TIP➡ In World War II the hotel served as the special pub for the U.S. Air Force's 48th Bomber Group; look for memorabilia on the walls of the bar. ⊠ *High St., CO10 9QA* ☎ *01787/247477* ▤ *01787/248286* ⊕ *www. theswanatlavenham.co.uk* ⇆ *49 rooms, 2 suites* ⌂ *Restaurant, minibars, cable TV, in-room data ports, 2 bars, babysitting, meeting room, some pets allowed (fee); no a/c* ▤ *AE, DC, MC, V.*

★ **£££–££££** ▥ **Lavenham Priory.** You can immerse yourself in Lavenham's Tudor history at this luxurious B&B in a sprawling house that dates in part to the 13th century. The beamed great hall, sitting room (with TV and VCR), and 3 acres of gardens are great places to relax, and a walled herb garden is the scene for evening drinks in warm weather. Prints and wood furnishings fill the bedrooms; each has oak floors and ancient timbered ceilings, and some have four-posters. Reserve well in advance. ⊠ *Water*

St., CO10 9RW ☎ *01787/247404* 🖶 *01787/248472* ⊕ *www.lavenhampriory.co.uk* ⌧ *5 rooms, 1 suite* ⌂ *Lounge; no a/c, no room phones, no kids under 10, no smoking* ⊟ *MC, V* ⎆ *BP.*

Bury St. Edmunds

★ ㉔ *10 mi north of Lavenham, 28 mi east of Cambridge.*

Bury St. Edmunds owes its name, and indeed its existence, to Edmund, the last king of East Anglia and medieval patron saint of England, who was hacked to death by marauding Danes in 869. He was subsequently canonized, and his shrine attracted pilgrims, settlement, and commerce. In the 11th century the erection of a great Norman abbey (now only ruins) confirmed the town's importance as a religious center. Robert Adam designed the town hall in 1774. The Georgian streetscape helps make the town one of the area's prettiest, and the nearby Greene King Westgate Brewery adds the smell of sweet hops to the air.

A walk along **Angel Hill** is a journey through the history of Bury St. Edmunds. Along one side, the Abbey Gate, cathedral, Norman Gate Tower, and St. Mary's church make up a continuous display of medieval architecture. Elegant Georgian houses line Angel Hill on the side opposite St. Mary's Church; these include the **Athenaeum**, an 18th-century social and cultural meeting place, which has a fine Adam-style ballroom. The splendid **Angel Hotel** (⌧ 3 Angel Hill) is the scene of Sam Weller's meeting with Job Trotter in Dickens's *Pickwick Papers*. Dickens stayed here while he was giving readings at the Athenaeum.

Originally three churches stood within the walls of the Abbey of St. Edmunds, but only two have survived, including **St. Mary's,** built in the 15th century. It has a blue-and-gold embossed "wagon" (barrel-shape) roof over the choir. Mary Tudor, Henry VIII's sister and queen of France, is buried here. ⌧ *Angel Hill at Honey Hill* ☎ *01284/706668* ⊙ *Daily 10–3; call to confirm.*

St. Edmundsbury Cathedral dates from the 15th century, but the brilliant paint on its ceiling and the gleaming stained-glass windows are the result of 19th-century restoration by the architect Sir Gilbert Scott. Don't miss the memorial (near the altar) to an event in 1214, when the barons of England gathered here to take an oath to force King John to grant the Magna Carta. The cathedral's original Abbey Gate was destroyed in a riot, and it was rebuilt in the 14th century with defense in mind—you can see the arrow slits. ■ TIP➡ **After your visit, stop by the Refectory, a modest café filled with locals.** ⌧ *Angel Hill* ☎ *01284/754933* ⊕ *www.stedscathedral.co.uk* 🖹 *Free, suggested donation £3* ⊙ *Daily 7:30–6.*

The **Abbey Ruins and Botanical Gardens** are all that remain of the Abbey of Bury St. Edmunds, which fell during Henry VIII's dissolution of the monasteries. The Benedic-

---

A HALF-PINT PUB?

Pop in for a pint of the local Greene King ale at **The Nutshell** (⌧ Skinner St. ☎ 01905/764867), Britain's smallest pub, measuring just 16 feet by 7½ feet.

tine abbey's enormous scale is evident in the surviving Norman Gate Tower on Angel Hill; besides this, only the fortified Abbot's Bridge over the River Lark and a few ruins remain. There are explanatory plaques amid the ruins, which are now the site of the Abbey Botanical Gardens, with roses, elegant hedges, and rare trees, including a Chinese tree of heaven planted in the 1830s. The **Bury St. Edmunds Tourist Information Centre** (⊠ 6 Angel Hill ☎ 01284/764667 ⊙ Easter–Oct., Mon.–Sat. 9:30–5:30, Sun. 10–3; Nov.–Easter, weekdays 10–4, Sat. 10-1) has a leaflet about the ruins and can arrange a guided tour. ⊠ *Angel Hill* ⊠ *Free* ⊙ *Weekdays 7:30 AM–½ hr before dusk, weekends 9 AM–dusk.*

Manor House Museum, a Georgian mansion, contains excellent art collections: paintings, furniture, costumes, and ceramics from the 17th through the 20th centuries. The clocks and watches in the horological collection are extraordinary. ⊠ *Honey Hill* ☎ *01284/757072* ⊕ *www. stedmundsbury.gov.uk* ⊠ *£2.50* ⊙ *Wed.–Sun. 11–4.*

The 12th-century **Moyse's Hall,** probably the oldest building in East Anglia, is a rare surviving example of a Norman house. The rooms hold local history and archaeological collections. One macabre display relates to the Red Barn murder, a local case that gained notoriety in a 19th-century play. ⊠ *Cornhill* ☎ *01284/706183* ⊕ *www.stedmundsbury. gov.uk* ⊠ *£2.50* ⊙ *Weekdays 10:30–4:30, weekends 11–4.*

OFF THE BEATEN PATH

ICKWORTH HOUSE – The creation of the eccentric Frederick Hervey, 4th earl of Bristol and bishop of Derry, this unusual 18th-century home was owned by the Hervey family until the 1960s. Inspired by his travels, Hervey wanted an Italianate palace and gardens. Today the two wings around a striking central rotunda contain a hotel (east wing) and paintings by William Hogarth, Titian, and Gainsborough (west wing). Behind the house, the rose gardens and vineyards spread out to reach 1,800 acres of woods. A stroll over the hills gives the best vistas of the house, which is 7 mi southwest of Bury St. Edmunds. ⊠ *Off A143, Horringer* ☎ *01284/735270* ⊕ *www.nationaltrust.org.uk* ⊠ *£6.70, gardens and park £3.10* ⊙ *House mid-Mar.–Sept., Fri.–Tues. 1–5; Oct., Fri.–Tues. 1–4:30. Garden mid-Mar.–Oct., daily 10–5; Nov.–mid-Dec., weekdays 10–4; Jan.–mid-Mar., daily 10–4. Park daily 8–8, or dusk if earlier.*

Where to Stay & Eat

££–£££ ✕ **Maison Bleue.** This French restaurant, with the same owners as the Great House hotel in nearby Lavenham, specializes in locally caught seafood and serves some meat dishes, too. The seafood depends on the day's catch, but mussels and grilled fillets of local trout and salmon are always available, as are cheeses imported from Paris. ⊠ *30 Churchgate St.* ☎ *01284/760623* ⚠ *Reservations essential* ⊟ *AE, MC, V* ⊙ *Closed Sun., Mon., Jan., and 2 wks in summer.*

£ ✕ **Harriet's Café Tearooms.** In an elegant dining room, Harriet's brings back the tearooms of yesteryear. Munch on a savory sandwich or have a full cream tea while listening to hits from the 1940s. ⊠ *57 Cornhill* ☎ *01284/756256* ⊟ *MC, V* ⊙ *No dinner.*

★ **£££££** ✕ ▣ **Ickworth Hotel.** You can live like nobility in the east wing of the Italianate Ickworth House, a National Trust property 7 mi southwest of Bury St. Edmunds. The splendid public rooms have stylish 1950s and

'60s furniture and striking modern art. This look extends to most bedrooms, though some still have period furnishings; all are luxe. There is no dress code and children are catered to with a free day-care room (for kids under 6) and a game center. Adults can dine in the more formal Frederick's restaurant, and the casual Café Inferno serves pizza. ⊠ *Off A143, Horringer IP29 5QE* ☎ *01284/735350* 🖷 *01284/736300* ⊕ *www. ickworthhotel.com* 🖙 *27 rooms, 11 apartments* ♿ *2 restaurants, room service, some kitchens, cable TV, in-room DVDs, Wi-Fi, tennis court, indoor pool, massage, spa, bicycles, croquet, horseback riding, lounge, babysitting, dry cleaning, laundry service, meeting rooms, some pets allowed, no-smoking rooms; no a/c* ⊟ *AE, DC, MC, V* ⫶⊙⫶ *BP.*

££££ ⤬🖼 **Angel Hotel.** This spruced-up former coaching inn in the heart of town has spacious, well-furnished rooms. Several have four-posters, and the Charles Dickens Room, where the author stayed, is done in perfect 19th-century English style (the bed is a bit small, however). Morning coffee and afternoon tea are served in the cozy lobby. Dine on English fare in the Abbeygate Restaurant (£££–££££) overlooking the abbey's main gate, or try brasserie-style dishes in the more informal Vaults, in the cellar. ⊠ *3 Angel Hill, IP33 1LT* ☎ *01284/753926* 🖷 *01284/ 750092* ⊕ *www.theangel.co.uk* 🖙 *66 rooms* ♿ *2 restaurants, cable TV with movies, in-room data ports, bar, business services, meeting rooms, no-smoking rooms; no a/c in some rooms* ⊟ *AE, DC, MC, V* ⫶⊙⫶ *BP.*

£££–££££ 🖼 **Ounce House.** Small and friendly, this Victorian B&B a three-minute walk from the abbey ruins has a great deal of charm. Print fabrics and wooden furniture furnish the stylish guest rooms. You can unwind in the antiques-filled drawing room and library, and have a drink from the honor bar. The house is close to Bury's restaurants. ⊠ *Northgate St., IP33 1HP* ☎ *01284/761779* 🖷 *01284/768315* ⊕ *www.ouncehouse.co. uk* 🖙 *4 rooms* ♿ *In-room data ports, bar, lounge; no a/c, no smoking* ⊟ *MC, V* ⫶⊙⫶ *BP.*

Nightlife & the Arts

The **Theatre Royal**, which presents touring shows, was built in 1819 and is a perfect example of Regency theater design. Guided tours (£2.50) can be booked at the box office. The theater reopens in spring 2007 after refurbishment. ⊠ *Westgate St.* ☎ *01284/769505* ⊙ *Apr.–Oct., guided tours Tues. and Thurs. 11:30 and 2:30, Sat. 11:30, except during rehearsals.*

COLCHESTER & THE SUFFOLK COAST

Colchester is the oldest town on record in England, dating back to the Iron Age, and the reminders of its long history are well worth visiting. The town also serves as a traditional base for exploring Constable Country, that quintessentially English rural landscape on the borders of Suffolk and Essex made famous by the early-19th-century painter John Constable. This area runs north and west of Colchester along the valley of the River Stour. The 40-mi Suffolk Heritage Coast, which wanders northward from Felixstowe up to Kessingland, is one of the most unspoiled shorelines in the country.

Colchester

⑳ *59 mi northeast of London, 51 mi southeast of Cambridge, 68 mi south of Norwich.*

Evidence of Colchester's four centuries of Roman history is visible everywhere in this ancient town. The Roman walls still stand, together with a Norman castle, a Victorian town hall, and Dutch-style houses built by refugee weavers from the Low Countries in the late 16th century. Archaeological research indicates a settlement at the head of the Colne estuary at least as early as 1100 BC. Two thousand years ago it was the domain of Cunobelin (Shakespeare's Cymbeline), who was king of the Catuvellauni. On Cunobelin's death, the Romans invaded in AD 43. The emperor Claudius made it the first Roman colony in Britain, renaming the town *Colonia Victricensis,* the Colony of Victory. The settlement was burned during the failed revolt in AD 60 by Boudicca, queen of the Iceni. The Romans relocated their administrative center to Londinium (now London) after the revolt but kept a military presence. The English Civil War saw further conflict in Colchester, as the city endured a three-month siege in 1648 before the Royalist forces surrendered. Colchester has always had a strategic importance and still has a military base; a tattoo (military spectacle) is held in even-numbered years.

Colchester was important enough for the Romans to build massive fortifications around it, and the **Roman Walls,** dating largely from the reign of Emperor Vespasian (AD 69–79), can still be seen, especially along Balkerne Hill (to the west of the town center), with its splendid Balkerne Gate. Most of the foundations lie beneath the neighboring Hole-in-the-Wall pub. Near the castle, the remains of a 3,000-seat **Roman amphitheater** (✉ Maidenburgh St.) are visible. The curve of the foundations is outlined in the paving stones of the roadway, and parts of the walls and floor have been preserved in a building, where they can be viewed alongside an image of how the amphitheater would have looked.

The castle built by William the Conqueror between 1076 and 1125, ☾ re-using brick and tiles from the ruins of the Roman town, is today the superb **Colchester Castle Museum.** All that remains is the keep, the largest the Normans built. The castle was constructed over the foundations of the huge Roman Temple of Claudius, and in the vaults you can descend through 1,000 years of history. The museum contains an ever-growing collection of prehistoric and Roman remains including

QUEEN OF THE ICENI

After King Prasutagus died around AD 60, his wife Boudicca became queen of the Iceni kingdom, which covered roughly the same area as modern-day Norfolk. Alas, the occupying Romans annexed Iceni. They flogged Boudicca and raped her daughters; in revenge the queen led an uprising, destroying first Roman Colchester, then London and St. Albans. By the time Boudicca met with the army of the Roman governor, Suetonius, her army outnumbered the occupiers. The queen, however, was defeated. With her flowing red hair and her chariot, the warrior queen has become a symbol of Britain.

the beautifully carved tombstones of Facilis and Longinus, two Roman soldiers. ⊠ *Castle Park* ☎ *01206/282939* ⊕ *www.colchestermuseums. org.uk* 🖾 *£4.70, guided tours £1.80* ⊙ *Mon.–Sat. 10–5, Sun. 11–5.*

★ ☾ The excellent interactive **Hollytrees Museum,** in a Georgian mansion near the castle, tells the story of the daily lives of local people through objects. There are chances to create a silhouette portrait or play with Victorian toys and there are occasional children's events, such as making puppets. ⊠ *Castle Park* ☎ *01206/282940* ⊕ *www.colchestermuseums. org.uk* 🖾 *Free* ⊙ *Mon.–Sat. 10–5, Sun. 11–5.*

Halfway down the broad High Street, which follows the line of the main Roman road, the splendid Edwardian **Town Hall** stands on the site of the original Moot (assembly) Hall. On its tower you can see four figures representing Colchester's main industries: fisheries, agriculture, the military, and engineering. The narrow medieval streets behind the Town Hall, off High Street, are called the **Dutch Quarter** because weavers— refugees from the Low Countries—settled here in the 16th century, when Colchester was the center of a thriving cloth trade.

Tymperleys Clock Museum, off Sir Isaac's Walk, displays a unique collection of beautiful, Colchester-made clocks in the wing of an Elizabethan house. ⊠ *Trinity St.* ☎ *01206/282943* ⊕ *www.colchestermuseums. org.uk* 🖾 *Free* ⊙ *June–Oct., Tues.–Sat. 10–1 and 2–5.*

Where to Stay & Eat

££–£££ ✕ **Warehouse Brasserie.** Colchester's most popular eating place has a pastel green and rich red split-level dining room with wooden tables and large wall mirrors. This cheerful interior contrasts with a fairly anonymous exterior and location: it's tucked away in a converted Methodist chapel, next to the Headgate Theatre down a cul-de-sac off St. John's Street. The fixed-price lunch and dinner menu (lunch Tuesday–Saturday, dinner Tuesday–Friday) mixes brasserie favorites with classic English dishes. ⊠ *12 Chapel St. N* ☎ *01206/765656* ▭ *MC, V* ⊙ *No dinner Sun. and Mon.*

££–£££ ✕🖼 **George Hotel.** This 500-year-old inn in the heart of downtown is now a part of the Swallow chain but has kept plenty of age-old charm. Many rooms incorporate original oak beams and are comfortably furnished in traditional style. The George Bar also retains its ancient beams, and in the cellar a section of Roman pavement and a 16th-century wall painting are on display. The Brasserie restaurant (££) has a good à la carte menu and is popular for afternoon tea or an evening pint and there is an attached oyster bar. ⊠ *116 High St., CO1 1TD* ☎ *01206/578494* 🖷 *01206/761732* ⊕ *www.swallow-hotels.com* ✎ *47 rooms* ⚘ *Restaurant, cable TV, bar, no-smoking rooms; no a/c in some rooms* ▭ *AE, DC, MC, V.*

Dedham

㉖ *8 mi northeast of Colchester, off A12 on B1029.*

Fodor'sChoice
★ Dedham is the heart of Constable Country. Here, gentle hills and the cornfields of Dedham Vale, set under the district's delicate, pale skies, inspired John Constable (1776–1837) to paint some of his most cele-

brated canvases. He went to school in Dedham, a picture-book village that did well from the wool trade in the 15th and 16th centuries and has retained a well-off air ever since. The architecture is a mix of timber-frame medieval and Georgian. The 15th-century church looms large over handsomely sturdy, pastel-color houses. Plans are afoot to build a Constable visitor center up the Stour valley, but until then it's still possible on quiet days to imagine yourself in a Constable painting.

Two miles northeast of Dedham, off A12, the Constable trail continues in **East Bergholt**, where Constable was born in 1776. Only the stables remain of the house that was his birthplace. As well as many other views of East Bergholt, Constable painted its village church, **St. Mary's**, where his parents lie buried. It has one unusual feature—a freestanding wooden bell house in place of a tower.

From Dedham, on the banks of the River Stour, you can rent a rowboat (☉ Easter–Sept., daily 10–5, weather permitting ⊠ £6 per hour ☎ 01206/323153), an idyllic way to travel the 2 mi downriver to **Flatford** where you can see Flatford Mill, one of the two water mills owned by Constable's father, and the subject of his most famous painting, *The Hay Wain* (1821). Near Flatford Mill is the 16th-century **Willy Lott's House** (not open to the public), which is instantly recognizable from *The Hay Wain*. Boats can also be rented in Flatford, near Bridge Cottage.

> **CHANGING TASTES**
>
> Constable's landscape paintings may be popular today, but *The Hay Wain*, now in London's National Gallery, did not sell after the Royal Academy displayed it. The artist sold only 20 paintings in England during his lifetime. He was elected to the Royal Academy with a majority of one vote only at age 52.

The National Trust owns Flatford Mill and the houses around it, including the thatched 16th-century **Bridge Cottage,** on the north bank of the Stour, which has a shop and a display about Constable's life. ⊠ *Off B1070, East Bergholt* ☎ *01206/298260* ⊕ *www.nationaltrust.org.uk* ⊠ *Free, guided tours or audio tour £2* ☉ *Jan. and Feb., weekends 11–3:30; Mar. and Apr., Wed.–Sun. 11–5; May–Sept., daily 10–5:30; Oct., daily 11–4; Nov. and Dec., Wed.–Sun. 11–3:30. Guided tours Apr.–Oct. on days open, at 11, 1, and 2:30.*

Where to Stay & Eat

★ **£££–£££££** ✕ **Le Talbooth.** A longtime favorite, this sophisticated restaurant in a Tudor house idyllically set beside the River Stour has a floodlighted terrace where food and drinks are served in summer and where jazz bands play on summer Sunday nights as swans glide by. Inside, original beams, leaded-glass windows, and a brick fireplace add to the sense of age. The superb English fare at lunch and dinner may include loin of Suffolk venison, local sea bass or whole roasted partridge. ⊠ *Gun Hill* ☎ *01206/ 323150* ☖ *Reservations essential* ⋒ *Jacket and tie* ▭ *AE, D, MC, V* ☉ *No dinner Sun. Nov.–June.*

££ ✕ **Marlborough Head.** Fine lunches, from marinated mussels to fillet of beef, are served with fine East Anglian ales at this early-18th-century pub opposite Constable's school. It gets busy during summer, so arrive early to ensure a table. ⊠ *Mill La.* ☎ *01206/323250* ▤ *AE, MC, V.*

£££ ✕▣ **Milsoms.** Owned by the Milsoms of Maison Talbooth fame, this hotel and restaurant in a Victorian house reflects their high standards while providing a modern style. Room decoration is understated, with heavy natural fibers and black-and-white photos. The busy split-level restaurant (££–£££; reservations essential) specializes in updated versions of classic British fare such as shepherds pie made with roast Suffolk mutton or lamb on flageolet bean puree. In warm weather, try sitting by the pond in the garden. ⊠ *Stratford Rd., CO7 6HW* ☎ *01206/322795* ▤ *01206/323689* ⊕ *www.milsom-hotels.co.uk* ➲ *15 rooms* ♢ *Restaurant, room service, minibars, cable TV, bar, lounge, dry cleaning, laundry service, meeting rooms, no-smoking rooms; no a/c* ▤ *AE, MC, V.*

£££££ ▣ **Maison Talbooth.** Constable painted the rich meadowlands in which this luxurious Victorian country-house hotel is set. Period antiques, print fabrics, and upholstered furniture decorate each of the elegant, spacious suites, with sumptuous bathrooms. Some rooms also have private access to outdoor hot tubs, available year-round. Guests are encouraged to eat in Le Talbooth restaurant, a short walk or free ride down the lane and owned by the same management. Continental or cooked breakfast is served in your bedroom. ⊠ *Stratford Rd., CO7 6HP* ☎ *01206/ 322367* ▤ *01206/322752* ⊕ *www.talbooth.com* ➲ *10 rooms* ♢ *Room service, some hot tubs, minibars, cable TV, croquet, lounge; no a/c* ▤ *AE, MC, V* ❖ *BP, CP.*

Woodbridge

 18 mi northeast of Dedham.

One of the first good ports of call on the Suffolk Heritage Coast, Woodbridge, off A12, is a pleasant town whose upper reaches center on a fine old market square with two great pubs, the Bull and the King's Head. Antiques shops fill the surrounding streets, but Woodbridge is at its best around its old quayside. Boatbuilding has been carried out here since the 16th century. The most prominent building is a white clapboard mill, which dates from the 18th century and is powered by the tides.

The visitor center at **Sutton Hoo** helps interpret one of Britain's most significant Anglo-Saxon archaeological sites. In 1938 a local archaeologist excavated three 7th-century burial mounds associated with King Raedwald of East Anglia. Traces of a buried ship were the most unique find; many artifacts uncovered are now in the British Museum in London. Later excavations revealed that this was the site of other burials, some royal. A replica of the 40-oar, 90-foot-long ship stands in the visitor center, which has artifacts and displays about

> **WORD OF MOUTH**
>
> "Suffolk is beautiful—I was born and raised in the county, and the Woodbridge area has so much to offer. A car will be vital, though, to make the most of it."   —Morgana

Anglo-Saxon society. Trails around the 245-acre site explore the area along the River Deben. Sutton Hoo is 2 mi east of Woodbridge. ⊠ *B1083* ☎ *01394/389700* ⊕ *www.nationaltrust.org.uk* ✎ *£5* ☉ *Apr.–June, Sept., and Oct., Wed.–Sun. 11–5; July–Sept., daily 11–5; Nov.–Mar., weekends 10–4.*

OFF THE
BEATEN
PATH

FRAMLINGHAM CASTLE – From the outside, this moated castle looks much as it would have in the 12th century. Upon entering, you'll notice that the keep is missing. (Nearby Orford Castle has an intact keep but no battlements.) An audio tour, included in the admission, leads you on a walk around the curtain wall, with its 13 towers. Most of the chimneys along the wall are fake; they were additions meant to give the impression to passersby that this was a great Tudor mansion. ■ TIP➔ **The open-air concerts and reenactments held in the summer are worth seeking out.** ⊠ *B1119* ☎ *01728/724189* ⊕ *www.english-heritage.org.uk* ✎ *£4.30* ☉ *Apr.–Sept., daily 10–6; Oct., daily 10–5; Nov.–Mar., daily 10–4.*

Where to Stay

★ **££££** ⬚ **Seckford Hall.** This magnificent Tudor manor house recalls the days of yore with its wood-panel walls, oak beams, fireplaces, and impressive antiques, including a 16th-century half-tester bed. The landscaped grounds are perfect for a stroll to admire the roses or the duck-filled lake. The main restaurant specializes in local lobster. ⊠ *Off A12, IP13 6NU* ☎ *01394/385678* 🖷 *01394/380610* ⊕ *www.seckford.co.uk* ⇆ *32 rooms* ⌕ *2 restaurants, room service, cable TV, golf privileges, indoor pool, gym, spa, hot tub, bar, lounge, laundry service, meeting rooms, some pets allowed (fee); no a/c* ⊟ *AE, DC, MC, V* ¶⊙↓ *BP.*

Orford

❷❽ *10 mi east of Woodbridge, 35 mi northeast of Colchester.*

Part of the Suffolk Heritage Coast, a 40-mi stretch that runs from Felixstowe northward to Kessingland, ancient Orford is a beautiful example of the coast's many Sites of Special Scientific Interest (legally protected nature preserves). There are numerous beaches, marshes, and broads, with an abundance of wildflowers and birds. You can reach other areas on minor roads running east off A12 north of Ipswich.

Small and squat, **Orford Castle** surveys the flatlands from atop a green mound favored by picnickers in summer. Its splendid triple-tower keep was built in 1160 as a coastal defense. Climb it for a view over what was once a thriving medieval port; the 6-mi shingle (coarse gravel) bank of Orford Ness eventually cut off direct access to the sea. ⊠ *B1084* ☎ *01394/450472* ⊕ *www.english-heritage.org.uk* ✎ *£4.30* ☉ *Apr.–Sept., daily 10–6; Oct.–Mar., Thurs.–Mon., 10–4.*

Just a boat ride beyond Orford Quay lies mysterious **Orford Ness,** Europe's biggest vegetated shingle (gravel) spit. A 5-mi-long path takes you through beaches and salt marshes to see migrating and native birds and to discover the secret past of the spit—from 1913 until the mid-1980s, it served as a military site. If you'd rather sit than walk, take the tractor-drawn trailer tour on the first Saturday of the month, July through

September (reservations essential). ⊠ *Orford Quay* ☎ *01394/450057* ⊕ *www.nationaltrust.org.uk* 🎫 *£6 including ferry crossing* ⊙ *Apr.–June and Oct., Sat. 10–2; July–Sept., Tues.–Sat. 10–2; last ferry at 5.*

Where to Stay & Eat

££ ✕ **Butley-Orford Oysterage.** What started as a little café that sold oysters and cups of tea has become a large, bustling, no-nonsense restaurant. It still specializes in oysters and smoked salmon, as well as smoked seafood platters and seasonal fish dishes. The actual smoking takes place in the adjacent smokehouse, and products are for sale in a shop around the corner. ⊠ *Market Hill* ☎ *01394/450277* 🖃 *MC, V* ⊙ *No dinner Sun.–Thurs. Nov.–Mar.*

★ **£££–££££** ✕ 🏠 **Crown and Castle.** Artsy, laid-back, and genuinely friendly, this contemporary hotel in an 18th-century building near Orford Castle is a little gem. Many rooms have bathrooms with sunflower-size showerheads; ask for one of these. The garden rooms are spacious. The Trinity Bistro (££–£££), run by food writer Ruth Watson, focuses on modern British fare, including plenty of fresh fish and local Butley oysters. In warm weather, the outdoor terrace is a great place for grandstand views of Orford Castle. ⊠ *Market Hill, IP12 2LJ* ☎ *01394/450205* 🖷 *01394/ 450176* ⊕ *www.crownandcastle.co.uk* ➳ *18 rooms* ౨ *Restaurant, in-room VCRs, bar, lobby lounge, some pets allowed, no-smoking rooms; no a/c* 🖃 *MC, V* ⧦I *BP.*

Aldeburgh

㉙ *20 mi north of Orford, 41 mi northeast of Colchester.*

Aldeburgh (pronounced orl-bruh) is a quiet seaside resort, except in June, when the town fills up with people attending the noted Aldeburgh Festival. Its beach is backed by a promenade lined with candy-color dwellings. Twentieth-century composer Benjamin Britten lived here for some time—he was born in the busy seaside resort of Lowestoft, 30 mi to the north. Britten grew interested in the story of Aldeburgh's native son, the poet George Crabbe (1754–1832), and turned his life story into the celebrated modern opera *Peter Grimes,* a piece that perfectly captures the atmosphere of the Suffolk coast.

The **Elizabethan Moot Hall,** built of flint and timber, stood in the center of a thriving 16th-century town when first erected. Now it's just a few steps from the beach, a mute witness to the erosive powers of the North Sea. ⊠ *Market Cross, Sea Front* ☎ *01728/454666* ⊕ *www. aldeburghmuseum.org.uk* 🎫 *£1* ⊙ *Easter–Apr. and Oct., weekends 2:30–5; May, Sept., and Oct., daily 2:30–5; June–Aug., daily noon–5.*

Where to Stay & Eat

££–£££ ✕ **152aldeburgh.** The Mediterranean influences the cooking at this restaurant and brasserie where seafood is the prime attraction. Bright colors, wood floors, and candlelight create a relaxed backdrop for dishes such as baked cod in herb butter, seafood risottos, and grilled duck breast. For picnic fixings or culinary souvenirs, stop by the adjacent delicatessen, which sells quiches, terrines, cold cuts, and cheeses. ⊠ *152 High St.* ☎ *01728/454594* 🖃 *MC, V.*

ff–fff ✕ **The Lighthouse.** An excellent value, this low-key brasserie relies exclu-
Fodor'sChoice sively on local produce and focuses on seafood, including oysters and
★ Cromer crabs. All the dishes are simply but imaginatively cooked, usually with an interesting sauce that might just as easily be Italian or Asian
as English. Desserts, such as the creamy bread-and-butter pudding, are
particularly good. ⊠ *77 High St.* ☎ *01728/453377* ⊟ *MC, V.*

f ✕ **The Fish and Chip Shop.** When frying time approaches, Aldeburgh's
most celebrated fish-and-chip shop always has a long line, especially in
summer. The Golden Galleon, along the road, is the version with seating, where you can bring wine or beer to enjoy with your succulent chips,
but for the full experience you should probably join the queue here. ⊠ *137
High St.* ☎ *01728/454685* ⊟ *No credit cards.*

ffff–fffff ▥ **Brudenell.** The best rooms at this bright, stylish contemporary seaside hotel face the water. Its restaurant serves fresh, uncomplicated
seafood dishes. The accommodating staff here is informal, helping
guests feel more relaxed. The White Lion hotel, dating to 1563, is the
Brudenell's historic sister property. ⊠ *Market Cross Pl., IP15 5BJ*
☎ *01728/452071* ⊠ *01728/454082* ⊕ *www.brudenellhotel.co.uk* ⇩ *42
rooms ⟁ Restaurant, room service, cable TV, in-room data ports, bar,
lounge, some pets allowed (fee); no a/c, no smoking* ⊟ *AE, MC, V* ¶◯¶ *BP.*

ffff–fffff ▥ **Wentworth Hotel.** The Pritt family has owned and managed the Wentworth since 1920, and their caring attention shows. Huge chairs fill the
public rooms on the ground floor and are a great place to sip coffee and
watch people stroll by. The bedrooms are done in pastel fabrics and seem
somewhat dated; sea-view rooms, which are worth the extra cost, come
equipped with binoculars. All rooms have a copy of the whimsical children's favorite *Orlando the Marmalade Cat,* by Kathleen Hale, which
is set in "Owlbarrow," a fictional town based on Aldeburgh. ⊠ *Wentworth Rd., IP15 5BD* ☎ *01728/452312* ⊠ *01728/454343* ⊕ *www.
wentworth-aldeburgh.com* ⇩ *37 rooms, 35 with bath ⟁ Restaurant,
room service, cable TV, in-room data ports, bar, lobby lounge, meeting
rooms, some pets allowed; no a/c, no smoking* ⊟ *MC, V* ¶◯¶ *BP.*

★ **ff** ▥ **Ocean House.** Juliet and Phil Brereton are your hosts at this redbrick
1860s house practically on the beach, which is an outstanding deal for
the price. Antiques and bric-a-brac decorate the public areas and bedrooms, and the two rooms with bath have views of the sea. Breakfast
is hearty and home-cooked, and the warm welcome is enhanced by open
fireplaces and an abundance of books and magazines. ⊠ *25 Crag Path,
IP15 5BS* ☎ *01728/452094* ⇩ *6 rooms, 2 with bath ⟁ Lounge, piano,
Ping-Pong, bicycles; no a/c, no smoking* ⊟ *No credit cards* ¶◯¶ *BP.*

Nightlife & the Arts

★ East Anglia's most important arts festival, and one of the best known
in Great Britain, is the **Aldeburgh Festival** (☎ 01728/687100, 01728/
453543 box office ⊕ www.aldeburgh.co.uk) held during two June
weeks in the small village of Snape, 5 mi west of Aldeburgh, at the Snape
Maltings Concert Hall. Founded by Benjamin Britten, the festival concentrates on music but includes related exhibitions, poetry readings, and
even walks. A less hectic calendar of concerts and events continues
through the year.

It's well worth a stop to take in the peaceful River Alde location of the **Snape Maltings** cultural center that includes art galleries and craft shops. You can pause at the tea shop or the Plough & Sail pub. Snape Maltings has special events year-round, such as the two-day Aldeburgh Folk Festival, held each July to celebrate traditional English folk music, and the Britten Festival in October. One-hour river cruise (£5) leave from Snape Bridge during high tide. ⊠ *Snape, near Saxmundham* ☎ *01728/688305* ⊕ *www.snapemaltings.co.uk* ☽ *Daily 10–5.*

Southwold

㉚ *15 mi north of Aldeburgh, 32 mi southeast of Norwich.*

This seaside town is an idyllic place to spend a day. Old-fashioned beach huts painted in bright colors huddle together against the wind on the shingle beach, which is lined with small pebbles, and up in the town center a pleasing ensemble of old houses faces the main street and surrounds the central green. The Church of St. Edmund dates to the 15th century. There aren't many "sights," but the whole town gives you the sensation of being transported back in time.

The **Southwold Museum** displays works of local archaeology, natural history, and pictures of the 17th-century Battle of Sole Bay. It's in a Dutch-gabled cottage, a style typical of Southwold's domestic architecture. ⊠ *Victoria St.* ☎ *01502/722375* ⊕ *www.southwoldmuseum.org* ☞ *Free, but donations welcome* ☽ *Easter–July, Sept., and Oct., daily 2–4; Aug., daily 10:30–noon and 2–4.*

> **OFF THE BEATEN PATH**
>
> **WALBERSWICK** – For many years this tranquil little village, on B1387, was the haunt of arty types (including, during 1914–15, the Scottish art nouveau architect Charles Rennie Mackintosh). The village is separated from Southwold by the mouth of the River Blyth, over which there's a footbridge (about 1 mi inland), but no main road bridge. On summer weekends, a boatman ferries foot passengers in a rowboat every few minutes. ☞ *Ferry £1* ☽ *Ferry May–Sept., weekends 9–12:30 and 2–5.*

Where to Stay & Eat

££££–£££££ ✕🏨 **Swan Hotel.** This 17th-century inn has spacious public rooms and decent-size bedrooms decorated in traditional English-country style. Seventeen secluded, quiet garden rooms are set around the old bowling green. The restaurant's dishes (£££–££££) are mainly traditional English fare, accompanied by an excellent wine list. Children under 5 are not allowed in the dining room after 7 PM. ⊠ *Market Pl., IP18 6EG* ☎ *01502/722186* 🖷 *01502/724800* ⊕ *www.adnams.co.uk* ⇨ *43 rooms, 41 with bath* ⚲ *Restaurant, croquet, bar, meeting rooms, some pets allowed; no a/c* ▭ *AE, DC, MC, V* ⫶◯⫶ *BP.*

£££ ✕🏨 **Crown Hotel.** Like the nearby Swan, the Crown is owned by the old family firm of Adnams brewery, the major employer in Southwold. Bedrooms are suitably small for a 17th-century building, but the antique furniture and friendly staff compensate. The maritime-theme Back Bar (££–£££) or the eclectic brasserie and wine bar provide a cozy place to dine. Seafood dishes are excellent, from panfried John Dory to smoked haddock. Children under 5 are not allowed in the restaurant after 7 PM.

✉ 90 High St., IP18 6DP ☏ 01502/722275 ⊟ 01502/727263 ⊕ www. adnams.co.uk ⇥ 14 rooms, 11 with bath ⚭ Restaurant, bar, meeting rooms; no a/c in some rooms ☰ AE, DC, MC, V ⦿ BP.

NORWICH TO NORTH NORFOLK

Norwich, unofficial capital of East Anglia and the heart of the eastern and northern part of East Anglia's "bump," is dominated by the 15th-century spire of its impressive cathedral. Norfolk's continuing isolation from the rest of the country, and its unspoiled landscape and architecture—bypassed by the Industrial Revolution—have proved to be a draw. Many of the flint-knapped (decorated with broken flint) houses in North Norfolk's newly trendy villages are now weekend or holiday homes. Windmills, churches, and waterways are the area's chief defining characteristics. A few miles inland from the Norfolk coast, the Broads begin, a national park made up of a network of shallow, reed-bordered lakes, many linked by wide rivers. Boating and fishing are great lures; rent a boat for a day or a week and the waterside pubs, churches, villages, and nature reserves are all within easy reach.

Norwich

63 mi northeast of Cambridge.

It used to be said that Norwich had a pub for each day of the year and a church in which to repent for every Sunday of the year. Although this is no longer true, real ales and steeples are still much in evidence in this pleasant city of about 130,000. Established by the Saxons because of its prime trading position on the rivers Yare and Wensum, the town has its heart in the triangle between the two waterways. The inner beltway follows the line of the old city wall, much of which is still visible. It's worth walking or driving around after dark to see the floodlit older buildings. By the time of the Norman Conquest, Norwich was one of the largest towns in England, although much was destroyed by the Normans to create a new town.

You can see the old flint buildings as you walk down the medieval streets and alleyways. Despite its concessions to modernity—some industrial sites and many shopping centers—the town remains historic and engaging. The University of East Anglia brings a cosmopolitan touch, including a lively arts scene, to an otherwise remote urban area. It's a good base from which to explore the Norfolk Broads and the coast.

Main Attractions

⟲ ㉟ **Norwich Castle.** The decorated stone facing of this castle, now a museum on the hill in the center of the city, makes it look like a children's book illustration. The castle is Norman (1130), but a stone keep replaced the original wooden bailey (wall) on the castle mound. The thick walls and other defenses attest to its military function. Today it houses three museum zones. Dioramas in Natural History show Norfolk plants and wildlife, and excellent interactive displays in Castle and Archaeology explore topics from ancient Egypt to life in Norman times. You can even try out a copy of Queen Boudicca's chariot to relive her attack on

City Hall **36**

Elm Hill **31**

Norwich
Castle **35**

Norwich
Cathedral **33**

Origins **39**

Pulls Ferry **34**

Sainsbury Centre
for the
Visual Arts **37**

St. Peter
Mancroft **38**

Tombland **32**

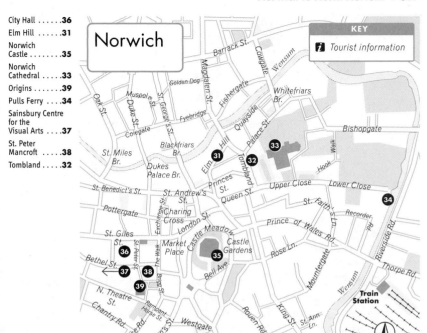

Roman Colchester. Art and Exhibitions includes a gallery devoted to the Norwich School of painters who, like John Constable, focused on the everyday landscape and seascape. This museum also holds glass, ceramics, and the world's largest teapot collection. Daily tours explore the castle's battlements or dungeons. ⊠ *Castle Meadow* ☎ *01603/ 493625* ⊕ *www.museums.norfolk.gov.uk* ⊡ *Entire museum £5.95, castle and archaeology £3.95, art and exhibitions £3.95; tours of the battlements or dungeons £1.20* ⊘ *Weekdays 10–4:30, Sat. 10–5, Sun. 1–5.*

★ ㉝ **Norwich Cathedral.** The grandest example of Norman architecture in Norwich has the second-largest monastic cloisters in Britain (Salisbury's are bigger). Although its spire, at 315 feet tall (also second only to Salisbury's), is visible from everywhere in the city, you cannot see the building itself until you pass through St. Ethelbert's Gate. The cathedral was begun in 1096 by Herbert de Losinga, who had come from Normandy in 1091 to be its first bishop; his splendid tomb is by the high altar. Distinctly Norman elements are the plain west front and dramatic crossing tower, with its austere, geometrical decoration. The remarkable length of the nave is immediately impressive; the similarly striking height of the vaulted ceiling makes it a strain to study the delightful colored bosses, which illustrate Bible stories with great vigor and detail. Binoculars can help, and the bosses in the cloisters are easier to appreciate. The grave of Norfolk-born nurse Edith Cavell, the British World War I heroine shot by the Germans in 1915, is at the east end of the cathedral. ⊠ *62 The Close* ☎ *01603/764385* ⊕ *www.cathedral.org.uk* ⊡ *Free* ⊙ *Mid-May–mid-Sept., daily 7:30–7; mid-Sept.–mid-May, daily 7:30–6; free guided tours Mon.–Sat. 10:45, 11:30, and 2:15.*

③⑦ Sainsbury Centre for the Visual Arts. A modern, hangarlike building designed by Norman Foster on the University of East Anglia campus holds the private art collection of the Sainsbury family, owners of a supermarket chain. It includes a remarkable quantity of tribal art and 20th-century works, especially art nouveau, and has pieces by Pablo Picasso and Alberto Giacometti. Buses 4, 5, 26, and 27 run from Norwich Castle Meadow to the university. ⊠ *Earlham Rd.* ☎ *01603/593199* ⊕ *www. scva.org.uk* ⊡ *£2* ⊙ *Tues. and Thurs.–Sun. 11–5, Wed. 11–8.*

Also Worth Seeing

③⑥ City Hall. Bronze Norwich lions guard the steps of the imposing—if severe—early-20th-century City Hall, which overlooks the Market Place. ⊠ *St. Peter St.*

③① Elm Hill. Off Tombland, this neighborhood is a cobbled and pleasing mixture of Tudor and Georgian houses that hold gift shops and tearooms.

☉ ③⑨ Origins. On three floors of the modern **Forum,** Origins provides an introduction to Norwich and the surrounding area via a 90-minute interactive tour. The museum delves back 2,000 years to show how the area's inhabitants and landscape have changed—from the Vikings and Romans to the U.S. servicemen and servicewomen who were here during World War II. You can drain a three-dimensional map of the fens, try the Norfolk dialect, and watch a film about the region on a wraparound screen. The shop stocks lots of made-in-Norfolk souvenirs, and the Forum also houses the Norwich Library, a tourist information center, a few places to eat, and an atrium space for entertainment. ⊠ *Between N. Theatre and Bethel Sts.* ☎ *01603/727920* ⊕ *www. theforumnorfolk.com* ⊡ *£5.95* ⊙ *Mon.–Sat. 10–5:15, Sun. 11–4:45.*

③④ Pulls Ferry. The Cathedral **Close** (grounds) is one of the most idyllic places in Norwich; past the mixture of medieval and Georgian houses, a path leads down to the ancient water gate, Pulls Ferry.

③⑧ St. Peter Mancroft. The elaborate church tower of 15th-century St. Peter Mancroft rises next to the Market Place. ⊠ *Bethel St.*

③② Tombland. Narrow lanes and alleys that used to be the main streets of medieval Norwich lead away from the market and end at Tombland by the cathedral. Neither a graveyard nor a plague pit, Tombland was the site of the Anglo-Saxon trading place, now a busy thoroughfare.

Where to Stay & Eat

★ ✕ **Adlard's Restaurant.** Wine enthusiast and chef David Adlard runs this **££££–£££££** relaxed contemporary restaurant with pine floors and white walls. Beautifully presented dishes such as roast turbot with skate terrine, white beans, and broccoli puree show his ability to bring classical French cooking up to date. Desserts such as coconut rice pudding with lime jelly compete against excellent cheeses. Choose from a small à la carte menu or one of the set menus for lunch or dinner. Lunch is good value. ✉ *79 Upper St. Giles St.* ☎ *01603/633522* ▭ *AE, DC, MC, V* ☉ *Closed Sun. and 1 wk after Christmas. No dinner Mon.*

£–££ ✗ **Adam and Eve.** Said to be Norwich's oldest pub, this place dates back to 1249. From noon until 7, the kitchen serves such hearty pub staples as beef-and-mushroom pie or cheese-and-ale soup from the short but solid bar menu. Theakston's and Adnams beer are available on tap, as is Addlestone's cider. ✉ *Bishopsgate* ☎ *01603/667423* ▭ *AE, MC, V.*

★ **£** ✗ **Britons Arms.** A converted pub, this cozy, thatched café and eatery has famously good homemade cakes as well as some pies and tarts. The 15th-century building has low ceilings and a garden in summer. ✉ *9 Elm Hill* ☎ *01603/623367* ▭ *MC, V* ☉ *Closed Sun.*

£ ✗ **Tree House.** Inventive global cuisine such as tofu in coconut-lime sauce, hearty salads, and tasty sweets are the specialties at this co-op vegetarian restaurant. The menu indicates sugar- and gluten-free dishes. ✉ *14 Dove St.* ☎ *01603/763258* ▭ *No credit cards.*

£££££ ⌂ **Dunston Hall Hotel & Country Club.** Gables and tall chimneys give this redbrick mansion built in 1859 an Elizabethan look, and extensive modern additions have transformed a country house into a luxurious retreat. The peaceful landscaped gardens and woodland are ideal for relaxing after a day's sightseeing. If you seek a sense of the past, ask for a four-poster bedroom or one of the small attic bedrooms with original low beamed ceilings. The hotel is 4 mi south of the city center, on the A140. ✉ *Ipswich Rd., NR14 8PQ* ☎ *01508/470444* 📠 *01508/471499* ⊕ *www.devereonline.co.uk* ⇆ *127 rooms, 3 suites* ♨ *3 restaurants, room service, cable TV, in-room data ports, driving range, 18-hole golf course, putting green, 2 tennis courts, indoor pool, gym, hot tub, sauna, steam room, billiards, babysitting, dry cleaning, laundry service, concierge, meeting rooms, no-smoking rooms; no a/c* ▭ *AE, DC, MC, V* ⦿ *BP.*

£££ ⌂ **Beeches Hotel.** Three handsome early Victorian houses in the Victorian Gardens make up this family-run hotel. The Governor's House has some rooms with terraces, and the Beeches House has a modern extension. All rooms are simply but pleasantly furnished, and several look out over the gardens and their ornate Gothic fountain and Italianate terrace. Rooms at the front can be noisy. The hotel is about a mile west of the city center. ✉ *2–6 Earlham Rd., NR2 3DB* ☎ *01603/621167* 📠 *01603/620151* ⊕ *www.mjbhotels.com* ⇆ *36 rooms* ♨ *Restaurant, room service, cable TV, bar, dry cleaning, laundry service; no a/c, no kids under 12, no smoking* ▭ *AE, DC, MC, V* ⦿ *BP.*

Nightlife & the Arts

Cinema City (✉ St. George's St. ☎ 01603/622047), Norwich's venue for art films, relocated to the Norwich Playhouse in 2005 pending the excavation of Roman remains discovered underneath the cinema. The **King of Hearts** (✉ 7–15 Fye Bridge St. ☎ 01603/766129), a restored medieval merchant's house, serves as a small arts center that presents chamber concerts, recitals, and poetry readings. It has a good café. **Norwich Arts Centre** (✉ St. Benedict's St. ☎ 01603/660352) puts on an eclectic program of live music, dance, and stand-up comedy. It too has a good café, with free Internet access.

The **Maddermarket Theatre** (⊠ St. John's Alley ☎ 01603/620917), patterned after Elizabethan theaters, has been the base of the Norwich Players, an amateur repertory company, since 1911. The theater closes in August. **Norwich Playhouse** (⊠ Gun Wharf, St. George's St. ☎ 01603/598598), a professional repertory group, performs everything from Shakespeare to world premieres of new plays; it also runs a bookshop. Norwich's biggest and best-known theater, the **Theatre Royal** (⊠ Theatre St. ☎ 01603/630000), hosts touring companies staging musicals, ballet, opera, and plays.

Sports & the Outdoors
Traffic on the River Yare is now mostly for pleasure rather than commerce, and a summer trip with **City Boats** (⊠ Elm Hill, Pulls Ferry, Station, Whitlingham Park, and Griffin Lane quays ☎ 01603/701701 ☎ £7–£8.50 ☉ Tours daily at 10:15, 11, 12:30, 1:30, 3) gives a fresh perspective on Norwich. Longer trips are available down the Rivers Wensum and Yare to the nearer Broads.

Broads Tours (☎ 01603/782207 Wroxham, 01692/670711 Potter Heigham), based at the quaysides in Wroxham, 7 mi northeast of Norwich, and Potter Heigham, 15 mi northeast of Norwich, offers day cruises in the Broads as well as half-day and full-day launch rental (lessons included). Major operators such as **Hoseasons** (☎ 01502/502588 or 0870/543–4434) rent boats by the week. The *Norada, Olive,* and *Hathor* are historic wherry yachts (sailing barges), and all may be chartered from the **Wherry Yacht Centre** (☎ 01603/782470) for luxurious cruises.

Explore the Norfolk Broads by bicycle with **Broadland Cycle Hire** (⊠ The Rhond, Hoverton ☎ 01603/783096), 8 mi northeast of Norwich. Rentals (£9 per day) are available from Easter through October. The company can recommend routes 7 to 20 mi from their base.

Shopping
The medieval lanes of Norwich, around Elm Hill and Tombland, contain the best antiques, book, and crafts stores. The **Mustard Shop** (⊠ 15 Royal Arcade ☎ 01603/627889) pays homage to Colman's Mustard, a company founded in Norwich in the early 19th century; it sells collectibles and more than 15 varieties of mustard. The **Norwich Antiques Centre** (⊠ 14 Tombland ☎ 01603/619129), opposite the cathedral, is an old house crammed full of shops. **Norwich Market** (⊠ Market Pl., Gentleman's Walk ☎ 01603/212414), the city's main outdoor market, is open daily; it sells everything from jewelry to clothes and food and has been the heart of the city for 900 years.

Blickling Hall

★ ⓐ *15 mi north of Norwich.*

Behind the wrought-iron entrance gate to Blickling Hall, two mighty yew hedges form an imposing allée, creating a magnificent frame for this perfectly symmetrical, Jacobean masterpiece. The redbrick mansion has towers and chimneys, baroque Dutch gables, and, in the center, a

Introducing Fens & Broads   11

CLOSE UP

East Anglia is its separateness, its desolate landscapes and isolated beaches. Of these, the fens (marshy lowlands) of northern Cambridgeshire and the Broads (expanded rivers) of Norfolk are the most dramatic—or depressing, depending on your mood. The water in the marshes and dikes reflects the arching sky, whose cloudscapes are ever-changing, stretching toward seemingly infinite horizons. The sunsets are to be treasured. The fens resemble areas of Holland across the North Sea, and, indeed, work on much of the drainage system here was carried out by Dutch engineers beginning in the 17th century.

In both Norfolk and Suffolk, the reed-bordered Broads make a gentle landscape of canals and lakes that are ideal for boating and are alive with birds and animals. Touring by car isn't really an option if you want to see something of the **Norfolk Broads** (⊕ www.broads-authority.gov.uk), because much of this area of shallow lakes linked by wide rivers is inaccessible by road. There are boat tours and people with their own launch can cruise through 150 mi of waterways. The Broads Authority (⇨ Visitor Information *in* East Anglia Essentials) maintains an extensive network of cycle paths and bike rental centers. Rentals are £10 per day, and each rental center can provide local maps and route advice. All centers are within 30 to 40 minutes' drive of Norwich. The Suffolk Heritage Coast includes 40 mi of unspoiled coastline, with marshes, beaches, and broads.

three-story timber clock tower. The grounds include a formal flower garden and parkland with woods that conceal a temple, an orangery, and a pyramid. Blickling belonged to a succession of historic figures, including Sir John Fastolf, the model for Shakespeare's Falstaff; Anne Boleyn's family; and finally, Lord Lothian, an ambassador to the United States. The Long Gallery (127 feet) has an intricate plasterwork ceiling with Jacobean emblems. Most of the interior is handsome but somewhat austere, although a sumptuous tapestry of Peter the Great at the Battle of Poltawa hangs in its own room. Next to the main entrance is the Buckinghamshire Arms, a pub. ✉ *B1354, Blickling* ☎ *01263/738030* ⊕ *www.nationaltrust.org.uk* 🖼 *£8, gardens only £5* ☉ *House Apr.–July, Sept., and Oct., Wed.–Sun. 1–5; Aug., Wed.–Mon. 1–5; Oct., Wed.–Sun. 1–4. Gardens Apr.–July, Sept., and Oct., Wed.–Sun. 10:15–5:15; Aug., Wed.–Mon. 10:15–5:15; Nov.–Mar., Thurs.–Sun. 11–4.*

Blakeney

 15 mi northeast of Blickling Hall, 27 mi northeast of Norwich.

The Norfolk coast begins to feel wild and remote near Blakeney, 15 mi west of Cromer. Driving the coast road from Cromer, you pass marshes, sandbanks, and coves, as well as villages. Blakeney is one of the most appealing, with harbors for small fishing boats and yachts. Once a

Popular Paths

EAST ANGLIA IS A WALKER'S DREAM, especially if a relatively flat trail appeals to you. The long-distance footpath known as the Peddar's Way follows the line of a pre-Roman road, running from near Thetford through heathland, pine forests, and arable fields, and on through rolling chalk lands to the Norfolk coast near Hunstanton. The Norfolk Coastal Path then continues eastward along the coast, joining at Cromer with the delightfully varied Weaver's Way, which passes through medieval weaving villages and deeply rural parts of the Norfolk Broads on its 56-mi route from Cromer to Great Yarmouth. Birders or anyone interested in birds should carry binoculars and a bird identification book, as both of these routes have abundant avian life—both local and migratory. Tourist information centers and the regional Web site ⊕ www.visiteastofengland. com have further details.

bustling port town exporting corn and salt, it enjoys a quiet existence today, and a reputation for wildlife viewing at Blakeney Point.

Blakeney Point, a thousand acres of grassy dunes, is home to nesting terns and about 500 common and gray seals. You can walk 3½ mi from Cley Beach to get here, but a boat trip from Blakeney or Morston Quay is fun and educational. An information center and a tearoom at Morston Quay open according to tides and weather. **Bishop's Boats** (⊠ Old Lifeboat House ☎ 01263/740753 ⊕ www.norfolksealtrips.co.uk) runs one- or two-hour trips daily from Morston quay and Blakeney harbor for £6 per person. ⊠ A149 ☎ 01263/740480 Apr.–Sept., 01263/740241 Oct.–Mar. ⊕ www.nationaltrust.org.uk ⊠ Free.

Where to Stay & Eat

★ **££££** ✕⊡ **Byfords.** In a market town 5 mi southeast of Blakeney, Byfords epitomizes the increasing trendiness of North Norfolk. The rooms are stylish and comfortable, with wooden beams, Egyptian cotton, elegantly modern hi-fi sound systems, and fresh flowers. The busy café by day turns into a restaurant (£–££) offering Mediterranean and English fare in the evening. There's also a mouth-wateringly good delicatessen—excellent for preparing a picnic. ⊠ 1–3 Shirehall Plain, Holt NR25 6BG ☎ 01263/711400 ⊕ www.byfords.org.uk ⌗ 9 rooms, 1 apartment ⚏ Restaurant, in-room DVDs; no a/c ☰ MC, V ⊙ CP.

££–££££ ✕⊡ **White Horse at Blakeney.** Fine food is the draw at this former coaching inn. Mussels, crabs, and fish appear on the menu, along with pub classics such as steak-and-ale pie and Whitby scampi-and-chips. The restaurant (££–£££; reservations essential) opens at 7 PM every day. A few of the pleasant, simply furnished rooms have sea views that are worth paying extra for. Good discounts are available midweek. ⊠ 4 High St., NR25 7TE ☎ 01263/740574 01263/741303 ⊕ www. blakeneywhitehorse.co.uk ⌗ 9 rooms, 1 suite ⚏ Restaurant, lounge, pub, Internet room; no a/c ☰ MC, V ⊙ Closed 2 wks in Jan. ⊙ BP.

Wells-next-the-Sea

42 *10 mi west of Blakeney, 37 mi northwest of Norwich.*

A quiet base from which to explore other towns such as shop–filled Burn-ham Market, the harbor town of Wells-next-the-Sea and the nearby coast-line remain untouched, with many excellent places for bird-watching and walking on the sandy beaches of Holkham Bay, near Holkham Hall. Today the town is a mile from the sea, but in Tudor times, when it was closer to the ocean, it served as one of the main ports of East Anglia. The remains of a medieval priory and two holy wells point to the town's past as a major pilgrimage destination in the Middle Ages. Along the nearby beach, a narrow-gauge steam train makes the short journey to Walsingham in summer.

Fodor'sChoice
★

The Palladian **Holkham Hall,** one of the most splendid mansions in Britain, is the seat of the Coke family, the earls of Leicester. In the late 18th cen-tury, Thomas Coke went on the fashionable grand tour of the Continent, returning with art treasures and de-termined to build a house accord-ing to the new Italian ideas. Centered by a grand staircase and modeled after the Baths of Diocletian, the entryway, the 60-foot-tall Marble Hall (mostly alabaster, in fact), may be the most spectacular room in Britain. Beyond this hall lie salons brilliant with gold and alabaster, each filled with works from Coke's collection of masterpieces, including paintings by Gainsborough, Sir An-thony Van Dyck, Peter Paul Rubens, Raphael, and other old masters. Surrounding this transplant from neoclassical Italy is extensive parkland landscaped by Capability Brown in 1762. The **Bygones Museum,** in the stable block, has more than 5,000 items, from gramophones to fire engines. ⊠ *Off A149* ☎ *01328/710227* ⊕ *www.holkham.co.uk* ✉ *Hall £6.50, museum £5, combined ticket £10; deer park and grounds free* ☉ *June–Sept., Thurs.–Mon. 1–5; call ahead for open days in late Mar., early Apr. and May.*

> **WORD OF MOUTH**
>
> "Wells is a working, small town, but one that still welcomes tourists. It is authentic, preten-sion-free, and interesting. It's real. Sandringham, the home of the Queen in the summer, is nearby, as are some other pretty towns. The sea is quite wild in places, but great for walks and blowing away the cobwebs." –Nigello

Where to Stay & Eat

★ **£££££** ✕🏨 **Hoste Arms.** Paul Whittome and his wife have turned a 17th-cen-tury former coaching inn into a small hotel and destination gastro-pub (££–£££). The menu lists such delights as Cromer crab, Burnham Creek oysters, and North Sea mussels, with light, Asian-influenced sauces. The hotel's style is traditional, with walled gardens, beamed ceilings, and log fires; the six modern rooms in the Zulu Wing are the exception. For less expensive accommodation try the nearby sister property, the Rail-way Inn, which has six small rooms with fewer amenities or try mid-week, when prices drop considerably. Burnham Market is a lovely town 6 mi west of Wells. ⊠ *The Green, B1155, Burnham Market PE31 8HD*

☎ *03128/738777* 🖷 *01328/730103* ⊕ *www.hostearms.co.uk* 🗫 *36 rooms* ↻ *3 restaurants, bar, meeting rooms, some pets allowed (fee), Internet room; no a/c* ☐ *AE, DC, MC, V* ⍨ *BP.*

££££ ✕🖭 **Crown Hotel.** Overlooking an expanse of green known as the Buttlands, the Crown contains stylish, bright guest rooms done with minimalist flair. The wonderful restaurant (££) serves local delights, with nods to Asia: flash-fried squid; bacon and black pudding; steamed North Sea cod with ginger, lemongrass, and lime; and apple and walnut pudding with clotted cream. The bar offers less expensive but no less innovative fare. ☒ *The Buttlands, NR23 1EX* ☎ *01328/710209* 🖷 *01328/711432* ⊕ *www.thecrownhotelwells.co.uk* 🗫 *9 rooms, 2 suites* ↻ *Restaurant, some in-room VCRs, in-room data ports, bar, lounge, babysitting, meeting rooms; no a/c* ☐ *MC, V* ⍨ *BP.*

££££ ✕🖭 **Victoria at Holkham.** A colorful, whimsical hideaway, the Victoria
Fodor'sChoice is adjacent to Holkham Hall and owned by the current earl of Leices-
★ ter. Guest rooms and public areas mix Victorian, colonial, and local themes, all with a touch of Asia. The ornately carved dark-wood furniture was handmade in India for the hotel. In the restaurant you can try game dishes and local seafood such as Cromer crabs, Brancaster mussels, and unusually good fish-and-chips. The dune-backed Holkham Beach (where the ending beach scene from *Shakespeare in Love* was filmed) is only a few minutes' walk away. ☒ *A149, NR23 1AB* ☎ *01328/ 711008* 🖷 *01328/711009* ⊕ *www.holkham.co.uk/victoria* 🗫 *9 rooms, 1 suite, 3 apartments* ↻ *Restaurant, room service, cable TV, in-room data ports, bar, Internet room; no a/c in some rooms* ☐ *AE, DC, MC, V* ⍨ *CP.*

Sports & the Outdoors

On Yer Bike Cycle Hire (☒ The Laurels, Nutwood Farm, Wighton ☎ 01328/820719 ⊕ www.norfolkcyclehire.co.uk) will deliver and collect bikes; rentals are £11 per day, and advance reservations are required.

Sandringham House

➍➌ *15 mi southwest of Wells-next-the-Sea, 8 mi northeast of King's Lynn, 43 mi northwest of Norwich.*

Sandringham House, not far from the old-fashioned but still popular seaside resort of Hunstanton, is one of the Queen's residences—it's where the Royal Family traditionally spends Christmas, as well as other vacations. The huge, redbrick Victorian mansion was clearly designed for enormous country-house parties, with a ballroom, billiard room, and bowling alley, as well as a shooting lodge on the grounds. The house and gardens close when the Queen is in residence, but the woodlands, nature walks, and museum of royal memorabilia (in the old stables) remain open, as does the church, medieval but in heavy Victorian disguise. Tours have access to most rooms but steer clear of personal effects of current royals. ☒ *Sandringham* ☎ *01553/772675* ⊕ *www. sandringhamestate.co.uk* 🖾 *House, gardens, and museum £8, gardens and museum £5.50* ⊙ *Apr.–mid-July, Aug., and Sept., daily 11–5; Oct., daily 11–4.*

Houghton Hall

44 *8 mi east of Sandringham, 35 mi northwest of Norwich.*

This grand Palladian pile, built by British prime minister Sir Robert Walpole in the 1720s, has been carefully restored by its current owner, the seventh marquess of Cholmondeley. The double-height Stone Hall and the sumptuous state rooms, perfect for gatherings of the powerful, reveal designer William Kent's preference for gilt, plush fabrics, stucco, and elaborate carvings. The Common Parlour, one of the original family rooms, is elegant but far simpler. New landscaping, including a 5-acre walled garden, is also part of the picture. ⊠ *Off A148, near Harpley* ☎ *01485/528569* ⊕ *www.houghtonhall.com* 🎫 *£7, park and grounds only £4.50* ⊗ *May–Sept., Wed., Thurs., Sun., and bank holiday Mon. 1:30–5; grounds open at 11; last admission at 4:30.*

King's Lynn

45 *12 mi southwest of Houghton Hall, 40 mi northwest of Norwich.*

As Bishop's Lynn, the town thrived as a port on the River Ouse, growing prosperous in the 15th century through the wool trade and other trade with the continent; a Flemish influence is apparent in the church brasses and the style of the town squares. When Bishop's Lynn became royal property, the name was changed to King's Lynn. Although part of the old center was rebuilt in the mid-20th century, enough remains of its Georgian town houses, guildhalls, and ancient quayside warehouses (including the 15th-century Hanseatic Warehouse on St. Margaret's Lane) that this is still one of the most English of English towns.

The 15th-century **Trinity Guildhall**, with its striking, checkered-stone front, contains some civic treasures in the **Regalia Rooms,** in the guildhall undercroft. A recorded audio tour calls attention to such items as the unique silver-and-enamel 14th-century chalice known as King John's Cup. You enter the rooms through the **Old Gaol House,** site of the town police station until 1954, whose cells form part of an engaging law-and-order museum. The Guildhall itself is not generally open to the public, except during the King's Lynn Festival in July and on occasional guided tours in summer. ⊠ *Saturday Market Pl.* ☎ *01533/774297* 🎫 *£2.40* ⊗ *Apr.–Oct., daily 10–5; Nov.–Mar., Fri.–Tues. 10–5.*

St. George's Guildhall, the largest surviving medieval guildhall in England, forms part of the **King's Lynn Arts Centre,** an arts and theater complex administered by the National Trust, and the focal point for the annual King's Lynn Festival. Galleries in refurbished barns hold interesting contemporary exhibitions, and the center has a crafts fair every December. The **Crofters Coffee House** (☎ *01553/773134*), in a brick-vaulted wine cellar underneath the guildhall, is a budget choice for breakfast, lunch, or afternoon tea. ⊠ *27–29 King St.* ☎ *01553/765565, 01553/764864 box office* ⊕ *www.kingslynnarts.co.uk* 🎫 *Free* ⊗ *Mar.–Oct., Tues.–Sat. 10–5; Nov.–Feb., Tues.–Sat. 10–4.*

CASTLE RISING – Giant defensive earthworks surround this 12th-century stone castle, which is 4 mi northeast of King's Lynn. The 120-foot-high walls, sadly lacking a roof after all these centuries, contain some well-preserved sections, especially the chapel and the kitchen. Owned by the Howard family since 1544, the castle is a fine example of a domestic keep. ✉ *A149* ☎ *01553/631330* ⊕ *www.castlerising.co.uk* 🔖 *£3.85* ⊙ *Apr.–Oct., daily 10–6 or dusk; Nov.–Mar., Wed.–Sun. 10–4.*

> **OFF THE**
> **BEATEN**
> **PATH**

Where to Stay & Eat

£££–££££ ✕ **Riverside Restaurant.** Part of the King's Lynn Arts Centre, this restaurant reflects the style of the original 15th-century warehouse, with its gnarled oak beams and redbrick walls. Lunches might include local mussels or fresh salmon; dinner is more elaborate, perhaps lobster and brandy soup followed by game casserole. When the weather allows, there are tables outside, overlooking the river. ✉ *27 King St.* ☎ *01553/773134* ▭ *MC, V* ⊙ *Closed Sun. and national holiday Mon.*

£££££ ✕▦ **Congham Hall.** Parkland surrounds this lovely Georgian manor house, 6 mi east of King's Lynn. Neutral colors and traditional print fabrics keep the bedrooms light and airy. Food is taken seriously here—the hotel grows the herbs and vegetables used in the kitchen, smokes its own fish, and collects honey. Cromer crab, Norfolk pheasant, and King's Lynn shrimp all appear on the menu (two-course menu £33.50). ✉ *A148, Grimston PE32 1AH* ☎ *01485/600250* 🖷 *01485/601191* ⊕ *www.conghamhallhotel.co.uk* 🛏 *12 rooms, 2 suites* ⚫ *Restaurant, lounge, babysitting, meeting rooms, helipad, some pets allowed, kennel, no-smoking rooms; no a/c* ▭ *AE, DC, MC, V* ¶⊙ *BP.*

£££ ▦ **Elizabeth Duke's Head.** The location couldn't be better: wake up on Tuesday morning and the front rooms at the pink-washed Duke's Head have prime views of the market below in full swing. In the oldest, 17th-century part of the hotel, where age bows the main staircase, no two guest rooms are alike. The floorboards may be creaky, but each room has comfortable beds and armchairs. ✉ *Tuesday Market Pl., PE30 1JS* ☎ *01553/774996* 🖷 *01553/763556* ⊕ *www.elizabethhotels.co.uk* 🛏 *70 rooms, 1 suite* ⚫ *2 restaurants, room TVs with movies, some in-room data ports, 2 bars, lounge, some pets allowed (fee), meeting rooms, no-smoking rooms; no a/c* ▭ *AE, MC, V* ¶⊙ *BP.*

Nightlife & the Arts

St. George's Guildhall is the venue for much of the **King's Lynn Festival** (☎ 01553/767557 ⊕ www.kl-festival.freeserve.co.uk), which takes place in July and encompasses concerts, exhibitions, theater, dance, films, literary events, and children's programs. The **Corn Exchange** (✉ Tuesday Market Pl. ☎ 01553/764864), a splendidly revamped 19th-century building, hosts concerts, theater, comedy, and crafts events.

LINCOLN, BOSTON & STAMFORD

The fens of northern Cambridgeshire pass imperceptibly into the three divisions of Lincolnshire: Holland, Kesteven, and Lindsey are all parts of the great county, divided administratively. Holland borders the Isle of Ely and the Soke of Peterborough. This marshland spreads far and wide south of the Wash. The chief attractions are two towns: Lincoln,

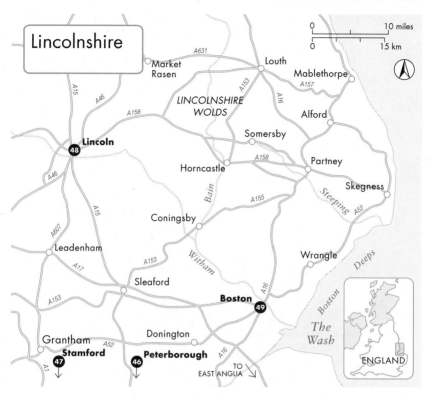

Lincolnshire

with its magnificent cathedral, and Stamford, to the southwest. En route to Lincoln is Peterborough, with its medieval cathedral.

The countryside around Lincoln, especially the Lincolnshire Wolds (chalk hills) to the northeast, consists of hills and copses, with dry-stone (unmortared) walls dividing well-tended fields. The unspoiled rural area of the Wolds is particularly worth a visit, whereas the long coastline with its miles of sandy beaches and its North Sea air has all the usual, if occasionally tacky, seaside facilities for families.

Peterborough

46 *22 mi southwest of King's Lynn, 38 mi north of Cambridge.*

Peterborough's main attraction, the cathedral, is best seen on a day trip from Cambridge. Much of the pedestrianized city center is marred by the commercial shopping center, the Queensgate.

The third building to rise on the site, **Peterborough Cathedral** was begun in 1118, and its history reflects some key events in English history. The first church was founded in 655 by Peada, a nobleman from the early English kingdom of Mercia in central Britain. It was destroyed by the Danes in 870 and reconstructed in 972, only to be burned down again, this time by mistake, in 1116. The next incarnation, consecrated in 1238 after 120 years of building, still towers over Peterborough. It has seen its fair share of strife, including occupation by Cromwell's forces, who fired muskets into the ceiling and broke most of the statues, stained-glass windows, choir stalls, and high altar. Although the cathedral has been left with few monuments, the result is a startlingly spacious interior into which light streams through the clear glass.

Three soaring arches, each 85 feet high, mark the outstanding west front. In the peaks of their gables are the figures of St. Peter, St. Paul, and St. Andrew. Inside, the nave ceiling, dating from 1220, is one of the most significant examples of Romanesque painting in Europe—note the monsters as well as figures of saints, bishops, and kings. Henry VIII buried Catherine of Aragon, his first wife, here after her death (by natural causes) in 1536. The last addition to the cathedral is the exquisitely vaulted New Building, built between 1496 and 1508. An exhibit in the north transept depicts the life of the cathedral throughout its long history.

In the Deanery gardens (seen by tour only), 18th- and 19th-century buildings surround an early Victorian garden. Tout Hill, the remains of a Norman fortification, is in the gardens. ⊠ *Little Prior's Gate, 12A Minster Precinct* ☎ *01733/355315* ⊕ *www.peterborough-cathedral.org.uk* 🎫 *Donation (£3.50) requested; tour £3.50, tower £4.50, garden £3.50* ⊙ *Weekdays 9–5, Sat. 9–3, Sun. 7:30–3.*

The **Peterborough Museum and Art Gallery,** a short walk from the cathedral, explores the history of Peterborough from the Jurassic period to the modern day, including both natural and social history. The art gallery displays contemporary art and crafts. ⊠ *Priestgate* ☎ *01733/343329* ⊕ *www.peterboroughheritage.org.uk* 🎫 *Free* ⊙ *Tues.–Sat. 10–5, Sun. noon–4.*

Stamford

47 *14 mi northwest of Peterborough, 47 mi northwest of Cambridge.*

Serene, honey-hued Stamford, on a hillside overlooking the River Welland, has a well-preserved center, in part because in 1967 it was designated England's first conservation area. This unspoiled town, which grew rich in the medieval wool and cloth trades, is a delightful place to study the harmonious mixture of Georgian and medieval architecture.

★ **Burghley House,** an architectural masterpiece that many consider the grandest house of the first Elizabethan age, is celebrated for its roof-scape bristling with pepper-pot chimneys and slate-roof towers. It was built between 1565 and 1587 to the design of William Cecil, first Baron Burghley, when he was Elizabeth I's high treasurer; his descendants still occupy the house. The interior was remodeled in the late 17th century with treasures from Europe. The house contains 18 sumptuous state rooms, with carvings by Grinling Gibbons and ceiling paintings by Antonio Verrio (including the dramatic Heaven Room and the Hell Staircase), as well as innumerable paintings and priceless porcelain. There's an 80-minute guided tour of the house on weekdays, or you can tour at your own pace on weekends. In the 18th century Capability Brown landscaped the grounds (where deer now roam and open-air Shakespeare and opera are staged in summer) creating the lake, the Lion Bridge, and the Gothic Revival Orangery, where you can have tea or lunch. The house was used in the 2005 filming of *Pride and Prejudice* and a recent chatelain, the sixth marquess of Exeter, was one of the Olympic runners whose life story inspired the 1981 film *Chariots of Fire*. In early September Burghley is host to the international Burghley Horse Trials. The house is a mile southeast of Stamford. ⊠ *Off A1* ☎ *01780/752451* ⊕ *www.burghley. co.uk* ⊠ *£8.20* ☽ *Apr.–Oct., Sat.–Thurs. 11–5.*

Lincoln

★ **48** *93 mi northwest of Cambridge, 97 mi northwest of Norwich, 53 mi north of Stamford.*

Celts, Romans, and Danes all had important settlements here, but it was the Normans who gave Lincoln its medieval stature after William the Conqueror founded Lincoln Castle as a stronghold in 1068. Four years later William appointed Bishop Remigius to run the huge diocese stretching from the Humber to the Thames, resulting in the construction of Lincoln Cathedral, the third largest in England after York Minster and St. Paul's. Since medieval times Lincoln's status has declined. However, its somewhat remote location (there are no major motorways or railways nearby) has helped preserve its traditional character.

In the city center you can walk under the 15th-century Stonebow arch on the site of an old Roman gate. Beyond the arch is the Guildhall, which houses the city's civic regalia. The River Witham flows unobtrusively under the incongruously named High Bridge, a low, vaulted Norman bridge topped by timber-frame houses from the 16th century. West of High Bridge, the river opens out into Brayford Pool, busy with river traffic and, less attractively, road traffic. Here you can rent different kinds of boats. From April through September cruisers show you the city from the River Witham (contact the Lincoln tourist office).

The cathedral is on the aptly named Steep Hill; to its south, narrow medieval streets cling to the hillside and invite exploration. Jew's House, on the Strait, dating from the early 12th century, is one of several well-preserved domestic buildings in this area.

★ Lincoln's crowning glory, the great **Cathedral of St. Mary,** was for hundreds of years the tallest building in Europe, but this magnificent medieval building is now among the least known of European cathedrals. The Norman bishop Remigius began work in 1072. The Romanesque church he built was irremediably damaged, first by fire, then by earthquake (in 1185), but you can still see parts of the ancient structure at the west front. The next great phase of building, initiated by Bishop Hugh of Avalon, is mainly 13th century in character. The west front, topped by two strikingly tall towers, gives tremendous breadth to the entrance. It is best seen from the 14th-century Exchequer Gate arch in front of the cathedral, or from the castle battlements beyond.

Inside, a breathtaking impression of space and unity belies the many centuries of building and rebuilding. The stained-glass window at the north end of the transept, known as the Dean's Eye, undergoing restoration, is one of the earliest (13th-century) traceried windows, whereas its opposite number at the south end shows a 14th-century sophistication in its interlaced designs. ■ TIP→ **Look for the Lincoln Imp upon the pillar nearest St. Hugh's shrine; an angel turned this creature to stone, according to legend.** Through a door on the north side is the chapter house, a 10-sided building that sometimes housed the medieval Parliament of England during the reigns of Edward I and Edward II. The chapter house is connected to the 13th-century cloister, notable for its amusing ceiling bosses. The cathedral library, a restrained building by Christopher Wren, was built onto the north side of the cloisters after the original library collapsed. Tours of the cathedral roof are fascinating. ⊠ *Minster Yard* ☎ *01522/544544* ⊕ *www.lincolncathedral.com* ⊠ *£4* ☉ *June–Aug., daily 7:15 AM–8 PM; Sept.–May, daily 7:15–6. Guided tours Oct.–Feb., daily at 11 and 2; Mar.–Sept., daily at 11, 1, and 3; roof tours weekdays at 2, Sat. 11 and 2.*

> **A STAND-IN ROLE**
>
> The dean of Lincoln's cathedral called *The Da Vinci Code*, the best-selling novel by Dan Brown, "a load of old tosh" but agreed to let parts of the movie be filmed there. In return, producers donated £100,000. The cathedral doubles for Westminster Abbey in the film. The real Westminster Abbey refused permission to film, though it has since announced *Da Vinci Code*-themed lectures and printed leaflets.

NEED A BREAK? After climbing Steep Hill, you'll need at least one of the 23 different teas or 15 coffees available at **Pimento** (⊠ 26/27 Steep St. ☎ 01522/569333). Choose a cake or snack to go along with your pick-me-up.

The **Minster Yard,** which surrounds the cathedral on three sides, contains buildings of different periods, including graceful Georgian architecture. A statue of Alfred, Lord Tennyson, who was born in Lincolnshire, stands on the green near the chapter house. The **Medieval Bishop's Palace,** on the south side of Minster Yard, has a garden and exhibits about the former administrative center of the diocese. ⊠ *Minster Yard* ☎ *01522/527468* ⊕ *www.english-heritage.org.uk* ⊠ *£3.60* ☉ *July and Aug., daily 10–6; Apr.–June, Sept., and Oct., daily 10–5; Nov.–Mar., Thurs.–Mon. 10–4.*

☾ **Lincoln Castle,** facing the cathedral across Exchequer Gate, was built on two great mounds by William the Conqueror in 1068, incorporating part of the remains of Roman garrison walls. The castle was a military base until the 17th century, after which it operated as a prison. In the extraordinary prison chapel you can see the cagelike stalls in which Victorian convicts listened to sermons. ■ TIP→ **One of the four surviving copies of the Magna Carta, signed by King John at Runnymede in 1215, is on display in the same building.** ⊠ *Castle Hill* ☎ *01522/511068* ⊕ *www.*

lincolnshire.gov.uk/lincolncastle ⌷ *£3.70* ⊙ *Apr.–Oct., Mon.–Sat. 9:30–5:30, Sun. 11–5:30; Nov.–Mar., Mon.–Sat. 9:30–4, Sun. 11–4.*

The Collection is made up of the **Usher Gallery,** an art gallery with paintings by Turner, Lowry, and Hitchens as well as some more contemporary works, and the modern **Archaeology Collection** next door, an interactive museum with a sound installation, games to play, and local artifacts spanning 3,000 years of history. Look out for good temporary exhibitions at the Usher Gallery. ⊠ *Danes Terr.* ☎ *01522/550990* ⊕ *www.thecollection.lincoln.museum* ⌷ *Free* ⊙ *Daily 10–5.*

Where to Stay & Eat

£££££ ✕ **Jew's House.** This intimate restaurant, with restrained tones and open stonework, is in one of Lincoln's oldest buildings, a rare survivor of 12th-century Norman domestic architecture that was originally the home of a Jewish merchant. The cosmopolitan fixed-price menu of continental specialties changes daily, and the restaurant is renowned for its fresh fish and rich desserts, all homemade. ⊠ *15 The Strait* ☎ *01522/524851* ⊟ *AE, DC, MC, V* ⊙ *Closed Sun. and Mon.*

££–£££ ✕ **Brown's Pie Shop.** More than you might imagine from the modest name, Brown's Pie Shop serves the best of traditional English cuisine: succulent beef, great puddings, and, of course, some very good, freshly made savory pies. ⊠ *33 Steep Hill* ☎ *01522/527330* ⊟ *AE, MC, V.*

££–£££ ✕ **Wig and Mitre.** This interesting downtown pub-café-restaurant stays open from 8 AM until 11 PM, with everything from breakfast to full evening meals. Produce comes from the local markets, and dishes may include crusted rack of lamb or venison with smoked bacon. ⊠ *30 Steep Hill* ☎ *01522/535190* ⊟ *AE, DC, MC, V.*

★ **£££–££££** ⌂ **White Hart.** Luxuriously furnished with a wealth of antiques, among them some fine clocks and china, the establishment has been a hotel for 600 years. Bedrooms are individually decorated in traditional style; many are outfitted with antiques and hardwoods such as walnut and mahogany abound. ⊠ *Bailgate, LN1 3AR* ☎ *01522/526222* ⊟ *01522/531798* ⊕*www.whitehart-lincoln.co.uk* ⇱*36 rooms, 12 suites* ⌕ *Restaurant, room service, some in-room data ports, bar, lounge, babysitting, dry cleaning, laundry service, meeting rooms, some pets allowed (fee), no-smoking rooms; no a/c* ⊟ *AE, MC, V* ⌸ *BP.*

££–£££ ⌂ **Bailhouse & Mews.** In a 14th-century Baronial hall near the cathedral, the welcoming Bailhouse & Mews offers good value accommodation, with four-poster beds in some rooms and plenty of antique features, such as flagstones and wooden beams. The gardens have a swimming pool and a stone chapel and you can help yourself to tea or coffee at any time from the kitchen. The hotel also has two self-catering cottages available in the grounds. ⊠ *34 Bailgate, LN1 3AP* ☎ *01522/520883* ⊟ *01522 521829* ⊕ *www.bailhouse.co.uk* ⇱ *10 rooms, 2 cottages* ⌕ *Wi-Fi, pool, lounge, no-smoking; no a/c* ⊟ *MC, V* ⌸ *BP.*

Nightlife & the Arts

The **Theatre Royal** (⊠ Clasketgate ☎ 01522/525555), a fine Victorian theater, previews shows before their London runs and hosts touring productions. Concerts are occasionally given on Sunday.

Shopping

Chain stores fill the Bailgate Mall and High Street. The best stores, however, are on Bailgate, Steep Hill, and the medieval streets leading directly down from the cathedral and castle. Just off Steep Hill, **The Cheese Society** (⊠ 1 St Martins La. ☎ 01522/511003) has a great selection of English and French cheeses and an attached café. **Cobb Hall Craft Centre** (⊠ St. Paul's La., off Bailgate), a small mall of crafts shops and workshops, sells clocks, candles, and ornaments. **David Hansord** (⊠ Castle Hill ☎ 01522/530044) specializes in antiques, especially scientific instruments. Steep Hill has good bookstores, antiques shops, and crafts and art galleries, including **Harding House Galleries** (⊠ Steep Hill ☎ 01522/523537).

Boston

 *31 mi southeast of Lincoln.*

This town on the River Witham prospered during the Middle Ages because of the wool trade with Flanders, and revived in the late 18th century after the fens were drained. It was from Boston that, in 1630, a group of Puritans including John Winthrop (the first governor of the Massachusetts Bay colony) set sail in search of religious freedom. They soon founded the Massachusetts city of the same name.

The town's leading landmark is the Boston Stump, the lantern tower of the 14th-century **Church of St. Botolph** (⊠ 1 Wormgate ☎ 01205/362992). With a height of 288 feet, the tower can be seen for 20 mi from both land and sea; it once housed a light that not only guided ships coming to the old port but also directed wayfarers crossing the treacherous marsh. Today it's also a directional beacon for aircraft.

The 15th-century guildhall, now the **Guildhall Museum,** contains the courtroom where the Pilgrims were tried and the cells where they were held. It is closed until late 2007 or early 2008; call for new opening information. ⊠ *St. Mary's Guildhall, South St.* ☎ *01205/365954.*

EAST ANGLIA ESSENTIALS

Transportation

BY AIR

Norwich International Airport serves domestic and European destinations. For information about Stansted Airport in Essex, north of London, *see* Airports *in* Smart Travel Tips.

🛫 **Norwich International Airport** ⊠ A140, Norwich ☎ 01603/428700 ⊕ www.norwichinternational.com.

BY BUS

National Express serves the region from London's Victoria Coach Station. Average travel times: 2½ hours to Bury St. Edmunds, 2 hours to Cambridge, 2 hours to Colchester, 4 hours to Lincoln, and 3 hours to Norwich. Information about local Norfolk service and county service is available from the Norfolk Bus Information Centre. First buses serve parts of the region. The largest bus company is Stagecoach. Traveline can answer public transportation questions.

CUTTING COSTS A FirstTourist ticket (available on the bus) from First gives a day's unlimited travel on the whole network for £9; a family pass for two parents and two children costs £20. Stagecoach sells Megarider tickets (£5) for seven days' travel within Cambridge.

FARES & SCHEDULES ▮ **First** ☎ 01603/760076 ⊕ www.firstgroup.com. **National Express** ☎ 0870/580–8080 ⊕ www.nationalexpress.com. **Norfolk Bus Information Centre** ☎ 0845/300–6116. **Stagecoach** ☎ 01223/423554 ⊕ www.stagecoachbus.com/cambridge. **Traveline** ☎ 0870/608–2608 ⊕ www.traveline.org.uk.

BY CAR

From London, Cambridge (54 mi) is off M11. At Exit 9, M11 connects with A11 to Norwich (114 mi); A14 off A11 goes to Bury St. Edmunds. A12 from London goes through east Suffolk via Colchester and Ipswich. For Lincoln (131 mi), take A1 via Huntingdon, Peterborough, and Grantham to A46 at Newark-on-Trent. A more scenic alternative is to leave A1 at Grantham and take A607 to Lincoln.

East Anglia has few fast main roads. The principal routes are those mentioned above. Once off the A roads, traveling within the region often means taking country lanes that have many twists and turns.

BY TRAIN

The entire region is served by trains from London's Liverpool Street station; in addition, there are trains to Cambridge, Ely, Lincoln, and Peterborough from King's Cross Station. Full information on trains to East Anglia is available from National Rail Enquiries. Average travel times are one hour to Colchester, 50–90 minutes to Cambridge, almost 2 hours and 50 minutes to Norwich, and 2 hours to Lincoln.

CUTTING COSTS An Anglia Plus Three-Day Pass costs $22 and allows unlimited travel in Norfolk, Suffolk, and part Cambridgeshire on any three days in a week.

FARES & SCHEDULES ▮ **Anglia Plus Three-Day Pass** ☎ 0845/6007245. **National Rail Enquiries** ☎ 0845/748–4950 ⊕ www.nationalrail.co.uk.

Contacts & Resources

EMERGENCIES

▮ **Ambulance, fire, police** ☎ 999. **Addenbrooke's Hospital** ✉ Hill's Rd., Cambridge ☎ 01223/245151. **Norfolk and Norwich Hospital** ✉ Brunswick Rd., Norwich ☎ 01603/286286.

INTERNET

Internet cafés are much less frequent in East Anglia than in larger cities, though an increasing number of hotels offer free Wi-Fi. Cambridge and Norwich, as university cities, both have a good number of Internet cafés, however. Public libraries usually also offer Internet access.

TOUR OPTIONS

BUS TOURS City Sightseeing operates open-top bus tours of Cambridge—the Backs, the colleges, the Imperial War Museum in Duxford, and the Grafton shopping center. Tours start from Cambridge train station but can be picked up at marked bus stops throughout the city. Buy tickets from the driver, the City Sightseeing office at Cambridge train station, or the Cambridge Tourist Information Centre for £8. Tours run mid-April–September, every 15 minutes, and October to mid-April, every 20 or 30 minutes. From June to the first week of September, hourlong tours run through Colchester daily from 10 to 6 for £5. Tours depart from the castle hourly. The 45-minute Norwich tour starts at St. Peter's Street outside City Hall, with several pick-up points. Tours (£6) run April–through October and leave on the hour from 10 to 4.

🏛 **City Sightseeing** ✉ Cambridge train station ☎ 01708/866000 ⊕ www.city-sightseeing.com 🖂 Colchester Castle ☎ 01708/866000 🖂 St Peter's St., Norwich ☎ 01263/587005.

WALKING TOURS Qualified guides for walking tours of the major towns, including Bury St. Edmunds, Cambridge, Ely, Colchester, Norwich, and Lincoln, can be booked through the respective tourist offices (⇨ Visitor Information). Those in Cambridge are particularly popular; book well in advance for tours (£8) that depart at 1:30 year-round and more frequently in summer. Ninety-minute audio tours of Lavenham are available for rental from the Lavenham Pharmacy, 99 High Street for £3.

VISITOR INFORMATION

🏛 **East of England Tourist Board** ✉ Toppesfield Hall, Market Pl., Hadleigh IP7 5DN ☎ 0870/225-4800 🖨 0870/225-4890 ⊕ www.visiteastofengland.com. **Broads Authority** ✉ 18 Colegate, Norwich NR3 1BQ ☎ 01603/610734 ⊕ www.broads-authority. gov.uk. **Aldeburgh** ✉ 152 High St., IP15 5AQ ☎ 01728/453637 ⊕ www.suffolkcoastal. gov.uk. **Boston** ✉ Market Pl. ☎ 01205/356656 ⊕ www.boston.gov.uk. **Bury St. Edmunds** ✉ 6 Angel Hill ☎ 01284/764667 ⊕ www.stedmundsbury.gov.uk. **Cambridge** ✉ Wheeler St., CB2 3QB ☎ 0871/226-8006, or 44/1223/464732 from abroad ⊕ www. visitcambridge.org. **Cambridge University** ⊕ www.cam.ac.uk. **Colchester** ✉ 1 Queen St. ☎ 01206/282920 ⊕ www.visitcolchester.co.uk. **Ely** ✉ Oliver Cromwell's House, 29 St. Mary's St., CB7 4HF ☎ 01353/662062 ⊕ www.ely.org.uk. **King's Lynn** ✉ The Custom House, Purfleet Quay, PE30 1HP ☎ 01553/763044 ⊕ www.west-norfolk.gov.uk. **Lavenham** ✉ Lady St. ☎ 01787/248207 ⊕ www.babergh-south-suffolk.gov.uk. **Lincoln** ✉ 9 Castle Hill ☎ 01522/873213 ⊕ www.lincoln.gov.uk. **Norwich** ✉ Forum, between N. Theatre and Bethel Sts. ☎ 01603/666071 ⊕ www.visitnorwich.co.uk. **Peterborough** ✉ 3 Minster Precincts, PE1 1XS ☎ 01733/452336 ⊕ www.visitpeterborough.com. **Saffron Walden** ✉ 1 Market Pl., Market Sq. ☎ 01799/510444 ⊕ www.uttlesford.gov.uk. **Southwold** ✉ 69 High St. ☎ 01502/724729. **Stamford** ✉ Stamford Arts Centre, St. Marys St. ☎ 01780/755611. **Sudbury** ✉ Town Hall, Market Hill ☎ 01787/881320 ⊕ www.babergh-south-suffolk.gov.uk. **Wells-next-the-Sea** ✉ Staithe St., NR23 1AN ☎ 01328/710885. **Woodbridge** ✉ Station Buildings ☎ 01394/382240 ⊕ www.suffolkcoastal.gov.uk.

Yorkshire

LEEDS, BRADFORD, HAWORTH, YORK,
WHITBY, CASTLE HOWARD

WORD OF MOUTH

"Evensong at York Minster is beautiful, so plan around it. Go early enough that you get to sit in the Choir, where you can see (as well as hear) everything that goes on—I'm guessing that being in the queue 15–20 minutes early should be fine."

—leonberger

"Robin Hood's Bay is very picturesque. No cars are allowed down the very steep main street . . . leave it at the top of the hill. Wear flat shoes! Don't just walk along the main street, but explore the little alleys. A path runs along the coastline. . . . An hour or so is all you will need, unless you get waylaid by the teashops."

—Morgana

Updated by
Christi
Daugherty

A HAUNTINGLY BEAUTIFUL REGION, Yorkshire is known for its wide–open spaces and dramatic landscapes that outlasted the blast of the Industrial Revolution in manufacturing towns such as Leeds and Bradford. The hills of the moors and dales glow pink with heather in summer, and turn black with it in winter. Hearty fishing villages and ruined monasteries cling to the edges of cliffs in one of England's last remaining wildernesses. Two of the region's biggest attractions are the result of human endeavor: the towering cathedral in medieval York and the sites associated with the Brontë sisters in the town of Haworth.

The most rugged land is the North York Moors, a vast, lonely area free of fences, and dotted with the fluffy sheep who wander at will in summer. (It is said that if the grazing sheep ever disappeared, the ancient forests would return.) Though the landscape is stunning in the summer sun, glowering storms can sweep across the moors from out of nowhere, leaving you lucky if you can see as far as the next cloud-swept ridge. Between the bleak moors and the rocky Pennine hills lie lush, green valleys known as the Yorkshire Dales, where the high rainfall produces luxuriant vegetation, swift rivers, sparkling streams, and waterfalls. The villages here, immortalized in the books of the late veterinarian Alf Wight (1916–95)—who wrote under the name James Herriot—are wonderfully peaceful, only bursting into life in summer as hundreds of hikers (or "ramblers" as they're known in England) appear over the hills.

The area is not all green fields and perfect villages—there's also a gritty, urban aspect to Yorkshire, whose manufacturing towns changed the course of British history. In West Yorkshire, once down-at-the-heels Leeds has remade itself with trendy restaurant and cafés, and its buzzing music industry and nightlife scene. Quieter and smaller, the walled city of York, dominated by Britain's most noble cathedral, York Minster Cathedral, is genteel, and as filled with history as it is with tourists.

Yorkshire is a big, diverse region, difficult to explore in a small amount of time. Those with limited time could visit York as a day trip from London; the fastest trains take just two hours. Proper exploration of the region—especially of the countryside—requires time and effort. But it's well worth it. This is the path less traveled.

Exploring Yorkshire

Yorkshire is the largest English region to explore (its fiercely proud inhabitants would say the only English region *worth* exploring). The industrial heartland is West Yorkshire, with the cities of Leeds and Bradford. What the tourist office likes to call Brontë Country—basically Haworth, home of the Brontë family—is just to the northwest, and northward spread the hills, valleys, and villages of the Yorkshire Dales, stomping ground of the late James Herriot, the much-loved writer. In the center of the region, York deserves special attention, as do its environs, from the spa town of Harrogate to magnificent Fountains Abbey.

Moving east to the coast, Yorkshire reveals itself to be a seaside holiday destination, although never one that will win prizes for summer-like weather. But fine beaches and a fascinating history await you in the

GREAT ITINERARIES

You could drive across Yorkshire in less than a day (as many do, on the way to Scotland), but you would have little time to sightsee. Three days allows a night in York, followed by a night in rural Yorkshire. However, with five to seven days you could stop longer in York and visit the coast, as well as get off the beaten track.

Numbers in the text correspond to numbers in the margin and on the Yorkshire and York maps.

IF YOU HAVE 3 DAYS

Start in ▣ **York** ⑫-㉕ ▸, the quintessential city of Yorkshire, and see several of the main medieval city sites, such as York Minster and the Shambles. Then head out to spectacular **Castle Howard** ⑩. Return to York about 4:30 in the afternoon and repair to Betty's tearoom. Next morning, continue to see York sights and then travel to Leeds to pick up a bus to ▣ **Haworth** ④ for a Brontë pilgrimage. (If you have a car, you can make a quick visit to stunning **Studley Royal and Fountains Abbey** ㉘.) Spend your final day in Haworth. Return to Leeds.

IF YOU HAVE 7 DAYS

Spend a morning in ▣ **Leeds** ① ▸ before heading out to the model 19th-century community of **Saltaire**. It's just a short drive to ▣ **Haworth** ④ for an overnight stop in Brontë Country; see the sights in the morning. After this, meander up through the Yorkshire Dales, via **Skipton** ⑥ before stopping for the night in ▣ **Grassington** ⑦. The next day, soak up more remote scenery as you tour the northern dales, Wensleydale, and Swaledale before hitting the main roads and heading south, via **Studley Royal and Fountains Abbey** ㉘, to the spa town of ▣ **Harrogate** ㉖. After all this driving, you have only a short journey to York the following day. Stay in ▣ **York** ⑫-㉕ for two nights, and then early on the morning of departure, aim for **Helmsley** ㊳ with a sightseeing stop at **Rievaulx Abbey** ㊴ and **Castle Howard** ⑩ before driving across the moors ▣ **Whitby** ㉟ for your overnight stop. The next day, return to York after a drive along the coast via **Robin Hood's Bay** ㉞ and **Scarborough** ㉝.

resort of Scarborough, the former whaling port of Whitby, and Robin Hood's Bay—a cliff-top, onetime smuggler's haunt. Finally, you can strike inland to the North York Moors National Park. Isolated stone villages, moorland walks, Rievaulx Abbey, and elegant Castle Howard are within easy reach.

About the Restaurants

Generally speaking, Yorkshire is not known for its cuisine, and bacon-based breakfasts and pork pies do tend to pale fairly quickly. Luckily, in the larger towns and cities, particularly in Leeds, a foodie culture has developed. Indian restaurants (called "curry restaurants") are very good in the north, particularly in and around Bradford. Out in the country-side, pubs are your best bet for dining. Many offer excellent home-cooked food and locally produced meat (especially lamb) and vegetables. Roast beef dinners generally come with Yorkshire pudding, the tasty, light bread that is called a popover in the United States and Canada. It's generally served with lots of gravy. Be sure to sample local cheeses, especially Wensleydale, which has a delicate flavor and honeyed aftertaste.

About the Hotels

Traditional hotels are limited primarily to major towns and cities; those in the country tend to be guesthouses. Many of the better guesthouses are at the edge of town, but some proprietors will pick you up at the main station if you're relying on public transportation—verify before booking.

Rooms fill quickly at seaside resorts in July and August, and some places in the moors and dales close in winter. Always call ahead to make sure a hotel is open and has space available. Hikers and budgeteers love the region's unique hostels. Many in this stretch of the country are in historic buildings, with views that even the most expensive hotels can't replicate, but you'll have to rough it. Tourist offices have reservation numbers and details on the best hostel options.

WHAT IT COSTS In pounds				
	££££££	££££	£££	££	£
RESTAURANTS	over £22	£18–£22	£13–£17	£7–£12	under £7
HOTELS	over £160	£120–£160	£90–£120	£60–£90	under £60

Restaurant prices are for a main course at dinner. Hotel prices are for two people in a standard double room in high season, including V.A.T., with no meals or, if indicated, CP (with continental breakfast), BP (Breakfast Plan, with full breakfast), or MAP (Modified American Plan, with breakfast and dinner).

Timing

To see the heather at its lushest, visit in summer (and be prepared for some chilly days). It's also the best time for the coast, when colorful regattas and arts festivals are under way. York Minster makes a splendid focal point for the prestigious York Early Music Festival in early July. Spring and fall bring their own rewards: far fewer crowds and crisp, clear days, although with an increased risk of rain and fog. The harsh winter is hard to call: with glistening snow and bright days, the coast, moors, and dales are beautiful, but storms and blizzards set in quickly. The tiny moorland roads become impassable, and villages can be cut off entirely. In winter, stick to York and the main towns.

WEST YORKSHIRE & BRONTË COUNTRY

The busy city of Leeds, easily reached from the west by the trans-Pennine M62 and from the south by the M1, provides an obvious starting point to a tour of West Yorkshire. From there you can strike out for the traditional wool towns, such as Saltaire, a UNESCO-protected gem, and the Magna museum at Rotherham, which draws long lines for its surprisingly interesting exploration of steel. But the main thrust of any visit to West Yorkshire is to the west of Leeds, where the gaunt hills north of the Calder Valley and south of the River Aire form the district im-

TOP REASONS TO GO

York Minster: The largest Gothic cathedral in England helps make York, which retains its ancient walls and narrow streets, one of the country's most-visited towns. The building's history is told in its crypt, brilliantly converted into a museum.

North York Moors: There's enough space for walkers to experience isolation amid the heather-covered hills that glow crimson and purple in late summer and early fall. Make way for the passing sheep.

Rievaulx Abbey: Heading down the tiny lane that leads to the ruins of one of the great Cistercian abbeys only serves to make it all more dramatic when the abbey's soaring arches appear out of the trees.

Whitby: This bustling coastal town set against a cliff was where Bram Stoker came to write *Dracula*. It comes into itself at night, when its gloomy clifftop church and skeletal abbey ruins loom over Whitby dramatically.

Robin Hood's Bay: Test your balance on the steep roads of this seaside village set in a ravine, and then breathe easy on the miles of outstanding beach.

mortalized by the mournful writings of the Brontë sisters. Haworth, an otherwise gray village, might have faded into obscurity were it not for the magnetism of the literary sisters. Every summer, thousands toil up the steep main street to visit their home town, but to truly understand their writing you need to go farther afield to the ruined farm of Top Withins, which is by legend, if not fact, Wuthering Heights.

Leeds

► ❶ *43 mi northeast of Manchester, 25 mi southwest of York.*

It may be one of the cultural centers of the north, but Leeds is still living down a reputation as a grim, northern industrial town. However, since 1990, the city has successfully transformed itself with green spaces and regenerations. Its Victorian buildings have been polished and restored, its old factories and warehouses converted into pricey loft housing and modern offices. Everywhere are cafés with outdoor tables defying the northern weather, sleek, modern bars and hotels, and upscale restaurants. Leeds University keeps the town young and hip, supporting the city's good music shops and funky clothing and jewelry boutiques.

One of the best examples of Victorian architecture is **City Square,** right in front of the train station. Busy streets surround the pedestrianized oasis where benches make a good place to get your bearings as you take in the 19th-century statues. On the east side is the 18th-century Mill Hill Chapel.

Park Row is an impressive row of restored 19th-century office buildings that leads to the fine, classical **Town Hall** (⊠ The Headrow ☎ 0113/247–8384). Built in 1853, the building, with its stone lions, enormous

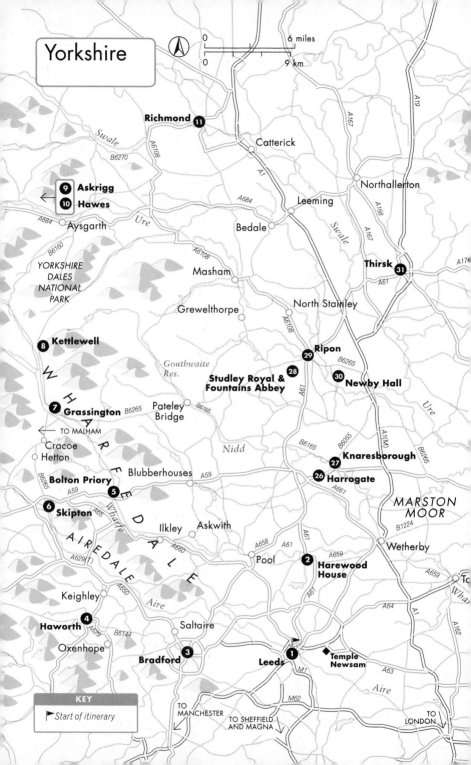

Yorkshire

0 — 6 miles
0 — 9 km

Richmond ⑪

Catterick

Northallerton

⑨ **Askrigg**
⑩ **Hawes**

Aysgarth

Swale

Leeming

Bedale

Ure

Thirsk ㉛

**YORKSHIRE
DALES
NATIONAL
PARK**

Masham

North Stainley

Grewelthorpe

⑧ **Kettlewell**

*Gouthwaite
Res.*

Ripon ㉙
㉘ **Studley Royal &
Fountains Abbey**

㉚ **Newby Hall**

⑦ **Grassington**

Pateley
Bridge

Nidd

Ure

← TO MALHAM

Cracoe
Hetton

Blubberhouses

Knaresborough ㉗

⑤

Bolton Priory

㉖ **Harrogate**

⑥ **Skipton**

Ilkley   Askwith

*MARSTON
MOOR*

AIREDALE

Pool

Wetherby

Keighley

Aire

② **Harewood
House**

*To
Wha*

④ **Haworth**

Saltaire

Oxenhope

③ **Bradford**

Leeds ①

◆ **Temple
Newsam**

Aire

TO
MANCHESTER

TO SHEFFIELD
AND MAGNA

TO
LONDON

KEY

▶ *Start of itinerary*

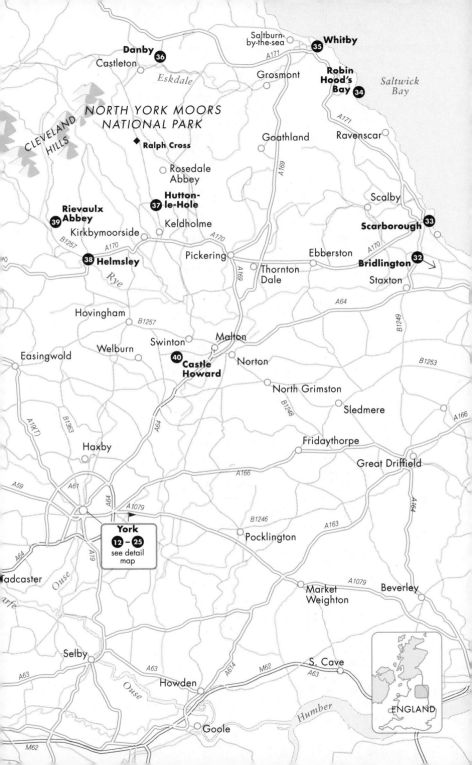

clock, sculptures, and massive columns, was the masterwork of local architect Cuthbert Broderick. Today it is a popular concert venue.

★ Next door to the Town Hall, the **City Art Gallery** is Yorkshire's most impressive art museum, with a strong core collection of works by Courbet, Sisley, Constable, Crome, and the internationally acclaimed Yorkshire sculptor Henry Moore, who studied at the Leeds School of Art. The graceful statue on the steps outside the gallery is Moore's *Reclining Woman.* More works by Moore are at the adjacent **Henry Moore Institute,** which also has regular exhibitions of modern sculpture. The **Craft Centre and Design Gallery,** also in the museum, exhibits and sells fine contemporary crafts. ⊠ *The Headrow* ☎ *0113/247–8248* ⊕ *www.leeds. gov.uk/artgallery* ⊠ *Free* ☉ *Mon., Tues., and Thurs.–Sat. 10–5, Wed. 10–8, Sun. 1–5.*

NEED A BREAK? | **Step down to the cozy, book-lined New Conservatory (⊠ The Albions, Albion Place, off Briggate ☎ 0113/246-1853) for fresh sandwiches, wraps, and cakes. You can also sit and relax with a cup of tea or coffee.**

Once the center of Leeds' decayed industrial area, two adjacent neighborhoods along the River Aire have been revitalized into a trendy area of pricey loft apartments, chic bars, and pleasant cafés. **Granary Wharf,** in the Canal Basin, reached via the Dark Arches where the River Aire flows under City Station, is a good place to go exploring design and crafts shops, music shops, and a regular festival market. **The Calls,** east of Granary Wharf by the river, has converted redbrick warehouses with more snazzy bars and restaurants that enliven the cobbled streets and quayside. This is definitely the area to wander at lunchtime, and when you're craving an afternoon coffee.

↻ Much of the vast, legendary arms and armor originally collected in the Tower of London fills the **Royal Armouries,** which occupies a redeveloped 13-acre dockland site, a 15-minute walk from the city center. Five theme galleries—War, Tournament, Self-Defense, Hunting, and Arms and Armor of the Orient—trace the history of weaponry. The state-of-the-art building is stunningly designed: expect a full-size elephant in armor, warriors on horseback, and floor-to-ceiling tents, as well as spirited interactive displays and live demonstrations. Shoot a crossbow, direct operations on a battlefield, experience a Wild West gunfight or an Elizabethan joust—it's your choice. ⊠ *Armouries Dr., off M1 or M621* ☎ *0113/ 220–1999* ⊕ *www.armouries.org.uk* ⊠ *Free* ☉ *Daily 10–5.*

The Leeds City Council uses **Temple Newsam,** a huge Elizabethan and Jacobean building, to display its impressive collections of furniture, paintings, and ceramics. The house was the birthplace in 1545 of Lord Darnley, the doomed husband of Mary, Queen of Scots. Surrounding the house is a public park with rose gardens, greenhouses, and miles of woodland walks, all originally laid out by Capability Brown in 1762. Temple Newsam is 4 mi east of Leeds on A63; Buses 18, 40, 88, and 163–165 leave from Leeds Central Bus Station every 30 minutes and stop at the Irwin Arms, a 10-minutes' walk from the site. ⊠ *Off Selby Rd.* ☎ *0113/264–7321* ⊕ *www.leeds.gov.uk/templenewsam* ⊠ *House*

£3.50, farm £3, joint ticket £5.50; parking £3.50 ⊘ Apr.–Oct., Tues.–Sun. and national holiday Mon. 10:30–5; Nov.–Mar., Tues.–Sun. and national holiday Mon. 10:30–4. Last admission 45 mins before closing.

Even the squeamish won't balk at the educational but entertaining exhibits in the **Thackray Medical Museum,** which present as much social as medical history. Interactive displays take you back to the slums of the 1840s, reveal the realities of surgery without anesthetics, and explore the experience of having a baby in Victorian times or today. The museum is a mile east of the city center and accessible by Buses 4, 4C, 42, 49, and 50. ⊠ *Beckett St.* ☏ *0113/244–4343* ⊕ *www.thackraymuseum. org* 🎟 *£5.50, parking £1* ⊘ *Daily 10–5; last admission 3.*

OFF THE BEATEN PATH

MAGNA – A 45-minute drive south from Leeds to Rotherham brings you squarely in view of Yorkshire's industrial past. The sheer scale of the former steelworks that houses Magna, a widely respected science museum, is impressive, but the power of the Big Melt show really hits the spot. Smoke, flames, and sparking electricity bring one of the original six arc furnaces roaring to life in a sound-and-light show. Steel workers lost their jobs in the 1970s and 1980s when the British coal and steel industries collapsed, and a permanent exhibit explores what happened to those workers afterwards. In summer, former steel workers give tours here. Four pavilions engagingly illustrate the elements of fire, earth, air, and water used in the production of steel. ⊠ *Junction 33 or 34 off M1, Sheffield Rd., Rotherham* ☏ *01709/720002* ⊕ *www.visitmagna.co.uk* 🎟 *£9* ⊘ *Daily 10–5.*

Where to Stay & Eat

£££££ ✕ **Pool Court at 42.** Elegant and tranquil, this restaurant in the revitalized warehouse district by the river is typical of the fashionable spots popular with northern food-fanciers. Good choices on the cosmopolitan contemporary menu include seafood and expertly prepared game, such as roasted pigeon with candied lemon and wild rice. Two-course meals go for £40; three courses cost £48. The adjacent, associated Brasserie Forty 4 (££–£££) is less formal and less expensive, but just as delicious. ⊠ *42–44 The Calls* ☏ *0113/244–4242, 0113/234–3232 Brasserie Forty 4* ▤ *AE, DC, MC, V* ⊘ *Closed Sun. No lunch Sat.*

£££–££££ ✕ **Anthony's.** This is the place that has been making the headlines. Based on the eclectic cuisine of the Fat Duck in Bray, this small, basement restaurant takes a lot of chances and is hugely rewarding to lovers of food fusion. Main courses change daily but can include risotto with white onion, espresso and Parmesan, or roasted duck with chocolate truffles. These unusual combinations work well in the formal, fine-dining setting. ⊠ *19 Boar La.* ☏ *0113/245–5922* ▤ *AE, DC, MC, V* ⊘ *Closed Sun. and Mon.*

££–£££ ✕ **Fourth Floor Restaurant.** If the Harvey Nichols department store has been a roaring success, it's partly because of the lure of its swank Fourth Floor eatery, a standout for both food and dramatic, high-tech design. The well-crafted modern British menu changes several times a week, but is sure to have stylish takes on dishes such as saffron risotto with spiced eggplant, char-grilled rib-eye steak, and the freshest lemon sole. ⊠ *Har-*

vey Nichols, 107–111 Briggate ☎ 0113/204–8000 ▤ AE, DC, MC, V ☉ No dinner Sun.–Wed.

£–££ ✕ **Whitelocks.** The city's oldest pub (1715), tucked away in an alley in the city center, recommends itself for traditional Yorkshire pudding and gravy, homemade pies, and real ale. The long, narrow bar has all the trappings of the Victorian era—stained glass, etched mirrors, copper-topped tables, and red plush banquettes. Service is brisk and friendly. ⊠ Turks Head Yard, off Briggate ☎ 0113/245–3950 ▤ AE, MC, V.

★ **£££–££££** ✕🏨 **Malmaison.** Passengers who used this building in its days as a tram and bus garage could hardly have envisioned its rebirth as a chic hotel exuding contemporary class and comfort. Guest rooms have color themes of subtle tones—plum, charcoal, yellow ocher—and are beautifully furnished with velvet pillows and floor-to-ceiling windows. The dark-panel brasserie (£££) concentrates on French food with a Mediterranean twist. ⊠ 1 Swinegate, LS1 4AG ☎ 0113/398–1000 🖷 0113/398–1002 ⊕ www.malmaison.com ⇱ 100 rooms ♨ Restaurant, cable TV, in-room broadband, gym, spa, bar, laundry service, meeting rooms ▤ AE, DC, MC, V.

£££££ 🏨 **42 The Calls.** This high-tech, high-comfort hotel in the trendy waterfront area was once an old grain mill. Each room shows creative flair but retains such original elements as skylights, exposed beams, and brickwork. Facilities are up-to-the-minute, including in-room CD players: some rooms even come with fishing rods (bring your own bait). ⊠ 42 The Calls, LS2 7EW ☎0113/244–0099 🖷0113/234–4100 ⊕www.the-calls.co.uk ⇱ 41 rooms ♨ 2 restaurants, room service, minibars, cable TV with movies, in-room broadband, bar, meeting rooms, some pets allowed, no-smoking rooms; no a/c ▤ AE, DC, MC, V.

££££ 🏨 **Quebecs.** The grand Leeds and County Liberal Club may have changed its identity when it became a boutique hotel, but the building has lost none of its Victorian verve. The sweeping oak staircase, lighted by tall stained-glass windows, leads up to classy bedrooms of different shapes and sizes, all sympathetically decorated in muted colors. The paneled Oak Room, an unusual circular design, is a must for a drink. Lower weekend rates include breakfast. ⊠ 9 Quebec St., LS1 2HA ☎ 0113/244–8989 🖷 0113/244–9090 ⊕ www.theetoncollection.com ⇱ 45 rooms, 6 suites ♨ Room service, in-room safes, minibars, cable TV, in-room broadband, bar, lounge, meeting rooms ▤ AE, DC, MC, V.

££ 🏨 **Aragon Hotel.** If you prefer to escape the rush of the city, one option is this late-19th-century gabled house with a large garden, a couple of miles from the city center. Chunky pine pieces furnish the colorful bedrooms, and breakfasts are excellent. The hotel is on the A61 Harrogate Road but set back from it. ⊠ 250 Stainbeck La., LS7 2PS ☎ 0113/275–9306 🖷 0113/275–7166 ⇱ 12 rooms ♨ Bar; no a/c, no smoking ▤ AE, DC, MC, V ﹖⃝ BP.

Nightlife & the Arts

NIGHTLIFE At fashionable café-bars all over Leeds, you can grab a bite or sip cappuccino or designer beer until late into the night. There's no shortage of clubs, either; Leeds has one of the best party scenes outside London. **The Atrium** (⊠ 6–9 The Grand Arcade ☎ 0113/242–6116) is the place for deep soul and funk. **Bar Norman** (⊠ 36 Call La. ☎ 0113/234–3988) has won the local in-crowd with its weird and wonderful design, including curved walls. Japanese food and music are other draws. The hot spot du jour is **brb@Call Lane** (⊠ 37 Call La. ☎ 0113/243–0315), where you can linger over a cocktail, snack on pizza, or catch its Monday film night. Upstairs the house music pounds out all night long. **Cuban Heels** (⊠ The Arches, 28–30 Assembly St. ☎ 0113/234–6115) kicks out salsa sounds most nights. **Mojo** (⊠ 18 Merrion St. ☎ 0113/244–6387) is a real rock-and-roll bar, with the music and the look to match.

THE ARTS   Opera North, a leading provincial opera company, has its home in Leeds at the **Grand Theatre** (⊠ 46 New Briggate ☎ 0113/222–6222); the opulent gold-and-plush auditorium is modeled on that of La Scala. Opera North also plays for free each summer at Temple Newsam.

The Victorian **Town Hall** (⊠ The Headrow ☎ 0113/224–3801) hosts an international concert season (October through May) that attracts top performers and conductors. In September it is the site of the fourth and final stage of the prestigious Leeds International Piano Competition.

The ultramodern **West Yorkshire Playhouse** (⊠ Playhouse Sq., Quarry Hill ☎ 0113/213–7700) was built on the slope of an old quarry. Its adaptable staging makes it eminently suitable for new and classic productions.

Shopping

For funky and cheap ethnic clothes, handmade gifts, artisan jewelry, and accessories, visit the shops inside the old, circular **Corn Exchange** (⊠ Call La. ☎ 0113/234–0363). **Harvey Nichols** (⊠ 107–111 Briggate ☎ 0113/204–8888), the department store regarded as the crucible of chic, contains an abundance of fashion and a great café-restaurant and bar. The city has some excellent markets, notably **Kirkgate Market** (⊠ 34 George St. ☎ 0113/214–5162 ⊘ Closed Wed. morning and Sun.), an Edwardian beauty that's the largest in the north of England. Specialty stores and designer boutiques fill the Victorian shopping arcades; the glistening **Victoria Quarter** (⊠ Briggate ☎ 0113/245–5333), with its 70 stores, epitomizes fin-de-siècle style and 21st-century chic.

Harewood House

★ ❷ *7 mi north of Leeds.*

The home of the earl of Harewood, a cousin of the Queen, Harewood House (pronounced *har*-wood) is a spectacular neoclassical mansion, built in 1759 by John Carr of York. Highlights include Robert Adam interiors, important paintings and ceramics, and a large, ravishingly beautiful collection of Chippendale furniture (Chippendale was born in nearby Otley), notably the magnificent State Bed. The Old Kitchen and Below Stairs exhibition illustrates life from the servants' point of view. Capability Brown designed the handsome grounds, and Charles Barry created a notable Italian garden with fountains in the 1840s. Also here are a bird garden with 120 rare and endangered species, an adventure playground, and a butterfly house. ⊠ *Junction of A61 and A659, Harewood ☎ 0113/218–1010 ⊕ www.harewood.org ☞ £11.30, bird garden and grounds only £8.80; prices are halved if you come by bus and £2 higher on weekends and holidays ⊘ House mid-Mar.–mid-Nov., daily*

10–5, last admission 4. Old Kitchen mid-Mar.–mid-Nov., daily noon–4. Bird garden and grounds mid-Feb.–mid-Nov., daily 10–6; mid-Nov.–mid-Dec., weekends 10–4; last admission 1 hr before dusk.

Bradford

❸ *17 mi southwest of Harewood House, 10 mi west of Leeds, 32 mi northeast of Manchester.*

Bradford was once a busy wool-market town, a trade at which it had excelled since the 16th century. Even as late as the 1960s, wool accounted for a substantial part of its economy, but as with all the West Yorkshire textile towns, recession and competition from new markets hit hard. Bradford tries to be likeable today, and although much of its grandeur has gone, the center still holds the odd Victorian building from its period of greatest prosperity: St. George's Hall on Bridge Street (1851) and the Wool Exchange on Market Street (1864) are two fine examples.

Most people come to Bradford for the museums, particularly the renowned **National Museum of Photography, Film, and Television**, which traces the history of photographic media. It's a huge and hugely entertaining place, with interactive models, machines, and related ephemera spread out over five galleries, encompassing the world's first negative, up-to-the-minute digital imaging, and all stages between. ■ TIP→ **The museum's popularity with children means you should come early or late in the day if you want to see the displays in peace.** The associated Pictureville cinema has a full repertory program. ⊠ *Pictureville, Prince's Way* ☎ *01274/ 202030 or 0870/701–0200* ⊕ *www.nmpft.org.uk* 🖾 *Museum free, IMAX movie £5.95, Pictureville screenings £5* ☉ *Tues.–Sun. and bank holidays 10–6.*

The **Industrial Museum and Horses at Work,** in a former spinning mill 3 mi northeast of the town center, outlines Bradford's history as a wool-producing town. Exhibits include workers' dwellings dating from the 1870s and a mill owner's house from the 19th century. Children love riding in the Shire horse-drawn tram. Moorside Road is off A658 Harrogate Road; take Bus 645, 646, or 613 from the city center. ⊠ *Moorside Rd., Eccleshill* ☎ *01274/435900* ⊕ *www.visitbradford.com* 🖾 *Free* ☉ *Tues.–Sat. and national holiday Mon. 10–5, Sun. noon–5.*

★ A UNESCO World Heritage Site, the former model town of **Saltaire** was built in the mid-19th century by textile magnate Sir Titus Salt, who was trying to create the ideal industrial world. When he decided to relocate his factories from the dark mills of Bradford to the countryside, he hoped to create a beautiful environment in which his workers would be happy. Fashioned in Italianate style, the town is remarkably well preserved, its former mills and houses now turned into shops, restaurants, and galleries. Salt's Mill, built in 1853, resembles a palazzo and was the largest factory in the world when it was built. Today it holds an art gallery and crafts and furniture shops. One-hour guided tours (£3) depart every Saturday at 2 PM and Sunday at 11 AM and 2 PM from the **tourist information center** (⊠ 2 Victoria Rd., Saltaire ☎ 01274/774993 ⊕ www.

saltaire.yorks.com/touristinfo). The **1853 Gallery** (✉ Salt's Mill, Victoria Rd. ☎ 01274/531163 ≣ Free ☉ Daily 10–6) holds a remarkable, permanent, retrospective exhibition of 400 works by Bradford-born artist David Hockney. There are two restaurants on-site. Saltaire is 4 mi north of Bradford, and there are regular bus and train services. Drivers should take A650 to Shipley and follow the signs.

Where to Stay & Eat

£ ✕ **Mumtaz.** Not only does this Kashmiri curry house draw big crowds but its successful line of ready-made curries, Indian breads, and blended teas can be found in local grocery stores, and as far south as Harrods department store in London. Try *biryani*, a saffron rice dish that blends onions, garlic, cardamom, cinnamon, yogurt, raisins, heaps of chilis, and your choice of meat, fish, or vegetables. Wash it down with a sweet mango or spicy masala lassi (yogurt drink)—alcohol is not served. ✉ *Great Horton Rd.* ☎ *01274/571861* ≣ *AE, DC, MC, V.*

£–££ ✕◻ **Beeties.** In the center of Saltaire, the well-preserved former model factory village, this onetime storage house and fish shop provides intimate accommodation away from downtown Bradford. Top-floor bedrooms are pleasantly furnished with pine pieces and colorful bedspreads. Below are a vibrant tapas bar and a more formal restaurant (*£–£££*) that focuses on fine Mediterranean-style food. ✉ *7 Victoria Rd., Saltaire BD18 3LA* ☎ *01274/595988* 🖨 *01274/582118* ⊕ *www.beeties.co.uk* ➥ *5 rooms* ⌕ *Restaurant, tapas bar, meeting rooms, no-smoking rooms; no a/c, no kids under 10* ≣ *MC, V* ⦿| *BP.*

Haworth: Heart of Brontë Country

★ ❹ *10 mi northwest of Bradford, 5 mi southwest of Keighley.*

Whatever Haworth might have been in the past, today it is Brontë country. This old stone-built village on the edge of the Yorkshire Moors long ago gave up its own personality and allowed itself to be taken over by the doomed sisters, their mournful books, and their millions of fans. In 1820, when Anne, Emily, and Charlotte were very young, their father moved them and their other three siblings away from their old home in Bradford to Haworth. The sisters—Emily (author of *Wuthering Heights,* 1847), Charlotte (*Jane Eyre,* 1847), and Anne (*The Tenant of Wildfell Hall,* 1848) were inevitably affected by the stark, dramatic countryside around them. These days, every street they ever walked down, every building they ever glanced at, has been turned into a Brontë memorial, shop, or museum.

> ### LANDSCAPE AS MUSE
>
> The rugged Yorkshire Moors helped inspire Emily Brontë's 1847 *Wuthering Heights*; if ever a work of fiction grew out of the landscape in which its author lived, it was surely this. "My sister Emily loved the moors," wrote Charlotte. "Flowers brighter than the rose bloomed in the blackest of the heath for her; out of a sullen hollow in a livid hillside her mind could make an Eden. She found in the bleak solitude many and dear delights; and not the least and best loved was liberty."

To reach Haworth by bus or train, buy a Metro Day Rover for bus and rail, and take the Metro train from Leeds train station to Keighley. There are about three hourly. From Keighley, take the Keighley & Worth Valley Railway for the trip to Haworth (weekends only; £6 round-trip), or Keighley and District Bus 663, 664, or 665 (Monday–Saturday, every 20 minutes; Sunday, every ½ hour). From Bradford station, Interchange buses run every ½ hour to Keighley.

The town's **information center** has information about accommodations, maps, books on the Brontës, and inexpensive leaflets to help you find your way to such outlying *Wuthering Heights* sites as Ponden Hall (Thrushcross Grange) and Ponden Kirk (Penistone Crag). ⊠ *2–4 West La.* ☎ *01535/642329* ☉ *Thurs.–Tues. 9:30–5; Wed. 10–5.*

Haworth's steep, cobbled **Main Street** has changed little in outward appearance since the early 19th century, but today acts as a funnel for the people who crowd into the points of interest: the **Black Bull** pub, where the reprobate Branwell, the Brontës' only brother, drank himself into an early grave; the **post office** from which Charlotte, Emily, and Anne sent their manuscripts to their London publishers; and the **church,** with its gloomy graveyard (Charlotte and Emily are buried inside the church; Anne is buried in Scarborough).

The best of the Brontë sights in Haworth is the **Brontë Parsonage Museum.** In the somber Georgian house in which the sisters grew up, it displays original furniture (some bought by Charlotte after the success of *Jane Eyre*), portraits, and books. The Brontës moved to this simple house when the Reverend Patrick Brontë was appointed to the local church, but tragedy soon struck—his wife, Maria, and their two eldest children died within five years (done in, some scholars assert, by water wells tainted by seepage from the neighboring graveyard). The museum contains enchanting mementos of the four surviving children, including Charlotte's wedding bonnet and the sisters' spidery, youthful graffiti on the nursery wall. Branwell painted several of the portraits on display. ⊠ *Church St.* ☎ *01535/642323* ⊕ *www.bronte.info* ⊠ *£5* ☉ *Apr.–Sept., daily 10–5:30; Oct.–Dec., Feb., and Mar., daily 11–5; last admission 30 mins before closing.*

If you have the time, you can pack a lunch and walk an hour or so along a field path, a lane, and a moorland track to the lovely, isolated waterfall that has, inevitably, been renamed the **Brontë Waterfall.** It was a favorite of the sisters, who wrote about it in poems and letters. **Top Withins,** a ruined, gloomy house on a bleak hilltop farm 3 mi from Haworth, is often taken to be the inspiration for Heathcliff's gloomy mansion, Wuthering Heights. Brontë scholars say it probably isn't; the ruins never looked the way the book describes them. Still, it's an inspirational walk across the moors. There and back from Haworth is a two-hour walk. Wherever you go, wear sturdy shoes and protective clothing: if you've read *Wuthering Heights,* you have a fairly good idea of what weather can be like on the Yorkshire Moors.

Haworth is on the **Keighley & Worth Valley Railway,** a gorgeous 5-mi-long branch line along which steam engines run between Keighley (3 mi north of Haworth) and Oxenhope. Kids like it even more on special days when there are family fairs en route. The **Museum of Rail Travel** (⊠ £1 ☉ Daily 11–4), at Ingrow along the line, exhibits vintage train cars. ⊠ *Railway Station, Keighley* ☎ *01535/645214, 01535/647777 for 24-hr information* ⊕ *www.kwvr.co.uk* ⊠ *£8 round-trip, £12 Day Rover ticket* ☉ *Sept.–June, weekends; July and Aug., daily; call for schedules.*

Where to Stay & Eat

££ ✕⊞ **Weavers.** Book well in advance to secure a room in this establishment converted from a number of old cottages in a fine village location. Weavers operates mainly as a restaurant (££–£££), but the few chintz-filled rooms have antique French beds and vivid bedspreads. Downstairs, the restaurant (closed Sunday night and Monday) serves traditional, organic Yorkshire fare, including smoked haddock soup and duck in brandy sauce, served with home-baked bread. ⊠ *15 West La., BD22 8DU* ☎ *01535/643822* 🖶 *01535/643822* ⊕ *www.weaversmallhotel. co.uk* ➥ *3 rooms* ⚐ *Restaurant, bar; no a/c* ▤ *AE, DC, MC, V* ☉ *Closed 1 wk at Christmas and 1 wk in summer* ⊙⚑ *BP.*

£ ✕⊞ **Aitches.** This intimate 19th-century stone house is close to the Brontë Parsonage on Haworth's main street. The guest rooms are modern, with pine pieces and colorful quilts and drapes. A fixed-price meal in the elegant small restaurant (££££), which is open to nonguests on Friday and Saturday only, might include pork cutlet with Stilton crumble followed by a traditional bread-and-butter pudding. ⊠ *11 West La., BD22 8DU* ☎ *01535/642501* ⊕ *www.aitches.co.uk* ➥ *5 rooms* ⚐ *Restaurant; no a/c, no room phones, no smoking* ▤ *MC, V* ⊙⚑ *BP.*

££ ⊞ **Old Registry.** The lovely theme guest rooms—Memories Room, Blue Heaven, Cherub Corner, and so on—in this creeper-covered Victorian house at the lower end of the main street are all individually decorated and equipped with CD players. One room has lavender-scented pillows, another has a green bed and gardening memorabilia, and there's an unusual three-poster bed in the attic room. All have large bathrooms and two have whirlpool baths. ⊠ *2–4 Main St., BD22 8DA* ☎⊞ *01535/ 646503* ⊕ *www.oldregistryhaworth.co.uk* ➥ *10 rooms* ⚐ *In-room VCR, some pets allowed; no a/c, no room phones, no smoking* ▤ *MC, V* ⊙⚑ *BP.*

THE YORKSHIRE DALES

The western equivalent of the North York Moors, the Yorkshire Dales are just as beautiful and nearly as wild. The word "dale" comes from the Viking word for "valley," which gives you an indication that, although the moors have steep hills, the dales are more rugged, with sharper, higher hills culminating in the mountains Pen-y-ghent, Ingleborough, and Whernside. These river valleys fall south and east from the Pennines, and beyond Skipton they present an almost wholly rural aspect. Ruined priories, narrow roads, drystone walls made without mortar, and babbling rivers make for a quintessentially English landscape, full of paths and trails to explore.

Bolton Priory

★ ❺ *12 mi north of Haworth, 18 mi north of Bradford, 24 mi northwest of Leeds.*

Some of the loveliest Wharfedale scenery comes into view around Bolton Priory, the ruins of an Augustinian priory, which sits on a grassy embankment inside a great curve of the River Wharfe. The priory is just a short walk or drive from the village of Bolton Abbey. You can wander through the 13th-century ruins or visit the priory church, which is still the local parish church. The duke of Devonshire owns the Bolton Abbey estate, including the ruins. Among the famous visitors enchanted by Bolton Priory were William Wordsworth and J. M. W. Turner; John Ruskin, the Victorian art critic, rated it the most beautiful of all English ruins.

Close to Bolton Priory, surrounded by romantic woodland scenery, the River Wharfe plunges between a narrow chasm in the rocks (called the Strid) before reaching **Barden Tower,** a medieval hunting lodge. This lodge is now a ruin and can be visited just as easily as Bolton Priory, in whose grounds it stands. You can ride the scenic 4-mi **Embsay & Bolton Abbey Steam Railway** (☎ 01756/710614, 01756/795189 recorded timetable), which has a station in Bolton Abbey. ✉ *B6160, off A59* ☎ *01756/718009* ⊕ *www.boltonabbey.com* ☜ *Free, parking £4* ☉ *Daily 9–dusk.*

Where to Stay & Eat

£££££ ✕▦ **Devonshire Arms.** Originally an 18th-century coaching inn, and still belonging to the dukes of Devonshire, this luxurious country-house hotel is near the River Wharfe, an easy walk from Bolton Abbey. The bedrooms are tastefully decorated with antiques and family memorabilia from the family home, Chatsworth House in Derbyshire. The Burlington restaurant (£££££) has a fixed-price menu of superb traditional fare that uses game and fish from the estate. The brasserie serves modestly priced fare (££). ✉ *Bolton Abbey, Skipton BD23 6AJ* ☎ *01756/ 710441, 01756/718111 reservation line* 🖷 *01756/710564* ⊕ *www. devonshirehotels.co.uk* ☜ *37 rooms, 3 suites* ⚭ *2 restaurants, in-room data ports, tennis court, pool, health club, sauna, fishing, 2 bars, meeting rooms, some pets allowed; no a/c* ⊟ *AE, DC, MC, V* ⏃ *BP.*

Skipton

❻ *6 mi west of Bolton Abbey, 12 mi north of Haworth, 22 mi west of Harrogate.*

Skipton in Airedale, capital of the limestone district of Craven, is a typical Dales market town with as many farmers as visitors milling in the streets. There are markets Monday, Wednesday, Friday, and Saturday, and shops selling local produce predominate.

★ **Skipton Castle,** built by the Normans in 1090 and unaltered since the Civil War (17th century), is the town's most prominent attraction and one of the best preserved of English medieval castles. After the Battle of Marston Moor during the Civil War, it remained the only Royalist stronghold in the north of England. So sturdy was the squat little for-

Over Hills & Dales

CLOSE UP

THE GREEN DALES, the changeable moors, the rugged North Sea coast: Yorkshire's landscapes are glorious to explore on foot, and they're crisscrossed by long-distance footpaths designed to take in the most charming villages and the most breathtaking views. There's no need to pack a backpack and head to the hills for days if you're not at experience hiker—even a brief walk can take you deep into the quiet of the countryside. The hardest part is deciding where to start. Short trails and longer paths meander across the Yorkshire Dales National Park, while the North York Moors have long, empty swaths of land for tramping, and craggy cliff walks follow the dramatic coastline. Top trails include the Cleveland Way (108 mi), from Helmsley to Filey; the hard-going coastal Lyke-Wake Walk (40 mi), from Osmotherley to Ravenscar; and the eastern section of the Coast-to-Coast Walk (190 mi), which starts or finishes in Robin Hood's Bay. The Dales Way (80 mi) connects Leeds and Bradford with the Lake District. And the exhausting but incredible Pennine Way, which runs from the Peak District to Scotland, crosses the Yorkshire Dales en route.

12

tification with its rounded battlements (in places the walls are 12 feet thick) that Oliver Cromwell ordered the roof be removed, as it had survived one bombardment after another during a three-year siege. When the castle's owner, Lady Anne Clifford, later asked if she could replace the roof, he allowed her do so, as long as it was not strong enough to withstand cannon fire. Today the buildings are still marvelously complete, and in the central courtyard, a yew tree, planted more than 300 years ago by Lady Anne herself, still flourishes. ⊠ *High St.* ☎ *01756/ 792442* ⊕ *www.skiptoncastle.co.uk* ☞ *£5.40* ☉ *Mar.–Sept., Mon.–Sat. 10–6, Sun. noon–6; Oct.–Feb., Mon.–Sat. 10–4, Sun. noon–4.*

Where to Stay & Eat

££££–£££££ ✕⌂ **Angel Inn.** Diners at the Angel clog the hidden-away hamlet of Hetton with their vehicles, such is the attraction of this locally renowned brasserie and more formal restaurant. Roasted lamb and duck are specialties (£££; reservations essential; no dinner Sunday). The ancient stone barn across the road has well-equipped guest rooms in unfussy country styles, from rustic to French. The inn is 5 mi north of Skipton. ⊠ *Off B6265, Hetton* ☎ *01756/730263* 🖷 *01756/730363* ⊕ *www. angelhetton.co.uk* ↙ *5 rooms* ⌂ *2 restaurants, bar, in-room safes, minibars, bar; no a/c, no-smoking* ▤ *AE, DC, MC, V* ⍥ *BP.*

Grassington

❼ *10 mi north of Skipton, 14 mi northwest of Ilkley, 25 mi west of Ripon.*

A small, stone village built around an ancient cobbled marketplace, Grassington makes a good base for exploring Upper Wharfedale. The Dales Way footpath passes through the village, and there's a good mix of guesthouses, stores, pubs, and cafés. In summer, facilities become

HIKING IN MALHAM

Avid summer hikers descend in droves on Malham to tour the remarkable limestone formations Malham Cove and Gordale Scar, and Malham Tarn. The three sites are on a circular walk of 8 mi that takes most people four to five hours. Those with less time should cut out the tarn (a small lake): a circular walk from the village to the limestone formations Malham Cove and Gordale Scar can be completed in just over two hours. Malham's **National Park Centre** (☎ 01729/830363 ⊕ www.yorkshiredales.org. uk ☉ Apr.–Oct., daily 10–5; Nov.–Mar., Fri.–Sun. 10–4) has displays and will give you ideas of what to do locally and in Yorkshire Dales National Park. You can get a list of B&B and pub accommodations, too.

Malham Cove, a huge, 300-foot-high natural rock amphitheater, is a mile north of the village and provides the easiest local walk, although following the path *up* to the top is a brutal climb, though rewarded by magnificent views.

At **Gordale Scar,** a deep natural chasm between overhanging limestone cliffs, the white waters of a moorland stream plunge 300 feet. It's a mile northeast of Malham by a lovely riverside path.

A walk of more than 3 mi leads north from Malham to **Malham Tarn,** an attractive lake in windswept isolation. There's a nature reserve on the west bank and an easy-to-follow trail on the east bank. Malham is 10 mi west of Grassington: take B6265 south 2 mi through Cracoe, then branch west onto the minor road past Hetton and Calton. Malham is also 12 mi northwest of Skipton, off A65.

overwhelmed by day-trippers and walkers. There are plenty of local walks, however, and if you're prepared to make a day of it, you can soon leave the crowds behind. The **National Park Centre** has guidebooks, maps, and bus schedules to help you enjoy a day in the Yorkshire Dales National Park. ⊠ *Colvend, Hebdon Rd.* ☎ *01756/752774* ⊕ *www. yorkshiredales.org.uk* ☉ *Apr.–Oct., daily 10–5; Nov.–Mar., Wed. and Fri.–Sun. 10–4.*

Where to Stay & Eat

£–££ ✕ **Devonshire Hotel.** This traditional Dales inn makes a comfortable and refined rural dining spot, with a fine assortment of upholstered chairs in the oak-panel and candlelighted dining room. Local lamb and dishes such as fish hotpot (stew with vegetables) and gammon (cured ham) steak appear on the menu alongside stir-frys and curries. ⊠ *Main St.* ☎ *01756/752525* ▭ *MC, V.*

££ ▦ **Ashfield House.** Three converted 17th-century stone cottages, once the homes of Grassington lead miners, make up this well-run small hotel off the main street. Expect a cheery welcome on arrival, soothingly decorated bedrooms with pine furniture and white walls, a cozy brick-and-beam sitting room, and a walled garden. It's worth asking ahead for the deliciously hearty set dinner (£22). ✉ *Summers Fold, BD23 5AE* ☎ *01756/752584* ⊕ *www.ashfieldhouse.co.uk* ➹ *7 rooms* ⚲ *Dining room, Internet room; no a/c, no room phones, no kids under 5, no smoking* ▭ *MC, V* ⦿ *BP.*

££ ▦ **Grassington Lodge.** Light and airy, this Victorian house has made the most of its original features with tasteful and uncluttered decoration. Bedrooms have beautiful quilts; the top-floor room has the biggest bed. A roaring log fire in the sitting room takes the edge off cold days. ✉ *8 Wood La., BD23 5LU* ☎ *01756/752518* ⊕ *www.grassingtonlodge. co.uk* ➹ *7 rooms* ⚲ *No a/c, no room phones, no kids under 12, no smoking* ▭ *No credit cards* ⊙ *Call ahead in winter* ⦿ *BP.*

Kettlewell

❽ *6 mi north of Grassington.*

Kettlewell is the main settlement in Upper Wharfedale and a fine base for an exploration of the local hills and valleys, with their stone-flagged pubs and riverside walks. A babbling river and the Dales Way hiking path pass through the quiet, gray-stone village. The town was called "Knapely" in its appearance in the film *Calendar Girls.*

Where to Stay & Eat

££ ✕▦ **Blue Bell Inn.** Horse brasses, tankards hanging from the rafters, ornamental plates, and high-back settles decorate this 17th-century coaching inn. Guest rooms are simply furnished with colorfully striped quilts. The reasonably priced menu (£–££) includes Dales lamb chops, grilled Wharfedale trout, and plenty for vegetarians. ✉ *BD23 5QX* ☎ *01756/ 760230* ⊕ *www.bluebellinn.co.uk* ➹ *9 rooms* ⚲ *Restaurant, bar, no-smoking rooms; no a/c, no room phones* ▭ *MC* ⦿ *BP.*

▌**EN ROUTE** From Kettlewell, it's just 4 mi north along B6160 to **Buckden,** the last village in Wharfedale. A minor road leads to the riverside hamlet of Hubberholme. Its stone chapel and ancient George Inn were favorites of Yorkshire-born author J. B. Priestley, who is buried in the churchyard. Back on B6160, you can go north through Kidstone Pass to Aysgarth in Wensleydale, where the River Ure plummets over a series of waterfalls.

Askrigg

❾ *16 mi north of Kettlewell.*

Askrigg would be just another typical Wensleydale village were it not for its association with the James Herriot TV series *All Creatures Great and Small,* which was filmed in and around it in the 1970s and 1980s. The tourist board pushes "Herriot Country" hard, but although Askrigg is a pleasant village, there's not much else to keep you here, apart from walks to a couple of local waterfalls. The **King's Arms Hotel** (✉ Market Pl. ☎ 01969/650817), a wood-panel, 18th-century coaching inn, was rechristened the Drover's Arms for its appearance in episodes of the Herriot TV series. The historic building has nook-and-cranny rooms, good local beer, and two restaurants.

Hawes

 *5 mi west of Askrigg.*

The best time to visit the so-called cheesiest town in Yorkshire is on Tuesday when farmers crowd into town for the weekly market. Hawes is the business center for Wensleydale's traditional cheese-making. Crumbly, white Wensleydale cheese has been made in the valley for centuries, and it is sold in local stores and at the market. Allow yourself time to wander the cobbled side streets, some of which are filled with antiques shops and tearooms.

The **Wensleydale Creamery Visitor Centre,** in a working dairy farm, includes a museum that tells the story of the famed local cheese so beloved by the cartoon characters Wallace and Gromit. You can watch production (best seen between 10 and 2) from the viewing gallery, and then taste the output in the

> ### WORD OF MOUTH
>
> "Yorkshire Dales . . . I do have a soft spot for Malham . . . and around Hawes. You might like to get hold of an Ordnance Survey map for the area. Hours of fun planning where to drive/go based on contours, other natural features, and small villages in the middle of nowhere where there's a 'PH' (pub) for lunch."
>
> –fuzzylogic

shop. A restaurant on-site has plenty of cheese samples as well, such as smoked, with ginger, or with apple pie. ✉ *Gayle La.* ☎ *01969/667664* ⊕ *www.wensleydale.co.uk/centre.htm* 🎦 *Museum £2.50* ⊗ *Apr.–Oct., daily 9–5:30; Nov.–Mar., daily 9:30–4:30.*

The Yorkshire Dales National Park Information Centre in the old train station contains the **Dales Countryside Museum,** which gives a picture of Dales life in past centuries. A traditional rope-making shop here also welcomes visitors. ✉ *Station Yard* ☎ *01969/667450* ⊕ *www. destinationdales.org* 🎦 *Museum £3* ⊗ *Daily 10–5.*

Richmond

⑪ *22 mi northeast of Hawes, 25 mi northwest of Ripon.*

Richmond tucks itself into a curve above the foaming River Swale, with a network of narrow Georgian streets and terraces opening onto a large cobbled marketplace. Despite appearances, it would be a mistake to date the town to the 18th century. The Normans swept in during the late 11th century, determined to subdue the local population and establish their rule in the north. This they did by building a mighty castle, around which the town grew, and throughout the Middle Ages Richmond was effectively a garrison town.

The immense keep of Norman **Richmond Castle** towers above the river, providing excellent views of the countryside. Built around 1071 by Alan Rufus, first earl of Richmond, it was used as a prison for William "the Lion" of Scotland 100 years later. The castle is a well-preserved monument of this era, retaining its thick curtain wall and chapel, and a great hall that has been restored to its medieval splendor; even the 14th-

12

century graffiti remains. There's a heritage garden, and a path along the river leads to the ruins of golden-stone Easby Abbey. One historical note: when Henry Tudor (son of Edmund Tudor, earl of Richmond) became Henry VII in 1485, he began calling his palace in Shene, southwest London, Richmond (Palace), after his family seat in Richmond. The name gradually became used to describe that area of London. ☎ *01748/822493* ⊕ *www.english-heritage.org.uk* ⌦ *£3.60* ☉ *Apr.–Sept., daily 10–6; Oct.–Mar., Thurs.–Mon. 10–4.*

The tiny Georgian **Theatre Royal**, a jewel box built in 1788, retains original features such as the wooden seating from the days of the 18th-century Shakespearean actor David Garrick. The museum holds scenery dating from 1836. ⌧ *Victoria Rd.* ☎ *01748/823710, 01748/825252 box office* ⊕ *www.georgiantheatreroyal.co.uk* ⌦ *Museum £2.50 suggested donation* ☉ *Museum mid-Feb.–Dec., Mon.–Sat. 10–4:30.*

Where to Stay & Eat

££–£££ ✕ **Frenchgate Café.** Blue wicker chairs and yellow walls capture a bit of the bright Mediterranean at this bistro-style café, just below the main cobbled square. Try one of the pastas, such as penne with smoked salmon and prawns. Cappuccino, scones, and sandwiches are available. ⌧ *29 Frenchgate* ☎ *01748/824949* ⊟ *AE, MC, V* ☉ *Closed Mon.*

££ ⌂ **Frenchgate Hotel.** This three-story Georgian town house on a quiet cobbled street has a secluded walled garden for summer days and a bright and welcoming interior, furnished with some flair. Public rooms hark back to the 17th century, but the decorative mice (symbol of local craftsman Mousey Thompson) hidden in the woodwork are more recent. Some of the spacious bedrooms have deep, roll-top baths. ⌧ *59–61 Frenchgate, DL10 7AE* ☎ *01748/822087* ⎙ *01748/823596* ⊕ *www. frenchgatehotel.com* ⇆ *11 rooms* ⌂ *Restaurant, bar; no a/c* ⊟ *MC, V* ⧎ *BP.*

YORK

▶ It would be unthinkable to visit North Yorkshire without first visiting the historic cathedral city of York, and not just because of its central location. Named "Eboracum" by the Romans, York was the military capital of Roman Britain, and traces of garrison buildings survive throughout the city. After the Roman Empire collapsed in the 5th century, the Saxons built "Eoforwic" upon the ruins of a fort, but were soon defeated by Vikings (who called the town Jorvik, and used it as a base from which to subjugate the countryside). The Normans came in the 11th century and emulated the Vikings by using the town as a military base. It was during Norman times that the foundations of York Minster, the largest medieval cathedral in England, were laid.

Because York was largely a backwater during the Industrial Revolution, much of the city's medieval and 18th-century architecture has survived, making the city an architectural time capsule and a delight to explore. The only changes the 19th century brought were large houses, built mostly on the outskirts of the city center. York is 48 mi southeast of Richmond,

25 mi northeast of Leeds, and 82 mi south of Newcastle. ■ TIP→ **The city is one of the most popular short-stay destinations in Britain and only two hours by train from London's Kings Cross Station.**

Exploring York

This is a fine city for walking, especially along the walls embracing the old center. At night many historic buildings are illuminated, too. You can get a free walking map from the tourist office in the train station; most hotels have maps in their lobbies. July and August are the town's busiest months, when tourists choke the narrow streets and cause long lines at the popular museums and restaurants. April, May, June, and September are less crowded, although the weather is unpredictable. April is also the time to see the embankments beneath the city walls filled with the pale gold ripple of daffodils.

The best way to explore York is to start at the Minster and head down the little medieval lane, Stonegate, which is lined with shops and leads directly to Betty's tea shop. From there you can swing right to find antiques shops, or left for more modern shops, and eventually the shopping area known as the Shambles, and the remains of the old castle. At any point, climb the steps to the top of the city walls for some perspective on where you are in town. The Ouse River, by the way, is more like an undeveloped canal, hidden away by buildings.

Main Attractions

★ ⑬ **City walls.** York's almost 3 mi of ancient stone walls are among the best preserved in England. A walk on the narrow paved path along the top leads you through 1,900 years of history, from the time the earthen ramparts were raised by the Romans and York's Viking kings to repel raiders, to their fortification by the Normans, to their current colorful landscaping by the city council. The walls are crossed periodically by York's distinctive fortified gates or "bars": the portcullis on Monk's Bar on Goodramgate is still in working order, and Walmgate Bar in the east is the only gate in England with an intact barbican. It also has scars from the cannon balls hurled at it during the Civil War. Bootham Bar in Exhibition Square was the defensive bastion for the north road, and Micklegate Bar, in the city's southwest corner, was traditionally the monarch's entrance. For a small fee, you can explore all of these gates. To access the path and the lookout towers, find a staircase at one of the many breaks in the walls. ⊕ *www.york.gov.uk/walls* 🎫 *Free* ☉ *Daily 8 AM–dusk.*

WHERE ARE THE GATES?

The Viking conquerors of northern England held the region for more than a century, and made York their capital. Many of the city's street names are still suffixed with the word "-gate" (Goodramgate and Micklegate, for example). "Gate" was the Viking word for "street." Adding to the confusion, the city's entrances, or gates, are called "bars," from an Old English term. As local tour guides like to say, "In York, our streets are called gates, our gates are called bars, and our bars are called pubs."

12

☼ ⓰ **Dig.** This new venture from the people behind the Jorvik Viking Centre is a great way to get young people inspired about history and archaeology. It's an ongoing archaeological dig in and beneath an old church; kids, supervised by knowledgable experts, help with the work. After your dig, record your findings and head to the lab to learn what archaeological finds discovered on the site reveal about how people lived in the past. It's an educational, fun, fascinating way to spend a couple of hours. ✉ *St. Saviour's Church, St. Saviourgate* ☎ *01904/543403* ⊕ *www.vikingjorvik.com* ✉ *£5.50; joint admission to Jorvik Viking Centre £11* ⏱ *Apr.–Oct., daily 10–5; Nov.–Mar., daily 10–4.*

㉒ **Guildhall.** The mid-15th-century guildhall, by the River Ouse, was a meeting place for the city's powerful guilds. It was also used for pageants and mystery plays (medieval dramas based on biblical stories and the lives of saints). Restoration after the damage done by World War II bombing has given it something of its erstwhile glory. The guildhall is behind the 18th-century Mansion House; you can visit it when no function is in progress. ✉ *St. Helen's Sq.* ☎ *01904/613161* ✉ *Free* ⏱ *May–Oct., weekdays 9–5, Sat. 10–5, Sun. 2–5; Nov.–Apr., weekdays 9–5.*

☼ ⓲ **Jorvik Viking Centre.** This exhibition re-creates a 10th-century Viking village. A mixture of museum and carnival ride, it requires you to "travel through time." You climb into a Disney-esque machine that propels you above straw huts and mannequins in Viking garb. Commentary is provided in 10 languages (click on the British flag to hear it in English). Kids will get a lot out of it, but adults are unlikely to learn anything new. A small collection of Viking-era artifacts is on display at the end of the ride. ✉ *Coppergate* ☎ *01904/643211, 01904/543403 advance booking* ⊕ *www.vikingjorvik.com* ✉ *£7.75; joint admission to Dig £11* ⏱ *Apr.–Oct., daily 10–5; Nov.–Mar., daily 10–4.*

☼ ㉕ **National Railway Museum.** For train-lovers one and all: here Britain's national collection of locomotives forms part of a massive train museum. Among the exhibits are gleaming giants of the steam era, including the *Mallard*, holder of the world speed record for a steam engine (126 mph). Passenger cars used by Queen Victoria are on display, as well as the only Japanese bullet train to be seen outside Japan. You can clamber aboard the trains, some of which are started up regularly to keep the engines working. ✉ *Leeman Rd.* ☎ *01904/621261, 01904/686286 information line* ⊕ *www.nrm.org.uk* ✉ *Free* ⏱ *Daily 10–6.*

⓯ **The Shambles.** York's best-preserved medieval street has half-timber stores and houses with overhangs so massive you could almost reach across the street from one second-floor window to another. Once the

---

THE YORK EYE

At the National Railway Museum, you can soar above the city on the Norwich Union Yorkshire Wheel, the observation wheel that is York's answer to the London Eye. It costs £6 for the 13-minute ride, which takes you up 175 feet for great views. It's open daily 10–6, and until 9 May through September. At this time no advance tickets were being sold, but check the museum's Web site, ⊕ www.nrm. org.uk, for an update.

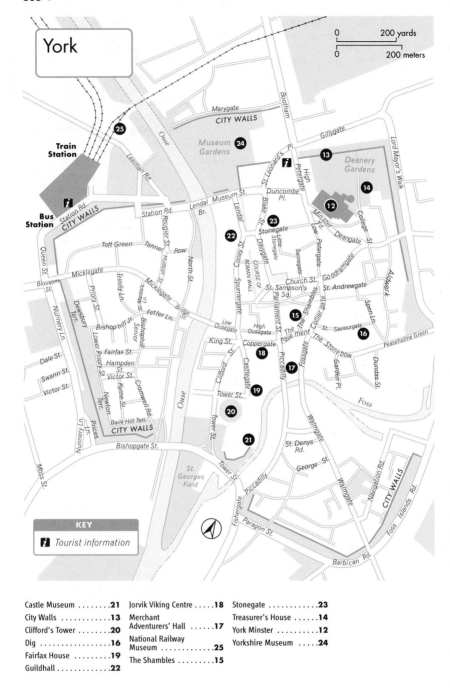

York

Train Station

Bus Station

KEY

i Tourist information

Castle Museum **21**
City Walls **13**
Clifford's Tower **20**
Dig **16**
Fairfax House **19**
Guildhall **22**

Jorvik Viking Centre **18**
Merchant
Adventurers' Hall **17**
National Railway
Museum **25**
The Shambles **15**

Stonegate **23**
Treasurer's House **14**
York Minster **12**
Yorkshire Museum **24**

city's street of butchers (meat hooks are still fastened outside some of the doors), today it's filled with touristy shops of scant interest to most visitors. Still, it's beautiful to walk down for the atmosphere.

㉓ Stonegate. This narrow, pedestrian-only street of Tudor and 18th-century storefronts and courtyards retains considerable charm. It has been in daily use for almost 2,000 years, since first being paved in Roman times. Today it's lined with jewelry stores, knickknack shops, tea shops, and ancient pubs. A passage just off Stonegate, at 52A, leads to the remnants of a 12th-century Norman stone house attached to a more recent structure. You can see the old Norman wall and window. Look out for the little red devil high up on a doorpost. Keep an eye out throughout the area for similar tiny statues that once acted as signs for businesses. The devil announced a printer's shop. ■ TIP→ **There's another statue at the intersection of Stonegate and High Petergate, where Minerva lounges on a stack of books. She once advertised a bookseller.**

NEED A BREAK? At the opposite end of Stonegate from the Minster, **Betty's** (⊠ 6–8 Helen's Sq., off Stonegate ☎ 01904/659142) has been a York institution since 1912. This tea-and-cakes salon in an attractive art nouveau building is more beloved for its history and ambience than for its food, which is only so-so. Still, it's a piece of history, and a good place to take a rest. Expect to wait 10 minutes for a table.

⑫ York Minster. Focal point of the city, this vast cathedral is the largest Gothic church in England and attracts almost as many visitors as London's Westminster Abbey. Inside, the effect created by its soaring pillars and lofty vaulted ceilings is almost overpowering. Come with binoculars if you wish to study the dazzling 128 stained-glass windows. Glowing with deep wine reds and cobalt blues, they are bested only by those in Chartres Cathedral in France. Mere statistics cannot convey the scale of the building; however, the central towers are 184 feet high, and the church is 534 feet long, 249 feet across its transepts, and 90 feet from floor to roof. Contributing to the cold, crushing splendor are the ornamentation of the 14th-century nave; the east window, one of the greatest pieces of medieval glazing in the world; the north transept's **Five Sisters** windows, five tall lancets of frosted 13th-century glass; the enormous choir screen portraying somewhat whimsical images of every king of England from William the Conqueror to Henry VI; and the imposing tracery of the **Rose Window**, commemorating the marriage of Henry VII and Elizabeth of York in 1486 (the event that ended the Wars of the Roses and began the Tudor dynasty). Don't miss the exquisite 13th-century **Chapter House** and the **Undercroft, Treasury, and Crypt.** Finds during the latest renovation date back to Roman times, and include a Saxon child's coffin. After exploring the interior, you might take the 275 winding steps to the roof of the great **Central Tower** (strictly for those with a head for heights), not only for the close-up view of the cathedral's detailed carving but for a panorama of York and the surrounding moors. ■ TIP→ **Attending Evensong here is a memorable experience.** ⊠ *Duncombe Pl.* ☎ *01904/557216* ⊕ *www.yorkminster. org* 🎫 *Minster £5, Undercroft, Treasury, and Crypt £3, Central Tower £3* ⊙ *Apr.–Oct., Mon.–Sat. 9–5:30, Sun. noon–3:45; Nov.–Mar., Mon.–Sat. 9:30–4:45, Sun. noon–3:45.*

Fodor'sChoice ★

Also Worth Seeing

㉑ Castle Museum. A former 18th-century debtors' prison, this quirky museum of everyday items presents detailed exhibitions and re-creations, including a Victorian street complete with crafts shops and a working water mill, as well as notable domestic, costume, and arms and armor displays. One treasure is the Coppergate Helmet, a 1,200-year-old Anglo-Saxon helmet discovered during excavations of the city; it's one of only three such objects found. You can also visit the cell where Dick Turpin, the 18th-century highwayman and folk hero, spent the night before his execution. ⊠ *Clifford St.* ☎ *01904/687687* ⊕ *www.yorkcastlemuseum.org.uk* ⌑ *£6.50* ☉ *Daily 9:30–5.*

⑳ Clifford's Tower. Apart from the city walls, this rather sad and battered looking keep is all that remains of the old York castle. The stone tower, which sits on a grassy mound surrounded by a parking lot, dates from the mid-12th century. The Norman version that preceded it was infamously destroyed in 1190. More than 150 Jews locked themselves inside with no food or water to protect themselves from a violent mob. After several days, they were forced to choose between starvation or murder. In the end, they committed mass suicide by setting their own prison aflame. ⊠ *Tower St.* ☎ *01904/646940* ⊕ *www.cliffordstower.com* ⌑ *£2.75* ☉ *Apr.–June and Sept., daily 10–6; July and Aug., daily 9:30–7; Oct.–Mar., daily 10–4.*

★ ⑲ Fairfax House. This elegant Georgian (1762) town house is a museum of decorative arts. The house is beautifully decorated with period furniture, crystal chandeliers, and silk wallpaper. ⊠ *Castlegate* ☎ *01904/655543* ⊕ *www.fairfaxhouse.co.uk* ⌑ *£4.75* ☉ *Mon.–Thurs. and Sat. 11–5, Sun. 1:30–5; last admission 4:30; Fri., guided tours 11 and 2.*

⑰ Merchant Adventurers' Hall. Built between 1357 and 1368 by a wealthy medieval guild, this is the largest half-timber hall in York. Portraits, silver, and furniture are on display, and the house itself is much of the attraction. A riverfront garden lies behind the hall. On most Saturdays, antiques fairs are held inside the building. ⊠ *Fossgate* ☎ *01904/654818* ⊕ *www.theyorkcompany.co.uk* ⌑ *£2.75* ☉ *Apr.–Sept., Mon.–Thurs. 9–5, Fri. and Sat. 9–3:30, Sun. noon–4; Oct.–Mar., Mon.–Sat. 9–3:30; closed 1st wk in Dec.*

⑭ Treasurer's House. Surprises await inside this large 17th-century house, the home from 1897 to 1930 of industrialist Frank Green. With a fine eye for texture, decoration, and pattern, Green created period rooms—including a medieval great hall—as a showcase for his collection of antique furniture. Delft tiles decorate the kitchen, copies of medieval stenciling cover the vibrant

> ### GET LOST
>
> The streets of York's city center are so unsuited to automobile traffic that most have been pedestrianized, so if you're driving, park at your hotel and strike out on foot. The old center is a compact, dense web of narrow streets and tiny medieval alleys called "snickleways." These provide shortcuts across the city center, but they're not on maps, so you never quite know where you'll end up, which in York is more often a pleasant surprise.

Red Room, and 17th-century stump work adorns the Tapestry Room. The "ghost" cellar is shown on the guided tour. ✉ *Minster Yard* ☎ *01904/624247* ⊕ *www.nationaltrust.org.uk* ✈ *House and garden £5; £7 with cellar tour* ⊗ *Apr.–Oct., Sat.–Thurs. 11–5; last admission 30 mins before closing.*

24 **Yorkshire Museum.** The natural and archaeological history of the county, including material on the Roman, Anglo-Saxon, and Viking aspects of York, is the focus of this museum. Also on display in the solid, Doric-style building is the 15th-century Middleham Jewel, a pendant gleaming with a large sapphire. The museum lies just outside the walled city, through Bootham Bar, one of York's old gates. ✉ *Museum Gardens, Museum St.* ☎ *01904/551805* ⊕ *www.yorkshiremuseum.org.uk* ✈ *£4* ⊗ *Daily 10–5.*

Where to Eat

££–££££ ✕ **Melton's.** Once a private house, this unpretentious but excellent restaurant has local art on the walls and an open kitchen. The seasonal menus are highly imaginative with modern English and European fare, such as venison with red wine and mulled pears, and roast partridge with marscapone and grilled polenta. Melton's is a 10 minutes' walk from York Minster. ✉ *7 Scarcroft Rd.* ☎ *01904/634341* ✍ *Reservations essential* ▤ *MC, V* ⊗ *Closed 3 wks at Christmas, and 1 wk in Aug. No lunch Mon; no dinner Sun.*

★ **££–£££** ✕ **Blue Bicycle.** York's best restaurant is in a building that once served as a brothel. Downstairs are evocative walled booths and at street level is a lively room with wood floors in a candlelight glow. The menu concentrates on local beef and seafood. You can start with crab cannelloni on spinach salad, and move on to seared salmon or the fillet of Yorkshire beef on smoked bacon mashed potatoes. The wine list is good, and the service couldn't be friendlier. ✉ *34 Fossgate* ☎ *01904/673990* ✍ *Reservations essential* ▤ *MC, V.*

££ ✕ **Café Concerto.** Music ephemera decorate this relaxed, intimate bistro in sight of York Minster, which prepares virtually any style of food you care to name, from Caribbean to continental. You might choose the Cuban spiced chicken with sweet potatoes, and then homemade cake and a cappuccino. ✉ *21 High Petergate* ☎ *01904/610478* ▤ *No credit cards.*

£ ✕ **Golden Slipper.** Although it's only a stone's throw from the busy minster, this warm and cozy place with book-lined walls resembles a country pub. Besides good homemade pies—try the pork, apple, and sage—there are stuffed baked potatoes and hot and cold sandwiches, all served until 7 PM, or 5 PM on weekends. ✉ *20 Goodramgate* ☎ *01904/651235* ▤ *MC, V.*

Where to Stay

★ **£££££** ⌂ **Middlethorpe Hall & Spa.** This splendidly restored 18th-century mansion, about 1½ mi from the city center, was the sometime home of the traveler and diarist Lady Mary Wortley Montagu (1689–1762). Antiques, paintings, and fresh flowers fill the traditionally decorated rooms, some in cottage-style accommodations around an 18th-century courtyard. The extensive grounds include a lake and a 17th-century dovecote. The Anglo-French menu of the wood-paneled restaurant changes seasonally but always has more than a hint of luxury—like the hotel itself. ⊠ *Bishopthorpe Rd., YO23 2GB* ☎ *01904/641241* 🖷 *01904/620176* ⊕ *www. middlethorpe.com* ➦ *23 rooms, 8 suites* ♿ *Restaurant, room TVs with movies, in-room data ports, indoor pool, gym, health club, sauna, spa, croquet, bar, laundry service, meeting rooms, free parking; no a/c, no kids under 8* ▭ *AE, MC, V* ⏍ *CP.*

££££ 🖵 **Dean Court Hotel.** The clergy of York Minster, just across the way, once found accommodations at this large Victorian house. Traditionally furnished rooms with plenty of print fabrics and plump sofas have fine views overlooking the minster. The restaurant serves good English cuisine, including a hearty Yorkshire breakfast. ⊠ *Duncombe Pl., YO1 7EF* ☎ *01904/625082* 🖷 *01904/620305* ⊕ *www.bw-deancourt.co.uk* ➦ *39 rooms* ♿ *Restaurant, coffee shop, room service, cable TV, in-room data ports, bar, meeting rooms, parking (fee), no-smoking rooms; no a/c* ▭ *AE, DC, MC, V* ⏍ *BP.*

££££ 🖵 **One3two.** This small Georgian town house manages to be plushly contemporary without sacrificing its period features. Bedrooms done in rich solid colors have teak beds and Egyptian cotton linens; the marble bathrooms have walk-in showers and deep bathtubs. You can take breakfast in the elegant, pumpkin-hue dining room, or have a champagne hamper delivered to your room. ⊠ *132 The Mount, YO24 1AS* ☎ *01904/ 600060* 🖷 *01904/676132* ⊕ *www.one3two.co.uk* ➦ *5 rooms* ♿ *Minibars, in-room data ports; no a/c, no smoking* ▭ *MC, V* ⏍ *BP.*

£££ 🖵 **Judge's Lodgings.** This Georgian mansion provided rooms for justices when they traveled up north from London's Inns of Court. The somewhat shabby-genteel lobby leads to the main salon—a delightful, cozy cocoon of pastels, overstuffed chairs, and gilded mirrors. The finest room in the house is the "Minster" with a sunken hot tub and a massive 7-foot fourposter (£130). ⊠ *9 Lendal, YO1 2AQ* ☎ *01904/638733* 🖷 *01904/ 679947* ⊕ *www.judgeslodgings.com* ➦ *14 rooms* ♿ *Restaurant, cable TV, bar, meeting rooms, free parking; no a/c* ▭ *AE, DC, MC, V* ⏍ *BP.*

£££ 🖵 **Mount Royale Hotel.** In a quiet country house in the upscale residential part of west York, near the racecourse, this hotel offers excellent service that is both professional and friendly. Outside near the pool, discover orange, lemon, and fig trees mingling with the sprays of flowers in the pristine English garden. Rooms are spacious and decorated simply with subtle colors; four have walk-in closets and verandas that lead to the garden. ■ TIP➔ **The modern European restaurant, Sous le Mont (££–££££), is one of York's most popular; if you drive, expect to fight for parking.** This hotel is too far from the city center to walk to. ⊠ *117–119 The Mount, YO24 1GU* ☎ *01904/628856, 01904/619444 for restaurant* 🖷 *01904/611171* ⊕ *www.mountroyale.co.uk* ➦ *23 rooms* ♿ *Restaurant, room service, cable TV, pool, bar, laundry service, meeting rooms; no a/c* ▭ *AE, DC, MC, V* ⏍ *BP.*

££–£££ 🖵 **The Hazelwood.** Only 400 yards from York Minster, this tall Victorian town house stands in a peaceful cul-de-sac, away from the noise of traffic. Reds and golds dominate bedrooms furnished with rich fabrics and handsome traditional wood pieces. The memorable breakfasts include black pudding, Danish pastries, and vegetarian sausages. ✉ *24–25 Portland St., YO31 7EH* ☎ *01904/626548* 🖶 *01904/628032* ⊕ *www.thehazelwoodyork.com* ➘ *14 rooms* ☖ *Free parking; no a/c, no room phones, no kids under 8, no smoking* ➾ *MC, V* ⵏⵎ *BP.*

££ 🏠 **Dairy Guest House.** Victorian stained glass, pine woodwork, and intricate plaster cornices are original features of this former dairy 200 yards from the city walls. Bedrooms, done in pleasant pastels, come with books and games, and the imaginative breakfasts (served 8:30–9:15) can accommodate vegetarians and vegans. The flower-filled internal courtyard is lovely. ✉ *3 Scarcroft Rd., YO23 1ND* ☎ *01904/639367* ⊕ *www.dairyguesthouse.co.uk* ➘ *5 rooms* ☖ *Some pets allowed; no a/c, no room phones, no smoking* ➾ *MC, V* ⵏⵎ *BP.*

£–££ 🏠 **Eastons.** Two Victorian houses knocked into one, this guesthouse retains a rich sense of the era. Dark colors enhance the marble fireplaces, wood paneling, tiling, antique furniture, and big sofas. Breakfast is substantial. It's easy to find parking on the street, which is just south of the city center, 300 yards from the city walls. ✉ *88–90 Bishopthorpe Rd., YO23 1JS* ☎ *01904/626646* 🖶 *01904/626165* ⊕ *www.eastons.ws* ➘ *10 rooms* ☖ *No a/c, no room phones, no kids under 5, no smoking* ➾ *No credit cards* ⵏⵎ *BP.*

Nightlife & the Arts

Nightlife

York is full of historic pubs where you can while away an hour over a pint. The **Black Swan** (✉ Peasholme Green ☎ 01904/686911) is the city's oldest pub, a 16th-century Tudor building. It's said to be haunted by a young girl that sits by the fireplace. The **Old White Swan** (✉ Goodramgate ☎ 01904/540911) is vast, spreading across five medieval, half-timbered buildings on busy Goodramgate. It's known for its good pub lunches, and its ghosts—it claims to be more haunted than the Black Swan. The **Snickleway Inn** (✉ Goodramgate ☎ 01904/656138) is in a 15th-century building with open fireplaces and a real sense of history.

The Arts

The **Early Music Festival** (☎ 01904/658338 festival office, 01904/621756 Tourist Information Centre ⊕ www.ncem.co.uk) is held each July. The **Viking Festival** (✉ Jorvik, Coppergate ☎ 01904/543402 ⊕ www.vikingjorvik.com) takes place each February. The celebrations, including a parade and long-ship regatta, end with the Jorvik Viking Combat reenactment, when Norsemen confront their Anglo-Saxon enemies.

In a lovely 18th-century building, the **York Theatre Royal** (✉ St. Leonard's Pl. ☎ 01904/623568) presents plays, music, poetry readings, and art exhibitions.

Shopping

The new and secondhand bookstores around Petergate, Stonegate, and the Shambles are excellent. The **Minster Gate Bookshop** (✉ 8 Minster Gate ☎ 01904/621812) sells secondhand books, old maps, and prints. **Mulberry Hall** (✉ Stonegate ☎ 01904/620736) is a sales center for all the famous names in fine bone china and crystal. It also has a neat café. The

York Antiques Centre (✉ 2 Lendal ☎ 01904/641445) has 25 shops selling antiques, bric-a-brac, books, and jewelry.

YORK ENVIRONS

West and north of York, a number of sights make easy, appealing day trips from the city: the spa town of Harrogate, atmospheric Knaresborough, the ruins of Fountain Abbey, the market town of Ripon and nearby Newby Hall, and Thirsk, with its James Herriot connection. If you're heading northwest from York to Harrogate, you might take the less direct B1224 across Marston Moor, where, in 1644, Oliver Cromwell won a decisive victory over the Royalists during the Civil War. A few miles beyond, at Wetherby, you can cut northwest along the A661 to Harrogate.

Harrogate

★ ㉖ *21 mi west of York, 11 mi south of Ripon, 16 mi north of Leeds.*

During the Regency and early Victorian periods, it became fashionable for the noble and wealthy to retire to a spa to "take the waters" for relaxation. In Yorkshire the trend reached its grandest heights in Harrogate, an elegant town that flourished during the 19th century. Today the Regency buildings, parks, and spas built during that time make Harrogate an absorbing getaway. At the edge of the town center, the 200-acre grassy parkland known as **The Stray** is a riot of color in spring. The **Valley Gardens**, southwest of the town center, include a boating lake, tennis courts, and a little café.

The **Royal Pump Room Museum** is in the octagonal structure built in 1842 over the original sulfur well that brought great prosperity to the town. You can still drink the evil-smelling (and nasty-tasting) spa waters here. The museum displays some equipment of spa days gone by, alongside a rather eccentric collection of fine 19th-century china, clothes, and bicycles. ✉ *Crown Pl.* ☎ *01423/556188* ⊕ *www.harrogate.gov.uk* 🎟 *£2.80* ☉ *Apr.–Oct., Mon.–Sat. 10–5, Sun. 2–5; Nov.–Mar., Mon.–Sat. 10–4, Sun. 2–4.*

★ The exotic and fully restored **Turkish Baths** (1897) allow you to experience what brought so many Victorians to Harrogate. After changing into your bathing suit, you can relax on luxurious lounge chairs in the mosaic-tile warming room. Move on to increasingly hot sauna rooms, then soak up eucalyptus mist in the steam room before braving the icy plunge pool. You can also book a massage or facial. Open hours are divided into women-only, men-only, and couples-only nights. Book in advance. ✉ *Parliament St.* ☎ *01423/556746* ⊕ *www.harrogate.gov.uk/ turkishbaths* 🎟 *£12 per bath and sauna session, massages and treatments additional* ☉ *Daily; call for schedules.*

Where to Stay & Eat

£ ✕ **Betty's.** The celebrated Yorkshire tearoom began life in Harrogate in the 1920s, when Swiss restaurateur Frederic Belmont brought his Alpine specialties to England. The elegant surroundings have changed little since then, and the same cakes and pastries are for sale, along with teas. A pianist plays nightly. ✉ *1 Parliament St.* ☎ *01423/502746* ▭ *MC, V.*

12

£££ ✗🍴 **Balmoral Hotel.** Luxurious contemporary and antique furniture, patterned wallpapers, and colorful ornaments and posters fill this mock-Tudor edifice. Ten pastel-hue bedrooms have mahogany, walnut, or oak four-poster beds, all frilled and draped. The lively Villu Toots restaurant (££–£££), known for its cocktail creations, reverts to a minimalist style; the contemporary menu is eclectic. Guests have access to a nearby health club. Prices rise when conventions meet in town. ✉ *Franklin Mt., HG1 5EJ* ☎ *01423/508208* 🖷 *01423/530652* ⊕ *www.balmoralhotel.co.uk* ⤴ *20 rooms, 1 suite* ♿ *Restaurant, bar, meeting rooms, some pets allowed; no a/c* ▭ *AE, MC, V* 🍽 *BP.*

£££ ✗🍴 **Hotel du Vin.** Tired of chintz? This hip hotel chain has taken over eight Georgian houses for its latest offering, using stripped wood floors, clubby leather armchairs, and a purple baize billiard table to set the tone. Bedrooms, clean-lined and modern, are done in beige and cream tones, with Egyptian linens and pampering bathrooms. The bar is a serious place to drink, and the popular bistro (£££) offers classics like roasted lamb, smoked salmon, and vegetarian linguine. ✉ *Prospect Pl., HG1 1LB* ☎ *01423/856800* 🖷 *01423/856801* ⊕ *www.hotelduvin.com* ⤴ *35 rooms, 8 suites* ♿ *Restaurant, in-room safes, cable TV, in-room data ports, gym, bar, meeting rooms; no a/c, no smoking* ▭ *AE, MC, V.*

Nightlife & the Arts

★ Harrogate's annual **International Festival** (☎ 01423/562303 ⊕ www.harrogate-festival.org.uk) of ballet, music, contemporary dance, film, comedy, street theater, and more takes place during two weeks at the end of July and beginning of August.

Knaresborough

㉗ *3 mi northeast of Harrogate, 17 mi west of York.*

At the bottom of a precipitously deep rocky gorge along the River Nidd, the little town of Knaresborough couldn't be more photogenic. It's best seen from a train, crossing the high viaduct above. Once you leave the train, there's a steep descent to the riverside. In summer you can rent a boat and paddle down the slow-moving river and wander its little marketplace, and year-round you can climb to the hilltop ruins of the castle where Richard II was imprisoned in 1399.

The touristy **Mother Shipton's Cave,** across the river from the main riverside attractions, is tucked in a pleasant park. The cave is, according to local lore, the birthplace of the titular 16th-century prophetess. Events supposedly foretold by her include the defeat of the Spanish Armada. The mineral-rich well beside her cave is famed for its ability to turn any object to stone in just a few hours. It's all good fun. ✉ *Prophesy House, High Bridge* ☎ *01423/864600* ⊕ *www.mothershipton.co.uk* 🎫 *£6* ⊙ *Mar.–Oct., daily 10–5:45; last admission 5.*

Studley Royal Water Garden & Fountains Abbey

★ **㉘** *9 mi northwest of Knaresborough, 4 mi southwest of Ripon.*

You can easily spend a day at this World Heritage Site, a 822-acre complex made up of an 18th-century water garden and deer park and the

The Monastic Past

THE SHEER NUMBER of once richly decorated monastic buildings here is a testament to the power of the Catholic monks of medieval Yorkshire. They became some of the richest in Europe by virtue of the international wool trade that they conducted, with the help of lay workers, from their vast religious estates. The buildings lie mostly in romantic ruins, a result of the dissolution of the monasteries during the 16th century, part of Henry VIII's struggle with the Catholic church over finances and his divorce request (the rejection of which he perceived as a calculated way to deny him a male heir). Henry's break with Rome was made official in 1534 with the Act of Supremacy, which made him head of the Church of England. By 1540, no monasteries or abbeys remained; the king confiscated all their property, distributed the lands, and destroyed or gave away many buildings. Today the ruined abbeys at Fountains, Rievaulx, and Whitby are top attractions where you can learn about the religious and business worlds of the great monasteries, and the political machinations that destroyed them. They serve as vivid reminders of what life was like in the Middle Ages.

majestic ruins of medieval Fountains Abbey. Here, a neoclassical vision of an ordered universe—with lakes, spectacular water terraces, classical temples, statues, and a grotto—blends with the glories of English Gothic architecture. The abbey, on the banks of the River Skell, was founded in 1132 and completed in the early 1500s. The Cistercian monks here, called "White Monks" for the color of their robes, devoted their lives to silence, prayer, and work. Of the surviving buildings, the lay brothers' echoing refectory and dormitory impresses most; the Gothic tower was a 16th-century addition. Fountains Mill, with sections dating back to 1140, displays reconstructed mill machinery (wool was the monks' large and profitable business). The 17th-century Fountains Hall, partially built with stones taken from the abbey, has an exhibition and video display. ⊠ *Off B6265* ☎ *01765/608888* ⊕ *www. fountainsabbey.org.uk* ⊠ *£5.50* ⊗ *Mar.–Oct., daily 10–6; Feb. and Nov., daily 10–4. Free guided tours of abbey and gardens Apr.–Oct., daily at 11, 1:30, and 2:30 (June–Aug. extra tour at 3:30); water garden tour Apr.–Oct., daily at 2.*

Ripon

 4 mi northeast of Fountains Abbey, 11 mi north of Harrogate, 24 mi northwest of York.

Ripon was thriving as early as the 9th century as an important market center. A relatively small church has been designated a cathedral since the mid-19th century, which makes Ripon, with only about 15,000 inhabitants, technically a city. Market day, Thursday, is probably the best day to stop by. Successive churches here were destroyed by the Vikings and the Normans, and the current **Ripon Cathedral,** dating from the 12th and 13th centuries, is notable for its finely carved choir stalls. The

12

Saxon crypt (AD 672), now an empty series of chambers, housed sacred relics. ✉ *Minster Rd.* ☎ *01765/602072* ⊕ *www.riponcathedral.org.uk* 💷 *£3 donation requested* ⊙ *Daily 8–5.*

Where to Stay

££££–£££££ 🏨 **Swinton Park.** The Cunliffe-Lister family operates part of its ancestral castle—a stately pile rebuilt in the 18th and 19th centuries with turret and battlements—as an upscale country-house hotel. The plush public rooms give you space to relax, and the traditionally decorated bedrooms are named and themed after towns in Yorkshire. Two hundred acres of parkland near Yorkshire Dales National Park guarantee seclusion and abundant outdoor pursuits. Chef-author Rosemary Shrager has a cooking school on the grounds. Masham is 8 mi north of Ripon and 35 mi north of Leeds and York. ✉ *Off A1, Swinton Park, Masham HG4 4JH* ☎ *01765/680900* 🖷 *01765/680901* ⊕ *www.swintonpark. com* 🛏 *26 rooms, 4 suites* 🍴 *Restaurant, cable TV, in-room data ports, gym, hot tub, fishing, mountain bikes, horseback riding, meeting rooms, some pets allowed (fee); no a/c* ▤ *AE, DC, MC, V* ⏐○⏐ *BP.*

Newby Hall

🐚 ㉚ *5 mi southeast of Ripon.*

An early-18th-century house redecorated later in the same century by Robert Adam for his patron William Weddell, Newby Hall contains fine decorative art of its period, particularly ornamental plasterwork and Chippendale furniture. The domed Sculpture Hall with Roman works, and the Tapestry Hall, with its priceless Gobelin tapestries, are gorgeous; both are Adams designs. The 25 acres of gardens are justifiably famous; a double herbaceous border, which runs down to the river, separates garden "rooms," each flowering during a different season. A miniature railroad, playground, and pedal boats amuse kids. ✉ *Skelton-on-Ure* ☎ *01423/322583* ⊕ *www.newbyhall.co.uk* 💷 *£8.20, gardens only £6.70* ⊙ *Apr.–Sept., Tues.–Sun. and national holiday Mon., house noon–5, grounds 11–5:30; last admission 30 mins before closing.*

Thirsk

㉛ *15 mi north of Newby Hall, 23 mi north of York.*

This busy market town on the western edge of the moors was a thriving place on the main east–west route from the dales to the coast. Lovely Georgian houses abound, and the cobbled medieval Market Place is handsome; Saturday and Monday are market days. Today Thirsk is best known as the place where veterinarian Alf Wight (who wrote about his experiences under the name James Herriot) had his practice. The popular
🐚 **World of James Herriot,** in the author's actual office, re-creates the operating room and the living spaces of the 1940s and 1950s; it also displays veterinary artifacts. The interactive displays upstairs appeal to kids and adults alike. ✉ *23 Kirkgate* ☎ *01845/524234* ⊕ *www. worldofjamesherriot.org* 💷 *£5* ⊙ *Apr.–Sept., daily 10–6; Oct.–Mar., daily 11–4; last admission 1 hr before closing.*

THE NORTH YORKSHIRE COAST

The North York Moors plummet down to the sea in spectacular cliffs that stretch down the coastline, creating a dramatic view of pink heather and white cliffs hundreds of feet above the dark sea. The red roofs of Robin Hood's Bay, the sharply curved bay at Whitby, and the gold and white buildings of Scarborough capture the imagination at first sight. Most coastal towns still support an active fishing industry, and every harbor offers fishing and leisure trips throughout summer. Beaches at Scarborough, Whitby, and Filey have patrolled areas: swim (in cold water) between the red-and-yellow flags, and don't swim when a red flag is flying. All the North Sea beaches are ideal for fossil hunting and seashell collecting.

Coastal Bridlington is about an hour's drive away from York. From here you can follow the main road north to Scarborough (A165), and on to Robin Hood's Bay and Whitby (A171). Otherwise, you can head directly across the moors to Whitby, which makes for a more wild and beautiful journey not to be taken lightly in winter.

Bridlington

32 *41 mi east of York.*

A fishing port with an ancient harbor, Bridlington is the lesser of the Yorkshire seaside towns, although it arguably has the best beach of them all—a wide arc of dark sand. Boat trips through the harbor and up the coast depart frequently in summer, or you can simply join the milling crowds that promenade up and down the tattered seafront, eating fish-and-chips, browsing at the cheap gift shops, and frequenting the rides at the battered amusement park. At **Flamborough Head** a huge bank of chalk cliffs plunges dramatically into the North Sea.

A coastal path over the cliff tops ends at the seabird reserve of **Bempton Cliffs,** where a colony of 7,000 rare puffins nest on the 400-foot-high cliffs between March and August. The reserve, off B1229, is open at all times, and the nearby visitor center provides orientation. Rent binoculars for a closer view of the puffins, shags, kittiwakes, gannets, guillemots, and razorbills that make the cliffs their home. ⊠ *Visitor Centre, Cliff La., Bempton* ☎ *01262/851179* ⊕ *www.rspb.org.uk* ✉ *Free, parking £3 Mar.–Sept.* ☉ *Visitor center Mar.–Nov., daily 10–5; Dec.–Feb., daily 9:30–4.*

**OFF THE
BEATEN
PATH**

BEVERLEY – A 20-mi drive southwest from Bridlington through wolds and flatlands brings you to this market town, well worth exploring for its old streets, timbered houses, and Georgian terraces. Of the city's 350 buildings of architectural or historical merit, the standout is **Beverley Minster** (⊠ Minster Yard North ☎ 01482/868540 ⊕ www.beverleyminster. co.uk ✉ £2 suggested donation ☉ Mon.–Sat. 9–dusk, Sun. noon–dusk), a lovely Gothic church, filled with elaborate carving.

Where to Eat

£–££ ✕ **Jerome's.** Wrought iron decorates this seafront café-restaurant, which keeps up with these multicultural times with a selection of good-value dishes from around Europe. Popular options are the Greek salad, the chef's roast, and the specialty ice creams (26 varieties). ⊠ *The Floral Pavilion, Royal Prince's Parade* ☎ *01262/671881* ⊟ *AE, DC, MC, V.*

Scarborough

❸❸ *17 mi north of Bridlington, 34 mi northeast of York.*

There is no Scarborough Fair, and historians are divided on whether there ever was one, but don't let that stop you from heading to this classic English seaside resort, where lemon-color Victorian houses top cliffs overlooking the dark blue sea. The older, more genteel side of Scarborough is in the southern half of town, with carefully laid-out crescents and squares, the ruins of its castle, and views across Cayton Bay. The northern side is a riot of tacky seaside arcades, ice-cream stands, bingo halls, and stores selling "rock" (luridly colored hard candy). The huddle of streets, alleyways, and red-roof cottages around the harbor give an idea of what the town was like before the resort days.

For nearly 900 years the rambling ruins of **Scarborough Castle** have dominated the northern headland. The Romans used the site as a signaling station in the fourth century, and archaeological digs have uncovered evidence that people lived here in the Bronze age. The current structure dates to 1136, when it was built by William de Gros to replace a wooden fort. Henry II later took the castle for himself because he believed it was virtually impossible to invade. He was right: although the castle was repeatedly besieged, it was never taken by force. The castle has spectacular views across the North Bay and the shore gardens. ⊠ *Castle Rd.* ☎ *01723/372451* ⊕ *www.english-heritage.org.uk* ⊠ *£3.40* ☉ *Apr.–Sept., daily 10–6; Oct.–Mar., Thurs.–Mon. 10–4.*

Most visitors to the little medieval church of **St. Mary** (⊠ Castle Rd. ☎ 01723/500541) are attracted by the churchyard's most famous occupant: Anne, the youngest Brontë sister. She was taken to Scarborough from Haworth when suffering from turberculosis in a futile effort to save her life by exposing her to the sea air. She died in 1849. The church is near the castle on the way into town.

Wood End was the vacation home of 20th-century writers Edith, Osbert, and Sacheverell Sitwell, and the west wing houses a library of their works as well as paintings. The rest of the early Victorian house, set in delightful grounds, holds the collections of the **Museum of Natural**

A SPA IS BORN

In 1626, Elizabeth Farrow came upon a stream of acidic water running from a cliff south of Scarborough. This led to the town's establishment as a hugely popular spa on a par with Harrogate. By the 18th century, when icy sea bathing came into vogue, no beaches were busier than Scarborough's. Donkeys and horses drew wheeled cabins called bathing machines into the surf and anchored there. The city's prosperity manifested itself in the handsome Regency and early Victorian residences and hotels you see today.

History. ⊠ *The Crescent* ☎ *01723/367326* 🖭 *£2.50* ⊙ *June–Sept.,*
Tues.–Sun. 10–5; Oct.–May, Wed. and weekends 11–4.

The **Rotunda Museum,** an extraordinary circular building, was constructed in 1829 for William Smith of the Scarborough Philosophical
Society to display his geological collection; it now contains important
archaeological and local history collections. ⊠ *Vernon Rd.* ☎ *01723/*
374839 🖭 *£2.50 includes admission to Wood End* ⊙ *June–Sept.,*
Tues.–Sun. 10–5; Oct.–May, Tues., Sat., and Sun. 11–4.

Recognizable by its white pyramids, **Scarborough Sea Life Centre** is a great—
if expensive—way to keep the kids entertained for an afternoon. Fish,
crabs, and sting rays are presented in an engaging way, with lots of marine habitats. ⊠ *Scalby Mills, North Bay* ☎ *01723/373414* ⊕ *www.*
sealifeeurope.com 🖭 *£9.50, parking £1 for 3 hrs* ⊙ *Mar.–Oct., daily*
10–6; Nov.–Feb., daily 10–4; last admission 1 hr before closing.

Where to Stay & Eat

£££–££££ ✕ **Lanterna Ristorante.** This attractive but unpretentious restaurant prides
itself on not being modern. Instead it offers classic Italian dishes including tender steak cooked with ham and cheese. Opt for seasonal specials
using fresh vegetables, fish, and white truffles (October to January). ⊠ *33*
Queen St. ☎ *01723/363616* ▤ *MC, V* ⊙ *Closed Sun. and 2 wks late*
Oct. No lunch in winter.

£ ✕ **The Golden Grid.** Everyone has to have fish-and-chips at least once
in Scarborough, and this harbor-front spot is a classic of its kind. Choose
an upstairs window table and tuck into freshly fried cod or haddock.
⊠ *4 Sandside* ☎ *01723/360922* ▤ *MC, V* ⊙ *No dinner weekdays*
in winter.

£££ ▦ **The Crown.** The centerpiece of the Regency Esplanade, this 19th-cen-
tury hotel overlooks South Bay and the castle headland. Built to accommodate fashionable visitors to Scarborough Spa, it has been considerably
refurbished; rooms are modern and done in muted colors. Rates drop
for some two-night stays. ⊠ *The Esplanade, YO11 2AG* ☎ *01723/*
357426 🖶 *01723/357404* ⊕ *www.scarboroughhotel.com* 🛏 *87 rooms*
△ *2 restaurants, pool, health club, hot tub, sauna, steam room, 2 bars,*
meeting rooms, some pets allowed; no a/c ▤ *AE, MC, V* ⦅◎⦆ *BP.*

Nightlife & the Arts

Scarborough is one of England's busy theater towns, especially for summer rep, with most of the activity buzzing around the **Stephen Joseph**
Theatre (⊠ Westborough ☎ 01723/370541). It presents productions
on two stages and also has a cinema, a restaurant, and a bar. The tourist
office also has box-office details.

Robin Hood's Bay

★ ❸❹ *15 mi northwest of Scarborough.*

This tiny fishing village squeezed into a steep narrow ravine is absolutely adorable, from its name right down to its tiny red-roof cottages
and steep cobbled roads. The village has no connection to the famous
medieval outlaw, though. It was once a smuggling center that passed
contraband up the streambed beneath the cottages, linked to one an-

12

other by secret passages. The attraction here is the town itself, with its winding stone staircases that eventually wander off across the headland. ■ TIP→ **Park in the pay lots at the top of the hill (put coins into a machine to get a sticker; do not under any circumstances attempt to drive down to the bottom of the hill).**

The **beach** is lovely, but mercurial—the tide rushes in quickly, so take care not to get cut off. Provided the tide is out, you can stroll for a couple of hours south from the town, along a rough stone shore full of rock pools, inlets, and sandy strands. A few stretches of sand are suitable for sunbathers. To the south, at the curiously named **Boggle Hole,** a ravine nestles an old water mill, now an atmospheric youth hostel (signs mark the way on the clifftop path). Farther south is **Ravenscar,** a Victorian village that never took off and now consists of little more than a hotel, which can be reached by a hazardous but exhilarating path up the cliff. The walk back, along the cliff, is less tricky but no less energetic.

Where to Stay & Eat

£–££ ✕ **Bay Hotel.** The village's most favored pub is this friendly Victorian retreat, perfectly positioned at the bottom of the village, on a rocky outcrop lapped by the sea. The bar is festooned with oak and brass; in winter, a roaring fire warms all comers. Whitby scampi and chestnut and butter-bean casserole are often on the menu. ⊠ *The Dock* ☎ *01947/880278* ▤ *MC, V.*

££££ ▦ **Raven Hall Hotel.** This superb Georgian hotel with landscaped grounds offers unrivaled coastal views from the headland of Ravenscar, 3 mi southeast of Robin Hood's Bay. All rooms have faux-medieval beds, and you should try your utmost to secure a room with a bay view. The hotel is known for its good sports facilities; the bar marks the traditional end of the punishing, long-distance Lyke-Wake Walk, so on occasion you may share the lounge with exhausted walkers. It's worth checking dinner and B&B deals year-round. ⊠ *Ravenscar YO13 0ET* ☎ *01723/870353* ⊕ *www.ravenhall.co.uk* ⇨ *53 rooms* △ *Restaurant, in-room data ports, 9-hole golf course, 2 tennis courts, indoor pool, gym, hair salon, sauna, croquet, bar, recreation room, meeting rooms; no a/c* ▤ *AE, MC, V* ⥏◎ *BP.*

££ ▦ **Orchard House.** At the very center of town, Orchard House is a relaxing place to stay, with views of the town and the sea from its patio and from some rooms. Owners Mike and Carolyn Parry are friendly and offer a simple but good breakfast in the sunny common space. ⊠ *The Bolts YO22 4SG* ☎ *01947/880912* ⊕ *www.robinhoodsbayaccomodation. co.uk* ⇨ *3 rooms* △ *No a/c* ▤ *No credit cards* ⥏◎ *BP.*

Sports & the Outdoors

Several superb long-distance walks start at, finish in, or run through Robin Hood's Bay. The coastal part of **Cleveland Way** (⊕ www.clevelandway. gov.uk) runs north (to Whitby) and south (to Scarborough). The village marks one end of the 190-mi **Coast-to-Coast Walk**; the other is at St. Bees Head on the Irish Sea. Walkers finish at the Bay Hotel, above the harbor. The trans-moor **Lyke-Wake Walk** (⊕ www.lykewakewalk.co.uk) finishes 3 mi away at Ravenscar. **Wellington Lodge** (⊠ Staintondale

☎ 01723/871234 ⊕ www.llamatreks.co.uk), 3 mi south of Ravenscar, schedules llama treks along the moors or the coast; you walk, and the llamas carry your lunch.

Whitby

 Fodor'sChoice ★

35 *7 mi northwest of Robin Hood's Bay, 20 mi northeast of Pickering.*

A scenic seaside town with a Gothic edge, Whitby is a busy tourist hub, but it handles that fact so well you might not notice (except at dinnertime, when it's hard to get a seat in a restaurant). The town curves around its perfectly symmetrical harbor and winds its way up the cliffs. The glassy waters of the slow-moving River Esk cut through the town. Fine Georgian houses dominate the west side of the river (known as West Cliff), and across the swing bridge, smaller 17th-century buildings mark the old town (known as East Cliff). Here cobbled Church Street is packed in summer with people exploring the alleyways lined with small shops.

Whitby came to prominence as a whaling port. The first ships sailed from here to Greenland in the mid-18th century, captained by local men such as William Scoresby. Herman Melville paid tribute to this inventor of the crow's nest in *Moby Dick.* Whaling brought Whitby wealth and shipbuilding made it famous: Captain James Cook (1728–79), explorer and navigator, sailed on his first ship from Whitby in 1747, and all four of his subsequent discovery vessels were built in in the town.

On top of the East Cliff—reached by climbing 199 stone steps—the Gothic church of **St. Mary** overlooks the town, while it in turn is watched over by the gaunt ruins of Whitby Abbey. Bram Stoker came to Whitby to write *Dracula,* at times finding inspiration in such moments as when pallbearers carried the dead up the long staircase to the spooky churchyard. The unusual–looking church with its ship's-deck roof, tripledecker pulpit, and enclosed box pews dates from the 12th century, although almost everything you see today is the result of 19th- and 20th-century renovations. The weather-beaten churchyard is filled with the crooked old gravestones of ancient mariners. ■ TIP➜ **Rather than walking the 199 steps, you can drive to the hilltop (follow signs) and park in the abbey's large parking lot for a small fee.** ☒ *Church La., East Cliff* ☎ 01947/603421 ☜ *Free, donation suggested* ☉ *Apr., daily 10–4; May–Aug., daily 10–5; Sept. and Oct., daily 10–3; Nov.–Mar., daily 10–2.*

★ The glorious ruins of **Whitby Abbey,** high on the East Cliff, dominate the area. The skeletal remains of the once grand church can even be seen from the hills of the moors. The cutting-edge abbess St. Hilda founded the abbey in AD 657—it is

A LOCAL HAUNT

Locals know perfectly well that St. Mary's church is an eerie sight—at night it is chillingly lit by low spotlights. Kids like to stand in between the lights and the church, casting huge scary shadows that can be seen from the town below. In Bram Stoker's *Dracula,* the count claimed Lucy as his victim in the churchyard. Even though the tale is entirely fiction, few like to linger up there after dark.

CLOSE UP

Whitby Jet

IN THE 19TH CENTURY Whitby became famous around the western world for jet, a very hard, black form of natural carbon, found in thin seams along the coast here and worked into jewelry and ornaments. Known since prehistoric times and sometimes used to ward off the evil eye, it reached the peak of its popularity in the 1850s when 1,400 men and boys, supplied by 200 miners, made a good living in jewelry workshops all over the town. The queen of Bavaria was impressed enough to order a chain more than 4 feet long. On the death of her husband, Albert, in 1861, Queen Victoria introduced jet into court circles and set the fashion for mourning memorabilia.

You can see fine examples in the Whitby Museum on St. Hilda's Terrace and in the shop displays in the old town along Church Street and parallel to Sandgate. If you buy a piece, keep it shiny with baby oil.

one of very few founded by a woman, and operated with a mixed population of monks and nuns. Caedmon (died circa 670), the first identifiable poet of the English language, was a monk here. Sacked by the Vikings in the 9th century, the monastery was refounded in the 11th century and enlarged in the 13th century, from which point these ruins date. It flourished until it was destroyed by Henry VIII. The visitor center is excellent, with exhibits on the lives of St. Hilda and Bram Stoker, artifacts from the site, interactive displays on the medieval abbey, and a tea shop. ✉ *Abbey La., East Cliff* ☎ *01947/603568* ⊕ *www.english-heritage.org.uk* ✆ *£4.20* ⊙ *Apr.–Sept., daily 10–6; Oct., daily 10–5; Nov.–Mar., Thurs.–Mon. 10–4.*

Filled with exhibits relating to the man and explorer, the **Captain Cook Memorial Museum** is in the 18th-century house belonging to shipowner John Walker. Cook lived here as an apprentice from 1746 to 1749. On display are mementos of his epic expeditions, including maps, diaries, and drawings. ✉ *Grape La.* ☎ *01947/601900* ⊕ *www.cookmuseumwhitby.co.uk* ✆ *£3* ⊙ *Apr.–Oct., daily 9:45–5; Mar., daily 11–3.*

The **Whitby Museum** is a quirky place whose attention wanders from local geology and natural history to archaeology, whaling, and trade routes in Asia. It's interesting for its old-fashioned approach—displays still have handwritten cards. ✉ *St. Hilda's La., Pannett Park* ☎ *01947/602908* ⊕ *www.durain.demon.co.uk* ✆ *£3* ⊙ *May–Sept., Mon.–Sat. 9:30–5:30, Sun. 2–5; Oct.–Apr., Tues. 10–1, Wed.–Sat. 10–4, Sun. 2–4.*

OFF THE BEATEN PATH

GOATHLAND – This moorland village, 8 mi southwest of Whitby, attracts walkers and people who want to see the fictional Aidensfield of the British TV series *Heartbeat*. Its cute 1865 train station served as Hogsmeade Station for students arriving at the school of wizardry in *Harry Potter and the Sorcerer's Stone*. The 18-mi **North Yorkshire Moors Railway** (✉ Pickering Station, Park St., Pickering ☎ 01751/472508, 01751/473535 recorded information ⊕ www.northyorkshiremoorsrailway.

com ☒£13.50 round-trip ☉ Late Mar.–early Nov., daily; early Nov.–Feb., some weekends and holiday periods), between Grosmont and Pickering, passes through neat towns and moorland. Steam-powered trains (like the one that takes Harry to Hogwarts) provide a great outing.

Where to Stay & Eat

£–££ ✕ **Magpie Café.** Whitby is full of fish-and-chip places, but this is the one that draws the biggest crowd with a well-stocked menu that includes plaice, cod, and haddock along with grilled fish and meat platters. The food is good and fans say it's worth the wait, which can stretch to an hour on busy nights. ☒ *14 Pier Rd.* ☎ *01947/602058* ⌕ *Reservations not accepted* ⊟ *MC, V* ☉ *Closed Jan.*

££ ✕☶ **White Horse and Griffin.** When looking for the perfect inn, you want an old building with character, a roaring fire, and food to thrill. This 18th-century establishment, in which Charles Dickens once slept and railway pioneer George Stephenson lectured, fills the bill. The tidy rooms, done in an uncluttered traditional style, are warmly decorated in muted colors, and downstairs the cozy bistro-bar (*££–£££*) serves a fine, changing menu with locally caught fish and game in season. ☒ *Church St., YO22 4BH* ☎ *01947/604857* ⌨ *01947/604857* ⊕ *www. whitehorseandgriffin.co.uk* ⤳ *10 rooms* ⌕ *Restaurant, bar, meeting rooms, some pets allowed; no a/c, no room phones, no smoking* ⊟ *MC, V* ⏉ *BP.*

££££ ☶ **Dunsley Hall Hotel.** Built as the home of a shipping magnate, this family-run Victorian country-house hotel has 4 acres of gardens and grounds. Stained- and leaded-glass windows and plenty of wood paneling complement rich carpets, rocking chairs, and leather armchairs. Bedrooms are spacious and the only intrusion is the occasional screech of a peacock. The hotel is 4 mi west of Whitby. ☒ *Dunsley YO21 3TL* ☎ *01947/ 893437* ⌨ *01947/893505* ⊕ *www.dunsleyhall.com* ⤳ *18 rooms* ⌕ *Restaurant, putting green, tennis court, indoor pool, gym, sauna, croquet, bar, meeting rooms; no a/c* ⊟ *AE, MC, V* ⏉ *BP.*

£ ☶ **Shepherd's Purse.** This splendid little complex in the cobbled old town consists of boutique-style guest rooms, an organic café that looks like a junk shop, and a health-food store. There are two less-expensive bedrooms above the stores and others in the galleried courtyard at the back. Although small, many rooms have four-poster or brass bedsteads; floors are wooden, the furniture is country style, and two rooms overlooking the courtyard have balconies. ☒ *95 Church St., YO22 4BH* ☎ *01947/820228* ⤳ *9 rooms, 5 with bath* ⌕ *Restaurant, meeting rooms, some pets allowed; no a/c, no room phones* ⊟ *MC, V* ⏉ *BP.*

Nightlife & the Arts

The **Whitby Regatta** (⊕ www.whitbyregatta.co.uk), held at the beginning of August, is a three-day jamboree of boat races, fair rides, lifeboat rescue displays, fireworks, and music. Music (but also traditional dance
★ and storytelling) predominates during **Whitby Folk Week** (⊕ www. folkwhitby.freeserve.co.uk), usually held the week before the late-August bank holiday, when pubs, sidewalks, and halls become venues for more than 600 traditional folk events by British performers.

THE NORTH YORK MOORS

The North York Moors are a dramatic swath of high moorland starting 25 mi north of the city of York and stretching east to the coast and west to the Cleveland Hills. Once covered in forest, of which a few pockets survive, the landscape changed when the monks at Rievaulx and Whitby abbeys began raising huge flocks of sheep in medieval times. Over the course of centuries, the sheep have kept the moors deforested, and still ensure that the pink heather on which they feed spreads lushly across the hills. A series of isolated, medieval "standing stones" that once acted as signposts on the paths between the abbeys are now handy for hikers.

For more than four decades the area has been designated a national park, ensuring the protection of the bleak moors and grassy valleys that shelter brownstone villages and hamlets. Minor roads and tracks crisscross the hills in all directions, and there's no single, obvious route through the region. Perhaps the most rewarding approach is west from the coast at Whitby, along the Esk Valley to Danby, which is also accessible on the Esk Valley branch train line between Middlesbrough and Whitby. From Danby, minor roads run south over the high moors reaching Hutton-le-Hole, beyond which main roads lead to interesting towns on the moors' edge, such as Helmsley. Completing the route in this direction leaves you with an easy side trip to Castle Howard before returning to nearby York.

Danby

 15 mi west of Whitby.

The old stone village of Danby nestles in a green valley, just a short walk from the tops of the moors. It's been settled since Viking times—Danby means "village where the Danes lived"—and these days it bumbles along in a semitourled way. There's a pub, and a cozy bakery with a tearoom, and if you bring hiking boots, within 10 minutes you can be above the village looking down, surrounded by moorland. To get here from Whitby, take A171 west and turn north for Danby after 12 mi, after which it's a 3-mi drive over Danby Low Moor to the village.

In a house on the eastern outskirts of Danby, the North York Moors National Park's **Moors Centre** has exhibitions, displays, and plenty of information. There's also a tearoom with picnic tables. The summer Moorsbus operates from the center for the 30-minutes' journey south to Hutton-le-Hole. ⊠ *Danby Lodge* ☎ *01439/772737* ⊕ *www.moors. uk.net* ⊠ *Free; parking £1.50* ☉ *Jan. and Feb., weekends 11–4; Mar., Nov., and Dec., daily 11–4; Apr.–Oct., daily 10–5.*

EN ROUTE

From Danby take the road due west for 2 mi to Castleton, and then turn south over the top of the moors toward Hutton-le-Hole. The narrow road offers magnificent views over North York Moors National Park, especially at the old stone **Ralph Cross** (5 mi), which marks the park's highest point. Drive carefully: sheep-dodging is a necessary art.

Hutton-le-Hole

③ *13 mi south of Danby.*

Similar to many other area villages, sleepy Hutton-le-Hole is a charming little place based around a wide village green, with fluffy sheep snoozing in the shade of stone cottages. Due to its frequent selection by guidebooks as *the* village to see in the area, it can be unbearably crowded in summer. You can always keep driving to either the nearby burg of Thorton-le-Dale or to the medieval market towns of Helmsley or Pickering.

⚮ The excellent 3-acre, open-air **Ryedale Folk Museum** interprets life in the Dales from prehistory onward through craft demonstrations and 13 historic buildings, including a medieval kiln, 16th-century cottages, and a 19th-century blacksmith's shop. ☎ *01751/417367* ⊕ *www. ryedalefolkmuseum.co.uk* ✑ *£4.75* ☉ *Early Mar.–Oct., daily 10–5:30; Nov.–Feb., daily 10–dusk; last admission 4:30.*

Helmsley

★ **③** *8 mi southwest of Hutton-le-Hole, 27 mi north of York.*

The picture-perfect market town of Helmsley, with its flowering window boxes, stone cottages, arched bridges across streams, and churchyard, is the perfect place to spend a relaxing afternoon. You can while away a few hours lingering in its tea shops and tiny boutiques, and exploring the craggy ruins of its Norman castle (destroyed during the Civil War). Market day is Friday.

Where to Stay & Eat

£££££ ✕▦ **Black Swan.** A splendid, relaxing base, this ivy-covered property sits on the edge of the market square. The building is a hybrid—part 16th-century coaching inn, part Georgian house. Cozy rooms overlook either the square or the fine walled garden at the back. The restaurant (*££–£££*) serves traditional British and local dishes. ⊠ *Market Pl., YO62 5BJ* ☎ *01439/770466, 0870/400–8112 for reservations* 🖹 *01439/ 770174* ✑ *45 rooms* ⚭ *Restaurant, cable TV, croquet, bar, meeting rooms, some pets allowed; no a/c* ▤ *AE, DC, MC, V* ⦿ *BP.*

££ ▦ **No. 54.** Tea and cakes provide a tasty welcome in this stone cottage just off market square. The small rooms are decorated in creamy hues, with comfortable beds and lots of light. Owner Lizzie Would knows everything about the area and is happy to help. She'll cook you a fine dinner for £22 if you book in advance. ⊠ *Bondgate, YO62 5EZ* ☎ *01439/ 771533* ⊕ *www.no54.co.uk* ✑ *3 rooms* ⚭ *Dining room; no a/c, no room phones* ▤ *No credit cards* ⦿ *BP.*

Sports & the Outdoors

Helmsley, on the southern edge of the moors, is the starting point of the **Cleveland Way** (⊕ www.clevelandway.co.uk), the long-distance moor-and-coastal footpath. Boots are donned at the old cross in the market square; it's 50 mi or so across the moors to the coast and then a similar distance south to Filey along the cliff tops. The footpath is 110 mi long and takes around nine days start to finish. The trail passes close to Rievaulx Abbey, a few miles outside town, and walking to Rievaulx is a good way to sample the trail. Maps are available at the tourist center in town, but the Rievaulx section is well sign-posted.

Rievaulx Abbey

39 *2 mi northwest of Helmsley.*

Fodor's Choice
★

The perfect marriage of architecture and countryside, Rievaulx (pronounced ree-*voh*) Abbey has a dramatic setting; its sweeping arches soar at the precise point where a forested hillside rushes down to the River Rye. A French Cistercian sect founded this abbey in 1132, and though its monks led a life of isolation and silence, they were active in the wool business. By the end of the 13th century the abbey was massively wealthy, with hundreds of lay workers and farmland filling the valley. The evocative ruins give a good indication of how vast the abbey once was. Tiny plaques indicate where the dormitories, kitchen, chapter house, and nave once stood. Medieval mosaic tiling can still be seen here and there, and part of the symmetrical cloisters remain. The Chapter House retains the original shrine of the first abbot, William, by the entrance. By the time of Henry VIII the abbey had shrunk dramatically; only 20 or so monks lived here when the king's soldiers arrived to destroy the building in 1538. After that, the earl of Rutland owned Rievaulx, and he destroyed what was left to the best of his ability. The abbey is a 1½-hour walk northwest from Helmsley by signposted footpath, or 2 mi by vehicle. ✉ *Off B1257* ☎ *01439/798228* ⊕ *www. english-heritage.org.uk* ✐ *£4.20* ☉ *Apr.–Sept., daily 10–6; Oct., daily 10–5; Nov.–Mar., Thurs.–Mon. 10–4.*

OFF THE
BEATEN
PATH

RIEVAULX TERRACE AND TEMPLES – From Rievaulx Abbey it's a short walk or drive up to the hill where Rievaulx Terraces have a magnificent view of the abbey. The long, grassy walkway on the hillside ends at the remains of several Tuscan- and Ionic-style classical temples, once maintained by the earl of Rutland. ✉ *Off B1257* ☎ *01439/798340* ⊕ *www. nationaltrust.org.uk* ✐ *£3.80* ☉ *Late Mar.–Sept., daily 10:30–6; Oct., daily 10:30–5; last admission 1 hr before closing.*

Castle Howard

40 *14 mi southeast of Rievaulx Abbey, 12 mi southeast of Helmsley, 15 mi*
Fodor's Choice *northeast of York.*
★

Standing serene among the Howardian Hills to the west of Malton, Castle Howard is an opulent stately home whose magnificent profile is punctuated by stone chimneys and a graceful central dome. Many people know it best as Brideshead, the home of the Flyte family in Evelyn Waugh's tale of aristocratic woe, *Brideshead Revisited,* because much of the 1981 TV series was filmed here. The house was designed for the Howard family (who still live here) by Sir John Vanbrugh (1664–1726). Considering its many theatrical, even flamboyant features, it seems fitting that Vanbrugh was praised more as a playwright than an architect (he also had careers as a soldier and adventurer). In 18th-century London, his plays were second in popularity only to Congreve's. This was Vanbrugh's first building design; his self-assurance knowing no bounds, he went on to create Blenheim Palace, the Versailles of England. For Castle Howard, however, Vanbrugh sought assistance, and turned to the brilliant Nicholas Hawksmoor (1661–1736), who at 18 had been under the tutelage of Christopher Wren. Hawksmoor encouraged adding bodies of water to the landscape, and he designed the imposing Mausoleum; many consider it a masterpiece equal to his churches in London.

The audacity of the great baroque house is startling, proclaiming the wealth and importance of the Howards. This was the first private residence in Britain built with a stone dome. A magnificent central hallway spanned by a hand-painted (in the 20th century) ceiling dwarfs all visitors, and there is no shortage of grandeur: vast family portraits, delicate marble fireplaces, immense and fading tapestries, huge pieces of Victorian silver on polished tables, and a great many marble busts. Outside, the stunning neoclassical landscape of carefully arranged woods, lakes, bridges, and obelisks led Horace Walpole, the 18th-century connoisseur, to comment that a pheasant at Castle Howard lives better than most dukes elsewhere. The grounds sprawl for miles, and hidden away among its hills and lakes (there's even a fanciful playground for children) are the Temple of the Four Winds and the Mausoleum, whose magnificence caused Walpole to quip that all who view it would wish to be buried alive. Hourly tours (included in the admission price) fill you in on more background and history. ⊠ *Off A64 and B1257, Coneysthorpe* ☎ *01653/648333* ⊕ *www.castlehoward.co.uk* ⊠ *£9.50, gardens only £6.50* ⊗ *House Mar.–Oct., daily 11–6, last admission 4. Grounds daily 10–6:30 or dusk, last admission 4:30.*

YORKSHIRE ESSENTIALS

Transportation

BY AIR

Leeds Bradford Airport, 8 mi northwest of Leeds, connects with domestic and European destinations. Manchester Airport, about 40 mi southwest of Leeds, is well served internationally.

Leeds Bradford International Airport ⊠ A658, Yeadon ☎ 0113/250-9696 ⊕ www.lbia.co.uk. **Manchester Airport** ⊠ Near Junctions 5 and 6 of M56 ☎ 0161/489-3000 ⊕ www.manairport.co.uk.

BY BUS

National Express serves the region from London's Victoria Coach Station. Average travel times are 4¼ hours to Leeds, 6 hours to York, and 8 hours to Scarborough.

Traveline and local tourist information centers can help you discover each district's own bus company. Timetable booklets for the Yorkshire Moors and Dales are widely available, and special summer services in both national parks provide bus connections. There are local Metro buses from Leeds and Bradford into the more remote parts of the Yorkshire Dales. Other companies are Harrogate & District for services to Ripon, Harrogate, and Leeds; Yorkshire Coastliner for Castle Howard, Scar-

12

borough, Whitby, Malton, and Leeds; and Arriva for Whitby, Scarborough, and Middlesbrough. In York, the main local bus operator is First.

CUTTING COSTS Many districts have Rover tickets; in York, the FirstWeek card (£10.50) gives a week's travel on all First bus services. With a West Yorkshire Day Rover you have a day's train and bus travel for £4.50; contact Metroline for details. The Moorsbus (information from any National Park office) runs every Sunday and bank-holiday Monday from April to the end of October, and daily from June to the end of September. It connects Danby, Hutton-le-Hole, Helmsley, Rievaulx Abbey, Rosedale Abbey, and Pickering and costs £3 for an all-day ticket. Note, though, that services are infrequent, and you may end up spending more time in the towns than you might wish.

FARES & SCHEDULES ☑ **Arriva** ☎ 0870/120-1088 ⊕ www.arriva.co.uk. **First** ☎ 01904/883000 ⊕ www.firstgroup.com. **Harrogate & District** ☎ 01423/566061. **Metroline** ☎ 0113/245-7676 ⊕ www.wymetro.com. **National Express** ☎ 0870/580-8080 ⊕ www.nationalexpress.com. **Traveline** ☎ 0870/608-2608 ⊕ www.traveline.org.uk. **Yorkshire Coastliner** ☎ 01653/692556 ⊕ www.yorkshirecoastliner.co.uk.

BY CAR

The M1, the principal route north from London, gets you to the region in about two hours, with longer travel times up into North Yorkshire. For York (193 mi) and the Scarborough areas, stay on M1 to Leeds (189 mi), then take A64. For the Yorkshire Dales, take M1 to Leeds, then A660 to A65 north and west to Skipton. For the North York Moors, either take B1363 north from York to Helmsley, or the A64 through Malton to Whitby. The trans-Pennine motorway, the M62, between Liverpool and Hull, crosses the bottom of this region. North of Leeds, A1 is the major north–south road, although narrow stretches, roadwork, and heavy traffic make this slow going at times.

ROAD CONDITIONS Some of the steep, narrow roads in the countryside off the main routes are difficult drives and can be perilous (or closed altogether) in winter. Main roads often closed by snowdrifts are the moorland A169 and the coast-and-moor A171. If you plan to drive in the dales or moors in winter, check the weather forecast in advance.

BY TRAIN

Great Northeastern Railways serves the region from London's King's Cross and Euston stations. Average travel times from King's Cross are 2½ hours to Leeds and 2 hours to York. It is possible to reach the North Yorkshire coast by train; journey time from London to Scarborough (change at York) is 4½ hours, to Whitby (change at Darlington and Middlesbrough) up to 6½ hours.

There is local service from Leeds to Skipton, and from York to Knaresborough and Harrogate and also to Scarborough (which has connections to the seaside towns of Filey and Bridlington). Whitby can be reached on the minor but attractive Esk Valley line from Middlesbrough. For train travel information in the region, call National Rail Enquiries.

CUTTING COSTS Two Regional Rover tickets for seven days' unlimited travel are available: North East (£73) and Coast and Peaks (£52.50). For the East Yorkshire area, which includes Scarborough, Bridlington, and York, an unlimited travel pass valid for four days (within an eight-day period) costs £32.50.

FARES & SCHEDULES **Great Northeastern Railways** ☎ 0845/722–5225 booking line, 44/19122–75959 from U.S. ⊕ www.gner.co.uk. **National Rail Enquiries** ☎ 0845/748–4950 ⊕ www.nationalrail.co.uk.

Contacts & Resources

DISCOUNTS & DEALS

The York Pass offers unlimited free entry to more than 30 attractions in or near the city (including Castle Howard), plus free transportation on City Sightseeing bus tours. You also get discounts on restaurants and theaters. Adult passes cost £19 (one day), £22.50 (two days), and £28.50 (three days), and can be purchased online, by phone, or at the York Tourist Information Centre.

York Pass ☎ 0870/242–9988 or 01904/621756 ⊕ www.yorkpass.com.

EMERGENCIES

Ambulance, fire, police ☎ 999. **Leeds General Infirmary** ⊠ Great George St., Leeds ☎ 0113/243–2799. **York District Hospital** ⊠ Wiggington Rd., York ☎ 01904/631313. **Whitby Hospital** ⊠ Spring Hill, Whitby ☎ 01947/604851.

INTERNET

Internet cafés are generally plentiful in cities like Leeds, but scarce in the countryside. Broadband is relatively rare in hotels (and virtually unheard of in guesthouses), and Wi-Fi is like gold dust.

Internet Cafés Internet Exchange ⊠ 29 Boar La., Leeds ☎ 0113/242–1093. **Internet Exchange** ⊠ 13 Stonegate, York ☎ 01904/638808. **Complete Computing** ⊠ 14 Northway, Scarborough ☎ 01723/500501.

SPORTS & THE OUTDOORS

BIKE TRAVEL Although the countryside is too hilly for extensive bicycle touring (except by experienced riders), you can rent bikes locally in several places. In York, where there are special bike paths, contact Europcar and pick up a cycling map from the tourist information center.

Bike Rentals Europcar ⊠ York Train Station, Station Rd., York ☎ 01904/656161.

NATIONAL PARKS For information about visitor centers, walks, and guided tours, contact Yorkshire Dales National Park and North York Moors National Park.

Yorkshire Dales National Park ☎ 01756/752745 ⊕ www.yorkshiredales.org.uk. **North York Moors National Park** ☎ 01439/770657 ⊕ www.moors.uk.net.

TOURS

BUS TOURS City Sightseeing runs frequent tours of York (£8.50), including stops at the minster, the Castle Museum, the Shambles, and Jorvik that allow you to get on and off the bus as you please.

City Sightseeing ☎ 01904/655585 ⊕ www.citysightseeing.co.uk.

WALKING TOURS The York Association of Voluntary Guides arranges short walking tours around the city, which depart daily at 10:15; there are additional tours at 2:15 PM April through October, and at 6:45 PM July and August. The tours are free, but a gratuity is appreciated. Yorktour also schedules walks of York.

🚹 **York Association of Voluntary Guides** ✉ De Grey Rooms, Exhibition Sq. ☎ 01904/640780. **Yorktour** ☎ 01423/321240 ⊕ www.eddiebrowntours.com.

VISITOR INFORMATION

The Yorkshire Tourist Board has information about the area. Local tourist information centers have varied opening hours. Many offices in the North York Moors and Yorkshire Dales open only in summer.

🚹 **Yorkshire Tourist Board** ✉ 312 Tadcaster Rd., York YO2 1GS ☎ 01904/707961 ⊕ www.yorkshirevisitor.com. **Beverley** ✉ 34 Butcher Row, HU17 0AB ☎ 01482/867430 ⊕ www.eastriding.gov.uk. **Bradford** ✉ City Hall, BD1 1HY ☎ 01274/433678 ⊕ www.visitbradford.com. **Bridlington** ✉ 25 Prince St., Humberside YO15 2NP ☎ 01262/673474 ⊕ www.eastriding.gov.uk. **Harrogate** ✉ Royal Baths, Crescent Rd., HG1 2RR ☎ 01423/537300 ⊕ www.harrogate.gov.uk. **Haworth** ✉ 2-4 West La., BD22 8EF ☎ 01535/642329. **Helmsley** ✉ Town Hall, Market Pl., YO62 5BL ☎ 01439/770173 ⊕ www.ryedale.gov.uk. **Knaresborough** ✉ 9 Castle Courtyard, Market Pl., HG5 8AE ☎ 01423/866886 ⊕ www.harrogate.gov.uke. **Leeds** ✉ Leeds City Station, LS1 1PL ☎ 0113/242-5242 ⊕ www.leeds.gov.uk. **Richmond** ✉ Friary Gardens, Victoria Rd., DL10 4AJ ☎ 01748/850252 ⊕ www.yorkshiredales.org. **Scarborough** ✉ Unit 3, Pavilion House, Valley Bridge Rd., YO11 1UZ ☎ 01723/383636 ⊕ www.discoveryorkshirecoast.com. **Skipton** ✉ 35 Coach St., BD23 1LQ ☎ 01756/792809 ⊕ www.skiptononline.co.uk. **Whitby** ✉ Langbourne Rd., YO21 1YN ☎ 01947/602674. **York** ✉ De Grey Rooms, Exhibition Sq., YO1 2HB ☎ 01904/621756 ⊕ www.visityork.org ✉ York Train Station ☎ 01904/621756.

The Northeast

DURHAM, HADRIAN'S WALL,
LINDISFARNE ISLAND

WORD OF MOUTH

"Add Durham to your collection of cathedrals. Because it was completed in such a short time . . . it is arguably the best example of Norman architecture on a massive scale. The location on the bluffs above the River Wear is awesome."

—jsmith

"Hadrian's Wall, Housesteads, and Vindolanda were the favorites of my whole family . . . . The museum at Vindolanda has incredible artifacts retrieved from the Roman garrison's garbage dump. The countryside also is amazing—you can imagine that the Romans stationed there thought they were at the end of the earth!"

—Marsha

Updated by
Christi
Daugherty

A DECIDED AIR OF REMOTENESS pervades much of England's northeast corner, although one village in this region—Allendale Town, southwest of Hexham—lays claim to being the geographical center of the British Isles. For many Britons the words "the Northeast" provoke a vision of somewhat bitter, near-Siberian isolation. The truth is a revelation. For although there are wind-hammered, wide-open spaces and empty roads that thread wild high moorland, the Northeast also has simple fishing towns, small villages of remarkable charm, and historic abbeys and castles that are all the more romantic for their often ruinous state. Even the remoteness can be relative. Suddenly, around the next bend of a country road, you may come across an imposing church, a tall monastery, or a gorgeous country house built by a Victorian-era millionaire. The value found in the shops and accommodations, the uncrowded beaches ideal for walking, and the friendliness of the people also add to the region's appeal. Still, outside of a few key sights, the Northeast is off the well-trodden tourist path.

Mainly composed of the two large counties of Durham and Northumberland, the Northeast includes English villages adjacent to the Scottish border area, renowned in ballads and romantic literature for feuds, raids, and battles. Hadrian's Wall, which marked the northern limit of the Roman Empire, stretches across prehistoric remains and moorland in this region. Much of it, remarkably, is still intact. Not far north of Hadrian's Wall are some of the most interesting parts of Northumberland National Park. Steel, coal, railroads, and shipbuilding made prosperous towns such as Newcastle upon Tyne—now re-creating itself as a cultural center—Darlington, and Middlesbrough.

The region's 100 mi of largely undeveloped coast is one of the least-visited and most dramatic in all Europe. Several outstanding castles perch on headlands and promontories along here, including Bamburgh, which according to legend was the site of Joyous Garde, the castle of Sir Lancelot du Lac. The island of Lindisfarne is a landmark of early Christendom. Fittingly, Durham Cathedral, the greatest ecclesiastical structure of the region, has memorably been described as "half church of God, half castle 'gainst the Scot." For almost 800 years, this great cathedral was the seat of bishops who raised their own armies and ruled the turbulent northern diocese as prince-bishops with quasi-royal authority.

Exploring the Northeast

Many people travel from the south to visit the historic cathedral city of Durham, not far east of the wooded foothill valleys of the Pennines. Farther north, Newcastle, with Gateshead, straddles the region's main river, the Tyne. This reviving industrial city is making a bid for attention with new cultural facilities. Nearby, the still-impressive Roman fortifications of Hadrian's Wall snake through superb scenery to the west, whereas to the north lies the wilderness of Northumberland National Park. Huge castles and offshore gems such as the Farne Islands and Holy Island, also known as Lindisfarne, stud the stunning, final 40 mi of England's eastern coast, starting an hour's drive north of Newcastle.

About the Restaurants

You can try fine local products here, but don't wait until 9 PM to have dinner or you can have a hard time getting a meal. Look for restaurants that serve game from the Kielder Forest, local lamb from the hillsides, salmon and trout from the rivers, and shellfish, crab and oysters from the coast. Oak-smoked kippers (herring) are a regional specialty, as are the lunchtime seafood sandwiches and the stotties (large bread buns) served for afternoon tea. You can sample Lindisfarne mead, a highly potent spirit produced on Holy Island and made of honey vatted with grape juice and mineral water. Less strong is Newcastle Brown ale, whose caramel overtones have found their way even into ice cream.

About the Hotels

The large hotel chains don't have much of a presence in the Northeast, outside the few large cities. Instead, you can expect to find country houses converted into welcoming hotels, old coaching inns that still greet guests after 300 years, and cozy bed-and-breakfasts convenient to hiking trails. Check ahead if you're contemplating budget accommodation in winter, as many such places will be closed.

WHAT IT COSTS In pounds				
	££££££	**££££**	**£££**	**££**	**£**
RESTAURANTS	over £22	£18–£22	£13–£17	£7–£12	under £7
HOTELS	over £160	£120–£160	£90–£119	£60–£89	under £60

Restaurant prices are for a main course at dinner. Hotel prices are for two people in a standard double room in high season, including V.A.T., with no meals or, if indicated, CP (with continental breakfast), BP (Breakfast Plan, with full breakfast), or MAP (Modified American Plan, with breakfast and dinner).

Timing

The best time to see the Northeast is in summer. This ensures that the museums—and the roads—will be open, and you can take advantage of the countryside walks that are one of the region's greatest pleasures. Rough seas and inclement weather make it extremely difficult to swim at any of the beaches except in July and August. At the end of June, Alnwick hosts its annual fair, with a costumed reenactment of a medieval fair, a market, and concerts. The Durham Regatta, England's oldest rowing event, also takes place in June. The Northumberland Traditional Music Festival is scheduled in venues throughout the county over two weeks in October. The Berwick Military Tattoo, a more intimate version of its Edinburgh counterpart, is at the end of August.

DURHAM, NEWCASTLE & ENVIRONS

Durham—the first major northeastern town on the main road up from London—is by far the region's most interesting historic city. Newcastle, however, along with Gateshead across the River Tyne, is the region's biggest, liveliest, and most cosmopolitan city. Most other towns in the area made their fortunes during the Industrial Revolution and have since subsided into relative decline. Several, such as Darlington, birthplace of

GREAT ITINERARIES

Although you can get a sense of the Northeast through an overnight stop en route to or from Scotland, spending four days here is well worth the time.

Numbers in the text correspond to numbers in the margin and on the Northeast and Durham maps.

IF YOU HAVE 2 DAYS

Base yourself in either 🔲 **Durham ❶–❺** ▶, with time to inspect the Norman cathedral and the castle to either side of the central Palace Green, or in smaller, quainter 🔲 **Alnwick ㉓**, with its cobbled square and magnificent riverside castle and garden. Drive inland between the two for at least a brief glimpse of **Hadrian's Wall**, ideally at **Housesteads Roman Fort ⓳**, and wind up at the monastic settlement on **Lindisfarne ㉘**.

IF YOU HAVE 4 DAYS

Having spent at least a half day exploring 🔲 **Durham ❶–❺** ▶, set aside a full day to follow the course of **Hadrian's Wall**. An overnight stop nearby in 🔲 **Hexham ⓰** enables you to see the excellent museums of Roman finds at **Vindolanda ⓲** and **Housesteads Roman Fort ⓳**. Then head east to overnight in 🔲 **Newcastle ⓮**, or drive northeast through the countryside to the little market town of 🔲 **Alnwick ㉓**. The next morning, walk from **Craster ㉔** to the splendidly bleak ruin of **Dunstanburgh Castle ㉕**. Visit one or two of the huge beaches to the north as you head to 🔲 **Bamburgh ㉗** for the night. Overlooking the windswept shore, its famous castle conjures up the days of chivalry as few others do. Whether you're heading back to Durham from there, or onward to Scotland, visit the wind-battered monastic outpost at **Lindisfarne ㉘**, a short distance north.

13

the modern railroad, do hold interesting relics of their 19th-century heyday. The land to the west, known as County Durham, toward the Pennine Hills, is far more scenic, and a daylong drive through the valleys of Teesdale and Weardale takes you past ruined castles, industrial heritage sites, isolated moorland villages, and tumbling waterfalls.

Durham

▶ *250 mi north of London, 15 mi south of Newcastle.*

The great medieval city of Durham, seat of County Durham, stands on a rocky spur, making it among the most dramatically sited cities in Britain. Despite the military advantages of its location, Durham was founded surprisingly late, probably in about the year 1000, growing up around a small Saxon church erected to house the remains of St. Cuthbert. It was the Normans, under William the Conqueror, who put Durham on the map, building the first defensive castle and beginning work on the cathedral. From here, Durham's prince-bishops, granted almost dictatorial local powers by William in 1072, kept a tight rein on the county, coining their own money and maintaining their own laws and courts; not until 1836 were these rights finally restored to the English Crown.

Together, the cathedral and castle, a World Heritage Site, rise high on a wooded peninsula almost entirely encircled by the River Wear (rhymes with "beer"). For centuries these two ancient structures have dominated Durham—now a thriving university town, the Northeast's equivalent to Oxford or Cambridge—and the surrounding countryside. Durham is more than its cathedral and castle, however. It's a great place to explore, with steep, narrow streets overlooked by perilously angled medieval houses and 18th-century town houses. In the most attractive part of the city, near the Palace Green and along the river, people go boating, anglers cast their lines, and strollers walk along the shaded paths. Between 10 and 4 on Monday through Saturday, cars are charged £2 (on top of parking charges) to enter the Palace Green area. Bus 40 links parking lots and the train and bus stations with the cathedral.

❷ Durham Castle. For almost 800 years the castle was the home of successive prince-bishops; from here, they ruled large tracts of northern England and kept the Scots at bay. Facing the cathedral across Palace Green, the castle commands a strategic position above the River Wear. It has required many renovations and repairs through the ages because of less-than-stable foundations, but it remains an impressive pile. Henry VIII first curtailed the bishops' independence, although it wasn't until the 19th century that the prince-bishops finally had their powers annulled. They abandoned the castle, turning it over to University College, one of several colleges of the University of Durham (founded 1832), the oldest in England after Oxford and Cambridge. You can visit the castle on a 45-minute guided tour. ⊠ *Palace Green* ☏ *0191/334–4106* ⊕ *www.durhamcastle.com* ☏*£5* ⊙ *Guided tours mid-Mar.–Sept., Mon.–Sat. 10–12:30 and 2–4, Sun. 10–noon and 2–4; Oct.–mid-Mar., Mon., Wed., and weekends 2–4.*

| NEED A BREAK? | Drop into the **Almshouse Café** (⊠ Palace Green ☏ 0191/386–1054), in an ancient almshouse between the cathedral and castle, for fat brownies or tasty cheesecake. These sweet treats are the perfect accompaniment to your tea. |

❶ Durham Cathedral. A Norman masterpiece in the heart of the city, the cathedral is an amazing vision of solidity and strength, a far cry from the airy lightness of later, Gothic cathedrals. Construction began in about 1090, and the main body was finished in about 1150. Durham reveals the essence of an almost entirely Norman, or Romanesque, edifice: the round arches of the nave and the deep zigzag patterns carved into them typify the heavy, gaunt style of Norman building. The technology of Durham, however, was revolutionary. This was the first European cathedral to be given a stone, rather than a wooden, roof. When you consider the means of construction available to its builders—the stones that form the ribs of the roof had to be hoisted by hand and set on a wooden structure, which was then knocked away—the achievement seems staggering.

*Fodor's*Choice ★

The origins of the cathedral go back to the 10th century. In 995 monks brought to this site the remains of St. Cuthbert, which had been removed from the monastery at Lindisfarne after a Viking raid in 875. Soon the

TOP REASONS TO GO

Castles, castles, castles: Fought over for centuries by the Scots and the English, and prey to Viking raiders, the Northeast was one of the most heavily fortified regions in England. Some of the most spectacular castles are along the dramatic, far Northeast coast, including Dunstanburgh and Bamburgh.

Medieval Durham: A splendid Norman cathedral that dates back to the 11th century is just one of the city's charms. Take a stroll on its ancient winding streets or along the River Wear; this is a fairy-tale town hewn from stone.

Hadrian's Wall: The ancient Roman wall is a wonder for the wild countryside around it and the resiliency of its stones. Museums and surviving forts help tell the story, and for an awe-inspiring

sense of history with stunning views, nothing beats a hike along part of the Hadrian's Wall Path national trail or a ride on Hadrian's Cycleway.

Lindisfarne (Holy Island): Just getting to this historic island is an unusual experience; you drive across a causeway that floods at high tide. This remote spot, a center of monastic learning from the 7th century, includes the ruins of Lindisfarne Priory and a Tudor fort-turned-Edwardian-home.

Alnwick Castle and Gardens: The imposing inland seat of the dukes of Northumberland is fascinating with its formidable walls and luxurious interiors. The current duchess's multimillion-dollar gardens have everything from interactive water sculptures to an enormous tree house.

13

wealth attracted by Cuthbert's shrine paid for the construction of a cathedral. The bishop's throne here was claimed to be the loftiest in medieval Christendom; the miter of the bishop is the only one to be encircled by a coronet, and his coat of arms is the only one to be crossed with a sword as well as a crosier. **Cuthbert's shrine** lies surrounded by columns of local marble, with the saint's remains buried below a simple slab. An unobtrusive tomb at the west end of the cathedral, in the handsome, Moorish-influenced **Galilee Chapel,** is the final resting place of the **Venerable Bede,** an 8th-century Northumbrian monk whose contemporary account of the English people made him the country's first reliable historian. He died in Jarrow in 735, and his remains were placed here in 1020.

Upon entering the cathedral, note the 12th-century bronze **Sanctuary Knocker,** shaped like the head of a ferocious mythological beast, mounted on the massive northwestern door. By grasping the ring clenched in the animal's mouth, medieval felons could claim sanctuary; cathedral records show that 331 criminals sought this protection between 1464 and 1524. The knocker is, in fact, a reproduction. The original is kept for security reasons in the cathedral **Treasury,** along with ancient illuminated manuscripts, fragments of St. Cuthbert's oak coffin, and more church treasures well worth a look. You can view a film and an exhibit about building the cathedral, and in good weather you can climb the **tower.**

668 <

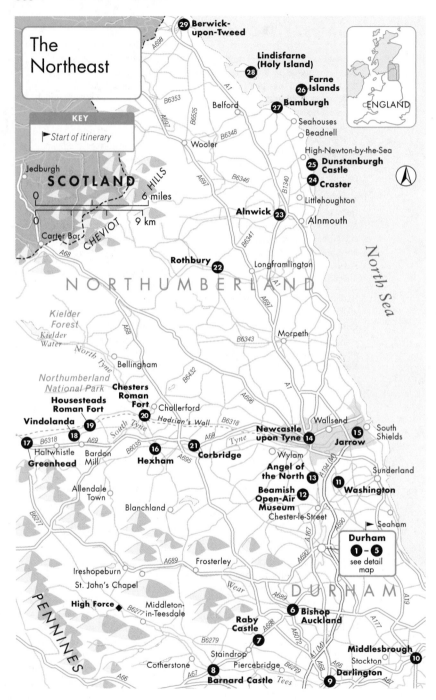

There's also a restaurant and a bookstore. ✉ *Palace Green* ☎ *0191/ 386–4266* ⊕ *www.durhamcathedral.co.uk* 🖂 *£3.50 donation requested; Treasury £2.50, tower £2.50, guided tours £4* ⊙ *Cathedral mid-June–early Sept., daily 7:30* AM–*8* PM; *early Sept.–mid-June, Mon.–Sat. 7:30–6:15, Sun. 7:45–5. Treasury and tower Mon.–Sat. 10–4:30, Sun. 2–4:30. Choral evensong service Tues.–Sat. 5:15, Sun. 3:30. Guided tours mid-Apr.–Sept., Mon.–Sat. 11 and 2:30.*

❹ **Framwellgate Bridge.** If you follow the far side of the Wear north from Prebends Footbridge, you can recross the river at this bridge, which dates from the 12th century. Many of the elegant town houses that line the narrow lanes back up to the cathedral now house departments of the University of Durham.

❸ **Prebends Footbridge.** Delightful views are the reward of a short stroll along the River Wear's leafy banks, especially as you cross this footbridge, reached from the southern end of Palace Green. J. M. W. Turner reveled in the view from here and painted a celebrated scene of Durham from the bridge.

> **ROW THEIR BOATS**
>
> The pretty River Wear winds through Durham, curving beneath the cathedral and castle. In mid-June each year the city hosts the prestigious Durham Regatta, Britain's oldest rowing event. Three hundred racing crews compete in events including races for single sculls and teams of eight.

❺ **University of Durham Oriental Museum.** The museum displays fine art and craft work from all parts of Asia. The collection of Chinese ceramics is noted, and don't miss the nearby 18-acre Botanic Gardens. ✉ *Elvet Hill, off South Rd. (A1050)* ☎ *0191/334–5694* ⊕ *www.dur.ac.uk/oriental. museum* 🖂 *£1.50* ⊙ *Weekdays 10–5, weekends noon–5.*

Where to Stay & Eat

During college vacations (late March through April, July through September, and December), reasonably priced accommodations are available at the **University of Durham** (☎ 0191/334–2886 🖶 0191/334–2892 ⊕ www.dur.ac.uk/conferences), in Durham Castle and in buildings throughout the city.

££–£££ ✕ **Bistro 21.** Relaxed and cottagey, Durham's most fashionable restaurant lies a couple of miles northwest from the center, in a superbly restored farmhouse. The eclectic and seasonal menu has such dishes as poached salmon and lamb with lemon polenta, as well as rich desserts. ✉ *Aykley Heads* ☎ *0191/384–4354* 🖃 *AE, DC, MC, V* ⊙ *Closed Sun.*

££ ✕🖭 **Seven Stars Inn.** Warm oranges and tartans in the public areas enhance the coziness of this good-value early-18th-century coaching inn. The simple bedrooms are done in creamy yellows and reds and have modern pine furniture. At the restaurant (££–£££), tuck into such dishes as rib-eye steak with black pudding and bacon or monkfish on herb mashed potatoes with saffron sauce, and finish with apple crumble or sticky toffee pudding. The inn is 2 mi south of the city and sits right on the road. ✉ *High St. N, Shincliffe Village DH1 2NU* ☎ *0191/384–8454* 🖶 *0191/*

Durham
Castle **2**

Durham
Cathedral **1**

Framwellgate
Bridge **4**

Prebends
Footbridge **3**

University
of Durham
Oriental
Museum **5**

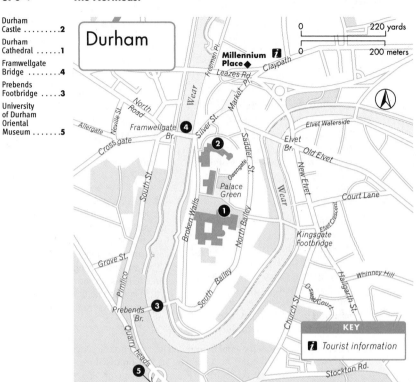

386–0640 ⊕ *landmark-inns.co.uk* ➥ *8 rooms* ⚒ *Restaurant, some pets allowed; no a/c* ⊟ *MC, V* ¶⊙| *BP.*

£££ ⊞ **Swallow Three Tuns.** This cheery 16th-century inn, now part of a hotel chain, has echoes of its solid country past. Some parts retain the old oak beams and fireplaces, and a colorful modern stained-glass ceiling illuminates other public rooms. The pastel modern bedrooms have a floral motif. Guests can use the indoor pool and health club at the nearby Swallow Royal County Hotel. Browns restaurant serves staples such as veal, steak, and salmon. ⊠ *New Elvet, DH1 3AQ* ☎ *0191/386–4326* 🖷 *0191/386–1406* ⊕ *www.swallow-hotels.com* ➥ *50 rooms* ⚒ *Restaurant, cable TV, piano bar, meeting rooms, free parking, some pets allowed; no a/c* ⊟ *AE, DC, MC, V* ¶⊙| *BP.*

★ **££** ⊞ **Georgian Town House.** Exactly as the name suggests, this friendly, family-run guesthouse, at the top of a cobbled street overlooking the cathedral and castle, makes the best of its Georgian exterior and details. Stylish modern furnishings, paintings, and stencils, evidence of the owner's hand, give all rooms a colorful individuality. Rooms at the back have the best view. ⊠ *10 Crossgate, DH1 4PS* 🖷🖷 *0191/386–8070* ⊕ *www. thegeorgiantownhouse.co.uk* ➥ *8 rooms* ⚒ *No-smoking rooms; no a/c* ⊟ *No credit cards* ⊙ *Closed last wk Dec.* ¶⊙| *BP.*

Nightlife & the Arts

Durham's nightlife is geared to the university set. The **Coach-and-Eight** (⊠ Bridge House, Framwellgate Bridge ☎ 0191/386–3284) can get noisy with students, but outdoor seating makes it appealing. The **Hogshead** (⊠ 58 Saddler St. ☎ 0191/386–9550) pub is a true student haunt.

Durham's **Gala Theatre** (⊠ Millennium Pl. ☎ 0191/332–4041) presents plays, concerts, and opera year-round.

Sports & the Outdoors

Brown's Boat House (⊠ Elvet Bridge ☎ 0191/386–3779) rents rowboats April through early November and offers short cruises all year. **Cycleforce** (⊠ 87 Claypath ☎ 0191/3840319) has mountain bikes for rent at £12 per day.

Shopping

Bramwells Jewellers (⊠ 24 Elvet Bridge ☎ 0191/386–8006) has its own store specialty, a pendant copy of the gold-and-silver cross of St. Cuthbert. The food and bric-a-brac stalls in **Durham Indoor Market** (⊠ Market Pl. ☎ 0191/384–6153), a Victorian arcade, are open Monday through Saturday 9 to 5.

Bishop Auckland

❻ *10 mi southwest of Durham.*

For 700 years, between the 12th and 19th centuries, the powerful prince-bishops of Durham had their country residence in Auckland Castle, in the town of Bishop Auckland. When finally deprived of their powers in 1836, the bishops left Durham and made Bishop Auckland their official home. Arguably the greatest of the prince-bishops of Durham's properties is the episcopal palace of **Auckland Castle**, which you enter through an elaborate stone arch. Much of what you see today dates mainly from the 16th century, although the limestone and marble chapel, with its dazzling stained-glass windows, was built in 1665 from the ruins of a 12th-century hall. ■ TIP➔ **Don't miss some of the palace's greatest treasures, paintings by the 17th-century Spanish artist Zurbarán of Jacob and his 12 sons.** The turreted 18th-century "deer house" on the parklike grounds is a reminder that the castle was once used as a hunting lodge by the prince-bishops. ⊠ *Off Market Pl.* ☎ *01388/601627* ⊕ *www.auckland-castle.co.uk* ☐ *£4* ☉ *Apr.–July and Sept., Mon. and Sun. 2–5; Aug., Mon., Wed., and Sun. 2–5; park daily 7 AM–sunset.*

Raby Castle

★ **❼** *7 mi southwest of Bishop Auckland, 19 mi southwest of Durham.*

The stone battlements and turrets of moated Raby Castle, once the seat of the powerful Nevills and currently the home of the 11th baron Barnard, stand amid a 200-acre deer park and ornamental gardens. Charles Nevill supported Mary, Queen of Scots in the 1659 uprising against Elizabeth I known as the Rising of the North; when the uprising failed, the estate was confiscated. Dating mostly from the 14th century (using stone plundered from Barnard Castle) and renovated in the

18th and 19th centuries, the luxuriously furnished castle has displays of art and other treasures, including an important Meissen collection. Rooms in wonderfully elaborate Gothic Revival, Regency, and Victorian styles are open for viewing. Victorian domestic ware fills the well-preserved medieval kitchens. ⊠ *A688, 1 mi north of Staindrop* ☎ *01833/660202* ⊕ *www.rabycastle.com* ⊠ *Castle, park, and gardens £9, park and gardens £4* ☉ *Castle May, June, and Sept., Wed. and Sun. 1–5; July and Aug., Sun.–Fri. 1–5. Park and gardens May and Sept., Wed. and Sun. 11–5:30; June–Aug., Sun.–Fri. 11–5:30.*

UPSTAIRS, DOWNSTAIRS

Gorgeous Raby Castle acts as a living museum for castle life through the centuries. It's especially good at juxtaposing life as a servant with life as a lord. In the lord's dining room, rich red carpets and patterned silk wallpaper glow under a soaring, intricately carved ceiling. Downstairs, the servants had their meals in the bare, low-ceilinged medieval servants' hall, sitting at a rough pine table on hard wooden benches. Ouch!

Barnard Castle

⑧ *6 mi southwest of Raby Castle, 25 mi southwest of Durham.*

The handsome market town of Barnard Castle has sights of its own and can also serve as a base for venturing into the Teesdale Valley to the northwest. Its unusual butter-market hall (known locally as Market Cross), surmounted by an old fire-alarm bell, marks the junction of the streets Thorngate, Newgate, and Market Place. Stores, pubs, and cafés line these thoroughfares. In 1838 Charles Dickens stayed at the **King's Head Inn** here while doing research for his novel *Nicholas Nickleby,* which deals with the abuse of children in boarding schools. The local tourist office has a free *In the Footsteps of Charles Dickens* leaflet.

The substantial ruins of **Barnard Castle,** which gave its name to the town, cling to an aerie overlooking the River Tees. Inside you can see parts of the 14th-century Great Hall and the cylindrical, 13th-century tower, built by the castle's original owners, the Anglo-Scottish Balliol family. ⊠ *Off Galgate* ☎ *01833/638212* ⊕ *www.english-heritage.org. uk* ⊠ *£3.40* ☉ *Apr.–Sept., daily 10–6; Oct., daily 10–4; Nov.–Mar., Thurs.–Mon. 10–4; call ahead in winter.*

★ The **Bowes Museum,** a vast French-inspired château a little more than a mile west of the town center, was built between 1862 and 1875 to house the art and artifacts accumulated by philanthropists John and Josephine Bowes. Highlights include paintings by Canaletto, El Greco, Francisco Goya, and François Boucher, and 18th-century French furniture. Ceramics, silver, glass, and toys are also on view, along with archaeological exhibits about County Durham. ■ **TIP→ Time your visit so you can see the extraordinary 18th-century life-size, mechanical silver swan in action. It sits on a stream of twisted glass and catches and swallows a silver fish every day at 2** PM**.** ⊠ *Up Newgate, follow signs from town center* ☎ *01833/690606* ⊕ *www.bowesmuseum.org.uk* ⊠ *£7* ☉ *Daily 11–5.*

OFF THE
BEATEN
PATH

HIGH FORCE – The Upper Teesdale Valley's elemental nature shows its most volatile aspect in the sprays of England's highest waterfall, the 72-foot High Force. From the roadside parking lot it's a 10-minute walk through woodland to the massive rocks over which the water tumbles. A precarious viewpoint puts you right above the falls, at their best in springtime after a rain. The waterfall is 15 mi northwest of Barnard Castle. A welcome pub on the main road, the **High Force** (✉ B6277 ☎ 01833/622222) , serves bar meals and home-brewed beer, a boon in this isolated stretch. ✉ *Off B6277* ☎ *01833/640209* 🎫 *£1; parking £1.50* ⊙ *Mid-Apr.–Oct., daily 9:30–5; Nov.–mid-Apr., open but unattended.*

13

Where to Eat

£ ✗ **Market Place Teashop.** A nicely old-fashioned air pervades this 17th-century building on the main square. Waitresses clad in striped uniforms serve such dishes as parsnip and bacon with Mornay sauce, or many vegetarian options, and afternoon tea comes in silver teapots. ✉ *29 Market Pl.* ☎ *01833/690110* ▤ *MC, V* ⊙ *Closed Sun. except afternoons Apr.–Oct. No dinner.*

Darlington

❾ *15 mi east of Barnard Castle, 21 mi south of Durham.*

Still rooted in its 19th-century industrial past, the town of Darlington gained fame in 1825, when George Stephenson piloted his steam-powered *Locomotion* along newly laid tracks the few miles to nearby Stockton, thus kick-starting the railway age. The story of the coming of the ★ ☺ railway is well told in the excellent **Darlington Railway Centre and Museum,** in the town's original train station, built in 1842 and now a (signposted) 20-minute walk outside the town center. The focus is on railroads in the Northeast, particularly around Darlington. On display are historic engines, including Stephenson's *Locomotion,* as well as photographs, documents, models, and paraphernalia associated with a 19th-century station. ✉ *North Rd. Station, Station Rd.* ☎ *01325/460532* ⊕ *www.drcm.org.uk* 🎫 *£2.50* ⊙ *Daily 10–5.*

Where to Stay & Eat

££ ✗▥ **George Hotel.** This sprawling 18th-century coaching inn, 4 mi west of Darlington in tiny Piercebridge, sits on the banks of the River Tees, with the road on the other side. Rooms are plain and white with dark wood furniture, and the restaurant (£–££), whose windows overlook the river, serves traditional dishes such as roast pork with apple-and-thyme stuffing. The George could use a bit of a spruce-up overall, but it's handy and has its charms. ✉ *B6275, Piercebridge-on-Tees, Darlington DL2 3SW* ☎ *01325/374576* 🖷 *01325/374577* ⊕ *www.thegeorgehotel.activehotels.com* 🛌 *35 rooms* ⚐ *Restaurant, 2 bars, dry cleaning, laundry service, some pets allowed, no-smoking rooms; no a/c* ▤ *AE, MC, V* ⑩ *BP.*

Middlesbrough

❿ *12 mi east of Darlington, 22 mi southeast of Durham.*

In 1802 only a handful of people lived in Middlesbrough, near the mouth of the River Tees. A few years later, with the discovery of iron ore, the area boomed. Steel mills opened up and down the river, and later chemical plants did much to boost the local economy but blighted the landscape. Today Middlesbrough is a modern city, with little to offer the average tourist, although a handful of sights are worth your time; the Institute of Modern Art, a gallery, was set to open in late 2006.

Middlesbrough's unusual **Transporter Bridge,** built in 1911, is the largest of its kind in the world, a vast structure like a giant's Erector-set model. The gantry system can carry up to 12 cars and 600 passengers across the river in two minutes, every 15 minutes. ☎ *01642/247563* ✉ *Pedestrians 30p, cars 80p* ☙ *Mon.–Sat. 5 AM–11 PM, Sun. 2–11.*

The **Captain Cook Birthplace Museum,** in the Middlesbrough suburb of Marton, vividly explores the life and times of Captain James Cook (1728–79), the celebrated circumnavigator and explorer. You can walk through Stewart Park to the modern museum building, which is near the site where Cook was born. Interactive displays, exhibits, and films cover Cook's remarkable voyages to Australia, New Zealand, Canada, Antarctica, and Hawaii, where he met an untimely death. ✉ *Stewart Park, off A174, south of city center, Marton* ☎ *01642/311211* ✉ *£2.40* ☙ *Mar.–Oct., Tues.–Sun. 10–5:30; Nov.–Mar., Tues.–Sun. 9–4; last admission 45 mins before closing.*

Where to Eat

££–£££ ✗ **Purple Onion.** A treat as idiosyncratic as its name, this antiques-decorated restaurant has a relaxed attitude and a wide-ranging modern menu. Try creative sandwiches and salads at lunch, and in the evening, chargrilled steaks, roasted lamb, or poached seafood. After-hours jazz and funk are played in the cellar bar. ✉ *72–80 Corporation Rd.* ☎ *01642/ 222250* ▤ *MC, V* ☙ *Closed Sun. and Mon.*

Washington

❶ *34 mi northwest of Middlesbrough, 12 mi north of Durham.*

The little town of Washington has a direct link to the history of the United States. **Washington Old Hall** is the ancestral home of the first U.S. president. George Washington's direct forebears, the de Wessyngtons, lived here between 1183 and 1288. Other family members resided in the house until 1613, when the property was rebuilt in its current form, using parts of the medieval manor. The stone house retains a Jacobean (17th-century) appearance, particularly in the fine wood paneling and the heavy furniture. ✉ *From A1(M), 5 mi west of Sunderland, follow signs to Washington New Town, District 4, and on to Washington Village* ☎ *0191/ 416–6879* ⊕ *www.nationaltrust.org.uk* ✉ *£4* ☙ *Apr.–Oct., Sun.–Wed. 11–5; last admission 4:30.*

Beamish Open-Air Museum

★ **❷** *8 mi west of Washington, 3 mi west of Chester-le-Street.*

The buildings moved to this sprawling, more-than-300-acre museum village from throughout the region explore the way people in the Northeast lived and worked in the 1820s and early 1900s, the periods just before and at the peak of industrialization. A streetcar takes you around the site and to the reconstructed 1920s shopping street (called a "high street" in Britain), with a dentist's operating room, a pub, and a grocery store. On the early-20th-century farm are local Durham Shorthorn cattle and Teeswater sheep. Other attractions include a small manor house from the early 1900s, a railroad station, a coal mine, and a transportation collection; in summer a steam train makes a short run. The gift store specializes in period souvenirs and local crafts. ■ TIP→ **Allow at least a half day if you come in summer; winter visits center on the reconstructed street, and admission prices are reduced.** ⊠ *Off A693, between Chester-le-Street and Stanley* ☎ *0191/370–4000* ⊕ *www.beamish.org.uk* ✆ *£16 Apr.–Oct., £6 Nov.–Mar.* ☉ *Apr.–Oct., daily 10–5; Nov.–mid-Dec. and Jan.–Mar., Tues.–Thurs. and weekends 10–4; last admission 3.*

Where to Stay & Eat

£££££
Fodor'sChoice
★
✕▦ **Lumley Castle Hotel.** This is a real Norman castle, right down to the dungeons and maze of dark flagstone corridors. Antiques, silks, and deep, rich fabrics furnish all the sumptuous rooms, which are designed with clever touches such as a bathroom hidden behind a bookcase. The rooms in the courtyard annex are less expensive. You can join in the merriment of the Friday and Saturday night Elizabethan banquets or dine in the Black Knight Restaurant (£££–£££££) on English fare such as monkfish with rosemary and garlic. A full breakfast is included in the price on weekends. The hotel is just east of town via the B1284. ⊠ *Chester-le-Street DH3 4NX* ☎ *0191/389–1111* 🖷 *0191/387–1437* ⊕ *www.lumleycastle.com* ➥ *59 rooms* ⚒ *Restaurant, cable TV, in-room data ports, billiards, bar, library, meeting rooms; no a/c* ▭ *AE, DC, MC, V.*

Angel of the North

★ ⓭ *6 mi north of Beamish Open-Air Museum.*

At the junction of A1(M) and A1 at Gateshead stands England's largest—and one of its most popular—sculptures, the powerful *Angel of the North.* Created by Antony Gormley in 1998, the rust-color steel sculpture is a sturdy, abstract human figure with airplane-like wings rather than arms. It stands 65 feet tall and has a horizontal wingspan of 175 feet. There's parking nearby, signposted on A167.

Newcastle upon Tyne

⓮ *8 mi north of Beamish Open-Air Museum, 16 mi north of Durham.*

Durham may have the glories of its castle, cathedral, and university, but the liveliest city of the Northeast is Newcastle. Settled since Roman times on the Tyne River, it made its fortune twice—first by exporting coal in the Elizabethan age and later by shipbuilding. As a 19th-century industrial center, Newcastle had few equals in Britain, showing off its wealth in grand Victorian buildings lining the broad streets. Some of these buildings remain (particularly on Grey Street), and after years of industrial decline, the city has reinvented itself as a regional center for culture and modern architecture. The Metro system makes getting around easy.

Much of the regeneration since the early 1990s has been based around the Gateshead Quays project on the historic quayside. Here the Baltic Centre for Contemporary Art and the pedestrian- and cyclist-only Millennium Bridge—the world's first tilting bridge, which opens and shuts like an eyelid—have risen from wasteland. Pricey loft housing (some in converted warehouses) and upscale restaurants and bars now stand alongside the surviving 17th-century houses. By the old quayside is the symbol of the city, the celebrated **Tyne Bridge** (1929), one of seven bridges spanning the river in the city.

Overlooking the Tyne River, the remains of the **Norman castle** recall the city's earlier status as a defensive stronghold. This was the "new castle," built in 1080, that gave the city its name. ⊠ *St. Nicholas St.* ☎ *0191/232-7938* ⊕ *www.castlekeep-newcastle.org.uk* ⊠ *£1.50* ⊙ *Apr.–Sept., daily 9:30–5:30; Oct.–Mar., daily 9:30–4:30; last admission 30 mins before closing.*

★ The Northeast's finest art museum, the **Laing Art Gallery** merits at least an hour's visit for its selection of British art. Some of the most extraordinary paintings are those by 19th-century local artist John Martin, who produced dramatic biblical landscapes. The Pre-Raphaelites are on show, too, and the Art on Tyneside exhibition traces 400 years of local arts, highlighting glassware, pottery, and engraving. ⊠ *Higham Pl. near John Dobson St.* ☎ *0191/232-7734* ⊕ *www.twmuseums.org.uk* ⊠ *Free* ⊙ *Mon.–Sat. 10–5, Sun. 2–5.*

NEED A BREAK? The popular art deco **Tyneside Coffee Rooms** (⊠ 10 Pilgrim St. ☎ 0191/261-9291), on the second floor above the cinema, make an intriguing place to stop for teas, coffee, and a snack. It's closed Sunday.

The buildings of the **University of Newcastle upon Tyne** contain some of the city's best museums. The **Museum of Antiquities** (⊕ www.ncl.ac.uk/antiquities) shows finds from Hadrian's Wall and has a reconstruction of the 1st-century Temple of Mithras at Carrawburgh. The **Shefton Museum of Greek Art and Archaeology** (⊕ www.ncl.ac.uk/sheftonmuseum) of the Department of Classics contains ancient arms and decorative pottery. ⊠ *The University* ☎ *0191/222-7849* ⊠ *Free* ⊙ *Museum of Antiquities Mon.–Sat. 10–5; Shefton Museum weekdays 10–4.*

☺ At the **Life Science Centre,** three high-tech shows and 60 kid-oriented exhibits bring science to life, from research on genes to travel to Mars. There's also a virtual reality arcade, and work is under way on a massive expansion of the museum, to be completed during 2007. ⊠ *Times Sq.* ☎ *0191/243-8223* ⊕ *www.lifesciencecentre.org.uk* ⊠ *£6.95* ⊙ *Mon.–Sat. 10–6, Sun. 11–6; last admission 4.*

★ ☺ The **Discovery Museum** tells Newcastle's story. Reconstructed streets and homes lead you from Roman times to the present day, and the Tyne galleries show off maritime and industrial achievements. *Turbinia* is a model of the 1897 ship that was the world's first to be powered by steam turbines. This museum is good for kids and history buffs. ⊠ *Blandford Sq.* ☎ *0191/232-6789* ⊕ *www.twmuseums.org.uk* ⊠ *Free* ⊙ *Mon.–Sat. 10–5, Sun. 2–5.*

The **Segedunum Roman Fort, Baths and Museum** includes the remains of the substantial Roman fort of Segedunum, built around AD 125 as an eastern extension to Hadrian's Wall, and part of the original wall as well as a reproduction section. It's a good introduction to Britain's Roman history. There's also a reconstructed Roman bath complex (check ahead for days when it's heated up). A museum with interactive displays interprets finds from the area, and an observation tower provides views of the site. The Wallsend Metro stop is a two-minute walk away. ⊠ *Buddle St., Wallsend* ☏ *0191/236–9347* ⊕ *www.twmuseums.org.uk* ⚄ *£3.50* ☉ *Apr.–Oct., daily 10–5; Nov.–Mar., daily 10–3:30.*

OFF THE
BEATEN
PATH

GEORGE STEPHENSON'S BIRTHPLACE – In 1781 the Father of the Railroads was born in this tiny stone cottage. Four families shared the house; the Stephensons lived in just one room, and it's this room that is open to the public, a modest tribute to the engineer who invented the steam locomotive. You can park your car in the village by the war memorial, a 10-minute walk away. ⊠ *4 mi west of Newcastle, 1½ mi south of A69, Wylam* ☏ *01661/853457* ⊕ *www.nationaltrust.org.uk* ⚄ *£1.50* ☉ *Apr.–Oct., Thurs., weekends, and national holidays 1–5.*

Where to Stay & Eat

★ **££££** ✕ **McCoy's Rooftop Restaurant.** You can select a Newcastle or Gateshead panorama when dining in this bright, airy restaurant at the top of the Baltic Centre. Choosing from the sophisticated fixed-price dinner menu, you might opt for the wild salmon with red wine and mushroom risotto and finish up with roast figs or chocolate and banana bread pudding. ⊠ *Baltic, Gateshead Quays* ☏ *0191/440–4949* ⚄ *Reservations essential* ⊟ *AE, DC, MC, V* ☉ *No dinner Sun.*

££££ ✕ **Treacle Moon.** Well-presented contemporary dishes with a Mediterranean touch are the specialty at this plush, modern, purple-painted restaurant centrally placed near the river. There's a good selection of unusual ice creams and sorbets, as well as house wines. The name comes from the poet Byron's description of his honeymoon at nearby Seaham; his words adorn the walls. ⊠ *5–7 The Side* ☏ *0191/232–5537* ⊟ *AE, DC, MC, V* ☉ *Closed Sun. No lunch.*

★ **£££££** ✕▥ **Seaham Hall.** Byron married Annabella Milbanke in this foursquare mansion in 1815; today the sumptuous contemporary interior filled with warm natural hues is a haven of luxury. Bedrooms have their own fireplaces, original artwork, large baths, and exotic flowers. At the equally elegant restaurant (£££££), indulge in dishes such as loin of venison and root vegetables flavored with chocolate. Make some time for the Serenity Spa, a retreat inspired by feng shui principles. Seaham is 15 mi south of the center of Newcastle, off A19. ⊠ *Lord Byron's Walk, Seaham SR7 7AG* ☏ *0191/516–1400* 🖷 *0191/516–1410* ⊕ *www.seaham-hall.com* ⚲ *19 suites* ⚄ *Restaurant, in-room data ports, indoor pool, gym, hot tub, spa, bar, meeting rooms* ⊟ *AE, DC, MC, V* ⚋ *CP.*

£££–££££ ✕▥ **Malmaison.** Converted from an old riverside warehouse, this member of a glamorous, design-conscious chain sits right beside the pedestrian Millennium Bridge. Bedrooms, done in a modern style, are spacious, and the huge beds piled high with pillows. The discreet art deco Brasserie & Bar (££–££££) presents French fare, such as grilled Toulouse sausage, in a room that overlooks the Tyne through arched windows. ⊠ *Quay-*

side, NE1 3DX ☎ *0191/245–5000* 🖷 *0191/245–4545* ⊕ *www. malmaison.com* ⇨ *116 rooms* ◇ *Restaurant, café, room service, cable TV with movies, in-room data ports, gym, spa, bar, laundry service, meeting rooms, some pets allowed* ⊟ *AE, DC, MC, V.*

★ ££ ✕▦ **Da Vinci's.** Italian flair prevails at this small hotel in the vibrant Jesmond district, a mile from the city center. Bedrooms are refreshingly simple and contemporary, with white walls and bed linen and blue carpets. Dine on Italian specialties in the popular restaurant. ⊠ *73 Osborne Rd., NE2 2AN* ☎ *0191/281–5284* 🖷 *0191/281–4103* ⊕ *www.davincis.co. uk* ⇨ *16 rooms* ◇ *Restaurant, café, bar; no a/c* ⊟ *AE, MC, V* ⦿ *CP.*

Nightlife & the Arts

Nightlife centers around the Quayside, or you might head for the prettily lighted, suburban Jesmond area, where lively bars and restaurants line Osborne Road. The **Offshore 44** (⊠ 40–44 Sandhill ☎ 0191/261–0921) is an old pub with a nautical theme. The upstairs terrace of the

★ **Pitcher and Piano** (⊠ 108 Quayside ☎ 0191/232–4110), a popular pub with enormous floor-to-ceiling windows, is the perfect viewing point for the Millennium Bridge and quayside. **Thirty 3i8ht** (⊠ Exchange Building, Lombard St. ☎ 0191/261–6463), a classy, contemporary bar, has a no-smoking area, good food, and live music.

The **Baltic Centre for Contemporary Art** (⊠ Gateshead Quays ☎ 0191/478–1810 ⊕ www.balticmill.com), formerly a grain warehouse and now the country's largest national gallery for contemporary art outside London, has changing exhibitions (there's no permanent collection).

★ The **Sage Gateshead** (⊠ West St., Gateshead Quays ☎ 0870/703–4555), hosts concerts—jazz, world, pop, classical, and folk, rock—in a curving, modern building designed by Norman Foster.

Theatre Royal (⊠ Grey St. ☎ 0870/905–5060), the region's most established theater, has high-quality productions and is also a venue for opera and dance.

Jarrow

⑮ *4 mi east of Newcastle.*

To British ears, the name "Jarrow" is linked to the "Jarrow Crusade," a protest march to London led by unemployed former workers from the town's steelworks and shipyards in the depths of the 1930s. In its heyday the shipyard at Jarrow on Tyneside employed 10,000 and prided itself on the 80,000 ships it had built for the British empire; the yard closed in 1934. Travelers are attracted here, however, by Jarrow's much more ancient history.

Bede's World holds substantial monastic ruins, a visitor center–museum, and the church of St. Paul, all reflecting the long tradition of religion and learning that began here in AD 681, when the first Saxon church was established on the site. The Venerable Bede, deemed to be England's earliest historian, moved into the monastery when he was seven and remained until his death in AD 735. In AD 731, he completed his *History of the English Church and People* without ever leaving the premises.

The museum explores the development of Northumbria, using excerpts from Bede's work as well as archaeological finds and reconstructions. You can gain a sense of medieval life from the reconstructed farm buildings and the rare breeds of pigs and cattle on the 11-acre Anglo-Saxon farm. St. Paul's contains the oldest dedicatory church inscription in Britain, a carved stone inscribed in AD 685. From the southern exit traffic circle at South Tyne tunnel, take A185 to South Shields and follow signs to St. Paul's Church and Jarrow Hall. ⊠ *Church Bank* ☎ *0191/489–2106* ⊕ *www.bedesworld.co.uk* ⊠ *£4.50* ☉ *Apr.–Oct., Mon.–Sat. 10–5:30, Sun. noon–5:30; Nov.–Mar., Mon.–Sat. 10–4:30, Sun. noon–4:30; last admission 1 hr before closing.*

13

HADRIAN'S WALL COUNTRY

A formidable line of Roman fortifications, Hadrian's Wall was the Romans' most ambitious construction in Britain. The land through which the old wall wanders is wild and inhospitable in places, but that seems only to add to the powerful sense of history it evokes. Museums and information centers along the wall make it possible to learn as much as you want about the Roman era.

Hadrian's Wall

Fodor'sChoice
★

73 mi from Wallsend, north of Newcastle, to Bowness-on-Solway, beyond Carlisle.

Dedicated to the Roman god Terminus, the massive span of Hadrian's Wall once marked the northern frontier of the Roman Empire. Today the remnants of the wall extend 73 mi from Wallsend ("Wall's End," north of Newcastle) in the east, to Bowness-on-Solway, beyond Carlisle, in the west. The wall's completion in just four years is a good indication of Roman determination and efficiency.

At Emperor Hadrian's command, three legions of soldiers began building the wall in AD 122, in response to repeated invasions from Scotland. During the Roman era, the wall stood 15 feet high and 9 feet thick; behind it lay the vallum, a ditch about 20 feet wide and 10 feet deep. Spaced at 5-mi intervals along the wall were 3- to 5-acre forts (such as those at Housesteads and Chesters), which could hold 500 to 1,000 soldiers. Every mile was marked by a thick-walled milecastle (a smaller fort that housed about 30 soldiers), and between each milecastle were two smaller turrets, each lodging four men who kept watch. For more than 250 years the Roman army used the wall to control travel and trade and to fortify Roman Britain against the barbarians to the north.

During the Jacobite Rebellion of 1745, the English dismantled much of the Roman wall and used its stone to pave the Military Road, now B6318. The most substantial stretches of the remaining wall are between Housesteads and Birdoswald (west of Greenhead). Running through the southern edge of Northumberland National Park and along the sheer escarpment of Whin Sill, this section is also an area of dramatic natural beauty. The ancient ruins, rugged cliffs, dramatic vistas, and spreading pastures make it a good area for hiking.

Today, the wall is a World Heritage Site, and excavating, interpreting, repairing, and generally managing the Roman remains is a Northumbrian growth industry. ■ TIP→ **At Chesters, Housesteads (the best-preserved fort), and Vindolanda, and at the Roman Army Museum near Greenhead, you get a good introduction to the life led by Roman soldiers on the frontier.** In summer most sites sponsor talks, Roman drama, and festivals; local tourist offices and the sites have details.

A special **Hadrian's Wall Bus** (☎ 01434/322002 ⊕ www.hadrians-wall.org) offers day passes (£6) for service between Wallsend and Carlisle, stopping at Newcastle, Hexham, and the major Roman forts. The service runs daily from late May to mid-September and on Sunday throughout the year. Another bus runs daily from Wallsend to Bowness, and another from Hexham to Vindolanda (£2.45).

> ### FAST WALL FACTS
>
> ■ No slaves were used to build the wall; it was built by skilled Roman masons with the labor of thousands of soldiers.
>
> ■ The wall was a multicultural military zone, with soldiers (and their families) coming from places such as Germany, Spain, and North Africa. Lively wall communities were made up of people with different languages and customs.
>
> ■ Only 5% of the Roman remains in the region around the wall have been excavated.

Sports & the Outdoors

BIKING **Hadrian's Cycleway** (⊕ www.cycle-routes.org/hadrianscycleway), between Tynemouth and Whitehaven, follows the river Tyne from the east coast until Newcastle, before chasing the entire length of Hadrian's Wall. It then continues west to the Irish Sea. Maps and guides are available at the Tourist Information Centre in Newcastle or online. **Eden's Lawn Cycle Hire** (✉ Eden's Lawn Garage, Haltwhistle ☎ 01434/320443) rents mountain bikes for £12 per day. Bikes in the **Bike Shop** (✉ 16–17 St. Mary's, Hexham ☎ 01434/601032) cost £15 per day.

HIKING **Hadrian's Wall Path** (☎ 01434/322022 ⊕ www.nationaltrail.co.uk/
★ hadrianswall), a national trail completed in 2003, runs the entire 73-mi length of the wall. If you don't have time for it all, you can walk a section or take one of the less challenging circular routes, detailed in leaflets at tourist information offices along the way. One of the most scenic but also most rugged sections is the 12-mi western stretch between Sewingshields (east of Housesteads) and Greenhead.

HORSEBACK Riding schools offer hour-long rides to full-day treks on horseback. For
RIDING a full list, contact the Hexham tourist information office; advance booking is essential in summer.

Hexham

🔟 *22 mi west of Newcastle, 31 mi northwest of Durham.*

The historic market town of Hexham makes the best base for visiting Hadrian's Wall. Just a few miles from the most significant remains, it retains enough interest in its medieval streets to warrant a stop in its own right. First settled in the 7th century, around a Benedictine monastery, Hexham later became a byword for monastic learning, famous for its book painting, sculpture, and liturgical singing.

★ Ancient **Hexham Abbey,** a site of Christian worship for more than 1,300 years, forms one side of the town's main square. Inside, you can climb the 35 worn stone "night stairs," which once led from the main part of the abbey to the canon's dormitory, to overlook the whole ensemble. Most of the current building dates from the 12th and 13th centuries, and much of the stone, including that of the Anglo-Saxon crypt, was taken from the Roman fort at Corbridge. The interior is alive with paintings; note the portraits on the 16th-century wooden rood screen and the four panels from a 15th-century Dance of Death in the sanctuary. ⊠ *Beaumont St.* ☎ *01434/602031* ⊕ *www.hexhamabbey.org.uk* ⊠ *Requested donation £2* ☉ *May–Sept., daily 9:30–7; Oct.–Apr., daily 9:30–5. Crypt daily at 11:30 and 3. No tours during services.*

Hexham's central **Market Place** has been the site since 1239 of a weekly market, held each Tuesday. Crowded stalls are set out under the long slate roof of the Shambles; other stalls, protected only by bright awnings, take their chances with the weather.

Dating from 1330, Hexham's **Old Gaol,** across Market Place from the abbey, houses fascinating exhibits about Border history. Photographs, models, a Border house interior, armor, and weapons tell the story of the "Middle March," the medieval administrative area governed by a warden and centered on Hexham. A glass elevator takes you to four floors, including the dungeon. ⊠ *Hallgate* ☎ *01434/652351* ⊠ *£3* ☉ *Apr.–Oct., daily 10–4:30; Nov., Feb., and Mar., Mon., Tues., and Sat. 10–4:30.*

Where to Stay & Eat

£££–£££££ ✕⌂ **Langley Castle Hotel.** Rescued from decline by a professor from the United States in the mid-1980s, this 14th-century castle with turrets and battlements is thoroughly lavish. Bedrooms within the castle, resplendent with tapestries and four-poster beds, have deep window seats set in the 7-foot-thick walls; those in the Castle View annex are more modest. The baronial restaurant (£30 fixed-price menu) serves an excellent menu of traditional English dishes. The hotel is 6 mi west of Hexham. ⊠ *Langley-on-Tyne NE47 5LU* ☎ *01434/688888* 🖷 *01434/684019* ⊕ *www.langleycastle.com* ⥱ *18 rooms* ⌂ *Restaurant, in-room data ports, sauna, 2 bars, meeting rooms; no a/c* ⊟ *AE, DC, MC, V* ⊫❙ *BP.*

££££ ✕⌂ **Lord Crewe Arms Hotel.** In a former role, this unusual hotel in a tiny stone village once provided guest accommodations for Blanchland Abbey. It's not the fanciest place but has medieval and Gothic touches, including a vault-roofed crypt with its own bar. Bedrooms are simply but pleasantly furnished; a number have oak-beam ceilings. The fixed-price menu (£32) of the hotel restaurant offers dishes such as roast partridge and rack of lamb in an herb-and-mustard crust. ⊠ *Off B6306, about 8 mi south of Hexham, Blanchland DH8 9SP* ☎ *01434/675251* 🖷 *01434/675337* ⊕ *www.lordcrewehotel.com* ⥱ *19 rooms* ⌂ *Restaurant, bar, meeting rooms; no a/c* ⊟ *AE, DC, MC, V* ⊫❙ *BP.*

£ ⊞ **Dene House.** This peaceful, stone-built former farmhouse on 9 acres of lovely countryside has beamed ceilings and homey rooms with pine pieces and colorful quilts. Breakfasts, taken in the cozy kitchen, include homemade bread and preserves. The house is 4 mi south of Hexham; follow signs for Dye House. ⊠ *B6303, Juniper, Hexham NE46 1SJ* 📠 *01434/673413* ⊕ *www.denehouse-hexham.co.uk* 🗢 *3 rooms, 1 with private bath* ⚲ *Lounge; no a/c, no room phones, no room TVs, no smoking* ⊟ *AE, MC, V* ⦿ *BP.*

Nightlife & the Arts

One of the Northeast's most adventurous arts venues, the **Queen's Hall Arts Centre** (⊠ Beaumont St. 📞 01434/652477) presents drama, dance, and exhibitions by local artists. It sponsors events such as the annual jazz festival (June), which has dozens of concerts in one weekend.

Greenhead

⑰ *18 mi west of Hexham, 49 mi northwest of Durham.*

Tiny Greenhead has an informative Hadrian's Wall site. The **Roman Army Museum,** at the garrison fort of Carvoran, near the village, makes an excellent introduction to Hadrian's Wall. Full-size models and excavations bring this remote outpost of the empire to life; authentic Roman graffiti adorn the walls of an excavated barracks. Opposite the museum, at Walltown Crags on the Pennine Way (a long-distance hiking route), are 400 yards of the best-preserved section of the wall. ⊠ *Off B6318, 1 mi northeast of Greenhead* 📞 *016977/47485* ⊕ *www.vindolanda.com* ⊠ *£3.95, joint ticket with Vindoland £7.50* ⊙ *Mid-Feb.–Mar., Oct., and Nov., daily 10–5; Apr.–Sept., daily 10–6.*

Where to Stay & Eat

★ ££ ✕ **Milecastle Inn.** The snug traditional bar and restaurant of this remote and peaceful 17th-century pub make an excellent place to dine. Fine local meat goes into its famous pies; take your pick from rabbit, venison, wild boar, and duckling. The inn is on the north side of Haltwhistle on B6318. ⊠ *Military Rd., Haltwhistle* 📞 *01434/321372* ⊟ *AE, MC, V.*

£–£££ ✕⊞ **Centre of Britain Hotel.** In a building dating in part to the 15th century, this hotel skillfully blends Scandinavian style with original features. Room 3 on the first floor has a sauna and whirlpool bath. The restaurant's fixed-price menu (££££) includes Norwegian dishes such as sweet cured herring on rye bread as well as local pork with apricot and sage sauce. ⊠ *Main St., 3 mi east of Greenhead, Haltwhistle NE49 0BH* 📞*01434/322422* 📠*01434/322655* ⊕*www.centre-of-britain.org.uk* 🗢*9 rooms* ⚲ *Restaurant, bar, laundry facilities, meeting rooms; no a/c* ⊟ *AE, DC, MC, V* ⦿ *BP.*

££ ⊞ **Holmhead Guest House.** This former farmhouse in open countryside is not only built *on* Hadrian's Wall but also *of* it. Stone arches and exposed beams add to the feeling of history. Rooms are small but comfortable, the beds covered with soft, white eiderdown. You can book a fixed-priced dinner that may include organic vegetables. There's also an apartment in a cottage and 8 hostel-style beds in a barn. ⊠ *Off A69 about 18 mi west of Hexham, CA6 7HY* 📠 *016977/47402* ⊕ *www.*

bandbhadrianswall.com ⬎4 *rooms, 8 beds, 1 apartment* ⌂ *Dining room; no a/c, no room TVs, no smoking* ▭ *MC, V* ⦿ *BP.*

Vindolanda

18 *8 mi east of Greenhead, 41 mi northwest of Durham.*

The great garrison fort of Vindolanda holds the remains of eight successive Roman forts and civilian settlements, which have provided intriguing information about daily life in a military compound. Most of the visible remains date from the 2nd and 3rd centuries, and excavations are always under way. There's a reconstructed Roman temple, house, and shop to explore, and the museum displays rare artifacts such as writing tablets. A full-size reproduction of a section of the wall gives a sense of its massiveness. ⊠ *Near Bardon Mill* ☎ *01434/344277* ⊕ *www.vindolanda.com* 🎫 *£4.95, joint ticket with Roman Army Museum £7.50* ⊙ *Mid-Nov.–mid-Jan., Wed.–Sun. 10–4; mid-Feb.–Mar., Oct., and Nov., daily 10–5; Apr.–Sept., daily 10–6; call to confirm times in winter.*

In Northumberland National Park, **Once Brewed National Park Visitor Centre**, ½ mi north of Vindolanda, has informative displays about Hadrian's Wall and can advise about local walks. It's also a national tourist information center. ⊠ *B6318* ☎ *01434/344396* ⊕ *www.northumberland-national-park.org.uk* 🎫 *Free* ⊙ *Mid-Mar.–Nov., daily 9:30–5.*

Housesteads Roman Fort

★ **19** *3 mi east of Vindolanda, 38 mi northwest of Durham.*

If you have time to visit only one Hadrian's Wall site, Housesteads Roman Fort, Britain's most complete example of a Roman fort, is your best bet. It includes an interpretive center, views of long sections of the wall, the excavated 5-acre fort itself, and a museum. The steep, 10-minute walk up from the parking lot by B6318 to the site rewards the effort, especially for the sight of the wall disappearing over hills and crags into the distance. Excavations have revealed granaries, gateways, barracks, a hospital, and the commandant's house. ⊠ *B6318, 3 mi northeast of Bardon Mill* ☎ *01434/ 344363* ⊕ *www.english-heritage. org.uk* 🎫 *£3.80* ⊙ *Apr.–Sept., daily 10–6; Oct.–Mar., daily 10–4.*

> **WORD OF MOUTH**
>
> "Probably the most spectacular stretch of the wall is near Housesteads Roman Fort near Hexham. If you can, park at Steel Rigg and hike a bit down to the fort, then grab a bus back. There are many other Roman ruins in the vicinity. It's worth at least a day."
>
> –Pausanias

Chesters Roman Fort

20 *7 mi east of Housestead, 4 mi north of Hexham, 35 mi northwest of Durham.*

This cavalry fort in a wooded valley on the banks of the North Tyne River was known as Cilurnum in Roman times, when it protected the point where Hadrian's Wall crossed the river. You approach the fort directly from the parking lot, and, although the site cannot compete with Housesteads in setting, the museum here holds a fascinating collection of Roman artifacts, including statues of river and water gods, altars, milestones, iron tools, weapons, and jewelry. The military bathhouse by the river is well preserved. ⊠ *B6318, ½ mi southwest of Chollerford* ☎ *01434/681379* ⊕ *www.english-heritage.org.uk* ⊠ *£3.80* ⊙ *Apr.–Sept., daily 9:30–5; Oct.–Mar., daily 10–4.*

Corbridge

㉑ *8 mi southeast of Chesters Roman Fort, 19 mi west of Newcastle, 29 mi northwest of Durham.*

A small town of honey-color stone houses and riverside walks, Corbridge is a prosperous-looking place with an abundance of welcoming pubs and attractive shops. In the yard of St. Andrew's Church by Market Place is the **Vicar's Pele,** built with stones taken from the Roman fort at Corbridge. This nearly 700-year-old fortified tower served as a refuge from Scottish raiders.

The ruins of the **Corbridge Roman Site,** occupied longer than any other fort on Hadrian's Wall, actually predate the wall by 40 years. The fort was strategically positioned at the junction of the east–west and north–south Roman routes—Stanegate ran west to Carlisle, Dere Street led north to Scotland and south to London. You can visit a museum rich in artifacts, and explore the remains of two giant granaries, as well as temples, houses, and garrison buildings. ⊠ *On a signposted back road ½ mi northwest of Corbridge* ☎ *01434/632349* ⊕ *www.english-heritage.org.uk* ⊠ *£3.50* ⊙ *Apr.–Sept., daily 10–6; Oct., daily 10–4; Nov.–Mar., weekends 10–4.*

Where to Stay

£–££ ⊞ **Town Barns.** The stone-built former home of the novelist Catherine Cookson (1906–88) has three spacious rooms, approached from a double staircase and galleried landing and furnished with yew and mahogany pieces. Get set up for the day with a packed lunch and return to a cozy fire in the evening. It's best to call ahead for winter opening information. ⊠ *Off Trinity Terr., NE45 5HP* ☎ *01434/633345* ⇨ *3 rooms* ♢ *No a/c, no smoking* ⊟ *No credit cards* ⊩⊙ *BP.*

Rothbury

㉒ *25 mi northeast of Corbridge, 9 mi southwest of Alnwick.*

The small market town of Rothbury, surrounded by stunning countryside, originally developed as a Victorian resort, attracting the gentry who roamed its hills and glades. Buildings from the era survive in the handsome center, although, as with many such towns, the sheer weight of modern traffic has blunted its appeal.

The helpful staff at the **Northumberland National Park Visitor Centre** can discuss walking routes through the Simonside Hills. It's also a national tourist information center. ⊠ *4 Bridge St.* ☎ *01669/620887* ⊕ *www. northumberland-national-park.org.uk* ⊙ *Apr.–Oct., daily 10–5.*

★ The turrets and towers of Tudor-style of **Cragside** look out over the edge of a forested hillside. This epitome of the Victorian country house was built between 1864 and 1895 by Lord Armstrong, an early electrical engineer and inventor, and designed by Richard Norman Shaw, a well-regarded late-Victorian architect. Among Armstrong's contemporaries it was called "the palace of a modern magician" because it contained so many of his inventions. This was the first house to be lighted by hydroelectricity; the grounds also hold an energy center with restored mid-Victorian machinery. There are Pre-Raphaelite paintings and an elaborate mock-Renaissance marble chimneypiece. The house is closed until April 2007, but the grounds are

> **WALK & BIKE**
>
> Wide vistas, quiet roads, and fresh air make hikes and bike rides appealing in the Northeast. Long-distance footpaths include the 90-mi Teesdale Way, which follows the River Tees through Barnard Castle and Middleton-in-Teesdale. Otherwise, the russet hills and dales of Northumberland National Park will please any serious walker. Bike routes to explore—in whole or in part—are the 220-mi Northumbria's Cycling Kingdom loop and the 81-mi Coast and Castles cycle route, which takes in Dunstanburgh and Bamburgh castles.

13

worth exploring. The gardens, including an enormous rock garden and a sculpture trail, are as impressive as the house; in June rhododendrons bloom in the 660-acre park surrounding the mansion. ■ TIP→ **Paths around the grounds are steep and distances can be long; wear comfortable footwear.** ⊠ *Off A697 and B6341, 1 mi north of Rothbury* ☎ *01669/620333* ⊕ *www.nationaltrust.org.uk* ✉ *Grounds £6.50; call for house price in 2007* ☉ *Grounds Apr.–Oct., Tues.–Sun. 10:30–6; Nov.–mid-Dec., Wed.–Sun. 11–4.*

Where to Stay & Eat

£££ ✕🏠 **Embleton Hall.** The 5 acres of beautiful grounds are reason enough to stay in this stone country mansion, parts of which date to 1730. Some lovely antiques and paintings decorate the individually furnished guest rooms. The chintz draperies and cut-glass chandeliers in the restaurant (£££–£££££) make perfect accompaniments to traditional English dishes such as noisettes of lamb with mint and rosemary sauce. There are less-expensive options in the bar. ⊠ *A697, 5 mi east of Rothbury, Longframlington NE65 8DT* ☎ *01665/570249* 🖷 *01665/570056* ⊕ *www.embletonhallmorpeth.co.uk* ⌧ *14 rooms* ⚭ *Restaurant, bar, meeting rooms, some pets allowed; no a/c* ▤ *AE, DC, MC, V* ⃝ *BP.*

THE FAR NORTHEAST COAST

Before England gives way to Scotland, extraordinary medieval fortresses and monasteries line the final 40 mi of the Northeast coast. Northumbria was an enclave where the flame of learning was kept alive during Europe's Dark Ages, most notably at Lindisfarne, home of saints and scholars. Castles abound, including the spectacularly sited Bamburgh and the desolate Dunstanburgh. The region also has some magnificent beaches that are far better for walking than swimming. The 3-mi walk from Seahouses to Bamburgh gives splendid views of the Farne Islands, and the 2-mi hike from Craster to Dunstanburgh Castle is unforgettable.

Alnwick

❷ *30 mi north of Newcastle, 46 mi north of Durham.*

Dominated by a grand castle, the little market town of Alnwick (pronounced *ann*-ick) is the best base from which to explore the dramatic coast and countryside of northern Northumberland. A weekly open-air market (every Saturday) has been held in Alnwick's cobbled **Market Place** for more than 800 years. Note the market cross, built on the base of an older cross; the town crier once made his proclamations from here. In the last week of June, this site is host to the **Alnwick Fair,** a festival noteworthy for the enthusiastic participation of locals in medieval costume.

★ The grandly scaled **Alnwick Castle,** on the edge of the town center, is still the home of the dukes of Northumberland, whose family, the regal Percys, dominated the Northeast for centuries. Known as "the Windsor of the North," it has been remodeled several times since the first occupant, Henry de Percy, adapted the original Norman keep. Nowadays the castle is in favor as a set for films such as *Robin Hood: Prince of Thieves, Elizabeth,* and the first two Harry Potter movies (in the first, the castle grounds appear as the exterior of Hogwarts School in scenes such as the Quidditch match). In

> **GARDEN VISION**
>
> A marvelous flight of fancy, the Alnwick Gardens represent the vision of the duchess of Northumberland. Work, begun in 2000, will continue through 2008. Centering on modern terraced fountains by Belgian designers Jacques and Peter Wirtz, the gardens include traditional features (shaded woodland walks) and funkier elements such as a Poison Garden and a labyrinth of towering bamboo.

contrast with the cold, formidable exterior, the interior has all the opulence of the palatial home it still is. You see only 6 of the more than 150 rooms, but among the treasures on show are a galleried library, Meissen dinner services, niches with larger-than-life-size marble statues, and Venetian-mosaic floors. The castle's extensive gardens are the big news, however: they include a modern, 260-foot-long stepped water cascade as well as rose and ornamental gardens and a large tree house. ⊠ *Above junction of Narrowgate and Bailiffgate* ☎*01665/510777* ⊕*www.alnwickcastle. com, www.alnwickgarden.com* ☒*Castle and garden £10, castle only £8.50, garden only £5* ⊙ *Castle Apr.–Oct., daily 11–5; last admission 4:15. Garden daily 10–dusk; last admission 45 mins before closing.*

Where to Stay & Eat

£££ ✕🏨 **White Swan Hotel.** The surprise feature of this comfortable, modernized, 18th-century coaching inn near the town square is that one lounge, the Olympic Suite, has been reconstructed with the paneling, stained glass, and mirrors of the *Olympic,* sister ship of the ill-fated *Titanic.* It's used as a function room, but guests can take a look. You can choose from the hearty dishes on the fixed-price menu (£20) in the Bondgate restaurant (dinner and Sunday lunch only); kipper pâté and steamed plum pudding help fill you up. ⊠ *Bondgate Within, NE66 1TD* ☎ *01665/602109* 🖷 *01665/510400* ⊕ *www.classiclodges.co.uk* ⇌ *57 rooms* ⚲ *Restaurant, bar, meeting rooms, some pets allowed; no a/c* ⊟ *AE, MC, V* ⵌ *BP.*

Shopping

The **House of Hardy** (☎ 01665/602771), just outside Alnwick (from downtown, take A1 south to just beyond the traffic circle on the left, clearly marked), is one of Britain's finest stores for country sports. It has a worldwide reputation for handcrafted fishing tackle.

13

Craster

㉔ *6 mi north of Alnwick.*

The tiny fishing village of Craster is known for its footpath to Dunstanburgh Castle—and for that great English breakfast delicacy, kippers: herring salted and smoked over smoldering oak shavings. You can visit the tar-blackened smokehouses and see the fish hanging in ranks; then cross the road to the pub to taste for yourself. **L. Robson & Sons** (⊠ Haven Hill ☎ 01665/576223) has been smoking fish for four generations. The smokehouse is open Monday through Saturday all year for kippers, smoked cod, and salmon.

Where to Eat

★ **£** ✕ **Jolly Fisherman.** You can feast in this traditional pub on the famous fresh crab sandwiches or kipper pâté. The splendid picture window provides views of crashing waves; on sunny days, the garden beckons. ⊠ *Haven Hill* ☎ *01665/576461* ⊟ *MC, V.*

Dunstanburgh Castle

㉕ *1 mi north of Craster.*

Perched romantically on a cliff 100 feet above the shore, the ruins of Dunstanburgh Castle can be reached along a windy, mile-long coastal footpath from Craster. Built in 1316 by the earl of Lancaster as a defense against the Scots (or perhaps as a symbol of Lancaster's deteriorating relationship with King Edward II), and later enlarged by John of Gaunt (the powerful duke of Lancaster who virtually ruled England in the late 14th century), the castle is known to many from the popular paintings by 19th-century artist J. M. W. Turner. Several handsome sandy bays indent the coastline immediately to the north. ☎ 01665/576231 ⊕ *www.english-heritage.org.uk* ⵌ £2.70 ⊙ *Apr.–Sept., daily 10–6; Oct., daily 10–4; Nov.–Mar., Thurs.–Mon. 10–4.*

Farne Islands

★ **㉖** *7 mi north of Craster, 13 mi northeast of Alnwick.*

Regular boat trips from the village of Seahouses provide access to the bleak, wind-tossed Farne Islands (owned by the National Trust), with their impressive colonies of seabirds, including puffins, kittiwakes, terns, shags, and guillemots, and barking groups of gray seals. Inner Farne, where St. Cuthbert, the great abbot of Lindisfarne, died in AD 687, has a tiny chapel. Cruises to Inner Farne (April, August, and September, at 10, 11, 1, and 2; May to July, afternoons only) and the rocky Staple Island (May to July, daily at 10 and 11) take 2½ hours each and include landfall in good weather. All boat services leave from Seahouses harbor. Six-hour trips (May to July) allow for a morning stroll on Inner Farne and an afternoon on Staple Island. Pack a lunch. ☎ 01665/ 721099 *National Trust information center, 01665/720308 boat trips, 01665/720884 Seahouses Tourist Information Centre (summer only)* ⊕ *www.farne-islands.com* ⌧ *Boat trips £10–£20, landing fees £3.80–£4.80, payable to wardens* ⊙ *Boat trips Apr.–Sept., daily, weather permitting.*

Bamburgh

㉗ *14 mi north of Alnwick.*

Tiny Bamburgh has a splendid castle, and several beaches are a few minutes' walk away. Especially stunning when floodlighted at night, **Bamburgh Castle** dominates the coastal view for miles, set atop a great crag to the north of Seahouses and overlooking a magnificent sweep of sand backed by high dunes. It was once believed to be the legendary Joyous Garde of Sir Lancelot du Lac, one of King Arthur's fabled knights. A fortification of some kind has stood here since the 6th century, but the Norman castle was damaged during the 15th century. Much of the castle—the home of the Armstrong family since 1894—was restored during the 18th and 19th centuries, including the Victorian Great Hall, although the great Norman keep (central tower) remains intact. Exhibits include armor, porcelain, jade, furniture, and paintings. ⊠ *3 mi north of Seahouses, Bamburgh* ☎ *01668/214515* ⊕ *www.bamburghcastle.com* ⌧ *£6* ⊙ *Mid-Mar.–Oct., daily 11–5; last admission 4:30.*

Where to Stay & Eat

££££–£££££ ✕▥ **Waren House Hotel.** Six acres of woodland surround this Georgian hotel on a quiet bay between Bamburgh and Holy Island. Public areas are furnished comfortably in period style, and guest rooms have comfortable beds and themed decoration (Gray, Victorian, and so on). The crisply elegant restaurant has romantic views of Holy Island when the trees are bare; two- to four-course dinners (£££££) might include zucchini and apple soup, local game or trout, and ginger cheesecake. ⊠ *Waren Mill, Belford NE70 7EE* ☎ *01668/214581* ⌸ *01668/214484* ⊕ *www.warenhousehotel.co.uk* ↄ *9 rooms, 3 suites* ⟨ *Restaurant, some pets allowed; no a/c, no kids under 15* ⊟ *AE, DC, MC, V* ⧉ *BP.*

££–£££ ✕▥ **Lord Crewe Arms.** This cozy, stone-walled inn with oak beams is in the heart of the village, close to Bamburgh Castle. It's an ideal spot for lunch while you're touring the area. Pine furnishings decorate the simple guest rooms, but the food (££), especially seafood dishes, is excellent. ⊠ *Front St., NE69 7BL* ☎ *01668/214243* ⌸ *01668/214273* ⊕ *www.lordcrewe.co.uk* ↄ *18 rooms* ⟨ *Restaurant, bar, some pets allowed; no a/c, no kids under 5* ⊟ *MC, V* ⊙ *Closed Jan. and weekdays in Dec. and Feb.* ⧉ *BP.*

Lindisfarne (Holy Island)

★ **㉘** *6 mi east of A1, north of Bamburgh; 22 mi north of Alnwick; 8 mi southeast of Berwick-upon-Tweed.*

Cradle of northern England's Christianity and home of St. Cuthbert, Lindisfarne (or Holy Island) has a religious history that dates from AD 635, when St. Aidan established a monastery here. Under its greatest abbot, the sainted Cuthbert, Lindisfarne became one of the foremost centers of learning in Christendom. ■ TIP→ **The island is reached from the mainland by a long drive along a causeway that floods at high tide, so you *must* check to find out when crossing is safe.** The times, which change daily, are displayed at the causeway and printed in local newspapers. Traffic can be heavy; allow at least a half hour for your return trip.

In the year 875, Vikings destroyed the Lindisfarne community; only a few monks managed to escape, carrying with them Cuthbert's bones, which they reburied in Durham. The sandstone Norman ruins of **Lindisfarne Priory,** reestablished in the 11th century by monks from Durham, remain both impressive and beautiful. A museum here displays Anglo-Saxon carvings. ✉ *Lindisfarne* ☎ *01289/389200* ⊕ *www.english-heritage.org.uk* 🎫 *£3.70* ◷ *Apr.–Sept., daily 10–6; Feb., Mar., and Oct., daily 10–4; Nov.–Jan., weekends 10–4.*

Reached by causeway from the mainland (during low tide), **Lindisfarne Castle** appears to grow out of the rocky pinnacle on which it was built 400 years ago, looking for all the world like a fairy-tale illustration. In 1903 architect Sir Edwin Lutyens converted the former Tudor fort into a private home that retains the original's ancient features. Across several fields from the castle is a walled garden designed by Gertrude Jekyll. ✉ *Lindisfarne* ☎ *01289/389244* ⊕ *www.nationaltrust.org.uk* 🎫 *£5.20, garden only £1* ◷ *Late Mar.–Oct., Tues.–Sun. 10:30–3 or noon–4:30; call for hrs.*

Berwick-upon-Tweed

㉙ *10 mi northwest of Lindisfarne, 30 mi northwest of Alnwick, 77 mi north of Durham.*

Although Berwick-upon-Tweed now lies just inside the border of England, historians estimate that it has changed hands between the Scots and the English 14 times. The market on Wednesday and Saturday draws customers from both sides of the border. The town's thick 16th-century walls, among the best-preserved in Europe, completely encircle the old town; a path follows the ramparts, and the views are rewarding. The parish church, Holy Trinity, was built during Cromwell's Puritan Commonwealth with stone from a castle.

In the **Barracks,** built between 1717 and 1721, three accommodation wings surround a square, with the decorated gatehouse forming the fourth side. An exhibition called "By Beat of Drum" depicts the life of the common soldier from the 1660s to the 1880s. Other displays highlight the history of the local regiment, the King's Own Scottish Borderers, and that of the town itself. ✉ *The Parade, off Church St. in town center* ☎ *01289/*

304493 ⊕ *www.english-heritage.org.uk* ✉ *£3.30* ☉ *Apr.–Sept., daily 10–6; Oct., daily 10–4; Nov.–Mar., Thurs.–Mon. 10–4.*

Where to Stay & Eat

£–££ ✗ **Town House.** Fresh quiches, pastries, and other snacks are your reward for seeking out this tricky-to-find spot: cross Buttermarket under the Guildhall and go through the old jail. ✉ *Marygate* ☎ *01289/307904* ⊟ *MC, V* ☉ *Closed Thurs. afternoon and Sun. No dinner.*

£££ ▦ **No. 1 Sallyport.** In the heart of town, this stylish, pampering B&B stands a mere 20 yards from the Elizabethan walls. The large rooms and suites (*££££*) are luxuriously decorated in contemporary style, with wood floors, leather or upholstered chairs and sofas, and comfortable beds covered in thick duvets. Breakfast is unbeatable, with choices from salmon fishcakes to kippers with eggs. Evening meals can be arranged. ✉ *1 Sallyport, TD15 1EZ* ☎ *01289/308827* ⊕ *www.1sallyport-be-dandbreakfast.com* ⇝ *2 rooms, 3 suites* ⚶ *Dining room, room TVs with movies, some pets allowed; no a/c* ⊟ *No credit cards* ⯁ *BP.*

££–£££ ▦ **Coach House.** Part of a cluster of attractive, well-converted farm buildings, this friendly country guesthouse 10 mi southwest of Berwick-upon-Tweed includes a 17th-century cottage. Spacious bedrooms, some of which have rare chestnut beams, vary in style from traditional to modern. You can relax by the fire in the lounge or try the books and games in the library. The breakfast menu seems unending. ✉ *A 697, Crookham, Cornhill-on-Tweed TD12 4TD* ☎ *01890/820293* ▤ *01890/820284* ⊕ *www.coachhousecrookham.com* ⇝ *9 rooms, 7 with bath* ⚶ *Dining room, refrigerators, bar, some pets allowed; no a/c* ⊟ *MC, V* ⯁ *BP.*

THE NORTHEAST ESSENTIALS

Transportation

BY AIR

Newcastle Airport, 5 mi northwest of the city center, is well served for domestic destinations and major European cities. Metro trains connect the airport to the center of Newcastle, with service approximately every 8 minutes at peak times; cost is £2 one-way. The airport is about 15 minutes by car from the city center.

🛈 **Newcastle Airport** ✉ Off A696 ☎ 0870/122–1488 ⊕ www.newcastleairport.com.

BY BUS

National Express and the low-cost Megabus both serve the region from London's Victoria Coach Station. Average travel times are 6¾ hours to Durham, 7 hours to Newcastle, and 7½ hours to Berwick-upon-Tweed. Connecting services to other parts of the region leave from Durham and Newcastle. For all bus inquiries, call Traveline or National Express, or visit the Megabus Web site. Book Megabus tickets online, since their phone number charges at a costly premium rate.

CUTTING COSTS The Northeast Explorer Pass (£6, one day) allows unlimited travel on most local bus and Metro train services and is available from the bus driver or local bus or metro stations.

FARES &
SCHEDULES You can pick up free regional public transport guides from the tourist information centers.

🚌 **Megabus** ☎ 0900/160-0900 ⊕ www.megabus.co.uk. **National Express** ☎ 0870/ 580-8080 ⊕ www.nationalexpress.com. **Traveline** ☎ 0870/608-2608 ⊕ www.traveline. org.uk.

BY CAR

The most direct north–south route through the Northeast is A1, linking London and Edinburgh via Newcastle (274 mi from London; five to six hours) and Berwick-upon-Tweed (338 mi from London; two hours past Newcastle). A697, which branches west off A1 north of Morpeth, is a more attractive road, leading past the 16th-century battlefield of Flodden. For Hexham and Hadrian's Wall, take the A69 west of Newcastle. For the coast, leave the A1 at Alnwick and follow the minor B1340 and B1339 for Craster, Seahouses, and Bamburgh. Holy Island is reached from a minor exit off the A1. A66 and A69 run east–west through the southern and middle parts of the region, respectively.

Many country roads provide quiet and scenic, if slower, alternatives to the main routes. Part of the Cheviot Hills, which run along the Northumbrian side of the Scottish border, is now a military firing range. Don't drive here when the warning flags are flying. The military, though, has restored the Roman road, Dere Street, which crosses this region. Try also B6318, which runs alongside Hadrian's Wall on the south side.

BY TRAIN

Great Northeastern Railways serves the region from London's King's Cross Station, en route to Scotland. Average travel times are 2½ hours to Darlington, 3 hours to Durham and Newcastle, and 3¾ hours to Berwick-upon-Tweed. From Newcastle, there is local service north to Alnwick and to Corbridge and Hexham on the east–west line to Carlisle. All journeys take approximately ½ hour.

FARES &
SCHEDULES 🚆 **Great Northeastern Railways** ☎ 0845/722-5225 or 0845/748-4950 ⊕ www.gner.co.uk.

Contacts & Resources

EMERGENCIES
🚑 **Ambulance, fire, police** ☎ 999. **Berwick Infirmary** ⊠ Infirmary Square, Berwick-upon-Tweed ☎ 01289/307484. **University Hospital of North Durham** ⊠ North Rd., Durham ☎ 0191/333-2333. **Newcastle General Hospital** ⊠ Westgate Rd. ☎ 0191/ 233-6161.

INTERNET
Beyond Newcastle and Durham Internet cafés are rare in the Northeast. Your best bet may be your hotel, or any good-size library. Most hotels in the region are not yet wired for broadband, much less Wi-Fi.

💻 Internet Cafés **Cafe Gulp** ⊠ Priestgate, Darlington ☎ 01325/389797. **Reality X** ⊠ 1 Framwelgate Bridge, Durham ☎ 0191/384-5700. **Kitschn** ⊠ 32 Acorn, Newcastle-upon-Tyne ☎ 0191/281-3377.

TOUR OPTIONS

North of England Tours specializes in general tours of northern England, and can help research family trees. Birdwatch Northumbria runs one-day and weekend tours in small groups throughout the year.

📋 **Birdwatch Northumbria** ☎ 01670/783451 ⊕ www.birdwatchnorthumbria.co.uk. **North of England Tours** ☎ 01325/308094 🖷 01325/315940 ⊕ www.northofenglandtours.co.uk.

WALKING TOURS Durham County Council Environment Department organizes a year-round program of guided walks, both in the town and countryside, which cost £2 to £3 per person. A daily walk at 2 PM (June to September) introduces you to the center of Newcastle. These walks are available through local tourist offices.

📋 **Durham County Council Environment Department** ☎ 0191/383-4144.

VISITOR INFORMATION

Northumbria Regional Tourist Board is open weekdays 8:30 to 5. Other tourist information centers are open Monday through Saturday 9:30 to 5:30, but times vary by season. The telephone for the Haltwhistle Tourist Information Centre serves as the Hadrian's Wall Information Line.

📋 **Hadrian's Wall Country** ⊕ www.hadrians-wall.org. **Northumbria Regional Tourist Board** ✉ Stella House, Goldcrest Way, Newburn Riverside, Newcastle-upon-Tyne NE15 8NY ☎ 01271/336182 ⊕ www.visitnorthumbria.com. **Alnwick** ✉ 2 the Shambles, NE66 1TN ☎ 01665/510665 ⊕ www.alnwick.gov.uk. **Barnard Castle** ✉ Woodleigh, Flatts Rd., DL12 8AA ☎ 01833/690909 ⊕ www.teesdalediscovery.com. **Berwick-upon-Tweed** ✉ 106 Marygate, TD15 1BN ☎ 01289/330733 ⊕ www.berwickonline.org.uk. **Bishop Auckland** ✉ Town Hall, Market Pl., DL14 7NP ☎ 01388/604922 ⊕ www.durham.gov.uk. **Darlington** ✉ 13 Horsemarket, DL1 5PW ☎ 01325/388666 ⊕ www.visitdarlington.net. **Durham** ✉ Millennium Pl., DH1 1WA ☎ 0191/384-3720 ⊕ www.durhamtourism.co.uk. **Hadrian's Wall** ⊕ www.hadrians-wall.org. **Haltwhistle** ✉ Railway Station, NE49 9HN ☎ 01434/322002. **Hexham** ✉ Wentworth Car Park, NE46 1QE ☎ 01434/652220 ⊕ www.hadrianswallcountry.org. **Middlesbrough** ✉ Old Town Hall Box Office, Albert Rd., Cleveland TS1 2QQ ☎ 01642/729700 or 01642/358088 ⊕ www.middlesbrough.gov.uk. **Newcastle upon Tyne** ✉ Central Arcade, 132 Grainger St., NE1 5AF ☎ 0191/277-8000 ✉ Main Concourse, Central Station ☎ 0191/277-8000 ⊕ www.visitnewcastlegateshead.com.

Wales

WORD OF MOUTH

"For British gardens at their most splendid and beautiful, go to Bodnant Garden. . . . It takes more than one visit to appreciate the whole beauty, but in late May/early June, see the famous Laburnum Arch . . . with flowers like golden raindrops. [Nearby] is Conwy with impressive Conwy Castle."

–JC

"Okay, I'm biased seeing as I live there, but South Wales is so beautiful in the summer! . . . I'm from Swansea and we have the Gower coast . . . miles and miles of stunning coastline and beaches. . . . Cardiff is near, of course, and so is Pembroke (with the castle where Henry VII was born—very historic). Tenby is a great little town, too."

–Lea_Lea

Updated by
Roger Thomas

WALES, KNOWN AS THE LAND OF SONG, is also a land of mountain and flood, where wild peaks challenge the sky and waterfalls thunder down steep, rocky chasms. It is a land of gray-stone castles, ruined abbeys, male-voice choirs, and a handful of cities. Pockets of the southeast and northeast were heavily industrialized in the 19th century, largely with mining and steelmaking, but long stretches of the coast and the mountainous interior remain areas of unmarred beauty. Small, self-contained Wales has three national parks (Snowdonia, including Snowdon, highest mountain in England and Wales; the Brecon Beacons; and the Pembrokeshire Coast) and five official Areas of Outstanding Natural Beauty (the Wye Valley, Gower Peninsula, Llŷn Peninsula, Isle of Anglesey, and Clwydian Range), as well as large tracts of unspoiled moor and mountain in mid-Wales, the least traveled part of the country. Riches of other sorts fill the country: medieval castles, seaside resorts, traditional market towns, the glorious Bodnant Garden and the National Botanic Garden, the stately houses of Powis and Plas Newydd, steam-powered trains running through Snowdonia and central Wales, and the cosmopolitan capital of Cardiff.

The 1941 film *How Green Was My Valley* depicted Wales as an industrial cauldron filled with coal mines. Although mining did take place in Wales, the picture was not accurate then and is certainly not accurate now, when the country has only one fully operational mine. One of the glories of visiting Wales is the drive through beautiful countryside from south to north without passing through any large towns. On such a drive, it's easy to believe that Wales has a population of about 2.9 million but is home to 5.5 million sheep. The country's 750 mi of coast consists mainly of sandy beaches, grassy headlands, cliffs, and estuaries.

The Welsh are a Celtic race. When, toward the middle of the AD first millennium, the Anglo-Saxons spread through Britain, they pushed the indigenous Celts farther back into their Welsh mountain strongholds. In fact, "Wales" comes from the Saxon word *Weallas,* which means "strangers," the name impertinently given by the new arrivals to the natives. The Welsh, however, have always called themselves *Y Cymry,* the companions. Not until the English king Edward I (1272–1307) waged a brutal campaign to conquer Wales was English supremacy established. Welsh hopes were finally crushed with the death in battle of Llywelyn ap Gruffudd, last native prince of Wales, in 1282.

Today Wales has achieved a measure of independence from its English neighbor. In a 1999 referendum, a narrow majority of the Welsh people voted for partial devolution for the country. Elections were held and the Welsh Assembly was born. Unlike the Scottish Parliament, the Welsh Assembly has no lawmaking powers, but it does have significant administrative responsibilities and considerable control over Welsh affairs. The Welsh Assembly is housed in a building on Cardiff Bay designed by the world-famous British architect Sir Richard Rogers.

The Welsh language continues to flourish. Although spoken by only a fifth of the population, it has a high profile within the country. Welsh-language schools are popular, there is a Welsh TV channel, and road

GREAT ITINERARIES

Although less than 200 mi from south to north, Wales is packed with scenic variety and a daunting number of places to visit. Many people make the mistake of thinking that they can see Wales in a day or so, but that's time only to scratch the surface.

Numbers in the text correspond to numbers in the margin and on the Wales and Cardiff maps.

IF YOU HAVE 3 DAYS

Start in **Cardiff** ㉒–㉙ ▶, Wales's capital city, and spend at least a half day here before you drive through the Brecon Beacons National Park to 🚂 **Llandrindod Wells** ⑯, a Victorian spa town. On day two, drive via Rhayader and the Elan Valley, Wales's "Lake District," to **Aberystwyth** ⑰; then travel along the north coast of Cardigan Bay to 🚂 **Porthmadog** ⑤ (accommodations are also in nearby Harlech and Portmeirion). For your final day, drive via **Blaenau Ffestiniog** ④ through the Snowdonia National Park to **Betws-y-Coed** ⑥ and, drop by to see the castle and town walls in **Conwy** ⑩ before leaving Wales via the A55 route to England.

IF YOU HAVE 9 DAYS

Travel to 🚂 **Cardiff** ㉒–㉙ ▶ for a full day's visit and overnight stop. On day two, drive via **Swansea** ㉝ to 🚂 **Tenby** ㉟, a resort at the southern gateway to the Pembrokeshire Coast National Park. Day three is taken up by a tour of this wild and beautiful seashore. Drive to 🚂 **St. David's** ㊲ in the far

west to visit the cathedral. You can walk a stretch of the coast path or explore **Fishguard** ㊳. Day four is taken up by more coastline on the way to **Cardigan** ㊴, and then a tour along the Vale of Teifi through Cilgerran to Drefach Felindre to explore the National Wool Museum. Continue on to 🚂 **Aberystwyth** ⑰ and overnight there. From Aberystwyth, drive along the Cardigan Bay coast via **Machynlleth** ⑱ to **Dolgellau** ⑲, then head inland through Snowdonia National Park to lakeside 🚂 **Bala** ③.

You see more mountains on day six on the way from Bala to **Blaenau Ffestiniog** ④, where you can visit the caverns that gave this town its past reputation as the "slate capital of North Wales." From here, follow the Vale of Ffestiniog west to **Porthmadog** ⑤; stop at Portmeirion, a mock-Italian village. Continue north to 🚂 **Caernarfon** ⑧ and its medieval castle. On day seven, make a short detour inland from Caernarfon to **Llanberis** ⑦ and Llanberis Pass in the heart of Snowdonia. Continue along the coast to **Conwy** ⑩, overnighting in the Victorian seaside resort of 🚂 **Llandudno** ⑪. Head south through **Denbigh** ⑫, **Ruthin** ⑬, **Llangollen** ②, **Chirk** ①, and **Welshpool** ㉑ on the way to 🚂 **Llandrindod Wells** ⑯. On your last day, visit **Hay-on-Wye** ⑭, the "town of books," then drive on through the mountains to **Brecon** ㉜ in the Brecon Beacons National Park.

14

signs are bilingual. Ironically, although in the 15th and 16th centuries the Tudor kings Henry VII and Henry VIII continued England's domination of the Welsh, principally by attempting to abolish the language, another Tudor monarch, Elizabeth I, ensured its survival by authorizing a Welsh translation of the Bible in 1588. Many older people say they owe their knowledge of Welsh to the Bible. You may see (and hear) Welsh throughout your travels, but everyone in Wales speaks English, too.

Exploring Wales

Wales has three main regions: south, mid, and north. The south is the most varied, for its boundaries include everything from Wales's capital city to unspoiled coastline, grassy mountains, and wooded valleys. It's a landscape of dramatic and sudden contrasts—within minutes of densely populated urban areas you can be among national parklands, moors and mountains. Mid-Wales is pure countryside, fringed on its western shores by the great arc of Cardigan Bay. Here you'll find Wales's rural heartland, an unhurried region of mountain lakes, quiet roads, hill sheep farms, and traditional market towns. North Wales is a mixture of high, rocky mountains, popular sandy beaches, and coastal hideaways. Although dominated by the rocky Snowdonia National Park, the north has a gentler, greener side along the border with England.

About the Restaurants

Today even many rural pubs are more interested in offering meals than serving pints of beer, so do consider these as a dining option. Don't overlook hotel restaurants in Wales; many, particularly those in country inns or hotels, are excellent.

About the Hotels

A 19th-century dictum, "I sleeps where I dines," still holds true in Wales, where good hotels and good restaurants often go together. Castles, country mansions, and even small railway stations are being transformed into interesting hotels and restaurants. Cozy traditional inns with low, beamed ceilings, wood paneling, and fireplaces remain Wales's pride, but they, as well as farmhouse accommodations, tend to be off the beaten track. Cardiff and Swansea have some large chain hotels, and, for luxury, Wales has a good choice of country-house hotels. An added attraction is that prices are generally lower than they are for equivalent properties in the Cotswolds, Scotland, or southeast England. A service charge may be added to the room cost; ask if it's included.

WHAT IT COSTS In pounds sterling				
££££	**£££**	**£££**	**££**	**£**
RESTAURANTS over £22	£18–£22	£13–£17	£7–£12	under £7
HOTELS over £160	£120–£160	£90–£119	£60–£89	under £60

Restaurant prices are for a main course at dinner. Hotel prices are for two people in a standard double room in high season, including V.A.T., with no meals or, if indicated, CP (with continental breakfast), BP (Breakfast Plan, with full breakfast), or MAP (Modified American Plan, with breakfast and dinner).

TOP REASONS TO GO

Castles. Wales is the "Land of Castles." With more than 400 historic sites, it has one of the highest concentrations of castles in Europe. They range from evocative ruins of the native Welsh princes, such as Criccieth Castle, through the fairy-tale Victorian extravaganza of Castell Coch to the huge, mighty fortresses of Caernarfon and Harlech.

Cardiff old and new. The capital of Wales is young and vibrant. Compare the stately architecture of Cardiff's neoclassical Civic Centre with the futuristic form of Wales Millennium Centre, the new arts complex on lively Cardiff Bay.

Coast and mountain walks. Hike along the coast at St. David's, one of the most magical sections of the long-distance Pembrokeshire Coast Path. Or take a hike to the top of Pen y Fan, the highest peak in the grassy Brecon Beacons National Park.

A ride on the rails. Wales has 13 mostly narrow-gauge railways that transport you at the more leisurely pace of a bygone era along scenic routes throughout the country. The rack-and-pinion Snowdon Mountain Railway takes you to the summit of the highest mountain in England and Wales.

Pump the pedals. Brecon is great for biking. From this attractive town, country roads lead into the national park; mountain bikers can climb grassy trails and tracks up into the hills.

14

Timing

The weather in Wales, as in the rest of Britain, is a lottery. It can be warm in spring and cool in summer; come prepared for rain or shine. Generally speaking, southwest Wales enjoys a milder climate than elsewhere in Britain, thanks to the moderating effects of the sea. Spring and autumn can be surprisingly dry and sunny (spring may arrive very early in Pembrokeshire, in the southwest). Book ahead for major festivals such as the literary Hay Festival, Brecon Jazz, Abergavenny Food Festival, and Llangollen's International Musical Eisteddfod.

NORTH WALES

IN THE REALM OF SNOWDONIA

Wales masses all its savage splendor and fierce beauty in the north. Dominating the area is Snowdon, at 3,560 feet, the highest peak in England and Wales. It is impossible to describe the magnificence of the view from the mountain on a clear day: to the northwest the Menai Strait, Anglesey, and beyond to the Irish Sea; to the south the mountains of Merionethshire, Harlech Castle, and the Cadair Idris mountain range; and all around towering masses of wild and barren rock. If you ascend the peak by the Snowdon Mountain Railway from Llanberis, telephone from the terminus to ascertain whether Snowdon is free from mist. You lose much when clouds encircle the monster's brow, as often happens.

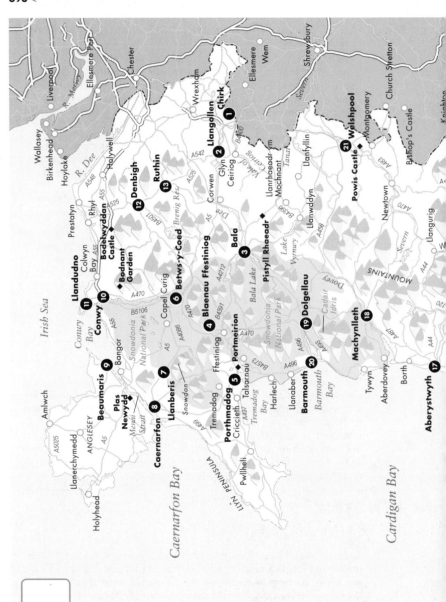

Wales

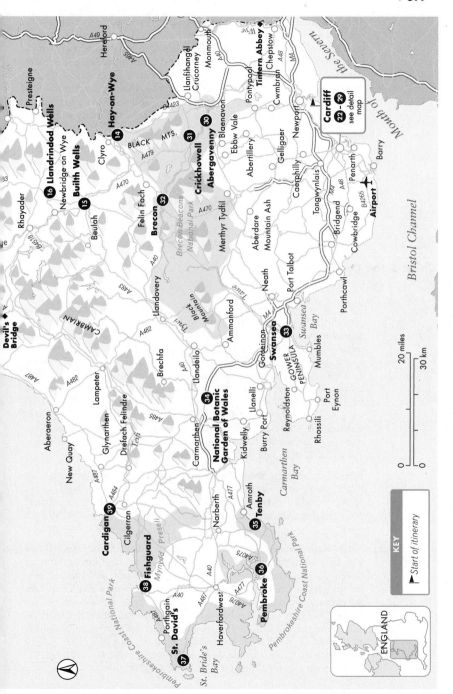

The peak gives its name to **Snowdonia National Park,** which extends southward all the way to Machynlleth in mid-Wales. The park consists of 840 square mi of rocky mountains, valleys clothed in oak woods, moorlands, lakes, and rivers, all guaranteeing natural beauty, and, to a lesser extent, solitude. As in other British national parks, much of the land is privately owned, so inside the park are towns, villages, and farms. The park has become a popular climbing center, and some fear that Snowdon itself is becoming worn away by the boots of too many walkers.

Along the sandy, north-facing coast, a string of seaside resorts has attracted people for well over a century. Llandudno, the dignified "Queen of the North Wales coast," was built in Victorian times as a seaside watering hole. Nearby Conwy, with its medieval castle and town walls, also deserves a look. If you prefer away-from-it-all seashore, there are two official Areas of Outstanding Beauty: the Isle of Anglesey (connected by bridge to mainland Wales), and the Llŷn Peninsula, dotted with quieter small resorts and coastal villages. Portmeirion, a mock-Italianate village, is a quite different kind of escape.

Chirk & the Ceiriog Valley

❶ *22 mi southwest of Chester, 60 mi southwest of Manchester.*

Chirk, poised on the border between England and Wales, is a handy gateway to the Ceiriog Valley, a narrowing vale that penetrates the silent, green foothills of the lofty Berwyn Mountains. The impressive medieval fortress of **Chirk Castle,** finished in its original form in 1310, has evolved into a grand home (albeit one with a medieval dungeon), complete with an 18th-century servants hall and interiors furnished in 16th- to 19th-century styles. Surrounding the castle are beautiful formal gardens and parkland. ✉ *Off B4500* ☎ *01691/777701* ⊕ *www.nationaltrust.org. uk* ✍ *£7, garden only £4.50* ☉ *Castle mid-Mar.–June, Wed.–Sun. noon–5; July and Aug., Tues.–Sun. noon–5; Sept. and Oct., Wed.–Sun. noon–4. Garden mid-Mar.–June, Wed.–Sun. 10–6; July and Aug., Tues.–Sun. 10–6; Sept. and Oct., Wed.–Sun. 10–4.*

West of Chirk is the **Vale of Ceiriog,** nicknamed Little Switzerland. Take B4500 west 6 mi through the lovely valley to the village of Glyn Ceiriog, at the foothills of the remote Berwyn Mountains. The area attracts pony trekkers, walkers, and anglers.

Where to Stay & Eat

££–£££ ✕🏠 **Golden Pheasant.** Antiques and Victorian-style fabrics furnish this well-kept 18th-century hotel east of the village of Glyn Ceiriog. You can have a drink in the bar with its fireplace, slate floor, and beamed ceiling, or relax in deep-cushion comfort in the lounge, which overlooks the countryside. There's a three-course, fixed-price menu in the restaurant (*£££££*), as well as a bar menu. Specialties include Ceiriog trout and game pie. ✉ *Off B4500, near Chirk, Glyn Ceiriog LL20 7BB* ☎ *01691/718281* ⊕ *www.goldenpheasanthotel.co.uk* 🖷 *01691/718479* ➪ *19 rooms* ⚐ *Restaurant, bar, lounge, some pets allowed (fee), no-smoking rooms; no a/c* ▭ *DC, MC, V* ⦿ *BP.*

£ 🏠 **Bron Heulog.** Carefully restored in period style as a guesthouse, this former home of a Victorian, liberal politician was built in 1861 and stands in 2 acres of gardens. Fireplaces, high ceilings, and an oak staircase are original elements of the large stone house. Rooms have showers. ✉ *Waterfall Rd., off B4396, Llanrhaeadr ym Mochnant SY10 0JX* ☎ *01691/780521* ⊕ *www.kraines.enta.net* ⤴ *4 rooms* ⚲ *No a/c, no room phones, no smoking* ▤ *MC, V* ❙⊙❙ *BP.*

EN ROUTE The peat-brown water of **Pistyll Rhaeadr,** the highest waterfall in Wales, thunders down a 290-foot double cascade. To get here, take B4500 south-west from Glyn Ceiriog, and then its unnumbered continuation, to reach Llanrhaeadr ym Mochnant, in the peaceful Tanat Valley. Here, in 1588, the Bible was translated into Welsh, thus ensuring the survival of the language. Turn northwest and go 4 mi up the road to the waterfall.

14

Llangollen

❷ *5 mi northwest of Chirk, 23 mi southwest of Chester.*

Llangollen's setting in a deep valley carved by the River Dee gives it a typically Welsh appearance. The bridge over the Dee, a 14th-century stone structure, is named in a traditional Welsh folk song as one of the "Seven Wonders of Wales." In July the popular International Musical Eisteddfod brings crowds to town. For a particularly scenic drive in this area, head for the Horseshoe Pass.

Plas Newydd (not to be confused with the grand estate on the Isle of Anglesey with the same name) was the home from 1778 to 1828 of Lady Eleanor Butler and Sarah Ponsonby, the eccentric Ladies of Llangollen, who set up a then-scandalous single-sex household, collected curios and magnificent wood carvings, and made it into a tourist attraction even during their lifetimes. The terraced gardens have original features such as a font from an abbey. ✉ *Hill St.* ☎ *01824/708223* 🖶 *01824/708258* ⊕ *www.llangollen.com* ✉ *£3* ⊙ *Easter–Oct., daily 10–5.*

From the **canal wharf** (☎ 01978/860702) you can take a horse-drawn boat or a narrow boat (a slender barge) along the Llangollen Canal to ♻ the largest navigable aqueduct in the world at Pontcysyllte. The **Llangollen Railway,** a restored standard-gauge steam line, runs for a few miles along the scenic Dee Valley. The terminus is near the town's bridge. ☎ *01978/860979, 01978/860702 recorded information* ⊕ *www.llangollen-railway.co.uk* ✉ *£8 round-trip* ⊙ *Apr.–Oct., daily 10–5; Nov.–Mar., weekends, limited service.*

Where to Stay

£ 🏠 **Oakmere.** This sandstone Victorian residence with landscaped grounds, a few minutes' walk from Llangollen center, succeeds in preserving its period flavor. Special features include tile or polished pine floors, 19th-century furniture in walnut and mahogany, a conservatory, and spacious, high-ceiling bedrooms. There are excellent views of the valley and mountains. ✉ *Regent St., LL20 8HS* ☎ *01978/861126* ⊕ *www.oakmere.llangollen.co.uk* ⤴ *6 rooms* ⚲ *Tennis court, lounge; no a/c, no room phones, no smoking* ▤ *No credit cards* ❙⊙❙ *BP.*

CLOSE UP

All Aboard: Steam Railways

WALES IS THE BEST PLACE in Britain for narrow-gauge steam railways, many of which wind through extraordinary landscapes. The Great Little Trains of Wales (⊕ www. greatlittletrainsofwales.co.uk) operate in spring, summer, and fall through the mountains of Snowdonia and central Wales (there are also a few lines in South Wales). The ride is just part of the fun; a good deal of history is associated with the old trains and train stations, some of which served industry before they became attractions for visitors. The Ffestiniog Railway, which links two British Rail lines at the old slate town of Blaenau Ffestiniog and Porthmadog, climbs the mountainside in Snowdonia National Park around an ascending loop. Snowdonia also has Britain's only alpine-style steam-rack railway, the Snowdon Mountain Railway, where little sloping boiler engines on a rack-and-pinion track push their trains 3,000 feet up from Llanberis to the summit of Snowdon.

Nightlife & the Arts

★ The six-day **International Musical Eisteddfod** (☎ 01978/862001 ⊕ www. international-eisteddfod.co.uk), held in early July, brings together amateur choirs and dancers—more than 12,000 participants in all—from all corners of the globe for a large, colorful folk arts festival. The tradition of the *eisteddfod,* held throughout Wales, goes back to the 12th century. Originally gatherings of bards, the *eisteddfodau* of today are more like competitions or festivals.

Sports & the Outdoors

There are easy walks along the banks of the River Dee or along part of the **Offa's Dyke Path** (⊕ www.offasdyke.demon.co.uk), which passes through hills, river valleys, and lowlands. This 177-mi-long National Trail follows the line of an ancient earthen wall, still surviving in parts, which was built along the border with England in the 8th century by King Offa of Mercia to keep out Welsh raiders.

Bala

❸ *18 mi southwest of Llangollen.*

The staunchly Welsh town of Bala makes a good base for exploring the eastern and southern sections of Snowdonia National Park as well as the gentler landscapes of borderland Wales. It stands at the head of Llŷn Tegid (Bala Lake), at 4 mi long the largest natural lake in Wales. This is a fine place for kayaking and windsurfing. The scenic, narrow-gauge

☾ **Bala Lake Railway** (☎ 01678/540666 🖷 01678/540535 ⊕ www.bala-lake-railway.co.uk), one of the Great Little Trains of Wales, runs along the lake's southern shore. The station in Llanuwchllyn has parking.

★ To experience Wales at its wildest, you can drive over **Bwlch y Groes** (Pass of the Cross), the highest road in Wales, whose sweeping panoramas are breathtaking. To get here, take the narrow road south from Bala through Cwm Hirnant and over the mountain to Lake Vyrnwy. Turn right at the lake and drive for a mile on B4393 before heading west on the mountain road.

Where to Stay & Eat

★ ✕▥ **Lake Vyrnwy Hotel.** Awesome views of mountain-ringed Lake Vyrnwy
££££–£££££ are just one asset of this country mansion within a 24,000-acre estate. For the ultimate sporting holiday, you can fish, bird-watch, play tennis, or take long hikes. Sailboats are also available. Leather chairs, log fires, and antiques add luxury, and the bedrooms are full of pampering touches. The sophisticated contemporary cuisine (£££££; three-course, fixed-price menu only) includes trout and duck from the reserve; partridge with saffron vegetables and a casserole of monkfish and scallops are typical dishes. ⊠ *Off B4393, Llanwddyn SY10 0LY* ☎ *01691/ 870692* 🖷 *01691/870259* ⊕ *www.lakevyrnwy.com* 🛏 *35 rooms* ♨ *Restaurant, tennis court, boating, fishing, bicycles, meeting rooms, some pets allowed (fee), kennel; no a/c* 🖃 *AE, DC, MC, V* ⲟ⃝ *BP.*

££ ▥ **Cyfie Farm.** This refurbished, ivy-clad 17th-century farmhouse in a tranquil area close to Lake Vyrnwy has oak beams and log fireplaces. The luxurious suites, in converted barns and stables, possess all the sophistication of those in a top hotel. ⊠ *Off B4393, near Llanfyllin, Llanfihangel-yng-Ngwynfa SY22 5JE* ☎ *01691/648451* ⊕ *www. cyfiefarm.co.uk* 🛏 *3 suites* ♨ *In-room DVDs, lounge, no-smoking rooms; no a/c, no room phones* 🖃 *No credit cards* ⲟ⃝ *BP.*

Blaenau Ffestiniog

❹ *22 mi northwest of Bala, 10 mi southwest of Betws-y-Coed.*

Most of the world's roofing tiles used to come from this former "slate capital of North Wales," and commercial quarrying continues here. On the hillsides around the town is the evidence of decades of mining. The enterprises that attract attention nowadays, however, remain the old slate mines, which opened to the public in the 1970s. The Ffestiniog Railway, which begins in Porthmadog, ends in the town, near the caverns.

At the **Llechwedd Slate Caverns,** you can take two trips: a tram ride through floodlighted tunnels where Victorian working conditions have been re-created, and a ride on Britain's deepest underground railway to a mine where you can walk by an eerie underground lake. Either tour gives a good idea of the difficult working conditions the miners endured. On the surface of this popular site are a re-created Victorian village, old workshops, and slate-splitting demonstrations. ⊠ *Off A470* ☎ *01766/ 830306* ⊕ *www.llechwedd-slate-caverns.co.uk* 🎫 *Tour £8.95, grounds free* ☉ *Mar.–Sept., daily 10–5:15; Oct.–Feb., daily 10–4:15.*

Porthmadog

❺ *12 mi southwest of Blaenau Ffestiniog, 16 mi south of Caernarfon.*

The little seaside town of Porthmadog, built as a harbor to export slate from Blaenau Ffestiniog, stands at the gateway to Llŷn, an unspoiled peninsula of beaches, wildflowers, and country lanes. Its location between Snowdonia and Llŷn, as well as the good beaches nearby and the many attractions around town, makes it a lively place in summer. A mile-long embankment known as the Cob serves as the eastern approach to Porthmadog.

The oldest Welsh narrow-gauge line (founded in the early 19th century to carry slate), the **Ffestiniog Railway** runs from a quayside terminus along the Cob and continues through a wooded vale into the mountains. Its northern terminus is Blaenau Ffestiniog, where you can visit the slate caverns. ☎ 01766/516000 ⊕ www.festrail.co.uk ➔ £16.50 round-trip ☉ Apr.–Nov., daily, plus limited winter service; call for exact times.

Fodor'sChoice ★ One not-to-be-missed site in North Wales is **Portmeirion**, a tiny fantasy-Italianate village on a private peninsula surrounded by hills, which is said to be loosely modeled after Portofino. Begun in 1926 by architect Clough Williams-Ellis (1883–1978), the village has a hotel, restaurant, town hall, shops (selling books, gifts, and Portmeirion pottery), rental cottages, and woodland walks; beaches are nearby. Williams-Ellis called it his "light-opera approach to architecture," and the result is magical, though distinctly un-Welsh. Royalty, political figures, artists, and other celebrities have stayed here, and the cult 1967 TV series *The Prisoner* was filmed here. Portmeirion is a short trip east of Porthmadog over the Cob. ⊠ Off A496 ☎ 01766/770000 ⊕ www.portmeirion-village. com ➔ £6 ☉ Daily 9:30–5:30.

North of Porthmadog is **Tremadog**, a handsome village that was the birthplace of T. E. Lawrence (1888–1935), better known as Lawrence of Arabia. In the Victorian seaside resort of **Criccieth**, a few miles west of Porthmadog on A497, a medieval castle with sweeping views crowns the headland. David Lloyd George, the prime minister of Britain from 1916 to 1922, grew up in Wales and lived here; a small museum in his childhood home honors him.

★ A wealth of legend, poetry, and song is conjured up by the13th-century **Harlech Castle**, built by Edward I to help subdue the Welsh; it's now a UNESCO World Heritage Site. The castle, on a rocky promontory, dominates the little coastal town of Harlech, 12 mi south of Porthmadog. Its mighty ruins, visible for miles and commanding wide views, are as dramatic as its history (though you have to imagine the sea, which has since receded, edging the castle site). Harlech was occupied by Owain Glyndŵr from 1404 to 1408 during his revolt against the English. The inspiring music of Ceiriog's song *Men of Harlech* reflects the heroic defense

CASTLE COUNTRY

More than 400 fortresses in Wales provide an inexhaustible supply of inspiration for any lover of history. These ancient strongholds, some of which were built by Edward I in the 13th century during his struggles with the rebellious Welsh, punctuate the landscape from south (Caerphilly) to north (Harlech, Beaumaris, Conwy), and include romantic ruins and well-preserved fortresses. To make the most of a visit, buy a guidebook or take a tour so that you can best appreciate the remains of a distant era. The great North Wales castles, such as Caernarfon, are particularly famous; four are World Heritage Sites.

of this castle in 1468 by Dafydd ap Eynion, who, summoned to surrender, replied: "I held a castle in France until every old woman in Wales heard of it, and I will hold a castle in Wales until every old woman in France hears of it!" Later in the 15th century the Lancastrians survived an eight-year siege during the Wars of the Roses here, and it was the last Welsh stronghold to fall in the 17th-century Civil War. ⊠ *Off B4573* ☎ *01766/780552* ⊕ *www.cadw.wales.gov.uk* ⊠ *£3* ⊗ *Apr., May, and Oct., daily 9:30–5; June–Sept., daily 9:30–6; Nov.–Mar., Mon.–Sat. 9:30–4, Sun. 11–4.*

Where to Stay & Eat

★ **£££££** ✕▥ **Hotel Maes-y-Neuadd.** Eight acres of gardens and parkland create a glorious setting for this luxurious country hotel in a manor house dating from the 14th century. Walls of local granite, oak-beam ceilings, and an inglenook fireplace add character; the updated bedrooms have different shapes and details but use prints and pastel fabrics. The restaurant's three-course, fixed-price menu (£££££) of Welsh, English, and French specialties uses herbs and vegetables grown in the hotel's own prolific walled garden to complement local meat, fish, and cheeses. The hotel is 3½ mi northeast of Harlech. ⊠ *Off B4573, Talsarnau LL47 6YA* ☎ *01766/780200 or 800/635–3602* 🖷 *01766/780211* ⊕ *www.neuadd. com* ⟲ *16 rooms* ⌂ *Restaurant, meeting room, some pets allowed (fee), no-smoking rooms; no a/c* ▤ *AE, DC, MC, V* ⎀⎁ *BP.*

★ **£££££** ✕▥ **Hotel Portmeirion.** One of the most elegant and unusual places to stay in Wales is also supremely relaxing. Clough Williams-Ellis built his Italianate fantasy village around this waterside Victorian mansion with a library and curved, colonnaded dining room. The hotel bedrooms are comfortable and richly decorated. Accommodation is also available in cottage suites around the village and in chic, minimalistic suites in Castell Deudraeth, a castellated 19th-century house. The restaurant (£££££), which serves breakfast and has a fixed-price dinner menu, highlights local foods with a sophisticated contemporary style. ⊠ *Off A496, Portmeirion LL48 6ET* ☎ *01766/770000* 🖷 *01766/771331* ⊕ *www. portmeirion-village.com* ⟲ *14 rooms in main hotel, 26 rooms in cottages, 11 suites in Castell Deudraeth* ⌂ *Restaurant, cable TV, in-room VCRs, tennis court, pool, meeting rooms, some pets allowed (fee), no-smoking rooms; no a/c* ▤ *AE, DC, MC, V* ⎀⎁ *BP.*

★ **£££** ✕▥ **Castle Cottage.** Close to Harlech's mighty castle, this friendly "restaurant with rooms" is a wonderful find. The emphasis is on the exceptional cuisine of chef-proprietor Glyn Roberts, who uses ingredients from salmon to Welsh lamb to create imaginative, beautifully presented contemporary dishes. There's a fixed-price dinner menu (£££££; no lunch). The hotel has three spacious modern rooms with four more in the annex, a former 16th-century pub. ⊠ *Near B4573, Harlech LL46 2YL* ☎ *01766/780479* 🖷 *01766/781251* ⊕ *www. castlecottageharlech.co.uk* ⟲ *7 rooms* ⌂ *Restaurant, in-room DVD/ VCR, no-smoking rooms; no a/c* ▤ *MC, V* ⎀⎁ *BP.*

£ ✕▥ **Yr Hen Fecws.** The name of this welcoming stone restaurant and bed-and-breakfast near the quayside means "the old bakehouse." Bold modern colors blend with traditional furnishings at the bistro-style restaurant (££–£££; dinner only), which serves dishes such as fresh wild bass with

14

ratatouille and pesto. Bedrooms have exposed slate walls, dark-wood furniture, and cheerful bed coverings. ⊠ *16 Lombard St., LL49 9AP* ☎ *01766/514625* ⊕ *www.henfecws.com* ⇨ *7 rooms* ♿ *Restaurant; no a/c, no smoking* ▭ *MC, V* ⑂ *BP.*

Betws-y-Coed

6 *25 mi northeast of Porthmadog, 19 mi south of Llandudno.*

The Rivers Llugwy and Conwy meet at Betws-y-Coed, a popular resort village set among wooded hills with excellent views of Snowdonia. Busy in summer, the village has a good selection of hotels and crafts shops. The chief landmark here is the ornate iron Waterloo Bridge (1815) over the Conwy, designed by Thomas Telford (1757–1834), and the magnificent Bodnant Garden south of the town of Conwy makes a delightful excursion. On the western (A5) approach to Betws-y-Coed are the **Swallow Falls** (small admission charge), a famous North Wales beauty spot where the River Llugwy tumbles down through a wooded chasm.

Where to Stay & Eat

££–£££ ✕ **Ty Gwyn.** The restaurant in this 17th-century coaching inn overlooking Waterloo Bridge on the outskirts of Betws-y-Coed is a delight for lovers of antiques, old beams, and rustic uneven floors. Fresh local produce is used, and there are good-value bar meals and a full à la carte menu. Wild pheasant terrine and jumbo prawns sautéed with fresh garlic and chili butter are good choices on the contemporary menu. ⊠ *A5* ☎ *01690/710383* ▭ *MC, V.*

££££ ✕⊞ **Tan-y-Foel Country House.** Hidden away on a wooded hillside outside Betws-y-Coed, this quiet, contemporary hideaway has views over the Conwy Valley and Snowdonia mountain range. The vibrant hues of the stylish interior contrast with the dark stone exterior, and many bedrooms have four-posters. Chef-owner Janet Pitman, a Master Chef of Great Britain, prepares exquisite food (£££££; fixed-price menu) with French influences. ⊠ *Off A5, Capel Garmon LL26 ORE* ☎ *01690/ 710507* 🖶 *01690/710681* ⊕ *www.tyfhotel.co.uk* ⇨ *6 rooms* ♿ *Restaurant, lounge; no a/c, no kids under 7, no smoking* ▭ *MC, V* ⑂ *BP.*

££ ⊞ **Pengwern Country House.** In Victorian times, this stone-and-slate country house on 2 acres of woodland was an artists' colony. Today the polished slate floors, beamed bedrooms, and traditional furnishings reflect the house's original charm. You can expect a warm welcome and good food (guests can arrange dinner here). The house is about a mile south of Betws-y-Coed. ⊠ *A5, Allt Dinas LL24 OHF* ⊕ *www. snowdoniaaccommodation.com* 🖶🖶 *01690/710480* ⇨ *3 rooms* ♿ *Dining room, lounge; no a/c, no smoking* ▭ *MC, V* ⑂ *BP.*

£–££ ⊞ **Aberconwy House.** This Victorian B&B, with its garden, and flower-covered, terraced patio, has panoramic views over Betws-y-Coed and Snowdonia. Built in 1850, the house retains original features such as marble fireplaces, but has large, new windows to make the most of the setting. The modern bedrooms are a good value for the price, and the proprietors are extremely hospitable. ⊠ *Off A470, Lôn Muriau LL24 OHD* ☎ *01690/710202* 🖶 *01690/710800* ⊕ *www.aberconwy-house. co.uk* ⇨ *8 rooms* ♿ *Lounge; no a/c, no smoking* ▭ *MC, V* ⑂ *BP.*

Llanberis

❼ *17 mi west of Betws-y-Coed, 7 mi southeast of Caernarfon.*

Llanberis, like Betws-y-Coed, is a focal point for people visiting Snowdonia National Park. The town stands beside twin lakes at the foot of the rocky **Llanberis Pass,** which cuts through the highest mountains in the park and is lined with slabs popular with rock climbers. There are hiking trails from the top of the pass, but the going can be rough for the inexperienced. Ask local advice before starting any ramble.

★ ☕ Llanberis's most famous attraction is the rack-and-pinion **Snowdon Mountain Railway,** with some of its track at a gradient of 1 in 5; the train terminates within 70 feet of the 3,560-foot-high summit. Snowdon, *Yr Wyddfa* in Welsh, is the highest peak south of Scotland and lies within the 840-square-mi national park. From May through September, weather permitting, trains go all the way to the summit; on a clear day, you can see as far as the Wicklow Mountains in Ireland, about 90 mi away. In 1998 the National Trust bought the mountain, ensuring its long-term protection. ☎ *0870/458–0033* ⊕ *www.snowdonrailway.co.uk* ✉ *£21 maximum round-trip fare* ☉ *Mar.–Oct., daily; schedule depends on customer demand.*

14

> ### TRAINING FOR EVEREST
>
> Lord Hunt, Sir Edmund Hillary and their team used the rock-strewn slopes of Snowdonia to train for the first successful ascent of Mount Everest in 1953. The Pen-y-Gwryd Hotel, a famous climbing inn just beyond the summit of Llanberis Pass, has memorabilia from those times.

On Lake Padarn in the Padarn Country Park, the old Dinorwig slate quarry serves as the **National Slate Museum,** dedicated to what was an important industry here: Welsh slate roofed many a building. The museum has quarry workshops and slate-splitting demonstrations, as well as restored worker housing, all of which convey the development of the industry and the challenges faced by those who worked in it. The narrow-gauge Llanberis Lake Railway runs from here. ⊠ *A4086* ☎ *01286/870630* ⊕ *www.nmgw.ac.uk* ✉ *Free* ☉ *Easter–Oct., daily 10–5; Nov.–Easter, Sun.–Fri. 10–4.*

Caernarfon

❽ *7 mi northwest of Llanberis, 26 mi southwest of Llandudno.*

The town of Caernarfon, which has a historic pedigree as a walled medieval settlement, has nothing to rival the considerable splendor of its castle and is now overrun with tourist buses. Still, don't miss the garrison church of St. Mary, built into the city walls.

★ Standing like a warning finger, the grim, majestic mass of **Caernarfon Castle,** "that most magnificent badge of our subjection," wrote Thomas Pennant (1726–98), looms over the waters of the River Seiont. It's a UNESCO World Heritage Site. Numerous bloody encounters were witnessed by these sullen walls, erected by Edward I in 1283 as a symbol of his determination to subdue the Welsh. The castle's towers, unlike those of Edward I's other castles, are polygonal and patterned with bands of different-color stone. In 1284 the monarch thought of a scheme to steal the Welsh throne. Knowing that the Welsh chieftains would accept no foreign prince, Edward promised to designate a ruler who could speak no word of English. His long-suffering queen, Eleanor of Castile was despatched to this cold stone fortress where she gave birth to a son. Edward presented the infant to the assembled chieftains as their prince "who spoke no English, had been born on Welsh soil, and whose first words would be spoken in Welsh." The ruse worked, and on that day was created the first prince of Wales of English lineage. This tradition still holds: in July 1969, Elizabeth II presented Prince Charles to the people of Wales as their prince from this castle. In the Queen's Tower, a museum charts the history of the local regiment, the Royal Welsh Fusiliers. ⊠ *Castle Hill* ☎ *01286/677617* ⊕ *www.caernarfon.com* ✆ *£4.75* ⊘ *Apr., May, and Oct., daily 9:30–5; June–Sept., daily 9:30–6; Nov.–Mar., Mon.–Sat. 9:30–4, Sun. 11–4.*

Outside Caernarfon, the **Segontium Roman Museum** tells the story of the Roman presence in Wales; it includes material from one of Britain's most famous Roman forts. The extensive excavation site of the fort is here, too. ⊠ *Beddgelert Rd. (A4085)* ☎ *01286/675625* ⊕ *www.segontium. org.uk/* ✆ *Free* ⊘ *Tues.–Sun. 10–4:30. Museum Tues.–Sun. 12:30–4:30. Also open national holiday Mon. 10:30–4:30.*

You can take a workshop tour and short trip on a coal-fired steam locomotive at the **Welsh Highland Railway–Rheilffordd Eryri,** a narrow-gauge line that operates on the route of an abandoned railway. The terminus is on the quay near Caernarfon Castle. ⊠ *St. Helens Rd.* ☎ *01766/516000* ⊕ *www.festrail.co.uk* ✆ *£16.50 round-trip* ⊘ *Apr.–Oct., daily 10–4; Nov.–Mar., limited weekend service.*

Where to Stay

££ 🖼 **Meifod Country House.** Former home of the high sheriff of Caernarfon, this opulent Victorian house has polished tile floors, wood-burning fireplaces, and bedrooms with features such as Victorian claw-foot baths and chandeliers. The atmosphere is luxurious but unpretentious, and the food (guests only) is good. The house stands in lush grounds less than 2 mi south of Caernarfon, making it a convenient base for exploring Snowdonia. ⊠ *Off A487, Bontnewydd LL55 2TY* ☎ *01286/ 673351* 🖨 *01286/6713256* ⊕ *www.meifodcountryhouse.co.uk* ⇖ *5 rooms* ⚴ *Dining room; no a/c, no smoking* ▭ *MC, V* ⍫ *BP.*

The Outdoors

Caernarfon Airparc operates Pleasure Flights in light aircraft over Snowdon, Anglesey, and Caernarfon; flights are 10 to 30 minutes. "Hands-on" flying lessons are offered daily (one-hour lesson £138), and there's an aviation museum (£5.50). ⊠ *Dinas Dinlle Beach Rd.* ☎ *01286/ 830800* ✆ *£29–£69 per seat* ⊘ *Daily 9–5.*

Beaumaris

9 *13 mi northeast of Caernarfon.*

Elegant Beaumaris is on the Isle of Anglesey, the largest island directly off the shore of Wales and England. It's linked to the mainland by the Britannia road and rail bridge and by Thomas Telford's remarkable chain suspension bridge, built in 1826 over the Menai Strait. Though its name means "beautiful marsh," Beaumaris has become a town of pretty cottages, Georgian row houses, and bright shops. The nearest main-line train station is in Bangor, about 6 mi away on the mainland; bus service operates between the station and Beaumaris. Ferries and catamarans to Ireland leave from Holyhead, on the island's western side.

The town dates from 1295, when Edward I commenced work on impressive **Beaumaris Castle,** the last and largest link in an "iron ring" of fortifications around North Wales built to contain the Welsh. Guarding the western approach to the Menai Strait, the unfinished castle (a World Heritage Site) is solid and symmetrical, with concentric lines of fortification, arrow slits, and a moat: a superb example of medieval defensive planning. ⊠ *Castle St.* ☎ *01248/810361* ⊕ *www.cadw.wales. gov.uk* ⊠ *£3* ⊙ *Apr., May, and Oct., daily 9:30–5; June–Sept., daily 9:30–6; Nov.–Mar., Mon.–Sat. 9:30–4, Sun. 11–4.*

🄲 The **Museum of Childhood Memories** is an Aladdin's cave of music boxes, magic lanterns (early optical projectors), trains, cars, toy soldiers, rocking horses, and mechanical savings banks. ⊠ *1 Castle St.* ☎ *01248/712498* ⊠ *£4* ⊙ *Easter–Oct., Mon.–Sat. 10:30–5; Sun. noon–5.*

On Castle Street, the **Tudor Rose,** a house dating from 1400, is an excellent example of Tudor timberwork. To learn about the grim life of a Victorian prisoner, head to the old **gaol,** built in 1829 by Joseph Hansom (1803–82), who was also the designer of the Hansom cab. ⊠ *Steeple La.* ☎ *01248/811691* ⊠ *£1.50* ⊙ *Easter–Sept., daily 10:30–5.*

The 14th-century **Church of St. Mary and St. Nicholas,** opposite the gaol in Steeple Lane, houses the stone coffin of Princess Joan, daughter of King John (1167–1216) and wife of Welsh leader Llewelyn the Great.

OFF THE BEATEN PATH

PLAS NEWYDD – Some historians rate this mansion on the Isle of Anglesey the finest house in Wales. Remodeled in the 18th century by James Wyatt (1747–1813) for the marquesses of Anglesey (who still live here), it stands on the Menai Strait about 7 mi southwest of Beaumaris (don't confuse it with the Plas Newydd at Llangollen). The interior has some fine 18th-century Gothic-Revival decorations. In 1936–40 the society artist Rex Whistler (1905–44) painted the mural in the dining room. A museum commemorates the Battle of Waterloo, where the first marquess, Wellington's cavalry commander, lost his leg. The woodland walk and garden are worth exploring, and you can ask about boat trips on the strait. The views of Snowdonia are magnificent. ⊠ *Off A4080, southwest of Britannia Bridge, Llanfairpwll* ☎ *01248/714795* ⊕ *www. nationaltrust.org.uk* ⊠ *House £6, garden only £4* ⊙ *House late Mar.–early Nov., Sat.–Wed. noon–5; last admission ½ hr before closing. Garden late Mar.–early Nov., Sat.–Wed. 11–5:30.*

The **Beaumaris Festival** (☎ 01248/810415) takes place annually late May through early June. The whole town is used as a site for special concerts, dance performances, and plays.

Where to Stay & Eat

£££ ✕🖼 **Ye Olde Bull's Head.** Originally a coaching inn built in 1472, this place is small and filled with history, and rooms are comfortably modern if not large. Samuel Johnson and Charles Dickens both stayed here. Eat in the stylish brasserie or the excellent oak-beam dining room (£££££; reservations essential), dating from 1617. Contemporary specialties on the fixed-price dinner menu include warm salad of pigeon breast with hazelnut oil, and the local widgeon (wild duck); seafood dishes win praise, too. ⊠ *Castle St., LL58 8AP* ☎ *01248/810329* 🖷 *01248/811294* ⊕ *www.bullsheadinn.co.uk* ⇆ *13 rooms* △ *Restaurant, bar; no a/c* ⊟ *AE, MC, V* ⫶⃝⃒ *BP.*

★ **££** 🖼 **Cleifiog.** This cozy gem of a Georgian house overlooks the Menai Strait just a short stroll from Beaumaris Castle. Its charms include contemporary comforts, wood-panel walls, limestone floors, and a magnificent staircase dating from 1680. ⊠ *Townsend, Beaumaris LL53 7DY* ☎ *01248/811507* ⊕ *www.cleifiogbandb.co.uk* ⇆ *3 rooms* △ *Lounge, in-room DVD, in-room data ports; no a/c, no room phones, no smoking* ⊟ *MC, V* ⫶⃝⃒ *BP.*

Conwy

★ ⑩ *23 mi east of Beaumaris, 48 mi northwest of Chester.*

The still-authentic medieval town of Conwy grew up around its castle on the west bank of the River Conwy. A ring of ancient but well-preserved walls, built in the 13th century to protect the English merchants who lived here, enclose the old town and add to the strong sense of history. It's well worth strolling the streets and walking on top of sections of the wall, which has 21 towers. A walk on the walls rewards with impressive views across huddled rooftops to the castle on the estuary, with mountains in the distance.

Fodor'sChoice Of all Edward I's fortresses, **Conwy Castle,** a mighty, many-turreted ★ stronghold built between 1283 and 1287, preserves most convincingly the spirit of medieval times. Along with Conwy's town walls, the castle is a UNESCO World Heritage Site. The eight large round towers and tall curtain wall, set on a rocky promontory, provide sweeping views of the area and the town walls. Although the castle is roofless (and floorless in places), you can read the signs, take a tour, or buy a guidebook to help you visualize the Great Hall and other chambers. Narrow stairs lead into towers such as the Chapel Tower. Conwy Castle can be approached on foot by a dramatic suspension bridge completed in 1825; engineer Thomas Telford designed the bridge with turrets to blend in with the fortress's presence. ⊠ *Castle Sq.* ☎ *01492/592358* ⊕ *www.cadw.wales.gov.uk* 🖾 *£4.50; £7 joint ticket with Plas Mawr* ☉ *Apr., May, and Oct., daily 9:30–5; June–Sept., daily 9:30–6; Nov.–Mar., Mon.–Sat. 9:30–4, Sun. 11–4.*

ON THE MENU

Talented chefs making use of the country's bountiful resources have put Wales firmly on the culinary map. Welsh Black beef and succulent Welsh lamb are world-renowned, and the supply of fish and seafood (including mussels and oysters) from coasts and rivers is excellent. Organic products are available to restaurants and the public from specialized companies, farm shops, and farmers' markets. Tŷ Nant Welsh springwater graces restaurant tables worldwide, and wines, such as Cariad, have won medals at French wine festivals; there's even a Welsh whisky.

Cheese making has undergone a remarkable revival. You can try traditionally named cheeses such as Llanboidy and Caws Cenarth or an extra-mature cheddar called Black Bomber. Contemporary cuisine has the buzz, but traditional dishes are worth seeking out. Cawl, for example, is a nourishing broth of lamb and vegetables, and laverbread is a distinctive-tasting pureed seaweed that's usually fried with eggs and bacon. For information on quality Welsh food, check out the Web site Wales—the True Taste (⊕ www. walesthetruetaste.com).

14

What is said to be the **smallest house in Britain** (✉ Lower Gate St. ☎ 01492/593484) is furnished in mid-Victorian Welsh style. The house, which is 6 feet wide and 10 feet high, was reputedly last occupied in 1900 by a fisherman who was more than 6 feet tall.

Plas Mawr, a jewel in the heart of Conwy, is the best-preserved Elizabethan town house in Britain. Built in 1576 by Robert Wynn (who later became both a member of Parliament and sheriff of Caernarfonshire), this richly decorated house with its ornamental plasterwork gives a unique insight into the lives of the Tudor gentry and their servants. ✉ *High St.* ☎ *01492/580167* ⊕ *www.cadw.wales.gov.uk* ✐ *£4.90; £7 joint ticket with Conwy Castle* ☉ *June–Aug., Tues.–Sun. 9:30–6; Sept., Tues.–Sun. 9:30–5; Oct., Tues.–Sun. 9:30–4.*

Built in the 14th century, **Aberconwy House** is the only surviving medieval merchant's house in Conwy. Each room in the restored building reflects different eras of its long history. ✉ *Castle St.* ☎ *01492/592246* ✐ *£3* ☉ *Mid-Mar.–Oct., Wed.–Mon. 11–5.*

FodorśChoice
★

With a reputation as the finest garden in Wales, **Bodnant Garden** remains a pilgrimage spot for horticulturists from around the world. Laid out in 1875, the 87 acres are particularly famed for rhododendron, camellias, and magnolias. ■ TIP➤ **Visit in May to see the laburnum arch that forms a huge tunnel of golden blooms.** The mountains of Snowdonia form a magnificent backdrop to the Italianate terraces, rock and rose gardens, and pinetum. The gardens are about 5 mi south of Conwy. ✉ *Off A470, Tal-y-Cafn* ☎ *01492/650460* ⊕ *www.nationaltrust.org.uk* ✐ *£6* ☉ *Mid-Mar.–Oct., daily 10–5.*

Where to Stay & Eat

££–£££ ✕ **Le Gallois.** Just off the coast road 4 mi west of Conwy, this small and unpretentious restaurant is a culinary oasis. The chef-proprietor offers a changing chalkboard menu using the best local produce. Dishes like juicy scallops with a beurre blanc, Conwy crab au gratin and local lamb cooked pink with a mint and Madeira sauce are the daily fare. ⊠ *Pant yr Afon, Penmaenmawr* ☎ *01492/623820* ⊟ *MC, V* ☺ *No lunch* ☺ *Closed Mon. and Tues.*

£££–££££ ✕🏨 **Castle Hotel.** Sitting snugly within Conwy's medieval walls, this former coaching inn has wooden beams, old fireplaces, and plenty of antiques. Illustrious former guests include William Wordsworth, Samuel Johnson, and Charlotte Brontë. The bedrooms are smallish but plushly luxurious, with elaborate modern bathrooms. Shakespeare's restaurant (£££–££££), decorated with Victorian paintings of scenes from the Bard's plays, serves excellent modern British cuisine, such as salmon on a creamy Conwy crab risotto. Don't miss the local mussels if they're on the menu. A bar menu is also available. ⊠ *High St., LL32 8DB* ☎ *01492/ 582800* 🖨 *01492/582300* ⊕ *www.castlewales.co.uk* ✍ *28 rooms* ⚘ *Restaurant, bar, lounge, meeting rooms, some pets allowed (fee), no-smoking rooms; no a/c* ⊟ *AE, MC, V* ❍| *BP.*

£££–££££ ✕🏨 **Sychnant Pass House.** In a peaceful location on a wooded hillside above Conwy, this hotel has all the qualities of a country house hotel but without any unnecessary formality. The enthusiastic owners, Bre and Graham Carrington-Sykes, provide a genuine welcome and good food with a set-price dinner menu (£££££). There are spacious sitting rooms with big comfortable sofas and well furnished bedrooms, some with French windows opening out on to an attractive decked terrace. The leisure facilities are excellent. ⊠ *Sychnant Pass Rd., LL32 8BJ* ☎ *01492/596868* 🖨 *01492/585486* ⊕ *www.sychnant-pass-house.co.uk* ✍ *10 rooms* ⚘ *Restaurant, coffee shop, indoor pool, gym, hot tub, sauna, some pets allowed, no-smoking rooms; no a/c* ⊟ *MC, V* ❍| *BP.*

Llandudno

⓫ *3 mi north of Conwy, 50 mi northwest of Chester.*

This appealingly old-fashioned North Wales seaside resort has a wealth of well-preserved Victorian architecture and an ornate amusement pier with entertainments, shops, and places to eat. Attractively painted hotels line the wide promenade (Llandudno has the largest choice of lodging in Wales). The shopping streets behind also look the part, thanks to their original canopied walkways. Llandudno has little in the way of garish arcades, preferring to stick to its faithful cable car that climbs to the summit of the Great Orme headland above the resort. There's also an aerial cable car to the top, as well as a large, dry ski slope (with an artificial surface you can ski on year-round) and toboggan run.

Llandudno was the summer home of the family of Dr. Liddell, the Oxford don and father of the immortal Alice, inspiration for Lewis Carroll's *Alice's Adventures in Wonderland*. The book's Walrus and the Carpenter may be based on two rocks on Llandudno's West Shore near the Liddell home, which Alice possibly described to Carroll. The Alice

🕐 in Wonderland connection is explored in the **Alice in Wonderland Centre,** where Alice's adventures come to life in displays of the best-known scenes from the book. Alice merchandise is for sale, too. ⊠ *3–4 Trinity Sq.* ☎*01492/860082* ⊕*www.wonderland.co.uk* ⬚*£2.95* ⊙*Easter–Oct., daily 10–5; Nov.–Easter, Mon.–Sat. 10–5.*

The prehistoric **Great Orme Mines** are at the summit of the Great Orme (*orme,* a Norse word meaning "sea monster"), with its views of the coast and mountains of Snowdonia. Copper was first mined here in the Bronze Age, and you can tour the ancient underground workings. ⊠ *Great Orme* ☎ *01492/870447* ⊕ *www.greatormemines.info* ⬚ *£5* ⊙ *Feb.–Oct., daily 10–5.*

Where to Stay & Eat

★ **£££££** ✕🖾 **Bodysgallen Hall.** Antiques, comfortable chairs by cheery fires, pictures, and polished wood distinguish one of Wales's most luxurious country-house hotels. The part 17th-, part 18th-century building is set in walled gardens 2 mi out of town. Bedrooms in the house combine elegance and practicality; seekers of privacy may prefer the cottage suites scattered around the estate and parkland. The outstanding restaurant (£££££; three-course, fixed-price menu at dinner) uses local ingredients in creative ways, such as beef with a wild mushroom pancake or partridge with panfried foie gras. ⊠ *Off A470, LL30 1RS* ☎ *01492/584466* 🖷 *01492/582519* ⊕ *www.bodysgallen.com* ⬌ *19 rooms, 16 cottage suites* ⌂ *Restaurant, cable TV, in-room VCRs, in-room data ports, tennis court, indoor pool, gym, sauna, spa, croquet, meeting rooms, some pets allowed, no-smoking rooms; no a/c in some rooms, no kids under 8* ⊟ *MC, V* ⦿ *BP.*

£££–£££££ ✕🖾 **St. Tudno Hotel.** From the outside, one of Britain's best small seaside hotels blends unobtrusively with its neighbors, but the interior contains opulently furnished guest rooms and public areas with plenty of print fabrics and chintz. The fine contemporary cuisine (££££) includes dishes such as braised fillet of halibut with vanilla and Pernod velouté and saddle of hare with spicy cabbage. ⊠ *Promenade, LL30 2LP* ☎ *01492/874411* 🖷 *01492/860407* ⊕ *www.st-tudno.co.uk* ⬌ *18 rooms* ⌂ *Restaurant, in-room VCRs, in-room data ports, indoor pool, bar, some pets allowed (fee), no-smoking rooms; no a/c in some rooms* ⊟ *AE, DC, MC, V* ⦿ *BP.*

££ 🖾 **Bryn Derwen Hotel.** Many hoteliers at British seaside resorts have not upgraded their accommodations and food, but this immaculate Victorian hotel exemplifies how it should be done. Fresh flowers, plush period furnishings in the public areas, and soothing, warm-hued bedrooms show the owners' attention to detail. Bryn Derwen offers truly excellent value for the price. ⊠*34 Abbey Rd., LL30 2EE* ⊕*www.bryn-derwen-hotel.co.uk* 🖷🖷 *01492/876804* ⬌ *9 rooms* ⌂ *Dining room, lounge; no a/c, no kids under 7, no smoking* ⊟ *MC, V* ⦿ *BP.*

EN ROUTE Inland from Rhyl, **Bodelwyddan Castle,** between Abergele and St. Asaph, is the Welsh home of London's National Portrait Gallery. Gardens, including a maze, aviary, and woodland walks, surround the Victorian castle. Galleries display Regency and Victorian portraits by artists such as John Singer Sargent, Thomas Lawrence, Dante Gabriel Rossetti, and Edwin Landseer. There are also hands-on galleries of Victorian amusements and inventions. ⊠ *Off A55, Bodelwyddan* ☎ *01745/584060* ⊕ *www.bodelwyddan-castle.co.uk* ⊠ *£5, grounds only £3* ⊙ *Apr.–Sept., daily 10:30–5; Oct.–Mar., Thurs. 9:30–5, weekends 10:30–4.*

Denbigh

⑫ *25 mi southeast of Llandudno.*

This market town (market day is Wednesday) was much admired by the great English literary figure and lexicographer Dr. Samuel Johnson (1709–84). A walk along the riverbank at Lawnt (a village just south of Denbigh), which he loved, brings you to a monumental urn placed in his honor. Not that it pleased him: "It looks like an intention to bury me alive," he thundered.

Denbigh Castle, begun in 1282 as one of Edward I's ring of castles built to control the Welsh, is known as "the hollow crown" because it is not much more than a shell—though an impressive one—set on high ground, dominating the town. H. M. Stanley (1841–1904), the intrepid 19th-century journalist and explorer who found Dr. Livingstone in Africa, was born in a cottage below the castle. ☎ *01745/813385* ⊕ *www. cadw.wales.gov.uk* ⊠ *£3* ⊙ *Apr.–Sept., weekdays 10–5:30, weekends 9:30–5:30.*

Ruthin

⑬ *8 mi southeast of Denbigh, 23 mi west of Chester.*

Once a stronghold of Welsh hero Owain Glyndŵr (circa 1354–1416), Ruthin is a delightful market town with elegant shops, good inns, and a fascinating architectural mix of medieval, Tudor, and Georgian buildings. The town also hosts medieval-style banquets and has a crafts complex with displays of the artisans' creations. The 17th-century **Myddleton Arms** in the town square has seven Dutch-style dormer windows, known as the "eyes of Ruthin," set into its red-tiled roof. You can tour **Ruthin Gaol,** where from 1654 to 1916 thousands of prisoners were incarcerated, and learn about prison conditions over the centuries. ⊠ *Clwyd St.* ☎ *01824/708250* ⊕ *www.ruthingaol.co.uk* ⊠ *£3* ⊙ *Apr.–Oct., daily 10–5; Nov.–Mar., Tues.–Sun. 10–5.*

Where to Stay

£ 🏨 **Eyarth Old Railway Station.** This Victorian railway station 2 mi south of Ruthin has been converted into an outstanding B&B. The modern bedrooms are spacious, with large windows looking out over the Vale of Clwyd. ⊠ *Off A525, Llanfair Dyffryn Clwyd LL15 2EE* ☎ *01824/ 703643* 🖶 *01824/707464* ⊕ *www.eyarthstation.co.uk* ⇦ *6 rooms* ⟷ *Pool, bar; no a/c* ☰ *MC, V* ⦿ *BP.*

MID-WALES
THE HISTORIC HEARTLAND

Traditional market towns and country villages, small seaside resorts, quiet roads, and rolling landscapes filled with sheep farms, forests, and lakes make up mid-Wales, the country's green and rural heart. Because this is Wales's quietest vacation region, lodgings are scattered thinly. Outside of one or two large centers, Aberystwyth and Llandrindod Wells, accommodations are mainly country inns, small hotels, and farmhouses. This area also has some splendid country-house hotels.

Although green is the predominant color here, the landscape differs around the region. The borderlands are gentle and undulating, rising to the west into high wild mountains. Farther north, around Dolgellau, mountainous scenery becomes even more pronounced in the southern section of the Snowdonia National Park. Mountains meet the sea along Cardigan Bay, a long coastline of headlands, peaceful sandy beaches, and beautiful estuaries that has long been a refuge from the crowd. In the 19th century, Tennyson, Darwin, Shelley, and Ruskin came to this area to work and relax; today, thousands more come to delight in the numerous antiquarian bookstores of Hay-on-Wye.

Hay-on-Wye

★ ⑭ *57 mi north of Cardiff, 25 mi north of Abergavenny.*

Bookshops and a mostly ruined castle dominate this town on the border of Wales and England. Hay is a lively place, especially on Sunday, when the rest of central Wales seems to be closed down. In 1961 Richard Booth established a small secondhand and antiquarian bookshop here. Other booksellers soon got in on the act, and bookshops now fill several houses, a movie theater, shops, and a pub. At last count, there were about 40 bookstores, all in a town of only 1,300 inhabitants. It's now the largest secondhand bookselling center in the world, and priceless 14th-century manuscripts rub spines with "job lots" selling for a few pounds. Hay also has antiques and crafts centers. Things buzz in early ★ summer during the 10-day **Hay Festival** (☎ 0870/990–1299 ⊕ www. hayfestival.com), a celebration of literature that attracts famous writers from all over the world.

NEED A BREAK?

After some hard browsing, take stop off at The Granary (✉ Broad St. ☎ 01497/ 820790), a wood-beamed former grain store by the clock tower. The chalkboard menu lists soups, lamb and spinach curry, and cheese and garlic toasties (open, toasted sandwiches).

Where to Stay & Eat

££–£££ ✕🏠 **Old Black Lion.** A 17th-century coaching inn close to Hay's center is ideal for a lunch break while you're ransacking the bookshops, or for an overnight stay in one of its country-style rooms. The oak-beamed bar serves food, and the breakfasts are especially good. The restaurant's (*££–££££*) sophisticated cooking has an international flavor and emphasizes local meats and produce. ✉ *Lion St., HR3 5AD* ☎ *01497/820841* 🖨 *01497/822960* ⊕ *www.oldblacklion.co.uk* 🛏 *10 rooms* ↻ *Restaurant, bar, lounge, no-smoking rooms; no a/c, no kids under 5* ▤ *MC, V* ⦿*l BP.*

Shopping

Boz Books (⊠ 13A Castle St. ☎ 01497/821277) specializes in 19th-century novels, including first editions of Dickens. A former movie theater houses the town's largest book outpost, the **Hay Cinema Bookshop** (⊠ Castle St. ☎ 01497/820071), which stocks 200,000 volumes on subjects from art to zoology at prices from 50 pence to £5, 000.

Builth Wells

⓯ *20 mi northwest of Hay-on-Wye, 60 mi north of Cardiff.*

Builth Wells, a farming town and former spa on the banks of the River Wye, hosts Wales's biggest rural gathering. The countryside around Builth and its neighbor, Llandrindod Wells, varies considerably. Some of the land is soft and rich, with green hills and lush valleys, but close by are the wildernesses of Mynydd Eppynt and the foothills of the Cambrian Mountains, the lofty "backbone of Wales."

★ The annual **Royal Welsh Agricultural Show** (☎ 01982/553683 ⊕ www. rwas.co.uk), held in late July, is not only Wales's prime gathering of farming folk but also a colorful countryside jamboree that attracts huge crowds.

Where to Stay & Eat

★ ✕⊡ **Lake Country House & Spa.** This is the place to go for total Victorian country elegance. Its 50 acres of sloping lawns and rhododendrons **££££–£££££** also contain a trout-filled lake. Comfortable and quiet, the hotel has first-class service and excellent contemporary cuisine (£££££; fixed-price dinner menu) such as salmon with char-grilled eggplant and spicy couscous. Period furniture and fine fabrics decorate the large bedrooms; some have four-poster beds. The hotel is in a peaceful former spa town about 8 mi southwest of Builth. ⊠ *Llangammarch Wells LD4 4BS* ☎ *01591/620202* 🖷 *01591/620457* ⊕ *www.lakecountryhouse.co.uk* 🖃 *18 rooms* ♨ *Restaurant, 9-hole golf course, putting green, tennis court, fishing, billiards, indoor pool, gym, hot tub, sauna, massage, croquet, bar, no-smoking rooms; no a/c* ▤ *AE, DC, MC, V* ⫶◉⫶ *BP.*

Llandrindod Wells

⓰ *7 mi north of Builth Wells, 67 mi north of Cardiff.*

Also known as Llandod, the old spa town of Llandrindod Wells preserves its Victorian layout and look, with turrets, cupolas, loggias, and balustrades, and greenery everywhere. On a branch-line rail route and with good bus service, Llandrindod makes a useful base for exploring the region, and the town itself is easily explored on foot. Cross over to South Crescent, passing the Glen Usk Hotel with its wrought-iron balustrade and the Victorian bandstand in the gardens opposite, and you soon reach Middleton Street, another Victorian

---

PLAYING DRESS-UP

During Llandrindod Wells's **Victorian Festival** (☎ 01597/823441 ⊕ www.victorianfestival.co.uk), in late August, shop assistants, hotel staff, and anyone else who cares to join in wear period costume and enjoy "old-style" entertainment.

thoroughfare. From there, head to Rock Park and the path that leads to the Pump Room. This historic building is now an alternative health center but visitors can freely "take the waters" that the Victorians found so beneficial here. On the other side of town, the lake, with its boathouse, café, and gift shop, has wooded hills on one side and a broad common on the other.

The **Radnorshire Museum,** in Memorial Gardens, presents the spa's development from Roman times and explains some Victorian "cures" in gruesome detail. ☎ 01597/824513 ✏ £1 ☉ *Apr.–Sept., Tues.–Sat. 10–5, Sun. 1–5; Oct.–Mar., Tues.–Fri. 10–4, Sat. 10–1.*

Where to Stay

££ ▦ **Guidfa House.** Friendly hosts Tony and Anne Millan run this stylish Georgian guesthouse with a welcoming log fire and bright, individually furnished bedrooms. Cordon Bleu–trained Anne prepares dinners (for guests only) from fresh local produce; the guinea fowl with apple brandy and mushroom sauce is delicious. All in all, this is an ideal base from which to explore the countryside. ☒ *Crossgates, near Llandrindod Wells, LD1 6RF* ☎ *01597/851241* 🖷 *01597/851875* ⊕ *www.guidfa-house.co.uk* ⛭ *6 rooms* ♿ *Dining room; no a/c, no room phones, no kids under 10* ▭ *MC, V* ⫶◎⫶ *BP.*

£–££ ▦ **Brynhir Farm.** You get a warm welcome at this immaculate, cream-washed farmhouse tucked into the hills on a 200-acre sheep and cattle farm. Country-style furnishings enhance the rooms. ☒ *Chapel Rd., Howey LD1 5PB* 🖷🖷 *01597/822425* ⊕ *www.brynhir.farm.btinternet.co.uk* ⛭ *5 rooms* ♿ *Dining room; no a/c, no room phones, no smoking* ▭ *MC, V* ⫶◎⫶ *BP.*

EN ROUTE From Llandrindod, take A4081/A470 to Rhayader, a good pony-trekking center and gateway town for the **Elan Valley,** Wales's Lake District. This 7-mi chain of lakes, winding between gray-green hills, was created in the 1890s by a system of dams designed to supply water to Birmingham, 73 mi to the east. From the Elan Valley, you can follow the narrow Cwmystwyth mountain road west to **Devil's Bridge,** a famous (and popular) beauty spot where three bridges set one on top of the other span a chasm over the raging River Mynach, before continuing on to Aberystwyth. (You can also take the steam-operated Vale of Rheidol Railway to this site from Aberystwyth.)

Aberystwyth

🅱 *41 mi northwest of Llandrindod Wells via A44, 118 mi northwest of Cardiff.*

Aberystwyth makes the best of several worlds as a seaside resort (complete with promenade and amusement pier) and a long-established university town that is home to the impressive National Library of Wales. It also has a small harbor and is a major shopping center for mid-Wales. More than 5,000 students expand the full-time population of 12,000. The town, midway along Cardigan Bay, came to prominence as a Victorian watering hole thanks to a curving beach set beneath a

The Language of Cymru

WELSH, THE NATIVE LANGUAGE of Wales (Cymru, in Welsh), is revered in the country, but it was not legally recognized in Britain until the 1960s. Today Welsh schoolchildren under 14 are required to take classes to learn the language, and Welsh is surviving more successfully than its Celtic cousin, Breton, which is spoken in northwestern France. Welsh may look daunting to pronounce, but it is a phonetic language; pronunciation is fairly easy once the alphabet is learned. Remember that "dd" is sounded like "th" in they, "f" sounds like "v" in save, and "ff" is the equivalent of the English "f" in forest. The "ll" sound has no English equivalent; the closest match is the "cl" sound in "close."

Terms that crop up frequently in Welsh are *bach* or *fach* (small), *craig* or *graig* (rock), *cwm* (valley; pronounced "cum"), *dyffryn* (valley), *eglwys* (church), *glyn* (glen), *llyn* (lake), *mawr* or *fawr* (great, big), *mynydd* or *fynydd* (mountain, moorland), *pentre* (village, homestead), *plas* (hall, mansion), and *pont* or *bont* (bridge).

---

prominent headland. Aberystwyth is a good gateway for exploring mid-Wales: few towns in Wales present such varied scenery within their immediate neighborhood, from the Devil's Bridge to the green Rheidol Valley.

The massive, neoclassical **National Library of Wales,** on a hill amid the buildings of the modern University of Wales, Aberystwyth, houses notable Welsh and other Celtic literary works among its more than 4.5 million printed volumes. This self-described national treasure house also has enormous archives of maps, photographs, films, and sound recordings. ■ TIP→ **Material doesn't circulate, but the public can do research; many people pursue genealogical history here (there's a family history center).** The gallery has art shows (works may be for sale, too), and exhibitions highlight Welsh and other subjects. Films and concerts are presented in the auditorium. ☒ *Off Penglais Rd.* ☎ *01970/632800* ⊕ *www. llgc.org.uk* ☒ *Free* ☉ *Weekdays 9:30–6, Sat. 9:30–5.*

The **Ceredigion Museum,** in a flamboyant 1905 Edwardian theater, has fine collections related to folk history. Highlights include a reconstructed mud-walled cottage from 1850, exhibits from the building's music-hall past, and items illustrating the region's seafaring, lead mining, and farming history. ☒ *Terrace Rd.* ☎ *01970/633088* ⊕ *museum.ceredigion. gov.uk* ☒ *Free* ☉ *Mon.–Sat. 10–5.*

The **castle,** at the southern end of the bay near the New Promenade, was built in 1277 and rebuilt in 1282 by Edward I. It was one of several strongholds to fall, in 1404, to the Welsh leader Owain Glyndŵr. Today it is a romantic ruin on a headland.

At the northern end of the beach promenade, a zigzag cliff path–nature trail at **Constitution Hill** leads to a view from the hilltop. An enjoyable way to reach the summit of Constitution Hill is by the **Aberystwyth Cliff Railway,** the longest electric cliff railway in Britain. Opened in 1896, it has been refurbished without diminishing its Victorian look. ☏ 01970/ 617642 ✆ £2.50 round-trip ⊗ Nov.–Feb., Wed.–Sun. 10–4; Mar.–Oct., daily 10–5.

At the 430-foot summit of Constitution Hill is the **Great Aberystwyth Camera Obscura** (☏ 01970/617642), a free modern version of a Victorian amusement: a massive 14-inch lens gives a bird's-eye view of the whole of Cardigan Bay and 26 Welsh mountain peaks.

At Aberystwyth Station you can hop on the narrow-gauge, steam-operated **Vale of Rheidol Railway** for an hour ride to the **Devil's Bridge,** where the rivers Rheidol and Mynach meet in a series of spectacular falls. Clamped between two rocky cliffs where a torrent of water pours unceasingly, this bridge well deserves its name—*Pont y Gwr Drwg,* or Bridge of the Evil One. There are actually three bridges (the oldest is 800 years old), and the walk down to the lowest bridge, "the devil's," is magnificent but strictly for the sure-footed. ☒ *Alexandra St.* ☏ *01970/625819* 🖨 *01970/623769* ⊕ *www.rheidolrailway.co.uk* ✆ *£12.50 round-trip* ⊗ *Easter–Oct.; call for schedule.*

OFF THE BEATEN PATH

LLANERCHAERON – This late-18th-century Welsh gentry estate in the Aeron Valley, 17 mi south of Aberystwyth, near Aberaeron, is a superb example of the early work of John Nash (1752–1835). Nash was the leading architect of the Regency and the designer of Brighton's Royal Pavilion. The estate survived with few changes until the present; it is a self-contained world with stables, barns, dairy, and brewery. The walled gardens are spectacular. ☒ *Off A482, Ciliau Aeron* ☏ *01545/570200* ⊕ *www.nationaltrust.org.uk* ✆ *£6* ⊗ *House mid-Mar.–July, Wed.–Sun. 11:30–4:30; Aug., daily 11:30–4:30; Sept. and Oct., Wed.–Sun. 11:30–4:30. Farm and garden mid-Mar.–July, Wed.–Sun. 11–5; Aug., daily 11–5; Sept. and Oct., Wed.–Sun. 11–5.*

Where to Stay & Eat

££–£££ ✕ **Gannets.** A simple, good-value bistro, Gannets specializes in hearty roasts and pies produced from locally supplied meat, fish, and game. Organically grown vegetables and a good French house wine are further draws for a university crowd. ☒ *7 St. James's Sq.* ☏ *01970/617164* ▤ *MC, V* ⊗ *Closed Sun.–Tues.*

££££ ✕▥ **Conrah Country Hotel.** Part of the appeal of this Edwardian country-house hotel on 20 acres of grounds is its air of seclusion, even though it's just 3 mi south of Aberystwyth. Traditional country furnishings and antiques decorate the house, and fresh flowers fill each room. The restaurant (£££££) is known for its imaginative British cuisine making use of local fish and meat. There's a three-course, prix-fixe menu at dinner. ☒ *A487, Chancery SY23 4DF* ☏ *01970/617941* 🖨 *01970/ 624546* ⊕ *www.conrah.co.uk* ⇄ *14 rooms* ⌂ *Restaurant, indoor pool, sauna, croquet; no a/c, no kids under 5* ▤ *AE, DC, MC, V* ⎟⊙⎟ *BP.*

£££–££££ ✕▥ **Harbourmaster Hotel.** A drive south on the coast road from Aberystwyth brings you to Aberaeron and the delights of this early-19th-century Georgian-style building, right on the harbor among colorfully painted structures. Modern design and strong colors dominate the public areas and bedrooms, which have wonderful harbor views. The

14

brasserie (££££) produces sophisticated fare such as roasted parsnip soup and Thai monkfish red curry. ⊠ *Quay Parade, 15 mi south of Aberystwyth, Aberaeron SA46 OBT* ☎ *01545/570755* 🖷 *01545/570762* ⊕ *www.harbour-master.com* ⇆ *9 rooms* ♨ *Restaurant, bar, some pets allowed (fee); no a/c, no kids under 5* ⊟ *MC, V* ¶◎¶ *BP.*

££–£££   ✕⊞ **Four Seasons.** This family-run hotel in the town center (no relation to the famous chain) is relaxed and friendly. The spacious rooms are very simply decorated. The restaurant (££) serves à la carte and three-course, prix-fixe menus at dinner; roast saddle of Welsh lamb is a specialty. ⊠ *50–54 Portland St., SY23 2DX* ☎ *01970/612120* 🖷 *01970/627458* ⊕ *www.fourseasonshotel.uk.com* ⇆ *16 rooms* ♨ *Restaurant; no a/c* ⊟ *AE, MC, V* ¶◎¶ *BP.*

Machynlleth

⑱ *18 mi northeast of Aberystwyth.*

Machynlleth, at the head of the beautiful Dovey Estuary, does not look like a typical Welsh country town. Its long and wide main street (Heol Maengwyn), lined with a mixed style of buildings from sober gray stone to well-proportioned Georgian, creates an atypical sense of openness and space. Machynlleth's busiest day is Wednesday, when the stalls of market traders fill the main street.

At the **Owain Glyndŵr Centre,** a small exhibition celebrates Wales's last native leader, who established a Welsh parliament at Machynlleth in the early 15th century. ⊠ *End of Heol Maengwyn* ☎ *01654/702827* 🖃 *Free* ☉ *Easter–Sept., Mon.–Sat. 10–5.*

In a former chapel that's now a cultural and performing-arts center is the **Y Tabernacl Museum of Modern Art,** a superb gallery with permanent displays, including works by noted contemporary Welsh artist Kyffin Williams. ⊠ *Heol Penrallt* ☎ *01654/703355* ⊕ *www.momawales.org.uk* 🖃 *Free* ☉ *Mon.–Sat. 10–4.*

☍ At the unique **Centre for Alternative Technology,** in an abandoned slate quarry in the forested hills just north of Machynlleth, a water-balanced cliff railway transports you to a futuristic, educational village equipped with all things green: alternative energy sources (solar roofs, wood-chip boilers), organic gardens, and a vegetarian café. Interactive displays present practical ideas about renewable resources, and the store is full of inspirational books and ecofriendly products. ⊠ *Off A487* ☎ *01654/702400* ⊕*www.cat.org.uk* 🖃*£8; lower prices in off-season* ☉ *June–Sept., daily 10–6; Oct.–May, daily 10–4:30.*

Where to Stay & Eat

★ **£££££**   ✕⊞ **Ynyshir Hall.** Idyllic gardens and grounds surround this supremely luxurious country retreat in a white-painted Georgian mansion near a wildlife reserve. Inside, the place glows: owner Rob Reen, an artist, displays his vibrant-hue work around the house. He and his wife, Joan, have decorated all surfaces in jewel-like tones. Antiques and Welsh pottery fill the public areas; the pampering guest rooms, named after artists (Hogarth, Matisse, Goya), have antique beds. The outstanding contemporary cuisine in the candlelit restaurant (£££££; fixed-price dinner menu) uses local favorites, from wild salmon and venison to farmhouse cheeses. ✉ *Off A487, southwest of Machynlleth, Eglwysfach SY20 8TA* ☎ *01654/781209 or 800/777–6536* 📠 *01654/781366* ⊕ *www. ynyshir-hall.co.uk* ➳ *9 rooms* ⟁ *Restaurant; no a/c, no kids under 9, no smoking* ▭ *AE, DC, MC, V* ⎮⊙⎮ *BP.*

££ ✕⊡ **Penhelig Arms.** The delightful little sailing center of Aberdovey is perched at the mouth of the Dovey Estuary, west of Machynlleth. This immaculate harborside inn has a terrace overlooking the harbor and bay, and most rooms have wonderful sea views. Meet the locals in the wood-panel Fisherman's Bar and dine in style in the fine restaurant (££££; three-course, fixed-price dinner menu), where local seafood is a specialty. ✉ *A493, Aberdovey LL35 0LT* ☎ *01654/767215* 📠 *01654/767690* ⊕ *www.penheligarms.com* ➳ *15 rooms* ⟁ *Restaurant, bar, no-smoking rooms; no a/c* ▭ *MC, V* ⎮⊙⎮ *BP.*

Outdoors

The 128-mi **Glyndŵr's Way** (✉ Tourist Office, Heol Maengwyn ☎ 01654/ 702401 ⊕ www.glyndwrsway.org.uk) walking route passes through Machynlleth before it turns east to climb above the Dovey with wonderful views north to Cadair Idris.

Dolgellau

⑲ *16 mi north of Machynlleth, 34 mi north of Aberystwyth.*

A solidly Welsh town with dark stone buildings and old coaching inns made of the local gray dolerite and slate, Dolgellau (pronounced dol-*geth*-lee) thrived with the wool trade until the mid-19th century. (Sheep are still auctioned here, but they're valued for meat rather than wool.) Prosperity left striking architecture, with buildings of different eras side by side on crooked streets that are a pre-Norman legacy. The town trail booklet, sold in the tourist office on Eldon Square, tells the story. Dolgellau, in a valley, has long been a popular base for people eager to walk the surrounding countryside. Look down the streets or above the buildings, and you'll see mountains rise up in the distance—a lovely sight.

The town became the center of the Welsh gold trade in the 19th century, when high-quality gold was discovered locally. A nugget of Dolgellau gold is used to make royal wedding rings. You can still try your luck and pan for gold in the Mawddach.

The **Museum of the Quakers,** in the town square, commemorates the area's strong links with the Quaker movement and the Quakers' emigration to the American colonies. ✉ *Eldon Sq.* ☎ *01341/422888* 🎟 *Free* ☉ *Easter–Oct., daily 10–6; Nov.–Easter, Thurs.–Mon. 10–5.*

To the south of Dolgellau rises the menacing bulk of **Cadair Idris** (2,927 feet); the name means "the Chair of Idris," though no one is completely sure who Idris was—probably a warrior bard. It is said that anyone sleeping for a night on a certain part of the mountain will awaken either a poet or a madman, or not at all.

14

Barmouth

 10 mi west of Dolgellau.

Barmouth, on the northern mouth of the Mawddach Estuary, is one of the few places along the Welsh coast that can be described as a full-fledged seaside resort, although it's now a bit tired. It has a 2-mi-long promenade, wide expanses of golden beach, and facilities for sea, river, and mountain-lake fishing. To appreciate the splendid location, walk along the footpath beside the railway bridge that crosses the mouth of the estuary: the bay stretches out on one side, and on the other are rugged, looming mountains and the river.

The arrival of the railroad in the 19th century made Barmouth a popular vacation spot. Alfred, Lord Tennyson was inspired to write *Crossing the Bar* by the spectacle of the Mawddach rushing to meet the sea. Charles Darwin worked on *The Origin of Species* and *The Descent of Man* in a house by the shore. Essayist and art critic John Ruskin was a frequent visitor and was trustee of the St. George's cottages built in 1871 by the Guild of St. George (Ruskin's organization, dedicated to founding agrarian communities) in 1871. Ruskin loved the walk from Barmouth up the river to Dolgellau.

Where to Stay & Eat

££££ ✕⊞ **Bae Abermaw.** Perched high above the sea with panoramic views across the bay, this traditional Victorian stone house encloses a surprisingly contemporary minimalist interior. Clean lines and pale natural tones make for a relaxed atmosphere. The excellent restaurant (£££–££££) serves dishes like local panfried steak of Welsh Black fillet with dauphinoise potatoes, port wine sauce, and baby vegetables. ⊠ *Panorama Rd., LL42 1DQ* ☎ *01341/280550* 🖷 *01341/281346* ⊕ *www.baeabermaw.com* ⟿ *14 rooms* ♻ *Restaurant, bar, lounge, meeting rooms, no-smoking rooms; no a/c* ⊟ *MC, V* ⦿ *BP.*

Welshpool

 48 mi east of Barmouth, 19 mi west of Shrewsbury.

The border town of Welshpool, "Trallwng" in Welsh, is famous as the home of Powis Castle, one of mid-Wales's greatest treasures, but it also has an appealing town center.

★ Continuously occupied since the 13th century, **Powis Castle** is one of the most opulent residential castles in Britain, with gardens that are equally renowned. Its battlements rear high on a hilltop, and Italian- and French-influenced terraced gardens surround the castle. Below gigantic yew hedges, the grounds fall steeply down to wide lawns and neat Elizabethan gardens. The interior contains many treasures: Greek vases; paintings by Thomas Gainsborough, Joshua Reynolds, and George Romney, among others; superb furniture; and the **Clive of India Museum,** with a good collection of Indian art. The tearoom is excellent. A timed-ticket system may be in effect on busy days. ⊠ *Off A483* ☎ *01938/551929* ⊕ *www.nationaltrust.org.uk* 🎟 *£9.60, gardens only £6.60* ☉ *Castle and* *museum Apr. and Sept., Thurs.–Mon. 1–5; July and Aug., Wed.–Mon. 1–5; Sept. and Oct., Thurs.–Mon. 1–4; Gardens Apr. and Oct., Thurs.–Mon. 11–6; July and Aug., Wed.–Sun. 11–6; Sept. and Oct., Thurs.–Sun. 11–4:30.*

The excellent **Powysland Museum,** in a converted warehouse on the banks of the Montgomery Canal, focuses on local history from the Stone Age to Victorian times. ✉ *Canal Wharf* 🖼 *01938/554656* 📧 *£1* 🕙 *May–Sept., Mon., Tues., Thurs., and Fri. 11–1 and 2–5, weekends 10–1 and 2–5; Oct.–Apr., Mon., Tues., Thurs., and Fri. 11–1 and 2–5, Sat. 2–5.*

SOUTH WALES

14

FROM CARDIFF TO CARDIGAN

The most diverse of Wales's three regions, the south covers not only the immediate region around Cardiff and the border of Wales and England, but also the southwest as far as the rugged coastline of Pembrokeshire. The very different natures of its two national parks reveals South Wales's scenic variety. The Brecon Beacons park, a short drive north of Cardiff, is an area of high, grassy mountains, lakes, and craggy limestone gorges. In contrast, the Pembrokeshire Coast National Park holds one of Europe's finest stretches of coastal natural beauty, with mile after mile of spectacular sea cliffs, beaches, headlands, and coves. Other pieces of the complicated South Wales jigsaw include traditional farmlands, cosmopolitan urban areas, rolling border country, wooded vales, and the former industrial valleys where coal was mined in huge quantities during the 19th and early 20th centuries.

Cardiff

► *20 mi west of the Second Severn Bridge, which carries the M4 motorway across the Severn Estuary into Wales.*

Home to the Welsh Assembly and with a population of 306,000, Cardiff is financially, industrially, and commercially the most important city in Wales. It's also one of Europe's youngest and most vibrant capital cities with an appealing blend of old and brand new. Attracting increasing numbers of tourists are its handsome Civic Centre, magnificent parklands, canopied shopping arcades, and a castle with abundant Victorian verve. These traditional sights stand alongside new landmarks like the Millennium Stadium and the dazzling waterfront regeneration of the one-time coal-exporting hub of Cardiff Bay. Here a dam across the Taff and Ely rivers has created a freshwater lake edged by 8 mi of prime waterfront, an area of promenades, shops, restaurants, attractions, and exciting modern buildings like the Wales Millennium Centre.

True to the Welsh tradition of vocal excellence, Cardiff is home base for Britain's adventurous and acclaimed Welsh National Opera. Cardiff is also the sporting center of Wales and the Welsh capital of rugby football. To hear crowds singing their support for the Welsh team is a stirring experience.

Main Attractions

Cardiff Bay. Panoramic bay views, promenades, shops, restaurants, museums, and prestigious buildings make Cardiff Bay well worth a visit. The revitalized dockland, 1 mi south of the city center, can be reached by bus, train, or taxi. The **Cardiff Bay Visitor Centre** a futuristic building known locally as "the Tube" (because of its shape), tells the story of the transformation of the bay area. Next door and overlooking the bay is the timber Norwegian seamen's church where Roald Dahl (noted author whose children's books include *James and the Giant Peach* and *Charlie and the Chocolate Factory*) was baptized. It's now known as the **Norwegian Church Arts Centre** and houses a performance space, a gallery, and a café. North of the visitor center is the **National Assembly Debating Chamber,** a canopied glass structure designed by Richard Rogers that perfectly complements the neighboring modern buildings. The lively exhibition about the workings of the National Assembly, however, is across the street in the imposing Victorian building, the **Pierhead.**

★ ❷ **Cardiff Castle.** In Bute Park, one section of the city's hundreds of acres of parkland, is an unusual historic site, with Roman, Norman, and Victorian associations. Parts of the walls are Roman, the solid keep is Norman, and the whole complex was restored and transformed into a Victorian ego flight by the third marquess of Bute. He employed William Burges (1827–81), an architect obsessed by the Gothic period, and Burges transformed the castle into an extravaganza of medieval color and careful craftsmanship. It is the perfect expression of the anything-goes Victorian spirit, and a reflection of the fortune made by the marquess in Cardiff's booming docklands. ⊠ *Bute Park* ☎ *029/2087–8100* ⊕ *www.cardiffcastle.com* ⊠ *Grounds and guided tour of castle £6.50; grounds only £3.30* ☉ *Mar.–Oct., daily 9:30–6; Nov.–Feb., daily 9:30–5; call for tour times.*

NEED A BREAK? **Café Minuet** (⊠ 42 Castle Arcade ☎ 029/2034-1794 ☉ Mon.-Sat. 11-6), in the Victorian shopping arcade opposite Cardiff Castle has pale wood floors and checked tablecloths and serves tasty rustic Italian food like homemade soups, pasta, and pizzas. Service is prompt and friendly.

★ ❷ **Castell Coch.** Perched on a hillside is the Red Castle, a turreted Victorian vision. It was built (on the site of a medieval stronghold) in the 1870s, about the time that Ludwig II of Bavaria was creating his fairy-tale castles, and it could almost be one of them. The castle was another collaboration of the third marquess of Bute and William Burges, builders of Cardiff Castle. Burges created everything—architecture, furnishings, murals—in a remarkable exercise in Victorian–Gothic whimsy. ⊠ *A470, 4 mi north of Cardiff, Tongwynlais* ☎ *029/2081–0101* ⊕ *www.cadw. wales.gov.uk* ⊠ *£3* ☉ *Apr., May, and Oct., daily 9:30–5; June–Sept., daily 9:30–6; Nov.–Mar., Mon.–Sat. 9:30–4, Sun. 11–4.*

Civic Centre. Two blocks north and east of Cardiff Castle is a well-designed complex of tree-lined avenues and Edwardian civic buildings with white Portland stone facades; Cathays Park is in the center. A Welsh dragon sits atop the domed City Hall, and inside the Marble Hall contains statues of Welsh heroes, including St. David, Henry Tudor, and Owain

Cardiff
Castle **26**

Castell Coch ..**24**

Llandaff **22**

Millennium
Stadium **27**

National
Museum
Cardiff **25**

St. David's
Centre **28**

St. Fagans
National
History
Museum **23**

Wales
Millennium
Centre **29**

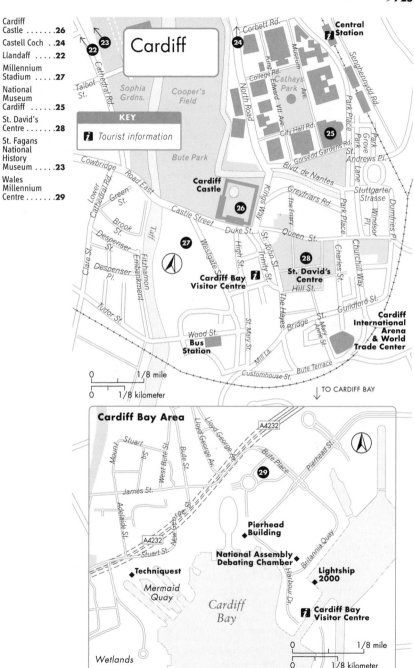

Glyndŵr (although he razed Cardiff in 1404). Neoclassical law courts and university campus buildings are also here. ⊠ *Bordered by North Rd. on the west and Park Pl. on the east.*

㉕ **National Museum Cardiff.** This splendid museum, next to City Hall in the
Fodor'sChoice Civic Centre, tells the story of Wales through its plants, rocks, archae-
★ ology, zoology, art, and industry. The Evolution of Wales gallery gives a dazzling run through Wales's existence using robotics and audiovisual effects. There's a fine collection of modern European art including the largest collection of French impressionist and postimpressionist works in the country. Allow at least half a day at the museum, and don't miss *La Parisienne* by Renoir. ⊠ *Cathays Park* 🕾 *029/2039–7951* ⊕ *www. nmgw.ac.uk* 🖾 *Free* ☉ *Tues.–Sun. 10–5.*

㉘ **St. David's Centre.** South of the Civic Centre are the shopping and business areas of Cardiff. A large, modern shopping mall holds **St. David's Hall,** one of Europe's best concert halls, with outstanding acoustics. People come here for classical music, jazz, rock, ballet, and even snooker championships. Nearby is the **Cardiff International Arena,** a multipurpose center for exhibitions, concerts, and conferences.

Also Worth Seeing

Caerphilly Castle. The largest and one of the most impressive fortresses in Wales was remarkable at the time of its 13th-century construction by an Anglo-Norman lord. The concentric fortification contained inner and outer defenses. More than 30 acres of grounds and a moat surrounds the castle, but Caerphilly is no longer on guard; some walls have toppled and others lean haphazardly. Exhibits in the gatehouse trace its turbulent history. The castle is 7 mi north of Cardiff. ⊠ *Access off A470–A468, Caerphilly* 🕾 *029/2088–3143* ⊕ *www.cadw.wales.gov.uk* 🖾 *£3* ☉ *Apr., May, and Oct., daily 9:30–5; June–Sept., daily 9:30–6; Nov.–Mar., Mon.–Sat. 9:30–4, Sun. 11–4.*

㉒ **Llandaff.** In a suburb that retains its village feeling, you can visit **Llandaff Cathedral,** which was repaired after serious bomb damage in World War II. The cathedral includes the work of a number of Pre-Raphaelites as well as *Christ in Majesty,* a 15-foot-tall aluminum figure by sculptor Jacob Epstein (1880–1959). To get here from Cardiff, cross the River Taff and follow Cathedral Road for about 2 mi. Guided tours available by arrangement. 🕾 *029/2056–4554* ⊕ *www.llandaffcathedral.org.uk.*

㉗ **Millennium Stadium.** The modern, 72,000-seat stadium stands beside the River Taff on the site of the famous Cardiff Arms Park, the spiritual home of Welsh rugby. The stadium's retractable roof enables it to be used for concerts and special events throughout the year, as well as for rugby. On a one-hour tour you can walk the players' tunnel and see the Royal Box, dressing rooms, pitch, and broadcasting suite. ⊠ *Entrance Gate 3, Westgate St.* 🕾 *029/2082–2228* ⊕ *www.millenniumstadium.com* 🖾 *£5.50* ☉ *Call for times.*

☾ ㉓ **St. Fagans National History Museum.** On 100 acres of parkland and gardens, this excellent, open-air museum has farmhouses, cottages, shops, a school, chapels, St. Fagans castle (a 16th-century manor house), and terraced houses that celebrate Wales's rich rural culture and show the evolution of building styles. All but two of the structures were brought here from places around Wales. Galleries display clothing and articles from daily life. There are farming demonstrations and special events that highlight ancient rural festivals. The museum is accessible from Junction 33 on the M4. ⊠ *St. Fagans* ☎ *029/2057–3500* ⊕ *www.nmgw. ac.uk* ☞ *Free* ☉ *Daily 10–5.*

Techniquest. A large science-discovery center on the waterfront, Techniquest has 160 interactive exhibits, a planetarium, and a science theater. ⊠ *Stuart St., Cardiff Bay* ☎ *029/2047–5475* ⊕ *www.techniquest.org* ☞ *£6.90* ☉ *Weekdays 9:30–4:30, weekends 10:30–5.*

OFF THE
BEATEN
PATH

TINTERN ABBEY – When Wordsworth penned "Lines Written a Few Miles Above Tintern Abbey," he had no idea of all the people who would flock to Tintern to gaze at the abbey's substantial ruins. Remote and hauntingly beautiful as the site is, Tintern's appeal is diminished in summer because of crowds, so visit early or late in the day to best appreciate the complex stonework and tracery of the Gothic church. The abbey, 5 mi north of Chepstow and 30 mi northeast of Cardiff, is on the lush banks of the River Wye. ⊠ *A466, Tintern* ☎ *01291/689251* ⊕ *www.cadw. wales.gov.uk* ☞ *£3.25* ☉ *Apr., May, and Oct., daily 9:30–5; June–Sept., daily 9:30–6; Nov.–Mar., Mon.–Sat. 9:30–4, Sun. 11–4.*

㉙ Wales Millennium Centre. This new, huge arts complex with a curving golden steel roof and purple slate walls, is a world-class stage for full-scale ballet, opera, and musical performances. The center contains dance and recording studios, an orchestral hall, and a 1,900-seat auditorium. Seven leading Welsh cultural organizations make this their home base, including the Welsh National Opera Company and the Dance Company of Wales. There are shops, bars, and restaurants; one-hour tours are available from WMC's guides. ⊠ *Cardiff Bay* ☎ *08700/402000* ⊕ *www. wmc.org.uk* ☞ *Free. Tours £5* ☉ *Call to arrange tour.*

Where to Stay & Eat

£££££ ✗ **Armless Dragon.** It's worth the five-minute drive from the city center to eat at this comfortable restaurant with a contemporary menu that changes daily. Dishes such as Monmouthshire woodland pork with smoked bacon and creamed leeks are created from seasonal, local ingredients. There are always vegetarian options and a good-value set-dinner menu (£14). ⊠ *97 Wyverne Rd.* ☎ *029/2038–2357* ⊕ *www. armlessdragon.co.uk* ☰ *AE, MC, V* ☉ *Closed Sun. and Mon.*

★ £££££ ✗ **Le Gallois.** Its minimalist furnishings and varied menu help make this sophisticated restaurant, close to Sophia Gardens, one of the city's most popular. The cooking is European in style and takes advantage of local ingredients. Try the venison with poached pear, celeriac and truffle purée, claret sauce, and chocolate oil. A good-value fixed-price menu is available at lunch, and there's a fixed-price dinner menu, too. ⊠ *8 Romilly Crescent* ☎ *029/2034–1264* ⊕ *www.legallois-ycymro.com* ☰ *AE, MC, V* ☉ *Closed Sun. and Mon.*

££–£££ ✗ **Da Venditto.** This stylish city-center restaurant specializes in pared-down, new-wave Italian cuisine with dishes like diver-caught scallops, skewered on a rosemary twig, and pancetta-wrapped monkfish with vegetable casserole. More traditional pasta dishes are also available. ⊠ *7–8 Park Pl., opposite New Theatre* ☎ *029/2023–0781* ⊕ *www.vendittogroup.co.uk* ⊟ *AE, MC, V* ⊗ *Closed Sun. and Mon.*

£–££ ✕ **Harry Ramsden's.** You can dine on the (reputedly) world's most famous fish-and-chips in a chandeliered, 200-seat dining room with wonderful views across Cardiff Bay. If you like live music with your meal, call to ask for dates of gala nights and sing-along evenings. ⊠ *Landsea House, Stuart St.* ☎ *029/2046–3334* ⊟ *AE, DC, MC, V.*

★ **£££££** ▥ **St. David's Hotel and Spa.** Natural light from a glass atrium floods this stylish, up-to-the-minute luxury hotel along the waterfront. Every room, done in soothing neutral tones with sleek modern furniture, has a private balcony and views over Cardiff Bay. You can indulge in a relaxing hydrotherapy spa treatment or feast at the Tides restaurant, under the guidance of noted London chef Marco Pierre White, which specializes in modern French fare. Special promotional deals are often available. ⊠ *Havannah St., CF10 6SD* ☎ *029/2045–4045* 🖷 *029/2048–7056* ⊕ *www.thestdavidshotel.com* ⇨ *132 rooms* ⚘ *Restaurant, cable TV, in-room data ports, indoor pool, gym, spa, business services, meeting rooms, no-smoking rooms* ⊟ *AE, DC, MC, V.*

££–£££££ ▥ **Jolyons Hotel.** Every room has different antiques, design, and fabrics at this sumptuous little boutique hotel close to the Millennium Centre. All the beds are king size. The lively Bar Cwtch (which means cuddle or cubbyhole in Welsh) has sofas you can sink into and a wood-burning stove. It's a great location from which to explore all the attractions of Cardiff Bay. ⊠ *Bute Cres., Cardiff Bay, CF10 5AN* ☎☎ *029/2048–8775* ⊕ *www.jolyons.co.uk* ⇨ *6 rooms* ⚘ *In-room DVD, Wi-Fi, bar; no a/c, no kids, no smoking* ⊟ *MC, V* ⊠ *BP.*

££ ▥ **Llanerch Vineyard.** The pine-furnished, country-style rooms in the farmhouse and converted outbuildings of this Vale of Glamorgan vineyard are only 15 minutes from Cardiff center, but you are deep in the green countryside here. You can walk in the surrounding vineyard and woodlands and arrange your own personal Welsh wine tasting. Take Junction 34 off M4 and follow the brown signs. ⊠ *Hensol, Pendoylan CF72 8GG* ☎ *01443/225877* 🖷 *01443/225546* ⊕ *www.llanerch-vineyard.co.uk* ⇨ *9 rooms* ⚘ *No a/c, no smoking* ⊟ *MC, V* ⊠ *BP.*

£–££ ▥ **Town House.** Cosmopolitan in style, this immaculate guesthouse near the city center (shops and castle are a short walk away) is well known as Cardiff's best B&B. The elegant Victorian building retains many original features and has neat, well-equipped bedrooms. You can have traditional British or American breakfasts in the formal dining room. ⊠ *70 Cathedral Rd., CF1 9LL* ☎ *029/2023–9399* 🖷 *029/2022–3214* ⊕ *www.thetownhousecardiff.co.uk* ⇨ *8 rooms* ⚘ *Lounge; no a/c, no smoking* ⊟ *MC, V* ⊠ *BP.*

Nightlife & the Arts

NIGHTLIFE   Cardiff's clubs and pubs support a lively nighttime scene. **Café Jazz** (⊠ 21 St. Mary St. ☎ 029/2038–7026) presents live jazz five nights a week and has TV screens in the bar and restaurant so you can view the on-stage action. **Clwb Ifor Bach** (⊠ Womanby St. ☎ 029/2023–2199), a distinctively Welsh club (its name means Little Ivor's Club), has three floors of eclectic music, from funk to folk to rock.

THE ARTS The big theaters present a full program of entertainment: drama and comedy, pop and the classics. The huge **Cardiff International Arena** (✉ Mary Ann St. ☎ 029/2022–4488) showcases artists who can draw huge crowds, from Tom Jones to Bob Dylan. **St. David's Hall** (✉ The Hayes ☎ 029/2087–8444), a popular venue, presents the Welsh Proms in July, attracting major international orchestras and soloists, and every two years hosts the prestigious Cardiff Singer of the World competition. It also stages rock, pop, jazz, and folk events.

New Theatre (✉ Park Pl. ☎ 029/2087–8889), a refurbished Edwardian playhouse, presents big names, including the Royal Shakespeare Company, the National Theatre, and the Northern Ballet.

Wales has one of Britain's four major opera companies, the outstanding **Welsh National Opera** (✉ Wales Millennium Centre, Cardiff Bay ☎ 029/2063–5000 for info, 08700/402000 for tickets). The company spends most of its time touring Wales and England.

Shopping

Canopied Victorian and Edwardian shopping arcades, lined with specialty stores, weave in and out of the city's modern shopping complexes. The **Cardiff Antiques Centre** (✉ Royal Arcade ☎ 029/2039–8891), in an 1856 arcade, is a good place to buy antique jewelry. Cardiff's traditional **covered market** (✉ The Hayes ☎ 029/2087–1214 ⊕ www.cardiff-market.co.uk) sells tempting fresh foods beneath its Victorian glass canopy. The **Learning Tree** (✉ Morgan Arcade ☎ 029/2022–5626 ⊕ www.tweedleandpip.co.uk) is a gem of a shop selling traditional toys and funky modern ones, educational games, books, and gifts for the discerning child up to age 11.

Abergavenny

30 *28 mi north of Cardiff.*

The market town of Abergavenny, near Brecon Beacons National Park, is a popular base for walkers and hikers. The popular **Abergavenny Food Festival** (☎ 01873/851643 general information, 01873/850805 tickets ⊕ www.abergavennyfoodfestival.com), held over a weekend in September, has lectures, discussions, demonstrations, and a food market. It's another sign of the growing interest in regional Welsh food.

Ruined **Abergavenny Castle**, built early in the 11th century, has a good local museum. The castle witnessed a tragic event on Christmas in 1176: the Norman knight William de Braose invited the neighboring Welsh chieftains to a feast and, in a crude attempt to gain control of the area, had them all slaughtered as they sat at dinner. Afterward, the Welsh attacked and virtually demolished the castle. Most of what now remains dates from the 13th and 14th centuries. The castle's 19th-century hunting lodge houses the museum, with exhibits about area history from the Iron Age to the present. The re-creation of a Victorian Welsh farmhouse kitchen includes old utensils and butter molds. ✉ *Castle Museum, Castle St.* ☎ *01873/854282* ▱ *Free* ⊙ *Mar.–Oct., Mon.–Sat. 11–1 and 2–5, Sun. 2–5; Nov.–Feb., Mon.–Sat. 11–1 and 2–4.*

14

West of Abergavenny lie the valleys—the Rhondda is the most famous—so well described by Richard Llewellyn in his 1939 novel *How Green Was My Valley* (the basis for the 1941 film). The slag heaps of the coal mines are green now, thanks to land reclamation schemes. The area southwest of Abergavenny, around the former iron- and coal-mining town of Blaenavon, has been named a World Heritage Site by UNESCO; it **Fodor'sChoice** provides a fascinating glimpse into Wales's industrial past. At the **Big ★ Pit: National Coal Museum,** ex-miners take you underground on a tour of an authentic coal mine for a look at the hard life of the South Wales miner. You can also see the pithead baths and workshops. ⊠ *Off A4043, Blaenavon* ☎ *01495/790311* ⊕ *www.nmgw.ac.uk* ⊠ *Free* ☺ *Feb.–Nov., daily 9:30–5; underground tours 10–3:30.*

The **Blaenavon Ironworks,** dating from 1789, trace the entire process of iron production in that era. Well-preserved blast furnaces, a water-balance lift used to transport materials to higher ground, and a terraced row of workers' cottages show how the business operated. ⊠ *A4043, Blaenavon* ☎ *01495/792615* ⊕ *www.blaenavontic.com* ⊠ *£2.50* ☺ *Apr.–Oct., daily 9:30–4:30.*

Where to Stay & Eat

£–£££ ✕ **Clytha Arms.** A converted house on the banks of the River Usk near Abergavenny serves imaginative modern food in a relaxed setting. Try the cracked whole crab seasoned with lemongrass, chili, and lime leaves. You can eat very cheaply in the bar (try the real ales) or pay a little more in the restaurant. ⊠ *Off B4598, Clytha* ☎ *01873/840206* ⊕ *www.clytha-arms.com* ⊟ *AE, MC, V* ☺ *Closed Mon.*

££££ ✕ **Allt-yr-Ynys Country House Hotel.** This 16th-century manor house in the foothills of the Black Mountains provides a winning blend of ancient charm and present-day comfort. Stone-tiled roofs, Jacobean oak paneling, decorative plasterwork ceilings, and exposed beams recall the past, whereas the comfortable public areas, pool, and hot tub pamper modern tastes. Most of the spacious, modern bedrooms are in converted stables and outbuildings, with views over mountains and woodland. The restaurant (£££) has a reputation for excellent modern British fare; try the braised Welsh lamb with rosemary and red-currant sauce. ⊠ *Off A465, 5 mi north of Abergavenny, Walterstone HR2 ODU* ☎ *01873/ 890307* 🖶 *01873/890539* ⊕ *www.allthotel.co.uk* ➮ *21 rooms* ⅙ *Restaurant, indoor pool, hot tub, sauna, bar, lounge, some pets allowed (fee), no-smoking rooms; no a/c* ⊟ *AE, MC, V* ⊠ *BP.*

Crickhowell

㉛ *5 mi northwest of Abergavenny.*

If you take A40 northwest out of Abergavenny, you pass Sugar Loaf mountain and come to Crickhowell, a charming town on the banks of the River Usk with little shops, an ancient bridge, and a ruined castle. **Tretower Court,** 3 mi northwest of Crickhowell, is a splendid example of a fortified medieval manor house. Nearby, and part of the site, are the ruins of a Norman castle. ⊠ *A479* ☎ *01874/730279* ⊕ *www.cadw.wales. gov.uk* ⊠ *£2.50* ☺ *Apr.–Sept., daily 10–5; Mar. and Oct., daily 10–5.*

Where to Stay & Eat

££–££££ ✗🏠 **Bear Hotel.** In the middle of town, this white-painted coaching inn with good food is full of character. The low-beamed bar, decorated with memorabilia from the days when stagecoaches stopped here, has a log fire in winter. Rooms in the hotel or in a modern addition in the former stable yard vary widely (some are fairly small); the most luxurious have four-poster beds and antiques. The Bear serves creative contemporary cuisine—excellent-value bar food and restaurant (££–£££) offerings such as scallops with Parma ham and venison on spinach. ✉ *A40, NP8 1BW* ☎ *01873/810408* 🖨 *01873/811696* ⊕ *www.bearhotel.co.uk* 🛏 *35 rooms* ♻ *Restaurant, bar; no a/c* ☰ *AE, MC, V* ❍❙ *BP.*

££ ✗🏠 **Ty Croeso Hotel.** A hillside location with views over the Usk Valley adds to the appeal of this hotel (its name means "House of Welcome") in an early-19th-century grey stone building. It has comfortable rooms with print fabrics, a lounge with a log fire, and imaginative food (££–£££) with a Welsh emphasis, such as Welsh beef flamed in whisky. ✉ *The Dardy, off B4558, NP8 1PU* ☎☎ *01873/810573* ⊕ *www.ty-croeso.co. uk* 🛏 *8 rooms* ♻ *Restaurant, bar, lounge; no a/c* ☰ *AE, MC, V* ❍❙ *BP.*

Brecon

㉜ *19 mi northwest of Abergavenny, 41 mi north of Cardiff.*

Brecon, a historic market town of narrow passageways, Georgian buildings, and pleasant riverside walks, is also the gateway to the Brecon Beacons National Park. It's particularly appealing on market days (Tuesday and Friday). You may want to purchase a hand-carved wooden love spoon similar to those on display in the Brecknock Museum.

Cavernous **Brecon Cathedral** (☎ 01874/623857 ⊕ www.breconcathedral. org.uk), with a heritage center that traces its history, stands on the hill above the middle of town. In the colonnaded Shire Hall built in 1842 is the **Brecknock Museum** (✉ Captain's Walk ☎ 01874/624121), with its items from rural life, art exhibits, superb collection of carved love spoons, and perfectly preserved 19th-century assize court.

The military exhibits in the **South Wales Borderers' Museum** span centuries of conflict; some relate to battles in which this regiment participated. The Zulu Room recalls the Borderers' defense of Rorke's Drift in the Anglo-Zulu war of 1879, an action dramatized in the 1964 film *Zulu,* starring Michael Caine. ✉ *The Watton, off Bulwark* ☎ *01874/613310* ⊕ *www.rrw.org. uk* 🎫 *£3* ⊙ *Oct.–Mar., weekdays 9–5; Apr.–Sept., weekdays 9–5, weekends 10–4.*

South of Brecon, the skyline fills with mountains, and wild, windswept uplands stretch to the horizon in the Brecon Beacons Na-

LOVE SPOONS

The rural Welsh custom of giving one's beloved a wooden spoon intricately hand-carved with symbols of love dates from the mid-17th century. Motifs include hearts, flowers, doves, intertwined vines, and chain links. These days you don't have to make the effort yourself as shops all over Wales sell the spoons as souvenirs.

14

HIKING & BIKING IN WALES

Hiking and walking are the most popular outdoor activities in Wales, and a great way to see the country. Long-distance paths include the Pembrokeshire Coast Path (which runs all along the spectacular shores of southwest Wales), the south–north Offa's Dyke Path, based on the border between England and Wales established by King Offa in the 8th century, and the Glyndŵr Way, a 128-mi-long highland route that traverses mid-Wales from the border town of Knighton via Machynlleth to Welshpool. Signposted footpaths in Wales's forested areas are short and easy to follow. Dedicated enthusiasts might prefer the wide-open spaces of the Brecon Beacons National Park or the mountains of Snowdonia.

Wales's reputation as both an on-road and off-road cycling mecca is well established. There's an amazing choice of scenic routes and terrain from challenging off-road tracks (⊕ www.mtbwales.com is for the serious cyclist) to long-distance road rides and gentle family trails; VisitWales has information to get your started.

CONTACTS & RESOURCES
Cycling Wales (⊕ www.cycling.visitwales.com). **Offa's Dyke Centre** (☎ 01547/528753 ⊕ www.offasdyke.demon.co.uk). **Pembrokeshire Coast Path** (⊕ www.nationaltrail.co.uk) **Ramblers' Association in Wales** (☎ 029/2034–3535 ⊕ www.ramblers.org.uk/wales).

tional Park. The **Brecon Beacons National Park Visitor Centre** on Mynydd Illtyd, a high, grassy stretch of upland west of A470, is an excellent source of information for attractions and activities within this 519-square-mi park of hills and open moorlands. It also gives wonderful panoramic views across to Pen-y-fan, at 2,907 feet the highest peak in South Wales. If you plan to explore Wales's high country on foot, come well equipped. Mist and rain can quickly descend, and the Beacons' summits are exposed to high winds. ✉ *Off A470, Libanus, Brecon LD3 8ER, 5½ mi southwest of Brecon* ☎ *01874/623366* ⊕ *www.breconbeacons.org* 🎟 *Free; fee for parking* ☉ *Daily 9:30–5; until 4:30 Nov.–Mar.*

Where to Stay & Eat

£ ✕ **Brecon Beacons National Park Visitor Centre Tearoom and Restaurant.** The spectacular view across the Beacons and high-quality homemade dishes make this a very popular spot. The parsnip and apple soup and the Welsh Black beef pie are among the good choices. You can indulge in a cream tea or fresh-baked cake, or just have coffee and enjoy the view. ✉ *Off A470, Libanus, Brecon* ☎ *01874/624979* ⊕ *www.breconbeacons.org* ☰ *MC, V* ☉ *No dinner.*

£££–££££ ✕🏨 **Felin Fach Griffin.** Old and new blend perfectly in this modern country-style inn with old wood floors, leather sofas, and terra-cotta–color stone walls hung with bright prints. Some bedrooms have four-posters. The excellent menu (£££) makes use of fresh local produce. Try the roast partridge with celeriac mash or the salmon fillet with fennel confit. ✉ *A470, east of Brecon, Felin Fach LD3 0UB* ☎ *01874/620111*

🕾 *01874/620120 ⊕ www.eatdrinksleep.ltd.uk ↩ 7 rooms ☖ Restaurant, no-smoking rooms; no a/c, no room TVs ▭ MC, V ⦿ BP.*

£–££ 🕮 **The Coach House.** This former coach house provides contemporary town-house accommodation. The friendly Welsh speaking owners are mines of local information on where to go and what to do in the Brecon Beacons, and at the end of a hectic day's activities can offer a relaxing holistic massage. Inventive Welsh breakfasts and evening meals are served in the small stylish restaurant. ⊠ *Orchard St., LD3 8AN* 🕾 *07050/691216* 🕭 *0705/691217* ⊕ *www.coachhousebrecon.co.uk* ↩ *7 rooms ☖ Restaurant, lounge, Wi-Fi, massage; no a/c, no smoking* ▭ *MC, V ⦿ BP.*

Nightlife & the Arts

Theatr Brycheiniog (⊠ Canal Wharf 🕾 01874/611622 ⊕ www.theatrbrycheiniog.co.uk), on the canal, is the town's impressive venue for the arts. It also has a gallery and waterfront bistro. Each summer, the town hosts **Brecon Jazz** (🕾 01874/611622 ⊕ www.breconjazz.co.uk), an international jazz festival that attracts top performers.

Sports

Crickhowell Adventure Gear (⊠ Ship St. 🕾 01874/611586), which also has a smaller shop in Crickhowell, sells outdoor gear such as clothes and climbing equipment.

Brecon is an ideal center for on- and off-road cycling. **Biped Cycles** (⊠ 4, Free St. 🕾🕾 01874/622296 ⊕ www.bipedcycles.co.uk) will rent you the right bike and equipment to take to the hills.

Swansea

③ *36 mi southwest of Brecon, 40 mi west of Cardiff.*

Swansea, the birthplace of poet Dylan Thomas (1914–53), marks the end of the industrial region of South Wales. Despite some undistinguished postwar architecture, Wales's second-largest city (population 224,000) has a number of appealing sights, including the waterfront pedestrian Sail Bridge, which has a 300-foot-high mast. Swansea was extensively bombed during World War II, and its old dockland has reemerged as the splendid **Maritime Quarter,** a modern marina with attractive housing and shops and a seafront that commands views across the sweep of Swansea Bay.

Housed in a construction of steel, slate, and glass grafted onto an historic redbrick building, the **National Waterfront Museum's** galleries have 15 theme areas. State-of-the-art interactive technology and artifacts bring Welsh industrial and maritime history to a 21st-century audience. ⊠ *Oystermouth Rd., Maritime Quarter* 🕾 *01792/638950* ⊕ *www.waterfrontmuseum.co.uk* 🎫 *Free* ⊗ *Daily 10–5.*

Founded in 1841, the **Swansea Museum** contains a quirky and eclectic collection that includes an Egyptian mummy, china, local archaeological exhibits, and the intriguing Cabinet of Curiosity, which holds artifacts from Swansea's past. The museum is close to the Maritime Quarter.

⊠ *Victoria Rd.* ☏ *01792/653763* ⊕ *www.swanseaheritage.net* ✉ *Free* ☉ *Tues.–Sun. 10–4:45.*

The **Dylan Thomas Centre,** on the banks of the Tawe close to the Maritime Quarter, is the National Literature Centre for Wales. The center houses a permanent Dylan Thomas exhibition, art gallery, restaurant and café-bookshop, and hosts literary events such as the annual Dylan Thomas Festival. The Wales Tourist Board has a leaflet for a Dylan Thomas Trail around South Wales for those interested in following in the poet's footsteps. ⊠ *Somerset Pl.* ☏ *01792/463980* ⊕ *www. dylanthomas.com* ✉ *Free* ☉ *Daily 10–4:30.*

Swansea's modern shopping center is nothing special, but the **covered market,** part of Quadrant Shopping Centre, is the best fresh-foods market in Wales. You can buy cockles from the Penclawdd beds on the nearby Gower Peninsula, and laverbread, that unique Welsh delicacy made from seaweed, which is usually served with bacon and eggs.

The **Egypt Centre** displays a substantial collection of ancient Egyptian artifacts, such as bead necklaces from the time of Tutankhamen and the beautiful painted coffin of a Theban musician. ⊠ *Taliesin Centre, University of Wales Swansea, Singleton Park* ☏ *01792/295960* ⊕ *www. swansea.ac.uk/egypt* ✉ *Free* ☉ *Tues.–Sat. 10–4.*

★　The 14-mi-long **Gower Peninsula,** only minutes away from Swansea's center, was the first part of Britain to be declared an area of Outstanding Natural Beauty. Its shores are a succession of sheltered sandy bays and awesome headlands. Actress Catherine Zeta-Jones was born here, in the Victorian seaside resort of Mumbles. ■ TIP→ **For the area's most breathtaking views, head to Rhossili on its western tip.**

Where to Stay & Eat

££–£££ ✕ **La Braseria.** This lively, welcoming spot resembles a Spanish restaurant, with its flamenco music, oak barrels, and whitewashed walls. Among the house specialties are sea bass in rock salt, roast suckling pig, and pheasant (in season). There's a good choice of 140 Spanish and French wines. ⊠ *28 Wind St.* ☏ *01792/469683* ⊕ *www.labraseria.com* ⊟ *AE, MC, V* ☉ *Closed Sun.*

★　✕🏨 **Fairyhill.** Luxuriously furnished public rooms, spacious bedrooms, **££££–£££££** and 24 acres of wooded grounds make this 18th-century country house in the western part of the scenic Gower Peninsula a restful retreat. The hotel is renowned for sophisticated cuisine and a well-chosen wine list; try the Welsh Black beef with beer batter onions or the seared scallops with black fettucine. There's a fixed-price dinner menu (£££££). ⊠ *Off B4295, 11 mi southwest of Swansea, Reynoldston SA3 1BS* ☏ *01792/ 390139* 🖷 *01792/391358* ⊕ *www.fairyhill.net* ➥ *8 rooms* ♿ *Restaurant, massage, croquet, helipad; no a/c, no kids* ⊟ *AE, MC, V* ⦵ *BP.*

£££–£££££ ✕🏨 **Morgans.** This old Victorian Port Authority building in the Maritime Quarter has been transformed into a strikingly modern hotel without losing any of its period features: moldings, pillars, stained glass, and wood floors. The rooms are immaculate with crisp cotton sheets and drapes of satin, silk, and suede. The stylish restaurant (£££–££££) serves dishes like seared fillet of local sea bass with buttered spinach and vanilla-bean sauce. Lighter treats at the café-bar include cockle, leek, and bacon risotto with Llanboidy cheese. ✉ *Somerset Pl., SA1 1RR* ☎ *01792/484848* 🖷 *01792/484849* ⊕ *www.morganshotel.co.uk* ↩ *20 rooms* ⟡ *Restaurant, café, room service, in-room DVD, bar; no smoking* ☰ *AE, MC, V.*

National Botanic Garden of Wales

★ ☕ ➌➍ *20 mi northwest of Swansea, 60 mi northwest of Cardiff.*

The first modern botanic garden in Britain, opened in 2000, celebrates conservation and education. It's based at Middleton Park, a 568-acre, 18th-century estate with seven lakes, cascades, fountains, and a Japanese garden. The garden's centerpiece is the Norman Foster–designed Great Glass House, the largest single-span greenhouse in the world, which blends into the curving landforms of the Tywi Valley. The interior landscape includes a 40-foot-deep ravine, 10,000 plants from all the Mediterranean climates of the world, and the interactive Bioverse. The garden is signposted off the main road between Swansea and Carmarthen. ✉ *Off A48 or B4310, Llanarthne* ☎ *01558/667148* ⊕ *www.gardenofwales.org.uk* 🖾 *£7* ⊙ *Apr.–Oct., daily 10–6; Nov.–Mar., daily 10–4:30.*

Tenby

➌➎ *53 mi west of Swansea.*

Pastel-color Georgian houses cluster around a harbor in this seaside resort, where two golden sandy beaches stretch below the hotel-lined cliff top. Medieval Tenby's ancient town walls still stand, enclosing narrow streets and passageways full of shops, inns, and places to eat. From the harbor you can take a boat trip to Caldey Island and visit the monastery, where monks make perfume.

The ruins of a castle stand on a headland overlooking the sea, close to the informative **Tenby Museum and Art Gallery** (✉ Castle Hill ☎ 01834/ 842809 ⊕ www.tenbymuseum.free-online.co.uk), which recalls the town's maritime history and its growth as a fashionable resort.

The late-15th-century **Tudor Merchant's House,** in town, shows how a prosperous trader would have lived in the Tenby of old. ✉ *Quay Hill* ☎ *01834/842279* ⊕ *www.nationaltrust.org.uk* 🖾 *£2.50* ⊙ *Apr.–Oct., Sun.–Fri. 11–5.*

Where to Stay

££££–£££££ 🖾 **Penally Abbey.** Built on the site of a 6th-century abbey on 5 acres of lush woodland overlooking the expanse of Camarthen Bay, this dignified 18th-century house is awash with period details. Bedrooms within the house are furnished with antiques and four-poster beds, whereas those in the adjoining St Deiniols Lodge are light and airy with a touch of urban chic. The hotel is relaxed rather than stuffy, but service is first-class. ✉ *Off A4139, 2 mi west of Tenby, Penally SA70 7PY* ☎ *01834/843033* 🖷 *01834/844714* ⊕ *www.penally-abbey.com* ↩ *17 rooms* ⟡ *Restaurant, indoor pool, billiards; no a/c* ☰ *AE, MC, V* ⥮ *BP.*

£–££   ⊞ **Ivy Bank Guest House.** This comfortable and immaculate Victorian house is just a five-minute stroll from the sea. The breakfast menu is extensive and the rooms are furnished with light flowery fabrics. ✉ *Harding St., Tenby SA70 7ll* ☎ *01834/842311* 📠 *01834/849053* ⊕ *www.ivybanktenby.co.uk* ↪ *5 rooms* ♿ *Some in-room VCRs, lounge; no smoking* ▭ *MC, V* ‖◯‖ *BP.*

Pembroke

36 *13 mi west of Tenby, 13 mi south of Haverfordwest.*

In Pembroke you are entering the heart of Pembrokeshire, one of the most curious regions of Wales. All around are English names such as Deeplake, New Hedges, and Rudbaxton. Locals more often than not don't understand Welsh, and South Pembrokeshire is known as "Little England beyond Wales." History is responsible: in the 11th century, the English conquered this region with the aid of the Normans, and the English and Normans intermarried and set about building castles.

One of the most magnificent Norman fortresses is massive **Pembroke Castle,** dating from 1190. Its walls remain stout, its gatehouse mighty, and the enormous cylindrical keep proved so impregnable to cannon fire in the Civil War that Cromwell's men had to starve out its Royalist defenders. You can climb the towers and walk the walls for fine views. This was the birthplace, in 1457, of Henry Tudor, who seized the throne of England as Henry VII in 1485, and whose son Henry VIII united Wales and England in 1536. ☎ *01646/681510* ⊕ *www.pembrokecastle.co.uk* 🎟 *£3.50* ☉ *Apr.–Sept., daily 9:30–6; Oct. and Mar., daily 10–5; Nov.–Feb., daily 10–4.*

St. David's

37 *25 mi northwest of Pembroke, 16 mi west of Fishguard.*

This tiny village holds what has been described as the holiest ground in Great Britain, the Cathedral of St. David and the shrine of the patron saint of Wales, who founded a monastic community here in the 6th century. The entire area around St. David's, steeped in sanctity and history, was a place of pilgrimage for many centuries, two journeys to St. David's equaling (in spiritual value) one to Rome. Here, on the savagely beautiful coastline, edged by the Pembrokeshire Coast Path—Pembrokeshire at its unspoiled best—you can almost recapture the feeling of those days nearly 1,500 years ago, when this shrine was very nearly the sole outpost of Christianity in the British Isles. If you have a day to spare, the 6.5-mi walk along the coastal path around the St David's headland from St Justinian to Caerfai Bay is magnificent.▮ **TIP→ Come in May and June to see the hedgerows and coastal path full of wild flowers.**

Unlike any other cathedral, the venerable 12th-century **St. David's Cathedral** (⊕ www.stdavidscathedral.org.uk) does not seek to dominate the surrounding countryside with its enormous mass; it is in a vast hollow. You must climb down 39 steps (called locally the Thirty-Nine Articles) to enter the cathedral. Its location helped protect the church from Viking raiders by hiding it from the view of invaders who came by sea. From the outside, purple-stoned St. David's has a simple austerity that harmonizes with the beautiful wind-swept countryside, but the interior is more intricate. Treasures include the fan vaulting in Bishop Vaughan's Chapel, the delicate carving on the choir stalls, and the oaken roof over the nave. Across the brook are the ruins of the medieval **Bishop's Palace.** ☎ 01437/720517 ⊕ www.cadw.wales.gov.uk ✉ £2.50 ☉ Nov.–Mar., Mon.–Sat. 9:30–4, Sun. 11–4; Apr.–Oct., daily 9:30–5.

Where to Stay & Eat

£££ ✕ **Morgan's Brasserie.** One choice sounds more delicious than the next at this classic bistro in the heart of town, which has an inventive menu based on local and organic ingredients. A blackboard lists daily specials, including Pembrokeshire-caught fish. Try the Welsh salt-marsh lamb, the Porthgain lobster with risotto, or sea bass on a bed of roasted vegetables. ✉ 20 Nun St. ☎ 01437/720508 ⊕ www.morgans-in-stdavids. co.uk ▤ MC, V.

£££££ ✕▦ **Warpool Court Hotel.** Overlooking a stunning stretch of coastline, this hotel sits on a bluff above St. Non's Bay, near a ruined chapel. Many rooms have sea views; decorative tiles adorn public areas and some bedrooms. The building dates from the 1860s, when it housed St. David's Cathedral Choir School. The well-equipped hotel offers contemporary cuisine (£££££; four-course, fixed-price menu at dinner), with fish, including home-smoked salmon, as a specialty; the dining room overlooks the water. ✉ Off Goat St., SA62 6BN ☎ 01437/720300 ✉ 01437/720676 ⊕ www.warpoolcourthotel.com ⇌ 25 rooms ♨ Restaurant, in-room data ports, tennis court, pool, gym, lounge; no a/c ▤ AE, MC, V �’⊙❙ BP.

Fishguard

38 16 mi northeast of St. David's, 26 mi north of Pembroke.

Fishguard is a town of three parts. The ferry terminal at Goodwick across the sheltered waters of Fishguard Bay sees activity throughout the year as boats sail to Rosslare, Ireland, across the Irish Sea. Fishguard's main town stands on high ground just south of Goodwick, separating the modern port from its old harbor in the Lower Town, where gabled cottages are grouped around the quayside. The Lower Town was the setting for the 1973 film of Dylan Thomas's play Under Milkwood, which starred Elizabeth Taylor and Welsh actor Richard Burton.

Cardigan & the Teifi Valley

39 18 mi northeast of Fishguard.

The little market town of Cardigan, with its ancient bridge, was the scene of a never-allowed-to-be-forgotten victory by the Welsh over the Norman army in 1136. The town is near the mouth of the Teifi, a river that runs through a wooded valley with traditional market towns and villages. The valley also contains reminders of the area's once-flourishing woolen industry. Wales's first eisteddfod, or folk festival, took place in Cardigan Castle in 1176. The eisteddfod tradition, based on the Welsh language and arts—a sort of Welsh cultural olympics remains strong in Wales, and events large and small are held here (mainly in summer months).

Cilgerran, a village a few miles south of Cardigan, has the dramatic ruins of 13th-century **Cilgerran Castle**, which stands above a deep, wooded gorge where the River Teifi flows. ⊠ *Off A478* ☎ *01239/615136* ⊕ *www. cadw.wales.gov.uk* 🎫 *£2.50* ⊗ *Apr.–late Oct., daily 9:30–6:30; late Oct.–Mar., daily 9:30–4.*

OFF THE BEATEN PATH

NATIONAL WOOL MUSEUM – Working exhibits and displays at this museum in what was once Wales's most important wool-producing area trace the evolution of the industry. The National Textile Collection is showcased. There are also crafts workshops and a woolen mill that produces reproduction fabrics. A shop sells the best of Welsh textiles. The museum is east of Cenarth, a few miles past Newcastle Emlyn. ⊠ *Off A484, Drefach Felindre* ☎ *01559/370929* ⊕ *www.nmgw.ac.uk* 🎫 *Free* ⊗ *Apr.–Sept., daily 10–5; Oct.–Mar., Tues.–Sat. 10–5.*

Where to Stay

££ 🏠 **Wervil Grange Farm.** Enjoy the rare experience of high-quality accommodation at an immaculate Georgian farmhouse on a traditional working farm rearing sheep and Welsh Black cattle. The rooms are beautifully furnished with antiques and fine fabrics patterned in flowers and stripes. There's free fishing on the farm and easy access to beach. ⊠ *Off A487, 8 mi northeast of Cardigan, Pentregat SA44 6HW* ☎ *01239/654252* 🛏 *6 rooms* ⚘ *Fishing, some pets allowed; no a/c, no smoking* ⊟ *No credit cards* ⊠ *BP.*

WALES ESSENTIALS

Transportation

BY AIR

London's Heathrow and Gatwick airports, with their excellent door-to-door motorway links with Wales, are convenient gateways (⇨ Airports *in* Smart Travel Tips). Manchester Airport, which offers many international flights, is an excellent gateway for North Wales, with a journey time to the Welsh border, via M56, of less than an hour. Cardiff International Airport, a 19-mi drive from the center of Cardiff, has direct flights to European destinations and Canada, with other connecting services worldwide via Amsterdam, and flights within the British Isles to London, Stansted, Manchester, Newcastle, Glasgow, Edinburgh, Aberdeen, Cork, and Dublin. A bus service runs from the airport to Cardiff's central train and bus stations.

AIRPORTS ⛢ **Cardiff International Airport** ⊠ A4226, Rhoose ☎ 01446/711111 ⊕ www.cwlfly. com. **Manchester Airport** ⊠ Near Junctions 5 and 6 of M56 ☎ 0161/489-3000 ⊕ www. manairport.co.uk.

BY BUS

Most parts of Wales are accessible by bus. National Express serves Wales from London's Victoria Coach Station and also direct from London's Heathrow and Gatwick airports. It also has routes into Wales from many major towns and cities in England and Scotland. Average travel times from London to Wales are 3½ hours to Cardiff, 4 hours to Swansea, 5½ hours to Aberystwyth, and 4½ hours to Llandudno.

The country's regional buses make travel around Wales quite easy; Traveline Cymru has information on all services. Wales's three national parks run summer bus services. The Snowdon Sherpa runs into and around Snowdonia and links with main rail and bus services. The Pembrokeshire Coastal Bus Service operates in the Pembrokeshire Coast National Park, and the Beacons Bus serves the Brecon Beacons National Park.

FARES & SCHEDULES

Beacons Bus ☎ 01873/853254 ⊕ www.breconbeacons.org. **National Express** ☎ 0870/580-8080 ⊕ www.nationalexpress.co.uk. **Pembrokeshire Coastal Service** ☎ 01437/776313 ⊕ www.pembrokeshiregreenways.co.uk. **Snowdon Sherpa** ☎ 0870/608-2608 ⊕ www.snowdonia-npa.gov.uk. **Traveline Cymru** ☎ 0870/608-2608 ⊕ www.traveline-cymru.org.uk.

BY CAR

Take the M4 from London for Cardiff (151 mi), Swansea (190 mi), and South Wales. Aberystwyth (211 mi from London) and Llandrindod Wells (204 mi) in mid-Wales are well served by major roads. The A40 is also an important route through central and South Wales. From London, M1/M6 is the most direct route to North Wales. A55, the coast road from Chester in England, goes through Bangor. Mid-Wales is reached by the M54, which links with the M6/M5/M1.

ROAD CONDITIONS

Distances in miles may not be great in Wales, but getting around takes time because there are few major highways. There is no single fast route from north to south (the mountains have discouraged that); A470 is good and scenic, and A487 runs along or near most of the coastline. Many smaller mountain roads are winding and difficult to maneuver, but they have magnificent views.

BY TRAIN

Travel time on the fast InterCity rail service from London's Paddington Station is about 2 hours to Cardiff and 3 hours to Swansea. InterCity trains also run between London's Euston Station and North Wales. Average travel times from Euston are 3¾ hours to Llandudno in North Wales (some direct trains, otherwise change at Crewe), and about 5 hours to Aberystwyth in mid-Wales (change at Birmingham).

Regional train service covers South Wales, western Wales, central Wales, the Conwy Valley, and the North Wales coast on many scenic routes, such as the Cambrian Coast Railway, running 70 mi between Aberystwyth and Pwllheli, and the Heart of Wales line, linking Swansea and Craven Arms, near Shrewsbury, 95 mi northeast.

CUTTING COSTS

For travel within Wales, ask about money-saving, unlimited-travel tickets (such as Freedom of Wales Flexi Pass, North and mid-Wales Rover, and the South Wales Flexi Rover), which include the use of bus services. Wanderer tickets are available from participating railways for unlimited travel on the narrow gauge Great Little Trains of Wales: a nine-day ticket is £55.

🚩 **Flexi Pass information** ☎ 0845/606–1660 ⊕ www.walesflexipass.co.uk. **Great Little Trains of Wales** ✉ Tallyllyn Railway, Wharf Station, Tywyn LL36 9EY ☎ 01654/710472 ⊕ www.greatlittletrainsofwales.co.uk. **National Rail Enquiries** ☎ 0845/748–4950 ⊕ www.nationalrail.co.uk. **Regional & Intercity Railways** ☎ 0845/748–4950 ⊕ www.thetrainline.com. **Snowdon Mountain Railway** ✉ Llanberis, Caernarfon LL55 4TY ☎ 01286/870223 ⊕ www.snowdonrailway.co.uk.

Contacts & Resources

DISCOUNTS & DEALS

The Cadw/Welsh Historic Monuments Explorer Pass is good for unlimited admission to most of Wales's historic sites. The seven-day pass costs £15.50 (single adult), £26 (two adults), or £32 (family ticket); the three-day pass costs £9.50, £16.50, and £23, respectively. Passes are available at any site covered by the Cadw program. All national museums and galleries in Wales are free.

🚩 **Cadw/Welsh Historic Monuments** ✉ Plas Carew, Unit 5-7, Cefn Coed, Parc Nantgarw, Treforest CF15 7QQ ☎ 01443/336000 ⊕ www.cadw.wales.gov.uk. **National Museums and Galleries of Wales** ⊕ www.nmgw.ac.uk.

EMERGENCIES

🚩 **Ambulance, fire, police** ☎ 999. **Bronglais Hospital** ✉ Caradog Rd., Aberystwyth ☎ 01970/623131. **Morriston Hospital** ✉ Heol Maes Eglwys, Cwm Rhydyceirw, Swansea ☎ 01792/702222. **University Hospital of Wales** ✉ Heath Park, Cardiff ☎ 029/2074-7747.

INTERNET

Travelers without personal computers can access the Internet at Internet cafés in many towns (use ⊕ www.upmystreet.com to check locations) and in some public libraries. Tourist information offices can also advise you. Wi-Fi hot spots exist only in the major urban centers.

🚩 **Internet Cafés PC 4 You** ✉ 8 Neville St., Cardiff ☎ 029/2022-0546. **Brecon Cyber Café** ✉ 10, Lion St., Brecon ☎ 01874/624942. **Directtech.co.uk** ✉ 5 Bodhyfryd Rd., Llandudno ☎ 01492/872092.

NATIONAL PARKS

🚩 **Brecon Beacons National Park** ✉ Plas-y-Ffynnon, Cambrian Way, Brecon LD3 7HP ☎ 01874/624437 ⊕ www.breconbeacons.org. **Pembrokeshire Coast National Park** ✉ Llannion Park, Pembroke Dock SA72 6DY ☎ 0845/345-7275 ⊕ www.pembrokeshirecoast.org.uk. **Snowdonia National Park** ✉ Penrhyndeudraeth LL48 6LF ☎ 01766/770274 ⊕ www.eryri-npa.gov.uk.

TOUR OPTIONS

A good way to see Wales is by local tour bus; in summer there's a large choice of day and half-day excursions to most parts of the country. In major resorts and cities you should ask for details at a tourist information center or bus station.

If you are interested in a personal guide, contact the Wales Official Tourist Guide Association. WOTGA uses only guides recognized by the Wales

Tourist Board and will create tailor-made tours. You can book a driver-guide or someone to accompany you as you drive.

🖪 **Wales Official Tourist Guide Association** ☏ 01633/774796 ⊕ www.walestourguides.com.

VISITOR INFORMATION

The Wales Tourist Board's Visit Wales Centre provides information and handles reservations; accommodations can also be booked online. Tourist information centers are normally open Monday through Saturday 10 to 5:30 and limited hours on Sunday, but vary by season.

🖪 **Visit Wales Centre** ⌂ Box 13, Bangor LL57 4WW ☏ 08701/211251 ⊕ www.visitwales.com. **Aberystwyth** ✉ Terrace Rd. ☏ 01970/612125. **Betws-y-Coed** ✉ Royal Oak Stables ☏ 01690/710426. **Caernarfon** ✉ Oriel Pendeitsh, opposite castle entrance ☏ 01286/672232. **Cardiff** national and city information ✉ The Old Library, The Hayes ☏ 029/2022–7281 ⊕ www.visitcardiff.info. **Llandrindod Wells** ✉ Auto Palace, Temple St. ☏ 01597/822600. **Llandudno** ✉ 1–2 Chapel St. ☏ 01492/876413. **Llanfair pwllgwyngyll** ✉ Station Site, Isle of Anglesey ☏ 01248/713177. **Llangollen** ✉ Y Chapel, Castle St. ☏ 01978/860828. **Machynlleth** ✉ Owain Glyndŵr Centre ☏ 01654/702401. **Ruthin** ✉ Craft Centre, Park Rd. ☏ 01824/703992. **Swansea** ✉ Plymouth St. ☏ 01792/468321 ⊕ www.visitswanseabay.com. **Tenby** ✉ Unit 2, The Gateway Complex ☏ 01834/842402. **Welshpool** ✉ Vicarage Gardens Car Park, Church St. ☏ 01938/552043.

14

UNDERSTANDING ENGLAND

ENGLAND & THE
PERFORMING ARTS

SPLENDID STONES &
ARCHITECTURE

BOOKS & MOVIES

CHRONOLOGY

ENGLISH VOCABULARY

ENGLAND & THE PERFORMING ARTS

ONE OF THE MAIN REASONS people want to visit England is the country's enviable reputation in the performing arts, whether it's music or drama, opera or ballet. The country is exactly what Shakespeare described, an "isle full of noises, sounds and sweet airs that give delight and hurt not." Although government subsidies often fall short of spiraling costs, numerous National Lottery grants have kept many a show on the road, and the performing-arts scene remains surprisingly healthy. There is a fluidity about the arts here that helps build their strength and appeal. An actor playing Lear with the Royal Shakespeare Company one day could appear in a television farce the next; an opera that has played to the small, exclusive audience at Glyndebourne reappears the next week at the Albert Hall as part of the BBC's Promenade Concerts, delighting not only the 7,000 in attendance, but millions more by radio. The performing arts largely transcend the social barriers that bedevil many aspects of English life, providing cultural nourishment for the widest spectrum of people.

The Theater

An evening at a play is a vital element of any trip to England. Most people head first for London's West End, the city's fabled "Theatreland." Here, you might catch Judi Dench and Vanessa Redgrave doing star turns, fabulous musical revivals, more than one Andrew Lloyd Webber extravaganza, and Agatha Christie's apparently immortal *The Mousetrap,* which opened in 1952.

Then there is that great mainstay, Shakespeare. His works provide a touchstone by which actors can measure themselves, and by which other people can measure them. Take *Hamlet,* for instance: occasionally a clutch of versions are staged at the same time. But that protracted procession of princes gives a fascinating lesson in the richness of talent available; indeed, the country's actors are among the nation's greatest treasures. However poor the play, the talents of the performers rarely fail. In the end, all the Hamlets have something to offer that seems to shed fresh light on the weary text. Simply put, Spain has its bullfights, Italy its opera, Britain its theater.

The pinnacle of the dramatic scene consists of two great national companies, the Royal National Theatre and the Royal Shakespeare Company (generally known as the RSC). They do have separate identities, though it is not always easy to pin down the ways in which they differ. The RSC is more prolific, performing at theaters in the West End and touring the country. It also performs at several stages at Stratford-upon-Avon; the main stage will be reconstructed beginning in mid-2007. The National Theatre plays in the three auditoriums in its concrete fortress on London's South Bank: the Olivier, the Lyttelton, and the Cottesloe, in descending order of size, the Olivier being huge and the Cottesloe studio-size. Of the two companies, the RSC is the more cohesive, with an impressive volume of work and a steadily developing style. The great majority of its offerings are works of Shakespeare and other English classics, with occasional ventures into musicals. The National ransacks world drama and also mounts some of the best stagings of American musicals anywhere beyond Broadway. It attracts more star performers than the RSC; the RSC relies largely on teamwork and creates stars from its own ranks.

As for the Bard of Bards, his fabled Globe Theatre, the most famous playhouse in the world, has risen again on the South Bank of the Thames in London, not 200 yards from where the original stood. England has always held special temptations for Shakespeare fans; the reconstructed Globe has added the thrill of seeing his plays performed in the neighborhood where he lived and on virtually the same kind of stage.

Beyond London, provincial theaters operate in most cities and large towns up and down the land, and many of them have developed national and international reputations. In Scarborough, a seaside town in Yorkshire, for example, the dramatist-director Alan Ayckbourn has run for years the Stephen Joseph Theatre, where he tries out his own plays. Most of these are transferred to London, appearing as often as not at the National Theatre. But the delight of regional theaters lies in their great diversity and local panache. In the town of Richmond, in Yorkshire, the charming Georgian Theatre Royal seats about 200 in rows and balconies that still reflect 18th-century class divisions. Porthcurno, near Penzance in Cornwall, has the cliff-top Minack Theatre, which overlooks the sea. The National Trust runs the lovely, still fully functioning, 1819 Theatre Royal in Bury St. Edmunds. There are woodland theaters, theaters in barns, and several in grand old country houses.

If you're traveling around the country, it's worth your time to find out what is on in any spot you may hit, especially in summer. At that time the acting fraternity takes to the open air and strives to outdo passing planes and nearby traffic. Notable venues include London's Regent's Park, which offers the best performances of the open-air theaters. There you can watch Shakespeare: to sit in the dusk, as Puck and Oberon plot their magic, and the actors gradually create a world of fantasy, is to take part in a national rite.

Opera

Dr. Samuel Johnson, who was a notable grouch, accused opera of being an exotic and irrational entertainment. Indeed, opera *is* irrational. It was born in the royal and ducal courts of Europe, where expense had no meaning. London's two main companies are poles apart. The Royal Opera at Covent Garden is socially the most

prestigious. This is the place for spectacles and productions to equal those presented anywhere. The English National Opera (ENO) at the Coliseum, beside Trafalgar Square, has a wider appeal, with classic operas sung in English. Seat prices for the ENO are generally much gentler than those at the Royal Opera, and the company consists mostly of British singers. The one drawback is that the auditorium sometimes dwarfs the voices.

Keep in mind that Britain has two other national opera companies: the Welsh National at Cardiff, and the Scottish National in Glasgow. They both embrace adventuresome artistic policies, attacking such blockbusters as Wagner's *Ring* and *The Trojans* by Berlioz. They also tour, the Welsh National especially, appearing in small towns around the country, even performing in movie houses. Opera North, a spin-off of the English National, is based in Leeds and is as venturesome as its begetter. Sadler's Wells, in north London, is a regular venue for regional opera as well as touring national and international dance companies.

Opera has always been an extravagant art form from a financial standpoint, but one company managed to build its own home in 1994. Glyndebourne, in deepest Sussex, relies entirely on sponsors and ticket sales, having no state subsidy. A visit there will cost you an arm and a leg, but you may feel like a guest at a superior house party.

Ballet

Ballet is a surprising art to flourish in England, and it does so only with a struggle. The Royal Ballet, the premier company, has one of its own veteran dancers, Monica Mason, as director. Few other companies present the classics with such seemingly effortless style.

The sibling Birmingham Royal Ballet is a dynamic company to watch, with its zesty director-choreographer David Bintley. The English National Ballet (ENB) goes from strength to strength in its mission to give ballet more mass appeal. You can catch the ENB performing its winter season at the London Coliseum, with summer shows at the Royal Albert Hall. Between times, it tours countrywide with a repertoire of classics. The Northern Ballet Theatre, based in Leeds, has popular appeal with its romantic take on such productions as *Wuthering Heights* and *Madame Butterfly*. If you want to catch some of these companies on tour in London, check out the performance schedules at Sadler's Wells and the Peacock Theatre.

Music

The country's amazingly vibrant musical life fills halls and theaters, churches and chapels throughout the land. In London, the three concert halls of the South Bank Centre, together with the Barbican, the Albert Hall, and the Wigmore Hall, provide the capital with venues for rich and varied musical fare. For example, every night for six weeks in summer, the Albert Hall is host of the BBC-sponsored "Proms," the biggest series of concerts in the world, involving 10 or more orchestras and dozens of other artists. Outside London, cities with fine resident orchestras include Birmingham (home to the noted City of Birmingham Symphony Orchestra), Liverpool, Manchester, and even the seaside town of Bournemouth.

Every week of the year you can attend performances of great choral works in concert halls, recitals of lieder in stately homes by candlelight, and lively madrigals from boats on moonlit rivers. It's not just the Welsh who can say, in Dylan Thomas's words, "Thank God we are a musical nation."

Arts Festivals

This is a land of festivals, mostly, though not exclusively, in summer. Whatever the size of the town, it will have a festival at some time. Some are of international scope, whereas others are small local wingdings. London may be the focus for annual film, dance, and music festivals, but the capital doesn't steal the whole show.

In Bath the International Festival, late May through mid-June, wins praise for its music especially. In Aldeburgh, a windswept East Anglian seaside town, the Festival of Music and the Arts, mid- to late June, honors the memory of Benjamin Britten and is mainly a music festival. Cheltenham has a musical celebration in July and an early to mid-October festival dedicated to literature, with readings, seminars, and lectures. York holds an early music festival in July and a Viking-related festival in February. Worcester, Hereford, and Gloucester take turns mounting the annual Three Choirs Festival in mid-August, the oldest in the world; this event has seen premieres of some notable music. Truro stages the Three Spires Festival in June in imitation. At Chichester in Sussex a summer drama festival has proved so popular that the town has built a theater especially for it. At Ludlow, Shakespeare is performed in summer in the open air, with the dramatic castle as backdrop.

All these festivals have the advantage of focusing a visit to a town and helping you to meet the locals, but be sure to book well in advance, because they are extremely popular. Year-round, England's performing arts offer one of the grandest and most unforgettable pageants in the world.

SPLENDID STONES & ARCHITECTURE

IN ENGLAND YOU CAN SEE STRUCTURES that go back to the dawn of history, in the hauntingly mysterious circles of mono-liths at Stonehenge or Avebury, or view the resurrected remains of Roman empire-builders preserved in towns such as Bath and Cirencester. On the other hand, you can startle your eyes with the very current, very controversial designs of contemporary architects in areas such as London's Dock-lands. Appreciating the wealth of the coun-try's architectural heritage does not require a degree in art history, but knowing a few hallmarks of particular styles can enhance your enjoyment of what you see. Here, then, is a primer of a millennium of ar-chitectural styles.

Norman

Duke William of Normandy brought the solid Norman style to Britain when he in-vaded and conquered England in 1066, al-though William's predecessor, King Edward (the Confessor) used the style in the building of Westminster Abbey a lit-tle earlier, in 1042. Until around 1200, it was favored for buildings of any impor-tance, and William's castles and churches soon dominated the countryside. Norman towers tended to be hefty and square, arches always round-top, and the vault-ing barrel-shape. Decoration was mostly geometrical, but within those limits, ornate. Norman motte and bailey castles had two connecting stockaded mounds, with the keep on the higher mound and other build-ings on the lower mound. *Best seen in the Tower of London and in the cathedrals of St. Albans, Ely, Gloucester, Durham, and Norwich, and at Tewkesbury Abbey.*

Gothic Early English

From 1130 to 1300, pointed arches began to supplant rounded ones, buttresses became heavier than the Norman variety, and win-dows lost their rounded tops to become more pointed and lancet shaped. Buildings climbed skyward, less squat and heavy, with the soaring effect accentuated by steep roofs and spires. *Best seen in the cathe-drals of York, Salisbury, Ely, Worcester, Wells (interior), and Canterbury (east end), and Westminster Abbey's Chapter House.*

Decorated. From the late 1100s until around 1400, elegance and ornament be-came fully integrated into architectural design, rather than applied to the surface of a solid, basic form. Windows filled more of the walls and were divided into sections by carved mullions. Vaulting grew increasingly complex, with ribs and or-namented bosses proliferating; spires be-came even more pointed; arches took on the ogee shape, with its unique double curve. This style was one of England's greatest gifts to world architecture. *Best seen at the cathedrals of Wells, Lincoln, Durham (east transept), and Ely (Lady Chapel and Octagon).*

Perpendicular. In later Gothic architecture, the emphasis on the vertical grew even more pronounced, as shown in features such as slender pillars, huge expanses of glass, and superb fan vaulting resembling the formalized branches of frozen trees. Walls were divided by panels. One of the chief areas in which to see Perpendicular architecture is East Anglia, where towns that grew rich from the wool trade built magnificent churches in the style. Houses, too, began to reflect prevailing taste. Per-pendicular Gothic lasted for well over two centuries from its advent around 1330. *Best seen at St. George's Chapel in Wind-sor, the cathedrals of Gloucester (cloister) and Hereford (chapter house), Henry VII's Chapel in Westminster Abbey, Bath Abbey, and King's College Chapel in Cambridge.*

Tudor

With the great period of cathedral build-ing over, from 1500 to 1560 the nation's attention turned to the construction of spacious homes characterized by this latest fashionable architectural style. The rapidly expanding, newly rich middle class, created by the two Tudor Henrys (VII and VIII) to challenge the power of the aristocracy, built spacious manor houses, often on the foundations of pillaged monasteries. Thus began the era of the great stately homes. Brick replaced stone as the most popular medium, and plasterwork and carved wood were used to display the elaborate motifs of the age.

Timber-frame and plaster buildings were also popular in this period for domestic and commercial use. Many "black-and-white" structures, as they are called, are copies made in later eras, but notable originals survive. (The Victorians are responsible for the fashion of painting half-timber buildings, of whatever era, black and white.) Wealthier individuals could afford to have the exposed wood beams carved or shaped; Little Moreton Hall, in Congleton near the Peak District, has wonderfully intricate patterns. Harvard House in Stratford-upon-Avon is another notable example of the style.

Another way the social climbers could make their mark, and ensure their place in the next world, was by building churches. Money earned in the wool trade funded splendid parish churches. Some of the most magnificent are in Suffolk, Norfolk, and the Cotswolds. *Domestic architecture is best seen at Hampton Court and St. James's Palace, London; for wool churches, Lavenham and Long Melford (though its tower is much later) in Suffolk, and Cirencester, Chipping Campden, Northleach, and Winchcombe in the Cotswolds.*

Renaissance Elizabethan

For a short period under Elizabeth I, 1560–1600, this development of Tudor style flourished as Italian influences began to seep into England, seen especially in symmetrical facades. The most notable example was Hardwick Hall in Derbyshire, built in the 1590s by Bess of Hardwick; the jingle that describes it goes "Hardwick Hall, more glass than wall." However grand the houses were, they were still on a human scale, warm and livable, built of a mellow amalgam of brick and stone. *Other great Elizabethan houses are Montacute in Somerset, Longleat in Wiltshire, and Burghley House in Cambridgeshire.*

Jacobean

At the beginning of the 17th century, for the first 15 years of the reign of James I (the name Jacobean is taken from the Latin word for James, Jacobus), architecture did not change noticeably. Windows were still large in proportion to the wall surfaces. Gables, in the style of the Netherlands, were popular. Carved decoration in wood and plaster (especially the geometrical patterning called "strapwork," another element of Dutch origin, which resembled intertwined leather belts) remained exuberant, now even more so.

A change was on the way, though. Inigo Jones (1573–1652), the first great modern British architect, attempted to synthesize the architectural heritage of England with current Italian theories. Two of his finest remaining buildings—the Banqueting House, Whitehall, and the Queen's House at Greenwich—epitomize his genius, which was to introduce to England the Italian-created Palladian style that would dominate the country's architecture for centuries. It uses the classical Greek orders: Doric, Ionic, and Corinthian. This was grandeur. But the classical style that proved so monumentally effective under a hot Mediterranean sun was somehow transformed here, domesticated and tamed. Columns and pediments decorated the facades, and huge frescoes provided acres of color to interior walls and ceilings, all in the Italian manner. These architectural elements had not yet been totally naturalized, however. There were in fact two quite distinct styles running concurrently: the comfortably domestic and the purer classical in public buildings. They were finally fused by the talent of Christopher Wren. *Jacobean is best seen at the Bodleian Library, Oxford; Chastleton House, near*

Stow-on-the Wold; Audley End, Essex; and Clare College, Cambridge.

Wren & the English Baroque

The work of Sir Christopher Wren (1632–1723) constituted an architectural era all by itself. Not only was he one of the world's greatest architects, but he was also given an unparalleled opportunity in 1666 when the disastrous Great Fire of London wiped out the center of the capital, destroying no fewer than 89 churches and 13,200 houses. Although Wren's great scheme for a modern city center was rejected, he did build 51 churches in London, the greatest of which was St. Paul's, completed in just 35 years. The range of Wren's designs is extremely wide, from simple classical shapes to the extravagantly dramatic baroque. He was also at home with domestic architecture, where his combinations of brick and stone produced a warm, homey effect. The influence of the Italian baroque can be seen in Sir John Vanbrugh's Blenheim Palace, where the facade echoes the piazza of St. Peter's in Rome, and at Vanbrugh's exuberant Castle Howard in Yorkshire. Nicholas Hawksmoor, Wren's pupil, designed some notable London churches and also the baroque Mausoleum at Castle Howard. The baroque had only a brief heyday in England; by 1725 the Palladian style was firmly in favor and the vast pile of Blenheim was being mocked by trendsetters. *Wren's ecclesiastical architecture is best seen at St. Paul's Cathedral (baroque with classical touches) and his other remaining London churches, his domestic style at Hampton Court Palace, Kensington Palace, the Royal Hospital in Chelsea, and the former Royal Naval College in Greenwich. English baroque is best seen at Blenheim Palace (Oxfordshire) and Castle Howard (Yorkshire).*

Palladian

In Britain, this style is often referred to as Georgian, so-called from the Hanoverian kings George I through IV, although it was introduced as early as Inigo Jones's time. During the 18th century, classical inspira-tion was thoroughly acclimatized. Though they looked completely at home among the hills, lakes, and trees of the English countryside, Palladian buildings were derived from the Roman-inspired designs of the Italian architectural theorist Andrea Palladio (1508–80), with pillared porticoes, triangular pediments, and strictly balanced windows. In domestic architecture, this large-scale classicism was usually modified to quiet simplicity, preserving mathematical proportions of windows, doors, and the exactly calculated volume of room space, to create a feeling of balance and harmony. The occasional departures from the classical manner at this time included the over-the-top Indian-style Royal Pavilion in Brighton, built for the prince regent (later George IV) by John Nash. The Regency style comes under the Palladian heading, though strictly speaking it lasted only for the few years of the actual Regency (1811–20). Architects such as the brilliant Robert Adam, who was born in Scotland but also worked in England, handled the Palladian style with more freedom than their counterparts elsewhere in Europe, and the United States took its cue from the British. *Among the best Palladian examples are Regent's Park Terraces (London), the library at Kenwood (London), the Royal Crescent and other streets in Bath, and Holkham Hall (Norfolk).*

Victorian

Elements of imaginative fantasy, already seen in the Palladian era, came to the fore during the long reign of Victoria (1837–1901). The country's vast profits made from the Industrial Revolution were spent lavishly. Civic building accelerated in all the major cities, with town halls modeled after medieval castles or French châteaux. The Victorians plundered the past for styles, with Gothic, about which the scholarly Victorians were very knowledgeable, leading the field. The supreme examples here are the Houses of Parliament by Charles Barry and Augustus Pugin, and the Albert Memorial by George Gilbert Scott, both in London. (To distinguish between the Victorian variety and a version of the style that flourished in the late 1700s, the earlier one is commonly spelled "Gothick.") But there were other styles in the running, including the attractively named, and self-explanatory, "Wrenaissance." *Other striking examples of Victorian architecture are Truro Cathedral, Manchester Town Hall, Ironbridge, and Cragside (Northumberland).*

Edwardian

Toward the end of the Victorian era, in the late 1800s, architecture calmed down considerably, with a return to a solid sort of classicism, and even to a muted baroque. The Arts and Crafts movement, especially the work of William Morris and work inspired by Morris, produced simpler designs, sometimes returning to medieval models. In an age of increasing mechanization, craftsmanship was emphasized. Architectural elements incorporated stylized natural motifs. *Best seen in Buckingham Palace and the Admiralty Arch in London. Kelmscott Manor (the interior of William Morris's Tudor home in the Thames Valley), Standen in East Grinstead (West Sussex), Rodmarton Manor near Tetbury (the Cotswolds), and Blackwell in Windermere (Cumbria) are notable Arts and Crafts houses.*

Modern

A furious public debate has raged here for years between traditionalists and the adherents of modernistic architecture. Britons tend to be strongly conservative when it comes to their environment. These arguments have been highlighted by the intervention of such notable figures as Prince Charles, who derides excessive modernism and who said, for instance, that the design for the Sainsbury Wing of the National Gallery in Trafalgar Square would be like "a carbuncle on a much-loved face." One reason for the strength of this attitude is that the country suffered from much ill-conceived development after World War II, when large areas of city centers had to be rebuilt after the devastation caused by German bombs. Town planners and ar-

chitects encumbered the country with badly built and worse-designed towers and shopping areas. Today, however, there appears to be an increased readiness to embrace the new, as designers draw people into user-friendly, fun buildings such as City Hall in London and the Baltic Centre for Contemporary Art in Newcastle.

The situation created in the '50s and '60s is slowly being reversed. High-rise apartment blocks are being taken down and replaced by more humanly scaled housing. Commercial areas in a number of cities are being rethought and slowly rebuilt. The emphasis has gradually moved to planning, design, and construction that pays more attention to the needs of inhabitants. A healthier attitude also exists toward the conservation of old buildings. As part of the postwar building splurge, older houses that should have been treasured were torn down wholesale. Happily, many of those that survived the wreckers' ball are now being restored and put back to use.

Nowadays, a number of architectural styles prevail. A predominant one draws largely on the past, with nostalgic echoes of the country cottage, and leans heavily on variegated brickwork and close attention to decorative detail. Urban centers have buildings in the most innovative styles, which are exciting and ecologically sensitive, too, using light to more thoughtful effect. These new designs have turned many fatigued or declining areas into destinations to see and be seen in.

In London, the Lloyd's of London tower in the City, by Sir Richard Rogers, designer of the Pompidou Center in Paris, began the trend toward modernism in the 1980s, but it took the millennium year to focus institutional minds on the creation of forward-looking images. The now-closed Millennium Dome, Rogers's tour de force, transformed the industrial blot of Greenwich peninsula; it may reopen in 2007 as O2, a performance venue. Sir Norman Foster's graceful Millennium Bridge has made equal headlines. Foster's glassy masterpiece, City Hall, near Tower Bridge, has been knocked as looking like a "glass testicle," but it is one of the boldest designs in London. Skyscrapers in the City of London are the exception rather than the rule, although the regenerated space of the old Docklands has allowed more room for imagination, as at Canary Wharf. Other buildings, such as Barclays Bank with its jukebox dome, and Swiss Re's "erotic gherkin" at 30 St. Mary Axe, the latter by Foster and looking akin to a glittering carousel pole, have begun to push height limitations established because of the proximity of historic buildings.

Other centers of modern architectural excellence include Manchester, with the Imperial War Museum North by Daniel Libeskind. Since the city center was bombed by the IRA in 1996, Manchester has received an impressive face-lift. Also in the north, Gateshead Quays is the spectacularly renovated industrial area around the River Tyne and Newcastle. The tilting Millennium Bridge in Newcastle is as dramatic as London's, and the city has opened the largest arts space in Europe, the Baltic Centre for Contemporary Art, with a vista that could rival Sydney Harbor's. Cornwall has the Eden Project, the world's largest conservatories, which are set in a former china clay pit and massed to make a giant glass crater.

Elsewhere, on a more sober scale, smaller public buildings are being built; schools and libraries, designed in a muted modernism, use traditional, natural materials, such as wood, stone, and brick. Numerous cultural institutions, particularly in London, have undergone innovative renovations, in part to add visitor-friendly, interactive technology. The Royal Opera House, Tate Modern and Tate Britain, the Great Court at the British Museum, the Queen's Gallery, and the Wellcome Wing at the Science Museum are among the most noteworthy projects that have embraced the new, with a subtle emphasis on complementing the old. Anyone with an interest in architecture should visit the headquarters of the Royal Institute of British Architects (RIBA) in Portland Place, London, for exhibits on buildings great and small, new and old. *Among other buildings to see are Richmond House and the Clore Building at Tate Britain (in London), the campus of Sussex University (outside Brighton), the Royal Regatta Building (Henley), the Sainsbury Centre for the Visual Arts (Norwich), the Lowry Centre (Manchester), and the Burrell Collection (Glasgow).*

BOOKS & MOVIES

Books

Many writers' names have become inextricably linked with the regions in which they set their books or plays. Hardy's Wessex, Daphne Du Maurier's Cornwall, Wordsworth's Lake District, Shakespeare's Arden, and Brontë Country are now evocative catchphrases, treasured by local tourist boards. However hackneyed the tags may be, you *can* still get a heightened insight about an area through the eyes of authors of genius, even though they may have written a century or more ago. Here are a few works that may provide you with an understanding of their authors' loved territory.

Thomas Hardy's novels *The Mayor of Casterbridge, Tess of the d'Urbervilles,* and *Far from the Madding Crowd* (and indeed almost everything he wrote) are solidly based on his Wessex (Dorset) homeland. Daphne Du Maurier had a deep love of Cornwall from her childhood; *Frenchman's Creek, Jamaica Inn,* and *The King's General* all capture the county's Celtic mood. The wildness of Exmoor in Devon is captured in the historical novel *Lorna Doone* by R. D. Blackmore. The Brontë sisters' *Wuthering Heights, The Tenant of Wildfell Hall,* and *Jane Eyre* breathe the sharp air of the moors around the writers' Haworth home. William Wordsworth, who was born at Cockermouth in the Lake District, depicts the area's rugged beauty in many of his poems, especially the *Lyrical Ballads.*

Virginia Woolf's visits to Vita Sackville-West at her ancestral home of Knole, in Sevenoaks, inspired the novel *Orlando.* The stately home is now a National Trust property. The country around Bateman's, near Burwash in East Sussex, the home where Rudyard Kipling lived for more than 30 years, was the inspiration for *Puck of Pook's Hill* and *Rewards and Fairies.* American writer Henry James lived at Lamb House in Rye, also in East Sussex, as did E. F. Benson, whose delicious Lucia novels take place in a thinly disguised version of the town. Bateman's and Lamb House are National Trust buildings.

A highly irreverent and very funny version of academic life, *Porterhouse Blue,* by Tom Sharpe, will guarantee that you look at Oxford and Cambridge with a totally different eye. John Fowles's *The French Lieutenant's Woman,* largely set in Lyme Regis, is full of local color about Dorset.

The late James Herriot's veterinary surgeon books, among them *All Creatures Great and Small,* give evocative accounts of life in the Yorkshire dales during much of the 20th century; the books were made into popular television shows. For a perceptive account of life in the English countryside, try Ronald Blythe's well-regarded *Akenfield: Portrait of an English Village.*

Mysteries are almost a way of life, partly because many of the best English mystery writers set their plots in their home territories. Modern whodunits by P. D. James and Ruth Rendell convey a fine sense of place, and Ellis Peters's Brother Cadfael stories re-create life in medieval Shrewsbury with a wealth of telling detail. Colin Dexter's Inspector Morse mysteries capture the flavor of Oxford's town and gown. There are also always the villages, vicarages, and scandals of Agatha Christie's "Miss Marple" books.

The fans of Arthurian legends can turn to some excellent, imaginative novels that not only tell the stories but also give fine descriptions of the countryside. Among them are *Sword at Sunset,* by Rosemary Sutcliffe, *The Once and Future King,* by T. H. White, and the four Merlin novels by Mary Stewart; *The Crystal Cave, The Hollow Hills, The Last Enchantment,* and *The Wicked Day.* Edward Rutherfurd's historical novels *Sarum, London,* and *The Forest* deal with British history with a grand sweep from the prehistoric past to the present.

An animal's close-to-the-earth viewpoint can reveal all kinds of countryside insights. *Watership Down*, a runaway bestseller about rabbits, was written by Richard Adam in the early '70s. *The Wind in the Willows*, by Kenneth Grahame, gives a vivid impression of the Thames Valley almost 100 years ago, which still holds largely true today. Devon, the northern part in particular, is the setting of Henry Williamson's *Tarka the Otter*, a beloved nature story published in the 1920s; many paths in the region are signposted as part of the Tarka Trail.

Those interested in writers and the surroundings that influenced their works should look at *A Literary Guide to London*, by Ed Glinert, and *The Oxford Literary Guide to the British Isles*, edited by Dorothy Eagle and Hilary Carnell (now out of print). One author currently in vogue is Jane Austen: Janeites will want to read Maggie Lane's *Jane Austen's World* and Nigel Nicolson's wonderful *World of Jane Austen*. For a vast portrait of everyone's favorite English author, dig into Peter Ackroyd's *Dickens*.

Good background books on English history are *The Oxford Illustrated History of Britain*, edited by Kenneth O. Morgan, and *The Story of England*, by Christopher Hibbert. *The Isles*, a history by Norman Davies, challenges conventional Anglocentric assumptions. *The English: A Portrait of a People*, by Jeremy Paxman, examines the concept of Englishness in a changing world. *The London Encyclopaedia*, by Ben Weinreb and Christopher Hibbert, now out of print, is invaluable as a source of information on the capital. Simon Schama's three-volume *History of Britain*, with handsome color illustrations, was written to accompany the BBC–History Channel television series. Peter Ackroyd's illustrated nonfiction *London: A Biography* captures the city's energy and its quirks from prehistory to the present.

The finest book on the country's stately homes is Nigel Nicolson's *Great Houses of Britain*, written for the National Trust (now out of print). Also spectacular is the picture book *Great Houses of Britain and Wales*, by Hugh Montgomery-Massingberd. *The Buildings of England*, written by Nikolaus Pevsner but much updated since his death, is part of a multivolume series, organized by county, which sets out to chronicle in detail every building of any importance. Pevsner's *Best Buildings of Britain* is a grand anthology with lush photographs. New Pevsner Architectural Guides continue to be published. For the golden era of Georgian architecture, check out John Summerson's definitive *Architecture in Britain 1530–1830*.

Simon Jenkins's *England's Thousand Best Churches*, with photographs, describes parish churches (not cathedrals) large and small. The same author's delightful *England's Thousand Best Houses*, also illustrated with photographs, has pithy descriptions (and star ratings) of small and large houses open to the public. Mark Girouard has written several books that are incomparable for their behind-the-scenes perspective on art and architecture: *Life in the English Country House* focuses on houses over the centuries, and *The Victorian Country House* addresses the lifestyles of the rich and famous of the 19th century. For the ultimate look at English villages, see *The Most Beautiful Villages of England*, by James Bentley, with ravishing photographs by Hugh Palmer.

There are many delightful travel books about Britain, including Susan Allen Toth's *England for All Seasons* and *My Love Affair with England*. Bill Bryson's *Notes from a Small Island* is perennially popular. Few of today's authors have managed to top the wit and perception of Henry James's magisterial *English Hours*. As for "the flower of cities all, " *London Perceived* is a classic text by the noted literary critic V. S. Pritchett, and John Russell's *London* is a superlative text written by a particularly eloquent art historian.

Movies

From *Wuthering Heights* to *Jane Eyre,* great classics of literature have been rendered into great classics of film. It's surprising to learn, however, how many of them were creations of Hollywood and not the British film industry (which had its heyday from the 1940s to the 1960s). From Laurence Olivier to Kenneth Branagh, noted director-actors have cross-pollinated the cinema in Britain and the United States.

Films have also produced another phenomenon: they can motivate travelers to visit specific locations and sights in a favorite film. VisitBritain (⊕ www.visitbritain.com) has recognized this by including a movies section on its Web site that identifies key locations and producing "movie maps" with the locations for certain films such as the Harry Potter series. Another Web site, ⊕ www.filmlondon.org.uk, has a section about recent movies filmed in the city.

A survey can begin with the dramas of Shakespeare: Olivier gave the world a memorable *Othello* and *Hamlet,* Orson Welles a moody *Macbeth,* Branagh gave up mod versions of *Hamlet* and *Much Ado About Nothing.* Leonardo DiCaprio graced Australian Baz Luhrmann's contemporary version of *Romeo and Juliet.* Going behind the scenes, so to speak, Tom Stoppard created the Oscar winner *Shakespeare in Love.* Charles Dickens has also provided the foundation for film favorites: David Lean's immortal *Great Expectations,* George Cukor's *David Copperfield,* and *A Christmas Carol,* with Alastair Sim as Scrooge, top this list, which continues to grow with additions such as Douglas McGrath's *Nicholas Nickleby.*

McGrath's *Emma,* starring Gwyneth Paltrow, and Ang Lee's *Sense and Sensibility,* starring Emma Thompson and Kate Winslet, are just two of the recent film versions of Jane Austen's works. Keira Knightley plays Elizabeth Bennet in the latest *Pride and Prejudice* (2005). *Pandaemonium,* about the youthful Wordsworth and Coleridge, is fanciful but has great Lake District scenery and some insight into the poets' early work.

Harry Potter and the Sorcerer's Stone (in Britain, *Harry Potter and the Philosopher's Stone*), based on the wildly popular children's books by J. K. Rowling, was filmed in many British locations, including London, Gloucester, the Cotswolds, Northumbria, and Yorkshire. The second movie, *Harry Potter and the Chamber of Secrets,* used some of the same settings as the first. *Harry Potter and the Prisoner of Azkaban* hit theaters in 2004, *Harry Potter and the Goblet of Fire* in 2005, and *Harry Potter and Order of the Phoenix* in 2007.

The *Da Vinci Code,* the adaptation of Dan Brown's bestselling novel released in 2006, includes scenes filmed in Britain. Lincoln Cathedral will stand in for Westminster Abbey, though. (*Fodor's Guide to the Da Vinci Code* fills you in on the novel's settings and can help you plan a trip.)

Of the film versions of Agatha Christie's books, one is especially treasured: *Murder, She Said,* which starred the inimitable Margaret Rutherford. With its quiet English village setting, harpsichord score, and the dotty Miss Marple as portrayed by Rutherford, this must be the most English of all Christie films.

Lovers of opulence, spectacle, and history have many choices—including Robert Bolt's classic version of Sir Thomas More's life and death, *A Man for All Seasons.* His *Lady Caroline Lamb* is surely the most beautiful historical film ever made. Richard Harris made a stirring Lord Protector in *Cromwell,* and the miniseries on Queen Elizabeth I, starring Glenda Jackson, is a great BBC addition to videos. Elizabeth's adversary came to breathless life in Vanessa Redgrave's rendition of *Mary, Queen of Scots,* certainly one of her finest performances. More recent and a chilling performance of tortuous times is Cate Blanchett as *Elizabeth.* The 2004 movie *Arthur,* with Clive Owen and Keira

Knightley, gives a new spin to Arthurian tales. In 2007, *Miss Potter* will explore the life of the beloved children's book writer and illustrator Beatrix Potter, who had a home in the Lake District; Renée Zellweger plays the lead.

Musicals? Near the top of anyone's list are four films set in England—three of them in Hollywood's England—that rank among the greatest musicals of all time: Walt Disney's *Mary Poppins*, George Cukor's *My Fair Lady*, Sir Carol Reed's Oscar-winner *Oliver!*, and—yeah, yeah, yeah!—the Beatles' *A Hard Day's Night*, a British production.

If you're seeking a look at contemporary England, you might view *My Beautiful Laundrette*, about Asians in London or *Secrets and Lies*, about a dysfunctional London family. Manchester's rocking music scene from the 1970s to early 1990s is the subject of the well-named *24 Hour Party People. Closer,* adapted from Patrick Marber's play, takes a dark look at love in modern London. Woody Allen set his 2005 drama *Match Point* in London; there are gorgeous shots of historic and modern locations.

You might lighten up with *The Full Monty,* about six former steelworkers in Sheffield who become strippers, or one of numerous romantic comedies: *Notting Hill,* with Julia Roberts and Hugh Grant; Hugh Grant again in *Four Weddings and a Funeral;* Gwyneth Paltrow in *Sliding Doors;* and Renée Zellweger (and Hugh Grant, again) in *Bridget Jones's Diary* and *Bridget Jones: The Edge of Reason.* Grant is also good in *About a Boy,* the film version of Nick Hornby's book about a cynical Londoner who learns about commitment. *Calendar Girls,* filmed in rural Yorkshire, follows the true story of middle-aged women who raise money for charity with an (almost) bare-all calendar.

Quintessentially British are some comedies of the 1950s and 1960s: Alec Guinness's *Kind Hearts and Coronets,* Peter Sellers's *The Mouse That Roared,* and Tony Richardson's Oscar-winner and cinematic style-setter, *Tom Jones,* starring Albert Finney, are best bets. In 2001 American director Robert Altman took a biting look at the country's class system in *Gosford Park,* a country-house murder mystery set in the 1930s that stars mostly British actors, including Jeremy Northam and Maggie Smith. A more staid, upstairs-downstairs look at the class system is the film of the novel *The Remains of the Day,* featuring Anthony Hopkins as the stalwart butler, with Emma Thompson. Today some people's visions of turn-of-the-last-century England have been captured by the Merchant and Ivory films, notably their *Howard's End,* which won many awards.

CHRONOLOGY

3000 BC   First building of Stonehenge (later building 2100–1900 BC)

54 BC–AD 43   Julius Caesar's exploratory invasion of England. Romans conquer England, led by Emperor Claudius

60   Boudicca, a native British queen, razes the first Roman London (Londinium)

122–27   Emperor Hadrian completes the Roman conquest and builds a wall across the north to keep back the Scottish Picts

300–50   Height of Roman colonization, administered from such towns as Verulamium (St. Albans), Colchester, Lincoln, and York

410   Roman rule of Britain ends, after waves of invasion by Jutes, Angles, and Saxons

ca. 490   Possible period for the legendary King Arthur, who may have led resistance to Anglo-Saxon invaders; in 500 the Battle of Badon is fought

550–700   Seven Anglo-Saxon kingdoms emerge—Essex, Wessex, Sussex, Kent, Anglia, Mercia, and Northumbria—to become the core of English social and political organization for centuries

597   St. Augustine arrives in Canterbury to Christianize Britain

871–99   Alfred the Great, king of Wessex, unifies the English against Viking invaders, who are then confined to the Northeast

1040   Edward the Confessor moves his court to Westminster and founds Westminster Abbey

1066   William, duke of Normandy, invades, defeats King Harold at the Battle of Hastings, and is crowned William I at Westminster in December

1086   Domesday Book completed, a survey of all taxpayers in England, drawn up to assist administration of the realm

1167   Oxford University founded

1170   Thomas à Becket murdered in Canterbury; his shrine becomes center for international pilgrimage

1189   Richard the Lionhearted embarks on the Third Crusade

1209   Cambridge University founded

1215   King John forced to sign Magna Carta at Runnymede. It promulgates basic principles of English law: no taxation except through Parliament, trial by jury, and property guarantees

1272–1307   Reign of Edward I, a great legislator; in 1282–83 he conquers Wales and reinforces his rule with a chain of massive castles

1337–1453   Edward III claims the French throne, starting the Hundred Years War. In spite of dramatic English victories—1346 at Crécy, 1356 at

Poitiers, 1415 at Agincourt—the long war of attrition ends with the French driving the English out from everywhere but Calais, which finally falls in 1558

1348–49 The Black Death (bubonic plague) reduces the population of Britain from around 4¼ million to around 2½ million; decades of social unrest follow

1399 Henry Bolingbroke (Henry IV) deposes and murders his cousin Richard II; beginning of the rivalry between houses of York and Lancaster

1402–10 The Welsh, led by Owain Glendŵr, rebel against English rule

1455–85 The Wars of the Roses; the York-Lancaster struggle erupts into civil war

1477 William Caxton prints first book in England

1485 Henry Tudor (Henry VII) defeats Richard III at the Battle of Bosworth and founds the Tudor dynasty; he suppresses private armies, develops administrative efficiency and royal absolutism

1530s Under Henry VIII the Reformation takes hold; he dissolves the monasteries and finally demolishes medieval England, replacing it with a restructured society. The land goes to wealthy merchant families, creating new gentry

1555 During the reign of papal supporter Mary I (reigned 1553–58), Protestant bishops Ridley and Latimer are burned in Oxford; in 1556 Archbishop Cranmer is burned

1558–1603 Reign of Elizabeth I: Protestantism reestablished; Drake, Raleigh, and other freebooters establish English claims in the West Indies and North America

1568 Mary, Queen of Scots, flees to England; in 1587 she is executed

1588 Spanish Armada fails to invade England

1603 James VI of Scotland, son of Mary, Queen of Scots and Lord Darnley, becomes James I of England

1605 Guy Fawkes and friends plot to blow up Parliament

1611 King James Authorized Version of the Bible published

1620 Pilgrims sail from Plymouth on the *Mayflower* and settle in what becomes New England

1629 Charles I dissolves Parliament, decides to rule alone

1642–49 Civil War between the Royalists and Parliamentarians (Cavaliers and Roundheads); the Parliamentarians win

1649 Charles I executed; England is a republic

1653 Oliver Cromwell becomes Lord Protector, establishing England's only dictatorship

1660   The Restoration: Charles II restored to the throne; accepts limits to royal power

1666   The Great Fire: London burns for three days; its medieval center is destroyed

1689   Accession of William III (of Orange) and his wife, Mary II, as joint monarchs; royal power further limited

1700s   Under the first four Georges, the Industrial Revolution develops and with it Britain's domination of world trade

1707   Union of English and Scots parliaments under Queen Anne

1714   The German Hanoverians succeed to the throne; George I's deficiency in English leads to the establishment of a council of ministers, the beginning of the cabinet system of government

1715, 1745–46   Two Jacobite rebellions fail to restore the House of Stuart to the throne; in 1746 Charles Edward Stuart (Bonnie Prince Charlie) is decisively defeated at Culloden Moor in Scotland

1756–63   Seven Years' War; Britain wins colonial supremacy from the French in Canada and India

1775–83   Britain loses the American colonies that become the United States

1795–1815   Britain and its allies defeat France in the Napoleonic Wars; in 1805, Admiral Lord Nelson is killed at Trafalgar; in 1815, Battle of Waterloo is fought

1801   Union with Ireland

1811–20   Prince Regent rules during his father's (George III) madness, the Regency period

1825   The Stockton to Darlington railway, the world's first passenger line with regular service, is established

1832   The Reform Bill extends the franchise, limiting the power of the great landowners

1837–1901   During the long reign of Victoria, Britain becomes the world's richest country, and the British Empire reaches its height; railways, canals, and telegraph lines draw Britain into one vast manufacturing net

1851   The Great Exhibition, Prince Albert's brainchild, is held in the Crystal Palace, Hyde Park

1861   Prince Albert dies from typhoid fever at 42

1887   Victoria celebrates her Golden Jubilee; in 1901 she dies, marking the end of an era

1914–18   World War I: fighting against Germany, Britain loses a whole generation, with 750, 000 men killed in trench warfare alone; enormous debts and inept diplomacy in the postwar years undermine Britain's position as a world power

1919   Ireland declares independence from England; bloody Black-and-Tan struggle is one result

1936   Edward VIII abdicates to marry American divorcée Wallis Simpson

1939–45   World War II: Britain declares war on Germany when Germany invades Poland in September 1939. London badly damaged during the Blitz, September '40–May '41; Britain's economy shattered

1945   Labour wins a landslide victory; stays in power for six years, transforming Britain into a welfare state

1952   Queen Elizabeth II accedes to the throne

1973   Britain joins the European Economic Community after referendum

1975   Britain begins to pump North Sea oil

1981   Marriage of Prince Charles and Lady Diana Spencer

1982   Falklands regained in war with Argentina

1987   Conservatives under Margaret Thatcher win a third term in office

1990   John Major takes over as prime minister

1991   The Persian Gulf War

1992   Great Britain and European countries join to form one European Community (EC), whose name changed to European Union in 1993

1994   The Channel Tunnel opens a direct rail link between Britain and Europe

1996   The Prince and Princess of Wales receive a divorce

1997   "New Labour" comes to power, with Tony Blair as prime minister. Diana, Princess of Wales, dies at 36 in a car crash in Paris. She is buried at Althorp in Northamptonshire

1999   London welcomes the new century on December 31, with the gala opening of the Millennium Dome in Greenwich

2001   The Millennium Dome closes. Prime Minister Tony Blair is elected to a second term

2002   Queen Elizabeth celebrates her Golden Jubilee. Queen Elizabeth (the Queen Mother) and Princess Margaret die. Euro coins and notes enter circulation as the currency of 12 European Union nations, but Britain continues to ponder adopting the euro

2003   Britain joins U.S. and coalition forces in invading Iraq

2005   Prince Charles and Camilla Parker Bowles wed in a civil ceremony. The ban on the traditional sport of fox hunting with hounds is put into effect. Tony Blair is elected to a historic third term as prime minister. London wins the bid for the 2012 Olympics in July; the same week, terrorists explode bombs in three tube stops and on one bus

ENGLISH VOCABULARY

Americans and the English may speak the same language, but some phrases definitely got lost in translation while traveling across the Atlantic.

British English	American English

Basic Terms & Everyday Items

bill	check
flat	apartment
lift	elevator
holiday	vacation
nappie	diaper
note	bill (currency)
plaster	Band-Aid
queue	line
row	argument
rubbish	trash
stalls	orchestra seats
toilet/loo/WC	bathroom
tin	can
torch	flashlight

Clothing

braces	suspenders
bum bag	fanny pack
dressing gown	robe
handbag	purse
jumper	sweater
pants/undies	underpants/briefs
rucksack	backpack
suspender	garter
tights	pantyhose
trainers	sneakers
trousers	pants
vest	undershirt
waistcoat	vest

Transportation

bonnet	hood
boot	trunk

British English	American English
coach	long-distance bus
pavement	sidewalk
petrol	gas
pram	baby carriage
puncture	flat
windscreen	windshield

Food

afters	dessert
aubergine	eggplant
banger	sausage
biscuit	cookie
chips	fries
courgette	zucchini
crisps	potato chips
jam	jelly
jelly	Jello
pips	seeds
pudding	dessert
rocket	arugula
spud	potato
starter	appetizer
sweet	candy

Slang

all right	hi there
bird	woman
bloke, chap	guy
cheers	thank you
chuffed	pleased
guv'nor, gaffer	boss
hard	tough
mate	buddy
ta	thank you
sound	good
wicked	cool

SMART TRAVEL TIPS

There are planners and there are those who, excuse the pun, fly by the seat of their pants. We happily place ourselves among the planners. Our writers and editors try to anticipate all the issues you may face before and during any journey, and then they do their research. This section is the product of their efforts. Use it to get excited about your trip to England and Wales, to inform your travel planning, or to guide you on the road should the seat of your pants start to feel threadbare.

AIR TRAVEL

Flying time to London is about 6½ hours from New York, 7½ hours from Chicago, 9½ hours from Dallas, 10 hours from Los Angeles, and 21½ hours from Sydney.

CARRIERS

British Airways is the national flag carrier and offers mostly nonstop flights from 18 U.S. cities to Heathrow and Gatwick airports outside London, along with flights to Manchester and Birmingham. It offers myriad add-on options that help bring down ticket costs. In addition, it has a vast program of discount airfare-hotel packages. Britain-based Virgin Atlantic is a strong competitor in terms of packages. London is a very popular destination, so many U.S. carriers have flights and packages there, too.

Because England is such a small country, internal air travel is much less important than it is in the United States. For trips of less than 200 mi, the train is often quicker, with rail stations more centrally located. Flying tends to cost more, but for longer trips, air travel has a considerable time advantage (you need to factor in time to get to and from the airport, though).

British Airways operates shuttle services between Heathrow or Gatwick and Manchester. Passengers can simply turn up and get a flight (usually hourly) without booking. bmi/British Midland operates from Heathrow to Leeds and Manchester, as well as to Washington, D.C., Chicago, Las Vegas, and major cities in eastern Canada; it also serves Chicago, Las Vegas, and Toronto from Manchester.

Air Travel
Airports
Bike Travel
Boat & Ferry Travel
Business Hours
Bus Travel
Car Rental
Car Travel
The Channel Tunnel
Computers on the Road
Cruise Travel
Customs & Duties
Discounts & Deals
Eating Out
Electricity
Emergencies
Etiquette & Behavior
Health
Holidays
Insurance
Lodging
Mail & Shipping
Media
Money Matters
Packing
Passports & Visas
Phones
Restrooms
Safety
Shopping
Sports & Outdoors
Taxes
Time
Tipping
Tours & Packages
Train Travel
Travel Agencies
Visitor Information
Web Sites

Low-cost airlines such as easyJet, bmi baby, and Ryanair offer flights within the United Kingdom as well as to cities in Ireland and continental Europe. Prices are low, but these airlines usually use satellite cities and fly out of smaller British airports such as Stansted and Luton (both near London). On the opposite end of the price spectrum, Maxjet and Eos offer more expensive service (between premium economy and business class) for travelers willing to pay for more comfortable flights.

⇘ To & from England **Aer Lingus** ☏ 800/474-7424, 0845/084-4444 in London ⊕ www.aerlingus.com to Heathrow, Gatwick. **American Airlines** ☏ 800/433-7300, 020/7365-0777 in London ⊕ www.aa.com to Heathrow, Gatwick, Manchester, Newcastle. **bmi/British Midland** ☏ 800/788-0555, 020/8745-7321 in London ⊕ www.flybmi.com. **British Airways** ☏ 800/247-9297, 0845/773-3377 in London ⊕ www.britishairways.com to Heathrow, Gatwick. **Continental** ☏ 800/231-0856, 0800/776464 in London ⊕ www.continental.com to Heathrow, Bristol, Gatwick. **Delta** ☏ 800/241-4141, 0800/414767 in London ⊕ www.delta.com to Gatwick. **Eos** ☏ 888/357-3677, 0800/019-6468 in London ⊕ www.eosairlines.com from New York to London Stansted. **Maxjet** ☏ 888/435-9629, 0800/023-4300 in London ⊕ www.maxjet.com from Washington and New York to London Stansted. **Northwest Airlines** ☏ 800/447-4747, 0870/507-4074 in London ⊕ www.nwa.com to Gatwick. **United** ☏ 800/538-2929, 0845/844-4777 in London ⊕ www.ual.com to Heathrow. **US Airways** ☏ 800/622-1015, 0845/600-3300 in London ⊕ www.usairways.com to Gatwick. **Virgin Atlantic** ☏ 800/862-8621, 01293/747-747 in London ⊕ www.virgin-atlantic.com to Heathrow, Gatwick.

⇘ Within England & to Europe **bmi baby** ☏ 0870/264-2229 in London ⊕ www.bmibaby.com. **easyJet** ☏ 0870/600-0000 in London ⊕ www.easyjet.com. **Ryanair** ☏ 0870/246-0000 in London ⊕ www.ryanair.com.

CHECK-IN & BOARDING

Double-check your flight times, especially if you made your reservations far in advance. Airlines change their schedules, and alerts may not reach you. Always **bring a government-issued photo ID to the airport** (even when it's not required, a passport is best), and **arrive when you need to and not before.** Check-in usually at least an hour before domestic flights and two to three hours for international flights. But many airlines have more stringent advance check-in requirements at some busy airports. The TSA estimates the waiting time for security at most major airports and publishes the information on its Web site. Note that if you aren't at the gate at least 10 minutes before your flight is scheduled to take off (sometimes earlier), you won't be allowed to board.

Don't stand in a line if you don't have to. Buy an e-ticket, check-in at an electronic kiosk, or—even better—check-in on your airline's Web site before you leave home. If you don't need to check luggage, you could bypass all but the security lines. These days, most domestic airline tickets are electronic; international tickets may be either electronic or paper.

You usually pay a surcharge (usually at least $25) to get a paper ticket, and its sole advantage is that it may be easier to endorse over to another airline if your flight is cancelled and the airline with which you booked can't accommodate you on another flight. With an e-ticket, the only thing you receive is an e-mailed receipt citing your itinerary and reservation and ticket numbers. Be sure to carry this with you as you'll need it to get past security. If you lose your receipt, though, you can simply print out another copy or ask the airline to do it for you at check-in.

Particularly during busy travel seasons and around holiday periods, if a flight is oversold, the gate agent will usually ask for volunteers and will offer some sort of compensation if you are willing to take a different flight. **Know your rights.** If you are bumped from a flight *involuntarily,* the airline must give you some kind of compensation if an alternate flight can't be found within one hour. If your flight is delayed because of something within the airline's control (so bad weather doesn't count), then the airline has a responsibility to get you to your destination on the same day, even if they have to book you on another airline and in an upgraded class if necessary. Read your airline's Contract of

Carriage; it's usually buried somewhere on the airline's Web site.

Be prepared to quickly adjust your plans by programming a few numbers into your cell: your airline, an airport hotel or two, your destination hotel, your car service, and/or your travel agent. Bring snacks, water, and sufficient diversions, and you'll be covered if you get stuck in the airport, on the tarmac, or even in the air during turbulence.

If you're flying to Europe from England, plan to arrive at the airport two hours in advance.

CUTTING COSTS

It's always good to **comparison shop.** Web sites (aka consolidators) and travel agents can have different arrangements with the airlines and offer different prices for exactly the same flight and day. Certain Web sites have tracking features that will e-mail you immediately when good deals are posted. Other people prefer to stick with one or two frequent-flier programs, racking up free trips and accumulating perks. On some airlines, perks include a special reservations number, early boarding, access to upgrades, and more roomy economy-class seating.

Check early and often. Start looking for cheap fares up to a year in advance, and keep looking until you see something you can live with; you never know when a good deal may pop up. That said, **jump on the good deals.** Waiting even a few minutes might mean paying more. For most people, saving money is more important than flexibility, so the more affordable nonrefundable tickets work. Just remember that you'll pay dearly (often as much as $100) if you must change your travel plans. Check on prices for departures at different times of the day and to and from alternate airports, and look for departures on Tuesday, Wednesday, and Thursday, typically the cheapest days to travel. Remember to **weigh your options,** though. A cheaper flight might have a long layover rather than being nonstop, or landing at a secondary airport might substantially increase your ground transportation costs.

Note that many airline Web sites—and most ads—show prices *without* taxes and surcharges. Don't buy until you know the full price. Government taxes add up quickly. Also **watch those ticketing fees.** Surcharges are usually added when you buy your ticket anywhere but on an airline's own Web site. (By the way, that includes on the phone–even if you call the airline directly—and for paper tickets regardless of how you book.)

If you're in England and you want to fly to Europe, check out Cheap Flights. It pools all flights available and then directs you to a phone number or site to purchase tickets.

Look into air passes. Many airlines, singly or in collaboration, offer discount air passes that allow foreigners to travel economically in a particular country or region. These visitor passes usually must be reserved and purchased before you leave home. Information about passes often can be found on most airlines' international Web pages, which tend to be aimed at travelers from outside the carrier's home country. Also, try typing the name of the pass into a search engine, or search for "pass" within the carrier's Web site.

🔢 Online Consolidators AirlineConsolidator.com ⊕ www.airlineconsolidator.com, for international tickets. Best Fares ⊕ www.bestfares.com; $59.90 annual membership. Cheap Flights ⊕ www. cheapflights.com. Cheap Tickets ⊕ www. cheaptickets.com. Expedia ⊕ www.expedia.com. Hotwire ⊕ www.hotwire.com. lastminute.com ⊕ www.lastminute.com specializes in last-minute travel; the main site is for the U.K., but it has a link to a U.S. site. Luxury Link ⊕ www.luxurylink.com has auctions (surprisingly good deals) as well as offers at the high-end side of travel. Orbitz ⊕ www. orbitz.com. Onetravel.com ⊕ www.onetravel.com. Priceline.com ⊕ www.priceline.com. Travelocity ⊕ www.travelocity.com.

🔢 Discount Airfares & Passes British Airways ☎ 800/247-9297, 0845/773-3377 in London ⊕ www.britishairways.com. DER Travel Services ✉ 9501 W. Devon Ave., Rosemont, IL 60018 ☎ 800/ 782-2424 📠 800/282-7474 for information, 800/ 860-9944 for brochures ⊕ www.der.com. Flight-Pass EuropebyAir, ☎ 888/387-2479 ⊕ www. europebyair.com.

ENJOYING THE FLIGHT

Get the seat you want. Avoid those on the aisle directly across from the lavatories. Most frequent fliers say those are even worse than the the seats that don't recline (e.g., those in the back row and those in front of a bulkhead). For more legroom, you can request emergency-aisle seats, but only do so if you're capable of moving the 35- to 60-point airplane exit door—a Federal Aviation Administration requirement of passengers in these seats. Seats behind a bulkhead also offer more legroom, but they don't have under-seat storage. Often, you can pick a seat when you buy your ticket on an airline's Web site. But it's not always a guarantee, particularly if the airline changes the plane after you book your ticket; check back before you leave. Seat-Guru.com has more information about specific seat configurations.

Fewer airlines are providing free food for passengers in economy class. **Don't go hungry.** If you're scheduled to fly during meal times, verify if your airline offers anything to eat; even when it does, be prepared to pay. If you have dietary concerns, request special meals. These can be vegetarian, low-cholesterol, or kosher, for example. It's a good idea to pack some healthful snacks and a small (plastic) bottle of water in your carry-on bag.

Ask the airline about its children's menus, activities, and fares. On some lines infants and toddlers fly for free if they sit on a parent's lap, and older children fly for half price in their own seats. Also inquire about policies involving car seats; having one may limit where you can sit. While you're at it, ask about seat-belt extenders for car seats. And note that you can't count on a flight attendant to automatically produce an extender; you may have to inquire about it again when you board.

HOW TO COMPLAIN

If your baggage goes astray or your flight goes awry, complain right away. Most carriers require that you **file a claim immediately.** The Aviation Consumer Protection Division of the Department of Transportation publishes *Fly-Rights,* which discusses airlines and consumer issues and is available online. You can also find articles and information on mytravelrights.com, the Web site of the nonprofit Consumer Travel Rights Center.

🔝 **Airline Complaints Office of Aviation Enforcement and Proceedings** (Aviation Consumer Protection Division) ☎ 202/366-2220 ⊕ airconsumer.ost. dot.gov. **Federal Aviation Administration Consumer Hotline** ☎ 866/835-5322 ⊕ www.faa.gov.

AIRPORTS

Most international flights to London arrive at either Heathrow Airport (LHR), 15 mi west of London, or at Gatwick Airport (LGW), 27 mi south of the capital. Most flights from the United States go to Heathrow, with Terminals 3 and 4 handling transatlantic flights (British Airways uses Terminal 4). Gatwick is London's second gateway, serving 21 U.S. destinations. A third, newer airport, Stansted (STN), is 35 mi northeast of the city. It handles mainly European and domestic traffic. Luton Airport (LLA), 30 mi north of the city, serves British and European destinations. Luton is the hub for the low-cost easyJet airline. Manchester (MAN) in northwest England handles some bmi/British Midland flights from the United States. Birmingham (BHX), in the Midlands, handles mainly European and British flights as well as flights from Chicago, Denver, Newark, New York, and Orlando. Bristol (BRS) has limited service from New York, as does Newcastle (NCL).

Heathrow and Gatwick are enormous and can seem like shopping malls where planes just happen to land. Heathrow in particular may tempt shoppers, with designer boutiques, jewelry stores, Harrods outlets, and enough perfume to scent half the world. Gatwick's shopping options are slightly less overwhelming, but can easily while away a few hours of flight delay. Both airports have bars and pubs, and other dining options. In 2006, Yotel was opening pod hotels in Heathrow and Gatwick with cabin-size rooms to be booked by four-hour blocks or overnight. By comparison, other airports, including Manchester, Birmingham, and London's Luton and Stansted, have much more limited shopping and dining options; a delay of a few hours may seem like years.

🔲 **Airlines & Airports** **Airline and Airport Links. com** ⊕ www.airlineandairportlinks.com has links to many of the world's airlines and airports. **Birmingham Airport** ☎ 0870/733–5511 ⊕ www.bhx.com. **Heathrow Airport** ☎ 0870/000–0123 ⊕ www.baa. co.uk/heathrow. **Gatwick Airport** ☎ 0870/000–2468 ⊕ www.baa.co.uk/gatwick. **Luton Airport** ☎ 01582/405100 ⊕ www.london-luton.co.uk. **Manchester Airport** ☎ 0161/489–3000 ⊕ www. manairport.co.uk. **Stansted Airport** ☎ 0870/000–0303 ⊕ www.baa.co.uk/stansted.

🔲 **Airline-Security Issues** **Transportation Security Agency** ⊕ www.tsa.gov/public has answers for almost every question that might come up.

TRANSFERS BETWEEN AIRPORTS

See London Essentials *in* Chapter 1 for information on transportation between the London airports.

GROUND TRANSPORTATION

See London Essentials *in* Chapter 1 for information on transportation between London and the airport. Essentials sections in other chapters cover ground transportation from other cities.

BIKE TRAVEL

Bikes are banned from freeways and most divided highways or main trunk roads, but on side roads and country lanes, the bike is one of the best ways to explore Britain. The National Cycle Network, a work in progress, covers about 7,000 mi of cycling and walking routes. Some routes are in towns and parts of the countryside; for example, in the Peak District National Park, bikes can be rented by the day for use on special traffic-free trails. Cyclists can legally use public bridleways—green, unsurfaced tracks reserved for horses, walkers, and cyclists. Some former railway lines have become popular bike paths, such as the Tarka Trail in North Devon and the Camel Trail in Cornwall. Bikes, from racing to mountain, are usually available for rental, and prices vary by area, anywhere from £3 to £5 an hour to £7–£20 for a full day. A deposit of £25 or more is often required. For night cycling, the law requires a full set of reflectors on the wheels and pedals, and lights at the back and front.

Sustrans (a nonprofit organization concerned with sustainable transportation) and the Cyclists' Touring Club (CTC, a national organization; ⇨ Sports & Outdoors) can provide route guides and information on cycling in England. For maps, the Landranger by Ordnance Survey series costs £6.49 a map and covers the country in scale 1:50,000 in more than 30 editions. In London, Stanfords bookshop stocks a vast selection of maps and has a telephone and Internet ordering service. The Highway Code booklet (£1.50), available at a service station, newsstand, or bookstore, contains information for cyclists.

Call tourist information offices for lists of local rental outlets, or contact the Britain Visitor Centre in London. The Yellow Pages classified telephone directory lists cycle rentals.

🔲 **Bike Maps & Travel Information** **Cyclists' Touring Club** ☎ 0870/873–0060 ⊕ www.ctc.org.uk. **Landranger by Ordnance Survey** ☎ 08456/050505 ⊕ www.ordnancesurvey.co.uk. **National Cycle Network (Sustrans)** ☎ 0117/926–8893 ⊕ www.sustrans.org.uk. **Stanfords** ✉ 12–14 Long Acre, London WC2E 9LP ☎ 020/7836–1321 ⊕ www. stanfords.co.uk.

🔲 **Bike Rentals** **Britain Visitor Centre** ✉ 1 Regent St., London SW1Y 4NX ☎ No phone ⊕ www. visitbritain.com. **Yellow Pages** ⊕ www.yell.co.uk.

BIKES IN FLIGHT

Most airlines accommodate bikes as luggage, provided they are dismantled and boxed; check with individual airlines about packing requirements. Some airlines sell bike boxes, which are often free at bike shops, for about $20 (bike bags can be considerably more expensive). International travelers often can substitute a bike for a piece of checked luggage at no charge; otherwise, the cost is about $100. Most U.S. and Canadian airlines charge $40–$80 each way.

BIKES ON TRAINS

Most trains allow bicycles on board for free or for up to £3 per journey. Bicycles are generally not allowed during rush hour (between 8 AM and 10 AM, and between 4:30 PM and 6:30 PM), particularly in cities. Train companies in London have been cracking down on that rule, so ask before taking your bike on with you, or you could face a fine. Folding bikes are always allowed by virtually every train company, as they take up little space.

BOAT & FERRY TRAVEL

Ferries, hovercraft, and Seacats (a kind of ferry) travel regular routes to France, Spain, Ireland, and Scandinavia. There are also numerous canal boats through the countryside and to the coast (⇨ Sports & Outdoors).

Hoverspeed provides fast travel to France and Belgium. P&O runs ferries between Belgium, Great Britain, Ireland, France, the Netherlands, and Spain. DFDS Seaways covers Denmark, Holland, Germany, Norway, Poland, and Sweden. Stena Line serves Ireland and the Netherlands.

FARES & SCHEDULES

For fares and schedules, contact ferry companies directly. Travelers checks (in pounds), cash, and major credit cards are accepted for payments. Prices vary; booking early ensures cheaper fares, but also ask about special deals. The Ferry Information Service can help with questions about routes and overviews of ferry companies. Seaview is a comprehensive online ferry- and cruise-booking portal for Great Britain and Continental Europe.

▨ Boat & Ferry Information **DFDS Seaways** ☏ 01255/240240 or 0870/533-3000 ⊕ www. dfdsseaways.co.uk. **Ferry Information Service** ☏ 020/7436-2449 ⊕ www.ferryinformationservice. co.uk. **Hoverspeed** ☏ 0870/240-8070 ⊕ www. hoverspeed.com. **P&O Irish Sea** ☏ 0870/242-4777 ⊕ www.poirishsea.com. **P&O North Sea** ☏ 0870/ 129-6002 ⊕ www.ponsf.com. **P&O Portsmouth** ☏ 0870/242-4999 ⊕ www.poportsmouth.com. **P&O Stena Line** ☏ 0870/600-0600 ⊕ www.posl. com. **Seaview** ⊕ www.seaview.co.uk. **Stena Line** ☏ 0870/570-7070 ⊕ www.stenaline.co.uk.

BUSINESS HOURS

BANKS & OFFICES

Most banks are open weekdays from 9:30 until 3:30 or 4:30. Some have Thursday evening hours, and a few are open Saturday morning. Many offices are open weekdays 9:30–5:30. *See* Mail & Shipping for post-office hours.

GAS STATIONS

Most gas stations (called petrol stations) in major cities and towns and on busy motorways are open seven days, 24 hours. In small towns or out in the countryside and off the motorways, hours vary considerably but are usually daily 8 AM to 8 PM.

MUSEUMS & SIGHTS

The major national museums and galleries are open daily from 9 until 6, including lunchtime, but have shorter hours on Sunday. Regional museums are usually closed Monday and have shorter hours in winter. In London, many museums are open late one evening a week, usually Wednesday or Thursday.

PHARMACIES

British pharmacies are called chemists. Independent chemist shops are generally open Monday through Saturday 9:30 to 5:30, although in larger cities some stay open until 10 PM; local newspapers list which pharmacies are open late. In London, the leading chain drugstore, Boots, is open until 6; the Oxford Street and Piccadilly Circus branches are open daily, and until 8 PM Thursday.

SHOPS

Usual business hours are Monday through Saturday 9 to 5:30, Sunday noon to 4. Outside the main centers, most shops close at 1 PM once a week, often Wednesday or Thursday. In small villages, many also close for lunch and do not open on Sunday at all. In large cities—especially London—department stores stay open late (usually until 7:30 or 8) one night a week, usually Thursday. On national holidays, most stores are closed, and over the Christmas holidays, most restaurants are closed as well (⇨ Holidays).

BUS TRAVEL

Britain has a comprehensive bus (short-haul) and coach (the British term for long-distance buses) network that offers an inexpensive way of seeing England and Wales. National Express is the major coach operator, and Victoria Coach Station in London is the hub of the National Express network, serving around 1,200 destinations within Great Britain and, via

Eurolines, continental Europe. Tickets (payable by most major credit cards; reservations are advisable) and information are available from any of the company's 2,500 agents nationwide, including offices at London's Heathrow and Gatwick airport coach stations. Green Line is the next-largest national service; although it serves fewer destinations, airports and major tourist towns are covered.

A newcomer on the bus travel scene, Megabus has been packing in budget travelers, with special cross-country fares for as little as £1 per person. Its double-decker buses serve cities across Britain. Though relatively new, it has been giving National Express a run for its money with rock-bottom fares, new buses, and a cheerful attitude. Megabus does not accommodate wheelchairs, and the company strictly limits luggage to one checked piece per person, and one piece of hand luggage. In London, the company's buses depart from the Green Line bus stand at Victoria Station.

Coach tickets can be as low as half the price of a train ticket, and buses are just as comfortable as trains. However, most bus services take twice as long as trains. Nearly all bus services have a no-smoking policy, and National Express has onboard refreshments and toilets. There is only one class of service.

Double-decker buses make up many of the extensive networks of local bus services, run by private companies. Check with the local bus station or tourist information center for bus schedules. Most companies offer day or week Explorer or Rover unlimited-travel tickets, and those in popular tourist areas invariably operate special scenic tours in summer. The top deck of a stately double-decker bus is a great place from which to view the countryside.

CUTTING COSTS

National Express offers discount Brit Explorer passes to non-British passport holders. The passes start at £79 for 7 days of travel, and must be bought in person at a Brit Explorer shop—these are scattered around the country including locations at Heathrow Airport and Victoria Station in London. A Discount Coach Card for students, 16–25, and over-50, which costs £10 and is good for one year, qualifies you for 20% to 30% discounts off many fares. Most companies offer a discount for children under 15.

Apex tickets (cheap advance-purchase tickets) save money on standard fares, and traveling midweek is cheaper than over weekends and at holiday periods. Tourist Trail Passes, sold by National Express, offer great savings if you plan to tour Britain; they can be bought in advance. Prices run from £49 for 2 days of unlimited travel within 3 days to £205 for 15 days of unlimited travel within two months.

FARES & SCHEDULES

You can find schedules online, pick them up from tourist information offices, or get them by phone from the various bus companies. Fares vary based on how close to the time of travel you book—Megabus tickets, for example, are cheaper if ordered in advance online—so contact the individual companies either online or by phone for ticket prices.

PAYING

Tickets for National Express can be bought from the Victoria, Heathrow, or Gatwick coach stations, or by phone with a credit card, or via the National Express Web site, or from most British travel agencies. Tickets for Megabus must be purchased online in advance, or by phone (avoid this, as the surcharge is at least 60p per minute). Surcharges for tickets bought online in advance rarely rise above £5.

Most companies will accept MasterCard and Visa for advance purchases, but cash only if you're purchasing your tickets on the bus on the day of travel.

RESERVATIONS

There are no surcharges for booking in advance; in fact, it's a much better idea, as busy routes and times can book up quickly. With most bus companies (National Express, Megabus, Green Line), if you pay in advance your receipt can be e-mailed to you, and your name is placed on a list given to the bus driver, who then checks you off when you arrive. This makes it easy for international travelers who cannot have their tickets mailed to them.

🚌 **Bus Information Green Line** ☎ 0870/608-7261 ⊕ www.greenline.co.uk. **Megabus** ☎ 0900/160-0900 ⊕ www.megabus.com, 60p per minute for calls from landlines in U.K. **National Express** ☎ 0870/580-8080 ⊕ www.nationalexpress.com. **Victoria Coach Station** ☎ 020/7730-3466 for station, 020/7730-3499 for booking ⊕ www.tfl.gov.uk/vcs.

CAR RENTAL

Request car seats and extras such as GPS when you book, and make sure that a confirmed reservation guarantees you a car. Agencies sometimes overbook, particularly for busy weekends and holiday periods. Rates are sometimes—but not always—better if you book in advance or reserve through a rental agency's Web site. There are other reasons to book ahead, though: for popular destinations, during busy times of the year, or to ensure that you get a certain type of car (vans, SUVs, exotic sports cars).

In England and Wales your own driver's license is acceptable. However, you may choose to get an International Driving Permit (IDP), which can be used only in conjunction with a valid driver's license and which translates your license into 10 languages. Check the AAA Web site for more info as well as for IDPs ($10) themselves. These permits are universally recognized, and having one in your wallet may save you a problem with the local authorities. Companies may not rent cars to people who are under 23 or over 75.

Rental rates vary widely, beginning at £25 ($48) a day and £160 ($300) a week for a midsized car, usually with manual transmission. Air-conditioning and unlimited mileage generally come with larger automatic transmission cars. As in the United States, prices are higher at times of heaviest use—summer, and holidays. Car seats for children usually cost about £20 ($36) extra. Adding one extra driver is usually included in the original rental price.

CUTTING COSTS

Really weigh your options. Find out if a credit card you carry or organization or frequent-renter program to which you belong has a discount program. And check that such discounts really are the best deal. You can often do better with special weekend or weekly rates offered by a rental agency. (And even if you only want to rent for five or six days, ask if you can get the weekly rate; it may very well be cheaper than the daily rate for that period of time.).

Price local car-rental companies as well as the majors. Also investigate wholesalers, which don't own fleets but rent in bulk from those that do and often offer better rates (note you must usually pay for such rentals before leaving home). Consider adding a car rental onto your air–hotel vacation package; the cost will often be cheaper than if you had rented the car separately on your own.

When traveling abroad, **look for guaranteed exchange rates,** which protect you against a falling dollar. With your rate locked in, you won't pay more, even if the price goes up in the local currency. (Note to self: not the best thing if the dollar is surging rather than plunging.)

Beware of hidden charges. Those great rental rates may not be so great when you add in taxes, surcharges, cancellation penalties, taxes, drop-off charges (if you're planning to pick up the car in one city and leave it in another), and surcharges (for being under or over a certain age, for additional drivers, or for driving over state or country borders or out of a specific radius from your point of rental).

Note that airport rental offices often add supplementary surcharges that you may avoid by renting from an agency whose office is just off airport property. Don't buy the tank of gas that's in the car when you rent it unless you plan to do a lot of driving. Avoid hefty refueling fees by filling the tank at a station well away from the rental agency (those nearby are often more expensive) just before you turn in the car.

🚗 **Local Agencies Dimple Car Hire** ☎ 020/8205-1200 🖷 020/7243-4408 ⊕ www.dimpleselfdrive.co.uk. **Easy Car** ☎ 0906/333-3333, 60p per minute within U.K. ⊕ www.easycar.com. **Enterprise** ☎ 020/7723-4800 🖷 020/7723-4368. **Europcar** ☎ 020/259-1600 ⊕ www.europcar.com.

🚗 Major Agencies **Alamo** ☎ 800/522-9696 ⊕ www.alamo.com. **Avis** ☎ 800/331-1084 ⊕ www. avis.com. **Budget** ☎ 800/472-3325 ⊕ www.budget. com. **Hertz** ☎ 800/654-3001 ⊕ www.hertz.com. **National Car Rental** ☎ 800/227-7368 ⊕ www. nationalcar.com.

🚗 Wholesalers **Auto Europe** ☎ 888/223-5555 ⊕ www.autoeurope.com. **Eurovacations** ☎ 877/ 471-3876 ⊕ www.eurovacations.com. **Europe by Car** ☎ 212/581-3040 in New York, 800/223-1516 ⊕ www.europebycar.com. **Kemwel** ☎ 877/820- 0668 ⊕ www.kemwel.com.

INSURANCE

Everyone who rents a car wonders about whether the insurance that the rental companies offer is worth the expense. No one—not even us—has a simple answer. This is particularly true abroad, where laws are different than at home.

If you own a car, your personal auto insurance may cover a rental to some degree, though not all policies protect you abroad; always read your policy's fine print. If you don't have auto insurance, then seriously consider buying the collision- or loss-damage waiver (CDW or LDW) from the car-rental company, which eliminates your liability for damage to the car. Some credit cards offer CDW coverage, but it's usually supplemental to your own insurance and rarely covers SUVs, minivans, luxury models, and the like. If your coverage is secondary, you may still be liable for loss-of-use costs from the car-rental company. But no credit-card insurance is valid unless you use that card for *all* transactions, from reserving to paying the final bill. All companies exclude car rental in some countries, so be sure to find out about the destination to which you are traveling.

Some countries require you to purchase CDW coverage or require car-rental companies to include it in quoted rates. Ask your rental company about issues like these in your destination. In most cases, it's cheaper to add a supplemental CDW plan to your comprehensive travel insurance policy (⇨ Trip Insurance *under* Things to Consider *in* Getting Started, *above*) than to purchase it from a rental company. That said, you don't want to pay for a supplement if you're required to buy insurance from the rental company.

Note that you can decline the insurance from the rental company and purchase it through a third-party provider such as Travel Guard (⊕ www.travelguard.com)— $9 per day for $35,000 of coverage. That's sometimes just under half the price of the CDW offered by some car-rental companies. Also, Diner's Club offers primary CDW coverage on all rentals reserved and paid for with the card. This means that Diner's Club's company—not your own car insurance—pays in case of an accident. It *doesn't* mean your car-insurance company won't raise your rates once it discovers you had an accident.

CAR TRAVEL

With more than 50 million inhabitants in England, and a road system designed in part for horse-drawn carriages, England can be a challenging place in which to drive. That's even without considering that people drive on the left side of the road, and the gear shift is on the wrong side entirely. In major cities such as London, Liverpool, Manchester, and Birmingham, it's best to rely on the comprehensive public transportation network. All those cities suffer from traffic congestion, and learning to drive within their borders is an art.

Outside the cities, a car can be very handy. Many sights are not easily reached without one—castles, for example, are rarely connected to any public transportation system. Small villages might have only one or two buses a day pass through them. If it's the deep countryside you want to see, and you don't feel like doing it on a package tour, consider driving. Away from the towns and cities you can find miles of small, little-used roads and lanes where driving can be a real pleasure. Driving between the tall hedgerows is a truly English experience that you're likely to find as exhilarating as it is (occasionally) scary. Just drive slowly when you need to, watch other drivers, and ignore the impatient honking of the locals. In a few hours, you may well be speeding along like a native.

EMERGENCY SERVICES

If your car breaks down, position the red hazard triangle (which should be in the trunk, or "boot" as it is called) a few paces away from the rear of the car. Leave the hazard warning lights on. On major highways, emergency roadside telephone booths are positioned within walking-distance intervals. Contact your car-rental company (there should be an emergency assistance phone number on the car's paperwork) or call the police for help. You can also call the British Automobile Association toll-free. You can join and receive assistance from the AA on the spot, but the charge (around £75) is higher than a simple membership fee. If you are a member of the AAA (American Automobile Association) or another association, check your membership details before you travel; reciprocal agreements may give you free roadside aid.

🚑 **Ambulance, fire, police** 🕾 999. **Automobile Association** 🕾 0800/085-2721 ⊕ www.theaa.co.uk.

GASOLINE

Gasoline is called petrol in England and is sold by the liter. The price you see posted at a petrol station is the price of a liter, and there are about four liters in a U.S. gallon. Petrol is becoming increasingly expensive; it was more than 90p ($1.60) per liter at press time. This means gas costs the equivalent of close to $7 a gallon. Supermarket pumps just outside the city centers frequently offer the best prices. Unleaded petrol is predominant, denoted by green stickers on fuel pumps and pump lines. Premium and super premium are the two varieties, and most cars run on regular premium. Diesel is prevalent; be sure not to use it by mistake. Along busy motorways, most large stations are open 24 hours a day, seven days a week. In rural areas, hours can vary. Most service stations accept major credit cards, and most are self-service.

PARKING

Parking regulations are strictly enforced everywhere, so look out for signs that display the rules where you're thinking of parking. If there are no signs on a street, it's free to park there. However, be sure there are no signs; many streets have centralized "pay and display" machines, in which you deposit the required money and get a ticket allowing you to park for a set period of time. You display that ticket in your front windshield. In London, parking meters are insatiable—£1 doesn't buy you 15 minutes—and some permit only a two-hour stay. Prices are considerably lower elsewhere, and in small towns you can usually find free parking, or lots that charge a nominal fee, such as £1 a day. In town centers, your best bet is usually to park in a public car lot. Square blue street signs with a white "P" in the center direct you to the nearest lot.

If you park on the street, follow these basic rules: do not park within 15 yards of an intersection. Do not park on double yellow lines or in bus lanes. Park as close to the curb as possible—England's narrow streets leave little room for cars to park. On "Red Routes"—busy roads with red lines painted on the street—you cannot park or even stop to let a passenger out of the car.

ROAD CONDITIONS

There's a very good network of highways (motorways) and divided highways (dual carriageways) throughout most of England and Wales, although in more remote areas (including parts of Wales), where unclassified roads join village to village and are little more than glorified agricultural cart tracks, travel is noticeably slower. Motorways (with the prefix M), shown in blue on most maps and road signs, are mainly two or three lanes in each direction. Other fast major roads (with the prefix A) are shown on maps in green and red. Sections of fast dual carriageway (with black-edged, thick outlines on maps) have both traffic lights and traffic circles, and right turns are sometimes permitted. Turnoffs are often marked by highway numbers, rather than place names, so know the road numbers.

The vast network of lesser roads, for the most part old coach and turnpike roads, might make your trip take twice the time but show you twice as much. Minor roads drawn in yellow or white, the former prefixed by *B,* the latter unlettered and unnumbered, are the ancient lanes and byways, a superb way of discovering the real England. Some of these (the white roads, in the main) are pothole-filled switchbacks, littered with blind corners and barely wide enough for one car. Should you take one of these, be prepared to reverse into a passing place if you meet an oncoming car or tractor.

ROAD MAPS

You should purchase maps and atlases in advance from bookstores, or buy them in England. Good planning maps are available from Britain's Automobile Association or the Royal Automobile Club. The excellent Ordnance Survey or Collins maps, available from newsstands and bookstores in Britain, cost about £5 for a paper foldout to £7 for a spiral-bound paperback.

◪ In the U.K. Automobile Association ☏ 0870/600-0371 ⊕ www.theaa.co.uk. **Royal Automobile Club** ☏ 0800/731-1104 ⊕ www.rac.co.uk.

RULES OF THE ROAD

The most important thing you can do while driving here is to remember to **drive on the left.** You may find it's easier than you expected, as the steering and mirrors on U.K. cars are designed for driving on the left. You use the side mirrors much more when driving this way, and if you have a standard transmission car, you have to shift gears with your left hand. Left-handed people will be in their element, but righties will have to work a bit. Study your map before leaving the rental car lot, and give yourself plenty of time to adjust. The use of seat belts is obligatory in the front and back seats. It is illegal to talk on a hand-held cell phone while driving.

If you plan to drive in Britain, **pick up a copy of the official Highway Code** (£1.50) at a service station, newsstand, or bookstore. Besides driving rules and illustrations of signs and road markings, this booklet contains information for motorcyclists, cyclists, and pedestrians. For license information, *see* Car Rental.

Speed limits are complicated, and there are speed cameras everywhere. Watch your speedometer. The speed limit (shown on circular red signs) is generally 30 mph in towns, 60 mph on two-lane highways, and 70 mph on motorways. At traffic circles (called "roundabouts"), you turn clockwise; you will see signs before the roundabout that indicate where each exiting road is headed. As cars enter the circle, they must yield to those already in the circle. If you're taking an exit all the way around the circle, stay to the center until just before your own exit. If your exit is the first one off the roundabout, stay to the outside and signal that you're taking the first turnoff. Go slow and don't be worried—the rules on roundabouts are fluid, and if you can't safely get to your own exit, the worst thing that happens is you go around again.

Pedestrians have the right-of-way on "zebra" crossings (black-and-white-stripe crosswalks between two orange-flashing globe lights). If there's a person waiting to cross the street, treat the crossing like a stop sign. The curb on each side of the zebra crossing has zigzag markings. It is illegal to park within zigzag areas or to pass another vehicle at a zebra crossing. At other crossings, pedestrians must yield to traffic, but they do have the right-of-way over traffic turning left—if they dare.

Drunk-driving laws are strictly enforced. The legal limit is 80 milligrams of alcohol, which means roughly two units of alcohol—two glasses of wine, one pint of beer, or one glass of whisky—but these amounts vary, depending on your body weight or the amount you have eaten that day. It's far safer to avoid alcohol if you're driving.

THE CHANNEL TUNNEL

Short of flying, taking the Channel Tunnel is the fastest way to cross the English Channel to France: 35 minutes from Folkestone to Calais, 60 minutes from motorway to motorway, or 2 hours and 40 minutes from London's Waterloo Station to Paris's Gare du Nord. The Belgian border is just a short drive northeast of Calais. High-speed Eurostar trains also connect London's Waterloo station with the town of Lille, in France, and with Brussels' Midi station in around 2½ hours. If purchased in advance, round-trip tickets from London to Belgium or France cost around £125.

🚄 Channel Tunnel Car Transport **Eurotunnel** ☎ 0870/535-3535 in U.K., 070/223210 in Belgium, 03-21-00-61-00 in France ⊕ www.eurotunnel.com. **French Motorail/Rail Europe** ☎ 0870/241-5415 ⊕ www.raileurope.co.uk/frenchmotorail.

🚄 Channel Tunnel Passenger Service **Eurostar** ☎ 0870/518-6186 in U.K. ⊕ www.eurostar.co.uk. **Rail Europe** ☎ 888/382-7245 in U.S., 0870/584-8848 U.K. inquiries and credit-card bookings ⊕ www.raileurope.com.

COMPUTERS ON THE ROAD

If you're traveling with a laptop, carry a spare battery and adapter. If you are going to use dial-up, get a telephone cord that's compatible with a British phone jack; these are widely available in Britain at airports and electronics stores. Never plug your computer into any socket before asking about surge protection. Some hotels do not have built-in current stabilizers, and extreme electrical fluctuations and surges can short your adapter or even destroy your computer. Before connecting your computer to a phone line, you may want to test the line as well. IBM sells an invaluable pen-size modem tester that plugs into a telephone jack to check whether the line is safe to use. More hotels are upgrading their Internet services and offering ISDN and Wi-Fi, and in cities Internet cafés are plentiful; even coffee shops may have access points.

CRUISE TRAVEL

The Cunard Line's *Queen Mary 2* has regular crossings, April through December, between Southampton, England, and Baltimore, Boston, and New York City; arrangements can include one-way airfare. For information about cruising England's rivers, lakes and canals, *see* Sports & Outdoors.

🚢 Cruise Lines **Cunard Line** ☎ 661/753-1000 or 800/728-6273 ⊕ www.cunard.com.

CUSTOMS & DUTIES

You're always allowed to bring goods of a certain value back home without having to pay any duty or import tax. There's also a limit on the amount of tobacco and liquor you can bring back duty-free, and some countries have separate limits for perfumes; for exact figures, check with your customs department. The values of so-called "duty-free" goods are included in these amounts. When you shop abroad, save all your receipts as customs inspectors may ask to see them as well as the items you purchased. If the total value of your goods is more than the duty-free limit, then you'll have to pay a tax (most often a flat percentage) on the value of everything beyond that limit.

Fresh meats, plants and vegetables, controlled drugs, and firearms and ammunition may not be brought into the United Kingdom. Pets from the United States or Canada with the proper documentation may be brought into the country without quarantine under the U.K. Pet Travel Scheme (PETS). The process takes about six months to complete and involves detailed steps.

You will face no customs formalities if you enter Scotland or Wales from any other part of the United Kingdom.

🛂 U.S. Information **U.S. Customs and Border Protection** ⊕ www.cbp.gov.

🛂 Information in England **HM Customs and Excise** ☎ 0208/929-0152, 0845/010-9000 advice service ⊕ www.hmce.gov.uk. **Pet Travel Scheme** ☎ 0870/241-1710 ⊕ www.defra.gov.uk/animalh/quarantine/index.htm.

DISCOUNTS & DEALS

DISCOUNT PASSES

If you plan to visit castles, gardens, and historic houses during your stay in England and Wales, **look into discount passes or organization memberships** that can provide significant savings. The National Trust, English Heritage, and the Historic Houses Association encompass hundreds of properties. English Heritage's Overseas Visitors Pass costs £18 for a 7-day pass and £22 for a 14-day pass for one adult. You can order it in advance by phone or online, or get the order form online and then submit it by fax or mail. If you are traveling within 21 days, you must purchase the pass at a participating property in England. The National Trust Touring Pass, for overseas visitors, must be purchased in advance of a visit; it is sold online or by phone but not at the properties. A 7-day pass is £17; a 14-day pass is £22. VisitBritain's Great British Heritage Pass is £28 for 4 days, £39 for one week, £52 for 15 days, and £70 for one month, and includes properties belonging to English Heritage and the National Trust. The pass is sold online and at major tourist information centers in Britain. Annual membership in the National Trust (the Royal Oak Foundation is the U.S. affiliate) is $50 a year if you join through the Royal Oak. English Heritage membership is £38, and the Historic Houses Association is £34. Many passes can be purchased online, and all offer free admission as well as a guide to the properties. Be sure to **match what the pass or membership offers against your itinerary** to see if it's worthwhile. For London Pass information, *see* London Essentials *in* Chapter 1. For passes specifically for Wales, *see* Wales Essentials *in* Chapter 14.

🇫 **English Heritage** ☎ 0870/333-1181 ⊕ www.english-heritage.org.uk. **Great Britain Heritage Pass** ⊕ www.gbheritagepass.com. **Historic Houses Association** ☎ 01464/896-688 ⊕ www.hha.org.uk. **Royal Oak Foundation** ☎ 212/480-2889 or 800/913-6565 ⊕ www.royal-oak.org.

EATING OUT

The stereotypical notion of English meals as parades of roast beef, overcooked vegetables, and stodgy puddings (desserts) is gradually being replaced—particularly in London and other major cities—with a more contemporary picture of the country as hot foodie territory. From trendy gastro-pubs to the see-and-be-seen dining shrines, England is shedding its tired image and becoming known for a global palate.

The restaurants reviewed in this book are the cream of the crop in each price category. Properties indicated by ✕🏠 are lodging establishments whose restaurants warrant a special trip. Price-category information is given in each chapter. In general, restaurant prices are high. If you're watching your budget, **seek out pubs and ethnic restaurants,** which offer excellent food at reasonable prices.

Was the service stellar or not up to snuff? Did the food give you shivers of delight or leave you cold? Did the prices and portions make you happy or sad? Rate restaurants and write your own reviews in Travel Ratings or start a discussion about your favorite places in Travel Talk on www.fodors.com. Your comments might even appear in our books. Yes, you, too, can be a correspondent!

CUTTING COSTS

Eating out in England's big cities in particular can be an expensive affair, but you can do it cheaply. Try local cafés, often called workers' cafés, where heaping plates of English comfort food (bacon sandwiches and stuffed baked potatoes, for example) are served. Fast-food outlets also offer cheap meals for those on a budget. England has plenty of the big names in fast food, as well as smaller places selling sandwiches, fish and chips, burgers, falafel, kebabs, and the like. Check out curry houses; Indian food is popular throughout the country. Marks & Spencer, Sainsbury's, Tesco, Waitrose, and Budgens are chain supermarkets with outlets throughout the country. They're good choices for groceries, sandwiches or picnic fixings.

MEALS & MEALTIMES

Cafés serving the traditional English breakfast of eggs, bacon, beans, half a grilled tomato, and strong tea are often the cheapest—and most authentic—places for breakfast. For lighter morning fare (or for real brewed coffee), try the continental-style sandwich bars and coffee shops offering croissants and other pastries.

At lunch, you can grab a sandwich between sights, pop into the local pub, or sit down in a restaurant. Dinner, too, has no set rules, but a three-course meal is standard in most mid-range or high-end restaurants. Pre- or posttheater menus, offering two or three courses for a set price, are usually a good value. Note that most pubs do not have any waitstaff and that you are expected to go to the bar, order a beverage and your meal, and inform them of your table number. Also, in cities, many pubs do not serve food after 3 PM, so they're usually a better lunch option than dinner.

On Sunday, for pure Englishness, a traditional roast beef, pork or lamb dinner still tops the list. Its typical accompaniment is Yorkshire pudding—a savory soufflé-like batter of eggs, milk, and flour oven-baked until crisp, then topped with a rich, dark gravy. Shepherd's pie, a classic pub dish, is made with diced or minced lamb and a mashed potato topping, and "bangers and mash" are English sausages with mashed potatoes and onion gravy. In the pubs, you'll also find a ploughman's lunch—crusty bread, English cheese (perhaps cheddar, blue Stilton, crumbly Cheshire, or smooth red Leicester), and pickles. And there's also fish-and-chips, usually made from cod or haddock deep-fried in a crispy batter and served with thick french fries. Take time for afternoon tea—whether with scones (with cream and jam, called a "cream tea") and pastries or just a hot cup of Assam or some other fancy tea, it's still a civilized respite.

You can eat your way around the country seeking out regional specialties. Every region has its own cheese, beer, cake, and candy—from the crumbly, sharp cheeses of the Yorkshire and Derbyshire dales to the hard cheddars of Somerset, the creamy goats' rounds in Wales, and the nutty Cornish yarg. In Devon and Cornwall, look for tooth-tingling fudge and toffee made with clotted cream.

Breakfast is generally served between 7:30 and 9, lunch between noon and 2, dinner or supper between 7:30 and 9:30, sometimes earlier, seldom later except in large cities. These days tea is rarely a proper meal anymore (it was once served between 4:30 at 6), and tea shops are often open all day in touristy areas (they're not found at all in non-touristy places). So you can have a cup and pastry or sandwich whenever you feel you need it. Sunday roasts at pubs last from 11 AM or noon to 3 or 4 PM.

As of 2007, there will be no smoking in pubs, clubs, and restaurants throughout Britain.

Unless otherwise noted, the restaurants listed in this guide are open daily for lunch and dinner.

PAYING

Credit cards are widely accepted in restaurants, but not in pubs, which generally still require cash (although a growing minority are taking plastic). Be sure that you **don't double pay a service charge.** Many restaurants exclude service charges from the printed menu (which the law obliges them to display outside), then add 10% to 15% to the check, or else stamp SERVICE NOT INCLUDED along the bottom, in which case you should add the 10% to 15% yourself. Just don't pay twice for service—some restaurateurs have been known to add service, but leave the total on the credit-card slip blank. Larger establishments generally accept major credit cards; pubs, small cafés, or ethnic restaurants may be cash-only.

For guidelines on tipping, *see* Tipping, *below.*

CATEGORY	LONDON	ELSEWHERE
$$$$	over£23	over £22
$$$	£20–£23	£18–£22
$$	£14–£19	£13–£17
$	£10–£13	£7–£12
¢	under £10	under £7

Prices are for a main course at dinner and are given in pounds.

PUBS

A common misconception among visitors to England is that pubs are bars. This is not exactly true. Pubs are also gathering places, conversation zones, even restaurants. In many pubs, alcohol is almost an afterthought. Pubs are, generally speaking, where people go to meet their friends and catch up on one another's lives. In small towns, pubs act almost as town halls. Many people in a pub drink soft drinks, tea, or coffee, rather than beer, and hard liquor is usually in short supply. Even if you don't drink alcohol, go to a pub and have an orange juice or a soda, relax and meet the locals. Traditionally pub hours are 11–11, with last orders called about 20 minutes before closing time, but laws have been relaxed recently. Some pubs now stay open until midnight or 1 AM.

Most pubs tend to be child-friendly, but others have restricted hours for children. If a pub serves food, it will generally allow children in during the day with adults. Some pubs are more strict than others, though, and will not admit anyone younger than 18. Some will allow children in during the day, but only until 6 PM. If you're in doubt, ask the bartender. However, that's usually not necessary, since family friendly pubs tend to be packed with kids, parents and all of their accoutrements, so you can just use your common sense. Some even have children's play areas with jungle gyms and toys.

RESERVATIONS & DRESS

Regardless of where you are, it's a good idea to make a reservation if you can. We only mention specifically when reservations are essential (there's no other way you'll ever get a table) or when they are not accepted. For popular restaurants, book as far ahead as you can (often 30 days), and reconfirm as soon as you arrive. (Large parties should always call ahead to check the reservations policy.) We mention dress only when men are required to wear a jacket or a jacket and tie.

WINES, BEER & SPIRITS

Although hundreds of varieties of beer are brewed around the country, the traditional brew is known as bitter and is not carbonated; it's usually served at room temperature. Fizzy American-style beer is called lager. There are also plenty of other potations: stouts like Guinness and Murphy's are thick, pitch-black brews you'll either love or hate; ciders, made from apples, are an alcoholic drink in Britain (Bulmer's and Strongbow are the names to remember); shandies are a mix of lager and lemon soda; and black-and-tans are a blend of lager and stout named for the distinctive uniforms worn by early-20th-century British troops. Real ales, which have a natural second fermentation in the cask, have a shorter shelf life (so many are brewed locally) but special flavor. Generally the selection and quality of cocktails is higher in a wine bar or café than in a pub. The legal drinking age is 18.

ELECTRICITY

Consider making a small investment in a universal adapter, which has several types of plugs in one lightweight, compact unit. Most laptops and mobile-phone chargers are dual voltage (i.e., they operate equally well on 110 and 220 volts) and so require only an adapter. These days the same is true more of small appliances such as hair dryers. Always check labels and manufacturer instructions to be sure. Don't use 110-volt outlets marked FOR SHAVERS ONLY for high-wattage appliances such as hair dryers. The electrical current in Great Britain is 240 volts (in line with the rest of Europe), 50 cycles alternating current (AC); wall outlets take three-pin plugs, and shaver sockets take two round, oversize prongs. Blackouts and brownouts are rare and are usually fixed in a few hours. For converters, adapters, and advice, contact the British Airways Travel Shop.

☑ **British Airways Travel Shop** ☒ 213 Piccadilly, W1J 9HQ ☎ 0845/606-0747. **Steve Kropla's Help for World Traveler's** ⊕ www.kropla.com has information on electrical and telephone plugs around the world. **Walkabout Travel Gear** ⊕ www.walkabouttravelgear.com has a good discussion about electricity under "adapters."

EMERGENCIES

If you need to report an emergency, dial 999 for police, fire, or ambulance. Be prepared to give the telephone number you're calling from. National Health Service hospitals give free, 24-hour treatment in Accident and Emergency sections, although delays can be an hour or more. Prescriptions are valid only if made out by doctors registered in the U.K. For additional information, *see* the Essentials sections at the end of each chapter.

☑ **Embassies American Embassy** ☒ 24 Grosvenor Sq., London W1 ☎ 020/7499-9000 ⊕ www.usembassy.org.uk; for passports, go to the **U.S. Passport Unit** ☒ 55 Upper Brook St., London W1 ☎ 020/7499-9000.

General Emergency Contacts **Ambulance, fire, police** ☎ 999.

ETIQUETTE & BEHAVIOR

Generally speaking, English people are soft-spoken, reserved, and ruthlessly polite. The spontaneity and outspokenness common in the United States can seem jarring in juxtaposition to their often quiet coolness. They also don't smile as much as North Americans, but there is a general consensus in England that this tendency to smile is one of the better things about "Yanks," as they call Americans, usually with some affection. Politeness and etiquette are still more ingrained in Britain than in the United States, and being on your best behavior when dealing with locals is always welcome.

Anti-Americanism is an issue throughout much of Europe, and it is possible, albeit unlikely, that Americans might encounter unkind comments about their nationality or government. You may be asked piercing questions about your own political beliefs. There is no right or wrong way to handle this, but do remember that these are sensitive times, and try not to take offense. Be polite and friendly, but if you don't want to talk about politics, say so and then walk away.

If you're visiting a family home, a simple bouquet of flowers is a welcome gift. If you're invited for a meal, bringing a bottle of wine is appropriate, if you wish, as is some candy for the children. In London and other urban centers, European-style kisses on one or two cheeks when meeting a woman friend are common. Elsewhere in the country, a warm handshake is the norm.

The English express gratitude more readily and frequently than Americans or Canadians. When buying a newspaper, for example, they may say "thank you" at least four times: When the shopkeeper takes the items, when he or she takes the money, when change is given, and when the item is bagged and handed to the customer. In most other countries, one "thank you" might cover all of that. Paradoxically, the country is known for service with a scowl—the person working the counter when you buy that newspaper might not say "thank you" once. Poor service is a constant subject of conversation among English residents of major cities, but in the countryside it's virtually unheard of. The person working the store counter might well talk your ear off. Expect to encounter both experiences.

BUSINESS ETIQUETTE

Punctuality is of prime importance, so **call ahead if you anticipate a late arrival.** Spouses do not generally attend business dinners, unless invited. If you invite someone to dine, it's usually assumed that you will pick up the tab. However, if you are the visitor, your host may insist on paying.

HEALTH

If you take prescription drugs, keep a supply in your carry-on luggage and make a list of all your prescriptions to keep on file at home while you are abroad. You will not be able to renew a U.S. prescription at a pharmacy in Britain. Prescriptions are accepted only if issued by a U.K.-registered physician.

The 1990s scare over Bovine Spongiform Encephalopathy (BSE), commonly known as Mad Cow Disease, is over. Extensive changes to the British beef industry effectively eliminated it from the country. Eating British beef is as safe as eating meat elsewhere in Europe. If you would like more information, contact the Centers for Disease Control and Prevention.

Health Warnings **National Centers for Disease Control & Prevention** (CDC) ☎ 877/394-8747 international travelers' health line ⊕ www.cdc.gov/travel. **World Health Organization** (WHO) ⊕ www.who.int.

HOLIDAYS

ENGLAND & WALES

Holidays are January 1, New Year's Day; Good Friday and Easter Monday; May Day (first Monday in May); spring and summer bank holidays (last Monday in May and August, respectively); December 25, Christmas Day; and December 26, Boxing Day (day after Christmas). If any of these holidays falls on a weekend, then the holiday is observed on the following Monday. During the Christmas holidays, many restaurants, as well as museums and other attractions, may close for at least a week—call to verify hours. Book hotels for Christmas travel well in advance, and check whether the hotel restaurant will be open.

INSURANCE

What kind of coverage do you honestly need? Do you even need trip insurance at all? Take a deep breath and read on.

We believe that comprehensive trip insurance is especially valuable if you're booking a very expensive or complicated trip (particularly to an isolated region) or if you're booking far in advance. Who knows what could happen six months down the road? But whether you get insurance has more to do with how comfortable you are assuming all that risk yourself.

Comprehensive travel policies typically cover trip cancellation and interruption, letting you cancel or cut your trip short because of a personal emergency, illness, or, in some cases, acts of terrorism in your destination. Such policies also cover evacuation and medical care. Some also cover you for trip delays because of bad weather or mechanical problems as well as for lost or delayed baggage. Another type of coverage to look for is financial default—that is, when your trip is disrupted because a tour operator, airline, or cruise line goes out of business. Generally you must buy this when you book your trip or shortly thereafter, and it's only available to you if your operator isn't on a list of excluded companies.

If you're going abroad, consider buying medical-only coverage at the very least. Neither Medicare nor some private insurers cover medical expenses anywhere outside of the United States besides Mexico and Canada (including time aboard a cruise ship, even if it leaves from a U.S. port). Medical-only policies typically reimburse you for medical care (excluding that related to preexisting conditions) and hospitalization abroad and provide for

evacuation. You still have to pay the bills and await reimbursement from the insurer, though.

Expect comprehensive travel insurance policies to cost about 4% to 7% of the total price of your trip (it's more like 12% if you're over age 70). A medical-only policy may or may not be cheaper than a comprehensive policy. Always read the fine print of your policy to make sure that you are covered for the risks that are of the most concern to you. Compare several policies to make sure you're getting the best price and range of coverage available.

Insurance Comparison Sites **Insure My Trip. com** ⊕ www.insuremytrip.com. **Square Mouth.com** ⊕ www.quotetravelinsurance.com.

Comprehensive Travel Insurers **Access America** ☎ 866/807-3982 ⊕ www.accessamerica.com. **CSA Travel Protection** ☎ 800/729-6021 ⊕ www. csatravelprotection.com. **HTH Worldwide** ☎ 610/ 254-8700 or 888/243-2358 ⊕ www.hthworldwide. com. **Travelex Insurance** ☎ 888/457-4602 ⊕ www.travelex-insurance.com. **Travel Guard International** ☎ 715/345-0505 or 800/826-4919 ⊕ www.travelguard.com. **Travel Insured International** ☎ 800/243-3174 ⊕ www.travelinsured.com.

Medical-Only Insurers **Wallach & Company** ☎ 800/237-6615 or 504/687-3166 ⊕ www.wallach. com. **International Medical Group** ☎ 800/628-4664 ⊕ www.imglobal.com. **International SOS** ☎ 215/942-8000 or 713/521-7611 ⊕ www. internationalsos.com.

LODGING

Did the resort look as good in real life as it did in the photos? Did you sleep like a baby, or were the walls paper thin? Did you get your money's worth? Rate hotels and write your own reviews in "Travel Ratings" or start a discussion about your favorite places in "Travel Talk" on www. fodors.com. Your comments might even appear in our books. Yes, you, too, can be a correspondent!

Hotels, bed-and-breakfasts, or small country houses—there's a style and price to suit most travelers. The lodgings listed are the cream of the crop in each price category. Wherever you stay, make reservations well in advance: England is popular.

Properties are assigned price categories based on a range that includes the cost of the least expensive standard double room in high season (excluding holidays) and the most expensive. Lodgings are indicated in the text by ⊡ . Properties indicated by ✕⊡ are lodging establishments whose restaurants warrant a special trip. Price-category information is given in each chapter. Unless otherwise noted, all lodgings listed have a private bathroom, air-conditioning, a room phone, and a television.

We always list the facilities that are available—but we don't specify whether they cost extra: when pricing accommodations, always ask what's included and what costs extra. Throughout Britain, lodging prices often include breakfast of some kind, but this is generally not the case in London.

Most hotels and other lodgings require you to give your credit-card details before they will confirm your reservation. If you don't feel comfortable e-mailing this information, ask if you can fax it (some places even prefer faxes). However you book, get confirmation in writing and have a copy of it handy when you check in.

Be sure you understand the hotel's cancellation policy. Some places allow you to cancel without any kind of penalty—even if you prepaid to secure a discounted rate—if you cancel at least 24 hours in advance. Others require you to cancel a week in advance or penalize you for the cost of one night. Small inns and B&Bs are most likely to require you to cancel far in advance. Most hotels allow children under a certain age to stay in their parents' room at no extra charge, but others charge for them as extra adults; find out the cutoff age for discounts.

Assume that hotels operate on the European Plan (**EP,** no meals) unless we specify that they use the Breakfast Plan (**BP,** with full breakfast), Continental Plan (**CP,** continental breakfast), Full American Plan (**FAP,** all meals), Modified American Plan (**MAP,** breakfast and dinner) or are **all-inclusive** (all meals and most activities).

CATEGORY	LONDON	ELSEWHERE
££££	over £250	over £160
£££	£180–£250	£120–£160
£££	£120–£179	£90–£119
££	£70–£119	£60–£89
£	under £70	under £60

Prices are for two people in a standard double room in high season, including V.A.T., and are given in pounds.

APARTMENT & HOUSE RENTALS

For a home base that is roomy enough for a family and comes with cooking facilities, consider renting furnished "flats" (the word for apartments in England). These can save you money, especially if you're traveling with a group, and provide more privacy than a hotel or a B&B. If you're interested in home exchange but don't feel like sharing, some home-exchange directories list rentals as well. If you deal directly with local agents, get a recommendation from someone who has used the company. Unlike with hotels, there's no accredited system for apartment-rental standards. The London Where to Stay section in Chapter 1 also has information about rentals. The National Trust rents historic cottages in rural locations by the week at often reasonable prices.

Also *see* Cottages *and* Historic Buildings. ⚑ **At Home Abroad** ☎ 212/421–9165 ⊕ www.athomeabroadinc.com. **Barclay International Group** ☎ 516/364–0064 or 800/845–6636 ⊕ www.barclayweb.com. **Hometours International** ☎ 865/690–8484 or 866/367–4668 ⊕ thor.he.net/~hometour/. **Interhome** ☎ 305/940–2299 or 800/882–6864 ⊕ www.interhome.us. **Suzanne B. Cohen & Associations** ☎ 207/622–0743 ⊕ www.villaeurope.com. **Vacation Home Rentals Worldwide** ☎ 201/767–9393 or 800/633–3284 ⊕ www.vhrww.com. **Villanet** ☎ 206/417–3444 or 800/964–1891 ⊕ www.rentavilla.com. **Villas International** ☎ 415/499–9490 or 800/221–2260 ⊕ www.villasintl.com. **Wimco** ☎ 800/449–1553 ⊕ www.wimco.com. ⚑ **Local Agents The Apartment Service** ☎ 020/8944–1444 🖷 020/8944–6744 ⊕ www.apartmentservice.com. **English Country Cottages** ☎ 0870/781100 ⊕ www.english-country-cottages.co.uk, from studio apartments to castles. **In the English Manner** ☎ 01559/371600 ⊕ www.english-manner.co.uk ✉ American agent ☎ 213/629–1811 or 800/422–0799, apartments and cottages. **Na-**

tional Trust ☎ 0870/458-4422 ⊕ www.
nationaltrustcottages.co.uk, houses and cottages.

BED & BREAKFASTS

A special English tradition, and the backbone of budget travel, B&Bs are usually in a family home. They vary in style and grace, but these days most have private bathrooms. They range from the ordinary to the truly elegant. Guesthouses are a slightly larger and sometimes more luxurious version of the same thing.

Tourist Information Centres around the country can help you find and book a B&B. Bed & Breakfast (GB) reservation service offers rooms in a range of prices and has discounts for families and off-peak reductions. It represents tourist board–accredited places in London, across the country, and in France. Wolsey Lodges, a consortium of more than 180 private homes mostly in Britain, includes many luxurious country homes and some more modest houses; some are historic. Guests are encouraged to dine with their hosts at least one night of their stay. For reservation services in London, *see* the Where to Stay section *in* Chapter 1.

🖪 **Reservation Services Bed & Breakfast.com** ☎ 512/322-2710 or 800/462-2632 ⊕ www.
bedandbreakfast.com also sends out an online newsletter. **Bed & Breakfast (GB)** ☎ 800/454-8704, 0871/781-0834 in U.K. ⊕ www.bedbreak.com. **Bulldog Club** ☎ 877/727-3004 in U.S. ⊕ www.
bulldogclub.com. **Host & Guest Service** ☎ 020/
7385-9922 in U.K. ⊕ www.host-guest.co.uk.
Wolsey Lodges ☎ 01473/822058, 01473/827500 for brochure ⊕ www.wolseylodges.com.

COTTAGES

Cottages and houses are available for weekly rental in all areas of the country. These vary from quaint older homes to brand-new buildings in scenic surroundings. For families and large groups, they offer the best value-for-money accommodations, but because they are often in isolated locations, a car is vital. Lists of rental properties are available free of charge from VisitBritain (⇨ Visitor Information). Some National Trust properties have cottages available on the estates of stately homes. Luxury Cottages Direct deals ex-

clusively in four- and five-star properties. You may find discounts of up to 50% on rentals during the off-season (October through March).

🖪 **Luxury Cottages Direct** ☎ 029/2021-2491 ⊕ www.luxury-cottages.co.uk. **National Trust** ☎ 0870/458-4422 ⊕ www.nationaltrust cottages.
co.uk. **Rural Retreats** ☎ 01386/701177 ⊕ www.
ruralretreats.co.uk.

FARMHOUSES

Farmhouses have become increasingly popular in recent years; their special appeal is the rustic, rural experience. Consider this option only if you are touring by car. Prices are generally very reasonable. Ask VisitBritain (⇨ Visitor Information) for the booklet "Stay on a Farm" or contact Farm Stay UK.

🖪 **Farm Stay UK** ☎ 024/7669-6909 🖷 024/
7669-6630 ⊕ www.farmstayuk.co.uk.

HISTORIC BUILDINGS

Want to spend your vacation in a Gothic banqueting house, an old lighthouse, a seaside castle, or maybe in an apartment at Hampton Court Palace? Several organizations, such as the Landmark Trust, National Trust (⇨ Cottages), and Vivat Trust have specially adapted historic buildings to rent. Celtic Castles represents castles and castle hotels in several countries including England. Rural Retreats renovates historic buildings including lighthouses around Britain. Stately Holiday Homes has rentals in houses and cottages in historic or rural settings. Most are self-catering (meaning that they include kitchens).

🖪 **Celtic Castles** ☎ 870/050-3232 ⊕ www.
celticcastles.com. **Landmark Trust** ☎ 01628/825925 ⊕ www.landmarktrust.org.uk. **Portmeirion Cottages** ☎ 01766/770000 ⊕ www.portmeirion-village.com. **Rural Retreats** ☎ 01386/701177 ⊕ www.ruralretreats.co.uk. **Stately Holiday Homes** ☎ 01638/674756 ⊕ www.statelyholidayhomes.co.
uk. **Vivat Trust** ☎ 020/7336-8825 from U.S., 0845/
090-0194 from U.K. ⊕ www.vivat.org.uk.

HOME EXCHANGES

With a direct home exchange, you stay in someone else's home while they stay in yours. Some outfits also deal with vacation homes, so you're not actually staying in someone's full-time residence, just their vacant weekend place.

▸ **Exchange Clubs HomeLink International** ☎ 813/975-9825 or 800/638-3841 ⊕ www.homelink.org; $80 yearly for Web-only membership; $125 with Web access and two directories. **Home Exchange.com** ☎ 800/877-8723 ⊕ www.homeexchange.com charges; $49.95 yearly for a 1-year online listing; this is a Web-based company with no catalog. **Intervac U.S.** ☎ 800/756-4663 ⊕ www.intervacus.com; $128.88 yearly for a listing, online access, and a catalog; $78.88 without catalog.

HOSTELS

Although the decor may be basic, some hostels in England and Wales are in extraordinary locations, and others are simply beautiful. Most hostels serve breakfast; dinner and/or shared cooking facilities may also be available. In some hostels, you aren't allowed to be in your room during the day, and there may be a curfew at night. Nevertheless, hostels provide a sense of community, with public rooms where travelers often gather to share stories.

Hostelling International (HI), the umbrella group for a number of national youth-hostel associations, offers single-sex, dorm-style beds and, at many hostels, rooms for couples and families. Membership in any HI national hostel association, open to travelers of all ages, allows you to stay in HI-affiliated hostels at member rates; one-year membership is about $28 for adults, £14 in the United Kingdom. Members have priority if the hostel is full; they're also eligible for discounts around the world, even on rail and bus travel in some countries. Members of the Boy Scouts may want to consider London's useful Baden-Powell House, which offers rooms for as little as $25 a night for Scouts and their families, and to non-Scouts for slightly more.

▸ **Baden-Powell House** ☎ 020/7584-7031 ⊕ www.scoutbase.org.uk/hq/bph/index.htm. **Hostelling International–USA** ☎ 301/495-1240 ⊕ www.hiusa.org. **YHA England and Wales** ☎ 0870/870-8808, 0870/770-8868, or 0162/959-2600 ⊕ www.yha.org.uk.

HOTELS

Weigh all your options (we can't say this enough). Join "frequent guest" programs. You may get preferential treatment in room choice and/or upgrades in your favorite chains. Check general travel sites and hotel Web sites because not all chains are represented on all travel sites. Always research or inquire about special packages and corporate rates. If you prefer to book by phone, note you can sometimes get a better price if you call the hotel's local toll-free number (if one is available) rather than the central reservations number.

Ask when rates go down. England's high season is June to September, so if you're trying to book, say, in late September, you might save considerably by changing your dates by a week or two to get a better price. Note, though, that many properties charge peak-season rates for your entire stay even if your travel dates straddle peak and nonpeak seasons. High-end chains catering to businesspeople are often busy only on weekdays and often drop rates dramatically on weekends to fill up rooms.

Watch out for hidden costs, including resort fees, energy surcharges, and "convenience" fees for such things as unlimited local phone service you won't use and a free newspaper—possibly written in a language you can't read. Always verify whether local hotel taxes are or are not included in the rates you are quoted, so that you'll know the real price of your stay. In some places, taxes can add 20% or more to your bill. If you're traveling overseas **look for price guarantees,** which protect you against a falling dollar.

England is a popular vacation destination, so be sure to reserve hotel rooms weeks (months for London) in advance. The country has everything from budget chain hotels to luxurious retreats in converted country houses. In many towns and cities you will find old inns that are former coaching inns, which served travelers as they journeyed around the country in horse-drawn carriages and stagecoaches. Most hotels have rooms with "en suite" bathrooms—as private bathrooms are called—although some older ones may have only washbasins; in this case, showers and bathtubs (and toilets) are usually just down the hall. When you book a room in the mid-to-lower price categories, it's best to confirm your request for a room with en suite facilities. Especially in London, rooms and bathrooms may be smaller than what you find in the United States. Tourist Information Centres will reserve rooms for you, usually for a small fee. A great many hotels offer special weekend and off-season bargain packages. All hotels listed have private bath unless otherwise noted.

HOTEL GRADING SYSTEM

Hotels in England are graded from one to five stars, and guesthouses, inns, and B&Bs are graded from one to five diamonds by VisitBritain in association with the Automobile Association (AA) and the Royal Automobile Association (RAC). Basically, the more stars or diamonds a property has, the more facilities it has, and the facilities will be of a higher standard.

In Wales, the star system is based on quality and comfort. It's a fairly good reflection of lodging from campsites to palatial hotels. Five stars are for the most luxurious hotels; one star is for fair and acceptable. Hostels are graded from one to three stars.

In 2006, VisitBritain, VisitScotland, the Wales Tourist Board, the AA, and the RAC agreed to rate accommodations by the same standards and to use a star system (one to five stars) for each category of lodging. Travelers can expect to start seeing the new ratings later in the year.

CUTTING COSTS

Youth hostels in rural areas favored by hikers and walkers attract all ages, and many have double rooms at excellent prices. Chains such as Premier Travel Inn offer low rates and reliable rooms, and are usually close to major sights and cities. At this writing VisitLondon.com, London's official Web site, was offering a lowest-price guarantee on hotel rooms. London-Town.com's London Visitor Information Centre provides free maps, tourist infor-

mation, and last-minute hotel bookings in the city, with savings of up to 50%. Its kiosk in Leicester Square is open daily 8 AM–11 PM. Lastminute.com offers deals on hotel rooms all over the United Kingdom. Hotel rates in major cities tend to be cheapest on weekends, while rural hotels are cheapest on weeknights. Early December and most of January have the lowest occupancy rates, so hotels offer cheaper rooms at these times.

Best Western and Choice Hotels Europe (Clarion, Comfort, and Quality brands) offer 10% off accommodation for people age 55 and over. Thistle Hotels discounts rooms up to 50% for seniors.

🔂 Local Resources **Choice Hotels** ☎ 800/645–6200. **Lastminute.com** ⊕ www.lastminute.com. **Premier Travel Inn** ☎ 0870/242–8000, 1582/567890 outside the U.K. ⊕ www.premiertravelinn.co.uk. **LondonTown.com's London Visitor Information Centre** ✉ Leicester Sq. ☎ 020/7292–2333 ⊕ www.londontown.com. **VisitLondon** ⊕ www.visitlondon.com.

🔂 Discount Hotel Rooms **Accommodations Express** ☎ 800/444–7666 or 800/277–1064. **Hotels.com** ☎ 800/219–4606 or 800/364–0291 ⊕ www.hotels.com. **Steigenberger Reservation Service** ☎ 800/223–5652 ⊕ www.srs-worldhotels.com. **Turbotrip.com** ☎ 800/473–7829 ⊕ w3.turbotrip.com.

MAIL & SHIPPING

Stamps may be bought from post offices (open weekdays 9 to 5:30, Saturday 9 to noon), from stamp machines outside post offices, and from news dealers' stores and newsstands. Mailboxes, known as post or letter boxes, are painted bright red; large tubular ones are set on the edge of sidewalks, and smaller boxes are set into post-office walls. Allow seven days for a letter to reach the United States and about 10 days to two weeks to Australia or New Zealand by airmail. Surface mail service can take up to four or five weeks. The useful Royal Mail Web site has information on everything from buying stamps to finding a post office.

Airmail letters up to 10 grams to North America cost 47p; postcards, 42p. The same rates apply to Australia and New Zealand. Letters within Britain are 30p for first-class, 20p for second-class. Always check rates before sending mail, because they are subject to change.

If you're uncertain where you'll be staying, **arrange to have your mail sent to American Express.** The service is free to cardholders and traveler's check holders; all others pay a small fee. You can also collect letters at any main or sub post office throughout Britain, so mail can reach you while you are traveling. Ask the sender to mark the envelope POSTE RESTANTE or TO BE CALLED FOR. The letter must be marked with the recipient's full name (as it appears on your passport), and you'll need your passport or another official form of identification for collection.

📮 **Royal Mail** ⊕ www.royalmail.com.

SHIPPING PARCELS

Most department stores and retail outlets can arrange to ship your goods back home. You should check your insurance for coverage of possible damage. If you want to ship goods yourself, use an overnight postal service, such as Federal Express, DHL, or Parcelforce. Shipping to North America, New Zealand, or Australia can take anywhere from overnight to a month, depending on how much you pay.

Contact the services listed below for information about the nearest office or package drop-off point.

📮 **Express Services DHL** ☎ 0870/110–0300 ⊕ www.dhl.co.uk. **Federal Express** ☎ 0800/ 123800 ⊕ www.fedex.com. **Parcelforce** ☎ 0870/ 850-1150 ⊕ www.parcelforce.co.uk.

MEDIA

NEWSPAPERS & MAGAZINES

The main serious national newspapers in England are the *Times,* the *Telegraph,* the *Independent,* and the *Guardian* (the *Observer* is the *Guardian*'s Sunday paper), which are known, collectively, as the "broadsheets." Each has a political viewpoint in both its news coverage and its opinion pages. The *Times* and *Telegraph* are more conservative, whereas the *Independent* and *Guardian* take a more left-wing approach. Tabloids, such as the *Sun,* the *Mirror,* and the *Daily Mail,* present a notably livelier version of the news, with

an emphasis on celebrities, nudity, sports, and scandal. They, too, have political agendas: the *Sun* and *Daily Mail* are both conservative, whereas the *Mirror* is liberal. This is more significant to the English than it likely will be for you—English people may make sweeping generalizations about one another based upon which newspaper is tucked under one's arm. Regardless of politics, you'll get more sports news from the tabloids, and more arts and entertainment news from the broadsheets. The newspapers all have Web sites full of articles, as well as news about what will be going on during your visit.

For detailed information about what's going on in London, pick up a copy of *Time Out* magazine. For countrywide information about shops, restaurants, and art events—or for inspiration in general— peruse the glossy monthly magazines: *Tatler, Country Living, Harpers & Queen, Vogue, Wallpaper, World of Interiors, House &Garden,* and *The Face.* Many of these are available in major cities around the world.

RADIO & TELEVISION

The main television channels are BBC1 and BBC2 from the British Broadcasting Corporation. BBC2 is considered the more eclectic and artsy, with a higher proportion of alternative humor, drama, and documentaries. The independent channels are ITV (Independent Television), which regionalizes into many companies across the country. Channel 4 is a mixture of mainstream and off-the-wall, whereas Channel 5 has more sports and films. You'll see big-budget highbrow productions on television occasionally (most often on the BBC), but there are also mainstream soaps such as *Eastenders* and *Coronation Street* (which the Queen is rumored to watch). Cable channels, many of which are available in hotel rooms, increase the diet of entertainment.

Radio has seen a similar explosion for every taste, from 24-hour classical music on Classic FM (100.9 FM), and rock on Capital FM (95.8 FM) and Branson's Virgin (105.8 FM), to nostalgic on Heart (106.2 FM) and talk on Talk Radio (1053

AM)—and that's just a sample of the independents. The BBC's Radio 1 (98.8 FM) is for the young and hip; 2 (89.1 FM) for middle-of-the-roadsters; 3 (91.3 FM) for classics, jazz, and arts; 4 (93.5 FM) for news, current affairs, drama (such as *The Archers* radio soap), and documentary; 5 Live (693 AM) for sports and news with phone-ins; and BBC World Service (648 AM) for the best of the BBC.

MONEY MATTERS

Prices in Britain are generally high, largely because the exchange rate is so unfavorable for other currencies, particularly the U.S. dollar. Prices are higher in London than elsewhere in the country, to the point where "London prices" is used as a warning in rural areas (as in "You wouldn't want to go there, they charge London prices"). A cup of coffee will run from 60p to £3, depending on where you buy it; a pint of beer is about £2.25 in the countryside and £3 in a city, and a ham sandwich costs £2.25–£3.50. A short taxi ride averages £8.

Banks rarely have every foreign currency on hand, and it may take as long as a week to order. If you're planning to exchange funds before leaving home, don't wait till the last minute.

Prices throughout this guide are given for adults. Substantially reduced fees are almost always available for children, students, and senior citizens. For information on taxes, *see* Taxes.

ATMS & BANKS

Your own bank will probably charge a fee for using ATMs abroad; the foreign bank you use may also charge a fee. Nevertheless, you'll usually get a better rate of exchange via an ATM than you will at a currency-exchange office or even when changing money in a bank. And extracting funds as you need them is a safer option than carrying around a large amount of cash.

Make sure before leaving home that your credit and debit cards have been programmed for ATM use abroad—ATMs in England and Wales accept PINs of four or fewer digits only; if your PIN is longer, ask about changing it. If you know your PIN as a word, learn the numerical equivalent, since most keypads in England show numbers only, not letters. Most ATMs are on both the Cirrus and Plus networks. ATMs are available at most main-street banks, at large supermarkets, such as Sainsbury's and Tesco's, some tube stops in London, and many rail stations. Major banks include Barclays, HSBC, and NatWest.

CREDIT CARDS

The Discover card is not accepted in Britain.

Throughout this guide, the following abbreviations are used: **AE**, American Express; **DC**, Diners Club; **MC**, MasterCard; and **V**, Visa.

It's a good idea to inform your credit-card company before you travel, especially if you're going abroad and don't travel internationally very often. Otherwise, the credit-card company might put a hold on your card owing to unusual activity—not a good thing halfway through your trip. Record all your credit-card numbers—as well as the phone numbers to call in the if your cards are lost or stolen—in a safe place so you're prepared should something go wrong. Both MasterCard and Visa have general numbers you can call (collect if you're abroad) if your card is lost, but you're better off calling the number of your issuing bank since MasterCard and Visa usually just transfer you to your bank; your bank's number is usually printed on your card.

If you plan to use your credit card for cash advances, you'll need to apply for a PIN at least two weeks before your trip. Although it's usually cheaper (and safer) to use a credit card abroad for large purchases (so you can cancel payments or be reimbursed if there's a problem) note that some credit-card companies *and* the banks that issue them add substantial percentages to all foreign transactions, whether they're done in a foreign currency or not. Check on these fees before leaving home so that there won't be any surprises when you get the bill.

Before you charge something, ask the merchant whether he or she plans to do a dynamic currency conversion (DCC). In such a transaction the credit-card *processor* (shop, restaurant, or hotel, not Visa or MasterCard) converts the currency and charges you in dollars. In most cases you'll pay the merchant a 3% fee for this service in addition to any credit-card company and issuing-bank foreign-transaction surcharges.

DCC programs are becoming increasingly widespread. Merchants who participate in them are supposed to ask whether you want to be charged in dollars or the local currency, but they don't always do so. And even if they do offer you a choice, they may well avoid mentioning the additional surcharges. The good news is that you *do* have a choice. And if this practice really gets your goat, you can avoid it entirely thanks to American Express; with its cards, DCC simply isn't an option.

🗷 Reporting Lost Cards **American Express** ☎ 800/992–3404 in U.S., 336/393–1111 collect from abroad ⊕ www.americanexpress.com. **Diners Club** ☎ 800/234–6377 in U.S., 303/799–1504 collect from abroad ⊕ www.dinersclub.com. **MasterCard** ☎ 800/622–7747 in U.S., 636/722–7111 collect from abroad ⊕ www.mastercard.com. **Visa** ☎ 800/847–2911 in U.S., 410/581–9994 collect from abroad ⊕ www.visa.com.

CURRENCY & EXCHANGE

The unit of currency in Britain is the pound sterling (£), divided into 100 pence (p). The bills (called notes in Britain) are 50, 20, 10, and 5 pounds. Scotland and the Channel Islands have their own bills, and the Channel Islands their own coins, too. Scottish bills are accepted in the rest of Britain, but you cannot use Channel Islands currency outside the islands. Coins are £2, £1, 50p, 20p, 10p, 5p, 2p, and 1p.

At the time of this writing, the exchange rate was about U.S. $1.85 to the pound.

For the most favorable rates, **change money through banks.** Although ATM transaction fees may be higher abroad than at home, ATM rates are excellent because they're based on wholesale rates offered only by major banks. You won't do

as well at exchange booths in airports or rail and bus stations, in hotels, in restaurants, or in stores. To avoid lines at airport exchange booths, get a bit of local currency before you leave home. British post offices exchange currency with no fee, and at decent rates.

🗷 Exchange Rate Information **Yahoo Finance** ⊕ finance.yahoo.com/currency. **Oanda.com** ⊕ www.oanda.com also allows you to print out a handy table with the current day's conversion rates. **XE.com** ⊕ www.xe.com.

TRAVELER'S CHECKS

Some consider this the currency of the cave man, and it's true that fewer establishments accept traveler's checks these days. Nevertheless, they're a cheap and secure way to carry extra money, particularly on trips to urban areas. Both Citibank (under the Visa brand) and American Express issue traveler's checks in the United States, but AmEx is better known and more widely accepted; you can also avoid hefty surcharges by cashing AmEx checks at AmEx offices. Whatever you do, keep track of all the serial numbers in case the checks are lost or stolen. Remember to **buy the traveler's checks in British pounds.**

American Express now offers a stored-value card called a Travelers Cheque Card, which you can use wherever American Express–credit cards are accepted, including ATMs. The card can carry a minimum of $300 and a maximum of $2,700, and it's a safe way to carry your funds. Although you can get replacement funds in 24 hours if your card is lost or stolen, it doesn't really strike us as a very good deal. In addition to a high initial cost ($14.95 to set up the card, plus $5 each time you "reload"), you still have to pay a 2% fee for each purchase in a foreign currency (similar to that of any credit card). Further, each time you use the card in an ATM you pay a transaction fee of $2.50 on top of the 2% transaction fee for the conversion—add it all up and it can be considerably more than you would pay for simply using your own ATM card. Regular traveler's checks are just as secure and cost less.

American Express ☎ 888/412-6945 in U.S., 801/945-9450 collect outside of U.S. to add value or speak to customer service ⊕ www.americanexpress.com.

PACKING

We realize that packing is a matter of style—a very personal thing—but there's a lot to be said for traveling light. The tips in this section will help you win the battle of the bulging bag.

Make a list. In a recent Fodor's survey, 29% of respondents said they make lists (and often pack) at least a week before a trip. Lists can be used at least twice—once to pack and once to repack at the end of your trip. You'll also have a record of the contents of your suitcase, just in case it disappears in transit.

Think it through. What's the weather like? Is this a business trip or a cruise or resort vacation? Going abroad? In some places and/or sights, traditions of dress may be more or less conservative than you're used to. As your itinerary comes together, jot activities down and note possible outfits next to each (don't forget those shoes and accessories).

Edit your wardrobe. Plan to wear everything twice (better yet, three times) and to do laundry along the way. Stick to one basic look—urban chic, sporty casual, etc. Build around one or two neutrals and an accent (e.g., black, white, and olive green). Women can freshen looks by changing scarves or jewelry. For a week's trip, you can look smashing with three bottoms, four or five tops, a sweater, and a jacket you can wear alone or over the sweater.

Be practical. Put comfortable shoes at the top of your list. (Did we need to tell you this?) Pack items that are lightweight, wrinkle resistant, compact, and washable. (Or this?) Try a simple wrinkling test: Intentionally fold a piece of fabric between your fingers for a couple minutes. If it refuses to crease, it will probably come out of your suitcase looking fresh. That said if you stack and then roll your clothes when packing, they'll wrinkle less.

Check weight and size limitations. In the United States you may be charged extra for checked bags weighing more than 50 pounds. Abroad some airlines don't allow you to check bags weighing more than 60 to 70 pounds, or they charge outrageous fees for every pound your luggage is over. Carry-on size limitations can be stringent, too.

Be prepared to lug it yourself. Unless you're on a guided tour or a cruise, select luggage that you can readily carry. Porters, like good butlers, are hard to find these days.

Lock it up. Several companies sell locks (about $10) approved by the Transportation Safety Administration that can be unlocked by all U.S. security personnel should they decide to search your bags. Alternatively, you can use simple plastic cable ties, which are sold at hardware stores in bundles.

Tag it. Always put tags on your luggage with some kind of contact information; use your business address if you don't want people to know your home address. Put the same information (and a copy of your itinerary) inside your luggage, too.

Don't check valuables. On U.S. flights, airlines are only liable for about $2,800 per person for bags. On international flights, the liability limit is around $635 per bag. But just try collecting from the airline for items like computers, cameras, and jewelry. It isn't going to happen; they aren't covered. And though comprehensive travel policies may cover luggage, the liability limit is often a pittance. Your home-owners' policy may cover you sufficiently when you travel—or not. Stash baubles and gizmos in your carry on—right near those prescription meds.

Report problems immediately. If your bags—or things in them—are damaged or go astray, file a written claim with your airline *before you leave the airport*. If the airline is at fault, it may give you money for essentials until your luggage arrives. Most lost bags are found within 48 hours, so alert the airline to your whereabouts for two or three days. If your bag was opened for security reasons in the United States and something is missing, file a claim with the TSA.

WHAT YOU'LL NEED IN ENGLAND

Britain can be cool, damp, and overcast, even in summer. You'll want a heavy coat for winter and a lightweight coat or warm jacket for summer. There's no time of year when a raincoat or umbrella won't come in handy. For the cities, **pack as you would for an American city:** coats and ties for expensive restaurants and nightspots, casual clothes elsewhere. Jeans are popular in Britain and are perfectly acceptable for sightseeing and informal dining. Casual blazers are popular here with men. For women, ordinary street dress is acceptable everywhere.

If you plan to stay in budget hotels, take your own soap. Many do not provide soap, and some give guests only one tiny bar per room.

PASSPORTS & VISAS

U.S. citizens need only a valid passport to enter Great Britain for stays of up to six months. Travelers should be prepared to show sufficient funds to support and accommodate themselves while in Britain (credit cards will usually suffice for this) and to show a return or onward ticket. Health certificates are not required.

PASSPORTS

We're always surprised at how few Americans have passports—only 25% at this writing, though the number is expected to grow in coming years, when it becomes impossible to reenter the United States from trips to neighboring Canada or Mexico without one. Remember this: a passport verifies both your identity and nationality—a great reason to have one.

U.S. passports are valid for 10 years. Applications are available online and at post offices as well as passport offices. The cost to apply is $97 for adults, $82 for children under 16; renewals are $67. Allow six weeks to process the paperwork for either a new or renewed passport. For an expediting fee of $60, you can reduce the time to about two weeks. If your trip is less than two weeks away, you can get a passport even more rapidly by going to a passport office with the necessary documentation. Private expediters can get things done in as little as 48 hours but charge hefty fees for their services. Children under 14 must appear in person to apply for or renew a passport; both parents must accompany the child (or send a notarized statement with their permission) and provide proof of their relationship to the child.

Before your trip, make two copies of your passport's data page (one for someone at home and another for you to carry separately). Or scan the page and e-mail it to someone at home and/or yourself.

🛂 **U.S. Passport Information** **U.S. Department of State** ☎ 877/487-2778 ⊕ travel.state.gov/passport.
🛂 **U.S. Passport & Visa Expediters** **A. Briggs Passport & Visa Expediters** ☎ 800/806-0581 or 202/464-3000 ⊕ www.abriggs.com. **American Passport Express** ☎ 800/455-5166 or 603/559-9888 ⊕ www.americanpassport.com. **Passport Express** ☎ 800/362-8196 or 401/272-4612 ⊕ www.passportexpress.com. **Travel Document Systems** ☎ 800/874-5100 or 202/638-3800 ⊕ www.traveldocs.com. **Travel the World Visas** ☎ 866/886-8472 or 301/495-7700 ⊕ www.world-visa.com.

PHONES

The good news is that you can now make a direct-dial telephone call from virtually any point on earth. The bad news? You can't always do so cheaply. Calling from a hotel is almost always the most expensive option; hotels usually add huge surcharges to all calls, particularly international ones. In some countries, you can phone from call centers or even the post office. Calling cards usually keep costs to a minimum, but only if you purchase them locally. And then there are mobile phones ⇨ *below*, which are sometimes more prevalent—particularly in the developing world—than land lines; as expensive as mobile phone calls can be, they are still usually a much cheaper option than calling from your hotel.

British Telecom runs the telephone service in Great Britain and is generally reliable. All calls (including local calls) made within the United Kingdom are charged according to the time of day. The standard rate applies weekdays 8 AM to 6 PM; a cheaper rate is in effect weekdays 6 PM to 8 AM and all day on weekends, when it's even cheaper. A local call before 6 PM costs 15p for three minutes; this doubles to 30p for the same from a pay phone. A daytime call to the United States will cost 24p a minute on a regular phone (weekends are cheaper), 80p on a pay phone.

AREA & COUNTRY CODES

The country code for Great Britain (and thus England) is 44. When dialing an English number from abroad, drop the initial 0 from the local area code. For example, let's say you're calling Buckingham Palace—020/7839–1377—from the United States. First, dial 011 (the international access code), then 44 (Great Britain's country code), then 20 (London's center city code—without its initial 0), then the remainder of the telephone number.

A word of warning: 0870 numbers are *not* toll-free numbers in Britain; in fact, numbers beginning with this or the 0900 (premium rate) prefix cost extra to call. The amount varies—and is usually relatively small when dialed from within the country—but can be excessive when dialed from outside Britain.

The country code is 1 for the United States.

DIRECTORY & OPERATOR ASSISTANCE

To call the U.K. operator, dial 100; to call the international operator, dial 155. For directory inquiries (information), dial 118500; for international directory assistance, dial 118505.

INTERNATIONAL CALLS

For direct overseas dialing from England, dial 00, then the country code, area code, and number. For the international operator, credit card, or collect calls, dial 155.

LOCAL CALLS

You do not need to dial the area code if you are making a call within the same area code.

LONG-DISTANCE CALLS

For long-distance calls within England (and Britain), dial the area code (which usually begins with 01, except in London), followed by the telephone number. The area code prefix is used only when you are dialing from outside the region. In provincial areas, the dialing codes for nearby towns are often posted in the phone booth.

LONG-DISTANCE SERVICES

AT&T, MCI, and Sprint access codes make calling long-distance relatively convenient, but you may find the local access number blocked in many hotel rooms. First ask the hotel operator to connect you. If the hotel operator balks, ask for an international operator, or dial the international operator yourself. One way to improve your odds of getting connected to your long-distance carrier is to travel with more than one company's calling card (a hotel may block Sprint, for example, but not MCI). If all else fails, call from a pay phone. If you are traveling for a longer period of time, consider renting a cell-phone from a local company.

Access Codes **AT&T Direct** In the U.K., there are AT&T access numbers to dial the U.S. using three different phone types: ☎ 0500/890011 Cable & Wireless, 0800/890011 British Telecom, 0800/013–0011 AT&T. **MCI WorldPhone** ☎ 0800/279–5088 in the U.K. for the U.S. via MCI. **Sprint International Access** ☎ 0800/890877.

MOBILE PHONES

If you have a multiband phone (some countries use different frequencies than what's used in the United States) and your service provider uses the world-standard GSM network (as do T-Mobile, Cingular, and Verizon), you can probably use your phone abroad. Roaming fees can steep, though: 99¢ a minute is considered reasonable. And overseas, you normally pay the toll charges for incoming calls. It's almost always cheaper to send a text message than to make a call since text messages have a very low set fee (often less than 5¢).

If you just want to make local calls, consider buying a new SIM card (note that your provider may have to unlock your phone for you to use a different SIM card) and a prepaid service plan in the destination. You'll then have a local number and can make local calls at local rates. If your trip is extensive you could also simply buy a new cell phone in your destination as the initial cost will be offset over time.

If you travel internationally frequently, save one of your old mobile phones or buy a cheap one on the Internet; ask your cellphone company to unlock it for you, and take it with you as a travel phone, buying a new SIM card with pay-as-you-go service in each destination. Another option in England is to rent a phone through your car-rental company.

🔲 **Cellular Abroad** ☎ 800/287–3020 or 310/829–6878 ⊕ www.cellularabroad.com rents cell phones and sells country-specific SIM cards and mobile phones that work in many countries. **Mobal** ☎ 888/888–9162 ⊕ www.mobalrental.com rents mobiles and sells GSM phones ($49 or $99) that will operate in 140 countries. Per-call rates vary throughout the world. **Planet Fone** ☎ 888/988–4777 ⊕ www.planetfone.com rents cell phones, but the per-minute rates are expensive.

PHONE CARDS

Public card phones operate with British Telecom (BT) chip cards that you can buy from post offices or newsstands. They are ideal for longer calls; are composed of units of 20p; and come in values of £3, £5, £10, and £20. To use a card phone, lift the receiver, insert your card, and dial the number. An indicator panel shows the number of units used. At the end of your call, the card will be returned. Where credit cards are taken, slide the card through, as indicated. Beware of buying cards that require you to dial a free phone number; some of these are not legitimate. It's better to get a BT card.

PUBLIC PHONES

There are three types of phones: those that accept (a) only coins, (b) only British Telecom (BT) phone cards, or (c) BT phone cards and credit cards.

The coin-operated phones are of the push-button variety; their workings vary, but there are usually instructions on each unit. Most take 10p, 20p, 50p, and £1 coins. Insert the coins *before* dialing (minimum charge is 20p). If you hear a repeated single tone after dialing, the line is busy; a continual tone means the number is unobtainable (or that you have dialed the wrong—or no—prefix). The indicator panel shows how much money is left; add

more whenever you like. If there is no answer, replace the receiver and your money will be returned.

RESTROOMS

Public restrooms are sparse in England. Most big cities maintain public facilities that are clean and modern. If there is an attendant, which is rare, you are expected to pay admission (usually 30p). Rail stations and department stores have public restrooms that occasionally charge a small fee, usually 20p. Most pubs, restaurants, and even fast-food chains reserve their bathrooms for customer use only. Hotels and museums are usually a good place to find clean, free facilities. Some upscale London establishments have attendants who expect a small tip—about £1. On the road, gas-station facilities are usually clean and free.

The Bathroom Diaries is a Web site that's flush with unsanitized info on restrooms the world over—each one located, reviewed, and rated.

🔲 Find a Loo **The Bathroom Diaries** ⊕ www.thebathroomdiaries.com.

SAFETY

England has a low incidence of violent crime. However, petty crime is on the rise, and tourists can be the target, although this problem is limited almost exclusively to city centers such as London, Birmingham, and Liverpool. Distribute your cash, credit cards, IDs, and other valuables between a deep front pocket, an inside jacket or vest pocket, and a hidden money pouch. Don't reach for the money pouch once you're in public.

When in a city center, if you're paying at a shop or a restaurant, **never put your wallet down or let your bag out of your hand.** When sitting on a chair in a public place, keep your purse on your lap. Always use the bag hooks in public toilet stalls instead of putting your bag on the floor where it may be snatched.

Don't wear expensive jewelry or watches, as they are easily lifted. **Store your passport in the hotel safe;** use your driver's license for identification. Don't leave anything in your car—take valuables with you and put everything else, even a coat, out of sight in your trunk.

Over the years there have been terrorist incidents in England and Northern Ireland, and although U.S. citizens are not targeted, some have been injured. In July 2005, a few days after London won the bid for the 2012 Olympics, bombs exploded in three tube (subway) stations and on one bus. Bomb threats are taken seriously. **Don't leave any bags unattended,** as they may be viewed as a security risk and taken away by the authorities. If you see any unattended bags on the train or tube, find a worker and report it. Never hesitate to get off of a tube, train, or bus if you feel unsafe or uncomfortable.

Women are unlikely to be harassed, but the usual precautions apply—be vigilant if walking alone at night and avoid dimly lighted or deserted areas. Avoid unlicensed minicabs.

GOVERNMENT ADVISORIES

The U.S. Department of State's Web site has more than just travel warnings and advisories. The consular information sheets issued for every country have general safety tips, entry requirements (though be sure to verify these with the country's embassy), and other useful details.

Consider registering online with the state department (https://travelregistration.state.gov/ibrs/), so the government will know to look for you should a crisis occur in the country you're visiting. If you travel frequently also look into the Registered Traveler program of the Transportation Security Administration (TSA; www.tsa.gov). The program, which is still being tested in five U.S. airports, is designed to cut down on gridlock at security checkpoints by allowing prescreened travelers to pass quickly through kiosks that scan an iris and/or a fingerprint. How sci-fi is that? ⛊ General Information & Warnings **Consular Affairs Bureau of Canada** ⊕ www.voyage.gc.ca. **U.K. Foreign & Commonwealth Office** ⊕ www.fco.gov.uk/travel. **U.S. Department of State** ⊕ www.travel.state.gov.

LOCAL SCAMS

Although scams do occur in Britain, they are not pervasive. Do, however, **watch out for pickpockets,** particularly in London and other large cities. They often work in pairs, with one distracting you in some way (asking for directions or bumping into you) while the other takes your valuables. Always take a licensed black taxi or call a car service (sometimes called minicabs) recommended by your hotel. Passengers have been robbed or overcharged by unlicensed drivers in fake cabs. Avoid using minicab services offered by drivers on the street. In most cases, they will drive an indirect route and overcharge you. Always buy theater tickets from a reputable dealer. If you are driving in from a British port, beware of thieves posing as fake customs officials. The thieves stop travelers after they have followed them away from the port. Then they flag them down and "confiscate illegal goods."

When withdrawing cash from an ATM, be sure to cover the number pad with one hand while inputting your PIN. Also, if you're getting money out of an ATM, beware of someone bumping into you to distract you. If anybody claims you've dropped money while getting cash from a machine, ignore him or her. This is a common distraction scam for a pickpocket. You may want to use ATMs inside banks rather than those outside them. In London, scams are most common at ATMs on Oxford Street and around Piccadilly Circus.

SHOPPING

Britain is a global market: Europe's best labels and fashion boutiques can be found in London and in many of the country's major cities, and several U.S. chain stores operate here as well. Department stores, including John Lewis, Selfridges, and Debenhams, have a wide range of everyday items and goods that make great gifts. Designer outlet malls have sprung up around the country, too. In any shopping excursion, seek out original designs, ethnic finds (from the many craft markets and fairs), and historical items, which you'll find in abundance, since nearly every village has at least one antiques shop. Take advantage of sales at the end of each season; the biggest are the post-Christmas sales that run through January.

KEY DESTINATIONS

London is the center of the English shopper's universe. Whatever department store, boutique, or specialty shop there is in the whole of the kingdom, you need look no farther than London's Oxford and Regent streets, Knightsbridge, and Kensington. Antiques hunters head for the capital's markets and auction rooms, particularly in the Portobello, Bermondsey, and Bond Street areas. For bespoke tailoring from top to toe, anything can be made to measure—at a price—on Savile Row and Jermyn Street. For fine china, department stores and specialty shops are fruitful hunting grounds. And for one-stop shopping for art, crafts, and beautiful clothes, head for Covent Garden.

To seek out England's most famous products on their home turf, you must travel beyond London. In Stoke-on-Trent, you can visit museums of pottery and china and purchase these items from the many stores and outlets. The Isle of Wight in the south produces designs to rival the Venetians' Murano glass. Hay-on-Wye, on the Welsh border, is a bibliophiles' center, full of bookshops.

SMART SOUVENIRS

Shops in museums, galleries, and stately homes around the country are often good choices for interesting merchandise, such as high-quality art reproductions, stationery, and beautifully packaged foods such as jam, toffee, and tea. Bookshops and antiques stores stock a plethora of unique and interesting souvenirs. In London, the Victoria & Albert Museum shop in London is a smart choice for British crafts and jewelry; for souvenirs with a historical bent, visit the British Museum shop.

WATCH OUT

For art or antiques more than 100 years old, get a Certificate of Age and Origin for customs from the Association of Art and Antique Dealers (LAPADA) or from the dealer selling the piece. Anything

more than 50 years old and valued at £39,600 or more needs a certificate, too. Beware of antique items that contain anything from an endangered species, such as tortoiseshell or ivory. You need a permit from the Department of Environment, Food and Rural Affairs to take such items out of Britain.

🗊 **Association of Art and Antiques Dealers** ☎ 020/7823-3511 ⊕ www.lapada.co.uk. **Department of Environment, Food and Rural Affairs** ☎ 0117/372-8433.

SPORTS & THE OUTDOORS

In addition to the associations listed below, VisitBritain and local Tourist Information Centres can recommend places to enjoy your favorite sport.

BIKING

The national body promoting cycle touring is the Cyclists' Touring Club (CTC: £33 a year, £12 for those under 26, £20 for those over 65, and £53 for a family of more than three). Members get free advice and route information, a B&B handbook, and a magazine. The CTC and VisitBritain (⇨ Visitor Information) publish a free guide, "Britain for Cyclists." Both the CTC and BTA provide lists of travel agencies specializing in cycling vacations. Also *see* Bike Travel for further information.

🗊 **Cyclists' Touring Club** ☎ 01483/417217 or 0870/873-0061 ⊕ www.ctc.org.uk.

BOATING

Boating can be a leisurely way to explore the countryside. For boat-rental operators along Britain's several hundred miles of historic canals and waterways, from the Norfolk Broads to the Lake District, contact the Association of Pleasure Craft Operators or Waterway Holidays UK. British Waterways has maps and other information. Waterway Holidays UK arranges boat accommodations of all kinds, from traditional narrow boats (small, slender barges) to motorboats and sailboats.

🗊 **Association of Pleasure Craft Operators** ☎ 01952/813572. **British Waterways** ☎ 01923/201120 ⊕ www.waterscape.com. **Waterway Holidays UK** ☎ 0870/241-5956 ⊕ www. waterwayholidaysuk.com.

GOLF

Originally invented in Scotland, golf is a beloved pastime all over England; it is also gaining popularity in Wales. Some courses take advantage of spectacular natural settings, from the ocean to mountain backdrops. Most courses are reserved for club members and adhere to strict rules of protocol and dress. However, many famous courses can be used by visiting golfers if they reserve well in advance. Package tours with companies such as Golf International and Owenoak International Golf Travel allow visitors into usually exclusive clubs. VisitBritain has a "Golf in Britain" map and brochure that covers 147 courses. For further information on courses, fees, and locations, try the Web sites UK Golf Guide and Golfcourses.org. 🎏 **Golf Courses** ⊕ www.golfcourses.org. **Golf International** ☎ 212/986–9176, 800/833–1389 in U.S. ⊕ www.golfinternational.com. **Owenoak International Golf Travel** ☎ 203/854–9000, 800/426–4498 in U.S. ⊕ www.owenoak.com. **UK Golf Guide** ⊕ www.uk-golfguide.com.

WALKING

Walking and hiking, from the slowest ramble to a mountainside climb requiring technical equipment, are enormously popular in England. Chapters in this book contain information about a number of long-distance paths; www.nationaltrail.co.uk has information about stunning National Trails. The Ramblers' Association publishes a magazine and a yearbook full of resources, and a list of B&Bs within 2 mi of selected long-distance footpaths. 🎏 **Countryside Commission** ☎ 01242/521381 ⊕ www.countryside.gov.uk and www.nationaltrail.co.uk. **Long Distance Walkers Association** ☎ 01753/866685 ⊕ www.ldwa.org.uk. **The Ramblers' Association** ☎ 020/7339–8500 ⊕ www.ramblers.org.uk.

TAXES

The British sales tax (V.A.T., Value Added Tax) is 17.5%. The tax is almost always included in quoted prices in shops, hotels, and restaurants. The most common exception is at high-end hotels, where prices often exclude V.A.T. Be sure to verify whether the room price includes V.A.T. Outside of hotels and rental car agencies, which have specific additional taxes, there is no other sales tax in England.

Most travelers can **get a V.A.T. refund** by either the Retail Export or the more cumbersome Direct Export method. Refunds apply for V.A.T. only on goods being taken out of Britain, and purchases must exceed a minimum limit (check with the store—generally £50–£100). Many large stores provide V.A.T.-refund services, but only if you request them; they will handle the paperwork. For the Retail Export method, you must ask the store to complete Form V.A.T. 407 (you must have identification—passports are best), to be given to customs at your last port of departure. Have the form stamped like any customs form by customs officials when you leave the country or, if you're visiting several European Union countries, when you leave the EU. Be ready to show customs officials what you've bought; budget extra time at the airport for this. After you're through passport control, take the form to a refund-service counter for an on-the-spot refund (if the retailer has an agreement with the firm running the counter; ask the store when you make your purchase), or mail it back to the store or a refund service from the airport or after you arrive home. The refund will be forwarded to you in about eight weeks, minus a service charge, either in the form of a credit to your charge card or as a British check, which American banks charge you to convert.

With the Direct Export method, the goods are mailed directly to your home; you must have a Form V.A.T. 407 certified by customs, police, or a notary public when you get home and then sent back to the store, which will refund your money. For inquiries, call the local Customs & Excise office listed in the telephone directory. Remember, V.A.T. refunds can't be processed after you arrive back home.

A service also processes refunds for most shops. You receive the total refund stated on the form. Global Refund is a Europe-wide service with 210,000 affiliated stores and more than 700 refund counters—located at major airports and border crossings. Its refund form is called a Tax Free Check. The service issues refunds in the form of cash, check, or credit-card adjustment. If you don't have time to wait at the refund counter, you can mail in the form to an office in Europe or Canada instead.

An airport departure tax of £20 (£10 for travel within U.K. and EU countries) per person is included in the price of your ticket.

🚩 **V.A.T. Refunds Global Refund** ☎ 800/566-9828 in U.S., 800/566-9828 in Canada ⊕ www. globalrefund.com. **Her Majesty's Customs & Excise office** ☎ 0845/010-9000 within U.K., 208/929-0152 from outside U.K. ⊕ http://customs.hmrc.gov.uk.

TIME

England sets its clocks by Greenwich Mean Time, five hours ahead of the U.S. East Coast. British summer time (GMT plus one hour) generally coincides with American daylight savings time adjustments.

TIPPING

Some restaurants, bars, and most hotels add a service charge of 10%–15% to the bill. In this case, you are not obliged to tip extra. If no service charge is indicated, add 10% to 15% to your total bill. Beware when signing credit-card slips that you fill in the correct total; some restaurants leave the gratuity entry empty even when they have levied a service charge. There's no need to tip at clubs (it's acceptable at posher establishments, though) unless you're being served at your table. Taxi drivers should also get 10%–15%. If you get help from a hotel concierge, a tip of £1 to £2 (more for a major service) is appropriate. You are not expected to tip theater or cinema ushers, elevator operators, or bartenders in pubs. Hairdressers and barbers should receive 10%–15%.

TOURS & PACKAGES

Guided tours are a good option when you don't want to do it all yourself. You travel along with a group (sometimes large, sometimes small), stay in pre-booked hotels, eat with your fellow travelers (sometimes included in the price of your tour, sometimes not), and follow a schedule. But not all guided tours are a "If This is Tuesday, It Must Be Belgium"

kind of experience. A knowledgable guide can take you places that you might never discover on your own. Tours aren't for everyone, but they can be just the thing for trips to places where making travel arrangements is difficult or time-consuming. Whenever you book a guided tour, find out what's included and what isn't. A "land-only" tour includes all your travel (by bus, in most cases) in the destination, but not necessarily your flights to or even within it. Also, in most cases, prices in tour brochures don't include fees and taxes. And remember that you'll be expected to tip your guide (in cash) at the end of the tour.

VACATION PACKAGES

Packages *are not* guided tours. Packages combine airfare, accommodations, and perhaps a rental car or other extras (theater tickets, guided excursions, boat trips, reserved entry to popular museums, transit passes), but they let you do your own thing. During busy periods, packages may be your only option because flights and rooms may be otherwise sold out. Packages will definitely save you time. They can also save you money, particularly in peak seasons, but—and this is a really big "but"—you should price each part of the package separately to be sure. And be aware that prices advertised on Web sites and in newspapers rarely include service charges or taxes, which can up your costs by hundreds of dollars.

Local tourism boards can provide information about lesser-known and small-niche operators that sell packages to just a few destinations. And don't always assume that you can get the best deal by booking everything yourself. Some packages and cruises are sold only through travel agents.

Each year consumers are stranded or lose their money when packagers—even large ones with excellent reputations—go out of business. How can you protect yourself? First, always pay with a credit card; if you have a problem, your credit-card company may help you resolve it. Second, buy trip insurance that covers default. Third, choose a company that belongs to the United States Tour Operators Association, whose members must set aside funds ($1 million) to cover defaults. Finally choose a company that also participates in the Tour Operator Program of the American Society of Travel Agents (ASTA), which will act as mediator in any disputes. You can also check on the tour operator's reputation among travelers by posting an inquiry on one of the Fodors.com forums.

▶ **Organizations** **American Society of Travel Agents (ASTA)** ☎ 703/739–2782 or 800/965–2782 24-hr hotline ⊕ www.astanet.com. **United States Tour Operators Association (USTOA)** ☎ 212/599–6599 ⊕ www.ustoa.com.

TRAIN TRAVEL

Operated by private companies, the train system in Britain is extensive and useful, though less than ideal. Some trains are old, and virtually all lines suffer from delays, schedule changes, and occasional crippling strikes. Worst of all, you can pay quite a lot for all of that. Work is under way to improve the situation, but resolution is years away. All major cities and even most small towns are served by trains, and despite the difficulties, rail travel is the most pleasant way to cover long distances.

When traveling by train, **make a reservation whenever possible;** there are always discounts for early booking. Book several weeks in advance and tickets can be half or one-third of what you might pay if you just showed up at the station on the day of travel. On long-distance runs, some rail lines have buffet cars; on others, you can purchase snacks from a mobile snack cart. Most train companies now have "quiet cars" on trains, where mobile-phone use is forbidden, and conversation is meant to be kept at a low volume.

CLASSES

Most rail lines have first-class and second-class cars. In virtually all cases, second class is perfectly comfortable. First class generally has superior seating and tables—but in many cases the only difference between first and second class is the size of the seats, which are marginally larger in first. First class usually costs two to three times the cost of second class, though, so it's usually not worth the cost. However,

first class is also usually quieter and less crowded, which can be priceless. Check with National Rail Enquiries for details.

CUTTING COSTS

To save money, **look into rail passes.** But be aware that if you don't plan to cover many miles, you may come out ahead by buying individual tickets. If you plan to travel a lot by train in England and Wales, **consider purchasing a BritRail Pass,** which gives unlimited travel over the entire British rail network and can save you money. But be aware that if you don't plan to cover many miles, you may come out ahead by buying individual tickets. You must **buy your BritRail Pass before you leave home.** They are available from most travel agents or from ACP Rail International, BritRail, DER, or Rail Europe; check their Web sites for complete details. Note that EurailPasses are not honored in Britain and that the rates listed here are subject to change.

BritRail passes come in two basic varieties. The Classic pass allows travel on consecutive days, and the FlexiPass allows a number of travel days within a set period of time. The cost (in U.S. dollars) of a BritRail Consecutive Pass adult ticket for 8 days is $311 standard and $469 first-class; for 15 days, $469 standard and $702 first-class; for 22 days, $592 and $891; and for a month, $702 and $1,054. The cost of a BritRail FlexiPass adult ticket for 4 days' travel in two months is $275 standard and $409 first-class; for 8 days' travel in two months, $399 standard and $598 first-class; and for 15 days' travel in two months, $604 standard and $901 first-class. Prices drop by about 25% for off-peak travel passes between October and March. Passes for students, seniors, and ages 16 to 25 are discounted, too.

For shorter journeys, try the London Plus Pass. This is an excellent deal, offering four days of first-class travel spread over eight days for $176. Two and seven days of travel are other options.

The England Flexipass, England Consecutive Pass, BritRail Pass Plus Ireland, and Freedom of Wales pass are other options, and you can purchase a Eurostar ticket for

Paris or Brussels in conjunction with a BritRail Pass.

Many travelers assume that rail passes guarantee them seats or sleeping accommodations on the trains they wish to ride. Not so. You need to **book seats ahead even if you are using a rail pass,** especially on trains that may be crowded, particularly in summer on popular routes.

There are also some discount passes for travel within regions; individual chapters in this book have information, or you can call National Rail Enquiries (⇨ Fares & Schedules).

🚈 Discount Passes **ACP Rail International** ☎ 866/938–7245 ⊕ www.acpmarketing.net. **BritRail** ☎ 877/677–1066 ⊕ www.britrail.net. **DER Travel Services** ☎ 800/782–2424 🖷 800/782–2424 for information, 800/860–9944 for brochures ⊕ www.der.com. **Rail Europe** ☎ 877/257–2887 ⊕ www.raileurope.com ☎ 416/482–1777 or 800/361–7245 🖷 0870/584–8848.

FARES & SCHEDULES

The best way to find out which train to take, which station to catch it at, and what times trains travel to your destination is to call National Rail Enquiries. It's a helpful, comprehensive, free service that covers all the country's rail lines. National Rail will help you choose the best train to take, and then connect you with the ticket office for that train company so that you can buy tickets.

Whenever possible, purchase your tickets at least two weeks in advance of your journey. Ticket prices are set on a sliding scale. The closer to the time of the journey, the more expensive the tickets. A single ticket from London to Cardiff, in Wales, can cost you £22 if you purchase it two weeks in advance, or more than £100 if you purchase it on the day you want to travel. Ticket prices are also more expensive during rush hour—so plan to travel after 9:30 AM, and before 4:30 PM or after 6:30 PM. That's just as well, since the crush of commuters makes traveling during rush hour unpleasant anyway.

If you want more information, the monthly *OAG Rail Guide* (about £7 and available from WH Smith branches and most larger main line rail stations) covers all national rail services and Eurostar, as well as buses, ferries, and rail-based tourist facilities. You can find timetables of rail services in Britain and some ferry services in the *Thomas Cook European Timetable,* issued monthly and available at travel agents and some bookstores in the United States.

🚈 Train Information **National Rail Enquiries** ☎ 0845/748–4950, 020/7278–5240 outside Britain ⊕ www.nationalrail.co.uk.

PAYING

Cash and credit cards are accepted by all train ticket offices, and over the phone.

RESERVATIONS

Reserving your ticket in advance is always recommended. Even a reservation 24 hours in advance can provide a substantial discount. Look into cheap day returns if you plan to travel a round-trip in one day.

TRAVEL AGENCIES

If you use an agent—brick-and-mortar or virtual—you'll pay a fee for the service. And know that the service you get from some online agents isn't comprehensive. For example Expedia or Travelocity don't search for prices on budget airlines like JetBlue, Southwest, or small foreign carriers. That said, some agents (online or not) *do* have access to fares that are difficult to find otherwise, and the savings can be more than make up for any surcharge.

A knowledgeable brick-and-mortar travel agent can be a godsend if you're booking a cruise, a package trip that's not available to you directly, an air pass, or a complicated itinerary including several overseas flights. What's more, travel agents who specialize in a destination may have exclusive access to certain deals and insider information on things such as charter flights. Agents who specialize in types of travelers (senior citizens, gays and lesbians, naturists) or types of trips (cruises, luxury travel, safaris) can also be invaluable. And complain about the surcharges all you like, but when things don't work out the way you'd hoped, it's nice to have an agent to put things right.

🔃 Agent Resources **American Society of Travel Agents** ☎ 703/739-2782 ⊕ www.travelsense.org. 🔃 Online Agents **Expedia** ⊕ www.expedia.com. **Onetravel.com** ⊕ www.onetravel.com. **Orbitz** ⊕ www.orbitz.com. **Priceline.com** ⊕ www. priceline.com. **Travelocity** ⊕ www.travelocity.com.

VISITOR INFORMATION

The Essentials section at the end of each chapter lists locations for local and regional tourist information centers. The main London Visitor Centre is at Waterloo International Terminal Arrivals Hall (daily 8:30 AM–10:30 PM), with branches at Heathrow Airport (Terminals 1, 2, and 3), Victoria train station, Gatwick, and elsewhere in the city. The Britain and London Visitor Centre (open June through October, weekdays 9:30 to 6:30, Saturday 9 to 5, Sunday 10 to 4; November through May, weekdays 9:30 to 6:30, weekends 10 to 4) provides details about travel, accommodations, and entertainment for the whole of Britain, but you need to visit the center in person to get information. London Line (accessible only in Britain) is Visit London's 24-hour phone service—it's a premium-rate (60p per minute at all times) recorded information line, with different numbers for theater, events, museums, sports, getting around, and so on. You may find that your guidebook, a newspaper, and a copy of the weekly *Time Out* magazine (it comes out each Tuesday) may be more helpful.

VisitBritain has a vast amount of information, both printed and on its Web site; you can even check out information online about film locations.

🔃 In London **Britain and London Visitor Centre** ✉ 1 Regent St., Piccadilly Circus, SW1Y 4NX ☎ No phone ⊕ www.visitbritain.com. **London Line** ☎ 09068/663344. **London Visitor Centre** ✉ Arrivals Hall, Waterloo International Terminal, Waterloo Rd. ☎ No phone ⊕ www.visitlondon.com. 🔃 In the U.S. **VisitBritain** ✉ 551 5th Ave., 7th fl., New York, NY 10176 ☎ 212/986-2200 or 800/462-2748 ⊕ www.visitbritain.com/usa ✉ 625 N. Michigan Ave., Suite 1510, Chicago, IL 60611 ☎ 800/462-2748.

WEB SITES

We're really proud of our Web site: Fodors.com is a great place to begin any journey. Scan "Travel Wire" for suggested itineraries, travel deals, restaurant and hotel openings, and other up-to-the-minute info. Check out "Booking" to research prices and book plane tickets, hotel rooms, rental cars, and vacation packages. Head to "Talk" for on-the-ground pointers from travelers who frequent our message boards. You can also link to loads of other travel-related resources.

After your trip, be sure to rate the places you visited and share your experiences and travel tips with us and other Fodorites in "Travel Ratings" and "Talk" on www. fodors.com.

RESOURCES

🔃 Currency Conversion **Google** ⊕ www.google. com does currency conversion. Just type in the amount you want to convert and an explanation of how you want it converted (e.g., "14 Swiss francs in dollars"), and then voila. **XE.com** ⊕ www.xe.com is a good currency conversion Web site. 🔃 Time Zones **Timeanddate.com** ⊕ www. timeanddate.com/worldclock can help you figure out the correct time anywhere in the world. 🔃 Weather **Accuweather.com** ⊕ www. accuweather.com is an independent weather-forecasting service with especially good coverage of hurricanes. **Weather.com** ⊕ www.weather.com is the Web site for the Weather Channel. 🔃 Other Resources **CIA World Factbook** ⊕ www. odci.gov/cia/publications/factbook/index.html has profiles of every country in the world. It's a good source if you need some quick facts and figures.

SPECIAL INTERESTS

Anyone planning to visit England's stately homes, castles, and gardens should study the Web sites of the National Trust (⊕ www.nationaltrust.org.uk) and English Heritage (⊕ www.english-heritage.org.uk). Gardens are the subject of VisitBritain's site at ⊕ www.visitbritain.com/gardens; also check out ⊕ www.ngs.org.uk, the site of Britain's National Gardens program, which organizes the opening of private gardens to the public. You can find information about more than 100 arts festivals from the British Arts Festivals Association

(⊕ www.artsfestivals.co.uk). 24 Hour Museum (⊕ www.24hourmuseum.org.uk) is a nonprofit, partly government-funded site packed with information about publicly funded museums (including special exhibits), art galleries, and historical sights. It includes theme trails and plenty of Web links. The official Web site of the British monarchy is ⊕ www.royal.gov.uk.

Many travelers wonder how to find out about London events and news in advance; sometimes a box-office phone call is needed. You can start by using *Time Out*'s weekly listings— ⊕ www.timeout. co.uk. For arts coverage and reviews, click on the daily newspaper site (⊕ www. thetimes.co.uk). Theatergoers should log on to ⊕ www.officiallondontheatre.co.uk, which provides a rundown of theater and opera events months down the road.

VISITOR INFORMATION

VisitBritain's U.S. Web site, ⊕ www. visitbritain.com/usa, focuses on information most helpful to England-bound U.S. travelers, from practical information to money-saving deals. Also useful are the official Web sites ⊕ www.enjoyengland.com and ⊕ www.visitwales.com. The official London Web site for visitors is ⊕ www. visitlondon.com. London's site for kids, ⊕ www.kidslovelondon.com, has interactive features and virtual tours. The British government's Foreign and Commonwealth Office runs ⊕ www.i-uk.com, with information about culture, business, and education in Britain, as well as tourism information.

INDEX

A

A la Ronde, *315*
Abbey Hotel 🏨, *291*
Abbey Museum, *48*
Abbey Road Studios, *79*
Abbey Ruins and Botanical
 Gardens, *585–586*
Abbot Hall, *532*
Abbotsbury, *254*
Abbotsbury Swannery, *254*
Aberconwy House, *711*
Abergavenny, *729–730*
Abergavenny Castle, *729*
Abergavenny Food Festival,
 729
Aberystwyth, *717–720*
Aberystwyth Cliff Railway,
 718–719
Achilles statue, *74*
ADC Theatre, *578*
Adlard's Restaurant ✕,
 598–599
Admiral Benbow Inn 🏨, *291*
Afflecks Palace (store), *500*
Agent Provocateur (shop),
 142
Agnès B (shop), *143*
Aintree Racecourse, *509*
Air travel, *761–765*
 Bath and the Cotswolds, 440
 East Anglia, 612
 Lake District, 558
 Lancashire and the Peaks, 521
 London, 146–149
 Northeast, 690
 Shakespeare Country, 385
 South, 257
 Southeast, 205
 Thames Valley, 358
 Wales, 738
 Welsh Borders, 481
 West Country, 317
 Yorkshire, 658
Aira Force, *551–552*
Albert Dock, *502*
Albert Memorial, *79*
Albion House, *334*
Alcester, *384*
Aldeburgh, *593–595*
Aldeburgh Festival, *594*
Alderminster, *383–384*
Alexander Keiller Museum,
 240
Alfie's Antique Market, *138*
Alice in Wonderland Centre,
 713

All Saints Church (Hereford),
 467
All Saints Church (Royal
 Tunbridge Wells), *196*
Allhallows Museum, *316*
Almeida Theatre, *133*
Almshouse Café ✕, *666*
Almshouses (Stratford-upon-
 Avon), *369*
Alnwick, *686–687*
Alnwick Castle, *686*
Alnwick Fair, *686*
Alnwick Gardens, *686*
Althorp, *358*
Alum Bay, *229*
Amberley Castle 🏨, *188–189*
Ambleside, *539–541*
American Air Museum, *571*
American Memorial Chapel,
 62
American Museum and
 Gardens, *398–399*
Anchor & Hope ✕, *99*
Angel Hill, *585*
Angel Hotel, *585*
Angel of the North, *675*
Angel Posting House and
 Livery ✕🏨, *192–193*
Anglican Cathedral, *505*
Anne of Cleves House,
 178–179
Anne Hathaway's Cottage,
 365–366
Annex 3 (bar), *124*
Apartment and house rentals,
 778–779
 London, 122–123
Apple Market, *52*
Apsley House, *74*
Aquarium of the Lakes, *536*
Aquariums, *72, 183, 255,
 300–301, 454, 536*
Architecture, *746–750*
 ⇨ *Also* Stately and historic
 homes
Arlington Row, *427*
Armitt Museum, *539*
Arnolfini, *268*
Arthurian Centre, *283–284*
Arts Theatre, *578*
Arundel, *188–189*
Arundel Castle, *188*
Arundel Festival, *189*
Ascot, *332*
Ascot Racecourse, *332*
Ashmolean Museum, *340*
Askrigg, *633*

Asprey (shop), *145*
Assembly Rooms, *395*
Aston Cantlow, *377*
Athelhampton House and
 Gardens, *251*
Athenaeum (Bury St.
 Edmunds), *585*
ATMs, *783*
Attingham Park, *473–474*
Auckland Castle, *671*
Audley End House and
 Gardens, *581*
Austen, Jane, *217, 220, 221,
 254, 395, 404*
Autumn in Malvern Festival,
 463
Avebury, *239–241*
Avebury Stone Circles,
 239–240
Avoncroft Museum of Historic
 Buildings, *448*
Aylesbury, *354–355*

B

Baddesley Clinton, *378*
Badminton Horse Trials, *271*
Bakewell, *514–515*
Bala, *702–703*
Bala Lake Railway, *702*
Baldry's ✕, *542*
Ballet, *131, 457, 499,
 744–745*
Balliol College, *340*
Balti cuisine, *455*
Baltic Centre for
 Contemporary Art, *678*
Bamburgh, *688*
Bamburgh Castle, *688*
Bancroft Gardens, *369–370*
Banerigg House 🏨, *543*
Bank of England, *65–66*
Banqueting House, *49*
Barbara Hepworth Museum
 and Sculpture Gardens, *286*
Barber Institute of Fine Art,
 448–449
Barbican (Plymouth), *300*
Barbican Centre, *128,
 129–130, 134*
Barbican House Museum, *178*
Barfly Club, *127*
Barmouth, *722*
Barnard Castle, *672–673*
Baron's Hall, *198*
Barracks (Berwick-upon-
 Tweed), *689–690*

Bartlett Street Antique Centre (Bath), *404*
Bassenthwaite Lake, *558*
Bateman's, *204–205*
Bath, *392–404*
Bath Abbey, *393–394*
Bath and the Cotswolds, *388–443*
Bath and environs, 392–407, 412
children, attractions for, 406–407, 412, 414, 423, 424, 438
The Cotswolds, 407–433
essential information, 440–443
Gloucester to the Forest of Dean, 433–440
hotels, 402–404, 405, 406, 410–411, 413, 415–418, 420–421, 422, 424, 425, 426, 427, 428–429, 431, 433, 435–437, 438–439, 440
itinerary suggestions, 391
nightlife and the arts, 404, 411, 429
outdoor activities and sports, 404, 412, 430, 437
restaurants, 400–402, 405, 406, 410, 413, 415, 416–418, 420–421, 425, 426, 427, 428–429, 431, 433, 435, 438–439, 440
shopping, 404, 412, 418, 422, 424, 430, 433, 436
Bath International Music Festival, *404*
Bath Literature Festival, *404*
Battersea Arts Centre (BAC), *134*
Battle, *176–177*
Battle Abbey, *176*
Bayswater (London), *105, 108–109*
Beaches, *174, 181, 253–254, 285–286, 310, 651*
Beamish Open-Air-Museum, *674–675*
Beatles, The, *79, 504–505, 510*
Beatles Shop, *510*
Beatles Story, *504*
Beatrix Potter Gallery, *547*
Beauchamp Chapel, *378*
Beauchamp Tower, *65*
Beaulieu, *244*
Beaulieu Abbey, *244*
Beaumaris, *709–710*
Beaumaris Castle, *709*
Beaumaris Festival, *710*

Beaumaris old gaol, *709*
Bed and breakfasts, *779*
London, 122–123
Bede's World, *678–679*
Beech House Hotel ☒, *533–534*
Beech Tree Guest House ☒, *546*
Beer, *316*
Beer Quarry Caves, *316*
Belas Knap, *412*
Belgrave Square, *79*
Bellamy's ✕, *95*
Bempton Cliffs, *648*
Berkeley Castle, *439–440*
Bermondsey (market), *145*
Bershka (store), *142*
Berwick-upon-Tweed, *689–690*
Betty's ✕, *639*
Betws-y-Coed, *706*
Beverley, *648*
Beverley Minster, *648*
Bewdley, *468–469*
Bicycling, *765–766, 790*
East Anglia, 578, 600, 604
Lake District, 541, 548, 555, 558
Lancashire and the Peaks, 523
Northeast, 671, 680, 685
Thames Valley, 330, 347, 353
Wales, 732, 733
West Country, 285, 315
Yorkshire, 660
Biddenden Winery and Cider Works, *203*
Bideford, *280*
Big Ben, *44*
Big Pit: National Coal Museum, *730*
Bilbury, *427*
Birds/bird-watching, *280, 439, 592, 602, 648, 687–688*
Birmingham, *446, 448–449, 451–458*
Birmingham Back to Backs, *449*
Birmingham Cathedral, *453*
Birmingham Museum and Art Gallery, *449*
Bishop Auckland, *671*
Bishop's Palace, *272*
Bishopstrow House ✕☒, *239*
Black Bull pub, *628*
Black Country Living Museum, *469*
Blackwell, *535*
Blackwell's (bookstore), *348*

Bladon, *351*
Blaenau Ffestiniog, *703*
Blaenavon Ironworks, *730*
Blakeney, *601–602*
Blakeney Point, *602*
Blandford Forum, *248*
Bleak House, *169*
Blenheim Palace, *347, 350–351*
Blickling Hall, *600–601*
Blists Hill Victorian Town, *475*
Bloody Tower, *64*
Bloomsbury (London), *55–59, 85, 88, 109–112*
Blue Bicycle ✕, *641*
Boating and boat travel, *766, 790*
East Anglia, 600
Lake District, 535, 538, 539, 540, 545–546, 551, 553, 555
Lancashire and the Peaks, 523
London, 152–153
Northeast, 671, 688
Shakespeare Country, 375–376, 385
South, 257
Thames Valley, 338, 347–348
Welsh Borders, 458, 469, 481
West Country, 279, 299–300, 317
Bodelwyddan Castle, *713–714*
Bodiam Castle, *204*
Bodmin, *298*
Bodnant Garden, *711*
Bodysgallen Hall ✕☒, *713*
Boggle Hole, *651*
Bolton Priory, *630*
Bookshop, The (Cambridge), *578*
Borough Market, *146*
Borrowdale, *555–557*
Borrowdale Fells, *555–556*
Boscastle, *282*
Boston, *612*
Boudicca, Queen, *588*
Bournemouth, *245–247*
Bournemouth International Centre, *245–246*
Bournemouth Live, *247*
Bourton-on-the-Water, *423–424*
Bovey Castle ☒, *307*
Bowes Museum, *673*
Bowness-on-Windermere, *534–538*
Bowood House and Gardens, *406–407*
Box Hill, *193*
Bradford, *626–627*

Brading, 228–229
Brading Roman Villa, 229
Brading: The Experience, 228
Bran Heulog, 701
Brantwood, 545
Braunton Burrows Biosphere
  Reserve, 280
Brecknock Museum, 731
Brecon, 731–733
Brecon Beacons National Park
  Visitor Centre, 732
Brecon Cathedral, 731
Brewery Arts Centre
  (Cirencester), 429
Brewery Arts Centre (Kendal),
  534
Bridge Cottage, 590
Bridge House, 539
Bridgewater Hall, 499
Bridgnorth, 476
Bridlington, 648–649
Brighton, 181–188
Brighton Festival, 187
Brighton Museum and Art
  Gallery, 182
Brighton Pier, 182
Bristol, 264–265, 268–271
£Bristol, 265
Bristol Old Vic, 271
Bristol Zoo Gardens, 269
British Airways London Eye,
  68
British Empire and
  Commonwealth Museum,
  268
British Library, 58–59
British Museum, 56, 58
Britons Arms ✕, 599
Britons Protection, The (pub),
  498
Britten Festival, 595
Brixham, 309
Broadlands, 226
Broads, 601
Broadstairs, 168–169
Broadway, 414–416
Brontë family, 627–628
Brontë Parsonage Museum,
  628
Brontë Waterfall, 628
Broughton Castle, 382–383
Brown's ✕, 460
Browns (shop), 143
Buckden, 633
Buckingham Palace, 41–42
Buckland Abbey, 303–304
Buckland Manor ✕⛌, 415
Buckler's Hard, 245
Building of Bath Museum, 399

Builth Wells, 716
Burford, 426–427
Burghley House, 608–609
Burwash, 204–205
Bury St. Edmunds, 585–587
Bus travel, 766–768
  Bath and the Cotswolds,
    440–441
  East Anglia, 612–613
  Lake District, 559
  Lancashire and the Peaks,
    521–522
  London, 149–150
  Northeast, 690–691
  Shakespeare Country, 385
  South, 257
  Southeast, 205
  Thames Valley, 358–359
  Wales, 738–739
  Welsh Borders, 481
  West Country, 317–318
  Yorkshire, 658–659
Busabe Eathai ✕, 88
Business hours, 766
Butler & Wilson (shop), 145
Butler's Wharf, 71
Butterfly Farm, 370
Buttermarket, 164
Buxton, 512–514
Buxton Festival, 514
Buxton Museum, 512
Buxton Opera House, 512,
  514
Buxton's Victorian Guesthouse
  ⛌, 513
Bwlch y Groes, 702–703
Byfords ✕⛌, 602
Bygones (antique store),
  461
Bygones Museum, 603

C

Cabinet War Rooms, 42
Cadair Idris, 721
Cadbury World, 453
Cadogan ⛌, 116
Caernarfon, 707–708
Caernarfon Castle, 707–708
Caerphilly Castle, 726
Café £ All Saints ✕, 467
Café Minuet ✕, 724
Café Parisien ✕, 398
Café René ✕, 398
Calendar of events, 29–32
Calls, The, 622
Cambridge, 564–579
Cambridge Folk Festival, 578
Canoeing, 297, 315, 404
Canterbury, 159, 162–167

Canterbury Cathedral,
  162–163
Canterbury Festival, 167
Canterbury Roman Museum,
  163–164
Canterbury Tales
  dramatization, 164
Capers ✕, 310
Captain Cook Birthplace
  Museum, 674
Captain Cook Memorial
  Museum, 653
Car rental, 768–769
Car travel, 769–771
  Bath and the Cotswolds, 441
  East Anglia, 613
  Lake District, 559
  Lancashire and the Peaks, 522
  London, 150
  Northeast, 691
  Shakespeare Country, 385–386
  South, 257–258
  Southeast, 205
  Thames Valley, 359
  Wales, 739
  Welsh Borders, 481
  West Country, 318
  Yorkshire, 659
Cardiff, 723–729
Cardiff Bay, 724
Cardiff Castle, 724
Cardiff International Arena,
  726, 729
Cardigan, 737–738
Cardynham House ✕⛌, 431
Carfax Tower, 340
Cargo (club), 125
Carisbrooke Castle, 230
Carling Academy Brixton
  (club), 126
Carlton House Terrace, 49
Carr Taylor Vineyards, 175
Castell Coch, 724
Casterbridge Hotel ⛌, 252
Castle Combe, 405
Castle Cottage ✕⛌, 705
Castle Drago, 306
Castle Howard, 657–658
Castle Museum (York), 640
Castle Rising, 606
Castlefield Urban Heritage
  Park, 488
Castlegate House Gallery, 557
Castlerigg Stone Circle, 553
Castles, 18
  Bath and the Cotswolds, 413,
    439–440
  East Anglia, 581, 592,
    596–597, 606, 610–611

Lake District, 533, 549
Lancashire and the Peaks, 519
*Northeast, 666, 671–672, 676,
    686, 687, 688, 689*
*Shakespeare Country, 379,
    380–381, 382–383*
South, 223, 230, 237, 248, 253
*Southeast, 170–171, 174–175,
    177, 178, 188, 198–199,
    200, 201–203, 204*
Thames Valley, 322–325, 351
*Wales, 700, 704–705, 707–708,
    709, 710, 713–714, 718,
    722–723, 724, 726, 729,
    736, 738*
*Welsh Borders, 464, 465,
    471–472, 476, 479*
*West Country, 277–278,
    282–283, 290, 293, 294,
    299, 305, 306, 309*
*Yorkshire, 630–631, 634–635,
    649, 657–658*
Castle, The ✕▦ , 277
Castleton, *519–520*
Cathedral Church of St.
    Andrew, 272
Cathedral Church of St. Mary
    (Truro), 295
Cathedral Close, 231
Cathedral of St. Mary
    (Lincoln), 609–610
Cathedral of St. Peter, 311
Caves
Bath and the Cotswolds, 438
*Lancashire and the Peaks,
    512–513, 516, 519*
Southeast, 175
Wales, 703
West Country, 273, 283, 316
Yorkshire, 645
Ceiriog Valley, *700–701*
Cenotaph, *50*
Centenary Square, 451
Central Library, 493
Centre for Alternative
    Technology, 720
Ceramica, 511
Ceredigion Museum, 718
Cerne Abbas, 252
Cerne Abbey, 252
Chagford, *306–307*
Chained Library, 466
Chalice Well, 274
Changing of the Guard, 42
Channel Tunnel, *771–772*
Chantry House, 335
Chapel of St. Edward, 48
Chapel of St. John the
    Evangelist, 64

Chapel Street (Penzance),
    289–290
Chapter House, *48*
Charlecote Park, *382*
Charles I, equestrian statue of,
    47
Charleston, *179*
Charlestown, *296*
Chartwell, *199*
Chastleton House, *421–422*
Chatsworth House, *518–519*
Chavenage, *432*
Chawton, *221*
Chedworth Roman Villa,
    427–428
Cheltenham, *408, 410–412*
Cheltenham Art Gallery and
    Museum, *410*
Cheltenham Racecourse, *412*
Cherhill Down, *239*
Cheshire Military Museum,
    479
Chesil Beach, *253–254*
Chester, *478–481*
Chester Castle, *479*
Chester Cathedral, *479*
Chester Crabwall Manor ✕▦ ,
    479–480
Chester Zoo, *479*
Chesters Roman Fort,
    683–684
Chewton Glen ✕▦ , *246*
Chez Bruce ✕ , *99*
Chichester, *189–191*
Chichester Cathedral, *189*
Chichester Festival Theatre,
    191
Chilham, *167*
Chipping Campden, *416–418*
Chirk, *700–701*
Chirk Castle, *700*
Christ Church (Oxford),
    340–341
Christ Church Picture Gallery,
    341
Christchurch Gate, *164*
Christ's College, *566*
Church of King Charles the
    Martyr, *196*
Church of St. Botolph, *612*
Church of St. John, *426*
Church of St. John the Baptist
    (Cirencester), *428*
Church of St. Mary (Tetbury),
    432
Church of St. Mary and St.
    Nicholas, *709*
Church of St. Mary the Virgin,
    172

Church of St. Mary's Redcliffe,
    268
Church of St. Peter and St.
    Paul (Lavenham), *584*
Churches and cathedrals
*Bath and the Cotswolds, 416,
    426, 428, 432, 434–435*
*East Anglia, 571–572, 580,
    581, 582, 584, 585, 590,
    597–598, 607–608, 609–610,
    612*
Lake District, 542
*Lancashire and the Peaks,
    493–494, 505, 506*
*London, 47–49, 50, 52, 61–62,
    64, 65, 71, 73*
Northeast, 666–667, 669
Shakespeare Country, 367, 381
*South, 213, 216, 228, 231,
    232–234, 237, 246, 247*
*Southeast, 162–163, 164, 167,
    172, 173, 189, 192, 193,
    196, 202*
*Thames Valley, 335, 340–341,
    343, 352, 358*
Wales, 709, 726, 731, 736–737
*Welsh Borders, 451, 453, 454,
    459, 465–466, 467, 471, 479*
*West Country, 268, 272, 274,
    276, 278, 295, 303, 311*
*Yorkshire, 639, 646–647, 648,
    649, 652*
Churchill Museum, 42
Cider Museum (Hereford),
    467
Cilgerran Castle, 738
Cinderford, *438*
Cinque Ports, 169
Circus, 394
Cirencester, *428–430*
City Art Gallery (Leeds), 622
City of Birmingham Symphony
    Orchestra, 458
City Hall (Norwich), 598
City Mill (Winchester), 216
City Museum (Winchester),
    212
City Square (Leeds), 619
City walls, 164, 478, 588,
    636
Civic Centre (Cardiff), 724,
    726
Clarence House, 49
Claridge's ▦ , 119
Clearwell Caves, 438
Cleifiog ▦ , 710
Cleopatra's Needle, 54
Cleveland Way, 651, 656–657
Clifford's Tower, 640

Clifton Suspension Bridge, 268
Climate, 28
Clink Prison, 71
Cliveden, 332–333
Cliveden ✕⊞, 333
Clock Tower, 44
Clockmakers' Company
Museum, 66
Cloisters, 48
Close (Winchester), 212
Clouds Hill, 248–249
Clovelly, 280–281
Clypping Ceremony, 430
Coach & Horses ✕, 90
Coalport China Museum, 475
Coast and Castles cycle route,
685
Coast-to-Coast Walk, 651
Cobb, The, 254
Cockermouth, 557
Cockermouth Summer Festival,
557
Colchester, 588–589
Colchester Castle Museum,
588–589
Coleford, 438–439
Coleridge Way, 278
Collection, The, 611
College Garden, 48
Collegiate Church of St. Mary,
378
Comedy Store (club), 125
Commandery, 460
Complete Works of
Shakespeare Festival, 375
Compton Verney, 382
Computers, traveling with,
772
Coniston, 544–546
Coniston Boating Centre, 546
Coniston Water, 544
Constable, John, 589–590
Constitution Hill, 718
Conwy, 710–712
Conwy Castle, 710
Corbridge, 684
Corbridge Roman Site, 684
Corfe Castle, 248–249
Corinium Museum, 428
Corn Exchange, 578, 606
Coronation Chair, 48
Corpus Christi College,
566–567
Cotehele House & Quay, 304
Cotswold Motor Museum and
Toy Collection, 423
Cotswold Water Park, 430
Cottage rentals, 779
Coughton Court, 385

Courtauld Institute Gallery, 52
Courtyard Theatre, 369
Covent Garden, 51–55,
91–92, 109–112
Covent Garden Hotel ⊞, 109
Covent Garden Piazza, 52
Coventry, 381
Coventry Cathedral, 381
Cowes, 227
Cox's Yard Tea Shop ✕, 370
Craft Centre and Design
Gallery, 622
Cragside, 685
Craster, 687
Crazy Bear (bar), 124
Credit cards, 783–784
Crescent (Buxton), 512
Criccieth, 704
Cricket, 135, 348, 458
Crickhowell, 730–731
Crown and Castle ✕⊞, 593
Crown Jewels, 65
Cruising, 772
Crypt, 62
Cuisine, national and local,
276, 455, 463, 515, 541,
575, 711
Cumberland Hotel, tea at,
246
Cumberland Pencil Museum,
553
Cumberland Terrace, 76
Currency exchange, 784–785
Curve, The, 129–130
Curzon Soho, 131
Custard Tart ✕, 163
Custom House, 312
Customs and duties, 772
Cuthbert's shrine, 667
Cutty Sark, 81

D

D-Day Museum, 222–223
Da Vinci's ✕⊞, 678
Dalemain, 550
Dales Countryside Museum,
634
Danby, 655
Dance, 131, 457, 499,
744–745
Dance Umbrella, 131
Dane John Mound, 164
Darlington, 673
Darlington Railway Centre and
Museum, 673
Dartington Hall, 309
Dartmoor National Park,
302–303
Dartmouth, 307–308

David Mellor (shop), 142
Deal, 170
Deal Castle, 170
Dean Heritage Centre, 437
Dean's Yard, 48
Dedham, 589–591
Denbigh, 714
Denbigh Castle, 714
Derwentwater, 553
Design Museum, 68–69
Devil's Bridge, 717, 719
Devon Guild of Craftsmen,
306
Devonshire Royal Hospital,
512
Diana Princess of Wales
Memorial Fountain, 75
Dickens Festival, 169
Dickens House Museum
(Broadstairs), 169
Dickens House Museum
(London), 58
Dickensian Christmas Festival,
202
Dig, 637
Dimbola Lodge, 229
Dingle, 471
Dinosaur Museum, 251
Dinosaurland Fossil Museum,
255–256
Discounts and deals, 152,
660, 740, 772–773
Discovery Museum
(Newcastle), 676
Divertimenti (shop), 142
Dockyard Museum, 268
Dolgellau, 721
Donkey-rides, 280
Donmar Warehouse, 134
Dora's Field, 541
Dorchester, 249–252
Dorchester Abbey, 352
Dorchester-on-Thames, 352
Dorking, 194
Dormy House Hotel ✕⊞, 415
Dorset Coast Path, 256
Dorset County Museum, 250
Dove Cottage, 542
Dove Cottage Tea Rooms and
Restaurant ✕, 542
Dover, 170–171
Dover Castle, 170–171
Downing Street, 49–50
Dozmury Pool, 298
Dr. Johnson's House, 66
Drunken Duck Inn ✕⊞,
547–548
Drusilla's Park, 177
Dudley, 469

Dunster, *277–278*
Dunster Castle, *277–278*
Durham, *665–667, 669–671*
Durham Castle, *666*
Durham Cathedral, *666–667, 669*
Durham Regatta, *669*
Dustanburgh Castle, *687*
Dutch Quarter (Colchester), *589*
Dylan Thomas Centre, *734*

E

Eagle and Child pub ✕ , *342*
Early Music Festival, *643*
East Anglia, *562–614*
Cambridge, 564–567, 570–579
children, attractions for, 583, 588–589, 596–597, 598, 610–611
Colchester and the Suffolk Coast, 587–596
Ely to Bury St. Edmunds, 579–587
essential information, 612–614
hotels, 576–577, 581, 583, 584–585, 586–587, 589, 591, 592, 593, 594, 595–596, 599, 602, 603–604, 606, 611
itinerary recommendations, 565
Lincoln, Boston and Stamford, 606–612
nightlife and the arts, 577–578, 587, 594–595, 599–600, 606, 611
Norwich to North Norfolk, 596–606
outdoor activities and sports, 578, 579, 600, 604
restaurants, 574–576, 580–581, 583, 584, 586–587, 589, 590–591, 593–594, 595–596, 598–599, 602, 603–604, 606, 611
shopping, 578–579, 600, 612
East Bergholt, *590*
East Grinstead, *194–195*
Eastbridge Hospital of St. Thomas, *164*
Eastgate Clock, *478*
Eastnor Castle, *464*
Edale, *520*
Eden Project, *296–297*
Egypt Centre, *734*
Egyptian House, *290*
Egyptian mummies, *56*
1853 Gallery, *627*
Elan Valley, *717*
Electric Brasserie ✕ , *95*

Electric Cinema, The, *131–132*
Electricity, *775*
Elgar Birthplace Museum, *462*
Elizabethan Banquet, *356*
Elizabethan Moot Hall, *593*
Elm Hill, *598*
Elterwater, *543–544*
Ely, *579–581*
Ely Cathedral, *580*
Emergencies, *775–776*
Bath and the Cotswolds, 442
car travel, 770
East Anglia, 613
Lake District, 560
Lancashire and the Peaks, 522
London, 152
Northeast, 691
Shakespeare Country, 386
South, 258
Southeast, 206
Thames Valley, 359
Wales, 740
Welsh Borders, 482
West Country, 318
Yorkshire, 660
Emma Bridgewater (shop), *142*
Emmanuel College, *567*
Enginuity exhibition, *474*
English National Ballet, *131*
Etiquette and behavior, *776*
Eton, *330–331*
Eton College, *331*
Evensong, *639*
Everton football club, *509*
Everyman Theatre (Cheltenham), *411*
Everyman Theatre (Liverpool), *509*
Ewelme, *338*
Exeter, *311–315*
Exeter Festival, *315*
Exmoor Coast Boat Cruises, *279*
Exmoor National Park, *278*
Explosion!, *223*
Express by Holiday Inn 🏨 , *508*
Eyeopener tours, *56*

F

Fairfax House, *640*
Fairyhill ✕🏨 , *734*
Falkland Arms ✕🏨 , *421*
Falmouth, *292–293*
Farm stays, *303, 537, 779*
Farne Islands, *687–688*

Fat Duck ✕ , *328*
Faversham, *168*
Feathers, The ✕🏨 , *349*
Fens, *601*
Ferries, *766*
Lake District, 535, 558
London, 81
Shakespeare Country, 385
South, 257
West Country, 293–294, 295, 317
Festival of Literature, *411*
Festivals and seasonal events, *745*
Bath and the Cotswolds, 404, 411, 439
East Anglia, 578, 594, 595, 606
Lake District, 534, 554–555, 556, 557
Lancashire and the Peaks, 498, 505, 514
Northeast, 669, 686
Shakespeare Country, 374–375
South, 235, 247
Southeast, 167, 169, 187, 189, 191, 202
Thames Valley, 330, 334, 336–337, 346–347, 348
Wales, 702, 710, 715, 716, 729
Welsh Borders, 462, 463, 473, 476
West Country, 271, 275, 297, 315
Yorkshire, 643, 645, 654
Ffestiniog Railway, *702, 704*
Film, *131–132, 499, 554–555, 626*
Fischer's ✕🏨 , *515*
Fishbourne Roman Palace, *190*
Fishguard, *737*
Fitzwilliam Museum, *567, 571*
Five Sumner Place 🏨 , *114*
Flamborough Head, *648*
Flatford, *590*
Flora London Marathon, *136*
Floris (shop), *144*
Football, *135, 499, 509*
Forest of Dean, *437*
Fortnum & Mason (shop), *144*
Fossils, *255–256, 315*
Foster's ✕ , *435*
Fountains, The, *75*
Fountains Abbey, *645–646*
Fowey, *297*
Fox, The ✕ , *249*
Fox & Goose ✕🏨 , *383–384*
Fox Talbot Museum, *406*
Foyles (bookstore), *139*
Framlingham Castle, *592*

Framwellgate Bridge, *669*
Frogmore House, *325*

G

Gainsborough statue, *582*
Gainsborough's House, *582*
Gala Theatre, *671*
Galilee Chapel, *667*
Gallery Café ✕, *58*
Galvin ✕, *85, 88*
Gardens, *19*
  Bath and the Cotswolds,
    398–399, 418–419, 420,
    430–431, 432
  East Anglia, *574, 581,*
    585–586
  Lake District, *538*
  Lancashire and the Peaks, *506,*
    518
  London, *48, 73, 75, 76, 78, 83*
  Northeast, *686*
  Shakespeare Country, *366, 367,*
    369–370, 377, 379
  South, *229, 237–238, 251*
  Southeast, *170, 177, 192, 193,*
    194, 203, 204
  Thames Valley, *325, 343,*
    348–349, 350–351, 354
  Wales, *711, 735*
  Welsh Borders, *471*
  West Country, *269, 277–278,*
    293, 294, 296, 301, 313
Garsington Opera, *347*
Gay Village (Manchester),
  498
Geevor Tin Mine, *288*
Georgian Town House ⌂,
  670
Gidleigh Park ✕⌂, *307*
Gilbert Collection, *52*
Gilpin Lodge ✕⌂, *537*
Gladstone Pottery Museum,
  511
Glass House ✕, *540*
Glastonbury, *274–275*
Glastonbury Abbey, *274*
Glastonbury Festival, *275*
Glastonbury Tor, *274*
Glenridding, *551*
Gloucester, *433–436*
Gloucester Cathedral,
  434–435
Gloucester Docks, *433–434*
Gloucester Folk Museum, *435*
Gloucestershire and
  Warwickshire Railway, *412*
Glyndebourne Opera House,
  180
Glyndŵr's Way, *721*

Goathland, *653–654*
God's House Tower, *225*
Gold Hill (Shaftesbury),
  236–237
Golden Gallery, *61–62*
Golden Hinde, *71–72*
Golf, *791*
Goodfellows Patisserie ✕,
  272
Goodrich, *465*
Goodrich Castle, *465*
Gordale Scar, *632*
Gordon Ramsey at Royal
  Hospital Road ✕, *88–89*
Gordon Square, *59*
Gower Peninsula, *734*
Granary, The ✕, *715*
Granary Wharf, *622*
Grand Café ✕, *344*
Grand Hotel ⌂, *186*
Grand National Experience,
  509
Grand Theatre (Leeds), *625*
Grange, *555*
Grasmere, *542–543*
Grasmere Gingerbread Shop,
  543
Grassington, *631–633*
Gratuities, *792*
Great Aberystwyth Camera
  Obscura, *719*
Great Brookham, *193*
Great Court, *56*
Great Dixter House &
  Gardens, *204*
Great Hall (Winchester), *212*
Great House (Lavenham)
  ✕⌂, *584*
Great Little Trains of Wales,
  702
Great Malvern, *462–463*
Great Milton, *352–353*
Great Orme Mines, *713*
Great St. Mary's, *571*
Green Room (Manchester),
  499
Greenhead, *682–683*
Greenhouse ✕, *94*
Greenwich, *80–82*
Greyfriars (Worcester), *460*
Grizedale Forest Park, *548*
Grosvenor Prints (shop), *145*
Guards Museum, *50*
Guesthouse West ⌂, *108*
Guild Chapel, *370*
Guildford (London), *191–193*
Guildford Cathedral, *192*
Guildford Museum, *192*
Guildhall (Exeter), *312*

Guildhall (London), *66*
Guildhall (Stratford-upon-
  Avon), *370*
Guildhall (Worcester), *460*
Guildhall (York), *637*
Guildhall Art Gallery, *66*
Guildhall of Corpus Christi,
  583
Guildhall Museum (Boston),
  612
Gulbenkian Theatre, *167*
Gyms, *135*

H

Haddon Hall, *515–516*
Hadrian's Wall, *679–680*
Hadrian's Wall Path, *680*
Hall's Croft, *366–367*
Hamley's (shop), *144*
Hampton Court Palace,
  82–83
Handel House Museum, *79*
Hans Fiebusch Studio, *189*
Hardwick Hall, *517*
Hardy, Thomas, *249, 250,*
  251, 252, 282
Hardy Monument, *254*
Hardy's Cottage, *250*
Harewood House, *625–626*
Harlech Castle, *704*
Harrods, *74, 138*
Harrogate, *644–645*
Harvard House, *370*
Hastings, *174–176*
Hastings Castle, *174–175*
Hatchards (bookstore), *139*
Hatfield House, *356*
Hawes, *634*
Hawkshead, *546–548*
Hawkshead Grammar School,
  547
Haworth, *627–629*
Hay Festival, *715*
Hay-on-Wye, *715–716*
Hay's Galleria, *72*
Hayward Gallery, *72, 130*
Hazlitt's ⌂, *110–111*
Health concerns, *776*
Hedingham Castle, *581*
Heights of Abraham Country
  Park and Caverns, *516*
Helens, *464–465*
Helmsley, *656–657*
Helvellyn, *552*
Henley Festival, *336–337*
Henley Royal Regatta, *337*
Henley-in-Arden, *377*
Henley-on-Thames, *334–337*
Henry Moore Institute, *622*

Henry VII Chapel, *48*
Henry Wood Promenade
  Concerts, *128*
Herbies ✕, *313*
Hereford, *466–467*
Hereford Cathedral, *466*
Heritage Vaults, *393–394*
Hermitage Rooms, *52, 54*
Heron Lodge 🏠, *374*
Herstmonceux Castle, *177*
Hever Castle, *198–199*
Hexham, *680–682*
Hexham Abbey, *681*
Hexham Market Place, *681*
Hibiscus ✕, *477*
Hidcote Bartrim, *419*
Hidcote Manor Garden,
  418–419
High Force, *673*
High Peak Trail, *516–517*
High Street Gate (Salisbury),
  233
Hill Top, *547*
Historic buildings, rentals of,
  779
Historic Dockyard
  (Rochester), *202*
HMS *Belfast*, *72*
HMS *Victory*, *221*
HMS *Warrior 1860*, *221*
Hoe (Plymouth), *300*
Holburne Museum, *394–395*
Holidays, *776–777*
Holkham Hall, *603*
Hollytrees Museum, *589*
Holy Island, *689*
Holy Trinity Church (Long
  Melford), *582*
Holy Trinity Church
  (Stratford-upon-Avon),
  367
Home exchanges, *779–780*
Honister Pass, *556–557*
Honiton, *316–317*
Hope Street Hotel 🏠, *507*
Horn of Plenty ✕🏠, *304*
Horse Guards Parade, *42*
Horse racing, *332, 412, 461,
  509*
Horseback riding, *244, 303,
  305, 306, 680*
Hoste Arms ✕🏠, *603–604*
Hostels, *780*
Hotel Barcelona ✕🏠, *314*
Hotel Maes-y-Neuadd ✕🏠,
  705
Hotel Portmeirion ✕🏠, *705*
Hotels, *780–781*
child-friendly, 120, 121, 330

price categories, 105, 158, 210,
  262, 322, 364, 390, 446,
  486, 526, 564, 618, 664,
  696, 778
⇨ *Also under specific areas*
Houghton Hall, *605*
House rentals, *778–779*
Houses of Parliament, *42, 44*
Housesteads Roman Fort,
  683
Howard's House ✕🏠, *234*
Howe Keld 🏠, *554*
Humblebee Wood, *412*
Huntingdon Hall, *461*
Hutton-le-Hole, *656*
Hyde Park, *74–75*

I

Ice-skating, *136*
Ickworth Hotel ✕🏠,
  586–587
Ickworth House, *586*
Ightham Mote, *201*
Ikon Gallery, *453–454*
Imperial War Museum
  (London), *69, 72*
Imperial War Museum
  Duxford, *571*
Imperial War Museum North
  (Manchester), *488–489*
Industrial Museum and Horses
  at Work, *626*
Institute of Contemporary Arts,
  49, 130
Insurance
  automobile, 769
  health/travel, 777
International Beatle Week,
  505
International Festival
  (Harrogate), *645*
International Festival of Music,
  411
International Jazz Festival,
  411
International Musical
  Eisteddfod, *702*
Ireland's Mansion, *470–471*
Iron Bridge, *474*
Ironbridge Gorge, *474–475*
Ironbridge Gorge Museum,
  474
Isle of Portland, *253–254*
Isle of Wight, *226–230*
Isles of Sicilly, *290*
Itinerary recommendations,
  22–27
⇨ *Also specific areas*
Ivy, The ✕, *91–92*

J

J Sheekey ✕, *92*
Jack the Ripper's London, *66*
Jacqueline Du Pre Music
  Building, *346*
Jane Austen Centre, *395*
Jane Austen Festival, *404*
Jane Austen's House, *221*
Jarrow, *678–679*
Jazz Café (club), *127*
Jennings Brewery, *557*
Jerwood Centre, *542*
Jesus College, *571*
Jewel Tower, *44*
Jewellery Quarter, *451,
  458*
Jigsaw (shop), *143*
John F. Kennedy Memorial,
  331
John Rylands Library, *493*
Jolly Fisherman ✕, *687*
Jorvik Viking Centre, *637*
JP Morgan Chase North
  American Gallery, *56*
Jubilee Market, *52*
Juniper ✕, *494*
Jurassic Coast, *315*

K

Keighley & Worth Valley
  Railway, *628–629*
Keith Harding's World of
  Mechanical Music, *426*
Kelmscott Manor, *351*
Kendal, *529, 532–534*
Kendal Museum, *532–533*
Kenilworth Castle, *380–381*
Kennett Stone Avenue, *240*
Kensington, *73–80, 99,
  113–116*
Kensington Gardens, *75*
Kensington Palace, *75–76*
Kentwell Hall, *583*
Kenwood House, *128*
Keswick, *552–555*
Keswick Film Club, *554–555*
Keswick Jazz Festival, *555*
Keswick-on-Derwentwater
  Launch Co., *553*
Kettle's Yard, *573*
Kettlewell, *633*
Kew Gardens, *83–84*
Kew Palace and Queen
  Charlotte's Cottage, *83*
Kilpeck, *465–466*
Kilpeck Church, *465–466*
King Edward's Grammar
  School, *370*

King Harry Ferry, *293–294, 295*
King's Arms Hotel, *633*
King's College, *571*
King's College Chapel, *571–572, 578*
King's Cross Station, *59*
King's Gate, *213*
King's Head Inn, *672*
Kings Lynn, *605–606*
King's Lynn Arts Centre, *605*
King's Lynn Festival, *606*
Kingston Lacy, *247–248*
Knaresborough, *645*
Knightsbridge, *73–80, 93–94, 116–118*
Knightsbridge Barracks, *74–75*
Knole, *199–201*
Koh Samui (shop), *143*
Korean Gallery, *58*
Kwela's ✕, *536–537*
Kynance Cove, *292*

L

L. Robson & Sons, *687*
Lacock, *405–406*
Lacock Abbey, *405–406*
Laing Art Gallery, *676*
Lake Country House & Spa ✕⬚, *716*
Lake District, *525–561*
children, attractions for, *535, 536, 538–539, 547, 549–550, 553*
essential information, *558–561*
hotels, *533–534, 537–538, 540, 543, 544, 546, 547–548, 550, 552, 554, 556–557, 558*
nightlife and the arts, *534, 554–555*
outdoor activities and sports, *538, 540–541, 543, 544, 546, 548, 555, 556*
Penrith and the Northern Lakes, *548–558*
restaurants, *533, 536–538, 540, 542–543, 544, 546, 547–548, 550, 552, 554, 556–557, 558*
shopping, *534, 538, 543, 550, 555*
Southern Lakes, *529, 532–548*
itinerary recommendations, *527*
Lake District National Park Visitor Centre at Brockhole, *538–539*
Lake Vyrnwy Hotel ✕⬚, *703*
Lakeside & Haverthwaite Railway Company, *536*

Lamb & Flag (pub), *100*
Lamb House, *172*
Lambeth Palace, *72*
Lancashire and the Peaks, *484–524*
children, attractions for, *491, 504, 516, 518*
essential information, *521–524*
hotels, *496–497, 507–508, 513–514, 515, 516, 519–520*
itinerary recommendations, *487*
Liverpool, *500–510*
Manchester, *486–500*
nightlife and the arts, *497–499, 508–509, 514*
outdoor activities and sports, *499, 509, 516–517, 520*
Peak District, *510–520*
restaurants, *494–495, 506–507, 513, 514–515, 516, 518–519*
shopping, *500, 510, 514*
Land Warfare Hall, *571*
Land's End, *288*
Lanes, The, *182–183*
Lanhydrock, *298*
Late Lounge £ Coccon (bar), *124–125*
Launceston, *299*
Launceston Castle, *299*
Lavenham, *583–585*
Lavenham Priory ⬚, *584–585*
Le Cercle ✕, *93*
Le Champignon Sauvage ✕, *410*
Le Gallois ✕, *727*
Le Gavroche ✕, *94*
Le Manoir aux Quat' Saisons ✕⬚, *353*
Le Petit Blanc (Birmingham) ✕, *455*
Le Petit Blanc (Oxford) ✕, *343–344*
Le Talbooth ✕, *590*
Ledbury, *463–464*
Leeds, *619, 622–625*
Leeds Castle, *202–203*
Legoland, *325, 328*
Leicester Square, *54*
L'Escargot ✕, *98*
Lesley Craze Gallery, *144*
Levens Hall, *533*
Lewes, *178–180*
Lewes Castle, *178*
Liberty (department store), *138*
Libraries, *58–59, 341–342, 466, 493, 573, 610, 718*
Library House ⬚, *475*

Library Theatre, *499*
Lichfield Cathedral, *451, 453*
Life Science Centre (Newcastle), *676*
Lighthouse, The ✕, *594*
Limestone, *429*
Lincoln, *609–612*
Lincoln Castle, *610–611*
Lincoln's Inn, *58*
Lindisfarne, *689*
Lindisfarne Castle, *689*
Lindisfarne Priory, *689*
Lindow Man, *58*
Lindsay House ✕, *98*
Lisson, *130*
Little Cloister, *48*
Little Hall (Lavenham), *583–584*
Liverpool, *500–510*
Liverpool Empire, *509*
Liverpool football club, *506*
Lizard Peninsula, *292*
Llanberis, *707*
Llandaff, *726*
Llandrindod Wells, *716–717*
Llandudno, *712–714*
Llanerchaeron, *719*
Llangollen, *701–702*
Llangollen Railway, *701*
Llechwedd Slate Caverns, *703*
Lloyds ✕, *165*
Locanda Locatelli ✕, *95*
Lodging, *777–781*
⇨ Also Hotels; *specific types of accommodations*
London, *33–154*
afternoon tea, *102–103*
Bayswater, *105, 108–109*
Belgravia, *116–118*
Bloomsbury, *55–59, 85, 88, 109–112*
Chelsea, *88–89, 116–118*
children, attractions for, *42, 46, 50, 52, 54–55, 58, 59, 60–61, 62, 64–66, 68, 69, 70–73, 74–75, 76, 78, 79, 80, 81, 82–83, 136*
City of London, *59–67, 89–91, 112–113*
Covent Garden, *51–55, 91–92, 109–112*
essential information, *146–154*
Hammersmith, *93*
hotels, *103–123*
itinerary recommendations, *35*
Kensington, *73–80, 99, 113–116*
Knightsbridge, *73–80, 93–94, 116–118*

Marylebone, *118–120*
Mayfair, *73–80, 94–95,*
118–120
nightlife and the arts, *123–135*
Notting Hill, *95–97, 105,*
108–109
outdoor activities and sports,
135–136
pubs, *99–102*
restaurants, *84–99*
St. James's, *97–98, 118–120*
Shepherd's Bush, *105, 108–109*
shopping, *136–146*
Soho, *51–55, 98, 109–112*
South Bank, *67–73, 99,*
120–121
Thames River, *80–84*
Victoria, *121–122*
Westminster, *7, 41–50,*
121–122
London Aquarium, *72*
London Brass-Rubbing Centre,
50
London Dungeon, *72–73*
London Silver Vaults (antique
store), *139*
London Zoo, *79*
London's Transport Museum,
54
Long Bridge, *233*
Long Man of Wilmington, *177*
Long Melford, *582–583*
Long Walk, *325*
Longleat House, *238–239*
Lord Chancellor's Residence,
44
Lord Leycester Hospital, *378*
Lords, *135*
Lost Gardens of Heligan, *296*
Lower Broadheath, *462*
Lower Slaughter, *424–425*
Lowry, The, *489, 499*
Lowry Hotel, The ⌂, *496*
Lucy's on a Plate ✕, *540*
Ludlow, *476–477*
Ludlow Castle, *476*
Ludlow Festival, *477*
Ludlow and the Marches Food
Festival, *476*
Lugger Hotel ✕⌂, *294*
Lumley Castle Hotel ✕⌂,
675
Lydford Gorge, *305*
Lyke-Wake Walk, *651*
Lyme Regis, *254–256*
Lyme Regis Fossil Shop, *256*
Lyndhurst, *243–244*
Lyndhurst, churchyard at, *243*
Lynmouth, *279–280*

Lynton, *279–280*
Lynton-Lynmouth cliff railway,
279

M

Machynlleth, *720–721*
Madame Tussaud's, *80*
Maddermarket Theatre, *600*
Magdalen College (Oxford),
341
Magdalene College
(Cambridge), *573*
Magna, *623*
Maiden Castle, *253*
Maids of Honour ✕, *84*
Mail and shipping, *781–782*
Main Street (Haworth), *628*
Malham Cove, *632*
Malham National Park, *632*
Malham Tarn, *632*
Malmaison ✕⌂, *624*
Malt House ✕, *451*
Manchester, *486–500*
Manchester Art Gallery, *490*
Manchester Cathedral,
493–494
Manchester City (football
club), *499*
Manchester Craft and Design
Centre, *500*
Manchester International
Festival, *498*
Manchester Town Hall, *488,*
493
Manchester United (football
club), *499*
Mandarin Oriental Hyde Park
⌂, *116*
Manor House Hotel ✕⌂, *405*
Manor House Museum, *586*
Mapledurham House,
337–338
Mappa Mundi, *466*
Marine Aquarium (Lyme
Regis), *255*
Maritime Museum (Buckler's
Hard), *245*
Maritime Quarter, *733*
Mark Addy pub ✕, *491*
Market Hall (Chipping
Campden), *416*
Market House (Tetbury), *432*
Market Restaurant ✕, *494*
Market Square (Dorchester),
249–250
Market Square (Salisbury),
233
Marks & Spencer (department
store), *500*

Marlborough, *241*
Marlow, *334*
Marlow Place, *334*
Marlowe, The, *167*
Martyrs' Memorial, *340*
Mary Arden's House, *376–377*
Mary Rose, *222*
Mathew Street (Liverpool),
504
Matlock, *516*
Matlock River Illuminations,
516
Maumbury Rings, *251*
Mausoleum of Halikarnassos,
56
Max Gate, *250*
Mayfair (London), *73–80,*
94–95, 118–120
Mayflower Park, *225*
Mayflower Steps, *301*
Mayflower Stone, *301*
Mayflower Theatre, *225*
Mayse's Hall, *586*
McCoy's Rooftop Restaurant
✕, *677*
MDC Opera Shop, *139*
Meal plans, *7, 778*
Media, *782–783*
Medieval Bishop's Palace, *610*
Medieval Jousting Tournament,
439
Melford Hall, *582–583*
Mendips, *504–505*
Merchant Adventurers' Hall,
640
Merchant's Steps, *301*
Merlin's Cave, *283*
Merseyside Maritime Museum,
503
Metropolitan Cathedral of
Christ the King, *506*
Micro Gallery, *45*
Middlesbrough, *673–674*
Middlethorpe Hall & Spa ⌂,
641–642
Midsummer House ✕, *575*
Mildenhall Treasure, *56*
Milecastle Inn ✕, *682*
Milestone Hotel & Apartments
⌂, *114*
Millenium Bridge, *60*
Millenium Mile, *60*
Millennium Stadium, *726*
Miller Howe ✕⌂, *537*
Minack Theatre, *292*
Minster Yard, *610*
Mock Turtle ✕, *183*
Model Railway Exhibition, *424*
Model Village, *424*

Mol's Coffee House, *313*
Momo ✕, *98*
Mompesson House, *231*
Money, *783–785*
Monk's House, *179*
Monument, *60*
Moors Centre, *655*
Moot Hall, *553*
Mop Fair, *375*
Moreton-on-Marsh, *419–421*
Moro ✕, *90–91*
Morwellham Quay, *304*
Mother Shipton's Cave, *645*
Mousehole, *288*
Mr. Underhill's ✕⬜, *477*
Much Marcle, *464–465*
Much Wenlock, *474*
Museum of Antiquities, *676*
Museum of Archaeology and
 Anthropology, *573–574*
Museum of Bath at Work, *399*
Museum of British Pewter,
 370
Museum of Canterbury,
 164–165
Museum of Childhood
 Memories, *709*
Museum of Costume, *395*
Museum of Dartmoor Life, *306*
Museum in Docklands, *66–67*
Museum of East Asian Art,
 399
Museum of Garden History, *73*
Museum of the History of
 Science, *343*
Museum Inn ✕⬜, *248*
Museum of Iron, *474*
Museum of the Jewellery
 Quarter, *453*
Museum of Lakeland Life, *532*
Museum of London, *60–61*
Museum of Natural History,
 649–650
Museum of the Quakers, *721*
Museum of Rail Travel, *629*
Museum of Science and
 Industry, *488, 490–491*
Museum of Worcester
 Porcelain, *459*
Museums
Bath and the Cotswolds,
 394–395, 397–399, 400, 406,
 408, 423, 428, 435, 437
East Anglia, 567, 571,
 573–574, 580, 583, 586,
 588–589, 595, 596–597, 598,
 603, 608, 611, 612
Lake District, 532–533, 539,
 542, 544, 549, 553

Lancashire and the Peaks,
 489–491, 493, 494, 499,
 502, 503–504, 511, 512
London, 42, 44–45, 46, 48, 50,
 52, 54–55, 56, 58, 60–61,
 66–67, 68–69, 71, 72, 73, 74,
 76, 78, 79, 81, 82
Northeast, 669, 672, 673,
 674–675, 676, 677, 678–679,
 681, 682, 683–684, 689
Shakespeare Country, 367,
 370–371, 376–377, 379, 382
South, 212, 221–223, 225, 228,
 230, 232, 240, 244, 245,
 246, 247–248, 250, 251,
 255–256
Southeast, 163–165, 169, 171,
 178, 182, 189, 190, 191,
 192, 196
Thames Valley, 335, 343, 357
Wales, 707, 708, 709, 717, 718,
 720, 721, 722–723, 726–727,
 730, 731, 733–734, 735, 738
Welsh Borders, 448–449, 453,
 459, 460, 462, 467, 469,
 474, 475, 479
West Country, 268, 274–275,
 276–277, 286, 290, 293,
 295, 301, 304, 306, 312,
 315, 316
Yorkshire, 622, 623, 626, 627,
 628, 629, 634, 635, 637,
 640, 641, 644, 649–650,
 653, 656
Music, *745*
Bath and the Cotswolds, 404,
 411
East Anglia, 594, 595
Lake District, 555
Lancashire and the Peaks, 498,
 509, 514
London, 128–129
Northeast, 671
Thames Valley, 346–347
Wales, 726, 729, 733
Welsh Borders, 458, 473
West Country, 271, 275, 315
Yorkshire, 625, 643
Music at Oxford, *346–347*
Myddleton Arms, *714*

N

Nash's House, *367*
National Assembly Debating
 Chamber, *724*
National Botanic Garden of
 Wales, *735*
National Film Theatre (NFT),
 132

National Gallery, *44–45*
National Library of Wales,
 718
National Marine Aquarium,
 300–301
National Maritime Museum,
 81
National Maritime Museum
 Cornwall, *293*
National Motor Museum, *244*
National Museum Cardiff, *726*
National Museum of
 Photography, Film, and
 Television, *626*
National parks
Lake District, 538–539, 560
Lancashire and the Peaks, 520,
 523
Northeast, 683, 684
Wales, 700, 715, 723, 732, 740
West Country, 278, 302–303
Yorkshire, 632, 655, 660
National Portrait Gallery, *45*
National Railway Museum,
 637
National Sea Life Centre, *454*
National Slate Museum, *707*
National Sound Archive, *59*
National Waterfront Museum,
 733
National Waterways Museum,
 435
National Wool Museum, *738*
Natural History Museum, *76*
Nature in Art, *435*
Needles, The, *229*
Nelson's Column, *47*
New Alresford, *219*
New College, *341*
New Conservatory ✕, *622*
New Forest, *243, 244*
New Hall ⬜ (Birmingham),
 456
New Place, *367*
New Room, *269*
New Royal Brierly Experience,
 469
New Theatre, *347*
New Theatre (Cardiff), *729*
Newby Hall, *647*
Newcastle upon Tyne,
 675–678
Newlyn, *289*
Newquay, *285*
Norfolk Broads, *601*
Norman castle (Newcastle),
 676
North Yorkshire Moors
 Railway, *653–654*

Northcott Theatre, *315*
Northeast, *662–692*
children, attractions for, 673,
676
Durham, Newcastle and
environs, 664–667, 669–679
essential information, 690–692
Far Northeast coast, 685–690
Hadrian's Wall country,
679–685
hotels, 669–670, 673, 675,
677–678, 681–683, 684, 685,
686–687, 688, 690
itinerary recommendations, 665
nightlife and the arts, 671, 678,
682
outdoor activities and sports,
671, 680
restaurants, 669, 673, 674, 675,
677–678, 681, 682, 685,
686–687, 688, 690
shopping, 671, 687
Northleach, *425–426*
Northumberland National Park
Visitor Centre, *684*
Northumbria's Cycling
Kingdom loop, *685*
Norwegian Church Arts
Centre, *724*
Norwich, *596–600*
Norwich Castle, *596–597*
Norwich Cathedral, *597–598*
Norwich Playhouse, *600*
Notting Hill, *80*
Nuffield Theatre, *226*
Number 1 Royal Crescent, *397*
Number 3 ⊡ , *275*
Nutshell, The (pub), *585*
Nymans Garden, *194*

O

Ocean House ⊡ , *594*
Offa's Dyke Path, *702*
Okehampton, *305–306*
Okehampton Castle, *305*
Old Bailey, *67*
Old Cottage Tea Shop ✕ , *306*
Old Dungeon Ghyll Hotel ⊡ ,
544
Old Fire Engine House ✕ ,
580–581
Old Fire Station, *347*
Old Gaol (Hexham), *681*
Old Grammar School
(Ledbury), *463*
Old House (Hereford), *467*
Old Malt House, *384*
Old Man of Coniston, *544,*
546

Old Mill (Salisbury), *233*
Old Nag's Head, *520*
Old Personage ⊡ , *345*
Old Post Office (Tintagel),
282
Old Rectory, The ⊡ , *282*
Old Royal Naval College, *82*
Old Sarum, *231–232*
Old Vic, The, *134*
Old Vicarage, The ⊡ , *540*
Oliver Cromwell's House, *580*
Once Brewed National Park
Visitor Centre, *683*
Open Air Theatre, *134*
Opera, *132, 347, 499, 729,*
744
Opera House (Manchester),
499
Orangery ✕ , *76*
Orford, *592–593*
Orford Castle, *592*
Orford Ness, *592–593*
Origins, *598*
Orrest Head, *536*
Osborne House, *227*
Other Place, The, *369*
Outdoor activities and sports,
17, 790–791
⇨ *Also specific activities;*
areas
Owain Glyndêwr Centre, *720*
Owlpen, *431*
Owlpen Manor, *431*
Oxford Coffee Concerts, *347*
Oxford Playhouse, *347*
Oxford Story Exhibition, *343*
Oxford University Cricket
Club, *348*
Oxford University Museum of
Natural History, *343*
Oxford's Eights Week, *348*
OXO Tower, *69*
Ozwald Boateng (shop), *143*

P

Packing, *785–786*
Packwood House, *377*
Padstow, *284–285*
Painswick, *430–431*
Painswick Rococo Garden,
430–431
Palaces
London, 41–42, 50, 75–76,
82–83
Southeast, 190
Thames Valley, 350–351
West Country, 272
Pallant House, *189*
Pantiles, *196*

Paris ✕ , *454*
Parliament Buildings, *42, 44*
Parthenon Marbles, *56*
Passports and visas, *786*
Patterdale, *551*
Paul Smith (shop), *143*
Pavilion, *512*
Peak Cavern, *519*
Peak District, *510–520*
Pear Tree Cottage ⊡ , *377*
Pembroke, *736*
Pembroke Castle, *736*
Pembroke College, *574*
Pembrokeshire Coast National
Park, *723*
Pendennis Castle, *293*
Penhaligon's (shop), *145*
Penlee House Gallery and
Museum, *290*
Pennine Way, *520*
Penrith, *549–550*
Penrith Castle, *549*
Penrith Museum, *549*
Penshurst Place, *197–198*
Penzance, *289–292*
Pepys Library, *573*
Percival David Foundation of
Chinese Art, *59*
Perranporth, *285–286*
Pershore, *461–462*
Pershore Abbey, *461*
Peterborough, *607–608*
Peterborough Cathedral,
607–608
Peterborough Museum and
Gallery, *608*
Peterhouse College, *574*
Petworth House, *191*
Peveril Castle, *519*
Pheasant, The ✕⊡ , *558*
Philharmonic (pub), *509*
Philharmonic Hall, *509*
Philpot Museum, *255*
Phones, *786–788*
Photographer's Gallery, *130*
Pickeral Inn ✕ , *572*
Pier Head, *503*
Pig's Ear, The ✕ , *88*
Pilgrim Fathers' Memorial,
225
Pimento ✕ , *610*
Pistyll Rhaeadr, *701*
Pitcher and Piano (pub), *678*
Pittville Pump Room, *408, 410*
Place, The, *131*
Place Below, The ✕ , *61*
Plas Mawr, *711*
Plas Newydd, *701, 709*
Plymouth, *299–302*

Plymouth Dome, *301*
Poets' Corner, *48*
Polesden Lacey, *193*
Polly Tearooms ✕, *234*
Poole's Cavern, *512–513*
Poppy's Tea Rooms ✕, *471*
Porlock, *278–279*
Porlock Hill, *279*
Porlock Weir, *278*
Port Isaac, *284*
Portchester Castle, *223*
Porterhouse (pub), *101*
Porthmadog, *703–706*
Porthole Eating House ✕, *536*
Portmeirion, *704*
Portobello Market, *146*
Portsmouth, *221–224*
Portsmouth Historic Dockyard, *221–222*
Potter, Beatrix, *539, 547, 551*
Potteries Museum and Art Gallery, *511*
Potters Café-Bistro ✕, *251*
Poultry Cross, *233*
Poundbury, *252*
Powderham Castle, *311–312*
Powis Castle, *722*
Powysland Museum, *723*
Prebends Footbridge, *669*
Prehistoric sites and artifacts, *232, 239–240, 241–242, 252, 271, 351, 352, 553, 591, 713*
Price categories
Bath and the Cotswolds, 390
dining, 85, 158, 210, 262, 322, 364, 390, 446, 486, 526, 564, 618, 664, 696, 774
East Anglia, 564
Lake District, 526
Lancashire and the Peaks, 486
lodging, 105, 158, 210, 262, 322, 364, 390, 446, 486, 526, 564, 618, 664, 696, 778
London, 85, 105
Northeast, 664
Shakespeare Country, 364
South, 210
Southeast, 158
Thames Valley, 322
Wales, 696
Welsh Borders, 446
West Country, 262
Yorkshire, 618
Priest's House Museum, *247*
Prime Meridian, *82*
Princess Diana Memorial Playground, *75*
Prior Park, *399–400*

Priory (Great Malvern), *462*
Prohibitian Bar & Grill ✕, *506*
Prospect of Whitby (pub), *101*
Providores & Tapa Room, The ✕, *85*
Pubs, *16, 99–102, 404, 498, 577, 585, 643, 774–775*
Pulls Ferry, *598*
Pulteney Bridge, *397*
Pump Room (Bath), *398*
Pumphouse: People's History Museum (Manchester), *491*
Punting, *347–348, 404, 578, 579*

Q

Quarry Park, *471*
Quay, The ✕, *313*
Quay House (Exeter), *313*
Queen Elizabeth Country Park, *224*
Queen Mary's Doll House, *324–325*
Queen Mary's Gardens, *76*
Queen Square, *397*
Queens' College, *572*
Queen's Gallery, *46*
Queen's Hall Arts Centre, *682*
Queen's Head Inn ✕🏠, *550*
Queen's House, *81*
Queensbury Hotel ✕🏠, *402*
Quince & Medlar ✕, *557*

R

Raby Castle, *671–672*
Radcliffe Camera and Bodleian Library, *341–342*
Radnorshire Museum, *717*
Ragley Hall, *384–385*
Ralph Cross, *655*
Ranger's House, *82*
Ravenscar, *651*
Reading Room, *56*
Read's ✕🏠, *168*
Regent's Park, *76, 78*
Regent's Park Open-Air Theatre, *76, 78*
Restaurant Margaux ✕, *371*
Restaurants, *773–775*
price categories, 85, 158, 210, 262, 322, 364, 390, 446, 486, 526, 564, 618, 664, 696, 774
⇨ *Also under specific areas*
Restrooms, *788*
Rheged, *549–550*
Riber Hall ✕🏠, *516*
Richmond, *634–635*

Richmond Castle, *634–635*
Ridgeway National Trail, *351*
Rievaulx Abbey, *657*
Rievaulx Terrace and Temples, *657*
Ripon, *646–647*
Ripon Cathedral, *646–647*
River & Rowing Museum, *335*
River Island (shop), *143*
Robin Hood's Bay, *650–652*
Rochester, *201–202*
Rochester Castle, *201–202*
Rochester Cathedral, *202*
Rodmarton Manor, *432*
Rollright Stones, *420*
Roman amphitheater (Colchester), *588*
Roman Army Museum, *682*
Roman artifacts
Bath and the Cotswolds, 397–398, 427–428
East Anglia, 588–589
Lancashire and the Peaks, 512
Northeast, 677, 679–680, 682, 683–684
South, 223, 225, 229, 250, 251
Southeast, 163–164, 170, 177, 190
Thames Valley, 356
Wales, 708
West Country, 313
Yorkshire, 635–641, 649
Roman baths, *397–398, 677*
Roman Painted House, *170*
Roman Theater, *356*
Roman Walls (Colchester), *588*
Romsey, *226*
Ronnie Scott's (club), *127*
Rookery, The 🏠, *112–113*
Rose Theatre, *69*
Rosetta Stone, *56*
Ross-on-Wye, *465*
Rosthwaite, *555*
Rothbury, *684–685*
Rotten Row, *74*
Rotunda Museum, *650*
Rougemont Gardens, *313*
Round Pond, *75*
Round Tower, *323*
Rousham Park House & Garden, *348–349*
Rowing, *337*
Rows, *478*
Royal Academy, *130*
Royal Albert Hall, *80, 128–129*
Royal Albert Memorial Museum, *312*

Royal Armouries (Leeds), 622

Royal Armouries (London), 64

Royal Ballet, 131

Royal Ceremonial Dress Collection, 75

Royal Citadel, 301

Royal Clarence Hotel ✕🖾, 314

Royal Cornwall Museum, 295

Royal Court Theatre (Liverpool), 509

Royal Court Theatre (London), 134

Royal Crescent Hotel ✕🖾, 402

Royal Exchange, 491, 493

Royal Exchange Theatre, 499

Royal family, 47

Royal Festival Hall, 131

Royal Liver Building, 503

Royal Mews, 325

Royal National Theatre, 134

Royal Naval Museum, 222

Royal Northern College of Music, 499

Royal Observatory, 82

Royal Opera House, 54

Royal Pavilion, 183

Royal Pump Room Museum (Harrogate), 644

Royal Shakespeare Company, 375

Royal Shakespeare Theatre, 367, 369

Royal Tunbridge Wells, 195–197

Royal Welsh Agricultural Show, 716

Royal Worcester Porcelain Factory, 459

Rugby, 726

Rules ✕, 92

Running, 136

Runnymeade, 331–332

Ruskin, John, 536, 544–545, 551

Ruskin Museum, 544–545

Russell-Cotes Art Gallery and Museum, 246

Ruthin, 714

Ruthin Gaol, 714

Rydal, 541

Rydal Mount, 541

Ryde, 228

Rye, 171–173

Rye Castle Museum, 171

Ryedale Folk Museum, 656

S

Saatchi Gallery, 130

Sadler's Wells, 131

Safety, 788–789

Saffron Walden, 581

Sage Gateshead, 678

Sainsbury African Galleries, 56

Sainsbury Centre for the Visual Arts, 598

St. Albans, 355–357

St. Albans Cathedral, 355–356

St. Alkmund's, 471

St. Anne's Church (Manchester), 494

St. Augustine's Abbey, 165

St. Bride's, 61

St. Chad, 471

St. Chad's Roman Catholic Cathedral, 454

St. Culbone, 278

St. David's, 736–737

St. David's Cathedral, 736–737

St. David's Centre, 726, 729

St. David's Hotel and Spa 🖾, 728

St. Edmundsbury Cathedral, 585

St. Fagans National History Museum, 726–727

St. George's, 271

St. George's Chapel, 324

St. George's Guildhall (King's Lynn), 605

St. George's Hall (Liverpool), 506

St. Giles's Hill, 217

St. Ives, 286–288

St. Ives Society of Artists Gallery, 287

St. James Church (Chipping Campden), 416

St. James Church (Taunton), 276

St. James's Palace, 50

St. James's Park, 46

St. John ✕, 89

St. John's College, 342, 572

St. John's House, 379–380

St. Just in Roseland, 294

St. Martin-in-the-Fields, 50, 129

St. Martin's Church, 340

St. Mary (Scarborough), 649

St. Mary (Whitby), 652

St. Mary Magdalene church, 276

St. Mary the Virgin (Althorp), 358

St. Mary the Virgin (Saffron Walden), 581

St. Mary-le-Bow, 61

St. Mary's (Bury St. Edmunds), 585

St. Mary's Church (Henley-on-Thames), 335

St. Mary's Church (Shrewsbury), 471

St. Mawes, 294–295

St. Mawes Castle, 294

St. Michael's Church, 274

St. Michael's Mount, 290

St. Olaves ✕, 313

St. Oswald's, 542

St. Paul's Cathedral (City of London), 61–62

St. Paul's Church (Soho's Actor's Church), 52

St. Peter ad Vincula, 65

St. Peter Mancroft, 598

St. Peter and St. Paul (Northleach), 426

St. Peter's Church (Winchcombe), 412

St. Peter's parish church (Bournemouth), 246

St. Smith's, Smith Square, 129

St. Swithun's Church, 213, 217

St. Thomas's Church, 233–234

Saints Way, 285

Salisbury, 230–236

Salisbury Cathedral, 232–233

Salisbury Festival, 235

Salisbury Playhouse, 235

Salisbury and South Wilshire Museum, 232

Saltaire, 626–627

Saltram, 301

Samling, The ✕🖾, 537

Sanctuary Knocker, 667

Sandringham House, 604

Sandwich, 169

Savill Garden, 325

Savoy, The 🖾, 110

Scafell Pike, 556

Scams, 789

Scarborough, 649–650

Scarborough Castle, 649

Scarborough Sea Life Centre, 650

Science Festival, 411

Science Museum, 78

Scuba diving, 292

Sculpture at Goodwood, 190

Sea Life Centre, 183

Seafood Bar ✕ , 293
Seafood Restaurant, The ✕▦ , 284–285
Seaham Hall ✕▦ , 677
Seatoller, 555
Seckford Hall ▦ , 592
Sedgemoor, 275
Segedunum Roman Fort, Baths and Museum, 677
Segontium Roman Museum, 708
Selfridges (department store), 138
Serpentine, 75
Serpentine Gallery, 130
Severn Studio, 545
Severn Valley Railway, 468
Sezincote, 419
Shaftesbury, 236–237
Shakespeare Birthplace Trust, 365
Shakespeare Centre, 369
Shakespeare Country, 361–387
children, attractions for, 370–371, 376–377, 379–380
essential information, 385–387
hotels, 372–374, 377, 380, 383–384
itinerary recommendations, 363
nightlife and the arts, 374–375
outdoor activities and sports, 375–376
restaurants, 371–372, 380, 381, 383–384
shopping, 376
Stratford-upon-Avon, 364–376
Shakespeare Countryside Museum, 376–377
Shakespeare Hotel ▦ , 372–373
Shakespeare Tree Garden, 366
Shakespeare's Birthplace, 369
Shakespeare's Globe Theatre, 69, 134–135
Shambles, The, 637, 639
Shambles, 468
Sharrow Bay, 552
Shaw's Corner, 356–357
Shefton Museum of Greek Art and Archaeology, 676
Sheila's Cottage ✕ , 539
Sheldonian Theatre, 342
Shelley's Hotel ▦ , 279–280
Sheppy's, 276–277
Sherborne, 237
Sherborne Abbey, 237
Sherborne Castle, 237

Shopping, 789–790
⇨ Also under specific areas
Shrewsbury, 470–473
Shrewsbury Abbey, 471
Shrewsbury Castle, 471–472
Shrewsbury International Music Festival, 473
Silbury Hill, 241
Silk Mill, 416
Simpsons ✕ , 454–455
Sir John Soane's Museum, 58
Sissinghurst Castle Garden, 203–204
Sizergh Castle, 533
Skipton, 630–631
Skipton Castle, 630–631
Slimbridge Wildfowl & Wetlands Trust, 439
Sloop Inn ✕ , 287
Smallest house in Britain, 711
Smeaton's Tower, 301
Smuggler's Adventure, 175
Snape Maltings, 595
Snowdon Mountain Railway, 702, 707
Snowdonia National Park, 700
Snowshill Manor, 414
Soho (London), 51–55
Soho Theatre, 135
Somerset House, 52, 54, 136
Somerset Rural Life Museum, 274–275
Sonning-on-Thames, 337
Soudley, 437
South, 208–259
children, attractions for, 217, 219, 223, 228, 238–239, 240, 244, 251, 255–256
essential information, 257–259
hotels, 218–219, 223–224, 225, 226, 227, 228, 229, 234–235, 237, 238, 239, 240–241, 243–244, 246–247, 248, 249, 251–252, 254, 256
Isle of Wight, 226–230
itinerary recommendations, 211
New Forest to Lyme Regis, 243–256
nightlife and the arts, 225–226, 235, 247
outdoor activities and sports, 224, 235, 244, 252, 256
restaurants, 217–218, 223, 225, 228, 234, 238, 239, 240, 243–244, 246–247, 248, 249, 251–252, 253, 254, 256

Salisbury to Stonehenge, 230–242
shopping, 219, 235–236
Winchester to Southampton, 211–226
South Bank, 67–73, 99, 120–121
South Bank Centre, 129
South Devon Railway, 308
South Wales Borderers Museum, 731
Southampton, 224–226
Southampton Maritime Museum, 225
Southeast, 155–207
Brighton to East Grinstead, 180–195
Canterbury to Dover, 159, 162–167
children, attractions for, 164–165, 170–171, 174–175, 177, 183, 204
essential information, 205–207
hotels, 166–167, 168, 169, 171, 172–174, 175–178, 179–180, 185–187, 188–189, 190–191, 192–193, 194–195, 197, 198, 202, 203–204
itinerary recommendations, 157
Masterpieces near Tunbridge Wells, 195–205
nightlife and the arts, 167, 169, 180, 187, 189, 191, 193, 202
outdoor activities and sports, 205
restaurants, 165–166, 167, 168, 172–174, 175, 176, 177, 179, 184–186, 188, 190, 192–193, 196–197, 198, 203
Rye to Glyndebourne, 171–180
shopping, 167, 173, 180, 187–188
Southwark Cathedral, 71
Southwold, 595–596
Southwold Museum, 595
Spaniards Inn (pub), 101
Speakers' Corner, 75
Speedwell Cavern, 519
Speke Hall and Gardens, 506
Spencer House, 50
Spinnaker Tower, 222
Square Orange Cafe ✕ , 554
SS Great Britain, 268
Stafford, The ▦ , 119
Stained Glass Museum, 580
Stamford, 608–609
Standen, 194
Stanton Drew Circles, 271
Stanway House, 413–414

Stately and historic homes, 18, 25–27
Bath and the Cotswolds, 394, 398–400, 406–407, 413–414, 419, 421–422, 432
East Anglia, 580, 581, 582–583, 586, 600–601, 603, 604, 608–609
Lake District, 532, 533, 539, 541, 545
Lancashire and the Peaks, 504–505, 506, 517, 518
London, 49, 50, 52, 58, 66, 74, 79, 82
Northeast, 685
Shakespeare Country, 365–367, 369, 370, 376–377, 378, 382, 384–385
South, 221, 226, 227, 231, 236, 237–238, 244, 247
Southeast, 169, 183, 189, 191, 193, 194, 197–198, 199, 200, 201, 204–205
Thames Valley, 334, 335, 348–349, 351, 354, 356–357, 358
Wales, 709, 711,n712, 719, 735
Welsh Borders, 464–465, 467, 470–471
West Country, 269, 282, 298, 301, 304, 311–312
Yorkshire, 622–623, 625–626, 640, 647, 649–650
Steine, 183
Stephen Joseph Theatre, 650
Stephenson, George, birthplace of, 677
Still & West Country House ✕ , 222
Stoke-on-Kent, 511
Stokesay Castle, 476
Stone Gallery, 61
Stonegate, 639
Stonehenge, 241–242
Stourbridge, 469
Stourhead, 237–238
Stourport Steamer Co, 469
Stow-on-the-Wold, 421–423
Stowe Landscape Gardens, 354
Stratford-upon-Avon, 364–376
Stratford-upon-Avon Shakespeare Birthday Celebrations, 374
Stray, The, 644
Stuart Crystal Visitor Centre and Factory Shop, 469

Studley Royal Water Garden, 645–646
Submarine World, 223
Sudbury, 582
Sudeley Castle, 413
Sun Hotel ✕⊡ , 546
Surfing, 285–286, 287
Sutton Hoo (Woodbridge), 591
Sutton Hoo Treasure (London), 56, 58
Swallow Falls, 706
Swan Theatre, 369
Swan-Upping, 334
Swansea, 733–735
Swansea Museum, 733–734
Swimming, 136
Symbols, 7
Symond's Yat, 465
Symphony Hall, 454

T

Tarn Hows, 547
Tate Britain, 46
Tate Liverpool, 503
Tate Modern, 71, 130
Tate St. Ives, 286–287
Taunton, 276–277
Taxes, 791–792
Taxis, 110
Tea, 17
Techniquest, 727
Teddy Bear Museum, 370–371
Teesdale Way, 685
Teifi Valley, 737–738
Temple, 59
Temple Bar, 62
Temple Newsam, 622–623
10 Downing Street, 49–50
Tenby, 735–736
Tenby Museum and Art Gallery, 735
Tennis, 136
Tenterden Vineyard, 172
Tetbury, 432–433
Tewkesbury, 436–437
Tewkesbury Abbey, 436
T'Gallants ⊡ , 296
Thackeray's House ✕ , 196
Thackray Medical Museum, 623
Thames Valley, 320–360
Blenham Palace to Althorp, 348–358
children, attractions for, 324–325, 328, 335, 343, 357
essential information, 358–360
Henley and beyond, 333–338

hotels, 329–330, 331, 332, 333, 334, 335–336, 337, 344–346, 349–350, 351–352, 353, 354–355, 357, 358
itinerary suggestions, 323
nightlife and the arts, 330, 336–337, 346–347
outdoor activities and sports, 330, 333, 337, 347–348
Oxford, 338–348
restaurants, 328–329, 331, 333, 334, 335–336, 337, 343–344, 349, 353, 354, 357, 358
shopping, 330, 348, 349
Windsor and environs, 322–325, 328–333
Theater, 21, 743–744
Bath and the Cotswolds, 404, 411
East Anglia, 578, 587, 600, 611
Lake District, 555
Lancashire and the Peaks, 499, 509
London, 132–135
Northeast, 671
Shakespeare Country, 375
Thames Valley, 330, 347
Wales, 729, 733
Welsh Borders, 458
West Country, 271, 292, 302, 315
Yorkshire, 625, 643, 650
Theatr Brycheiniog, 733
Theatre by the Lake, 555
Theatre Museum, 54–55
Theatre Royal (Bath), 398, 404
Theatre Royal (Bury St. Edmunds), 587
Theatre Royal (Lincoln), 611
Theatre Royal (Newcastle upon Tyne), 678
Theatre Royal (Norwich), 600
Theatre Royal (Plymouth), 302
Theatre Royal (Richmond), 635
Theatre Royal (Windsor), 330
Thermae Bath Spa, 400
Thinktank, 453
Thirst, 647
Thomas Hardy Society, 252
Thornbury Castle ✕⊡ , 440
Three Counties Show, 462
Tickle Manor Tea Room ✕ , 584
Time, 792
Timing the trip, 28
Tintagel, 282–284

Tintagel Castle, *282–283*
Tintern Abbey, *727*
Tipping, *792*
Tom Aikens ✕, *89*
Tomb of the Unknown Warrior, *48*
Tombland, *598*
Top Withins, *628*
Topsham, *315*
Topsham Museum, *315*
Topshop (shop), *143*
Torbay, *309–311*
Totnes, *308–309*
Totnes Castle, *308*
Tours and packages, *792–793*
Bath and the Cotswolds, 442
East Anglia, 613–614
Lake District, 560–561
Lancashire and the Peaks, 523
London, 152–154
Northeast, 692
Shakespeare Country, 386–387
South, 258–259
Southeast, 206
Thames Valley, 360
Wales, 740–741
Welsh Borders, 482
West Country, 319
Yorkshire, 660–661
Tower Bridge, *62*
Tower of London, *62, 64–65*
Town Hall (Birmingham), *454*
Town Hall (Colchester), *589*
Town Hall (Leeds), *619, 622, 625*
Trafalgar Square, *46–47*
Trafalgar Tavern ✕, *81*
Train travel and railroads, *793–794*
Bath and the Cotswolds, 412, 424, 441
East Anglia, 613
Lake District, 536, 559–560
Lancashire and the Peaks, 522
London, 150
Northeast, 673, 677, 691
Shakespeare Country, 386
South, 258
Southeast, 205–206
Thames Valley, 359
Wales, 701, 702, 704, 707, 708, 718–719, 739–740
Welsh Borders, 468, 482
West Country, 279, 309, 318
Yorkshire, 628–629, 630, 637, 653–654, 659–660
Traitors' Gate, *64*
Tram travel, *522*
Transporter Bridge, *674*

Travel agencies, *794–795*
Traveler's checks, *784–785*
Treasurer's House, *640–641*
Trelissick, *293–294*
Tremadog, *704*
Tresanton Hotel ✕☷, *294–295*
Tretower Court, *730*
Tricycle Theatre, *135*
Trinity Chapel, *163*
Trinity College, *572–573*
Trinity Guildhall, *605*
Trinity Hall College, *574*
Trouble House ✕, *433*
Trout Inn ✕, *344*
Truro, *295–296*
Tudor Merchant's House, *735*
Tudor Rose, *709*
Tuesday market (Moreton-on-Marsh), *419*
Tunbridge Wells Museum and Art Gallery, *196*
Turkish Bath, *644*
Turk's Head, *290*
Turnbull & Asser (shop), *143*
Tutankhamun Exhibition, *251*
20 Forthlin Road, *505*
Two Toads ✕, *432*
Tymperleys Clock Museum, *589*
Tyne Bridge, *676*
Tyneside Coffee Rooms ✕, *676*
Tyntesfield, *269*

U

Uffington, *351–352*
Uffington Castle, *351*
Ullswater, *550–552*
Ullswater Steamers, *551*
Undercroft (Warwick) ✕, *379*
Undercroft (Westminster Abbey), *48*
Underground tube travel, *151*
Union Chapel (club), *126*
Union Hotel, *290*
University Botanic Gardens, *574*
University Church of St. Mary the Virgin, *343*
University of Durham Oriental Museum, *669*
University of Newcastle upon Tyne, *676*
University of Oxford Botanic Garden, *343*
Upper Slaughter, *424–425*
Urbis, *494*

V

Vale of Ceiriog, *700*
Vale of Rheidol Railway, *719*
Vale of the White Horse, *351*
Valley Gardens, *644*
V.A.T. (Value Added Tax), *791–792*
Ventnor, *229*
Ventnor Botanic Gardens, *229*
Verulamium Museum, *356*
Verulamium Park, *356*
Vicar's Close, *273*
Vicar's Pele, *683*
Victoria & Albert Museum, *78*
Victoria at Holkham ✕☷, *604*
Victoria Miro Gallery, *130–131*
Victoria Quarter (shopping arcade), *625*
Victoria Tower, *44*
Viking Festival, *643*
Vindolanda, *683*
Vineyards, *172, 175, 203, 586*
Virginia Water, *325*
Visitor information, *795*
⇨ *Also specific areas*
Volk's Electric Railway, *183*

W

Waddesdon Manor, *354*
Wainwright, Alfred, *532*
Walberswick, *595*
Wales, *693–741*
children, attractions for, 701, 702, 704, 707, 708, 709, 713, 718–719, 720, 726–727, 733, 735
essential information, 738–741
hotels, 700–701, 703, 705–706, 708, 710, 712, 713, 714, 715, 716, 717, 719–721, 722, 728, 730, 731, 732–733, 734–736, 737, 738
itinerary recommendations, 695
Mid-Wales, 714–723
nightlife and the arts, 702, 710, 728–729, 733
North Wales, 697, 700–714
outdoor activities and sports, 702, 708, 721, 733
restaurants, 700, 703, 705–706, 710, 712, 713, 715, 716, 719–721, 722, 727–728, 730, 731, 732–733, 734–735, 737
shopping, 716, 729
South Wales, 723–738
Wales Millennium Centre, *727*

Walker Art Gallery, *503–504*
Walking, *20, 791*
Bath and the Cotswolds, 397,
425, 434, 437
East Anglia, 602, 614
Lake District, 536, 540–541,
543, 544, 545, 546, 548,
552, 555–556, 560–561
Lancashire and the Peaks,
516–517, 520
London, 66, 154
Northeast, 680, 685, 692
Shakespeare Country, 376
South, 244, 252, 256
Southeast, 195
Thames Valley, 336, 351, 353
Wales, 700, 702, 721, 732
Welsh Borders, 464, 474
West Country, 271, 277, 278,
280, 285, 303, 305
Yorkshire, 631, 632, 633,
651–652, 656–657, 660–661
Wallace Collection, *78*
Walmar Castle and Gardens,
170
Wardens' Way, *424–425*
Warwick, *378–380*
Warwick Castle, *379*
Warwickshire Doll Museum,
379
Washington, *674*
Washington Old Hall, *674*
Watercress Line, *219*
Waterfalls, *551, 555, 628,*
632, 673, 701, 706
Watershed Media Centre, *271*
Watershed Media Centre café-
restaurant ✕, *268*
Weald and Downland Open
Air Museum, *190*
Weather, *28*
Weavers' Houses, *165*
Web sites, *795–796*
Wedgwood Visitor Centre,
511
Welford-on-Avon, *384*
Well dressing, *517*
Wellington Arch, *74, 80*
Wellington Barracks, *50*
Wellington Museum, *74*
Wells, *272–274*
Wells-next-to-Sea, *603–604*
Welsh Borders, *444–483*
Birmingham, 446, 448–449,
451–458
children, attractions for, 453,
454, 468, 469, 474, 479
essential information, 481–483

hotels, 456–457, 460–463, 464,
465, 467, 468, 472–473,
475, 477, 479–480
itinerary recommendations, 447
nightlife and the arts, 457–458,
461, 463, 473, 477
outdoor activities and sports,
458, 461, 474, 481
restaurants, 454–456, 460,
462–463, 464, 467, 468,
472, 475, 477, 479–480
shopping, 458, 461, 467, 469,
473, 480
Shrewsbury to Chester,
470–481
Worcester to Dudley, 458–469
Welsh Highland Railway-
Rheilffordd Eryri, *708*
Welsh National Opera, *729*
Welshpool, *722–723*
Wenlock Edge, *474*
Wenlock Priory, *474*
Wensleydale Creamery Visitor
Centre, *634*
Wesley Café ✕, *44*
West Country, *260–319*
Bristol to North Devon,
264–281
children, attractions for, 265,
268, 274–275, 288, 293,
300–301, 309
Cornwall, 281–299
Dartmouth, Torbay and Exeter,
307–317
essential information, 317–319
hotels, 262, 270–271, 273–274,
275, 277, 278–280, 281,
282, 284–285, 287–288, 291,
293, 294–296, 297, 298,
299, 302, 304, 305, 307,
308–309, 310–311, 314–315,
316
itinerary recommendations, 263
nightlife and the arts, 271, 275,
292, 302, 309, 315
outdoor activities and sports,
271, 285, 292, 297, 303,
305, 306, 315
Plymouth and Dartmoor,
299–307
restaurants, 262, 269–270,
273–274, 277, 278–279, 281,
284–285, 287, 291, 293,
294–296, 297, 299, 301–302,
304, 305, 307, 308–309,
310, 313–314, 316
shopping, 309, 315, 317
West Gate Museum, *165*

West Kennett Long Barrow,
241
West Yorkshire Playhouse, *625*
Westgate, *217*
Westminster Abbey, *47–49*
Westonbirt National
Arboretum, *432*
Weymouth, *253*
Whispering Gallery, *61*
Whitby, *652–654*
Whitby Abbey, *652–653*
Whitby Folk Week, *654*
Whitby Museum, *653*
Whitby Regatta, *654*
White Cliffs, *170*
White Cube, *131*
White Hart (Lincoln) 🖼, *611*
White Hart (London pub),
101–102
White Horse (pub), *102*
White Moss House ✕🖼, *543*
White Swan 🖼, *373–374*
Whitechapel Art Gallery, *131*
Whitworth Art Gallery, *493*
Wigmore Hall, *129*
William Herschel Museum,
400
Willy Lott's House, *590*
Wilmington, *177–178*
Wilton, *236*
Wilton House, *236*
Wimborne Minster, *247–248*
Winchcombe, *412–413*
Winchelsea, *173–174*
Winchester, *212–213,*
216–219
Winchester Cathedral, *213,*
216, 217
Winchester College, *217*
Windemere, *534–538*
Windermere Lake Cruises, *535*
Windermere Steamboat
Centre, *535*
Windsor, *322–325, 328–330*
Windsor Castle, *322–325*
Windsor Festival, *330*
Windsor Great Park, *325*
Winnats Pass, *520*
Wisley, *192*
Witley Court, *468*
Woburn Abbey, *357–358*
Woburn Safari Park, *357*
Wolseley, The ✕, *97*
Wood End, *649–650*
Woodbridge, *591–592*
Woodstock, *349–350*
Wookey Hole Caves, *273*
Worcester, *459–461*

Worcester Cathedral, *459*
Worcester Racecourse, *461*
Wordsworth, William, *541,
542, 547, 551, 557*
Wordsworth House, *557*
Wordsworth Museum, *542*
World of Beatrix Potter, *535*
World of James Herriot, *647*
World Museum Liverpool,
504
Wrekin volcano, *474*
Wykeham Arms ✕🖭 , *218*

Y

Y Tabernacl Museum of
Modern Art, *720*
Yalbury Cottage ✕🖭 ,
251–252
Yang Sing ✕ , *495*
Yauatcha ✕ , *98*
Ynyshir Hall ✕🖭 , *720–721*
York, *635–644*

York Minster, *639*
York Theatre Royal, *643*
Yorkshire, *615–661*
*children, attractions for, 622,
623, 626, 628–629, 637,
647, 656*
essential information, 658–661
*hotels, 624, 630, 631, 632–633,
635, 641–643, 645, 647,
650, 651, 654, 656*
itinerary recommendations, 617
*nightlife and the arts, 624–625,
643, 645, 650, 654*
North York Moors, 655–658
*North Yorkshire Coast,
648–654*
*outdoor activities and sports,
651–652, 656–657, 660*
*restaurants, 623–624, 630,
631, 632, 633, 635, 641,
644–645, 648–649, 650, 651,
654, 656*

shopping, 625, 643–644
*West Yorkshire and Brontë
Country, 618–619,
622–629*
York, 635–644
York environs, 644–647
Yorkshire Dales, 629–635
Yorkshire Museum, *641*
Ypres Tower, *172*

Z

Zetter Rooms 🖭 , *111*
Zoos/safari parks
London, 79
South, 238–239
Southeast, 177
Thames Valley, 357
Welsh Borders, 479
West Country, 269

PHOTO CREDITS

ABOUT OUR WRITERS

Longtime contributor Robert Andrews loves warm beer and soggy moors, but hates shopping malls and the sort of weather when you're not sure if it's raining—all of which he found in abundance while updating the South, West Country, and Bath & the Cotswolds. He writes and revises other guidebooks and has penned his own guide to Devon and Cornwall.

A native New Yorker, Ferne Arfin has been living in London and writing about travel for more than 20 years. A contributor to the *Sunday Telegraph* and Fodor's Travel Wire, Ferne wrote about the Templars in London for *Fodor's Guide to The Da Vinci Code*. She updated London Shopping—perfect work for a Chelsea shophound.

Texan by birth and Anglophile at heart, Christi Daugherty now lives in London, where she works as a freelance writer and editor. Her Fodor's territory was Smart Travel Tips and Where to Stay in London, and chapters from the Southeast to Yorkshire. She has written and edited guidebooks to Dublin, New Orleans, Paris, and other cities.

Londoner Adam Gold is passionate about sussing out the city's most intriguing places, dispensing advice on where to grab a glorious pub lunch or find a bar that serves bespoke cocktails. Fittingly, he updated London Nightlife and the Pubs sections of the London chapter. He writes and edits for national newspapers and magazines.

Julius Honnor, who revised the Sports & the Outdoors and Arts sections in the London chapter, lives in the city. His Fodor's territory also included the Lake District and East Anglia, where he made many great discoveries. His work for other guidebooks has taken him to Italy and other places around the globe.

Writer and editor Kate Hughes spent her formative years in Yorkshire and studied classical literature in Liverpool. She enjoyed traveling in the Peak District but also checked out the urban pleasures of Manchester and Liverpool as she updated the Welsh Borders and Lancashire & the Peaks chapters.

Always hoping to entertain—and surprise—his readers, Fodor's contributor Roger Thomas spends almost every minute tracking down the latest and the best of Wales. He has to: he's editor of *A View of Wales* magazine.

A Londoner born and bred, Alex Wijeratna updated the London Where to Eat section. With his English/Sri Lankan roots, Alex knows that the real flavor of London is found in its ethnic diversity. He has written for newspapers including the *Daily Mail* and the *Times*.